Collins
French
Dictionary

HarperCollins Publishers
Westerhill Road
Bishopbriggs
Glasgow
G64 2QT
Great Britain

First Edition 2005

Previously published as Collins Pocket
French Dictionary

© William Collins Sons & Co. Ltd. 1990
© HarperCollins Publishers 1995, 1998,
2001

ISBN 0-00-718378-X

Collins® and Bank of English® are
registered trademarks of HarperCollins
Publishers Limited

www.collins.co.uk

A catalogue record for this book is
available from the British Library

HarperCollins Publishers, Inc.
10 East 53rd Street, New York, NY 10022

ISBN 0-06-093751-3

Library of Congress Cataloging-in-
Publication Data has been applied for

www.harpercollins.com

First HarperCollins edition published
2000

HarperCollins books may be purchased
for educational, business, or sales
promotional use. For information,
please write to: Special Markets
Department, HarperCollins Publishers
Inc., 10 East 53rd Street, New York, NY
10022

Typeset by Morton Word Processing
Ltd, Scarborough

Printed in Italy by Amadeus S.r.l.

Acknowledgements
We would like to thank those authors
and publishers who kindly gave
permission for copyright material to be
used in the Collins Word Web. We
would also like to thank Times
Newspapers Ltd for providing valuable
data.

editors/rédaction
Pierre-Henri Cousin • Lorna Sinclair Knight
Catherine E. Love • Jean-François Allain • Claude Nimmo
Bob Grossmith • Jean-Benoit Ormal-Grenon
Cécile Aubinière-Robb • Claire Calder • Christine Penman

editorial staff/secrétariat de rédaction
Val McNulty • John Podbielski

series editor/collection dirigée par
Lorna Sinclair Knight

INTRODUCTION

We are delighted that you have decided to buy the Collins French Dictionary, and hope you will enjoy and benefit from using it at home, at school, on holiday or at work.

The innovative use of colour guides you quickly and efficiently to the word you want, and the comprehensive wordlist provides a wealth of modern and idiomatic phrases not normally found in a dictionary this size.

In addition, the supplement provides you with guidance on using the dictionary, along with entertaining ways of improving your dictionary skills.

We hope that you will enjoy using it and that it will significantly enhance your language studies.

Note on trademarks

COMMENT UTILISER VOTRE ROBERT & COLLINS MINI

Les informations contenues dans ce dictionnaire sont présentées à l'aide de plusieurs polices de caractères, de symboles, abréviations, parenthèses et crochets. Les conventions et symboles utilisés sont expliqués dans les sections qui suivent.

Entrées

Les mots que vous cherchez dans le dictionnaire (les 'entrées') sont classés par ordre alphabétique. Ils sont imprimés en couleur pour pouvoir être repérés rapidement. Les deux entrées figurant en haut de page indiquent le premier et le dernier mot qui apparaissent sur la page en question.

Des informations sur l'emploi ou sur la forme de certaines entrées sont données entre parenthèses, après la transcription phonétique. Ces indications apparaissent sous forme abrégée et en italique (ex: *(fam)*, *(COMM)*).

Plusieurs mots appartenant à la même famille peuvent être regroupés dans un même article (ex: **ronger, rongeur**). Dans la partie anglais-français et pour les préfixes de la partie français-anglais, la graphie de l'entrée principale est reprise par un tilde: ~ dans les sous-entrées (ex: **accept, ~ance**). Les sous-entrées apparaissent en caractères rouges, légèrement plus petits que ceux de l'entrée.

Les expressions courantes dans lesquelles apparaît l'entrée sont indiquées par des caractères romains gras (ex **avoir du retard**).

Transcription phonétique

La transcription phonétique symbolisant la prononciation de chaque entrée est indiquée entre crochets immédiatement après l'entrée (ex **fumer** [fyme]; **knead** [niːd]). La liste des symboles phonétiques figure aux pages xiii et xiv.

Traductions

Les traductions interchangeables sont séparées par une virgule; lorsque plusieurs sens coexistent, ces traductions sont séparées par un point-virgule. Vous trouverez souvent entre parenthèses d'autres mots en italique qui précèdent les traductions. Ces mots fournissent certains des contextes dans lesquels l'entrée est susceptible d'être utilisée (ex **rough** *(voice)* ou *(weather)*) ou offrent des synonymes (ex **rough** *(violent)*).

'Mots-clés'

Une importance particulière est accordée à certains mots français et anglais qui sont considérés comme des "mots-clés" dans chacune des langues. Cela peut être dû à leur utilisation très fréquente ou au fait qu'ils ont divers types d'usages (ex **vouloir, plus; get, that**). Une combinaison de losanges et de chiffres vous aident à distinguer différentes catégories grammaticales et différents sens. D'autres renseignements utiles apparaissent en italique et entre parenthèses dans la langue de l'utilisateur.

Données grammaticales

Les catégories grammaticales sont données sous forme abrégée et en italique après la transcription phonétique des entrées (ex *vt, adv, conj*).

Le genre des noms français est indiqué de la manière suivante: *nm* pour un nom masculin et *nf* pour un nom féminin. Le féminin et le pluriel irréguliers sont également indiqués (**directeur, trice; cheval, aux**).

Le masculin et le féminin des adjectifs sont mentionnés lorsque ces deux formes sont différentes (ex **noir, e**). Lorsque l'adjectif a un féminin ou un pluriel irrégulier, ces formes sont clairement indiquées (ex **net, nette**). Les pluriels irréguliers des noms et les formes irrégulières des verbes anglais sont indiqués entre parenthèses, avant la catégorie grammaticale (ex **man** ... (*pl* **men**) *n*; **give** (*pt* **gave**, *pp* **given**) *vt*).

USING YOUR COLLINS FRENCH DICTIONARY

A wealth of information is presented in the dictionary, using various typefaces, sizes of type, symbols, abbreviations and brackets. The conventions and symbols used are explained in the following sections.

Headwords

The words you look up in a dictionary — "headwords" — are listed alphabetically. They are printed in **colour** for rapid identification. The two headwords appearing at the top of each page indicate the first and last word dealt with on the page in question.

Information about the usage or form of certain headwords is given in brackets after the phonetic spelling. This usually appears in abbreviated form and in italics (e.g. (*fam*), (*COMM*)).
Where appropriate, words related to headwords are grouped in the same entry (**ronger, rongeur; accept, acceptance**) in a slightly smaller coloured type than the headword.

Common expressions in which the headword appears are shown in black bold roman type (e.g. **avoir du retard**).

Phonetic spellings

The phonetic spelling of each headword (indicating its pronunciation) is given in square brackets immediately after the headword (e.g. **fumer** [fyme]; **knead** [niːd]). A list of the phonetic symbols is given on pages xiii and xiv.

Translations

Headword translations are given in ordinary type and, where more than one meaning or usage exists, these are separated by a semi-colon. You will often find other words in italics in brackets before the translations. These offer suggested contexts in which the headword might appear (e.g. **rough** (*voice*) or (*weather*)) or provide synonyms (e.g. **rough** (*violent*)).

"Key" words

Special status is given to certain French and English words which are considered as "key" words in each language. They may, for example, occur very frequently or have several types of usage (e.g. **vouloir, plus; get, that**). A combination of lozenges and numbers helps you to distinguish different parts of speech and different meanings. Further helpful information is provided in brackets and in italics in the relevant language for the user.

Grammatical information

Parts of speech are given in abbreviated form in italics after the phonetic spellings of headwords (e.g. *vt, adv, conj*).

Genders of French nouns are indicated as follows: *nm* for a masculine and *nf* for a feminine noun. Feminine and irregular plural forms of nouns are also shown (**directeur, trice; cheval, aux**).

Adjectives are given in both masculine and feminine forms where these forms are different (e.g. **noir, e**). Clear information is provided where adjectives have an irregular feminine or plural form (e.g. **net, nette**).

ABRÉVIATIONS

ABBREVIATIONS

adjectif, locution adjective	adj	adjective, adjectival phrase
abréviation	ab(b)r	abbreviation
adverbe, locution adverbiale	adv	adverb, adverbial phrase
administration	ADMIN	administration
agriculture	AGR	agriculture
anatomie	ANAT	anatomy
architecture	ARCHIT	architecture
article défini	art déf	definite article
article indéfini	art indéf	indefinite article
attribut	attrib	predicative
l'automobile	AUT(O)	the motor car and motoring
auxiliaire	aux	auxiliary
aviation, voyages aériens	AVIAT	flying, air travel
biologie	BIO(L)	biology
botanique	BOT	botany
anglais de Grande-Bretagne	BRIT	British English
commerce, finance, banque	COMM	commerce, finance, banking
comparatif	compar	comparative
informatique	COMPUT	computing
conditionnel	cond	conditional
chimie	CHEM	chemistry
conjonction	conj	conjunction
construction	CONSTR	building
nom utilisé comme adjectif, ne peut s'employer ni comme attribut, ni après le nom qualifié	cpd	compound element: used as an adjective and which cannot follow the noun it qualifies
cuisine, art culinaire	CULIN	cookery
article défini	def art	definite article
déterminant: article démonstratif ou indéfini etc	dét	determiner: article, demonstrative etc
diminutif	dimin	diminutive
économie	ECON	economics
électricité, électronique	ELEC	electricity, electronics
exclamation, interjection	excl	exclamation, interjection
féminin	f	feminine
langue familière (! emploi vulgaire)	fam(!)	informal usage (! very offensive)
emploi figuré	fig	figurative use
(verbe anglais) dont la particule est inséparable du verbe dans la plupart des sens	fus	(phrasal verb) where the particle cannot be separated from main verb in most or all senses
généralement	gén, gen	generally
géographie, géologie	GEO	geography, geology
géométrie	GEOM	geometry
impersonnel	impers	impersonal
article indéfini	indef art	indefinite article
langue familière (! emploi vulgaire)	inf(!)	informal usage (! particularly offensive)
infinitif	infin	infinitive
informatique	INFORM	computing

ABRÉVIATIONS ABBREVIATIONS

invariable	**inv**	invariable
irrégulier	**irreg**	irregular
domaine juridique	**JUR**	law
grammaire, linguistique	**LING**	grammar, linguistics
masculin	**m**	masculine
mathématiques, algèbre	**MATH**	mathematics, calculus
médecine	**MÉD, MED**	medical term, medicine
masculin ou féminin, suivant le sexe	**m/f**	either masculine or feminine depending on sex
domaine militaire, armée	**MIL**	military matters
musique	**MUS**	music
nom	**n**	noun
navigation, nautisme	**NAVIG, NAUT**	sailing, navigation
nom ou adjectif numéral	**num**	numeral adjective or noun
	o.s.	oneself
péjoratif	**péj, pej**	derogatory, pejorative
photographie	**PHOT(O)**	photography
physiologie	**PHYSIOL**	physiology
pluriel	**pl**	plural
politique	**POL**	politics
participe passé	**pp**	past participle
préposition	**prép, prep**	preposition
pronom	**pron**	pronoun
psychologie, psychiatrie	**PSYCH**	psychology, psychiatry
temps du passé	**pt**	past tense
quelque chose	**qch**	
quelqu'un	**qn**	
religions, domaine ecclésiastique	**REL**	religions, church service
	sb	somebody
enseignement, système scolaire et universitaire	**SCOL**	schooling, schools and universities
singulier	**sg**	singular
	sth	something
subjonctif	**sub**	subjunctive
sujet (grammatical)	**su(b)j**	(grammatical) subject
superlatif	**superl**	superlative
techniques, technologie	**TECH**	technical term, technology
télécommunications	**TEL**	telecommunications
télévision	**TV**	television
typographie	**TYP(O)**	typography, printing
anglais des USA	**US**	American English
verbe	**vb**	verb
verbe ou groupe verbal à fonction intransitive	**vi**	verb or phrasal verb used intransitively
verbe ou groupe verbal à fonction transitive	**vt**	verb or phrasal verb used transitively
zoologie	**ZOOL**	zoology
marque déposée	**®**	registered trademark
indique une équivalence culturelle	**≈**	introduces a cultural equivalent

TRANSCRIPTION PHONÉTIQUE

CONSONNES		CONSONANTS
NB. **p, b, t, d, k, g** sont suivis d'une aspiration en anglais.		NB. **p, b, t, d, k, g** are not aspirated in French.
poupée	p	*puppy*
bombe	b	*baby*
tente thermal	t	*tent*
dinde	d	*daddy*
coq qui képi	k	*cork kiss chord*
gag bague	g	*gag guess*
sale ce nation	s	*so rice kiss*
zéro rose	z	*cousin buzz*
tache chat	ʃ	*sheep sugar*
gilet juge	ʒ	*pleasure beige*
	tʃ	*church*
	dʒ	*judge general*
fer phare	f	*farm raffle*
valve	v	*very rev*
	θ	*thin maths*
	ð	*that other*
lent salle	l	*little ball*
rare rentrer	R	
	r	*rat rare*
maman femme	m	*mummy comb*
non nonne	n	*no ran*
agneau vigne	ɲ	
	ŋ	*singing bank*
hop!	h	*hat reheat*
yeux paille pied	j	*yet*
nouer oui	w	*wall bewail*
huile lui	ɥ	
	x	*loch*

DIVERS		MISCELLANEOUS
pour l'anglais: le r final se prononce en liaison devant une voyelle	ʳ	in English transcription: final r can be pronounced before a vowel
pour l'anglais: précède la syllabe accentuée	ˈ	in French wordlist and transcription: no liaison

PHONETIC TRANSCRIPTION

Voyelles

NB. La mise en équivalence
de certains sons n'indique
qu'une ressemblance
approximative.

Vowels

NB. The pairing of some vowel
sounds only indicates
approximate equivalence.

ici v*ie* l*y*re	i iː	h*ee*l b*ea*d
	ɪ	h*i*t p*i*ty
jou*er* ét*é*	e	s*e*t t*e*nt
l*ait* jou*et* m*er*ci	ɛ	
pl*a*t *a*mour	a æ	b*a*t *a*pple
b*a*s p*â*te	ɑ ɑː	*a*fter c*a*r c*a*lm
	ʌ	f*u*n c*ou*sin
l*e* prem*ier*	ə	*o*ver *a*bove
b*eu*rre p*eu*r	œ	
p*eu* d*eu*x	ø ɜː	*u*rn f*er*n w*or*k
or h*o*mme	ɒ	w*a*sh p*o*t
m*o*t *eau* g*au*che	o ɔː	b*or*n c*or*k
gen*ou* r*ou*e	u ʊ	f*u*ll s*oo*t
	uː	b*oo*n l*ew*d
r*ue* *u*rne	y	

Diphtongues

Diphthongs

ɪə	b*ee*r t*ie*r
ɛə	t*ea*r f*ai*r th*e*re
eɪ	d*a*te pl*ai*ce d*ay*
aɪ	l*i*fe b*uy* cr*y*
aʊ	*ow*l f*ou*l n*ow*
əʊ	l*ow* n*o*
ɔɪ	b*oi*l b*oy* *oi*ly
ʊə	p*oo*r t*ou*r

Nasales

Nasal Vowels

mat*in* pl*ein*	ɛ̃
br*un*	œ̃
s*ang* *an* d*ans*	ɑ̃
n*on* p*on*t	ɔ̃

A, a

a [a] *vb voir* **avoir**

MOT-CLÉ

à [a] (*à + le* = **au**, *à + les* = **aux**) *prép* **1**
(*endroit, situation*) at, in; **être à Paris/au
Portugal** to be in Paris/Portugal; **être à la
maison/à l'école** to be at home/at
school; **à la campagne** in the country,
c'est à 10 km/à 20 minutes (d'ici) it's
10 km/20 minutes away

2 (*direction*) to; **aller à Paris/au Portugal**
to go to Paris/Portugal; **aller à la
maison/à l'école** to go home/to school;
à la campagne to the country

3 (*temps*): **à 3 heures/minuit** at 3
o'clock/midnight; **au printemps/mois de
juin** in the spring/the month of June

4 (*attribution, appartenance*) to; **le livre est
à Paul/à lui/à nous** this book is Paul's/
his/ours; **donner qch à qn** to give sth to
sb

5 (*moyen*) with; **se chauffer au gaz** to
have gas heating; **à bicyclette** on a *ou* by
bicycle; **à la main/machine** by hand/
machine

6 (*provenance*) from; **boire à la bouteille**
to drink from the bottle

7 (*caractérisation, manière*): **l'homme aux
yeux bleus** the man with the blue eyes;
à la russe the Russian way

8 (*but, destination*): **tasse à café** coffee
cup; **maison à vendre** house for sale

9 (*rapport, évaluation, distribution*): **100
km/unités à l'heure** 100 km/units per
ou an hour; **payé à l'heure** paid by the
hour; **cinq à six** five to six

---

abaisser [abese] *vt* to lower, bring down;
(*manette*) to pull down; **s'~** *vi* to go
down; (*fig*) to demean o.s.

abandon [abɑ̃dɔ̃] *nm* abandoning; giving
up; withdrawal; **être à l'~** to be in a state
of neglect

abandonner [abɑ̃dɔne] *vt* (*personne*) to
abandon; (*projet, activité*) to abandon,
give up; (SPORT) to retire *ou* withdraw
from; (*céder*) to surrender; **s'~ à** (*paresse,
plaisirs*) to give o.s. up to

abasourdir [abazuʀdiʀ] *vt* to stun, stagger

abat-jour [abaʒuʀ] *nm inv* lampshade

abats [aba] *nmpl* (*de bœuf, porc*) offal *sg*;
(*de volaille*) giblets

abattement [abatmɑ̃] *nm*: **~ fiscal** ≈ tax
allowance

abattoir [abatwaʀ] *nm* slaughterhouse

abattre [abatʀ] *vt* (*arbre*) to cut down, fell;
(*mur, maison*) to pull down; (*avion, personne*) to shoot down; (*animal*) to shoot,
kill; (*fig*) to wear out, tire out; to demoral-
ize; **s'~** *vi* to crash down; **ne pas se
laisser ~** to keep one's spirits up, not to
let things get one down; **s'~ sur** to beat
down on; (*fig*) to rain down on

abbaye [abei] *nf* abbey

abbé [abe] *nm* priest; (*d'une abbaye*) abbot

abcès [apsɛ] *nm* abscess

abdiquer [abdike] *vi* to abdicate

abdominaux [abdɔmino] *nmpl*: **faire des
~** to do exercises for one's abdominals,
do one's abdominals

abeille [abɛj] *nf* bee

aberrant, e [abeʀɑ̃, ɑ̃t] *adj* absurd,

aberration [abeʀasjɔ̃] *nf* aberration

abêtir [abetiʀ] *vt* to make morons of (*ou* a
moron of)

abîme [abim] *nm* abyss, gulf

abîmer [abime] *vt* to spoil, damage; **s'~**

vi to get spoilt *ou* damaged

ablation [ablasjɔ̃] *nf* removal

aboiement [abwamã] *nm* bark, barking

abois [abwa] *nmpl:* **aux ~** at bay

abolir [abɔliʀ] *vt* to abolish

abominable [abɔminabl] *adj* abominable

abondance [abɔ̃dɑ̃s] *nf* abundance

abondant, e [abɔ̃dɑ̃, ɑ̃t] *adj* plentiful, abundant, copious; **abonder** *vi* to abound, be plentiful; **abonder dans le sens de qn** to concur with sb

abonné, e [abɔne] *nm/f* subscriber; season ticket holder

abonnement [abɔnmɑ̃] *nm* subscription; *(transports, concerts)* season ticket

abonner [abɔne] *vt:* **s'~ à** to subscribe to, take out a subscription to

abord [abɔʀ] *nm:* **au premier ~** at first sight, initially; **~s** *nmpl (environs)* surroundings; **d'~** first

abordable [abɔʀdabl] *adj (prix)* reasonable; *(personne)* approachable

aborder [abɔʀde] *vi* to land ♦ *vt (sujet, difficulté)* to tackle; *(personne)* to approach; *(rivage etc)* to reach

aboutir [abutiʀ] *vi (négociations etc)* to succeed; **~ à** to end up at; **n'~ à rien** to come to nothing

aboyer [abwaje] *vi* to bark

abréger [abʀeʒe] *vt* to shorten

abreuver [abʀœve]: **s'~** *vi* to drink; **abreuvoir** *nm* watering place

abréviation [abʀevjasjɔ̃] *nf* abbreviation

abri [abʀi] *nm* shelter; **être à l'~** to be under cover; **se mettre à l'~** to shelter

abricot [abʀiko] *nm* apricot

abriter [abʀite] *vt* to shelter; **s'~** *vt* to shelter, take cover

abrupt, e [abʀypt] *adj* sheer, steep; *(ton)* abrupt

abruti, e [abʀyti] *adj* stunned, dazed ♦ *nm/f (fam)* idiot, moron; **~ de travail** overworked

absence [apsɑ̃s] *nf* absence; *(MÉD)* blackout; **avoir des ~s** to have mental blanks

absent, e [apsɑ̃, ɑ̃t] *adj* absent ♦ *nm/f* absentee; **absenter**: **s'absenter** *vi* to take time off work; *(sortir)* to leave, go out

absolu, e [apsɔly] *adj* absolute; **absolument** *adv* absolutely

absorbant, e [apsɔʀbɑ̃, ɑ̃t] *adj* absorbent

absorber [apsɔʀbe] *vt* to absorb; *(gén MÉD: manger, boire)* to take

abstenir [apstəniʀ] *vb:* **s'~ de qch/de faire** to refrain from sth/from doing

abstraction [apstʀaksjɔ̃] *nf* abstraction

abstrait, e [apstʀɛ, ɛt] *adj* abstract

absurde [apsyʀd] *adj* absurd

abus [aby] *nm* abuse; **~ de confiance** breach of trust; **abuser** *vi* to go too far, overstep the mark; **abuser de** *(duper)* to take advantage of; **abusif, -ive** *adj* exorbitant; *(punition)* excessive

acabit [akabi] *nm:* **de cet ~** of that type

académie [akademi] *nf* academy; *(SCOL: circonscription)* ≈ regional education authority

Académie française

i The **Académie française** *was founded by Cardinal Richelieu in 1635 during the reign of Louis XIII. It consists of forty elected scholars and writers who are known as "les Quarante" or "les Immortels". One of the Académie's functions is to regulate the development of the French language and its recommendations are frequently the subject of lively public debate. It has produced several editions of its famous dictionary and awards various literary prizes.*

acajou [akaʒu] *nm* mahogany

acariâtre [akaʀjɑtʀ] *adj* cantankerous

accablant, e [akablɑ̃, ɑ̃t] *adj (chaleur)* oppressive; *(témoignage, preuve)* overwhelming

accablement [akabləmɑ̃] *nm* despondency

accabler [akable] *vt* to overwhelm, overcome; **~ qn d'injures** to heap *ou* shower abuse on sb

accalmie [akalmi] *nf* lull

accaparer [akapaʀe] *vt* to monopolize; (*suj: travail etc*) to take up (all) the time *ou* attention of

accéder [aksede]: **~ à** *vt* (*lieu*) to reach; (*accorder: requête*) to grant, accede to

accélérateur [akseleʀatœʀ] *nm* accelerator

accélération [akseleʀasjɔ̃] *nf* acceleration

accélérer [akseleʀe] *vt* to speed up ♦ *vi* to accelerate

accent [aksɑ̃] *nm* accent; (*PHONÉTIQUE, fig*) stress; **mettre l'~ sur** (*fig*) to stress; **~ aigu/grave/circonflexe** acute/grave/circumflex accent; **accentuer** *vt* (*LING*) to accent; (*fig*) to accentuate, emphasize; **s'accentuer** *vi* to become more marked *ou* pronounced

acceptation [aksɛptasjɔ̃] *nf* acceptance

accepter [aksɛpte] *vt* to accept; **~ de faire** to agree to do

accès [aksɛ] *nm* (*à un lieu*) access; (*MÉD: de toux*) fit; (: *de fièvre*) bout; **d'~ facile** easily accessible; **facile d'~** easy to get to; **~ de colère** fit of anger; **accessible** *adj* accessible; (*livre, sujet*). **accessible à qn** within the reach of sb

accessoire [aksɛswaʀ] *adj* secondary; incidental ♦ *nm* accessory; (*THÉÂTRE*) prop

accident [aksidɑ̃] *nm* accident; **par ~** by chance; **~ de la route** road accident; **~ du travail** industrial injury *ou* accident; **accidenté, e** *adj* damaged; injured; (*relief, terrain*) uneven; hilly; **accidentel, le** *adj* accidental

acclamations [aklamasjɔ̃] *nfpl* cheers

acclamer [aklame] *vt* to cheer, acclaim

acclimater [aklimate]: **s'~** *vi* (*personne*) to adapt (o.s.)

accolade [akɔlad] *nf* (*amicale*) embrace; (*signe*) brace

accommodant, e [akɔmɔdɑ̃, ɑ̃t] *adj* accommodating, easy-going

accommoder [akɔmɔde] *vt* (*CULIN*) to prepare; **s'~ de** *vt* to put up with; (*se contenter de*) to make do with

accompagnateur, -trice [akɔ̃paɲatœʀ, tʀis] *nm/f* (*MUS*) accompanist; (*de voyage: guide*) guide; (*de voyage organisé*) courier

accompagner [akɔ̃paɲe] *vt* to accompany, be *ou* go *ou* come with; (*MUS*) to accompany

accompli, e [akɔ̃pli] *adj* accomplished

accomplir [akɔ̃pliʀ] *vt* (*tâche, projet*) to carry out; (*souhait*) to fulfil; **s'~** *vi* to be fulfilled

accord [akɔʀ] *nm* agreement; (*entre des styles, tons etc*) harmony; (*MUS*) chord; **d'~!** OK!; **se mettre d'~** to come to an agreement; **être d'~ (pour faire qch)** to agree (to do sth)

accordéon [akɔʀdeɔ̃] *nm* (*MUS*) accordion

accorder [akɔʀde] *vt* (*faveur, délai*) to grant; (*harmoniser*) to match; (*MUS*) to tune; **s'~** *vt* to get on together; to agree

accoster [akɔste] *vt* (*NAVIG*) to draw alongside ♦ *vi* to berth

accotement [akɔtmɑ̃] *nm* verge (*BRIT*), shoulder

accouchement [akuʃmɑ̃] *nm* delivery, (child)birth; labour

accoucher [akuʃe] *vi* to give birth, have a baby; **~ d'un garçon** to give birth to a boy; **accoucheur** *nm*: (*médecin*) **accoucheur** obstetrician

accouder [akude]: **s'~** *vi* to rest one's elbows on/against; **accoudoir** *nm* armrest

accoupler [akuple] *vt* to couple; (*pour la reproduction*) to mate; **s'~** *vt* to mate

accourir [akuʀiʀ] *vi* to rush *ou* run up

accoutrement [akutʀəmɑ̃] (*péj*) *nm* (*tenue*) outfit

accoutumance [akutymɑ̃s] *nf* (*gén*) adaptation; (*MÉD*) addiction

accoutumé, e [akutyme] *adj* (*habituel*) customary, usual

accoutumer [akutyme] *vt*: **s'~ à** to get accustomed *ou* used to

accréditer [akʀedite] *vt* (*nouvelle*) to substantiate

accroc [akʀo] *nm* (*déchirure*) tear; (*fig*) hitch, snag

accrochage [akrɔʃaʒ] nm (AUTO) collision; (dispute) clash, brush

accrocher [akrɔʃe] vt (fig) to catch, attract; **s'~** (se disputer) to have a clash ou brush; **~ qch à** (suspendre) to hang sth (up) on; (attacher: remorque) to hitch sth (up) to; **~ qch (à)** (déchirer) to catch sth (on); **~ un passant** (heurter) to hit a pedestrian; **s'~ à** (rester pris à) to catch on; (agripper, fig) to hang on ou cling to

accroissement [akrwasmɑ̃] nm increase

accroître [akrwatr]: **s'~** vi to increase

accroupir [akrupir]: **s'~** vi to squat, crouch (down)

accru, e [akry] pp de **accroître**

accueil [akœj] nm welcome; **comité d'~** reception committee; **accueillir** vt to welcome; (aller chercher) to meet, collect

acculer [akyle] vt: **~ qn à** ou **contre** to drive sb back against

accumuler [akymyle] vt to accumulate, amass; **s'~** vi to accumulate; to pile up

accusation [akyzasjɔ̃] nf (gén) accusation; (JUR) charge; (partie): **l'~** the prosecution

accusé, e [akyze] nm/f accused; defendant; **~ de réception** acknowledgement of receipt

accuser [akyze] vt to accuse; (fig) to emphasize, bring out; to show; **~ qn de** to accuse sb of; (JUR) to charge sb with; **~ réception de** to acknowledge receipt of

acerbe [asɛrb] adj caustic, acid

acéré, e [asere] adj sharp

acharné, e [aʃarne] adj (efforts) relentless; (lutte, adversaire) fierce, bitter

acharner [aʃarne] vb: **s'~ contre** to set o.s. against; (suj: malchance) to dog; **s'~ à faire** to try doggedly to do; (persister) to persist in doing

achat [aʃa] nm purchase; **faire des ~s** to do some shopping; **faire l'~ de qch** to purchase sth

acheminer [aʃ(ə)mine] vt (courrier) to forward, dispatch; **s'~ vers** to head for

acheter [aʃ(ə)te] vt to buy, purchase; (soudoyer) to buy; **~ qch à** (marchand) to buy

ou purchase sth from; (ami etc: offrir) to buy sth for; **acheteur, -euse** nm/f buyer; shopper; (COMM) buyer

achever [aʃ(ə)ve] vt to complete, finish; (blessé) to finish off; **s'~** vi to end

acide [asid] adj sour, sharp; (CHIMIE) acid(ic) ♦ nm (CHIMIE) acid; **acidulé, e** adj slightly acid

acier [asje] nm steel; **aciérie** nf steelworks sg

acné [akne] nf acne

acolyte [akɔlit] (péj) nm associate

acompte [akɔ̃t] nm deposit

à-côté [akote] nm side-issue; (argent) extra

à-coup [aku] nm: **par ~~s** by fits and starts

acoustique [akustik] nf (d'une salle) acoustics pl

acquéreur [akerœr] nm buyer, purchaser

acquérir [akerir] vt to acquire

acquis, e [aki, iz] pp de **acquérir** ♦ nm (accumulated) experience; **son aide nous est ~e** we can count on her help

acquit [aki] vb voir **acquérir** ♦ nm (quittance) receipt; **par ~ de conscience** to set one's mind at rest

acquitter [akite] vt (JUR) to acquit; (facture) to pay, settle; **s'~ de** vt (devoir) to discharge; (promesse) to fulfil

âcre [akr] adj acrid, pungent

acrobate [akrɔbat] nm/f acrobat; **acrobatie** nf acrobatics sg

acte [akt] nm act, action; (THÉÂTRE) act; **prendre ~ de** to note, take note of; **faire ~ de candidature** to apply; **faire ~ de présence** to put in an appearance; **~ de naissance** birth certificate

acteur [aktœr] nm actor

actif, -ive [aktif, iv] adj active ♦ nm (COMM) assets pl; (fig): **avoir à son ~** to have to one's credit; **population active** working population

action [aksjɔ̃] nf (gén) action; (COMM) share; **une bonne ~** a good deed; **actionnaire** nm/f shareholder; **actionner** vt (mécanisme) to activate; (machine) to operate

activer [aktive] *vt* to speed up; **s'~** *vi* to bustle about; to hurry up

activité [aktivite] *nf* activity; **en ~** (*volcan*) active; (*fonctionnaire*) in active life

actrice [aktʀis] *nf* actress

actualiser [aktɥalize] *vt* to bring up to date

actualité [aktɥalite] *nf* (*d'un problème*) topicality; (*événements*): **l'~** current events; **les ~s** *nfpl* (*CINÉMA, TV*) the news; **d'~** topical

actuel, le [aktɥɛl] *adj* (*présent*) present; (*d'actualité*) topical; **à l'heure ~le** at the present time; **actuellement** *adv* at present, at the present time

acuité [akɥite] *nf* acuteness

acuponcteur [akypɔ̃ktœʀ] *nm* acupuncturist

acuponcture [akypɔ̃ktyʀ] *nf* acupuncture

adaptateur [adaptatœʀ] *nm* (*ÉLEC*) adapter

adapter [adapte] *vt* to adapt; **s'~ (à)** (*suj: personne*) to adapt (to); **~ qch à** (*approprier*) to adapt sth to (to fit); **~ qch sur/ dans/à** (*fixer*) to fit sth on/into/to

additif [aditif] *nm* additive

addition [adisjɔ̃] *nf* addition; (*au café*) bill; **additionner** *vt* to add (up)

adepte [adɛpt] *nm/f* follower

adéquat, e [adekwa(t), at] *adj* appropriate, suitable

adhérent, e [adeʀɑ̃, ɑ̃t] *nm/f* member

adhérer [adeʀe]: **~ à** *vt* (*coller*) to adhere *ou* stick to; (*se rallier à*) to join; **adhésif, -ive** *adj* adhesive, sticky; **ruban adhésif** sticky *ou* adhesive tape; **adhésion** *nf* joining; (*fait d'être membre*) membership; (*accord*) support

adieu, x [adjø] *excl* goodbye ♦ *nm* farewell

adjectif [adʒɛktif] *nm* adjective

adjoindre [adʒwɛ̃dʀ] *vt*: **~ qch à** to attach sth to; (*ajouter*) to add sth to; **s'~** *vt* (*collaborateur etc*) to take on, appoint; **adjoint, e** *nm/f* assistant; **adjoint au maire** deputy mayor; **directeur adjoint** assistant

manager

adjudant [adʒydɑ̃] *nm* (*MIL*) warrant officer

adjuger [adʒyʒe] *vt* (*prix, récompense*) to award; (*lors d'une vente*) to auction (off); **s'~** *vt* to take for o.s.

adjurer [adʒyʀe] *vt*: **~ qn de faire** to implore *ou* beg sb to do

admettre [admɛtʀ] *vt* (*laisser entrer*) to admit; (*candidat: SCOL*) to pass; (*tolérer*) to allow, accept; (*reconnaître*) to admit, acknowledge

administrateur, -trice [administʀatœʀ, tʀis] *nm/f* (*COMM*) director; (*ADMIN*) administrator

administration [administʀasjɔ̃] *nf* administration; **l'A~** ≃ the Civil Service

administrer [administʀe] *vt* (*firme*) to manage, run; (*biens, remède, sacrement etc*) to administer

admirable [admiʀabl] *adj* admirable, wonderful

admirateur, -trice [admiʀatœʀ, tʀis] *nm/f* admirer

admiration [admiʀasjɔ̃] *nf* admiration

admirer [admiʀe] *vt* to admire

admis, e [admi, iz] *pp de* **admettre**

admissible [admisibl] *adj* (*candidat*) eligible; (*comportement*) admissible, acceptable

admission [admisjɔ̃] *nf* admission; acknowledgement; **demande d'~** application for membership

ADN *sigle m* (= *acide désoxyribonucléique*) DNA

adolescence [adɔlesɑ̃s] *nf* adolescence

adolescent, e [adɔlesɑ̃, ɑ̃t] *nm/f* adolescent, teenager

adonner [adɔne]: **s'~ à** *vt* (*sport*) to devote o.s. to; (*boisson*) to give o.s. over to

adopter [adɔpte] *vt* to adopt; **adoptif, -ive** *adj* (*parents*) adoptive; (*fils, patrie*) adopted

adorable [adɔʀabl] *adj* delightful, adorable

adorer [adɔʀe] *vt* to adore; (*REL*) to worship

adosser [adose] *vt*: ~ **qch à** *ou* **contre** to stand sth against; **s'~ à** *ou* **contre** to lean with one's back against

adoucir [adusiʀ] *vt* (*goût, température*) to make milder; (*avec du sucre*) to sweeten; (*peau, voix*) to soften; (*caractère*) to mellow

adresse [adʀɛs] *nf* (*domicile*) address; (*dextérité*) skill, dexterity; ~ **électronique** email address

adresser [adʀese] *vt* (*lettre: expédier*) to send; (: *écrire l'adresse sur*) to address; (*injure, compliments*) to address; **s'~ à** (*parler à*) to speak to, address; (*s'informer auprès de*) to go and see; (: *bureau*) to enquire at; (*suj: livre, conseil*) to be aimed at; ~ **la parole à** to speak to, address

adroit, e [adʀwa, wat] *adj* skilful, skilled

adulte [adylt] *nm/f* adult, grown-up ♦ *adj* (*chien, arbre*) fully-grown, mature; (*attitude*) adult, grown-up

adultère [adylteʀ] *nm* (*acte*) adultery

advenir [advəniʀ] *vi* to happen

adverbe [advɛʀb] *nm* adverb

adversaire [advɛʀseʀ] *nm/f* (*SPORT, gén*) opponent, adversary

adverse [advɛʀs] *adj* opposing

aération [aeʀasjɔ̃] *nf* airing; (*circulation de l'air*) ventilation

aérer [aeʀe] *vt* to air; (*fig*) to lighten; **s'~** *vi* to get some (fresh) air

aérien, ne [aeʀjɛ̃, jɛn] *adj* (*AVIAT*) air *cpd*, aerial; (*câble, métro*) overhead; (*fig*) light; **compagnie ~ne** airline

aéro... [aeʀɔ] *préfixe*: **aérobic** *nm* aerobics *sg*; **aérogare** *nf* airport (buildings); (*en ville*) air terminal; **aéroglisseur** *nm* hovercraft; **Aéronavale** *nf* ≃ Fleet Air Arm (*BRIT*), ≃ Naval Air Force (*US*); **aérophagie** *nf* (*MÉD*) wind, aerophagia (*MÉD*); **aéroport** *nm* airport; **aéroporté, e** *adj* airborne, airlifted; **aérosol** *nm* aerosol

affable [afabl] *adj* affable

affaiblir [afebliʀ] **s'~** *vi* to weaken

affaire [afɛʀ] *nf* (*problème, question*) matter; (*criminelle, judiciaire*) case; (*scandaleuse etc*) affair; (*entreprise*) business; (*marché, transaction*) deal; business *no pl*; (*occasion intéressante*) bargain; **~s** *nfpl* (*intérêts publics et privés*) affairs; (*activité commerciale*) business *sg*; (*effets personnels*) things, belongings; **ce sont mes ~s** (*cela me concerne*) that's my business; **ça fera l'~** that will do (nicely); **se tirer d'~** to sort it *ou* things out for o.s.; **avoir ~ à** (*être en contact*) to be dealing with; **les A~s étrangères** Foreign Affairs; **affairer: s'affairer** *vi* to busy o.s., bustle

affaisser [afese]: **s'~** *vi* (*terrain, immeuble*) to subside, sink; (*personne*) to collapse

affaler [afale] *vb*: **s'~ (dans/sur)** to collapse *ou* slump (into/onto)

affamé, e [afame] *adj* starving

affectation [afɛktasjɔ̃] *nf* (*nomination*) appointment; (*manque de naturel*) affectation

affecter [afɛkte] *vt* to affect; ~ **qch à** to allocate *ou* allot sth to; ~ **qn à** to appoint sb to; (*diplomate*) to post sb to

affectif, -ive [afɛktif, iv] *adj* emotional

affection [afɛksjɔ̃] *nf* affection; (*mal*) ailment; **affectionner** *vt* to be fond of; **affectueux, -euse** *adj* affectionate

affermir [afɛʀmiʀ] *vt* to consolidate, strengthen; (*muscles*) to tone up

affichage [afiʃaʒ] *nm* billposting; (*électronique*) display

affiche [afiʃ] *nf* poster; (*officielle*) notice; (*THÉÂTRE*) bill

afficher [afiʃe] *vt* (*affiche*) to put up; (*réunion*) to put up a notice about; (*électroniquement*) to display; (*fig*) to exhibit, display; **"défense d'~"** "stick no bills"

affilée [afile]: **d'~** *adv* at a stretch

affiler [afile] *vt* to sharpen

affilier [afilje]: **s'~ à** *vt* (*club, société*) to join

affiner [afine] *vt* to refine

affirmatif, -ive [afiʀmatif, iv] *adj* affirmative

affirmation [afiʀmasjɔ̃] *nf* assertion

affirmer [afiʀme] *vt* to assert

affligé, e [afliʒe] *adj* distressed, grieved; ~

de (*maladie, tare*) afflicted with

affliger [afliʒe] *vt* (*peiner*) to distress, grieve

affluence [aflyãs] *nf* crowds *pl*; **heures d'~** rush hours; **jours d'~** busiest days

affluent [aflyã] *nm* tributary

affluer [aflye] *vi* (*secours, biens*) to flood in, pour in; (*sang*) to rush, flow

affolant, e [afɔlã, ãt] *adj* frightening

affolement [afɔlmã] *nm* panic

affoler [afɔle] *vt* to throw into a panic; **s'~** *vi* to panic

affranchir [afrãʃiʀ] *vt* to put a stamp *ou* stamps on; (*à la machine*) to frank (*BRIT*), meter (*US*); (*fig*) to free, liberate; **affranchissement** *nm* postage

affréter [afrete] *vt* to charter

affreux, -euse [afrø, øz] *adj* dreadful, awful

affront [afrõ] *nm* affront; **affrontement** *nm* clash, confrontation

affronter [afrõte] *vt* to confront, face

affubler [afyble] (*péj*) *vt*: **~ qn de** to rig *ou* deck sb out in

affût [afy] *nm*: **à l'~ (de)** (*gibier*) lying in wait (for); (*fig*) on the look-out (for)

affûter [afyte] *vt* to sharpen, grind

afin [afɛ̃]: **~ que** *conj* so that, in order that; **~ de faire** in order to do, so as to do

africain, e [afrikɛ̃, ɛn] *adj*, *nm/f* African

Afrique [afrik] *nf*: **l'~** Africa; **l'~ du Sud** South Africa

agacer [agase] *vt* to irritate

âge [ɑʒ] *nm* age; **quel ~ as-tu?** how old are you?; **prendre de l'~** to be getting on (in years); **âgé, e** *adj* old, elderly; **âgé de 10 ans** 10 years old

agence [aʒãs] *nf* agency, office; (*succursale*) branch; **~ de voyages** travel agency; **~ immobilière** estate (*BRIT*) *ou* real estate (*US*) agent's (office)

agencer [aʒãse] *vt* to put together; (*local*) to arrange, lay out

agenda [aʒɛ̃da] *nm* diary

agenouiller [aʒ(ə)nuje]: **s'~** *vi* to kneel (down)

agent [aʒã] *nm* (*aussi*: **~ de police**) policeman; (*ADMIN*) official, officer; **~ d'assurances** insurance broker

agglomération [aglɔmeʀasjɔ̃] *nf* town; built-up area; **l'~ parisienne** the urban area of Paris

aggloméré [aglɔmeʀe] *nm* (*bois*) chipboard

aggraver [agʀave]: **s'~** *vi* to worsen

agile [aʒil] *adj* agile, nimble

agir [aʒiʀ] *vi* to act; **il s'agit de** (*ça traite de*) it is about; (*il est important de*) it's a matter *ou* question of

agitation [aʒitasjɔ̃] *nf* (hustle and) bustle; (*trouble*) agitation, excitement; (*politique*) unrest, agitation

agité, e [aʒite] *adj* fidgety, restless; (*troublé*) agitated, perturbed; (*mer*) rough

agiter [aʒite] *vt* (*bouteille, chiffon*) to shake; (*bras, mains*) to wave; (*préoccuper, exciter*) to perturb; **s'~** *vi* (*enfant, élève*) to fidget

agneau, x [aɲo] *nm* lamb

agonie [agɔni] *nf* mortal agony, death pangs *pl*; (*fig*) death throes *pl*

agrafe [agʀaf] *nf* (*de vêtement*) hook, fastener; (*de bureau*) staple; **agrafer** *vt* to fasten; to staple; **agrafeuse** *nf* stapler

agrandir [agʀãdiʀ] *vt* to enlarge; **s'~** *vi* (*ville, famille*) to grow, expand; (*trou, écart*) to get bigger; **agrandissement** *nm* (*PHOTO*) enlargement

agréable [agʀeabl] *adj* pleasant, nice

agréé, e [agʀee] *adj*: **concessionnaire ~** registered dealer

agréer [agʀee] *vt* (*requête*) to accept; **~ à** to please, suit; **veuillez ~ ...** (*formule épistolaire*) yours faithfully

agrégation [agʀegasjɔ̃] *nf* highest teaching diploma in France; **agrégé, e** *nm/f* holder of the *agrégation*

agrément [agʀemã] *nm* (*accord*) consent, approval; **agrémenter** *vt* to embellish, adorn

agresser [agʀese] *vt* to attack; **agresseur** *nm* aggressor, attacker; (*POL, MIL*) aggressor; **agressif, -ive** *adj* aggressive

agricole [agʀikɔl] *adj* agricultural; **agriculteur** *nm* farmer; **agriculture** *nf* agriculture, farming

agripper [agʀipe] *vt* to grab, clutch; **s'~ à** to cling (on) to, clutch, grip

agroalimentaire [agʀoalimɑ̃tɛʀ] *nm* farm-produce industry

agrumes [agʀym] *nmpl* citrus fruit(s)

aguerrir [ageʀiʀ] *vt* to harden

aguets [agɛ] *nmpl*: **être aux ~** to be on the look out

aguicher [agiʃe] *vt* to entice

ahuri, e [ayʀi] *adj* (*stupéfait*) flabbergasted

ai [ɛ] *vb voir* **avoir**

aide [ɛd] *nm/f* assistant; carer ♦ *nf* assistance, help; (*secours financier*) aid; **à l'~ de** (*avec*) with the help *ou* aid of; **appeler (qn) à l'~** to call for help (from sb); **~ familiale** home help, mother's help; **~ judiciaire** ♦ *nf* legal aid; **~ sociale** ♦ *nf* (*assistance*) state aid; **aide-mémoire** *nm inv* memoranda pages *pl*; (key facts) handbook; **aide-soignant, e** *nm/f* auxiliary nurse

aider [ede] *vt* to help; **s'~ de** (*se servir de*) to use, make use of

aie *etc* [ɛ] *vb voir* **avoir**

aïe [aj] *excl* ouch!

aïeul, e [ajœl] *nm/f* grandparent, grandfather(-mother)

aïeux [ajø] *nmpl* grandparents; (*ancêtres*) forebears, forefathers

aigle [ɛgl] *nm* eagle

aigre [ɛgʀ] *adj* sour, sharp; (*fig*) sharp, cutting; **aigre-doux, -ce** *adj* (*sauce*) sweet and sour; **aigreur** *nf* sourness; sharpness; **aigreurs d'estomac** heartburn *sg*; **aigrir** *vt* (*personne*) to embitter; (*caractère*) to sour

aigu, ë [egy] *adj* (*objet, douleur*) sharp; (*son, voix*) high-pitched, shrill; (*note*) high(-pitched)

aiguille [eguij] *nf* needle; (*de montre*) hand; **~ à tricoter** knitting needle

aiguiller [eguije] *vt* (*orienter*) to direct; **aiguilleur du ciel** *nm* air-traffic controller

aiguillon [eguijɔ̃] *nm* (*d'abeille*) sting; **aiguillonner** *vt* to spur *ou* goad on

aiguiser [egize] *vt* to sharpen; (*fig*) to stimulate; (: *sens*) to excite

ail [aj, o] *nm* garlic

aile [ɛl] *nf* wing; **aileron** *nm* (*de requin*) fin; **ailier** *nm* winger

aille *etc* [aj] *vb voir* **aller**

ailleurs [ajœʀ] *adv* elsewhere, somewhere else; **partout/nulle part ~** everywhere/nowhere else; **d'~** (*du reste*) moreover, besides; **par ~** (*d'autre part*) moreover, furthermore

aimable [ɛmabl] *adj* kind, nice

aimant [ɛmɑ̃] *nm* magnet

aimer [eme] *vt* to love; (*d'amitié, affection, par goût*) to like; (*souhait*): **j'~ais ...** I would like ...; **bien ~ qn/qch** to like sb/sth; **j'~ais mieux faire** I'd much rather do

aine [ɛn] *nf* groin

aîné, e [ene] *adj* elder, older; (*le plus âgé*) eldest, oldest ♦ *nm/f* oldest child *ou* one, oldest boy *ou* son/girl *ou* daughter

ainsi [ɛ̃si] *adv* (*de cette façon*) like this, in this way, thus; (*ce faisant*) thus, so; **~ que** (*comme*) (just) as; (*et aussi*) as well as; **pour ~ dire** so to speak; **et ~ de suite** and so on

aïoli [ajɔli] *nm* garlic mayonnaise

air [ɛʀ] *nm* air; (*mélodie*) tune; (*expression*) look, air; **prendre l'~** to get some (fresh) air; **avoir l'~** (*sembler*) to look, appear; **avoir l'~ de** to look like; **avoir l'~ de faire** to look as though one is doing, appear to be doing; **en l'~** (*promesses*) empty

aisance [ɛzɑ̃s] *nf* ease; (*richesse*) affluence

aise [ɛz] *nf* comfort; **être à l'~** *ou* **à son ~** to be comfortable; (*pas embarrassé*) to be at ease; (*financièrement*) to be comfortably off; **se mettre à l'~** to make o.s. comfortable; **être mal à l'~** to be uncomfortable; (*gêné*) to be ill at ease; **en faire à son ~** to do as one likes; **aisé, e** *adj* easy; (*assez riche*) well-to-do, well-off

aisselle [ɛsɛl] *nf* armpit

ait [ε] *vb voir* **avoir**

ajonc [aʒɔ̃] *nm* gorse *no pl*

ajourner [aʒuʀne] *vt* (*réunion*) to adjourn; (*décision*) to defer, postpone

ajouter [aʒute] *vt* to add

ajusté, e [aʒyste] *adj*: **bien ~** (*robe etc*) close-fitting

ajuster [aʒyste] *vt* (*régler*) to adjust; (*vêtement*) to alter; (*coup de fusil*) to aim; (*cible*) to aim at; (*TECH, gén: adapter*): **~ qch à** to fit sth to

alarme [alaʀm] *nf* alarm; **donner l'~** to give *ou* raise the alarm; **alarmer** *vt* to alarm; **s'alarmer** *vi* to become alarmed; **alarmiste** *adj, nm/f* alarmist

album [albɔm] *nm* album

albumine [albymin] *nf* albumin; **avoir de l'~** to suffer from albuminuria

alcool [alkɔl] *nm*: **l'~** alcohol; **un ~** a spirit, a brandy; **bière sans ~** non-alcoholic *ou* alcohol-free beer; **~ à brûler** methylated spirits (*BRIT*), wood alcohol (*US*); **~ à 90°** surgical spirit; **alcoolique** *adj, nm/f* alcoholic; **alcoolisé, e** *adj* alcoholic; **une boisson non alcoolisée** a soft drink; **alcoolisme** *nm* alcoholism; **alcootest** ® *nm* Breathalyser ®; (*test*) breath-test

aléas [alea] *nmpl* hazards; **aléatoire** *adj* uncertain; (*INFORM*) random

alentour [alɑ̃tuʀ] *adv* around, round about; **~s** *nmpl* (*environs*) surroundings; **aux ~s de** in the vicinity *ou* neighbourhood of, round about; (*temps*) round about

alerte [alεʀt] *adj* agile, nimble; brisk, lively ♦ *nf* alert; warning; **~ à la bombe** bomb scare; **alerter** *vt* to alert

algèbre [alʒεbʀ] *nf* algebra

Alger [alʒe] *n* Algiers

Algérie [alʒeʀi] *nf*: **l'~** Algeria; **algérien, ne** *adj* Algerian ♦ *nm/f*: **Algérien, ne** Algerian

algue [alg] *nf* (*gén*) seaweed *no pl*; (*BOT*) alga

alibi [alibi] *nm* alibi

aliéné, e [aljene] *nm/f* insane person, lunatic (*péj*)

aligner [aliɲe] *vt* to align, line up; (*idées, chiffres*) to string together; (*adapter*): **~ qch sur** to bring sth into alignment with; **s'~** (*soldats etc*) to line up; **s'~ sur** (*POL*) to align o.s. on

aliment [alimɑ̃] *nm* food; **alimentaire** *adj*: **denrées alimentaires** foodstuffs; **alimentation** *nf* (*commerce*) food trade; (*magasin*) grocery store; (*régime*) diet; (*en eau etc, de moteur*) supplying; (*INFORM*) feed; **alimenter** *vt* to feed; (*TECH*): **alimenter (en)** to supply (with); to feed (with); (*fig*) to sustain, keep going

alinéa [alinea] *nm* paragraph

aliter [alite]: **s'~** *vi* to take to one's bed

allaiter [alete] *vt* to (breast-)feed, nurse; (*suj: animal*) to suckle

allant [alɑ̃] *nm* drive, go

alléchant, e [aleʃɑ̃, ɑ̃t] *adj* (*odeur*) mouth-watering; (*offre*) enticing

allécher [aleʃe] *vt*: **~ qn** to make sb's mouth water; to tempt *ou* entice sb

allée [ale] *nf* (*de jardin*) path; (*en ville*) avenue, drive; **~s et venues** comings and goings

allégé, e [aleʒe] *adj* (*yaourt etc*) low-fat

alléger [aleʒe] *vt* (*voiture*) to make lighter; (*chargement*) to lighten; (*souffrance*) to alleviate, soothe

allègre [a(l)lεgʀ] *adj* lively, cheerful

alléguer [a(l)lege] *vt* to put forward (as proof *ou* an excuse)

Allemagne [almaɲ] *nf*: **l'~** Germany; **allemand, e** *adj* German ♦ *nm/f*: **Allemand, e** German ♦ *nm* (*LING*) German

aller [ale] *nm* (*trajet*) outward journey; (*billet: aussi*: **~ simple**) single (*BRIT*) *ou* one-way (*US*) ticket ♦ *vi* (*gén*) to go; **~ à** (*convenir*) to suit; (*suj: forme, pointure etc*) to fit; **~ (bien) avec** (*couleurs, style etc*) to go (well) with; **je vais y ~/me fâcher** I'm going to go/to get angry; **~ voir** to go and see, go to see; **allez!** come on!; **allons!** come now!; **comment allez-vous?**

how are you?; **comment ça va?** how are you?; (*affaires etc*) how are things?; **il va bien/mal** he's well/not well, he's fine/ill; **ça va bien/mal** (*affaires etc*) it's going well/not going well; **~ mieux** to be better; **s'en ~** (*partir*) to be off, go, leave; (*disparaître*) to go away; **~ retour** return journey (*BRIT*), round trip; (*billet*) return (ticket) (*BRIT*), round trip ticket (*US*)

allergique [alɛʀʒik] *adj*: **~ à** allergic to

alliage [aljaʒ] *nm* alloy

alliance [aljɑ̃s] *nf* (*MIL, POL*) alliance; (*bague*) wedding ring

allier [alje] *vt* (*POL, gén*) to ally; (*fig*) to combine; **s'~** to become allies; to combine

allô [alo] *excl* hullo, hallo

allocation [alɔkasjɔ̃] *nf* allowance; **~ (de) chômage** unemployment benefit; **~s familiales** ≃ child benefit

allocution [a(l)lɔkysjɔ̃] *nf* short speech

allonger [alɔ̃ʒe] *vt* to lengthen, make longer; (*étendre: bras, jambe*) to stretch (out); **s'~** *vi* to get longer; (*se coucher*) to lie down, stretch out; **~ le pas** to hasten one's step(s)

allouer [alwe] *vt* to allocate, allot

allumage [alymaʒ] *nm* (*AUTO*) ignition

allume-cigare [alymsigaʀ] *nm inv* cigar lighter

allumer [alyme] *vt* (*lampe, phare, radio*) to put *ou* switch on; (*pièce*) to put *ou* switch the light(s) on in; (*feu*) to light; **s'~** *vi* (*lumière, lampe*) to come *ou* go on

allumette [alymɛt] *nf* match

allure [alyʀ] *nf* (*vitesse*) speed, pace; (*démarche*) walk, (*aspect, air*) look; **avoir de l'~** to have style; **à toute ~** at top speed

allusion [a(l)lyzjɔ̃] *nf* allusion; (*sous-entendu*) hint; **faire ~ à** to allude *ou* refer to; to hint at

---

MOT-CLÉ

alors [alɔʀ] *adv* **1** (*à ce moment-là*) then, at that time; **il habitait alors à Paris** he lived in Paris at that time

2 (*par conséquent*) then; **tu as fini? alors je m'en vais** have you finished? I'm going then; **et alors?** so what?; **alors que** *conj* **1** (*au moment où*) when, as; **il est arrivé alors que je partais** he arrived as I was leaving

2 (*pendant que*) while, when; **alors qu'il était à Paris, il a visité ...** while *ou* when he was in Paris, he visited ...

3 (*tandis que*) whereas, while; **alors que son frère travaillait dur, lui se reposait** while his brother was working hard, HE would rest

---

alouette [alwɛt] *nf* (sky)lark

alourdir [aluʀdiʀ] *vt* to weigh down, make heavy

aloyau [alwajo] *nm* sirloin

Alpes [alp] *nfpl*: **les ~** the Alps

alphabet [alfabɛ] *nm* alphabet; (*livre*) ABC (book); **alphabétique** *adj* alphabetical; **alphabétiser** *vt* to teach to read and write; (*pays*) to eliminate illiteracy in

alpinisme [alpinism] *nm* mountaineering, climbing; **alpiniste** *nm/f* mountaineer, climber

Alsace [alzas] *nf* Alsace; **alsacien, ne** *adj* Alsatian ♦ *nm/f*: **Alsacien, ne** Alsatian

altérer [alteʀe] *vt* (*vérité*) to distort; **s'~** *vi* to deteriorate

alternateur [altɛʀnatœʀ] *nm* alternator

alternatif, -ive [altɛʀnatif, iv] *adj* alternating; **alternative** *nf* (*choix*) alternative; **alternativement** *adv* alternately; **alterner** *vi* to alternate

Altesse [altɛs] *nf* Highness

altitude [altityd] *nf* altitude, height

alto [alto] *nm* (*instrument*) viola

aluminium [alyminjɔm] *nm* aluminium (*BRIT*), aluminum (*US*)

amabilité [amabilite] *nf* kindness

amadouer [amadwe] *vt* to mollify, soothe

amaigrir [amegʀiʀ] *vt* to make thin(ner); **amaigrissant, e** *adj* (*régime*) slimming

amalgame [amalgam] (*péj*) *nm* (strange) mixture

amande [amɑ̃d] *nf* (*de l'amandier*) almond; **amandier** *nm* almond (tree)

amant [amɑ̃] *nm* lover

amarrer [amaʀe] *vt* (*NAVIG*) to moor; (*gén*) to make fast

amas [amɑ] *nm* heap, pile; **amasser** *vt* to amass; **s'amasser** *vi* (*foule*) to gather

amateur [amatœʀ] *nm* amateur; **en ~** (*péj*) amateurishly; **~ de musique/sport** *etc* music/sport *etc* lover

amazone [amazon] *nf*: **en ~** sidesaddle

ambassade [ɑ̃basad] *nf* embassy; **l'~ de France** the French Embassy; **ambassadeur, -drice** *nm/f* ambassador(-dress)

ambiance [ɑ̃bjɑ̃s] *nf* atmosphere

ambiant, e [ɑ̃bjɑ̃, jɑ̃t] *adj* (*air, milieu*) surrounding; (*température*) ambient

ambigu, ë [ɑ̃bigy] *adj* ambiguous

ambitieux, -euse [ɑ̃bisjø, jøz] *adj* ambitious

ambition [ɑ̃bisjɔ̃] *nf* ambition

ambulance [ɑ̃bylɑ̃s] *nf* ambulance; **ambulancier, -ière** *nm/f* ambulance man/woman (*BRIT*), paramedic (*US*)

ambulant, e [ɑ̃bylɑ̃, ɑ̃t] *adj* travelling, itinerant

âme [ɑm] *nf* soul

amélioration [ameljɔʀasjɔ̃] *nf* improvement

améliorer [ameljɔʀe] *vt* to improve; **s'~** *vi* to improve, get better

aménager [amenaʒe] *vt* (*agencer, transformer*) to fit out; to lay out; (: *quartier, territoire*) to develop; (*installer*) to fix up, put in; **ferme aménagée** converted farmhouse

amende [amɑ̃d] *nf* fine; **faire ~ honorable** to make amends

amener [am(ə)ne] *vt* to bring; (*causer*) to bring about; **s'~** *vi* to show up (*fam*), turn up

amenuiser [amənɥize]: **s'~** *vi* (*chances*) to grow slimmer, lessen

amer, amère [amɛʀ] *adj* bitter

américain, e [ameʀikɛ̃, ɛn] *adj* American ♦ *nm/f*: **A~, e** American

Amérique [ameʀik] *nf*: **l'~** America; **l'~ centrale/latine** Central/Latin America; **l'~ du Nord/du Sud** North/South America

amertume [amɛʀtym] *nf* bitterness

ameublement [amœbləmɑ̃] *nm* furnishing; (*meubles*) furniture

ameuter [amøte] *vt* (*peuple*) to rouse

ami, e [ami] *nm/f* friend; (*amant/maîtresse*) boyfriend/girlfriend ♦ *adj*: **pays/groupe ~** friendly country/group

amiable [amjabl]: **à l'~** *adv* (*JUR*) out of court; (*gén*) amicably

amiante [amjɑ̃t] *nm* asbestos

amical, e, -aux [amikal, o] *adj* friendly; **amicalement** *adv* in a friendly way; (*formule épistolaire*) regards

amidon [amidɔ̃] *nm* starch

amincir [amɛ̃siʀ] *vt*: **~ qn** to make sb thinner ou slimmer; (*suj: vêtement*) to make sb look slimmer

amincissant, e [amɛ̃sisɑ̃, ɑ̃t] *adj*: **régime ~** (slimming) diet; **crème ~e** slimming cream

amiral, -aux [amiʀal, o] *nm* admiral

amitié [amitje] *nf* friendship; **prendre en ~** to befriend; **~s, Christèle** best wishes, Christèle; **présenter ses ~s à qn** to send sb one's best wishes

ammoniaque [amɔnjak] *nf* ammonia (water)

amnistie [amnisti] *nf* amnesty

amoindrir [amwɛ̃dʀiʀ] *vt* to reduce

amollir [amɔliʀ] *vt* to soften

amonceler [amɔ̃s(ə)le] *vt* to pile *ou* heap up; **s'~** *vi* to pile *ou* heap up; (*fig*) to accumulate

amont [amɔ̃]: **en ~** *adv* upstream

amorce [amɔʀs] *nf* (*sur un hameçon*) bait; (*explosif*) cap; primer; priming; (*fig: début*) beginning(s), start; **amorcer** *vt* to start

amorphe [amɔʀf] *adj* passive, lifeless

amortir [amɔʀtiʀ] *vt* (*atténuer: choc*) to absorb, cushion; (*bruit, douleur*) to deaden; (*COMM: dette*) to pay off; **~ un achat** to make a purchase pay for itself; **amortisseur** *nm* shock absorber

amour [amuʀ] *nm* love; **faire l'~** to make love; **amouracher: s'amouracher de** (*péj*) *vt* to become infatuated with; **amoureux, -euse** *adj* (*regard, tempérament*) amorous; (*vie, problèmes*) love *cpd*; (*personne*): **amoureux (de qn)** in love (with sb) ♦ *nmpl* courting couple(s); **amour-propre** *nm* self-esteem, pride

amovible [amɔvibl] *adj* removable, detachable

ampère [ɑ̃pɛʀ] *nm* amp(ere)

amphithéâtre [ɑ̃fiteɑtʀ] *nm* amphitheatre; (*d'université*) lecture hall *ou* theatre

ample [ɑ̃pl] *adj* (*vêtement*) roomy, ample; (*gestes, mouvement*) broad; (*ressources*) ample; **amplement** *adv*: **c'est amplement suffisant** that's more than enough; **ampleur** *nf* (*de dégâts, problème*) extent

amplificateur [ɑ̃plifikatœʀ] *nm* amplifier

amplifier [ɑ̃plifje] *vt* (*fig*) to expand, increase

ampoule [ɑ̃pul] *nf* (*électrique*) bulb; (*de médicament*) phial; (*aux mains, pieds*) blister; **ampoulé, e** (*péj*) *adj* pompous, bombastic

amputer [ɑ̃pyte] *vt* (*MÉD*) to amputate; (*fig*) to cut *ou* reduce drastically

amusant, e [amyzɑ̃, ɑ̃t] *adj* (*divertissant, spirituel*) entertaining, amusing; (*comique*) funny, amusing

amuse-gueule [amyzgœl] *nm inv* appetizer, snack

amusement [amyzmɑ̃] *nm* (*divertissement*) amusement; (*jeu etc*) pastime, diversion

amuser [amyze] *vt* (*divertir*) to entertain, amuse; (*égayer, faire rire*) to amuse; **s'~** *vi* (*jouer*) to play; (*se divertir*) to enjoy o.s., have fun; (*fig*) to mess around

amygdale [amidal] *nf* tonsil

an [ɑ̃] *nm* year; **avoir quinze ~s** to be fifteen (years old); **le jour de l'~, le premier de l'~, le nouvel ~** New Year's Day

analogique [analɔʒik] *adj* (*INFORM, montre*) analog

analogue [analɔg] *adj*: **~ (à)** analogous (to), similar (to)

analphabète [analfabɛt] *nm/f* illiterate

analyse [analiz] *nf* analysis; (*MÉD*) test; **analyser** *vt* to analyse; to test

ananas [anana(s)] *nm* pineapple

anarchie [anaʀʃi] *nf* anarchy

anatomie [anatɔmi] *nf* anatomy

ancêtre [ɑ̃sɛtʀ] *nm/f* ancestor

anchois [ɑ̃ʃwa] *nm* anchovy

ancien, ne [ɑ̃sjɛ̃, jɛn] *adj* old; (*de jadis, de l'antiquité*) ancient; (*précédent, ex-*) former, old; (*par l'expérience*) senior ♦ *nm/f* (*dans une tribu*) elder; **~-combattant** ♦ *nm* war veteran; **anciennement** *adv* formerly; **ancienneté** *nf* (*ADMIN*) (length of) service; (*privilèges obtenus*) seniority

ancre [ɑ̃kʀ] *nf* anchor; **jeter/lever l'~** to cast/weigh anchor; **ancrer** *vt* (*CONSTR: câble etc*) to anchor; (*fig*) to fix firmly

Andorre [ɑ̃dɔʀ] *nf* Andorra

andouille [ɑ̃duj] *nf* (*CULIN*) *sausage made of chitterlings*; (*fam*) clot, nit

âne [ɑn] *nm* donkey, ass; (*péj*) dunce

anéantir [aneɑ̃tiʀ] *vt* to annihilate, wipe out; (*fig*) to obliterate, destroy

anémie [anemi] *nf* anaemia; **anémique** *adj* anaemic

ânerie [ɑnʀi] *nf* stupidity; (*parole etc*) stupid *ou* idiotic comment *etc*

anesthésie [anɛstezi] *nf* anaesthesia; **faire une ~ locale/générale à qn** to give sb a local/general anaesthetic

ange [ɑ̃ʒ] *nm* angel; **être aux ~s** to be over the moon

angélus [ɑ̃ʒelys] *nm* angelus; (*cloches*) evening bells *pl*

angine [ɑ̃ʒin] *nf* throat infection; **~ de poitrine** angina

anglais, e [ɑ̃glɛ, ɛz] *adj* English ♦ *nm/f*: **A~, e** Englishman(-woman) ♦ *nm* (*LING*) English; **les A~** the English; **filer à l'~e** to take French leave

angle [ɑ̃gl] *nm* angle; (*coin*) corner; **~ droit** right angle

Angleterre [ɑ̃glətɛʀ] *nf*: **l'~** England

anglo... [ɑ̃glɔ] *préfixe* Anglo-, anglo(-);

anglophone *adj* English-speaking

angoisse [ãgwas] *nf* anguish, distress; **angoissé, e** *adj* (*personne*) distressed; **angoisser** *vt* to harrow, cause anguish to ♦ *vi* to worry, fret

anguille [ãgij] *nf* eel

anicroche [anikʀɔʃ] *nf* hitch, snag

animal, e, -aux [animal, o] *adj, nm* animal

animateur, -trice [animatœʀ, tʀis] *nm/f* (*de télévision*) host; (*de groupe*) leader, organizer

animation [animasjɔ̃] *nf* (*voir animé*) busyness; liveliness; (*CINÉMA: technique*) animation; **~s culturelles** cultural activities

animé, e [anime] *adj* (*lieu*) busy, lively; (*conversation, réunion*) lively, animated

animer [anime] *vt* (*ville, soirée*) to liven up; (*mener*) to lead; **s'~** *vi* to liven up

anis [ani(s)] *nm* (*CULIN*) aniseed; (*BOT*) anise

ankyloser [ãkiloze]: **s'~** *vi* to get stiff

anneau, x [ano] *nm* (*de rideau, bague*) ring; (*de chaîne*) link

année [ane] *nf* year

annexe [aneks] *adj* (*problème*) related; (*document*) appended; (*salle*) adjoining ♦ *nf* (*bâtiment*) annex(e); (*jointe à une lettre*) enclosure

anniversaire [anivɛʀsɛʀ] *nm* birthday; (*d'un événement, bâtiment*) anniversary

annonce [anɔ̃s] *nf* announcement; (*signe, indice*) sign; (*aussi: ~ publicitaire*) advertisement; **les petites ~s** the classified advertisements, the small ads

annoncer [anɔ̃se] *vt* to announce; (*être le signe de*) to herald; **s'~ bien/difficile** to look promising/difficult; **annonceur, -euse** *nm/f* (*publicitaire*) advertiser; (*TV, RADIO: speaker*) speaker

annuaire [anɥɛʀ] *nm* yearbook, annual; **~ téléphonique** (telephone) directory, phone book

annuel, le [anɥɛl] *adj* annual, yearly

annuité [anɥite] *nf* annual instalment

annulation [anylasjɔ̃] *nf* cancellation

annuler [anyle] *vt* (*rendez-vous, voyage*) to cancel, call off; (*jugement*) to quash (*BRIT*), repeal (*US*); (*MATH, PHYSIQUE*) to cancel out

anodin, e [anɔdɛ̃, in] *adj* (*blessure*) harmless; (*détail*) insignificant, trivial

anonymat [anɔnima] *nm* anonymity

anonyme [anɔnim] *adj* anonymous; (*fig*) impersonal

ANPE *sigle f* (= *Agence nationale pour l'emploi*) national employment agency

anorexie [anɔʀɛksi] *nf* anorexia

anormal, e, -aux [anɔʀmal, o] *adj* abnormal

anse [ãs] *nf* (*de panier, tasse*) handle

antan [ãtã]: **d'~** *adj* of long ago

antarctique [ãtaʀktik] *adj* Antarctic ♦ *nm*: **l'A~** the Antarctic

antécédents [ãtesedã] *nmpl* (*MÉD etc*) past history *sg*

antenne [ãtɛn] *nf* (*de radio*) aerial; (*d'insecte*) antenna, feeler; (*poste avancé*) outpost; (*petite succursale*) sub-branch; **passer à l'~** to go on the air

antérieur, e [ãteʀjœʀ] *adj* (*d'avant*) previous, earlier; (*de devant*) front

anti... [ãti] *préfixe* anti...; **antialcoolique** *adj* anti-alcohol; **antlatomlque** *adj*: **abri antiatomique** fallout shelter; **antibiotique** *nm* antibiotic; **antibrouillard** *adj*: **phare antibrouillard** fog lamp (*BRIT*) *ou* light (*US*)

anticipation [ãtisipasjɔ̃] *nf*: **livre/film d'~** science fiction book/film

anticipé, e [ãtisipe] *adj*: **avec mes remerciements ~s** thanking you in advance *ou* anticipation

anticiper [ãtisipe] *vt* (*événement, coup*) to anticipate, foresee

anti...: anticonceptionnel, le *adj* contraceptive; **anticorps** *nm* antibody; **antidépresseur** *nm* antidepressant; **antidote** *nm* antidote; **antigel** *nm* antifreeze; **antihistaminique** *nm* antihistamine

antillais, e [ãtijɛ, ɛz] *adj* West Indian, Caribbean ♦ *nm/f*: **A~, e** West Indian, Caribbean

Antilles [ãtij] *nfpl*: **les ~** the West Indies

antilope [ɑ̃tilɔp] *nf* antelope
anti...: antimite(s) *adj*, *nm*: **(produit)
antimite(s)** mothproofer; moth repellent;
antipathique *adj* unpleasant, disagreeable; **antipelliculaire** *adj* anti-dandruff
antipodes [ɑ̃tipɔd] *nmpl* (*fig*): **être aux ~
de** to be the opposite extreme of
antiquaire [ɑ̃tikɛʀ] *nm/f* antique dealer
antique [ɑ̃tik] *adj* antique; (*très vieux*) ancient, antiquated; **antiquité** *nf* (*objet*) antique; **l'Antiquité** Antiquity; **magasin
d'antiquités** antique shop
anti...: antirabique *adj* rabies *cpd*; **antirouille** *adj inv* anti-rust *cpd*; **antisémite**
adj anti-Semitic; **antiseptique** *adj*, *nm*
antiseptic; **antivol** *adj*, *nm*: **(dispositif)
antivol** anti-theft device
antre [ɑ̃tʀ] *nm* den, lair
anxiété [ɑ̃ksjete] *nf* anxiety
anxieux, -euse [ɑ̃ksjø, jøz] *adj* anxious,
worried
AOC *sigle f* (= *appellation d'origine contrôlée*)
label guaranteeing the quality of wine

AOC

i AOC *is the highest French wine classification. It indicates that the wine
meets strict requirements concerning the
vineyard of origin, the type of vine grown,
the method of production, and the volume
of alcohol present.*

août [u(t)] *nm* August
apaiser [apeze] *vt* (*colère, douleur*) to
soothe; (*personne*) to calm (down), pacify;
s'~ *vi* (*tempête, bruit*) to die down, subside; (*personne*) to calm down
apanage [apanaʒ] *nm*: **être l'~ de** to be
the privilege *ou* prerogative of
aparté [aparte] *nm* (*entretien*) private conversation; **en ~** in an aside
apathique [apatik] *adj* apathetic
apatride [apatʀid] *nm/f* stateless person
apercevoir [apɛʀsəvwaʀ] *vt* to see; **s'~ de**
vt to notice; **s'~ que** to notice that
aperçu [apɛʀsy] *nm* (*vue d'ensemble*) general survey

apéritif [aperitif] *nm* (*boisson*) aperitif; (*réunion*) drinks *pl*
à-peu-près [apøpʀɛ] (*péj*) *nm inv* vague
approximation
apeuré, e [apœʀe] *adj* frightened, scared
aphte [aft] *nm* mouth ulcer
apiculture [apikyltyʀ] *nf* beekeeping, apiculture
apitoyer [apitwaje] *vt* to move to pity; **s'~
(sur)** to feel pity (for)
aplanir [aplaniʀ] *vt* to level; (*fig*) to
smooth away, iron out
aplatir [aplatiʀ] *vt* to flatten; **s'~** *vi* to become flatter; (*écrasé*) to be flattened; **s'~
devant qn** (*fig: s'humilier*) to crawl to sb
aplomb [aplɔ̃] *nm* (*équilibre*) balance, equilibrium; (*fig*) self-assurance; nerve; **d'~**
steady
apogée [apɔʒe] *nm* (*fig*) peak, apogee
apologie [apɔlɔʒi] *nf* vindication, praise
a posteriori [apɔsteʀjɔʀi] *adv* after the
event
apostrophe [apɔstʀɔf] *nf* (*signe*) apostrophe
apostropher [apɔstʀɔfe] *vt* (*interpeller*) to
shout at, address sharply
apothéose [apɔteoz] *nf* pinnacle (of
achievement); (*MUS*) grand finale
apôtre [apotʀ] *nm* apostle
apparaître [apaʀɛtʀ] *vi* to appear
apparat [apaʀa] *nm*: **tenue d'~** ceremonial dress
appareil [apaʀɛj] *nm* (*outil, machine*) piece
of apparatus, device; (*électrique, ménager*)
appliance; (*avion*) (aero)plane, aircraft *inv*;
(*téléphonique*) phone; (*dentier*) brace (*BRIT*),
braces (*US*); **"qui est à l'~?"** "who's
speaking?"; **dans le plus simple ~** in
one's birthday suit; **appareiller** *vi* (*NAVIG*) to cast off, get under way ♦ *vt* (*assortir*) to match up; **appareil(-photo)** *nm*
camera
apparemment [apaʀamɑ̃] *adv* apparently
apparence [apaʀɑ̃s] *nf* appearance; **en ~**
apparently

apparent, e [aparã, ãt] *adj* visible; (*évident*) obvious; (*superficiel*) apparent

apparenté, e [aparãte] *adj*: ~ **à** related to; (*fig*) similar to

apparition [aparisjɔ̃] *nf* appearance; (*surnaturelle*) apparition

appartement [apartəmã] *nm* flat (*BRIT*), apartment (*US*)

appartenir [apartənir]: ~ **à** *vt* to belong to; **il lui appartient de** it is his duty to

apparu, e [apary] *pp de* **apparaître**

appât [apa] *nm* (*PÊCHE*) bait; (*fig*) lure, bait; **appâter** *vt* to lure

appauvrir [apovrir] *vt* to impoverish

appel [apɛl] *nm* call; (*nominal*) roll call; (: *SCOL*) register; (*MIL: recrutement*) call-up; **faire ~ à** (*invoquer*) to appeal to; (*avoir recours à*) to call on; (*nécessiter*) to call for, require; **faire ~** (*JUR*) to appeal; **faire l'~** to call the register; to call the register; **sans ~** (*fig*) final, irrevocable; **~ d'offres** (*COMM*) invitation to tender; **faire un ~ de phares** to flash one's headlights; **~ (téléphonique)** (tele)phone call

appelé [ap(ə)le] *nm* (*MIL*) conscript

appeler [ap(ə)le] *vt* to call; (*faire venir: médecin etc*) to call, send for; **s'~** *vi*: **elle s'appelle Gabrielle** her name is Gabrielle, she's called Gabrielle; **comment ça s'appelle?** what is it called?; **être appelé à** (*fig*) to be destined to

appendice [apɛ̃dis] *nm* appendix; **appendicite** *nf* appendicitis

appentis [apãti] *nm* lean-to

appesantir [apəzãtir]: **s'~** *vi* to grow heavier; **s'~ sur** (*fig*) to dwell on

appétissant, e [apetisã, ãt] *adj* appetizing, mouth-watering

appétit [apeti] *nm* appetite; **bon ~!** enjoy your meal!

applaudir [aplodir] *vt* to applaud ♦ *vi* to applaud, clap; **applaudissements** *nmpl* applause *sg*, clapping *sg*

application [aplikasjɔ̃] *nf* application

applique [aplik] *nf* wall lamp

appliquer [aplike] *vt* to apply; (*loi*) to enforce; **s'~** *vi* (*élève etc*) to apply o.s.; **s'~ à** to apply to

appoint [apwɛ̃] *nm* (*extra*) contribution *ou* help; **chauffage d'~** extra heating

appointements [apwɛ̃tmã] *nmpl* salary *sg*

apport [apɔr] *nm* (*approvisionnement*) supply; (*contribution*) contribution

apporter [apɔrte] *vt* to bring

apposer [apoze] *vt* (*signature*) to affix

appréciable [apresjabl] *adj* appreciable

apprécier [apresje] *vt* to appreciate; (*évaluer*) to estimate, assess

appréhender [apreãde] *vt* (*craindre*) to dread; (*arrêter*) to apprehend; **appréhension** *nf* apprehension, anxiety

apprendre [aprãdr] *vt* to learn; (*événement, résultats*) to learn of, hear of; **~ qch à qn** (*informer*) to tell sb (of) sth; (*enseigner*) to teach sb sth; **~ à faire qch** to learn to do sth; **~ à qn à faire qch** to teach sb to do sth; **apprenti, e** *nm/f* apprentice; **apprentissage** *nm* learning; (*COMM, SCOL: période*) apprenticeship

apprêté, e [aprete] *adj* (*fig*) affected

apprêter [aprete] *vt*: **s'~ à faire qch** to get ready to do sth

appris, e [apri, iz] *pp de* **apprendre**

apprivoiser [aprivwaze] *vt* to tame

approbation [aprɔbasjɔ̃] *nf* approval

approchant, e [aprɔʃã, ãt] *adj* similar; **quelque chose d'~** something like that

approche [aprɔʃ] *nf* approach

approcher [aprɔʃe] *vi* to approach, come near ♦ *vt* to approach; (*rapprocher*): **~ qch (de qch)** to bring *ou* put sth near (to sth); **s'~ de** *vi* to approach, go *ou* come near to; **~ de** (*lieu, but*) to draw near to; (*quantité, moment*) to approach

approfondir [aprɔfɔ̃dir] *vt* to deepen; (*question*) to go further into

approprié, e [aprɔprije] *adj*: **~ (à)** appropriate (to), suited to

approprier [aprɔprije]: **s'~** *vt* to appropriate, take over

approuver [apruve] *vt* to agree with;

(*trouver louable*) to approve of

approvisionner [apʀɔvizjɔne] *vt* to supply; (*compte bancaire*) to pay funds into; **s'~ en** to stock up with

approximatif, -ive [apʀɔksimatif, iv] *adj* approximate, rough; (*termes*) vague

appt *abr* = **appartement**

appui [apɥi] *nm* support; **prendre ~ sur** to lean on; (*objet*) to rest on; **l'~ de la fenêtre** the windowsill, the window ledge; **appui(e)-tête** *nm inv* headrest

appuyer [apɥije] *vt* (*poser*): **~ qch sur/contre** to lean *ou* rest sth on/against; (*soutenir: personne, demande*) to support, back (up) ♦ *vi*: **~ sur** (*bouton, frein*) to press, push; (*mot, détail*) to stress, emphasize; **s'~ sur** to lean on; (*fig: compter sur*) to rely on

âpre [ɑpʀ] *adj* acrid, pungent; **~ au gain** grasping

après [apʀe] *prép* after ♦ *adv* afterwards; **2 heures ~** 2 hours later; **~ qu'il est** *ou* **soit parti** after he left; **~ avoir fait** after having done; **d'~** (*selon*) according to; **~ coup** after the event, afterwards; **~ tout** (*au fond*) after all; **et (puis) ~?** so what?; **après-demain** *adv* the day after tomorrow; **après-guerre** *nm* post-war years *pl*; **après-midi** *nm ou nf inv* afternoon; **après-rasage** *nm inv* aftershave; **après-shampooing** *nm inv* conditioner; **après-ski** *nm inv* snow boot

à-propos [apʀopo] *nm* (*d'une remarque*) aptness; **faire preuve d'~-~** to show presence of mind

apte [apt] *adj* capable; (*MIL*) fit

aquarelle [akwaʀɛl] *nf* watercolour

aquarium [akwaʀjɔm] *nm* aquarium

arabe [aʀab] *adj* Arabic; (*désert, cheval*) Arabian; (*nation, peuple*) Arab ♦ *nm/f*: **A~** Arab ♦ *nm* (*LING*) Arabic

Arabie [aʀabi] *nf*: **l'~ (Saoudite)** Saudi Arabia

arachide [aʀaʃid] *nf* (*plante*) groundnut (plant); (*graine*) peanut, groundnut

araignée [aʀeɲe] *nf* spider

arbitraire [aʀbitʀɛʀ] *adj* arbitrary

arbitre [aʀbitʀ] *nm* (*SPORT*) referee; (: *TENNIS, CRICKET*) umpire; (*fig*) arbiter, judge; (*JUR*) arbitrator; **arbitrer** *vt* to referee; to umpire; to arbitrate

arborer [aʀbɔʀe] *vt* to bear, display

arbre [aʀbʀ] *nm* tree; (*TECH*) shaft; **~ généalogique** family tree

arbuste [aʀbyst] *nm* small shrub

arc [aʀk] *nm* (*arme*) bow; (*GÉOM*) arc; (*ARCHIT*) arch; **en ~ de cercle** semi-circular

arcade [aʀkad] *nf* arch(way); **~s** *nfpl* (*série*) arcade *sg*, arches

arcanes [aʀkan] *nmpl* mysteries

arc-boutant [aʀkbutɑ̃] *nm* flying buttress

arceau, x [aʀso] *nm* (*métallique etc*) hoop

arc-en-ciel [aʀkɑ̃sjɛl] *nm* rainbow

arche [aʀʃ] *nf* arch; **~ de Noé** Noah's Ark

archéologie [aʀkeɔlɔʒi] *nf* arch(a)eology; **archéologue** *nm/f* arch(a)eologist

archet [aʀʃe] *nm* bow

archevêque [aʀʃəvɛk] *nm* archbishop

archi... [aʀʃi] (*fam*) *préfixe* tremendously; **archicomble** (*fam*) *adj* chock-a-block; **archiconnu, e** (*fam*) *adj* enormously well-known

archipel [aʀʃipɛl] *nm* archipelago

architecte [aʀʃitɛkt] *nm* architect

architecture [aʀʃitɛktyʀ] *nf* architecture

archives [aʀʃiv] *nfpl* (*collection*) archives

arctique [aʀktik] *adj* Arctic ♦ *nm*: **l'A~** the Arctic

ardemment [aʀdamɑ̃] *adv* ardently, fervently

ardent, e [aʀdɑ̃, ɑ̃t] *adj* (*soleil*) blazing; (*amour*) ardent, passionate; (*prière*) fervent

ardeur [aʀdœʀ] *nf* ardour (*BRIT*), ardor (*US*); (*du soleil*) heat

ardoise [aʀdwaz] *nf* slate

ardu, e [aʀdy] *adj* (*travail*) arduous; (*problème*) difficult

arène [aʀɛn] *nf* arena; **~s** *nfpl* (*amphithéâtre*) bull-ring *sg*

arête [aʀɛt] *nf* (*de poisson*) bone; (*d'une montagne*) ridge

argent [aʀʒɑ̃] *nm* (*métal*) silver; (*monnaie*)

money; **~ de poche** pocket money; **~ liquide** ready money, (ready) cash; **argenté, e** *adj* (*couleur*) silver, silvery; **en métal argenté** silver-plated; **argenterie** *nf* silverware

argentin, e [aʀʒɑ̃tɛ̃, in] *adj* Argentinian, Argentine

Argentine [aʀʒɑ̃tin] *nf*: **l'~** Argentina, the Argentine

argile [aʀʒil] *nf* clay

argot [aʀɡo] *nm* slang; **argotique** *adj* slang *cpd*; (*très familier*) slangy

argument [aʀɡymɑ̃] *nm* argument

argumentaire [aʀɡymɑ̃tɛʀ] *nm* sales leaflet

argumenter [aʀɡymɑ̃te] *vi* to argue

argus [aʀɡys] *nm* guide to second-hand car etc prices

aride [aʀid] *adj* arid

aristocratie [aʀistɔkʀasi] *nf* aristocracy; **aristocratique** *adj* aristocratic

arithmétique [aʀitmetik] *adj* arithmetic(al) ♦ *nf* arithmetic

armateur [aʀmatœʀ] *nm* shipowner

armature [aʀmatyʀ] *nf* framework; (*de tente etc*) frame; **soutien-gorge à/sans ~** underwired/unwired bra

arme [aʀm] *nf* weapon; **~s** *nfpl* (~*ment*) weapons, arms; (*blason*) (coat of) arms; **~ à feu** firearm

armée [aʀme] *nf* army; **~ de l'air** Air Force; **~ de terre** Army

armement [aʀməmɑ̃] *nm* (*matériel*) arms *pl*, weapons *pl*

armer [aʀme] *vt* to arm; (*arme à feu*) to cock; (*appareil-photo*) to wind on; **~ qch de** to reinforce sth with; **s'~ de** to arm o.s. with

armistice [aʀmistis] *nm* armistice; **l'A~** ≈ Remembrance (*BRIT*) *ou* Veterans (*US*) Day

armoire [aʀmwaʀ] *nf* (tall) cupboard; (*penderie*) wardrobe (*BRIT*), closet (*US*)

armoiries [aʀmwaʀi] *nfpl* coat *sg* of arms

armure [aʀmyʀ] *nf* armour *no pl*, suit of armour; **armurier** *nm* gunsmith

arnaque [aʀnak] (*fam*) *nf* swindling; **c'est de l'~** it's a rip-off; **arnaquer** (*fam*) *vt* to swindle

aromates [aʀɔmat] *nmpl* seasoning *sg*, herbs (and spices)

aromathérapie [aʀɔmateʀapi] *nf* aromatherapy

aromatisé, e [aʀɔmatize] *adj* flavoured

arôme [aʀom] *nm* aroma

arpenter [aʀpɑ̃te] *vt* (*salle, couloir*) to pace up and down

arpenteur [aʀpɑ̃tœʀ] *nm* surveyor

arqué, e [aʀke] *adj* arched; (*jambes*) bandy

arrache-pied [aʀaʃpje]: **d'~~** *adv* relentlessly

arracher [aʀaʃe] *vt* to pull out; (*page etc*) to tear off, tear out; (*légumes, herbe*) to pull up; (*bras etc*) to tear off; **s'~** *vt* (*article recherché*) to fight over; **~ qch à qn** to snatch sth from sb; (*fig*) to wring sth out of sb

arraisonner [aʀɛzɔne] *vt* (*bateau*) to board and search

arrangeant, e [aʀɑ̃ʒɑ̃, ɑ̃t] *adj* accommodating, obliging

arrangement [aʀɑ̃ʒmɑ̃] *nm* agreement, arrangement

arranger [aʀɑ̃ʒe] *vt* (*gén*) to arrange; (*réparer*) to fix, put right; (*régler: différend*) to settle, sort out; (*convenir à*) to suit, be convenient for; **s'~** *vi* (*se mettre d'accord*) to come to an agreement; **je vais m'~** I'll manage; **ça va s'~** it'll sort itself out

arrestation [aʀɛstasjɔ̃] *nf* arrest

arrêt [aʀɛ] *nm* stopping; (*de bus etc*) stop; (*JUR*) judgment, decision; **à l'~** stationary; **tomber en ~ devant** to stop short in front of; **sans ~** (*sans interruption*) nonstop; (*très fréquemment*) continually; **~ de travail** stoppage (of work); **~ maladie** sick leave

arrêté [aʀete] *nm* order, decree

arrêter [aʀete] *vt* to stop; (*chauffage etc*) to turn off, switch off; (*fixer: date etc*) to appoint, decide on; (*criminel, suspect*) to arrest; **s'~** *vi* to stop; **~ de faire** to stop

doing
arrhes [aʀ] *nfpl* deposit *sg*
arrière [aʀjɛʀ] *nm* back; (SPORT) fullback
♦ *adj inv*: **siège/roue ~** back *ou* rear
seat/wheel; **à l'~** behind, at the back; **en
~** behind; (*regarder*) back, behind; (*tomber, aller*) backwards; **arriéré, e** *adj* (*péj*)
backward ♦ *nm* (*d'argent*) arrears *pl*;
arrière-goût *nm* aftertaste; **arrière-
grand-mère** *nf* great-grandmother;
arrière-grand-père *nm* great-grand-
father; **arrière-pays** *nm inv* hinterland;
arrière-pensée *nf* ulterior motive; mental reservation; **arrière-plan** *nm* background; **arrière-saison** *nf* late autumn;
arrière-train *nm* hindquarters *pl*
arrimer [aʀime] *vt* to secure; (*cargaison*) to
stow
arrivage [aʀivaʒ] *nm* consignment
arrivée [aʀive] *nf* arrival; (*ligne d'~*) finish
arriver [aʀive] *vi* to arrive; (*survenir*) to
happen, occur; **il arrive à Paris à 8h** he
gets to *ou* arrives in Paris at 8; **~ à** (*atteindre*) to reach; **~ à faire qch** to succeed
in doing sth; **en ~ à** (*finir par*) to come to;
il arrive que it happens that; **il lui arrive
de faire** he sometimes does; **arriviste**
nm/f go-getter
arrobase [aʀɔbaz] *nf* (INFORM) @, 'at' sign
arrogance [aʀɔgɑ̃s] *nf* arrogance
arrogant, e [aʀɔgɑ̃, ɑ̃t] *adj* arrogant
arrondir [aʀɔ̃diʀ] *vt* (*forme, objet*) to
round; (*somme*) to round off
arrondissement [aʀɔ̃dismɑ̃] *nm* (ADMIN)
≈ district
arroser [aʀoze] *vt* to water; (*victoire*) to celebrate (over a drink); (CULIN) to baste;
arrosoir *nm* watering can
arsenal, -aux [aʀsənal, o] *nm* (NAVIG) naval dockyard; (MIL) arsenal; (*fig*) gear
art [aʀ] *nm* art
artère [aʀtɛʀ] *nf* (ANAT) artery; (*rue*) main
road
arthrite [aʀtʀit] *nf* arthritis
artichaut [aʀtiʃo] *nm* artichoke
article [aʀtikl] *nm* article; (COMM) item, ar-

ticle; **à l'~ de la mort** at the point of
death; **~s de luxe** luxury goods
articulation [aʀtikylasjɔ̃] *nf* articulation;
(ANAT) joint
articuler [aʀtikyle] *vt* to articulate
artifice [aʀtifis] *nm* device, trick
artificiel, le [aʀtifisjɛl] *adj* artificial
artisan [aʀtizɑ̃] *nm* artisan, (self-employed)
craftsman; **artisanal, e, -aux** *adj* of *ou*
made by craftsmen; (*péj*) cottage industry
cpd; **de fabrication artisanale** home-
made; **artisanat** *nm* arts and crafts *pl*
artiste [aʀtist] *nm/f* artist; (*de variétés*) entertainer; (*musicien etc*) performer; **artistique** *adj* artistic
as[1] [a] *vb voir* **avoir**
as[2] [ɑs] *nm* ace
ascendance [asɑ̃dɑ̃s] *nf* (*origine*) ancestry
ascendant, e [asɑ̃dɑ̃, ɑ̃t] *adj* upward
♦ *nm* influence
ascenseur [asɑ̃sœʀ] *nm* lift (BRIT), elevator
(US)
ascension [asɑ̃sjɔ̃] *nf* ascent; (*de montagne*) climb; **l'A~** (REL) the Ascension

| Ascension |

i **La fête de l'Ascension** *is a French
public holiday, usually in May. As it
falls on a Thursday, many people take Friday off work and enjoy a long weekend;
see also* **faire le pont**.

aseptisé, e (*péj*) *adj* sanitized
aseptiser [asɛptize] *vt* (*ustensile*) to sterilize; (*plaie*) to disinfect
asiatique [azjatik] *adj* Asiatic, Asian
♦ *nm/f*: **A~** Asian
Asie [azi] *nf*: **l'~** Asia
asile [azil] *nm* (*refuge*) refuge, sanctuary;
(POL): **droit d'~** (political) asylum; **~ (de
vieillards)** old people's home
aspect [aspɛ] *nm* appearance, look; (*fig*)
aspect, side; **à l'~ de** at the sight of
asperge [aspɛʀʒ] *nf* asparagus *no pl*
asperger [aspɛʀʒe] *vt* to spray, sprinkle
aspérité [asperite] *nf* bump, protruding

bit (of rock *etc*)

asphalte [asfalt] *nm* asphalt

asphyxier [asfiksje] *vt* to suffocate, asphyxiate; (*fig*) to stifle

aspirateur [aspiʀatœʀ] *nm* vacuum cleaner; **passer l'~** to vacuum

aspirer [aspiʀe] *vt* (*air*) to inhale; (*liquide*) to suck (up); (*suj: appareil*) to suck up; **~ à** to aspire to

aspirine [aspiʀin] *nf* aspirin

assagir [asaʒiʀ]: **s'~** *vi* to quieten down, settle down

assaillir [asajiʀ] *vt* to assail, attack

assainir [aseniʀ] *vt* (*logements*) to clean up; (*eau, air*) to purify

assaisonnement [asɛzɔnmɑ̃] *nm* seasoning

assaisonner [asɛzɔne] *vt* to season

assassin [asasɛ̃] *nm* murderer; assassin; **assassiner** *vt* to murder; (*esp POL*) to assassinate

assaut [aso] *nm* assault, attack; **prendre d'~** to storm, assault; **donner l'~** to attack

assécher [aseʃe] *vt* to drain

assemblage [asɑ̃blaʒ] *nm* (*action*) assembling; (*de couleurs, choses*) collection

assemblée [asɑ̃ble] *nf* (*réunion*) meeting; (*assistance*) gathering; (*POL*) assembly

assembler [asɑ̃ble] *vt* (*joindre, monter*) to assemble, put together; (*amasser*) to gather (together), collect (together); **s'~** *vi* to gather

assener, asséner [asene] *vt*: **~ un coup à qn** to deal sb a blow

assentiment [asɑ̃timɑ̃] *nm* assent, consent

asseoir [aswaʀ] *vt* (*malade, bébé*) to sit up; (*personne debout*) to sit down; (*autorité, réputation*) to establish; **s'~** *vi* to sit (o.s.) down

assermenté, e [asɛʀmɑ̃te] *adj* sworn, on oath

asservir [asɛʀviʀ] *vt* to subjugate, enslave

assez [ase] *adv* (*suffisamment*) enough, sufficiently; (*passablement*) rather, quite,

fairly; **~ de pain/livres** enough *ou* sufficient bread/books; **vous en avez ~?** have you got enough?; **j'en ai ~!** I've had enough!

assidu, e [asidy] *adj* (*appliqué*) assiduous, painstaking; (*ponctuel*) regular

assied *etc* [asje] *vb voir* **asseoir**

assiéger [asjeʒe] *vt* to besiege

assiérai *etc* [asjeʀe] *vb voir* **asseoir**

assiette [asjɛt] *nf* plate; (*contenu*) plate(ful); **il n'est pas dans son ~** he's not feeling quite himself; **~ à dessert** dessert plate; **~ anglaise** assorted cold meats; **~ creuse** (soup) dish, soup plate; **~ plate** (dinner) plate

assigner [asiɲe] *vt*: **~ qch à** (*poste, part, travail*) to assign sth to

assimiler [asimile] *vt* to assimilate, absorb; (*comparer*): **~ qch/qn à** to liken *ou* compare sth/sb to

assis, e [asi, iz] *pp de* **asseoir** ♦ *adj* sitting (down), seated; **~e** *nf* (*fig*) basis, foundation; **assises** *nfpl* (*JUR*) assizes

assistance [asistɑ̃s] *nf* (*public*) audience; (*aide*) assistance; **enfant de l'A~ publique** child in care

assistant, e [asistɑ̃, ɑ̃t] *nm/f* assistant; (*d'université*) probationary lecturer; **~(e) social(e)** social worker

assisté, e [asiste] *adj* (*AUTO*) power assisted; **~ par ordinateur** computer-assisted

assister [asiste] *vt* (*aider*) to assist; **~ à** (*scène, événement*) to witness; (*conférence, séminaire*) to attend, be at; (*spectacle, match*) to be at, see

association [asɔsjasjɔ̃] *nf* association

associé, e [asɔsje] *nm/f* associate; (*COMM*) partner

associer [asɔsje] *vt* to associate; **s'~** *vi* to join together; **s'~ à qn pour faire** to join (forces) with sb to do; **s'~ à** (*couleurs, qualités*) to be combined with; (*opinions, joie de qn*) to share in; **~ qn à** (*profits*) to give sb a share of; (*affaire*) to make sb a partner in; (*joie, triomphe*) to include sb in;

~ qch à (*allier à*) to combine sth with
assoiffé, e [aswafe] *adj* thirsty
assombrir [asɔ̃bRiR] *vt* to darken; (*fig*) to fill with gloom
assommer [asɔme] *vt* (*étourdir, abrutir*) to knock out, stun
Assomption [asɔ̃psjɔ̃] *nf*: **l'~** the Assumption

┌─────────────────────┐
│ Assomption   │
└─────────────────────┘

🛈　La fête de l'Assomption *on August 15 is a French national holiday. Traditionally, large numbers of holidaymakers set out on this date, frequently causing chaos on the roads; see also faire le* **pont**.

---

assorti, e [asɔRti] *adj* matched, matching; (*varié*) assorted; **~ à** matching; **assortiment** *nm* assortment, selection
assortir [asɔRtiR] *vt* to match; **~ qch à** to match sth with; **~ qch de** to accompany sth with
assoupi, e [asupi] *adj* dozing, sleeping
assoupir [asupiR]: **s'~** *vi* to doze off
assouplir [asupliR] *vt* to make supple; (*fig*) to relax; **assouplissant** *nm* (*fabric*) softener
assourdir [asuRdiR] *vt* (*bruit*) to deaden, muffle; (*suj: bruit*) to deafen
assouvir [asuviR] *vt* to satisfy, appease
assujettir [asyʒetiR] *vt* to subject
assumer [asyme] *vt* (*fonction, emploi*) to assume, take on
assurance [asyRɑ̃s] *nf* (*certitude*) assurance; (*confiance en soi*) (self-)confidence; (*contrat*) insurance (policy); (*secteur commercial*) insurance; **~ maladie** health insurance; **~ tous risques** (*AUTO*) comprehensive insurance; **~s sociales** ≈ National Insurance (*BRIT*), ≈ Social Security (*US*); **assurance-vie** *nf* life assurance *ou* insurance
assuré, e [asyRe] *adj* (*certain: réussite, échec*) certain, sure; (*air*) assured; (*pas*) steady ♦ *nm/f* insured (person); **assurément** *adv* assuredly, most certainly

assurer [asyRe] *vt* (*FIN*) to insure; (*victoire etc*) to ensure; (*frontières, pouvoir*) to make secure; (*service*) to provide, operate; **s'~ (contre)** (*COMM*) to insure o.s. (against); **s'~ de/que** (*vérifier*) to make sure of/that; **s'~ (de)** (*aide de qn*) to secure; **~ à qn que** to assure sb that; **~ qn de** to assure sb of; **assureur** *nm* insurer
asthmatique [asmatik] *adj, nm/f* asthmatic
asthme [asm] *nm* asthma
asticot [astiko] *nm* maggot
astiquer [astike] *vt* to polish, shine
astre [astR] *nm* star
astreignant, e [astRɛɲɑ̃, ɑ̃t] *adj* demanding
astreindre [astRɛ̃dR] *vt*: **~ qn à faire** to compel *ou* force sb to do; **s'~** *vi*: **s'~ à faire** to force o.s. to do
astrologie [astRɔlɔʒi] *nf* astrology
astronaute [astRonot] *nm/f* astronaut
astronomie [astRɔnɔmi] *nf* astronomy
astuce [astys] *nf* shrewdness, astuteness; (*truc*) trick, clever way; **astucieux, -euse** *adj* clever
atelier [atalje] *nm* workshop; (*de peintre*) studio
athée [ate] *adj* atheistic ♦ *nm/f* atheist
Athènes [aten] *n* Athens
athlète [atlɛt] *nm/f* (*SPORT*) athlete; **athlétisme** *nm* athletics *sg*
atlantique [atlɑ̃tik] *adj* Atlantic ♦ *nm*: **l'(océan) A~** the Atlantic (Ocean)
atlas [atlas] *nm* atlas
atmosphère [atmɔsfɛR] *nf* atmosphere
atome [atom] *nm* atom; **atomique** *adj* atomic, nuclear
atomiseur [atɔmizœR] *nm* atomizer
atout [atu] *nm* trump; (*fig*) asset
âtre [ɑtR] *nm* hearth
atroce [atRɔs] *adj* atrocious
attabler [atable]: **s'~** *vi* to sit down at (the) table
attachant, e [ataʃɑ̃, ɑ̃t] *adj* engaging, lovable, likeable
attache [ataʃ] *nf* clip, fastener; (*fig*) tie

attacher [ataʃe] *vt* to tie up; (*étiquette*) to attach, tie on; (*ceinture*) to fasten ♦ *vi* (*poêle, riz*) to stick; **s'~ à** (*par affection*) to become attached to; **s'~ à faire** to endeavour to do; **~ qch à** to tie *ou* attach sth to

attaque [atak] *nf* attack; (*cérébrale*) stroke; (*d'épilepsie*) fit; **~ à main armée** armed attack

attaquer [atake] *vt* to attack; (*en justice*) to bring an action against, sue ♦ *vi* to attack; **s'~ à** ♦ *vt* (*personne*) to attack; (*problème*) to tackle

attardé, e [atarde] *adj* (*enfant*) backward; (*passants*) late

attarder [atarde]: **s'~** *vi* to linger

atteindre [atɛ̃dʀ] *vt* to reach; (*blesser*) to hit; (*émouvoir*) to affect; **atteint, e** *adj* (*MÉD*): **être atteint de** to be suffering from; **atteinte** *nf*: **hors d'atteinte** out of reach; **porter atteinte à** to strike a blow at

atteler [at(ə)le] *vt* (*cheval, bœufs*) to hitch up; **s'~ à** (*travail*) to buckle down to

attelle [atɛl] *nf* splint

attenant, e [at(ə)nɑ̃, ɑ̃t] *adj.* **~ (à)** adjoining

attendant [atɑ̃dɑ̃] *adv*: **en ~** meanwhile, in the meantime

attendre [atɑ̃dʀ] *vt* (*gén*) to wait for; (*être destiné ou réservé à*) to await, be in store for ♦ *vi* to wait; **s'~ à (ce que)** to expect (that); **~ un enfant** to be expecting a baby; **~ de faire/d'être** to wait until one does/is; **attendez qu'il vienne** wait until he comes; **~ qch de** to expect sth of

attendrir [atɑ̃dʀiʀ] *vt* to move (to pity); (*viande*) to tenderize; **attendrissant, e** *adj* moving, touching

attendu, e [atɑ̃dy] *adj* (*visiteur*) expected; (*événement*) long-awaited; **~ que** considering that, since

attentat [atɑ̃ta] *nm* assassination attempt; **~ à la bombe** bomb attack; **~ à la pudeur** indecent assault *no pl*

attente [atɑ̃t] *nf* wait; (*espérance*) expecta-

tion

attenter [atɑ̃te]: **~ à** *vt* (*liberté*) to violate; **~ à la vie de qn** to make an attempt on sb's life

attentif, -ive [atɑ̃tif, iv] *adj* (*auditeur*) attentive; (*examen*) careful; **~ à** careful to

attention [atɑ̃sjɔ̃] *nf* attention; (*prévenance*) attention, thoughtfulness *no pl*; **à l'~ de** for the attention of; **faire ~ (à)** to be careful (of); **faire ~ (à ce) que** to be *ou* make sure that; **~! carefull!, watch out!**; **attentionné, e** *adj* thoughtful, considerate

atténuer [atenɥe] *vt* (*douleur*) to alleviate, ease; (*couleurs*) to soften

atterrer [atere] *vt* to dismay, appal

atterrir [ateʀiʀ] *vi* to land; **atterrissage** *nm* landing

attestation [atɛstasjɔ̃] *nf* certificate

attester [atɛste] *vt* to testify to

attirail [atiʀaj] (*fam*) *nm* gear; (*péj*) paraphernalia

attirant, e [atiʀɑ̃, ɑ̃t] *adj* attractive, appealing

attirer [atiʀe] *vt* to attract; (*appâter*) to lure, entice; **~ qn dans un coin** to draw sb into a corner; **~ l'attention de qn** to attract sb's attention; **~ l'attention de qn sur** to draw sb's attention to; **s'~ des ennuis** to bring trouble upon o.s., get into trouble

attiser [atize] *vt* (*feu*) to poke (up)

attitré, e [atitʀe] *adj* (*habituel*) regular, usual; (*agréé*) accredited

attitude [atityd] *nf* attitude; (*position du corps*) bearing

attouchements [atuʃmɑ̃] *nmpl* (*sexuels*) fondling *sg*

attraction [atʀaksjɔ̃] *nf* (*gén*) attraction; (*de cabaret, cirque*) number

attrait [atʀɛ] *nm* appeal, attraction

attrape-nigaud [atʀapnigo] (*fam*) *nm* con

attraper [atʀape] *vt* (*gén*) to catch; (*habitude, amende*) to get, pick up; (*fam: duper*) to con; **se faire ~** (*fam*) to be told off

attrayant, e [atʀɛjɑ̃, ɑ̃t] *adj* attractive

attribuer [atʀibɥe] *vt* (*prix*) to award; (*rôle, tâche*) to allocate, assign; (*imputer*): ~ **qch à** to attribute sth to; **s'~** *vt* (*s'approprier*) to claim for o.s.; **attribut** *nm* attribute

attrister [atʀiste] *vt* to sadden

attroupement [atʀupmɑ̃] *nm* crowd

attrouper [atʀupe]: **s'~** *vi* to gather

au [o] *prép* +*dét* = **à** +**le**

aubaine [obɛn] *nf* godsend

aube [ob] *nf* dawn, daybreak; **à l'~** at dawn *ou* daybreak

aubépine [obepin] *nf* hawthorn

auberge [obɛʀʒ] *nf* inn; ~ **de jeunesse** youth hostel

aubergine [obɛʀʒin] *nf* aubergine

aubergiste [obɛʀʒist] *nm/f* inn-keeper, hotel-keeper

aucun, e [okœ̃, yn] *dét* no, *tournure négative* +any; (*positif*) any ♦ *pron* none, *tournure négative* +any; any(one); ~ **sans ~ doute** without any doubt; **plus qu'~ autre** more than any other; ~ **des deux** neither of the two; ~ **d'entre eux** none of them; **aucunement** *adv* in no way, not in the least

audace [odas] *nf* daring, boldness; (*péj*) audacity; **audacieux, -euse** *adj* daring, bold

au-delà [od(ə)la] *adv* beyond ♦ *nm*: **l'~~** the hereafter; **~~ de** beyond

au-dessous [odsu] *adv* underneath; below; **~~ de** under(neath), below; (*limite, somme etc*) below, under; (*dignité, condition*) below

au-dessus [odsy] *adv* above; **~~ de** above

au-devant [od(ə)vɑ̃]: **~~ de** *prép*: **aller ~~ de** (*personne, danger*) to go (out) and meet; (*souhaits de qn*) to anticipate

audience [odjɑ̃s] *nf* audience; (*JUR: séance*) hearing

audimat ® [odimat] *nm* (*taux d'écoute*) ratings *pl*

audio-visuel, le [odjovizɥel] *adj* audio-visual

auditeur, -trice [oditœʀ, tʀis] *nm/f* lis-tener

audition [odisjɔ̃] *nf* (*ouïe, écoute*) hearing; (*JUR: de témoins*) examination; (*MUS, THÉÂTRE: épreuve*) audition

auditoire [oditwaʀ] *nm* audience

auge [oʒ] *nf* trough

augmentation [ɔgmɑ̃tasjɔ̃] *nf* increase; ~ **(de salaire)** rise (in salary) (*BRIT*), (pay) raise (*US*)

augmenter [ɔgmɑ̃te] *vt* (*gén*) to increase; (*salaire, prix*) to increase, raise, put up; (*employé*) to increase the salary of ♦ *vi* to increase

augure [ogyʀ] *nm*: **de bon/mauvais ~** good/ill omen; **augurer** *vt*: **augurer bien de** to augur well for

aujourd'hui [oʒuʀdɥi] *adv* today

aumône [omon] *nf inv* alms *sg*; **aumô-nier** *nm* chaplain

auparavant [oparavɑ̃] *adv* before(hand)

auprès [opʀɛ]: ~ **de** *prép* next to, close to; (*recourir, s'adresser*) to; (*en comparaison de*) compared with

auquel [okel] *prép* +*pron* = **à** +**lequel**

aurai *etc* [ɔʀe] *vb voir* **avoir**

auréole [ɔʀeɔl] *nf* halo; (*tache*) ring

aurons *etc* [ɔʀɔ̃] *vb voir* **avoir**

aurore [ɔʀɔʀ] *nf* dawn, daybreak

ausculter [ɔskylte] *vt* to sound (the chest of)

aussi [osi] *adv* (*également*) also, too; (*de comparaison*) as ♦ *conj* therefore, conse-quently; ~ **fort que** as strong as; **moi ~** me too

aussitôt [osito] *adv* straight away, im-mediately; ~ **que** as soon as

austère [ostɛʀ] *adj* austere

austral, e [ɔstʀal] *adj* southern

Australie [ɔstʀali] *nf*: **l'~** Australia; **aus-tralien, ne** *adj* Australian ♦ *nm/f*: **Aus-tralien, ne** Australian

autant [otɑ̃] *adv* so much; (*comparatif*): ~ **(que)** as much (as); (*nombre*) as many (as); ~ **(de)** so much (*ou* many); as much (*ou* many); ~ **partir** we (*ou* you *etc*) may as well leave; ~ **dire que ...** one might as well say that ...; **pour ~** for all that; **d'~ plus/mieux (que)** all the more/the better (since)

autel [otɛl] *nm* altar

auteur [otœʀ] *nm* author

authenticité [otɑ̃tisite] *nf* authenticity

authentique [otɑ̃tik] *adj* authentic, genuine

auto [oto] *nf* car

auto...: autobiographie *nf* autobiography; **autobronzant** *nm* self-tanning cream (*or* lotion *etc*); **autobus** *nm* bus; **autocar** *nm* coach

autochtone [otɔktɔn] *nm/f* native

auto...: autocollant, e *adj* self-adhesive; (*enveloppe*) self-seal ♦ *nm* sticker; **auto-couchettes** *adj*: **train auto-couchettes** car sleeper train; **autocuiseur** *nm* pressure cooker; **autodéfense** *nf* self-defence; **autodidacte** *nm/f* self-taught person; **auto-école** *nf* driving school; **autographe** *nm* autograph

automate [ɔtɔmat] *nm* (*machine*) (automatic) machine

automatique [ɔtɔmatik] *adj* automatic ♦ *nm*: **l'~** direct dialling; **automatiquement** *adv* automatically; **automatiser** *vt* to automate

automne [ɔtɔn] *nm* autumn (*BRIT*), fall (*US*)

automobile [ɔtɔmɔbil] *adj* motor *cpd* ♦ *nf* (motor) car; **automobiliste** *nm/f* motorist

autonome [ɔtɔnɔm] *adj* autonomous; **autonomie** *nf* autonomy; (*POL*) self-government, autonomy

autopsie [ɔtɔpsi] *nf* post-mortem (examination), autopsy

autoradio [otoʀadjo] *nm* car radio

autorisation [ɔtɔʀizasjɔ̃] *nf* permission, authorization; (*papiers*) permit

autorisé, e [ɔtɔʀize] *adj* (*opinion, sources*) authoritative

autoriser [ɔtɔʀize] *vt* to give permission for, authorize; (*fig*) to allow (of)

autoritaire [ɔtɔʀitɛʀ] *adj* authoritarian

autorité [ɔtɔʀite] *nf* authority; **faire ~** to

be authoritative

autoroute [otoʀut] *nf* motorway (*BRIT*), highway (*US*); **~ de l'information** (*INFORM*) information superhighway

auto-stop [otostɔp] *nm*: **faire de l'~-~** to hitch-hike; **prendre qn en ~-~** to give sb a lift; **auto-stoppeur, -euse** *nm/f* hitch-hiker

autour [otuʀ] *adv* around; **~ de** around; **tout ~** all around

---

MOT-CLÉ

autre [otʀ] *adj* **1** (*différent*) other, different; **je préférerais un autre verre** I'd prefer another *ou* a different glass

2 (*supplémentaire*) other; **je voudrais un autre verre d'eau** I'd like another glass of water

3: autre chose something else; **autre part** somewhere else; **d'autre part** on the other hand

♦ *pron*: **un autre** another (one); **nous/vous autres** us/you; **d'autres** others; **l'autre** the other (one); **les autres** the others; (*autrui*) others; **l'un et l'autre** both of them; **se détester l'un l'autre/les uns les autres** to hate each other *ou* one another; **d'une semaine à l'autre** from one week to the next; (*incessamment*) any week now; (*entre autres* among other things

---

autrefois [otʀəfwa] *adv* in the past

autrement [otʀəmɑ̃] *adv* differently; (*d'une manière différente*) in another way; (*sinon*) otherwise; **~ dit** in other words

Autriche [otʀiʃ] *nf*: **l'~** Austria; **autrichien, ne** *adj* Austrian ♦ *nm/f*: **Autrichien, ne** Austrian

autruche [otʀyʃ] *nf* ostrich

autrui [otʀɥi] *pron* others

auvent [ovɑ̃] *nm* canopy

aux [o] *prép* +*dét* = **à +les**

auxiliaire [ɔksiljɛʀ] *adj*, *nm/f* auxiliary

auxquelles [okɛl] *prép* +*pron* = **à +lesquelles**

auxquels [okɛl] _prép_ +_pron_ = **à** +**lesquels**
avachi, e [avaʃi] _adj_ limp, flabby
aval [aval] _nm_: **en ~** downstream, down-river
avalanche [avalɑ̃ʃ] _nf_ avalanche
avaler [avale] _vt_ to swallow
avance [avɑ̃s] _nf_ (_de troupes etc_) advance; progress; (_d'argent_) advance; (_sur un concurrent_) lead; **~s** _nfpl_ (_amoureuses_) advances; **(être) en ~** (to be) early; (_sur un programme_) (to be) ahead of schedule; **à l'~, d'~** in advance
avancé, e [avɑ̃se] _adj_ advanced; (_travail_) well on, well under way
avancement [avɑ̃smɑ̃] _nm_ (_professionnel_) promotion
avancer [avɑ̃se] _vi_ to move forward, advance; (_projet, travail_) to make progress; (_montre, réveil_) to be fast; to gain ♦ _vt_ to move forward, advance; (_argent_) to advance; (_montre, pendule_) to put forward; **s'~** _vi_ to move forward, advance; (_fig_) to commit o.s.
avant [avɑ̃] _prép, adv_ before ♦ _adj inv_: **siège/roue ~** front seat/wheel ♦ _nm_ (_d'un véhicule, bâtiment_) front; (_SPORT: joueur_) forward; **~ qu'il (ne) fasse/de faire** before he does/doing; **~ tout** (_surtout_) above all; **à l'~** (_dans un véhicule_) in (the) front; **en ~** forward(s); **en ~ de** in front of
avantage [avɑ̃taʒ] _nm_ advantage; **~s sociaux** fringe benefits; **avantager** _vt_ (_favoriser_) to favour; (_embellir_) to flatter; **avantageux, -euse** _adj_ (_prix_) attractive
avant...: **avant-bras** _nm inv_ forearm; **avantcoureur** _adj inv_: **signe avantcoureur** advance indication _ou_ sign; **avant-dernier, -ière** _adj, nm/f_ next to last, last but one; **avant-goût** _nm_ foretaste; **avant-guerre** _nm_ pre-war years; **avant-hier** _adv_ the day before yesterday; **avant-première** _nf_ (_de film_) preview; **avant-projet** _nm_ (preliminary) draft; **avant-propos** _nm_ foreword; **avant-veille** _nf_: **l'avant-veille** two days before

avare [avaʀ] _adj_ miserly, avaricious ♦ _nm/f_ miser; **~ de** (_compliments etc_) sparing of
avarié, e [avaʀje] _adj_ (_aliment_) rotting
avaries [avaʀi] _nfpl_ (_NAVIG_) damage _sg_
avec [avɛk] _prép_ with; (_à l'égard de_) to(wards), with; **et ~ ça?** (_dans magasin_) anything else?
avenant, e [av(ə)nɑ̃, ɑ̃t] _adj_ pleasant; **à l'~** in keeping
avènement [avɛnmɑ̃] _nm_ (_d'un changement_) advent, coming
avenir [avniʀ] _nm_ future; **à l'~** in future; **politicien d'~** politician with prospects _ou_ a future
aventure [avɑ̃tyʀ] _nf_ adventure; (_amoureuse_) affair; **aventurer: s'aventurer** _vi_ to venture; **aventureux, -euse** _adj_ adventurous, venturesome; (_projet_) risky, chancy
avenue [avny] _nf_ avenue
avérer [aveʀe]: **s'~** _vb_ +_attrib_ to prove (to be)
averse [avɛʀs] _nf_ shower
averti, e [avɛʀti] _adj_ (well-)informed
avertir [avɛʀtiʀ] _vt_: **~ qn (de qch/que)** to warn sb (of sth/that); (_renseigner_) to inform sb (of sth/that); **avertissement** _nm_ warning; **avertisseur** _nm_ horn, siren
aveu, x [avø] _nm_ confession
aveugle [avœgl] _adj_ blind ♦ _nm/f_ blind man/woman; **aveuglément** _adv_ blindly; **aveugler** _vt_ to blind
aviateur, -trice [avjatœʀ, tʀis] _nm/f_ aviator, pilot
aviation [avjasjɔ̃] _nf_ aviation; (_sport_) flying; (_MIL_) air force
avide [avid] _adj_ eager; (_péj_) greedy, grasping
avilir [aviliʀ] _vt_ to debase
avion [avjɔ̃] _nm_ (aero)plane (_BRIT_), (air)plane (_US_); **aller (quelque part) en ~** to go (somewhere) by plane, fly (somewhere); **par ~** by airmail; **~ à réaction** jet (plane)
aviron [aviʀɔ̃] _nm_ oar; (_sport_): **l'~** rowing
avis [avi] _nm_ opinion; (_notification_) notice; **à mon ~** in my opinion; **changer d'~** to

change one's mind; **jusqu'à nouvel ~** until further notice

avisé, e [avize] *adj* sensible, wise; **bien/mal ~ de** well-/ill-advised to

aviser [avize] *vt* (*informer*): **~ qn de/que** to advise *ou* inform sb of/that ♦ *vi* to think about things, assess the situation; **nous ~ons sur place** we'll work something out once we're there; **s'~ de qch/que** to become suddenly aware of sth/that; **s'~ de faire** to take it into one's head to do

avocat, e [avɔka, at] *nm/f* (*JUR*) barrister (*BRIT*), lawyer ♦ *nm* (*CULIN*) avocado (pear); **~ de la défense** counsel for the defence; **~ général** assistant public prosecutor

avoine [avwan] *nf* oats *pl*

MOT-CLÉ

avoir [avwaʀ] *nm* assets *pl*, resources *pl*; (*COMM*) credit

♦ *vt* **1** (*posséder*) to have; **elle a 2 enfants/une belle maison** she has (got) 2 children/a lovely house; **il a les yeux bleus** he has (got) blue eyes

2 (*âge, dimensions*) to be; **il a 3 ans** he is 3 (years old); **le mur a 3 mètres de haut** the wall is 3 metres high, *voir aussi* **faim; peur** *etc*

3 (*fam: duper*) to do, have; **on vous a eu!** you've been done *ou* had!

4: en avoir contre qn to have a grudge against sb; **en avoir assez** to be fed up; **j'en ai pour une demi-heure** it'll take me half an hour

♦ *vb aux* **1** to have; **avoir mangé/dormi** to have eaten/slept

2 (*avoir +à +infinitif*): **avoir à faire qch** to have to do sth; **vous n'avez qu'à lui demander** you only have to ask him

♦ *vb impers* **1: il y a** (+ *singulier*) there is; (+ *pluriel*) there are; **qu'y-a-t-il?, qu'est-ce qu'il y a?** what's the matter?, what is it?; **il doit y avoir une explication** there must be an explanation; **il n'y a qu'à ...**

we (*ou* you *etc*) will just have to ...

2 (*temporel*): **il y a 10 ans** 10 years ago; **il y a 10 ans/longtemps que je le sais** I've known it for 10 years/a long time; **il y a 10 ans qu'il est arrivé** it's 10 years since he arrived

---

avoisiner [avwazine] *vt* to be near *ou* close to; (*fig*) to border *ou* verge on

avortement [avɔʀtəmɑ̃] *nm* abortion

avorter [avɔʀte] *vi* (*MÉD*) to have an abortion; (*fig*) to fail

avoué, e [avwe] *adj* avowed ♦ *nm* (*JUR*) ≈ solicitor

avouer [avwe] *vt* (*crime, défaut*) to confess (to); **~ avoir fait/que** to admit *ou* confess to having done/that

avril [avʀil] *nm* April

---

poisson d'avril

i The traditional prank on April 1 in France is to stick a cut-out paper fish, known as a **poisson d'avril**, to someone's back without being caught.

---

axe [aks] *nm* axis; (*de roue etc*) axle; (*fig*) main line; **axer** *vt*: **axer qch sur** to centre sth on

ayons *etc* [ɛjɔ̃] *vb voir* **avoir**

azote [azɔt] *nm* nitrogen

B, b

baba [baba] *nm*: **~ au rhum** rum baba

babines [babin] *nfpl* chops

babiole [babjɔl] *nf* (*bibelot*) trinket; (*vétille*) trifle

bâbord [bɑbɔʀ] *nm*: **à ~** to port, on the port side

baby-foot [babifut] *nm* table football

baby-sitting [babisitiŋ] *nm*: **faire du ~-~** to baby-sit

bac [bak] *abr m* = **baccalauréat** ♦ *nm* (*récipient*) tub

baccalauréat [bakalɔʀea] *nm* high school

diploma

---
baccalauréat
---

i In France the **baccalauréat** or **bac** is the school-leaving certificate taken at a lycée at the age of seventeen or eighteen, enabling entry to university. Different subject combinations are available from the broad subject range studied.

---

bâche [baʃ] *nf* tarpaulin

bachelier, -ière [baʃəlje, jɛʀ] *nm/f* holder of the baccalauréat

bâcler [bakle] *vt* to botch (up)

badaud, e [bado, od] *nm/f* idle onlooker, stroller

badigeonner [badiʒɔne] *vt* (*barbouiller*) to daub

badiner [badine] *vi*: ~ **avec qch** to treat sth lightly

baffe [baf] (*fam*) *nf* slap, clout

baffle [bafl] *nm* speaker

bafouer [bafwe] *vt* to deride, ridicule

bafouiller [bafuje] *vi, vt* to stammer

bâfrer [bɑfʀe] (*fam*) *vi* to guzzle

bagages [bagaʒ] *nmpl* luggage *sg*; ~ **à main** hand-luggage

bagarre [bagaʀ] *nf* fight, brawl; **bagarrer: se bagarrer** *vi* to have a fight *ou* scuffle, fight

bagatelle [bagatɛl] *nf* trifle

bagne [baɲ] *nm* penal colony

bagnole [baɲɔl] (*fam*) *nf* car

bagout [bagu] *nm*: **avoir du** ~ to have the gift of the gab

bague [bag] *nf* ring; ~ **de fiançailles** engagement ring

baguette [bagɛt] *nf* stick; (*cuisine chinoise*) chopstick; (*de chef d'orchestre*) baton; (*pain*) stick of (French) bread; ~ **magique** magic wand

baie [bɛ] *nf* (*GÉO*) bay; (*fruit*) berry; ~ **(vitrée)** picture window

baignade [bɛɲad] *nf* bathing; **"~ interdite"** "no bathing"

baigner [bɛɲe] *vt* (*bébé*) to bath; **se** ~ *vi* to have a swim, go swimming *ou* bathing

baignoire [bɛɲwaʀ] *nf* bath(tub)

bail [baj, bo] (*pl* **baux**) *nm* lease

bâillement [bɑjmɑ̃] *nm* yawn

bâiller [bɑje] *vi* to yawn; (*être ouvert*) to gape

bâillonner [bɑjɔne] *vt* to gag

bain [bɛ̃] *nm* bath; **prendre un** ~ to have a bath; **se mettre dans le** ~ (*fig*) to get into it *ou* things; ~ **de soleil: prendre un** ~ **de soleil** to sunbathe; **~s de mer** sea bathing *sg*; **bain-marie** *nm*: **faire chauffer au bain-marie** (*boîte etc*) to immerse in boiling water

baiser [beze] *nm* kiss ♦ *vt* (*main, front*) to kiss; (*fam!*) to screw (!)

baisse [bɛs] *nf* fall, drop; **être en** ~ to be falling, be declining

baisser [bese] *vt* to lower; (*radio, chauffage*) to turn down ♦ *vi* to fall, drop, go down; (*vue, santé*) to fail, dwindle; **se** ~ *vi* to bend down

bal [bal] *nm* dance; (*grande soirée*) ball; ~ **costumé** fancy-dress ball

balade [balad] (*fam*) *nf* (*à pied*) walk, stroll; (*en voiture*) drive; **balader: se balader** *vi* to go for a walk *ou* stroll; to go for a drive; **baladeur** *nm* personal stereo, Walkman ®

balafre [balafʀ] *nf* (*cicatrice*) scar

balai [balɛ] *nm* broom, brush; **balai-brosse** *nm* (long-handled) scrubbing brush

balance [balɑ̃s] *nf* scales *pl*; (*signe*): **la B~** Libra

balancer [balɑ̃se] *vt* to swing; (*fam: lancer*) to fling, chuck; (: *jeter*) to chuck out; **se** ~ *vi* to swing, rock; **se** ~ **de** (*fam*) not to care about

balançoire [balɑ̃swaʀ] *nf* swing; (*sur pivot*) seesaw

balayer [baleje] *vt* (*feuilles etc*) to sweep up, brush up; (*pièce*) to sweep; (*objections*) to sweep aside; (*suj: radar*) to scan; **balayeur, -euse** *nm/f* roadsweeper

balbutier [balbysje] vi, vt to stammer
balcon [balkɔ̃] nm balcony; (THÉÂTRE) dress circle
baleine [balɛn] nf whale
balise [baliz] nf (NAVIG) beacon; (marker) buoy; (AVIAT) runway light, beacon; (AUTO, SKI) sign, marker; **baliser** vt to mark out (with lights etc)
balivernes [balivɛrn] nfpl nonsense sg
ballant, e [balɑ̃, ɑ̃t] adj dangling
balle [bal] nf (de fusil) bullet; (de sport) ball; (fam: franc) franc
ballerine [bal(ə)rin] nf (danseuse) ballet dancer; (chaussure) ballet shoe
ballet [balɛ] nm ballet
ballon [balɔ̃] nm (de sport) ball; (jouet, AVIAT) balloon; ~ **de football** football
ballot [balo] nm bundle; (péj) nitwit
ballottage [balɔtaʒ] nm (POL) second ballot
ballotter [balɔte] vt: **être ballotté** to be thrown about
balnéaire [balneɛr] adj seaside cpd; **station ~** seaside resort
balourd, e [balur, urd] adj clumsy
balustrade [balystrad] nf railings pl, handrail
bambin [bɑ̃bɛ̃] nm little child
bambou [bɑ̃bu] nm bamboo
ban [bɑ̃] nm: **mettre au ~ de** to outlaw from; **~s** nmpl (de mariage) banns
banal, e [banal] adj banal, commonplace; (péj) trite; **banalité** nf banality
banane [banan] nf banana; (sac) waistbag, bum-bag
banc [bɑ̃] nm seat, bench; (de poissons) shoal; **~ d'essai** (fig) testing ground
bancaire [bɑ̃kɛr] adj banking; (chèque, carte) bank cpd
bancal, e [bɑ̃kal] adj wobbly
bandage [bɑ̃daʒ] nm bandage
bande [bɑ̃d] nf (de tissu etc) strip; (MÉD) bandage; (motif) stripe; (magnétique etc) tape; (groupe) band; (: péj) bunch; **faire ~ à part** to keep to o.s.; **~ dessinée** comic strip; **~ sonore** sound track

bandeau, x [bɑ̃do] nm headband; (sur les yeux) blindfold
bander [bɑ̃de] vt (blessure) to bandage; **~ les yeux à qn** to blindfold sb
banderole [bɑ̃drɔl] nf banner, streamer
bandit [bɑ̃di] nm bandit; **banditisme** nm violent crime, armed robberies pl
bandoulière [bɑ̃duljɛr] nf: **en ~** (slung ou worn) across the shoulder
banlieue [bɑ̃ljø] nf suburbs pl; **lignes / quartiers de ~** suburban lines/areas; **trains de ~** commuter trains
banlieusard, e nm/f (suburban) commuter
bannière [banjɛr] nf banner
bannir [banir] vt to banish
banque [bɑ̃k] nf bank; (activités) banking; **~ d'affaires** merchant bank, **banque route** nf bankruptcy
banquet [bɑ̃kɛ] nm dinner; (d'apparat) banquet
banquette [bɑ̃kɛt] nf seat
banquier [bɑ̃kje] nm banker
banquise [bɑ̃kiz] nf ice field
baptême [batɛm] nm christening; baptism; **~ de l'air** first flight
baptiser [batize] vt to baptize, christen
baquet [bakɛ] nm tub, bucket
bar [bar] nm bar
baraque [barak] nf shed; (fam) house; **baraqué, e** (fam) adj well-built, hefty; **baraquements** nmpl (provisoires) huts
baratin [baratɛ̃] (fam) nm smooth talk, patter; **baratiner** vt to chat up
barbare [barbar] adj barbaric; **barbarie** nf barbarity

barbe [baʀb] *nf* beard; **la ~!** (*fam*) damn it!; **quelle ~!** (*fam*) what a drag *ou* bore!; **à la ~ de qn** under sb's nose; **~ à papa** candy-floss (*BRIT*), cotton candy (*US*)

barbelé [baʀbəle] *adj, nm*: **(fil de fer) ~** barbed wire *no pl*

barber [baʀbe] (*fam*) *vt* to bore stiff

barbiturique [baʀbityʀik] *nm* barbiturate

barboter [baʀbɔte] *vi* (*enfant*) to paddle

barbouiller [baʀbuje] *vt* to daub; **avoir l'estomac barbouillé** to feel queasy

barbu, e [baʀby] *adj* bearded

barda [baʀda] (*fam*) *nm* kit, gear

barder [baʀde] (*fam*) *vi*: **ça va ~** sparks will fly, things are going to get hot

barème [baʀɛm] *nm* (*SCOL*) scale; (*table de référence*) table

baril [baʀi(l)] *nm* barrel; (*poudre*) keg

bariolé, e [baʀjɔle] *adj* gaudily-coloured

baromètre [baʀɔmɛtʀ] *nm* barometer

baron, ne [baʀɔ̃] *nm/f* baron(ess)

baroque [baʀɔk] *adj* (*ART*) baroque; (*fig*) weird

barque [baʀk] *nf* small boat

barquette [baʀkɛt] *nf* (*pour repas*) tray; (*pour fruits*) punnet

barrage [baʀaʒ] *nm* dam; (*sur route*) roadblock, barricade

barre [baʀ] *nf* bar; (*NAVIG*) helm; (*écrite*) line, stroke

barreau, x [baʀo] *nm* bar; (*JUR*): **le ~** the Bar

barrer [baʀe] *vt* (*route etc*) to block; (*mot*) to cross out; (*chèque*) to cross (*BRIT*); (*NAVIG*) to steer; **se ~** (*fam*) *vi* to clear off

barrette [baʀɛt] *nf* (*pour cheveux*) (hair) slide (*BRIT*) *ou* clip (*US*)

barricader [baʀikade]: **se ~** *vi* to barricade o.s.

barrière [baʀjɛʀ] *nf* fence; (*obstacle*) barrier; (*porte*) gate

barrique [baʀik] *nf* barrel, cask

bar-tabac [baʀtaba] *nm* bar (which sells tobacco and stamps)

bas, basse [bɑ, bɑs] *adj* low ♦ *nm* bottom, lower part; (*vêtement*) stocking ♦ *adv*

low; (*parler*) softly; **au ~ mot** at the lowest estimate; **en ~** down below; (*d'une liste, d'un mur etc*) at/to the bottom; (*dans une maison*) downstairs; **en ~ de** at the bottom of; **un enfant en ~ âge** a young child; **à ~ ...!** down with ...!; **~ morceaux** *nmpl* (*viande*) cheap cuts

basané, e [bazane] *adj* tanned

bas-côté [bakote] *nm* (*de route*) verge (*BRIT*), shoulder (*US*)

bascule [baskyl] *nf*: **(jeu de) ~** seesaw; **(balance à) ~** scales *pl*; **fauteuil à ~** rocking chair

basculer [baskyle] *vi* to fall over, topple (over); (*benne*) to tip up ♦ *vt* (*contenu*) to tip out; (*benne*) to tip up

base [bɑz] *nf* base; (*POL*) rank and file; (*fondement, principe*) basis; **de ~** basic; **à ~ de café** *etc* coffee *etc* -based; **~ de données** database; **baser** *vt* to base; **se baser sur** *vt* (*preuves*) to base one's argument on

bas-fond [bafɔ̃] *nm* (*NAVIG*) shallow; **~-~s** *nmpl* (*fig*) dregs

basilic [bazilik] *nm* (*CULIN*) basil

basket [basket] *nm* trainer (*BRIT*), sneaker (*US*); (*aussi*: **~-ball**) basketball

basque [bask] *adj, nm/f* Basque

basse [bɑs] *adj voir* **bas** ♦ *nf* (*MUS*) bass; **basse-cour** *nf* farmyard

bassin [basɛ̃] *nm* (*pièce d'eau*) pond, pool; (*de fontaine, GÉO*) basin; (*ANAT*) pelvis; (*portuaire*) dock

bassine [basin] *nf* (*ustensile*) basin; (*contenu*) bowl(ful)

basson [basɔ̃] *nm* bassoon

bas-ventre [bavɑ̃tʀ] *nm* (lower part of the) stomach

bat [ba] *vb voir* **battre**

bataille [bataj] *nf* (*MIL*) battle; (*rixe*) fight; **batailler** *vi* to fight

bâtard, e [bɑtaʀ, aʀd] *nm/f* illegitimate child, bastard (*pej*)

bateau, x [bato] *nm* boat, ship; **bateau-mouche** *nm* passenger pleasure boat (on the Seine)

bâti, e [bɑti] *adj*: **bien ~** well-built

batifoler [batifɔle] *vi* to frolic about

bâtiment [bɑtimɑ̃] *nm* building; (NAVIG) ship, vessel; (*industrie*) building trade

bâtir [bɑtiʀ] *vt* to build

bâtisse [bɑtis] *nf* building

bâton [bɑtɔ̃] *nm* stick; **à ~s rompus** informally

bats [ba] *vb voir* **battre**

battage [bataʒ] *nm* (*publicité*) (hard) plugging

battant [batɑ̃, ɑ̃t] *nm*: **porte à double ~** double door

battement [batmɑ̃] *nm* (*de cœur*) beat; (*intervalle*) interval (*between classes, trains*); **10 minutes de ~** 10 minutes to spare

batterie [batʀi] *nf* (MIL, ÉLEC) battery; (MUS) drums *pl*, drum kit; **~ de cuisine** pots and pans *pl*, kitchen utensils *pl*

batteur [batœʀ] *nm* (MUS) drummer; (*appareil*) whisk

battre [batʀ] *vt* to beat; (*blé*) to thresh; (*passer au peigne fin*) to scour; (*cartes*) to shuffle ♦ *vi* (*cœur*) to beat; (*volets etc*) to bang, rattle; **se ~** *vi* to fight; **~ la mesure** to beat time; **~ son plein** to be at its height, be going full swing; **~ des mains** to clap one's hands

battue [baty] *nf* (*chasse*) beat; (*policière etc*) search, hunt

baume [bom] *nm* balm

baux [bo] *nmpl de* **bail**

bavard, e [bavaʀ, aʀd] *adj* (very) talkative; gossipy; **bavarder** *vi* to chatter; (*commérer*) to gossip; (*divulguer un secret*) to blab

bave [bav] *nf* dribble; (*de chien etc*) slobber; (*d'escargot*) slime; **baver** *vi* to dribble; (*chien*) to slobber; **en baver** (*fam*) to have a hard time (of it); **baveux, -euse** *adj* (*omelette*) runny; **bavoir** *nm* bib

bavure [bavyʀ] *nf* smudge; (*fig*) hitch; (*policière etc*) blunder

bayer [baje] *vi*: **~ aux corneilles** to stand gaping

bazar [bazaʀ] *nm* general store; (*fam*) jumble; **bazarder** (*fam*) *vt* to chuck out

BCBG *sigle adj* (= *bon chic bon genre*) preppy, smart and trendy

BCE *sigle f* (= *Banque centrale européenne*) ECB

BD *sigle f* = **bande dessinée**

bd *abr* = **boulevard**

béant, e [beɑ̃, ɑ̃t] *adj* gaping

béat, e [bea, at] *adj*: **~ d'admiration** struck dumb with admiration; **béatitude** *nf* bliss

beau (bel), belle [bo, bɛl] (*mpl* **beaux**) *adj* beautiful, lovely; (*homme*) handsome; (*femme*) beautiful ♦ *adv*: **il fait beau** the weather's fine; **un ~jour** one (fine) day; **de plus belle** more than ever, even more; **on a ~essayer** however hard we try; **bel et bien** well and truly

---
MOT-CLÉ
---

beaucoup [boku] *adv* **1** a lot; **il boit beaucoup** he drinks a lot; **il ne boit pas beaucoup** he doesn't drink much *ou* a lot
2 (*suivi de plus, trop etc*) much, a lot, far; **il est beaucoup plus grand** he is much *ou* a lot *ou* far taller
3: **beaucoup de** (*nombre*) many, a lot of; (*quantité*) a lot of; **beaucoup d'étudiants / de touristes** a lot of *ou* many students/tourists; **beaucoup de courage** a lot of courage; **il n'a pas beaucoup d'argent** he hasn't got much *ou* at lot of money
4: **de beaucoup** by far

beau...: **beau-fils** *nm* son-in-law; (*remariage*) stepson; **beau-frère** *nm* brother-in-law; **beau-père** *nm* father-in-law; (*remariage*) stepfather

beauté [bote] *nf* beauty; **de toute ~** beautiful; **finir qch en ~** to complete sth brilliantly

beaux-arts [bozaʀ] *nmpl* fine arts

beaux-parents [bopaʀɑ̃] *nmpl* wife's/ husband's family, in-laws

bébé [bebe] *nm* baby

bec [bɛk] *nm* beak, bill; (*de théière*) spout; (*de casserole*) lip; (*fam*) mouth; **~ de gaz** (street) gaslamp; **~ verseur** pouring lip

bécane [bekan] (*fam*) *nf* bike
bec-de-lièvre [bɛkdəljɛvʀ] *nm* harelip
bêche [bɛʃ] *nf* spade; **bêcher** *vt* to dig
bécoter [bekɔte]: **se ~** *vi* to smooch
becqueter [bekte] (*fam*) *vt* to eat
bedaine [bədɛn] *nf* paunch
bedonnant, e [bədɔnã, ãt] *adj* potbellied
bée [be] *adj*: **bouche ~** gaping
beffroi [befʀwa] *nm* belfry
bégayer [begeje] *vt*, *vi* to stammer
bègue [bɛg] *nm/f*: **être ~** to have a stammer
beige [bɛʒ] *adj* beige
beignet [bɛɲe] *nm* fritter
bel [bɛl] *adj voir* **beau**
bêler [bele] *vi* to bleat
belette [bəlɛt] *nf* weasel
belge [bɛlʒ] *adj* Belgian ♦ *nm/f*: **B~** Belgian
Belgique [bɛlʒik] *nf*: **la ~** Belgium
bélier [belje] *nm* ram; (*signe*): **le B~** Aries
belle [bɛl] *adj voir* **beau** ♦ *nf* (*SPORT*) decider; **belle-fille** *nf* daughter-in-law; (*remariage*) stepdaughter; **belle-mère** *nf* mother-in-law; stepmother; **belle-sœur** *nf* sister-in-law
belliqueux, -euse [belikø, øz] *adj* aggressive, warlike
belvédère [belvedɛʀ] *nm* panoramic viewpoint (*or small building there*)
bémol [bemɔl] *nm* (*MUS*) flat
bénédiction [benediksjɔ̃] *nf* blessing
bénéfice [benefis] *nm* (*COMM*) profit; (*avantage*) benefit; **bénéficier: bénéficier de** *vt* to enjoy; (*situation*) to benefit by *ou* from; **bénéfique** *adj* beneficial
bénévole [benevɔl] *adj* voluntary, unpaid
bénin, -igne [benɛ̃, iɲ] *adj* minor, mild; (*tumeur*) benign
bénir [beniʀ] *vt* to bless; **bénit, e** *adj* consecrated; **eau bénite** holy water
benjamin, e [bɛ̃ʒamɛ̃, in] *nm/f* youngest child
benne [bɛn] *nf* skip; (*de téléphérique*) (cable) car; **~ basculante** tipper (*BRIT*), dump truck (*US*)

BEP *sigle m* (= *brevet d'études professionnelles*) *technical school certificate*
béquille [bekij] *nf* crutch; (*de bicyclette*) stand
berceau, x [bɛʀso] *nm* cradle, crib
bercer [bɛʀse] *vt* to rock, cradle; (*suj: musique etc*) to lull; **~ qn de** (*promesses etc*) to delude sb with; **berceuse** *nf* lullaby
béret (basque) [beʀe (bask(ə))] *nm* beret
berge [bɛʀʒ] *nf* bank
berger, -ère [bɛʀʒe, ɛʀ] *nm/f* shepherd(-ess); **~ allemand** alsatian (*BRIT*), German shepherd
berlingot [bɛʀlɛ̃go] *nm* (*bonbon*) boiled sweet, humbug (*BRIT*)
berlue [bɛʀly] *nf*: **j'ai la ~** I must be seeing things
berner [bɛʀne] *vt* to fool
besogne [bəzɔɲ] *nf* work *no pl*, job
besoin [bəzwɛ̃] *nm* need; **avoir ~ de qch/faire qch** to need sth/to do sth; **au ~** if need be; **le ~** (*pauvreté*) need, want; **être dans le ~** to be in need *ou* want; **faire ses ~s** to relieve o.s.
bestiaux [bɛstjo] *nmpl* cattle
bestiole [bɛstjɔl] *nf* (*tiny*) creature
bétail [betaj] *nm* livestock, cattle *pl*
bête [bɛt] *nf* animal; (*bestiole*) insect, creature ♦ *adj* stupid, silly; **il cherche la petite ~** he's being pernickety *ou* overfussy; **~ noire** pet hate
bêtement [bɛtmã] *adv* stupidly
bêtise [betiz] *nf* stupidity; (*action*) stupid thing (to say *ou* do)
béton [betɔ̃] *nm* concrete; **(en) ~** (*alibi, argument*) cast iron; **~ armé** reinforced concrete; **bétonnière** *nf* cement mixer
betterave [bɛtʀav] *nf* beetroot (*BRIT*), beet (*US*); **~ sucrière** sugar beet
beugler [bøgle] *vi* to bellow; (*radio etc*) to blare ♦ *vt* (*chanson*) to bawl out
Beur [bœʀ] *nm/f person of North African origin living in France*
beurre [bœʀ] *nm* butter; **beurrer** *vt* to butter; **beurrier** *nm* butter dish
beuverie [bøvʀi] *nf* drinking session

bévue [bevy] *nf* blunder
Beyrouth [beʀut] *n* Beirut
bi... [bi] *préfixe* bi..., two-
biais [bjɛ] *nm* (*moyen*) device, expedient;
(*aspect*) angle; **en ~, de ~** (*obliquement*)
at an angle; **par le ~ de** by means of;
biaiser *vi* (*fig*) to sidestep the issue
bibelot [biblo] *nm* trinket, curio
biberon [bibʀɔ̃] *nm* (feeding) bottle; **nour-rir au ~** to bottle-feed
bible [bibl] *nf* bible
biblio... [bibl] *préfixe*: **bibliobus** *nm* mo-bile library van; **bibliographie** *nf* bibli-ography; **bibliothécaire** *nm/f* librarian;
bibliothèque *nf* library; (*meuble*) book-case
blc ® [bik] *nm* Biro ®
bicarbonate [bikaʀbɔnat] *nm*: **~ (de sou-de)** bicarbonate of soda
biceps [bisɛps] *nm* biceps
biche [biʃ] *nf* doe
bichonner [biʃɔne] *vt* to pamper
bicolore [bikɔlɔʀ] *adj* two-coloured
bicoque [bikɔk] (*péj*) *nf* shack
bicyclette [bisiklɛt] *nf* bicycle
bide [bid] (*fam*) *nm* (*ventre*) belly; (*THÉÂTRE*)
flop
bldet [bidɛ] *nm* bidet
bldon [bidɔ̃] *nm* can ♦ *adj inv* (*fam*) pho-ney
bidonville [bidɔ̃vil] *nm* shanty town
bidule [bidyl] (*fam*) *nm* thingumajig

MOT-CLÉ
---

bien [bjɛ̃] *nm* 1 (*avantage, profit*): **faire du
bien à qn** to do sb good; **dire du bien
de** to speak well of; **c'est pour son bien**
it's for his own good
2 (*possession, patrimoine*) possession, prop-erty; **son bien le plus précieux** his most
treasured possession; **avoir du bien** to
have property; **biens (de consommation
etc)** (consumer *etc*) goods
3 (*moral*): **le bien** good; **distinguer le
bien du mal** to tell good from evil
♦ *adv* 1 (*de façon satisfaisante*) well; **elle**

travaille/mange bien she works/eats
well; **croyant bien faire, je/il ...** thinking
I/he was doing the right thing, I/he ...;
c'est bien fait! it serves him (*ou* her *etc*)
right!
2 (*valeur intensive*) quite; **bien jeune** quite
young; **bien assez** quite enough; **bien
mieux** (very) much better; **j'espère bien
y aller** I do hope to go; **je veux bien le
faire** (*concession*) I'm quite willing to do
it; **il faut bien le faire** it has to be done
3: **bien du temps/des gens** quite a
time/a number of people
♦ *adj inv* 1 (*en bonne forme, à l'aise*): **je
me sens bien** I feel fine; **je ne me sens
pas bien** I don't feel well; **on est bien
dans ce fauteuil** this chair is very com-fortable
2 (*joli, beau*) good-looking; **tu es bien
dans cette robe** you look good in that
dress
3 (*satisfaisant*) good; **elle est bien, cette
maison/secrétaire** it's a good house/
she's a good secretary
4 (*moralement*) right; (: *personne*) good,
nice; (*respectable*) respectable; **ce n'est
pas bien de ...** it's not right to ...; **elle
est bien, cette femme** she's a nice wo-man, she's a good sort; **des gens biens**
respectable people
5 (*en bons termes*): **être bien avec qn** to
be on good terms with sb
♦ *préfixe*: **bien-aimé** *adj*, *nm/f* beloved;
bien-être *nm* well-being; **bienfaisance**
nf charity; **bienfaisant, e** *adj* (*chose*)
beneficial; **bienfait** *nm* act of generosity,
benefaction; (*de la science etc*) benefit;
bienfaiteur, -trice *nm/f* benefactor/
benefactress; **bien-fondé** *nm* soundness;
bien-fonds *nm* property; **bienheureux,
-euse** *adj* happy; (*REL*) blessed, blest;
bien que *conj* (al)though; **bien sûr** *adv*
certainly

---

bienséant, e [bjɛ̃seɑ̃, ɑ̃t] *adj* seemly
bientôt [bjɛ̃to] *adv* soon; **à ~** see you

soon

bienveillant, e [bjɛ̃vɛjɑ̃, ɑ̃t] *adj* kindly

bienvenu, e [bjɛ̃vny] *adj* welcome; **bienvenue** *nf*: **souhaiter la bienvenue à** to welcome; **bienvenue à** welcome to

bière [bjɛʀ] *nf* (*boisson*) beer; (*cercueil*) bier; **~ (à la) pression** draught beer; **~ blonde** lager; **~ brune** brown ale

biffer [bife] *vt* to cross out

bifteck [biftɛk] *nm* steak

bifurquer [bifyʀke] *vi* (*route*) to fork; (*véhicule*) to turn off

bigarré, e [bigaʀe] *adj* multicoloured; (*disparate*) motley

bigorneau, x [bigɔʀno] *nm* winkle

bigot, e [bigo, ɔt] (*péj*) *adj* bigoted

bigoudi [bigudi] *nm* curler

bijou, x [biʒu] *nm* jewel; **bijouterie** *nf* jeweller's (shop); **bijoutier, -ière** *nm/f* jeweller

bikini [bikini] *nm* bikini

bilan [bilɑ̃] *nm* (*fig*) (net) outcome; (: *de victimes*) toll; (*COMM*) balance sheet(s); **un ~ de santé** a (medical) checkup; **faire le ~ de** to assess, review; **déposer son ~** to file a bankruptcy statement

bile [bil] *nf* bile; **se faire de la ~** (*fam*) to worry o.s. sick

bilieux, -euse [biljø, øz] *adj* bilious; (*fig*: *colérique*) testy

bilingue [bilɛ̃g] *adj* bilingual

billard [bijaʀ] *nm* (*jeu*) billiards *sg*; (*table*) billiard table; **~ américain** pool

bille [bij] *nf* (*gén*) ball; (*du jeu de ~s*) marble

billet [bijɛ] *nm* (*aussi*: **~ de banque**) (bank)note; (*de cinéma, de bus etc*) ticket; (*courte lettre*) note; **~ Bige** cheap rail ticket for under-26s; **billetterie** *nf* ticket office; (*distributeur*) ticket machine; (*BANQUE*) cash dispenser

billion [biljɔ̃] *nm* billion (*BRIT*), trillion (*US*)

billot [bijo] *nm* block

bimensuel, le [bimɑ̃sɥɛl] *adj* bimonthly

binette [binɛt] *nf* hoe

bio... [bjɔ] *préfixe* bio...; **biochimie** *nf* biochemistry; **biodiversité** *nf* biodiversity; **bioéthique** *nf* bioethics *sg*; **biographie** *nf* biography; **biologie** *nf* biology; **biologique** *adj* biological; (*produits, aliments*) organic; **biologiste** *nm/f* biologist

Birmanie [biʀmani] *nf* Burma

bis [bis] *adv*: **12 ~** 12a *ou* A ♦ *excl, nm* encore

bisannuel, le [bizanɥɛl] *adj* biennial

biscornu, e [biskɔʀny] *adj* twisted

biscotte [biskɔt] *nf* toasted bread (*sold in packets*)

biscuit [biskɥi] *nm* biscuit; **~ de savoie** sponge cake

bise [biz] *nf* (*fam*: *baiser*) kiss; (*vent*) North wind; **grosses ~s (de)** (*sur lettre*) love and kisses (from)

bisou [bizu] (*fam*) *nm* kiss

bissextile [bisɛkstil] *adj*: **année ~** leap year

bistouri [bisturi] *nm* lancet

bistro(t) [bistro] *nm* bistro, café

bitume [bitym] *nm* asphalt

bizarre [bizaʀ] *adj* strange, odd

blafard, e [blafaʀ, aʀd] *adj* wan

blague [blag] *nf* (*propos*) joke; (*farce*) trick; **sans ~!** no kidding!; **blaguer** *vi* to joke

blaireau, x [blɛʀo] *nm* (*ZOOL*) badger; (*brosse*) shaving brush

blairer [blɛʀe] (*fam*) *vt*: **je ne peux pas le ~** I can't bear *ou* stand him

blâme [blɑm] *nm* blame; (*sanction*) reprimand; **blâmer** *vt* to blame

blanc, blanche [blɑ̃, blɑ̃ʃ] *adj* white; (*non imprimé*) blank ♦ *nm/f* white, white man(-woman) ♦ *nm* (*couleur*) white; (*espace non écrit*) blank; (*aussi*: **~ d'œuf**) (egg-)white; (*aussi*: **~ de poulet**) breast, white meat; (*aussi*: **vin ~**) white wine; **~ cassé** off-white; **chèque en ~** blank cheque; **à ~** (*chauffer*) white-hot; (*tirer, charger*) with blanks; **blanc-bec** *nm* greenhorn; **blanche** *nf* (*MUS*) minim (*BRIT*), half-note (*US*); **blancheur** *nf* whiteness

blanchir [blɑ̃ʃiʀ] *vt* (*gén*) to whiten; (*linge*) to launder; (*CULIN*) to blanch; (*fig*: *discul-*

per) to clear ♦ *vi* to grow white; (*cheveux*) to go white; **blanchisserie** *nf* laundry

blason [blazɔ̃] *nm* coat of arms

blasphème [blasfɛm] *nm* blasphemy

blazer [blazɛʀ] *nm* blazer

blé [ble] *nm* wheat; **~ noir** buckwheat

bled [blɛd] (*péj*) *nm* hole

blême [blɛm] *adj* pale

blessant, e [blesɑ̃, ɑ̃t] *adj* (*offensant*) hurtful

blessé, e [blese] *adj* injured ♦ *nm/f* injured person, casualty

blesser [blese] *vt* to injure; (*délibérément: MIL etc*) to wound; (*offenser*) to hurt; **se ~** to injure o.s.; **se ~ au pied** *etc* to injure one's foot *etc*; **blessure** *nf* (*accidentelle*) injury; (*intentionnelle*) wound

bleu, e [blø] *adj* blue; (*biftek*) very rare ♦ *nm* (*couleur*) blue; (*contusion*) bruise; (*vêtement: aussi:* **~s**) overalls *pl*; **~ marine** navy blue; **bleuet** *nm* cornflower; **bleuté, e** *adj* blue-shaded

blinder [blɛ̃de] *vt* to armour; (*fig*) to harden

bloc [blɔk] *nm* (*de pierre etc*) block; (*de papier à lettres*) pad; (*ensemble*) group, block; **serré à ~** tightened right down; **en ~** as a whole; **~ opératoire** operating *ou* theatre block; **~ sanitaire** toilet block; **blocage** *nm* (*des prix*) freezing; (*PSYCH*) hang-up; **bloc-notes** *nm* note pad

blocus [blɔkys] *nm* blockade

blond, e [blɔ̃, blɔ̃d] *adj* fair, blond; (*sable, blés*) golden; **~ cendré** ash blond; **blonde** *nf* (*femme*) blonde; (*bière*) lager; (*cigarette*) Virginia cigarette

bloquer [blɔke] *vt* (*passage*) to block; (*pièce mobile*) to jam; (*crédits, compte*) to freeze; **se ~** to jam; (*PSYCH*) to have a mental block

blottir [blɔtiʀ]: **se ~** *vi* to huddle up

blouse [bluz] *nf* overall

blouson [bluzɔ̃] *nm* blouson jacket; **~ noir** (*fig*) ≈ rocker

blue-jean [bludʒin] *nm* (pair of) jeans

bluff [blœf] *nm* bluff; **bluffer** *vi* to bluff

bobard [bɔbaʀ] (*fam*) *nm* tall story

bobine [bɔbin] *nf* reel; (*ÉLEC*) coil

bocal, -aux [bɔkal, o] *nm* jar

bock [bɔk] *nm* glass of beer

body [bɔdi] *nm* body(suit); (*SPORT*) leotard

bœuf [bœf] *nm* ox; (*CULIN*) beef

bof! [bɔf] (*fam*) *excl* don't care!; (*pas terrible*) nothing special

bogue [bɔg] *nm*: **le ~ de l'an 2000** the millennium bug

bohème [bɔɛm] *adj* happy-go-lucky, unconventional; **bohémien, ne** *nm/f* gipsy

boire [bwaʀ] *vt* to drink; (*s'imprégner de*) to soak up; **~ un coup** (*fam*) to have a drink

bois [bwa] *nm* wood; **de ~, en ~** wooden; **boisé, e** *adj* woody, wooded

boisson [bwasɔ̃] *nf* drink

boîte [bwat] *nf* box; (*fam: entreprise*) firm; **aliments en ~** canned *ou* tinned (*BRIT*) foods; **~ aux lettres** letter box; **~ d'allumettes** box of matches; (*vide*) matchbox; **~ (de conserve)** can *ou* tin (*BRIT*) (of food); **~ de nuit** night club; **~ de vitesses** gear box; **~ postale** PO Box; **~ vocale** (*TEL*) voice mail

boiter [bwate] *vi* to limp; (*fig: raisonnement*) to be shaky

boîtier [bwatje] *nm* case

boive *etc* [bwav] *vb voir* **boire**

bol [bɔl] *nm* bowl; **un ~ d'air** a breath of fresh air; **j'en ai ras le ~** (*fam*) I'm fed up with this; **avoir du ~** (*fam*) to be lucky

bolide [bɔlid] *nm* racing car; **comme un ~** at top speed, like a rocket

bombardement [bɔ̃baʀdəmɑ̃] *nm* bombing

bombarder [bɔ̃baʀde] *vt* to bomb; **~ qn de** (*cailloux, lettres*) to bombard sb with

bombe [bɔ̃b] *nf* bomb; (*atomiseur*) (aerosol) spray; **bombé, e** *adj* (*forme*) rounded; **bomber** *vt*: **bomber le torse** to swell out one's chest

---

MOT-CLÉ

bon, bonne [bɔ̃, bɔn] *adj* **1** (*agréable, satisfaisant*) good; **un bon repas/restaurant** a good meal/restaurant; **être bon en maths** to be good at maths

2 (*charitable*): **être bon (envers)** to be good (to)
3 (*correct*) right; **le bon numéro / moment** the right number/moment
4 (*souhaits*): **bon anniversaire** happy birthday; **bon voyage** have a good trip; **bonne chance** good luck; **bonne année** happy New Year; **bonne nuit** good night
5 (*approprié, apte*): **bon à / pour** fit to/for
6: **bon enfant** *adj inv* accommodating, easy-going; **bonne femme** (*péj*) woman; **de bonne heure** early; **bon marché** *adj inv* cheap ♦ *adv* cheap; **bon mot** witticism; **bon sens** common sense; **bon vivant** jovial chap; **bonnes œuvres** charitable works, charities
♦ *nm* **1** (*billet*) voucher; (*aussi*: **bon cadeau**) gift voucher; **bon d'essence** petrol coupon; **bon du Trésor** Treasury bond
2: **avoir du bon** to have its good points; **pour de bon** for good
♦ *adv*: **il fait bon** it's *ou* the weather is fine; **sentir bon** to smell good; **tenir bon** to stand firm
♦ *excl* good!; **ah bon?** really?; *voir aussi* **bonne**

bonbon [bɔ̃bɔ̃] *nm* (boiled) sweet
bonbonne [bɔ̃bɔn] *nf* demijohn
bond [bɔ̃] *nm* leap; **faire un ~** to leap in the air
bondé, e [bɔ̃de] *adj* packed (full)
bondir [bɔ̃diʀ] *vi* to leap
bonheur [bɔnœʀ] *nm* happiness; **porter ~ (à qn)** to bring (sb) luck; **au petit ~** haphazardly; **par ~** fortunately
bonhomie [bɔnɔmi] *nf* goodnaturedness
bonhomme [bɔnɔm] (*pl* **bonshommes**) *nm* fellow; **~ de neige** snowman
bonifier [bɔnifje] *vt* to improve
boniment [bɔnimɑ̃] *nm* patter *no pl*
bonjour [bɔ̃ʒuʀ] *excl, nm* hello; (*selon l'heure*) good morning/afternoon; **c'est simple comme ~!** it's easy as pie!
bonne [bɔn] *adj voir* **bon** ♦ *nf* (*domestique*)

maid; **bonnement** *adv*: **tout bonnement** quite simply
bonnet [bɔne] *nm* hat; (*de soutien-gorge*) cup; **~ de bain** bathing cap
bonshommes [bɔ̃zɔm] *nmpl de* **bonhomme**
bonsoir [bɔ̃swaʀ] *excl* good evening
bonté [bɔ̃te] *nf* kindness *no pl*
bonus [bɔnys] *nm* no-claims bonus
bord [bɔʀ] *nm* (*de table, verre, falaise*) edge; (*de rivière, lac*) bank; (*de route*) side; (**monter**) **à ~** (to go) on board; **par-dessus ~** to throw overboard; **le commandant de / les hommes du ~** the ship's master/crew; **au ~ de la mer** at the seaside; **être au ~ des larmes** to be on the verge of tears
bordeaux [bɔʀdo] *nm* Bordeaux (wine)
♦ *adj inv* maroon
bordel [bɔʀdɛl] *nm* brothel; (*fam!*) bloody mess (*!*)
bordelais, e [bɔʀdəlɛ, ɛz] *adj* of *ou* from Bordeaux
border [bɔʀde] *vt* (*être le long de*) to line; (*qn dans son lit*) to tuck up; (*garnir*): **~ qch de** to edge sth with
bordereau, x [bɔʀdəʀo] *nm* (*formulaire*) slip
bordure [bɔʀdyʀ] *nf* border; **en ~ de** on the edge of
borgne [bɔʀɲ] *adj* one-eyed
borne [bɔʀn] *nf* boundary stone; (*aussi*: **~ kilométrique**) kilometre-marker; ≈ milestone; **~s** *nfpl* (*fig*) limits; **dépasser les ~s** to go too far
borné, e [bɔʀne] *adj* (*personne*) narrow-minded
borner [bɔʀne] *vt*: **se ~ à faire** (*se contenter de*) to content o.s. with doing; (*se limiter à*) to limit o.s. to doing
bosquet [bɔskɛ] *nm* grove
bosse [bɔs] *nf* (*de terrain etc*) bump; (*enflure*) lump; (*du bossu, du chameau*) hump; **avoir la ~ des maths** *etc* (*fam*) to have a gift for maths *etc*; **il a roulé sa ~** (*fam*) he's been around

bosser [bɔse] (*fam*) *vi* (*travailler*) to work; (*travailler dur*) to slave (away)

bossu, e [bɔsy] *nm/f* hunchback

botanique [bɔtanik] *nf* botany ♦ *adj* botanic(al)

botte [bɔt] *nf* (*soulier*) (high) boot; (*gerbe*): **~ de paille** bundle of straw; **~ de radis** bunch of radishes; **~s de caoutchouc** wellington boots; **botter** *vt*: **ça me botte** (*fam*) I fancy that

bottin [bɔtɛ̃] *nm* directory

bottine [bɔtin] *nf* ankle boot

bouc [buk] *nm* goat; (*barbe*) goatee; **~ émissaire** scapegoat

boucan [bukɑ̃] (*fam*) *nm* din, racket

bouche [buʃ] *nf* mouth; **rester ~ bée** to stand open-mouthed; **le ~ à ~** the kiss of life; **~ d'égout** manhole; **~ d'incendie** fire hydrant; **~ de métro** métro entrance

bouché, e [buʃe] *adj* (*temps, ciel*) overcast; **c'est ~** there's no future in it

bouchée [buʃe] *nf* mouthful; **~s à la reine** chicken vol-au-vents

boucher, -ère [buʃe] *nm/f* butcher ♦ *vt* (*trou*) to fill up; (*obstruer*) to block (up); **se ~** *vi* (*tuyau etc*) to block up, get blocked up; **j'ai le nez bouché** my nose is blocked, **se ~ le nez** to hold one's nose; **boucherie** *nf* butcher's (shop); (*fig*) slaughter

bouche-trou [buʃtru] *nm* (*fig*) stop-gap

bouchon [buʃɔ̃] *nm* stopper; (*de tube*) top; (*en liège*) cork; (*fig: embouteillage*) holdup; (*PÊCHE*) float

boucle [bukl] *nf* (*forme, figure*) loop; (*objet*) buckle; **~ (de cheveux)** curl; **~ d'oreille** earring

bouclé, e [bukle] *adj* (*cheveux*) curly

boucler [bukle] *vt* (*fermer: ceinture etc*) to fasten; (*terminer*) to finish off; (*fam: enfermer*) to shut away; (*quartier*) to seal off ♦ *vi* to curl

bouclier [buklije] *nm* shield

bouddhiste [budist] *nm/f* Buddhist

bouder [bude] *vi* to sulk ♦ *vt* to stay away from

boudin [budɛ̃] *nm*: **~ (noir)** black pudding; **~ blanc** white pudding

boue [bu] *nf* mud

bouée [bwe] *nf* buoy; **~ (de sauvetage)** lifebuoy

boueux, -euse [bwø, øz] *adj* muddy

bouffe [buf] (*fam*) *nf* grub (*fam*), food

bouffée [bufe] *nf* (*de cigarette*) puff; **une ~ d'air pur** a breath of fresh air

bouffer [bufe] (*fam*) *vi* to eat

bouffi, e [bufi] *adj* swollen

bougeoir [buʒwaR] *nm* candlestick

bougeotte [buʒɔt] *nf*: **avoir la ~** (*fam*) to have the fidgets

bouger [buʒe] *vi* to move; (*dent etc*) to be loose; (*s'activer*) to get moving ♦ *vt* to move; **les prix/les couleurs n'ont pas bougé** prices/colours haven't changed

bougie [buʒi] *nf* candle; (*AUTO*) spark(ing) plug

bougon, ne [bugɔ̃, ɔn] *adj* grumpy

bougonner [bugɔne] *vi, vt* to grumble

bouillabaisse [bujabɛs] *nf* type of fish soup

bouillant, e [bujɑ̃, ɑ̃t] *adj* (*qui bout*) boiling; (*très chaud*) boiling (hot)

bouillie [buji] *nf* (*de bébé*) cereal; **en ~** (*fig*) crushed

bouillir [bujiR] *vi, vt* to boil; **~ d'impatience** to seethe with impatience

bouilloire [bujwaR] *nf* kettle

bouillon [bujɔ̃] *nm* (*CULIN*) stock *no pl*; **bouillonner** *vi* to bubble; (*fig: idées*) to bubble up

bouillotte [bujɔt] *nf* hot-water bottle

boulanger, -ère [bulɑ̃ʒe, ɛR] *nm/f* baker; **boulangerie** *nf* bakery; **boulangerie-pâtisserie** *nf* baker's and confectioner's (shop)

boule [bul] *nf* (*gén*) ball; **~s** *nfpl* (*jeu*) bowls; **se mettre en ~** (*fig: fam*) to fly off the handle, to blow one's top; **jouer aux ~s** to play bowls; **~ de neige** snowball

bouleau, x [bulo] *nm* (silver) birch

bouledogue [buldɔg] *nm* bulldog

boulet [bulɛ] *nm* (*aussi*: **~ de canon**) can-

nonball
boulette [bulɛt] *nf* (*de viande*) meatball
boulevard [bulvar] *nm* boulevard
bouleversant, e [bulvɛrsɑ̃, ɑ̃t] *adj* (*scène, récit*) deeply moving
bouleversement [bulvɛrsəmɑ̃] *nm* upheaval
bouleverser [bulvɛrse] *vt* (*émouvoir*) to overwhelm; (*causer du chagrin*) to distress; (*pays, vie*) to disrupt; (*papiers, objets*) to turn upside down
boulon [bulɔ̃] *nm* bolt
boulot, te [bulo, ɔt] *adj* plump, tubby
♦ *nm* (*fam: travail*) work
boum [bum] *nm* bang ♦ *nf* (*fam*) party
bouquet [bukɛ] *nm* (*de fleurs*) bunch (of flowers), bouquet; (*de persil etc*) bunch; **c'est le ~!** (*fam*) that takes the biscuit!
bouquin [bukɛ̃] (*fam*) *nm* book; **bouquiner** (*fam*) *vi* to read; **bouquiniste** *nm/f* bookseller
bourbeux, -euse [burbø, øz] *adj* muddy
bourbier [burbje] *nm* (quag)mire
bourde [burd] (*fam*) *nf* (*erreur*) howler; (*gaffe*) blunder
bourdon [burdɔ̃] *nm* bumblebee; **bourdonner** *vi* to buzz
bourg [bur] *nm* small market town
bourgeois, e [burʒwa, waz] (*péj*) *adj* ≈ (upper) middle class; **bourgeoisie** *nf* ≈ upper middle classes *pl*
bourgeon [burʒɔ̃] *nm* bud
Bourgogne [burgɔɲ] *nf*: **la ~** Burgundy ♦ *nm*: **b~** burgundy (wine)
bourguignon, ne [burgiɲɔ̃, ɔn] *adj* of *ou* from Burgundy, Burgundian
bourlinguer [burlɛ̃ge] (*fam*) *vi* to knock about a lot, get around a lot
bourrade [burad] *nf* shove, thump
bourrage [buraʒ] *nm*: **~ de crâne** brainwashing; (*SCOL*) cramming
bourrasque [burask] *nf* squall
bourratif, -ive [buratif, iv] (*fam*) *adj* filling, stodgy (*pej*)
bourré, e [bure] *adj* (*fam: ivre*) plastered, tanked up (*BRIT*); (*rempli*): **~ de** crammed

full of
bourreau, x [buro] *nm* executioner; (*fig*) torturer; **~ de travail** workaholic
bourrelet [burlɛ] *nm* fold *ou* roll (of flesh)
bourrer [bure] *vt* (*pipe*) to fill; (*poêle*) to pack; (*valise*) to cram (full)
bourrique [burik] *nf* (*âne*) ass
bourru, e [bury] *adj* surly, gruff
bourse [burs] *nf* (*subvention*) grant; (*porte-monnaie*) purse; **la B~** the Stock Exchange
boursier, -ière [bursje, jɛr] *nm/f* (*étudiant*) grant holder
boursoufler [bursufle]: **se ~** *vi* to swell (up)
bous [bu] *vb voir* **bouillir**
bousculade [buskylad] *nf* (*hâte*) rush; (*cohue*) crush; **bousculer** *vt* (*heurter*) to knock into; (*fig*) to push, rush
bouse [buz] *nf* dung *no pl*
bousiller [buzije] (*fam*) *vt* (*appareil*) to wreck
boussole [busɔl] *nf* compass
bout [bu] *vb voir* **bouillir** ♦ *nm* bit; (*d'un bâton etc*) tip; (*d'une ficelle, table, rue, période*) end; **au ~ de** at the end of, after; **pousser qn à ~** to push sb to the limit; **venir à ~ de** to manage to finish
boutade [butad] *nf* quip, sally
boute-en-train [butɑ̃trɛ̃] *nm inv* (*fig*) live wire
bouteille [butɛj] *nf* bottle; (*de gaz butane*) cylinder
boutique [butik] *nf* shop
bouton [butɔ̃] *nm* button; (*sur la peau*) spot; (*BOT*) bud; **~ d'or** buttercup; **boutonner** *vt* to button up; **boutonnière** *nf* buttonhole; **bouton-pression** *nm* press stud
bouture [butyr] *nf* cutting
bovins [bɔvɛ̃] *nmpl* cattle *pl*
bowling [bulin] *nm* (tenpin) bowling; (*salle*) bowling alley
box [bɔks] *nm* (*d'écurie*) loose-box; (*JUR*): **~ des accusés** dock
boxe [bɔks] *nf* boxing; **boxeur** *nm* boxer

boyaux [bwajo] *nmpl* (*viscères*) entrails, guts

BP *abr* = **boîte postale**

bracelet [bʀaslɛ] *nm* bracelet

braconnier [bʀakɔnje] *nm* poacher

brader [bʀade] *vt* to sell off; **braderie** *nf* cut-price shop/stall

braguette [bʀagɛt] *nf* fly *ou* flies *pl* (*BRIT*), zipper (*US*)

brailler [bʀaje] *vi* to bawl, yell

braire [bʀɛʀ] *vi* to bray

braise [bʀɛz] *nf* embers *pl*

brancard [bʀɑ̃kaʀ] *nm* (*civière*) stretcher; **brancardier** *nm* stretcher-bearer

branchages [bʀɑ̃ʃaʒ] *nmpl* boughs

branche [bʀɑ̃ʃ] *nf* branch

branché, e [bʀɑ̃ʃe] (*fam*) *adj* trendy

brancher [bʀɑ̃ʃe] *vt* to connect (up); (*en mettant la prise*) to plug in

brandir [bʀɑ̃diʀ] *vt* to brandish

branle [bʀɑ̃l] *nm*: **mettre en ~** to set in motion; **branle-bas** *nm inv* commotion

braquer [bʀake] *vi* (*AUTO*) to turn (the wheel) ♦ *vt* (*revolver etc*): **~ qch sur** to aim sth at, point sth at; (*mettre en colère*): **~ qn** to put sb's back up

bras [bʀa] *nm* arm; **~ dessus, ~ dessous** arm in arm; **se retrouver avec qch sur les ~** (*fam*) to be landed with sth; **~ droit** (*fig*) right hand man; **~ de fer** arm wrestling

brasier [bʀazje] *nm* blaze, inferno

bras-le-corps [bʀalkɔʀ] *adv*: **à ~-~-~** (a)round the waist

brassard [bʀasaʀ] *nm* armband

brasse [bʀas] *nf* (*nage*) breast-stroke

brassée [bʀase] *nf* armful

brasser [bʀase] *vt* to mix; **~ l'argent/les affaires** to handle a lot of money/business

brasserie [bʀasʀi] *nf* (*restaurant*) café-restaurant; (*usine*) brewery

brave [bʀav] *adj* (*courageux*) brave; (*bon, gentil*) good, kind

braver [bʀave] *vt* to defy

bravo [bʀavo] *excl* bravo ♦ *nm* cheer

bravoure [bʀavuʀ] *nf* bravery

break [bʀɛk] *nm* (*AUTO*) estate car

brebis [bʀəbi] *nf* ewe; **~ galeuse** black sheep

brèche [bʀɛʃ] *nf* breach, gap; **être toujours sur la ~** (*fig*) to be always on the go

bredouille [bʀəduj] *adj* empty-handed

bredouiller [bʀəduje] *vi, vt* to mumble, stammer

bref, brève [bʀɛf, ɛv] *adj* short, brief ♦ *adv* in short; **d'un ton ~** sharply, curtly; **en ~** in short, in brief

Brésil [bʀezil] *nm* Brazil; **brésilien, -ne** *adj* Brazilian ♦ *nm/f*: **Brésilien, ne** Brazilian

Bretagne [bʀətaɲ] *nf* Brittany

bretelle [bʀətɛl] *nf* (*de vêtement, de sac*) strap; (*d'autoroute*) slip road (*BRIT*), entrance/exit ramp (*US*); **~s** *nfpl* (*pour pantalon*) braces (*BRIT*), suspenders (*US*)

breton, ne [bʀətɔ̃, ɔn] *adj* Breton ♦ *nm/f*: **B~, ne** Breton

breuvage [bʀœvaʒ] *nm* beverage, drink

brève [bʀɛv] *adj voir* **bref**

brevet [bʀəvɛ] *nm* diploma, certificate; **~ (d'invention)** patent; **breveté, e** *adj* patented

bribes [bʀib] *nfpl* (*de conversation*) snatches; **par ~** piecemeal

bricolage [bʀikɔlaʒ] *nm*: **le ~** do-it-yourself

bricole [bʀikɔl] *nf* (*babiole*) trifle

bricoler [bʀikɔle] *vi* (*petits travaux*) to do DIY jobs; (*passe-temps*) to potter about ♦ *vt* (*réparer*) to fix up; **bricoleur, -euse** *nm/f* handyman(-woman), DIY enthusiast

bride [bʀid] *nf* bridle; **tenir qn en ~** to keep a tight rein on sb

bridé, e [bʀide] *adj*: **yeux ~s** slit eyes

bridge [bʀidʒ] *nm* (*CARTES*) bridge

brièvement [bʀijɛvmɑ̃] *adv* briefly

brigade [bʀigad] *nf* (*POLICE*) squad; (*MIL*) brigade; **brigadier** *nm* sergeant

brigandage [bʀigɑ̃daʒ] *nm* robbery

briguer [bʀige] *vt* to aspire to

brillamment [bʀijamɑ̃] *adv* brilliantly

brillant, e [bʀijɑ̃, ɑ̃t] *adj* (*remarquable*) bright; (*luisant*) shiny, shining

briller [bʀije] *vi* to shine

brimer [bʀime] *vt* to bully

brin [bʀɛ̃] *nm* (*de laine, ficelle etc*) strand; (*fig*): **un ~ de** a bit of; **~ d'herbe** blade of grass; **~ de muguet** sprig of lily of the valley

brindille [bʀɛ̃dij] *nf* twig

brio [bʀijo] *nm*: **avec ~** with panache

brioche [bʀijɔʃ] *nf* brioche (bun); (*fam*: *ventre*) paunch

brique [bʀik] *nf* brick; (*de lait*) carton

briquer [bʀike] *vt* to polish up

briquet [bʀike] *nm* (cigarette) lighter

brise [bʀiz] *nf* breeze

briser [bʀize] *vt* to break; **se ~** *vi* to break

britannique [bʀitanik] *adj* British ♦ *nm/f*: **B~** British person, Briton; **les B~s** the British

brocante [bʀɔkɑ̃t] *nf* junk, second-hand goods *pl*; **brocanteur, -euse** *nm/f* junk-shop owner; junk dealer

broche [bʀɔʃ] *nf* brooch; (*CULIN*) spit; (*MÉD*) pin; **à la ~** spit-roasted

broché, e [bʀɔʃe] *adj* (*livre*) paper-backed

brochet [bʀɔʃe] *nm* pike *inv*

brochette [bʀɔʃet] *nf* (*ustensile*) skewer; (*plat*) kebab

brochure [bʀɔʃyʀ] *nf* pamphlet, brochure, booklet

broder [bʀɔde] *vt* to embroider ♦ *vi* to embroider the facts; **broderie** *nf* embroidery

broncher [bʀɔ̃ʃe] *vi*: **sans ~** without flinching, without turning a hair

bronches [bʀɔ̃ʃ] *nfpl* bronchial tubes; **bronchite** *nf* bronchitis

bronze [bʀɔ̃z] *nm* bronze

bronzer [bʀɔ̃ze] *vi* to get a tan; **se ~** to sunbathe

brosse [bʀɔs] *nf* brush; **coiffé en ~** with a crewcut; **~ à cheveux** hairbrush; **~ à dents** toothbrush; **~ à habits** clothesbrush; **brosser** *vt* (*nettoyer*) to brush; (*fig*:

tableau etc) to paint; **se brosser les dents** to brush one's teeth

brouette [bʀuet] *nf* wheelbarrow

brouhaha [bʀuaa] *nm* hubbub

brouillard [bʀujaʀ] *nm* fog

brouille [bʀuj] *nf* quarrel

brouiller [bʀuje] *vt* (*œufs, message*) to scramble; (*idées*) to mix up; (*rendre trouble*) to cloud; (*désunir: amis*) to set at odds; **se ~** *vi* (*vue*) to cloud over; (*gens*) to fall out

brouillon, ne [bʀujɔ̃, ɔn] *adj* (*sans soin*) untidy; (*qui manque d'organisation*) disorganized ♦ *nm* draft; (**papier**) **~** rough paper

broussailles [bʀusaj] *nfpl* undergrowth *sg*; **broussailleux, -euse** *adj* bushy

brousse [bʀus] *nf*: **la ~** the bush

brouter [bʀute] *vi* to graze

broutille [bʀutij] *nf* trifle

broyer [bʀwaje] *vt* to crush; **~ du noir** to be down in the dumps

bru [bʀy] *nf* daughter-in-law

brugnon [bʀyɲɔ̃] *nm* (*BOT*) nectarine

bruiner [bʀɥine] *vb impers*: **il bruine** it's drizzling, there's a drizzle

bruire [bʀɥiʀ] *vi* (*feuilles*) to rustle

bruit [bʀɥi] *nm*: **un ~** a noise, a sound; (*fig: rumeur*) a rumour; **le ~** noise; **sans ~** without a sound, noiselessly; **~ de fond** background noise; **bruitage** *nm* sound effects *pl*

brûlant, e [bʀylɑ̃, ɑ̃t] *adj* burning; (*liquide*) boiling (hot)

brûlé, e [bʀyle] *adj* (*fig: démasqué*) blown ♦ *nm*: **odeur de ~** smell of burning

brûle-pourpoint [bʀylpuʀpwɛ̃]: **à ~-~** *adv* point-blank

brûler [bʀyle] *vt* to burn; (*suj: eau bouillante*) to scald; (*consommer: électricité, essence*) to use; (*feu rouge, signal*) to go through ♦ *vi* to burn; (*jeu*): **tu brûles!** you're getting hot!; **se ~** to burn o.s.; (*s'ébouillanter*) to scald o.s.

brûlure [bʀylyʀ] *nf* (*lésion*) burn; **~s d'estomac** heartburn *sg*

brume [bʀym] *nf* mist; **brumisateur** *nm* atomizer

brun, e [bʀœ̃, bʀyn] *adj* (*gén, bière*) brown; (*cheveux, tabac*) dark; **elle est ~e** she's got dark hair

brunch [bʀœntʃ] *nm* brunch

brunir [bʀynir] *vi* to get a tan

brushing [bʀœʃiŋ] *nm* blow-dry

brusque [bʀysk] *adj* abrupt; **brusquer** *vt* to rush

brut, e [bʀyt] *adj* (*minerai, soie*) raw; (*diamant*) rough; (*COMM*) gross; **(pétrole) ~** crude (oil)

brutal, e, -aux [bʀytal, o] *adj* brutal; **brutaliser** *vt* to handle roughly, manhandle

Bruxelles [bʀysɛl] *n* Brussels

bruyamment [bʀyjamɑ̃] *adv* noisily

bruyant, e [bʀyjɑ̃, ɑ̃t] *adj* noisy

bruyère [bʀyjɛʀ] *nf* heather

BTS *sigle m* (= *brevet de technicien supérieur*) *vocational training certificate taken at the end of a higher education course*

bu, e [by] *pp de* **boire**

buccal, e, -aux [bykal, o] *adj*: **par voie ~e** orally

bûche [byʃ] *nf* log; **prendre une ~** (*fig*) to come a cropper; **de Noël** Yule log

bûcher [byʃe] *nm* (*funéraire*) pyre; (*supplice*) stake ♦ *vi* (*fam*) to swot (*BRIT*), slave (away) ♦ *vt* (*fam*) to swot up (*BRIT*), slave away at; **bûcheron** *nm* woodcutter; **bûcheur, -euse** (*fam*) *adj* hard-working

budget [bydʒɛ] *nm* budget

buée [bɥe] *nf* (*sur une vitre*) mist

buffet [byfɛ] *nm* (*meuble*) sideboard; (*de réception*) buffet; **~ (de gare)** (station) buffet, snack bar

buffle [byfl] *nm* buffalo

buis [bɥi] *nm* box tree; (*bois*) box(wood)

buisson [bɥisɔ̃] *nm* bush

buissonnière [bɥisɔnjɛʀ] *adj*: **faire l'école ~** to skip school

bulbe [bylb] *nm* (*BOT, ANAT*) bulb

Bulgarie [bylgaʀi] *nf* Bulgaria

bulle [byl] *nf* bubble

bulletin [byltɛ̃] *nm* (*communiqué, journal*) bulletin; (*SCOL*) report; **~ d'informations** news bulletin; **~ de salaire** pay-slip; **~ (de vote)** ballot paper; **~ météorologique** weather report

bureau, x [byʀo] *nm* (*meuble*) desk; (*pièce, service*) office; **~ de change** (foreign) exchange office *ou* bureau; **~ de poste** post office; **~ de tabac** tobacconist's (shop); **~ de vote** polling station; **bureaucratie** [byʀokʀasi] *nf* bureaucracy

burin [byʀɛ̃] *nm* cold chisel; (*ART*) burin

burlesque [byʀlɛsk] *adj* ridiculous; (*LITTÉRATURE*) burlesque

bus¹ [by] *vb voir* **boire**

bus² [bys] *nm* bus

busqué, e [byske] *adj* (*nez*) hook(ed)

buste [byst] *nm* (*torse*) chest; (*seins*) bust

but¹ [by] *vb voir* **boire**

but² [by(t)] *nm* (*cible*) target; (*fig*) goal, aim; (*FOOTBALL etc*) goal; **de ~ en blanc** point-blank; **avoir pour ~ de faire** to aim to do; **dans le ~ de** with the intention of

butane [bytan] *nm* (*camping*) butane; (*usage domestique*) Calor gas ®

buté, e [byte] *adj* stubborn, obstinate

buter [byte] *vi*: **~ contre** (*cogner*) to bump into; (*trébucher*) to stumble against; **se ~** *vi* to get obstinate, dig in one's heels; **~ contre une difficulté** (*fig*) to hit a snag

butin [bytɛ̃] *nm* booty, spoils *pl*; (*d'un vol*) loot

butiner [bytine] *vi* (*abeilles*) to gather nectar

butte [byt] *nf* mound, hillock; **être en ~ à** to be exposed to

buvais *etc* [byve] *vb voir* **boire**

buvard [byvaʀ] *nm* blotter

buvette [byvɛt] *nf* bar

buveur, -euse [byvœʀ, øz] *nm/f* drinker

C, c

c' [s] *dét voir* **ce**

CA *sigle m* = **chiffre d'affaires**

ça [sa] *pron* (*pour désigner*) this; (: *plus loin*) that; (*comme sujet indéfini*) it; **comment ~ va?** how are you?; **~ va?** (*d'accord?*) OK?, all right?; **où ~?** where's that?; **pourquoi ~?** why's that?; **qui ~?** who's that?; **~ alors!** well really!; **~ fait 10 ans (que)** it's 10 years (since); **c'est ~** that's right; **~ y est** that's it

çà [sa] *adv*: **~ et là** here and there

cabane [kaban] *nf* hut, cabin

cabaret [kabaʁɛ] *nm* night club

cabas [kaba] *nm* shopping bag

cabillaud [kabijo] *nm* cod *inv*

cabine [kabin] *nf* (*de bateau*) cabin; (*de piscine etc*) cubicle; (*de camion, train*) cab; (*d'avion*) cockpit; **~ d'essayage** fitting room; **~ (téléphonique)** call *ou* (tele)phone box

cabinet [kabinɛ] *nm* (*petite pièce*) closet; (*de médecin*) surgery (*BRIT*), office (*US*); (*de notaire etc*) office; (: *clientèle*) practice; (*POL*) Cabinet; **~s** *nmpl* (w.-c.) toilet *sg*; **~ d'affaires** business consultancy; **~ de toilette** toilet

câble [kabl] *nm* cable

cabosser [kabɔse] *vt* to dent

cabrer [kabʁe]: **se ~** *vi* (*cheval*) to rear up

cabriole [kabʁijɔl] *nf*: **faire des ~s** to caper about

cacahuète [kakaɥɛt] *nf* peanut

cacao [kakao] *nm* cocoa

cache [kaʃ] *nm* mask, card (for masking)

cache-cache [kaʃkaʃ] *nm*: **jouer à ~-~** to play hide-and-seek

cachemire [kaʃmiʁ] *nm* cashmere

cache-nez [kaʃne] *nm inv* scarf, muffler

cacher [kaʃe] *vt* to hide, conceal; **se ~** *vi* (*volontairement*) to hide; (*être caché*) to be hidden *ou* concealed; **~ qch à qn** to hide *ou* conceal sth from sb

cachet [kaʃɛ] *nm* (*comprimé*) tablet; (*de la poste*) postmark; (*rétribution*) fee; (*fig*) style, character; **cacheter** *vt* to seal

cachette [kaʃɛt] *nf* hiding place; **en ~** on the sly, secretly

cachot [kaʃo] *nm* dungeon

cachotterie [kaʃɔtʁi] *nf*: **faire des ~s** to be secretive

cactus [kaktys] *nm* cactus

cadavre [kadavʁ] *nm* corpse, (dead) body

Caddie ®, **caddy** [kadi] *nm* (*supermarket*) trolley

cadeau, x [kado] *nm* present, gift; **faire un ~ à qn** to give sb a present *ou* gift; **faire ~ de qch à qn** to make a present of sth to sb, give sb sth as a present

cadenas [kadna] *nm* padlock

cadence [kadɑ̃s] *nf* (*tempo*) rhythm; (*de travail etc*) rate; **en ~** rhythmically

cadet, te [kadɛ, ɛt] *adj* younger; (*le plus jeune*) youngest ♦ *nm/f* youngest child *ou* one

cadran [kadʁɑ̃] *nm* dial; **~ solaire** sundial

cadre [kadʁ] *nm* frame; (*environnement*) surroundings *pl* ♦ *nm/f* (*ADMIN*) managerial employee, executive; **dans le ~ de** (*fig*) within the framework *ou* context of

cadrer [kadʁe] *vi*: **~ avec** to tally *ou* correspond with ♦ *vt* to centre

cafard [kafaʁ] *nm* cockroach; **avoir le ~** (*fam*) to be down in the dumps

café [kafe] *nm* coffee; (*bistro*) café ♦ *adj inv* coffee(-coloured); **~ au lait** white coffee; **~ noir** black coffee; **~ tabac** tobacconist's *ou* newsagent's serving coffee and spirits; **cafetière** *nf* (*pot*) coffee-pot

cafouiller [kafuje] (*fam*) *vi* to get into a shambles

cage [kaʒ] *nf* cage; **~ d'escalier** (stair)well; **~ thoracique** rib cage

cageot [kaʒo] *nm* crate

cagibi [kaʒibi] (*fam*) *nm* (*débarras*) box room

cagnotte [kaɲɔt] *nf* kitty

cagoule [kagul] *nf* (*passe-montagne*) balaclava

cahier [kaje] *nm* notebook; **~ de brouillons** roughbook, jotter; **~ d'exercices** exercise book

cahot [kao] *nm* jolt, bump

caïd [kaid] *nm* big chief, boss

caille [kaj] *nf* quail

cailler [kaje] *vi* (*lait*) to curdle; **ça caille** (*fam*) it's freezing; **caillot** *nm* (blood) clot

caillou, x [kaju] *nm* (little) stone; **cailloteux, -euse** *adj* (*route*) stony

Caire [kɛʀ] *nm*: **le ~** Cairo

caisse [kɛs] *nf* box; (*tiroir où l'on met la recette*) till; (*où l'on paye*) cash desk (*BRIT*), check-out; (*de banque*) cashier's desk; **~ d'épargne** savings bank; **~ de retraite** pension fund; **~ enregistreuse** cash register; **caissier, -ière** *nm/f* cashier

cajoler [kaʒɔle] *vt* (*câliner*) to cuddle; (*amadouer*) to wheedle, coax

cake [kɛk] *nm* fruit cake

calandre [kalɑ̃dʀ] *nf* radiator grill

calanque [kalɑ̃k] *nf* rocky inlet

calcaire [kalkɛʀ] *nm* limestone ♦ *adj* (*eau*) hard; (*GÉO*) limestone *cpd*

calciné, e [kalsine] *adj* burnt to ashes

calcul [kalkyl] *nm* calculation; **le ~** (*SCOL*) arithmetic; **~ (biliaire)** (gall)stone; **calculatrice** *nf* calculator; **calculer** *vt* to calculate, work out; **calculette** *nf* pocket calculator

cale [kal] *nf* (*de bateau*) hold; (*en bois*) wedge; **~ sèche** dry dock

calé, e [kale] (*fam*) *adj* clever, bright

caleçon [kalsɔ̃] *nm* (*d'homme*) boxer shorts; (*de femme*) leggings

calembour [kalɑ̃buʀ] *nm* pun

calendrier [kalɑ̃dʀije] *nm* calendar; (*fig*) timetable

calepin [kalpɛ̃] *nm* notebook

caler [kale] *vt* to wedge ♦ *vi* (*moteur, véhicule*) to stall

calfeutrer [kalføtʀe] *vt* to (make) draughtproof; **se ~** *vi* to make o.s. snug and comfortable

calibre [kalibʀ] *nm* calibre

alifourchon [kalifuʀʃɔ̃]: **à ~** *adv* astride

câlin, e [kɑlɛ̃, in] *adj* cuddly, cuddlesome; (*regard, voix*) tender; **câliner** *vt* to cuddle

calmant [kalmɑ̃] *nm* tranquillizer, sedative; (*pour la douleur*) painkiller

calme [kalm] *adj* calm, quiet ♦ *nm* calm(ness), quietness; **calmer** *vt* to calm (down); (*douleur, inquiétude*) to ease, soothe; **se calmer** *vi* to calm down

calomnie [kalɔmni] *nf* slander; (*écrite*) libel; **calomnier** *vt* to slander; to libel

calorie [kalɔʀi] *nf* calorie

calotte [kalɔt] *nf* (*coiffure*) skullcap; (*fam: gifle*) slap; **~ glaciaire** (*GÉO*) icecap

calquer [kalke] *vt* to trace; (*fig*) to copy exactly

calvaire [kalvɛʀ] *nm* (*croix*) wayside cross, calvary; (*souffrances*) suffering

calvitie [kalvisi] *nf* baldness

camarade [kamaʀad] *nm/f* friend, pal; (*POL*) comrade; **camaraderie** *nf* friendship

cambouis [kɑ̃bwi] *nm* dirty oil *ou* grease

cambrer [kɑ̃bʀe]: **se ~** *vi* to arch one's back

cambriolage [kɑ̃bʀijɔlaʒ] *nm* burglary; **cambrioler** *vt* to burgle (*BRIT*), burglarize (*US*); **cambrioleur, -euse** *nm/f* burglar

camelote [kamlɔt] (*fam*) *nf* rubbish, trash, junk

caméra [kameʀa] *nf* (*CINÉMA, TV*) camera; (*d'amateur*) cine-camera

caméscope ® [kameskɔp] *nm* camcorder ®

camion [kamjɔ̃] *nm* lorry (*BRIT*), truck; **~ de dépannage** breakdown (*BRIT*) *ou* tow (*US*) truck; **camion-citerne** *nm* tanker; **camionnette** *nf* (small) van; **camionneur** *nm* (*chauffeur*) lorry (*BRIT*) *ou* truck driver; (*entrepreneur*) haulage contractor (*BRIT*), trucker (*US*)

camisole [kamizɔl] *nf*: **~ (de force)** straitjacket

camomille [kamɔmij] *nf* camomile; (*boisson*) camomile tea

camoufler [kamufle] *vt* to camouflage; (*fig*) to conceal, cover up

camp [kɑ̃] *nm* camp; (*fig*) side; ~ **de va-cances** children's holiday camp (*BRIT*), summer camp (*US*)

campagnard, e [kɑ̃paɲaʀ, aʀd] *adj* country *cpd*

campagne [kɑ̃paɲ] *nf* country, country-side; (*MIL, POL, COMM*) campaign; **à la ~** in the country

camper [kɑ̃pe] *vi* to camp ♦ *vt* to sketch; **se ~ devant** to plant o.s. in front of; **campeur, -euse** *nm/f* camper

camping [kɑ̃piŋ] *nm* camping; **(terrain de) ~** campsite, camping site; **faire du ~** to go camping; **camping-car** *nm* camper, motorhome (*US*); **camping-gaz** ® *nm inv* camp(ing) stove

Canada [kanada] *nm*: **le ~** Canada; **ca-nadien, ne** *adj* Canadian ♦ *nm/f*: **Cana-dien, ne** Canadian; **canadienne** *nf* (*veste*) fur-lined jacket

canaille [kanɑj] (*péj*) *nf* scoundrel

canal, -aux [kanal, o] *nm* canal; (*naturel*) channel; **canalisation** *nf* (*tuyau*) pipe; **canaliser** *vt* to canalize; (*fig*) to channel

canapé [kanape] *nm* settee, sofa

canard [kanaʀ] *nm* duck; (*fam: journal*) rag

canari [kanaʀi] *nm* canary

cancans [kɑ̃kɑ̃] *nmpl* (malicious) gossip *sg*

cancer [kɑ̃sɛʀ] *nm* cancer; (*signe*): **le C~** Cancer; ~ **de la peau** skin cancer

cancre [kɑ̃kʀ] *nm* dunce

candeur [kɑ̃dœʀ] *nf* ingenuousness, guile-lessness

candidat, e [kɑ̃dida, at] *nm/f* candidate; (*à un poste*) applicant, candidate; **candi-dature** *nf* (*POL*) candidature; (*à poste*) ap-plication; **poser sa candidature à un poste** to apply for a job

candide [kɑ̃did] *adj* ingenuous, guileless

cane [kan] *nf* (female) duck

caneton [kantɔ̃] *nm* duckling

canette [kanɛt] *nf* (*de bière*) (flip-top) bot-tle

canevas [kanvɑ] *nm* (*COUTURE*) canvas

caniche [kaniʃ] *nm* poodle

canicule [kanikyl] *nf* scorching heat

canif [kanif] *nm* penknife, pocket knife

canine [kanin] *nf* canine (tooth)

caniveau, x [kanivo] *nm* gutter

canne [kan] *nf* (walking) stick; ~ **à pêche** fishing rod; ~ **à sucre** sugar cane

cannelle [kanɛl] *nf* cinnamon

canoë [kanɔe] *nm* canoe; (*sport*) canoeing

canon [kanɔ̃] *nm* (*arme*) gun; (*HISTOIRE*) cannon; (*d'une arme: tube*) barrel; (*fig, norme*) model; (*MUS*) canon

canot [kano] *nm* ding(h)y; ~ **de sauveta-ge** lifeboat; ~ **pneumatique** inflatabl ding(h)y; **canotier** *nm* boater

cantatrice [kɑ̃tatʀis] *nf* (opera) singer

cantine [kɑ̃tin] *nf* canteen

cantique [kɑ̃tik] *nm* hymn

canton [kɑ̃tɔ̃] *nm* district consisting of sev eral communes; (*en Suisse*) canton

cantonade [kɑ̃tɔnad]: **à la ~** *adv* t everyone in general

cantonner [kɑ̃tɔne]: **se ~ à** *vt* to confin o.s. to

cantonnier [kɑ̃tɔnje] *nm* roadmender

canular [kanylaʀ] *nm* hoax

caoutchouc [kautʃu] *nm* rubber

cap [kap] *nm* (*GÉO*) cape; (*promontoire* headland; (*fig: tournant*) watershed; (*N VIG*): **changer de ~** to change course **mettre le ~ sur** to head *ou* steer for

CAP *sigle m* (= *Certificat d'aptitude profe sionnelle*) *vocational training certifica taken at secondary school*

capable [kapabl] *adj* able, capable; ~ **d qch/faire** capable of sth/doing

capacité [kapasite] *nf* (*compétence*) abilit (*JUR, contenance*) capacity

cape [kap] *nf* cape, cloak; **rire sous ~** t laugh up one's sleeve

CAPES [kapɛs] *sigle m* (= *Certifica d'aptitude pédagogique à l'enseignement s condaire*) *teaching diploma*

capillaire [kapilɛʀ] *adj* (*soins, lotion*) ha *cpd*; (*vaisseau etc*) capillary

capitaine [kapitɛn] *nm* captain

capital, e, -aux [kapital, o] *adj* (*œuvre* major; (*question, rôle*) fundamental ♦ *n* capital; (*fig*) stock; **d'une importance ~e** of capital importance; *voir aussi* **capitaux**; **~ (social)** authorized capital; **capitale** *nf* (*ville*) capital; (*lettre*) capital (letter); **capitalisme** *nm* capitalism; **capitaliste** *adj*, *nm/f* capitalist; **capitaux** *nmpl* (*fonds*) capital *sg*

apitonné, e [kapitɔne] *adj* padded

aporal, -aux [kapɔral, o] *nm* lance corporal

apot [kapo] *nm* (*AUTO*) bonnet (*BRIT*), hood (*US*)

apote [kapɔt] *nf* (*de voiture*) hood (*BRIT*), top (*US*); (*fam*) condom

apoter [kapɔte] *vi* (*négociations*) to founder

âpre [kɑpʀ] *nf* caper

aprice [kapʀis] *nm* whim, caprice; **faire des ~s** to make a fuss; **capricieux, -euse** *adj* (*fantasque*) capricious, whimsical; (*enfant*) awkward

apricorne [kapʀikɔʀn] *nm*: **le ~** Capricorn

apsule [kapsyl] *nf* (*de bouteille*) cap; (*BOT etc, spatiale*) capsule

apter [kapte] *vt* (*ondes radio*) to pick up; (*fig*) to win, capture

aptivant, e [kaptivɑ̃, ɑ̃t] *adj* captivating

aptivité [kaptivite] *nf* captivity

apturer [kaptyʀe] *vt* to capture

apuche [kapyʃ] *nf* hood

apuchon [kapyʃɔ̃] *nm* hood; (*de stylo*) cap, top

apucine [kapysin] *nf* (*BOT*) nasturtium

aquet [kakɛ] *nm*: **rabattre le ~ à qn** (*fam*) to bring sb down a peg or two

aqueter [kakte] *vi* to cackle

ar [kaʀ] *nm* coach ♦ *conj* because, for

arabine [kaʀabin] *nf* rifle

aractère [kaʀaktɛʀ] *nm* (*gén*) character; **avoir bon/mauvais ~** to be good-/ill-natured; **en ~s gras** in bold type; **en petits ~s** in small print; **~s d'imprimerie** (block) capitals; **caractériel, le** *adj* (*traits*) (of) character; (*enfant*) emotionally disturbed

caractérisé, e [kaʀakteʀize] *adj* sheer, downright

caractériser [kaʀakteʀize] *vt* to be characteristic of

caractéristique [kaʀakteʀistik] *adj*, *nf* characteristic

carafe [kaʀaf] *nf* (*pour eau, vin ordinaire*) carafe

caraïbe [kaʀaib] *adj* Caribbean ♦ *n*: **les C~s** the Caribbean (Islands)

carambolage [kaʀɑ̃bɔlaʒ] *nm* multiple crash, pileup

caramel [kaʀamɛl] *nm* (*bonbon*) caramel, toffee; (*substance*) caramel

carapace [kaʀapas] *nf* shell

caravane [kaʀavan] *nf* caravan; **caravaning** *nm* caravanning

carbone [kaʀbɔn] *nm* carbon; (*double*) carbon (copy); **carbonique** *adj*: **gaz carbonique** carbon dioxide; **neige carbonique** dry ice; **carbonisé, e** *adj* charred

carburant [kaʀbyʀɑ̃] *nm* (motor) fuel

carburateur [kaʀbyʀatœʀ] *nm* carburettor

carcan [kaʀkɑ̃] *nm* (*fig*) yoke, shackles *pl*

carcasse [kaʀkas] *nf* carcass; (*de véhicule etc*) shell

cardiaque [kaʀdjak] *adj* cardiac, heart *cpd* ♦ *nm/f* heart patient; **être ~** to have heart trouble

cardigan [kaʀdigɑ̃] *nm* cardigan

cardiologue [kaʀdjɔlɔg] *nm/f* cardiologist, heart specialist

carême [kaʀɛm] *nm*: **le C~** Lent

carence [kaʀɑ̃s] *nf* (*manque*) deficiency

caresse [kaʀɛs] *nf* caress

caresser [kaʀese] *vt* to caress; (*animal*) to stroke

cargaison [kaʀgɛzɔ̃] *nf* cargo, freight

cargo [kaʀgo] *nm* cargo boat, freighter

caricature [kaʀikatyʀ] *nf* caricature

carie [kaʀi] *nf*: **la ~ (dentaire)** tooth decay; **une ~** a bad tooth

carillon [kaʀijɔ̃] *nm* (*air, de pendule*) chimes *pl*

caritatif, -ive [kaʀitatif, iv] *adj*: **organisation caritative** charity

carnassier, -ière [kaʀnasje, jɛʀ] *adj* carnivorous

carnaval [kaʀnaval] *nm* carnival

carnet [kaʀnɛ] *nm* (*calepin*) notebook; (*de tickets, timbres etc*) book; ~ **de chèques** cheque book; ~ **de notes** school report

carotte [kaʀɔt] *nf* carrot

carpette [kaʀpɛt] *nf* rug

carré, e [kaʀe] *adj* square; (*fig: franc*) straightforward ♦ *nm* (MATH) square; **mètre/kilomètre** ~ square metre/kilometre

carreau, x [kaʀo] *nm* (*par terre*) (floor) tile; (*au mur*) (wall) tile; (*de fenêtre*) (window) pane; (*motif*) check, square; (CARTES: *couleur*) diamonds *pl*; **tissu à ~x** checked fabric

carrefour [kaʀfuʀ] *nm* crossroads *sg*

carrelage [kaʀlaʒ] *nm* (*sol*) (tiled) floor

carrelet [kaʀlɛ] *nm* (*poisson*) plaice

carrément [kaʀemɑ̃] *adv* (*franchement*) straight out, bluntly; (*sans hésiter*) straight; (*intensif*) completely; **c'est ~ impossible** it's completely impossible

carrière [kaʀjɛʀ] *nf* (*métier*) career; (*de roches*) quarry; **militaire de** ~ professional soldier

carrossable [kaʀɔsabl] *adj* suitable for (motor) vehicles

carrosse [kaʀɔs] *nm* (horse-drawn) coach

carrosserie [kaʀɔsʀi] *nf* body, coachwork *no pl*

carrure [kaʀyʀ] *nf* build; (*fig*) stature, calibre

cartable [kaʀtabl] *nm* satchel, (school)bag

carte [kaʀt] *nf* (*de géographie*) map; (*marine, du ciel*) chart; (*d'abonnement, à jouer*) card; (*au restaurant*) menu; (*aussi*: ~ **de visite**) (visiting) card; **à la** ~ (*au restaurant*) à la carte; **donner** ~ **blanche à qn** to give sb a free rein; ~ **bancaire** cash card; ~ **de crédit** credit card; ~ **de fidélité** loyalty card; ~ **d'identité** identity card; ~ **de séjour** residence permit; ~ **grise** (AUTO) ≃ (car) registration book, logbook; ~ **postale** postcard; ~ **routière** road map; ~ **té-**

léphonique phonecard

carter [kaʀtɛʀ] *nm* sump

carton [kaʀtɔ̃] *nm* (*matériau*) cardboard; (*boîte*) (cardboard) box; **faire un** ~ (*fam*) to score a hit; ~ **(à dessin)** portfolio

carton-pâte *nm* pasteboard

cartouche [kaʀtuʃ] *nf* cartridge; (*de cigarettes*) carton

cas [kɑ] *nm* case; **ne faire aucun** ~ **de** to take no notice of; **en aucun** ~ on no account; **au** ~ **où** in case; **en** ~ **de** in case of, in the event of; **en** ~ **de besoin** if need be; **en tout** ~ in any case, at any rate; ~ **de conscience** matter of conscience

casanier, -ière [kazanje, jɛʀ] *adj* stay-at-home

cascade [kaskad] *nf* waterfall, cascade; (*fig*) stream, torrent; **cascadeur, -euse** *nm/f* stuntman(-girl)

case [kɑz] *nf* (*hutte*) hut; (*compartiment*) compartment; (*sur un formulaire, de mots croisés etc*) box

caser [kɑze] (*fam*) *vt* (*placer*) to put (away); (*loger*) to put up; **se** ~ *vi* (*se marier*) to settle down; (*trouver un emploi*) to find a (steady) job

caserne [kazɛʀn] *nf* barracks *pl*

cash [kaʃ] *adv*: **payer** ~ to pay cash down

casier [kazje] *nm* (*pour courrier*) pigeonhole; (*compartiment*) compartment; (*à clé*) locker; ~ **judiciaire** police record

casino [kazino] *nm* casino

casque [kask] *nm* helmet; (*chez le coiffeur*) (hair-)drier; (*pour audition*) (head-)phones *pl*, headset

casquette [kaskɛt] *nf* cap

cassant, e [kasɑ̃, ɑ̃t] *adj* brittle; (*fig: ton*) curt, abrupt

cassation [kasasjɔ̃] *nf*: **cour de** ~ final court of appeal

casse [kɑs] (*fam*) *nf* (*pour voitures*): **mettre à la** ~ to scrap; (*dégâts*): **il y a eu de la** ~ there were a lot of breakages; **casse-cou** *adj inv* daredevil, reckless; **casse-croûte** *nm inv* snack; **casse-noix** *nm inv*

inv nutcrackers *pl*; **casse-pieds** (*fam*) *adj inv*: **il est casse-pieds** he's a pain in the neck

asser [kɑse] *vt* to break; (*JUR*) to quash; **se ~** *vi* to break; **~ les pieds à qn** (*fam*: *irriter*) to get on sb's nerves; **se ~ la tête** (*fam*) to go to a lot of trouble

asserole [kasʀɔl] *nf* saucepan

asse-tête [kɑstɛt] *nm inv* (*difficultés*) headache (*fig*)

assette [kasɛt] *nf* (*bande magnétique*) cassette; (*coffret*) casket

asseur [kasœʀ] *nm* hooligan

assis [kasis] *nm* blackcurrant

assoulet [kasulɛ] *nm* bean and sausage hot-pot

assure [kasyʀ] *nf* break, crack

astor [kastɔʀ] *nm* beaver

astrer [kastʀe] *vt* (*mâle*) to castrate; (: *cheval*) to geld; (*femelle*) to spay

atalogue [katalɔg] *nm* catalogue

ataloguer [katalɔge] *vt* to catalogue, to list; (*péj*) to put a label on

atalyseur [katalizœʀ] *nm* catalyst; **catalytique** *adj*: **pot catalytique** catalytic convertor

atastrophe [katastʀɔf] *nf* catastrophe, disaster; **catastrophé, e** (*fam*) *adj* stunned

atch [katʃ] *nm* (all-in) wrestling

atéchisme [kateʃism] *nm* catechism

atégorie [kategɔʀi] *nf* category; **catégorique** *adj* categorical

athédrale [katedʀal] *nf* cathedral

atholique [katɔlik] *adj*, *nm/f* (Roman) Catholic; **pas très ~** a bit shady *ou* fishy

atimini [katimini]: **en ~** *adv* on the sly

auchemar [koʃmaʀ] *nm* nightmare

ause [koz] *nf* cause; (*JUR*) lawsuit, case; **à ~ de** because of, owing to; **(et) pour ~** and for (a very) good reason; **être en ~** (*intérêts*) to be at stake; **remettre en ~** to challenge; **causer** *vt* to cause ♦ *vi* to talk, talk; **causerie** *nf* (*conférence*) talk; **causette** *nf*: **faire la causette** to have a chat

caution [kosjɔ̃] *nf* guarantee, security; (*JUR*) bail (bond); (*fig*) backing, support; **libéré sous ~** released on bail; **cautionner** *vt* (*répondre de*) to guarantee; (*soutenir*) to support

cavalcade [kavalkad] *nf* (*fig*) stampede

cavalier, -ière [kavalje, jɛʀ] *adj* (*désinvolte*) offhand ♦ *nm/f* rider; (*au bal*) partner ♦ *nm* (*ÉCHECS*) knight

cave [kav] *nf* cellar

caveau, x [kavo] *nm* vault

caverne [kavɛʀn] *nf* cave

CCP *sigle m* = **compte chèques postaux**

CD *sigle m* (= *compact disc*) CD

CD-ROM [sedeʀɔm] *sigle m* CD-ROM

CE *n abr* (= *Communauté Européenne*) EC

┌─────────────┐
│ *MOT-CLÉ* │
└─────────────┘

ce, cette [sə, sɛt] (*devant nm* **cet** + *voyelle ou h aspiré*; *pl* **ces**) *dét* (*proximité*) this; these *pl*; (*non-proximité*) that; those *pl*; **cette maison(-ci/là)** this/that house; **cette nuit** (*qui vient*) tonight; (*passée*) last night

♦ *pron* 1: **c'est** it's *ou* it is; **c'est un peintre** he's *ou* he is a painter; **ce sont des peintres** they're *ou* they are painters; **c'est le facteur** (*à la porte*) it's the postman; **qui est-ce?** who is it?; (*en désignant*) who is he/she?; **qu'est-ce?** what is it?

2: **ce qui, ce que** what; (*chose qui*): **il est bête, ce qui me chagrine** he's stupid, which saddens me; **tout ce qui bouge** everything that *ou* which moves; **tout ce que je sais** all I know; **ce dont j'ai parlé** what I talked about; **ce que c'est grand!** it's so big!; *voir aussi* **-ci**; **est-ce que**; **n'est-ce pas**; **c'est-à-dire**

---

ceci [səsi] *pron* this

cécité [sesite] *nf* blindness

céder [sede] *vt* (*donner*) to give up ♦ *vi* (*chaise, barrage*) to give way; (*personne*) to give in; **~ à** to yield to, give in to

CEDEX [sedɛks] *sigle m* (= *courrier*

d'entreprise à distribution exceptionnelle) post-al service for bulk users

cédille [sedij] *nf* cedilla

cèdre [sɛdʀ] *nm* cedar

CEI *abr m* (= *Communauté des États Indépendants*) CIS

ceinture [sɛ̃tyʀ] *nf* belt; *(taille)* waist; ~ **de sécurité** safety *ou* seat belt

cela [s(ə)la] *pron* that; *(comme sujet indéfini)* it; **quand/où ~?** when/where (was that)?

célèbre [selebʀ] *adj* famous; **célébrer** *vt* to celebrate

céleri [selʀi] *nm*: ~**(-rave)** celeriac; ~ **(en branche)** celery

célibat [seliba] *nm* (*homme*) bachelorhood; (*femme*) spinsterhood; (*prêtre*) celibacy; **célibataire** *adj* single, unmarried ♦ *nm* bachelor ♦ *nf* unmarried woman

celle(s) [sɛl] *pron voir* **celui**

cellier [selje] *nm* storeroom (*for wine*)

cellule [selyl] *nf* (*gén*) cell

cellulite [selylit] *nf* excess fat, cellulite

┌─────────────────┐
│ *MOT-CLÉ* │
└─────────────────┘

celui, celle [səlɥi, sɛl] (*mpl* **ceux**, *fpl* **celles**) *pron* **1**: **celui-ci/là, celle-ci/là** this one/that one; **ceux-ci, celles-ci** these (ones); **ceux-là, celles-là** those (ones); **celui de mon frère** my brother's; **celui du salon/du dessous** the one in (*ou* from) the lounge/below

2: **celui qui bouge** the one which *ou* that moves; (*personne*) the one who moves; **celui que je vois** the one (which *ou* that) I see; the one (whom) I see; **celui dont je parle** the one I'm talking about

3 (*valeur indéfinie*): **celui qui veut** whoever wants

cendre [sɑ̃dʀ] *nf* ash; ~**s** *nfpl* (*d'un défunt*) ashes; **sous la** ~ (*CULIN*) in (the) embers; **cendrier** *nm* ashtray

cène [sɛn] *nf*: **la** ~ (Holy) Communion

censé, e [sɑ̃se] *adj*: **être** ~ **faire** to be supposed to do

censeur [sɑ̃sœʀ] *nm* (*SCOL*) deputy-head

(*BRIT*), vice-principal (*US*); (*CINÉMA, POL*) censor

censure [sɑ̃syʀ] *nf* censorship; **censure** *vt* (*CINÉMA, PRESSE*) to censor; (*POL*) to cen-sure

cent [sɑ̃] *num* a hundred, one hundred; **centaine** *nf*: **une centaine (de)** about a hundred, a hundred or so; **des centaines (de)** hundreds (of); **centenaire** *adj* hundred-year-old ♦ *nm* (*anniversaire*) cen-tenary; (*monnaie*) cent **centième** *num* hundredth; **centigrade** *nm* centigrade **centilitre** *nm* centilitre; **centime** *nm* centime; **centimètre** *nm* centimetre; (*ru-ban*) tape measure, measuring tape

central, e, -aux [sɑ̃tʀal, o] *adj* centr-♦ *nm*: ~ **(téléphonique)** (telephone) ex-change; **centrale** *nf* power station

centre [sɑ̃tʀ] *nm* centre; ~ **commercia** shopping centre; **centre-ville** *nm* tow centre, downtown (area) (*US*)

centuple [sɑ̃typl] *nm*: **le** ~ **de qch** a hun-dred times sth; **au** ~ a hundredfold

cep [sɛp] *nm* (vine) stock

cèpe [sɛp] *nm* (edible) boletus

cependant [s(ə)pɑ̃dɑ̃] *adv* however

céramique [seʀamik] *nf* ceramics *sg*

cercle [sɛʀkl] *nm* circle; ~ **vicieux** viciou circle

cercueil [sɛʀkœj] *nm* coffin

céréale [seʀeal] *nf* cereal; ~**s** *nfpl* brea fast cereal

cérémonie [seʀemɔni] *nf* ceremony; **san** ~ informally

cerf [sɛʀ] *nm* stag

cerfeuil [sɛʀfœj] *nm* chervil

cerf-volant [sɛʀvɔlɑ̃] *nm* kite

cerise [s(ə)ʀiz] *nf* cherry; **cerisier** *n* cherry (tree)

cerne [sɛʀn] *nm*: **avoir des** ~**s** to hav shadows *ou* dark rings under one's eyes

cerner [sɛʀne] *vt* (*MIL etc*) to surround; (*fi* problème*) to delimit, define

certain, e [sɛʀtɛ̃, ɛn] *adj* certain ♦ *dét* ce tain; **d'un** ~ **âge** past one's prime, not young; **un** ~ **temps** (quite) some time; ~

♦ *pron* some; **certainement** *adv* (*probablement*) most probably *ou* likely; (*bien sûr*) certainly, of course

ertes [sɛʀt] *adv* (*sans doute*) admittedly; (*bien sûr*) of course

ertificat [sɛʀtifika] *nm* certificate

ertifier [sɛʀtifje] *vt*: **~ qch à qn** to assure sb of sth; **copie certifiée conforme (à l'original)** certified copy of the original

ertitude [sɛʀtityd] *nf* certainty

erveau, x [sɛʀvo] *nm* brain

ervelas [sɛʀvəla] *nm* saveloy

ervelle [sɛʀvɛl] *nf* (*ANAT*) brain; (*CULIN*) brains

es [se] *dét voir* **ce**

ES *sigle m* (= *Collège d'enseignement secondaire*) ~ (junior) secondary school (*BRIT*)

esse [sɛs]: **sans ~** *adv* (*tout le temps*) continually, constantly; (*sans interruption*) continuously; **il n'a eu de ~ que** he did not rest until; **cesser** *vt* to stop ♦ *vi* to stop, cease; **cesser de faire** to stop doing; **cessez-le-feu** *nm inv* ceasefire

est-à-dire [sɛtadiʀ] *adv* that is (to say)

et, cette [sɛt] *dét voir* **ce**

eux [sø] *pron voir* **celui**

FC *abr* (= chlorofluorocarbon) CFC

FDT *sigle f* (= *Confédération française démocratique du travail*) French trade union

GT *sigle f* (= *Confédération générale du travail*) French trade union

hacun, e [ʃakœ, yn] *pron* each; (*indéfini*) everyone, everybody

hagrin [ʃagʀɛ̃] *nm* grief, sorrow; **avoir du ~** to be grieved; **chagriner** *vt* to grieve

hahut [ʃay] *nm* uproar; **chahuter** *vt* to rag, bait ♦ *vi* to make an uproar

haine [ʃɛn] *nf* chain; (*RADIO, TV:* stations) channel; **~s** *nfpl* (*AUTO*) (snow) chains; **travail à la ~** production line work; **~ (de montage)** production *ou* assembly line; **~ de montagnes** mountain range; **~ (hi-fi)** hi-fi system; **~ laser** CD player; **~ (stéréo)** stereo (system); **chaînette** *nf* (small) chain

hair [ʃɛʀ] *nf* flesh; **avoir la ~ de poule** to

have goosepimples *ou* gooseflesh; **bien en ~** plump, well-padded; **en ~ et en os** in the flesh; **~ à saucisse** sausage meat

chaire [ʃɛʀ] *nf* (*d'église*) pulpit; (*d'université*) chair

chaise [ʃɛz] *nf* chair; **~ longue** deckchair

châle [ʃal] *nm* shawl

chaleur [ʃalœʀ] *nf* heat; (*fig: accueil*) warmth; **chaleureux, -euse** *adj* warm

chaloupe [ʃalup] *nf* launch; (*de sauvetage*) lifeboat

chalumeau, x [ʃalymo] *nm* blowlamp, blowtorch

chalutier [ʃalytje] *nm* trawler

chamailler [ʃamaje]: **se ~** *vi* to squabble, bicker

chambouler [ʃɑ̃bule] (*fam*) *vt* to disrupt, turn upside down

chambre [ʃɑ̃bʀ] *nf* bedroom; (*POL, COMM*) chamber; **faire ~ à part** to sleep in separate rooms; **~ à air** (*de pneu*) (inner) tube; **~ à coucher** bedroom; **~ à un lit/deux lits** (*à l'hôtel*) single-/twin-bedded room; **~ d'amis** spare *ou* guest room; **~ noire** (*PHOTO*) dark room; **chambrer** *vt* (*vin*) to bring to room temperature

chameau, x [ʃamo] *nm* camel

chamois [ʃamwa] *nm* chamois

champ [ʃɑ̃] *nm* field; **~ de bataille** battlefield; **~ de courses** racecourse; **~ de tir** rifle range

champagne [ʃɑ̃paɲ] *nm* champagne

champêtre [ʃɑ̃pɛtʀ] *adj* country *cpd*, rural

champignon [ʃɑ̃piɲɔ̃] *nm* mushroom; (*terme générique*) fungus; **~ de Paris** button mushroom

champion, ne [ʃɑ̃pjɔ̃, jɔn] *adj, nm/f* champion; **championnat** *nm* championship

chance [ʃɑ̃s] *nf*: **la ~** luck; **~s** *nfpl* (*probabilités*) chances; **avoir de la ~** to be lucky; **il a des ~s de réussir** he's got a good chance of passing

chanceler [ʃɑ̃s(ə)le] *vi* to totter

chancelier [ʃɑ̃səlje] *nm* (*allemand*) chancellor

chanceux, -euse [ʃɑ̃sø, øz] *adj* lucky
chandail [ʃɑ̃daj] *nm* (thick) sweater
Chandeleur [ʃɑ̃dlœʀ] *nf*: **la ~** Candlemas
chandelier [ʃɑ̃dəlje] *nm* candlestick
chandelle [ʃɑ̃dɛl] *nf* (tallow) candle; **dîner aux ~s** candlelight dinner
change [ʃɑ̃ʒ] *nm* (*devises*) exchange
changement [ʃɑ̃ʒmɑ̃] *nm* change; **~ de vitesses** gears *pl*
changer [ʃɑ̃ʒe] *vt* (*modifier*) to change, alter; (*remplacer*, COMM) to change ♦ *vi* to change, alter; **se ~** *vi* to change (o.s.); **~ de** (*remplacer: adresse, nom, voiture etc*) to change one's; (*échanger: place, train etc*) to change; **~ d'avis** to change one's mind; **~ de vitesse** to change gear
chanson [ʃɑ̃sɔ̃] *nf* song
chant [ʃɑ̃] *nm* song; (*art vocal*) singing; (*d'église*) hymn
chantage [ʃɑ̃taʒ] *nm* blackmail; **faire du ~** to use blackmail
chanter [ʃɑ̃te] *vt*, *vi* to sing; **si cela lui chante** (*fam*) if he feels like it; **chanteur, -euse** *nm/f* singer
chantier [ʃɑ̃tje] *nm* (building) site; (*sur une route*) roadworks *pl*; **mettre en ~** to put in hand; **~ naval** shipyard
chantilly [ʃɑ̃tiji] *nf voir* **crème**
chantonner [ʃɑ̃tɔne] *vi*, *vt* to sing to oneself, hum
chanvre [ʃɑ̃vʀ] *nm* hemp
chaparder [ʃapaʀde] (*fam*) *vt* to pinch
chapeau, x [ʃapo] *nm* hat; **~!** well done!
chapelet [ʃaplɛ] *nm* (REL) rosary
chapelle [ʃapɛl] *nf* chapel
chapelure [ʃaplyʀ] *nf* (dried) breadcrumbs *pl*
chapiteau, x [ʃapito] *nm* (*de cirque*) marquee, big top
chapitre [ʃapitʀ] *nm* chapter
chaque [ʃak] *dét* each, every; (*indéfini*) every
char [ʃaʀ] *nm* (MIL): **~ (d'assaut)** tank; **~ à voile** sand yacht
charabia [ʃaʀabja] (*péj*) *nm* gibberish
charade [ʃaʀad] *nf* riddle; (*mimée*) charade

charbon [ʃaʀbɔ̃] *nm* coal; **~ de bois** cha[r]
coal
charcuterie [ʃaʀkytʀi] *nf* (*magasin*) po[r]
butcher's shop and delicatessen; (*produit.*
cooked pork meats *pl*; **charcutier, -ièr**
nm/f pork butcher
chardon [ʃaʀdɔ̃] *nm* thistle
charge [ʃaʀʒ] *nf* (*fardeau*) load, burde[n]
(*explosif, ÉLEC, MIL, JUR*) charge; (*rôle, mi*
sion) responsibility; **~s** *nfpl* (*du loyer*) se[r]
vice charges; **à la ~ de** (*dépendant de*) de
pendent upon; (*aux frais de*) chargeab[le]
to; **prendre en ~** to take charge of; (*su*
véhicule) to take on; (*dépenses*) to ta[ke]
care of; **~s sociales** social security cont[ri]
butions
chargé, e [ʃaʀʒe] *adj* (*emploi du temp*
journée) full, heavy
chargement [ʃaʀʒəmɑ̃] *nm* (*objets*) load
charger [ʃaʀʒe] *vt* (*voiture, fusil, caméra*) [to]
load; (*batterie*) to charge ♦ *vi* (MIL etc) [to]
charge; **se ~ de** *vt* to see to; **~ qn d[e]**
(faire) qch to put sb in charge of (doin[g]
sth
chariot [ʃaʀjo] *nm* trolley; (*charrette*) wa[g]
gon
charité [ʃaʀite] *nf* charity
charmant, e [ʃaʀmɑ̃, ɑ̃t] *adj* charming
charme [ʃaʀm] *nm* charm; **charmer** *vt* [to]
charm
charnel, le [ʃaʀnɛl] *adj* carnal
charnière [ʃaʀnjɛʀ] *nf* hinge; (*fi*
turning-point
charnu, e [ʃaʀny] *adj* fleshy
charpente [ʃaʀpɑ̃t] *nf* frame(work); **cha**
pentier *nm* carpenter
charpie [ʃaʀpi] *nf*: **en ~** (*fig*) in shreds [o]
ribbons
charrette [ʃaʀɛt] *nf* cart
charrier [ʃaʀje] *vt* (*entraîner: fleuve*) to ca[r]
ry (along); (*transporter*) to cart, carry
charrue [ʃaʀy] *nf* plough (BRIT), plow (US
charter [ʃaʀtɛʀ] *nm* (*vol*) charter flight
chasse [ʃas] *nf* hunting; (*au fusil*) shoo[t]
ing; (*poursuite*) chase; (*aussi*: **~ d'ea[u]**
flush; **~ gardée** private hunting groun[d]

pl; **prendre en ~** to give chase to; **tirer la ~ (d'eau)** to flush the toilet, pull the chain; **~ à courre** hunting; **chasse-neige** *nm inv* snowplough (*BRIT*), snow-plow (*US*); **chasser** *vt* to hunt; (*expulser*) to chase away *ou* out, drive away *ou* out; **chasseur, -euse** *nm/f* hunter ♦ *nm* (*avion*) fighter

châssis [ʃasi] *nm* (*AUTO*) chassis; (*cadre*) frame

chat [ʃa] *nm* cat

châtaigne [ʃatɛɲ] *nf* chestnut; **châtaignier** *nm* chestnut (tree)

châtain [ʃatɛ̃] *adj inv* (*cheveux*) chestnut (brown); (*personne*) chestnut-haired

château, x [ʃato] *nm* (*forteresse*) castle; (*résidence royale*) palace; (*manoir*) mansion; **~ d'eau** water tower; **~ fort** stronghold, fortified castle

châtier [ʃatje] *vt* to punish; **châtiment** *nm* punishment

chaton [ʃatɔ̃] *nm* (*ZOOL*) kitten

chatouiller [ʃatuje] *vt* to tickle; **chatouilleux, -euse** *adj* ticklish; (*fig*) touchy, over-sensitive

chatoyer [ʃatwaje] *vi* to shimmer

châtrer [ʃatʀe] *vt* (*mâle*) to castrate; (: *cheval*) to geld; (*femelle*) to spay

chatte [ʃat] *nf* (she-)cat

chaud, e [ʃo, ʃod] *adj* (*gén*) warm; (*très ~*) hot; **il fait ~** it's warm; it's hot; **avoir ~** to be warm; to be hot; **ça me tient ~** it keeps me warm; **rester au ~** to stay in the warm

chaudière [ʃodjɛʀ] *nf* boiler

chaudron [ʃodʀɔ̃] *nm* cauldron

chauffage [ʃofaʒ] *nm* heating; **~ central** central heating

chauffard [ʃofaʀ] *nm* (*péj*) reckless driver

chauffe-eau [ʃofo] *nm inv* water-heater

chauffer [ʃofe] *vt* to heat ♦ *vi* to heat up, warm up; (*trop ~: moteur*) to overheat; **se ~** *vi* (*au soleil*) to warm o.s.

chauffeur [ʃofœʀ] *nm* driver; (*privé*) chauffeur

chaume [ʃom] *nm* (*du toit*) thatch; **chau-**

mière *nf* (thatched) cottage

chaussée [ʃose] *nf* road(way)

chausse-pied [ʃospje] *nm* shoe-horn

chausser [ʃose] *vt* (*bottes, skis*) to put on; (*enfant*) to put shoes on; **~ du 38/42** to take size 38/42

chaussette [ʃosɛt] *nf* sock

chausson [ʃosɔ̃] *nm* slipper; (*de bébé*) bootee; **~ (aux pommes)** (apple) turn-over

chaussure [ʃosyʀ] *nf* shoe; **~s à talon** high-heeled shoes; **~s de marche** walking shoes/boots; **~s de ski** ski boots

chauve [ʃov] *adj* bald; **chauve-souris** *nf* bat

chauvin, e [ʃovɛ̃, in] *adj* chauvinistic

chaux [ʃo] *nf* lime; **blanchi à la ~** white-washed

chavirer [ʃaviʀe] *vi* to capsize

chef [ʃɛf] *nm* head, leader; (*de cuisine*) chef; **~ d'accusation** charge; **~ d'entreprise** company head; **~ d'état** head of state; **~ de famille** head of the family; **~ de gare** station master; **~ d'orchestre** conductor; **~ de service** department head; **chef-d'œuvre** *nm* masterpiece; **chef-lieu** *nm* county town

chemin [ʃ(ə)mɛ̃] *nm* path; (*itinéraire, direction, trajet*) way; **en ~** on the way; **~ de fer** railway (*BRIT*), railroad (*US*); **par ~ de fer** by rail

cheminée [ʃ(ə)mine] *nf* chimney; (*à l'intérieur*) chimney piece, fireplace; (*de bateau*) funnel

cheminement [ʃ(ə)minmɑ̃] *nm* progress

cheminot [ʃ(ə)mino] *nm* railwayman

chemise [ʃ(ə)miz] *nf* shirt; (*dossier*) folder; **~ de nuit** nightdress

chemisier [ʃ(ə)mizje, jɛʀ] *nm* blouse

chenal, -aux [ʃanal, o] *nm* channel

chêne [ʃɛn] *nm* oak (tree); (*bois*) oak

chenil [ʃ(ə)nil] *nm* kennels *pl*

chenille [ʃ(ə)nij] *nf* (*ZOOL*) caterpillar

chèque [ʃɛk] *nm* cheque (*BRIT*), check (*US*); **~ sans provision** bad cheque; **~ de**

voyage traveller's cheque; **chéquier** [ʃekje] nm cheque book

cher, -ère [ʃɛʁ] adj (aimé) dear; (coûteux) expensive, dear ♦ adv: **ça coûte ~** it's expensive

chercher [ʃɛʁʃe] vt to look for; (gloire etc) to seek; **aller ~** to go for, go and fetch; **~ à faire** to try to do; **chercheur, -euse** nm/f researcher, research worker

chère [ʃɛʁ] adj voir **cher**

chéri, e [ʃeʁi] adj beloved, dear; **(mon) ~** darling

chérir [ʃeʁiʁ] vt to cherish

cherté [ʃɛʁte] nf: **la ~ de la vie** the high cost of living

chétif, -ive [ʃetif, iv] adj (enfant) puny

cheval, -aux [ʃ(ə)val, o] nm horse; (AUTO): **~ (vapeur)** horsepower no pl; **faire du ~** to ride; **à ~** on horseback; **à ~ sur** astride; (fig) overlapping; **~ de course** racehorse

chevalet [ʃ(ə)valɛ] nm easel

chevalier [ʃ(ə)valje] nm knight

chevalière [ʃ(ə)valjɛʁ] nf signet ring

chevalin, e [ʃ(ə)valɛ̃, in] adj: **boucherie ~e** horse-meat butcher's

chevaucher [ʃ(ə)voʃe] vi (aussi: **se ~**) to overlap (each other) ♦ vt to be astride, straddle

chevaux [ʃəvo] nmpl de **cheval**

chevelu, e [ʃəv(ə)ly] (péj) adj long-haired

chevelure [ʃəv(ə)lyʁ] nf hair no pl

chevet [ʃ(ə)vɛ] nm: **au ~ de qn** at sb's bedside; **lampe de ~** bedside lamp

cheveu, x [ʃ(ə)vø] nm hair; **~x** nmpl (chevelure) hair sg; **avoir les ~x courts** to have short hair

cheville [ʃ(ə)vij] nf (ANAT) ankle; (de bois) peg; (pour une vis) plug

chèvre [ʃɛvʁ] nf (she-)goat

chevreau, x [ʃəvʁo] nm kid

chèvrefeuille [ʃɛvʁəfœj] nm honeysuckle

chevreuil [ʃəvʁœj] nm roe deer inv; (CULIN) venison

chevronné, e [ʃəvʁɔne] adj seasoned

chez [ʃe] prép **1** (à la demeure de) at; (: direction) to; **chez qn** at/to sb's house ou place; **chez moi** at home; (direction) home

2 (+profession) at; (: direction) to; **chez le boulanger/dentiste** at ou to the baker's/dentist's

3 (dans le caractère, l'œuvre de) in; **chez les renards/Racine** in foxes/Racine

chez-soi [ʃeswa] nm inv home

chic [ʃik] adj inv chic, smart; (fam: généreux) nice, decent ♦ nm stylishness; **~ (alors)!** (fam) great!; **avoir le ~ de** to have the knack of

chicane [ʃikan] nf (querelle) squabble; **chicaner** vi (ergoter): **chicaner sur** to quibble about

chiche [ʃiʃ] adj niggardly, mean ♦ excl (à un défi) you're on!

chichis [ʃiʃi] (fam) nmpl fuss sg

chicorée [ʃikɔʁe] nf (café) chicory; (salade) endive

chien [ʃjɛ̃] nm dog; **~ de garde** guard dog; **chien-loup** nm wolfhound

chiendent [ʃjɛ̃dɑ̃] nm couch grass

chienne [ʃjɛn] nf dog, bitch

chier [ʃje] (fam!) vi to crap (!)

chiffon [ʃifɔ̃] nm (piece of) rag; **chiffonner** vt to crumple; (fam: tracasser) to concern

chiffre [ʃifʁ] nm (représentant un nombre) figure, numeral; (montant, total) total, sum; **en ~s ronds** in round figures; **~ d'affaires** turnover; **chiffrer** vt (dépense) to put a figure to, assess; (message) to (en)code, cipher; **se chiffrer à** to add up to, amount to

chignon [ʃiɲɔ̃] nm chignon, bun

Chili [ʃili] nm: **le ~** Chile; **chilien, ne** adj Chilean ♦ nm/f: **Chilien, ne** Chilean

chimie [ʃimi] nf chemistry; **chimique** adj chemical; **produits chimiques** chemicals

chimpanzé [ʃɛ̃pɑ̃ze] nm chimpanzee

Chine [ʃin] *nf*: **la ~** China; **chinois, e** *adj* Chinese ♦ *nm/f*: **Chinois, e** Chinese ♦ *nm* (*LING*) Chinese

chiot [ʃjo] *nm* pup(py)

chiper [ʃipe] (*fam*) *vt* to pinch

chipoter [ʃipɔte] (*fam*) *vi* (*ergoter*) to quibble

chips [ʃips] *nfpl* crisps (*BRIT*), (potato) chips (*US*)

chiquenaude [ʃiknod] *nf* flick, flip

chirurgical, e, -aux [ʃiryrʒikal, o] *adj* surgical

chirurgie [ʃiryrʒi] *nf* surgery; **~ esthétique** plastic surgery; **chirurgien, ne** *nm/f* surgeon

chlore [klɔr] *nm* chlorine

choc [ʃɔk] *nm* (*heurt*) impact, shock; (*collision*) crash; (*moral*) shock; (*affrontement*) clash

chocolat [ʃɔkɔla] *nm* chocolate; **~ au lait** milk chocolate; **~ (chaud)** hot chocolate

chœur [kœr] *nm* (*chorale*) choir; (*OPÉRA, THÉÂTRE*) chorus; **en ~** in chorus

choisir [ʃwazir] *vt* to choose, select

choix [ʃwa] *nm* choice, selection; **avoir le ~** to have the choice; **premier ~** (*COMM*) class one; **de ~** choice, selected; **au ~** as you wish

chômage [ʃomaʒ] *nm* unemployment; **mettre au ~** to make redundant, put out of work; **être au ~** to be unemployed *ou* out of work; **chômeur, -euse** *nm/f* unemployed person

chope [ʃɔp] *nf* tankard

choper [ʃɔpe] (*fam*) *vt* (*objet, maladie*) to catch

choquer [ʃɔke] *vt* (*offenser*) to shock; (*deuil*) to shake

chorale [kɔral] *nf* choir

choriste [kɔrist] *nm/f* choir member; (*OPÉRA*) chorus member

chose [ʃoz] *nf* thing; **c'est peu de ~** it's nothing (really)

chou, x [ʃu] *nm* cabbage; **mon petit ~** (my) sweetheart; **~ à la crème** choux bun; **~x de Bruxelles** Brussels sprouts;

chouchou, te (*fam*) *nm/f* darling; (*SCOL*) teacher's pet; **choucroute** *nf* sauerkraut

chouette [ʃwet] *nf* owl ♦ *adj* (*fam*) great, smashing

chou-fleur [ʃuflœr] *nm* cauliflower

choyer [ʃwaje] *vt* (*dorloter*) to cherish; (: *excessivement*) to pamper

chrétien, ne [kretjɛ̃, jen] *adj, nm/f* Christian

Christ [krist] *nm*: **le ~** Christ; **christianisme** *nm* Christianity

chrome [krom] *nm* chromium; **chromé, e** *adj* chromium-plated

chronique [krɔnik] *adj* chronic ♦ *nf* (*de journal*) column, page; (*historique*) chronicle; (*RADIO, TV*): **la ~ sportive** the sports review

chronologique [krɔnɔlɔʒik] *adj* chronological

chronomètre [krɔnɔmetr] *nm* stopwatch; **chronométrer** *vt* to time

chrysanthème [krizɑ̃tem] *nm* chrysanthemum

chuchotement [ʃyʃɔtmɑ̃] *nm* whisper

chuchoter [ʃyʃɔte] *vt, vi* to whisper

chut [ʃyt] *excl* sh!

chute [ʃyt] *nf* fall; (*déchet*) scrap; **faire une ~ (de 10 m)** to fall (10 m); **~ (d'eau)** waterfall; **la ~ des cheveux** hair loss; **~ libre** free fall; **~s de pluie/neige** rain/snowfalls

Chypre [ʃipr] *nm/f* Cyprus

-ci [si] *adv voir* **par** ♦ *dét*: **ce garçon-~/-là** this/that boy; **ces femmes-~/-là** these/those women

cible [sibl] *nf* target

ciboulette [sibulet] *nf* (small) chive

cicatrice [sikatris] *nf* scar; **cicatriser** *vt* to heal

ci-contre [sikɔ̃tr] *adv* opposite

ci-dessous [sidəsu] *adv* below

ci-dessus [sidəsy] *adv* above

cidre [sidr] *nm* cider

Cie *abr* (= *compagnie*) Co.

ciel [sjel] *nm* sky; (*REL*) heaven; **cieux** *nmpl* (*REL*) heaven *sg*; **à ~ ouvert** open-air; (*mine*) open-cast

cierge [sjɛʀʒ] *nm* candle

cieux [sjø] *nmpl de* **ciel**

cigale [sigal] *nf* cicada

cigare [sigaʀ] *nm* cigar

cigarette [sigaʀɛt] *nf* cigarette

ci-gît [siʒi] *adv +vb* here lies

cigogne [sigɔɲ] *nf* stork

ci-inclus, e [siɛ̃kly, yz] *adj, adv* enclosed

ci-joint, e [siʒwɛ̃, ɛ̃t] *adj, adv* enclosed

cil [sil] *nm* (eye)lash

cime [sim] *nf* top; (*montagne*) peak

ciment [simɑ̃] *nm* cement

cimetière [simtjɛʀ] *nm* cemetery; (*d'église*) churchyard

cinéaste [sineast] *nm/f* film-maker

cinéma [sinema] *nm* cinema; **cinématographique** *adj* film *cpd*, cinema *cpd*

cinglant, e [sɛ̃glɑ̃, ɑ̃t] *adj* (*remarque*) biting

cinglé, e [sɛ̃gle] (*fam*) *adj* crazy

cinq [sɛ̃k] *num* five; **cinquantaine** *nf*: **une cinquantaine (de)** about fifty; **avoir la cinquantaine** (*âge*) to be around fifty; **cinquante** *num* fifty; **cinquantenaire** *adj, nm/f* fifty-year-old; **cinquième** *num* fifth

cintre [sɛ̃tʀ] *nm* coat-hanger

cintré, e [sɛ̃tʀe] *adj* (*chemise*) fitted

cirage [siʀaʒ] *nm* (shoe) polish

circonflexe [siʀkɔ̃flɛks] *adj*: **accent ~** circumflex accent

circonscription [siʀkɔ̃skʀipsjɔ̃] *nf* district; **~ électorale** (*d'un député*) constituency

circonscrire [siʀkɔ̃skʀiʀ] *vt* (*sujet*) to define, delimit; (*incendie*) to contain

circonstance [siʀkɔ̃stɑ̃s] *nf* circumstance; (*occasion*) occasion; **~s atténuantes** mitigating circumstances

circuit [siʀkɥi] *nm* (*ÉLEC, TECH*) circuit; (*trajet*) tour, (round) trip

circulaire [siʀkylɛʀ] *adj, nf* circular

circulation [siʀkylasjɔ̃] *nf* circulation; (*AUTO*): **la ~** (the) traffic

circuler [siʀkyle] *vi* (*sang, devises*) to circulate; (*véhicules*) to drive (along); (*passants*) to walk along; (*train, bus*) to run; **faire ~** (*nouvelle*) to spread (about), circulate; (*badauds*) to move on

cire [siʀ] *nf* wax; **ciré** *nm* oilskin; **cirer** *vt* to wax, polish

cirque [siʀk] *nm* circus; (*fig*) chaos, bedlam; **quel ~!** what a carry-on!

cisaille(s) [sizaj] *nf(pl)* (gardening) shears *pl*

ciseau, x [sizo] *nm*: **~ (à bois)** chisel; **~x** *nmpl* (*paire de ~x*) (pair of) scissors

ciseler [siz(ə)le] *vt* to chisel, carve

citadin, e [sitadɛ̃, in] *nm/f* city dweller

citation [sitasjɔ̃] *nf* (*d'auteur*) quotation; (*JUR*) summons *sg*

cité [site] *nf* town; (*plus grande*) city; **~ universitaire** students' residences *pl*

citer [site] *vt* (*un auteur*) to quote (from); (*nommer*) to name; (*JUR*) to summon

citerne [sitɛʀn] *nf* tank

citoyen, ne [sitwajɛ̃, jɛn] *nm/f* citizen

citron [sitʀɔ̃] *nm* lemon; **~ vert** lime; **citronnade** *nf* still lemonade

citrouille [sitʀuj] *nf* pumpkin

civet [sivɛ] *nm*: **~ de lapin** rabbit stew

civière [sivjɛʀ] *nf* stretcher

civil, e [sivil] *adj* (*mariage, poli*) civil; (*non militaire*) civilian; **en ~** in civilian clothes; **dans le ~** in civilian life

civilisation [sivilizasjɔ̃] *nf* civilization

clair, e [klɛʀ] *adj* light; (*pièce*) light, bright; (*eau, son, fig*) clear ♦ *adv*: **voir ~** to see clearly; **tirer qch au ~** to clear sth up, clarify sth; **mettre au ~** (*notes etc*) to tidy up; **~ de lune** ♦ *nm* moonlight; **clairement** *adv* clearly

clairière [klɛʀjɛʀ] *nf* clearing

clairon [klɛʀɔ̃] *nm* bugle; **claironner** *vt* (*fig*) to trumpet, shout from the rooftops

clairsemé, e [klɛʀsəme] *adj* sparse

clairvoyant, e [klɛʀvwajɑ̃, ɑ̃t] *adj* perceptive, clear-sighted

clandestin, e [klɑ̃dɛstɛ̃, in] *adj* clandestine, secret; (*mouvement*) underground; (*travailleur*) illegal; **passager ~** stowaway

clapier [klapje] *nm* (rabbit) hutch

clapoter [klapɔte] *vi* to lap

claque [klak] *nf* (*gifle*) slap; **claquer** *vi* (*porte*) to bang, slam; (*fam: mourir*) to snuff it ♦ *vt* (*porte*) to slam, bang; (*doigts*) to snap; (*fam: dépenser*) to blow; **il claquait des dents** his teeth were chattering; **être claqué** (*fam*) to be dead tired; **se claquer un muscle** to pull *ou* strain a muscle; **claquettes** *nfpl* tap-dancing *sg*

clarinette [klaʀinɛt] *nf* clarinet

clarté [klaʀte] *nf* (*luminosité*) brightness; (*d'un son, de l'eau*) clearness; (*d'une explication*) clarity

classe [klas] *nf* class; (*SCOL: local*) class(room); (: *leçon, élèves*) class; **aller en ~** to go to school; **classement** *nm* (*rang: SCOL*) placing; (: *SPORT*) placing; (*liste: SCOL*) class list (in order of merit); (: *SPORT*) placings *pl*

classer [klase] *vt* (*idées, livres*) to classify; (*papiers*) to file; (*candidat*) to grade; (*JUR: affaire*) to close; **se ~ premier/dernier** to come first/last; (*SPORT*) to finish first/last; **classeur** *nm* (*cahier*) file

classique [klasik] *adj* classical; (*sobre: coupe etc*) classic(al); (*habituel*) classic

clause [kloz] *nf* clause

clavecin [klav(ə)sɛ̃] *nm* harpsichord

clavicule [klavikyl] *nf* collarbone

clavier [klavje] *nm* keyboard

clé [kle] *nf* key; (*MUS*) clef; (*de mécanicien*) spanner (*BRIT*), wrench (*US*); **prix ~s en main** (*d'une voiture*) on-the-road price; **~ anglaise** (monkey) wrench; **~ de contact** ignition key

clef [kle] *nf* = **clé**

clément, e [klemɑ̃, ɑ̃t] *adj* (*temps*) mild; (*indulgent*) lenient

clerc [klɛʀ] *nm*: **~ de notaire** solicitor's clerk

clergé [klɛʀʒe] *nm* clergy

cliché [kliʃe] *nm* (*fig*) cliché; (*négatif*) negative; (*photo*) print

client, e [klijɑ̃, klijɑ̃t] *nm/f* (*acheteur*) customer, client; (*d'hôtel*) guest, patron; (*du docteur*) patient; (*de l'avocat*) client; **clientèle** *nf* (*du magasin*) customers *pl*, clien-

tèle; (*du docteur, de l'avocat*) practice

cligner [kliɲe] *vi*: **~ des yeux** to blink (one's eyes); **~ de l'œil** to wink; **clignotant** *nm* (*AUTO*) indicator; **clignoter** *vi* (*étoiles etc*) to twinkle; (*lumière*) to flicker

climat [klima] *nm* climate

climatisation [klimatizasjɔ̃] *nf* air conditioning; **climatisé, e** *adj* air-conditioned

clin d'œil [klɛ̃dœj] *nm* wink; **en un ~** in a flash

clinique [klinik] *nf* private hospital

clinquant, e [klɛ̃kɑ̃, ɑ̃t] *adj* flashy

clip [klip] *nm* (*boucle d'oreille*) clip-on; (**vidéo**) **~** (pop) video

cliquer [klike] *vt*: **~ sur** to click on

cliqueter [klik(ə)te] *vi* (*ferraille*) to jangle; (*clés*) to jingle

clochard, e [klɔʃaʀ, aʀd] *nm/f* tramp

cloche [klɔʃ] *nf* (*d'église*) bell; (*fam*) clot; **cloche-pied: à cloche-pied** *adv* on one leg, hopping (along); **clocher** *nm* church tower; (*en pointe*) steeple ♦ *vi* (*fam*) to be *ou* go wrong; **de clocher** (*péj*) parochial

cloison [klwazɔ̃] *nf* partition (wall)

cloître [klwatʀ] *nm* cloister; **cloîtrer** *vt*: **se cloîtrer** to shut o.s. up *ou* away

clone [klɔn] *nm* clone ♦ *vt* cloner

cloque [klɔk] *nf* blister

clore [klɔʀ] *vt* to close; **clos, e** *adj* voir **maison; huis**

clôture [klotyʀ] *nf* closure; (*barrière*) enclosure

clou [klu] *nm* nail; **~s** *nmpl* (*passage ~té*) pedestrian crossing; **pneus à ~s** studded tyres; **le ~ du spectacle** the highlight of the show; **~ de girofle** clove; **clouer** *vt* to nail down *ou* up; **clouer le bec à qn** (*fam*) to shut sb up

clown [klun] *nm* clown

club [klœb] *nm* club

CMU *nf* (= *couverture maladie universelle*) system of free health care for those on low incomes

CNRS *sigle m* (= *Centre nationale de la recherche scientifique*) ≃ SERC (*BRIT*), ≃ NSF (*US*)

coaguler [kɔagyle] *vt, vi* (*aussi: se ~*:

sang) to coagulate

coasser [kɔase] *vi* to croak

cobaye [kɔbaj] *nm* guinea-pig

coca [kɔka] *nm* Coke ®

cocaïne [kɔkain] *nf* cocaine

cocasse [kɔkas] *adj* comical, funny

coccinelle [kɔksinɛl] *nf* ladybird (*BRIT*), ladybug (*US*)

cocher [kɔʃe] *vt* to tick off

cochère [kɔʃɛʀ] *adj f*: **porte ~** carriage entrance

cochon, ne [kɔʃɔ̃, ɔn] *nm* pig ♦ *adj* (*fam*) dirty, smutty; **~ d'Inde** guinea pig; **cochonnerie** (*fam*) *nf* (*saleté*) filth; (*marchandise*) rubbish, trash

cocktail [kɔktɛl] *nm* cocktail; (*réception*) cocktail party

coco [kɔko] *nm voir* **noix**

cocorico [kɔkɔʀiko] *excl, nm* cock-a-doodle-do

cocotier [kɔkɔtje] *nm* coconut palm

cocotte [kɔkɔt] *nf* (*en fonte*) casserole; **~ (minute)** pressure cooker; **ma ~** (*fam*) sweetie (pie)

cocu [kɔky] (*fam*) *nm* cuckold

code [kɔd] *nm* code ♦ *adj*: **phares ~s** dipped lights; **se mettre en ~(s)** to dip one's (head)lights; **~ à barres** bar code; **~ civil** Common Law; **~ de la route** highway code; **~ pénal** penal code; **~ postal** (*numéro*) post (*BRIT*) ou zip (*US*) code

cœur [kœʀ] *nm* heart; (*CARTES: couleur*) hearts *pl*; (: *carte*) heart; **avoir bon ~** to be kind-hearted; **avoir mal au ~** to feel sick; **en avoir le ~ net** to be clear in one's own mind (about it); **par ~** by heart; **de bon ~** willingly; **cela lui tient à ~** that's (very) close to his heart

coffre [kɔfʀ] *nm* (*meuble*) chest; (*d'auto*) boot (*BRIT*), trunk (*US*); **coffre(-fort)** *nm* safe; **coffret** *nm* casket

cognac [kɔɲak] *nm* brandy, cognac

cogner [kɔɲe] *vi* to knock; **se ~ la tête** to bang one's head

cohérent, e [kɔeʀɑ̃, ɑ̃t] *adj* coherent, consistent

cohorte [kɔɔʀt] *nf* troop

cohue [kɔy] *nf* crowd

coi, coite [kwa, kwat] *adj*: **rester ~** to remain silent

coiffe [kwaf] *nf* headdress

coiffé, e [kwafe] *adj*: **bien/mal ~** with tidy/untidy hair

coiffer [kwafe] *vt* (*fig: surmonter*) to cover, top; **se ~** *vi* to do one's hair; **~ qn** to do sb's hair; **coiffeur, -euse** *nm/f* hairdresser; **coiffeuse** *nf* (*table*) dressing table; **coiffure** *nf* (*cheveux*) hairstyle, hairdo; (*art*): **la coiffure** hairdressing

coin [kwɛ̃] *nm* corner; (*pour ~cer*) wedge; **l'épicerie du ~** the local grocer; **dans le ~** (*aux alentours*) in the area, around about; (*habiter*) locally; **je ne suis pas du ~** I'm not from here; **au ~ du feu** by the fireside; **regard en ~** sideways glance

coincé, e [kwɛ̃se] *adj* stuck, jammed; (*fig: inhibé*) inhibited, hung up (*fam*)

coincer [kwɛ̃se] *vt* to jam; (*fam: attraper*) to pinch

coïncidence [kɔɛ̃sidɑ̃s] *nf* coincidence

coïncider [kɔɛ̃side] *vi* to coincide

coing [kwɛ̃] *nm* quince

col [kɔl] *nm* (*de chemise*) collar; (*encolure, cou*) neck; (*de montagne*) pass; **~ de l'utérus** cervix; **~ roulé** polo-neck

colère [kɔlɛʀ] *nf* anger; **une ~** a fit of anger; **(se mettre) en ~** (to get) angry; **coléreux, -euse** *adj*, **colérique** *adj* quick-tempered, irascible

colifichet [kɔlifiʃɛ] *nm* trinket

colimaçon [kɔlimasɔ̃] *nm*: **escalier en ~** spiral staircase

colin [kɔlɛ̃] *nm* hake

colique [kɔlik] *nf* diarrhoea

colis [kɔli] *nm* parcel

collaborateur, -trice [kɔ(l)labɔʀatœʀ, tʀis] *nm/f* (*aussi POL*) collaborator; (*d'une revue*) contributor

collaborer [kɔ(l)labɔʀe] *vi* to collaborate; **~ à** to collaborate on; (*revue*) to contribute to

collant, e [kɔlɑ̃, ɑ̃t] *adj* sticky; (*robe etc*)

clinging, skintight; (*péj*) clinging ♦ *nm* (*bas*) tights *pl*; (*de danseur*) leotard

collation [kɔlasjɔ̃] *nf* light meal

colle [kɔl] *nf* glue; (*à papiers peints*) (wallpaper) paste; (*fam: devinette*) teaser, riddle; (*SCOL: fam*) detention

collecte [kɔlɛkt] *nf* collection; **collectif, -ive** *adj* collective; (*visite, billet*) group *cpd*

collection [kɔlɛksjɔ̃] *nf* collection; (*ÉDITION*) series; **collectionner** *vt* to collect; **collectionneur, -euse** *nm/f* collector

collectivité [kɔlɛktivite] *nf* group; **~s locales** (*ADMIN*) local authorities

collège [kɔlɛʒ] *nm* (*école*) (secondary) school; (*assemblée*) body; **collégien** *nm* schoolboy; **collégienne** *nf* schoolgirl

---

collège

🛈 *The* **collège** *is a state secondary school for children aged between eleven and fifteen. Pupils follow a nationally prescribed curriculum consisting of a common core and various options. Schools are free to arrange their own timetable and choose their own teaching methods. Before leaving the* **collège***, pupils are assessed by examination and course work for their* **brevet des collèges.**

---

collègue [kɔ(l)lɛg] *nm/f* colleague

coller [kɔle] *vt* (*papier, timbre*) to stick (on); (*affiche*) to stick up; (*enveloppe*) to stick down; (*morceaux*) to stick *ou* glue together; (*fam: mettre, fourrer*) to stick, shove; (*SCOL: fam*) to keep in ♦ *vi* (*être collant*) to be sticky; (*adhérer*) to stick; **~ à** to stick to; **être collé à un examen** (*fam*) to fail an exam

collet [kɔlɛ] *nm* (*piège*) snare, noose; (*cou*): **prendre qn au ~** to grab sb by the throat

collier [kɔlje] *nm* (*bijou*) necklace; (*de chien, TECH*) collar

collimateur [kɔlimatœR] *nm*: **avoir qn/qch dans le ~** (*fig*) to have sb/sth in

one's sights

colline [kɔlin] *nf* hill

collision [kɔlizjɔ̃] *nf* collision, crash; **entrer en ~ (avec)** to collide (with)

colloque [kɔ(l)lɔk] *nm* symposium

collyre [kɔliR] *nm* eye drops

colmater [kɔlmate] *vt* (*fuite*) to seal off; (*brèche*) to plug, fill in

colombe [kɔlɔ̃b] *nf* dove

Colombie [kɔlɔ̃bi] *nf*: **la ~** Colombia

colon [kɔlɔ̃] *nm* settler

colonel [kɔlɔnɛl] *nm* colonel

colonie [kɔlɔni] *nf* colony; **~ (de vacances)** holiday camp (*for children*)

colonne [kɔlɔn] *nf* column; **se mettre en ~ par deux** to get into twos; **~ (vertébrale)** spine, spinal column

colorant [kɔlɔRɑ̃, ɑ̃t] *nm* colouring

colorer [kɔlɔRe] *vt* to colour

colorier [kɔlɔRje] *vt* to colour (in)

coloris [kɔlɔRi] *nm* colour, shade

colporter [kɔlpɔRte] *vt* to hawk, peddle

colza [kɔlza] *nm* rape(seed)

coma [kɔma] *nm* coma; **être dans le ~** to be in a coma

combat [kɔ̃ba] *nm* fight, fighting *no pl*, **~ de boxe** boxing match; **combattant** *nm*: **ancien combattant** war veteran; **combattre** *vt* to fight; (*épidemie, ignorance*) to combat, fight against

combien [kɔ̃bjɛ̃] *adv* (*quantité*) how much; (*nombre*) how many; **~ de** (*quantité*) how much; (*nombre*) how many; **~ de temps** how long; **~ ça coûte/pèse?** how much does it cost/weigh?; **on est le ~ aujourd'hui?** (*fam*) what's the date today?

combinaison [kɔ̃binɛzɔ̃] *nf* combination; (*astuce*) device, scheme; (*de femme*) slip; (*de plongée*) wetsuit; (*bleu de travail*) boiler suit (*BRIT*), coveralls *pl* (*US*)

combine [kɔ̃bin] *nf* trick; (*péj*) scheme, fiddle (*BRIT*)

combiné [kɔ̃bine] *nm* (*aussi:* **~ téléphonique**) receiver

combiner [kɔ̃bine] *vt* (*grouper*) to combine; (*plan, horaire*) to work out, devise

comble [kɔbl] *adj* (*salle*) packed (full)
♦ *nm* (*du bonheur, plaisir*) height; **~s** *nmpl*
(*CONSTR*) attic *sg*, loft *sg*; **c'est le ~!** that
beats everything!
combler [kɔble] *vt* (*trou*) to fill in; (*besoin,
lacune*) to fill; (*déficit*) to make good; (*satisfaire*) to fulfil
combustible [kɔbystibl] *nm* fuel
comédie [kɔmedi] *nf* comedy; (*fig*) playacting *no pl*; **faire la ~** (*fam*) to make a
fuss; **~ musicale** musical; **comédien, ne**
nm/f actor(-tress)

Comédie française

i Founded in 1680 by Louis XIV, the
Comédie française *is the French national theatre. Subsidized by the state, the
company performs mainly in the Palais
Royal in Paris and stages mainly classical
French plays.*

comestible [kɔmestibl] *adj* edible
comique [kɔmik] *adj* (*drôle*) comical;
(*THÉÂTRE*) comic ♦ *nm* (*artiste*) comic, comedian
comité [kɔmite] *nm* committee; **~ d'entreprise** works council
commandant [kɔmɑdɑ] *nm* (*gén*) commander, commandant; (*NAVIG, AVIAT*) captain
commande [kɔmɑd] *nf* (*COMM*) order; **~s**
nfpl (*AVIAT etc*) controls; **sur ~** to order;
commandement *nm* command; (*REL*)
commandment; **commander** *vt* (*COMM*)
to order; (*diriger, ordonner*) to command;
commander à qn de faire to command
ou order sb to do
commando [kɔmɑdo] *nm* commando
(squad)

MOT-CLÉ

comme [kɔm] *prép* **1** (*comparaison*) like;
tout comme son père just like his father;
fort comme un bœuf as strong as an ox;
joli comme tout ever so pretty
2 (*manière*) like; **faites-le comme ça** do it

like this, do it this way; **comme ci,
comme ça** so-so, middling
3 (*en tant que*) as a; **donner comme prix**
to give as a prize; **travailler comme secrétaire** to work as a secretary
♦ *conj* **1** (*ainsi que*) as; **elle écrit comme
elle parle** she writes as she talks; **comme
si** as if
2 (*au moment où, alors que*) as; **il est parti
comme j'arrivais** he left as I arrived
3 (*parce que, puisque*) as; **comme il était
en retard, il ...** as he was late, he ...
♦ *adv*: **comme il est fort/c'est bon!** he's
so strong/it's so good!

commémorer [kɔmemɔre] *vt* to commemorate
commencement [kɔmɑsmɑ] *nm* beginning, start
commencer [kɔmɑse] *vt, vi* to begin,
start; **~ à** *ou* **de faire** to begin *ou* start
doing
comment [kɔmɑ] *adv* how; **~?** (*que dites-
vous*) pardon?
commentaire [kɔmɑtɛr] *nm* (*remarque*)
comment, remark; (*exposé*) commentary
commenter [kɔmɑte] *vt* (*jugement, événement*) to comment (up)on; (*RADIO, TV*:
match, manifestation) to cover
commérages [kɔmeraʒ] *nmpl* gossip *sg*
commerçant, e [kɔmɛrsɑ, ɑt] *nm/f* shopkeeper, trader
commerce [kɔmɛrs] *nm* (*activité*) trade,
commerce; (*boutique*) business; **~ électronique** e-commerce; **commercial, e,
-aux** *adj* commercial, trading; (*péj*) commercial; **les commerciaux** the sales
people; **commercialiser** *vt* to market
commère [kɔmɛr] *nf* gossip
commettre [kɔmɛtr] *vt* to commit
commis [kɔmi] *nm* (*de magasin*) (shop) assistant; (*de banque*) clerk
commissaire [kɔmisɛr] *nm* (*de police*) ≈
(police) superintendent; **commissaire-
priseur** *nm* auctioneer; **commissariat**
nm police station

ommission [kɔmisjɔ̃] nf (comité, pourcentage) commission; (message) message; (course) errand; **~s** nfpl (achats) shopping sg

ommode [kɔmɔd] adj (pratique) convenient, handy; (facile) easy; (personne): **pas ~** awkward (to deal with) ♦ nf chest of drawers; **commodité** nf convenience

ommotion [kɔmosjɔ̃] nf: **~ (cérébrale)** concussion; **commotionné, e** adj shocked, shaken

ommun, e [kɔmœ̃, yn] adj common; (pièce) communal, shared; (effort) joint; **ça sort du ~** it's out of the ordinary; **le ~ des mortels** the common run of people; **en ~** (faire) jointly; **mettre en ~** to pool, share; voir aussi **communs**

ommunauté [kɔmynote] nf community

ommune [kɔmyn] nf (ADMIN) commune, ≈ district; (: urbaine) ≈ borough

ommunicatif, -ive [kɔmynikatif, iv] adj (rire) infectious; (personne) communicative

ommunication [kɔmynikasjɔ̃] nf communication; **~ (téléphonique)** (telephone) call

ommunier [kɔmynje] vi (REL) to receive communion

ommunion [kɔmynjɔ̃] nf communion

ommuniquer [kɔmynike] vt (nouvelle, dossier) to pass on, convey; (peur etc) to communicate ♦ vi to communicate; **se ~ à** (se propager) to spread to

ommunisme [kɔmynism] nm communism; **communiste** adj, nm/f communist

ommuns [kɔmœ̃] nmpl (bâtiments) outbuildings

ommutateur [kɔmytatœʀ] nm (ÉLEC) (change-over) switch, commutator

ompact, e [kɔ̃pakt] adj (dense) dense; (appareil) compact

ompagne [kɔ̃paɲ] nf companion

ompagnie [kɔ̃paɲi] nf (firme, MIL) company; **tenir ~ à qn** to keep sb company; **fausser ~ à qn** to give sb the slip, slip ou sneak away from sb; **~ aérienne** airline (company)

compagnon [kɔ̃paɲɔ̃] nm companion

comparable [kɔ̃paʀabl] adj: **~ (à)** comparable (to)

comparaison [kɔ̃paʀɛzɔ̃] nf comparison

comparaître [kɔ̃paʀɛtʀ] vi: **~ (devant)** to appear (before)

comparer [kɔ̃paʀe] vt to compare; **~ qch/qn à** ou **et** (pour choisir) to compare sth/sb with ou and; (pour établir une similitude) to compare sth/sb to

compartiment [kɔ̃paʀtimɑ̃] nm compartment

comparution [kɔ̃paʀysjɔ̃] nf (JUR) appearance

compas [kɔ̃pa] nm (GÉOM) (pair of) compasses pl; (NAVIG) compass

compatible [kɔ̃patibl] adj compatible

compatir [kɔ̃patiʀ] vi to sympathize

compatriote [kɔ̃patʀijɔt] nm/f compatriot

compensation [kɔ̃pɑ̃sasjɔ̃] nf compensation

compenser [kɔ̃pɑ̃se] vt to compensate for, make up for

compère [kɔ̃pɛʀ] nm accomplice

compétence [kɔ̃petɑ̃s] nf competence

compétent, e [kɔ̃petɑ̃, ɑ̃t] adj (apte) competent, capable

compétition [kɔ̃petisjɔ̃] nf (gén) competition; (SPORT: épreuve) event; **la ~ automobile** motor racing

complainte [kɔ̃plɛ̃t] nf lament

complaire [kɔ̃plɛʀ]: **se ~** vi: **se ~ dans** to take pleasure in

complaisance [kɔ̃plɛzɑ̃s] nf kindness; **pavillon de ~** flag of convenience

complaisant, e [kɔ̃plɛzɑ̃, ɑ̃t] adj (aimable) kind, obliging

complément [kɔ̃plemɑ̃] nm complement; (reste) remainder; **~ d'information** (ADMIN) supplementary ou further information; **complémentaire** adj complementary; (additionnel) supplementary

complet, -ète [kɔ̃plɛ, ɛt] adj complete; (plein: hôtel etc) full ♦ nm (aussi: **~-veston**) suit; **pain ~** wholemeal bread; **complètement** adv completely;

compléter vt (porter à la quantité voulue) to complete; (augmenter: connaissances, études) to complement, supplement; (: garde-robe) to add to; se compléter (caractères) to complement one another

complexe [kɔ̃plɛks] adj, nm complex; complexé, e adj mixed-up, hung-up

complication [kɔ̃plikasjɔ̃] nf complexity, intricacy; (difficulté, ennui) complication

complice [kɔ̃plis] nm accomplice; complicité nf complicity

compliment [kɔ̃plimɑ̃] nm (louange) compliment; ~s nmpl (félicitations) congratulations

compliqué, e [kɔ̃plike] adj complicated, complex; (personne) complicated

compliquer [kɔ̃plike] vt to complicate; se ~ to become complicated

complot [kɔ̃plo] nm plot

comportement [kɔ̃pɔrtəmɑ̃] nm behaviour

comporter [kɔ̃pɔrte] vt (consister en) to consist of, comprise; (inclure) to have; se ~ vi to behave

composant [kɔ̃pozɑ̃] nm, composante [kɔ̃pozɑ̃t] nf component

composé [kɔ̃poze] nm compound

composer [kɔ̃poze] vt (musique, texte) to compose; (mélange, équipe) to make up; (numéro) to dial; (constituer) to make up, form ♦ vi (transiger) to come to terms; se ~ de to be composed of, be made up of; compositeur, -trice nm/f (MUS) composer; composition nf composition; (SCOL) test

composter [kɔ̃pɔste] vt (billet) to punch

compote [kɔ̃pɔt] nf stewed fruit no pl; ~ de pommes stewed apples

compréhensible [kɔ̃preɑ̃sibl] adj comprehensible; (attitude) understandable

compréhensif, -ive [kɔ̃preɑ̃sif, iv] adj understanding

comprendre [kɔ̃prɑ̃dr] vt to understand; (se composer de) to comprise, consist of

compresse [kɔ̃prɛs] nf compress

compression [kɔ̃presjɔ̃] nf compression;

(de personnes) reduction

comprimé [kɔ̃prime] nm tablet

comprimer [kɔ̃prime] vt to compress; (fig: crédit etc) to reduce, cut down

compris, e [kɔ̃pri, iz] pp de comprendre ♦ adj (inclus) included; ~ entre (situé) contained between; l'électricité ~e/non ~e, y/non ~ l'électricité including/excluding electricity; 100 F tout ~ 100 F all inclusive ou all-in

compromettre [kɔ̃prɔmɛtr] vt to compromise; compromis nm compromise

comptabilité [kɔ̃tabilite] nf (activité) accounting, accountancy; (comptes) accounts pl, books pl; (service) accounts office

comptable [kɔ̃tabl] nm/f accountant

comptant [kɔ̃tɑ̃] adv: payer ~ to pay cash; acheter ~ to buy for cash

compte [kɔ̃t] nm count; (total, montant) count, (right) number; (bancaire, facture) account; ~s nmpl (FINANCE) account books; (fig) explanation sg; en fin de ~ all things considered; s'en tirer à bon ~ to get off lightly; pour le ~ de on behalf of; pour son propre ~ for one's own benefit; tenir ~ de to take account of; travailler à son ~ to work for oneself; rendre ~ (à qn) de qch to give (sb) an account of sth; voir aussi rendre ~ à rebours countdown; ~ chèques postaux Post Office account; ~ courant current account; ~ rendu account, report; (de film, livre) review; compte-gouttes nm inv dropper

compter [kɔ̃te] vt to count; (facturer) to charge for; (avoir à son actif, comporter) to have; (prévoir) to allow, reckon; (penser, espérer): ~ réussir to expect to succeed ♦ vi to count; (être économe) to economize; (figurer): ~ parmi to be ou rank among; ~ sur to count (up)on; ~ avec qch/qn to reckon with ou take account of sth/sb; sans ~ que besides which

compteur [kɔ̃tœr] nm meter; ~ de vitesse speedometer

omptine [kɔ̃tin] *nf* nursery rhyme

omptoir [kɔ̃twaʀ] *nm (de magasin)* counter; *(bar)* bar

ompulser [kɔ̃pylse] *vt* to consult

omte [kɔ̃t] *nm* count; **comtesse** *nf* countess

on, ne [kɔ̃, kɔn] *(fam!) adj* damned *ou* bloody *(BRIT)* stupid *(!)*

oncéder [kɔ̃sede] *vt* to grant; *(défaite, point)* to concede

oncentré, e [kɔ̃sɑ̃tʀe] *adj (lait)* condensed ♦ *nm:* **~ de tomates** tomato purée

oncentrer [kɔ̃sɑ̃tʀe] *vt* to concentrate; **se ~** *vi* to concentrate

oncept [kɔ̃sɛpt] *nm* concept

onception [kɔ̃sɛpsjɔ̃] *nf* conception; *(d'une machine etc)* design; *(d'un problème, de la vie)* approach

oncerner [kɔ̃sɛʀne] *vt* to concern; **en ce qui me concerne** as far as I am concerned

oncert [kɔ̃sɛʀ] *nm* concert; **de ~** *(décider)* unanimously; **concerter: se concerter** *vi* to put their *etc* heads together

oncession [kɔ̃sesjɔ̃] *nf* concession; **concessionnaire** *nm/f* agent, dealer

oncevoir [kɔ̃s(ə)vwaʀ] *vt (idée, projet)* to conceive (of); *(comprendre)* to understand; *(enfant)* to conceive; **bien/mal conçu** well-/badly-designed

oncierge [kɔ̃sjɛʀʒ] *nm/f* caretaker

onciliabules [kɔ̃siljabyl] *nmpl (private)* discussions, confabulations

oncilier [kɔ̃silje] *vt* to reconcile; **se ~** *vt* to win over

oncis, e [kɔ̃si, iz] *adj* concise

oncitoyen, ne [kɔ̃sitwajɛ̃, jɛn] *nm/f* fellow citizen

oncluant, e [kɔ̃klyɑ̃, ɑ̃t] *adj* conclusive

onclure [kɔ̃klyʀ] *vt* to conclude; **conclusion** *nf* conclusion

onçois *etc* [kɔ̃swa] *vb voir* **concevoir**

oncombre [kɔ̃kɔ̃bʀ] *nm* cucumber

oncorder [kɔ̃kɔʀde] *vi* to tally, agree

oncourir [kɔ̃kuʀiʀ] *vi (SPORT)* to com-

pete; **~ à** *(effet etc)* to work towards

concours [kɔ̃kuʀ] *nm* competition; *(SCOL)* competitive examination; *(assistance)* aid, help; **~ de circonstances** combination of circumstances; **~ hippique** horse show

concret, -ète [kɔ̃kʀɛ, ɛt] *adj* concrete

concrétiser [kɔ̃kʀetize]: **se ~** *vi* to materialize

conçu, e [kɔ̃sy] *pp de* **concevoir**

concubinage [kɔ̃kybinaʒ] *nm (JUR)* cohabitation

concurrence [kɔ̃kyʀɑ̃s] *nf* competition; **faire ~ à** to be in competition with; **jusqu'à ~ de** up to

concurrent, e [kɔ̃kyʀɑ̃, ɑ̃t] *nm/f (SPORT, ÉCON etc)* competitor; *(SCOL)* candidate

condamner [kɔ̃dane] *vt (blâmer)* to condemn; *(JUR)* to sentence; *(porte, ouverture)* to fill in, block up; **~ qn à 2 ans de prison** to sentence sb to 2 years' imprisonment

condensation [kɔ̃dɑ̃sasjɔ̃] *nf* condensation

condenser [kɔ̃dɑ̃se] *vt* to condense; **se ~** *vi* to condense

condisciple [kɔ̃disipl] *nm/f* fellow student

condition [kɔ̃disjɔ̃] *nf* condition; **~s** *nfpl (tarif, prix)* terms; *(circonstances)* conditions; **à ~ de** *ou* **que** provided that; **conditionnel, le** *nm* conditional (tense)

conditionnement [kɔ̃disjɔnmɑ̃] *nm (emballage)* packaging

conditionner [kɔ̃disjɔne] *vt (déterminer)* to determine; *(COMM: produit)* to package; **air conditionné** air conditioning

condoléances [kɔ̃dɔleɑ̃s] *nfpl* condolences

conducteur, -trice [kɔ̃dyktœʀ, tʀis] *nm/f* driver ♦ *nm (ÉLEC etc)* conductor

conduire [kɔ̃dɥiʀ] *vt* to drive; *(délégation, troupeau)* to lead; **se ~** *vi* to behave; **~ à** to lead to; **~ qn quelque part** to take sb somewhere; to drive sb somewhere

conduite [kɔ̃dɥit] *nf (comportement)* behaviour; *(d'eau, de gaz)* pipe; **sous la ~ de** led by; **~ à gauche** left-hand drive

cône [kon] *nm* cone

confection [kɔ̃feksjɔ̃] *nf* (*fabrication*) making; (*COUTURE*): **la ~** the clothing industry

confectionner [kɔ̃feksjɔne] *vt* to make

conférence [kɔ̃feʀɑ̃s] *nf* conference; (*exposé*) lecture; **~ de presse** press conference; **conférencier, -ière** *nm/f* speaker, lecturer

confesser [kɔ̃fese] *vt* to confess; **se ~** *vi* (*REL*) to go to confession; **confession** *nf* confession; (*culte: catholique etc*) denomination

confiance [kɔ̃fjɑ̃s] *nf* (*en l'honnêteté de qn*) confidence, trust; (*en la valeur de qch*) faith; **avoir ~ en** to have confidence *ou* faith in, trust; **faire ~ à qn** to trust sb; **mettre qn en ~** to win sb's trust; **~ en soi** self-confidence

confiant, e [kɔ̃fjɑ̃, jɑ̃t] *adj* confident; trusting

confidence [kɔ̃fidɑ̃s] *nf* confidence; **confidentiel, le** *adj* confidential

confier [kɔ̃fje] *vt*: **~ à qn** (*objet, travail*) to entrust to sb; (*secret, pensée*) to confide to sb; **se ~ à qn** to confide in sb

confins [kɔ̃fɛ̃] *nmpl*: **aux ~ de** on the borders of

confirmation [kɔ̃fiʀmasjɔ̃] *nf* confirmation

confirmer [kɔ̃fiʀme] *vt* to confirm

confiserie [kɔ̃fizʀi] *nf* (*magasin*) confectioner's *ou* sweet shop; **~s** *nfpl* (*bonbons*) confectionery *sg*

confisquer [kɔ̃fiske] *vt* to confiscate

confit, e [kɔ̃fi, it] *adj*: **fruits ~s** crystallized fruits ♦ *nm*: **~ d'oie** conserve of goose

confiture [kɔ̃fityʀ] *nf* jam; **~ d'oranges** (orange) marmalade

conflit [kɔ̃fli] *nm* conflict

confondre [kɔ̃fɔ̃dʀ] *vt* (*jumeaux, faits*) to confuse, mix up; (*témoin, menteur*) to confound; **se ~** *vi* to merge; **se ~ en excuses** to apologize profusely; **confondu, e** *adj* (*stupéfait*) speechless, overcome

conforme [kɔ̃fɔʀm] *adj*: **~ à** (*loi, règle*) in accordance with; **conformément** *adv*: **conformément à** in accordance with;

conformer *vt*: **se conformer à** to conform to

confort [kɔ̃fɔʀ] *nm* comfort; **tout ~** (*COMM*) with all modern conveniences; **confortable** *adj* comfortable

confrère [kɔ̃fʀɛʀ] *nm* colleague

confronter [kɔ̃fʀɔ̃te] *vt* to confront

confus, e [kɔ̃fy, yz] *adj* (*vague*) confused; (*embarrassé*) embarrassed; **confusion** *nf* (*voir confus*) confusion; embarrassment; (*voir confondre*) confusion, mixing up

congé [kɔ̃ʒe] *nm* (*vacances*) holiday; **en ~** on holiday; **semaine de ~** week of prendre **~ de qn** to take one's leave of sb; **donner son ~ à** to give in one's notice; **~ de maladie** sick leave; **~ de maternité** maternity leave; **~s payés** paid holiday

congédier [kɔ̃ʒedje] *vt* to dismiss

congélateur [kɔ̃ʒelatœʀ] *nm* freezer

congeler [kɔ̃ʒ(ə)le] *vt* to freeze; **les produits congelés** frozen foods

congestion [kɔ̃ʒɛstjɔ̃] *nf* congestion; **~ cérébrale** stroke; **congestionner** *vt* (*rue*) to congest; (*visage*) to flush

congrès [kɔ̃gʀɛ] *nm* congress

conifère [kɔnifɛʀ] *nm* conifer

conjecture [kɔ̃ʒɛktyʀ] *nf* conjecture

conjoint, e [kɔ̃ʒwɛ̃, wɛ̃t] *adj* joint ♦ *nm* spouse

conjonction [kɔ̃ʒɔ̃ksjɔ̃] *nf* (*LING*) conjunction

conjonctivite [kɔ̃ʒɔ̃ktivit] *nf* conjunctivitis

conjoncture [kɔ̃ʒɔ̃ktyʀ] *nf* circumstances *pl*; **la ~ actuelle** the present (economic) situation

conjugaison [kɔ̃ʒygɛzɔ̃] *nf* (*LING*) conjugation

conjuguer [kɔ̃ʒyge] *vt* (*LING*) to conjugate; (*efforts etc*) to combine

conjuration [kɔ̃ʒyʀasjɔ̃] *nf* conspiracy

conjurer [kɔ̃ʒyʀe] *vt* (*sort, maladie*) to avert; (*implorer*) to beseech, entreat

connaissance [kɔnɛsɑ̃s] *nf* (*savoir*) knowledge *no pl*; (*personne connue*) acquaintance; **être sans ~** to be unconscious

perdre/reprendre ~ to lose/regain consciousness; **à ma ~** to (the best of) my knowledge; **faire la ~ de qn** to meet sb
onnaisseur [kɔnɛsœʀ, øz] *nm* connoisseur
onnaître [kɔnɛtʀ] *vt* to know; (*éprouver*) to experience; (*avoir: succès*) to have, enjoy; **~ de nom/vue** to know by name/sight; **ils se sont connus à Genève** they (first) met in Geneva; **s'y ~ en qch** to know a lot about sth
onnecter [kɔnɛkte] *vt* to connect; **se ~** (*INFORM*) to log on
onnerie [kɔnʀi] (*fam!*) *nf* stupid thing (to do/say)
onnu, e [kɔny] *adj* (*célèbre*) well-known
onquérir [kɔkeʀiʀ] *vt* to conquer
onsacrer [kɔsakʀe] *vt* (*employer*) to devote, dedicate; (*REL*) to consecrate
onscience [kɔsjɑs] *nf* conscience; **avoir/prendre ~ de** to be/become aware of; **perdre ~** to lose consciousness; **avoir mauvaise ~** to have a guilty conscience; **consciencieux, -euse** *adj* conscientious; **conscient, e** *adj* conscious
onscrit [kɔskʀi] *nm* conscript
onsécutif, -ive [kɔsekytif, iv] *adj* consecutive; **~ à** following upon
onseil [kɔsɛj] *nm* (*avis*) piece of advice; (*assemblée*) council; **des ~s** advice; **prendre ~ (auprès de qn)** to take advice (from sb); **~ d'administration** board (of directors); **le ~ des ministres** ≈ the Cabinet; **~ municipal** town council
onseiller, -ère [kɔseje, ɛʀ] *nm/f* adviser ♦ *vt* (*personne*) to advise; (*méthode, action*) to recommend, advise; **~ à qn de** to advise sb to; **~ municipal** town councillor
onsentement [kɔsɑtmɑ] *nm* consent
onsentir [kɔsɑtiʀ] *vt* to agree, consent
onséquence [kɔsekɑs] *nf* consequence; **en ~** (*donc*) consequently; (*de façon appropriée*) accordingly; **conséquent, e** *adj* logical, rational; (*fam: important*) substantial; **par conséquent** consequently
onservateur, -trice [kɔsɛʀvatœʀ, tʀis]

nm/f (*POL*) conservative; (*de musée*) curator ♦ *nm* (*pour aliments*) preservative
conservatoire [kɔsɛʀvatwaʀ] *nm* academy
conserve [kɔsɛʀv] *nf* (*gén pl*) canned *ou* tinned (*BRIT*) food; **en ~** canned, tinned (*BRIT*)
conserver [kɔsɛʀve] *vt* (*faculté*) to retain, keep; (*amis, livres*) to keep; (*préserver, aussi CULIN*) to preserve
considérable [kɔsideʀabl] *adj* considerable, significant, extensive
considération [kɔsideʀasjɔ] *nf* consideration; (*estime*) esteem
considérer [kɔsideʀe] *vt* to consider; **~ qch comme** to regard sth as
consigne [kɔsiɲ] *nf* (*de gare*) left luggage (office) (*BRIT*), checkroom (*US*); (*ordre, instruction*) instructions *pl*; **~ (automatique)** left-luggage locker; **consigner** *vt* (*note, pensée*) to record; (*punir: élève*) to put in detention; (*COMM*) to put a deposit on
consistant, e [kɔsistɑ, ɑt] *adj* (*mélange*) thick; (*repas*) solid
consister [kɔsiste] *vi*: **~ en/à faire** to consist of/in doing
consœur [kɔsœʀ] *nf* (*lady*) colleague
console [kɔsɔl] *nf*: **~ de jeux** games console
consoler [kɔsɔle] *vt* to console
consolider [kɔsɔlide] *vt* to strengthen; (*fig*) to consolidate
consommateur, -trice [kɔsɔmatœʀ, tʀis] *nm/f* (*ÉCON*) consumer; (*dans un café*) customer
consommation [kɔsɔmasjɔ] *nf* (*boisson*) drink; (*ÉCON*) consumption
consommer [kɔsɔme] *vt* (*suj: personne*) to eat *ou* drink, consume; (*: voiture, machine*) to use, consume; (*mariage*) to consummate ♦ *vi* (*dans un café*) to (have a) drink
consonne [kɔsɔn] *nf* consonant
conspirer [kɔspiʀe] *vi* to conspire
constamment [kɔstamɑ] *adv* constantly
constant, e [kɔstɑ, ɑt] *adj* constant; (*personne*) steadfast

constat [kɔstal] *nm* (*de police, d'accident*) report; ~ **(à l')amiable** *jointly-agreed statement for insurance purposes*; ~ **d'échec** acknowledgement of failure

constatation [kɔstatasjɔ̃] *nf* (*observation*) (observed) fact, observation

constater [kɔstate] *vt* (*remarquer*) to note; (*ADMIN, JUR: attester*) to certify

consterner [kɔstɛʀne] *vt* to dismay

constipé, e [kɔstipe] *adj* constipated

constitué, e [kɔstitɥe] *adj*: ~ **de** made up *ou* composed of

constituer [kɔstitɥe] *vt* (*équipe*) to set up; (*dossier, collection*) to put together; (*suj: éléments: composer*) to make up, constitute; (*représenter, être*) to constitute; **se ~ prisonnier** to give o.s. up; **constitution** *nf* (*composition*) composition, make-up; (*santé, POL*) constitution

constructeur [kɔstʀyktœʀ] *nm* manufacturer, builder

constructif, -ive [kɔstʀyktif, iv] *adj* constructive

construction [kɔstʀyksjɔ̃] *nf* construction, building

construire [kɔstʀɥiʀ] *vt* to build, construct

consul [kɔsyl] *nm* consul; **consulat** *nm* consulate

consultant, e [kɔsyltɑ̃, ɑ̃t] *adj, nm* consultant

consultation [kɔsyltasjɔ̃] *nf* consultation; **~s** *nfpl* (*POL*) talks; **heures de ~** (*MÉD*) surgery (*BRIT*) *ou* office (*US*) hours

consulter [kɔsylte] *vt* to consult ♦ *vi* (*médecin*) to hold surgery (*BRIT*), be in (the office) (*US*); **se ~** *vi* to confer

consumer [kɔsyme] *vt* to consume; **se ~** *vi* to burn

contact [kɔtakt] *nm* contact; **au ~ de** (*air, peau*) on contact with; (*gens*) through contact with; **mettre/couper le ~** (*AUTO*) to switch on/off the ignition; **entrer en** *ou* **prendre ~ avec** to get in touch *ou* contact with; **contacter** *vt* to contact, get in touch with

contagieux, -euse [kɔtaʒjø, jøz] *adj* infectious; (*par le contact*) contagious

contaminer [kɔtamine] *vt* to contaminate

conte [kɔt] *nm* tale; ~ **de fées** fairy tale

contempler [kɔtɑple] *vt* to contemplate, gaze at

contemporain, e [kɔtɑpɔʀɛ̃, ɛn] *adj, nm/f* contemporary

contenance [kɔt(ə)nɑs] *nf* (*d'un récipient*) capacity; (*attitude*) bearing, attitude; **perdre ~** to lose one's composure

conteneur [kɔt(ə)nœʀ] *nm* container

contenir [kɔt(ə)niʀ] *vt* to contain; (*avoir une capacité de*) to hold; **se ~** *vi* to contain o.s.

content, e [kɔtɑ̃, ɑ̃t] *adj* pleased, glad; ~ **de** pleased with; **contenter** *vt* to satisfy, please; **se contenter de** to content o.s. with

contentieux [kɔtɑsjø] *nm* (*COMM*) litigation; (*service*) litigation department

contenu [kɔt(ə)ny] *nm* (*d'un récipient*) contents *pl*; (*d'un texte*) content

conter [kɔte] *vt* to recount, relate

contestable [kɔtestabl] *adj* questionable

contestation [kɔtestasjɔ̃] *nf* (*POL*) protest

conteste [kɔtest]: **sans ~** *adv* unquestionably, indisputably; **contester** *vt* to question, contest ♦ *vi* (*POL, gén*) to protest, rebel (against established authority)

contexte [kɔtɛkst] *nm* context

contigu, ë [kɔtigy] *adj*: ~ **(à)** adjacent (to)

continent [kɔtinɑ̃] *nm* continent

continu, e [kɔtiny] *adj* continuous; **faire la journée ~e** to work without taking a full lunch break; **(courant) ~** direct current, DC

continuel, le [kɔtinɥɛl] *adj* (*qui se répète*) constant, continual; (*continu*) continuous

continuer [kɔtinɥe] *vt* (*travail, voyage etc*) to continue (with), carry on (with), go on (with); (*prolonger: alignement, rue*) to continue ♦ *vi* (*vie, bruit*) to continue, go on; to; **à** *ou* **de faire** to go on *ou* continue doing

contorsionner [kɔtɔʀsjɔne]: **se ~** *vi* to

contort o.s., writhe about

contour [kɔ̃tuʀ] *nm* outline, contour;
contourner *vt* to go round; (*difficulté*) to
get round

contraceptif, -ive [kɔ̃tʀaseptif, iv] *adj,
nm* contraceptive; **contraception** *nf*
contraception

contracté, e [kɔ̃tʀakte] *adj* tense

contracter [kɔ̃tʀakte] *vt* (*muscle etc*) to
tense, contract; (*maladie, dette*) to contract; (*assurance*) to take out; **se ~** *vi*
(*muscles*) to contract

contractuel, le [kɔ̃tʀaktɥel] *nm/f* (*agent*)
traffic warden

contradiction [kɔ̃tʀadiksjɔ̃] *nf* contradiction; **contradictoire** *adj* contradictory,
conflicting

contraignant, e [kɔ̃tʀɛɲɑ̃, ɑ̃t] *adj* restrict-
ing

contraindre [kɔ̃tʀɛ̃dʀ] *vt*: **~ qn à faire** to
compel sb to do; **contrainte** *nf* constraint

contraire [kɔ̃tʀɛʀ] *adj, nm* opposite; **~ à**
contrary to; **au ~** on the contrary

contrarier [kɔ̃tʀaʀje] *vt* (*personne: irriter*) to
annoy; (*fig: projets*) to thwart, frustrate;
contrariété *nf* annoyance

contraste [kɔ̃tʀast] *nm* contrast

contrat [kɔ̃tʀa] *nm* contract; **~ de travail**
employment contract

contravention [kɔ̃tʀavɑ̃sjɔ̃] *nf* parking
ticket

contre [kɔ̃tʀ] *prép* against; (*en échange*) (in
exchange) for; **par ~** on the other hand

contrebande [kɔ̃tʀabɑ̃d] *nf* (*trafic*) contraband, smuggling; (*marchandise*) contraband, smuggled goods *pl*; **faire la ~ de**
to smuggle; **contrebandier, -ière** *nm/f*
smuggler

contrebas [kɔ̃tʀaba]: **en ~** *adv* (down)
below

contrebasse [kɔ̃tʀabas] *nf* (double) bass

contre...: **contrecarrer** *vt* to thwart;
contrecœur: **à contrecœur** *adv*
(be)grudgingly, reluctantly; **contrecoup**
nm repercussions *pl*; **contredire** *vt* (*per-*

sonne) to contradict; (*faits*) to refute

contrée [kɔ̃tʀe] *nf* (*région*) region; (*pays*)
land

contrefaçon [kɔ̃tʀafasɔ̃] *nf* forgery

contrefaire [kɔ̃tʀafɛʀ] *vt* (*document, signature*) to forge, counterfeit

contre...: **contre-indication** (*pl*
contre-indications) *nf* (MÉD) contra-
indication; **"contre-indication en cas
d'eczéma"** "should not be used by
people with eczema"; **contre-indiqué, e**
adj (MÉD) contraindicated; (*déconseillé*) un-
advisable, ill-advised; **contre-jour**: **à
contre-jour** *adv* against the sunlight

contremaître [kɔ̃tʀamɛtʀ] *nm* foreman

contrepartie [kɔ̃tʀaparti] *nf*: **en ~** in return

contre-pied [kɔ̃tʀapje] *nm*: **prendre le
~-~ de** (*opinion*) to take the opposing
view of; (*action*) to take the opposite
course to

contre-plaqué [kɔ̃tʀaplake] *nm* plywood

contrepoids [kɔ̃tʀapwa] *nm* counter-
weight, counterbalance

contrepoison [kɔ̃tʀapwazɔ̃] *nm* antidote

contrer [kɔ̃tʀe] *vt* to counter

contresens [kɔ̃tʀasɑ̃s] *nm* (*erreur*) misin-
terpretation; (*de traduction*) mistranslation;
à ~ the wrong way

contretemps [kɔ̃tʀatɑ̃] *nm* hitch; **à ~**
(*fig*) at an inopportune moment

contrevenir [kɔ̃tʀav(a)niʀ]: **~ à** *vt* to
contravene

contribuable [kɔ̃tʀibɥabl] *nm/f* taxpayer

contribuer [kɔ̃tʀibɥe]: **~ à** *vt* to contribute
towards; **contribution** *nf* contribution;
contributions directes/indirectes direct/
indirect taxation; **mettre à contribution**
to call upon

contrôle [kɔ̃tʀol] *nm* checking *no pl*,
check; (*des prix*) monitoring, control; (*test*)
test, examination; **perdre le ~ de** (*véhicule*) to lose control of; **~ continu** (SCOL)
continuous assessment; **~ d'identité**
identity check

contrôler [kɔ̃tʀole] *vt* (*vérifier*) to check;

(*surveiller: opérations*) to supervise; (: *prix*) to monitor, control; (*maîtriser, COMM: firme*) to control; **se** ~ *vi* to control o.s.; **contrôleur, -euse** *nm/f* (*de train*) (ticket) inspector; (*de bus*) (bus) conductor(-tress)
contrordre [kɔ̃tRɔRdR] *nm:* **sauf** ~ unless otherwise directed
controversé, e [kɔ̃tRɔvɛRse] *adj* (*personnage, question*) controversial
contusion [kɔ̃tyzjɔ̃] *nf* bruise, contusion
convaincre [kɔ̃vɛ̃kR] *vt:* ~ **qn (de qch)** to convince sb (of sth); ~ **qn (de faire)** to persuade sb (to do)
convalescence [kɔ̃valesɑ̃s] *nf* convalescence
convenable [kɔ̃vnabl] *adj* suitable; (*assez bon, respectable*) decent
convenance [kɔ̃vnɑ̃s] *nf:* **à ma/votre** ~ to my/your liking; ~**s** *nfpl* (*normes sociales*) proprieties
convenir [kɔ̃vniR] *vi* to be suitable; ~ **à** to suit; ~ **de** (*bien-fondé de qch*) to admit (to), acknowledge; (*date, somme etc*) to agree upon; ~ **que** (*admettre*) to admit that; ~ **de faire** to agree to do
convention [kɔ̃vɑ̃sjɔ̃] *nf* convention; ~**s** *nfpl* (*convenances*) convention *sg;* ~ **collective** (*ÉCON*) collective agreement; **conventionné, e** *adj* (*ADMIN*) applying charges laid down by the state
convenu, e [kɔ̃vny] *pp de* **convenir** ♦ *adj* agreed
conversation [kɔ̃vɛRsasjɔ̃] *nf* conversation
convertir [kɔ̃vɛRtiR] *vt:* ~ **qn (à)** to convert sb (to); **se** ~ **(à)** to be converted (to); ~ **qch en** to convert sth into
conviction [kɔ̃viksjɔ̃] *nf* conviction
convienne *etc* [kɔ̃vjɛn] *vb voir* **convenir**
convier [kɔ̃vje] *vt:* ~ **qn à** (*dîner etc*) to (cordially) invite sb to
convive [kɔ̃viv] *nm/f* guest (*at table*)
convivial, e, -aux [kɔ̃vivjal, jo] *adj* (*INFORM*) user-friendly
convocation [kɔ̃vɔkasjɔ̃] *nf* (*document*) notification to attend; (: *JUR*) summons *sg*
convoi [kɔ̃vwa] *nm* convoy; (*train*) train

convoiter [kɔ̃vwate] *vt* to covet
convoquer [kɔ̃vɔke] *vt* (*assemblée*) to convene; (*subordonné*) to summon; (*candidat*) to ask to attend
convoyeur [kɔ̃vwajœR] *nm:* ~ **de fonds** security guard
coopération [kɔɔpeRasjɔ̃] *nf* co-operation; (*ADMIN*): **la C~** ≈ Voluntary Service Overseas (*BRIT*), ≈ Peace Corps (*US*)
coopérer [kɔɔpere] *vi:* ~ **(à)** to co-operate (in)
coordonnées [kɔɔRdɔne] *nfpl:* **donnez moi vos** ~ (*fam*) can I have your details please?
coordonner [kɔɔRdɔne] *vt* to coordinate
copain [kɔpɛ̃] (*fam*) *nm* mate, pal; (*petit ami*) boyfriend
copeau, x [kɔpo] *nm* shaving
copie [kɔpi] *nf* copy; (*SCOL*) script, paper; **copier** *vt, vi* to copy; **copier sur** to copy from; **copieur** *nm* (photo)copier
copieux, -euse [kɔpjø, jøz] *adj* copious
copine [kɔpin] (*fam*) *nf* mate, pal; (*petite amie*) girlfriend
copropriété [kɔpRɔpRijete] *nf* co-ownership, joint ownership
coq [kɔk] *nm* cock, rooster; **coq-à-l'âne** *nm inv* abrupt change of subject
coque [kɔk] *nf* (*de noix, mollusque*) shell; (*de bateau*) hull; **à la** ~ (*CULIN*) (soft) boiled
coquelicot [kɔkliko] *nm* poppy
coqueluche [kɔklyʃ] *nf* whooping-cough
coquet, te [kɔkɛ, ɛt] *adj* appearance-conscious; (*logement*) smart, charming
coquetier [kɔk(ə)tje] *nm* egg-cup
coquillage [kɔkijaʒ] *nm* (*mollusque*) shellfish *inv;* (*coquille*) shell
coquille [kɔkij] *nf* shell; (*TYPO*) misprint; **St Jacques** scallop
coquin, e [kɔkɛ̃, in] *adj* mischievous, roguish; (*polisson*) naughty
cor [kɔR] *nm* (*MUS*) horn; (*MÉD*): ~ **(au pied**) corn
corail, -aux [kɔRaj, o] *nm* coral *no pl*
Coran [kɔRɑ̃] *nm:* **le** ~ the Koran

orbeau, x [kɔrbo] *nm* crow

orbeille [kɔrbɛj] *nf* basket; **~ à papier** waste paper basket *ou* bin

orbillard [kɔrbijar] *nm* hearse

orde [kɔrd] *nf* rope; *(de violon, raquette)* string; **usé jusqu'à la ~** threadbare; **~ à linge** washing *ou* clothes line; **~ à sauter** skipping rope; **~s vocales** vocal cords

ordée *nf (d'alpinistes)* rope, roped party

ordialement [kɔrdjalmɑ̃] *adv (formule épistolaire)* (kind) regards

ordon [kɔrdɔ̃] *nm* cord, string; **~ ombilical** umbilical cord; **~ sanitaire/de police** sanitary/police cordon

ordonnerie [kɔrdɔnri] *nf* shoe repairer's (shop); **cordonnier** *nm* shoe repairer

orée [kɔre] *nf*: **la ~ du Sud/du Nord** South/North Korea

oriace [kɔrjas] *adj* tough

orne [kɔrn] *nf* horn; *(de cerf)* antler

ornée [kɔrne] *nf* cornea

orneille [kɔrnɛj] *nf* crow

ornemuse [kɔrnəmyz] *nf* bagpipes *pl*

ornet [kɔrnɛ] *nm* (paper) cone; *(de glace)* cornet, cone

orniche [kɔrniʃ] *nf (route)* coast road

ornichon [kɔrniʃɔ̃] *nm* gherkin

ornouailles [kɔrnwaj] *nf* Cornwall

orporation [kɔrpɔrasjɔ̃] *nf* corporate body

orporel, le [kɔrpɔrɛl] *adj* bodily; *(punition)* corporal

orps [kɔr] *nm* body; **à ~ perdu** headlong; **prendre ~** to take shape; **~ à ~ ♦** *adv* hand-to-hand ♦ *nm* clinch; **le ~ électoral** the electorate; **le ~ enseignant** the teaching profession

orpulent, e [kɔrpylɑ̃, ɑ̃t] *adj* stout

orrect, e [kɔrɛkt] *adj* correct; *(fam: acceptable: salaire, hôtel)* reasonable, decent; **correcteur, -trice** *nm/f (SCOL)* examiner; **correction** *nf (voir corriger)* correction; *(voir correct)* correctness; *(coups)* thrashing; **correctionnel, le** *adj (JUR)*: **tribunal correctionnel** ≃ criminal court

orrespondance [kɔrɛspɔ̃dɑ̃s] *nf* correspondence; *(de train, d'avion)* connection; **cours par ~** correspondence course; **vente par ~** mail-order business

correspondant, e [kɔrɛspɔ̃dɑ̃, ɑ̃t] *nm/f* correspondent; *(TÉL)* person phoning *(ou* being phoned)

correspondre [kɔrɛspɔ̃dr] *vi* to correspond, tally; **~ à** to correspond to; **~ avec qn** to correspond with sb

corrida [kɔrida] *nf* bullfight

corridor [kɔridɔr] *nm* corridor

corrigé [kɔriʒe] *nm (SCOL: d'exercise)* correct version

corriger [kɔriʒe] *vt (devoir)* to correct; *(punir)* to thrash; **~ qn de** *(défaut)* to cure sb of

corroborer [kɔrɔbɔre] *vt* to corroborate

corrompre [kɔrɔ̃pr] *vt* to corrupt; *(acheter: témoin etc)* to bribe

corruption [kɔrypsjɔ̃] *nf* corruption; *(de témoins)* bribery

corsage [kɔrsaʒ] *nm* bodice; *(chemisier)* blouse

corsaire [kɔrsɛr] *nm* pirate

corse [kɔrs] *adj, nm/f* Corsican ♦ *nf*: **la C~** Corsica

corsé, e [kɔrse] *adj (café)* full-flavoured; *(sauce)* spicy; *(problème)* tough

corset [kɔrsɛ] *nm* corset

cortège [kɔrtɛʒ] *nm* procession

cortisone [kɔrtizɔn] *nf* cortisone

corvée [kɔrve] *nf* chore, drudgery *no pl*

cosmétique [kɔsmetik] *nm* beauty care product

cosmopolite [kɔsmɔpɔlit] *adj* cosmopolitan

cossu, e [kɔsy] *adj (maison)* opulent(-looking)

costaud, e [kɔsto, od] *(fam) adj* strong, sturdy

costume [kɔstym] *nm (d'homme)* suit; *(de théâtre)* costume; **costumé, e** *adj* dressed up; **bal costumé** fancy dress ball

cote [kɔt] *nf (en Bourse)* quotation; **~ d'alerte** danger *ou* flood level

côte [kot] *nf (rivage)* coast(line); *(pente)*

hill; (*ANAT*) rib; (*d'un tricot, tissu*) rib, ribbing *no pl*; **côte à côte** side by side; **la C~ (d'Azur)** the (French) Riviera

coté, e [kɔte] *adj*: **être bien ~** to be highly rated

côté [kote] *nm* (*gén*) side; (*direction*) way, direction; **de chaque ~ (de)** on each side (of); **de tous les ~s** from all directions; **de quel ~ est-il parti?** which way did he go?; **de ce/de l'autre ~** this/the other way; **du ~ de** (*provenance*) from; (*direction*) towards; (*proximité*) near; **de ~** (*regarder*) sideways; (*mettre*) aside; **mettre de l'argent de ~** to save some money; **à ~** (*right*) nearby; (*voisins*) next door; **à ~ de** beside, next to; (*en comparaison*) compared to; **être aux ~s de** to be by the side of

coteau, x [kɔto] *nm* hill

côtelette [kotlɛt] *nf* chop

côtier, -ière [kotje, jɛR] *adj* coastal

cotisation [kɔtizasjɔ̃] *nf* subscription, dues *pl*; (*pour une pension*) contributions *pl*

cotiser [kɔtize] *vi*: **~ (à)** to pay contributions (to); **se ~** *vi* to club together

coton [kɔtɔ̃] *nm* cotton; **~ hydrophile** cotton wool (*BRIT*), absorbent cotton (*US*); **Coton-Tige** ® *nm* cotton bud

côtoyer [kotwaje] *vt* (*fréquenter*) to rub shoulders with

cou [ku] *nm* neck

couchant [kuʃɑ̃] *adj*: **soleil ~** setting sun

couche [kuʃ] *nf* layer; (*de peinture, vernis*) coat; (*de bébé*) nappy (*BRIT*), diaper (*US*); **~ d'ozone** ozone layer; **~s sociales** social levels *ou* strata

couché, e [kuʃe] *adj* lying down; (*au lit*) in bed

coucher [kuʃe] *nm* (*du soleil*) setting ♦ *vt* (*personne*) to put to bed; (: *loger*) to put up; (*objet*) to lay on its side ♦ *vi* to sleep; **se ~** *vi* (*pour dormir*) to go to bed; (*pour se reposer*) to lie down; (*soleil*) to set; **~ de soleil** sunset

couchette [kuʃɛt] *nf* couchette; (*pour voyageur, sur bateau*) berth

coucou [kuku] *nm* cuckoo

coude [kud] *nm* (*ANAT*) elbow; (*de tuyau, de la route*) bend; **~ à ~** shoulder to shoulder, side by side

coudre [kudʀ] *vt* (*bouton*) to sew on ♦ *vi* to sew

couenne [kwan] *nf* (*de lard*) rind

couette [kwɛt] *nf* duvet, quilt; **~s** *nfpl* (*cheveux*) bunches

couffin [kufɛ̃] *nm* Moses basket

couler [kule] *vi* to flow, run; (*fuir: stylo, récipient*) to leak; (*nez*) to run; (*sombrer: bateau*) to sink ♦ *vt* (*cloche, sculpture*) to cast; (*bateau*) to sink; (*faire échouer: personne*) to bring down

couleur [kulœʀ] *nf* colour (*BRIT*), color (*US*); (*CARTES*) suit; **film/télévision en ~** colo(u)r film/television

couleuvre [kulœvʀ] *nf* grass snake

coulisse [kulis] *nf*: **~s** *nfpl* (*THÉÂTRE*) wings; (*fig*): **dans les ~s** behind the scenes; **coulisser** *vi* to slide, run

couloir [kulwaʀ] *nm* corridor, passage; (*d'avion*) aisle; (*de bus*) gangway; **~ aérien/de navigation** air/shipping lane

coup [ku] *nm* (*heurt, choc*) knock; (*affectif*) blow, shock; (*agressif*) blow; (*avec arme à feu*) shot; (*de l'horloge*) stroke; (*tennis, golf*) stroke; (*boxe*) blow; (*fam: fois*) time; **~ de coude** nudge (with the elbow); **~ de tonnerre** clap of thunder; **~ de sonnette** ring of the bell; **donner un ~ de balai** to give the floor a sweep; **boire un ~** (*fam*) to have a drink; **être dans le ~** to be in on it; **du ~ ...** as a result; **d'un seul ~** (*subitement*) suddenly; (*à la fois*) at one go; **du premier ~** first time; **du même ~** at the same time; **à tous les ~s** (*fam*) every time; **tenir le ~** to hold out; **après ~** afterwards; **à ~ sûr** definitely, without fail; **~ sur ~** in quick succession; **sur le ~** outright; **sous le ~ de** (*surprise etc*) under the influence of; **en ~ de vent** in a tearing hurry; **~ de chance** stroke of luck; **~ de couteau** stab (of a knife); **~ d'État** coup; **~ de feu** shot; **~ de fil** (*fam*) phone call; **~ de frein** (sharp) braking *no pl*; **~ de main**: **donner un ~ de main à qn** to give sb a (helping) hand; **~ d'œil** glance; **~ de pied** kick; **~ de poing** punch; **~ de soleil** sunburn *no pl*; **~ de téléphone** phone call; **~ de tête** (*fig*) (sudden) impulse

coupable [kupabl] *adj* guilty ♦ *nm/f* (*gén*) culprit; (*JUR*) guilty party

coupe [kup] *nf* (*verre*) goblet; (*à fruits*) dish; (*SPORT*) cup; (*de cheveux, de vêtement*) cut; (*graphique, plan*) (cross) section

coupe-papier [kuppapje] *nm inv* paper knife

couper [kupe] *vt* to cut; (*retrancher*) to cut (out); (*route, courant*) to cut off; (*appétit*) to take away; (*vin à table*) to dilute ♦ *vi* to cut; (*prendre un raccourci*) to take a short-cut; **se ~** *vi* (*se blesser*) to cut o.s.; **~ la parole à qn** to cut sb short

couple [kupl] *nm* couple

couplet [kuple] *nm* verse

coupole [kupɔl] *nf* dome

coupon [kupɔ̃] *nm* (*ticket*) coupon; (*reste de tissu*) remnant; **coupon-réponse** *nm* reply coupon

coupure [kupyʀ] *nf* cut; (*billet de banque*) note; (*de journal*) cutting; **~ de courant** power cut

cour [kuʀ] *nf* (*de ferme, jardin*) (court)yard; (*d'immeuble*) back yard; (*JUR, royale*) court; **faire la ~ à qn** to court sb; **~ d'assises** court of assizes; **~ de récréation** playground; **~ martiale** court-martial

courage [kuʀaʒ] *nm* courage, bravery; **courageux, -euse** *adj* brave, courageous

couramment [kuʀamɑ̃] *adv* commonly; (*parler*) fluently

courant, e [kuʀɑ̃, ɑ̃t] *adj* (*fréquent*) common; (*COMM, gén: normal*) standard; (*en cours*) current ♦ *nm* current; (*fig*) movement; (*: d'opinion*) trend; **être au ~ (de)** (*fait, nouvelle*) to know (about); **mettre qn au ~ (de)** to tell sb (about); (*nouveau travail etc*) to teach sb the basics (of); **se te-**

nir au ~ (de) (*techniques etc*) to keep o.s. up-to-date (on); **dans le ~ de** (*pendant*) in the course of; **le 10 ~** (*COMM*) the 10th inst.; **~ d'air** draught; **~ électrique** (electric) current, power

courbature [kuʀbatyʀ] *nf* ache

courbe [kuʀb] *adj* curved ♦ *nf* curve; **courber** *vt* to bend; **se courber** *vi* (*personne*) to bend (down), stoop

coureur, -euse [kuʀœʀ, øz] *nm/f* (*SPORT*) runner (*ou* driver); (*péj*) womanizer; manhunter; **~ automobile** racing driver

courge [kuʀʒ] *nf* (*CULIN*) marrow; **courgette** *nf* courgette (*BRIT*), zucchini (*US*)

courir [kuʀiʀ] *vi* to run ♦ *vt* (*SPORT*: *épreuve*) to compete in; (*risque*) to run; (*danger*) to face; **~ les magasins** to go round the shops; **le bruit court que** the rumour is going round that

couronne [kuʀɔn] *nf* crown; (*de fleurs*) wreath, circlet

courons *etc* [kuʀɔ̃] *vb voir* **courir**

courrier [kuʀje] *nm* mail, post; (*lettres à écrire*) letters *pl*; **~ électronique** E-mail

courroie [kuʀwa] *nf* strap; (*TECH*) belt

courrons *etc* [kuʀɔ̃] *vb voir* **courir**

cours [kuʀ] *nm* (*leçon*) class; (*: particulier*) lesson; (*série de leçons, cheminement*) course; (*écoulement*) flow; (*COMM*: *de devises*) rate; (*: de denrées*) price; **donner libre ~ à** to give free expression to; **avoir ~** (*SCOL*) to have a free class *ou* lecture; **en ~** (*année*) current; (*travaux*) in progress; **en ~ de route** on the way; **au ~ de** in the course of, during; **~ d'eau** waterway; **~ du soir** night school; **~ intensif** crash course

course [kuʀs] *nf* running; (*SPORT*: *épreuve*) race; (*d'un taxi*) journey, trip; (*commission*) errand; **~s** *nfpl* (*achats*) shopping *sg*; **faire des ~s** to do some shopping

court, e [kuʀ, kuʀt(ə)] *adj* short ♦ *adv* short ♦ *nm*: **~ (de tennis)** (tennis) court; **à ~ de** short of; **prendre qn de ~** to catch sb unawares; **court-circuit** *nm* short-circuit

courtier, -ère [kuʀtje, jɛʀ] *nm/f* broker

courtiser [kuʀtize] *vt* to court, woo

courtois, e [kuʀtwa, waz] *adj* courteous; **courtoisie** *nf* courtesy

couru, e [kuʀy] *pp de* **courir**

cousais *etc* [kuze] *vb voir* **coudre**

couscous [kuskus] *nm* couscous

cousin, e [kuzɛ̃, in] *nm/f* cousin

coussin [kusɛ̃] *nm* cushion

cousu, e [kuzy] *pp de* **coudre**

coût [ku] *nm* cost; **le ~ de la vie** the cost of living; **coûtant** *adj m*: **au prix coûtant** at cost price

couteau, x [kuto] *nm* knife

coûter [kute] *vt, vi* to cost; **combien ça coûte?** how much is it?, what does it cost?; **coûte que coûte** at all costs; **coûteux, -euse** *adj* costly, expensive

coutume [kutym] *nf* custom

couture [kutyʀ] *nf* sewing; (*profession*) dressmaking; (*points*) seam; **couturier** *nm* fashion designer; **couturière** *nf* dressmaker

couvée [kuve] *nf* brood, clutch

couvent [kuvã] *nm* (*de sœurs*) convent; (*de frères*) monastery

couver [kuve] *vt* to hatch; (*maladie*) to be coming down with ♦ *vi* (*feu*) to smoulder; (*révolte*) to be brewing

couvercle [kuvɛʀkl] *nm* lid; (*de bombe aérosol etc, qui se visse*) cap, top

couvert, e [kuvɛʀ, ɛʀt] *pp de* **couvrir** ♦ *adj* (*ciel*) overcast ♦ *nm* place setting; (*place à table*) place; **~s** *nmpl* (*ustensiles*) cutlery *sg*; **~ de** covered with *ou* in; **mettre le ~** to lay the table

couverture [kuvɛʀtyʀ] *nf* blanket; (*de livre, assurance, fig*) cover; (*presse*) coverage; **~ chauffante** electric blanket

couveuse [kuvøz] *nf* (*de maternité*) incubator

couvre-feu [kuvʀəfø] *nm* curfew

couvre-lit [kuvʀəli] *nm* bedspread

couvreur [kuvʀœʀ] *nm* roofer

couvrir [kuvʀiʀ] *vt* to cover; **se ~** *vi* (*s'habiller*) to cover up; (*se coiffer*) to put on one's hat; (*ciel*) to cloud over

cow-boy [kɔbɔj] *nm* cowboy

crabe [kʀab] *nm* crab

cracher [kʀaʃe] *vi, vt* to spit

crachin [kʀaʃɛ̃] *nm* drizzle

crack [kʀak] *nm* (*fam: as*) ace

craie [kʀɛ] *nf* chalk

craindre [kʀɛ̃dʀ] *vt* to fear, be afraid of; (*être sensible à: chaleur, froid*) to be easily damaged by

crainte [kʀɛ̃t] *nf* fear; **de ~ de/que** for fear of/that; **craintif, -ive** *adj* timid

cramoisi, e [kʀamwazi] *adj* crimson

crampe [kʀãp] *nf* cramp

crampon [kʀãpɔ̃] *nm* (*de chaussure de football*) stud; (*de chaussure de course*) spike; (*d'alpinisme*) crampon; **cramponner** *vb*: **se cramponner (à)** to hang *ou* cling on (to)

cran [kʀã] *nm* (*entaille*) notch; (*de courroie*) hole; (*fam: courage*) guts *pl*; **~ d'arrêt** safety catch

crâne [kʀan] *nm* skull

crâner [kʀane] (*fam*) *vi* to show off

crapaud [kʀapo] *nm* toad

crapule [kʀapyl] *nf* villain

craquement [kʀakmã] *nm* crack, snap; (*du plancher*) creak, creaking *no pl*

craquer [kʀake] *vi* (*bois, plancher*) to creak; (*fil, branche*) to snap; (*couture*) to come apart; (*fig: accusé*) to break down; (: *fam*) to crack up ♦ *vt* (*allumette*) to strike; **j'ai craqué** (*fam*) I couldn't resist it

crasse [kʀas] *nf* grime, filth; **crasseux, -euse** *adj* grimy, filthy

cravache [kʀavaʃ] *nf* (riding) crop

cravate [kʀavat] *nf* tie

crawl [kʀol] *nm* crawl; **dos ~é** backstroke

crayon [kʀɛjɔ̃] *nm* pencil; **~ à bille** ballpoint pen; **~ de couleur** crayon, colouring pencil; **crayon-feutre** (*pl* **crayons-feutres**) *nm* felt(-tip) pen

créancier, -ière [kʀeãsje, jɛʀ] *nm/f* creditor

création [kʀeasjɔ̃] *nf* creation

créature [kʀeatyʀ] *nf* creature

crèche [kʀɛʃ] *nf* (*de Noël*) crib; (*garderie*) crèche, day nursery

crédit [kʀedi] *nm* (*gén*) credit; **~s** *nmpl* (*fonds*) funds; **payer/acheter à ~** to pay/buy on credit *ou* on easy terms; **faire ~ à qn** to give sb credit; **créditer** *vt*: **créditer un compte (de)** to credit an account (with)

crédule [kʀedyl] *adj* credulous, gullible

créer [kʀee] *vt* to create

crémaillère [kʀemajɛʀ] *nf*: **pendre la ~** to have a house-warming party

crématoire [kʀematwaʀ] *adj*: **four ~** crematorium

crème [kʀɛm] *nf* cream; (*entremets*) cream dessert ♦ *adj inv* cream(-coloured); **un (café) ~** ≃ a white coffee; **~ anglaise** (egg) custard; **~ chantilly** whipped cream; **~ fouettée** = **crème chantilly**; **crémerie** *nf* dairy; **crémeux, -euse** *adj* creamy

créneau, x [kʀeno] *nm* (*de fortification*) crenel(le); (*dans marché*) gap, niche; (*AUTO*): **faire un ~** to reverse into a parking space (*between two cars alongside the kerb*)

crêpe [kʀɛp] *nf* (*galette*) pancake ♦ *nm* (*tissu*) crêpe; **crêpé, e** *adj* (*cheveux*) backcombed; **crêperie** *nf* pancake shop *ou* restaurant

crépiter [kʀepite] *vi* (*friture*) to sputter, splutter; (*fire*) to crackle

crépu, e [kʀepy] *adj* frizzy, fuzzy

crépuscule [kʀepyskyl] *nm* twilight, dusk

cresson [kʀesɔ̃] *nm* watercress

crête [kʀɛt] *nf* (*de coq*) comb, (*de vague, montagne*) crest

creuser [kʀøze] *vt* (*trou, tunnel*) to dig; (*sol*) to dig a hole in; (*fig*) to go (deeply) into; **ça creuse** that gives you a real appetite; **se ~ la cervelle** (*fam*) to rack one's brains

creux, -euse [kʀø, kʀøz] *adj* hollow ♦ *nm* hollow; **heures creuses** slack periods; (*électricité, téléphone*) off-peak periods; **avoir un ~** (*fam*) to be hungry

crevaison [kʀəvɛzɔ̃] *nf* puncture

crevasse [kʀəvas] *nf* (*dans le sol, la peau*) crack; (*de glacier*) crevasse

crevé, e [kʀəve] (*fam*) *adj* (*fatigué*) all in, exhausted

crever [kʀəve] *vt* (*ballon*) to burst ♦ *vi* (*pneu*) to burst; (*automobiliste*) to have a puncture (*BRIT*) *ou* a flat (tire) (*US*); (*fam*) to die

crevette [kʀəvɛt] *nf*: **~ (rose)** prawn; **~ grise** shrimp

cri [kʀi] *nm* cry, shout; (*d'animal: spécifique*) cry, call; **c'est le dernier ~** (*fig*) it's the latest fashion

criant, e [kʀijɑ̃, kʀijɑ̃t] *adj* (*injustice*) glaring

criard, e [kʀijaʀ, kʀijaʀd] *adj* (*couleur*) garish, loud; (*voix*) yelling

crible [kʀibl] *nm* riddle; **passer qch au ~** (*fig*) to go over sth with a fine-tooth comb; **criblé, e** *adj*: **criblé de** riddled with; (*de dettes*) crippled with

cric [kʀik] *nm* (*AUTO*) jack

crier [kʀije] *vi* (*pour appeler*) to shout, cry (out); (*de douleur etc*) to scream, yell ♦ *vt* (*injure*) to shout (out), yell (out)

crime [kʀim] *nm* crime; (*meurtre*) murder; **criminel, le** *nm/f* criminal; (*assassin*) murderer

crin [kʀɛ̃] *nm* (*de cheval*) hair *no pl*

crinière [kʀinjɛʀ] *nf* mane

crique [kʀik] *nf* creek, inlet

criquet [kʀike] *nm* grasshopper

crise [kʀiz] *nf* crisis; (*MÉD*) attack; (: *d'épilepsie*) fit; **piquer une ~ de nerfs** to go hysterical; **~ cardiaque** heart attack; **~ de foie** bilious attack

crisper [kʀispe] *vt* (*poings*) to clench; **se ~** *vi* (*visage*) to tense; (*personne*) to get tense

crisser [kʀise] *vi* (*neige*) to crunch; (*pneu*) to screech

cristal, -aux [kʀistal, o] *nm* crystal; **cristallin, e** *adj* crystal-clear

critère [kʀitɛʀ] *nm* criterion

critiquable [kʀitikabl] *adj* open to criticism

critique [kʀitik] *adj* critical ♦ *nm/f* (*de théâtre, musique*) critic ♦ *nf* criticism; (*THÉÂTRE etc: article*) review

critiquer [kʀitike] *vt* (*dénigrer*) to criticize; (*évaluer*) to assess, examine (critically)

croasser [kʀɔase] *vi* to caw

Croatie [kʀɔasi] *nf* Croatia

croc [kʀo] *nm* (*dent*) fang; (*de boucher*) hook; **croc-en-jambe** *nm*: **faire un croc-en-jambe à qn** to trip sb up

croche [kʀɔʃ] *nf* (*MUS*) quaver (*BRIT*), eighth note (*US*); **croche-pied** *nm* = **croc-en-jambe**

crochet [kʀɔʃɛ] *nm* hook; (*détour*) detour; (*TRICOT: aiguille*) crochet hook; (: *technique*) crochet; **vivre aux ~s de qn** to live *ou* sponge off sb

crochu, e [kʀɔʃy] *adj* (*nez*) hooked; (*doigts*) claw-like

crocodile [kʀɔkɔdil] *nm* crocodile

croire [kʀwaʀ] *vt* to believe; **se ~ fort** to think one is strong; **~ que** to believe *ou* think that; **~ à, ~ en** to believe in

croîs [kʀwa] *vb voir* **croître**

croisade [kʀwazad] *nf* crusade

croisé, e [kʀwaze] *adj* (*veste*) double-breasted

croisement [kʀwazmɑ̃] *nm* (*carrefour*) crossroads *sg*; (*BIO*) crossing; (: *résultat*) crossbreed

croiser [kʀwaze] *vt* (*personne, voiture*) to pass; (*route*) to cross, cut across; (*BIO*) to cross; **se ~** *vi* (*personnes, véhicules*) to pass each other; (*routes, lettres*) to cross; (*regards*) to meet; **~ les jambes/bras** to cross one's legs/fold one's arms

croisière [kʀwazjɛʀ] *nf* cruise

croissance [kʀwasɑ̃s] *nf* growth

croissant [kʀwasɑ̃] *nm* (*à manger*) croissant; (*motif*) crescent

croître [kʀwatʀ] *vi* to grow

croix [kʀwa] *nf* cross; **~ gammée** swastika; **la C~ Rouge** the Red Cross

croque-monsieur [kʀɔkməsjø] *nm inv* toasted ham and cheese sandwich

croquer [kʀɔke] *vt* (*manger*) to crunch; (: *fruit*) to munch; (*dessiner*) to sketch; **chocolat à ~** plain dessert chocolate

croquis [kʀɔki] *nm* sketch

cross [kʀɔs] *nm*: **faire du ~ (à pied)** to do cross-country running

crosse [kʀɔs] *nf* (*de fusil*) butt; (*de revolver*) grip

crotte [kʀɔt] *nf* droppings *pl*; **crotté, e** *adj* muddy, mucky; **crottin** *nm* dung, manure; (*fromage*) (small round) cheese (*made of goat's milk*)

crouler [kʀule] *vi* (*s'effondrer*) to collapse; (*être délabré*) to be crumbling

croupe [kʀup] *nf* rump; **en ~** pillion

croupir [kʀupiʀ] *vi* to stagnate

croustillant, e [kʀustijɑ̃, ɑ̃t] *adj* crisp

croûte [kʀut] *nf* crust; (*du fromage*) rind; (*MÉD*) scab; **en ~** (*CULIN*) in pastry

croûton [kʀutɔ̃] *nm* (*CULIN*) crouton; (*bout du pain*) crust, heel

croyable [kʀwajabl] *adj* credible

croyant, e [kʀwajɑ̃, ɑ̃t] *nm/f* believer

CRS *sigle fpl* (= *Compagnies républicaines de sécurité*) state security police force ♦ *sigle m* member of the CRS

cru, e [kʀy] *pp de* **croire** ♦ *adj* (*non cuit*) raw; (*lumière, couleur*) harsh; (*paroles*) crude ♦ *nm* (*vignoble*) vineyard; (*vin*) wine; **un grand ~** a great vintage; **jambon ~** Parma ham

crû [kʀy] *pp de* **croître**

cruauté [kʀyote] *nf* cruelty

cruche [kʀyʃ] *nf* pitcher, jug

crucifix [kʀysifi] *nm* crucifix; **crucifixion** *nf* crucifixion

crudités [kʀydite] *nfpl* (*CULIN*) salads

crue [kʀy] *nf* (*inondation*) flood

cruel, le [kʀyɛl] *adj* cruel

crus *etc* [kʀy] *vb voir* **croire**; **croître**

crûs *etc* [kʀy] *vb voir* **croître**

crustacés [kʀystase] *nmpl* shellfish

Cuba [kyba] *nf* Cuba; **cubain, e** *adj* Cuban ♦ *nm/f*: **Cubain, e** Cuban

cube [kyb] *nm* cube; (*jouet*) brick; **mètre ~** cubic metre; **2 au ~** 2 cubed

cueillette [kœjɛt] *nf* picking; *(quantité)* crop, harvest

cueillir [kœjiʀ] *vt (fruits, fleurs)* to pick, gather; *(fig)* to catch

cuiller [kɥijɛʀ], **cuillère** [kɥijɛʀ] *nf* spoon; **~ à café** coffee spoon; *(CULIN)* teaspoonful; **~ à soupe** soup-spoon; *(CULIN)* tablespoonful; **cuillerée** *nf* spoonful

cuir [kɥiʀ] *nm* leather; **~ chevelu** scalp

cuire [kɥiʀ] *vt (aliments)* to cook; *(au four)* to bake ♦ *vi* to cook; **bien cuit** *(viande)* well done; **trop cuit** overdone

cuisant, e [kɥizɑ̃, ɑ̃t] *adj (douleur)* stinging; *(fig: souvenir, échec)* bitter

cuisine [kɥizin] *nf (pièce)* kitchen; *(art culinaire)* cookery, cooking; *(nourriture)* cooking, food; **faire la ~** to cook; **cuisiné, e** *adj*: **plat cuisiné** ready-made meal *ou* dish; **cuisiner** *vt* to cook; *(fam)* to grill ♦ *vi* to cook; **cuisinier, -ière** *nm/f* cook; **cuisinière** *nf (poêle)* cooker

cuisse [kɥis] *nf* thigh; *(CULIN)* leg

cuisson [kɥisɔ̃] *nf* cooking

cuit, e [kɥi, kɥit] *pp de* **cuire**

cuivre [kɥivʀ] *nm* copper; **les ~s** *(MUS)* the brass

cul [ky] *(fam!)* *nm* arse (!)

culbute [kylbyt] *nf* somersault; *(accidentelle)* tumble, fall

culminant, e [kylminɑ̃, ɑ̃t] *adj*: **point ~** highest point

culminer [kylmine] *vi* to reach its highest point

culot [kylo] *(fam)* *nm (effronterie)* cheek

culotte [kylɔt] *nf (de femme)* knickers *pl (BRIT)*, panties *pl*

culpabilité [kylpabilite] *nf* guilt

culte [kylt] *nm (religion)* religion; *(hommage, vénération)* worship; *(protestant)* service

cultivateur, -trice [kyltivatœʀ, tʀis] *nm/f* farmer

cultivé, e [kyltive] *adj (personne)* cultured, cultivated

cultiver [kyltive] *vt* to cultivate; *(légumes)* to grow, cultivate

culture [kyltyʀ] *nf* cultivation; *(connaissances etc)* culture; **les ~s intensives** intensive farming; **~ physique** physical training; **culturel, le** *adj* cultural; **culturisme** *nm* body-building

cumin [kymɛ̃] *nm* cumin

cumuler [kymyle] *vt (emplois)* to hold concurrently; *(salaires)* to draw concurrently

cupide [kypid] *adj* greedy, grasping

cure [kyʀ] *nf (MÉD)* course of treatment

curé [kyʀe] *nm* parish priest

cure-dent [kyʀdɑ̃] *nm* toothpick

cure-pipe [kyʀpip] *nm* pipe cleaner

curer [kyʀe] *vt* to clean out

curieusement [kyʀjøzmɑ̃] *adv* curiously

curieux, -euse [kyʀjø, jøz] *adj (indiscret)* curious, inquisitive; *(étrange)* strange, curious ♦ *nmpl (badauds)* onlookers; **curiosité** *nf* curiosity; *(site)* unusual feature

curriculum vitae [kyʀikylɔmvite] *nm inv* curriculum vitae

curseur [kyʀsœʀ] *nm (INFORM)* cursor

cutané, e [kytane] *adj* skin

cuti-réaction [kytiʀeaksjɔ̃] *nf (MÉD)* skintest

cuve [kyv] *nf* vat; *(à mazout etc)* tank

cuvée [kyve] *nf* vintage

cuvette [kyvɛt] *nf (récipient)* bowl, basin; *(GÉO)* basin

CV *sigle m (AUTO)* = **cheval vapeur**; *(COMM)* = **curriculum vitae**

cyanure [sjanyʀ] *nm* cyanide

cybercafé [sibɛʀkafe] *nm* cybercafé

cyclable [siklabl] *adj*: **piste ~** cycle track

cyclable [siklabl] *adj*: **piste ~** cycle track

cycle [sikl] *nm* cycle; **cyclisme** *nm* cycling; **cycliste** *nm/f* cyclist ♦ *adj* cycle *cpd*; **coureur cycliste** racing cyclist

cyclomoteur [siklomɔtœʀ] *nm* moped

cyclone [siklon] *nm* hurricane

cygne [siɲ] *nm* swan

cylindre [silɛ̃dʀ] *nm* cylinder; **cylindrée** *nf (AUTO)* (cubic) capacity

cymbale [sɛ̃bal] *nf* cymbal

cynique [sinik] *adj* cynical

cystite [sistit] *nf* cystitis

D, d

d' [d] *prép voir* **de**

dactylo [daktilo] *nf* (*aussi:* **~graphe**) typist; (*aussi:* **~graphie**) typing; **dactylographier** *vt* to type (out)

dada [dada] *nm* hobby-horse

daigner [deɲe] *vt* to deign

daim [dɛ̃] *nm* (fallow) deer *inv*; (*cuir suédé*) suede

dalle [dal] *nf* paving stone, slab

daltonien, ne [daltɔnjɛ̃, jɛn] *adj* colour-blind

dam [dã] *nm*: **au grand ~ de** much to the detriment (*ou* annoyance) of

dame [dam] *nf* lady; (*CARTES, ÉCHECS*) queen; **~s** *nfpl* (*jeu*) draughts *sg* (*BRIT*), checkers *sg* (*US*)

damner [dane] *vt* to damn

dancing [dãsiŋ] *nm* dance hall

Danemark [danmark] *nm* Denmark

danger [dãʒe] *nm* danger; **dangereux, -euse** *adj* dangerous

danois, e [danwa, waz] *adj* Danish ♦ *nm/f*: **D~, e** Dane ♦ *nm* (*LING*) Danish

---MOT-CLÉ---

dans [dã] *prép* **1** (*position*) in; (*à l'intérieur de*) inside; **c'est dans le tiroir/le salon** it's in the drawer/lounge; **dans la boîte** in *ou* inside the box; **marcher dans la ville** to walk about the town

2 (*direction*) into; **elle a couru dans le salon** she ran into the lounge

3 (*provenance*) out of, from; **je l'ai pris dans le tiroir/salon** I took it out of *ou* from the drawer/lounge; **boire dans un verre** to drink out of *ou* from a glass

4 (*temps*) in; **dans 2 mois** in 2 months, in 2 months' time

5 (*approximation*) about; **dans les 20 F** about 20F

danse [dãs] *nf*: **la ~** dancing; **une ~** a

dance; **la ~ classique** ballet; **danser** *vi, vt* to dance; **danseur, -euse** *nm/f* ballet dancer; (*au bal etc*) dancer; (: *cavalier*) partner

dard [daʀ] *nm* (*d'animal*) sting

date [dat] *nf* date; **de longue ~** long-standing; **~ de naissance** date of birth; **~ de péremption** expiry date; **~ limite** deadline; **dater** *vt, vi* to date; **dater de** to date from; **à dater de** (as) from

datte [dat] *nf* date

dauphin [dofɛ̃] *nm* (*ZOOL*) dolphin

davantage [davãtaʒ] *adv* more; (*plus longtemps*) longer; **~ de** more

---MOT-CLÉ---

de, d' [də] (*de + le = du, de + les = des*) *prép* **1** (*appartenance*) of; **le toit de la maison** the roof of the house; **la voiture d'Elisabeth/de mes parents** Elizabeth's/my parents' car

2 (*provenance*) from; **il vient de Londres** he comes from London; **elle est sortie du cinéma** she came out of the cinema

3 (*caractérisation, mesure*): **un mur de brique/bureau d'acajou** a brick wall/mahogany desk; **un billet de 50 F** a 50F note; **une pièce de 2 m de large** *ou* **large de 2 m** a room 2m wide, a 2m-wide room; **un bébé de 10 mois** a 10-month-old baby; **12 mois de crédit/travail** 12 months' credit/work; **augmenter de 10 F** to increase by 10F; **de 14 à 18** from 14 to 18

♦ *dét* **1** (*phrases affirmatives*) some (*souvent omis*); **du vin, de l'eau, des pommes** (some) wine, (some) water, (some) apples; **des enfants sont venus** some children came; **pendant des mois** for months

2 (*phrases interrogatives et négatives*) any; **a-t-il du vin?** has he got any wine?; **il n'a pas de pommes/d'enfants** he hasn't (got) any apples/children, he has no apples/children

dé [de] nm (à jouer) die ou dice; (aussi: ~ à coudre) thimble

dealer [dilœʀ] (fam) nm (drug) pusher

déambuler [deãbyle] vi to stroll about

débâcle [debɑkl] nf rout

déballer [debale] vt to unpack

débandade [debɑ̃dad] nf (dispersion) scattering

débarbouiller [debaʀbuje] vt to wash; **se ~** vi to wash (one's face)

débarcadère [debaʀkadɛʀ] nm wharf

débardeur [debaʀdœʀ] nm (maillot) tank top

débarquer [debaʀke] vt to unload, land ♦ vi to disembark; (fig: fam) to turn up

débarras [debaʀɑ] nm (pièce) lumber room; (placard) junk cupboard; **bon ~!** good riddance!; **débarrasser** vt to clear; **se débarrasser de** vt to get rid of; **débarrasser qn de** (vêtements, paquets) to relieve sb of

débat [deba] nm discussion, debate; **débattre** vt to discuss, debate; **se débattre** vi to struggle

débaucher [deboʃe] vt (licencier) to lay off, dismiss; (entraîner) to lead astray, debauch

débile [debil] (fam) adj (idiot) dim-witted

débit [debi] nm (d'un liquide, fleuve) flow; (d'un magasin) turnover (of goods); (élocution) delivery; (bancaire) debit; **~ de boissons** drinking establishment; **~ de tabac** tobacconist's; **débiter** vt (compte) to debit; (couper: bois, viande) to cut up; (péj: dire) to churn out; **débiteur, -trice** nm/f debtor ♦ adj in debit; (compte) debit cpd

déblayer [debleje] vt to clear

débloquer [deblɔke] vt (prix, crédits) to free

déboires [debwaʀ] nmpl setbacks

déboiser [debwaze] vt to deforest

déboîter [debwate] vt (AUTO) to pull out; **se ~ le genou** etc to dislocate one's knee etc

débonnaire [debɔnɛʀ] adj easy-going, good-natured

bordé, e [debɔʀde] adj: **être ~ (de)** (travail, demandes) to be snowed under (with)

déborder [debɔʀde] vi to overflow; (lait etc) to boil over; **~ (de) qch** (dépasser) to extend beyond sth

débouché [debuʃe] nm (pour vendre) outlet; (perspective d'emploi) opening

déboucher [debuʃe] vt (évier, tuyau etc) to unblock; (bouteille) to uncork ♦ vi: **~ de** to emerge from; **~ sur** (études) to lead on to

débourser [debuʀse] vt to pay out

déboussolé, e [debusɔle] (fam) adj disorientated

debout [d(ə)bu] adv: **être ~** (personne) to be standing, up; (: levé, éveillé) to be up; **se mettre ~** to stand up; **se tenir ~** to stand; **~!** stand up!; (du lit) get up!; **cette histoire ne tient pas ~** this story doesn't hold water

déboutonner [debutɔne] vt to undo, unbutton

débraillé, e [debʀaje] adj slovenly, untidy

débrancher [debʀɑ̃ʃe] vt to disconnect; (appareil électrique) to unplug

débrayage [debʀɛjaʒ] nm (AUTO) clutch; **débrayer** vi (AUTO) to declutch; (cesser le travail) to stop work

débris [debʀi] nmpl fragments; **des ~ de verre** bits of glass

débrouillard, e [debʀujaʀ, aʀd] (fam) adj smart, resourceful

débrouiller [debʀuje] vt to disentangle, untangle; **se ~** vi to manage; **débrouillez-vous** you'll have to sort things out yourself

début [deby] nm beginning, start; **~s** nmpl (de carrière) début sg; **~ juin** in early June; **débutant, e** nm/f beginner, novice; **débuter** vi to begin, start; (faire ses débuts) to start out

deçà [dəsa]: **en ~ de** prép this side of

décadence [dekadɑ̃s] nf decline

décaféiné, e [dekafeine] adj decaffeinated

décalage [dekalaʒ] nm gap; **~ horaire** time difference

décaler [dekale] *vt* to shift

décalquer [dekalke] *vt* to trace

décamper [dekɑ̃pe] *(fam) vi* to clear out *ou* off

décaper [dekape] *vt (surface peinte)* to strip

décapiter [dekapite] *vt* to behead; *(par accident)* to decapitate

décapotable [dekapɔtabl] *adj* convertible

décapsuleur [dekapsylœʀ] *nm* bottle-opener

décarcasser [dekaʀkase]: **se ~** *(fam) vi* to flog o.s. to death

décédé, e [desede] *adj* deceased

décéder [desede] *vi* to die

déceler [des(ə)le] *vt (trouver)* to discover, detect

décembre [desɑ̃bʀ] *nm* December

décemment [desamɑ̃] *adv* decently

décennie [deseni] *nf* decade

décent, e [desɑ̃, ɑ̃t] *adj* decent

déception [desɛpsjɔ̃] *nf* disappointment

décerner [deseʀne] *vt* to award

décès [desɛ] *nm* death

décevant, e [des(ə)vɑ̃, ɑ̃t] *adj* disappointing

décevoir [des(ə)vwaʀ] *vt* to disappoint

déchaîner [deʃene] *vt (violence)* to unleash; *(enthousiasme)* to arouse; **se ~** *(tempête)* to rage; *(personne)* to fly into a rage

déchanter [deʃɑ̃te] *vi* to become disillusioned

décharge [deʃaʀʒ] *nf (dépôt d'ordures)* rubbish tip *ou* dump; *(électrique)* electrical discharge; **décharger** *vt (marchandise, véhicule)* to unload; *(tirer)* to discharge; **se décharger** *vi (batterie)* to go flat; **décharger qn de** *(responsabilité)* to release sb from

décharné, e [deʃaʀne] *adj* emaciated

déchausser [deʃose] *vt (skis)* to take off; **se ~** *vi* to take off one's shoes; *(dent)* to come *ou* work loose

déchéance [deʃeɑ̃s] *nf (physique)* degeneration; *(morale)* decay

déchet [deʃɛ] *nm (reste)* scrap; **~s** *nmpl* *(ordures)* refuse *sg*, rubbish *sg*; **~s nucléaires** nuclear waste

déchiffrer [deʃifʀe] *vt* to decipher

déchiqueter [deʃik(ə)te] *vt* to tear *ou* p to pieces

déchirant, e [deʃiʀɑ̃, ɑ̃t] *adj* hear rending

déchirement [deʃiʀmɑ̃] *nm (chagri* wrench, heartbreak; *(gén pl: conflit)* ri split

déchirer [deʃiʀe] *vt* to tear; *(en morceau* to tear up; *(arracher)* to tear out; *(fig: co flit)* to tear (apart); **se ~** *vi* to tear, ri **se ~ un muscle** to tear a muscle

déchirure [deʃiʀyʀ] *nf (accroc)* tear, rip; **musculaire** torn muscle

déchoir [deʃwaʀ] *vi (personne)* to low o.s., demean o.s.

déchu, e [deʃy] *adj (roi)* deposed

décidé, e [deside] *adj (personne, air)* d termined; **c'est ~** it's decided; **décidé ment** *adv* really

décider [deside] *vt:* **~ qch** to decide sth; **se ~ (à faire)** to decide (to do make up one's mind (to do); **se ~ pot** to decide on *ou* in favour of; **~ de faire que** to decide to do/that; **~ qn (à fai qch)** to persuade sb (to do sth)

décimal, e, -aux [desimal, o] *adj* dec mal; **décimale** *nf* decimal

décimètre [desimɛtʀ] *nm* decimetre

décisif, -ive [desizif, iv] *adj* decisive

décision [desizjɔ̃] *nf* decision

déclaration [deklaʀasjɔ̃] *nf* declaratio *(discours: POL etc)* statement; **~ (d'impôt** ≈ tax return

déclarer [deklaʀe] *vt* to declare; *(déce naissance)* to register; **se ~** *vi (feu)* break out

déclencher [deklɑ̃ʃe] *vt (mécanisme etc)* release; *(sonnerie)* to set off; *(attaqu grève)* to launch; *(provoquer)* to trigger o **se ~** *vi (sonnerie)* to go off

déclic [deklik] *nm (bruit)* click

décliner [dekline] *vi* to decline ♦ *vt (invit tion)* to decline; *(nom, adresse)* to state

décocher [dekɔʃe] vt (coup de poing) to throw; (flèche, regard) to shoot

décoiffer [dekwafe] vt: ~ **qn** to mess up sb's hair; **je suis toute décoiffée** my hair is in a real mess

déçois etc [deswa] vb voir **décevoir**

décollage [dekɔlaʒ] nm (AVIAT) takeoff

décoller [dekɔle] vt to unstick ♦ vi (avion) to take off; **se ~** vi to come unstuck

décolleté, e [dekɔlte] adj low-cut ♦ nm low neck(line); (plongeant) cleavage

décolorer [dekɔlɔre]: **se ~** vi to fade; **se faire ~ les cheveux** to have one's hair bleached

décombres [dekɔ̃bʀ] nmpl rubble sg, debris sg

décommander [dekɔmɑ̃de] vt to cancel; **se ~** vi to cry off

décomposé, e [dekɔ̃poze] adj (pourri) decomposed; (visage) haggard, distorted

décompte [dekɔ̃t] nm deduction; (facture) detailed account

déconcerter [dekɔ̃sɛʀte] vt to disconcert, confound

déconfit, e [dekɔ̃fi, it] adj crestfallen

décongeler [dekɔ̃ʒ(ə)le] vt to thaw

déconner [dekɔne] (fam) vi to talk rubbish

déconseiller [dekɔ̃seje] vt: ~ **qch (à qn)** to advise (sb) against sth; **c'est déconseillé** it's not recommended

décontracté, e [dekɔ̃trakte] adj relaxed, laid-back (fam)

décontracter [dekɔ̃trakte]: **se ~** vi to relax

déconvenue [dekɔ̃v(ə)ny] nf disappointment

décor [dekɔʀ] nm décor; (paysage) scenery; ~**s** nmpl (THÉÂTRE) scenery sg, décor sg; (CINÉMA) set sg; **décorateur** nm (interior) decorator; **décoration** nf decoration; **décorer** vt to decorate

décortiquer [dekɔʀtike] vt to shell; (fig: texte) to dissect

découcher [dekuʃe] vi to spend the night away from home

découdre [dekudʀ]: **se ~** vi to come un-

stitched

découler [dekule] vi: ~ **de** to ensue ou follow from

découper [dekupe] vt (papier, tissu etc) to cut up; (viande) to carve; (article) to cut out; **se ~ sur** to stand out against

décourager [dekuraʒe] vt to discourage; **se ~** vi to lose heart, become discouraged

décousu, e [dekuzy] adj unstitched; (fig) disjointed, disconnected

découvert, e [dekuvɛʀ, ɛʀt] adj (tête) bare, uncovered; (lieu) open, exposed ♦ nm (bancaire) overdraft; **découverte** nf discovery; **faire la découverte de** to discover

découvrir [dekuvʀiʀ] vt to discover; (enlever ce qui couvre) to uncover; (dévoiler) to reveal; **se ~** vi (chapeau) to take off one's hat; (vêtement) to take something off; (ciel) to clear

décret [dekʀe] nm decree; **décréter** vt to decree

décrié, e [dekʀije] adj disparaged

décrire [dekʀiʀ] vt to describe

décrocher [dekʀɔʃe] vt (détacher) to take down; (téléphone) to take off the hook; (: pour répondre) to lift the receiver; (fam: contrat etc) to get, land ♦ vi (fam: abandonner) to drop out; (: cesser d'écouter) to switch off

décroître [dekʀwatʀ] vi to decrease, decline

décrypter [dekʀipte] vt to decipher

déçu, e [desy] pp de **décevoir**

décupler [dekyple] vt, vi to increase tenfold

dédaigner [dedeɲe] vt to despise, scorn; (négliger) to disregard, spurn; **dédaigneux, -euse** adj scornful, disdainful; **dédain** nm scorn, disdain

dédale [dedal] nm maze

dedans [dədɑ̃] adv inside; (pas en plein air) indoors, inside ♦ nm inside; **au ~** inside

dédicacer [dedikase] vt: ~ **(à qn)** to sign (for sb), autograph (for sb)

dédier [dedje] vt to dedicate

dédire [dediʀ]: **se ~** vi to go back on one's word, retract

dédommagement [dedɔmaʒmɑ̃] nm compensation

dédommager [dedɔmaʒe] vt: **~ qn (de)** to compensate sb (for)

dédouaner [dedwane] vt to clear through customs

dédoubler [deduble] vt (classe, effectifs) to split (into two)

déduire [dedɥiʀ] vt: **~ qch (de)** (ôter) to deduct sth (from); (conclure) to deduce ou infer sth (from)

déesse [deɛs] nf goddess

défaillance [defajɑ̃s] nf (syncope) black-out; (fatigue) (sudden) weakness no pl; (technique) fault, failure; **~ cardiaque** heart failure

défaillir [defajiʀ] vi to feel faint; (mémoire etc) to fail

défaire [defɛʀ] vt to undo; (installation) to take down, dismantle; **se ~** vi to come undone; **se ~ de** to get rid of

défait, e [defɛ, ɛt] adj (visage) haggard, ravaged; **défaite** nf defeat

défalquer [defalke] vt to deduct

défaut [defo] nm (moral) fault, failing, defect; (tissus) fault, flaw; (manque, carence): **~ de** shortage of; **prendre qn en ~** to catch sb out; **faire ~** (manquer) to be lacking; **à ~ de** for lack ou want of

défavorable [defavɔʀabl] adj unfavourable (BRIT), unfavorable (US)

défavoriser [defavɔʀize] vt to put at a disadvantage

défection [defɛksjɔ̃] nf defection, failure to give support

défectueux, -euse [defɛktɥø, øz] adj faulty, defective

défendre [defɑ̃dʀ] vt to defend; (interdire) to forbid; **se ~** vi to defend o.s.; **~ à qn qch/de faire** to forbid sb sth/to do; **il se défend** (fam: se débrouille) he can hold his own; **se ~ de/contre** (se protéger) to protect o.s. from/against; **se ~ de** (se garder

de) to refrain from

défense [defɑ̃s] nf defence; (d'éléphant et tusk; **"~ de fumer"** "no smoking"

déférer [defere] vt (JUR) to refer; **~ à** (r_ quête, décision) to defer to

déferler [defɛʀle] vi (vagues) to break; (fi_ foule) to surge

défi [defi] nm challenge; **lancer un ~ à q**_ to challenge sb; **sur un ton de ~** de_ antly

déficit [defisit] nm (COMM) deficit; **défic_ taire** adj in deficit

défier [defje] vt (provoquer) to challeng_ (mort, autorité) to defy

défigurer [defigyʀe] vt to disfigure

défilé [defile] nm (GÉO) (narrow) gorge _ pass; (soldats) parade; (manifestants) pr_ cession, march; **~ de mode** fashion pa_ ade

défiler [defile] vi (troupes) to march pas_ (sportifs) to parade; (manifestants) _ march; (visiteurs) to pour, stream; **se** _ vi: **il s'est défilé** (fam) he wriggled out _ it

définir [definiʀ] vt to define

définitif, -ive [definitif, iv] adj (final) fina_ definitive; (pour longtemps) permanen_ definitive; (refus) definite; **définitive** _ **en définitive** eventually; (somme toute) _ fact; **définitivement** adv (part_ s'installer) for good

défoncer [defɔ̃se] vt (porte) to smash in _ down; **se ~** (fam) vi (travailler) to wo_ like a dog; (drogué) to get high

déformer [defɔʀme] vt to put out _ shape; (pensée, fait) to distort; **se ~** vi _ lose its shape

défouler [defule]: **se ~** vi to unwind, l_ off steam

défraîchir [defʀeʃiʀ]: **se ~** vi to fade

défricher [defʀiʃe] vt to clear (for cultiv_ tion)

défunt, e [defœ̃, œ̃t] nm/f deceased

dégagé, e [degaʒe] adj (route, ciel) clea_ **sur un ton ~** casually

dégagement [degaʒmɑ̃] nm: **voie de ~**

slip road

dégager [degaʒe] vt (exhaler) to give off; (délivrer) to free, extricate; (désencombrer) to clear; (isoler: idée, aspect) to bring out; **se ~** vi (passage, ciel) to clear

dégarnir [degaʀniʀ] vt (vider) to empty, clear; **se ~** vi (tempes, crâne) to go bald

dégâts [dega] nmpl damage sg

dégel [deʒɛl] nm thaw; **dégeler** vt to thaw (out)

dégénérer [deʒeneʀe] vi to degenerate

dégingandé, e [deʒɛ̃gɑ̃de] adj gangling

dégivrer [deʒivʀe] vt (frigo) to defrost; (vitres) to de-ice

dégonflé, e [degɔ̃fle] adj (pneu) flat

dégonfler [degɔ̃fle] vt (pneu, ballon) to let down, deflate; **se ~** vi (fam) to chicken out

dégouliner [deguline] vi to trickle, drip

dégourdi, e [deguʀdi] adj smart, resourceful

dégourdir [deguʀdiʀ] vt: **se ~ les jambes** to stretch one's legs (fig)

dégoût [degu] nm disgust, distaste; **dégoûtant, e** adj disgusting; **dégoûté, e** adj disgusted; **dégoûté de** sick of; **dégoûter** vt to disgust; **dégoûter qn de qch** to put sb off sth

dégrader [degʀade] vt (MIL: officier) to degrade; (abîmer) to damage, deface; **se ~** vi (relations, situation) to deteriorate

dégrafer [degʀafe] vt to unclip, unhook

degré [dəgʀe] nm degree

dégressif, -ive [degʀesif, iv] adj on a decreasing scale

dégringoler [degʀɛ̃gɔle] vi to tumble (down)

dégrossir [degʀosiʀ] vt (fig: projet) to work out roughly

déguenillé, e [deg(ə)nije] adj ragged, tattered

déguerpir [degɛʀpiʀ] vi to clear off

dégueulasse [degœlas] (fam) adj disgusting

dégueuler [degœle] (fam) vi to throw up

déguisement [degizmɑ̃] nm (pour

s'amuser) fancy dress

déguiser [degize]: **se ~** vi (se costumer) to dress up; (pour tromper) to disguise o.s.

dégustation [degystasjɔ̃] nf (de fromages etc) sampling; **~ de vins** wine-tasting session

déguster [degyste] vt (vins) to taste; (fromages etc) to sample; (savourer) to enjoy, savour

dehors [dəɔʀ] adv outside; (en plein air) outdoors ♦ nm outside ♦ nmpl (apparences) appearances; **mettre** ou **jeter ~** (expulser) to throw out; **au ~** outside; **au ~ de** outside; **en ~ de** (hormis) apart from

déjà [deʒa] adv already; (auparavant) before, already

déjeuner [deʒœne] vi to (have) lunch; (le matin) to have breakfast ♦ nm lunch

déjouer [deʒwe] vt (complot) to foil

delà [dəla] adv: **en ~ (de), au ~ (de)** beyond

délabrer [delabʀe]: **se ~** vi to fall into decay, become dilapidated

délacer [delase] vt (chaussures) to undo

délai [dele] nm (attente) waiting period; (sursis) extension (of time); (temps accordé) time limit; **sans ~** without delay; **dans les ~s** within the time limit

délaisser [delese] vt to abandon, desert

délasser [delase] vt to relax; **se ~** vi to relax

délavé, e [delave] adj faded

délayer [deleje] vt (CULIN) to mix (with water etc); (peinture) to thin down

delco [delko] nm (AUTO) distributor

délecter [delɛkte]: **se ~** vi to revel ou delight in

délégué, e [delege] nm/f representative

déléguer [delege] vt to delegate

délibéré, e [delibeʀe] adj (conscient) deliberate

délibérer [delibeʀe] vi to deliberate

délicat, e [delika, at] adj delicate; (plein de tact) tactful; (attention) thoughtful; **délicatement** adv delicately; (avec douceur) gently

délice [delis] *nm* delight

délicieux, -euse [delisjø, jøz] *adj (au goût)* 'delicious; *(sensation)* delightful

délimiter [delimite] *vt (terrain)* to delimit, demarcate

délinquance [delēkãs] *nf* criminality

délirant, e [delirã, ãt] *(fam) adj* wild

délirer [deline] *vi* to be delirious; **tu délires!** *(fam)* you're crazy!

délit [deli] *nm (criminal)* offence

délivrer [delivre] *vt (prisonnier)* to (set) free, release; *(passeport)* to issue

déloger [delɔʒe] *vt (objet coincé)* to dislodge

déloyal, e, -aux [delwajal, o] *adj (ami)* disloyal; *(procédé)* unfair

deltaplane [deltaplan] *nm* hang-glider

déluge [delyʒ] *nm (pluie)* downpour; *(biblique)* Flood

déluré, e [delyre] *(péj) adj* forward, pert

demain [d(ə)mē] *adv* tomorrow

demande [d(ə)mãd] *nf (requête)* request; *(revendication)* demand; *(d'emploi)* application; *(ÉCON)*: **la ~** demand; **"~s d'emploi"** *(annonces)* "situations wanted"; **~ en mariage** proposal (of marriage)

demandé, e [d(ə)mãde] *adj (article etc)*: **très ~** (very) much in demand

demander [d(ə)mãde] *vt* to ask for; *(chemin, heure etc)* to ask; *(nécessiter)* to require, demand; **se si/pourquoi** *etc* to wonder whether/why *etc*; **~ qch à qn** to ask sb for sth; **~ un service à qn** to ask sb a favour; **~ à qn de faire** to ask sb to do; **demandeur, -euse** *nm/f*: **demandeur d'emploi** job-seeker; **~ d'asile** asylum-seeker

démangeaison [demãʒɛzɔ̃] *nf* itching; **avoir des ~s** to be itching

démanger [demãʒe] *vi* to itch

démanteler [demãt(ə)le] *vt* to break up

démaquillant [demakijã] *nm* make-up remover

démaquiller [demakije] *vt*: **se ~** to remove one's make-up

démarche [demarʃ] *nf (allure)* gait, walk;

(intervention) step; *(fig: intellectuell* thought processes *pl*; **faire les ~s néces saires (pour obtenir qch)** to take the ne cessary steps (to obtain sth)

démarcheur, -euse [demarʃœr. ø *nm/f (COMM)* door-to-door salesman woman)

démarque [demark] *nf (article)* markdow

démarrage [demaraʒ] *nm* start

démarrer [demare] *vi (conducteur)* to sta (up); *(véhicule)* to move off; *(travaux)* get moving; **démarreur** *nm (AUTO)* sta ter

démêlant [demelã] *nm* conditioner

démêler [demele] *vt* to untangle; **dé mêlés** *nmpl* problems

déménagement [demenaʒmã] *nm* mov **camion de ~** removal van

déménager [demenaʒe] *vt (meubles)* (re)move ♦ *vi* to move (house); **démé nageur** *nm* removal man

démener [dem(ə)ne]: **se ~** *vi (se dépense* to exert o.s.; *(pour obtenir qch)* to go great lengths

dément, e [demã, ãt] *adj (fou)* mad, cr zy; *(fam)* brilliant, fantastic

démentiel, le [demãsjɛl] *adj* insane

démentir [demãtir] *vt* to refute; **~ que** deny that

démerder [demɛrde] *(fam)*: **se ~** *vi* sort things out for o.s.

démesuré, e [dem(ə)zyre] *adj* immode ate

démettre [demɛtr] *vt*: **~ qn de** *(fonctio poste)* to dismiss sb from; **se ~ l'épau** *etc* to dislocate one's shoulder *etc*

demeurant [d(ə)mœrã]: **au ~** *adv* for that

demeure [d(ə)mœr] *nf* residence; **de meurer** *vi (habiter)* to live; *(rester)* to r main

demi, e [dəmi] *adj* half ♦ *nm (bière)* half-pint *(0,25 litres)* ♦ *préfixe*: **~...** hal semi..., demi-; **trois heures/bouteilles ~es** three and a half hours/bottles, thr hours/bottles and a half; **il est 2 heure**

et ~e/midi et ~ it's half past 2/half past 12; à ~ half-; à la ~e (heure) on the half-hour; demi-cercle nm semicircle; en demi-cercle ♦ adj semicircular ♦ adv in a half circle; demi-douzaine nf half-dozen, half a dozen; demi-finale nf semifinal; demi-frère nm half-brother; demi-heure nf half-hour, half an hour; demi-journée nf half-day, half a day; demi-litre nm half-litre, half a litre; demi-livre nf half-pound, half a pound; demi-mot adv: à demi-mot without having to spell things out; demi-pension nf (à l'hôtel) half-board; demi-pensionnaire nm/f: être demi-pensionnaire to take school lunches; demi-place nf half-fare

démis, e [demi, iz] adj (épaule etc) dislocated

demi-sel [dəmisεl] adj inv (beurre, fromage) slightly salted

demi-sœur [dəmisœʀ] nf half-sister

démission [demisjɔ̃] nf resignation; donner sa ~ to give ou hand in one's notice; démissionner vi to resign

demi-tarif [dəmitaʀif] nm half-price; voyager à ~-~ to travel half-fare

demi-tour [dəmituʀ] nm about-turn; faire ~-~ to turn (and go) back

démocratie [demɔkʀasi] nf democracy; démocratique adj democratic

démodé, e [demɔde] adj old-fashioned

demoiselle [d(ə)mwazεl] nf (jeune fille) young lady; (célibataire) single lady, maiden lady; ~ d'honneur bridesmaid

démolir [demɔliʀ] vt to demolish

démon [demɔ̃] nm (enfant turbulent) devil, demon; le D~ the Devil

démonstration [demɔ̃stʀasjɔ̃] nf demonstration

démonté, e [demɔ̃te] adj (mer) raging, wild

démonter [demɔ̃te] vt (machine etc) to take down, dismantle

démontrer [demɔ̃tʀe] vt to demonstrate

démordre [demɔʀdʀ] vi: ne pas ~ de to refuse to give up, stick to

démouler [demule] vt to turn out

démuni, e [demyni] adj (sans argent) impoverished; ~ de without

démunir [demyniʀ] vt: ~ qn de to deprive sb of; se ~ de to part with, give up

dénaturer [denatyʀe] vt (goût) to alter; (pensée, fait) to distort

dénicher [denife] (fam) vt (objet) to unearth; (restaurant etc) to discover

dénier [denje] vt to deny

dénigrer [denigʀe] vt to denigrate, run down

dénivellation [denivelasjɔ̃] nf (pente) slope

dénombrer [denɔ̃bʀe] vt to count

dénomination [denɔminasjɔ̃] nf designation, appellation

dénommé, e [denɔme] adj: un ~ Dupont a certain Mr Dupont

dénoncer [denɔ̃se] vt to denounce

dénouement [denumɑ̃] nm outcome

dénouer [denwe] vt to unknot, undo; se ~ vi (nœud) to come undone

dénoyauter [denwajote] vt to stone

denrée [dɑ̃ʀe] nf: ~s (alimentaires) foodstuffs

dense [dɑ̃s] adj dense; densité nf density

dent [dɑ̃] nf tooth; ~ de lait/sagesse milk/wisdom tooth; dentaire adj dental

dentelé, e [dɑ̃t(ə)le] adj jagged, indented

dentelle [dɑ̃tεl] nf lace no pl

dentier [dɑ̃tje] nm denture

dentifrice [dɑ̃tifʀis] nm toothpaste

dentiste [dɑ̃tist] nm/f dentist

dentition [dɑ̃tisjɔ̃] nf teeth

dénuder [denyde] vt to bare

dénué, e [denɥe] adj: ~ de devoid of; dénuement nm destitution

déodorant [deɔdɔʀɑ̃] nm deodorant

déontologie [deɔ̃tɔlɔʒi] nf code of practice

dépannage [depanaʒ] nm: service de ~ (AUTO) breakdown service

dépanner [depane] vt (voiture, télévision) to fix, repair; (fig) to bail out, help out; dépanneuse nf breakdown lorry (BRIT), tow truck (*US*)

dépareillé, e [depaʀeje] *adj* (*collection, service*) incomplete; (*objet*) odd

départ [depaʀ] *nm* departure; (*SPORT*) start; **au ~** at the start; **la veille de son ~** the day before he leaves/left

départager [depaʀtaʒe] *vt* to decide between

département [depaʀtəmã] *nm* department

département

i France is divided into 96 administrative units called **départements**. These local government divisions are headed by a state-appointed **préfet**, and administered by an elected **Conseil général**. Départements are usually named after prominent geographical features such as rivers or mountain ranges; see also **DOM-TOM**.

dépassé, e [depase] *adj* superseded, outmoded; **il est complètement ~** he's completely out of his depth, he can't cope

dépasser [depase] *vt* (*véhicule, concurrent*) to overtake; (*endroit*) to pass, go past; (*somme, limite*) to exceed; (*fig: en beauté etc*) to surpass, outshine ♦ *vi* (*jupon etc*) to show

dépaysé, e [depeize] *adj* disoriented

dépaysement [depeizmã] *nm* (*changement*) change of scenery

dépecer [depəse] *vt* to joint, cut up

dépêche [depɛʃ] *nf* dispatch

dépêcher [depeʃe]: **se ~** *vi* to hurry

dépeindre [depɛ̃dʀ] *vt* to depict

dépendance [depãdãs] *nf* dependence; (*bâtiment*) outbuilding

dépendre [depãdʀ]: **~ de** *vt* to depend on; (*financièrement etc*) to be dependent on

dépens [depã] *nmpl*: **aux ~ de** at the expense of

dépense [depãs] *nf* spending *no pl*, expense, expenditure *no pl*; **dépenser** *vt*

to spend; (*energie*) to expend, use up; **s[e]** **dépenser** *vi* to exert o.s.; **dépensier, -ière** *adj*: **il est dépensier** he's a spen[d]thrift

dépérir [depeʀiʀ] *vi* (*personne*) to wast[e] away; (*plante*) to wither

dépêtrer [depetʀe] *vt*: **se ~ de** to extricat[e] o.s. from

dépeupler [depœple]: **se ~** *vi* to becom[e] depopulated

dépilatoire [depilatwaʀ] *adj* depilatory[,] hair-removing

dépister [depiste] *vt* to detect; (*voleur*) t[o] track down

dépit [depi] *nm* vexation, frustration; **en [~]** **de** in spite of; **en ~ du bon sens** con[-]trary to all good sense; **dépité, e** *a[dj]* vexed, frustrated

déplacé, e [deplase] *adj* (*propos*) out o[f] place, uncalled-for

déplacement [deplasmã] *nm* (*voyag[e]*) trip, travelling *no pl*

déplacer [deplase] *vt* (*table, voiture*) t[o] move, shift; **se ~** *vi* to move; (*voyager*) t[o] travel; **se ~ une vertèbre** to slip a disc

déplaire [deplɛʀ] *vt*: **ça me déplaît** [I] don't like this, I dislike this; **se ~** *vi* to b[e] unhappy; **déplaisant, e** *adj* disagreeabl[e]

dépliant [deplijã] *nm* leaflet

déplier [deplije] *vt* to unfold

déplorer [deplɔʀe] *vt* to deplore

déployer [deplwaje] *vt* (*carte*) to open ou[t]; (*ailes*) to spread; (*troupes*) to deploy

déporter [depɔʀte] *vt* (*exiler*) to depor[t]; (*dévier*) to carry off course

déposer [depoze] *vt* (*gén: mettre, poser*) t[o] lay *ou* put down; (*à la banque, à la con[-]signe*) to deposit; (*passager*) to drop (off[)], set down; (*roi*) to depose; (*plainte*) t[o] lodge; (*marque*) to register; **se ~** *vi* t[o] settle; **dépositaire** *nm/f* (*COMM*) agen[t]; **déposition** *nf* statement

dépôt [depo] *nm* (*à la banque, sédimen[t]*) deposit; (*entrepôt*) warehouse, store

dépotoir [depɔtwaʀ] *nm* dumping groun[d], rubbish dump

dépouiller [depuje] *vt* (*documents*) to go through, peruse; ~ **qn/qch de** to strip sb/sth of; ~ **le scrutin** to count the votes

dépourvu, e [depurvy] *adj*: ~ **de** lacking in, without; **prendre qn au** ~ to catch sb unprepared

déprécier [depresje]: **se** ~ *vi* to depreciate

dépression [depresjɔ̃] *nf* depression; ~ **(nerveuse)** (nervous) breakdown

déprimant, e [deprimã, ãt] *adj* depressing

déprimer [deprime] *vi* to be/get depressed

MOT-CLÉ

---

depuis [dəpɥi] *prép* **1** (*point de départ dans le temps*) since; **il habite Paris depuis 1983/l'an dernier** he has been living in Paris since 1983/last year; **depuis quand le connaissez-vous?** how long have you known him?

2 (*temps écoulé*) for; **il habite Paris depuis 5 ans** he has been living in Paris for 5 years; **je le connais depuis 3 ans** I've known him for 3 years

3 (*lieu*): **il a plu depuis Metz** it's been raining since Metz; **elle a téléphoné depuis Valence** she rang from Valence

4 (*quantité, rang*) from; **depuis les plus petits jusqu'aux plus grands** from the youngest to the oldest

♦ *adv* (*temps*) since (then); **je ne lui ai pas parlé depuis** I haven't spoken to him since (then)

depuis que *conj* (ever) since; **depuis qu'il m'a dit ça** (ever) since he said that to me

---

député, e [depyte] *nm/f* (*POL*) ≈ Member of Parliament (*BRIT*), ≈ Member of Congress (*US*)

députer [depyte] *vt* to delegate

déraciner [derasine] *vt* to uproot

dérailler [deraje] *vi* (*train*) to be derailed; **faire** ~ to derail

déraisonner [derezɔne] *vi* to talk nonsense, rave

dérangement [derãʒmã] *nm* (*gêne*) trouble; (*gastrique etc*) disorder; **en** ~ (*téléphone, machine*) out of order

déranger [derãʒe] *vt* (*personne*) to trouble, bother; (*projets*) to disrupt, upset; (*objets, vêtements*) to disarrange; **se** ~ *vi*: **surtout ne vous dérangez pas pour moi** please don't put yourself out on my account; **est-ce que cela vous dérange si ...?** do you mind if ...?

déraper [derape] *vi* (*voiture*) to skid; (*personne, semelles*) to slip

dérégler [deregle] *vt* (*mécanisme*) to put out of order; (*estomac*) to upset

dérider [deride]: **se** ~ *vi* to brighten up

dérision [derizjɔ̃] *nf*: **tourner en** ~ to deride; **dérisoire** *adj* derisory

dérive [deriv] *nf*: **aller à la** ~ (*NAVIG, fig*) to drift

dérivé, e [derive] *nm* (*TECH*) by-product

dériver [derive] *vt* (*MATH*) to derive; (*cours d'eau etc*) to divert ♦ *vi* (*bateau*) to drift; ~ **de** to derive from

dermatologue [dermatɔlɔg] *nm/f* dermatologist

dernier, -ière [dernje, jer] *adj* last; (*le plus récent*) latest, last; **lundi/le mois** ~ last Monday/month; **c'est le** ~ **cri** it's the very latest thing; **en** ~ last; **ce** ~ the latter; **dernièrement** *adv* recently

dérobé, e [derɔbe] *adj*: **à la** ~e surreptitiously

dérober [derɔbe] *vt* to steal; **se** ~ *vi* (*s'esquiver*) to slip away; **se** ~ **à** (*justice, regards*) to hide from; (*obligation*) to shirk

dérogation [derɔgasjɔ̃] *nf* (special) dispensation

déroger [derɔʒe]: ~ **à** *vt* to go against, depart from

dérouiller [deruje] *vt*: **se** ~ **les jambes** to stretch one's legs (*fig*)

déroulement [derulmã] *nm* (*d'une opération etc*) progress

dérouler [derule] *vt* (*ficelle*) to unwind; **se**

~ *vi (avoir lieu)* to take place; *(se passer)* to go (off); **tout s'est déroulé comme prévu** everything went as planned

dérouter [deʀute] *vt (avion, train)* to re-route, divert; *(étonner)* to disconcert, throw (out)

derrière [dɛʀjɛʀ] *adv, prép* behind ♦ *nm (d'une maison)* back; *(postérieur)* behind, bottom; **les pattes de ~** the back *ou* hind legs; **par ~** from behind; *(fig)* behind one's back

des [de] *dét voir* **de** ♦ *prép* +*dét* = **de** +**les**

dès [de] *prép* from; **~ que** as soon as; **~ son retour** as soon as he was *(ou* is) back

désabusé, e [dezabyze] *adj* disillusioned

désaccord [dezakɔʀ] *nm* disagreement; **désaccordé, e** *adj (MUS)* out of tune

désaffecté, e [dezafɛkte] *adj* disused

désagréable [dezagreabl] *adj* unpleasant

désagréger [dezagreʒe]: **se ~** *vi* to disintegrate, break up

désagrément [dezagremɑ̃] *nm* annoyance, trouble *no pl*

désaltérer [dezaltere] *vt*: **se ~** to quench one's thirst

désapprobateur, -trice [dezapʀɔbatœʀ, tʀis] *adj* disapproving

désapprouver [dezapʀuve] *vt* to disapprove of

désarmant, e [dezaʀmɑ̃, ɑ̃t] *adj* disarming

désarroi [dezaʀwa] *nm* disarray

désastre [dezastʀ] *nm* disaster; **désastreux, -euse** *adj* disastrous

désavantage [dezavɑ̃taʒ] *nm* disadvantage; **désavantager** *vt* to put at a disadvantage

descendre [desɑ̃dʀ] *vt (escalier, montagne)* to go *(ou* come) down; *(valise, paquet)* to take *ou* get down; *(étagère etc)* to lower; *(fam: abattre)* to shoot down ♦ *vi* to go *(ou* come) down; *(passager: s'arrêter)* to get out, alight; **~ à pied/en voiture** to walk/drive down; **~ du train** to get out of *ou* get off the train; **~ de cheval** to dismount; **~ à l'hôtel** to stay at a hotel

descente [desɑ̃t] *nf* descent, going down; *(chemin)* way down; *(SKI)* downhill (race); **~ de lit** bedside rug; **~ (de police)** (police) raid

description [dɛskʀipsjɔ̃] *nf* description

désemparé, e [dezɑ̃paʀe] *adj* bewildered, distraught

désemplir [dezɑ̃pliʀ] *vi*: **ne pas ~** to be always full

déséquilibre [dezekilibʀ] *nm (position)*: **en ~** unsteady; *(fig: des forces, du budget)* imbalance; **déséquilibré, e** *nm/f (PSYCH)* unbalanced person; **déséquilibrer** *vt* to throw off balance

désert, e [dezɛʀ, ɛʀt] *adj* deserted ♦ *nm* desert; **déserter** *vi, vt* to desert; **désertique** *adj* desert *cpd*

désespéré, e [dezɛspeʀe] *adj* desperate

désespérer [dezɛspeʀe] *vi*: **~ (de)** to despair (of); **désespoir** *nm* despair; **en désespoir de cause** in desperation

déshabiller [dezabije] *vt* to undress; **se ~** *vi* to undress (o.s.)

déshériter [dezeʀite] *vt* to disinherit; **déshérités** *nmpl*: **les déshérités** the underprivileged

déshonneur [dezɔnœʀ] *nm* dishonour

déshydraté, e [dezidʀate] *adj* dehydrated

desiderata [deziderata] *nmpl* requirements

désigner [dezine] *vt (montrer)* to point out, indicate; *(dénommer)* to denote; *(candidat etc)* to name

désinfectant, e [dezɛ̃fɛktɑ̃, ɑ̃t] *adj, nm* disinfectant

désinfecter [dezɛ̃fɛkte] *vt* to disinfect

désintégrer [dezɛ̃tegʀe]: **se ~** *vi* to disintegrate

désintéressé, e [dezɛ̃teʀese] *adj* disinterested, unselfish

désintéresser [dezɛ̃teʀese] *vt*: **se ~ (de)** to lose interest (in)

désintoxication [dezɛ̃tɔksikasjɔ̃] *nf*: **faire une cure de ~** to undergo treatment for alcoholism *(ou* drug addiction)

désinvolte [dezɛ̃vɔlt] _adj_ casual, off-hand; **désinvolture** _nf_ casualness

désir [deziR] _nm_ wish; (_sensuel_) desire; **désirer** _vt_ to want, wish for; (_sexuellement_) to desire; **je désire ...** (_formule de politesse_) I would like ...

désister [deziste]: **se ~** _vi_ to stand down, withdraw

désobéir [dezɔbeiR] _vi_: **~ (à qn/qch)** to disobey (sb/sth); **désobéissant, e** _adj_ disobedient

désobligeant, e [dezɔbliʒɑ̃, ɑ̃t] _adj_ disagreeable

désodorisant [dezɔdɔRizɑ̃] _nm_ air freshener, deodorizer

désœuvré, e [dezœvRe] _adj_ idle

désolé, e [dezɔle] _adj_ (_paysage_) desolate; **je suis ~** I'm sorry

désoler [dezɔle] _vt_ to distress, grieve

désopilant, e [dezɔpilɑ̃, ɑ̃t] _adj_ hilarious

désordonné, e [dezɔRdɔne] _adj_ untidy

désordre [dezɔRdR] _nm_ disorder(liness), untidiness; (_anarchie_) disorder; **en ~** in a mess, untidy

désorienté, e [dezɔRjɑ̃te] _adj_ disorientated

désormais [dezɔRmɛ] _adv_ from now on

désossé, e [dezɔse] _adj_ (_viande_) boned

desquelles [dekɛl] _prép_ +_pron_ = **de +lesquelles**

desquels [dekɛl] _prép_ +_pron_ = **de +lesquels**

desséché, e [deseʃe] _adj_ dried up

dessécher [deseʃe]: **se ~** _vi_ to dry out

dessein [desɛ̃] _nm_: **à ~** intentionally, deliberately

desserrer [deseRe] _vt_ to loosen; (_frein_) to release

dessert [desɛR] _nm_ dessert, pudding

desserte [desɛRt] _nf_ (_table_) side table; (_transport_): **la ~ du village est assurée par autocar** there is a coach service to the village

desservir [desɛRviR] _vt_ to serve; (_débarrasser_): **~ (la table)** to clear the table

dessin [desɛ̃] _nm_ (_œuvre, art_) drawing; (_motif_) pattern, design; **~ animé** cartoon (film); **~ humoristique** cartoon; **dessinateur, -trice** _nm/f_ drawer; (_de bandes dessinées_) cartoonist; (_industriel_) draughtsman(-woman) (_BRIT_), draftsman(-woman) (_US_); **dessiner** _vt_ to draw; (_concevoir_) to design

dessous [d(ə)su] _adv_ underneath, beneath ♦ _nm_ underside ♦ _nmpl_ (_sous-vêtements_) underwear _sg_; **en ~, par ~** underneath; **au-~ (de)** below; (_peu digne de_) beneath; **avoir le ~** to get the worst of it; **les voisins du ~** the downstairs neighbours; **dessous-de-plat** _nm inv_ tablemat

dessus [d(ə)sy] _adv_ on top; (_collé, écrit_) on it ♦ _nm_ top; **en ~** above; **par ~** ♦ _adv_ over it ♦ _prép_ over; **au-~ (de)** above; **avoir le ~** to get the upper hand; **dessus-de-lit** _nm inv_ bedspread

destin [destɛ̃] _nm_ fate; (_avenir_) destiny

destinataire [destinatɛR] _nm/f_ (_POSTES_) addressee; (_d'un colis_) consignee

destination [destinasjɔ̃] _nf_ (_lieu_) destination; (_usage_) purpose; **à ~ de** bound for, travelling to

destinée [destine] _nf_ fate; (_existence, avenir_) destiny

destiner [destine] _vt_: **~ qch à qn** (_envisager de donner_) to intend sb to have sth; (_adresser_) to intend sth for sb; **être destiné à** (_usage_) to be meant for

désuet, -ète [desɥɛ, ɛt] _adj_ outdated, outmoded

détachant [detaʃɑ̃] _nm_ stain remover

détachement [detaʃmɑ̃] _nm_ detachment

détacher [detaʃe] _vt_ (_enlever_) to detach, remove; (_délier_) to untie; (_ADMIN_): **~ qn (auprès de** _ou_ **à)** to post sb (to); **se ~** _vi_ (_se séparer_) to come off; (: _page_) to come out; (_se défaire_) to come undone; **se ~ sur** to stand out against; **se ~ de** (_se désintéresser_) to grow away from

détail [detaj] _nm_ detail; (_COMM_): **le ~** retail; **en ~** in detail; **au ~** (_COMM_) retail; **détaillant** _nm_ retailer; **détaillé, e** _adj_ (*plan, explications*) detailed; (*facture*) item-ized; **détailler** vt (*expliquer*) to explain in detail

détaler [detale] (*fam*) vi (*personne*) to take off

détartrant [detaʀtʀɑ̃] nm scale remover

détaxé, e [detakse] adj: **produits ~s** tax-free goods

détecter [detɛkte] vt to detect

détective [detɛktiv] nm: **~ (privé)** private detective

déteindre [detɛ̃dʀ] vi (*au lavage*) to run, lose its colour

détendre [detɑ̃dʀ] vt (*corps, esprit*) to re-lax; **se ~** vi (*ressort*) to lose its tension; (*personne*) to relax

détenir [det(ə)niʀ] vt (*record, pouvoir, se-cret*) to hold; (*prisonnier*) to detain, hold

détente [detɑ̃t] nf relaxation

détention [detɑ̃sjɔ̃] nf (*d'armes*) posses-sion; (*captivité*) detention; **~ préventive** custody

détenu, e [det(ə)ny] nm/f prisoner

détergent [detɛʀʒɑ̃] nm detergent

détériorer [deteʀjɔʀe] vt to damage; **se ~** vi to deteriorate

déterminé, e [detɛʀmine] adj (*résolu*) de-termined; (*précis*) specific, definite

déterminer [detɛʀmine] vt (*fixer*) to deter-mine; **se ~ à faire qch** to make up one's mind to do sth

déterrer [detɛʀe] vt to dig up

détestable [detɛstabl] adj foul, detestable

détester [detɛste] vt to hate, detest

détonner [detɔne] vi (*fig*) to clash

détour [detuʀ] nm detour; (*tournant*) bend, curve; **ça vaut le ~** it's worth the trip; **sans ~** (*fig*) plainly

détourné, e [detuʀne] adj (*moyen*) round-about

détournement [detuʀnəmɑ̃] nm: **~ d'avion** hijacking

détourner [detuʀne] vt to divert; (*par la force*) to hijack; (*yeux, tête*) to turn away; (*de l'argent*) to embezzle; **se ~** vi to turn away

détracteur, -trice [detʀaktœʀ, tʀis] nm/f disparager, critic

détraquer [detʀake] vt to put out of or-der; (*estomac*) to upset; **se ~** vi (*machine*) to go wrong

détrempé, e [detʀɑ̃pe] adj (*sol*) sodden, waterlogged

détresse [detʀɛs] nf distress

détriment [detʀimɑ̃] nm: **au ~ de** to the detriment of

détritus [detʀity(s)] nmpl rubbish sg, ref-use sg

détroit [detʀwa] nm strait

détromper [detʀɔ̃pe] vt to disabuse

détruire [detʀɥiʀ] vt to destroy

dette [dɛt] nf debt

DEUG sigle m (= *diplôme d'études universi-taires générales*) diploma taken after 2 years at university

deuil [dœj] nm (*perte*) bereavement; (*pé-riode*) mourning; **être en ~** to be in mourning

deux [dø] num two; **tous les ~** both; **ses ~ mains** both his hands, his two hands; **~ fois** twice; **deuxième** num second; **deuxièmement** adv secondly; **deux-pièces** nm inv (*tailleur*) two-piece suit, (*de bain*) two-piece (swimsuit); (*apparte-ment*) two-roomed flat (*BRIT*) ou apart-ment (*US*); **deux-points** nm inv colon sg, **deux-roues** nm inv two-wheeled vehicle

devais etc [dəvɛ] vb voir **devoir**

dévaler [devale] vt to hurtle down

dévaliser [devalize] vt to rob, burgle

dévaloriser [devalɔʀize] vt to depreciate, **se ~** vi to depreciate

dévaluation [devalɥasjɔ̃] nf devaluation

devancer [d(ə)vɑ̃se] vt (*coureur, rival*) to get ahead of; (*arriver*) to arrive before (*prévenir: questions, désirs*) to anticipate

devant [d(ə)vɑ̃] adv in front; (*à distance: en avant*) ahead ♦ prép in front of; (*en avant*) ahead of; (*avec mouvement: passer*) past (*en présence de*) before, in front of; (*étant donné*) in view of ♦ nm front; **prendre les ~s** to make the first move; **les pattes de**

~ the front legs, the forelegs; **par ~** (*boutonner*) at the front; (*entrer*) the front way; **aller au-~ de qn** to go out to meet sb; **aller au-~ de** (*désirs de qn*) to anticipate

devanture [d(ə)vɑ̃tyʀ] *nf* (*étalage*) display; (*vitrine*) (shop) window

déveine [devɛn] (*fam*) *nf* rotten luck *no pl*

développement [dev(ə)lɔpmɑ̃] *nm* development; **pays en voie de ~** developing countries

développer [dev(ə)lɔpe] *vt* to develop; **se ~** *vi* to develop

devenir [dəv(ə)niʀ] *vb +attrib* to become; **que sont-ils devenus?** what has become of them?

dévergondé, e [devɛʀɡɔ̃de] *adj* wild, shameless

déverser [devɛʀse] *vt* (*liquide*) to pour (out); (*ordures*) to tip (out); **se ~ dans** (*fleuve*) to flow into

dévêtir [devetiʀ]: **se ~** *vi* to undress

devez *etc* [dəve] *vb voir* **devoir**

déviation [devjasjɔ̃] *nf* (AUTO) diversion (BRIT), detour (US)

devienne *etc* [dəvjɛn] *vb voir* **devenir**

dévier [devje] *vt* (*fleuve, circulation*) to divert; (*coup*) to deflect ♦ *vi* to veer (off course)

devin [dəvɛ̃] *nm* soothsayer, seer

deviner [d(ə)vine] *vt* to guess; (*apercevoir*) to distinguish; **devinette** *nf* riddle

devins *etc* [dəvɛ̃] *vb voir* **devenir**

devis [d(ə)vi] *nm* estimate, quotation

dévisager [devizaʒe] *vt* to stare at

devise [dəviz] *nf* (*formule*) motto, watchword; **~s** *nfpl* (*argent*) currency *sg*

deviser [dəvize] *vi* to converse

dévisser [devise] *vt* to unscrew, undo

dévoiler [devwale] *vt* to unveil

devoir [d(ə)vwaʀ] *nm* duty; (SCOL) homework *no pl*; (: *en classe*) exercise ♦ *vt* (*argent, respect*): **~ qch (à qn)** to owe (sb) sth; (+*infin*: *obligation*): **il doit le faire** he has to do it, he must do it; (: *intention*): **le nouveau centre commercial doit**

ouvrir en mai the new shopping centre is due to open in May; (: *probabilité*): **il doit être tard** it must be late

dévolu [devɔly] *nm*: **jeter son ~ sur** to fix one's choice on

dévorer [devɔʀe] *vt* to devour

dévot, e [devo, ɔt] *adj* devout, pious; **dévotion** *nf* devoutness

dévoué, e [devwe] *adj* devoted

dévouement [devumɑ̃] *nm* devotion

dévouer [devwe]: **se ~** *vi* (*se sacrifier*): **se ~ (pour)** to sacrifice o.s. (for); (*se consacrer*): **se ~ à** to devote *ou* dedicate o.s. to

dévoyé, e [devwaje] *adj* delinquent

devrai *etc* [dəvʀe] *vb voir* **devoir**

diabète [djabɛt] *nm* diabetes *sg*; **diabétique** *nm/f* diabetic

diable [djɑbl] *nm* devil

diabolo [djabɔlo] *nm* (*boisson*) lemonade with fruit cordial

diagnostic [djagnɔstik] *nm* diagnosis *sg*; **diagnostiquer** *vt* to diagnose

diagonal, e, -aux [djagɔnal, o] *adj* diagonal; **diagonale** *nf* diagonal; **en diagonale** diagonally

diagramme [djagʀam] *nm* chart, graph

dialecte [djalɛkt] *nm* dialect

dialogue [djalɔg] *nm* dialogue

diamant [djamɑ̃] *nm* diamond

diamètre [djamɛtʀ] *nm* diameter

diapason [djapazɔ̃] *nm* tuning fork

diaphragme [djafʀagm] *nm* diaphragm

diapo [djapo] (*fam*) *nf* slide

diapositive [djapozitiv] *nf* transparency, slide

diarrhée [djaʀe] *nf* diarrhoea

dictateur [diktatœʀ] *nm* dictator; **dictature** *nf* dictatorship

dictée [dikte] *nf* dictation

dicter [dikte] *vt* to dictate

dictionnaire [diksjɔnɛʀ] *nm* dictionary

dicton [diktɔ̃] *nm* saying, dictum

dièse [djɛz] *nm* sharp

diesel [djezɛl] *nm* diesel ♦ *adj inv* diesel

diète [djɛt] *nf* (*jeûne*) starvation diet; (*régime*) diet; **diététique** *adj*: **magasin dié-**

tétique health food shop

dieu, x [djø] *nm* god; **D~** God; **mon D~!** good heavens!

diffamation [difamasjɔ̃] *nf* slander; (*écrite*) libel

différé [difeʀe] *nm* (*TV*): **en ~** (pre-)recorded

différemment [difeʀamɑ̃] *adv* differently

différence [difeʀɑ̃s] *nf* difference; **à la ~ de** unlike; **différencier** *vt* to differentiate; **différend** *nm* difference (of opinion), disagreement

différent, e [difeʀɑ̃, ɑ̃t] *adj* (*dissemblable*) different; **~ de** different from; (*divers*) different, various

différer [difeʀe] *vt* to postpone, put off ♦ *vi*: **~ (de)** to differ (from)

difficile [difisil] *adj* difficult; (*exigeant*) hard to please; **difficilement** *adv* with difficulty

difficulté [difikylte] *nf* difficulty; **en ~** (*bateau, alpiniste*) in difficulties

difforme [difɔʀm] *adj* deformed, misshapen

diffuser [difyze] *vt* (*chaleur*) to diffuse; (*émission, musique*) to broadcast; (*nouvelle*) to circulate; (*COMM*) to distribute

digérer [diʒeʀe] *vt* to digest; (*fam: accepter*) to stomach, put up with; **digestif** *nm* (after-dinner) liqueur; **digestion** *nf* digestion

digne [diɲ] *adj* dignified; **~ de** worthy of; **~ de foi** trustworthy; **dignité** *nf* dignity

digue [dig] *nf* dike, dyke

dilapider [dilapide] *vt* to squander

dilemme [dilem] *nm* dilemma

dilettante [diletɑ̃t] *nm/f*: **faire qch en ~** to dabble in sth

diligence [diliʒɑ̃s] *nf* stagecoach

diluer [dilɥe] *vt* to dilute

diluvien, ne [dilyvjɛ̃, jɛn] *adj*: **pluie ~ne** torrential rain

dimanche [dimɑ̃ʃ] *nm* Sunday

dimension [dimɑ̃sjɔ̃] *nf* (*grandeur*) size; (~s) dimensions

diminué, e [diminɥe] *adj*: **il est très ~**

depuis son accident he's not at all the man he was since his accident

diminuer [diminɥe] *vt* to reduce, decrease; (*ardeur etc*) to lessen; (*dénigrer*) to belittle ♦ *vi* to decrease, diminish; **diminutif** *nm* (*surnom*) pet name; **diminution** *nf* decreasing, diminishing

dinde [dɛ̃d] *nf* turkey

dindon [dɛ̃dɔ̃] *nm* turkey

dîner [dine] *nm* dinner ♦ *vi* to have dinner

dingue [dɛ̃g] (*fam*) *adj* crazy

dinosaure [dinɔzɔʀ] *nm* dinosaur

diplomate [diplɔmat] *adj* diplomatic ♦ *nm* diplomat; (*fig*) diplomatist; **diplomatie** *nf* diplomacy

diplôme [diplom] *nm* diploma; **avoir des ~s** to have qualifications; **diplômé, e** *adj* qualified

dire [diʀ] *nm*: **au ~ de** according to ♦ *vt* to say; (*secret, mensonge, heure*) to tell; **~ qch à qn** to tell sb sth; **~ à qn qu'il fasse** *ou* **de faire** to tell sb to do; **on dit que** they say that; **ceci dit** that being said; **si cela lui dit** (*plaire*) if he fancies it; **que dites-vous de** (*penser*) what do you think of; **on dirait que** it looks (*ou* sounds *etc*) as if; **dis/dites (donc)!** I say!

direct, e [diʀɛkt] *adj* direct ♦ *nm* (*TV*): **en ~** live; **directement** *adv* directly

directeur, -trice [diʀɛktœʀ, tʀis] *nm/f* (*d'entreprise*) director; (*de service*) manager(-eress); (*d'école*) head(teacher) (*BRIT*), principal (*US*)

direction [diʀɛksjɔ̃] *nf* (*sens*) direction; (*d'entreprise*) management; (*AUTO*) steering; **"toutes ~s"** "all routes"

dirent [diʀ] *vb voir* **dire**

dirigeant, e [diʀiʒɑ̃, ɑ̃t] *adj* (*classe*) ruling ♦ *nm/f* (*d'un parti etc*) leader

diriger [diʀiʒe] *vt* (*entreprise*) to manage, run; (*véhicule*) to steer; (*orchestre*) to conduct; (*recherches, travaux*) to supervise; **se ~** *vi* (*s'orienter*) to find one's way; **se ~ vers** *ou* **sur** to make *ou* head for

dis *etc* [di] *vb voir* **dire**

discernement [disɛʀnamɑ̃] *nm* (*bon sens*)

discernment, judgement

discerner [disɛRne] vt to discern, make out

discipline [disiplin] nf discipline; **discipliner** vt to discipline

discontinu, e [diskɔ̃tiny] adj intermittent

discontinuer [diskɔ̃tinɥe] vi: **sans ~** without stopping, without a break

discordant, e [diskɔʀdɑ̃, ɑ̃t] adj discordant

discothèque [diskɔtek] nf (boîte de nuit) disco(thèque)

discours [diskuʀ] nm speech

discret, -ète [diskʀe, ɛt] adj discreet; (parfum, maquillage) unobtrusive; **discrétion** nf discretion; **à discrétion** as much as one wants

discrimination [diskʀiminasjɔ̃] nf discrimination; **sans ~** indiscriminately

disculper [diskylpe] vt to exonerate

discussion [diskysjɔ̃] nf discussion

discutable [diskytabl] adj debatable

discuté, e [diskyte] adj controversial

discuter [diskyte] vt (débattre) to discuss; (contester) to question, dispute ♦ vi to talk; (protester) to argue; **~ de** to discuss

dise etc [diz] vb voir **dire**

diseuse [dizøz] nf: **~ de bonne aventure** fortuneteller

disgracieux, -euse [disgʀasjø, jøz] adj ungainly, awkward

disjoindre [disʒwɛ̃dʀ] vt to take apart; **se ~** vi to come apart

disjoncteur [disʒɔ̃ktœʀ] nm (ÉLEC) circuit breaker

disloquer [dislɔke]: **se ~** vi (parti, empire) to break up

disons [dizɔ̃] vb voir **dire**

disparaître [dispaʀetʀ] vi to disappear; (se perdre: traditions etc) to die out; **faire ~** (tache) to remove; (douleur) to get rid of

disparition [dispaʀisjɔ̃] nf disappearance; **espèce en voie de ~** endangered species

disparu, e [dispaʀy] nm/f missing person ♦ adj: **être porté ~** to be reported missing

dispensaire [dispɑ̃sɛʀ] nm community clinic

dispenser [dispɑ̃se] vt: **~ qn de** to exempt sb from; **se ~ de** vt (corvée) to get out of

disperser [dispɛʀse] vt to scatter; **se ~** vi to break up

disponibilité [dispɔnibilite] nf availability; **disponible** adj available

dispos [dispo] adj m: **(frais et) ~** fresh (as a daisy)

disposé, e [dispoze] adj: **bien/mal ~** (humeur) in a good/bad mood; **~ à** (prêt à) willing ou prepared to

disposer [dispoze] vt to arrange ♦ vi: **vous pouvez ~** you may leave; **~ de** to have (at one's disposal); **se ~ à faire** to prepare to do, be about to do

dispositif [dispozitif] nm device; (fig) system, plan of action

disposition [dispozisjɔ̃] nf (arrangement) arrangement, layout; (humeur) mood; **prendre ses ~s** to make arrangements; **avoir des ~s pour la musique** etc to have a special aptitude for music etc; **à la ~ de qn** at sb's disposal; **je suis à votre ~** I am at your service

disproportionné, e [dispʀopɔʀsjɔne] adj disproportionate, out of all proportion

dispute [dispyt] nf quarrel, argument; **disputer** vt (match) to play; (combat) to fight; **se disputer** vi to quarrel

disquaire [diskɛʀ] nm/f record dealer

disqualifier [diskalifje] vt to disqualify

disque [disk] nm (MUS) record; (forme, pièce) disc; (SPORT) discus; **~ compact** compact disc; **~ dur** hard disk; **disquette** nf floppy disk, diskette

disséminer [disemine] vt to scatter

disséquer [diseke] vt to dissect

dissertation [disɛʀtasjɔ̃] nf (SCOL) essay

dissimuler [disimyle] vt to conceal

dissipé, e [disipe] adj (élève) undisciplined, unruly

dissiper [disipe] vt to dissipate; (fortune)

to squander; **se ~** *vi* (*brouillard*) to clear, disperse

dissolvant [disɔlvɑ̃] *nm* nail polish remover

dissonant, e [disɔnɑ̃, ɑ̃t] *adj* discordant

dissoudre [disudʀ] *vt* to dissolve; **se ~** *vi* to dissolve

dissuader [disɥade] *vt*: **~ qn de faire** to dissuade sb from doing; **dissuasion** *nf*: **force de dissuasion** deterrent power

distance [distɑ̃s] *nf* distance; (*fig: écart*) gap; **à ~**: at *ou* from a distance; **distancer** *vt* to outdistance

distant, e [distɑ̃, ɑ̃t] *adj* (*réservé*) distant; **~ de** (*lieu*) far away from

distendre [distɑ̃dʀ]: **se ~** *vi* to distend

distillerie [distilʀi] *nf* distillery

distinct, e [distɛ̃(kt), ɛ̃kt] *adj* distinct; **distinctement** *adv* distinctly, clearly; **distinctif, -ive** *adj* distinctive

distingué, e [distɛ̃ge] *adj* distinguished

distinguer [distɛ̃ge] *vt* to distinguish

distraction [distʀaksjɔ̃] *nf* (*inattention*) absent-mindedness; (*passe-temps*) distraction, entertainment

distraire [distʀɛʀ] *vt* (*divertir*) to entertain, divert; (*déranger*) to distract; **se ~** *vi* to amuse *ou* enjoy o.s.; **distrait, e** *adj* absent-minded

distrayant, e [distʀɛjɑ̃, ɑ̃t] *adj* entertaining

distribuer [distʀibɥe] *vt* to distribute, hand out; (*CARTES*) to deal (out); (*courrier*) to deliver; **distributeur** *nm* (*COMM*) distributor; (*automatique*) (vending) machine; (: *de billets*) (cash) dispenser; **distribution** *nf* distribution; (*postale*) delivery; (*choix d'acteurs*) casting, cast

dit, e [di, dit] *pp de* **dire** ♦ *adj* (*fixé*): **le jour ~** the arranged day; (*surnommé*): **X, ~ Pierrot** X, known as Pierrot

dites [dit] *vb voir* **dire**

divaguer [divage] *vi* to ramble; (*fam*) to rave

divan [divɑ̃] *nm* divan

diverger [divɛʀʒe] *vi* to diverge

divers, e [divɛʀ, ɛʀs] *adj* (*varié*) diverse, varied; (*différent*) different, various; **~es personnes** various *ou* several people

diversifier [divɛʀsifje] *vt* to vary

diversité [divɛʀsite] *nf* (*variété*) diversity

divertir [divɛʀtiʀ]: **se ~** *vi* to amuse *ou* enjoy o.s.; **divertissement** *nm* distraction, entertainment

divin, e [divɛ̃, in] *adj* divine

diviser [divize] *vt* to divide; **division** *nf* division

divorce [divɔʀs] *nm* divorce; **divorcé, e** *nm/f* divorcee; **divorcer** *vi* to get a divorce, get divorced

divulguer [divylge] *vt* to divulge, disclose

dix [dis] *num* ten; **dixième** *num* tenth

dizaine [dizɛn] *nf*: **une ~ (de)** about ten, ten or so

do [do] *nm* (*note*) C; (*en chantant la gamme*) do(h)

docile [dɔsil] *adj* docile

dock [dɔk] *nm* dock; **docker** *nm* docker

docteur [dɔktœʀ] *nm* doctor; **doctorat** *nm* doctorate; **doctoresse** *nf* lady doctor

doctrine [dɔktʀin] *nf* doctrine

document [dɔkymɑ̃] *nm* document; **documentaire** *adj, nm* documentary; **documentaliste** *nm/f* (*SCOL*) librarian; **documentation** *nf* documentation, literature; **documenter** *vt*: **se documenter (sur)** to gather information (on)

dodo [dɔdo] *nm* (*langage enfantin*): **aller faire ~** to go to beddy-byes

dodu, e [dɔdy] *adj* plump

dogue [dɔg] *nm* mastiff

doigt [dwa] *nm* finger; **à deux ~s de** within an inch of; **~ de pied** toe; **doigté** *nm* (*MUS*) fingering; (*fig: habileté*) diplomacy, tact

doit *etc* [dwa] *vb voir* **devoir**

doléances [dɔleɑ̃s] *nfpl* grievances

dollar [dɔlaʀ] *nm* dollar

domaine [dɔmɛn] *nm* estate, property; (*fig*) domain, field

domestique [dɔmɛstik] *adj* domestic

♦ *nm/f* servant, domestic; **domestiquer** *vt* to domesticate

omicile [dɔmisil] *nm* home, place of residence; **à** ~ at home; **livrer à** ~ to deliver; **domicilié, e** *adj*: **"domicilié à ..."** "address ..."

ominant, e [dɔminɑ̃, ɑ̃t] *adj* (*opinion*) predominant

ominer [dɔmine] *vt* to dominate; (*sujet*) to master; (*surpasser*) to outclass, surpass; (*surplomber*) to tower above, dominate ♦ *vi* to be in the dominant position; **se** ~ *vi* to control o.s.

omino [dɔmino] *nm* domino

ommage [dɔmaʒ] *nm*: ~**s** (*dégâts*) damage *no pl*; **c'est** ~! what a shame!; **c'est** ~ **que** it's a shame *ou* pity that; **dommages-intérêts** *nmpl* damages

ompter [dɔ̃(p)te] *vt* to tame; **dompteur, -euse** *nm/f* trainer

OM-TOM [dɔmtɔm] *sigle m* (= *départements et territoires d'outre-mer*) French overseas departments and territories

on [dɔ̃] *nm* gift; (*charité*) donation; **avoir des** ~**s pour** to have a gift *ou* talent for; **elle a le** ~ **de m'énerver** she's got a knack of getting on my nerves

onc [dɔ̃k] *conj* therefore, so; (*après une digression*) so, then

onjon [dɔ̃ʒɔ̃] *nm* keep

onné, e [dɔne] *adj* (*convenu: lieu, heure*) given; (*pas cher: fam*): **c'est** ~ it's a gift; **étant** ~ **...** given ...; **données** *nfpl* data

onner [dɔne] *vt* to give; (*vieux habits etc*) to give away; (*spectacle*) to put on; ~ **qch à qn** to give sb sth, give sth to sb; ~ **sur** (*suj: fenêtre, chambre*) to look (out) onto; **ça donne soif/faim** it makes you (feel) thirsty/hungry; **se** ~ **à fond** to give one's all; **se** ~ **du mal** to take (great) trouble; **s'en** ~ **à cœur joie** (*fam*) to have a great time

---

MOT-CLÉ

ont [dɔ̃] *pron relatif* **1** (*appartenance: objets*) whose, of which; (*appartenance: êtres animés*) whose; **la maison dont le toit est rouge** the house the roof of which is red, the house whose roof is red; **l'homme dont je connais la sœur** the man whose sister I know

2 (*parmi lesquel(le)s*): **2 livres, dont l'un est ...** 2 books, one of which is ...; **il y avait plusieurs personnes, dont Gabrielle** there were several people, among them Gabrielle; **10 blessés, dont 2 grièvement** 10 injured, 2 of them seriously

3 (*complément d'adjectif, de verbe*): **le fils dont il est si fier** the son he's so proud of; **ce dont je parle** what I'm talking about

---

doré, e [dɔʀe] *adj* golden; (*avec dorure*) gilt, gilded

dorénavant [dɔʀenavɑ̃] *adv* henceforth

dorer [dɔʀe] *vt* to gild; **(faire)** ~ (*CULIN*) to brown

dorloter [dɔʀlɔte] *vt* to pamper

dormir [dɔʀmiʀ] *vi* to sleep; (*être endormi*) to be asleep

dortoir [dɔʀtwaʀ] *nm* dormitory

dorure [dɔʀyʀ] *nf* gilding

dos [do] *nm* back; (*de livre*) spine; **"voir au** ~**"** "see over"; **de** ~ from the back

dosage [dozaʒ] *nm* mixture

dose [doz] *nf* dose; **doser** *vt* to measure out; **il faut savoir doser ses efforts** you have to be able to pace yourself

dossard [dosaʀ] *nm* number (*worn by competitor*)

dossier [dosje] *nm* (*documents*) file; (*de chaise*) back; (*PRESSE*) feature; **un** ~ **scolaire** a school report

dot [dɔt] *nf* dowry

doter [dɔte] *vt*: ~ **de** to equip with

douane [dwan] *nf* customs *pl*; **(droits de)** ~ (customs) duty; **douanier, -ière** *adj* customs *cpd* ♦ *nm* customs officer

double [dubl] *adj, adv* double ♦ *nm* (*2 fois plus*): **le** ~ **(de)** twice as much (*ou* many) (as); (*autre exemplaire*) duplicate, copy;

(*sosie*) double; (*TENNIS*) doubles *sg*; **en ~ (exemplaire)** in duplicate; **faire ~ emploi** to be redundant

double-cliquer [dublklike] *vi* (*INFORM*) to double-click

doubler [duble] *vt* (*multiplier par 2*) to double; (*vêtement*) to line; (*dépasser*) to overtake, pass; (*film*) to dub; (*acteur*) to stand in for ♦ *vi* to double

doublure [dublyʀ] *nf* lining; (*CINÉMA*) stand-in

douce [dus] *adj voir* **doux**; **douceâtre** *adj* sickly sweet; **doucement** *adv* gently; (*lentement*) slowly; **doucereux, -euse** (*péj*) *adj* sugary; **douceur** *nf* softness; (*de quelqu'un*) gentleness; (*de climat*) mildness

douche [duʃ] *nf* shower; **doucher: se doucher** *vi* to have *ou* take a shower

doudoune [dudun] *nf* padded jacket

doué, e [dwe] *adj* gifted, talented; **être ~ pour** to have a gift for

douille [duj] *nf* (*ÉLEC*) socket

douillet, te [duje, ɛt] *adj* cosy; (*péj: à la douleur*) soft

douleur [dulœʀ] *nf* pain; (*chagrin*) grief, distress; **douloureux, -euse** *adj* painful

doute [dut] *nm* doubt; **sans ~** no doubt; (*probablement*) probably; **sans aucun ~** without a doubt; **douter** *vt* to doubt; **douter de** (*sincérité de qn*) to have (one's) doubts about; (*réussite*) to be doubtful of; **se douter de qch/que** to suspect sth/that; **je m'en doutais** I suspected as much; **douteux, -euse** *adj* (*incertain*) doubtful; (*péj*) dubious-looking

Douvres [duvʀ] *n* Dover

doux, douce [du, dus] *adj* soft; (*sucré*) sweet; (*peu fort: moutarde, clément: climat*) mild; (*pas brusque*) gentle

douzaine [duzɛn] *nf* (*12*) dozen; (*environ 12*): **une ~ (de)** a dozen or so

douze [duz] *num* twelve; **douzième** *num* twelfth

doyen, ne [dwajɛ̃, jɛn] *nm/f* (*en âge*) most senior member; (*de faculté*) dean

dragée [dʀaʒe] *nf* sugared almond

draguer [dʀage] *vt* (*rivière*) to dredge; (*fam*) to try to pick up

dramatique [dʀamatik] *adj* dramatic; (*tragique*) tragic ♦ *nf* (*TV*) (television) drama

dramaturge [dʀamatyʀʒ] *nm* dramatist, playwright

drame [dʀam] *nm* drama

drap [dʀa] *nm* (*de lit*) sheet; (*tissu*) woollen fabric

drapeau, x [dʀapo] *nm* flag

drap-housse [dʀaus] *nm* fitted sheet

dresser [dʀese] *vt* (*mettre vertical, monter*) to put up, erect; (*liste*) to draw up; (*animal*) to train; **se ~** *vi* (*obstacle*) to stand; (*personne*) to draw o.s. up; **~ qn contre qn** to set sb against sb; **~ l'oreille** to prick up one's ears

drogue [dʀɔg] *nf* drug; **la ~** drugs *pl*; **drogué, e** *nm/f* drug addict; **droguer** *vt* (*victime*) to drug; **se droguer** *vi* (*aux stupéfiants*) to take drugs; (*péj: de médicaments*) to dose o.s. up; **droguerie** *nf* hardware shop; **droguiste** *nm* keeper *ou* owner of a hardware shop

droit, e [dʀwa, dʀwat] *adj* (*non courbe*) straight; (*vertical*) upright, straight; (*fig: loyal*) upright, straight(forward); (*opposé à gauche*) right, right-hand ♦ *adv* straight ♦ *nm* (*prérogative*) right; (*taxe*) duty, tax (: *d'inscription*) fee; (*JUR*): **le ~** law; **avoir le ~ de** to be allowed to; **avoir ~ à** to be entitled to; **être dans son ~** to be within one's rights; **à ~e** on the right; (*direction*) (to the) right; **~s d'auteur** royalties; **~ de l'homme** human rights; **~s d'inscription** enrolment fee; **droite** *nf* (*POL*): **la droite** the right (wing); **droitier, -ière** *nm/f* right-handed person; **droiture** *nf* uprightness, straightness

drôle [dʀol] *adj* funny; **une ~ d'idée** funny idea; **drôlement** (*fam*) *adv* (*très*) terribly, awfully

dromadaire [dʀɔmadɛʀ] *nm* dromedary

dru, e [dʀy] *adj* (*cheveux*) thick, bushy; (*pluie*) heavy

du [dy] *dét voir* **de** ♦ *prép* +*dét* = **de + le**

dû, due [dy] vb voir devoir ♦ adj (somme) owing, owed; (causé par): ~ à due to ♦ nm due

duc [dyk] nm duke; duchesse nf duchess

dûment [dymɑ̃] adv duly

dune [dyn] nf dune

Dunkerque [dœ̃kɛʀk] n Dunkirk

duo [dɥo] nm (MUS) duet

dupe [dyp] nf dupe ♦ adj: (ne pas) être ~ de (not) to be taken in by

duplex [dypleks] nm (appartement) split-level apartment, duplex

duplicata [dyplikata] nm duplicate

duquel [dykɛl] prép +pron = de +lequel

dur, e [dyʀ] adj (pierre, siège, travail, problème) hard; (voix, climat) harsh; (sévère) hard, harsh; (cruel) hard(-hearted); (porte, col) stiff; (viande) tough ♦ adv hard ♦ nm (fam: meneur) tough nut; ~ d'oreille hard of hearing

durant [dyʀɑ̃] prép (au cours de) during; (pendant) for; des mois ~ for months

durcir [dyʀsiʀ] vt, vi to harden; se ~ vi to harden

durée [dyʀe] nf length; (d'une pile etc) life; de courte ~ (séjour) short

durement [dyʀmɑ̃] adv harshly

durer [dyʀe] vi to last

dureté [dyʀte] nf hardness; harshness; stiffness; toughness

durit ® [dyʀit] nf (car radiator) hose

dus etc [dy] vb voir devoir

duvet [dyvɛ] nm down; (sac de couchage) down-filled sleeping bag

DVD sigle m (= digital versatile disc) DVD

dynamique [dinamik] adj dynamic; dynamisme nm dynamism

dynamite [dinamit] nf dynamite

dynamo [dinamo] nf dynamo

dysenterie [disɑ̃tʀi] nf dysentery

dyslexie [disleksi] nf dyslexia, word-blindness

E, e

eau, x [o] nf water; ~x nfpl (MÉD) waters; prendre l'~ to leak, let in water; tomber à l'~ (fig) to fall through; ~ courante running water; ~ de Javel bleach; ~ de toilette toilet water; ~ douce fresh water; ~ gazeuse sparkling (mineral) water; ~ minérale mineral water; ~ plate still water; ~ potable drinking water; eau-de-vie nf brandy; eau-forte nf etching

ébahi, e [ebai] adj dumbfounded

ébattre [ebatʀ]: s'~ vi to frolic

ébaucher [eboʃe] vt to sketch out, outline; s'~ vi to take shape

ébène [ebɛn] nf ebony; ébéniste nm cabinetmaker

éberlué, e [ebɛʀlye] adj astounded

éblouir [ebluiʀ] vt to dazzle

éborgner [ebɔʀɲe] vt to blind in one eye

éboueur [ebwœʀ] nm dustman (BRIT), garbageman (US)

ébouillanter [ebujɑ̃te] vt to scald; (CULIN) to blanch

éboulement [ebulmɑ̃] nm rock fall

ébouler [ebule]: s'~ vi to crumble, collapse; éboulis nmpl fallen rocks

ébouriffé, e [ebuʀife] adj tousled

ébranler [ebʀɑ̃le] vt to shake; (affaiblir) to weaken; s'~ vi (partir) to move off

ébrécher [ebʀeʃe] vt to chip

ébriété [ebʀijete] nf: en état d'~ in a state of intoxication

ébrouer [ebʀue]: s'~ vi to shake o.s.

ébruiter [ebʀɥite] vt to spread, disclose

ébullition [ebylisjɔ̃] nf boiling point

écaille [ekaj] nf (de poisson) scale; (matière) tortoiseshell; écailler vt (poisson) to scale; s'écailler vi to flake ou peel (off)

écarlate [ekaʀlat] adj scarlet

écarquiller [ekaʀkije] vt: ~ les yeux to stare wide-eyed

écart [ekaʀ] nm gap; à l'~ out of the way; à l'~ de away from; faire un ~ (voi-

ture) to swerve; **~ de conduite** misdemeanour

écarté, e [ekaʀte] *adj* (*lieu*) out-of-the-way, remote; (*ouvert*): **les jambes ~es** legs apart; **les bras ~s** arms outstretched

écarter [ekaʀte] *vt* (*séparer*) to move apart, separate; (*éloigner*) to push back, move away; (*ouvrir: bras, jambes*) to spread, open; (: *rideau*) to draw (back); (*éliminer: candidat, possibilité*) to dismiss; **s'~** *vi* to part; (*s'éloigner*) to move away; **s'~ de** to wander from

écervelé, e [esɛʀvəle] *adj* scatterbrained, featherbrained

échafaud [eʃafo] *nm* scaffold

échafaudage [eʃafodaʒ] *nm* scaffolding

échafauder [eʃafode] *vt* (*plan*) to construct

échalote [eʃalɔt] *nf* shallot

échancrure [eʃɑ̃kʀyʀ] *nf* (*de robe*) scoop neckline

échange [eʃɑ̃ʒ] *nm* exchange; **en ~ de** in exchange *ou* return for; **échanger** *vt*: **échanger qch (contre)** to exchange sth (for); **échangeur** *nm* (*AUTO*) interchange

échantillon [eʃɑ̃tijɔ̃] *nm* sample

échappement [eʃapmɑ̃] *nm* (*AUTO*) exhaust

échapper [eʃape]: **~ à** *vt* (*gardien*) to escape (from); (*punition, péril*) to escape; **s'~** *vi* to escape; **~ à qn** (*détail, sens*) to escape sb; (*objet qu'on tient*) to slip out of sb's hands; **laisser ~** (*cri etc*) to let out; **l'~ belle** to have a narrow escape

écharde [eʃaʀd] *nf* splinter (of wood)

écharpe [eʃaʀp] *nf* scarf; **avoir le bras en ~** to have one's arm in a sling

échasse [eʃas] *nf* stilt

échassier [eʃasje] *nm* wader

échauffer [eʃofe] *vt* (*moteur*) to overheat; **s'~** *vi* (*SPORT*) to warm up; (*dans la discussion*) to become heated

échéance [eʃeɑ̃s] *nf* (*d'un paiement: date*) settlement date; (*fig*) deadline; **à brève ~** in the short term; **à longue ~** in the long run

échéant [eʃeɑ̃]: **le cas ~** *adv* if the case arises

échec [eʃɛk] *nm* failure; (*ÉCHECS*): **~ e mat/au roi** checkmate/check; **~s** *nmp* (*jeu*) chess *sg*; **tenir en ~** to hold i check

échelle [eʃɛl] *nf* ladder; (*fig, d'une carte* scale

échelon [eʃ(ə)lɔ̃] *nm* (*d'échelle*) rung; (*AL MIN*) grade; **échelonner** *vt* to space out

échevelé, e [eʃəv(ə)le] *adj* tousled, di shevelled

échine [eʃin] *nf* backbone, spine

échiquier [eʃikje] *nm* chessboard

écho [eko] *nm* echo; **échographie** *n* **passer une échographie** to have a scan

échoir [eʃwaʀ] *vi* (*dette*) to fall due; (*délai* to expire; **~ à** to fall to

échouer [eʃwe] *vi* to fail; **s'~** *vi* to ru aground

échu, e [eʃy] *pp de* **échoir**

éclabousser [eklabuse] *vt* to splash

éclair [eklɛʀ] *nm* (*d'orage*) flash of ligh ning, lightning *no pl*; (*gâteau*) éclair

éclairage [eklɛʀaʒ] *nm* lighting

éclaircie [eklɛʀsi] *nf* bright interval

éclaircir [eklɛʀsiʀ] *vt* to lighten; (*fig: my tère*) to clear up; (: *point*) to clarify; **s'~** (*ciel*) to clear; **s'~ la voix** to clear one throat; **éclaircissement** *nm* (*sur u point*) clarification

éclairer [eklɛʀe] *vt* (*lieu*) to light (up (*personne: avec une lampe etc*) to light th way for; (*fig: problème*) to shed light c ♦ *vi*: **~ mal/bien** to give a poor/goo light; **s'~ à la bougie** to use candlelight

éclaireur, -euse [eklɛʀœʀ, øz] *nm* (*scout*) (boy) scout/(girl) guide ♦ *nm* (*MI* scout

éclat [ekla] *nm* (*de bombe, de verre*) frag ment; (*du soleil, d'une couleur etc*) brigh ness, brilliance; (*d'une cérémonie*) splen dour; (*scandale*): **faire un ~** to cause commotion; **~s de voix** shouts; **~ de ri** roar of laughter

éclatant, e [eklatɑ̃, ɑ̃t] *adj* brilliant

éclater [eklate] vi (pneu) to burst; (bombe) to explode; (guerre) to break out; (groupe, parti) to break up; ~ **en sanglots/de rire** to burst out sobbing/laughing

éclipser: **s'~** vi to slip away

éclore [eklɔʀ] vi (œuf) to hatch; (fleur) to open (out)

écluse [eklyz] nf lock

écœurant, e [ekœʀɑ̃, ɑ̃t] adj (gâteau etc) sickly; (fig) sickening

écœurer [ekœʀe] vt: ~ **qn** (nourriture) to make sb feel sick; (conduite, personne) to disgust sb

école [ekɔl] nf school; **aller à l'~** to go to school; ~ **maternelle/primaire** nursery/primary school; ~ **publique** state school; **écolier, -ière** nm/f schoolboy(-girl)

école maternelle

ⓘ Nursery school (l'**école maternelle**) is publicly funded in France and, though not compulsory, is attended by most children between the ages of two and six. Statutory education begins with primary school (l'**école primaire**) from the age of six to ten or eleven.

écologie [ekɔlɔʒi] nf ecology; **écologique** adj environment-friendly; **écologiste** nm/f ecologist

éconduire [ekɔ̃dɥiʀ] vt to dismiss

économe [ekɔnɔm] adj thrifty ♦ nm/f (de lycée etc) bursar (BRIT), treasurer (US)

économie [ekɔnɔmi] nf economy; (gain: d'argent, de temps etc) saving; (science) economics sg; ~**s** nfpl (pécule) savings; **économique** adj (avantageux) economical; (ÉCON) economic; **économiser** vt, vi to save; **économiseur** nm (INFORM): ~ **d'écran** screensaver

écoper [ekɔpe] vi to bale out; ~ **de 3 ans de prison** (fig: fam) to get sentenced to 3 years

écorce [ekɔʀs] nf bark; (de fruit) peel

écorcher [ekɔʀʃe] vt: **s'~ le genou/la main** to graze one's knee/one's hand;

écorchure nf graze

écossais, e [ekɔsε, εz] adj Scottish ♦ nm/f: **É~, e** Scot

Écosse [ekɔs] nf: l'~ Scotland

écosser [ekɔse] vt to shell

écoulement [ekulmɑ̃] nm (d'eau) flow

écouler [ekule] vt (objet) to sell; **s'~** vi (eau) to flow (out); (temps) to pass (by)

écourter [ekuʀte] vt to curtail, cut short

écoute [ekut] nf (RADIO, TV): **temps/heure d'~** listening (ou viewing) time/hour; **rester à l'~ (de)** to stay tuned in (to); ~**s téléphoniques** phone tapping sg

écouter [ekute] vt to listen to; **écouteur** nm (TÉL) receiver; (RADIO) headphones pl, headset

écoutille [ekutij] nf hatch

écran [ekʀɑ̃] nm screen; **petit ~** television; ~ **total** sunblock

écrasant, e [ekʀazɑ̃, ɑ̃t] adj overwhelming

écraser [ekʀaze] vt to crush; (piéton) to run over; **s'~** vi to crash; **s'~ contre** to crash into

écrémé, e [ekʀeme] adj (lait) skimmed

écrevisse [ekʀəvis] nf crayfish inv

écrier [ekʀije]: **s'~** vi to exclaim

écrin [ekʀɛ̃] nm case, box

écrire [ekʀiʀ] vt to write; **s'~** to write to each other; **ça s'écrit comment?** how is it spelt?; **écrit** nm (examen) written paper; **par écrit** in writing

écriteau, x [ekʀito] nm notice, sign

écriture [ekʀityʀ] nf writing; l'**É~, les É~s** the Scriptures

écrivain [ekʀivɛ̃] nm writer

écrou [ekʀu] nm nut

écrouer [ekʀue] vt to imprison

écrouler [ekʀule]: **s'~** vi to collapse

écru, e [ekʀy] adj (couleur) off-white, écru

ECU [eky] sigle m ECU

écueil [ekœj] nm reef; (fig) pitfall

éculé, e [ekyle] adj (chaussure) down-at-heel; (fig: péj) hackneyed

écume [ekym] nf foam; **écumer** vt (CULIN) to skim; **écumoire** nf skimmer

écureuil [ekyRœj] *nm* squirrel

écurie [ekyRi] *nf* stable

écusson [ekysɔ̃] *nm* badge

écuyer, -ère [ekɥije, jɛR] *nm/f* rider

eczéma [ɛgzema] *nm* eczema

édenté, e [edɑ̃te] *adj* toothless

EDF *sigle f* (= *Électricité de France*) national electricity company

édifice [edifis] *nm* edifice, building

édifier [edifje] *vt* to build, erect; (*fig*) to edify

Édimbourg [edɛ̃buR] *n* Edinburgh

éditer [edite] *vt* (*publier*) to publish; (*annoter*) to edit; **éditeur, -trice** *nm/f* publisher; **édition** *nf* edition; (*industrie du livre*) publishing

édredon [edRədɔ̃] *nm* eiderdown

éducateur, -trice [edykatœR, tRis] *nm/f* teacher; (*in special school*) instructor

éducatif, -ive [edykatif, iv] *adj* educational

éducation [edykasjɔ̃] *nf* education; (*familiale*) upbringing; (*manières*) (good) manners *pl*; **~ physique** physical education

édulcorant [edylkɔRɑ̃] *nm* sweetener

éduquer [edyke] *vt* to educate; (*élever*) to bring up

effacé, e [efase] *adj* unassuming

effacer [efase] *vt* to erase, rub out; **s'~** *vi* (*inscription etc*) to wear off; (*pour laisser passer*) to step aside

effarant, e [efaRɑ̃, ɑ̃t] *adj* alarming

effarer [efaRe] *vt* to alarm

effaroucher [efaRuʃe] *vt* to frighten *ou* scare away

effectif, -ive [efɛktif, iv] *adj* real ♦ *nm* (SCOL) (pupil) numbers *pl*; (*entreprise*) staff, workforce; **effectivement** *adv* (*réellement*) actually, really; (*en effet*) indeed

effectuer [efɛktɥe] *vt* (*opération*) to carry out; (*trajet*) to make

efféminé, e [efemine] *adj* effeminate

effervescent, e [efɛRvesɑ̃, ɑ̃t] *adj* effervescent

effet [efɛ] *nm* effect; (*impression*) impression; **~s** *nmpl* (*vêtements etc*) things; **faire**

~ (*médicament*) to take effect; **faire bon/ mauvais ~ sur qn** to make a good/bad impression on sb; **en ~** indeed; **~ de serre** greenhouse effect

efficace [efikas] *adj* (*personne*) efficient; (*action, médicament*) effective; **efficacité** *nf* efficiency; effectiveness

effilocher [efilɔʃe]: **s'~** *vi* to fray

efflanqué, e [eflɑ̃ke] *adj* emaciated

effleurer [eflœRe] *vt* to brush (against); (*sujet*) to touch upon; (*suj: idée, pensée*) **ça ne m'a pas effleuré** it didn't cross my mind

effluves [eflyv] *nmpl* exhalation(s)

effondrer [efɔ̃dRe]: **s'~** *vi* to collapse

efforcer [efɔRse]: **s'~ de** *vt*: **s'~ de faire** to try hard to do

effort [efɔR] *nm* effort

effraction [efRaksjɔ̃] *nf*: **s'introduire par ~ dans** to break into

effrayant, e [efRejɑ̃, ɑ̃t] *adj* frightening

effrayer [efReje] *vt* to frighten, scare

effréné, e [efRene] *adj* wild

effriter [efRite]: **s'~** *vi* to crumble

effroi [efRwa] *nm* terror, dread *no pl*

effronté, e [efRɔ̃te] *adj* cheeky

effroyable [efRwajabl] *adj* horrifying, appalling

effusion [efyzjɔ̃] *nf* effusion; **sans ~ de sang** without bloodshed

égal, e, -aux [egal, o] *adj* equal; (*constant: vitesse*) steady ♦ *nm/f* equal; **être ~ à** (*prix, nombre*) to be equal to; **ça lui est ~** it's all the same to him, he doesn't mind; **sans ~** matchless, unequalled; **d'~ à ~** as equals; **également** *adv* equally; (*aussi*) too, as well; **égaler** *vt* to equal; **égaliser** *vt* (*sol, salaires*) to level (out); (*chances*) to equalize ♦ *vi* (SPORT) to equalize; **égalité** *nf* equality; **être à égalité** to be level

égard [egaR] *nm*: **~s** consideration *sg*; **à cet ~** in this respect; **par ~ pour** out of consideration for; **à l'~ de** towards

égarement [egaRmɑ̃] *nm* distraction

égarer [egaRe] *vt* to mislay; **s'~** *vi* to get

lost, lose one's way; (*objet*) to go astray

égayer [egeje] *vt* to cheer up; (*pièce*) to brighten up

églantine [eglɑ̃tin] *nf* wild *ou* dog rose

églefin [egləfɛ̃] *nm* haddock

église [egliz] *nf* church; **aller à l'~** to go to church

égoïsme [egɔism] *nm* selfishness; **égoïste** *adj* selfish

égorger [egɔʀʒe] *vt* to cut the throat of

égosiller [egozije]: **s'~** *vi* to shout o.s. hoarse˙

égout [egu] *nm* sewer

égoutter [egute] *vi* to drip; **s'~** *vi* to drip; **égouttoir** *nm* draining board; (*mobile*) draining rack

égratigner [egratiɲe] *vt* to scratch; **égratignure** *nf* scratch

Égypte [eʒipt] *nf*: **l'~** Egypt; **égyptien, ne** *adj* ·Egyptian ♦ *nm/f*: **Égyptien, ne** Egyptian

eh [e] *excl* hey!; **~ bien** well

éhonté, e [eɔ̃te] *adj* shameless, brazen

éjecter [eʒɛkte] *vt* (*TECH*) to eject; (*fam*) to kick *ou* chuck out

élaborer [elabɔʀe] *vt* to elaborate; (*projet, stratégie*) to work out; (*rapport*) to draft

élan [elɑ̃] *nm* (*ZOOL*) elk, moose; (*SPORT*) run up; (*fig: de tendresse etc*) surge; **prendre de l'~** to gather speed

élancé, e [elɑ̃se] *adj* slender

élancement [elɑ̃smɑ̃] *nm* shooting pain

élancer [elɑ̃se]: **s'~** *vi* to dash, hurl o.s.

élargir [elaʀʒiʀ] *vt* to widen; **s'~** *vi* to widen; (*vêtement*) to stretch

élastique [elastik] *adj* elastic ♦ *nm* (*de bureau*) rubber band; (*pour la couture*) elastic *no pl*

électeur, -trice [elɛktœʀ, tʀis] *nm/f* elector, voter

élection [elɛksjɔ̃] *nf* election

électorat [elɛktɔʀa] *nm* electorate

électricien, ne [elɛktʀisjẽ, jɛn] *nm/f* electrician

électricité [elɛktʀisite] *nf* electricity; **.allumer/éteindre l'~** to put on/off the light

électrique [elɛktʀik] *adj* electric(al)

électrocuter [elɛktʀɔkyte] *vt* to electrocute

électroménager [elɛktʀomenaʒe] *adj, nm*: **appareils ~s, l'~** domestic (electrical) appliances

électronique [elɛktʀɔnik] *adj* electronic ♦ *nf* electronics *sg*

électrophone [elɛktʀɔfɔn] *nm* record player

élégance [elegɑ̃s] *nf* elegance

élégant, e [elegɑ̃, ɑ̃t] *adj* elegant

élément [elemɑ̃] *nm* element; (*pièce*) component, part; **~s de cuisine** kitchen units; **élémentaire** *adj* elementary

éléphant [elefɑ̃] *nm* elephant

élevage [el(ə)vaʒ] *nm* breeding; (*de bovins*) cattle rearing; **truite d'~** farmed trout

élévation [elevasjɔ̃] *nf* (*hausse*) rise

élevé, e [el(ə)ve] *adj* high; **bien/mal ~** well-/ill-mannered

élève [elɛv] *nm/f* pupil

élever [el(ə)ve] *vt* (*enfant*) to bring up, raise; (*animaux*) to breed; (*hausser: taux, niveau*) to raise; (*édifier: monument*) to put up, erect; **s'~** *vi* (*avion*) to go up; (*niveau, température*) to rise; **s'~ à** (*suj: frais, dégâts*) to amount to, add up to; **s'~ contre qch** to rise up against sth; **~ la voix** to raise one's voice; **éleveur, -euse** *nm/f* breeder

élimé, e [elime] *adj* threadbare

éliminatoire [eliminatwaʀ] *nf* (*SPORT*) heat

éliminer [elimine] *vt* to eliminate

élire [eliʀ] *vt* to elect

elle [el] *pron* (*sujet*) she; (*: chose*) it; (*complément*) her; it; **~s** (*sujet*) they; (*complément*) them; **~-même** herself; itself; **~s-mêmes** themselves; *voir aussi* **il**

élocution [elɔkysjɔ̃] *nf* delivery; **défaut d'~** speech impediment

éloge [elɔʒ] *nm* (*gén no pl*) praise; **faire l'~ de** to praise; **élogieux, -euse** *adj* laudatory, full of praise

éloigné, e [elwaɲe] *adj* distant, far-off;

(*parent*) distant; **éloignement** *nm* (*distance, aussi fig*) distance

éloigner [elwaɲe] *vt* (*échéance*) to put off, postpone; (*soupçons, danger*) to ward off; (*objet*): **~ qch (de)** to move *ou* take sth away (from); (*personne*): **~ qn (de)** to take sb away *ou* remove sb (from); **s'~ (de)** (*personne*) to go away (from); (*véhicule*) to move away (from); (*affectivement*) to become estranged (from); **ne vous éloignez pas!** don't go too far away!

élu, e [ely] *pp de* **élire ♦** *nm/f* (POL) elected representative

éluder [elyde] *vt* to evade

Élysée [elize] *nm*: (**le palais de**) **l'~** the Élysee Palace (*the French president's residence*)

émacié, e [emasje] *adj* emaciated

émail, -aux [emaj, o] *nm* enamel

émaillé, e [emaje] *adj* (*fig*): **~ de** dotted with

émanciper [emãsipe]: **s'~** *vi* (*fig*) to become emancipated *ou* liberated

émaner [emane]: **~ de** *vt* to come from

emballage [ãbalaʒ] *nm* (*papier*) wrapping; (*boîte*) packaging

emballer [ãbale] *vt* to wrap (up); (*dans un carton*) to pack (up); (*fig: fam*) to thrill (to bits); **s'~** *vi* (*moteur*) to race; (*cheval*) to bolt; (*fig: personne*) to get carried away

embarcadère [ãbaʀkadɛʀ] *nm* wharf, pier

embarcation [ãbaʀkasjɔ̃] *nf* (small) boat, (small) craft *inv*

embardée [ãbaʀde] *nf*: **faire une ~** to swerve

embarquement [ãbaʀkəmã] *nm* (*de passagers*) boarding; (*de marchandises*) loading

embarquer [ãbaʀke] *vt* (*personne*) to embark; (*marchandise*) to load; (*fam*) to cart off **♦** *vi* (*passager*) to board; **s'~** *vi* to board; **s'~ dans** (*affaire, aventure*) to embark upon

embarras [ãbaʀa] *nm* (*gêne*) embarrassment; **mettre qn dans l'~** to put sb in

an awkward position; **vous n'avez que l'~ du choix** the only problem is choosing

embarrassant, e [ãbaʀasã, ãt] *adj* embarrassing

embarrasser [ãbaʀase] *vt* (*encombrer*) to clutter (up); (*gêner*) to hinder, hamper; **~ qn** to put sb in an awkward position; **s'~ de** to burden o.s. with

embauche [ãboʃ] *nf* hiring; **embaucher** *vt* to take on, hire

embaumer [ãbome] *vt*: **~ la lavande** *etc* to be fragrant with (the scent of) lavender *etc*

embellie [ãbeli] *nf* brighter period

embellir [ãbelir] *vt* to make more attractive; (*une histoire*) to embellish **♦** *vi* to grow lovelier *ou* more attractive

embêtements [ãbetmã] *nmpl* trouble *sg*

embêter [ãbete] *vt* to bother; **s'~** *vi* (*s'ennuyer*) to be bored

emblée [ãble]: **d'~** *adv* straightaway

embobiner [ãbɔbine] *vt* (*fam*) to get round

emboîter [ãbwate] *vt* to fit together; **s'~ (dans)** to fit (into); **~ le pas à qn** to follow in sb's footsteps

embonpoint [ãbɔ̃pwɛ̃] *nm* stoutness

embouchure [ãbuʃyʀ] *nf* (GÉO) mouth

embourber [ãbuʀbe]: **s'~** *vi* to get stuck in the mud

embourgeoiser [ãbuʀʒwaze]: **s'~** *vi* to become middle-class

embouteillage [ãbutejaʒ] *nm* traffic jam

emboutir [ãbutir] *vt* (*heurter*) to crash into, ram

embranchement [ãbʀãʃmã] *nm* (*routier*) junction

embraser [ãbʀaze]: **s'~** *vi* to flare up

embrassades [ãbʀasad] *nfpl* hugging and kissing

embrasser [ãbʀase] *vt* to kiss; (*sujet, période*) to embrace, encompass; **s'~** to kiss (each other)

embrasure [ãbʀazyʀ] *nf*: **dans l'~ de la porte** in the door(way)

embrayage [ãbʀɛjaʒ] *nm* clutch

embrayer [ãbʀeje] *vi (AUTO)* to let in the clutch

embrocher [ãbʀɔʃe] *vt* to put on a spit

embrouiller [ãbʀuje] *vt* to muddle up; *(fils)* to tangle (up); **s'~** *vi (personne)* to get in a muddle

embruns [ãbʀœ̃] *nmpl* sea spray *sg*

embryon [ãbʀijɔ̃] *nm* embryo

embûches [ãbyʃ] *nfpl* pitfalls, traps

embué, e [ãbɥe] *adj* misted up

embuscade [ãbyskad] *nf* ambush

éméché, e [emeʃe] *adj* tipsy, merry

émeraude [em(ə)ʀod] *nf* emerald

émerger [emɛʀʒe] *vi* to emerge; *(faire saillie, aussi fig)* to stand out

émeri [em(ə)ʀi] *nm*: **toile** *ou* **papier ~** emery paper

émerveillement [emɛʀvejmã] *nm* wonder

émerveiller [emɛʀveje] *vt* to fill with wonder; **s'~ de** to marvel at

émettre [emɛtʀ] *vt (son, lumière)* to give out, emit; (*message etc: RADIO*) to transmit; *(billet, timbre, emprunt)* to issue; *(hypothèse, avis)* to voice, put forward ♦ *vi* to broadcast

émeus *etc* [emø] *vb voir* **émouvoir**

émeute [emøt] *nf* riot

émietter [emjete] *vt* to crumble

émigrer [emigʀe] *vi* to emigrate

émincer [emɛ̃se] *vt* to cut into thin slices

éminent, e [eminã, ãt] *adj* distinguished

émission [emisjɔ̃] *nf (RADIO, TV)* programme, broadcast; *(d'un message)* transmission; *(de timbre)* issue

emmagasiner [ãmagazine] *vt (amasser)* to store up

emmanchure [ãmãʃyʀ] *nf* armhole

emmêler [ãmele] *vt* to tangle (up); *(fig)* to muddle up; **s'~** *vi* to get in a tangle

emménager [ãmenaʒe] *vi* to move in; **~ dans** to move into

emmener [ãm(ə)ne] *vt* to take (with one); *(comme otage, capture)* to take away; **~ qn au cinéma** to take sb to the cinema

emmerder [ãmɛʀde] *(fam!) vt* to bug, bother; **s'~** *vi* to be bored stiff

emmitoufler [ãmitufle]: **s'~** *vi* to wrap up (warmly)

émoi [emwa] *nm* commotion

émotif, -ive [emɔtif, iv] *adj* emotional

émotion [emosjɔ̃] *nf* emotion

émousser [emuse] *vt* to blunt; *(fig)* to dull

émouvoir [emuvwaʀ] *vt* to move; **s'~** *vi* to be moved; *(s'indigner)* to be roused

empailler [ãpaje] *vt* to stuff

empaqueter [ãpakte] *vt* to parcel up

emparer [ãpaʀe]: **s'~ de** *vt (objet)* to seize, grab; *(comme otage, MIL)* to seize; *(suj: peur etc)* to take hold of

empâter [ãpate]: **s'~** *vi* to thicken out

empêchement [ãpɛʃmã] *nm* (unexpected) obstacle, hitch

empêcher [ãpeʃe] *vt* to prevent; **~ qn de faire** to prevent *ou* stop sb (from) doing; **il n'empêche que** nevertheless; **il n'a pas pu s'~ de rire** he couldn't help laughing

empereur [ãpʀœʀ] *nm* emperor

empester [ãpeste] *vi* to stink, reek

empêtrer [ãpetʀe] *vt*: **s'~ dans** *(fils etc)* to get tangled up in

emphase [ãfaz] *nf* pomposity, bombast

empiéter [ãpjete] *vi*: **~ sur** to encroach upon

empiffrer [ãpifʀe]: **s'~** *(fam) vi* to stuff o.s.

empiler [ãpile] *vt* to pile (up)

empire [ãpiʀ] *nm* empire; *(fig)* influence

empirer [ãpiʀe] *vi* to worsen, deteriorate

emplacement [ãplasmã] *nm* site

emplettes [ãplet] *nfpl* shopping *sg*

emplir [ãpliʀ] *vt* to fill; **s'~ (de)** to fill (with)

emploi [ãplwa] *nm* use; *(COMM, ÉCON)* employment; *(poste)* job, situation; **mode d'~** directions for use; **~ du temps** timetable, schedule

employé, e [ãplwaje] *nm/f* employee; **~ de bureau** office employee *ou* clerk

employer [ãplwaje] *vt* to use; (*ouvrier, main-d'œuvre*) to employ; **s'~ à faire** to apply *ou* devote o.s. to doing; **employeur, -euse** *nm/f* employer
empocher [ãpɔʃe] *vt* to pocket
empoigner [ãpwaɲe] *vt* to grab
empoisonner [ãpwazɔne] *vt* to poison; (*empester: air, pièce*) to stink out; (*fam*): ~ **qn** to drive sb mad
emporté, e [ãpɔrte] *adj* quick-tempered
emporter [ãpɔrte] *vt* to take (with one); (*en dérobant ou enlevant, emmener: blessés, voyageurs*) to take away; (*entraîner*) to carry away; **s'~** *vi* (*de colère*) to lose one's temper; **l'~ (sur)** to get the upper hand (of); **plats à ~** take-away meals
empreint, e [ãprɛ̃, ɛ̃t] *adj*: ~ **de** (*regret, jalousie*) marked with; **empreinte** *nf*: **empreinte (de pas)** footprint; **empreinte (digitale)** fingerprint
empressé, e [ãprese] *adj* attentive
empressement [ãpresmã] *nm* (*hâte*) eagerness
empresser [ãprese]: **s'~** *vi*: **s'~ auprès de qn** to surround sb with attentions; **s'~ de faire** (*se hâter*) to hasten to do
emprise [ãpriz] *nf* hold, ascendancy
emprisonnement [ãprizɔnmã] *nm* imprisonment
emprisonner [ãprizɔne] *vt* to imprison
emprunt [ãprœ̃] *nm* loan
emprunté, e [ãprœ̃te] *adj* (*fig*) ill-at-ease, awkward
emprunter [ãprœ̃te] *vt* to borrow; (*itinéraire*) to take, follow
·ému, e [emy] *pp de* **émouvoir** ♦ *adj* (*gratitude*) touched; (*compassion*) moved

---
MOT-CLÉ

en [ã] *prép* **1** (*endroit, pays*) in; (*direction*) to; **habiter en France/ville** to live in France/town; **aller en France/ville** to go to France/town
2 (*moment, temps*) in; **en été/juin** in summer/June
3 (*moyen*) by; **en avion/taxi** by plane/taxi

4 (*composition*) made of; **c'est en verre** it's (made of) glass; **un collier en argent** a silver necklace
5 (*description, état*): **une femme (habillée) en rouge** a woman (dressed) in red; **peindre qch en rouge** to paint sth red; **en T/étoile** T/star-shaped; **en chemise/chaussettes** in one's shirt-sleeves/socks; **en soldat** as a soldier; **cassé en plusieurs morceaux** broken into several pieces; **en réparation** being repaired, under repair; **en vacances** on holiday; **en deuil** in mourning; **le même en plus grand** the same but *ou* only bigger
6 (*avec gérondif*) while, on, by; **en dormant** while sleeping, as one sleeps; **en sortant** on going out, as he *etc* went out; **sortir en courant** to run out
♦ *pron* **1** (*indéfini*): **j'en ai/veux** I have/want some; **en as-tu?** have you got any?; **je n'en veux pas** I don't want any; **j'en ai 2** I've got 2; **combien y en a-t-il?** how many (of them) are there?; **j'en ai assez** I've got enough (of it *ou* them); (*j'en ai marre*) I've had enough
2 (*provenance*) from there; **j'en viens** I've come from there
3 (*cause*): **il en est malade/perd le sommeil** he is ill/can't sleep because of it
4 (*complément de nom, d'adjectif, de verbe*): **j'en connais les dangers** I know its *ou* the dangers; **j'en suis fier/ai besoin** I am proud of it/need it

ENA *sigle f* (= *École Nationale d'Administration*) *one of the Grandes Écoles*
encadrement [ãkadrəmã] *nm* (*cadres*) managerial staff
encadrer [ãkadre] *vt* (*tableau, image*) to frame; (*fig: entourer*) to surround; (*personnel, soldats etc*) to train
encaissé, e [ãkese] *adj* (*vallée*) steep-sided; (*rivière*) with steep banks
encaisser [ãkese] *vt* (*chèque*) to cash; (*argent*) to collect; (*fam: coup, défaite*) to take
encart [ãkar] *nm* insert

en-cas [ɑ̃kɑ] *nm* snack
encastré, e [ɑ̃kastʀe] *adj*: **four ~** built-in oven
enceinte [ɑ̃sɛ̃t] *adj f*: **~ (de 6 mois)** (6 months) pregnant ♦ *nf* (*mur*) wall; (*espace*) enclosure; (*aussi*: **~ acoustique**) (loud)speaker
encens [ɑ̃sɑ̃] *nm* incense
encercler [ɑ̃sɛʀkle] *vt* to surround
enchaîner [ɑ̃ʃene] *vt* to chain up; (*mouvements, séquences*) to link (together) ♦ *vi* to carry on
enchanté, e [ɑ̃ʃɑ̃te] *adj* (*ravi*) delighted; (*magique*) enchanted; **~ (de faire votre connaissance)** pleased to meet you
enchantement [ɑ̃ʃɑ̃tmɑ̃] *nm* delight; (*magie*) enchantment
enchère [ɑ̃ʃɛʀ] *nf* bid; **mettre/vendre aux ~s** to put up for (sale by)/sell by auction
enchevêtrer [ɑ̃ʃ(ə)vetʀe]: **s'~** *vi* to get in a tangle
enclencher [ɑ̃klɑ̃ʃe] *vt* (*mécanisme*) to engage; **s'~** *vi* to engage
enclin, e [ɑ̃klɛ̃, in] *adj*: **~ à** inclined *ou* prone to
enclos [ɑ̃klo] *nm* enclosure
enclume [ɑ̃klym] *nf* anvil
encoche [ɑ̃kɔʃ] *nf* notch
encoignure [ɑ̃kɔɲyʀ] *nf* corner
encolure [ɑ̃kɔlyʀ] *nf* (*cou*) neck
encombrant, e [ɑ̃kɔ̃bʀɑ̃, ɑ̃t] *adj* cumbersome, bulky
encombre [ɑ̃kɔ̃bʀ]: **sans ~** *adv* without mishap *ou* incident; **encombrement** *nm*: **être pris dans un encombrement** to be stuck in a traffic jam
encombrer [ɑ̃kɔ̃bʀe] *vt* to clutter (up); (*gêner*) to hamper; **s'~ de** (*bagages etc*) to load *ou* burden o.s. with
encontre [ɑ̃kɔ̃tʀ]: **à l'~ de** *prép* against, counter to

MOT-CLÉ
---

encore [ɑ̃kɔʀ] *adv* **1** (*continuation*) still; **il y travaille encore** he's still working on it;

pas encore not yet
2 (*de nouveau*) again; **j'irai encore demain** I'll go again tomorrow; **encore une fois** (once) again; **encore deux jours** two more days
3 (*intensif*) even, still; **encore plus fort/mieux** even louder/better, louder/better still
4 (*restriction*) even so *ou* then, only; **encore pourrais-je le faire si ...** even so, I might be able to do it if ...; **si encore** if only **encore que** *conj* although

---

encouragement [ɑ̃kuʀaʒmɑ̃] *nm* encouragement
encourager [ɑ̃kuʀaʒe] *vt* to encourage
encourir [ɑ̃kuʀiʀ] *vt* to incur
encrasser [ɑ̃kʀase] *vt* to make filthy
encre [ɑ̃kʀ] *nf* ink; **encrier** *nm* inkwell
encroûter [ɑ̃kʀute]: **s'~** (*fam*) *vi* (*fig*) to get into a rut, get set in one's ways
encyclopédie [ɑ̃siklɔpedi] *nf* encyclopaedia
endetter [ɑ̃dete]: **s'~** *vi* to get into debt
endiablé, e [ɑ̃djable] *adj* (*danse*) furious
endimanché, e [ɑ̃dimɑ̃ʃe] *adj* in one's Sunday best
endive [ɑ̃div] *nf* chicory *no pl*
endoctriner [ɑ̃dɔktʀine] *vt* to indoctrinate
endommager [ɑ̃dɔmaʒe] *vt* to damage
endormi, e [ɑ̃dɔʀmi] *adj* asleep
endormir [ɑ̃dɔʀmiʀ] *vt* to put to sleep; (*suj: chaleur etc*) to send to sleep; (*MÉD: dent, nerf*) to anaesthetize; (*fig: soupçons*) to allay; **s'~** *vi* to fall asleep, go to sleep
endosser [ɑ̃dose] *vt* (*responsabilité*) to take, shoulder; (*chèque*) to endorse; (*uniforme, tenue*) to put on, don
endroit [ɑ̃dʀwa] *nm* place; (*opposé à l'envers*) right side; **à l'~** (*vêtement*) the right way out; (*objet posé*) the right way round
enduire [ɑ̃dɥiʀ] *vt* to coat
enduit [ɑ̃dɥi] *nm* coating
endurance [ɑ̃dyʀɑ̃s] *nf* endurance
endurant, e [ɑ̃dyʀɑ̃, ɑ̃t] *adj* tough, hardy

endurcir [ɑ̃dyʀsiʀ]: **s'~** *vi* (*physiquement*) to become tougher; (*moralement*) to become hardened

endurer [ɑ̃dyʀe] *vt* to endure, bear

énergétique [enɛʀʒetik] *adj* (*aliment*) energy-giving

énergie [enɛʀʒi] *nf* (*PHYSIQUE*) energy; (*TECH*) power; (*morale*) vigour, spirit; **énergique** *adj* energetic, vigorous; (*mesures*) drastic, stringent

énervant, e [enɛʀvɑ̃, ɑ̃t] *adj* irritating, annoying

énerver [enɛʀve] *vt* to irritate, annoy; **s'~** *vi* to get excited, get worked up

enfance [ɑ̃fɑ̃s] *nf* childhood

enfant [ɑ̃fɑ̃] *nm/f* child; ~ **de chœur** *nm* (*REL*) altar boy; **enfantillage** (*péj*) *nm* childish behaviour *no pl*; **enfantin, e** *adj* (*puéril*) childlike; (*langage, jeu etc*) children's *cpd*

enfer [ɑ̃fɛʀ] *nm* hell

enfermer [ɑ̃fɛʀme] *vt* to shut up; (*à clef, interner*) to lock up

enfiévré, e [ɑ̃fjevʀe] *adj* feverish

enfiler [ɑ̃file] *vt* (*vêtement*) to slip on, slip into; (*perles*) to string; (*aiguille*) to thread

enfin [ɑ̃fɛ̃] *adv* at last; (*en énumérant*) lastly; (*toutefois*) still; (*pour conclure*) in a word; (*somme toute*) after all

enflammer [ɑ̃flame]: **s'~** *vi* to catch fire; (*MÉD*) to become inflamed

enflé, e [ɑ̃fle] *adj* swollen

enfler [ɑ̃fle] *vi* to swell (up)

enfoncer [ɑ̃fɔ̃se] *vt* (*clou*) to drive in; (*faire pénétrer*): ~ **qch dans** to push (*ou* drive) sth into; (*forcer: porte*) to break open; **s'~** *vi* to sink; **s'~ dans** to sink into; (*forêt, ville*) to disappear into

enfouir [ɑ̃fwiʀ] *vt* (*dans le sol*) to bury; (*dans un tiroir etc*) to tuck away

enfourcher [ɑ̃fuʀʃe] *vt* to mount

enfreindre [ɑ̃fʀɛ̃dʀ] *vt* to infringe, break

enfuir [ɑ̃fɥiʀ]: **s'~** *vi* to run away *ou* off

enfumer [ɑ̃fyme] *vt* (*pièce*) to fill with smoke

engageant, e [ɑ̃gaʒɑ̃, ɑ̃t] *adj* attractive, appealing

engagement [ɑ̃gaʒmɑ̃] *nm* commitment

engager [ɑ̃gaʒe] *vt* (*embaucher*) to take on; (: *artiste*) to engage; (*commencer*) to start; (*lier*) to bind, commit; (*impliquer*) to involve; (*investir*) to invest, lay out; (*inciter*) to urge; (*introduire: clé*) to insert; **s'~** *vi* (*promettre*) to commit o.s.; (*MIL*) to enlist; (*débuter: conversation etc*) to start (up); **s'~ à faire** to undertake to do; **s'~ dans** (*rue, passage*) to turn into; (*fig: affaire, discussion*) to enter into, embark on

engelures [ɑ̃ʒlyʀ] *nfpl* chilblains

engendrer [ɑ̃ʒɑ̃dʀe] *vt* to breed, create

engin [ɑ̃ʒɛ̃] *nm* machine; (*outil*) instrument; (*AUT*) vehicle; (*AVIAT*) aircraft *inv*

englober [ɑ̃glɔbe] *vt* to include

engloutir [ɑ̃glutiʀ] *vt* to swallow up

engoncé, e [ɑ̃gɔ̃se] *adj*: ~ **dans** cramped in

engorger [ɑ̃gɔʀʒe] *vt* to obstruct, block

engouement [ɑ̃gumɑ̃] *nm* (sudden) passion

engouffrer [ɑ̃gufʀe] *vt* to swallow up, devour; **s'~ dans** to rush into

engourdir [ɑ̃guʀdiʀ] *vt* to numb; (*fig*) to dull, blunt; **s'~** *vi* to go numb

engrais [ɑ̃gʀɛ] *nm* manure; ~ **(chimique)** (chemical) fertilizer

engraisser [ɑ̃gʀese] *vt* to fatten (up)

engrenage [ɑ̃gʀənaʒ] *nm* gears *pl*, gearing; (*fig*) chain

engueuler [ɑ̃gœle] (*fam*) *vt* to bawl at

enhardir [ɑ̃aʀdiʀ]: **s'~** *vi* to grow bolder

énigme [enigm] *nf* riddle

enivrer [ɑ̃nivʀe] *vt*: **s'~** to get drunk

enjambée [ɑ̃ʒɑ̃be] *nf* stride

enjamber [ɑ̃ʒɑ̃be] *vt* to stride over

enjeu, x [ɑ̃ʒø] *nm* stakes *pl*

enjôler [ɑ̃ʒole] *vt* to coax, wheedle

enjoliver [ɑ̃ʒɔlive] *vt* to embellish; **enjoliveur** *nm* (*AUTO*) hub cap

enjoué, e [ɑ̃ʒwe] *adj* playful

enlacer [ɑ̃lase] *vt* (*étreindre*) to embrace, hug

enlaidir [ɑ̃lediʀ] *vt* to make ugly ♦ *vi* to

become ugly

enlèvement [ɑ̃lɛvmɑ̃] *nm* (*rapt*) abduction, kidnapping

enlever [ɑ̃l(ə)ve] *vt* (*ôter*: *gén*) to remove; (: *vêtement, lunettes*) to take off; (*emporter*: *ordures etc*) to take away; (*kidnapper*) to abduct, kidnap; (*obtenir*: *prix, contrat*) to win; (*prendre*): **~ qch à qn** to take sth (away) from sb

enliser [ɑ̃lize] **s'~** *vi* to sink, get stuck

enneigé, e [ɑ̃neʒe] *adj* (*route, maison*) snowed-up; (*paysage*) snowy

ennemi, e [ɛnmi] *adj* hostile; (*MIL*) enemy *cpd* ♦ *nm/f* enemy

ennui [ɑ̃nɥi] *nm* (*lassitude*) boredom; (*difficulté*) trouble *no pl*; **avoir des ~s** to have problems; **ennuyer** *vt* to bother; (*lasser*) to bore; **s'ennuyer** *vi* to be bored; **ennuyeux, -euse** *adj* boring, tedious; (*embêtant*) annoying

énoncé [enɔ̃se] *nm* (*de problème*) terms *pl*

énoncer [enɔ̃se] *vt* (*faits*) to set out, state

enorgueillir [ɑ̃nɔʀgœjiʀ] **s'~ de** *vt* to pride o.s. on

énorme [enɔʀm] *adj* enormous, huge; **énormément** *adv* enormously; **énormément de neige/gens** an enormous amount of snow/number of people; **énormité** *nf* (*propos*) outrageous remark

enquérir [ɑ̃keʀiʀ] **s'~ de** *vt* to inquire about

enquête [ɑ̃kɛt] *nf* (*de journaliste, de police*) investigation; (*judiciaire, administrative*) inquiry; (*sondage d'opinion*) survey; **enquêter** *vi* to investigate

enquiers *etc* [ɑ̃kje] *vb voir* **enquérir**

enquiquiner [ɑ̃kikine] (*fam*) *vt* to annoy, irritate, bother

enraciné [ɑ̃ʀasine] *adj* deep-rooted

enragé, e [ɑ̃ʀaʒe] *adj* (*MÉD*) rabid, with rabies; (*fig*) fanatical

enrageant, e [ɑ̃ʀaʒɑ̃, ɑ̃t] *adj* infuriating

enrager [ɑ̃ʀaʒe] *vi* to be in a rage

enrayer [ɑ̃ʀeje] *vt* to check, stop

enregistrement [ɑ̃ʀ(ə)ʒistʀəmɑ̃] *nm* recording; **~ des bagages** (*à l'aéroport*) baggage check-in

enregistrer [ɑ̃ʀ(ə)ʒistʀe] *vt* (*MUS etc*) to record; (*fig*: *mémoriser*) to make a mental note of; (*bagages*: *à l'aéroport*) to check in

enrhumer [ɑ̃ʀyme] *vt*: **s'~, être enrhumé** to catch a cold

enrichir [ɑ̃ʀiʃiʀ] *vt* to make rich(er); (*fig*) to enrich; **s'~** *vi* to get rich(er)

enrober [ɑ̃ʀɔbe] *vt*: **~ qch de** to coat sth with

enrôler [ɑ̃ʀole] *vt* to enlist; **s'~ (dans)** to enlist (in)

enrouer [ɑ̃ʀwe] **s'~** *vi* to go hoarse

enrouler [ɑ̃ʀule] *vt* (*fil, corde*) to wind (up)

ensanglanté, e [ɑ̃sɑ̃glɑ̃te] *adj* covered with blood

enseignant, e [ɑ̃sɛɲɑ̃, ɑ̃t] *nm/f* teacher

enseigne [ɑ̃sɛɲ] *nf* sign; **~ lumineuse** neon sign

enseignement [ɑ̃sɛɲ(ə)mɑ̃] *nm* teaching; (*ADMIN*) education

enseigner [ɑ̃sɛɲe] *vt, vi* to teach; **~ qch à qn** to teach sb sth

ensemble [ɑ̃sɑ̃bl] *adv* together ♦ *nm* (*groupement*) set; (*vêtements*) outfit; (*totalité*): **l'~ du/de la** the whole *ou* entire; (*unité, harmonie*) unity; **impression/idée d'~** overall *ou* general impression/idea; **dans l'~** (*en gros*) on the whole

ensemencer [ɑ̃s(ə)mɑ̃se] *vt* to sow

ensevelir [ɑ̃səv(ə)liʀ] *vt* to bury

ensoleillé, e [ɑ̃sɔleje] *adj* sunny

ensommeillé, e [ɑ̃sɔmeje] *adj* drowsy

ensorceler [ɑ̃sɔʀsəle] *vt* to enchant, bewitch

ensuite [ɑ̃sɥit] *adv* then, next; (*plus tard*) afterwards, later

ensuivre [ɑ̃sɥivʀ] **s'~** *vi* to follow, ensue; **et tout ce qui s'ensuit** and all that goes with it

entaille [ɑ̃taj] *nf* cut; (*sur un objet*) notch

entamer [ɑ̃tame] *vt* (*pain, bouteille*) to start; (*hostilités, pourparlers*) to open

entasser [ɑ̃tase] *vt* (*empiler*) to pile up, heap up; **s'~** *vi* (*s'amonceler*) to pile up; **s'~ dans** (*personnes*) to cram into

entendre [ɑ̃tɑ̃dʀ] vt to hear; (*comprendre*) to understand; (*vouloir dire*) to mean; **s'~** vi (*sympathiser*) to get on; (*se mettre d'accord*) to agree; **j'ai entendu dire que** I've heard (it said) that

entendu, e [ɑ̃tɑ̃dy] adj (*réglé*) agreed; (*au courant: air*) knowing; **(c'est) ~** all right, agreed; **bien ~** of course

entente [ɑ̃tɑ̃t] nf understanding; (*accord, traité*) agreement; **à double ~** (*sens*) with a double meaning

entériner [ɑ̃teʀine] vt to ratify, confirm

enterrement [ɑ̃tɛʀmɑ̃] nm (*cérémonie*) funeral, burial

enterrer [ɑ̃teʀe] vt to bury

entêtant, e [ɑ̃tɛtɑ̃, ɑ̃t] adj heady

entêté, e [ɑ̃tete] adj stubborn

en-tête [ɑ̃tɛt] nm heading; **papier à ~-~** headed notepaper

entêter [ɑ̃tete]: **s'~** vi: **s'~ (à faire)** to persist (in doing)

enthousiasme [ɑ̃tuzjasm] nm enthusiasm; **enthousiasmer** vt to fill with enthusiasm; **s'enthousiasmer (pour qch)** to get enthusiastic (about sth); **enthousiaste** adj enthusiastic

enticher [ɑ̃tiʃe]: **s'~ de** vt to become infatuated with

entier, -ère [ɑ̃tje, jɛʀ] adj whole; (*total: satisfaction etc*) complete; (*fig: caractère*) unbending ♦ nm (MATH) whole; **en ~** totally; **lait ~** full-cream milk; **entièrement** adv entirely, wholly

entonner [ɑ̃tɔne] vt (*chanson*) to strike up

entonnoir [ɑ̃tɔnwaʀ] nm funnel

entorse [ɑ̃tɔʀs] nf (MÉD) sprain; (*fig*): **~ au règlement** infringement of the rule

entortiller [ɑ̃tɔʀtije] vt (*enrouler*) to twist, wind; (*fam: cajoler*) to get round

entourage [ɑ̃tuʀaʒ] nm circle; (*famille*) circle of family/friends; (*ce qui enclôt*) surround

entourer [ɑ̃tuʀe] vt to surround; (*apporter son soutien à*) to rally round; **~ de** to surround with

entracte [ɑ̃tʀakt] nm interval

entraide [ɑ̃tʀɛd] nf mutual aid; **s'~r** vi to help each other

entrain [ɑ̃tʀɛ̃] nm spirit; **avec/sans ~** spiritedly/half-heartedly

entraînement [ɑ̃tʀɛnmɑ̃] nm training

entraîner [ɑ̃tʀene] vt (*charrier*) to carry ou drag along; (TECH) to drive; (*emmener: personne*) to take (off); (*influencer*) to lead; (SPORT) to train; (*impliquer*) to entail; **s'~** vi (SPORT) to train; **s'~ à qch/à faire** to train o.s. for sth/to do; **~ qn à faire** (*inciter*) to lead sb to do; **entraîneur, -euse** nm/f (SPORT) coach, trainer ♦ nm (HIPPISME) trainer

entraver [ɑ̃tʀave] vt (*action, progrès*) to hinder

entre [ɑ̃tʀ] prép between; (*parmi*) among(st); **l'un d'~ eux/nous** one of them/us; **~ eux** among(st) themselves; **entrebâillé, e** adj half-open, ajar; **entrechoquer: s'entrechoquer** vi to knock ou bang together; **entrecôte** nf entrecôte ou rib steak; **entrecouper** vt: **entrecouper qch de** to intersperse sth with; **entrecroiser: s'entrecroiser** vi to intertwine

entrée [ɑ̃tʀe] nf entrance; (*accès: au cinéma etc*) admission; (*billet*) (admission) ticket; (CULIN) first course

entre...: **entrefaites: sur ces entrefaites** adv at this juncture; **entrefilet** nm paragraph (*short article*); **entrejambes** nm crotch; **entrelacer** vt to intertwine; **entremêler: s'entremêler** vi to become entangled; **entremets** nm (cream) dessert; **entremise** nf intervention; **par l'entremise de** through

entreposer [ɑ̃tʀəpoze] vt to store, put into storage

entrepôt [ɑ̃tʀəpo] nm warehouse

entreprenant, e [ɑ̃tʀəpʀənɑ̃, ɑ̃t] adj (*actif*) enterprising; (*trop galant*) forward

entreprendre [ɑ̃tʀəpʀɑ̃dʀ] vt (*se lancer dans*) to undertake; (*commencer*) to begin ou start (upon)

entrepreneur [ɑ̃tʀəpʀənœʀ, øz] nm: **~**

(en bâtiment) (building) contractor
entreprise [ɑ̃tʀəpʀiz] *nf* (*société*) firm, concern; (*action*) undertaking, venture
entrer [ɑ̃tʀe] *vi* to go (*ou* come) in, enter ♦ *vt* (*INFORM*) to enter, input; **(faire)** ~ **qch dans** to get sth into; ~ **dans** (*gén*) to enter; (*pièce*) to enter; (*club*) to join; (*heurter*) to run into; ~ **à l'hôpital** to go into hospital; **faire** ~ (*visiteur*) to show in
entresol [ɑ̃tʀəsɔl] *nm* mezzanine
entre-temps [ɑ̃tʀətɑ̃] *adv* meanwhile
entretenir [ɑ̃tʀət(ə)niʀ] *vt* to maintain; (*famille, maîtresse*) to support, keep; ~ **qn (de)** to speak to sb (about)
entretien [ɑ̃tʀətjɛ̃] *nm* maintenance; (*discussion*) discussion, talk; (*pour un emploi*) interview
entrevoir [ɑ̃tʀəvwaʀ] *vt* (*à peine*) to make out; (*brièvement*) to catch a glimpse of
entrevue [ɑ̃tʀəvy] *nf* (*audience*) interview
entrouvert, e [ɑ̃tʀuvɛʀ, ɛʀt] *adj* half-open
énumérer [enymeʀe] *vt* to list, enumerate
envahir [ɑ̃vaiʀ] *vt* to invade; (*suj: inquiétude, peur*) to come over; **envahissant, e** (*péj*) *adj* (*personne*) interfering, intrusive
enveloppe [ɑ̃v(ə)lɔp] *nf* (*de lettre*) envelope; (*crédits*) budget; **envelopper** *vt* to wrap; (*fig*) to envelop, shroud
envenimer [ɑ̃v(ə)nime] *vt* to aggravate
envergure [ɑ̃vɛʀgyʀ] *nf* (*fig*) scope; (*personne*) calibre
enverrai *etc* [ɑ̃veʀe] *vb voir* **envoyer**
envers [ɑ̃vɛʀ] *prép* towards, to ♦ *nm* other side; (*d'une étoffe*) wrong side; **à l'**~ (*verticalement*) upside down; (*pull*) back to front; (*chaussettes*) inside out
envie [ɑ̃vi] *nf* (*sentiment*) envy; (*souhait*) desire, wish; **avoir** ~ **de (faire)** to feel like (doing); (*plus fort*) to want (to do); **avoir** ~ **que** to wish for that; **cette glace me fait** ~ I fancy some of that ice cream; **envier** *vt* to envy; **envieux, -euse** *adj* envious
environ [ɑ̃viʀɔ̃] *adv*: ~ **3 h/2 km** (around) about 3 o'clock/2 km; *voir aussi* **environs**
environnant, e [ɑ̃viʀɔnɑ̃, ɑ̃t] *adj* surrounding

environnement [ɑ̃viʀɔnmɑ̃] *nm* environment
environs [ɑ̃viʀɔ̃] *nmpl* surroundings; **aux** ~ **de** (round) about
envisager [ɑ̃vizaʒe] *vt* to contemplate, envisage; ~ **de faire** to consider doing
envoi [ɑ̃vwa] *nm* (*paquet*) parcel, consignment; **coup d'**~ (*SPORT*) kick-off
envoler [ɑ̃vɔle]: **s'**~ *vi* (*oiseau*) to fly away; (*avion*) to take off; (*papier, feuille*) to blow away; (*fig*) to vanish (into thin air)
envoûter [ɑ̃vute] *vt* to bewitch
envoyé, e [ɑ̃vwaje] *nm/f* (*POL*) envoy; (*PRESSE*) correspondent
envoyer [ɑ̃vwaje] *vt* to send; (*lancer*) to hurl, throw; ~ **chercher** to send for; ~ **promener qn** (*fam*) to send sb packing
Éole [eɔl] *sigle m* (= est-ouest-liaison-express) *Paris high-speed, east-west subway service*
épagneul [epaɲœl] *nm/f* spaniel
épais, se [epɛ, ɛs] *adj* thick; **épaisseur** *nf* thickness
épancher [epɑ̃ʃe]: **s'**~ *vi* to open one's heart
épanouir [epanwiʀ]: **s'**~ *vi* (*fleur*) to bloom, open out; (*visage*) to light up; (*personne*) to blossom
épargne [epaʀɲ] *nf* saving
épargner [epaʀɲe] *vt* to save; (*ne pas tuer ou endommager*) to spare ♦ *vi* to save; ~ **qch à qn** to spare sb sth
éparpiller [epaʀpije] *vt* to scatter; **s'**~ *vi* to scatter; (*fig*) to dissipate one's efforts
épars, e [epaʀ, aʀs] *adj* scattered
épatant, e [epatɑ̃, ɑ̃t] (*fam*) *adj* super
épater [epate] (*fam*) *vt* (*étonner*) to amaze; (*impressionner*) to impress
épaule [epol] *nf* shoulder
épauler [epole] *vt* (*aider*) to back up, support; (*arme*) to raise (to one's shoulder) ♦ *vi* to (take) aim
épaulette [epolɛt] *nf* (*MIL*) epaulette; (*rembourrage*) shoulder pad
épave [epav] *nf* wreck
épée [epe] *nf* sword
épeler [ep(ə)le] *vt* to spell

éperdu, e [epɛʀdy] *adj* distraught, over-come; (*amour*) passionate

éperon [epʀɔ̃] *nm* spur

épervier [epɛʀvje] *nm* sparrowhawk

épi [epi] *nm* (*de blé, d'orge*) ear; (*de maïs*) cob

épice [epis] *nf* spice

épicé, e [epise] *adj* spicy

épicer [epise] *vt* to spice

épicerie [episʀi] *nf* grocer's shop; (*den-rées*) groceries *pl*; **~ fine** delicatessen; **épi-cier, -ière** *nm/f* grocer

épidémie [epidemi] *nf* epidemic

épiderme [epidɛʀm] *nm* skin

épier [epje] *vt* to spy on, watch closely

épilepsie [epilɛpsi] *nf* epilepsy

épiler [epile] *vt* (*jambes*) to remove the hair from; (*sourcils*) to pluck

épilogue [epilɔg] *nm* (*fig*) conclusion, dé-nouement; **épiloguer** *vi*: **épiloguer sur** to hold forth on

épinards [epinaʀ] *nmpl* spinach *sg*

épine [epin] *nf* thorn, prickle; (*d'oursin etc*) spine; **~ dorsale** backbone; **épineux, -euse** *adj* thorny

épingle [epɛ̃gl] *nf* pin; **~ à cheveux** hair-pin; **~ de nourrice** *ou* **de sûreté** safety pin; **épingler** *vt* (*badge, décoration*): **épin-gler qch sur** to pin sth on(to); (*fam*) to catch, nick

épique [epik] *adj* epic

épisode [epizɔd] *nm* episode; **film/roman à ~s** serial; **épisodique** *adj* occasional

éploré, e [eplɔʀe] *adj* tearful

épluche-légumes [eplyʃlegym] *nm inv* (potato) peeler

éplucher [eplyʃe] *vt* (*fruit, légumes*) to peel; (*fig*) to go over with a fine-tooth comb; **épluchures** *nfpl* peelings

éponge [epɔ̃ʒ] *nf* sponge; **éponger** *vt* (*li-quide*) to mop up; (*surface*) to sponge; (*fig: déficit*) to soak up

épopée [epɔpe] *nf* epic

époque [epɔk] *nf* (*de l'histoire*) age, era; (*de l'année, la vie*) time; **d'~** (*meuble*) per-iod *cpd*

époumoner [epumɔne]: **s'~** *vi* to shout o.s. hoarse

épouse [epuz] *nf* wife; **épouser** *vt* to marry

épousseter [epuste] *vt* to dust

époustouflant, e [epustuflɑ̃, ɑ̃t] (*fam*) *adj* staggering, mind-boggling

épouvantable [epuvɑ̃tabl] *adj* appalling, dreadful

épouvantail [epuvɑ̃taj] *nm* scarecrow

épouvante [epuvɑ̃t] *nf* terror; **film d'~** horror film; **épouvanter** *vt* to terrify

époux [epu] *nm* husband ♦ *nmpl* (mar-ried) couple

éprendre [epʀɑ̃dʀ]: **s'~ de** *vt* to fall in love with

épreuve [epʀœv] *nf* (*d'examen*) test; (*mal-heur, difficulté*) trial, ordeal; (*PHOTO*) print; (*TYPO*) proof; (*SPORT*) event; **à toute ~** un-failing; **mettre à l'~** to put to the test

épris, e [epʀi, iz] *pp de* **éprendre**

éprouvant, e [epʀuvɑ̃, ɑ̃t] *adj* trying, testing

éprouver [epʀuve] *vt* (*tester*) to test; (*mar-quer, faire souffrir*) to afflict, distress; (*res-sentir*) to experience

éprouvette [epʀuvɛt] *nf* test tube

épuisé, e [epɥize] *adj* exhausted; (*livre*) out of print; **épuisement** *nm* exhaustion

épuiser [epɥize] *vt* (*fatiguer*) to exhaust, wear *ou* tire out; (*stock, sujet*) to exhaust; **s'~** *vi* to wear *ou* tire o.s. out, exhaust o.s.

épuisette [epɥizɛt] *nf* shrimping net

épurer [epyʀe] *vt* (*liquide*) to purify; (*parti etc*) to purge

équateur [ekwatœʀ] *nm* equator; (**la ré-publique de**) **l'É~** Ecuador

équation [ekwasjɔ̃] *nf* equation

équerre [ekɛʀ] *nf* (*à dessin*) (set) square

équilibre [ekilibʀ] *nm* balance; **garder/perdre l'~** to keep/lose one's balance; **être en ~** to be balanced; **équilibré, e** *adj* well-balanced; **équilibrer** *vt* to bal-ance; **s'équilibrer** *vi* (*poids*) to balance; (*fig: défauts etc*) to balance each other out

quipage [ekipaʒ] nm crew

quipe [ekip] nf team

quipé, e [ekipe] adj: **bien/mal ~** well-/poorly-equipped; **équipée** nf escapade

quipement [ekipmɑ̃] nm equipment; **~s** nmpl (installations) amenities, facilities

quiper [ekipe] vt to equip; **~ qn/qch de** to equip sb/sth with

quipier, -ière [ekipje, jɛʀ] nm/f team member

quitable [ekitabl] adj fair

quitation [ekitasjɔ̃] nf (horse-)riding; **faire de l'~** to go riding

quivalent, e [ekivalɑ̃, ɑ̃t] adj, nm equivalent

quivaloir [ekivalwaʀ]: **~ à** vt to be equivalent to

quivoque [ekivɔk] adj equivocal, ambiguous; (louche) dubious ♦ nf (incertitude) doubt

rable [eʀabl] nm maple

rafler [eʀafle] vt to scratch; **éraflure** nf scratch

raillé, e [eʀaje] adj (voix) rasping

re [eʀ] nf era; **en l'an 1050 de notre ~** in the year 1050 A.D.

rection [eʀɛksjɔ̃] nf erection

reinter [eʀɛ̃te] vt (exhauster) to exhaust, wear out; (critiquer) to pull to pieces

riger [eʀiʒe] vt (monument) to erect

rmite [eʀmit] nm hermit

roder [eʀɔde] vt to erode

rotique [eʀɔtik] adj erotic

rrer [eʀe] vi to wander

rreur [eʀœʀ] nf mistake, error; **faire ~** to be mistaken; **par ~** by mistake; **~ judiciaire** miscarriage of justice

rudit, e [eʀydi, it] adj erudite, learned

ruption [eʀypsjɔ̃] nf eruption; (MÉD) rash

s [ɛ] vb voir **être**

s [ɛs] prép: **licencié ~ lettres/sciences** ≈ Bachelor of Arts/Science

scabeau, x [ɛskabo] nm (tabouret) stool; (échelle) stepladder

scadron [ɛskadʀɔ̃] nm squadron

scalade [ɛskalad] nf climbing no pl; (POL

etc) escalation; **escalader** vt to climb

escale [ɛskal] nf (NAVIG: durée) call; (endroit) port of call; (AVIAT) stop(over); **faire ~ à** (NAVIG) to put in at; (AVIAT) to stop over at; **vol sans ~** nonstop flight

escalier [ɛskalje] nm stairs pl; **dans l'~** on the stairs; **~ roulant** escalator

escamoter [ɛskamɔte] vt (esquiver) to get round, evade; (faire disparaître) to conjure away

escapade [ɛskapad] nf: **faire une ~** to go on a jaunt; (s'enfuir) to run away ou off

escargot [ɛskaʀgo] nm snail

escarpé, e [ɛskaʀpe] adj steep

escarpin [ɛskaʀpɛ̃] nm low-fronted shoe, court shoe (BRIT)

escient [ɛsjɑ̃] nm: **à bon ~** advisedly

esclaffer [ɛsklafe]: **s'~** vi to guffaw

esclandre [ɛsklɑ̃dʀ] nm scene, fracas

esclavage [ɛsklavaʒ] nm slavery

esclave [ɛsklav] nm/f slave

escompte [ɛskɔ̃t] nm discount; **escompter** vt (fig) to expect

escorte [ɛskɔʀt] nf escort; **escorter** vt to escort

escrime [ɛskʀim] nf fencing

escrimer [ɛskʀime]: **s'~** vi: **s'~ à faire** to wear o.s. out doing

escroc [ɛskʀo] nm swindler, conman; **escroquer** [ɛskʀɔke] vt: **escroquer qch (à qn)** to swindle sth (out of sb); **escroquerie** nf swindle

espace [ɛspas] nm space

espacer vt to space out; **s'~** vi (visites etc) to become less frequent

espadon [ɛspadɔ̃] nm swordfish inv

espadrille [ɛspadʀij] nf rope-soled sandal

Espagne [ɛspaɲ] nf: **l'~** Spain; **espagnol, e** adj Spanish ♦ nm/f: **Espagnol, e** Spaniard ♦ nm (LING) Spanish

escouade [ɛskwad] nf squad

espèce [ɛspɛs] nf (BIO, BOT, ZOOL) species inv; (gén: sorte) sort, kind, type; (péj): **~ de maladroit!** you clumsy oaf!; **~s** nfpl (COMM) cash sg; **en ~** in cash

espérance [ɛspeʀɑ̃s] nf hope; **~ de vie**

life expectancy

espérer [espeʀe] *vt* to hope for; **j'espère (bien)** I hope so; **~ que/faire** to hope that/to do

espiègle [espjɛgl] *adj* mischievous

espion, ne [espjɔ̃, jɔn] *nm/f* spy; **espionnage** *nm* espionage, spying; **espionner** *vt* to spy (up)on

esplanade [esplanad] *nf* esplanade

espoir [espwaʀ] *nm* hope

esprit [espʀi] *nm* (*intellect*) mind; (*humour*) wit; (*mentalité, d'une loi etc, fantôme etc*) spirit; **faire de l'~** to try to be witty; **reprendre ses ~s** to come to; **perdre l'~** to lose one's mind

esquimau, de, x [eskimo, od] *adj* Eskimo ♦ *nm/f:* **E~, de** Eskimo ♦ *nm:* **E~** ® ice lolly (*BRIT*), popsicle (*US*)

esquinter [eskɛ̃te] (*fam*) *vt* to mess up

esquisse [eskis] *nf* sketch; **esquisser** *vt* to sketch; **esquisser un sourire** to give a vague smile

esquiver [eskive] *vt* to dodge; **s'~** *vi* to slip away

essai [ese] *nm* (*tentative*) attempt, try; (*de produit*) testing; (*RUGBY*) try; (*LITTÉRATURE*) essay; **~s** *nmpl* (*AUTO*) trials; **~ gratuit** (*COMM*) free trial; **à l'~** on a trial basis

essaim [esɛ̃] *nm* swarm

essayer [eseje] *vt* to try; (*vêtement, chaussures*) to try (on); (*méthode, voiture*) to try (out) ♦ *vi* to try; **~ de faire** to try *ou* attempt to do

essence [esɑ̃s] *nf* (*de voiture*) petrol (*BRIT*), gas(oline) (*US*); (*extrait de plante*) essence; (*espèce: d'arbre*) species *inv*

essentiel, le [esɑ̃sjɛl] *adj* essential; **c'est l'~** (*ce qui importe*) that's the main thing; **l'~ de** the main part of

essieu, x [esjø] *nm* axle

essor [esɔʀ] *nm* (*de l'économie etc*) rapid expansion

essorer [esɔʀe] *vt* (*en tordant*) to wring (out); (*par la force centrifuge*) to spin-dry; **essoreuse** *nf* spin-dryer

essouffler [esufle] **s'~** *vi* to get out of

breath

essuie-glace [esɥiglas] *nm inv* windscreen (*BRIT*) *ou* windshield (*US*) wiper

essuyer [esɥije] *vt* to wipe; (*fig: échec*) ♦ suffer; **s'~** *vi* (*après le bain*) to dry o.s.; **la vaisselle** to dry up

est¹ [ɛ] *vb voir* **être**

est² [ɛst] *nm* east ♦ *adj inv* east; (*régio* east(ern); **à l'~** in the east; (*direction*) the east, east(wards); **à l'~ de** (to th east of

estampe [ɛstɑ̃p] *nf* print, engraving

est-ce que [ɛskə] *adv:* **~ c'est cher c'était bon?** is it expensive/was it good **quand est-ce qu'il part?** when does h leave?, when is he leaving?; *voir aussi* **qu**

esthéticienne [ɛstetisjɛn] *nf* beautician

esthétique [ɛstetik] *adj* attractive

estimation [ɛstimasjɔ̃] *nf* valuatio (*chiffre*) estimate

estime [ɛstim] *nf* esteem, regard; **estim** *vt* (*respecter*) to esteem; (*expertiser: bij etc*) to value; (*évaluer: coût etc*) to asses estimate; (*penser*): **estimer que/être** consider that/o.s. to be

estival, e, -aux [ɛstival, o] *adj* summe cpd

estivant, e [ɛstivɑ̃, ɑ̃t] *nm/f* (summe holiday-maker

estomac [ɛstɔma] *nm* stomach

estomaqué, e [ɛstɔmake] (*fam*) *adj* fla bergasted

estomper [ɛstɔ̃pe] **s'~** *vi* (*sentiments*) soften; (*contour*) to become blurred

estrade [ɛstʀad] *nf* platform, rostrum

estragon [ɛstʀagɔ̃] *nm* tarragon

estuaire [ɛstɥɛʀ] *nm* estuary

et [e] *conj* and; **~ lui?** what about him?; **alors!** so what!

étable [etabl] *nf* cowshed

établi [etabli] *nm* (work)bench

établir [etabliʀ] *vt* (*papiers d'identité, fo ture*) to make out; (*liste, programme*) draw up; (*entreprise*) to set up; (*réputatio usage, fait, culpabilité*) to establish; **s'~** to be established; **s'~ (à son compte)**

set up in business; **s'~ à/près de** to settle in/near

ablissement [etablismã] *nm* (*entreprise,*
institution) establishment; **~ scolaire**
school, educational establishment

age [etaʒ] *nm* (*d'immeuble*) storey, floor;
à l'~ upstairs; **au 2ème ~** on the 2nd
(*BRIT*) *ou* 3rd (*US*) floor

agère [etaʒɛʀ] *nf* (*rayon*) shelf; (*meuble*)
shelves *pl*

ai [ete] *nm* stay, prop

ain [etɛ̃] *nm* pewter *no pl*

ais *etc* [ete] *vb voir* **être**

al [etal] *nm* stall

alage [etalaʒ] *nm* display; (*devanture*)
display window; **faire ~ de** to show off,
parade

aler [etale] *vt* (*carte, nappe*) to spread
(out); (*peinture*) to spread; (*échelonner*:
paiements, vacances) to spread, stagger;
(*marchandises*) to display; (*connaissances*)
to parade; **s'~** *vi* (*liquide*) to spread out;
(*fam*) to fall flat on one's face; **s'~ sur**
(*suj: paiements etc*) to be spread out over

alon [etalɔ̃] *nm* (*cheval*) stallion

anche [etɑ̃ʃ] *adj* (*récipient*) watertight;
(*montre, vêtement*) waterproof; **étancher**
vt: **étancher sa soif** to quench one's
thirst

ang [etɑ̃] *nm* pond

ant [etɑ̃] *vb voir* **être; donné**

ape [etap] *nf* stage; (*lieu d'arrivée*) stopping place; (: *CYCLISME*) staging point

at [eta] *nm* (*POL, condition*) state; **en mau-**
vais ~ in poor condition; **en ~ (de mar-**
che) in (working) order, **remettre en ~**
to repair; **hors d'~** out of order; **être en**
~/hors d'~ de faire to be in a/in no fit
state to do; **être dans tous ses ~s** to be
in a state; **faire ~ de** (*alléguer*) to put forward; **l'É~** the State; **~ civil** civil status; **~**
des lieux inventory of fixtures; **étatiser**
vt to bring under state control; **état-**
major *nm* (*MIL*) staff; **États-Unis** *nmpl*:
les États-Unis the United States

au, x [eto] *nm* vice (*BRIT*), vise (*US*)

étayer [eteje] *vt* to prop *ou* shore up

etc. [ɛtsetera] *adv* etc

et c(a)etera [ɛtsetera] *adv* et cetera, and
so on

été [ete] *pp de* **être ♦** *nm* summer

éteindre [etɛ̃dʀ] *vt* (*lampe, lumière, radio*)
to turn *ou* switch off; (*cigarette, feu*) to put
out, extinguish; **s'~** *vi* (*feu, lumière*) to go
out; (*mourir*) to pass away; **éteint, e** *adj*
(*fig*) lacklustre, dull; (*volcan*) extinct

étendard [etɑ̃daʀ] *nm* standard

étendre [etɑ̃dʀ] *vt* (*pâte, liquide*) to spread;
(*carte etc*) to spread out; (*linge*) to hang
up; (*bras, jambes*) to stretch out; (*fig:*
agrandir) to extend; **s'~** *vi* (*augmenter, se*
propager) to spread; (*terrain, forêt etc*) to
stretch; (*s'allonger*) to stretch out; (*se*
coucher) to lie down; (*fig: expliquer*) to
elaborate

étendu, e [etɑ̃dy] *adj* extensive; **étendue**
nf (*d'eau, de sable*) stretch, expanse; (*im-*
portance) extent

éternel, le [etɛʀnɛl] *adj* eternal

éterniser [etɛʀnize]: **s'~** *vi* to last for
ages; (*visiteur*) to stay for ages

éternité [etɛʀnite] *nf* eternity; **ça a duré**
une ~ it lasted for ages

éternuement [etɛʀnymã] *nm* sneeze

éternuer [etɛʀnɥe] *vi* to sneeze

êtes [ɛt(z)] *vb voir* **être**

éthique [etik] *adj* ethical

ethnie [ɛtni] *nf* ethnic group

éthylisme [etilism] *nm* alcoholism

étiez [etje] *vb voir* **être**

étinceler [etɛ̃s(ə)le] *vi* to sparkle

étincelle [etɛ̃sɛl] *nf* spark

étiqueter [etik(ə)te] *vt* to label

étiquette [etikɛt] *nf* label; (*protocole*): **l'~**
etiquette

étirer [etiʀe]: **s'~** *vi* (*personne*) to stretch;
(*convoi, route*): **s'~ sur** to stretch out over

étoffe [etɔf] *nf* material, fabric

étoffer [etɔfe] *vt* to fill out; **s'~** *vi* to fill
out

étoile [etwal] *nf* star; **à la belle ~** in the
open; **~ de mer** starfish; **~ filante** shoot-

ing star; **étoilé, e** *adj* starry

étonnant, e [etɔnɑ̃, ɑ̃t] *adj* amazing

étonnement [etɔnmɑ̃] *nm* surprise, amazement

étonner [etɔne] *vt* to surprise, amaze; **s'~ que/de** to be amazed that/at; **cela m'~ait (que)** (*j'en doute*) I'd be very surprised (if)

étouffant, e [etufɑ̃, ɑ̃t] *adj* stifling

étouffée [etufe] **: à l'~** *adv* (CULIN: *légumes*) steamed; (: *viande*) braised

étouffer [etufe] *vt* to suffocate; (*bruit*) to muffle; (*scandale*) to hush up ♦ *vi* to suffocate; **s'~** *vi* (*en mangeant etc*) to choke; **on étouffe** it's stifling

étourderie [eturdəri] *nf* (*caractère*) absent-mindedness *no pl*; (*faute*) thoughtless blunder

étourdi, e [eturdi] *adj* (*distrait*) scatter-brained, heedless

étourdir [eturdir] *vt* (*assommer*) to stun, daze; (*griser*) to make dizzy *ou* giddy; **étourdissement** *nm* dizzy spell

étourneau, x [eturno] *nm* starling

étrange [etrɑ̃ʒ] *adj* strange

étranger, -ère [etrɑ̃ʒe, ɛr] *adj* foreign; (*pas de la famille, non familier*) strange ♦ *nm/f* foreigner; stranger ♦ *nm*: **à l'~** abroad

étrangler [etrɑ̃gle] *vt* to strangle; **s'~** *vi* (*en mangeant etc*) to choke

┌─────────────┐
│ *MOT-CLÉ* │
└─────────────┘

être [etr] *nm* being; **être humain** human being

♦ *vb +attrib* **1** (*état, description*) to be; **il est instituteur** he is *ou* he's a teacher; **vous êtes grand/intelligent/fatigué** you are *ou* you're tall/clever/tired

2 (*+à: appartenir*) to be; **le livre est à Paul** the book is Paul's *ou* belongs to Paul; **c'est à moi/eux** it is *ou* it's mine/theirs

3 (*+de: provenance*): **il est de Paris** he is from Paris; (: *appartenance*): **il est des nôtres** he is one of us

4 (*date*): **nous sommes le 10 janvier** i the 10th of January (today)

♦ *vi* to be; **je ne serai pas ici demain** won't be here tomorrow

♦ *vb aux* **1** to have; to be; **être arrivé allé** to have arrived/gone; **il est parti** has left, he has gone

2 (*forme passive*) to be; **être fait par** to made by; **il a été promu** he has be promoted

3 (*+à: obligation*): **c'est à réparer** it nee repairing; **c'est à essayer** it should tried

♦ *vb impers* **1**: **il est +adjectif** it is *+adje tive*; **il est impossible de le faire** it's in possible to do it

2 (*heure, date*): **il est 10 heures, c'est heures** it is *ou* it's 10 o'clock

3 (*emphatique*): **c'est moi** it's me; **c'est lui de le faire** it's up to him to do it

étreindre [etrɛ̃dr] *vt* to clutch, gr (*amoureusement, amicalement*) to embrac **s'~** *vi* to embrace

étrenner [etrene] *vt* to use (*ou* wear) the first time; **étrennes** *nfpl* Christm box *sg*

étrier [etrije] *nm* stirrup

étriqué, e [etrike] *adj* skimpy

étroit, e [etrwa, wat] *adj* narro (*vêtement*) tight; (*fig: liens, collaboratic* close; **à l'~** cramped; **~ d'esprit** narro minded

étude [etyd] *nf* studying; (*ouvrage, rapp* study; (SCOL: *salle de travail*) study roo **~s** *nfpl* (SCOL) studies; **être à l'~** (*pr etc*) to be under consideration; **faire d ~s (de droit/médecine)** to study (la medicine)

étudiant, e [etydjɑ̃, jɑ̃t] *nm/f* student

étudier [etydje] *vt, vi* to study

étui [etɥi] *nm* case

étuve [etyv] *nf* steamroom

étuvée [etyve]: **à l'~** *adv* braised

eu, eue [y] *pp de* **avoir**

euh [ø] *excl* er

uro [øʀo] *nm* euro

uroland [øʀɔlɑ̃d] *nm* Euroland

urope [øʀɔp] *nf*: **l'~** Europe; **européen,
ne** *adj* European ♦ *nm/f*: **Européen, ne**
European

us *etc* [y] *vb voir* **avoir**

ux [ø] *pron* (*sujet*) they; (*objet*) them

vacuer [evakɥe] *vt* to evacuate

vader [evade]: **s'~** *vi* to escape

valuer [evalɥe] *vt* (*expertiser*) to appraise,
evaluate; (*juger approximativement*) to estimate

vangile [evɑ̃ʒil] *nm* gospel

vanouir [evanwiʀ]: **s'~** *vi* to faint; (*disparaître*) to vanish, disappear; **évanouissement** *nm* (*syncope*) fainting fit

vaporer [evapɔʀe]: **s'~** *vi* to evaporate

vasé, e [evaze] *adj* (*manches, jupe*) flared

vasif, -ive [evazif, iv] *adj* evasive

vasion [evazjɔ̃] *nf* escape

vêché [eveʃe] *nm* bishop's palace

veil [evεj] *nm* awakening; **être en ~** to
be alert; **éveillé, e** *adj* awake; (*vif*) alert,
sharp; **éveiller** *vt* to (a)waken; (*soupçons
etc*) to arouse; **s'éveiller** *vi* to (a)waken;
(*fig*) to be aroused

vénement [evenmɑ̃] *nm* event

ventail [evɑ̃taj] *nm* fan; (*choix*) range

ventaire [evɑ̃tεʀ] *nm* stall, stand

venter [evɑ̃te] *vt* (*secret*) to uncover; **s'~**
vi (*parfum*) to go stale

ventualité [evɑ̃tɥalite] *nf* eventuality;
possibility; **dans l'~ de** in the event of

ventuel, le [evɑ̃tɥεl] *adj* possible; **éven-
tuellement** *adv* possibly

vêque [evεk] *nm* bishop

vertuer [evεʀtɥe]: **s'~** *vi*: **s'~ à faire** to
try very hard to do

viction [eviksjɔ̃] *nf* (*de locataire*) eviction

videmment [evidamɑ̃] *adv* (*bien sûr*) of
course; (*certainement*) obviously

vidence [evidɑ̃s] *nf* obviousness; (*fait*)
obvious fact; **de toute ~** quite obviously
au evidently; **être en ~** to be clearly visible; **mettre en ~** (*fait*) to highlight; **évident, e** *adj* obvious, evident; **ce n'est**

pas évident! (*fam*) it's not that easy!

évider [evide] *vt* to scoop out

évier [evje] *nm* (kitchen) sink

évincer [evɛ̃se] *vt* to oust

éviter [evite] *vt* to avoid; **~ de faire** to
avoid doing; **~ qch à qn** to spare sb sth

évolué, e [evɔlɥe] *adj* advanced

évoluer [evɔlɥe] *vi* (*enfant, maladie*) to develop; (*situation, moralement*) to evolve,
develop; (*aller et venir*) to move about;
évolution *nf* development, evolution

évoquer [evɔke] *vt* to call to mind, evoke;
(*mentionner*) to mention

ex... [εks] *préfixe* ex-

exact, e [εgza(kt), εgzakt] *adj* exact; (*correct*) correct; (*ponctuel*) punctual; **l'heure
~e** the right *ou* exact time; **exactement**
adv exactly

ex aequo [εgzeko] *adj* equally placed; **arriver ~** to finish neck and neck

exagéré, e [εgzaʒeʀe] *adj* (*prix etc*) excessive

exagérer [εgzaʒeʀe] *vt* to exaggerate ♦ *vi*
to exaggerate; (*abuser*) to go too far

exalter [εgzalte] *vt* (*enthousiasmer*) to excite, elate

examen [εgzamɛ̃] *nm* examination; (*SCOL*)
exam(ination); **à l'~** under consideration

examinateur, -trice [εgzaminatœʀ, tʀis]
nm/f examiner

examiner [εgzamine] *vt* to examine

exaspérant, e [εgzaspeʀɑ̃, ɑ̃t] *adj* ex-
asperating

exaspérer [εgzaspeʀe] *vt* to exasperate

exaucer [εgzose] *vt* (*vœu*) to grant

excédent [εksedɑ̃] *nm* surplus; **en ~** surplus; **~ de bagages** excess luggage

excéder [εksede] *vt* (*dépasser*) to exceed;
(*agacer*) to exasperate

excellent, e [εkselɑ̃, ɑ̃t] *adj* excellent

excentrique [εksɑ̃tʀik] *adj* eccentric

excepté, e [εksεpte] *adj, prép*: **les élèves
~s, ~ les élèves** except for the pupils

exception [εksεpsjɔ̃] *nf* exception; **à l'~
de** except for, with the exception of; **d'~**
(*mesure, loi*) special, exceptional; **excep-**

tionnel, le *adj* exceptional; **exception-nellement** *adv* exceptionally

excès [ɛksɛ] *nm* surplus ♦ *nmpl* excesses; **faire des ~** to overindulge; **~ de vitesse** speeding *no pl*; **excessif, -ive** *adj* excessive

excitant, e [ɛksitɑ̃, ɑ̃t] *adj* exciting ♦ *nm* stimulant; **excitation** *nf* (*état*) excitement

exciter [ɛksite] *vt* to excite; (*suj: café etc*) to stimulate; **s'~** *vi* to get excited

exclamation [ɛksklamasjɔ̃] *nf* exclamation

exclamer [ɛksklame]: **s'~** *vi* to exclaim

exclure [ɛksklyʀ] *vt* (*faire sortir*) to expel; (*ne pas compter*) to exclude, leave out; (*rendre impossible*) to exclude, rule out; **il est exclu que** it's out of the question that ...; **il n'est pas exclu que ...** it's not impossible that ...; **exclusif, -ive** *adj* exclusive; **exclusion** *nf* exclusion; **à l'exclusion de** with the exclusion *ou* exception of; **exclusivité** *nf* (*COMM*) exclusive rights *pl*; **film passant en exclusivité à** film showing only at

excursion [ɛkskyʀsjɔ̃] *nf* (*en autocar*) excursion, trip; (*à pied*) walk, hike

excuse [ɛkskyz] *nf* excuse; **~s** *nfpl* (*regret*) apology *sg*, apologies; **excuser** *vt* to excuse; **s'excuser (de)** to apologize (for); **"excusez-moi"** "I'm sorry"; (*pour attirer l'attention*) "excuse me"

exécrable [ɛgzekʀabl] *adj* atrocious

exécuter [ɛgzekyte] *vt* (*tuer*) to execute; (*tâche etc*) to execute, carry out; (*MUS: jouer*) to perform, execute; **s'~** *vi* to comply; **exécutif, -ive** *adj, nm* (*POL*) executive; **exécution** *nf* execution; **mettre à exécution** to carry out

exemplaire [ɛgzɑ̃plɛʀ] *nm* copy

exemple [ɛgzɑ̃pl] *nm* example; **par ~** for instance, for example; **donner l'~** to set an example

exempt, e [ɛgzɑ̃, ɑ̃(p)t] *adj*: **~ de** (*dispensé de*) exempt from; (*sans*) free from

exercer [ɛgzɛʀse] *vt* (*pratiquer*) to exercise, practise; (*influence, contrôle*) to exert; (*former*) to exercise, train; **s'~** *vi* (*sportif, mu-*

sicien) to practise

exercice [ɛgzɛʀsis] *nm* exercise

exhaustif, -ive [ɛgzostif, iv] *adj* exhau tive

exhiber [ɛgzibe] *vt* (*montrer: papiers, cert* *cat*) to present, produce; (*péj*) to displa flaunt; **s'~** *vi* to parade; (*suj: exhibitio niste*) to expose o.s.; **exhibitionnis** [ɛgzibisjɔnist] *nm/f* flasher

exhorter [ɛgzɔʀte] *vt* to urge

exigeant, e [ɛgziʒɑ̃, ɑ̃t] *adj* demandin (*péj*) hard to please

exigence [ɛgziʒɑ̃s] *nf* demand, requir ment

exiger [ɛgziʒe] *vt* to demand, require

exigu, ë [ɛgzigy] *adj* cramped, tiny

exil [ɛgzil] *nm* exile; **exiler** *vt* to exi **s'exiler** *vi* to go into exile

existence [ɛgzistɑ̃s] *nf* existence

exister [ɛgziste] *vi* to exist; **il existe u des** there is a/are (some)

exonérer [ɛgzɔneʀe] *vt*: **~ de** to exem from

exorbitant, e [ɛgzɔʀbitɑ̃, ɑ̃t] *adj* exor tant

exorbité, e [ɛgzɔʀbite] *adj*: **yeux ~s** bu ing eyes

exotique [ɛgzɔtik] *adj* exotic; **yaourt a fruits ~s** tropical fruit yoghurt

expatrier [ɛkspatʀije] *vt*: **s'~** to lea one's country

expectative [ɛkspɛktativ] *nf*: **être da l'~** to be still waiting

expédient [ɛkspedjɑ̃, jɑ̃t] (*péj*) *nm*: **viv d'~s** to live by one's wits

expédier [ɛkspedje] *vt* (*lettre, paquet*) send; (*troupes*) to dispatch; (*fam: trav etc*) to dispose of, dispatch; **expédite -trice** *nm/f* sender; **expédition** *nf* ser ing; (*scientifique, sportive, MIL*) expedition

expérience [ɛkspeʀjɑ̃s] *nf* (*de la vie*) perience; (*scientifique*) experiment

expérimenté, e [ɛkspeʀimɑ̃te] *adj* exp ienced

expérimenter [ɛkspeʀimɑ̃te] *vt* to te out, experiment with

xpert, e [ɛkspɛʀ, ɛʀt] *adj, nm* expert; **expert-comptable** *nm* ≃ chartered accountant (*BRIT*), ≃ certified public accountant (*US*)

xpertise [ɛkspɛʀtiz] *nf* (*évaluation*) expert evaluation

xpertiser [ɛkspɛʀtize] *vt* (*objet de valeur*) to value; (*voiture accidentée etc*) to assess damage to

xpier [ɛkspje] *vt* to expiate, atone for

xpirer [ɛkspiʀe] *vi* (*prendre fin, mourir*) to expire; (*respirer*) to breathe out

xplicatif, -ive [ɛksplikatif, iv] *adj* explanatory

xplication [ɛksplikasjɔ̃] *nf* explanation; (*discussion*) discussion; (*dispute*) argument; **~ de texte** (*SCOL*) critical analysis

xplicite [ɛksplisit] *adj* explicit

xpliquer [ɛksplike] *vt* to explain; **s'~** to explain (o.s.); **s'~ avec qn** (*discuter*) to explain o.s. to sb; **son erreur s'explique** one can understand his mistake

xploit [ɛksplwa] *nm* exploit, feat; **exploitant, e** *nm/f*: **exploitant (agricole)** farmer

xploitation *nf* exploitation; (*d'une entreprise*) running; **~ agricole** farming concern; **exploiter** *vt* (*personne, don*) to exploit; (*entreprise, ferme*) to run, operate; (*mine*) to exploit, work

xplorer [ɛksplɔʀe] *vt* to explore

xploser [ɛksploze] *vi* to explode, blow up; (*engin explosif*) to go off; (*personne: de colère*) to flare up; **explosif, -ive** *adj, nm* explosive; **explosion** *nf* explosion

xportateur, -trice [ɛkspɔʀtatœʀ, tʀis] *adj* export *cpd*, exporting ♦ *nm* exporter

xportation [ɛkspɔʀtasjɔ̃] *nf* (*action*) exportation; (*produit*) export

xporter [ɛkspɔʀte] *vt* to export

xposant [ɛkspozɑ̃] *nm* exhibitor

xposé, e [ɛkspoze] *nm* talk ♦ *adj*: **~ au sud** facing south

xposer [ɛkspoze] *vt* (*marchandise*) to display; (*peinture*) to exhibit, show; (*parler de*) to explain, set out; (*mettre en danger,*

orienter, *PHOTO*) to expose; **exposition** *nf* (*manifestation*) exhibition; (*PHOTO*) exposure

exprès¹ [ɛkspʀɛ] *adv* (*délibérément*) on purpose; (*spécialement*) specially

exprès², -esse [ɛkspʀɛs] *adj* (*ordre, défense*) express, formal ♦ *adj inv* (*PTT*) express ♦ *adv* express

express [ɛkspʀɛs] *adj, nm*: **(café) ~** espresso (coffee); **(train) ~** fast train

expressément [ɛkspʀesemɑ̃] *adv* (*spécialement*) specifically

expressif, -ive [ɛkspʀesif, iv] *adj* expressive

expression [ɛkspʀesjɔ̃] *nf* expression

exprimer [ɛkspʀime] *vt* (*sentiment, idée*) to express; (*jus, liquide*) to press out; **s'~** *vi* (*personne*) to express o.s

exproprier [ɛkspʀɔpʀije] *vt* to buy up by compulsory purchase, expropriate

expulser [ɛkspylse] *vt* to expel; (*locataire*) to evict; (*SPORT*) to send off

exquis, e [ɛkski, iz] *adj* exquisite

extase [ɛkstaz] *nf* ecstasy; **extasier: s'extasier sur** *vt* to go into raptures over

extension [ɛkstɑ̃sjɔ̃] *nf* (*fig*) extension

exténuer [ɛkstenɥe] *vt* to exhaust

extérieur, e [ɛksteʀjœʀ] *adj* (*porte, mur etc*) outer, outside; (*au dehors: escalier, w.-c.*) outside; (*commerce*) foreign; (*influences*) external; (*apparent: calme, gaieté etc*) surface *cpd* ♦ *nm* (*d'une maison, d'un récipient etc*) outside, exterior; (*apparence*) exterior; **à l'~** outside; (*à l'étranger*) abroad; **extérieurement** *adv* on the outside; (*en apparence*) on the surface

exterminer [ɛkstɛʀmine] *vt* to exterminate, wipe out

externat [ɛkstɛʀna] *nm* day school

externe [ɛkstɛʀn] *adj* external, outer ♦ *nm/f* (*MÉD*) non-resident medical student (*BRIT*), extern (*US*); (*SCOL*) day pupil

extincteur [ɛkstɛ̃ktœʀ] *nm* (fire) extinguisher

extinction [ɛkstɛ̃ksjɔ̃] *nf*: **~ de voix** loss of voice

extorquer [ɛkstɔrke] *vt* to extort
extra [ɛkstra] *adj inv* first-rate; *(fam)* fantastic ♦ *nm inv* extra help
extrader [ɛkstrade] *vt* to extradite
extraire [ɛkstrɛr] *vt* to extract; **extrait** *nm* extract
extraordinaire [ɛkstraɔrdinɛr] *adj* extraordinary; *(POL: mesures etc)* special
extravagant, e [ɛkstravagɑ̃, ɑ̃t] *adj* extravagant
extraverti, e [ɛkstravɛrti] *adj* extrovert
extrême [ɛkstrɛm] *adj, nm* extreme; **extrêmement** *adv* extremely; **extrême-onction** *nf* last rites *pl*; **Extrême-Orient** *nm* Far East
extrémité [ɛkstremite] *nf* end; *(situation)* straits *pl*, plight; *(geste désespéré)* extreme action; **~s** *nfpl (pieds et mains)* extremities
exubérant, e [ɛgzyberɑ̃, ɑ̃t] *adj* exuberant
exutoire [ɛgzytwar] *nm* outlet, release

F, f

F *abr* = **franc**
fa [fa] *nm inv (MUS)* F; *(en chantant la gamme)* fa
fable [fabl] *nf* fable
fabricant [fabrikɑ̃, ɑ̃t] *nm* manufacturer
fabrication [fabrikasjɔ̃] *nf* manufacture
fabrique [fabrik] *nf* factory; **fabriquer** *vt* to make; *(industriellement)* to manufacture; *(fig)*: **qu'est-ce qu'il fabrique?** *(fam)* what is he doing?
fabulation [fabylasjɔ̃] *nf* fantasizing
fac [fak] *(fam) abr f (SCOL)* = **faculté**
façade [fasad] *nf* front, façade
face [fas] *nf* face; *(fig: aspect)* side ♦ *adj*: **le côté ~** heads; **en ~ de** opposite; *(fig)* in front of; **de ~** *(voir)* face on; **~ à** facing; *(fig)* faced with, in the face of; **faire ~ à** to face; **~ à ~** *adv* facing each other ♦ *nm inv* encounter
fâché, e [fɑʃe] *adj* angry; *(désolé)* sorry
fâcher [fɑʃe] *vt* to anger; **se ~** *vi* to get

angry; **se ~ avec** *(se brouiller)* to fall o
with
fâcheux, -euse [fɑʃø, øz] *adj* unfort
nate, regrettable
facile [fasil] *adj* easy; *(caractère)* eas
going; **facilement** *adv* easily
facilité *nf* easiness; *(disposition, don)* ap
tude; **facilités de paiement** easy term
faciliter *vt* to make easier
façon [fasɔ̃] *nf (manière)* way; *(d'une ro
etc)* making-up, cut; **~s** *nfpl (péj)* fuss s
de ~ à/à ce que so as to/that; **de tout
~** anyway, in any case
façonner [fasɔne] *vt (travailler: matière)*
shape, fashion
facteur, -trice [faktœr] *nm/f* postman
woman) *(BRIT)*, mailman(-woman) *(U*
♦ *nm (MATH, fig: élément)* factor
factice [faktis] *adj* artificial
faction [faksjɔ̃] *nf* faction; **être de ~** to l
on guard (duty)
facture [faktyr] *nf (à payer: gén)* bill; i
voice
facturer [faktyre] *vt* to invoice
facultatif, -ive [fakyltatif, iv] *adj* optiona
faculté [fakylte] *nf (intellectuel*
d'université) faculty; *(pouvoir, possibili*
power
fade [fad] *adj* insipid
fagot [fago] *nm* bundle of sticks
faible [fɛbl] *adj* weak; *(voix, lumière, ver*
faint; *(rendement, revenu)* low ♦ *nm (po*
quelqu'un) weakness, soft spot; **faibless**
nf weakness; **faiblir** *vi* to weaken; *(*
mière) to dim; *(vent)* to drop
faïence [fajɑ̃s] *nf* earthenware *no pl*
faignant, e [fɛɲɑ̃, ɑ̃t] *nm/f* = **fainéant, e**
faille [faj] *vb voir* **falloir** ♦ *nf (GÉO)* fau
(fig) flaw, weakness
faillir [fajir] *vi*: **j'ai failli tomber** I alm
ou very nearly fell
faillite [fajit] *nf* bankruptcy
faim [fɛ̃] *nf* hunger; **avoir ~** to be hungi
rester sur sa ~ *(aussi fig)* to be le
wanting more
fainéant, e [fɛneɑ̃, ɑ̃t] *nm/f* idler, loafer

aire [fɛʀ] *vt* **1** (*fabriquer, être l'auteur de*) to make; **faire du vin/une offre/un film** to make wine/an offer/a film; **faire du bruit** to make a noise

2 (*effectuer: travail, opération*) to do; **que faites-vous?** (*quel métier etc*) what do you do?; (*quelle activité: au moment de la question*) what are you doing?; **faire la lessive** to do the washing

3 (*études*) to do; (*sport, musique*) to play; **faire du droit/du français** to do law/French; **faire du rugby/piano** to play rugby/the piano

4 (*simuler*): **faire le malade/l'ignorant** to act the invalid/the fool

5 (*transformer, avoir un effet sur*): **faire de qn un frustré/avocat** to make sb frustrated/a lawyer; **ça ne me fait rien** (*m'est égal*) I don't care *ou* mind; (*me laisse froid*) it has no effect on me; **ça ne fait rien** it doesn't matter; **faire que** (*impliquer*) to mean that

6 (*calculs, prix, mesures*): **2 et 2 font 4** 2 and 2 are *ou* make 4; **ça fait 10 m/15 F** it's 10 m/15F; **je vous le fais 10 F** I'll let you have it for 10F

7: qu'a-t-il fait de sa valise? what has he done with his case?

8: ne faire que: il ne fait que critiquer (*sans cesse*) all he (ever) does is criticize; (*seulement*) he's only criticizing

9 (*dire*) to say; **"vraiment?" fit-il** "really?" he said

10 (*maladie*) to have; **faire du diabète** to have diabetes *sg*

♦ *vi* **1** (*agir, s'y prendre*) to act, do; **il faut faire vite** we (*ou* you *etc*) must act quickly; **comment a-t-il fait pour?** how did he manage to?; **faites comme chez vous** make yourself at home

2 (*paraître*) to look; **faire vieux/démodé** to look old/old-fashioned; **ça fait bien** it looks good

♦ *vb substitut* to do; **ne le casse pas**

comme je l'ai fait don't break it as I did; **je peux le voir? - faites!** can I see it? - please do!

♦ *vb impers* **1**: **il fait beau** *etc* the weather is fine *etc*; *voir aussi* **jour**; **froid** *etc*

2 (*temps écoulé, durée*): **ça fait 2 ans qu'il est parti** it's 2 years since he left; **ça fait 2 ans qu'il y est** he's been there for 2 years

♦ *vb semi-aux* **1**: **faire** +*infinitif* (*action directe*) to make; **faire tomber/bouger qch** to make sth fall/move; **faire démarrer un moteur/chauffer de l'eau** to start up an engine/heat some water; **cela fait dormir** it makes you sleep; **faire travailler les enfants** to make the children work *ou* get the children to work

2 (*indirectement, par un intermédiaire*): **faire réparer qch** to get *ou* have sth repaired; **faire punir les enfants** to have the children punished

se faire *vi* **1** (*vin, fromage*) to mature

2: cela se fait beaucoup/ne se fait pas it's done a lot/not done

3: se faire +*nom ou pron*: **se faire une jupe** to make o.s. a skirt; **se faire des amis** to make friends; **se faire du souci** to worry; **il ne s'en fait pas** he doesn't worry

4: se faire +*adj* (*devenir*): **se faire vieux** to be getting old; (*délibérément*): **se faire beau** to do o.s. up

5: se faire à (*s'habituer*) to get used to; **je n'arrive pas à me faire à la nourriture/au climat** I can't get used to the food/climate

6: se faire +*infinitif*: **se faire examiner la vue/opérer** to have one's eyes tested/to have an operation; **se faire couper les cheveux** to get one's hair cut; **il va se faire tuer/punir** he's going to get himself killed/get (himself) punished; **il s'est fait aider** he got somebody to help him; **il s'est fait aider par Simon** he got Simon to help him; **se faire faire un vêtement** to get a garment made for o.s.

7 (*impersonnel*): **comment se fait-il/ faisait-il que?** how is it/was it that?

faire-part [fɛʀpaʀ] *nm inv* announcement (*of birth, marriage etc*)

faisable [fəzabl] *adj* feasible

faisan, e [fəzɑ̃, an] *nm/f* pheasant; **faisandé, e** *adj* high (*bad*)

faisceau, x [fɛso] *nm* (*de lumière etc*) beam

faisons [fəzɔ̃] *vb voir* **faire**

fait, e [fɛ, fɛt] *adj* (*mûr: fromage, melon*) ripe ♦ *nm* (*événement*) event, occurrence; (*réalité, donnée*) fact; **être au ~ (de)** to be informed (of); **au ~** (*à propos*) by the way; **en venir au ~** to get to the point; **du ~ de ceci/qu'il a menti** because of *ou* on account of this/his having lied; **de ce ~** for this reason; **en ~** in fact; **prendre qn sur le ~** to catch sb in the act; **~ divers** news item

faîte [fɛt] *nm* top; (*fig*) pinnacle, height

faites [fɛt] *vb voir* **faire**

faitout [fɛtu] *nm*, **fait-tout** [fɛtu] *nm inv* stewpot

falaise [falɛz] *nf* cliff

falloir [falwaʀ] *vb impers*: **il faut qu'il parte/a fallu qu'il parte** (*obligation*) he has to *ou* must leave/had to leave; **il a fallu le faire** it had to be done; **il faut faire attention** you have to be careful; **il me faudrait 100 F** I would need 100 F; **il vous faut tourner à gauche après l'église** you have to turn left past the church; **nous avons ce qu'il (nous) faut** we have what we need; **s'en ~: il s'en est fallu de 100 F/5 minutes** we/they *etc* were 100 F short/5 minutes late (*ou* early); **il s'en faut de beaucoup qu'il soit** he is far from being; **il s'en est fallu de peu que cela n'arrive** it very nearly happened

falsifier [falsifje] *vt* to falsify, doctor

famé, e [fame] *adj*: **mal ~** disreputable, of ill repute

famélique [famelik] *adj* half-starved

fameux, -euse [famø, øz] *adj* (*illustre*) famous; (*bon: repas, plat etc*) first-rate, first class; (*valeur intensive*) real, downright

familial, e, -aux [familjal, jo] *adj* family *cpd*

familiarité [familjaʀite] *nf* familiarity; **~s** *nfpl* (*privautés*) familiarities

familier, -ère [familje, jɛʀ] *adj* (*connu*) familiar; (*atmosphère*) informal, friendly; (*LING*) informal, colloquial ♦ *nm* regular (visitor)

famille [famij] *nf* family; **il a de la ~ à Paris** he has relatives in Paris

famine [famin] *nf* famine

fanatique [fanatik] *adj* fanatical ♦ *nm/f* fanatic; **fanatisme** *nm* fanaticism

faner [fane]: **se ~** *vi* to fade

fanfare [fɑ̃faʀ] *nf* (*orchestre*) brass band; (*musique*) fanfare

fanfaron, ne [fɑ̃faʀɔ̃, ɔn] *nm/f* braggart

fantaisie [fɑ̃tezi] *nf* (*spontanéité*) fancy, imagination; (*caprice*) whim ♦ *adj*: **bijou** costume jewellery; **fantaisiste** (*péj*) *adj* unorthodox, eccentric

fantasme [fɑ̃tasm] *nm* fantasy

fantasque [fɑ̃task] *adj* whimsical, capricious

fantastique [fɑ̃tastik] *adj* fantastic

fantôme [fɑ̃tom] *nm* ghost, phantom

faon [fɑ̃] *nm* fawn

farce [faʀs] *nf* (*viande*) stuffing; (*blague*) (practical) joke; (*THÉÂTRE*) farce; **farcir** *vt* (*viande*) to stuff

fardeau, x [faʀdo] *nm* burden

farder [faʀde]: **se ~** *vi* to make (o.s.) up

farfelu, e [faʀfəly] *adj* hare-brained

farine [faʀin] *nf* flour; **farineux, -euse** *adj* (*sauce, pomme*) floury

farouche [faʀuʃ] *adj* (*timide*) shy, timid

fart [faʀt] *nm* (ski) wax

fascicule [fasikyl] *nm* volume

fascination [fasinasjɔ̃] *nf* fascination

fasciner [fasine] *vt* to fascinate

fascisme [faʃism] *nm* fascism

fasse *etc* [fas] *vb voir* **faire**

faste [fast] *nm* splendour

fastidieux, -euse [fastidjø, jøz] *adj* tedious, tiresome

fastueux, -euse [fastɥø, øz] *adj* sumptuous, luxurious

fatal, e [fatal] *adj* fatal; (*inévitable*) inevitable; **fatalité** *nf* (*destin*) fate; (*coïncidence*) fateful coincidence

fatidique [fatidik] *adj* fateful

fatigant, e [fatigɑ̃, ɑ̃t] *adj* tiring; (*agaçant*) tiresome

fatigue [fatig] *nf* tiredness, fatigue; **fatigué, e** *adj* tired; **fatiguer** *vt* to tire, make tired; (*fig: agacer*) to annoy ♦ *vi* (*moteur*) to labour, strain; **se fatiguer** to get tired

fatras [fatrɑ] *nm* jumble, hotchpotch

faubourg [fobur] *nm* suburb

fauché, e [foʃe] (*fam*) *adj* broke

faucher [foʃe] *vt* (*herbe*) to cut; (*champs, blés*) to reap; (*fig: véhicule*) to mow down; (*fam: voler*) to pinch

faucille [fosij] *nf* sickle

faucon [fokɔ̃] *nm* falcon, hawk

faudra [fodra] *vb voir* **falloir**

faufiler [fofile]: **se ~** *vi*: **se ~ dans** to edge one's way into; **se ~ parmi/entre** to thread one's way among/between

faune [fon] *nf* (*ZOOL*) wildlife, fauna

faussaire [fosɛr] *nm* forger

fausse [fos] *adj voir* **faux**; **faussement** *adv* (*accuser*) wrongly, wrongfully; (*croire*) falsely

fausser [fose] *vt* (*objet*) to bend, buckle; (*fig*) to distort; **~ compagnie à qn** to give sb the slip

faut [fo] *vb voir* **falloir**

faute [fot] *nf* (*erreur*) mistake, error; (*mauvaise action*) misdemeanour; (*FOOTBALL etc*) offence; (*TENNIS*) fault; **c'est de sa/ma ~** it's his/my fault; **être en ~** to be in the wrong; **~ de** (*temps, argent*) for *ou* through lack of; **sans ~** without fail; **~ de frappe** typing error; **~ de goût** error of taste; **~ professionnelle** professional misconduct *no pl*

fauteuil [fotœj] *nm* armchair; **~ roulant** wheelchair

fauteur [fotœr] *nm*: **~ de troubles** trouble-maker

fautif, -ive [fotif, iv] *adj* (*responsable*) at fault, in the wrong; (*incorrect*) incorrect, inaccurate; **il se sentait ~** he felt guilty

fauve [fov] *nm* wildcat ♦ *adj* (*couleur*) fawn

faux¹ [fo] *nf* scythe

faux², fausse [fo, fos] *adj* (*inexact*) wrong; (*voix*) out of tune; (*billet*) fake, forged; (*sournois, postiche*) false ♦ *adv* (*MUS*) out of tune ♦ *nm* (*copie*) fake, forgery; (*opposé au vrai*): **le ~** falsehood; **faire ~ bond à qn** to stand sb up; **fausse alerte** false alarm; **fausse couche** miscarriage; **~ frais** *nmpl* extras, incidental expenses; **~ pas** tripping *no pl*; (*fig*) faux pas; **~ témoignage** (*délit*) perjury; **fauxfilet** *nm* sirloin; **faux-monnayeur** *nm* counterfeiter, forger

faveur [favœr] *nf* favour; **traitement de ~** preferential treatment; **en ~ de** in favour of

favorable [favorabl] *adj* favourable

favori, te [favɔri, it] *adj, nm/f* favourite

favoriser [favɔrize] *vt* to favour

fax [faks] *nm* fax; **faxer** *vt* to fax

FB *abr* (= *franc belge*) BF

fébrile [febril] *adj* feverish, febrile

fécond, e [fekɔ̃, ɔ̃d] *adj* fertile; **féconder** *vt* to fertilize; **fécondité** *nf* fertility

fécule [fekyl] *nf* potato flour; **féculent** *nm* starchy food

fédéral, e, -aux [federal, o] *adj* federal

fée [fe] *nf* fairy; **féerique** *adj* magical, fairytale *cpd*

feignant, e [fɛɲɑ̃, ɑ̃t] *nm/f* = **fainéant, e**

feindre [fɛ̃dr] *vt* to feign; **~ de faire** to pretend to do

feinte [fɛ̃t] *nf* (*SPORT*) dummy

fêler [fele] *vt* to crack

félicitations [felisitasjɔ̃] *nfpl* congratulations

féliciter [felisite] *vt*: **~ qn (de)** to congratulate sb (on)

félin, e [felɛ̃, in] *nm* (big) cat

fêlure [felyʀ] *nf* crack

femelle [fəmɛl] *adj, nf* female

féminin, e [feminɛ̃, in] *adj* feminine; (*sexe*) female; (*équipe, vêtements etc*) women's ♦ *nm* (*LING*) feminine; **féministe** [feminist] *adj* feminist

femme [fam] *nf* woman; (*épouse*) wife; ~ **au foyer** housewife; ~ **de chambre** chambermaid; ~ **de ménage** cleaning lady

fémur [femyʀ] *nm* femur, thighbone

fendre [fɑ̃dʀ] *vt* (*couper en deux*) to split; (*fissurer*) to crack; (*traverser: foule, air*) to cleave through; **se** ~ *vi* to crack

fenêtre [f(ə)nɛtʀ] *nf* window

fenouil [fənuj] *nm* fennel

fente [fɑ̃t] . *nf* (*fissure*) crack; (*de boîte à lettres etc*) slit

féodal, e, -aux [feɔdal, o] *adj* feudal

fer [fɛʀ] *nm* iron; ~ **à cheval** horseshoe; ~ **(à repasser)** iron; ~ **forgé** wrought iron

ferai *etc* [fəʀe] *vb voir* faire

fer-blanc [fɛʀblɑ̃] *nm* tin(plate)

férié, e [feʀje] *adj*: **jour** ~ public holiday

ferions *etc* [faʀjɔ̃] *vb voir* faire

ferme [fɛʀm] *adj* firm ♦ *adv* (*travailler etc*) hard ♦ *nf* (*exploitation*) farm; (*maison*) farmhouse

fermé, e [fɛʀme] *adj* closed, shut; (*gaz, eau etc*) off; (*fig: milieu*) exclusive

fermenter [fɛʀmɑ̃te] *vi* to ferment

fermer [fɛʀme] *vt* to close, shut; (*cesser l'exploitation de*) to close down, shut down; (*eau, électricité, robinet*) to put off, turn off; (*aéroport, route*) to close ♦ *vi* to close, shut; (*magasin: définitivement*) to close down, shut down; **se** ~ *vi* to close, shut

fermeté [fɛʀməte] *nf* firmness

fermeture [fɛʀmətyʀ] *nf* closing; (*dispositif*) catch; **heures de** ~ closing times; ~ **éclair** ® zip (fastener) (*BRIT*), zipper (*US*)

fermier [fɛʀmje, jɛʀ] *nm* farmer; **fermière** *nf* woman farmer; (*épouse*) farmer's wife

fermoir [fɛʀmwaʀ] *nm* clasp

féroce [feʀɔs] *adj* ferocious, fierce

ferons [fəʀɔ̃] *vb voir* faire

ferraille [feʀaj] *nf* scrap iron; **mettre à la** ~ to scrap

ferrer [feʀe] *vt* (*cheval*) to shoe

ferronnerie [feʀɔnʀi] *nf* ironwork

ferroviaire [feʀɔvjɛʀ] *adj* rail(way) *cpd* (*BRIT*), rail(road) *cpd* (*US*)

ferry(boat) [feʀe(bot)] *nm* ferry

fertile [fɛʀtil] *adj* fertile; ~ **en incidents** eventful, packed with incidents

féru, e [feʀy] *adj*: ~ **de** with a keen interest in

fervent, e [fɛʀvɑ̃, ɑ̃t] *adj* fervent

fesse [fɛs] *nf* buttock; **fessée** *nf* spanking

festin [festɛ̃] *nm* feast

festival [festival] *nm* festival

festivités [festivite] *nfpl* festivities

festoyer [festwaje] *vi* to feast

fêtard [fetaʀ, aʀd] (*fam*) *nm* high liver, merry-maker

fête [fɛt] *nf* (*religieuse*) feast; (*publique*) holiday; (*réception*) party; (*kermesse*) fête, fair (*du nom*) feast day, name day; **faire la** ~ to live it up; **faire** ~ **à qn** to give sb a warm welcome; **les** ~**s (de fin d'année)** the festive season; **la salle des** ~**s** the village hall; ~ **foraine** (fun) fair; **fêter** *vt* to celebrate; (*personne*) to have a celebration for

feu, x [fø] *nm* (*gén*) fire; (*signal lumineux*) light; (*de cuisinière*) ring; ~**x** *nmpl* (*AUTO*) (traffic) lights; **au** ~! (*incendie*) fire!; **à** ~ **doux/vif** over a slow/brisk heat; **à petit** ~ (*CULIN*) over a gentle heat; (*fig*) slowly; **faire** ~ to fire; **prendre** ~ to catch fire; **mettre le** ~ **à** to set fire to; **faire du** ~ to make a fire; **avez-vous du** ~? (*pour cigarette*) have you (got) a light?; ~ **arrière** rear light; ~ **d'artifice** (*spectacle*) firework(s) *pl*; ~ **de joie** bonfire; ~**x de joie** bonfire; ~**x de route** headlights; ~**x de position** sidelights; ~**x de croisement** dipped (*BRIT*) ou dimmed (*US*) headlights; ~**x de brouillard** fog-lamps; ~**x d'artifice** fireworks; **feu de route** headlights orange red/green/amber (*BRIT*) ou yellow (*US*) light; ~**x de brouillard** fog-lamps; ~**x de croisement** dipped (*BRIT*) ou dimmed (*US*) headlights; ~**x de position** sidelights; ~**x de route** headlights

feuillage [fœjaʒ] *nm* foliage, leaves *pl*

feuille [fœj] nf (d'arbre) leaf; (de papier) sheet; ~ **de maladie** medical expenses claim form; ~ **de paie** pay slip

feuillet [fœjɛ] nm leaf

feuilleté, e [fœjte] adj: **pâte ~** flaky pastry

feuilleter [fœjte] vt (livre) to leaf through

feuilleton [fœjtɔ̃] nm serial

feutre [føtʀ] nm felt; (chapeau) felt hat; (aussi: **stylo-~**) felt-tip pen; **feutré, e** adj (atmosphère) muffled

fève [fɛv] nf broad bean

février [fevʀije] nm February

FF abr (= franc français) FF

fiable [fjabl] adj reliable

fiançailles [fjɑ̃saj] nfpl engagement sg

fiancé, e [fjɑ̃se] nm/f fiancé(e) ♦ adj: **être ~ (à)** to be engaged (to)

fiancer [fjɑ̃se]: **se ~** vi to become engaged

fibre [fibʀ] nf fibre; ~ **de verre** fibreglass, glass fibre

ficeler [fis(ə)le] vt to tie up

ficelle [fisɛl] nf string no pl; (morceau) piece ou length of string

fiche [fiʃ] nf (pour fichier) (index) card; (formulaire) form; (ÉLEC) plug

ficher [fiʃe] vt (dans un fichier) to file; (PO-LICE) to put on file; (fam: faire) to do; (: donner) to give; (: mettre) to stick ou shove; **se ~ de** (fam: se gausser) to make fun of; **fiche(-moi) le camp** (fam) clear off; **fiche-moi la paix** (fam) leave me alone; **je m'en fiche!** (fam) I don't care!

fichier [fiʃje] nm file

fichu, e [fiʃy] pp de **ficher** (fam) ♦ adj (fam: fini, inutilisable) bust, done for; (: intensif) wretched, darned ♦ nm (foulard) (head)scarf; **mal ~** (fam) feeling lousy

fictif, -ive [fiktif, iv] adj fictitious

fiction [fiksjɔ̃] nf fiction; (fait imaginé) invention

fidèle [fidɛl] adj faithful ♦ nm/f (REL): **les ~s** (à l'église) the congregation sg; **fidélité** nf fidelity

fier¹ [fje]: **se ~ à** vt to trust

fier², fière [fjɛʀ] adj proud; **fierté** nf pride

fièvre [fjɛvʀ] nf fever; **avoir de la ~/39 de ~** to have a high temperature/a temperature of 39ºC; **fiévreux, -euse** adj feverish

figé, e [fiʒe] adj (manières) stiff; (société) rigid; (sourire) set

figer [fiʒe]: **se ~** vi (huile) to congeal; (personne) to freeze

fignoler [fiɲɔle] (fam) vt to polish up

figue [fig] nf fig; **figuier** nm fig tree

figurant, e [figyʀɑ̃, ɑ̃t] nm/f (THÉÂTRE) walk-on; (CINÉMA) extra

figure [figyʀ] nf (visage) face; (forme, personnage) figure; (illustration) picture, diagram

figuré, e [figyʀe] adj (sens) figurative

figurer [figyʀe] vi to appear ♦ vt to represent; **se ~ que** to imagine that

fil [fil] nm (brin, fig: d'une histoire) thread; (électrique) wire; (d'un couteau) edge; **au ~ des années** with the passing of the years; **au ~ de l'eau** with the stream ou current; **coup de ~** (fam) phone call; ~ **à coudre** (sewing) thread; ~ **de fer** wire; ~ **de fer barbelé** barbed wire

filament [filamɑ̃] nm (ÉLEC) filament

filandreux, -euse [filɑ̃dʀø, øz] adj stringy

filature [filatyʀ] nf (fabrique) mill; (policière) shadowing no pl, tailing no pl

file [fil] nf line; (AUTO) lane; **en ~ indienne** in single file; **à la ~** (d'affilée) in succession; ~ **(d'attente)** queue (BRIT), line (US)

filer [file] vt (tissu, toile) to spin; (prendre en filature) to shadow, tail; (fam: donner): ~ **qch à qn** to slip sb sth ♦ vi (bas) to run; (aller vite) to fly past; (fam: partir) to make ou be off; ~ **doux** to toe the line

filet [filɛ] nm net; (CULIN) fillet; (d'eau, de sang) trickle; ~ **(à provisions)** string bag

filiale [filjal] nf (COMM) subsidiary

filière [filjɛʀ] nf (carrière) path; **suivre la ~** (dans sa carrière) to work one's way up (through the hierarchy)

filiforme [filifɔʀm] *adj* spindly

filigrane [filigʀan] *nm* (*d'un billet, timbre*) watermark

fille [fij] *nf* girl; (*opposé à fils*) daughter; **vieille ~** old maid; **fillette** *nf* (little) girl

filleul, e [fijœl] *nm/f* godchild, godson/ daughter

film [film] *nm* (*pour photo*) (roll of) film; (*œuvre*) film, picture, movie; **~ d'épouvante** horror film; **~ policier** thriller

filon [filɔ̃] *nm* vein, lode; (*fig*) lucrative line, money spinner

fils [fis] *nm* son; **à papa** daddy's boy

filtre [filtʀ] *nm* filter; **filtrer** *vt* to filter; (*fig: candidats, visiteurs*) to screen

fin¹ [fɛ̃] *nf* end; **~s** *nfpl* (*but*) ends; **prendre ~** to come to an end; **mettre ~ à** to put an end to; **à la ~** in the end, eventually; **en ~ de compte** in the end; **sans ~** endless; **~ juin** at the end of June

fin², e [fɛ̃, fin] *adj* (*papier, couche, fil*) thin; (*cheveux, visage*) fine; (*taille*) neat, slim; (*esprit, remarque*) subtle ♦ *adv* (*couper*) finely; **~ prêt** quite ready; **~es herbes** mixed herbs

final, e [final, o] *adj* final ♦ *nm* (*MUS*) finale; **finale** *nf* final; **quarts de finale** quarter finals; **finalement** *adv* finally, in the end; (*après tout*) after all

finance [finɑ̃s]: **~s** *nfpl* (*situation*) finances; (*activités*) finance *sg*; **moyennant ~** for a fee; **financer** *vt* to finance; **financier, -ière** *adj* financial

finaud, e [fino, od] *adj* wily

finesse [fines] *nf* thinness; (*raffinement*) fineness; (*subtilité*) subtlety

fini, e [fini] *adj* finished; (*MATH*) finite ♦ *nm* (*d'un objet manufacturé*) finish

finir [finiʀ] *vt* to finish ♦ *vi* to finish, end; **~ par faire** to end up *ou* finish up doing; **~ de faire** to finish doing; (*cesser*) to stop doing; **il finit par m'agacer** he's beginning to get on my nerves; **en ~ avec** to be *ou* have done with; **il va mal ~** he will come to a bad end

finition [finisjɔ̃] *nf* (*résultat*) finish

finlandais, e [fɛ̃lɑ̃dɛ, ɛz] *adj* Finnish ♦ *nm/f*: **F~, e** Finn

Finlande [fɛ̃lɑ̃d] *nf*: **la ~** Finland

fiole [fjɔl] *nf* phial

firme [fiʀm] *nf* firm

fis [fi] *vb voir* **faire**

fisc [fisk] *nm* tax authorities *pl*; **fiscal, e, -aux** *adj* tax *cpd*, fiscal; **fiscalité** *nf* tax system

fissure [fisyʀ] *nf* crack; **fissurer** *vt* to crack; **se fissurer** *vi* to crack

fiston [fistɔ̃] (*fam*) *nm* son, lad

fit [fi] *vb voir* **faire**

fixation [fiksasjɔ̃] *nf* (*attache*) fastening; (*PSYCH*) fixation

fixe [fiks] *adj* fixed; (*emploi*) steady, regular ♦ *nm* (*salaire*) basic salary; **à heure ~** at a set time; **menu à prix ~** set menu

fixé, e [fikse] *adj*: **être ~ (sur)** (*savoir à quoi s'en tenir*) to have made up one's mind (about)

fixer [fikse] *vt* (*attacher*): **~ qch (à/sur)** to fix *ou* fasten sth (to/onto); (*déterminer*) to fix, set; (*regarder*) to stare at; **se ~** *vi* (*s'établir*) to settle down; **se ~ sur** (*suj: attention*) to focus on

flacon [flakɔ̃] *nm* bottle

flageoler [flaʒɔle] *vi* (*jambes*) to sag

flageolet [flaʒɔle] *nm* (*CULIN*) dwarf kidney bean

flagrant, e [flagʀɑ̃, ɑ̃t] *adj* flagrant, blatant; **en ~ délit** in the act

flair [flɛʀ] *nm* sense of smell; (*fig*) intuition; **flairer** *vt* (*humer*) to sniff (at); (*détecter*) to scent

flamand, e [flamɑ̃, ɑ̃d] *adj* Flemish ♦ *nm* (*LING*) Flemish ♦ *nm/f*: **F~, e** Fleming; **les F~s** the Flemish

flamant [flamɑ̃] *nm* flamingo

flambant [flɑ̃bɑ̃, ɑ̃t] *adv*: **~ neuf** brand new

flambé, e [flɑ̃be] *adj* (*CULIN*) flambé

flambeau, x [flɑ̃bo] *nm* (flaming) torch

flambée [flɑ̃be] *nf* blaze; (*fig: des prix*) explosion

flamber [flɑ̃be] *vi* to blaze (up)

flamboyer [flɑ̃bwaje] *vi* to blaze (up)

flamme [flɑm] *nf* flame; (*fig*) fire, fervour; **en ~s** on fire, ablaze

flan [flɑ̃] *nm* (*CULIN*) custard tart *ou* pie

flanc [flɑ̃] *nm* side; (*MIL*) flank

flancher [flɑ̃ʃe] (*fam*) *vi* to fail, pack up

flanelle [flanɛl] *nf* flannel

flâner [flɑne] *vi* to stroll; **flânerie** *nf* stroll

flanquer [flɑ̃ke] *vt* to flank; (*fam: mettre*) to chuck, shove; (: *jeter*): **~ par terre/à la porte** to fling to the ground/chuck out

flaque [flak] *nf* (*d'eau*) puddle; (*d'huile, de sang etc*) pool

flash [flaʃ] (*pl* **~es**) *nm* (*PHOTO*) flash; **~ (d'information)** newsflash

flasque [flask] *adj* flabby

flatter [flate] *vt* to flatter; **se ~ de qch** to pride o.s. on sth; **flatterie** *nf* flattery *no pl*; **flatteur, -euse** *adj* flattering

fléau, x [fleo] *nm* scourge

flèche [flɛʃ] *nf* arrow; (*de clocher*) spire; **monter en ~** (*fig*) to soar, rocket; **partir en ~** to be off like a shot; **fléchette** *nf* dart

fléchir [fleʃiʀ] *vt* (*corps, genou*) to bend; (*fig*) to sway, weaken ♦ *vi* (*fig*) to weaken, flag

flemmard, e [flemaʀ, aʀd] (*fam*) *nm/f* lazybones *sg*, loafer

flemme [flɛm] *nf* (*fam*) laziness; **j'ai la ~ de le faire** I can't be bothered doing it

flétrir [fletʀiʀ]: **se ~** *vi* to wither

fleur [flœʀ] *nf* flower; (*d'un arbre*) blossom; **en ~** (*arbre*) in blossom; **à ~s** flowery

fleuri, e [flœʀi] *adj* (*jardin*) in flower *ou* bloom; (*tissu, papier*) flowery

fleurir [flœʀiʀ] *vi* (*rose*) to flower; (*arbre*) to blossom; (*fig*) to flourish ♦ *vt* (*tombe*) to put flowers on; (*chambre*) to decorate with flowers

fleuriste [flœʀist] *nm/f* florist

fleuve [flœv] *nm* river

flexible [flɛksibl] *adj* flexible

flic [flik] (*fam: péj*) *nm* cop

flipper [flipœʀ] *nm* pinball (machine)

flirter [flœʀte] *vi* to flirt

flocon [flɔkɔ̃] *nm* flake

flopée [flɔpe] (*fam*) *nf*: **une ~ de** loads of, masses of

floraison [flɔʀɛzɔ̃] *nf* flowering

flore [flɔʀ] *nf* flora

florissant, e [flɔʀisɑ̃, ɑ̃t] *adj* (*économie*) flourishing

flot [flo] *nm* flood, stream; **~s** *nmpl* (*de la mer*) waves; **être à ~** (*NAVIG*) to be afloat; **entrer à ~s** to stream *ou* pour in

flottant, e [flɔtɑ̃, ɑ̃t] *adj* (*vêtement*) loose

flotte [flɔt] *nf* (*NAVIG*) fleet; (*fam: eau*) water; (: *pluie*) rain

flottement [flɔtmɑ̃] *nm* (*fig*) wavering, hesitation

flotter [flɔte] *vi* to float; (*nuage, odeur*) to drift; (*drapeau*) to fly; (*vêtements*) to hang loose; (*fam: pleuvoir*) to rain; **faire ~** to float; **flotteur** *nm* float

flou, e [flu] *adj* fuzzy, blurred; (*fig*) woolly, vague

fluctuation [flyktɥasjɔ̃] *nf* fluctuation

fluet, te [flɥɛ, ɛt] *adj* thin, slight

fluide [flɥid] *adj* fluid; (*circulation etc*) flowing freely ♦ *nm* fluid

fluor [flyɔʀ] *nm*: **dentifrice au ~** fluoride toothpaste

fluorescent, e [flyɔʀesɑ̃, ɑ̃t] *adj* fluorescent

flûte [flyt] *nf* flute; (*verre*) flute glass; (*pain*) long loaf; **~!** drat it!; **~ à bec** recorder

flux [fly] *nm* incoming tide; (*écoulement*) flow; **le ~ et le reflux** the ebb and flow

FM *sigle f* (= *fréquence modulée*) FM

foc [fɔk] *nm* jib

foi [fwa] *nf* faith; **digne de ~** reliable; **être de bonne/mauvaise ~** to be sincere/insincere; **ma ~ ...** well ...

foie [fwa] *nm* liver; **crise de ~** stomach upset

foin [fwɛ̃] *nm* hay; **faire du ~** (*fig: fam*) to kick up a row

foire [fwaʀ] *nf* fair; (*fête foraine*) (fun) fair; **faire la ~** (*fig: fam*) to whoop it up; **~ (exposition)** trade fair

fois [fwa] *nf* time; **une/deux ~** once/

twice; **2 ~ 2** 2 times 2; **une ~** (*passé*) once; (*futur*) sometime; **une ~ pour toutes** once and for all; **une ~ que** once; **des ~** (*parfois*) sometimes; **à la ~** (*ensemble*) at once

foison [fwazɔ̃] *nf*: **à ~** in plenty; **foisonner** *vi* to abound

fol [fɔl] *adj voir* **fou**

folie [fɔli] *nf* (*d'une décision, d'un acte*) madness, folly; (*état*) madness, insanity; **la ~ des grandeurs** delusions of grandeur; **faire des ~s** (*en dépenses*) to be extravagant

folklorique [fɔlklɔrik] *adj* folk *cpd*; (*fam*) weird

folle [fɔl] *adj, nf voir* **fou**; **follement** *adv* (*très*) madly, wildly

foncé, e [fɔ̃se] *adj* dark

foncer [fɔ̃se] *vi* to go darker; (*fam: aller vite*) to tear *ou* belt along; **~ sur** to charge at

foncier, -ère [fɔ̃sje, jɛʀ] *adj* (*honnêteté etc*) basic, fundamental; (*COMM*) real estate *cpd*

fonction [fɔ̃ksjɔ̃] *nf* function; (*emploi, poste*) post, position; **~s** *nfpl* (*professionnelles*) duties; **voiture de ~** company car; **en ~ de** (*par rapport à*) according to; **faire ~ de** to serve as; **la ~ publique** the state *ou* civil (*BRIT*) service; **fonctionnaire** *nm/f* state employee, local authority employee; (*dans l'administration*) ≃ civil servant; **fonctionner** *vi* to work, function

fond [fɔ̃] *nm* (*d'un récipient, trou*) bottom; (*d'une salle, scène*) back; (*d'un tableau, décor*) background; (*opposé à la forme*) content; (*SPORT*): **le ~** long distance (running); **au ~ de** at the bottom of; at the back of; **à ~** (*connaître, soutenir*) thoroughly; (*appuyer, visser*) right down *ou* home; **à ~ (de train)** (*fam*) full tilt; **dans le ~, au ~** (*en somme*) basically, really; **de ~ en comble** from top to bottom; *voir aussi* **fonds**; **~ de teint** foundation (cream)

fondamental, e, -aux [fɔ̃damɑ̃tal, o] *adj* fundamental

fondant, e [fɔ̃dɑ̃, ɑ̃t] *adj* (*neige*) melting; (*poire*) that melts in the mouth

fondateur, -trice [fɔ̃datœʀ, tʀis] *nm/f* founder

fondation [fɔ̃dasjɔ̃] *nf* founding; (*établissement*) foundation; **~s** *nfpl* (*d'une maison*) foundations

fondé, e [fɔ̃de] *adj* (*accusation etc*) well-founded; **être ~ à** to have grounds for *ou* good reason to

fondement [fɔ̃dmɑ̃] *nm*: **sans ~** (*rumeur etc*) groundless, unfounded

fonder [fɔ̃de] *vt* to found; (*fig*) to base; **se ~ sur** (*suj: personne*) to base o.s. on

fonderie [fɔ̃dʀi] *nf* smelting works *sg*

fondre [fɔ̃dʀ] *vt* (*aussi:* **faire ~**) to melt; (*dans l'eau*) to dissolve; (*fig: mélanger*) to merge, blend ♦ *vi* (*à la chaleur*) to melt; (*dans l'eau*) to dissolve; (*fig*) to melt away; (*se précipiter*): **~ sur** to swoop down on; **~ en larmes** to burst into tears

fonds [fɔ̃] *nm* (*COMM*): **~ (de commerce)** business ♦ *nmpl* (*argent*) funds

fondu, e [fɔ̃dy] *adj* (*beurre, neige*) melted; (*métal*) molten; **fondue** *nf* (*CULIN*) fondue

font [fɔ̃] *vb voir* **faire**

fontaine [fɔ̃ten] *nf* fountain; (*source*) spring

fonte [fɔ̃t] *nf* melting; (*métal*) cast iron; **la ~ des neiges** the (spring) thaw

foot [fut] (*fam*) *nm* football

football [futbol] *nm* football, soccer; **footballeur** *nm* footballer

footing [futiŋ] *nm* jogging; **faire du ~** to go jogging

for [fɔʀ] *nm*: **dans son ~ intérieur** in one's heart of hearts

forain, e [fɔʀɛ̃, ɛn] *adj* fairground *cpd* ♦ *nm* (*marchand*) stallholder; (*acteur*) fairground entertainer

forçat [fɔʀsa] *nm* convict

force [fɔʀs] *nf* strength; (*PHYSIQUE, MÉCANIQUE*) force; **~s** *nfpl* (*physiques*) strength *sg*; (*MIL*) forces; **à ~ d'insister** by dint of insisting; **as he** (*ou* **I** *etc*) **kept on**

nsisting; **de ~** forcibly, by force; **les ~s de l'ordre** the police

rcé, e [fɔʀse] adj forced; **c'est ~** (fam) t's inevitable; **forcément** adv inevitably; **pas forcément** not necessarily

rcené, e [fɔʀsəne] nm/f maniac

rcer [fɔʀse] vt to force; (voix) to strain ♦ vi (SPORT) to overtax o.s.; **~ la dose** (fam) to overdo it; **se ~ (à faire)** to force ..s. (to do)

rcir [fɔʀsiʀ] vi (grossir) to broaden out

rer [fɔʀe] vt to drill, bore

restier, -ère [fɔʀestje, jɛʀ] adj forest pd

rêt [fɔʀe] nf forest

rfait [fɔʀfe] nm (COMM) all-in deal ou rice; **forfaitaire** adj inclusive

rge [fɔʀʒ] nf forge, smithy; **forger** vt to orge; (fig: prétexte) to contrive, make up; **orgeron** nm (black)smith

rmaliser [fɔʀmalize]: **se ~** vi: **se ~ (de)** o take offence (at)

rmalité [fɔʀmalite] nf formality; **simple** mere formality

rmat [fɔʀma] nm size; **formater** vt (dis- ue), to format

rmation [fɔʀmasjɔ̃] nf (développement) orming; (apprentissage) training; **~ per- nanente** continuing education; **~ profes- ionnelle** vocational training

rme [fɔʀm] nf (gén) form; (d'un objet) hape, form; **~s** nfpl (bonnes manières) roprieties; (d'une femme) figure sg; **être n ~** (SPORT etc) to be on form; **en bon- e et due ~** in due form

rmel, le [fɔʀmɛl] adj (catégorique) defi- ite, positive; **formellement** adv (absolu- ent) positively; **formellement interdit** rictly forbidden

rmer [fɔʀme] vt to form; (éduquer) to ain; **se ~** vi to form

rmidable [fɔʀmidabl] adj tremendous

rmulaire [fɔʀmylɛʀ] nm form

rmule [fɔʀmyl] nf (gén) formula; (expres- on) phrase; **~ de politesse** polite hrase; (en fin de lettre) letter ending; **for-**

muler vt (émettre: désir) to formulate

fort, e [fɔʀ, fɔʀt] adj strong; (intensité, ren- dement) high, great; (corpulent) stout; (doué) good, able ♦ adv (serrer, frapper) hard; (parler) loud(ly); (beaucoup) greatly, very much; (très) very ♦ nm (édifice) fort; (point ~) strong point, forte; **~e tête** re- bel; **forteresse** nf stronghold

fortifiant [fɔʀtifjɑ̃, jɑ̃t] nm tonic

fortifier [fɔʀtifje] vt to strengthen, fortify

fortiori [fɔʀsjɔʀi]: **à ~** adv all the more so

fortuit, e [fɔʀtɥi, it] adj fortuitous, chance cpd

fortune [fɔʀtyn] nf fortune; **faire ~** to make one's fortune; **de ~** makeshift; **for- tuné, e** adj wealthy

fosse [fos] nf (grand trou) pit; (tombe) grave

fossé [fose] nm ditch; (fig) gulf, gap

fossette [fosɛt] nf dimple

fossile [fosil] nm fossil

fossoyeur [foswajœʀ] nm gravedigger

fou (fol), folle [fu, fɔl] adj mad; (déréglé etc) wild, erratic; (fam: extrême, très grand) terrific, tremendous ♦ nm/f madman(- woman) ♦ nm (du roi) jester; **être ~de** to be mad ou crazy about; **avoir le ~rire** to have the giggles

foudre [fudʀ] nf: **la ~** lightning

foudroyant, e [fudʀwajɑ̃, ɑ̃t] adj (progrès) lightning cpd; (succès) stunning; (maladie, poison) violent

foudroyer [fudʀwaje] vt to strike down; **être foudroyé** to be struck by lightning; **~ qn du regard** to glare at sb

fouet [fwe] nm whip; (CULIN) whisk; **de plein ~** (se heurter) head on; **fouetter** vt to whip; (crème) to whisk

fougère [fuʒɛʀ] nf fern

fougue [fug] nf ardour, spirit; **fougueux, -euse** adj fiery

fouille [fuj] nf search; **~s** nfpl (archéologi- ques) excavations; **fouiller** vt to search; (creuser) to dig ♦ vi to rummage; **fouillis** nm jumble, muddle

fouiner [fwine] vi (péj): **~ dans** to nose

around *ou* about in
foulard [fulaʀ] *nm* scarf
foule [ful] *nf* crowd; **la ~** crowds *pl*; **une ~ de** masses of
foulée [fule] *nf* stride
fouler [fule] *vt* to press; (*sol*) to tread upon; **se ~ la cheville** to sprain one's ankle; **ne pas se ~** not to overexert o.s.; **il ne se foule pas** he doesn't put himself out; **foulure** *nf* sprain
four [fuʀ] *nm* oven; (*de potier*) kiln; (*THÉÂTRE: échec*) flop
fourbe [fuʀb] *adj* deceitful
fourbu, e [fuʀby] *adj* exhausted
fourche [fuʀʃ] *nf* pitchfork
fourchette [fuʀʃɛt] *nf* fork; (*STATISTIQUE*) bracket, margin
fourgon [fuʀɡɔ̃] *nm* van; (*RAIL*) wag(g)on; **fourgonnette** *nf* (small) van
fourmi [fuʀmi] *nf* ant; **~s** *nfpl* (*fig*) pins and needles; **fourmilière** *nf* ant-hill; **fourmiller** *vi* to swarm
fournaise [fuʀnɛz] *nf* blaze; (*fig*) furnace, oven
fourneau, x [fuʀno] *nm* stove
fournée [fuʀne] *nf* batch
fourni, e [fuʀni] *adj* (*barbe, cheveux*) thick; (*magasin*): **bien ~ (en)** well stocked (with)
fournir [fuʀniʀ] *vt* to supply; (*preuve, exemple*) to provide, supply; (*effort*) to put in; **fournisseur, -euse** *nm/f* supplier; **fournisseur m d'accès** service provider; **fourniture** *nf* supply(ing); **fournitures scolaires** school stationery
fourrage [fuʀaʒ] *nm* fodder
fourré, e [fuʀe] *adj* (*bonbon etc*) filled; (*manteau etc*) fur-lined ♦ *nm* thicket
fourrer [fuʀe] (*fam*) *vt* to stick, shove; **se ~ dans/sous** to get into/under; **fourre-tout** *nm inv* (*sac*) holdall; (*fig*) rag-bag
fourrière [fuʀjɛʀ] *nf* pound
fourrure [fuʀyʀ] *nf* fur; (*sur l'animal*) coat
fourvoyer [fuʀvwaje]: **se ~** *vi* to go astray, stray
foutre [futʀ] (*fam!*) *vt* = **ficher**; **foutu, e** (*fam!*) *adj* = **fichu, e**

foyer [fwaje] *nm* (*maison*) home; (*famil* family; (*de cheminée*) hearth; (*de jeunes e* (social) club; (*résidence*) hostel; (*salo* foyer; **lunettes à double ~** bi-focals
fracas [fʀaka] *nm* (*d'objet qui tombe*) cra* **fracassant, e** *adj* (*succès*) thunderir **fracasser** *vt* to smash
fraction [fʀaksjɔ̃] *nf* fraction; **fractionn** *vt* to divide (up), split (up)
fracture [fʀaktyʀ] *nf* fracture; **~ du crâ** fractured skull; **fracturer** *vt* (*coffre, s* *rure*) to break open; (*os, membre*) to fra ture
fragile [fʀaʒil] *adj* fragile, delicate; (* frail; **fragilité** *nf* fragility
fragment [fʀaɡmɑ̃] *nm* (*d'un objet*) fra ment, piece
fraîche [fʀɛʃ] *adj voir* **frais**; **fraîcheur** coolness; (*d'un aliment*) freshness; **fraîch** *vi* to get cooler; (*vent*) to freshen
frais, fraîche [fʀɛ, fʀɛʃ] *adj* fresh; (*fro* cool ♦ *adv* (*récemment*) newly, fresh ♦ *nm*: **mettre au ~** to put in a cool pla ♦ *nmpl* (*gén*) expenses; (*COMM*) costs; **fait ~** it's cool; **servir ~** serve chille **prendre le ~** to take a breath of cool a **faire des ~** to go to a lot of expense **de scolarité** school fees (*BRIT*), tuiti (*US*); **~ généraux** overheads
fraise [fʀɛz] *nf* strawberry; **~ des bois** w strawberry
framboise [fʀɑ̃bwaz] *nf* raspberry
franc, franche [fʀɑ̃, fʀɑ̃ʃ] *adj* (*person* frank, straightforward; (*visage*) open; (* *refus*) clear; (*: coupure*) clean; (*inter* downright ♦ *nm* franc
français, e [fʀɑ̃sɛ, ɛz] *adj* French ♦ *nm* **F~, e** Frenchman(-woman) ♦ *nm* (*LIN* French; **les F~** the French
France [fʀɑ̃s] *nf*: **la ~** France
franche [fʀɑ̃ʃ] *adj voir* **franc**; **franch** **ment** *adv* frankly; (*nettement*) definit (*tout à fait: mauvais etc*) downright
franchir [fʀɑ̃ʃiʀ] *vt* (*obstacle*) to clear, over; (*seuil, ligne, rivière*) to cross; (*distar* to cover

franchise [fʀɑ̃ʃiz] nf frankness; (douanière) exemption; (ASSURANCES) excess

franc-maçon [fʀɑ̃masɔ̃] nm freemason

franco [fʀɑ̃ko] adv (COMM): ~ **(de port)** postage paid

francophone [fʀɑ̃kɔfɔn] adj French-speaking

franc-parler [fʀɑ̃paʀle] nm inv outspokenness; **avoir son ~-~** to speak one's mind

frange [fʀɑ̃ʒ] nf fringe

frangipane [fʀɑ̃ʒipan] nf almond paste

franquette [fʀɑ̃kɛt]: **à la bonne ~** adv without any fuss

frappant, e [fʀapɑ̃, ɑ̃t] adj striking

frappé, e [fʀape] adj iced

frapper [fʀape] vt to hit, strike; (étonner) to strike; **~ dans ses mains** to clap one's hands; **frappé de stupeur** dumbfounded

frasques [fʀask] nfpl escapades

fraternel, le [fʀatɛʀnɛl] adj brotherly, fraternal; **fraternité** nf brotherhood

fraude [fʀod] nf fraud; (SCOL) cheating; **passer qch en ~** to smuggle sth in (ou out); **~ fiscale** tax evasion; **frauder** vi, vt to cheat; **frauduleux, -euse** adj fraudulent

frayer [fʀeje] vt to open up, clear ♦ vi to spawn; **se ~ un chemin dans la foule** to force one's way through the crowd

frayeur [fʀejœʀ] nf fright

fredonner [fʀədɔne] vt to hum

freezer [fʀizœʀ] nm freezing compartment

frein [fʀɛ̃] nm brake; **mettre un ~ à** (fig) to curb, check; **~ à main** handbrake; **freiner** vi to brake ♦ vt (progrès etc) to check

frêle [fʀɛl] adj frail, fragile

frelon [fʀəlɔ̃] nm hornet

frémir [fʀemiʀ] vi (de peur, d'horreur) to shudder; (de colère) to shake; (feuillage) to quiver

frêne [fʀɛn] nm ash

frénétique [fʀenetik] adj frenzied, frenetic

fréquemment [fʀekamɑ̃] adv frequently

fréquent, e [fʀekɑ̃, ɑ̃t] adj frequent

fréquentation [fʀekɑ̃tasjɔ̃] nf frequenting;

~s nfpl (relations) company sg

fréquenté, e [fʀekɑ̃te] adj: **très ~** (very) busy; **mal ~** patronized by disreputable elements

fréquenter [fʀekɑ̃te] vt (lieu) to frequent; (personne) to see; **se ~** to see each other

frère [fʀɛʀ] nm brother

fresque [fʀɛsk] nf (ART) fresco

fret [fʀɛ(t)] nm freight

frétiller [fʀetije] vi (poisson) to wriggle

fretin [fʀətɛ̃] nm: **menu ~** small fry

friable [fʀijabl] adj crumbly

friand, e [fʀijɑ̃, fʀijɑ̃d] adj: **~ de** very fond of ♦ nm: **~ au fromage** cheese puff

friandise [fʀijɑ̃diz] nf sweet

fric [fʀik] (fam) nm cash, bread

friche [fʀiʃ]: **en ~** adj, adv (lying) fallow

friction [fʀiksjɔ̃] nf (massage) rub, rubdown; (TECH, fig) friction; **frictionner** vt to rub (down)

frigidaire ® [fʀiʒidɛʀ] nm refrigerator

frigide [fʀiʒid] adj frigid

frigo [fʀigo] (fam) nm fridge

frigorifié, e [fʀigɔʀifje] (fam) adj: **être ~** to be frozen stiff

frigorifique [fʀigɔʀifik] adj refrigerating

frileux, -euse [fʀilø, øz] adj sensitive to (the) cold

frime [fʀim] (fam) nf: **c'est de la ~** it's a lot of eyewash, it's all put on; **frimer** (fam) vi to show off

frimousse [fʀimus] nf (sweet) little face

fringale [fʀɛ̃gal] (fam) nf: **avoir la ~** to be ravenous

fringant, e [fʀɛ̃gɑ̃, ɑ̃t] adj dashing

fringues [fʀɛ̃g] (fam) nfpl clothes

fripé, e [fʀipe] adj crumpled

fripon, ne [fʀipɔ̃, ɔn] adj roguish, mischievous ♦ nm/f rascal, rogue

fripouille [fʀipuj] nf scoundrel

frire [fʀiʀ] vt, vi: **faire ~** to fry

frisé, e [fʀize] adj (cheveux) curly; (personne) curly-haired

frisson [fʀisɔ̃] nm (de froid) shiver; (de peur) shudder; **frissonner** vi (de fièvre, froid) to shiver; (d'horreur) to shudder

frit, e [fʀi, fʀit] *pp* de **frire**; **frite** *nf*: (**pommes**) **frites** chips (*BRIT*), French fries; **friteuse** *nf* chip pan; **friture** *nf* (*huile*) (deep) fat; (*plat*): **friture** (**de poissons**) fried fish

frivole [fʀivɔl] *adj* frivolous

froid, e [fʀwa, fʀwad] *adj, nm* cold; **il fait ~** it's cold; **avoir/prendre ~** to be/catch cold; **être en ~ avec** to be on bad terms with; **froidement** *adv* (*accueillir*) coldly; (*décider*) coolly

froideur [fʀwadœʀ] *nf* coldness

froisser [fʀwase] *vt* to crumple (up), crease; (*fig*) to hurt, offend; **se ~** to crumple, crease; (*personne*) to take offence; **se ~ un muscle** to strain a muscle

frôler [fʀole] *vt* to brush against; (*suj: projectile*) to skim past; (*fig*) to come very close to

fromage [fʀɔmaʒ] *nm* cheese; **~ blanc** soft white cheese

froment [fʀɔmɑ̃] *nm* wheat

froncer [fʀɔ̃se] *vt* to gather; **~ les sourcils** to frown

frondaisons [fʀɔ̃dɛzɔ̃] *nfpl* foliage *sg*

front [fʀɔ̃] *nm* forehead, brow; (*MIL*) front; **de ~** (*se heurter*) head-on; (*rouler*) together (*i.e. 2 or 3 abreast*); (*simultanément*) at once; **faire ~ à** to face up to

frontalier, -ère [fʀɔ̃talje, jɛʀ] *adj* border *cpd*, frontier *cpd*

frontière [fʀɔ̃tjɛʀ] *nf* frontier, border

frotter [fʀɔte] *vi* to rub, scrape ♦ *vt* to rub; (*pommes de terre, plancher*) to scrub; **~ une allumette** to strike a match

fructifier [fʀyktifje] *vi* to yield a profit

fructueux, -euse [fʀyktɥø, øz] *adj* fruitful

frugal, e, -aux [fʀygal, o] *adj* frugal

fruit [fʀɥi] *nm* fruit *gen no pl*; **~ de la passion** passion fruit; **~s de mer** seafood(s); **~s secs** dried fruit *sg*; **fruité, e** *adj* fruity; **fruitier, -ère** *adj*: **arbre fruitier** fruit tree

fruste [fʀyst] *adj* unpolished, uncultivated

frustrer [fʀystʀe] *vt* to frustrate

FS *abr* (= *franc suisse*) SF

fuel(-oil) [fjul(ɔjl)] *nm* fuel oil; (*domestiqu* heating oil

fugace [fygas] *adj* fleeting

fugitif, -ive [fyʒitif, iv] *adj* (*fugace*) fleetir ♦ *nm/f* fugitive

fugue [fyg] *nf*: **faire une ~** to run awa abscond

fuir [fɥiʀ] *vt* to flee from; (*éviter*) to sh ♦ *vi* to run away; (*gaz, robinet*) to leak

fuite [fɥit] *nf* flight; (*écoulement, divulgatio* leak; **être en ~** to be on the run; **mett en ~** to put to flight

fulgurant, e [fylgyʀɑ̃, ɑ̃t] *adj* lightnin *cpd*, dazzling

fulminer [fylmine] *vi* to thunder forth

fumé, e [fyme] *adj* (*CULIN*) smoked; (*ver* tinted; **fumée** *nf* smoke

fumer [fyme] *vi* to smoke; (*soupe*) steam ♦ *vt* to smoke

fûmes *etc* [fym] *vb voir* **être**

fumet [fymɛ] *nm* aroma

fumeur, -euse [fymœʀ, øz] *nm/f* smoke

fumeux, -euse [fymø, øz] (*péj*) *a* woolly, hazy

fumier [fymje] *nm* manure

fumiste [fymist] *nm/f* (*péj: paresseux*) shir er

funèbre [fynɛbʀ] *adj* funeral *cpd*; (*fig*: *mosphère*) gloomy

funérailles [fyneʀɑj] *nfpl* funeral *sg*

funeste [fynɛst] *adj* (*erreur*) disastrous

fur [fyʀ]: **au ~ et à mesure** *adv* as o goes along; **au ~ et à mesure que** as

furet [fyʀɛ] *nm* ferret

fureter [fyʀ(ə)te] (*péj*) *vi* to nose about

fureur [fyʀœʀ] *nf* fury; **être en ~** to be furiated; **faire ~** to be all the rage

furibond, e [fyʀibɔ̃, ɔ̃d] *adj* furious

furie [fyʀi] *nf* fury; (*femme*) shrew, vixe **en ~** (*mer*) raging; **furieux, -euse** *a* furious

furoncle [fyʀɔ̃kl] *nm* boil

furtif, -ive [fyʀtif, iv] *adj* furtive

fus [fy] *vb voir* **être**

fusain [fyzɛ̃] *nm* (*ART*) charcoal

fuseau, x [fyzo] *nm* (*pour filer*) spind

(pantalon) (ski) pants; **~ horaire** time zone
∎sée [fyze] *nf* rocket; **~ éclairante** flare
∎ser [fyze] *vi (rires etc)* to burst forth
∎sible [fyzibl] *nm (ÉLEC: fil)* fuse wire;
(: fiche) fuse
∎sil [fyzi] *nm (de guerre, à canon rayé)* rifle,
gun; *(de chasse, à canon lisse)* shotgun,
gun; **fusillade** *nf* gunfire *no pl*, shooting
no pl; **fusiller** *vt* to shoot; **fusil-
mitrailleur** *nm* machine gun
∎sionner [fyzjɔne] *vi* to merge
∎t [fy] *vb voir* **être**
∎t [fy] *vb voir* **être** ♦ *nm (tonneau)* barrel,
cask
∎té, e [fyte] *adj* crafty; **Bison ~** ® *TV
and radio traffic monitoring service*
∎tile [fytil] *adj* futile; frivolous
∎tur, e [fytyR] *adj, nm* future
∎yant, e [fɥijã, ãt] *vb voir* **fuir** ♦ *adj (regard etc)* evasive; *(lignes etc)* receding
∎yard, e [fɥijar, ard] *nm/f* runaway

G, g

∎âcher [gɑʃe] *vt (gâter)* to spoil; *(gaspiller)*
to waste; **gâchis** *nm* waste *no pl*
∎adoue [gadu] *nf* sludge
∎affe [gaf] *nf* blunder; **faire ~** *(fam)* to be
careful
∎age [gaʒ] *nm (dans un jeu)* forfeit; *(fig: de
fidélité, d'amour)* token
∎ageure [gaʒyR] *nf*: **c'est une ~** it's attempting the impossible
∎agnant, e [gaɲã, ãt] *nm/f* winner
∎agne-pain [gɑɲpɛ̃] *nm inv* job
∎agner [gaɲe] *vt* to win; *(somme d'argent,
revenu)* to earn; *(aller vers, atteindre)* to
reach; *(envahir: sommeil, peur)* to overcome; *(: mal)* to spread to ♦ *vi* to win;
(fig) to gain; **~ du temps/de la place** to
gain time/save space; **~ sa vie** to earn
one's living
∎i, e [ge] *adj* cheerful; *(un peu ivre)* merry; **gaiement** *adv* cheerfully; **gaieté** *nf*
cheerfulness; **de gaieté de cœur** with a
light heart

gaillard [gajaR, aRd] *nm (strapping)* fellow
gain [gɛ̃] *nm (revenu)* earnings *pl*; *(bénéfice:
gén pl)* profits *pl*
gaine [gɛn] *nf (corset)* girdle; *(fourreau)*
sheath
gala [gala] *nm* official reception; **de ~**
(soirée etc) gala
galant, e [galã, ãt] *adj (courtois)* courteous, gentlemanly; *(entreprenant)* flirta-
tious, gallant; *(scène, rendez-vous)* romantic
galère [galɛR] *nf* gallery; **quelle ~!** *(fam)* it's
a real grind!; **galérer** *(fam) vi* to slog
away, work hard; *(rencontrer les difficultés)*
to have a hassle
galerie [galRi] *nf* gallery; *(THÉÂTRE)* circle;
(de voiture) roof rack; *(fig: spectateurs)*
audience; **~ de peinture** (private) art gallery; **~ marchande** shopping arcade
galet [galɛ] *nm* pebble
galette [galɛt] *nf* flat cake; **~ des Rois**
cake eaten on Twelfth Night
galipette [galipɛt] *nf* somersault
Galles [gal] *nfpl*: **le pays de ~** Wales;
gallois, e *adj* Welsh ♦ *nm/f*: **Gallois, e**
Welshman(-woman) ♦ *nm (LING)* Welsh
galon [galɔ̃] *nm (MIL)* stripe; *(décoratif)*
piece of braid
galop [galo] *nm* gallop; **galoper** *vi* to gallop
galopin [galɔpɛ̃] *nm* urchin, ragamuffin
gambader [gɑ̃bade] *vi (animal, enfant)* to
leap about
gambas [gɑ̃bas] *nfpl* Mediterranean
prawns
gamin, e [gamɛ̃, in] *nm/f* kid ♦ *adj* childish
gamme [gam] *nf (MUS)* scale; *(fig)* range
gammé, e [game] *adj*: **croix ~e** swastika
gang [gɑ̃g] *nm (de criminels)* gang
gant [gɑ̃] *nm* glove; **~ de toilette** face flannel *(BRIT)*, face cloth
garage [gaRaʒ] *nm* garage; **garagiste**
nm/f garage owner; *(employé)* garage
mechanic
garantie [gaRɑ̃ti] *nf* guarantee; **(bon de) ~**

guarantee *ou* warranty slip

garantir [gaʀɑ̃tiʀ] *vt* to guarantee

garce [gaʀs] *(fam) nf* bitch

garçon [gaʀsɔ̃] *nm* boy; *(célibataire):* **vieux ~** bachelor; *(serveur):* **~ (de café)** waiter; **~ de courses** messenger; **~ d'honneur** best man; **garçonnière** *nf* bachelor flat

garde [gaʀd(ə)] *nm (de prisonnier)* guard; *(de domaine etc)* warden; *(soldat, sentinelle)* guardsman ♦ *nf (soldats)* guard; **de ~** on duty; **monter la ~** to stand guard; **mettre en ~** to warn; **prendre (à) ~** to be careful (of); **~ champêtre** ♦ *nm* rural policeman; **~ du corps** ♦ *nm* bodyguard; **~ des enfants** ♦ *nf (après divorce)* custody of the children; **~ à vue** ♦ *nf (JUR)* ≃ police custody; **garde-à-vous** *nm:* **être/se mettre au garde-à-vous** to be at/stand to attention; **garde-barrière** *nm/f* level-crossing keeper; **garde-boue** *nm inv* mudguard; **garde-chasse** *nm* game-keeper; **garde-malade** *nf* home nurse; **garde-manger** *nm inv (armoire)* meat safe; *(pièce)* pantry, larder

garder [gaʀde] *vt (conserver)* to keep; *(surveiller: enfants)* to look after; (*: immeuble, lieu, prisonnier*) to guard; **se ~** *vi (aliment: se conserver)* to keep; **se ~ de faire** to be careful not to do; **~ le lit/la chambre** to stay in bed/indoors; **pêche/chasse gardée** private fishing/hunting (ground)

garderie [gaʀdəʀi] *nf* day nursery, crèche

garde-robe [gaʀdəʀɔb] *nf* wardrobe

gardien, ne [gaʀdjɛ̃, jɛn] *nm/f (garde)* guard; *(de prison)* warder; *(de domaine, réserve)* warden; *(de musée etc)* attendant; *(de phare, cimetière)* keeper; *(d'immeuble)* caretaker; *(fig)* guardian; **~ de but** goal-keeper; **~ de la paix** policeman; **~ de nuit** night watchman

gare [gaʀ] *nf* station; **~ routière** bus station

garer [gaʀe] *vt* to park; **se ~** *vi* to park

gargariser [gaʀgaʀize]: **se ~** *vi* to gargle

gargote [gaʀgɔt] *nf* cheap restaurant

gargouille [gaʀguj] *nf* gargoyle

gargouiller [gaʀguje] *vi* to gurgle

garnement [gaʀnəmɑ̃] *nm* rascal, scally-wag

garni, e [gaʀni] *adj (plat)* served with vegetables *(and chips or rice etc)*

garnison [gaʀnizɔ̃] *nf* garrison

garniture [gaʀnityʀ] *nf (CULIN)* vegetable *pl;* **~ de frein** brake lining

gars [gɑ] *(fam) nm* guy

Gascogne [gaskɔɲ] *nf* Gascony; **le golfe de ~** the Bay of Biscay

gas-oil [gazɔjl] *nm* diesel (oil)

gaspiller [gaspije] *vt* to waste

gastronome [gastʀɔnɔm] *nm/f* gourmet; **gastronomie** *nf* gastronomy; **gastronomique** *adj* gastronomic

gâteau, x [gɑto] *nm* cake; **~ sec** biscuit

gâter [gɑte] *vt* to spoil; **se ~** *vi (dent, fruit)* to go bad; *(temps, situation)* to change for the worse

gâterie [gɑtʀi] *nf* little treat

gâteux, -euse [gɑtø, øz] *adj* senile

gauche [goʃ] *adj* left, left-hand; *(maladroit)* awkward, clumsy ♦ *nf (POL)* left (wing); **bras ~** the left arm; **le côté ~** the left-hand side; **à ~** on the left; *(direction)* (to the) left; **gaucher, -ère** *adj* left-handed; **gauchiste** *nm/f* leftist

gaufre [gofʀ] *nf* waffle

gaufrette [gofʀɛt] *nf* wafer

gaulois, e [golwa, waz] *adj* Gallic ♦ *nm/f:* **G~, e** Gaul

gaver [gave] *vt* to force-feed; **se ~ de** to stuff o.s. with

gaz [gaz] *nm inv* gas

gaze [gaz] *nf* gauze

gazer [gaze] *(fam) vi:* **ça gaze?** how's things?

gazette [gazɛt] *nf* news sheet

gazeux, -euse [gazø, øz] *adj (boisson)* fizzy; *(eau)* sparkling

gazoduc [gazodyk] *nm* gas pipeline

gazon [gazɔ̃] *nm (herbe)* grass; *(pelouse)* lawn

gazouiller [gazuje] *vi* to chirp; *(enfant)* to babble

geai [ʒɛ] *nm* jay

géant, e [ʒeã, ãt] *adj* gigantic; (*COMM*) giant-size ♦ *nm/f* giant

geindre [ʒɛ̃dʀ] *vi* to groan, moan

gel [ʒɛl] *nm* frost

gélatine [ʒelatin] *nf* gelatine

gelée [ʒ(ə)le] *nf* jelly; (*gel*) frost

geler [ʒ(ə)le] *vt*, *vi* to freeze; **il gèle** it's freezing

gélule [ʒelyl] *nf* (*MÉD*) capsule

gelures [ʒəlyʀ] *nfpl* frostbite *sg*

Gémeaux [ʒemo] *nmpl*: **les ~** Gemini

gémir [ʒemiʀ] *vi* to groan, moan

gênant, e [ʒɛnã, ãt] *adj* (*irritant*) annoying; (*embarrassant*) embarrassing

gencive [ʒãsiv] *nf* gum

gendarme [ʒãdaʀm] *nm* gendarme; **gendarmerie** *nf* military police force in countryside and small towns; *their police station or barracks*

gendre [ʒãdʀ] *nm* son-in-law

gêné, e [ʒene] *adj* embarrassed

gêner [ʒene] *vt* (*incommoder*) to bother; (*encombrer*) to be in the way; (*embarrasser*): **~ qn** to make sb feel ill-at-ease

général, e, -aux [ʒeneral, o] *adj, nm* general; **en ~** usually, in general; **générale** *nf*: **(répétition) générale** final dress rehearsal; **généralement** *adv* generally; **généraliser** *vt, vi* to generalize; **se généraliser** *vi* to become widespread; **généraliste** *nm/f* general practitioner, G.P.

génération [ʒeneʀasjɔ̃] *nf* generation

généreux, -euse [ʒeneʀø, øz] *adj* generous

générique [ʒeneʀik] *nm* (*CINÉMA*) credits *pl*

générosité [ʒeneʀozite] *nf* generosity

genêt [ʒ(ə)nɛ] *nm* broom *no pl* (*shrub*)

génétique [ʒenetik] *adj* genetic; **génétiquement** *adv*: **génétiquement modifié** genetically-modified

Genève [ʒ(ə)nɛv] *n* Geneva

génial, e, -aux [ʒenjal, jo] *adj* of genius; (*fam: formidable*) fantastic, brilliant

génie [ʒeni] *nm* genius; (*MIL*): **le ~** the Engineers *pl*; **~ civil** civil engineering

genièvre [ʒənjɛvʀ] *nm* juniper

génisse [ʒenis] *nf* heifer

génital, e, -aux [ʒenital, o] *adj* genital; **les parties ~es** the genitals

génoise [ʒenwaz] *nf* sponge cake

genou, x [ʒ(ə)nu] *nm* knee; **à ~x** on one's knees; **se mettre à ~x** to kneel down

genre [ʒãʀ] *nm* kind, type, sort; (*LING*) gender; **avoir bon ~** to look a nice sort; **avoir mauvais ~** to be coarse-looking; **ce n'est pas son ~** it's not like him

gens [ʒã] *nmpl* (*f in some phrases*) people *pl*

gentil, le [ʒãti, ij] *adj* kind; (*enfant: sage*) good; (*endroit etc*) nice; **gentillesse** *nf* kindness; **gentiment** *adv* kindly

géographie [ʒeɔgʀafi] *nf* geography

geôlier [ʒolje, jɛʀ] *nm* jailer

géologie [ʒeɔlɔʒi] *nf* geology

géomètre [ʒeɔmɛtʀ] *nm/f* (*arpenteur*) (land) surveyor

géométrie [ʒeɔmetʀi] *nf* geometry; **géométrique** *adj* geometric

géranium [ʒeʀanjɔm] *nm* geranium

gérant, e [ʒeʀã, ãt] *nm/f* manager(-eress)

gerbe [ʒɛʀb] *nf* (*de fleurs*) spray; (*de blé*) sheaf

gercé, e [ʒɛʀse] *adj* chapped

gerçure [ʒɛʀsyʀ] *nf* crack

gérer [ʒeʀe] *vt* to manage

germain, e [ʒɛʀmɛ̃, ɛn] *adj*: **cousin ~** first cousin

germe [ʒɛʀm] *nm* germ; **germer** *vi* to sprout; (*semence*) to germinate

geste [ʒɛst] *nm* gesture

gestion [ʒɛstjɔ̃] *nf* management

gibier [ʒibje] *nm* (*animaux*) game

giboulée [ʒibule] *nf* sudden shower

gicler [ʒikle] *vi* to spurt, squirt

gifle [ʒifl] *nf* slap (in the face); **gifler** *vt* to slap (in the face)

gigantesque [ʒigãtɛsk] *adj* gigantic

gigogne [ʒigɔɲ] *adj*: **lits ~s** truckle (*BRIT*) *ou* trundle beds

gigot [ʒigo] *nm* leg (of mutton *ou* lamb)

gigoter [ʒigɔte] *vi* to wriggle (about)
gilet [ʒile] *nm* waistcoat; (*pull*) cardigan; ~ **de sauvetage** life jacket
gin [dʒin] *nm* gin; ~**-tonic** gin and tonic
gingembre [ʒɛ̃ʒɑ̃bʀ] *nm* ginger
girafe [ʒiʀaf] *nf* giraffe
giratoire [ʒiʀatwaʀ] *adj*: **sens** ~ roundabout
girofle [ʒiʀɔfl] *nf*: **clou de** ~ clove
girouette [ʒiʀwɛt] *nf* weather vane *ou* cock
gitan, e [ʒitɑ̃, an] *nm/f* gipsy
gîte [ʒit] *nm* (*maison*) home; (*abri*) shelter; ~ **(rural)** holiday cottage *ou* apartment
givre [ʒivʀ] *nm* (hoar) frost; **givré, e** *adj* covered in frost; (*fam: fou*) nuts; **orange givrée** orange sorbet (*served in peel*)
glace [glas] *nf* ice; (*crème glacée*) ice cream; (*miroir*) mirror; (*de voiture*) window
glacé, e [glase] *adj* (*mains, vent, pluie*) freezing; (*lac*) frozen; (*boisson*) iced
glacer [glase] *vt* to freeze; (*gâteau*) to ice; (*fig*): ~ **qn** (*intimider*) to chill sb; (*paralyser*) to make sb's blood run cold
glacial, e [glasjal, jo] *adj* icy
glacier [glasje] *nm* (*GÉO*) glacier; (*marchand*) ice-cream maker
glacière [glasjɛʀ] *nf* icebox
glaçon [glasɔ̃] *nm* icicle; (*pour boisson*) ice cube
glaïeul [glajœl] *nm* gladiolus
glaise [glez] *nf* clay
gland [glɑ̃] *nm* acorn; (*décoration*) tassel
glande [glɑ̃d] *nf* gland
glander [glɑ̃de] (*fam*) *vi* to fart around (*!*)
glauque [glok] *adj* dull blue-green
glissade [glisad] *nf* (*par jeu*) slide; (*chute*) slip; **faire des** ~**s sur la glace** to slide on the ice
glissant, e [glisɑ̃, ɑ̃t] *adj* slippery
glissement [glismɑ̃] *nm*: ~ **de terrain** landslide
glisser [glise] *vi* (*avancer*) to glide *ou* slide along; (*coulisser, tomber*) to slide; (*déraper*) to slip; (*être glissant*) to be slippery ♦ *vt* to slip; **se** ~ **dans** to slip into

global, e, -aux [glɔbal, o] *adj* overall
globe [glɔb] *nm* globe
globule [glɔbyl] *nm* (*du sang*) corpuscle
globuleux, -euse [glɔbylø, øz] *adj*: **yeu** ~ protruding eyes
gloire [glwaʀ] *nf* glory; **glorieux, -eus** *adj* glorious
glousser [gluse] *vi* to cluck; (*rire*) t chuckle; **gloussement** *nm* cluck; chuck
glouton, ne [glutɔ̃, ɔn] *adj* gluttonous
gluant, e [glyɑ̃, ɑ̃t] *adj* sticky, gummy
glucose [glykoz] *nm* glucose
glycine [glisin] *nf* wisteria
goal [gol] *nm* goalkeeper
GO *sigle* (= **grandes ondes**) LW
gobelet [gɔble] *nm* (*en étain, verre, argen* tumbler; (*d'enfant, de pique-nique*) beake (*à dés*) cup
gober [gɔbe] *vt* to swallow (whole)
godasse [gɔdas] (*fam*) *nf* shoe
godet [gɔdɛ] *nm* pot
goéland [gɔelɑ̃] *nm* (sea)gull
goélette [gɔelɛt] *nf* schooner
gogo [gɔgo]: **à** ~ *adv* galore
goguenard, e [gɔɡ(ə)naʀ, aʀd] *adj* moch ing
goinfre [gwɛ̃fʀ] *nm* glutton
golf [gɔlf] *nm* golf; (*terrain*) golf course
golfe [gɔlf] *nm* gulf; (*petit*) bay
gomme [gɔm] *nf* (*à effacer*) rubber (*BRIT* eraser; **gommer** *vt* to rub out (*BRIT* erase
gond [gɔ̃] *nm* hinge; **sortir de ses** ~**s** (*fi* to fly off the handle
gondoler [gɔ̃dɔle]: **se** ~ *vi* (*planche*) warp; (*métal*) to buckle
gonflé, e [gɔ̃fle] *adj* swollen; **il est** (*fam: courageux*) he's got some nerve; (*i* *pertinent*) he's got a nerve
gonfler [gɔ̃fle] *vt* (*pneu, ballon: en soufflar* to blow up; (*: avec une pompe*) to pum up; (*nombre, importance*) to inflate ♦ *vi* swell (up); (*CULIN: pâte*) to rise; **gonfle** *nm* pump
gonzesse [gɔ̃zɛs] (*fam*) *nf* chick, bi (*BRIT*)

oret [gɔʀɛ] nm piglet

orge [gɔʀʒ] nf (ANAT) throat; (vallée) gorge

orgé, e [gɔʀʒe] adj: ~ **de** filled with; (eau) saturated with; **gorgée** nf (petite) sip; (grande) gulp

orille [gɔʀij] nm gorilla; (fam) bodyguard

osier [gozje] nm throat

osse [gɔs] (fam) nm/f kid

oudron [gudʀɔ̃] nm tar; **goudronner** vt to tar(mac) (BRIT), asphalt (US)

ouffre [gufʀ] nm abyss, gulf

oujat [guʒa] nm boor

oulot [gulo] nm neck; **boire au** ~ to drink from the bottle

oulu, e [guly] adj greedy

ourd, e [guʀ, guʀd] adj numb (with cold)

ourde [guʀd] nf (récipient) flask; (fam) (clumsy) clot ou oaf ♦ adj oafish

ourdin [guʀdɛ̃] nm club, bludgeon

ourer [guʀe] (fam): **se** ~ vi to boob

ourmand, e [guʀmɑ̃, ɑ̃d] adj greedy; **gourmandise** [guʀmɑ̃diz] nf greed; (bon-bon) sweet

ourmet [guʀmɛ] nm gourmet

ourmette [guʀmɛt] nf chain bracelet

ousse [gus] nf: ~ **d'ail** clove of garlic

oût [gu] nm taste; **avoir bon** ~ to taste good; **de bon** ~ tasteful; **de mauvais** ~ tasteless; **prendre** ~ **à** to develop a taste ou a liking for

oûter [gute] vt (essayer) to taste; (appré-cier) to enjoy ♦ vi to have (afternoon) tea ♦ nm (afternoon) tea

outte [gut] nf drop; (MÉD) gout; (alcool) brandy; **tomber** ~ **à** ~ to drip; **goutte-à-goutte** nm (MÉD) drip

outtelette [gut(ə)lɛt] nf droplet

outtière [gutjɛʀ] nf gutter

ouvernail [guvɛʀnaj] nm rudder; (barre) helm, tiller

ouvernante [guvɛʀnɑ̃t] nf governess

ouvernement [guvɛʀnəmɑ̃] nm govern-ment

ouverner [guvɛʀne] vt to govern

grabuge [gʀabyʒ] (fam) nm mayhem

grâce [gʀas] nf (charme) grace; (faveur) fa-vour; (JUR) pardon; **~s** nfpl (REL) grace sg; **faire** ~ **à qn de qch** to spare sb sth; **ren-dre** ~**(s) à** to give thanks to; **demander** ~ to beg for mercy; ~ **à** thanks to; **gra-cier** vt to pardon; **gracieux, -euse** adj graceful

grade [gʀad] nm rank; **monter en** ~ to be promoted

gradin [gʀadɛ̃] nm tier; step; **~s** nmpl (de stade) terracing sg

gradué, e [gʀadɥe] adj: **verre** ~ measur-ing jug

graduel, le [gʀadɥɛl] adj gradual

graduer [gʀadɥe] vt (effort etc) to increase gradually; (règle, verre) to graduate

graffiti [gʀafiti] nmpl graffiti

grain [gʀɛ̃] nm (gén) grain; (NAVIG) squall; ~ **de beauté** beauty spot; ~ **de café** cof-fee bean; ~ **de poivre** peppercorn; ~ **de poussière** speck of dust; ~ **de raisin** grape

graine [gʀɛn] nf seed

graissage [gʀesaʒ] nm lubrication, greas-ing

graisse [gʀɛs] nf fat; (lubrifiant) grease; **graisser** vt to lubricate, grease; (tacher) to make greasy; **graisseux, -euse** adj greasy

grammaire [gʀa(m)mɛʀ] nf grammar; **grammatical, e, -aux** adj grammatical

gramme [gʀam] nm gramme

grand, e [gʀɑ̃, gʀɑ̃d] adj (haut) tall; (gros, vaste, large) big, large; (long) long; (plus âgé) big; (adulte) grown-up; (sens abstraits) great ♦ adv: ~ **ouvert** wide open; **au** ~ **air** in the open (air); **les** ~**s blessés** the severely injured; ~ **ensemble** housing scheme; ~ **magasin** department store; ~**e personne** grown-up; ~**e surface** hyper-market; ~**es écoles** prestige schools of university level; ~**es lignes** (RAIL) main lines; ~**es vacances** summer holidays; **grand-chose** [gʀɑ̃ʃoz] nm/f inv: **pas grand-chose** not much; **Grande-**

Bretagne *nf* (Great) Britain; **grandeur** *nf* (*dimension*) size; **grandeur nature** life-size; **grandiose** *adj* imposing; **grandir** *vi* to grow ♦ *vt*: **grandir qn** (*suj: vêtement, chaussure*) to make sb look taller; **grand-mère** *nf* grandmother; **grand-messe** *nf* high mass; **grand-peine**: **à grand-peine** *adv* with difficulty; **grand-père** *nm* grandfather; **grand-route** *nf* main road; **grands-parents** *nmpl* grandparents

grange [gʀɑ̃ʒ] *nf* barn

granit(e) [gʀanit] *nm* granite

graphique [gʀafik] *adj* graphic ♦ *nm* graph

grappe [gʀap] *nf* cluster; **~ de raisin** bunch of grapes

gras, se [gʀɑ, gʀɑs] *adj* (*viande, soupe*) fatty; (*personne*) fat; (*surface, main*) greasy; (*plaisanterie*) coarse; (*TYPO*) bold ♦ *nm* (*CULIN*) fat; **faire la ~se matinée** to have a lie-in (*BRIT*), sleep late (*US*); **grassement** *adv*: **grassement payé** handsomely paid; **grassouillet, te** *adj* podgy, plump

gratifiant, e [gʀatifjɑ̃, jɑ̃t] *adj* gratifying, rewarding

gratin [gʀatɛ̃] *nm* (*plat*) cheese-topped dish; (*croûte*) cheese topping; **gratiné, e** *adj* (*CULIN*) au gratin

gratis [gʀatis] *adv* free

gratitude [gʀatityd] *nf* gratitude

gratte-ciel [gʀatsjɛl] *nm inv* skyscraper

gratte-papier [gʀatpapje] (*péj*) *nm inv* penpusher

gratter [gʀate] *vt* (*avec un outil*) to scrape; (*enlever: avec un outil*) to scrape off; (: *avec un ongle*) to scratch; (*enlever avec un ongle*) to scratch off ♦ *vi* (*irriter*) to be scratchy; (*démanger*) to itch; **se ~** to scratch (o.s.)

gratuit, e [gʀatɥi, ɥit] *adj* (*entrée, billet*) free; (*fig*) gratuitous

gravats [gʀava] *nmpl* rubble *sg*

grave [gʀav] *adj* (*maladie, accident*) serious, bad; (*sujet, problème*) serious, grave; (*air*) grave, solemn; (*voix, son*) deep, low-pitched; **gravement** *adv* seriously; (*parler, regarder*) gravely

graver [gʀave] *vt* to engrave

gravier [gʀavje] *nm* gravel *no pl*; **gravillons** *nmpl* loose chippings *ou* gravel *sg*

gravir [gʀaviʀ] *vt* to climb (up)

gravité [gʀavite] *nf* (*de maladie, d'acciden⟨* seriousness; (*de sujet, problème*) gravity

graviter [gʀavite] *vi* to revolve

gravure [gʀavyʀ] *nf* engraving; (*reprodu⟨* *tion*) print

gré [gʀe] *nm*: **de bon ~** willingly; **contr⟨** **le ~ de qn** against sb's will; **de so⟨** **(plein) ~** of one's own free will; **bon ⟨** **mal ~** like it or not; **de ~ ou de forc⟨** whether one likes it or not; **savoir ~ à q⟨** **de qch** to be grateful to sb for sth

grec, grecque [gʀɛk] *adj* Greek; (*class⟨* *que: vase etc*) Grecian ♦ *nm/f*: **G~, Gre⟨** **que** Greek ♦ *nm* (*LING*) Greek

Grèce [gʀɛs] *nf*: **la ~** Greece

greffe [gʀɛf] *nf* (*BOT, MÉD: de tissu*) graf⟨ (*MÉD: d'organe*) transplant; **greffer ⟨** (*BOT, MÉD: tissu*) to graft; (*MÉD: organe*) ⟨ transplant

greffier [gʀefje, jɛʀ] *nm* clerk of the court⟨

grêle [gʀɛl] *adj* (very) thin ♦ *nf* ha⟨

grêler [gʀele] *vb impers*: **il grêle** it's hailin⟨

grêlon [gʀɛlɔ̃] *nm* hailstone

grelot [gʀəlo] *nm* little bell

grelotter [gʀələte] *vi* to shiver

grenade [gʀənad] *nf* (*explosive*) grenad⟨ (*BOT*) pomegranate; **grenadine** *nf* gren⟨ dine

grenat [gʀəna] *adj inv* dark red

grenier [gʀənje] *nm* attic; (*de ferme*) loft

grenouille [gʀənuj] *nf* frog

grès [gʀɛ] *nm* sandstone; (*poterie*) ston⟨ ware

grésiller [gʀezije] *vi* to sizzle; (*RADIO*) ⟨ crackle

grève [gʀɛv] *nf* (*d'ouvriers*) strike; (*plag⟨* shore; **se mettre en/faire ~** to go on/⟨ on strike; **~ de la faim** hunger strike; ⟨ **du zèle** work-to-rule (*BRIT*), slowdow⟨ (*US*); **~ sauvage** wildcat strike

gréviste [gʀevist] *nm/f* striker

gribouiller [gʀibuje] *vt* to scribble, scraw⟨

grièvement [gʀijevmɑ̃] *adv* seriously

griffe [gʀif] *nf* claw; (*de couturier*) label; **griffer** *vt* to scratch

griffonner [gʀifɔne] *vt* to scribble

grignoter [gʀiɲɔte] *vt* (*personne*) to nibble at; (*souris*) to gnaw at ♦ *vi* to nibble

gril [gʀil] *nm* steak *ou* grill pan; **faire cuire au ~** to grill; **grillade** *nf* (*viande etc*) grill

grillage [gʀijaʒ] *nm* (*treillis*) wire netting; (*clôture*) wire fencing

grille [gʀij] *nf* (*clôture*) wire fence; (*portail*) (metal) gate; (*d'égout*) (metal) grate; (*fig*) grid

grille-pain [gʀijpɛ̃] *nm inv* toaster

griller [gʀije] *vt* (*pain*) to toast; (*viande*) to grill; (*fig: ampoule etc*) to blow; **faire ~** to toast; to grill; (*châtaignes*) to roast; **~ un feu rouge** to jump the lights

grillon [gʀijɔ̃] *nm* cricket

grimace [gʀimas] *nf* grimace; (*pour faire rire*): **faire des ~s** to pull *ou* make faces

grimper [gʀɛ̃pe] *vi, vt* to climb

grincer [gʀɛ̃se] *vi* (*objet métallique*) to grate; (*plancher, porte*) to creak; **~ des dents** to grind one's teeth

grincheux, -euse [gʀɛ̃ʃø, øz] *adj* grumpy

grippe [gʀip] *nf* flu, influenza; **grippé, e** *adj*: **être grippé** to have flu

gris, e [gʀi, gʀiz] *adj* grey; (*ivre*) tipsy

grisaille [gʀizaj] *nf* greyness, dullness

griser [gʀize] *vt* to intoxicate

grisonner [gʀizɔne] *vi* to be going grey

grisou [gʀizu] *nm* firedamp

grive [gʀiv] *nf* thrush

grivois, e [gʀivwa, waz] *adj* saucy

Groenland [gʀɔɛnlɑ̃d] *nm* Greenland

grogner [gʀɔɲe] *vi* to growl; (*fig*) to grumble; **grognon, ne** *adj* grumpy

groin [gʀwɛ̃] *nm* snout

grommeler [gʀɔm(ə)le] *vi* to mutter to o.s.

gronder [gʀɔ̃de] *vi* to rumble; (*fig: révolte*) to be brewing ♦ *vt* to scold; **se faire ~** to get a telling-off

groom [gʀum] *nm* bellboy

gros, se [gʀo, gʀos] *adj* big, large; (*obèse*) fat; (*travaux, dégâts*) extensive; (*épais*) thick; (*rhume, averse*) heavy ♦ *adv*: **risquer/gagner ~** to risk/win a lot ♦ *nm/f* fat man/woman ♦ *nm* (*COMM*): **le ~** the wholesale business; **prix de ~** wholesale price; **par ~ temps/grosse mer** in rough weather/heavy seas; **en ~** roughly; (*COMM*) wholesale; **~ lot** jackpot; **~ mot** coarse word; **~ plan** (*PHOTO*) close-up; **~ sel** cooking salt; **~ titre** headline; **~se caisse** big drum

groseille [gʀozɛj] *nf*: **~ (rouge/blanche)** red/white currant; **~ à maquereau** gooseberry

grosse [gʀos] *adj voir* **gros**; **grossesse** *nf* pregnancy; **grosseur** *nf* size; (*tumeur*) lump

grossier, -ière [gʀosje, jɛʀ] *adj* coarse; (*insolent*) rude; (*dessin*) rough; (*travail*) roughly done; (*imitation, instrument*) crude; (*évident: erreur*) gross; **grossièrement** *adv* (*sommairement*) roughly; (*vulgairement*) coarsely; **grossièretés** *nfpl*: **dire des grossièretés** to use coarse language

grossir [gʀosiʀ] *vi* (*personne*) to put on weight ♦ *vt* (*exagérer*) to exaggerate; (*au microscope*) to magnify; (*suj: vêtement*): **~ qn** to make sb look fatter

grossiste [gʀosist] *nm/f* wholesaler

grosso modo [gʀosomɔdo] *adv* roughly

grotesque [gʀɔtɛsk] *adj* (*extravagant*) grotesque; (*ridicule*) ludicrous

grotte [gʀɔt] *nf* cave

grouiller [gʀuje] *vi*: **~ de** to be swarming with; **se ~** (*fam*) ♦ *vi* to get a move on; **grouillant, e** *adj* swarming

groupe [gʀup] *nm* group; **le ~ des 7** Group of 7; **~ sanguin** blood group; **groupement** *nm* (*action*) grouping; (*groupe*) group; **grouper** *vt* to group; **se grouper** *vi* to gather

grue [gʀy] *nf* crane

grumeaux [gʀymo] *nmpl* lumps

guenilles [gənij] *nfpl* rags

guenon [gənɔ̃] *nf* female monkey

guépard [gepaʀ] *nm* cheetah

guêpe [gɛp] *nf* wasp

guêpier [gepje] *nm* (*fig*) trap

guère [gɛʀ] *adv* (*avec adjectif, adverbe*): **ne ... ~** hardly; (*avec verbe*): **ne ... ~** (*pas beaucoup*) *tournure négative +much*; (*pas souvent*) hardly ever; (*pas longtemps*) *tournure négative +(very) long*; **il n'y a ~ que/de** there's hardly anybody (*ou* anything) but/hardly any; **ce n'est ~ difficile** it's hardly difficult; **nous n'avons ~ de temps** we have hardly any time

guéridon [geʀidɔ̃] *nm* pedestal table

guérilla [geʀija] *nf* guerrilla warfare

guérillero [geʀijeʀo] *nm* guerrilla

guérir [geʀiʀ] *vt* (*personne, maladie*) to cure; (*membre, plaie*) to heal ♦ *vi* (*malade, maladie*) to be cured; (*blessure*) to heal; **guérison** *nf* (*de maladie*) curing; (*de membre, plaie*) healing; (*de malade*) recovery; **guérisseur, -euse** *nm/f* healer

guerre [gɛʀ] *nf* war; **~ civile** civil war; **en ~** at war; **faire la ~ à** to wage war against; **guerrier, -ière** *adj* warlike ♦ *nm/f* warrior

guet [gɛ] *nm*: **faire le ~** to be on the watch *ou* look-out; **guet-apens** [getapɑ̃] *nm* ambush; **guetter** *vt* (*épier*) to watch (intently); (*attendre*) to watch (out) for; (*hostilement*) to be lying in wait for

gueule [gœl] *nf* (*d'animal*) mouth; (*fam: figure*) face; (: *bouche*) mouth; **ta ~!** (*fam*) shut up!; **~ de bois** (*fam*) hangover; **gueuler** (*fam*) *vi* to bawl; **gueuleton** (*fam*) *nm* blow-out

gui [gi] *nm* mistletoe

guichet [giʃɛ] *nm* (*de bureau, banque*) counter; **les ~s** (*à la gare, au théâtre*) the ticket office *sg*; **~ automatique** cash dispenser (*BRIT*), automatic telling machine (*US*)

guide [gid] *nm* guide ♦ *nf* (*éclaireuse*) girl guide; **guider** *vt* to guide

guidon [gidɔ̃] *nm* handlebars *pl*

guignol [giɲɔl] *nm* ≃ Punch and Judy show; (*fig*) clown

guillemets [gijmɛ] *nmpl*: **entre ~** in inverted commas

guillotiner [gijɔtine] *vt* to guillotine

guindé, e [gɛ̃de] *adj* (*personne, air*) stiff, starchy; (*style*) stilted

guirlande [giʀlɑ̃d] *nf* (*fleurs*) garland; **~ de Noël** tinsel garland; **~ lumineuse** string of fairy lights; **~ de papier** paper chain

guise [giz] *nf*: **à votre ~** as you wish *ou* please; **en ~ de** by way of

guitare [gitaʀ] *nf* guitar

gym [ʒim] *nf* (*exercices*) gym; **gymnase** *nm* gym(nasium); **gymnaste** *nm/f* gymnast; **gymnastique** *nf* gymnastics *sg*; (*au réveil etc*) keep-fit exercises *pl*

gynécologie [ʒinekɔlɔʒi] *nf* gynaecology; **gynécologique** *adj* gynaecological; **gynécologue** *nm/f* gynaecologist

H, h

habile [abil] *adj* skilful; (*malin*) clever; **habileté** [abilte] *nf* skill, skilfulness; cleverness

habillé, e [abije] *adj* dressed; (*chic*) dressy

habillement [abijmɑ̃] *nm* clothes *pl*

habiller [abije] *vt* to dress; (*fournir en vêtements*) to clothe; **s'~** *vi* to dress (o.s.); (*se déguiser, mettre des vêtements chic*) to dress up

habit [abi] *nm* outfit; **~s** *nmpl* (*vêtements*) clothes; **~ (de soirée)** evening dress; (*pour homme*) tails *pl*

habitant, e [abitɑ̃, ɑ̃t] *nm/f* inhabitant; (*d'une maison*) occupant; **loger chez l'~** to stay with the locals

habitation [abitasjɔ̃] *nf* house; **~s à loyer modéré** (block of) council flats

habiter [abite] *vt* to live in ♦ *vi*: **~ à/dans** to live in

habitude [abityd] *nf* habit; **avoir l'~ de faire** to be in the habit of doing; (*expérience*) to be used to doing; **d'~** usually; **comme d'~** as usual

habitué, e [abitɥe] *nm/f* (*de maison*) regular visitor; (*de café*) regular (customer)

habituel, le [abitɥɛl] adj usual

habituer [abitɥe] vt: ~ **qn à** to get sb used to; **s'~ à** to get used to

hache ['aʃ] nf axe

hacher ['aʃe] vt (viande) to mince; (persil) to chop; **hachis** nm mince no pl; **hachis Parmentier** ≈ shepherd's pie

hachisch ['aʃiʃ] nm hashish

hachoir ['aʃwaʀ] nm (couteau) chopper; (appareil) (meat) mincer; (planche) chopping board

hagard, e ['agaʀ, aʀd] adj wild, distraught

haie ['ɛ] nf hedge; (SPORT) hurdle

haillons ['ajɔ̃] nmpl rags

haine ['ɛn] nf hatred

haïr ['aiʀ] vt to detest, hate

hâlé, e ['ɑle] adj (sun)tanned, sunburnt

haleine [alɛn] nf breath; **hors d'~** out of breath; **tenir en ~** (attention) to hold spellbound; (incertitude) to keep in suspense; **de longue ~** long-term

haleter ['alte] vt to pant

hall ['ol] nm hall

halle ['al] nf (covered) market; **~s** nfpl (d'une grande ville) central food market sg

hallucinant, e [alysinɑ̃, ɑ̃t] adj staggering

hallucination [alysinasjɔ̃] nf hallucination

halte ['alt] nf stop, break; (endroit) stopping place ♦ excl stop!; **faire ~** to stop

haltère [altɛʀ] nm dumbbell, barbell; **~s** nmpl: (**poids et**) **~s** (activité) weightlifting sg; **haltérophilie** nf weightlifting

hamac ['amak] nm hammock

hamburger ['ɑ̃buʀɡœʀ] nm hamburger

hameau, x ['amo] nm hamlet

hameçon [amsɔ̃] nm (fish) hook

hanche ['ɑ̃ʃ] nf hip

hand-ball ['ɑ̃dbal] nm handball

handicapé, e ['ɑ̃dikape] nm/f physically (ou mentally) handicapped person; **~ moteur** spastic

hangar ['ɑ̃gaʀ] nm shed; (AVIAT) hangar

hanneton ['antɔ̃] nm cockchafer

hanter ['ɑ̃te] vt to haunt

hantise ['ɑ̃tiz] nf obsessive fear

'happer ['ape] vt to snatch; (suj: train etc) to hit

'haras ['aʀɑ] nm stud farm

'harassant, e ['aʀasɑ̃, ɑ̃t] adj exhausting

'harcèlement ['aʀsɛlmɑ̃] nm harassment; **~ sexuel** sexual harassment

'harceler ['aʀsəle] vt to harass; **~ qn de questions** to plague sb with questions

'hardi, e ['aʀdi] adj bold, daring

'hareng ['aʀɑ̃] nm herring

'hargne ['aʀɲ] nf aggressiveness; **'hargneux, -euse** adj aggressive

'haricot ['aʀiko] nm bean; **~ blanc** haricot bean; **~ vert** green bean; **~ rouge** kidney bean

harmonica [aʀmɔnika] nm mouth organ

harmonie [aʀmɔni] nf harmony; **harmonieux, -euse** adj harmonious; (couleurs, couple) well-matched

'harnacher ['aʀnaʃe] vt to harness

'harnais ['aʀnɛ] nm harness

'harpe ['aʀp] nf harp

'harponner ['aʀpɔne] vt to harpoon; (fam) to collar

'hasard ['azaʀ] nm: **le ~** chance, fate; **un ~** a coincidence; **au ~** (aller) aimlessly; (choisir) at random; **par ~** by chance; **à tout ~** (en cas de besoin) just in case; (en espérant trouver ce qu'on cherche) on the off chance (BRIT); **'hasarder** vt (mot) to venture; **se hasarder à faire** to risk doing

'hâte ['ɑt] nf haste; **à la ~** hurriedly, hastily; **en ~** posthaste, with all possible speed; **avoir ~ de** to be eager ou anxious to; **'hâter** vt to hasten; **se hâter** vi to hurry; **'hâtif, -ive** adj (travail) hurried; (décision, jugement) hasty

'hausse ['os] nf rise, increase; **être en ~** to be going up; **'hausser** vt to raise; **hausser les épaules** to shrug (one's shoulders)

'haut, e ['o, 'ot] adj high; (grand) tall ♦ adv high ♦ nm top (part); **de 3 m de ~** 3 m high, 3 m in height; **des ~s et des bas** ups and downs; **en ~ lieu** in high places; **à ~e voix, (tout) ~** aloud, out loud; **du ~ de** from the top of; **de ~ en bas** from top to bottom; **plus ~** higher up, further up; *(dans un texte)* above; *(parler)* louder; **en ~** *(être/aller)* at/to the top; *(dans une maison)* upstairs; **en ~ de** at the top of

'**hautain, e** ['otɛ̃, ɛn] *adj* haughty

'**hautbois** ['obwa] *nm* oboe

'**haut-de-forme** ['odfɔʀm] *nm* top hat

'**hauteur** ['otœʀ] *nf* height; **à la ~ de** *(accident)* near; *(fig: tâche, situation)* equal to; **à la ~** *(fig)* up to it

'**haut...: 'haut-fourneau** *nm* blast *ou* smelting furnace; '**haut-le-cœur** *nm inv* retch, heave; '**haut-parleur** *nm* (loud)speaker

'**havre** ['avʀ] *nm* haven

'**Haye** ['ɛ] *n*: **la ~** the Hague

'**hayon** ['ɛjɔ̃] *nm* hatchback

hebdo [ɛbdo] *(fam) nm* weekly

hebdomadaire [ɛbdɔmadɛʀ] *adj, nm* weekly

hébergement [ebɛʀʒəmɑ̃] *nm* accommodation

héberger [ebɛʀʒe] *vt (touristes)* to accommodate, lodge; *(amis)* to put up; *(réfugiés)* to take in

hébété, e [ebete] *adj* dazed

hébreu, x [ebʀø] *adj m, nm* Hebrew

hécatombe [ekatɔ̃b] *nf* slaughter

hectare [ɛktaʀ] *nm* hectare

'**hein** ['ɛ̃] *excl* eh?

'**hélas** ['elas] *excl* alas! ♦ *adv* unfortunately

'**héler** ['ele] *vt* to hail

hélice [elis] *nf* propeller

hélicoptère [elikɔptɛʀ] *nm* helicopter

helvétique [ɛlvetik] *adj* Swiss

hématome [ematom] *nm* nasty bruise

hémicycle [emisikl] *nm (POL)*: **l'~** ≃ the benches (of the Commons) *(BRIT)*, ≃ the floor (of the House of Representatives) *(US)*

hémisphère [emisfɛʀ] *nm*: **l'~ nord/sud** the northern/southern hemisphere

hémorragie [emɔʀaʒi] *nf* bleeding *no pl*, haemorrhage

hémorroïdes [emɔʀɔid] *nfpl* piles, haemorrhoids

'**hennir** ['eniʀ] *vi* to neigh, whinny; '**hennissement** *nm* neigh, whinny

hépatite [epatit] *nf* hepatitis

herbe [ɛʀb] *nf* grass; *(CULIN, MÉD)* herb; **~s de Provence** mixed herbs; **en ~** unripe; *(fig)* budding; **herbicide** *nm* weed-killer; **herboriste** *nm/f* herbalist

'**hère** ['ɛʀ] *nm*: **pauvre ~** poor wretch

héréditaire [eʀeditɛʀ] *adj* hereditary

'**hérisser** ['eʀise] *vt*: **~ qn** *(fig)* to ruffle sb; **se ~** *vi* to bristle, bristle up; '**hérisson** *nm* hedgehog

héritage [eʀitaʒ] *nm* inheritance; *(coutumes, système)* heritage, legacy

hériter [eʀite] *vi*: **~ de qch (de qn)** to inherit sth (from sb); **héritier, -ière** [eʀitje, jɛʀ] *nm/f* heir(-ess)

hermétique [ɛʀmetik] *adj* airtight; watertight; *(fig: obscur)* abstruse; *(: impénétrable)* impenetrable

hermine [ɛʀmin] *nf* ermine

'**hernie** ['ɛʀni] *nf* hernia

héroïne [eʀɔin] *nf* heroine; *(drogue)* heroin

héroïque [eʀɔik] *adj* heroic

'**héron** ['eʀɔ̃] *nm* heron

'**héros** ['eʀo] *nm* hero

hésitant [ezitɑ̃, ɑ̃t] *adj* hesitant

hésitation [ezitasjɔ̃] *nf* hesitation

hésiter [ezite] *vi*: **~ (à faire)** to hesitate (to do)

hétéroclite [eteʀɔklit] *adj* heterogeneous; *(objets)* sundry

hétérogène [eteʀɔʒɛn] *adj* heterogeneous

hétérosexuel, le [eteʀɔsɛkɥɛl] *adj* heterosexual

'**hêtre** ['ɛtʀ] *nm* beech

heure [œʀ] *nf* hour; *(SCOL)* period; *(moment)* time; **c'est l'~** it's time; **quelle ~ est-il?** what time is it?; **2 ~s (du matin)** 2 o'clock (in the morning); **être à l'~** to be on time; *(montre)* to be right; **mettre à l'~** to set right; **à une ~ avancée (de la nuit)** at a late hour of the night; **à toute ~** at any time; **24 ~s sur 24** round the clock, 24 hours a day; **à l'~ qu'il est** at this time (of day); by now; **sur l'~** at once; **~ de pointe** rush hour; (*téléphone*) peak period; **~ d'affluence** rush hour; **~s creuses** slack periods; (*pour électricité, téléphone etc*) off-peak periods; **~s supplémentaires** overtime *sg*

heureusement [œRøzmɑ̃] *adv* (*par bonheur*) fortunately, luckily

heureux, -euse [œRø, øz] *adj* happy; (*chanceux*) lucky, fortunate

heurter [ˈœRte] *vt* (*mur*) to strike, hit; (*personne*) to collide with; **se ~ à** *vt* (*fig*) to come up against

heurts [ˈœR] *nmpl* (*fig*) clashes

hexagone [egzagɔn] *nm* hexagon; (*la France*) France (*because of its shape*)

hiberner [ibeRne] *vi* to hibernate

hibou, x [ˈibu] *nm* owl

hideux, -euse [ˈidø, øz] *adj* hideous

hier [jeR] *adv* yesterday; **~ soir** last night, yesterday evening; **toute la journée d'~** all day yesterday; **toute la matinée d'~** all yesterday morning

hiérarchie [ˈjeRaRʃi] *nf* hierarchy

hi-fi [ˈifi] *adj inv* hi-fi ♦ *nf* hi-fi

hilare [ilaR] *adj* mirthful

hindou, e [ɛ̃du] *adj* Hindu ♦ *nm/f*: **H~, e** Hindu

hippique [ipik] *adj* equestrian, horse *cpd*; **un club ~** a riding centre; **un concours ~** a horse show; **hippisme** *nm* (horse)riding

hippodrome [ipɔdRom] *nm* racecourse

hippopotame [ipɔpɔtam] *nm* hippopotamus

hirondelle [iRɔ̃dɛl] *nf* swallow

hirsute [iRsyt] *adj* (*personne*) shaggy-haired; (*barbe*) shaggy; (*tête*) tousled

hisser [ˈise] *vt* to hoist, haul up; **se ~** *vi* to heave o.s. up

histoire [istwaR] *nf* (*science, événements*) history; (*anecdote, récit, mensonge*) story; (*affaire*) business *no pl*; **~s** *nfpl* (*chichis*) fuss *no pl*; (*ennuis*) trouble *sg*; **historique** *adj* historical; (*important*) historic

'hit-parade [ˈitpaRad] *nm*: **le ~-~** the charts

hiver [iveR] *nm* winter; **hivernal, e, -aux** *adj* winter *cpd*; (*glacial*) wintry; **hiverner** *vi* to winter

HLM *nm ou f* (= *habitation à loyer modéré*) council flat; **des HLM** council housing

'hobby [ˈɔbi] *nm* hobby

'hocher [ˈɔʃe] *vt*: **~ la tête** to nod; (*signe négatif ou dubitatif*) to shake one's head

'hochet [ˈɔʃɛ] *nm* rattle

'hockey [ˈɔkɛ] *nm*: **~ (sur glace/gazon)** (ice/field) hockey

'hold-up [ˈɔldœp] *nm inv* hold-up

'hollandais, e [ˈɔlɑ̃dɛ, ɛz] *adj* Dutch ♦ *nm* (*LING*) Dutch ♦ *nm/f*: **H~, e** Dutchman(-woman); **les H~** the Dutch

'Hollande [ˈɔlɑ̃d] *nf*: **la ~** Holland

'homard [ˈɔmaR] *nm* lobster

homéopathique [ɔmeɔpatik] *adj* homoeopathic

homicide [ɔmisid] *nm* murder; **~ involontaire** manslaughter

hommage [ɔmaʒ] *nm* tribute; **~s** *nmpl*: **présenter ses ~s** to pay one's respects; **rendre ~ à** to pay tribute *ou* homage to

homme [ɔm] *nm* man; **~ d'affaires** businessman; **~ d'État** statesman; **~ de main** hired man; **~ de paille** stooge; **~ politique** politician; **homme-grenouille** *nm* frogman

homo...: homogène *adj* homogeneous; **homologue** *nm/f* counterpart; **homologué, e** *adj* (*SPORT*) ratified; (*tarif*) authorized; **homonyme** *nm* (*LING*) homonym; (*d'une personne*) namesake; **homosexuel, le** *adj* homosexual

'Hongrie [ˈɔ̃gRi] *nf*: **la ~** Hungary; **'hongrois, e** *adj* Hungarian ♦ *nm/f*: **Hongrois, e** Hungarian ♦ *nm* (*LING*) Hungarian

honnête [ɔnɛt] *adj* (*intègre*) honest; (*juste, satisfaisant*) fair; **honnêtement** *adv* honestly; **honnêteté** *nf* honesty

honneur [ɔnœR] *nm* honour; (*mérite*) credit; **en l'~ de** in honour of; (*événement*) on the occasion of; **faire ~ à** *(engagements)* to honour; *(famille)* to be a credit to; *(fig: repas etc)* to do justice to

honorable [ɔnɔrabl] *adj* worthy, honourable; *(suffisant)* decent

honoraire [ɔnɔRER] *adj* honorary; **professeur ~** professor emeritus; **honoraires** [ɔnɔRER] *nmpl* fees *pl*

honorer [ɔnɔre] *vt* to honour; *(estimer)* to hold in high regard; *(faire honneur à)* to do credit to; **honorifique** [ɔnɔrifik] *adj* honorary

'**honte** ['ɔt] *nf* shame; **avoir ~ de** to be ashamed of; **faire ~ à qn** to make sb (feel) ashamed; '**honteux, -euse** *adj* ashamed; *(conduite, acte)* shameful

hôpital, -aux [ɔpital, o] *nm* hospital

'**hoquet** ['ɔkɛ] *nm*: **avoir le ~** to have (the) hiccoughs; '**hoqueter** *vi* to hiccough

horaire [ɔRER] *adj* hourly ♦ *nm* timetable, schedule; **~s** *nmpl* *(d'employé)* hours; **~ souple** flexitime

horizon [ɔRizɔ̃] *nm* horizon

horizontal, e, -aux [ɔRizɔ̃tal, o] *adj* horizontal

horloge [ɔRlɔʒ] *nf* clock; **l'~ parlante** the speaking clock; **horloger, -ère** *nm/f* watchmaker; clockmaker

'**hormis** ['ɔRmi] *prép* save

horoscope [ɔRɔskɔp] *nm* horoscope

horreur [ɔRœR] *nf* horror; **quelle ~!** how awful!; **avoir ~ de** to loathe *ou* detest; **horrible** *adj* horrible; **horrifier** *vt* to horrify

horripiler [ɔRipile] *vt* to exasperate

'**hors** ['ɔR] *prép*: **~ de** out of; **~ pair** outstanding; **~ de propos** inopportune; **être ~ de soi** to be beside o.s.; **~ d'usage** out of service; '**hors-bord** *nm inv* speedboat *(with outboard motor)*; '**hors-d'œuvre** *nm inv* hors d'œuvre; '**hors-jeu** *nm inv* offside; '**hors-la-loi** *nm inv* outlaw; '**hors-taxe** *adj (boutique, articles)* duty-free

hortensia [ɔRtɑ̃sja] *nm* hydrangea

hospice [ɔspis] *nm (de vieillards)* home

hospitalier, -ière [ɔspitalje, jɛR] *adj (accueillant)* hospitable; *(MÉD: service, centre)* hospital *cpd*

hospitaliser [ɔspitalize] *vt* to take/send to hospital, hospitalize

hospitalité [ɔspitalite] *nf* hospitality

hostie [ɔsti] *nf* host *(REL)*

hostile [ɔstil] *adj* hostile; **hostilité** *nf* hostility

hosto [ɔsto] *(fam) nm* hospital

hôte [ot] *nm (maître de maison)* host; *(invité)* guest

hôtel [otɛl] *nm* hotel; **aller à l'~** to stay in a hotel; **~ de ville** town hall; **~ (particulier)** (private) mansion; **hôtelier, -ière** *adj* hotel *cpd* ♦ *nm/f* hotelier; **hôtellerie** *nf* hotel business

hôtesse [otɛs] *nf* hostess; **~ de l'air** air stewardess; **~ (d'accueil)** receptionist

'**hotte** ['ɔt] *nf (panier)* basket *(carried on the back)*; **~ aspirante** cooker hood

'**houblon** ['ublɔ̃] *nm (BOT)* hop; *(pour la bière)* hops *pl*

'**houille** ['uj] *nf* coal; **~ blanche** hydro-electric power

'**houle** ['ul] *nf* swell; '**houleux, -euse** *adj* stormy

'**houligan** ['uligɑ̃] *nm* hooligan

'**hourra** ['uRA] *excl* hurrah!

'**houspiller** ['uspije] *vt* to scold

'**housse** ['us] *nf* cover

'**houx** ['u] *nm* holly

HTML *sigle m* HTML

'**hublot** ['yblo] *nm* porthole

'**huche** ['yʃ] *nf*: **~ à pain** bread bin

'**huer** ['ɥe] *vt* to boo

huile [ɥil] *nf* oil; **~ solaire** suntan oil; **huiler** *vt* to oil; **huileux, -euse** *adj* oily

huis [ɥi] *nm*: **à ~ clos** in camera

huissier [ɥisje] *nm* usher; *(JUR)* ≈ bailiff

'**huit** ['ɥi(t)] *num* eight; **samedi en ~** a week on Saturday; **dans ~ jours** in a week; '**huitaine** *nf*: **une huitaine (de jours)** a week *ou* so; '**huitième** *num* eighth

huître [ɥitR] *nf* oyster

main, e [ymɛ̃, ɛn] *adj* human; (*compa-*
issant) humane ♦ *nm* human (being);
umanitaire *adj* humanitarian; **humani-**
é *nf* humanity
mble [ɑ̃bl] *adj* humble
mecter [ymɛkte] *vt* to dampen
umer ['yme] *vt* (*plat*) to smell; (*parfum*)
o inhale
meur [ymœʀ] *nf* mood; **de bonne/**
nauvaise ~ in a good/bad mood
mide [ymid] *adj* damp; (*main, yeux*)
noist; (*climat, chaleur*) humid; (*saison,*
oute) wet
milier [ymilje] *vt* to humiliate
milité [ymilite] *nf* humility, humbleness
moristique [ymɔʀistik] *adj* humorous
mour [ymuʀ] *nm* humour; **avoir de l'~**
o have a sense of humour; **~ noir** black
umour
uppé, e ['ype] (*fam*) *adj* posh
urlement ['yʀləmɑ̃] *nm* howling *no pl*,
owl, yelling *no pl*, yell
urler ['yʀle] *vi* to howl, yell
rluberlu [yʀlybɛʀly] (*péj*) *nm* crank
utte ['yt] *nf* hut
bride [ibʀid] *adj, nm* hybrid
dratant, e [idʀatɑ̃, ɑ̃t] *adj* (*crème*)
noisturizing
draulique [idʀolik] *adj* hydraulic
dravion [idʀavjɔ̃] *nm* seaplane
drogène [idʀɔʒɛn] *nm* hydrogen
droglisseur [idʀɔɡlisœʀ] *nm* hydro-
lane
ène [jɛn] *nf* hyena
giénique [iʒenik] *adj* hygienic
mne [imn] *nm* hymn; **~ national** nation-
l anthem
permarché [ipɛʀmaʀʃe] *nm* hyper-
narket
permétrope [ipɛʀmetʀɔp] *adj* long-
ghted
pertension [ipɛʀtɑ̃sjɔ̃] *nf* high blood
ressure
pnose [ipnoz] *nf* hypnosis; **hypnotiser**
t to hypnotize; **hypnotiseur** *nm* hyp-
otist

hypocrisie [ipɔkʀizi] *nf* hypocrisy; **hypo-**
crite *adj* hypocritical
hypothèque [ipɔtɛk] *nf* mortgage
hypothèse [ipɔtɛz] *nf* hypothesis
hystérique [isteʀik] *adj* hysterical

I, i

iceberg [ajsbɛʀɡ] *nm* iceberg
ici [isi] *adv* here; **jusqu'~** as far as this;
(*temps*) so far; **d'~ demain** by tomorrow;
d'~ là by then, in the meantime; **d'~ peu**
before long
icône [ikon] *nf* icon
idéal, e, -aux [ideal, o] *adj* ideal ♦ *nm*
ideal; **idéaliste** *adj* idealistic ♦ *nm/f*
idealist
idée [ide] *nf* idea; **avoir dans l'~ que** to
have an idea that; **~ fixe** obsession; **~ re-**
çue generally accepted idea; **~s noires**
black *ou* dark thoughts
identifier [idɑ̃tifje] *vt* to identify; **s'~ à**
(*héros etc*) to identify with
identique [idɑ̃tik] *adj*: **~ (à)** identical (to)
identité [idɑ̃tite] *nf* identity
idiot, e [idjo, idjɔt] *adj* idiotic ♦ *nm/f* idiot;
idiotie *nf* idiotic thing
idole [idɔl] *nf* idol
if [if] *nm* yew
igloo [iglu] *nm* igloo
ignare [iɲaʀ] *adj* ignorant
ignifugé, e [iɲifyʒe] *adj* fireproof
ignoble [iɲɔbl] *adj* vile
ignorant, e [iɲɔʀɑ̃, ɑ̃t] *adj* ignorant
ignorer [iɲɔʀe] *vt* not to know; (*personne*)
to ignore
il [il] *pron* he; (*animal, chose, en tournure im-*
personnelle) it; **~s** they; *voir aussi* **avoir**
île [il] *nf* island; **l'~ Maurice** Mauritius; **les**
~s anglo-normandes the Channel Is-
lands; **les ~s Britanniques** the British
Isles
illégal, e, -aux [i(l)legal, o] *adj* illegal
illégitime [i(l)leʒitim] *adj* illegitimate
illettré, e [i(l)letʀe] *adj, nm/f* illiterate

illimité, e [i(l)limite] *adj* unlimited

illisible [i(l)lizibl] *adj* illegible; (*roman*) unreadable

illogique [i(l)lɔʒik] *adj* illogical

illumination [i(l)lyminasjɔ̃] *nf* illumination; (*idée*) flash of inspiration

illuminer [i(l)lymine] *vt* to light up; (*monument, rue: pour une fête*) to illuminate; (*: au moyen de projecteurs*) to floodlight

illusion [i(l)lyzjɔ̃] *nf* illusion; **se faire des ~s** to delude o.s.; **faire ~** to delude *ou* fool people; **illusionniste** *nm/f* conjuror

illustration [i(l)lystrasjɔ̃] *nf* illustration

illustre [i(l)lystʀ] *adj* illustrious

illustré, e [i(l)lystʀe] *adj* illustrated ♦ *nm* comic

illustrer [i(l)lystʀe] *vt* to illustrate; **s'~** to become famous, win fame

îlot [ilo] *nm* small island, islet

ils [il] *pron voir* **il**

image [imaʒ] *nf* (*gén*) picture; (*métaphore*) image; **~ de marque** brand image; (*fig*) public image; **imagé, e** *adj* (*texte*) full of imagery; (*langage*) colourful

imaginaire [imaʒinɛʀ] *adj* imaginary

imagination [imaʒinasjɔ̃] *nf* imagination; **avoir de l'~** to be imaginative

imaginer [imaʒine] *vt* to imagine; (*inventer: expédient*) to devise, think up; **s'~** *vt* (*se figurer: scène etc*) to imagine, picture; **s'~ que** to imagine that

imbattable [ɛ̃batabl] *adj* unbeatable

imbécile [ɛ̃besil] *adj* idiotic ♦ *nm/f* idiot; **imbécillité** *nf* idiocy; (*action*) idiotic thing; (*film, livre, propos*) rubbish

imbiber [ɛ̃bibe] *vt* to soak; **s'~ de** to become saturated with

imbu, e [ɛ̃by] *adj*: **~ de** full of

imbuvable [ɛ̃byvabl] *adj* undrinkable; (*personne: fam*) unbearable

imitateur, -trice [imitatœʀ, tʀis] *nm/f* (*gén*) imitator; (*MUSIC-HALL*) impersonator

imitation [imitasjɔ̃] *nf* imitation; (*de personnalité*) impersonation

imiter [imite] *vt* to imitate; (*contrefaire*) to forge; (*ressembler à*) to look like

immaculé, e [imakyle] *adj* (*linge, surfa réputation*) spotless; (*blancheur*) immac late

immangeable [ɛ̃mɑ̃ʒabl] *adj* inedible

immatriculation [imatʀikylasjɔ̃] *nf* reg tration

immatriculer [imatʀikyle] *vt* to regist **faire/se faire ~** to register

immédiat, e [imedja, jat] *adj* immédia ♦ *nm*: **dans l'~** for the time being; i **médiatement** *adv* immediately

immense [i(m)mɑ̃s] *adj* immense

immerger [imɛʀʒe] *vt* to immerse, s merge

immeuble [imœbl] *nm* building; (*à use d'habitation*) block of flats

immigration [imigʀasjɔ̃] *nf* immigration

immigré, e [imigʀe] *nm/f* immigrant

imminent, e [iminɑ̃, ɑ̃t] *adj* imminent

immiscer [imise]: **s'~** *vi*: **s'~ dans** to terfere in *ou* with

immobile [i(m)mɔbil] *adj* still, motionle

immobilier, -ière [imɔbilje, jɛʀ] *adj* property *cpd* ♦ *nm*: **l'~** the property bu ness

immobiliser [imɔbilize] *vt* (*gén*) to imm bilize; (*circulation, véhicule, affaires*) to br to a standstill; **s'~** (*personne*) to sta still; (*machine, véhicule*) to come to a ha

immonde [i(m)mɔ̃d] *adj* foul

immoral, e, -aux [i(m)mɔʀal, o] *adj* moral

immortel, le [imɔʀtɛl] *adj* immortal

immuable [imɥabl] *adj* unchanging

immunisé, e [im(m)ynize] *adj*: **~ con** immune to

immunité [imynite] *nf* immunity

impact [ɛ̃pakt] *nm* impact

impair, e [ɛ̃pɛʀ] *adj* odd ♦ *nm* faux p blunder

impardonnable [ɛ̃paʀdɔnabl] *adj* unp donable, unforgivable

imparfait, e [ɛ̃paʀfɛ, ɛt] *adj* imperfect

impartial, e, -aux [ɛ̃paʀsjal, jo] *adj* partial, unbiased

impasse [ɛ̃pas] *nf* dead end, cul-de-s

(fig) deadlock

▪passible [ɛpasibl] *adj* impassive

▪patience [ɛpasjɑ̃s] *nf* impatience

▪patient, e [ɛpasjɑ̃, jɑ̃t] *adj* impatient; mpatienter: **s'impatienter** *vi* to get impatient

▪peccable [ɛpekabl] *adj (parfait)* perfect; *(propre)* impeccable; *(fam)* smashing

▪pensable [ɛpɑ̃sabl] *adj (événement hypothétique)* unthinkable; *(événement qui a eu lieu)* unbelievable

▪per [ɛpɛʀ] *(fam) nm* raincoat

▪pératif, -ive [ɛperatif, iv] *adj* imperative **♦** *nm (LING)* imperative; **~s** *nmpl (exigences: d'une fonction, d'une charge)* requirements; *(: de la mode)* demands

▪pératrice [ɛperatʀis] *nf* empress

▪perceptible [ɛpɛʀseptibl] *adj* imperceptible

▪périal, e, -aux [ɛperjal, jo] *adj* imperial; **impériale** *nf* top deck

▪périeux, -euse [ɛperjø, jøz] *adj (caractère, ton)* imperious; *(obligation, besoin)* pressing, urgent

▪périssable [ɛperisabl] *adj* undying

▪perméable [ɛpɛʀmeabl] *adj* waterproof; *(fig)*: **~ à** impervious to **♦** *nm* raincoat

▪pertinent, e [ɛpɛʀtinɑ̃, ɑ̃t] *adj* impertinent

▪perturbable [ɛpɛʀtyʀbabl] *adj (personne, caractère)* unperturbable; *(sang-froid, gaieté, sérieux)* unshakeable

▪pétueux, -euse [ɛpetɥø, øz] *adj* impetuous

▪pitoyable [ɛpitwajabl] *adj* pitiless, merciless

▪planter [ɛplɑ̃te] **s'~** *vi* to be set up

▪pliquer [ɛplike] *vt* to imply; **~ qn (dans)** to implicate sb (in)

▪poli, e [ɛpɔli] *adj* impolite, rude

▪populaire [ɛpɔpylɛʀ] *adj* unpopular

▪portance [ɛpɔʀtɑ̃s] *nf* importance; **sans ~** unimportant

▪portant, e [ɛpɔʀtɑ̃, ɑ̃t] *adj* important; *(en quantité: somme, retard)* considerable,

sizeable; *(: dégâts)* extensive; *(péj: airs, ton)* self-important **♦** *nm*: **l'~** the important thing

importateur, -trice [ɛpɔʀtatœʀ, tʀis] *nm/f* importer

importation [ɛpɔʀtasjɔ̃] *nf* importation; *(produit)* import

importer [ɛpɔʀte] *vt (COMM)* to import; *(maladies, plantes)* to introduce **♦** *vi (être important)* to matter; **il importe qu'il fasse** it is important that he should do; **peu m'importe** *(je n'ai pas de préférence)* I don't mind; *(je m'en moque)* I don't care; **peu importe (que)** it doesn't matter (if); *voir aussi* **n'importe**

importun, e [ɛpɔʀtœ̃, yn] *adj* irksome, importunate; *(arrivée, visite)* inopportune, ill-timed **♦** *nm* intruder; **importuner** *vt* to bother

imposable [ɛpozabl] *adj* taxable

imposant, e [ɛpozɑ̃, ɑ̃t] *adj* imposing

imposer [ɛpoze] *vt (taxer)* to tax; **s'~** *(être nécessaire)* to be imperative; **~ qch à qn** to impose sth on sb; **en ~ à** to impress; **s'~ comme** to emerge as; **s'~ par** to win recognition through

impossibilité [ɛposibilite] *nf* impossibility; **être dans l'~ de faire qch** to be unable to do sth

impossible [ɛposibl] *adj* impossible; **il m'est ~ de le faire** it is impossible for me to do it, I can't possibly do it; **faire l'~** to do one's utmost

imposteur [ɛpostœʀ] *nm* impostor

impôt [ɛpo] *nm* tax; **~s** *nmpl (contributions)* (income) tax *sg*; **payer 1000 F d'~s** to pay 1,000F in tax; **~ foncier** land tax; **~ sur le chiffre d'affaires** corporation *(BRIT) ou* corporate *(US)* tax; **~ sur le revenu** income tax

impotent, e [ɛpotɑ̃, ɑ̃t] *adj* disabled

impraticable [ɛpʀatikabl] *adj (projet)* impracticable, unworkable; *(piste)* impassable

imprécis, e [ɛpʀesi, iz] *adj* imprecise

imprégner [ɛpʀeɲe] *vt (tissu)* to impregnate; *(lieu, air)* to fill; **s'~ de** *(fig)* to absorb

imprenable [ɛ̃pʀənabl] *adj* (*forteresse*) impregnable; **vue** ~ unimpeded outlook

imprésario [ɛ̃pʀesaʀjo] *nm* manager

impression [ɛ̃pʀesjɔ̃] *nf* impression; (*d'un ouvrage, tissu*) printing; **faire bonne** ~ to make a good impression; **impressionnant, e** *adj* (*imposant*) impressive; (*bouleversant*) upsetting; **impressionner** *vt* (*frapper*) to impress; (*bouleverser*) to upset

imprévisible [ɛ̃pʀevizibl] *adj* unforeseeable

imprévoyant, e [ɛ̃pʀevwajɑ̃, ɑ̃t] *adj* lacking in foresight; (*en matière d'argent*) improvident

imprévu, e [ɛ̃pʀevy] *adj* unforeseen, unexpected ♦ *nm* (*incident*) unexpected incident; **des vacances pleines d'~** holidays full of surprises; **en cas d'~** if anything unexpected happens; **sauf** ~ unless anything unexpected crops up

imprimante [ɛ̃pʀimɑ̃t] *nf* printer

imprimé [ɛ̃pʀime] *nm* (*formulaire*) printed form; (*POSTES*) printed matter *no pl*; (*tissu*) printed fabric; ~ **à fleur** floral print

imprimer [ɛ̃pʀime] *vt* to print; (*publier*) to publish; **imprimerie** *nf* printing; (*établissement*) printing works *sg*; **imprimeur** *nm* printer

impromptu, e [ɛ̃pʀɔ̃pty] *adj* (*repas, discours*) impromptu; (*départ*) sudden; (*visite*) surprise

impropre [ɛ̃pʀɔpʀ] *adj* inappropriate; ~ **à** unfit for

improviser [ɛ̃pʀɔvize] *vt, vi* to improvise

improviste [ɛ̃pʀɔvist]: **à l'~** *adv* unexpectedly, without warning

imprudence [ɛ̃pʀydɑ̃s] *nf* (*d'une personne, d'une action*) carelessness *no pl*; (*d'une remarque*) imprudence *no pl*; **commettre une** ~ to do something foolish

imprudent, e [ɛ̃pʀydɑ̃, ɑ̃t] *adj* (*conducteur, geste, action*) careless; (*remarque*) unwise, imprudent; (*projet*) foolhardy

impudent, e [ɛ̃pydɑ̃, ɑ̃t] *adj* impudent

impudique [ɛ̃pydik] *adj* shameless

impuissant, e [ɛ̃pyisɑ̃, ɑ̃t] *adj* helpless (*sans effet*) ineffectual; (*sexuellement*) impotent

impulsif, -ive [ɛ̃pylsif, iv] *adj* impulsive

impulsion [ɛ̃pylsjɔ̃] *nf* (*ÉLEC, instinct*) in pulse; (*élan, influence*) impetus

impunément [ɛ̃pynemɑ̃] *adv* with impu nity

inabordable [inabɔʀdabl] *adj* (*cher*) proh bitive

inacceptable [inaksɛptabl] *adj* unaccep able

inaccessible [inaksesibl] *adj* inaccessible

inachevé, e [inaʃ(ə)ve] *adj* unfinished

inactif, -ive [inaktif, iv] *adj* inactive; (*r mède*) ineffective; (*BOURSE: marché*) sla ♦ *nm*: **les ~s** the non-working populatio

inadapté, e [inadapte] *adj* (*gén*): ~ **à n** adapted to, unsuited to; (*PSYCH*) mala justed

inadéquat, e [inadekwa(t), kwat] *adj* i adequate

inadmissible [inadmisibl] *adj* inadm sible

inadvertance [inadvɛʀtɑ̃s]: **par** ~ *adv* i advertently

inaltérable [inalteʀabl] *adj* (*matièr* stable; (*fig*) unfailing; ~ **à** unaffected by

inanimé, e [inanime] *adj* (*matière*) inar mate; (*évanoui*) unconscious; (*sans vi* lifeless

inanition [inanisjɔ̃] *nf*: **tomber d'~** faint with hunger (and exhaustion)

inaperçu, e [inapɛʀsy] *adj*: **passer** ~ go unnoticed

inapte [inapt] *adj*: ~ **à** incapable of; (*M* unfit for

inattaquable [inatakabl] *adj* (*texte, preuv* irrefutable

inattendu, e [inatɑ̃dy] *adj* unexpected

inattentif, -ive [inatɑ̃tif, iv] *adj* inatte tive; ~ **à** (*dangers, détails*) heedless c **inattention** *nf*: **faute d'inattention** ca less mistake

inauguration [inogyʀasjɔ̃] *nf* inauguratic

inaugurer [inogyʀe] *vt* (*monument*) to u

veil; (*exposition, usine*) to open; (*fig*) to inaugurate

navouable [inavwabl] *adj* shameful; (*bénéfices*) undisclosable

ncalculable [ɛ̃kalkylabl] *adj* incalculable

ncandescence [ɛ̃kɑ̃desɑ̃s] *nf*: **porter à ~** to heat white-hot

ncapable [ɛ̃kapabl] *adj* incapable; **~ de faire** incapable of doing; (*empêché*) unable to do

ncapacité [ɛ̃kapasite] *nf* (*incompétence*) incapability; (*impossibilité*) incapacity; **dans l'~ de faire** unable to do

ncarcérer [ɛ̃kaʀseʀe] *vt* to incarcerate, imprison

ncarné, e [ɛ̃kaʀne] *adj* (*ongle*) ingrown

ncarner [ɛ̃kaʀne] *vt* to embody, personify; (*THÉÂTRE*) to play

ncassable [ɛ̃kasabl] *adj* unbreakable

ncendiaire [ɛ̃sɑ̃djɛʀ] *adj* incendiary; (*fig: discours*) inflammatory

ncendie [ɛ̃sɑ̃di] *nm* fire; **~ criminel** arson *no pl*; **~ de forêt** forest fire; **incendier** *vt* (*mettre le feu à*) to set fire to, set alight; (*brûler complètement*) to burn down; **se faire incendier** (*fam*) to get a rocket

ncertain, e [ɛ̃sɛʀtɛ̃, ɛn] *adj* uncertain; (*temps*) unsettled; (*imprécis: contours*) indistinct, blurred; **incertitude** *nf* uncertainty

ncessamment [ɛ̃sesamɑ̃] *adv* very shortly

ncident [ɛ̃sidɑ̃, ɑ̃t] *nm* incident; **~ de parcours** minor hitch *ou* setback; **~ technique** technical difficulties *pl*

ncinérer [ɛ̃sineʀe] *vt* (*ordures*) to incinerate; (*mort*) to cremate

ncisive [ɛ̃siziv] *nf* incisor

nciter [ɛ̃site] *vt*: **~ qn à (faire) qch** to encourage sb to do sth; (*à la révolte etc*) to incite sb to do sth

nclinable [ɛ̃klinabl] *adj*: **siège à dossier ~** reclining seat

nclinaison [ɛ̃klinɛzɔ̃] *nf* (*déclivité: d'une route etc*) incline; (: *d'un toit*) slope; (*état penché*) tilt

nclination [ɛ̃klinasjɔ̃] *nf* (*penchant*) inclination; **~ de (la) tête** nod (of the head); **~ (de buste)** bow

incliner [ɛ̃kline] *vt* (*pencher*) to tilt ♦ *vi*: **~ à qch/à faire** to incline towards sth/doing; **s'~ (devant)** to bow (before); (*céder*) to give in *ou* yield (to); **~ la tête** to give a slight bow

inclure [ɛ̃klyʀ] *vt* to include; (*joindre à un envoi*) to enclose; **jusqu'au 10 mars inclus** until 10th March inclusive

incognito [ɛ̃kɔɲito] *adv* incognito ♦ *nm*: **garder l'~** to remain incognito

incohérent, e [ɛ̃kɔeʀɑ̃, ɑ̃t] *adj* (*comportement*) inconsistent; (*geste, langage, texte*) incoherent

incollable [ɛ̃kɔlabl] *adj* (*riz*) non-stick; **il est ~** (*fam*) he's got all the answers

incolore [ɛ̃kɔlɔʀ] *adj* colourless

incommoder [ɛ̃kɔmɔde] *vt* (*chaleur, odeur*): **~ qn** to bother sb

incomparable [ɛ̃kɔ̃paʀabl] *adj* incomparable

incompatible [ɛ̃kɔ̃patibl] *adj* incompatible

incompétent, e [ɛ̃kɔ̃petɑ̃, ɑ̃t] *adj* incompetent

incomplet, -ète [ɛ̃kɔ̃plɛ, ɛt] *adj* incomplete

incompréhensible [ɛ̃kɔ̃pʀeɑ̃sibl] *adj* incomprehensible

incompris, e [ɛ̃kɔ̃pʀi, iz] *adj* misunderstood

inconcevable [ɛ̃kɔ̃s(ə)vabl] *adj* inconceivable

inconciliable [ɛ̃kɔ̃siljabl] *adj* irreconcilable

inconditionnel, le [ɛ̃kɔ̃disjɔnɛl] *adj* unconditional; (*partisan*) unquestioning ♦ *nm/f* (*d'un homme politique*) ardent supporter; (*d'un écrivain, d'un chanteur*) ardent admirer; (*d'une activité*) fanatic

inconfort [ɛ̃kɔ̃fɔʀ] *nm* discomfort; **inconfortable** *adj* uncomfortable

incongru, e [ɛ̃kɔ̃gʀy] *adj* unseemly

inconnu, e [ɛ̃kɔny] *adj* unknown ♦ *nm/f* stranger ♦ *nm*: **l'~** the unknown; **inconnue** *nf* unknown factor

inconsciemment [ɛ̃kɔ̃sjamɑ̃] *adv* unconsciously

inconscient, e [ɛ̃kɔ̃sjɑ̃, jɑ̃t] *adj* unconscious; *(irréfléchi)* thoughtless, reckless; *(sentiment)* subconscious ♦ *nm* (PSYCH): **l'~** the unconscious; **~ de** unaware of

inconsidéré, e [ɛ̃kɔ̃sidere] *adj* ill-considered .

inconsistant, e [ɛ̃kɔ̃sistɑ̃, ɑ̃t] *adj (fig)* flimsy, weak

inconsolable [ɛ̃kɔ̃sɔlabl] *adj* inconsolable

incontestable [ɛ̃kɔ̃testabl] *adj* indisputable

incontinent, e [ɛ̃kɔ̃tinɑ̃, ɑ̃t] *adj* incontinent

incontournable [ɛ̃kɔ̃turnabl] *adj* unavoidable

incontrôlable [ɛ̃kɔ̃trolabl] *adj* unverifiable; *(irrépressible)* uncontrollable

inconvenant, e [ɛ̃kɔ̃v(ə)nɑ̃, ɑ̃t] *adj* unseemly, improper

inconvénient [ɛ̃kɔ̃venjɑ̃] *nm* disadvantage, drawback; **si vous n'y voyez pas d'~** if you have no objections

incorporer [ɛ̃kɔrpɔre] *vt*: **~ (à)** to mix in (with); **~ (dans)** *(paragraphe etc)* to incorporate (in); (MIL: *appeler*) to recruit (into); **il a très bien su s'~ à notre groupe** he was very easily incorporated into our group

incorrect, e [ɛ̃kɔrɛkt] *adj (impropre, inconvenant)* improper; *(défectueux)* faulty; *(inexact)* incorrect; *(impoli)* impolite; *(déloyal)* underhand

incorrigible [ɛ̃kɔriʒibl] *adj* incorrigible

incrédule [ɛ̃kredyl] *adj* incredulous; *(REL)* unbelieving

increvable [ɛ̃krəvabl] *(fam) adj* tireless

incriminer [ɛ̃krimine] *vt (personne)* to incriminate; *(action, conduite)* to bring under attack; *(bonne foi, honnêteté)* to call into question

incroyable [ɛ̃krwajabl] *adj* incredible

incruster [ɛ̃kryste] *vt* (ART) to inlay; **s'~** *vi (invité)* to take root

inculpé, e [ɛ̃kylpe] *nm/f* accused

inculper [ɛ̃kylpe] *vt*: **~ (de)** to charge

(with)

inculquer [ɛ̃kylke] *vt*: **~ qch à** to inculca sth in *ou* instil sth into

inculte [ɛ̃kylt] *adj* uncultivated; *(esprit, pe ple)* uncultured

Inde [ɛ̃d] *nf*: **l'~** India

indécent, e [ɛ̃desɑ̃, ɑ̃t] *adj* indecent

indéchiffrable [ɛ̃deʃifrabl] *adj* indecipher able

indécis, e [ɛ̃desi, iz] *adj (par nature)* ind cisive; *(temporairement)* undecided

indéfendable [ɛ̃defɑ̃dabl] *adj* indefensib

indéfini, e [ɛ̃defini] *adj (imprécis, incertai* undefined; *(illimité,* LING) indefinite; i **définiment** *adv* indefinitely; **indéfini** **sable** *adj* indefinable

indélébile [ɛ̃delebil] *adj* indelible

indélicat, e [ɛ̃delika, at] *adj* tactless

indemne [ɛ̃dɛmn] *adj* unharmed; **inder niser** *vt*: **indemniser qn (de)** to cor pensate sb (for)

indemnité [ɛ̃dɛmnite] *nf (dédommagemer* compensation *no pl*; *(allocation)* allo ance; **indemnité de licenciement** redu dancy payment

indépendamment [ɛ̃depɑ̃damɑ̃] *adv* i dependently; **~ de** *(abstraction faite de)* respective of; *(en plus de)* over and abov

indépendance [ɛ̃depɑ̃dɑ̃s] *nf* indepe dence

indépendant, e [ɛ̃depɑ̃dɑ̃, ɑ̃t] *adj* inc pendent; **~ de** independent of

indescriptible . [ɛ̃deskriptibl] *adj* inc scribable

indésirable [ɛ̃dezirabl] *adj* undesirable

indestructible [ɛ̃destryktibl] *adj* inc structible

indétermination [ɛ̃determinasjɔ̃] *nf (i solution: chronique)* indecision; (: *temp raire)* indecisiveness

indéterminé, e [ɛ̃determine] *adj (da cause, nature)* unspecified; *(forme, longue quantité)* indeterminate

index [ɛ̃dɛks] *nm (doigt)* index finger; *(d livre etc)* index; **mettre à l'~** to blackl **indexé, e** *adj* (ÉCON): **indexé (su**

index-linked (to)

ndic [ɛ̃dik] (fam) nm (POLICE) grass

dicateur [ɛ̃dikatœʀ] nm (POLICE) informer; (TECH) gauge, indicator

dicatif, -ive [ɛ̃dikatif, iv] adj: **à titre ~** for (your) information ♦ nm (LING) indicative; (RADIO) theme ou signature tune; (TÉL) dialling code

dication [ɛ̃dikasjɔ̃] nf indication; (renseignement) information no pl; **~s** nfpl (directives) instructions

dice [ɛ̃dis] nm (marque, signe) indication, sign; (POLICE: lors d'une enquête) clue; (JUR: présomption) piece of evidence; (SCIENCE, ÉCON, TECH) index

dicible [ɛ̃disibl] adj inexpressible

dien, ne [ɛ̃djɛ̃, jɛn] adj Indian ♦ nm/f: **I~, ne** Indian

différemment [ɛ̃difeʀamɑ̃] adv (sans distinction) equally (well)

différence [ɛ̃difeʀɑ̃s] nf indifference

différent, e [ɛ̃difeʀɑ̃, ɑ̃t] adj (peu intéressé) indifferent; **ça m'est ~** it doesn't matter to me; **elle m'est ~e** I am indifferent to her

digence [ɛ̃diʒɑ̃s] nf poverty

digène [ɛ̃diʒɛn] adj native, indigenous; (des gens du pays) local ♦ nm/f native

digeste [ɛ̃diʒɛst] adj indigestible

digestion [ɛ̃diʒɛstjɔ̃] nf indigestion no pl

digne [ɛ̃diɲ] adj unworthy

digner [ɛ̃diɲe] vt: **s'~ (de ou contre)** to get indignant (at)

diqué, e [ɛ̃dike] adj (date, lieu) agreed; (traitement) appropriate; (conseillé) advisable

diquer [ɛ̃dike] vt (suj: pendule, aiguille) to show; (: étiquette, panneau) to show, indicate; (renseigner sur) to point out, tell; (déterminer: date, lieu) to give, state; (signaler, dénoter) to indicate, point to; **~ qch/qn à qn** (montrer du doigt) to point sth/sb out to sb; (faire connaître: médecin, restaurant) to tell sb of sth/sb

direct, e [ɛ̃diʀɛkt] adj indirect

discipliné, e [ɛ̃disipline] adj undisci-plined

indiscret, -ète [ɛ̃diskʀɛ, ɛt] adj indiscreet

indiscutable [ɛ̃diskytabl] adj indisputable

indispensable [ɛ̃dispɑ̃sabl] adj indispensable, essential

indisposé, e [ɛ̃dispoze] adj indisposed

indisposer [ɛ̃dispoze] vt (incommoder) to upset; (déplaire à) to antagonize; (énerver) to irritate

indistinct, e [ɛ̃distɛ̃(kt), ɛ̃kt] adj indistinct; **indistinctement** adv (voir, prononcer) indistinctly; (sans distinction) indiscriminately

individu [ɛ̃dividy] nm individual; **individuel, le** adj (gén) individual; (responsabilité, propriété, liberté) personal; **chambre individuelle** single room; **maison individuelle** detached house

indolore [ɛ̃dɔlɔʀ] adj painless

indomptable [ɛ̃dɔ̃(p)tabl] adj untameable; (fig) invincible

Indonésie [ɛ̃dɔnezi] nf Indonesia

indu, e [ɛ̃dy] adj: **à une heure ~e** at some ungodly hour

induire [ɛ̃dɥiʀ] vt: **~ qn en erreur** to lead sb astray, mislead sb

indulgent, e [ɛ̃dylʒɑ̃, ɑ̃t] adj (parent, regard) indulgent; (juge, examinateur) lenient

industrialisé, e [ɛ̃dystʀijalize] adj industrialized

industrie [ɛ̃dystʀi] nf industry; **industriel, le** adj industrial ♦ nm industrialist

inébranlable [inebʀɑ̃labl] adj (masse, colonne) solid; (personne, certitude, foi) unshakeable

inédit, e [inedi, it] adj (correspondance, livre) hitherto unpublished; (spectacle, moyen) novel, original; (film) unreleased

ineffaçable [inefasabl] adj indelible

inefficace [inefikas] adj (remède, moyen) ineffective; (machine, employé) inefficient

inégal, e, -aux [inegal, o] adj unequal; (irrégulier) uneven; **inégalable** adj matchless; **inégalé, e** adj (record) unequalled; (beauté) unrivalled; **inégalité** nf inequality

inépuisable [inepɥizabl] adj inexhaustible

inerte [inɛʀt] *adj (immobile)* lifeless; *(sans réaction)* passive

inespéré, e [inespeʀe] *adj* unexpected, unhoped-for

inestimable [inɛstimabl] *adj* priceless; *(fig: bienfait)* invaluable

inévitable [inevitabl] *adj* unavoidable; *(fatal, habituel)* inevitable

inexact, e [inɛgza(kt), akt] *adj* inaccurate

inexcusable [inɛkskyzabl] *adj* unforgivable

inexplicable [inɛksplikabl] *adj* inexplicable

in extremis [inɛkstʀemis] *adv* at the last minute ♦ *adj* last-minute

infaillible [ɛ̃fajibl] *adj* infallible

infâme [ɛ̃fɑm] *adj* vile

infarctus [ɛ̃faʀktys] *nm*: ~ **(du myocarde)** coronary (thrombosis)

infatigable [ɛ̃fatigabl] *adj* tireless

infect, e [ɛ̃fɛkt] *adj* revolting; *(personne)* obnoxious; *(temps)* foul

infecter [ɛ̃fɛkte] *vt (atmosphère, eau)* to contaminate; *(MÉD)* to infect; **s'~** to become infected *ou* septic; **infection** *nf* infection; *(puanteur)* stench

inférieur, e [ɛ̃feʀjœʀ] *adj* lower; *(en qualité, intelligence)* inferior; ~ **à** *(somme, quantité)* less *ou* smaller than; *(moins bon que)* inferior to

infernal, e, -aux [ɛ̃fɛʀnal, o] *adj (insupportable: chaleur, rythme)* infernal; *(: enfant)* horrid; *(satanique, effrayant)* diabolical

infidèle [ɛ̃fidɛl] *adj* unfaithful

infiltrer [ɛ̃filtʀe] *vb*: **s'~ dans** to get into; *(liquide)* to seep through; *(fig: groupe, ennemi)* to infiltrate

infime [ɛ̃fim] *adj* minute, tiny

infini, e [ɛ̃fini] *adj* infinite ♦ *nm* infinity; **à l'~** endlessly; **infiniment** *adv* infinitely; **infinité** *nf*: **une infinité de** an infinite number of

infinitif [ɛ̃finitif, iv] *nm* infinitive

infirme [ɛ̃fiʀm] *adj* disabled ♦ *nm/f* disabled person

infirmerie [ɛ̃fiʀməʀi] *nf* medical room

infirmier, -ière [ɛ̃fiʀmje] *nm/f* nurse; **infirmière chef** sister

infirmité [ɛ̃fiʀmite] *nf* disability

inflammable [ɛ̃flamabl] *adj* (in)flammable

inflation [ɛ̃flasjɔ̃] *nf* inflation

infliger [ɛ̃fliʒe] *vt*: ~ **qch (à qn)** to inflict sth (on sb); *(amende, sanction)* to impose sth (on sb)

influençable [ɛ̃flyɑ̃sabl] *adj* easily influenced

influence [ɛ̃flyɑ̃s] *nf* influence; **influencer** *vt* to influence; **influent, e** *adj* influential

informateur, -trice [ɛ̃fɔʀmatœʀ, tʀis] *nm/f (POLICE)* informer

informaticien, ne [ɛ̃fɔʀmatisjɛ̃, jɛn] *nm/f* computer scientist

information [ɛ̃fɔʀmasjɔ̃] *nf (renseignement)* piece of information; *(PRESSE, TV: nouvelle)* item of news; *(diffusion de renseignements, INFORM)* information; *(JUR)* inquiry, investigation; ~**s** *nfpl (TV)* news *sg*

informatique [ɛ̃fɔʀmatik] *nf (technique)* data processing; *(science)* computer science ♦ *adj* computer *cpd*; **informatiser** *vt* to computerize

informe [ɛ̃fɔʀm] *adj* shapeless

informer [ɛ̃fɔʀme] *vt*: ~ **qn (de)** to inform sb (of); **s'~ (de/si)** to inquire *ou* find out (about/whether *ou* if)

infos [ɛ̃fo] *nfpl*: **les** ~ the news *sg*

infraction [ɛ̃fʀaksjɔ̃] *nf* offence; ~ **à** violation *ou* breach of; **être en** ~ to be in breach of the law

infranchissable [ɛ̃fʀɑ̃ʃisabl] *adj* impassable, *(fig)* insuperable

infrarouge [ɛ̃fʀaʀuʒ] *adj* infrared

infrastructure [ɛ̃fʀastʀyktyʀ] *nf (AVIAT, MIL)* ground installations *pl*; *(ÉCON: touristique etc)* infrastructure

infuser [ɛ̃fyze] *vt, vi (thé)* to brew; *(tisane)* to infuse; **infusion** *nf (tisane)* herb tea

ingénier [ɛ̃ʒenje]: **s'~** *vi*: **s'~ à faire** to strive to do

ingénierie [ɛ̃ʒeniʀi] *nf* engineering; ~ **génétique** genetic engineering

ingénieur [ɛ̃ʒenjœr] *nm* engineer; **ingénieur du son** sound engineer

ingénieux, -euse [ɛ̃ʒenjø, jøz] *adj* ingenious, clever

ingénu, e [ɛ̃ʒeny] *adj* ingenuous, artless

ingérer [ɛ̃ʒere] *vb*: **s'~ dans** to interfere in

ingrat, e [ɛ̃gra, at] *adj* (*personne*) ungrateful; (*travail, sujet*) thankless; (*visage*) unprepossessing

ingrédient [ɛ̃gredjɑ̃] *nm* ingredient

ingurgiter [ɛ̃gyrʒite] *vt* to swallow

inhabitable [inabitabl] *adj* uninhabitable

inhabité, e [inabite] *adj* uninhabited

inhabituel, le [inabituɛl] *adj* unusual

inhibition [inibisjɔ̃] *nf* inhibition

inhumain, e [inymɛ̃, ɛn] *adj* inhuman

inhumation [inymasjɔ̃] *nf* burial

inhumer [inyme] *vt* to inter, bury

inimaginable [inimaʒinabl] *adj* unimaginable

ininterrompu, e [inɛ̃terɔ̃py] *adj* (*file, série*) unbroken; (*flot, vacarme*) uninterrupted, non-stop; (*effort*) unremitting, continuous; (*suite, ligne*) unbroken

initial, e, -aux [inisjal, jo] *adj* initial; **initiale** *nf* initial; **initialiser** *vt* to initialize

initiation [inisjasjɔ̃] *nf*: **~ à** introduction to

initiative [inisjativ] *nf* initiative

initier [inisje] *vt*: **~ qn à** to initiate sb into; (*faire découvrir: art, jeu*) to introduce sb to

injecté, e [ɛ̃ʒɛkte] *adj*: **yeux ~s de sang** bloodshot eyes

injecter [ɛ̃ʒɛkte] *vt* to inject; **injection** *nf* injection; **à injection** (*AUTO*) fuel injection *cpd*

injure [ɛ̃ʒyr] *nf* insult, abuse *no pl*; **injurier** *vt* to insult, abuse; **injurieux, -euse** *adj* abusive, insulting

injuste [ɛ̃ʒyst] *adj* unjust, unfair; **injustice** *nf* injustice

inlassable [ɛ̃lɑsabl] *adj* tireless

inné, e [i(n)ne] *adj* innate, inborn

innocent, e [inɔsɑ̃, ɑ̃t] *adj* innocent; **innocenter** *vt* to clear, prove innocent

innombrable [i(n)nɔ̃brabl] *adj* innumerable

innommable [i(n)nɔmabl] *adj* unspeakable

innover [inɔve] *vi* to break new ground

inoccupé, e [inɔkype] *adj* unoccupied

inodore [inɔdɔr] *adj* (*gaz*) odourless; (*fleur*) scentless

inoffensif, -ive [inɔfɑ̃sif, iv] *adj* harmless, innocuous

inondation [inɔ̃dasjɔ̃] *nf* flood

inonder [inɔ̃de] *vt* to flood; **~ de** to flood with

inopiné, e [inɔpine] *adj* unexpected; (*mort*) sudden

inopportun, e [inɔpɔrtœ̃, yn] *adj* ill-timed, untimely

inoubliable [inublijabl] *adj* unforgettable

inouï, e [inwi] *adj* unheard-of, extraordinary

inox [inɔks] *nm* stainless steel

inqualifiable [ɛ̃kalifjabl] *adj* unspeakable

inquiet, -ète [ɛ̃kjɛ, ɛkjɛt] *adj* anxious; **inquiétant, e** *adj* wørrying, disturbing; **inquiéter** *vt* to worry; **s'inquiéter** to worry; **s'inquiéter de** to worry about; (*s'enquérir de*) to inquire about; **inquiétude** *nf* anxiety

insaisissable [ɛ̃sezisabl] *adj* (*fugitif, ennemi*) elusive; (*différence, nuance*) imperceptible

insalubre [ɛ̃salybr] *adj* insalubrious

insatisfaisant, e [ɛ̃satisfəzɑ̃, ɑ̃t] *adj* unsatisfactory

insatisfait, e [ɛ̃satisfɛ, ɛt] *adj* (*non comblé*) unsatisfied; (*mécontent*) dissatisfied

inscription [ɛ̃skripsjɔ̃] *nf* inscription; (*immatriculation*) enrolment

inscrire [ɛ̃skrir] *vt* (*marquer: sur son calepin etc*) to note *ou* write down; (*: sur un mur, une affiche etc*) to write; (*: dans la pierre, le métal*) to inscribe; (*mettre: sur une liste, un budget etc*) to put down; **s'~** (*pour une excursion etc*) to put one's name down; **s'~ (à)** (*club, parti*) to join; (*université*) to register *ou* enrol (at); (*examen, concours*) to register (for); **~ qn à** (*club, parti*) to enrol sb at

insecte [ɛ̃sɛkt] *nm* insect; **insecticide** *nm* insecticide

insensé, e [ɛ̃sɑ̃se] *adj* mad

insensibiliser [ɛ̃sɑ̃sibilize] *vt* to anaesthetize

insensible [ɛ̃sɑ̃sibl] *adj* (*nerf, membre*) numb; (*dur, indifférent*) insensitive

inséparable [ɛ̃separabl] *adj* inseparable ♦ *nm*: ~s (*oiseaux*) lovebirds

insigne [ɛ̃siɲ] *nm* (*d'un parti, club*) badge; (*d'une fonction*) insignia ♦ *adj* distinguished

insignifiant, e [ɛ̃siɲifjɑ̃, jɑ̃t] *adj* insignificant; trivial

insinuer [ɛ̃sinɥe] *vt* to insinuate; **s'~ dans** (*fig*) to worm one's way into

insipide [ɛ̃sipid] *adj* insipid

insister [ɛ̃siste] *vi* to insist; (*continuer à sonner*) to keep on trying; ~ **sur** (*détail, sujet*) to lay stress on

insolation [ɛ̃sɔlasjɔ̃] *nf* (*MÉD*) sunstroke *no pl*

insolent, e [ɛ̃sɔlɑ̃, ɑ̃t] *adj* insolent

insolite [ɛ̃sɔlit] *adj* strange, unusual

insomnie [ɛ̃sɔmni] *nf* insomnia *no pl*

insonoriser [ɛ̃sɔnɔrize] *vt* to soundproof

insouciant, e [ɛ̃susjɑ̃, jɑ̃t] *adj* carefree; ~ **du danger** heedless of (the) danger

insoumis, e [ɛ̃sumi, iz] *adj* (*caractère, enfant*) rebellious, refractory; (*contrée, tribu*) unsubdued

insoupçonnable [ɛ̃supsɔnabl] *adj* unsuspected; (*personne*) above suspicion

insoupçonné, e [ɛ̃supsɔne] *adj* unsuspected

insoutenable [ɛ̃sut(ə)nabl] *adj* (*argument*) untenable; (*chaleur*) unbearable

inspecter [ɛ̃spɛkte] *vt* to inspect; **inspecteur, -trice** *nm/f* inspector; **inspecteur d'Académie** (regional) director of education; **inspecteur des finances** ≈ tax inspector (*BRIT*), ≈ Internal Revenue Service agent (*US*); **inspection** *nf* inspection

inspirer [ɛ̃spire] *vt* (*gén*) to inspire ♦ *vi* (*aspirer*) to breathe in; **s'~ de** (*suj: artiste*) to draw one's inspiration from

instable [ɛ̃stabl] *adj* unstable; (*meuble, équilibre*) unsteady; (*temps*) unsettled

installation [ɛ̃stalasjɔ̃] *nf* installation; ~**s** *nfpl* facilities

installer [ɛ̃stale] *vt* (*loger, placer*) to put; (*meuble, gaz, électricité*) to put in; (*rideau, étagère, tente*) to put up; (*appartement*) to fit out; **s'~** (*s'établir: artisan, dentiste etc*) to set o.s. up; (*se loger*) to settle; (*emménager*) to settle in; (*sur un siège, à un emplacement*) to settle (down); (*fig: maladie, grève*) to take a firm hold

instance [ɛ̃stɑ̃s] *nf* (*ADMIN: autorité*) authority; **affaire en ~** matter pending; **être en ~ de divorce** to be awaiting a divorce

instant [ɛ̃stɑ̃] *nm* moment, instant; **dans un ~** in a moment; **à l'~** this instant; **pour l'~** for the moment, for the time being

instantané, e [ɛ̃stɑ̃tane] *adj* (*lait, café*) instant; (*explosion, mort*) instantaneous ♦ *nm* snapshot

instar [ɛ̃star]: **à l'~ de** *prép* following the example of, like

instaurer [ɛ̃stɔre] *vt* to institute; (*couvre-feu*) to impose

instinct [ɛ̃stɛ̃] *nm* instinct; **instinctivement** *adv* instinctively

instit [ɛ̃stit] (*fam*) *nm/f* (primary school) teacher

instituer [ɛ̃stitɥe] *vt* to establish

institut [ɛ̃stity] *nm* institute; ~ **de beauté** beauty salon; **Institut universitaire de technologie** ≈ polytechnic

instituteur, -trice [ɛ̃stitytœr, tris] *nm/f* (primary school) teacher

institution [ɛ̃stitysjɔ̃] *nf* institution; (*collège*) private school

instructif, -ive [ɛ̃stryktif, iv] *adj* instructive

instruction [ɛ̃stryksjɔ̃] *nf* (*enseignement, savoir*) education; (*JUR*) (preliminary) investigation and hearing; ~**s** *nfpl* (*ordres, mode d'emploi*) instructions; ~ **civique** civics *sg*

instruire [ɛ̃stʀɥiʀ] vt (élèves) to teach; (recrues) to train; (JUR: affaire) to conduct the investigation for; **s'~** to educate o.s.; **instruit, e** adj educated

instrument [ɛ̃stʀymɑ̃] nm instrument; **~ à cordes/vent** stringed/wind instrument; **~ de mesure** measuring instrument; **~ de musique** musical instrument; **~ de travail** (working) tool

insu [ɛ̃sy] nm: **à l'~ de qn** without sb knowing (it)

insubmersible [ɛ̃sybmɛʀsibl] adj unsinkable

insuffisant, e [ɛ̃syfizɑ̃, ɑ̃t] adj (en quantité) insufficient; (en qualité) inadequate; (sur une copie) poor

insulaire [ɛ̃sylɛʀ] adj island cpd; (attitude) insular

insuline [ɛ̃sylin] nf insulin

insulte [ɛ̃sylt] nf insult; **insulter** vt to insult

insupportable [ɛ̃sypɔʀtabl] adj unbearable

insurger [ɛ̃syʀʒe] vb: **s'~ (contre)** to rise up ou rebel (against)

insurmontable [ɛ̃syʀmɔ̃tabl] adj (difficulté) insuperable; (aversion) unconquerable

insurrection [ɛ̃syʀɛksjɔ̃] nf insurrection

intact, e [ɛ̃takt] adj intact

intangible [ɛ̃tɑ̃ʒibl] adj intangible; (principe) inviolable

intarissable [ɛ̃taʀisabl] adj inexhaustible

intégral, e, -aux [ɛ̃tegʀal, o] adj complete; **texte ~** unabridged version; **bronzage ~** all-over suntan; **intégralement** adv in full; **intégralité** nf whole; **dans son intégralité** in full; **intégrant, e** adj: **faire partie intégrante de** to be an integral part of

intègre [ɛ̃tɛgʀ] adj upright

intégrer [ɛ̃tegʀe] vt: **bien s'~** to integrate well

intégrisme [ɛ̃tegʀism] nm fundamentalism

intellectuel, le [ɛ̃telɛktɥɛl] adj intellectual

♦ nm/f intellectual; (péj) highbrow

intelligence [ɛ̃teliʒɑ̃s] nf intelligence; (compréhension): **l'~ de** the understanding of; (complicité): **regard d'~** glance of complicity; (accord): **vivre en bonne ~ avec qn** to be on good terms with sb

intelligent, e [ɛ̃teliʒɑ̃, ɑ̃t] adj intelligent

intelligible [ɛ̃teliʒibl] adj intelligible

intempéries [ɛ̃tɑ̃peʀi] nfpl bad weather sg

intempestif, -ive [ɛ̃tɑ̃pɛstif, iv] adj untimely

intenable [ɛ̃t(ə)nabl] adj (chaleur) unbearable

intendant, e [ɛ̃tɑ̃dɑ̃] nm/f (MIL) quartermaster; (SCOL) bursar

intense [ɛ̃tɑ̃s] adj intense; **intensif, -ive** adj intensive; **un cours intensif** a crash course

intenter [ɛ̃tɑ̃te] vt: **~ un procès contre** ou **à** to start proceedings against

intention [ɛ̃tɑ̃sjɔ̃] nf intention; (JUR) intent; **avoir l'~ de faire** to intend to do; **à l'~ de** for; (renseignement) for the benefit of; (film, ouvrage) aimed at; **à cette ~** with this aim in view; **intentionné, e** adj: **bien intentionné** well-meaning ou -intentioned; **mal intentionné** ill-intentioned

interactif, -ive [ɛ̃teʀaktif, iv] adj (COMPUT) interactive

intercalaire [ɛ̃teʀkalɛʀ] nm divider

intercaler [ɛ̃teʀkale] vt to insert

intercepter [ɛ̃teʀsepte] vt to intercept; (lumière, chaleur) to cut off

interchangeable [ɛ̃teʀʃɑ̃ʒabl] adj interchangeable

interclasse [ɛ̃teʀklɑs] nm (SCOL) break (between classes)

interdiction [ɛ̃teʀdiksjɔ̃] nf ban; **~ de stationner** no parking; **~ de fumer** no smoking

interdire [ɛ̃teʀdiʀ] vt to forbid; (ADMIN) to ban, prohibit; (: journal, livre) to ban; **~ à 'qn de faire** to forbid sb to do; (suj: empêchement) to prevent sb from doing

interdit, e [ɛ̃tɛʀdi, it] *adj* (*stupéfait*) taken aback

intéressant, e [ɛ̃teʀesɑ̃, ɑ̃t] *adj* interesting; (*avantageux*) attractive

intéressé, e [ɛ̃teʀese] *adj* (*parties*) involved, concerned; (*amitié, motifs*) self-interested

intéresser [ɛ̃teʀese] *vt* (*captiver*) to interest; (*toucher*) to be of interest to; (ADMIN: *concerner*) to affect, concern; **s'~ à** to be interested in

intérêt [ɛ̃teʀe] *nm* interest; (*égoïsme*) self-interest; **tu as ~ à accepter** it's in your interest to accept; **tu as ~ à te dépêcher** you'd better hurry

intérieur, e [ɛ̃teʀjœʀ] *adj* (*mur, escalier, poche*) inside; (*commerce, politique*) domestic; (*cour, calme, vie*) inner; (*navigation*) inland ♦ *nm* (*d'une maison, d'un récipient etc*) inside; (*d'un pays, aussi décor, mobilier*) interior; **à l'~ (de)** inside; **intérieurement** *adv* inwardly

intérim [ɛ̃teʀim] *nm* interim period; **faire de l'~** to temp; **assurer l'~ (de)** to deputize (for); **par ~** interim

intérimaire [ɛ̃teʀimɛʀ] *adj* (*directeur, ministre*) acting; (*secrétaire, personnel*) temporary ♦ *nm/f* (*secrétaire*) temporary secretary, temp (BRIT)

interlocuteur, -trice [ɛ̃tɛʀlɔkytœʀ, tʀis] *nm/f* speaker; **son ~** the person he was speaking to

interloquer [ɛ̃tɛʀlɔke] *vt* to take aback

intermède [ɛ̃tɛʀmɛd] *nm* interlude

intermédiaire [ɛ̃tɛʀmedjɛʀ] *adj* intermediate; (*solution*) temporary ♦ *nm/f* intermediary; (COMM) middleman; **sans ~** directly; **par l'~ de** through

interminable [ɛ̃tɛʀminabl] *adj* endless

intermittence [ɛ̃tɛʀmitɑ̃s] *nf*: **par ~** sporadically, intermittently

internat [ɛ̃tɛʀna] *nm* (SCOL) boarding school

international, e, -aux [ɛ̃tɛʀnasjɔnal, o] *adj, nm/f* international

interne [ɛ̃tɛʀn] *adj* internal ♦ *nm/f* (SCOL) boarder; (MÉD) houseman

interner [ɛ̃tɛʀne] *vt* (POL) to intern; (MÉD) to confine to a mental institution

Internet [ɛ̃tɛʀnɛt] *nm* Internet

interpeller [ɛ̃tɛʀpəle] *vt* (*appeler*) to call out to; (*apostropher*) to shout at; (POLICE, POL) to question; (*concerner*) to concern

interphone [ɛ̃tɛʀfɔn] *nm* intercom; (*d'immeuble*) entry phone

interposer [ɛ̃tɛʀpoze] *vt*: **s'~** to intervene; **par personnes interposées** through a third party

interprétation [ɛ̃tɛʀpʀetasjɔ̃] *nf* interpretation

interprète [ɛ̃tɛʀpʀɛt] *nm/f* interpreter; (*porte-parole*) spokesperson

interpréter [ɛ̃tɛʀpʀete] *vt* to interpret; (*jouer*) to play; (*chanter*) to sing

interrogateur, -trice [ɛ̃teʀɔgatœʀ, tʀis] *adj* questioning, inquiring

interrogatif, -ive [ɛ̃teʀɔgatif, iv] *adj* (LING) interrogative

interrogation [ɛ̃teʀɔgasjɔ̃] *nf* question; (*action*) questioning; (SCOL) (written or oral) test

interrogatoire [ɛ̃teʀɔgatwaʀ] *nm* (POLICE) questioning *no pl*; (JUR, *aussi fig*) cross-examination

interroger [ɛ̃teʀɔʒe] *vt* to question; (IN-FORM) to consult; (SCOL) to test

interrompre [ɛ̃teʀɔ̃pʀ] *vt* (*gén*) to interrupt; (*négociations*) to break off; (*match*) to stop; **s'~** to break off; **interrupteur** *nm* switch; **interruption** *nf* interruption; (*pause*) break; **sans interruption** without stopping

intersection [ɛ̃tɛʀsɛksjɔ̃] *nf* intersection

interstice [ɛ̃tɛʀstis] *nm* crack; (*de volet*) slit

interurbain, e [ɛ̃teʀyʀbɛ̃, ɛn] *adj* (TÉL) long-distance

intervalle [ɛ̃tɛʀval] *nm* (*espace*) space; (*de temps*) interval; **à deux jours d'~** two days apart

intervenir [ɛ̃tɛʀvəniʀ] *vi* (*gén*) to intervene; **~ auprès de qn** to intervene with sb

ntervention [ɛ̃tɛʀvɑ̃sjɔ̃] *nf* intervention; (*discours*) speech; **~ chirurgicale** (surgical) operation

ntervertir [ɛ̃tɛʀvɛʀtiʀ] *vt* to invert (the order of), reverse

nterview [ɛ̃tɛʀvju] *nf* interview

ntestin [ɛ̃tɛstɛ̃, in] *nm* intestine

ntime [ɛ̃tim] *adj* intimate; (*vie*) private; (*conviction*) inmost; (*dîner, cérémonie*) quiet ♦ *nm/f* close friend; **un journal ~** a diary

ntimider [ɛ̃timide] *vt* to intimidate

ntimité [ɛ̃timite] *nf*: **dans l'~** in private; (*sans formalités*) with only a few friends, quietly

ntitulé, e [ɛ̃tityle] *adj* entitled

ntolérable [ɛ̃tɔleʀabl] *adj* intolerable

ntox [ɛ̃tɔks] (*fam*) *nf* brainwashing

ntoxication [ɛ̃tɔksikasjɔ̃] *nf*: **~ alimentaire** food poisoning

ntoxiquer [ɛ̃tɔksike] *vt* to poison; (*fig*) to brainwash

ntraduisible [ɛ̃tʀadɥizibl] *adj* untranslatable; (*fig*) inexpressible

ntraitable [ɛ̃tʀɛtabl] *adj* inflexible, uncompromising

ntranet [ɛ̃tʀanɛt] *nm* intranet

ntransigeant, e [ɛ̃tʀɑ̃ziʒɑ̃, ɑ̃t] *adj* intransigent

ntransitif, -ive [ɛ̃tʀɑ̃zitif, iv] *adj* (*LING*) intransitive

ntrépide [ɛ̃tʀepid] *adj* dauntless

ntrigue [ɛ̃tʀig] *nf* (*scénario*) plot; **intriguer** *vt* to puzzle, intrigue

ntrinsèque [ɛ̃tʀɛ̃sɛk] *adj* intrinsic

ntroduction [ɛ̃tʀɔdyksjɔ̃] *nf* introduction

ntroduire [ɛ̃tʀɔdɥiʀ] *vt* to introduce; (*visiteur*) to show in; (*aiguille, clef*): **~ qch dans** to insert *ou* introduce sth into; **s'~ (dans)** to get in(to); (*dans un groupe*) to get o.s. accepted (into)

ntrouvable [ɛ̃tʀuvabl] *adj* which cannot be found; (*COMM*) unobtainable

ntroverti, e [ɛ̃tʀɔvɛʀti] *nm/f* introvert

ntrus, e [ɛ̃tʀy, yz] *nm/f* intruder

ntrusion [ɛ̃tʀyzjɔ̃] *nf* intrusion

ntuition [ɛ̃tɥisjɔ̃] *nf* intuition

inusable [inyzabl] *adj* hard-wearing

inusité, e [inyzite] *adj* rarely used

inutile [inytil] *adj* useless; (*superflu*) unnecessary; **inutilement** *adv* unnecessarily; **inutilisable** *adj* unusable

invalide [ɛ̃valid] *adj* disabled ♦ *nm*: **~ de guerre** disabled ex-serviceman

invasion [ɛ̃vazjɔ̃] *nf* invasion

invectiver [ɛ̃vɛktive] *vt* to hurl abuse at

invendable [ɛ̃vɑ̃dabl] *adj* unsaleable; (*COMM*) unmarketable; **invendus** *nmpl* unsold goods

inventaire [ɛ̃vɑ̃tɛʀ] *nm* inventory; (*COMM: liste*) stocklist; (: *opération*) stocktaking *no pl*

inventer [ɛ̃vɑ̃te] *vt* to invent; (*subterfuge*) to devise, invent; (*histoire, excuse*) to make up, invent; **inventeur** *nm* inventor; **inventif, -ive** *adj* inventive; **invention** *nf* invention

inverse [ɛ̃vɛʀs] *adj* opposite ♦ *nm* opposite; **dans l'ordre ~** in the reverse order; **en sens ~** in (*ou* from) the opposite direction; **dans le sens ~ des aiguilles d'une montre** anticlockwise; **tu t'es trompé, c'est l'~** you've got it wrong, it's the other way round; **inversement** *adv* conversely; **inverser** *vt* to invert, reverse; (*ÉLEC*) to reverse

investigation [ɛ̃vɛstigasjɔ̃] *nf* investigation

investir [ɛ̃vɛstiʀ] *vt* to invest; **investissement** *nm* investment; **investiture** *nf* nomination

invétéré, e [ɛ̃vetere] *adj* inveterate

invisible [ɛ̃vizibl] *adj* invisible

invitation [ɛ̃vitasjɔ̃] *nf* invitation

invité, e [ɛ̃vite] *nm/f* guest

inviter [ɛ̃vite] *vt* to invite

invivable [ɛ̃vivabl] *adj* unbearable

involontaire [ɛ̃vɔlɔ̃tɛʀ] *adj* (*mouvement*) involuntary; (*insulte*) unintentional; (*complice*) unwitting

invoquer [ɛ̃vɔke] *vt* (*Dieu, muse*) to call upon, invoke; (*prétexte*) to put forward (as an excuse); (*loi, texte*) to refer to

invraisemblable [ɛ̃vʀɛsɑ̃blabl] *adj* (*fait,*

nouvelle) unlikely, improbable; (*insolence, habit*) incredible

iode [jɔd] *nm* iodine

irai *etc* [iʀe] *vb voir* **aller**

Irak [iʀak] *nm* Iraq; **irakien, ne** *adj* Iraqi ♦ *nm/f*: **Irakien, ne** Iraqi

Iran [iʀɑ̃] *nm* Iran; **iranien, ne** *adj* Iranian ♦ *nm/f*: **Iranien, ne** Iranian

irascible [iʀasibl] *adj* short-tempered

irions *etc* [iʀjɔ̃] *vb voir* **aller**

iris [iʀis] *nm* iris

irlandais, e [iʀlɑ̃dɛ, ɛz] *adj* Irish ♦ *nm/f*: **Irlandais, e** Irishman(-woman); **les Irlandais** the Irish

Irlande [iʀlɑ̃d] *nf* Ireland; **~ du Nord** Northern Ireland; **la République d'~** the Irish Republic

ironie [iʀɔni] *nf* irony; **ironique** *adj* ironical; **ironiser** *vi* to be ironical

irons *etc* [iʀɔ̃] *vb voir* **aller**

irradier [iʀadje] *vt* to irradiate

irraisonné, e [iʀezɔne] *adj* irrational

irrationnel, le [iʀasjɔnɛl] *adj* irrational

irréalisable [iʀealizabl] *adj* unrealizable; (*projet*) impracticable

irrécupérable [iʀekypeʀabl] *adj* beyond repair; (*personne*) beyond redemption

irréductible [iʀedyktibl] *adj* (*volonté*) indomitable; (*ennemi*) implacable

irréel, le [iʀeɛl] *adj* unreal

irréfléchi, e [iʀefleʃi] *adj* thoughtless

irrégularité [iʀegylaʀite] *nf* irregularity; (*de travail, d'effort, de qualité*) unevenness *no pl*

irrégulier, -ière [iʀegylje, jɛʀ] *adj* irregular; (*travail, effort, qualité*) uneven; (*élève, athlète*) erratic

irrémédiable [iʀemedjabl] *adj* irreparable

irremplaçable [iʀɑ̃plasabl] *adj* irreplaceable

irréparable [iʀepaʀabl] *adj* (*objet*) beyond repair; (*dommage etc*) irreparable

irréprochable [iʀepʀɔʃabl] *adj* irreproachable, beyond reproach; (*tenue*) impeccable

irrésistible [iʀezistibl] *adj* irresistible; (*be-

soin, désir, preuve, logique) compelling; (*amusant*) hilarious

irrésolu, e [iʀezɔly] *adj* (*personne*) irresolute; (*problème*) unresolved

irrespectueux, -euse [iʀɛspɛktɥø, øz] *adj* disrespectful

irrespirable [iʀɛspiʀabl] *adj* unbreathable; (*fig*) oppressive

irresponsable [iʀɛspɔ̃sabl] *adj* irresponsible

irriguer [iʀige] *vt* to irrigate

irritable [iʀitabl] *adj* irritable

irriter [iʀite] *vt* to irritate

irruption [iʀypsjɔ̃] *nf*: **faire ~ (chez qn)** to burst in (on sb)

Islam [islam] *nm* Islam; **islamique** *adj* Islamic; **islamiste** *adj* (*militant*) Islamic; (*mouvement*) Islamic fundamentalist ♦ *nm/f* Islamic fundamentalist

Islande [islɑ̃d] *nf* Iceland

isolant, e [izɔlɑ̃, ɑ̃t] *adj* insulating; (*insonorisant*) soundproofing

isolation [izɔlasjɔ̃] *nf* insulation

isolé, e [izɔle] *adj* isolated; (*contre le froid*) insulated

isoler [izɔle] *vt* to isolate; (*prisonnier*) to put in solitary confinement; (*ville*) to cut off, isolate; (*contre le froid*) to insulate; **s'~** *vi* to isolate o.s.; **isoloir** [izɔlwaʀ] *nm* polling booth

Israël [isʀaɛl] *nm* Israel; **israélien, ne** *adj* Israeli ♦ *nm/f*: **Israélien, ne** Israeli; **israélite** *adj* Jewish ♦ *nm/f*: **Israélite** Jew (Jewess)

issu, e [isy] *adj*: **~ de** (*né de*) descended from; (*résultant de*) stemming from; **issue** *nf* (*ouverture, sortie*) exit; (*solution*) way out, solution; (*dénouement*) outcome; **à l'issue de** at the conclusion *ou* close of; **voie sans issue** dead end; **issue de secours** emergency exit

Italie [itali] *nf* Italy; **italien, ne** *adj* Italian ♦ *nm/f*: **Italien, ne** Italian ♦ *nm* (*LING*) Italian

italique [italik] *nm*: **en ~** in italics

itinéraire [itineʀeʀ] *nm* itinerary, route; ~

bis diversion

IUT sigle m = **Institut universitaire de technologie**

IVG sigle f (= interruption volontaire de grossesse) abortion

ivoire [ivwar] nm ivory

ivre [ivr] adj drunk; **~ de** (colère, bonheur) wild with; **ivresse** nf drunkenness; **ivrogne** nm/f drunkard

J, j

j' [ʒ] pron voir **je**

jacasser [ʒakase] vi to chatter

jacinthe [ʒasɛ̃t] nf hyacinth

jadis [ʒadis] adv long ago

jaillir [ʒajir] vi (liquide) to spurt out; (cris, responses) to burst forth

jais [ʒɛ] nm jet; **(d'un noir) de ~** jet-black

jalousie [ʒaluzi] nf jealousy; (store) slatted blind

jaloux, -ouse [ʒalu, uz] adj jealous

jamais [ʒamɛ] adv never; (sans négation) ever; **ne ... ~** never; **à ~** for ever

jambe [ʒɑ̃b] nf leg

jambon [ʒɑ̃bɔ̃] nm ham; **~ blanc** boiled ou cooked ham; **jambonneau, x** nm knuckle of ham

jante [ʒɑ̃t] nf (wheel) rim

janvier [ʒɑ̃vje] nm January

Japon [ʒapɔ̃] nm Japan; **japonais, e** adj Japanese ♦ nm/f: **Japonais, e** Japanese ♦ nm (LING) Japanese

japper [ʒape] vi to yap, yelp

jaquette [ʒakɛt] nf (de cérémonie) morning coat

jardin [ʒardɛ̃] nm garden; **~ d'enfants** nursery school; **jardinage** nm gardening; **jardiner** vi to do some gardening; **jardinier, -ière** nm/f gardener; **jardinière** nf planter; (de fenêtre) window box; **jardinière de légumes** mixed vegetables

jargon [ʒargɔ̃] nm (baragouin) gibberish; (langue professionnelle) jargon

jarret [ʒarɛ] nm back of knee; (CULIN) knuckle, shin

jarretelle [ʒartɛl] nf suspender (BRIT), garter (US)

jarretière [ʒartjɛr] nf garter

jaser [ʒaze] vi (médire) to gossip

jatte [ʒat] nf basin, bowl

jauge [ʒoʒ] nf (instrument) gauge; **~ d'essence** petrol gauge; **~ d'huile** (oil) dipstick

jaune [ʒon] adj, nm yellow ♦ adv (fam): **rire ~** to laugh on the other side of one's face; **~ d'œuf** (egg) yolk; **jaunir** vi, vt to turn yellow; **jaunisse** nf jaundice

Javel [ʒavɛl] nf voir **eau**

javelot [ʒavlo] nm javelin

J.-C. abr = **Jésus-Christ**

je, j' [ʒə] pron I

jean [dʒin] nm jeans pl

Jésus-Christ [ʒezykri(st)] n Jesus Christ; **600 avant/après ~-~** ou **J.-C.** 600 B.C./A.D.

jet¹ [ʒɛ] nm (lancer: action) throwing no pl; (: résultat) throw; (jaillissement: d'eaux) jet; (: de sang) spurt; **~ d'eau** spray

jet² [dʒɛt] nm (avion) jet

jetable [ʒ(ə)tabl] adj disposable

jetée [ʒəte] nf jetty; (grande) pier

jeter [ʒ(ə)te] vt (gén) to throw; (se défaire de) to throw away ou out; **se ~ dans** to flow into; **~ qch à qn** to throw sth to sb; (de façon agressive) to throw sth at sb; **~ un coup d'œil (à)** to take a look (at); **~ un sort à qn** to cast a spell on sb; **se ~ sur qn** to rush at sb

jeton [ʒ(ə)tɔ̃] nm (au jeu) counter; (de téléphone) token

jette etc [ʒɛt] vb voir **jeter**

jeu, x [ʒø] nm (divertissement, TECH: d'une pièce) play; (TENNIS: partie, FOOTBALL etc: façon de jouer) game; (THÉÂTRE etc) acting; (série d'objets, jouet) set; (CARTES) hand; (au casino): **le ~** gambling; **être en ~** to be at stake; **entrer/mettre en ~** to come/bring into play; **~ de cartes** pack of cards; **~ d'échecs** chess set; **~ de hasard** game of chance; **~ de mots** pun; **~ de**

société parlour game; **~ télévisé** television quiz; **~ vidéo** video game

jeudi [ʒødi] *nm* Thursday

jeun [ʒœ̃]: **à ~** *adv* on an empty stomach; **être à ~** to have eaten nothing; **rester à ~** not to eat anything

jeune [ʒœn] *adj* young; **les ~s** young people; **~ fille** girl; **~ homme** young man; **~s mariés** newly-weds

jeûne [ʒøn] *nm* fast

jeunesse [ʒœnes] *nf* youth; *(aspect)* youthfulness

joaillerie [ʒɔajʀi] *nf* jewellery; *(magasin)* jeweller's; **joaillier, -ière** *nm/f* jeweller

jogging [dʒɔgiŋ] *nm* jogging; *(survêtement)* tracksuit; **faire du ~** to go jogging

joie [ʒwa] *nf* joy

joindre [ʒwɛ̃dʀ] *vt* to join; *(à une lettre):* **~ qch à** to enclose sth with; *(contacter)* to contact, get in touch with; **se ~ à** to join; **~ les mains** to put one's hands together

joint, e [ʒwɛ̃, ɛ̃t] *adj:* **pièce ~e** enclosure ♦ *nm* joint; *(ligne)* join; **~ de culasse** cylinder head gasket; **~ de robinet** washer

joli, e [ʒɔli] *adj* pretty, attractive; **c'est du ~!** *(ironique)* that's very nice!; **c'est bien ~, mais ...** that's all very well but ...

jonc [ʒɔ̃] *nm* (bul)rush

jonction [ʒɔ̃ksjɔ̃] *nf* junction

jongleur, -euse [ʒɔ̃glœʀ, øz] *nm/f* juggler

jonquille [ʒɔ̃kij] *nf* daffodil

Jordanie [ʒɔʀdani] *nf:* **la ~** Jordan

joue [ʒu] *nf* cheek

jouer [ʒwe] *vt* to play; *(somme d'argent, réputation)* to stake, wager; *(simuler: sentiment)* to affect, feign ♦ *vi* to play; *(THÉÂTRE, CINÉMA)* to act; *(au casino)* to gamble; *(bois, porte: se voiler)* to warp; *(clef, pièce: avoir du jeu)* to be loose; **~ sur** *(miser)* to gamble on; **~ de** *(MUS)* to play; **~ à** *(jeu, sport, roulette)* to play; **~ un tour à qn** to play a trick on sb; **~ serré** to play a close game; **~ la comédie** to put on an act; **bien joué!** well done!; **on joue Hamlet au théâtre X** Hamlet is on at the X theatre

jouet [ʒwe] *nm* toy; **être le ~ de** *(illusion etc)* to be the victim of

joueur, -euse [ʒwœʀ, øz] *nm/f* player; **être beau ~** to be a good loser

joufflu, e [ʒufly] *adj* chubby-cheeked

joug [ʒu] *nm* yoke

jouir [ʒwiʀ] *vi* *(sexe: fam)* to come ♦ *vt:* **~ de** to enjoy; **jouissance** *nf* pleasure; *(JUR)* use

joujou [ʒuʒu] *(fam) nm* toy

jour [ʒuʀ] *nm* day; *(opposé à la nuit)* day, daytime; *(clarté)* daylight; *(fig: aspect)* light; *(ouverture)* gap; **au ~ le ~** from day to day; **de nos ~s** these days; **du ~ au lendemain** overnight; **il fait ~** it's daylight; **au grand ~** *(fig)* in the open; **mettre au ~** to disclose; **mettre à ~** to update; **donner le ~ à** to give birth to; **voir le ~** to be born; **~ férié** public holiday; **~ de fête** holiday; **~ ouvrable** week-day, working day

journal, -aux [ʒuʀnal, o] *nm* (news)paper; *(spécialisé)* journal; *(intime)* diary; **~ de bord** log; **~ télévisé** television news *sg*

journalier, -ière [ʒuʀnalje, jɛʀ] *adj* daily; *(banal)* everyday

journalisme [ʒuʀnalism] *nm* journalism; **journaliste** *nm/f* journalist

journée [ʒuʀne] *nf* day; **faire la ~ continue** to work over lunch

journellement [ʒuʀnɛlmɑ̃] *adv* daily

joyau, x [ʒwajo] *nm* gem, jewel

joyeux, -euse [ʒwajø, øz] *adj* joyful, merry; **~ Noël!** merry Christmas!; **~ anniversaire!** happy birthday!

jubiler [ʒybile] *vi* to be jubilant, exult

jucher [ʒyʃe] *vt, vi* to perch

judas [ʒyda] *nm* *(trou)* spy-hole

judiciaire [ʒydisjɛʀ] *adj* judicial

judicieux, -euse [ʒydisjø, jøz] *adj* judicious

judo [ʒydo] *nm* judo

juge [ʒyʒ] *nm* judge; **~ d'instruction** examining *(BRIT)* ou committing *(US)* mag istrate; **~ de paix** justice of the peace; **~ de touche** linesman

jugé [ʒyʒe]: **au ~** adv by guesswork

jugement [ʒyʒmɑ̃] nm judgment; (JUR: au pénal) sentence; (: au civil) decision

jugeote [ʒyʒɔt] (fam) nf commonsense

juger [ʒyʒe] vt to judge; (estimer) to consider; **~ qn/qch satisfaisant** to consider sb/sth (to be) satisfactory; **~ bon de faire** to see fit to do; **~ de** to appreciate

juif, -ive [ʒɥif, ʒɥiv] adj Jewish ♦ nm/f: **J~, -ive** Jew (Jewess)

juillet [ʒɥije] nm July

---

14 juillet

In France, le 14 juillet is a national holiday commemorating the storming of the Bastille during the French Revolution, celebrated by parades, music, dancing and firework displays. In Paris, there is a military parade along the Champs-Élysées, attended by the President.

---

juin [ʒɥɛ̃] nm June

jumeau, -elle, x [ʒymo, ɛl] adj, nm/f twin

jumeler [ʒym(ə)le] vt to twin

jumelle [ʒymɛl] adj, nf voir **jumeau; ~s** nfpl (appareil) binoculars

jument [ʒymɑ̃] nf mare

jungle [ʒɛ̃gl] nf jungle

jupe [ʒyp] nf skirt

jupon [ʒypɔ̃] nm waist slip

juré, e [ʒyʀe] nm/f juror

jurer [ʒyʀe] vt (obéissance etc) to swear, vow ♦ vi (dire des jurons) to swear, curse; (dissoner): **~ (avec)** to clash (with); **~ de faire/que** to swear to do/that; **~ de qch** (s'en porter garant) to swear to sth

juridique [ʒyʀidik] adj legal

juron [ʒyʀɔ̃] nm curse, swearword

jury [ʒyʀi] nm jury; (ART, SPORT) panel of judges; (SCOL) board of examiners

jus [ʒy] nm juice; (de viande) gravy, (meat) juice; **~ de fruit** fruit juice

jusque [ʒysk]: **jusqu'à** prép (endroit) as far

as, (up) to; (moment) until, till; (limite) up to; **~ sur/dans** up to; (y compris) even on/in; **jusqu'à ce que** until; **jusqu'à présent** so far; **jusqu'où?** how far?

justaucorps [ʒystokɔʀ] nm leotard

juste [ʒyst] adj (équitable) just, fair; (légitime) just; (exact) right; (pertinent) apt; (étroit) tight; (insuffisant) on the short side ♦ adv rightly, correctly; (chanter) in tune; (exactement, seulement) just; **~ assez/au-dessus** just enough/above; **au ~** exactly; **le ~ milieu** the happy medium; **c'était ~** it was a close thing; **justement** adv justly; (précisément) just, precisely; **justesse** nf (précision) accuracy; (d'une remarque) aptness; (d'une opinion) soundness; **de justesse** only just

justice [ʒystis] nf (équité) fairness, justice; (ADMIN) justice; **rendre ~ à qn** to do sb justice; **justicier, -ière** nm/f righter of wrongs

justificatif, -ive [ʒystifikatif, iv] adj (document) supporting; **pièce justificative** written proof

justifier [ʒystifje] vt to justify; **~ de** to prove

juteux, -euse [ʒytø, øz] adj juicy

juvénile [ʒyvenil] adj youthful

K, k

K [kɑ] nm (INFORM) K

kaki [kaki] adj inv khaki

kangourou [kɑ̃guʀu] nm kangaroo

karaté [kaʀate] nm karate

karting [kaʀtiŋ] nm go-carting, karting

kascher [kaʃɛʀ] adj kosher

kayak [kajak] nm canoe, kayak; **faire du ~** to go canoeing

képi [kepi] nm kepi

kermesse [kɛʀmɛs] nf fair; (fête de charité) bazaar, (charity) fête

kidnapper [kidnape] vt to kidnap

kilo [kilo] nm = **kilogramme**

kilo...: kilogramme nm kilogramme; **ki-**

lométrage *nm* number of kilometres travelled, ≃ mileage; **kilomètre** *nm* kilometre; **kilométrique** *adj* (*distance*) in kilometres

kinésithérapeute [kineziteʀapøt] *nm/f* physiotherapist

kiosque [kjɔsk] *nm* kiosk, stall; **~ à musique** bandstand

kir [kiʀ] *nm* kir (*white wine with blackcurrant liqueur*)

kit [kit] *nm*: **en ~** in kit form

klaxon [klaksɔn] *nm* horn; **klaxonner** *vi, vt* to hoot (*BRIT*), honk (*US*)

km *abr* = **kilomètre**

km/h *abr* (= *kilomètres/heure*) ≃ mph

K.-O. (*fam*) *adj inv* shattered, knackered

Kosovo [kɔsɔvo] *nm* Kosovo

k-way ® [kawɛ] *nm* (lightweight nylon) cagoule

kyste [kist] *nm* cyst

L, l

l' [l] *art déf voir* **le**

la [la] *art déf voir* **le** ♦ *nm* (*MUS*) A; (*en chantant la gamme*) la

là [la] *adv* there; (*ici*) here; (*dans le temps*) then; **elle n'est pas ~** she isn't here; **c'est ~ que** this is where; **~ où** where; **de ~** (*fig*) hence; **par ~** (*fig*) by that; *voir aussi* **-ci; ce; celui; là-bas** *adv* there

label [label] *nm* stamp, seal

labeur [labœʀ] *nm* toil *no pl*, toiling *no pl*

labo [labo] (*fam*) *nm* (= *laboratoire*) lab

laboratoire [labɔʀatwaʀ] *nm* laboratory; **~ de langues** language laboratory

laborieux, -euse [labɔʀjø, jøz] *adj* (*tâche*) laborious

labour [labuʀ] *nm* ploughing *no pl*; **~s** *nmpl* (*champs*) ploughed fields; **cheval de ~** plough- *ou* cart-horse; **labourer** *vt* to plough

labyrinthe [labiʀɛ̃t] *nm* labyrinth, maze

lac [lak] *nm* lake

lacer [lase] *vt* to lace *ou* do up

lacérer [laseʀe] *vt* to tear to shreds

lacet [lasɛ] *nm* (*de chaussure*) lace; (*d route*) sharp bend; (*piège*) snare

lâche [lɑʃ] *adj* (*poltron*) cowardly; (*desser* loose, slack ♦ *nm/f* coward

lâcher [lɑʃe] *vt* to let go of; (*ce qui tombe abandonner*) to drop; (*oiseau, animal: libé rer*) to release, set free; (*fig: mot, remarque* to let slip, come out with ♦ *vi* (*freins*) ▪ fail; **~ les amarres** (*NAVIG*) to cast off (th moorings); **~ prise** to let go

lâcheté [lɑʃte] *nf* cowardice

lacrymogène [lakʀimɔʒɛn] *adj*: **gaz ~** teargas

lacté, e [lakte] *adj* (*produit, régime*) mi *cpd*

lacune [lakyn] *nf* gap

là-dedans [ladədɑ̃] *adv* inside (there), it; (*fig*) in that

là-dessous [ladsu] *adv* underneath, u der there; (*fig*) behind that

là-dessus [ladsy] *adv* on there; (*fig: s* ces mots*) at that point; (: *à ce sujet*) abo that

ladite [ladit] *dét voir* **ledit**

lagune [lagyn] *nf* lagoon

là-haut [lao] *adv* up there

laïc [laik] *adj*, *nm/f* = **laïque**

laid, e [lɛ, lɛd] *adj* ugly; **laideur** *nf* ug ness *no pl*

lainage [lɛnaʒ] *nm* (*vêtement*) woollen ga ment; (*étoffe*) woollen material

laine [lɛn] *nf* wool

laïque [laik] *adj* lay, civil; (*SCOL*) state c ♦ *nm/f* layman(-woman)

laisse [lɛs] *nf* (*de chien*) lead, leash; **te en ~** to keep on a lead *ou* leash

laisser [lese] *vt* to leave ♦ *vb aux*: **~ ◀ faire** to let sb do; **se ~ aller** to let o go; **laisse-toi faire** let me (*ou* him *etc*) ◀ it; **laisser-aller** *nm* carelessness, slover ness; **laissez-passer** *nm inv* pass

lait [lɛ] *nm* milk; **frère/sœur de ~** fost brother/sister; **~ condensé/concentr** evaporated/condensed milk; **~ démaqu** **lant** cleansing milk; **laitage** *nm* da product; **laiterie** nf dairy; **laitier, -ière** adj dairy cpd ♦ nm/f milkman (dairy-woman)

laiton [lɛtɔ̃] nm brass

laitue [lety] nf lettuce

laïus [lajys] (péj) nm spiel

lambeau, x [lɑ̃bo] nm scrap; **en ~x** in tatters, tattered

lambris [lɑ̃bʀi] nm panelling no pl

lame [lam] nf blade; (vague) wave; (lamelle) strip; **~ de fond** ground swell no pl; **~ de rasoir** razor blade; **lamelle** nf thin strip ou blade

lamentable [lamɑ̃tabl] adj appalling

lamenter [lamɑ̃te] vb: **se ~ (sur)** to moan (over)

lampadaire [lɑ̃padɛʀ] nm (de salon) standard lamp; (dans la rue) street lamp

lampe [lɑ̃p] nf lamp; (TECH) valve; **~ à souder** blowlamp; **~ de chevet** bedside lamp; **~ de poche** torch (BRIT), flashlight (US)

lampion [lɑ̃pjɔ̃] nm Chinese lantern

lance [lɑ̃s] nf spear; **~ d'incendie** fire hose

lancée [lɑ̃se] nf: **être/continuer sur sa ~** to be under way/keep going

lancement [lɑ̃smɑ̃] nm launching

lance-pierres [lɑ̃spjɛʀ] nm inv catapult

lancer [lɑ̃se] nm (SPORT) throwing no pl, throw ♦ vt to throw; (émettre, projeter) to throw out, send out; (produit, fusée, bateau, artiste) to launch; (injure) to hurl, fling; **se ~** vi (prendre de l'élan) to build up speed; (se précipiter): **se ~ sur** ou **contre** to rush at; **se ~ dans** (discussion) to launch into; (aventure) to embark on; **~ qch à qn** to throw sth to sb; (de façon agressive) to throw sth at sb; **~ du poids** putting the shot

lancinant, e [lɑ̃sinɑ̃, ɑ̃t] adj (douleur) shooting

landau [lɑ̃do] nm pram (BRIT), baby carriage (US)

lande [lɑ̃d] nf moor

langage [lɑ̃gaʒ] nm language

langouste [lɑ̃gust] nf crayfish inv; **lan-**

goustine nf Dublin Bay prawn

langue [lɑ̃g] nf (ANAT, CULIN) tongue; (LING) language; **tirer la ~ (à)** to stick out one's tongue (at); **de ~ française** French-speaking; **~ maternelle** native language, mother tongue; **~ vivante/étrangère** modern/foreign language

langueur [lɑ̃gœʀ] nf languidness

languir [lɑ̃giʀ] vi to languish; (conversation) to flag; **faire ~ qn** to keep sb waiting

lanière [lanjɛʀ] nf (de fouet) lash; (de sac, bretelle) strap

lanterne [lɑ̃tɛʀn] nf (portable) lantern; (électrique) light, lamp; (de voiture) (side)light

laper [lape] vt to lap up

lapidaire [lapidɛʀ] adj (fig) terse

lapin [lapɛ̃] nm rabbit; (peau) rabbitskin; (fourrure) cony; **poser un ~ à qn** (fam) to stand sb up

Laponie [lapɔni] nf Lapland

laps [laps] nm: **~ de temps** space of time, time no pl

laque [lak] nf (vernis) lacquer; (pour cheveux) hair spray

laquelle [lakɛl] pron voir **lequel**

larcin [laʀsɛ̃] nm theft

lard [laʀ] nm (bacon) (streaky) bacon; (graisse) fat

lardon [laʀdɔ̃] nm: **~s** chopped bacon

large [laʀʒ] adj wide, broad; (fig) generous ♦ adv: **calculer/voir ~** to allow extra/think big ♦ nm (largeur): **5 m de ~** 5 m wide ou in width; (mer): **le ~** the open sea; **au ~ de** off; **~ d'esprit** broad-minded; **largement** adv widely; (de loin) greatly; (au moins) easily; (généreusement) generously; **c'est largement suffisant** that's ample; **largesse** nf generosity; **largesses** nfpl (dons) liberalities; **largeur** nf (qu'on mesure) width; (impression visuelle) wideness, width; (d'esprit) broadness

larguer [laʀge] vt to drop; **~ les amarres** to cast off (the moorings)

larme [laʀm] nf tear; (fam: goutte) drop; **en ~s** in tears; **larmoyer** vi (yeux) to water; (*se plaindre*) to whimper

larvé, e [laʀve] *adj (fig)* latent

laryngite [laʀɛʒit] *nf* laryngitis

las, lasse [lɑ, lɑs] *adj* weary

laser [lazeʀ] *nm*: **(rayon)** ~ laser (beam); **chaîne** ~ compact disc (player); **disque** ~ compact disc

lasse [lɑs] *adj voir* **las**

lasser [lɑse] *vt* to weary, tire; **se** ~ **de** *vt* to grow weary *ou* tired of

latéral, e, -aux [lateʀal, o] *adj* side *cpd*, lateral

latin, e [latɛ̃, in] *adj* Latin ♦ *nm/f*: **L~, e** Latin ♦ *nm* (*LING*) Latin

latitude [latityd] *nf* latitude

latte [lat] *nf* lath, slat; (*de plancher*) board

lauréat, e [lɔʀea, at] *nm/f* winner

laurier [lɔʀje] *nm* (*BOT*) laurel; (*CULIN*) bay leaves *pl*

lavable [lavabl] *adj* washable

lavabo [lavabo] *nm* washbasin; **~s** *nmpl* (*toilettes*) toilet *sg*

lavage [lavaʒ] *nm* washing *no pl*, wash; ~ **de cerveau** brainwashing *no pl*

lavande [lavɑ̃d] *nf* lavender

lave [lav] *nf* lava *no pl*

lave-linge [lavlɛ̃ʒ] *nm inv* washing machine

laver [lave] *vt* to wash; (*tache*) to wash off; **se** ~ *vi* to have a wash, wash; **se** ~ **les mains/dents** to wash one's hands/clean one's teeth; ~ **qn de** (*accusation*) to clear sb of; **laverie** *nf*: **laverie (automatique)** launderette; **lavette** *nf* dish cloth; (*fam*) drip; **laveur, -euse** *nm/f* cleaner; **lave-vaisselle** *nm inv* dishwasher; **lavoir** *nm* wash house; (*évier*) sink

laxatif, -ive [laksatif, iv] *adj, nm* laxative

layette [lɛjet] *nf* baby clothes

MOT-CLÉ
---

le [lə], **la, l'** (*pl* **les**) *art déf* **1** the; **le livre/la pomme/l'arbre** the book/the apple/the tree; **les étudiants** the students

2 (*noms abstraits*): **le courage/l'amour/la jeunesse** courage/love/youth

3 (*indiquant la possession*): **se casser** *jambe etc* to break one's leg *etc*; **levez main** put your hand up; **avoir les yeu gris/le nez rouge** to have grey eyes/red nose

4 (*temps*): **le matin/soir** in the morning evening; mornings/evenings; **le jeudi** *e* (*d'habitude*) on Thursdays *etc*; (*ce jeudi etc*) on (the) Thursday

5 (*distribution, évaluation*) a, an; **10 F** **mètre/kilo** 10F a *ou* per metre/kilo; **tiers/quart de** a third/quarter of

♦ *pron* **1** (*personne: mâle*) him; (*personn femelle*) her; (: *pluriel*) them; **je le/la/le vois** I can see him/her/them

2 (*animal, chose: singulier*) it; (: *plurie* them; **je le (***ou*** la) vois** I can see it; **je le vois** I can see them

3 (*remplaçant une phrase*): **je ne le sava pas** I didn't know (about it); **il était rich et ne l'est plus** he was once rich but *n* longer is

---

lécher [leʃe] *vt* to lick; (*laper: lait, eau*) lick *ou* lap up; **lèche-vitrines** *nm*: **fai du lèche-vitrines** to go window shopping

leçon [l(ə)sɔ̃] *nf* lesson; **faire la** ~ **à** (*f* to give a lecture to; **~s de conduite** dri ing lessons

lecteur, -trice [lɛktœʀ, tʀis] *nm/f* reade (*d'université*) foreign language assista ♦ *nm* (*TECH*): ~ **de cassettes/CD** ca sette/CD player; ~ **de disquette** disk dri

lecture [lɛktyʀ] *nf* reading

ledit [lədi], **ladite** (*mpl* **lesdits**, *fpl* **le dites**) *dét* the aforesaid

légal, e, -aux [legal, o] *adj* legal; **léga** ser *vt* to legalize; **légalité** *nf* law

légendaire [leʒɑ̃dɛʀ] *adj* legendary

légende [leʒɑ̃d] *nf* (*mythe*) legend; (carte, plan) key; (*de dessin*) caption

léger, -ère [leʒe, ɛʀ] *adj* light; (*bruit, tard*) slight; (*personne: superficiel*) thoug less; (: *volage*) free and easy; **à la légè** (*parler, agir*) rashly, thoughtlessly;

gèrement adv (s'habiller, bouger) lightly; (un peu) slightly; **manger légèrement** to eat a light meal; **légèreté** nf lightness; (d'une remarque) flippancy

Légion d'honneur

Created by Napoleon in 1802 to reward service to the state, **la Légion d'honneur** is a prestigious French order headed by the President of the Republic, the Grand Maître. Members receive an annual tax-free payment.

gislatif, -ive [leʒislatif, iv] adj legislative; **législatives** nfpl general election sg

gitime [leʒitim] adj (JUR) lawful, legitimate; (fig) rightful, legitimate; **en état de ~ défense** in self-defence

gs [leg] nm legacy

guer [lege] vt: **~ qch à qn** (JUR) to bequeath sth to sb

gume [legym] nm vegetable

ndemain [lɑ̃dmɛ̃] nm: **le ~** the next ou following day; **le ~ matin/soir** the next ou following morning/evening; **le ~ de** the day after

nt, e [lɑ̃, lɑ̃t] adj slow; **lentement** adv slowly; **lenteur** nf slowness no pl

ntille [lɑ̃tij] nf (OPTIQUE) lens sg; (CULIN) lentil

opard [leɔpaʀ] nm leopard

pre [lɛpʀ] nf leprosy

MOT-CLÉ

quel, laquelle [lakɛl, lakɛl] (mpl **lesquels**, fpl **lesquelles**) (à + lequel = **auquel**, de + lequel = **duquel** etc) pron 1 (interrogatif) which, which one

2 (relatif: personne: sujet) who; (: objet, après préposition) whom; (: chose) which

♦ adj: **auquel cas** in which case

s [le] dét voir **le**

sbienne [lɛsbjɛn] nf lesbian

sdites [ledit], **lesdits** [ledi] dét pl voir **ledit**

léser [leze] vt to wrong

lésiner [lezine] vi: **ne pas ~ sur les moyens** (pour mariage etc) to push the boat out

lésion [lezjɔ̃] nf lesion, damage no pl

lesquelles, lesquels [lekɛl] pron pl voir **lequel**

lessive [lesiv] nf (poudre) washing powder; (linge) washing no pl, wash; **lessiver** vt to wash; (fam: fatiguer) to tire out, exhaust

lest [lɛst] nm ballast

leste [lɛst] adj sprightly, nimble

lettre [lɛtʀ] nf letter; **~s** nfpl (littérature) literature sg; (SCOL) arts (subjects); **à la ~** literally; **en toutes ~s** in full

leucémie [løsemi] nf leukaemia

MOT-CLÉ

leur [lœʀ] adj possessif their; **leur maison** their house; **leurs amis** their friends

♦ pron 1 (objet indirect) (to) them; **je leur ai dit la vérité** I told them the truth; **je le leur ai donné** I gave it to them, I gave them it

2 (possessif): **le(la) leur, les leurs** theirs

leurre [lœʀ] nm (fig: illusion) delusion; (: duperie) deception; **leurrer** vt to delude, deceive

leurs [lœʀ] adj voir **leur**

levain [ləvɛ̃] nm leaven

levé, e [ləve] adj: **être ~** to be up; **levée** nf (POSTES) collection

lever [l(ə)ve] vt (vitre, bras etc) to raise; (soulever de terre, supprimer: interdiction, siège) to lift; (impôts, armée) to levy ♦ vi to rise ♦ nm: **au ~** on getting up; **se ~** vi to get up; (soleil) to rise; (jour) to break; (brouillard) to lift; **~ de soleil** sunrise; **~ du jour** daybreak

levier [ləvje] nm lever

lèvre [lɛvʀ] nf lip

lévrier [levʀije] nm greyhound

levure [l(ə)vyʀ] nf yeast; **~ chimique** baking powder

lexique [lɛksik] *nm* vocabulary; (*glossaire*) lexicon

lézard [lezaʀ] *nm* lizard

lézarde [lezaʀd] *nf* crack

liaison [ljezɔ̃] *nf* (*rapport*) connection; (*transport*) link; (*amoureuse*) affair; (*PHONÉTIQUE*) liaison; **entrer/être en ~ avec** to get/be in contact with

liane [ljan] *nf* creeper

liant, e [ljɑ̃, ljɑ̃t] *adj* sociable

liasse [ljas] *nf* wad, bundle

Liban [libɑ̃] *nm*: **le ~** (the) Lebanon; **libanais, e** *adj* Lebanese ♦ *nm/f*: **Libanais, e** Lebanese

libeller [libele] *vt* (*chèque, mandat*): **~ (au nom de)** to make out (to); (*lettre*) to word

libellule [libelyl] *nf* dragonfly

libéral, e, -aux [liberal, o] *adj, nm/f* liberal; **profession ~e** (liberal) profession

libérer [libere] *vt* (*délivrer*) to free, liberate; (*relâcher: prisonnier*) to discharge, release; (: *d'inhibitions*) to liberate; (*gaz*) to release; **se ~** (*de rendez-vous*) to get out of previous engagements

liberté [libɛʀte] *nf* freedom; (*loisir*) free time; **~s** *nfpl* (*privautés*) liberties; **mettre/être en ~** to set/be free; **en ~ provisoire/surveillée/conditionnelle** on bail/probation/parole

libraire [libʀɛʀ] *nm/f* bookseller

librairie [libʀeʀi] *nf* bookshop

libre [libʀ] *adj* free; (*route, voie*) clear; (*place, salle*) free; (*ligne*) not engaged; (*SCOL*) non-state; **~ de qch/de faire** free from sth/to do; **~ arbitre** free will; **libre-échange** *nm* free trade; **libre-service** *nm* self-service store

Libye [libi] *nf*: **la ~** Libya

licence [lisɑ̃s] *nf* (*permis*) permit; (*diplôme*) degree; (*liberté*) liberty; **licencié, e** *nm/f* (*SCOL*): **licencié ès lettres/en droit** ≈ Bachelor of Arts/Law

licenciement [lisɑ̃simɑ̃] *nm* redundancy

licencier [lisɑ̃sje] *vt* (*débaucher*) to make redundant, lay off; (*renvoyer*) to dismiss

licite [lisit] *adj* lawful

lie [li] *nf* dregs *pl*, sediment

lié, e [lje] *adj*: **très ~ avec** very friendl[y] with *ou* close to

liège [ljɛʒ] *nm* cork

lien [ljɛ̃] *nm* (*corde, fig: affectif*) bond; (*ra[p]port*) link, connection; **~ de parent[é]** family tie

lier [lje] *vt* (*attacher*) to tie up; (*joindre*) [to] link up; (*fig: unir, engager*) to bind; **se ~ avec** to make friends with; **~ qch à** [to] tie *ou* link sth to; **~ conversation avec** [to] strike up a conversation with

lierre [ljɛʀ] *nm* ivy

liesse [ljɛs] *nf*: **être en ~** to be celebrat[ing *ou* jubilant

lieu, x [ljø] *nm* place; **~x** *nmpl* (*locaux*) premises; (*endroit: d'un accident etc*) scen[e] *sg*; **en ~ sûr** in a safe place; **en premier [~]** in the first place; **en dernier ~** last[ly]; **avoir ~** to take place; **tenir ~ de** to ser[ve] as; **donner ~ à** to give rise to; **au ~ [de]** instead of; **lieu-dit** (*pl* **lieux-dits**) *nm* l[o-] cality

lieutenant [ljøt(ə)nɑ̃] *nm* lieutenant

lièvre [ljɛvʀ] *nm* hare

ligament [ligamɑ̃] *nm* ligament

ligne [liɲ] *nf* (*gén*) line; (*TRANSPORTS: li[ai-]son*) service; (: *trajet*) route; (*silhouett[e]*) figure; **entrer en ~ de compte** to co[me] into it

lignée [liɲe] *nf* line, lineage

ligoter [ligɔte] *vt* to tie up

ligue [lig] *nf* league; **liguer** *vt*: **se ligu[er]** **contre** (*fig*) to combine against

lilas [lila] *nm* lilac

limace [limas] *nf* slug

limande [limɑ̃d] *nf* dab

lime [lim] *nf* file; **~ à ongles** nail file; **[li-]mer** *vt* to file

limier [limje] *nm* bloodhound; (*détectiv[e]*) sleuth

limitation [limitasjɔ̃] *nf*: **~ de vitess[e]** speed limit

limite [limit] *nf* (*de terrain*) boundary; (*p[ar-]tie ou point extrême*) limit; **vitesse/charg[e**

RANÇAIS-ANGLAIS 159

limoger → logement

~ maximum speed/load; **cas** ~ border-
line case; **date** ~ deadline; **limiter** vt
(restreindre) to limit, restrict; (délimiter) to
border; **limitrophe** adj border cpd
limoger [limɔʒe] vt to dismiss
limon [limɔ̃] nm silt
limonade [limɔnad] nf lemonade
lin [lɛ̃] nm (tissu) linen
linceul [lɛ̃sœl] nm shroud
linge [lɛ̃ʒ] nm (serviettes etc) linen; (lessive)
washing; (aussi: ~ **de corps**) underwear;
lingerie nf lingerie, underwear
lingot [lɛ̃go] nm ingot
linguistique [lɛ̃ɡɥistik] adj linguistic ♦ nf
linguistics sg
lion, ne [ljɔ̃, ljɔn] nm/f lion (lioness);
(signe): **le L~** Leo; **lionceau, x** nm lion
cub
liqueur [likœʀ] nf liqueur
liquidation [likidasjɔ̃] nf (vente) sale
liquide [likid] adj liquid ♦ nm liquid;
(COMM): **en** ~ in ready money ou cash;
liquider vt to liquidate; (COMM: articles)
to clear, sell off; **liquidités** nfpl (COMM)
liquid assets
lire [liʀ] nf (monnaie) lira ♦ vt, vi to read
lis [lis] nm = **lys**
lisible [lizibl] adj legible
lisière [lizjɛʀ] nf (de forêt) edge
lisons [lizɔ̃] vb voir **lire**
lisse [lis] adj smooth
liste [list] nf list; **faire la** ~ **de** to list; ~
électorale electoral roll; **listing** nm (IN-
FORM) printout
lit [li] nm bed; **petit** ~, **lit à une place** single bed; **grand** ~, **lit à deux places** double bed; **faire son** ~ to make one's bed;
aller/se mettre au ~ to go to/get into
bed; ~ **de camp** campbed; ~ **d'enfant**
cot (BRIT), crib (US)
literie [litʀi] nf bedding, bedclothes pl
litière [litjɛʀ] nf litter
litige [litiʒ] nm dispute
litre [litʀ] nm litre
littéraire [literɛʀ] adj literary ♦ nm/f arts
student; **elle est très** ~ (she's very literary)

littéral, e, -aux [literal, o] adj literal
littérature [literatyʀ] nf literature
littoral, -aux [litɔral, o] nm coast
liturgie [lityrʒi] nf liturgy
livide [livid] adj livid, pallid
livraison [livrɛzɔ̃] nf delivery
livre [livʀ] nm book ♦ nf (poids, monnaie)
pound; ~ **de bord** logbook; ~ **de poche**
paperback
livré, e [livʀe] adj: ~ **à soi-même** left to
o.s. ou one's own devices; **livrée** nf livery
livrer [livʀe] vt (COMM) to deliver; (otage,
coupable) to hand over; (secret, information)
to give away; **se** ~ **à** (se confier) to confide in; (se rendre, s'abandonner) to give
o.s. up to; (faire: pratiques, actes) to indulge in; (enquête) to carry out
livret [livʀɛ] nm booklet; (d'opéra) libretto;
~ **de caisse d'épargne** (savings) bank-
book; ~ **de famille** (official) family record
book; ~ **scolaire** (school) report book
livreur, -euse [livʀœʀ, øz] nm/f delivery
boy ou man/girl ou woman
local, e, -aux [lɔkal, o] adj local ♦ nm (salle) premises pl; voir aussi **locaux**; **localiser** vt (repérer) to locate, place; (limiter) to
confine; **localité** nf locality
locataire [lɔkatɛʀ] nm/f tenant; (de
chambre) lodger
location [lɔkasjɔ̃] nf (par le locataire, le
loueur) renting; (par le propriétaire) renting
out, letting; (THÉÂTRE) booking office; **"~
de voitures"** "car rental"; **habiter en** ~
to live in rented accommodation; **prendre une** ~ **(pour les vacances)** to rent a
house etc (for the holidays)
locaux [lɔko] nmpl premises
locomotive [lɔkɔmɔtiv] nf locomotive, engine
locution [lɔkysjɔ̃] nf phrase
loge [lɔʒ] nf (THÉÂTRE: d'artiste) dressing
room; (: de spectateurs) box; (de concierge,
franc-maçon) lodge
logement [lɔʒmɑ̃] nm accommodation no
pl (BRIT), accommodations pl (US); (appartement) flat (BRIT), apartment (US); (héber-

gement) housing *no pl*

loger [lɔʒe] *vt* to accommodate ♦ *vi* to live; **se ~ dans** (*suj: balle, flèche*) to lodge itself in; **trouver à se ~** to find accommodation; **logeur, -euse** *nm/f* landlord(-lady)

logiciel [lɔʒisjɛl] *nm* software

logique [lɔʒik] *adj* logical ♦ *nf* logic

logis [lɔʒi] *nm* abode, dwelling

logo [lɔgo] *nm* logo

loi [lwa] *nf* law; **faire la ~** to lay down the law

loin [lwɛ̃] *adv* far; (*dans le temps: futur*) a long way off; (: *passé*) a long time ago; **plus ~** further; **~ de** far from; **au ~** far off; **de ~** from a distance; (*fig: de beaucoup*) by far

lointain, e [lwɛ̃tɛ̃, ɛn] *adj* faraway, distant; (*dans le futur, passé*) distant; (*cause, parent*) remote, distant ♦ *nm*: **dans le ~** in the distance

loir [lwaʀ] *nm* dormouse

loisir [lwaziʀ] *nm*: **heures de ~** spare time; **~s** *nmpl* (*temps libre*) leisure *sg*; (*activités*) leisure activities; **avoir le ~ de faire** to have the time *ou* opportunity to do; **à ~** at leisure

londonien, ne [lɔ̃dɔnjɛ̃, jɛn] *adj* London *cpd*, of London ♦ *nm/f*: **L~, ne** Londoner

Londres [lɔ̃dʀ] *n* London

long, longue [lɔ̃, lɔ̃g] *adj* long ♦ *adv*: **en savoir ~** to know a great deal ♦ *nm*: **de 3 m de ~** 3 m long, 3 m in length; **ne pas faire ~ feu** not to last long; **(tout) le ~ de** (all) along; **tout au ~ de** (*année, vie*) throughout; **de ~ en large** (*marcher*) to and fro, up and down; *voir aussi* **longue**

longer [lɔ̃ʒe] *vt* to go (*ou* walk *ou* drive) along(side); (*suj: mur, route*) to border

longiligne [lɔ̃ʒiliɲ] *adj* long-limbed

longitude [lɔ̃ʒityd] *nf* longitude

longtemps [lɔ̃tɑ̃] *adv* (for) a long time, (for) long; **avant ~** before long; **pour ou pendant ~** for a long time; **mettre ~ à faire** to take a long time to do

longue [lɔ̃g] *adj voir* **long** ♦ *nf*: **à la ~** in

the end; **longuement** *adv* (*longtemps*) fo[r] a long time; (*en détail*) at length

longueur [lɔ̃gœʀ] *nf* length; **~s** *nfpl* (*fig: d'un film etc*) tedious parts; **en ~** length[-] wise; **tirer en ~** to drag on; **à ~ de jour[-] née** all day long; **~ d'onde** wavelength

longue-vue [lɔ̃gvy] *nf* telescope

look [luk] (*fam*) *nm* look, image

lopin [lɔpɛ̃] *nm*: **~ de terre** patch of land

loque [lɔk] *nf* (*personne*) wreck; **~s** *nfp[l]* (*habits*) rags

loquet [lɔkɛ] *nm* latch

lorgner [lɔʀɲe] *vt* to eye; (*fig*) to hav[e] one's eye on

lors [lɔʀ]: **~ de** *prép* at the time of; during

lorsque [lɔʀsk] *conj* when, as

losange [lɔzɑ̃ʒ] *nm* diamond

lot [lo] *nm* (*part*) share; (*de ~erie*) prize; (*fig[:] destin*) fate, lot; (*COMM, INFORM*) batch; **l[e] gros ~** the jackpot

loterie [lɔtʀi] *nf* lottery

loti, e [lɔti] *adj*: **bien/mal ~** well-/bad[ly] off

lotion [losjɔ̃] *nf* lotion

lotissement [lɔtismɑ̃] *nm* housing deve[l-] opment; (*parcelle*) plot, lot

loto [lɔto] *nm* lotto

> Loto
>
> Le Loto *is a state-run national lottery with large cash prizes. Participants se-lect 7 numbers out of 49. The more correc[t] numbers, the greater the prize. The draw i[s] televised twice weekly.*

lotte [lɔt] *nf* monkfish

louable [lwabl] *adj* commendable

louanges [lwɑ̃ʒ] *nfpl* praise *sg*

loubard [lubaʀ] (*fam*) *nm* lout

louche [luʃ] *adj* shady, fishy, dubious ♦ *n[f]* ladle; **loucher** *vi* to squint

louer [lwe] *vt* (*maison: suj: propriétaire*) t[o] let, rent (out); (: *locataire*) to rent; (*voitu[re] etc: entreprise*) to hire out (*BRIT*), ren[t] (out); (: *locataire*) to hire, rent; (*réserve[r]*) to book; (*faire l'éloge de*) to praise; **"à ~[**

"to let" (BRIT), "for rent" (US)

loup [lu] nm wolf

loupe [lup] nf magnifying glass

louper [lupe] (fam) vt (manquer) to miss; (examen) to flunk

lourd, e [luʀ, luʀd] adj, adv heavy; ~ **de** (conséquences, menaces) charged with; **il fait ~** the weather is close, it's sultry; **lourdaud, e** (péj) adj clumsy; **lourdement** adv heavily; **lourdeur** nf weight; **lourdeurs d'estomac** indigestion

loutre [lutʀ] nf otter

louveteau, x [luv(ə)to] nm wolf-cub; (scout) cub (scout)

louvoyer [luvwaje] vi (fig) to hedge, evade the issue

loyal, e, -aux [lwajal, o] adj (fidèle) loyal, faithful; (fair-play) fair; **loyauté** nf loyalty, faithfulness; fairness

loyer [lwaje] nm rent

lu, e [ly] pp de **lire**

lubie [lybi] nf whim, craze

lubrifiant [lybʀifjɑ̃, jɑ̃t] nm lubricant

lubrifier [lybʀifje] vt to lubricate

lubrique [lybʀik] adj lecherous

lucarne [lykaʀn] nf skylight

lucide [lysid] adj lucid; (accidenté) conscious

lucratif, -ive [lykʀatif, iv] adj lucrative, profitable; **à but non ~** non profit-making

lueur [lɥœʀ] nf (pâle) (faint) light; (chatoyante) glimmer no pl; (fig) glimmer; gleam

luge [lyʒ] nf sledge (BRIT), sled (US)

lugubre [lygybʀ] adj gloomy, dismal

MOT-CLÉ

lui [lɥi] pron **1** (objet indirect: mâle) (to) him; (: femelle) (to) her; (: chose, animal) (to) it; **je lui ai parlé** I have spoken to him (ou to her); **il lui a offert un cadeau** he gave him (ou her) a present

2 (après préposition, comparatif: personne) him; (: chose, animal) it; **elle est contente de lui** she is pleased with him; **je la**

connais mieux que lui I know her better than he does; I know her better than him

3 (sujet, forme emphatique) he; **lui, il est à Paris** HE is in Paris

4: lui-même himself; itself

---

luire [lɥiʀ] vi to shine; (en rougeoyant) to glow

lumière [lymjɛʀ] nf light; **mettre en ~** (fig) to highlight; ~ **du jour** daylight

luminaire [lyminɛʀ] nm lamp, light

lumineux, -euse [lyminø, øz] adj luminous; (éclairé) illuminated; (ciel, couleur) bright; (rayon) of light, light cpd; (fig: regard) radiant

lunatique [lynatik] adj whimsical, temperamental

lundi [lœ̃di] nm Monday; ~ **de Pâques** Easter Monday

lune [lyn] nf moon; ~ **de miel** honeymoon

lunette [lynɛt] nf: **~s ♦** nfpl glasses, spectacles; (protectrices) goggles; ~ **arrière** (AUTO) rear window; **~s de soleil** sunglasses

lus etc [ly] vb voir **lire**

lustre [lystʀ] nm (de plafond) chandelier; (fig: éclat) lustre; **lustrer** vt to shine

lut [ly] vb voir **lire**

luth [lyt] nm lute

lutin [lytɛ̃] nm imp, goblin

lutte [lyt] nf (conflit) struggle; (sport) wrestling; **lutter** vi to fight, struggle

luxe [lyks] nm luxury; **de ~** luxury cpd

Luxembourg [lyksɑ̃buʀ] nm: **le ~** Luxembourg

luxer [lykse] vt: **se ~ l'épaule** to dislocate one's shoulder

luxueux, -euse [lyksɥø, øz] adj luxurious

luxure [lyksyʀ] nf lust

luxuriant, e [lyksyʀjɑ̃, jɑ̃t] adj luxuriant

lycée [lise] nm secondary school; **lycéen, ne** nm/f secondary school pupil

lyophilisé, e [ljɔfilize] adj (café) freeze-dried

lyrique [liʀik] adj lyrical; (OPÉRA) lyric; **artiste ~** opera singer

lys [lis] *nm* lily

M, m

M *abr* = **Monsieur**

m' [m] *pron voir* **me**

ma [ma] *adj voir* **mon**

macaron [makaʀɔ̃] *nm* (*gâteau*) macaroon; (*insigne*) (round) badge

macaronis [makaʀɔni] *nmpl* macaroni *sg*

macédoine [masedwan] *nf*: ~ **de fruits** fruit salad; ~ **de légumes** mixed vegetables

macérer [maseʀe] *vi, vt* to macerate; (*dans du vinaigre*) to pickle

mâcher [mɑʃe] *vt* to chew; **ne pas** ~ **ses mots** not to mince one's words

machin [maʃɛ̃] (*fam*) *nm* thing(umajig)

machinal, e, -aux [maʃinal, o] *adj* mechanical, automatic; **machinalement** *adv* mechanically, automatically

machination [maʃinasjɔ̃] *nf* frame-up

machine [maʃin] *nf* machine; (*locomotive*) engine; ~ **à écrire** typewriter; ~ **à laver/ coudre** washing/sewing machine; ~ **à sous** fruit machine

macho [matʃo] (*fam*) *nm* male chauvinist

mâchoire [mɑʃwaʀ] *nf* jaw

mâchonner [mɑʃɔne] *vt* to chew (at)

maçon [masɔ̃] *nm* builder; (*poseur de briques*) bricklayer; **maçonnerie** *nf* (*murs*) brickwork; (*pierres*) masonry, stonework

maculer [makyle] *vt* to stain

Madame [madam] (*pl* **Mesdames**) *nf*: ~ **X** Mrs X; **occupez-vous de** ~/ **Monsieur/Mademoiselle** please serve this lady/gentleman/(young) lady; **bonjour** ~/**Monsieur/Mademoiselle** good morning; (*ton déférent*) good morning Madam/Sir/Madam; (*le nom est connu*) good morning Mrs/Mr/Miss X; ~/ **Monsieur/Mademoiselle!** (*pour appeler*) Madam/Sir/Miss!; ~/**Monsieur/Mademoiselle** (*sur lettre*) Dear Madam/Sir/ Madam; **chère** ~/**cher Monsieur/chère**

Mademoiselle Dear Mrs/Mr/Miss X; **Mesdames** Ladies

madeleine [madlɛn] *nf* madeleine; *small sponge cake*

Mademoiselle [madmwazɛl] (*pl* **Mesdemoiselles**) *nf* Miss; *voir aussi* **Madame**

madère [madɛʀ] *nm* Madeira (wine)

magasin [magazɛ̃] *nm* (*boutique*) shop; (*entrepôt*) warehouse; **en** ~ (*COMM*) in stock

magazine [magazin] *nm* magazine

Maghreb [magʀɛb] *nm*: **le** ~ North Africa; **maghrébin, e** *adj* North African ♦ *nm/f*: **Maghrébin, e** North African

magicien, ne [maʒisjɛ̃, jɛn] *nm/f* magician

magie [maʒi] *nf* magic; **magique** *adj* magic; (*enchanteur*) magical

magistral, e, -aux [maʒistʀal, o] *adj* (*œuvre, adresse*) masterly; (*ton*) authoritative; **cours** ~ lecture

magistrat [maʒistʀa] *nm* magistrate

magnat [magna] *nm* tycoon

magnétique [maɲetik] *adj* magnetic

magnétiser [maɲetize] *vt* to magnetize; (*fig*) to mesmerize, hypnotize

magnétophone [maɲetɔfɔn] *nm* tape recorder; ~ **à cassettes** cassette recorder

magnétoscope [maɲetɔskɔp] *nm* videotape recorder

magnifique [maɲifik] *adj* magnificent

magot [mago] (*fam*) *nm* (*argent*) pile (of money); (*économies*) nest egg

magouille [maguj] (*fam*) *nf* scheming; **magouiller** (*fam*) *vi* to scheme

magret [magʀɛ] *nm*: ~ **de canard** duck steaklet

mai [mɛ] *nm* May

---

mai

i **Le premier mai** *is a public holiday in France marking union demonstrations in the United States in 1886 to secure the eight-hour working day. It is traditional to exchange and wear sprigs of lily of the valley.* **Le 8 mai** *is a public holiday in*

France commemorating the surrender of the German army to Eisenhower on May 7, 1945. There are parades of ex-servicemen in most towns. The social up-heavals of May and June 1968, marked by student demonstrations, strikes and rioting, are generally referred to as "les événements de mai 68". *De Gaulle's government survived, but reforms in education and a move towards decentralization ensued.*

maigre [mɛgʀ] *adj* (very) thin, skinny; (*viande*) lean; (*fromage*) low-fat; (*végétation*) thin, sparse; (*fig*) poor, meagre, skimpy; **jours ~s** days of abstinence, fish days; **maigreur** *nf* thinness; **maigrir** *vi* to get thinner, lose weight; **maigrir de 2 kilos** to lose 2 kilos

maille [maj] *nf* stitch; **avoir ~ à partir avec qn** to have a brush with sb; **~ à l'endroit/à l'envers** plain/purl stitch

maillet [majɛ] *nm* mallet

maillon [majɔ̃] *nm* link

maillot [majo] *nm* (*aussi:* **~ de corps**) vest; (*de sportif*) jersey; **~ de bain** swimsuit; (*d'homme*) bathing trunks *pl*

main [mɛ̃] *nf* hand; **à la ~** in one's hand; **se donner la ~** to hold hands; **donner** *ou* **tendre la ~ à qn** to hold out one's hand to sb; **serrer la ~ à qn** to shake hands with sb; **sous la ~** to *ou* at hand; **à remettre en ~s propres** to be delivered personally; **mettre la dernière ~ à** to put the finishing touches to; **se faire/perdre la ~** to get one's hand in/lose one's touch; **avoir qch bien en ~** to have (got) the hang of sth; **main-d'œuvre** *nf* manpower, labour; **main-forte**: **prêter main-forte à qn** to come to sb's assistance; **mainmise** *nf* (*fig*): **mainmise sur** complete hold on

maint, e [mɛ̃, mɛ̃t] *adj* many a; **~s** many; **à ~es reprises** time and (time) again

maintenant [mɛ̃t(ə)nɑ̃] *adv* now; (*actuellement*) nowadays

maintenir [mɛ̃t(ə)niʀ] *vt* (*retenir, soutenir*) to support; (*contenir: foule etc*) to hold back; (*conserver, affirmer*) to maintain; **se ~** *vi* (*prix*) to keep steady; (*amélioration*) to persist

maintien [mɛ̃tjɛ̃] *nm* (*sauvegarde*) maintenance; (*attitude*) bearing

maire [mɛʀ] *nm* mayor; **mairie** *nf* (*bâtiment*) town hall; (*administration*) town council

mais [mɛ] *conj* but; **~ non!** of course not!; **~ enfin** but after all; (*indignation*) look here!

maïs [mais] *nm* maize (*BRIT*), corn (*US*)

maison [mɛzɔ̃] *nf* house; (*chez-soi*) home; (*COMM*) firm ♦ *adj inv* (*CULIN*) home-made; (*fig*) in-house, own; **à la ~** at home; (*direction*) home; **~ close** *ou* **de passe** brothel; **~ de repos** convalescent home; **~ de santé** mental home; **~ des jeunes** ≃ youth club; **~ mère** parent company; **maisonnée** *nf* household, family; **maisonnette** *nf* small house, cottage

┌─────────────────────────────────────┐
│ **maisons des jeunes et de la culture** │
└─────────────────────────────────────┘

ⓘ **Maisons des jeunes et de la culture** *are centres for young people which organize a wide range of sporting and cultural activities, and are also engaged in welfare work. The centres are, in part, publicly financed.*

maître, -esse [mɛtʀ, mɛtʀɛs] *nm/f* master (mistress); (*SCOL*) teacher, schoolmaster(-mistress) ♦ *nm* (*peintre etc*) master; (*titre*): **M~** Maître, *term of address gen for a barrister* ♦ *adj* (*principal, essentiel*) main; **être ~ de** (*soi, situation*) to be in control of; **une maîtresse femme** a managing woman; **~ chanteur** blackmailer; **~ d'école** schoolmaster; **~ d'hôtel** (*domestique*) butler; (*d'hôtel*) head waiter; **~ nageur** lifeguard; **maîtresse** *nf* (*amante*) mistress; **maîtresse (d'école)** teacher, (school)mistress; **maîtresse de maison**

hostess; (*ménagère*) housewife

maîtrise [metriz] *nf* (*aussi*: ~ **de soi**) self-control, self-possession; (*habileté*) skill, mastery; (*suprématie*) mastery, command; (*diplôme*) ≃ master's degree; **maîtriser** *vt* (*cheval, incendie*) to (bring under) control; (*sujet*) to master; (*émotion*) to control, master; **se maîtriser** to control o.s.

maïzena ® [maizena] *nf* cornflour

majestueux, -euse [maʒɛstɥø, øz] *adj* majestic

majeur, e [maʒœr] *adj* (*important*) major; (*JUR*) of age ♦ *nm* (*doigt*) middle finger; **en ~e partie** for the most part; **la ~e partie de** most of

majoration [maʒɔʀasjɔ̃] *nf* rise, increase

majorer [maʒɔʀe] *vt* to increase

majoritaire [maʒɔʀitɛʀ] *adj* majority *cpd*

majorité [maʒɔʀite] *nf* (*gén*) majority; (*parti*) party in power; **en ~** mainly

majuscule [maʒyskyl] *adj, nf*: **(lettre) ~** capital (letter)

mal [mal, mo] (*pl* **maux**) *nm* (*opposé au bien*) evil; (*tort, dommage*) harm; (*douleur physique*) pain, ache; (*~adie*) illness, sickness *no pl* ♦ *adv* badly ♦ *adj* bad, wrong; **être ~ à l'aise** to be uncomfortable; **être ~ avec qn** to be on bad terms with sb; **il a ~ compris** he misunderstood; **dire/ penser du ~ de** to speak/think ill of; **ne voir aucun ~ à** to see no harm in, see nothing wrong in; **faire ~ à qn** to hurt sb; **se faire ~** to hurt o.s.; **se donner du ~ pour faire qch** to go to a lot of trouble to do sth; **ça fait ~** it hurts; **j'ai ~ au dos** my back hurts; **avoir ~ à la tête/à la gorge/aux dents** to have a headache/a sore throat/toothache; **avoir le ~ du pays** to be homesick; *voir aussi* **cœur**; **maux**; **~ de mer** seasickness; **~ en point** in a bad state

malade [malad] *adj* ill, sick; (*poitrine, jambe*) bad; (*plante*) diseased ♦ *nm/f* invalid, sick person; (*à l'hôpital etc*) patient; **tomber ~** to fall ill; **être ~ du cœur** to have heart trouble *ou* a bad heart; **~**

mental mentally sick *ou* ill person; **maladie** *nf* (*spécifique*) disease, illness; (*mauvaise santé*) illness, sickness; **maladif, -ive** *adj* sickly; (*curiosité, besoin*) pathological

maladresse [maladrɛs] *nf* clumsiness *no pl*; (*gaffe*) blunder

maladroit, e [maladrwa, wat] *adj* clumsy

malaise [malɛz] *nm* (*MÉD*) feeling of faintness; (*fig*) uneasiness, malaise; **avoir un ~** to feel faint

malaisé, e [maleze] *adj* difficult

malaria [malarja] *nf* malaria

malaxer [malakse] *vt* (*pétrir*) to knead; (*mélanger*) to mix

malchance [malʃɑ̃s] *nf* misfortune, ill luck *no pl*; **par ~** unfortunately; **malchanceux, -euse** *adj* unlucky

mâle [mal] *adj* (*aussi ÉLEC, TECH*) male; (*viril: voix, traits*) manly ♦ *nm* male

malédiction [malediksjɔ̃] *nf* curse

mal...: **malencontreux, -euse** *adj* unfortunate, untoward; **mal-en-point** *adj inv* in a sorry state; **malentendant, e** *nm/f*: **les malentendants** the hard of hearing; **malentendu** *nm* misunderstanding; **malfaçon** *nf* fault; **malfaisant, e** *adj* evil, harmful; **malfaiteur** *nm* lawbreaker, criminal; (*voleur*) burglar, thief; **malfamé, e** *adj* disreputable

malgache [malgaʃ] *adj* Madagascan, Malagasy ♦ *nm/f*: **M~** Madagascan, Malagasy ♦ *nm* (*LING*) Malagasy

malgré [malgre] *prép* in spite of, despite; **~ tout** all the same

malhabile [malabil] *adj* clumsy, awkward

malheur [malœr] *nm* (*situation*) adversity, misfortune; (*événement*) misfortune; (: *très grave*) disaster, tragedy; **faire un ~** to be a smash hit; **malheureusement** *adv* unfortunately; **malheureux, -euse** *adj* (*triste*) unhappy, miserable; (*infortuné, regrettable*) unfortunate; (*malchanceux*) unlucky; (*insignifiant*) wretched ♦ *nm/f* poor soul; **les malheureux** the destitute

malhonnête [malɔnɛt] *adj* dishonest; **malhonnêteté** *nf* dishonesty

malice [malis] *nf* mischievousness; *(méchanceté)*: **par ~** out of malice *ou* spite; **sans ~** guileless; **malicieux, -euse** *adj* mischievous

malin, -igne [malɛ̃, maliɲ] *adj (futé: f gén: maline)* smart, shrewd; *(MÉD)* malignant

malingre [malɛ̃gʀ] *adj* puny

malle [mal] *nf* trunk; **mallette** *nf* (small) suitcase; *(porte-documents)* attaché case

malmener [malməne] *vt* to manhandle; *(fig)* to give a rough handling to

malodorant, e [malɔdɔʀɑ̃, ɑ̃t] *adj* foul- *ou* ill-smelling

malotru [malɔtʀy] *nm* lout, boor

malpoli, e [malpɔli] *adj* impolite

malpropre [malpʀɔpʀ] *adj* dirty

malsain, e [malsɛ̃, ɛn] *adj* unhealthy

malt [malt] *nm* malt

Malte [malt] *nf* Malta

maltraiter [maltʀete] *vt* to manhandle, ill-treat

malveillance [malvejɑ̃s] *nf (animosité)* ill will; *(intention de nuire)* malevolence

malversation [malvɛʀsasjɔ̃] *nf* embezzlement

maman [mamɑ̃] *nf* mum(my), mother

mamelle [mamɛl] *nf* teat

mamelon [mam(ə)lɔ̃] *nm (ANAT)* nipple

mamie [mami] *(fam) nf* granny

mammifère [mamifɛʀ] *nm* mammal

mammouth [mamut] *nm* mammoth

manche [mɑ̃ʃ] *nf (de vêtement)* sleeve; *(d'un jeu, tournoi)* round; *(GÉO)*: **la M~** the Channel ♦ *nm (d'outil, casserole)* handle; *(de pelle, pioche etc)* shaft; **à ~s courtes/longues** short-/long-sleeved

manchette [mɑ̃ʃɛt] *nf (de chemise)* cuff; *(coup)* forearm blow; *(titre)* headline

manchot [mɑ̃ʃo, ɔt] *nm* one-armed man; armless man; *(ZOOL)* penguin

mandarine [mɑ̃daʀin] *nf* mandarin (orange), tangerine

mandat [mɑ̃da] *nm (postal)* postal *ou* money order; *(d'un député etc)* mandate; *(procuration)* power of attorney, proxy; *(POLICE)* warrant; **~ d'arrêt** warrant for ar-

rest; **mandataire** *nm/f (représentant)* representative; *(JUR)* proxy

manège [manɛʒ] *nm* riding school; *(à la foire)* roundabout, merry-go-round; *(fig)* game, ploy

manette [manɛt] *nf* lever, tap; **~ de jeu** joystick

mangeable [mɑ̃ʒabl] *adj* edible, eatable

mangeoire [mɑ̃ʒwaʀ] *nf* trough, manger

manger [mɑ̃ʒe] *vt* to eat; *(ronger: suj: rouille etc)* to eat into *ou* away ♦ *vi* to eat; **donner à ~ à** *(enfant)* to feed; **mangeur, -euse** *nm/f* eater; **gros mangeur** big eater

mangue [mɑ̃g] *nf* mango

maniable [manjabl] *adj (outil)* handy; *(voiture, voilier)* easy to handle

maniaque [manjak] *adj* finicky, fussy ♦ *nm/f (méticuleux)* fusspot; *(fou)* maniac

manie [mani] *nf (tic)* odd habit; *(obsession)* mania; **avoir la ~ de** to be obsessive about

manier [manje] *vt* to handle

manière [manjɛʀ] *nf (façon)* way, manner; **~s** *nfpl (attitude)* manners; *(chichis)* fuss *sg*; **de ~ à** so as to; **de cette ~** in this way *ou* manner; **d'une certaine ~** in a way; **de toute ~** in any case

maniéré, e [manjeʀe] *adj* affected

manif [manif] *(fam) nf* demo

manifestant, e [manifɛstɑ̃, ɑ̃t] *nm/f* demonstrator

manifestation [manifɛstasjɔ̃] *nf (de joie, mécontentement)* expression, demonstration; *(symptôme)* outward sign; *(culturelle etc)* event; *(POL)* demonstration

manifeste [manifɛst] *adj* obvious, evident ♦ *nm* manifesto; **manifester** *vt (volonté, intentions)* to show, indicate; *(joie, peur)* to express, show ♦ *vi* to demonstrate; **se manifester** *vi (émotion)* to show *ou* express itself; *(difficultés)* to arise; *(symptômes)* to appear

manigance [manigɑ̃s] *nf* scheme; **manigancer** *vt* to plot

manipulation [manipylasjɔ̃] *nf* handling;

(*POL, génétique*) manipulation
manipuler [manipyle] *vt* to handle; (*fig*) to manipulate
manivelle [manivɛl] *nf* crank
mannequin [mankɛ̃] *nm* (*COUTURE*) dummy; (*MODE*) model
manœuvre [manœvʀ] *nf* (*gén*) manoeuvre (*BRIT*), maneuver (*US*) ♦ *nm* labourer; **manœuvrer** *vt* to manoeuvre (*BRIT*), maneuver (*US*); (*levier, machine*) to operate ♦ *vi* to manoeuvre
manoir [manwaʀ] *nm* manor *ou* country house
manque [mɑ̃k] *nm* (*insuffisance*): **~ de** lack of; (*vide*) emptiness, gap; (*MÉD*) withdrawal; **être en état de ~** to suffer withdrawal symptoms
manqué, e [mɑ̃ke] *adj* failed; **garçon ~** tomboy
manquer [mɑ̃ke] *vi* (*faire défaut*) to be lacking; (*être absent*) to be missing; (*échouer*) to fail ♦ *vt* to miss ♦ *vb impers*: **il (nous) manque encore 100 F** we are still 100 F short; **il manque des pages (au livre)** there are some pages missing (from the book); **il/cela me manque** I miss him/this; **~ à** (*règles etc*) to be in breach of, fail to observe; **~ de** to lack; **je ne ~ai pas de le lui dire** I'll be sure to tell him; **il a manqué (de) se tuer** he very nearly got killed
mansarde [mɑ̃saʀd] *nf* attic; **mansardé, e** *adj*: **chambre mansardée** attic room
manteau, x [mɑ̃to] *nm* coat
manucure [manykyʀ] *nf* manicurist
manuel, le [manɥɛl] *adj* manual ♦ *nm* (*ouvrage*) manual, handbook
manufacture [manyfaktyʀ] *nf* factory; **manufacturé, e** *adj* manufactured
manuscrit, e [manyskʀi, it] *adj* handwritten ♦ *nm* manuscript
manutention [manytɑ̃sjɔ̃] *nf* (*COMM*) handling
mappemonde [mapmɔ̃d] *nf* (*plane*) map of the world; (*sphère*) globe
maquereau, x [makʀo] *nm* (*ZOOL*)

mackerel *inv*; (*fam*) pimp
maquette [makɛt] *nf* (*à échelle réduite*) (scale) model; (*d'une page illustrée*) paste-up
maquillage [makijaʒ] *nm* making up; (*crème etc*) make-up
maquiller [makije] *vt* (*personne, visage*) to make up; (*truquer: passeport, statistique*) to fake; (: *voiture volée*) to do over (*respray etc*); **se ~** *vi* to make up (one's face)
maquis [maki] *nm* (*GÉO*) scrub; (*MIL*) maquis, underground fighting *no pl*
maraîcher, -ère [maʀeʃe, ɛʀ] *adj*: **cultures maraîchères** market gardening *sg* ♦ *nm/f* market gardener
marais [maʀɛ] *nm* marsh, swamp
marasme [maʀasm] *nm* stagnation, slump
marathon [maʀatɔ̃] *nm* marathon
maraudeur [maʀodœʀ, øz] *nm* prowler
marbre [maʀbʀ] *nm* marble
marc [maʀ] *nm* (*de raisin, pommes*) marc; **~ de café** coffee grounds *pl ou* dregs *pl*
marchand, e [maʀʃɑ̃, ɑ̃d] *nm/f* shopkeeper, tradesman(-woman); (*au marché*) stallholder; (*de vins, charbon*) merchant ♦ *adj*: **prix/valeur ~(e)** market price/value; **~(e) de fruits** fruiterer (*BRIT*), fruit seller (*US*); **~(e) de journaux** newsagent; **~(e) de légumes** greengrocer (*BRIT*), produce dealer (*US*); **~(e) de poissons** fishmonger; **marchander** *vi* to bargain, haggle; **marchandise** *nf* goods *pl*, merchandise *no pl*
marche [maʀʃ] *nf* (*d'escalier*) step; (*activité*) walking; (*promenade, trajet, allure*) walk; (*démarche*) walk, gait; (*MIL etc*) march; (*fonctionnement*) running; (*des événements*) course; **dans le sens de la ~** (*RAIL*) facing the engine; **en ~** (*monter etc*) while the vehicle is moving *ou* in motion; **mettre en ~** to start; **se mettre en ~** (*personne*) to get moving; (*machine*) to start; **être en état de ~** to be in working order; **~ à suivre** (correct) procedure; **~ arrière** reverse (gear); **faire ~ arrière** to reverse; (*fig*) to backtrack, back-pedal

marché [maʀʃe] *nm* market; (*transaction*) bargain, deal; **faire du ~ noir** to buy and sell on the black market; **~ aux puces** flea market; **M~ commun** Common Market

marchepied [maʀʃəpje] *nm* (RAIL) step

marcher [maʀʃe] *vi* to walk; (MIL) to march; (*aller: voiture, train, affaires*) to go; (*prospérer*) to go well; (*fonctionner*) to work, run; (*fam: consentir*) to go along, agree; (: *croire naïvement*) to be taken in; **faire ~ qn** (*taquiner*) to pull sb's leg; (*tromper*) to lead sb up the garden path; **marcheur, -euse** *nm/f* walker

mardi [maʀdi] *nm* Tuesday; **M~ gras** Shrove Tuesday

mare [maʀ] *nf* pond; (*flaque*) pool

marécage [maʀekaʒ] *nm* marsh, swamp; **marécageux, -euse** *adj* marshy

maréchal, -aux [maʀeʃal, o] *nm* marshal; **maréchal-ferrant** [maʀeʃalferã, maʀeʃo-] (*pl* **maréchaux-ferrants**) *nm* blacksmith, farrier

marée [maʀe] *nf* tide; (*poissons*) fresh (sea) fish; **~ haute/basse** high/low tide; **~ montante/descendante** rising/ebb tide; **~ noire** oil slick

marelle [maʀɛl] *nf* hopscotch

margarine [maʀɡaʀin] *nf* margarine

marge [maʀʒ] *nf* margin; **en ~ de** (*fig*) on the fringe of; **~ bénéficiaire** profit margin

marginal, e, -aux [maʀʒinal, o] *nm/f* (*original*) eccentric; (*déshérité*) dropout

marguerite [maʀɡəʀit] *nf* . marguerite, (oxeye) daisy; (*d'imprimante*) daisy-wheel

mari [maʀi] *nm* husband

mariage [maʀjaʒ] *nm* marriage; (*noce*) wedding; **~ civil/religieux** registry office (BRIT) *ou* civil/church wedding

marié, e [maʀje] *adj* married ♦ *nm* (bride)groom; **les ~s** the bride and groom; **les (jeunes) ~s** the newly-weds; **mariée** *nf* bride

marier [maʀje] *vt* to marry; (*fig*) to blend; **se ~** *vr* to get married; **se ~ (avec)** to marry

marin, e [maʀɛ̃, in] *adj* sea *cpd*, marine ♦ *nm* sailor

marine [maʀin] *adj* voir **marin** ♦ *adj inv* navy (blue) ♦ *nm* (MIL) marine ♦ *nf* navy; **~ de guerre** navy; **~ marchande** merchant navy

mariner [maʀine] *vt*: **faire ~** to marinade

marionnette [maʀjɔnɛt] *nf* puppet

maritalement [maʀitalmã] *adv*: **vivre ~** to live as husband and wife

maritime [maʀitim] *adj* sea *cpd*, maritime

mark [maʀk] *nm* mark

marmelade [maʀməlad] *nf* stewed fruit, compote; **~ d'oranges** marmalade

marmite [maʀmit] *nf* (cooking-)pot

marmonner [maʀmɔne] *vt, vi* to mumble, mutter

marmot [maʀmo] (*fam*) *nm* kid

marmotter [maʀmɔte] *vt* to mumble

Maroc [maʀɔk] *nm*: **le ~** Morocco; **marocain, e** [maʀɔkɛ̃, ɛn] *adj* Moroccan ♦ *nm/f*: **Marocain, e** Moroccan

maroquinerie [maʀɔkinʀi] *nf* (*articles*) fine leather goods *pl*; (*boutique*) shop selling fine leather goods

marquant, e [maʀkã, ãt] *adj* outstanding

marque [maʀk] *nf* mark; (COMM: *de nourriture*) brand; (: *de voiture, produits manufacturés*) make; (*de disques*) label; **de ~** (*produits*) high-class; (*visiteur etc*) distinguished, well-known; **une grande ~ de vin** a well-known brand of wine; **~ de fabrique** trademark; **~ déposée** registered trademark

marquer [maʀke] *vt* to mark; (*inscrire*) to write down; (*bétail*) to brand; (SPORT: *but etc*) to score; (: *joueur*) to mark; (*accentuer: taille etc*) to emphasize; (*manifester: refus, intérêt*) to show ♦ *vi* (*événement*) to stand out, be outstanding; (SPORT) to score

marqueterie [maʀkɛtʀi] *nf* inlaid work, marquetry

marquis [maʀki] *nm* marquis, marquess; **marquise** *nf* marchioness; (*auvent*) glass canopy ·*ou* awning

marraine [maʀɛn] *nf* godmother

marrant, e [maʀɑ̃, ɑ̃t] *(fam) adj* funny
marre [maʀ] *(fam) adv:* **en avoir ~ de** to
be fed up with
marrer [maʀe]: **se ~** *(fam) vi* to have a
(good) laugh
marron [maʀɔ̃] *nm (fruit)* chestnut ♦ *adj
inv* brown; **~s glacés** candied chestnuts;
marronnier *nm* chestnut (tree)
mars [maʀs] *nm* March
Marseille [maʀsɛj] *n* Marseilles

┌─────────────────┐
│ **Marseillaise** │
└─────────────────┘

ⓘ **La Marseillaise** *has been France's national anthem since 1879. The words
of the "Chant de guerre de l'armée du
Rhin", as the song was originally called,
were written to an anonymous tune by the
army captain Rouget de Lisle in 1792.
Adopted as a marching song by the bat-
talion of Marseilles, it was finally popu-
larized as the Marseillaise.*

marsouin [maʀswɛ̃] *nm* porpoise
marteau, x [maʀto] *nm* hammer; **être ~**
(fam) to be nuts; **marteau-piqueur** *nm*
pneumatic drill
marteler [maʀtəle] *vt* to hammer
martien, ne [maʀsjɛ̃, jɛn] *adj* Martian, of
ou from Mars
martyr, e [maʀtiʀ] *nm/f* martyr; **martyre**
nm martyrdom; *(fig: sens affaibli)* agony,
torture; **martyriser** *vt (REL)* to martyr;
(fig) to bully; *(enfant)* to batter, beat
marxiste [maʀksist] *adj, nm/f* Marxist
mascara [maskaʀa] *nm* mascara
masculin, e [maskylɛ̃, in] *adj* masculine;
(sexe, population) male; *(équipe, vêtements)*
men's; *(viril)* manly ♦ *nm* masculine;
masculinité *nf* masculinity
masochiste [mazɔʃist] *adj* masochistic
masque [mask] *nm* mask; **masquer** *vt*
(cacher: paysage, porte) to hide, conceal;
(dissimuler: vérité, projet) to mask, obscure
massacre [masakʀ] *nm* massacre, slaughter; **massacrer** *vt* to massacre, slaughter; *(fam: texte etc)* to murder

massage [masaʒ] *nm* massage
masse [mas] *nf* mass; *(ÉLEC)* earth; *(maillet)*
sledgehammer; *(péj):* **la ~** 'the masses *pl*;
une ~ de *(fam)* masses *ou* loads of; **en ~**
♦ *adv (acheter)* in bulk; *(en foule)* en masse
♦ *adj (exécutions, production)* mass *cpd*
masser [mase] *vt (assembler: gens)* to
gather; *(pétrir)* to massage; **se ~** *vi (foule)*
to gather; **masseur, -euse** *nm/f*
masseur(-euse)
massif, -ive [masif, iv] *adj (porte)* solid,
massive; *(visage)* heavy, large; *(bois, or)*
solid; *(dose)* massive; *(déportations etc)*
mass *cpd* ♦ *nm (montagneux)* massif; *(de
fleurs)* clump, bank
massue [masy] *nf* club, bludgeon
mastic [mastik] *nm (pour vitres)* putty;
(pour fentes) filler
mastiquer [mastike] *vt (aliment)* to chew,
masticate
mat, e [mat] *adj (couleur, métal)* mat(t);
(bruit, son) dull ♦ *adj inv (ÉCHECS):* **être ~**
to be checkmate
mât [mɑ] *nm (NAVIG)* mast; *(poteau)* pole,
post
match [matʃ] *nm* match; **faire ~ nul** to
draw; **~ aller** first leg; **~ retour** second
leg, return match
matelas [mat(ə)lɑ] *nm* mattress; **~ pneumatique** air bed *ou* mattress; **matelas-
sé, e** *adj (vêtement)* padded; *(tissu)*
quilted
matelot [mat(ə)lo] *nm* sailor, seaman
mater [mate] *vt (personne)* to bring to
heel, subdue; *(révolte)* to put down
matérialiser [mateʀjalize]: **se ~** *vi* to
materialize
matérialiste [mateʀjalist] *adj* materialistic
matériaux [mateʀjo] *nmpl* material(s)
matériel, le [mateʀjɛl] *adj* material ♦ *nm*
equipment *no pl*; *(de camping etc)* gear *no
pl*; *(INFORM)* hardware
maternel, le [mateʀnɛl] *adj (amour, geste)*
motherly, maternal; *(grand-père, oncle)*
maternal; **maternelle** *nf (aussi:* **école
maternelle)** (state) nursery school

aternité [matɛʀnite] *nf* (*établissement*) maternity hospital; (*état de mère*) motherhood, maternity; (*grossesse*) pregnancy; **congé de ~** maternity leave

athématique [matematik] *adj* mathematical; **mathématiques** *nfpl* (*science*) mathematics *sg*

aths [mat] (*fam*) *nfpl* maths

atière [matjɛʀ] *nf* matter; (*COMM, TECH*) material, matter *no pl*; (*fig: d'un livre etc*) subject matter, material; (*SCOL*) subject; **en ~ de** as regards; **~s grasses** fat content *sg*; **~s premières** raw materials

---

ôtel Matignon

L'hôtel Matignon *is the Paris office and residence of the French Prime Minister. By extension, the term "Matignon" is often used to refer to the Prime Minister or his staff.*

---

atin [matɛ̃] *nm, adv* morning; **du ~ au soir** from morning till night; **de bon** *ou* **grand ~** early in the morning; **matinal, e, -aux** *adj* (*toilette, gymnastique*) morning *cpd*; **être matinal** (*personne*) to be up early; to be an early riser; **matinée** *nf* morning; (*spectacle*) matinée

atou [matu] *nm* tom(cat)

atraque [matʀak] *nf* (*de policier*) truncheon (*BRIT*), billy (*US*)

atricule [matʀikyl] *nm* (*MIL*) regimental number; (*ADMIN*) reference number

atrimonial, e, -aux [matʀimɔnjal, jo] *adj* marital, marriage *cpd*

audire [modiʀ] *vt* to curse; **maudit, e** (*fam*) *adj* (*satané*) blasted, confounded

augréer [mogʀee] *vi* to grumble

aussade [mosad] *adj* sullen; (*temps*) gloomy

auvais, e [mɔvɛ, ɛz] *adj* bad; (*faux*): **le ~ numéro/moment** the wrong number/moment; (*méchant, malveillant*) malicious; **il fait ~** the weather is bad; **la mer est ~e** the sea is rough; **~ plaisant** hoaxer; **~e herbe** weed; **~e langue** gos-sip, scandalmonger (*BRIT*); **~e passe** bad patch

mauve [mov] *adj* mauve

maux [mo] *nmpl de* **mal**; **~ de ventre** stomachache *sg*

maximum [maksimɔm] *adj, nm* maximum; **au ~** (*le plus possible*) as much as one can; (*tout au plus*) at the (very) most *ou* maximum; **faire le ~** to do one's level best

mayonnaise [majɔnez] *nf* mayonnaise

mazout [mazut] *nm* (*fuel*) oil

Me *abr =* **Maître**

me, m' [m(ə)] *pron* (*direct: téléphoner, attendre etc*) me; (*indirect: parler, donner etc*) (to) me; (*réfléchi*) myself

mec [mɛk] (*fam*) *nm* bloke, guy

mécanicien, ne [mekanisjɛ̃, jɛn] *nm/f* mechanic; (*RAIL*) (train *ou* engine) driver

mécanique [mekanik] *adj* mechanical ♦ *nf* (*science*) mechanics *sg*; (*mécanisme*) mechanism; **ennui ~** engine trouble *no pl*

mécanisme [mekanism] *nm* mechanism

méchamment [meʃamɑ̃] *adv* nastily, maliciously, spitefully

méchanceté [meʃɑ̃ste] *nf* nastiness, maliciousness; **dire des ~s à qn** to say spiteful things to sb

méchant, e [meʃɑ̃, ɑ̃t] *adj* nasty, malicious, spiteful; (*enfant: pas sage*) naughty; (*animal*) vicious

mèche [meʃ] *nf* (*de cheveux*) lock; (*de lampe, bougie*) wick; (*d'un explosif*) fuse; **de ~ avec** in league with

méchoui [meʃwi] *nm* barbecue of a whole roast sheep

méconnaissable [mekɔnesabl] *adj* unrecognizable

méconnaître [mekɔnetʀ] *vt* (*ignorer*) to be unaware of; (*mésestimer*) to misjudge

mécontent, e [mekɔ̃tɑ̃, ɑ̃t] *adj*: **~ (de)** discontented *ou* dissatisfied *ou* displeased (with); (*contrarié*) annoyed (at); **mécontentement** *nm* dissatisfaction, discontent, displeasure; (*irritation*) annoyance

médaille [medaj] nf medal

médaillon [medajɔ̃] nm (bijou) locket

médecin [med(ə)sɛ̃] nm doctor; **~ légiste** forensic surgeon

médecine [med(ə)sin] nf medicine

média [medja] nmpl: **les ~** the media; **médiatique** adj media cpd; **médiatisé, e** adj reported in the media; **ce procès a été très médiatisé** (péj) this trial was turned into a media event

médical, e, -aux [medikal, o] adj medical; **passer une visite ~e** to have a medical

médicament [medikamɑ̃] nm medicine, drug

médiéval, e, -aux [medjeval, o] adj medieval

médiocre [medjɔkʀ] adj mediocre, poor

médire [mediʀ] vi: **~ de** to speak ill of; **médisance** nf scandalmongering (BRIT)

méditer [medite] vi to meditate

Méditerranée [mediteʀane] nf: **la (mer) ~** the Mediterranean (Sea); **méditerranéen, ne** adj Mediterranean ♦ nm/f: **Méditerranéen, ne** native ou inhabitant of a Mediterranean country

méduse [medyz] nf jellyfish

meeting [mitiŋ] nm (POL, SPORT) rally

méfait [mefɛ] nm (faute) misdemeanour, wrongdoing; **~s** nmpl (ravages) ravages, damage sg

méfiance [mefjɑ̃s] nf mistrust, distrust

méfiant, e [mefjɑ̃, jɑ̃t] adj mistrustful, distrustful

méfier [mefje]: **se ~** vi to be wary; to be careful; **se ~ de** to mistrust, distrust, be wary of

mégarde [megaʀd] nf: **par ~** (accidentellement) accidentally; (par erreur) by mistake

mégère [meʒɛʀ] nf shrew

mégot [mego] (fam) nm cigarette end

meilleur, e [mɛjœʀ] adj, adv better ♦ nm: **le ~** the best; **le ~ des deux** the better of the two; **~ marché** (inv) cheaper; **meilleure** nf: **la meilleure** the best (one)

mélancolie [melɑ̃kɔli] nf melancho gloom; **mélancolique** adj melancho melancholy

mélange [melɑ̃ʒ] nm mixture; **mélang** vt to mix; (vins, couleurs) to blend; (me en désordre) to mix up, muddle (up)

mélasse [melas] nf treacle, molasses sg

mêlée [mele] nf mêlée, scramble; (RUG scrum(mage)

mêler [mele] vt (unir) to mix; (embrouil to muddle (up), mix up; **se ~** vi to m mingle; **se ~ à** (personne: se joindre) join; (: s'associer à) to mix with; **se ~** (suj: personne) to meddle with, interfe in; **mêle-toi de ce qui te regarde!** mi your own business!

mélodie [melɔdi] nf melody; **mélodieu -euse** adj melodious

melon [m(ə)lɔ̃] nm (BOT) (honeydew) m on; (aussi: **chapeau ~**) bowler (hat)

membre [mɑ̃bʀ] nm (ANAT) limb; (pe sonne, pays, élément) member ♦ adj me ber cpd

mémé [meme] (fam) nf granny

MOT-CLÉ

---

même [mɛm] adj 1 (avant le nom) sar en même temps at the same time

2 (après le nom: renforcement): **il est** loyauté même he is loyalty itself; **ce se ses paroles/celles-là mêmes** they his very words/the very ones

♦ pron: **le(la) même** the same one

♦ adv 1 (renforcement): **il n'a même p pleuré** he didn't even cry; **même lui** dit even HE said it; **ici même** at this v place

2: **à même**: **à même la bouteille** straie from the bottle; **à même la peau** next the skin; **être à même de faire** to be i position to do, be able to do

3: **de même**: **faire de même** to do li wise; **lui de même** so does (ou did ou he; **de même que** just as; **il en va même pour** the same goes for

émo [memo] (*fam*) *nm* memo

émoire [memwaʀ] *nf* memory ♦ *nm* (*SCOL*) dissertation, paper; **~s** *nmpl* (*souvenirs*) memoirs; **à la ~ de** to the *ou* in memory of; **de ~** from memory; **~ norte/vive** (*INFORM*) ROM/RAM

émorable [memɔʀabl] *adj* memorable, unforgettable

enace [mənas] *nf* threat; **menacer** *vt* to threaten

énage [menaʒ] *nm* (*travail*) housekeeping, housework; (*couple*) married couple; (*famille, ADMIN*) household; **faire le ~** to do the housework; **ménagement** *nm* care and attention; **ménager, -ère** *adj* household *cpd*, domestic ♦ *vt* (*traiter: personne*) to handle with tact; (*utiliser*) to use sparingly; (*prendre soin de*) to take (great) care of, look after; (*organiser*) to arrange; **ménager qch à qn** (*réserver*) to have sth in store for sb; **ménagère** *nf* housewife

endiant, e [mādjā, jāt] *nm/f* beggar

endier [mādje] *vi* to beg ♦ *vt* to beg (for)

ener [m(ə)ne] *vt* to lead; (*enquête*) to conduct; (*affaires*) to manage ♦ *vi*: **~ à/ dans** (*emmener*) to take to/into; **~ qch à bien** to see sth through (to a successful conclusion), complete sth successfully

eneur, -euse [mənœʀ, øz] *nm/f* leader; (*péj*) agitator

éningite [menēʒit] *nf* meningitis *no pl*

énopause [menopoz] *nf* menopause

enottes [mənɔt] *nfpl* handcuffs

ensonge [mãsɔ̃ʒ] *nm* lie; (*action*) lying *no pl*; **mensonger, -ère** *adj* false

ensualité [mãsɥalite] *nf* (*traite*) monthly payment

ensuel, le [mãsɥɛl] *adj* monthly

ensurations [mãsyʀasjɔ̃] *nfpl* measurements

ental, e, -aux [mãtal, o] *adj* mental; **mentalité** *nf* mentality

enteur, -euse [mãtœʀ, øz] *nm/f* liar

enthe [mãt] *nf* mint

ention [mãsjɔ̃] *nf* (*annotation*) note,

comment; (*SCOL*) grade; **~ bien** *etc* ≈ grade B *etc* (*ou* upper 2nd class *etc*) pass (*BRIT*), ≈ pass with (high) honors (*US*); (*ADMIN*): **"rayer les ~s inutiles"** "delete as appropriate"; **mentionner** *vt* to mention

mentir [mãtiʀ] *vi* to lie

menton [mãtɔ̃] *nm* chin

menu, e [məny] *adj* (*personne*) slim, slight; (*frais, difficulté*) minor ♦ *adv* (*couper, hacher*) very fine ♦ *nm* menu; **~ touristique/gastronomique** economy/ gourmet's menu

menuiserie [mənɥizʀi] *nf* (*métier*) joinery, carpentry; (*passe-temps*) woodwork; **menuisier** *nm* joiner, carpenter

méprendre [mepʀãdʀ]: **se ~** *vi*: **se ~ sur** to be mistaken (about)

mépris [mepʀi] *nm* (*dédain*) contempt, scorn; **au ~ de** regardless of, in defiance of; **méprisable** *adj* contemptible, despicable; **méprisant, e** *adj* scornful; **méprise** *nf* mistake, error; **mépriser** *vt* to scorn, despise; (*gloire, danger*) to scorn, spurn

mer [mɛʀ] *nf* sea; (*marée*) tide; **en ~** at sea; **en haute** *ou* **pleine ~** off shore, on the open sea; **la ~ du Nord/Rouge** the North/Red Sea

mercenaire [mɛʀsənɛʀ] *nm* mercenary, hired soldier

mercerie [mɛʀsəʀi] *nf* (*boutique*) haberdasher's shop (*BRIT*), notions store (*US*)

merci [mɛʀsi] *excl* thank you ♦ *nf*: **à la ~ de qn/qch** at sb's mercy/the mercy of sth; **~ beaucoup** thank you very much; **~ de** thank you for; **sans ~** merciless(ly)

mercredi [mɛʀkʀədi] *nm* Wednesday

mercure [mɛʀkyʀ] *nm* mercury

merde [mɛʀd] (*fam!*) *nf* shit (*!*) ♦ *excl* (bloody) hell (*!*)

mère [mɛʀ] *nf* mother; **~ célibataire** unmarried mother

merguez [mɛʀgɛz] *nf* merguez sausage (*type of spicy sausage from N Africa*)

méridional, e, -aux [meʀidjɔnal, o] *adj*

southern ♦ *nm/f* Southerner
meringue [mərɛ̃g] *nf* meringue
mérite [merit] *nm* merit; **avoir du ~ (à faire qch)** to deserve credit (for doing sth); **mériter** *vt* to deserve
merlan [mɛrlɑ̃] *nm* whiting
merle [mɛrl] *nm* blackbird
merveille [mɛrvɛj] *nf* marvel, wonder; **faire ~** to work wonders; **à ~** perfectly, wonderfully; **merveilleux, -euse** *adj* marvellous, wonderful
mes [me] *adj voir* **mon**
mésange [mezɑ̃ʒ] *nf* tit(mouse)
mésaventure [mezavɑ̃tyr] *nf* misadventure, misfortune
Mesdames [medam] *nfpl de* **Madame**
Mesdemoiselles [medmwazɛl] *nfpl de* **Mademoiselle**
mesquin, e [mɛskɛ̃, in] *adj* mean, petty; **mesquinerie** *nf* meanness; (*procédé*) mean trick
message [mesaʒ] *nm* message; **messager, -ère** *nm/f* messenger; **messagerie** *nf* (INTERNET): **messagerie électronique** bulletin board
messe [mɛs] *nf* mass
Messieurs [mesjø] *nmpl de* **Monsieur**
mesure [m(ə)zyr] *nf* (*évaluation, dimension*) measurement; (*récipient*) measure; (MUS: *cadence*) time, tempo; (: *division*) bar; (*retenue*) moderation; (*disposition*) measure, step; **sur ~** (*costume*) made-to-measure; **dans la ~ où** insofar as, inasmuch as; **à ~ que** as; **être en ~ de** to be in a position to; **dans une certaine ~** to a certain extent
mesurer [məzyre] *vt* to measure; (*juger*) to weigh up, assess; (*modérer: ses paroles etc*) to moderate; **se ~ avec** to have a confrontation with; **il mesure 1 m 80** he's 1 m 80 tall
met [me] *vb voir* **mettre**
métal, -aux [metal, o] *nm* metal; **métallique** *adj* metallic
météo [meteo] *nf* (*bulletin*) weather report
météorologie [meteɔrɔlɔʒi] *nf* meteorology

méthode [metɔd] *nf* method; (*livre, ouv‑ ge*) manual, tutor
méticuleux, -euse [metikylø, øz] ◀ meticulous
métier [metje] *nm* (*profession: gén*) jc (: *manuel*) trade; (*artisanal*) craft; (*tech que, expérience*) (acquired) skill *ou* te‑ nique; (*aussi:* **~ à tisser**) (weaving) loo **avoir du ~** to have practical experience
métis, se [metis] *adj, nm/f* half-cas half-breed
métrage [metraʒ] *nm*: **long/moyen/co ~** full-length/medium-length/short film
mètre [mɛtr] *nm* metre; (*règle*) (met rule; (*ruban*) tape measure; **métrique** ◀ metric
métro [metro] *nm* underground (BR subway
métropole [metrɔpɔl] *nf* (*capitale*) met polis; (*pays*) home country
mets [me] *nm* dish
metteur [metœr] *nm*: **~ en scè** (THÉÂTRE) producer; (CINÉMA) director

---
MOT-CLÉ
---

mettre [mɛtr] *vt* **1** (*placer*) to put; **met en bouteille/en sac** to bottle/put bags *ou* sacks; **mettre en charge (po** to charge (with), indict (for)
2 (*vêtements*): *revêtir*) to put on; (: *por* to wear; **mets ton gilet** put your cai gan on; **je ne mets plus mon mantea** no longer wear my coat
3 (*faire fonctionner: chauffage, électricité*) put on; (: *reveil, minuteur*) to set; (*insta gaz, eau*) to put in, lay on; **mettre marche** to start up
4 (*consacrer*): **mettre du temps à fa qch** to take time to do sth *ou* over sth
5 (*noter, écrire*) to say, put (dow **qu'est-ce qu'il a mis sur la carte?** w did he say *ou* write on the card?; **met au pluriel ...** put ... into the plural
6 (*supposer*): **mettons que ...** let's s pose *ou* say that ...
7: y mettre du sien to pull one's weig

se mettre vi 1 (se placer): **vous pouvez
vous mettre là** you can sit (ou stand)
there; **où ça se met?** where does it go?;
se mettre au lit to get into bed; **se mettre au piano** to sit down at the piano; **se
mettre de l'encre sur les doigts** to get
ink on one's fingers
2 (s'habiller): **se mettre en maillot de
bain** to get into ou put on a swimsuit;
n'avoir rien à se mettre to have nothing
to wear
3: **se mettre à** to begin, start; **se mettre
à faire** to begin ou start doing ou to do;
se mettre au piano to start learning the
piano; **se mettre au travail/à l'étude** to
get down to work/one's studies

euble [mœbl] nm piece of furniture; **des
~s** furniture; **meublé** nm furnished flatlet
(BRIT) ou room; **meubler** vt to furnish
eugler [mœgle] vi to low, moo
eule [mœl] nf (de foin, blé) stack; (de
fromage) round; (à broyer) millstone
eunier [mœnje, jɛʀ] nm miller; **meu-
nière** nf miller's wife
eure etc [mœʀ] vb voir **mourir**
eurtre [mœʀtʀ] nm murder; **meurtrier,
ière** adj (arme etc) deadly; (fureur, in-
stincts) murderous ♦ nm/f murderer(-
ress)
eurtrir [mœʀtʀiʀ] vt to bruise; (fig) to
wound; **meurtrissure** nf bruise
eus etc [mœ] vb voir **mouvoir**
eute [mœt] nf pack
exicain, e [mɛksikɛ̃, ɛn] adj Mexican
♦ nm/f: **M~, e** Mexican
exico [mɛksiko] n Mexico City
exique [mɛksik] nm: **le ~** Mexico
gr abr = **Monseigneur**
[mi] nm (MUS) E; (en chantant la gamme)
mi ♦ préfixe: **~...** half(-); mid-; **à la ~-
anvier** in mid-January; **à ~-hauteur** halfway up; **mi-bas** nm inv knee sock
auler [mjole] vi to mew
che [miʃ] nf round ou cob loaf
-chemin [miʃmɛ̃]: **à ~-~** adv halfway,

midway
mi-clos, e [miklo, kloz] adj half-closed
micro [mikʀo] nm mike, microphone; (IN-
FORM) micro
microbe [mikʀɔb] nm germ, microbe
micro...: **micro-onde** nf: **four à micro-
ondes** microwave oven; **micro-
ordinateur** nm microcomputer; **microscope** nm microscope; **microscopique**
adj microscopic
midi [midi] nm midday, noon; (moment du
déjeuner) lunchtime; (sud) south; **à ~** at
12 (o'clock) ou midday ou noon; **le M~**
the South (of France), the Midi
mie [mi] nf crumb (of the loaf)
miel [mjɛl] nm honey; **mielleux, -euse**
adj (personne) unctuous, syrupy
mien, ne [mjɛ̃, mjɛn] pron: **le(la) ~(ne),
les ~(ne)s** mine; **les ~s** my family
miette [mjɛt] nf (de pain, gâteau) crumb;
(fig: de la conversation etc) scrap; **en ~s** in
pieces ou bits

MOT-CLÉ
---

mieux [mjø] adv 1 (d'une meilleure façon):
mieux (que) better (than); **elle
travaille/mange mieux** she works/eats
better; **elle va mieux** she is better
2 (de la meilleure façon) best; **ce que je
sais le mieux** what I know best; **les livres les mieux faits** the best made
books
3: **de mieux en mieux** better and better
♦ adj 1 (plus à l'aise, en meilleure forme)
better; **se sentir mieux** to feel better
2 (plus satisfaisant) better; **c'est mieux
ainsi** it's better like this; **c'est le mieux
des deux** it's the better of the two; **le(la)
mieux, les mieux** the best; **demandez-
lui, c'est le mieux** ask him, it's the best
thing
3 (plus joli) better-looking
4: **au mieux** at best; **au mieux avec** on
the best of terms with; **pour le mieux** for
the best
♦ nm 1 (progrès) improvement

2: de mon/ton mieux as best I/you can (*ou* could); **faire de son mieux** to do one's best

mièvre [mjɛvʀ] *adj* mawkish (*BRIT*), sickly sentimental

mignon, ne [miɲɔ̃, ɔn] *adj* sweet, cute

migraine [migʀɛn] *nf* headache; (*MÉD*) migraine

mijoter [miʒɔte] *vt* to simmer; (*préparer avec soin*) to cook lovingly; (*fam: tramer*) to plot, cook up ♦ *vi* to simmer

mil [mil] *num* = **mille**

milieu, x [miljø] *nm* (*centre*) middle; (*BIO, GÉO*) environment; (*entourage social*) milieu; (*provenance*) background; (*pègre*): **le ~** the underworld; **au ~ de** in the middle of; **au beau** *ou* **en plein ~ (de)** right in the middle (of); **un juste ~** a happy medium

militaire [militɛʀ] *adj* military, army *cpd* ♦ *nm* serviceman

militant, e [militɑ̃, ɑ̃t] *adj, nm/f* militant

militer [milite] *vi* to be a militant

mille [mil] *num* a *ou* one thousand ♦ *nm* (*mesure*): **~ (marin)** nautical mile; **mettre dans le ~** (*fig*) to be bang on target; **millefeuille** *nm* cream *ou* vanilla slice; **millénaire** *nm* millennium ♦ *adj* thousand-year-old; (*fig*) ancient; **mille-pattes** *nm inv* centipede

millésimé, e [milezime] *adj* vintage *cpd*

millet [mijɛ] *nm* millet

milliard [miljaʀ] *nm* milliard, thousand million (*BRIT*), billion (*US*); **milliardaire** *nm/f* multimillionaire (*BRIT*), billionaire (*US*)

millier [milje] *nm* thousand; **un ~ (de)** a thousand or so, about a thousand; **par ~s** in (their) thousands, by the thousand

milligramme [miligʀam] *nm* milligramme

millimètre [milimɛtʀ] *nm* millimetre

million [miljɔ̃] *nm* million; **deux ~s de** two million; **millionnaire** *nm/f* millionaire

mime [mim] *nm/f* (*acteur*) mime(r) ♦ *nm* (*art*) mime, miming; **mimer** *vt* to mime;

(*singer*) to mimic, take off

mimique [mimik] *nf* (*grimace*) (funn face; (*signes*) gesticulations *pl*, sign la guage *no pl*

minable [minabl] *adj* (*décrépit*) shabby looking); (*médiocre*) pathetic

mince [mɛ̃s] *adj* thin; (*personne, taille*) slim slender; (*fig: profit, connaissances*) sligh small, weak ♦ *excl*: **~ alors!** drat it!, da it! (*US*); **minceur** *nf* thinness; (*d'une p sonne*) slimness, slenderness; **mincir** *vi* get slimmer

mine [min] *nf* (*physionomie*) expressio look; (*allure*) exterior, appearance; crayon) lead; (*gisement, explosif, fig: soure* mine; **avoir bonne ~** (*personne*) to lo well; (*ironique*) to look an utter idi **avoir mauvaise ~** to look unwell poorly; **faire ~ de faire** to make a pi tence of doing; **~ de rien** although y wouldn't think so

miner [mine] *vt* (*saper*) to undermir erode; (*MIL*) to mine

minerai [minʀɛ] *nm* ore

minéral, e, -aux [mineʀal, o] *adj, r* mineral

minéralogique [mineʀalɔʒik] *adj*: **num ro ~** registration number

minet, te [mine, ɛt] *nm/f* (*chat*) pussy-c (*péj*) young trendy

mineur, e [minœʀ] *adj* minor ♦ *nm/f* (J minor, person under age ♦ *nm* (*travaille* miner

miniature [minjatyʀ] *adj, nf* miniature

minibus [minibys] *nm* minibus

mini-cassette [minikasɛt] *nf* cassette (corder)

minier, -ière [minje, jɛʀ] *adj* mining

mini-jupe [miniʒyp] *nf* mini-skirt

minime [minim] *adj* minor, minimal

minimiser [minimize] *vt* to minimize; (to play down

minimum [minimɔm] *adj, nm* minimu **au ~** (*au moins*) at the very least

ministère [ministɛʀ] *nm* (*aussi REL*) m istry; (*cabinet*) government

inistre [ministʀ] *nm* (*aussi REL*) minister
Minitel ® [minitel] *nm* videotext terminal
and service

Minitel

Minitel *is a personal computer terminal supplied free of change by France-
Télécom to telephone subscribers. It serves
as a computerized telephone directory as
well as giving access to various services,
including information on train timetables,
the stock market and situations vacant.
Services are accessed by phoning the relevant number and charged to the subscriber's phone bill.*

---

inoritaire [minɔʀitɛʀ] *adj* minority
inorité [minɔʀite] *nf* minority; **être en ~**
to be in the *ou* a minority
inuit [minɥi] *nm* midnight
inuscule [minyskyl] *adj* minute, tiny
♦ *nf*: (**lettre**) **~** small letter
inute [minyt] *nf* minute; **à la ~** (just)
this instant; (*faire*) there and then; **minuter** *vt* to time; **minuterie** *nf* time switch
inutieux, -euse [minysjø, jøz] *adj* (*personne*) meticulous; (*travail*) minutely detailed
irabelle [miʀabɛl] *nf* (cherry) plum
iracle [miʀɑkl] *nm* miracle
irage [miʀaʒ] *nm* mirage
ire [miʀ] *nf*: **point de ~** (*fig*) focal point
iroir [miʀwaʀ] *nm* mirror
iroiter [miʀwate] *vi* to sparkle, shimmer;
faire ~ qch à qn to paint sth in glowing
colours for sb, dangle sth in front of sb's
eyes
is, e [mi, miz] *pp de* **mettre** ♦ *adj*: **bien
~** well-dressed
ise [miz] *nf* (*argent: au jeu*) stake; (*tenue*)
clothing, attire; **être de ~** to be acceptable *ou* in season; **~ au point** (*fig*) clarification; **~ de fonds** capital outlay; **~ en
examen** charging, indictment; **~ en plis**
set; **~ en scène** production
iser [mize] *vt* (*enjeu*) to stake, bet; **~ sur**

(*cheval, numéro*) to bet on; (*fig*) to bank
ou count on
misérable [mizeʀabl] *adj* (*lamentable, malheureux*) pitiful, wretched; (*pauvre*)
poverty-stricken; (*insignifiant, mesquin*) miserable ♦ *nm/f* wretch
misère [mizɛʀ] *nf* (*extreme*) poverty, destitution; **~s** *nfpl* (*malheurs*) woes, miseries;
(*ennuis*) little troubles; **salaire de ~** starvation wage
missile [misil] *nm* missile
mission [misjɔ̃] *nf* mission; **partir en ~**
(*ADMIN, POL*) to go on an assignment;
missionnaire *nm/f* missionary
mit [mi] *vb voir* **mettre**
mité, e [mite] *adj* moth-eaten
mi-temps [mitɑ̃] *nf inv* (*SPORT: période*)
half; (: *pause*) half-time; **à ~-~** part-time
miteux, -euse [mitø, øz] *adj* (*lieu*) seedy
mitigé, e [mitiʒe] *adj*: **sentiments ~s**
mixed feelings
mitonner [mitɔne] *vt* to cook with loving
care; (*fig*) to cook up quietly
mitoyen, ne [mitwajɛ̃, jɛn] *adj* (*mur*) common, party *cpd*
mitrailler [mitʀaje] *vt* to machine-gun;
(*fig*) to pelt, bombard; (: *photographier*) to
take shot after shot of; **mitraillette** *nf*
submachine gun; **mitrailleuse** *nf*
machine gun
mi-voix [mivwa]: **à ~-~** *adv* in a low *ou*
hushed voice
mixage [miksaʒ] *nm* (*CINÉMA*) (sound) mixing
mixer [miksœʀ] *nm* (food) mixer
mixte [mikst] *adj* (*gén*) mixed; (*SCOL*)
mixed, coeducational
mixture [mikstyʀ] *nf* mixture; (*fig*) concoc-
tion
Mlle (*pl* **Mlles**) *abr* = **Mademoiselle**
MM *abr* = **Messieurs**
Mme (*pl* **Mmes**) *abr* = **Madame**
mobile [mɔbil] *adj* mobile; (*pièce de
machine*) moving ♦ *nm* (*motif*) motive;
(*œuvre d'art*) mobile
mobilier, -ière [mɔbilje, jɛʀ] *nm* furniture

mobiliser [mɔbilize] *vt* to mobilize
mocassin [mɔkasɛ̃] *nm* moccasin
moche [mɔʃ] *(fam) adj (laid)* ugly; *(mauvais)* rotten
modalité [mɔdalite] *nf* form, mode; **~s de paiement** methods of payment
mode [mɔd] *nf* fashion ♦ *nm (manière)* form, mode; **à la ~** fashionable, in fashion; **~ d'emploi** directions *pl* (for use)
modèle [mɔdɛl] *adj, nm* model; *(qui pose: de peintre)* sitter; **~ déposé** registered design; **~ réduit** small-scale model; **modeler** *vt* to model
modem [mɔdɛm] *nm* modem
modéré, e [mɔdere] *adj, nm/f* moderate
modérer [mɔdere] *vt* to moderate; **se ~** *vi* to restrain o.s.
moderne [mɔdɛrn] *adj* modern ♦ *nm (style)* modern style; *(meubles)* modern furniture; **moderniser** *vt* to modernize
modeste [mɔdɛst] *adj* modest; **modestie** *nf* modesty
modifier [mɔdifje] *vt* to modify, alter; **se ~** *vi* to alter
modique [mɔdik] *adj* modest
modiste [mɔdist] *nf* milliner
module [mɔdyl] *nm* module
moelle [mwal] *nf* marrow; **~ épinière** spinal cord
moelleux, -euse [mwalø, øz] *adj* soft; *(gâteau)* light and moist
mœurs [mœr] *nfpl (conduite)* morals; *(manières)* manners; *(pratiques sociales, mode de vie)* habits
mohair [mɔɛr] *nm* mohair
moi [mwa] *pron* me; *(emphatique)*: **~, je ...** for my part, I ..., I myself ...; **à ~** mine; **moi-même** *pron* myself; *(emphatique)* I myself
moindre [mwɛ̃dr] *adj* lesser; lower; **le(la) ~, les ~s** the least, the slightest; **merci – c'est la ~ des choses!** thank you – it's a pleasure!
moine [mwan] *nm* monk, friar
moineau, x [mwano] *nm* sparrow

MOT-CLÉ

moins [mwɛ̃] *adv* **1** *(comparatif)*: **moins (que)** less (than); **moins grand que les** tall than, not as tall as; **moins je travaille, mieux je me porte** the less I work, the better I feel
2 *(superlatif)*: **le moins** (the) least; **c'est ce que j'aime le moins** it's what I like (the) least; **le(la) moins doué(e)** the least gifted; **au moins, du moins** at least; **pour le moins** at the very least
3: **moins de** *(quantité)* less (than); *(nombre)* fewer (than); **moins de sable/d'eau** less sand/water; **moins de livres/gens** fewer books/people; **moins de 2 ans** less than 2 years; **moins de midi** not yet midday
4: **de moins, en moins**: **100 F/3 jours de moins** 100F/3 days less; **3 livres en moins** 3 books fewer; 3 books too few; **de l'argent en moins** less money; **le soleil en moins** but for the sun, minus the sun; **de moins en moins** less and less
5: **à moins de, à moins que** unless; **à moins de faire** unless we do *(ou he do etc)*; **à moins que tu ne fasses** unless you do; **à moins d'un accident** barring any accident
♦ *prép*: **4 moins 2** 4 minus 2; **il est moins 5** it's 5 to; **il fait moins 5** it's 5 (degrees) below (freezing), it's minus 5

---

mois [mwa] *nm* month
moisi [mwazi] *nm* mould, mildew; **odeur de ~** musty smell; **moisir** *vi* to go mouldy; **moisissure** *nf* mould *no pl*
moisson [mwasɔ̃] *nf* harvest; **moissonner** *vt* to harvest, reap; **moissonneuse** *nf (machine)* harvester
moite [mwat] *adj* sweaty, sticky
moitié [mwatje] *nf* half; **la ~** half; **la ~ de** half (of); **la ~ du temps** half the time; **la ~ de** halfway through; **à ~** *(avant le verbe)* half-; *(avant l'adjectif)* half-; **à ~ prix** (at) half-price; **~ moitié** half-and-half

moka [mɔka] *nm* coffee gateau

mol [mɔl] *adj voir* **mou**

molaire [mɔlɛʀ] *nf* molar

molester [mɔleste] *vt* to manhandle, maul (about)

molle [mɔl] *adj voir* **mou; mollement** *adv* (*péj: travailler*) sluggishly; (*protester*) feebly

mollet [mɔlɛ] *nm* calf ♦ *adj m:* **œuf ~** soft-boiled egg

molletonné, e [mɔltɔne] *adj* fleece-lined

mollir [mɔliʀ] *vi* (*fléchir*) to relent; (*substance*) to go soft

mollusque [mɔlysk] *nm* mollusc

môme [mom] (*fam*) *nm/f* (*enfant*) brat

moment [mɔmɑ̃] *nm* moment; **ce n'est pas le ~** this is not the (right) time; **pour un bon ~** for a good while; **pour le ~** for the moment, for the time being; **au ~ de** at the time of; **au ~ où** just as; **à tout ~** (*peut arriver etc*) at any time *ou* moment; (*constamment*) constantly, continually; **en ce ~** at the moment; at present; **sur le ~** at the time; **par ~s** now and then, at times; **du ~ où** *ou* **que** seeing that, since; **momentané, e** *adj* temporary, momentary; **momentanément** *adv* (*court instant*) for a short while

momie [mɔmi] *nf* mummy

mon, ma [mɔ̃, ma] (*pl* **mes**) *adj* my

Monaco [mɔnako] *nm* Monaco

monarchie [mɔnaʀʃi] *nf* monarchy

monastère [mɔnastɛʀ] *nm* monastery

monceau, x [mɔ̃so] *nm* heap

mondain, e [mɔ̃dɛ̃, ɛn] *adj* (*vie*) society *cpd*

monde [mɔ̃d] *nm* world; (*haute société*): **le ~** (high) society; **il y a du ~** (*beaucoup de gens*) there are a lot of people; (*quelques personnes*) there are some people; **beaucoup/peu de ~** many/few people; **mettre au ~** to bring into the world; **pas le moins du ~** not in the least; **se faire un ~ de qch** to make a great deal of fuss about sth; **mondial, e, -aux** *adj* (*population*) world *cpd*; (*influence*) world-wide; **mondialement** *adv* throughout the world

monégasque [mɔnegask] *adj* Monegasque, of *ou* from Monaco

monétaire [mɔnetɛʀ] *adj* monetary

moniteur, -trice [mɔnitœʀ, tʀis] *nm/f* (*SPORT*) instructor(-tress); (*de colonie de vacances*) supervisor ♦ *nm* (*écran*) monitor

monnaie [mɔnɛ] *nf* (*ÉCON, gén: moyen d'échange*) currency; (*petites pièces*): **avoir de la ~** to have (some) change; **une pièce de ~** a coin; **faire de la ~** to get (some) change; **avoir/faire la ~ de 20 F** to have change of/get change for 20 F; **rendre à qn la ~ (sur 20 F)** to give sb the change (out of *ou* from 20 F); **monnayer** *vt* to convert into cash; (*talent*) to capitalize on

monologue [mɔnɔlɔg] *nm* monologue, soliloquy; **monologuer** *vi* to soliloquize

monopole [mɔnɔpɔl] *nm* monopoly

monotone [mɔnɔtɔn] *adj* monotonous

Monsieur [məsjø] (*pl* **Messieurs**) *titre* Mr ♦ *nm* (*homme quelconque*): **un/le m~** a/ the gentleman; **~, ...** (*en tête de lettre*) Dear Sir, ...; *voir aussi* **Madame**

monstre [mɔ̃stʀ] *nm* monster ♦ *adj* (*fam: colossal*) monstrous; **un travail ~** a fantastic amount of work; **monstrueux, -euse** *adj* monstrous

mont [mɔ̃] *nm:* **par ~s et par vaux** up hill and down dale; **le M~ Blanc** Mont Blanc

montage [mɔ̃taʒ] *nm* (*assemblage: d'appareil*) assembly; (*PHOTO*) photomontage; (*CINÉMA*) editing

montagnard, e [mɔ̃taɲaʀ, aʀd] *adj* mountain *cpd* ♦ *nm/f* mountain-dweller

montagne [mɔ̃taɲ] *nf* (*cime*) mountain; (*région*): **la ~** the mountains *pl*; **~s russes** big dipper *sg*, switchback *sg*; **montagneux, -euse** *adj* mountainous; (*basse montagne*) hilly

montant, e [mɔ̃tɑ̃, ɑ̃t] *adj* rising; **pull à col ~** high-necked jumper ♦ *nm* (*somme, total*) (sum) total, (total) amount; (*de fenêtre*) upright; (*de lit*) post

monte-charge [mɔ̃tʃaʀʒ] *nm inv* goods

lift, hoist

montée [mɔ̃te] *nf* (*des prix, hostilités*) rise; (*escalade*) climb; (*côte*) hill; **au milieu de la ~** halfway up

monter [mɔ̃te] *vt* (*escalier, côte*) to go (*ou* come) up; (*valise, paquet*) to take (*ou* bring) up; (*étagère*) to raise; (*tente, échafaudage*) to put up; (*machine*) to assemble; (*CINÉMA*) to edit; (*THÉÂTRE*) to put on, stage; (*société etc*) to set up ♦ *vi* to go (*ou* come) up; (*prix, niveau, température*) to go up, rise; (*passager*) to get on; **se ~ à** (*frais etc*) to add up to, come to; **~ à pied** to walk up, go up on foot; **~ dans le train/l'avion** to get into the train/plane, board the train/plane; **~ sur** to climb up onto; **~ à cheval** (*faire du cheval*) to ride, go riding

montre [mɔ̃tʀ] *nf* watch; **contre la ~** (*SPORT*) against the clock; **montre-bracelet** *nf* wristwatch

montrer [mɔ̃tʀe] *vt* to show; **~ qch à qn** to show sb sth

monture [mɔ̃tyʀ] *nf* (*cheval*) mount; (*de lunettes*) frame; (*d'une bague*) setting

monument [mɔnymɑ̃] *nm* monument; **~ aux morts** war memorial

moquer [mɔke]: **se ~ de** *vt* to make fun of, laugh at; (*fam: se désintéresser de*) not to care about; (*tromper*): **se ~ de qn** to take sb for a ride; **moquerie** *nf* mockery

moquette [mɔket] *nf* fitted carpet

moqueur, -euse [mɔkœʀ, øz] *adj* mocking

moral, e, -aux [mɔʀal, o] *adj* moral ♦ *nm* morale; **avoir le ~** (*fam*) to be in good spirits; **avoir le ~ à zéro** (*fam*) to be really down; **morale** *nf* (*mœurs*) morals *pl*; (*valeurs*) moral standards *pl*, morality; (*d'une fable etc*) moral; **faire la morale à** to lecture, preach at; **moralité** *nf* morality; (*de fable*) moral

morceau, x [mɔʀso] *nm* piece, bit; (*d'une œuvre*) passage, extract; (*MUS*) piece; (*CULIN: de viande*) cut; (*de sucre*) lump; **mettre en ~x** to pull to pieces *ou* bits; **manger**

un ~ to have a bite (to eat)

morceler [mɔʀsəle] *vt* to break up, divide up

mordant, e [mɔʀdɑ̃, ɑ̃t] *adj* (*ton, remarque*) scathing, cutting; (*ironie, froid*) biting ♦ *nm* (*style*) bite, punch

mordiller [mɔʀdije] *vt* to nibble at, chew at

mordre [mɔʀdʀ] *vt* to bite ♦ *vi* (*poisson*) to bite; **~ sur** (*fig*) to go over into, overlap into; **~ à l'hameçon** to bite, rise to the bait

mordu, e [mɔʀdy] (*fam*) *nm/f* enthusiast; **un ~ de jazz** a jazz fanatic

morfondre [mɔʀfɔ̃dʀ]: **se ~** *vi* to mope

morgue [mɔʀg] *nf* (*arrogance*) haughtiness; (*lieu: de la police*) morgue; (: *l'hôpital*) mortuary

morne [mɔʀn] *adj* dismal, dreary

morose [mɔʀoz] *adj* sullen, morose

mors [mɔʀ] *nm* bit

morse [mɔʀs] *nm* (*ZOOL*) walrus; (*TÉ*) Morse (code)

morsure [mɔʀsyʀ] *nf* bite

mort¹ [mɔʀ] *nf* death

mort², e [mɔʀ, mɔʀt] *pp de* **mourir** ♦ *adj* dead ♦ *nm/f* (*défunt*) dead man/woman; (*victime*): **il y a eu plusieurs ~s** several people were killed, there were several killed; **~ de peur/fatigue** frightened to death/dead tired

mortalité [mɔʀtalite] *nf* mortality, death rate

mortel, le [mɔʀtɛl] *adj* (*poison etc*) deadly, lethal; (*accident, blessure*) fatal; (*silence, ennemi*) deadly; (*péché*) mortal; (*fam: ennuyeux*) deadly boring

mortier [mɔʀtje] *nm* (*gén*) mortar

mort-né, e [mɔʀne] *adj* (*enfant*) stillborn

mortuaire [mɔʀtɥeʀ] *adj*: **avis ~** death announcement

morue [mɔʀy] *nf* (*ZOOL*) cod *inv*

mosaïque [mɔzaik] *nf* mosaic

Moscou [mɔsku] *n* Moscow

mosquée [mɔske] *nf* mosque

mot [mo] *nm* word; (*message*) line, note;

à ~ word for word; ~ **d'ordre** watchword; ~ **de passe** password; ~**s croisés** crossword (puzzle) sg

motard [mɔtar, ard] nm biker; (policier) motorcycle cop

motel [mɔtɛl] nm motel

moteur, -trice [mɔtœr, tris] adj (ANAT, PHYSIOL) motor; (TECH) driving; (AUTO): **à 4 roues motrices** 4-wheel drive ♦ nm engine, motor; **à ~** power-driven, motor cpd; ~ **de recherche** search engine

motif [mɔtif] nm (cause) motive; (décoratif) design, pattern, motif; **sans ~** groundless

motivation [mɔtivasjɔ̃] nf motivation

motiver [mɔtive] vt to motivate; (justifier) to justify, account for

moto [mɔto] nf (motor)bike; **motocycliste** nm/f motorcyclist

motorisé, e [mɔtɔrize] adj (personne) having transport ou a car

motrice [mɔtris] adj voir **moteur**

motte [mɔt] nf: ~ **de terre** lump of earth, clod (of earth); ~ **de beurre** lump of butter

mou (mol), molle [mu, mɔl] adj soft; (personne) lethargic; (protestations) weak ♦ nm: **avoir du mou** to be slack

moucharder [muʃarde] (fam) vt (SCOL) to sneak on; (POLICE) to grass on

mouche [muʃ] nf fly

moucher [muʃe]: **se ~** vi to blow one's nose

moucheron [muʃrɔ̃] nm midge

mouchoir [muʃwar] nm handkerchief, hanky, ~ **en papier** tissue, paper hanky

moudre [mudr] vt to grind

moue [mu] nf pout; **faire la ~** to pout; (fig) to pull a face

mouette [mwɛt] nf (sea)gull

moufle [mufl] nf (gant) mitt(en)

mouillé, e [muje] adj wet

mouiller [muje] vt (humecter) to wet, moisten; (tremper): ~ **qn/qch** to make sb/sth wet ♦ vi (NAVIG) to lie ou be at anchor; **se ~** to get wet; (fam: prendre des risques) to commit o.s.

moulant, e [mulɑ̃, ɑ̃t] adj figure-hugging

moule [mul] nf mussel ♦ nm (CULIN) mould; ~ **à gâteaux** ♦ nm cake tin (BRIT) ou pan (US)

moulent [mul] vb voir **moudre; mouler**

mouler [mule] vt (suj: vêtement) to hug, fit closely round

moulin [mulɛ̃] nm mill; ~ **à café/à poivre** coffee/pepper mill; ~ **à légumes** (vegetable) shredder; ~ **à paroles** (fig) chatterbox; ~ **à vent** windmill

moulinet [mulinɛ] nm (de canne à pêche) reel; (mouvement): **faire des ~s avec qch** to whirl sth around

moulinette ® [mulinɛt] nf (vegetable) shredder

moulu, e [muly] pp de **moudre**

mourant, e [murɑ̃, ɑ̃t] adj dying

mourir [murir] vi to die; (civilisation) to die out; ~ **de froid/faim** to die of exposure/hunger; ~ **de faim/d'ennui** (fig) to be starving/be bored to death; ~ **d'envie de faire** to be dying to do

mousse [mus] nf (BOT) moss; (de savon) lather; (écume: sur eau, bière) froth, foam; (CULIN) mousse ♦ nm (NAVIG) ship's boy; ~ **à raser** shaving foam

mousseline [muslin] nf muslin; **pommes ~** mashed potatoes

mousser [muse] vi (bière, détergent) to foam; (savon) to lather; **mousseux, -euse** adj frothy ♦ nm: **(vin) mousseux** sparkling wine

mousson [musɔ̃] nf monsoon

moustache [mustaʃ] nf moustache; ~**s** nfpl (du chat) whiskers pl; **moustachu, e** adj with a moustache

moustiquaire [mustikɛr] nf mosquito net

moustique [mustik] nm mosquito

moutarde [mutard] nf mustard

mouton [mutɔ̃] nm sheep inv; (peau) sheepskin; (CULIN) mutton

mouvement [muvmɑ̃] nm movement; (fig: impulsion) gesture; **avoir un bon ~** to make a nice gesture; **en ~** in motion; on the move; **mouvementé, e** adj (vie, *poursuite*) eventful; (*réunion*) turbulent

mouvoir [muvwaʀ]: **se ~** *vi* to move

moyen, ne [mwajɛ̃, jɛn] *adj* average; (*tailles, prix*) medium; (*de grandeur moyenne*) medium-sized ♦ *nm* (*façon*) means *sg*, way; **~s** *nmpl* (*capacités*) means; **très ~** (*résultats*) pretty poor; **je n'en ai pas les ~s** I can't afford it; **au ~ de** by means of; **par tous les ~s** by every possible means, every possible way; **par ses propres ~s** all by oneself; **~ âge** Middle Ages; **~ de transport** means of transport

moyennant [mwajenɑ̃] *prép* (*somme*) for; (*service, conditions*) in return for; (*travail, effort*) with

moyenne [mwajɛn] *nf* average; (*MATH*) mean; (*SCOL: à l'examen*) pass mark; **en ~** on (an) average; **~ d'âge** average age

Moyen-Orient [mwajɛnɔʀjɑ̃] *nm*: **le ~-~** the Middle East

moyeu, x [mwajø] *nm* hub

MST *sigle f* (= *maladie sexuellement transmissible*) STD

MTC *sigle m* (= *mécanisme du taux de change*) ERM

mû, mue [my] *pp de* **mouvoir**

muer [mɥe] *vi* (*oiseau, mammifère*) to moult; (*serpent*) to slough; (*jeune garçon*): **il mue** his voice is breaking; **se ~ en** to transform into

muet, te [mɥe, mɥɛt] *adj* dumb; (*fig*): **~ d'admiration** *etc* speechless with admiration *etc*; (*CINÉMA*) silent ♦ *nm/f* mute

mufle [myfl] *nm* muzzle; (*fam: goujat*) boor

mugir [myʒiʀ] *vi* (*taureau*) to bellow; (*vache*) to low; (*fig*) to howl

muguet [mygɛ] *nm* lily of the valley

mule [myl] *nf* (*ZOOL*) (she-)mule

mulet [mylɛ] *nm* (*ZOOL*) (he-)mule

multinationale [myltinasjɔnal] *nf* multinational

multiple [myltipl] *adj* multiple, numerous; (*varié*) many, manifold; **multiplier** *vt* to multiply; **se multiplier** *vi* to multiply

municipal, e, -aux [mynisipal, o] *adj*

(élections, stade) municipal; (*conseil*) town *cpd*; **piscine/bibliothèque ~e** public swimming pool/library; **municipalité** *nf* (*ville*) municipality; (*conseil*) town council

munir [myniʀ] *vt*: **~ qch de** to equip sth with; **se ~ de** to arm o.s. with

munitions [mynisjɔ̃] *nfpl* ammunition *sg*

mur [myʀ] *nm* wall; **~ du son** sound barrier

mûr, e [myʀ] *adj* ripe; (*personne*) mature

muraille [myʀɑj] *nf* (high) wall

mural, e, -aux [myʀal, o] *adj* wall *cpd*; (*art*) mural

mûre [myʀ] *nf* blackberry

muret [myʀɛ] *nm* low wall

mûrir [myʀiʀ] *vi* (*fruit, blé*) to ripen; (*abcès*) to come to a head; (*fig: idée, personne*) to mature ♦ *vt* (*projet*) to nurture; (*personne*) to (make) mature

murmure [myʀmyʀ] *nm* murmur; **murmurer** *vi* to murmur

muscade [myskad] *nf* (*aussi:* **noix (de) ~**) nutmeg

muscat [myska] *nm* (*raisins*) muscat grape; (*vin*) muscatel (wine)

muscle [myskl] *nm* muscle; **musclé, e** *adj* muscular; (*fig*) strong-arm

museau, x [myzo] *nm* muzzle; (*CULIN*) brawn

musée [myze] *nm* museum; (*de peinture*) art gallery

museler [myz(ə)le] *vt* to muzzle

musette [myzɛt] *nf* (*sac*) lunchbag

musical, e, -aux [myzikal, o] *adj* musical

music-hall [myzikol] *nm* (*salle*) variety theatre; (*genre*) variety

musicien, ne [myzisjɛ̃, jɛn] *adj* musical ♦ *nm/f* musician

musique [myzik] *nf* music; **~ d'ambiance** background music

musulman, e [myzylmɑ̃, an] *adj, nm* Moslem, Muslim

mutation [mytasjɔ̃] *nf* (*ADMIN*) transfer

muter [myte] *vt* to transfer, move

mutilé, e [mytile] *nm/f* disabled person (*through loss of limbs*)

mutiler [mytile] *vt* to mutilate, maim

mutin, e [mytɛ̃, in] *adj* (*air, ton*) mischievous, impish ♦ *nm/f* (*MIL, NAVIG*) mutineer; **mutinerie** *nf* mutiny

mutisme [mytism] *nm* silence

mutuel, le [mytɥɛl] *adj* mutual; **mutuelle** *nf* voluntary insurance premiums for back-up health cover

myope [mjɔp] *adj* short-sighted

myosotis [mjɔzɔtis] *nm* forget-me-not

myrtille [miʀtij] *nf* bilberry

mystère [mistɛʀ] *nm* mystery; **mystérieux, -euse** *adj* mysterious

mystifier [mistifje] *vt* to fool

mythe [mit] *nm* myth

mythologie [mitɔlɔʒi] *nf* mythology

N, n

n' [n] *adv voir* **ne**

nacre [nakʀ] *nf* mother of pearl

nage [naʒ] *nf* swimming; (*manière*) style of swimming, stroke; **traverser/s'éloigner à la ~** to swim across/away; **en ~** bathed in sweat; **nageoire** *nf* fin; **nager** *vi* to swim; **nageur, -euse** *nm/f* swimmer

naguère [nagɛʀ] *adv* formerly

naïf, -ïve [naif, naiv] *adj* naïve

nain, e [nɛ̃, nɛn] *nm/f* dwarf

naissance [nesɑ̃s] *nf* birth; **donner ~ à** to give birth to; (*fig*) to give rise to

naître [nɛtʀ] *vi* to be born; (*fig*): **~ de** to arise from, be born out of; **il est né en 1960** he was born in 1960; **faire ~** (*fig*) to give rise to, arouse

naïve [naiv] *adj voir* **naïf**

naïveté [naivte] *nf* naïvety

nana [nana] (*fam*) *nf* (*fille*) chick, bird (*BRIT*)

nantir [nɑ̃tiʀ] *vt*: **~ qn de** to provide sb with; **les nantis** (*péj*) the well-to-do

nappe [nap] *nf* tablecloth; (*de pétrole, gaz*) layer; **~ phréatique** ground water; **napperon** *nm* table-mat

naquit *etc* [naki] *vb voir* **naître**

narcodollars [naʀkodɔlaʀ] *nmpl* drug money *sg*

narguer [naʀge] ♦ *vt* to taunt

narine [naʀin] *nf* nostril

narquois, e [naʀkwa, waz] *adj* mocking

natal, e [natal] *adj* native; **natalité** *nf* birth rate

natation [natasjɔ̃] *nf* swimming

natif, -ive [natif, iv] *adj* native

nation [nasjɔ̃] *nf* nation; **national, e, -aux** *adj* national; **(route) nationale** ≃ A road (*BRIT*), ≃ state highway (*US*); **nationaliser** *vt* to nationalize; **nationalisme** *nm* nationalism; **nationalité** *nf* nationality

natte [nat] *nf* (*cheveux*) plait; (*tapis*) mat

naturaliser [natyʀalize] *vt* to naturalize

nature [natyʀ] *nf* nature ♦ *adj, adv* (*CULIN*) plain, without seasoning or sweetening; (*café, thé*) black, without sugar; (*yaourt*) natural; **payer en ~** to pay in kind; **~ morte** still-life; **naturel, le** *adj* (*gén, aussi enfant*) natural ♦ *nm* (*absence d'affectation*) naturalness; (*caractère*) disposition, nature; **naturellement** *adv* naturally; (*bien sûr*) of course

naufrage [nofʀaʒ] *nm* (ship)wreck; **faire ~** to be shipwrecked

nauséabond, e [nozeabɔ̃, ɔ̃d] *adj* foul

nausée [noze] *nf* nausea

nautique [notik] *adj* nautical, water *cpd*; **sports ~s** water sports

naval, e [naval] *adj* naval; (*industrie*) shipbuilding

navet [navɛ] *nm* turnip; (*péj: film*) rubbishy film

navette [navɛt] *nf* shuttle; **faire la ~ (entre)** to go to and fro *ou* shuttle (between)

navigateur [navigatœʀ, tʀis] *nm* (*NAVIG*) seafarer; (*INFORM*) browser

navigation [navigasjɔ̃] *nf* navigation, sailing

naviguer [navige] *vi* to navigate, sail

navire [naviʀ] *nm* ship

navrer [navʀe] *vt* to upset, distress; **je suis navré** I'm so sorry

ne, n' [n(ə)] *adv voir* **pas**; **plus**; **jamais** *etc*; *(sans valeur négative: non traduit)*: **c'est plus loin que je ~ le croyais** it's further than I thought

né, e [ne] *pp (voir naître)*: **~ en 1960** born in 1960; **~e Scott** née Scott

néanmoins [neɑ̃mwɛ̃] *adv* nevertheless

néant [neɑ̃] *nm* nothingness; **réduire à ~** to bring to nought; *(espoir)* to dash

nécessaire [nesesɛʀ] *adj* necessary ♦ *nm* necessary; *(sac)* kit; **je vais faire le ~** I'll see to it; **~ de couture** sewing kit; **nécessité** *nf* necessity; **nécessiter** *vt* to require

nécrologique [nekʀɔlɔʒik] *adj*: **rubrique ~** obituary column

nectar [nɛktaʀ] *nm* nectar

néerlandais, e [neɛʀlɑ̃dɛ, ɛz] *adj* Dutch

nef [nɛf] *nf (d'église)* nave

néfaste [nefast] *adj (nuisible)* harmful; *(funeste)* ill-fated

négatif, -ive [negatif, iv] *adj* negative ♦ *nm (PHOTO)* negative

négligé, e [negliʒe] *adj (en désordre)* slovenly ♦ *nm (tenue)* negligee

négligeable [negliʒabl] *adj* negligible

négligent, e [negliʒɑ̃, ɑ̃t] *adj* careless, negligent

négliger [negliʒe] *vt (tenue)* to be careless about; *(avis, précautions)* to disregard; *(épouse, jardin)* to neglect; **~ de faire** to fail to do, not bother to do

négoce [negɔs] *nm* trade

négociant [negɔsjɑ̃, jɑ̃t] *nm* merchant

négociation [negɔsjasjɔ̃] *nf* negotiation

négocier [negɔsje] *vi, vt* to negotiate

nègre [nɛgʀ] *(péj) nm (écrivain)* ghost (writer)

neige [nɛʒ] *nf* snow; **neiger** *vi* to snow

nénuphar [nenyfaʀ] *nm* water-lily

néon [neɔ̃] *nm* neon

néo-zélandais, e [neozelɑ̃dɛ, ɛz] *adj* New Zealand *cpd* ♦ *nm/f*: **N~-Z~**, e New Zealander

nerf [nɛʀ] *nm* nerve; **être sur les ~s** to be all keyed up; **allons, du ~!** come on,

buck up!; **nerveux, -euse** *adj* nervous; *(irritable)* touchy, nervy; *(voiture)* nippy, responsive; **nervosité** *nf* excitability, tenseness; *(irritabilité passagère)* irritability

nervure [nɛʀvyʀ] *nf* vein

n'est-ce pas [nɛspa] *adv* isn't it?, won't you? *etc, selon le verbe qui précède*

Net [nɛt] *nm (Internet)*: **le ~** the Net

net, nette [nɛt] *adj (sans équivoque, distinct)* clear; *(évident: amélioration, différence)* marked, distinct; *(propre)* neat, clean, *(COMM: prix, salaire)* net ♦ *adv (refuser)* flatly ♦ *nm*: **mettre au ~** to copy out; **s'arrêter ~** to stop dead; **nettement** *adv* clearly, distinctly; *(incontestablement)* decidedly, distinctly; **netteté** *nf* clearness

nettoyage [netwajaʒ] *nm* cleaning; **~ à sec** dry cleaning

nettoyer [netwaje] *vt* to clean

neuf¹ [nœf] *num* nine

neuf², neuve [nœf, nœv] *adj* new ♦ *nm*: **remettre à ~** to do up (as good as new), refurbish; **quoi de ~?** what's new?

neutre [nøtʀ] *adj* neutral; *(LING)* neuter

neuve [nœv] *adj voir* **neuf²**

neuvième [nœvjɛm] *num* ninth

neveu, x [n(ə)vø] *nm* nephew

névrosé, e [nevʀoze] *adj, nm/f* neurotic

nez [ne] *nm* nose; **~ à ~ avec** face to face with; **avoir du ~** to have flair

ni [ni] *conj*: **~ ... ~** neither ... nor; **je n'aime ~ les lentilles ~ les épinards** I like neither lentils nor spinach; **il n'a dit ~ oui ~ non** he didn't say either yes or no; **elles ne sont venues ~ l'une ~ l'autre** neither of them came

niais, e [njɛ, njɛz] *adj* silly, thick

niche [niʃ] *nf (du chien)* kennel; *(de mur)* recess, niche; **nicher** *vi* to nest

nid [ni] *nm* nest; **~ de poule** pothole

nièce [njɛs] *nf* niece

nier [nje] *vt* to deny

nigaud, e [nigo, od] *nm/f* booby, fool

Nil [nil] *nm*: **le ~** the Nile

n'importe [nɛ̃pɔʀt] *adv*: **~ qui/quoi/o~** anybody/anything/anywhere; **~ quan**

any time; ~ **quel/quelle** any; ~ **lequel/laquelle** any (one); ~ **comment** (*sans soin*) carelessly

niveau, x [nivo] *nm* level; (*des élèves, études*) standard; ~ **de vie** standard of living

niveler [niv(ə)le] *vt* to level

NN *abr* (= *nouvelle norme*) *revised standard of hotel classification*

noble [nɔbl] *adj* noble; **noblesse** *nf* nobility; (*d'une action etc*) nobleness

noce [nɔs] *nf* wedding; (*gens*) wedding party (*ou* guests *pl*); **faire la** ~ (*fam*) to go on a binge

nocif, -ive [nɔsif, iv] *adj* harmful, noxious

nocturne [nɔktyʀn] *adj* nocturnal ♦ *nf* late-night opening

Noël [nɔɛl] *nm* Christmas

nœud [nø] *nm* knot; (*ruban*) bow; ~ **papillon** bow tie

noir, e [nwaʀ] *adj* black; (*obscur, sombre*) dark ♦ *nm/f* black man/woman ♦ *nm*: **dans le** ~ in the dark; **travail au** ~ moonlighting; **travailler au** ~ to work on the side; **noircir** *vt, vi* to blacken; **noire** *nf* (*MUS*) crotchet (*BRIT*), quarter note (*US*)

noisette [nwazɛt] *nf* hazelnut

noix [nwa] *nf* walnut; (*CULIN*): **une** ~ **de beurre** a knob of butter; ~ **de cajou** cashew nut; ~ **de coco** coconut; **à la** ~ (*fam*) worthless

nom [nɔ̃] *nm* name; (*LING*) noun; ~ **de famille** surname; ~ **de jeune fille** maiden name; ~ **déposé** trade name; ~ **propre** proper noun

nomade [nɔmad] *nm/f* nomad

nombre [nɔ̃bʀ] *nm* number; **venir en** ~ to come in large numbers; **depuis** ~ **d'années** for many years; **au** ~ **de mes amis** among my friends; **nombreux, -euse** *adj* many, numerous; (*avec nom sg: foule etc*) large; **peu nombreux** few

nombril [nɔ̃bʀi(l)] *nm* navel

nommer [nɔme] *vt* to name; (*élire*) to appoint, nominate; **se** ~: **il se nomme Pascal** his name's Pascal, he's called Pascal

non [nɔ̃] *adv* (*réponse*) no; (*avec loin, sans, seulement*) not; ~ **(pas) que** not that; **moi** ~ **plus** neither do I, I don't either; **c'est bon** ~? (*exprimant le doute*) it's good, isn't it?

non-alcoolisé, e [nɔ̃alkɔlize] *adj* non-alcoholic

nonante [nɔnɑ̃t] (*BELGIQUE, SUISSE*) *num* ninety

non-fumeur [nɔ̃fymœʀ, øz] *nm* non-smoker

non-sens [nɔ̃sɑ̃s] *nm* absurdity

nonchalant, e [nɔ̃ʃalɑ̃, ɑ̃t] *adj* nonchalant

nord [nɔʀ] *nm* North ♦ *adj* northern; north; **au** ~ (*situation*) in the north; (*direction*) to the north; **au** ~ **de** (to the) north of; **nord-est** *nm* North-East; **nord-ouest** *nm* North-West

normal, e, -aux [nɔʀmal, o] *adj* normal; **c'est tout à fait** ~ it's perfectly natural; **vous trouvez ça** ~? does it seem right to you?; **normale** *nf*: **la normale** the norm, the average; **normalement** *adv* (*en général*) normally

normand, e [nɔʀmɑ̃, ɑ̃d] *adj* of Normandy

Normandie [nɔʀmɑ̃di] *nf* Normandy

norme [nɔʀm] *nf* norm; (*TECH*) standard

Norvège [nɔʀvɛʒ] *nf* Norway; **norvégien, ne** *adj* Norwegian ♦ *nm/f*: **Norvégien, ne** Norwegian ♦ *nm* (*LING*) Norwegian

nos [no] *adj voir* **notre**

nostalgie [nɔstalʒi] *nf* nostalgia; **nostalgique** *adj* nostalgic

notable [nɔtabl] *adj* (*fait*) notable, noteworthy; (*marqué*) noticeable, marked ♦ *nm* prominent citizen

notaire [nɔtɛʀ] *nm* solicitor

notamment [nɔtamɑ̃] *adv* in particular, among others

note [nɔt] *nf* (*écrite, MUS*) note; (*SCOL*) mark (*BRIT*), grade; (*facture*) bill; ~ **de service** memorandum

noté, e [nɔte] *adj*: **être bien/mal** ~ (*employé etc*) to have a good/bad record

noter [nɔte] *vt* (*écrire*) to write down; (*re-*

marquer) to note, notice; (*devoir*) to mark, grade

notice [nɔtis] *nf* summary, short article; (*brochure*) leaflet, instruction book

notifier [nɔtifje] *vt*: **~ qch à qn** to notify sb of sth, notify sth to sb

notion [nɔsjɔ̃] *nf* notion, idea

notoire [nɔtwaʀ] *adj* widely known; (*en mal*) notorious

notre [nɔtʀ] (*pl* **nos**) *adj* our

nôtre [notʀ] *pron*: **le ~, la ~, les ~s** ours ♦ *adj* ours; **les ~s** ours; (*alliés etc*) our own people; **soyez des ~s** join us

nouer [nwe] *vt* to tie, knot; (*fig: alliance etc*) to strike up

noueux, -euse [nwø, øz] *adj* gnarled

nouilles [nuj] *nfpl* noodles

nourrice [nuʀis] *nf* (*gardienne*) child-minder

nourrir [nuʀiʀ] *vt* to feed; (*fig: espoir*) to harbour, nurse; **se ~** to eat; **se ~ de** to feed (o.s.) on; **nourrissant, e** *adj* nourishing, nutritious; **nourrisson** *nm* (un-weaned) infant; **nourriture** *nf* food

nous [nu] *pron* (*sujet*) we; (*objet*) us; **nous-mêmes** *pron* ourselves

nouveau (nouvel), -elle, x [nuvo, nuvɛl] *adj* new ♦ *nm*: **y a-t-il du ~?** is there anything new on this? ♦ *nm/f* new pupil (*ou* employee); **de ~, à ~** again; **~ venu, nouvelle venue** newcomer; **~x mariés** newly-weds; **nouveau-né, e** *nm/f* newborn baby; **nouveauté** *nf* novelty; (*objet*) new thing *ou* article

nouvel [nuvɛl] *adj voir* **nouveau; N~ An** New Year

nouvelle [nuvɛl] *adj voir* **nouveau** ♦ *nf* (piece of) news *sg*; (*LITTÉRATURE*) short story; **les ~s** the news; **je suis sans ~s de lui** I haven't heard from him; **Nouvelle-Calédonie** *nf* New Caledonia; **nouvellement** *adv* recently, newly; **Nouvelle-Zélande** *nf* New Zealand

novembre [nɔvɑ̃bʀ] *nm* November

novice [nɔvis] *adj* inexperienced

noyade [nwajad] *nf* drowning *no pl*

noyau, x [nwajo] *nm* (*de fruit*) stone; (*BIO, PHYSIQUE*) nucleus; (*fig: centre*) core; **noyauter** *vt* (*POL*) to infiltrate

noyer [nwaje] *nm* walnut (tree); (*bois*) wal-nut ♦ *vt* to drown; (*moteur*) to flood; **se ~** *vi* to be drowned, drown; (*suicide*) to drown o.s.

nu, e [ny] *adj* naked; (*membres*) naked, bare; (*pieds, mains, chambre, fil électrique*) bare ♦ *nm* (*ART*) nude; **tout ~** stark naked; **se mettre ~** to strip; **mettre à ~** to bare

nuage [nɥaʒ] *nm* cloud; **nuageux, -euse** *adj* cloudy

nuance [nɥɑ̃s] *nf* (*de couleur, sens*) shade; **il y a une ~ (entre)** there's a slight differ-ence (between); **nuancer** *vt* (*opinion*) to bring some reservations *ou* qualifications to

nucléaire [nykleɛʀ] *adj* nuclear ♦ *nm*: **le ~** nuclear energy

nudiste [nydist] *nm/f* nudist

nuée [nɥe] *nf*: **une ~ de** a cloud *ou* host *ou* swarm of

nues [ny] *nfpl*: **tomber des ~** to be taken aback; **porter qn aux ~** to praise sb to the skies

nuire [nɥiʀ] *vi* to be harmful; **~ à** to harm, do damage to; **nuisible** *adj* harmful; **ani-mal nuisible** pest

nuit [nɥi] *nf* night; **il fait ~** it's dark; **cette ~** (*hier*) last night; (*aujourd'hui*) tonight; **~ blanche** sleepless night

nul, nulle [nyl] *adj* (*aucun*) no; (*minime*) nil, non-existent; (*non valable*) null; (*péj*) useless, hopeless ♦ *pron* none, no one; **match** *ou* **résultat ~** draw; **~le part** no-where; **nullement** *adv* by no means; **nullité** *nf* (*personne*) nonentity

numérique [nymeʀik] *adj* numerical; (*affichage*) digital

numéro [nymeʀo] *nm* number; (*spectacle*) act, turn; (*PRESSE*) issue, number; **~ de té-léphone** (tele)phone number; **~ vert** ≈ freefone ℝ number (*BRIT*), ≈ toll-free number (*US*); **numéroter** *vt* to number

u-pieds [nypje] *adj inv, adv* barefoot

que [nyk] *nf* nape of the neck

u-tête [nytɛt] *adj inv, adv* bareheaded

utritif, -ive [nytʀitif, iv] *adj* (*besoins, va-*
leur) nutritional; (*nourrissant*) nutritious

ʼlon [nilɔ̃] *nm* nylon

O, o

sis [ɔazis] *nf* oasis

éir [ɔbeiʀ] *vi* to obey; **~ à** to obey;
obéissance *nf* obedience; **obéissant,**
e *adj* obedient

èse [ɔbɛz] *adj* obese; **obésité** *nf*
obesity

jecter [ɔbʒɛkte] *vt* (*prétexter*) to plead,
out forward as an excuse; **~ (à qn) que**
o object (to sb) that; **objecteur** *nm*: **ob-**
ecteur de conscience conscientious ob-
ector

jectif, -ive [ɔbʒɛktif, iv] *adj* objective
♦ *nm* objective; (*PHOTO*) lens *sg*, objective;
objectivité *nf* objectivity

jection [ɔbʒɛksjɔ̃] *nf* objection

jet [ɔbʒɛ] *nm* object; (*d'une discussion, re-*
cherche) subject; **être ou faire l'~ de** (*dis-*
cussion) to be the subject of; (*soins*) to be
given *ou* shown; **sans ~** purposeless;
groundless; **~ d'art** objet d'art; **~s trou-**
és lost property *sg* (*BRIT*), lost-and-found
sg (*US*); **~s de valeur** valuables

ligation [ɔbligasjɔ̃] *nf* obligation;
(*COMM*) bond, debenture; **obligatoire**
adj compulsory, obligatory; **obligatoire-**
ment *adv* necessarily; (*fam: sans aucun*
doute) inevitably

ligé, e [ɔbliʒe] *adj* (*redevable*): **être très**
~ à qn to be most obliged to sb

ligeance [ɔbliʒɑ̃s] *nf*: **avoir l'~ de ...**
o be kind *ou* good enough to ...; **obli-**
geant, e *adj* (*personne*) obliging, kind

liger [ɔbliʒe] *vt* (*contraindre*): **~ qn à fai-**
e to force *ou* oblige sb to do; **je suis**
ien obligé I have to

lique [ɔblik] *adj* oblique; **en ~** diagon-

ally; **obliquer** *vi*: **obliquer vers** to turn
off towards

oblitérer [ɔblitere] *vt* (*timbre-poste*) to cancel

obnubiler [ɔbnybile] *vt* to obsess

obscène [ɔpsɛn] *adj* obscene

obscur, e [ɔpskyʀ] *adj* dark; (*méconnu*)
obscure; **obscurcir** *vt* to darken; (*fig*) to
obscure; **s'obscurcir** *vi* to grow dark;
obscurité *nf* darkness; **dans l'obscurité**
in the dark, in darkness

obsédé, e [ɔpsede] *nm/f*: **un ~ (sexuel)** a
sex maniac

obséder [ɔpsede] *vt* to obsess, haunt

obsèques [ɔpsɛk] *nfpl* funeral *sg*

observateur, -trice [ɔpsɛʀvatœʀ, tʀis]
adj observant, perceptive ♦ *nm/f* observer

observation [ɔpsɛʀvasjɔ̃] *nf* observation;
(*d'un règlement etc*) observance; (*reproche*)
reproof; **être en ~** (*MÉD*) to be under observation

observatoire [ɔpsɛʀvatwaʀ] *nm* observatory

observer [ɔpsɛʀve] *vt* (*regarder*) to observe, watch; (*scientifiquement; aussi*
règlement etc) to observe; (*surveiller*) to
watch; (*remarquer*) to observe, notice; **fai-**
re ~ qch à qn (*dire*) to point out sth to
sb

obsession [ɔpsesjɔ̃] *nf* obsession

obstacle [ɔpstakl] *nm* obstacle;
(*ÉQUITATION*) jump, hurdle; **faire ~ à** (*pro-*
jet) to hinder, put obstacles in the path of

obstiné, e [ɔpstine] *adj* obstinate

obstiner [ɔpstine]: **s'~** *vi* to insist, dig
one's heels in; **s'~ à faire** to persist (ob-
stinately) in doing

obstruer [ɔpstʀye] *vt* to block, obstruct

obtenir [ɔptəniʀ] *vt* to obtain, get; (*résul-*
tat) to achieve, obtain; **~ de pouvoir fai-**
re to obtain permission to do

obturateur [ɔptyʀatœʀ, tʀis] *nm* (*PHOTO*)
shutter

obus [ɔby] *nm* shell

occasion [ɔkazjɔ̃] *nf* (*aubaine, possibilité*)
opportunity; (*circonstance*) occasion;

(*COMM: article non neuf*) secondhand buy; (: *acquisition avantageuse*) bargain; **à plusieurs ~s** on several occasions; **à l'~** sometimes, on occasions; **d'~** secondhand; **occasionnel, le** *adj* (*non régulier*) occasional; **occasionnellement** *adv* occasionally, from time to time

occasionner [ɔkazjɔne] *vt* to cause

occident [ɔksidɑ̃] *nm*: **l'O~** the West; **occidental, e, -aux** *adj* western; (*POL*) Western ♦ *nm/f* Westerner

occupation [ɔkypasjɔ̃] *nf* occupation

occupé, e [ɔkype] *adj* (*personne*) busy; (*place*) taken; (*toilettes*) engaged; (*ligne*) engaged(*BRIT*), busy(*US*); (*MIL, POL*) occupied

occuper [ɔkype] *vt* to occupy; (*poste*) to hold; **s'~ de** (*être responsable de*) to be in charge of; (*se charger de*: *affaire*) to take charge of, deal with; (: *clients etc*) to attend to; **s'~ (à qch)** to occupy o.s. *ou* keep o.s. busy (with sth)

occurrence [ɔkyrɑ̃s] *nf*: **en l'~** in this case

océan [ɔseɑ̃] *nm* ocean

octante [ɔktɑ̃t] *adj* (*regional*) eighty

octet [ɔktɛ] *nm* byte

octobre [ɔktɔbr] *nm* October

octroyer [ɔktrwaje]: **s'~** *vt* (*vacances etc*) to treat o.s. to

oculiste [ɔkylist] *nm/f* eye specialist

odeur [ɔdœr] *nf* smell

odieux, -euse [ɔdjø, jøz] *adj* hateful

odorant, e [ɔdɔrɑ̃, ɑ̃t] *adj* fragrant

odorat [ɔdɔra] *nm* (sense of) smell

œil [œj] (*pl* **yeux**) *nm* eye; **à l'~** (*fam*) for free; **à l'~ nu** with the naked eye; **tenir qn à l'~** to keep an eye *ou* a watch on sb; **avoir l'~ à** to keep an eye on; **fermer les yeux (sur)** (*fig*) to turn a blind eye (to); **voir qch d'un bon/mauvais ~** to look on sth favourably/unfavourably

œillères [œjɛr] *nfpl* blinkers (*BRIT*), blinders (*US*)

œillet [œjɛ] *nm* (*BOT*) carnation

œuf [œf, *pl* ø] *nm* egg; **~ à la coque/sur le plat/dur** boiled/fried/hard-boiled egg;

~ de Pâques Easter egg; **~s brouill..** scrambled eggs

œuvre [œvr] *nf* (*tâche*) task, undertakin.. (*livre, tableau etc*) work; (*ensemble de* production artistique*) works *pl* ♦ *n..* (*CONSTR*): **le gros ~** the shell; **~ (de bie..** faisance)** charity; **mettre en ~** (*moye..* to make use of; **~ d'art** work of art

offense [ɔfɑ̃s] *nf* insult; **offenser** *vt* to.. fend, hurt

offert, e [ɔfɛr, ɛrt] *pp de* **offrir**

office [ɔfis] *nm* (*agence*) bureau, agenc.. (*REL*) service ♦ *nm ou nf* (*pièce*) pant.. **faire ~ de** to act as; **d'~** automatically; **du tourisme** tourist bureau

officiel, le [ɔfisjɛl] *adj, nm/f* official

officier [ɔfisje] *nm* officer

officieux, -euse [ɔfisjø, jøz] *adj* unoffic..

offrande [ɔfrɑ̃d] *nf* offering

offre [ɔfr] *nf* offer; (*aux enchères*) bid; (*A.. MIN*: *soumission*) tender; (*ÉCON*): **l'~ et.. demande** supply and demand; "~ d'emploi" "situations vacant"; **~ d'e.. ploi** job advertised

offrir [ɔfrir] *vt*: **~ (à qn)** to offer (to s.. (*faire cadeau de*) to give (to sb) **s'~** (*vacances, voiture*) to treat o.s. to; **~ (à.. de faire qch** to offer to do sth (for s.. **~ à boire à qn** (*chez soi*) to offer sb.. drink

offusquer [ɔfyske] *vt* to offend

OGM *sigle m* (= *organisme génétiquem..* modifié*) GMO

oie [wa] *nf* (*ZOOL*) goose

oignon [ɔɲɔ̃] *nm* onion; (*de tulipe etc*) bu..

oiseau, x [wazo] *nm* bird; **~ de proie** b.. of prey

oisif, -ive [wazif, iv] *adj* idle

oléoduc [ɔleɔdyk] *nm* (oil) pipeline

olive [ɔliv] *nf* (*BOT*) olive; **olivier** *nm* ol.. (tree)

OLP *sigle f* (= *Organisation de libération* la Palestine*) PLO

olympique [ɔlɛ̃pik] *adj* Olympic

ombragé, e [ɔbraʒe] *adj* shaded, sha.. **ombrageux, -euse** *adj* (*person..*

touchy, easily offended

mbre [5bʀ] *nf* (*espace non ensoleillé*) shade; (~ *portée, tache*) shadow; **à l'~** in the shade; **dans l'~** (*fig*) in the dark; **~ à paupières** eyeshadow; **ombrelle** *nf* parasol, sunshade

melette [ɔmlɛt] *nf* omelette; **~ norvé-gienne** baked Alaska

mettre [ɔmɛtʀ] *vt* to omit, leave out

mnibus [ɔmnibys] *nm* slow *ou* stopping train

moplate [ɔmɔplat] *nf* shoulder blade

MOT-CLÉ

n [5] *pron* **1** (*indéterminé*) you, one; **on peut le faire ainsi** you *ou* one can do it like this, it can be done like this

2 (*quelqu'un*): **on les a attaqués** they were attacked; **on vous demande au té-léphone** there's a phone call for you, you're wanted on the phone

3 (*nous*) we; **on va y aller demain** we're going tomorrow

4 (*les gens*) they; **autrefois, on croyait ...** they used to believe ...

5: on ne peut plus

♦ *adv*: **on ne peut plus stupide** as stupid as can be

---

ncle [5kl] *nm* uncle

nctueux, -euse [5ktɥø, øz] *adj* creamy, smooth

nde [5d] *nf* wave; **sur les ~s** on the radio; **sur ~s courtes** on short wave *sg*; **moyennes/longues ~s** medium/long wave *sg*

ndée [5de] *nf* shower

n-dit [5di] *nm inv* rumour

nduler [5dyle] *vi* to undulate; (*cheveux*) to wave

néreux, -euse [ɔneʀø, øz] *adj* costly

ngle [5gl] *nm* nail

nt [5] *vb voir* **avoir**

NU *sigle f* (= *Organisation des Nations Unies*) UN

nze ['5z] *num* eleven; **onzième** *num*

eleventh

OPA *sigle f* = **offre publique d'achat**

opaque [ɔpak] *adj* opaque

opéra [ɔpeʀa] *nm* opera; (*édifice*) opera house

opérateur, -trice [ɔpeʀatœʀ, tʀis] *nm/f* operator; **~ (de prise de vues)** camera-man

opération [ɔpeʀasj5] *nf* operation; (*COMM*) dealing

opératoire [ɔpeʀatwaʀ] *adj* (*choc etc*) post-operative

opérer [ɔpeʀe] *vt* (*personne*) to operate on; (*faire, exécuter*) to carry out, make ♦ *vi* (*re-mède: faire effet*) to act, work; (*MÉD*) to operate; **s'~** *vi* (*avoir lieu*) to occur, take place; **se faire ~** to have an operation

opérette [ɔpeʀet] *nf* operetta, light opera

ophtalmologiste [ɔftalmɔlɔʒist] *nm/f* ophthalmologist, optician

opiner [ɔpine] *vi*: **~ de la tête** to nod as-sent

opinion [ɔpinj5] *nf* opinion; **l'~ (publique)** public opinion

opportun, e [ɔpɔʀtœ̃, yn] *adj* timely, op-portune; **opportuniste** *nm/f* opportunist

opposant, e [ɔpozɑ̃, ɑ̃t] *nm/f* opponent

opposé, e [ɔpoze] *adj* (*direction*) opposite; (*faction*) opposing; (*opinions, intérêts*) con-flicting; (*contre*): **~ à** opposed to, against ♦ *nm*: **l'~** the other *ou* opposite side (*ou* direction); (*contraire*) the opposite; **à l'~** (*fig*) on the other hand; **à l'~ de** (*fig*) con-trary to, unlike

opposer [ɔpoze] *vt* (*personnes, équipes*) to oppose; (*couleurs*) to contrast; **s'~** *vi* (*équipes*) to confront each other; (*opinions*) to conflict; (*couleurs, styles*) to contrast; **s'~ à** (*interdire*) to oppose; **~ qch à** (*comme obstacle, défense*) to set sth against; (*comme objection*) to put sth for-ward against

opposition [ɔpozisj5] *nf* opposition; **par ~ à** as opposed to, in contrast with; **entrer en ~ avec** to come into conflict with; **fai-re ~ à un chèque** to stop a cheque

oppressant, e [ɔpresɑ̃, ɑ̃t] *adj* oppressive
oppresser [ɔprese] *vt* to oppress; **oppression** [ɔpresjɔ̃] *nm* oppression
opprimer [ɔprime] *vt* to oppress
opter [ɔpte] *vi*: ~ **pour** to opt for
opticien, ne [ɔptisjɛ̃, jɛn] *nm/f* optician
optimisme [ɔptimism] *nm* optimism; **optimiste** *nm/f* optimist ♦ *adj* optimistic
option [ɔpsjɔ̃] *nf* option; **matière à ~** (*SCOL*) optional subject
optique [ɔptik] *adj* (*nerf*) optic; (*verres*) optical ♦ *nf* (*fig: manière de voir*) perspective
opulent, e [ɔpylɑ̃, ɑ̃t] *adj* wealthy, opulent; (*formes, poitrine*) ample, generous
or [ɔR] *nm* gold ♦ *conj* now, but; **en ~** (*objet*) gold *cpd*; **une affaire en ~** a real bargain; **il croyait gagner ~ il a perdu** he was sure he would win and yet he lost
orage [ɔRaʒ] *nm* (thunder)storm; **orageux, -euse** *adj* stormy
oral, e, -aux [ɔRal, o] *adj, nm* oral; **par voie ~e** (*MÉD*) orally
orange [ɔRɑ̃ʒ] *nf* orange ♦ *adj inv* orange; **orangeade** *nf* orangeade; **orangé, e** *adj* orangey, orange-coloured; **oranger** *nm* orange tree
orateur [ɔRatœR, tRis] *nm* speaker
orbite [ɔRbit] *nf* (*ANAT*) (eye-)socket; (*PHYSIQUE*) orbit
orchestre [ɔRkɛstR] *nm* orchestra; (*de jazz*) band; (*places*) stalls *pl* (*BRIT*), orchestra (*US*); **orchestrer** *vt* to orchestrate
orchidée [ɔRkide] *nf* orchid
ordinaire [ɔRdinɛR] *adj* ordinary; (*qualité*) standard; (*péj: commun*) common ♦ *nm* ordinary; (*menus*) everyday fare ♦ *nf* (*essence*) ≈ two-star (petrol) (*BRIT*), ≈ regular gas (*US*); **d'~** usually, normally; **comme à l'~** as usual
ordinateur [ɔRdinatœR] *nm* computer
ordonnance [ɔRdɔnɑ̃s] *nf* (*MÉD*) prescription; (*MIL*) orderly, batman (*BRIT*)
ordonné, e [ɔRdɔne] *adj* tidy, orderly
ordonner [ɔRdɔne] *vt* (*agencer*) to organize, arrange; (*donner un ordre*): ~ **à qn de faire** to order sb to do; (*REL*) to ordain;

(*MÉD*) to prescribe
ordre [ɔRdR] *nm* order; (*propreté et soin*) ◄ derliness, tidiness; (*nature*): **d'~ pratiqu** of a practical nature; **~s** *nmpl* (*REL*) h◄ orders; **mettre en ~** to tidy (up), put order; **à l'~ de qn** payable to sb; **êt aux ~s de qn/sous les ~s de qn** to at sb's disposal/under sb's command; **ju qu'à nouvel ~** until further notice; ◄ **premier ~** first-rate; **~ du jour** (*d'une r◄ nion*) agenda; **à l'~ du jour** (*fig*) topical
ordure [ɔRdyR] *nf* filth *no pl*; **~s** *nfpl* (*◄ layures, déchets*) rubbish *sg*, refuse *sg*; **ménagères** household refuse
oreille [ɔRɛj] *nf* ear; **avoir de l'~** to ha a good ear (for music)
oreiller [ɔReje] *nm* pillow
oreillons [ɔRɛjɔ̃] *nmpl* mumps *sg*
ores [ɔR]: **d'~ et déjà** *adv* already
orfèvrerie [ɔRfɛvRəRi] *nf* goldsmith's (silversmith's) trade; (*ouvrage*) gold (*ou* ◄ ver) plate
organe [ɔRgan] *nm* organ; (*porte-par◄* representative, mouthpiece
organigramme [ɔRganigRam] *nm* (*table hiérarchique*) organization chart; (*schém* flow chart
organique [ɔRganik] *adj* organic
organisateur, -trice [ɔRganizatœR, tⁿ *nm/f* organizer
organisation [ɔRganizasjɔ̃] *nf* organizati
organiser [ɔRganize] *vt* to organi◄ (*mettre sur pied: service etc*) to set up; **s** to get organized
organisme [ɔRganism] *nm* (*BIO*) organis (*corps, ADMIN*) body
organiste [ɔRganist] *nm/f* organist
orgasme [ɔRgasm] *nm* orgasm, climax
orge [ɔRʒ] *nf* barley
orgue [ɔRg] *nm* organ; **~s** *nfpl* (*MUS*) ◄ gan *sg*
orgueil [ɔRgœj] *nm* pride; **orgueille◄ -euse** *adj* proud
Orient [ɔRjɑ̃] *nm*: **l'~** the East, the Orie◄ **oriental, e, -aux** *adj* (*langue, produit*) iental; (*frontière*) eastern

rientation [ɔʀjɑ̃tasjɔ̃] *nf* (*de recherches*) orientation; (*d'une maison etc*) aspect; (*d'un journal*) leanings *pl*; **avoir le sens de l'~** to have a (good) sense of direction; ~ **professionnelle** careers advisory service

rienté, e [ɔʀjɑ̃te] *adj* (*fig: article, journal*) slanted; **bien/mal ~** (*appartement etc*) well/ badly positioned; ~ **au sud** facing south, with a southern aspect

rienter [ɔʀjɑ̃te] *vt* (*tourner: antenne*) to direct, turn; (*personne, recherches*) to direct; (*fig: élève*) to orientate; **s'~** (*se repérer*) to find one's bearings; **s'~ vers** (*fig*) to turn towards

rigan [ɔʀigɑ̃] *nm* oregano

riginaire [ɔʀiʒinɛʀ] *adj*: **être ~ de** to be a native of

riginal, e, -aux [ɔʀiʒinal, o] *adj* original; (*bizarre*) eccentric ♦ *nm/f* eccentric ♦ *nm* (*document etc, ART*) original

rigine [ɔʀiʒin] *nf* origin; **dès l'~** at *ou* from the outset; **à l'~** originally; **originel, le** *adj* original

rme [ɔʀm] *nm* elm

rnement [ɔʀnəmɑ̃] *nm* ornament

rner [ɔʀne] *vt* to decorate, adorn

rnière [ɔʀnjɛʀ] *nf* rut

rphelin, e [ɔʀfəlɛ̃, in] *adj* orphan(ed) ♦ *nm/f* orphan; ~ **de père/mère** fatherless/motherless; **orphelinat** *nm* orphanage

rteil [ɔʀtɛj] *nm* toe; **gros ~** big toe

rthographe [ɔʀtɔgʀaf] *nf* spelling

rtie [ɔʀti] *nf* (stinging) nettle

s [ɔs] *nm* bone; **tomber sur un ~** (*fam*) to hit a snag

sciller [ɔsile] *vi* (*au vent etc*) to rock; (*fig*): ~ **entre** to waver *ou* fluctuate between

sé, e [oze] *adj* daring, bold

seille [ozɛj] *nf* sorrel

ser [oze] *vi, vt* to dare; ~ **faire** to dare (to) do

sier [ozje] *nm* willow; **d'~, en ~** wicker(work)

sature [ɔsatyʀ] *nf* (*ANAT*) frame, skeletal structure; (*fig*) framework

osseux, -euse [ɔsø, øz] *adj* bony; (*tissu, maladie, greffe*) bone *cpd*

ostensible [ɔstɑ̃sibl] *adj* conspicuous

otage [ɔtaʒ] *nm* hostage; **prendre qn comme ~** to take sb hostage

OTAN *sigle f* (= *Organisation du traité de l'Atlantique Nord*) NATO

otarie [ɔtaʀi] *nf* sea-lion

ôter [ote] *vt* to remove; (*soustraire*) to take away; ~ **qch à qn** to take sth (away) from sb; ~ **qch de** to remove sth from

otite [ɔtit] *nf* ear infection

ou [u] *conj* or; ~ ... ~ either ... or; ~ **bien** or (else)

MOT-CLÉ
---

où [u] *pron relatif* **1** (*position, situation*) where, that (*souvent omis*); **la chambre où il était** the room (that) he was in, the room where he was; **la ville où je l'ai rencontré** the town where I met him; **la pièce d'où il est sorti** the room he came out of; **le village d'où je viens** the village I come from; **les villes par où il est passé** the towns he went through

2 (*temps, état*) that (*souvent omis*); **le jour où il est parti** the day (that) he left; **au prix où c'est** at the price it is

♦ *adv* **1** (*interrogation*) where; **où est-il/ va-t-il?** where is he/is he going?; **par où?** which way?; **d'où vient que ...?** how come ...?

2 (*position*) where; **je sais où il est** I know where he is; **où que l'on aille** wherever you go

---

ouate ['wat] *nf* cotton wool (*BRIT*), cotton (*US*)

oubli [ubli] *nm* (*acte*): **l'~ de** forgetting; (*trou de mémoire*) lapse of memory; (*négligence*) omission, oversight; **tomber dans l'~** to sink into oblivion

oublier [ublije] *vt* to forget; (*laisser quelque part: chapeau etc*) to leave behind; (*ne pas voir: erreurs etc*) to miss

oubliettes [ublijɛt] *nfpl* dungeon *sg*

ouest [wɛst] *nm* west ♦ *adj inv* west; (*région*) western; **à l'~** in the west; (*direction*) (to the) west, westwards; **à l'~ de** (to the) west of

ouf ['uf] *excl* phew!

oui ['wi] *adv* yes

ouï-dire ['widiʀ] : **par ~-~** *adv* by hearsay

ouïe [wi] *nf* hearing; **~s** *nfpl* (*de poisson*) gills

ouille ['uj] *excl* ouch!

ouragan [uʀagɑ̃] *nm* hurricane

ourlet [uʀlɛ] *nm* hem

ours [uʀs] *nm* bear; **~ brun/blanc** brown/polar bear; **~ (en peluche)** teddy (bear)

oursin [uʀsɛ̃] *nm* sea urchin

ourson [uʀsɔ̃] *nm* (bear-)cub

ouste [ust] *excl* hop it!

outil [uti] *nm* tool; **outiller** *vt* to equip

outrage [utʀaʒ] *nm* insult; **~ à la pudeur** indecent conduct *no pl*; **outrager** *vt* to offend gravely

outrance [utʀɑ̃s] : **à ~** *adv* excessively, to excess

outre [utʀ] *prép* besides ♦ *adv* : **passer ~ à** to disregard, take no notice of; **en ~** besides, moreover; **~ mesure** to excess; (*manger, boire*) immoderately; **outre-Atlantique** *adv* across the Atlantic; **outre-Manche** *adv* across the Channel; **outre-mer** *adv* overseas; **outrepasser** *vt* to go beyond, exceed

ouvert, e [uvɛʀ, ɛʀt] *pp de* **ouvrir** ♦ *adj* open; (*robinet, gaz etc*) on; **ouvertement** *adv* openly; **ouverture** *nf* opening; (*MUS*) overture; **ouverture d'esprit** open-mindedness

ouvrable [uvʀabl] *adj* : **jour ~** working day, weekday

ouvrage [uvʀaʒ] *nm* (*tâche, de tricot etc*) work *no pl*; (*texte, livre*) work; **ouvragé, e** *adj* finely embroidered (*ou* worked *ou* carved)

ouvre-boîte(s) [uvʀəbwat] *nm inv* tin (*BRIT*) *ou* can opener

ouvre-bouteille(s) [uvʀəbutɛj] *nm inv* bottle-opener

ouvreuse [uvʀøz] *nf* usherette

ouvrier, -ière [uvʀije, ijɛʀ] *nm/f* worke♦ ♦ *adj* working-class; (*conflit*) industria♦ (*mouvement*) labour *cpd*; **classe ouvrièr♦** working class

ouvrir [uvʀiʀ] *vt* (*gén*) to open; (*brèch♦ passage, MÉD: abcès*) to open up; (*co♦ mencer l'exploitation de, créer*) to open (up♦ (*eau, électricité, chauffage, robinet*) to tur♦ on ♦ *vi* to open; to open up; **s'~** *vi* ♦ open; **s'~ à qn** to open one's heart to s♦ **~ l'appétit à qn** to whet sb's appetite

ovaire [ɔvɛʀ] *nm* ovary

ovale [ɔval] *adj* oval

ovni [ɔvni] *sigle m* (= *objet volant non ide♦ tifié*) UFO

oxyder [ɔkside] : **s'~** *vi* to become ox♦ dized

oxygène [ɔksiʒɛn] *nm* oxygen

oxygéné, e [ɔksiʒene] *adj* : **eau ~e** hydr♦ gen peroxide

oxygéner [ɔksiʒene] : **s'~** (*fam*) *vi* to g♦ some fresh air

ozone [ozon] *nf* ozone; **la couche d'♦** the ozone layer

P, p

pacifique [pasifik] *adj* peaceful ♦ *nm* : **P~, l'océan P~** the Pacific (Ocean)

pacotille [pakɔtij] *nf* cheap junk

pack [pak] *nm* pack

pacte [pakt] *nm* pact, treaty

pagaie [pagɛ] *nf* paddle

pagaille [pagaj] *nf* mess, shambles *sg*

pagayer *vi* to paddle

page [paʒ] *nf* page ♦ *nm* page (boy); **à ~** (*fig*) up-to-date; **~ d'accueil** (*INFOR♦* home page

paiement [pemɑ̃] *nm* payment

païen, ne [pajɛ̃, pajɛn] *adj, nm/f* paga♦ heathen

paillasson [pajasɔ̃] *nm* doormat

paille [pɑj] *nf* straw

aillettes [pɑjet] *nfpl* (*décoratives*) sequins, spangles

ain [pɛ̃] *nm* (*substance*) bread; (*unité*) loaf (of bread); (*morceau*): **~ de savon** *etc* bar of soap *etc*; **~ au chocolat** chocolate-filled pastry; **~ aux raisins** currant bun; **~ bis/complet** brown/wholemeal (*BRIT*) *ou* wholewheat (*US*) bread; **~ d'épice** gingerbread; **~ de mie** sandwich loaf; **~ grillé** toast

air, e [pɛʀ] *adj* (*nombre*) even ♦ *nm* peer; **aller de ~** to go hand in hand *ou* together; **jeune fille au ~** au pair; **paire** *nf* pair

aisible [pezibl] *adj* peaceful, quiet

aître [pɛtʀ] *vi* to graze

aix [pɛ] *nf* peace; **faire/avoir la ~** to make/have peace; **fiche-lui la ~!** (*fam*) leave him alone!

akistan [pakistɑ̃] *nm*: **le ~** Pakistan

alace [palas] *nm* luxury hotel

alais [palɛ] *nm* palace; (*ANAT*) palate

âle [pɑl] *adj* pale; **bleu ~** pale blue

alestine [palɛstin] *nf*: **la ~** Palestine

alet [palɛ] *nm* disc; (*HOCKEY*) puck

aletot [palto] *nm* (thick) cardigan

alette [palɛt] *nf* (*de peintre*) palette; (*produits*) range

âleur [palœʀ] *nf* paleness

alier [palje] *nm* (*d'escalier*) landing; (*fig*) level, plateau; **par ~s** in stages

âlir [paliʀ] *vi* to turn *ou* go pale; (*couleur*) to fade

alissade [palisad] *nf* fence

allier [palje]: **~ à** *vt* to offset, make up for

almarès [palmaʀɛs] *nm* record (of achievements); (*SPORT*) list of winners

alme [palm] *nf* (*de plongeur*) flipper; **palmé, e** *adj* (*pattes*) webbed

almier [palmje] *nm* palm tree; (*gâteau*) heart-shaped biscuit made of flaky pastry

âlot, te [palo, ɔt] *adj* pale, peaky

alourde [paluʀd] *nf* clam

alper [palpe] *vt* to feel, finger

alpitant, e [palpitɑ̃, ɑ̃t] *adj* thrilling

palpiter [palpite] *vi* (*cœur, pouls*) to beat; (: *plus fort*) to pound, throb

paludisme [palydism] *nm* malaria

pamphlet [pɑ̃flɛ] *nm* lampoon, satirical tract

pamplemousse [pɑ̃pləmus] *nm* grapefruit

pan [pɑ̃] *nm* section, piece ♦ *excl* bang!

panache [panaʃ] *nm* plume; (*fig*) spirit, panache

panaché, e [panaʃe] *adj*: **glace ~e** mixed-flavour ice cream ♦ *nm* (*bière*) shandy

pancarte [pɑ̃kaʀt] *nf* sign, notice

pancréas [pɑ̃kʀeas] *nm* pancreas

pané, e [pane] *adj* fried in breadcrumbs

panier [panje] *nm* basket; **mettre au ~** to chuck away; **~ à provisions** shopping basket; **panier-repas** *nm* packed lunch

panique [panik] *nf, adj* panic; **paniquer** *vi* to panic

panne [pan] *nf* breakdown; **être/tomber en ~** to have broken down/break down; **être en ~ d'essence** *ou* **sèche** to have run out of petrol (*BRIT*) *ou* gas (*US*); **~ d'électricité** *ou* **de courant** power *ou* electrical failure

panneau, x [pano] *nm* (*écriteau*) sign, notice; **~ d'affichage** notice board; **~ de signalisation** roadsign

panoplie [panɔpli] *nf* (*jouet*) outfit; (*fig*) array

panorama [panɔrama] *nm* panorama

panse [pɑ̃s] *nf* paunch

pansement [pɑ̃smɑ̃] *nm* dressing, bandage; **~ adhésif** sticking plaster

panser [pɑ̃se] *vt* (*plaie*) to dress, bandage; (*bras*) to put a dressing on, bandage; (*cheval*) to groom

pantalon [pɑ̃talɔ̃] *nm* trousers *pl*, pair of trousers; **~ de ski** ski pants *pl*

panthère [pɑ̃tɛʀ] *nf* panther

pantin [pɑ̃tɛ̃] *nm* puppet

pantois [pɑ̃twa] *adj m*: **rester ~** to be flabbergasted

pantoufle [pɑ̃tufl] *nf* slipper

paon [pɑ̃] *nm* peacock

papa [papa] *nm* dad(dy)

pape [pap] *nm* pope

paperasse [papʀas] (*péj*) *nf* bumf *no pl*, papers *pl*; **paperasserie** (*péj*) *nf* paperwork *no pl*; (*tracasserie*) red tape *no pl*

papeterie [papetʀi] *nf* (*magasin*) stationer's (shop)

papi *nm* (*fam*) granddad

papier [papje] *nm* paper; (*article*) article; **~s** *nmpl* (*aussi*: **~s d'identité**) (identity) papers; **~ à lettres** writing paper, notepaper; **~ carbone** carbon paper; **~ (d')aluminium** aluminium (*BRIT*) *ou* aluminum (*US*) foil, tinfoil; **~ de verre** sandpaper; **~ hygiénique** *ou* **de toilette** toilet paper; **~ journal** newspaper; **~ peint** wallpaper

papillon [papijɔ̃] *nm* butterfly; (*fam: contravention*) (parking) ticket; **~ de nuit** moth

papillote [papijɔt] *nf*: **en ~** cooked in tinfoil

papoter [papɔte] *vi* to chatter

paquebot [pak(ə)bo] *nm* liner

pâquerette [pakʀɛt] *nf* daisy

Pâques [pɑk] *nm, nfpl* Easter

paquet [pakɛ] *nm* packet; (*colis*) parcel; (*fig: tas*): **~ de pile** *ou* heap of; **paquet-cadeau** *nm*: **faites-moi un paquet-cadeau** gift-wrap it for me

par [paʀ] *prép* by; **finir** *etc* **~** to end *etc* with; **~ amour** out of love; **passer ~ Lyon/la côte** to go via *ou* through Lyons/along the coast; **~ la fenêtre** (*jeter, regarder*) out of the window; **3 ~ jour/personne** 3 a *ou* per day/head; **2 ~ 2** in twos; **~ ici** this way; (*dans le coin*) round here; **~-ci, ~-là** here and there; **~ temps de pluie** in wet weather

parabolique [paʀabɔlik] *adj*: **antenne ~** parabolic *ou* dish aerial

parachever [paʀaʃ(ə)ve] *vt* to perfect

parachute [paʀaʃyt] *nm* parachute; **parachutiste** *nm/f* parachutist; (*MIL*) paratrooper

parade [paʀad] *nf* (*spectacle, défilé*) parad (*ESCRIME, BOXE*) parry

paradis [paʀadi] *nm* heaven, paradise

paradoxe [paʀadɔks] *nm* paradox

paraffine [paʀafin] *nf* paraffin

parages [paʀaʒ] *nmpl*: **dans les ~ (de)** the area *ou* vicinity (of)

paragraphe [paʀagʀaf] *nm* paragraph

paraître [paʀɛtʀ] *vb +attrib* to seem, loo appear ♦ *vi* to appear; (*être visible*) show; .(*PRESSE, ÉDITION*) to be publishe come out, appear ♦ *vb impers*: **il para que** it seems *ou* appears that, they sa that; **chercher à ~** to show off

parallèle [paʀalɛl] *adj* parallel; (*non offici* unofficial ♦ *nm* (*comparaison*): **faire un entre** to draw a parallel between ♦ parallel (line)

paralyser [paʀalize] *vt* to paralyse

paramédical, e, -aux [paʀamedikal, *adj*: **personnel ~** paramedics *pl*, param dical workers *pl*

paraphrase [paʀafʀɑz] *nf* paraphrase

parapluie [paʀaplɥi] *nm* umbrella

parasite [paʀazit] *nm* parasite; **~s** *nm* (*TÉL*) interference *sg*

parasol [paʀasɔl] *nm* parasol, sunshade

paratonnerre [paʀatɔnɛʀ] *nm* lightnin conductor

paravent [paʀavɑ̃] *nm* folding screen

parc [paʀk] *nm* (*public*) park, gardens (*de château etc*) grounds *pl*; (*d'enfa* playpen; (*ensemble d'unités*) stock; (*de v tures etc*) fleet; **~ d'attractions** ther park; **~ de stationnement** car park

parcelle [paʀsɛl] *nf* fragment, scrap; *terrain*) plot, parcel

parce que [paʀskə] *conj* because

parchemin [paʀʃəmɛ̃] *nm* parchment

parcmètre [paʀkmɛtʀ] *nm* parking mete

parcourir [paʀkuʀiʀ] *vt* (*trajet, distance*) cover; (*article, livre*) to skim *ou* glan through; (*lieu*) to go all over, travel and down; (*suj: frisson*) to run through

parcours [paʀkuʀ] *nm* (*trajet*) journey; (*néraire*) route

par-derrière [paʀdɛʀjɛʀ] *adv* round the back; **dire du mal de qn ~-~** to speak ill of sb behind his back

par-dessous [paʀd(ə)su] *prép, adv* under(neath)

pardessus [paʀdəsy] *nm* overcoat

par-dessus [paʀd(ə)sy] *prép* over (the top of) ♦ *adv* over (the top); **~-~ le marché** on top of all that; **~-~ tout** above all; **en avoir ~-~ la tête** to have had enough

par-devant [paʀd(ə)vɑ̃] *adv* (*passer*) round the front

pardon [paʀdɔ̃] *nm* forgiveness *no pl* ♦ *excl* sorry!; (*pour interpeller etc*) excuse me!; **demander ~ à qn (de)** to apologize to sb (for); **je vous demande ~** I'm sorry; (*pour interpeller*) excuse me; **pardonner** *vt* to forgive; **pardonner qch à qn** to forgive sb for sth

pare...: pare-balles *adj inv* bulletproof; **pare-brise** *nm inv* windscreen (*BRIT*), windshield (*US*); **pare-chocs** *nm inv* bumper

paré, e [paʀe] *adj* ready, all set

pareil, le [paʀɛj] *adj* (*identique*) the same, alike; (*similaire*) similar; (*tel*): **un courage/livre ~** such courage/a book, courage/a book like this; **de ~s livres** such books; **ne pas avoir son(sa) ~(le)** to be second to none; **~ à** the same as; (*similaire*) similar to; **sans ~** unparalleled, unequalled

parent, e [paʀɑ̃, ɑ̃t] *nm/f*: **un(e) ~(e)** a relative *ou* relation; **~s** *nmpl* (*père et mère*) parents; **parenté** *nf* (*lien*) relationship

parenthèse [paʀɑ̃tɛz] *nf* (*ponctuation*) bracket, parenthesis; (*digression*) parenthesis, digression; **entre ~s** in brackets; (*fig*) incidentally

parer [paʀe] *vt* to adorn; (*éviter*) to ward off; **~ au plus pressé** to attend to the most urgent things first

paresse [paʀɛs] *nf* laziness; **paresseux, -euse** *adj* lazy

parfaire [paʀfɛʀ] *vt* to perfect

parfait, e [paʀfɛ, ɛt] *adj* perfect ♦ *nm* (*LING*) perfect (tense); **parfaitement** *adv* perfectly ♦ *excl* (most) certainly

parfois [paʀfwa] *adv* sometimes

parfum [paʀfœ̃] *nm* (*produit*) perfume, scent; (*odeur: de fleur*) scent, fragrance; (*goût*) flavour; **parfumé, e** *adj* (*fleur, fruit*) fragrant; (*femme*) perfumed; **parfumé au café** coffee-flavoured; **parfumer** *vt* (*suj: odeur, bouquet*) to perfume; (*crème, gâteau*) to flavour; **parfumerie** *nf* (*produits*) perfumes *pl*; (*boutique*) perfume shop

pari [paʀi] *nm* bet; **parier** *vt* to bet

Paris [paʀi] *n* Paris; **parisien, ne** *adj* Parisian; (*GÉO, ADMIN*) Paris *cpd* ♦ *nm/f*: **Parisien, ne** Parisian

parjure [paʀʒyʀ] *nm* perjury

parking [paʀkiŋ] *nm* (*lieu*) car park

parlant, e [paʀlɑ̃, ɑ̃t] *adj* (*regard*) eloquent; (*CINÉMA*) talking; **les chiffres sont ~s** the figures speak for themselves

parlement [paʀləmɑ̃] *nm* parliament; **parlementaire** *adj* parliamentary ♦ *nm/f* member of parliament; **parlementer** *vi* to negotiate, parley

parler [paʀle] *vi* to speak, talk; (*avouer*) to talk; **~ (à qn) de** to talk *ou* speak (to sb) about; **~ le/en français** to speak French/in French; **~ affaires** to talk business; **sans ~ de** (*fig*) not to mention, to say nothing of; **tu parles!** (*fam: bien sûr*) you bet!

parloir [paʀlwaʀ] *nm* (*de prison, d'hôpital*) visiting room

parmi [paʀmi] *prép* among(st)

paroi [paʀwa] *nf* wall; (*cloison*) partition; **~ rocheuse** rock face

paroisse [paʀwas] *nf* parish

parole [paʀɔl] *nf* (*faculté*): **la ~** speech; (*mot, promesse*) word; **~s** *nfpl* (*MUS*) words, lyrics; **tenir ~** to keep one's word; **prendre la ~** to speak; **demander la ~** to ask for permission to speak; **je te crois sur ~** I'll take your word for it

parquer [paʀke] *vt* (*voiture, matériel*) to park; (*bestiaux*) to pen (in *ou* up)

parquet [paʀke] *nm* (*parquet*) floor; (*JUR*):

le ~ the Public Prosecutor's department
parrain [paʀɛ̃] *nm* godfather; **parrainer**
vt (*suj: entreprise*) to sponsor
pars [paʀ] *vb voir* **partir**
parsemer [paʀsəme] *vt* (*suj: feuilles, papiers*) to be scattered over; ~ **qch de** to
scatter sth with
part [paʀ] *nf* (*qui revient à qn*) share; (*fraction, partie*) part; **prendre ~ à** (*débat etc*)
to take part in; (*soucis, douleur de qn*) to
share in; **faire ~ de qch à qn** to announce sth to sb, inform sb of sth; **pour
ma ~** as for me, as far as I'm concerned;
à ~ entière full; **de la ~ de** (*au nom de*)
on behalf of; (*donné par*) from; **de toute(s) ~(s)** from all sides *ou* quarters; **de ~
et d'autre** on both sides, on either side;
d'une ~ ... d'autre ~ on the one hand
... on the other hand; **d'autre ~** (*de plus*)
moreover; **à ~** *adv* (*séparément*) separately; (*de côté*) aside ♦ *prép* apart from, except for; **faire la ~ des choses** to make
allowances
partage [paʀtaʒ] *nm* (*fractionnement*) dividing up; (*répartition*) sharing (out) *no pl*,
share-out
partager [paʀtaʒe] *vt* to share; (*distribuer,
répartir*) to share (out); (*morceler, diviser*) to
divide (up); **se ~** *vt* (*héritage etc*) to share
between themselves *ou* ourselves
partance [paʀtɑ̃s]: **en ~** *adv*: **en ~ pour**
(bound) for
partenaire [paʀtənɛʀ] *nm/f* partner
parterre [paʀtɛʀ] *nm* (*de fleurs*) (flower)
bed; (*THÉÂTRE*) stalls *pl*
parti [paʀti] *nm* (*POL*) party; (*décision*)
course of action; (*personne à marier*)
match; **tirer ~ de** to take advantage of,
turn to good account; **prendre ~ (pour/
contre)** to take sides *ou* a stand (for/
against); ~ **pris** bias
partial, e, -aux [paʀsjal, jo] *adj* biased,
partial
participant, e [paʀtisipɑ̃, ɑ̃t] *nm/f* participant; (*à un concours*) entrant
participation [paʀtisipasjɔ̃] *nf* participation; (*financière*) contribution
participer [paʀtisipe]: ~ **à** *vt* (*course, réunion*) to take part in; (*frais etc*) to contribute to; (*chagrin, succès de qn*) to share (in)
particularité [paʀtikylaʀite] *nf* (*distinctive*) characteristic
particulier, -ière [paʀtikylje, jɛʀ] *adj*
(*spécifique*) particular; (*spécial*) special, particular; (*personnel, privé*) private; (*étrange*)
peculiar, odd ♦ *nm* (*individu: ADMIN*) private individual; ~ **à** peculiar to; **en ~**
(*surtout*) in particular, particularly; (*en
privé*) in private; **particulièrement** *adv*
particularly
partie [paʀti] *nf* (*gén*) part; (*JUR etc: protagonistes*) party; (*de cartes, tennis etc*) game;
une ~ de pêche a fishing party *ou* trip;
en ~ partly, in part; **faire ~ de** (*s chose*) to be part of; **prendre qn à ~**
take sb to task; **en grande ~** largely,
the main; ~ **civile** (*JUR*) party claiming *d*
mages in a criminal case
partiel, le [paʀsjɛl] *adj* partial ♦ *nm* (*SCO*)
class exam
partir [paʀtiʀ] *vi* (*gén*) to go; (*quitter*)
go, leave; (*tache*) to go, come out; ~
(*lieu: quitter*) to leave; (: *commencer à*)
start from; **à ~ de** from
partisan, e [paʀtizɑ̃, an] *nm/f* partis
♦ *adj*: **être ~ de qch/de faire** to be in
vour of sth/doing
partition [paʀtisjɔ̃] *nf* (*MUS*) score
partout [paʀtu] *adv* everywhere; ~ **où**
allait everywhere *ou* wherever he went
paru [paʀy] *pp de* **paraître**
parure [paʀyʀ] *nf* (*bijoux etc*) finery *no*
jewellery *no pl*; (*assortiment*) set
parution [paʀysjɔ̃] *nf* publication
parvenir [paʀvəniʀ]: ~ **à** *vt* (*atteindre*)
reach; (*réussir*): ~ **à faire** to manage
do, succeed in doing; ~ **à ses fins**
achieve one's ends
pas¹ [pɑ] *nm* (*enjambée, DANSE*) step; (*
lure, mesure*) pace; (*bruit*) (foot)step; (*tra*
footprint; ~ **à ~** step by step; **au ~**

walking pace; **faire les cent ~** to pace up and down; **faire les premiers ~** to make the first move; **sur le ~ de la porte** on the doorstep

---

MOT-CLÉ

---

pas² [pɑ] adv 1 (en corrélation avec ne, non etc) not; **il ne pleure pas** he does not ou doesn't cry; he's not ou isn't crying; **il n'a pas pleuré/ne pleurera pas** he did not ou didn't/will not ou won't cry; **ils n'ont pas de voiture/d'enfants** they haven't got a car/any children, they have no car/children; **il m'a dit de ne pas le faire** he told me not to do it; **non pas que ...** not that ...

2 (employé sans ne etc): **pas moi** not me; not I, I don't (ou can't etc); **une pomme pas mûre** an apple which isn't ripe; **pas plus tard qu'hier** only yesterday; **pas du tout** not at all

3: **pas mal** not bad; not badly; **pas mal de** quite a lot of

---

passage [pɑsaʒ] nm (fait de passer) voir **passer**; (lieu, prix de la traversée, extrait) passage; (chemin) way; **de ~** (touristes) passing through; **~ à niveau** level crossing; **~ clouté** pedestrian crossing; **"~ interdit"** "no entry"; **~ souterrain** subway (BRIT), underpass

passager, -ère [pɑsaʒe, ɛʀ] adj passing ♦ nm/f passenger; **~ clandestin** stowaway

passant, e [pɑsɑ̃, ɑ̃t] adj (rue, endroit) busy ♦ nm/f passer-by; **en ~** in passing

passe¹ [pɑs] nf (SPORT, NAVIG) pass; **être en ~ de faire** to be on the way to doing; **être dans une mauvaise ~** to be going through a rough patch

passe² [pɑs] nm (~-partout) master ou skeleton key

passé, e [pɑse] adj (révolu) past; (dernier: semaine etc) last; (couleur) faded ♦ prép after ♦ nm past; (LING) past (tense); **~ de mode** out of fashion; **~ composé** perfect (tense); **~ simple** past historic

passe-partout [pɑspaʀtu] nm inv master ou skeleton key ♦ adj inv all-purpose

passeport [pɑspɔʀ] nm passport

passer [pɑse] vi (aller) to go; (voiture, piétons: défiler) to pass (by), go by; (facteur, laitier etc) to come, call; (pour rendre visite) to call ou drop in; (film, émission) to be on; (temps, jours) to pass, go by; (couleur) to fade; (mode) to die out; (douleur) to pass, go away; (SCOL) to go up (to the next class) ♦ vt (frontière, rivière etc) to cross; (douane) to go through; (examen) to sit, take; (visite médicale etc) to have; (journée, temps) to spend; (enfiler: vêtement) to slip on; (film, pièce) to show, put on; (disque) to play, put on; (marché, accord) to agree on; **se ~** vi (avoir lieu: scène, action) to take place; (se dérouler: entretien etc) to go; (s'écouler: semaine etc) to pass, go by; (arriver): **que s'est-il passé?** what happened?; **~ qch à qn** (sel etc) to pass sth to sb; (prêter) to lend sb sth; (lettre, message) to pass sth on to sb; (tolérer) to let sb get away with sth; **~ par** to go through; **~ avant qch/qn** (fig) to come before sth/sb; **~ un coup de fil à qn** (fam) to give sb a ring; **laisser ~** (air, lumière, personne) to let through; (occasion) to let slip, miss; (erreur) to overlook; **~ la seconde** (AUTO) to change into second; **~ le balai/l'aspirateur** to sweep up/hoover; **je vous passe M. X** (je vous mets en communication avec lui) I'm putting you through to Mr X; (je lui passe l'appareil) here is Mr X, I'll hand you over to Mr X; **se ~ de** to go ou do without

passerelle [pɑsʀɛl] nf footbridge; (de navire, avion) gangway

passe-temps [pɑstɑ̃] nm inv pastime

passible [pɑsibl] adj: **~ de** liable to

passif, -ive [pɑsif, iv] adj passive

passion [pɑsjɔ̃] nf passion; **passionnant, e** adj fascinating; **passionné, e** adj (personne) passionate; (récit) impassioned; **être passionné de** to have a passion for; **passionner** vt (personne) to fascinate, grip; **se passionner pour** (_sport_) to have a passion for

passoire [paswaʀ] _nf_ sieve; (_à légumes_) colander; (_à thé_) strainer

pastèque [pastɛk] _nf_ watermelon

pasteur [pastœʀ] _nm_ (_protestant_) minister, pastor

pasteurisé, e [pastœʀize] _adj_ pasteurized

pastille [pastij] _nf_ (_à sucer_) lozenge, pastille

patate [patat] _nf_ (_fam: pomme de terre_) spud; **~ douce** sweet potato

patauger [patoʒe] _vi_ to splash about

pâte [pat] _nf_ (_à tarte_) pastry; (_à pain_) dough; (_à frire_) batter; **~s** _nfpl_ (_macaroni etc_) pasta _sg_; **~ à modeler** modelling clay, Plasticine ® (_BRIT_); **~ brisée** shortcrust pastry; **~ d'amandes** almond paste; **~ de fruits** crystallized fruit _no pl_; **~ feuilletée** puff _ou_ flaky pastry

pâté [pate] _nm_ (_charcuterie_) pâté; (_tache_) ink blot; (_de sable_) sandpie; **~ de maisons** block (of houses); **~ en croûte** ≈ pork pie

pâtée [pate] _nf_ mash, feed

patente [patɑ̃t] _nf_ (_COMM_) trading licence

paternel, le [patɛʀnɛl] _adj_ (_amour, soins_) fatherly; (_ligne, autorité_) paternal

pâteux, -euse [patø, øz] _adj_ pasty; (_langue_) coated

pathétique [patetik] _adj_ moving

patience [pasjɑ̃s] _nf_ patience

patient, e [pasjɑ̃, jɑ̃t] _adj, nm/f_ patient; **patienter** _vi_ to wait

patin [patɛ̃] _nm_ skate; (_sport_) skating; **~s (à glace)** (ice) skates; **~s à roulettes** roller skates

patinage [patinaʒ] _nm_ skating

patiner [patine] _vi_ to skate; (_roue, voiture_) to spin; **se ~** _vi_ (_meuble, cuir_) to acquire a sheen; **patineur, -euse** _nm/f_ skater; **patinoire** _nf_ skating rink, (ice) rink

pâtir [patiʀ] : **~ de** _vt_ to suffer because of

pâtisserie [patisʀi] _nf_ (_boutique_) cake shop; (_gâteau_) cake, pastry; (_à la maison_) pastry- _ou_ cake-making, baking; **pâtissier, -ière** _nm/f_ pastrycook

patois [patwa, waz] _nm_ dialect, patois

patraque [patʀak] (_fam_) _adj_ peaky, off colour

patrie [patʀi] _nf_ homeland

patrimoine [patʀimwan] _nm_ (_culture_) heritage

patriotique [patʀijɔtik] _adj_ patriotic

patron, ne [patʀɔ̃, ɔn] _nm/f_ boss; (_REL_) patron saint ♦ _nm_ (_COUTURE_) pattern; **patronat** _nm_ employers _pl_; **patronner** _vt_ to sponsor, support

patrouille [patʀuj] _nf_ patrol

patte [pat] _nf_ (_jambe_) leg; (_pied: de chien, chat_) paw; (: _d'oiseau_) foot

pâturage [patyʀaʒ] _nm_ pasture

paume [pom] _nf_ palm

paumé, e [pome] (_fam_) _nm/f_ drop-out

paumer [pome] (_fam_) _vt_ to lose

paupière [popjɛʀ] _nf_ eyelid

pause [poz] _nf_ (_arrêt_) break; (_en parlant, MUS_) pause

pauvre [povʀ] _adj_ poor; **pauvreté** _n_ (_état_) poverty

pavaner [pavane] : **se ~** _vi_ to strut about

pavé, e [pave] _adj_ (_cour_) paved; (_chaussée_) cobbled ♦ _nm_ (_bloc_) paving stone; cobblestone

pavillon [pavijɔ̃] _nm_ (_de banlieue_) small (detached) house; pavilion; (_drapeau_) flag

pavoiser [pavwaze] _vi_ (_fig_) to rejoice, exu

pavot [pavo] _nm_ poppy

payant, e [pejɑ̃, ɑ̃t] _adj_ (_spectateurs etc_) paying; (_fig: entreprise_) profitable; (_effort_) which pays off; **c'est ~** you have to pay there is a charge

paye [pɛj] _nf_ pay, wages _pl_

payer [peje] _vt_ (_créancier, employé, loyer_) pay; (_achat, réparations, fig: faute_) to pa for ♦ _vi_ to pay; (_métier_) to be well-pai (_tactique etc_) to pay off; **il me l'a fait ~ 1 F** he charged me 10 F for it; **~ qch à q** to buy sth for sb, buy sb sth; **se ~ la têt de qn** (_fam_) to take the mickey out of sb

pays [pei] _nm_ country; (_région_) region; **d ~** local

paysage [peizaʒ] _nm_ landscape

paysan, ne [peizɑ̃, an] nm/f farmer; (péj) peasant ♦ adj (agricole) farming; (rural) country

Pays-Bas [peiba] nmpl: **les ~-~** the Netherlands

PC nm (INFORM) PC ♦ sigle m = **parti communiste**

P.D.G. sigle m = **président directeur géneral**

péage [peaʒ] nm toll; (endroit) tollgate

peau, x [po] nf skin; **gants de ~** fine leather gloves; **être bien/mal dans sa ~** to be quite at ease/ill-at-ease; **~ de chamois** (chiffon) chamois leather, shammy; **Peau-Rouge** nm/f Red Indian, redskin

pêche [pɛʃ] nf (sport, activité) fishing; (poissons pêchés) catch; (fruit) peach; **~ à la ligne** (en rivière) angling

péché [peʃe] nm sin

pécher [peʃe] vi (REL) to sin

pêcher [peʃe] nm peach tree ♦ vi to go fishing ♦ vt (attraper) to catch; (être pêcheur de) to fish for

pécheur, -eresse [peʃœʀ, peʃʀɛs] nm/f sinner

pêcheur [peʃœʀ] nm fisherman; (à la ligne) angler

pécule [pekyl] nm savings pl, nest egg

pédagogie [pedagɔʒi] nf educational methods pl, pedagogy; **pédagogique** adj educational

pédale [pedal] nf pedal

pédalo [pedalo] nm pedal-boat

pédant, e [pedɑ̃, ɑ̃t] (péj) adj pedantic

pédestre [pedɛstʀ] adj: **randonnée ~** ramble; **sentier ~** pedestrian footpath

pédiatre [pedjatʀ] nm/f paediatrician, child specialist

pédicure [pedikyʀ] nm/f chiropodist

pègre [pɛgʀ] nf underworld

peignais etc [peɲɛ] vb voir **peindre**; **peigner**

peigne [peɲ] nm comb; **peigner** vt to comb (the hair of); **se peigner** vi to comb one's hair

peignoir nm dressing gown; **peignoir de**

bain bathrobe

peindre [pɛ̃dʀ] vt to paint; (fig) to portray, depict

peine [pɛn] nf (affliction) sorrow, sadness no pl; (mal, effort) trouble no pl, effort; (difficulté) difficulty; (JUR) sentence; **avoir de la ~** to be sad; **faire de la ~ à qn** to distress ou upset sb; **prendre la ~ de faire** to go to the trouble of doing; **se donner de la ~** to make an effort; **ce n'est pas la ~ de faire** there's no point in doing, it's not worth doing; **à ~** scarcely, hardly, barely; **à ~ ... que** hardly ... than; **~ capitale** ou **de mort** capital punishment, death sentence; **peiner** vi (personne) to work hard; (moteur, voiture) to labour ♦ vt to grieve, sadden

peintre [pɛ̃tʀ] nm painter; **~ en bâtiment** house painter

peinture [pɛ̃tyʀ] nf painting; (matière) paint; (surfaces peintes: aussi: **~s**) paintwork; **"~ fraîche"** "wet paint"

péjoratif, -ive [peʒɔʀatif, iv] adj pejorative, derogatory

pelage [pəlaʒ] nm coat, fur

pêle-mêle [pɛlmɛl] adv higgledy-piggledy

peler [pəle] vt, vi to peel

pèlerin [pɛlʀɛ̃] nm pilgrim

pèlerinage [pɛlʀinaʒ] nm pilgrimage

pelle [pɛl] nf shovel; (d'enfant, de terrassier) spade

pellicule [pelikyl] nf film; **~s** nfpl (MÉD) dandruff sg

pelote [p(ə)lɔt] nf (de fil, laine) ball

peloton [p(ə)lɔtɔ̃] nm group, squad; (CYCLISME) pack; **~ d'exécution** firing squad

pelotonner [p(ə)lɔtɔne]: **se ~** vi to curl (o.s.) up

pelouse [p(ə)luz] nf lawn

peluche [p(ə)lyʃ] nf: **(animal en) ~** fluffy animal, soft toy; **chien/lapin en ~** fluffy dog/rabbit

pelure [p(ə)lyʀ] nf peeling, peel no pl

pénal, e, -aux [penal, o] adj penal; **pénalité** nf penalty

penaud, e [pəno, od] adj sheepish, contrite

penchant [pɑ̃ʃɑ̃] *nm* (*tendance*) tendency, propensity; (*faible*) liking, fondness

pencher [pɑ̃ʃe] *vi* to tilt, lean over ♦ *vt* to tilt; **se ~** *vi* to lean over; (*se baisser*) to bend down; **se ~ sur** (*fig: problème*) to look into; **~ pour** to be inclined to favour

pendaison [pɑ̃dɛzɔ̃] *nf* hanging

pendant [pɑ̃dɑ̃] *prép* (*au cours de*) during; (*indique la durée*) for; **~ que** while

pendentif [pɑ̃dɑ̃tif] *nm* pendant

penderie [pɑ̃dʀi] *nf* wardrobe

pendre [pɑ̃dʀ] *vt*, *vi* to hang; **se ~** (*se suicider*) to hang o.s.; **~ la crémaillère** to have a house-warming party

pendule [pɑ̃dyl] *nf* clock ♦ *nm* pendulum

pénétrer [penetʀe] *vi*, *vt* to penetrate; **~ dans** to enter

pénible [penibl] *adj* (*travail*) hard; (*sujet*) painful; (*personne*) tiresome; **péniblement** *adv* with difficulty

péniche [peniʃ] *nf* barge

pénicilline [penisilin] *nf* penicillin

péninsule [penɛ̃syl] *nf* peninsula

pénis [penis] *nm* penis

pénitence [penitɑ̃s] *nf* (*peine*) penance; (*repentir*) penitence; **pénitencier** *nm* penitentiary

pénombre [penɔ̃bʀ] *nf* (*faible clarté*) half-light; (*obscurité*) darkness

pensée [pɑ̃se] *nf* (*démarche, doctrine*) thinking *no pl*; (*fleur*) pansy; **en ~** in one's mind

penser [pɑ̃se] *vi*, *vt* to think; **~ à** (*ami, vacances*) to think of *ou* about; (*réfléchir à: problème, offre*) to think about *ou* over; (*prévoir*) to think of; **faire ~ à** to remind one of; **~ faire qch** to be thinking of doing sth, intend to do sth; **pensif, -ive** *adj* pensive, thoughtful

pension [pɑ̃sjɔ̃] *nf* (*allocation*) pension; (*prix du logement*) board and lodgings, bed and board; (*école*) boarding school; **~ alimentaire** (*de divorcée*) maintenance allowance, alimony; **~ complète** full board; **~ (de famille)** boarding house, guest-house; **pensionnaire** *nm/f* (*SCOL*) boarder; **pensionnat** *nm* boarding school

pente [pɑ̃t] *nf* slope; **en ~** sloping

Pentecôte [pɑ̃tkot] *nf*: **la ~** Whitsu (*BRIT*), Pentecost

pénurie [penyʀi] *nf* shortage

pépé [pepe] (*fam*) *nm* grandad

pépin [pepɛ̃] *nm* (*BOT: graine*) pip; (*ennu* snag, hitch

pépinière [pepinjɛʀ] *nf* nursery

perçant, e [pɛʀsɑ̃, ɑ̃t] *adj* (*cri*) piercing shrill; (*regard*) piercing

percée [pɛʀse] *nf* (*trouée*) opening; (*Mé technologique*) breakthrough

perce-neige [pɛʀsəneʒ] *nm inv* snowdrop

percepteur [pɛʀsɛptœʀ, tʀis] *nm* tax co lector

perception [pɛʀsɛpsjɔ̃] *nf* perceptio (*bureau*) tax office

percer [pɛʀse] *vt* to pierce; (*ouverture et* to make; (*mystère, énigme*) to penetra ♦ *vi* to break through; **perceuse** *nf* drill

percevoir [pɛʀsəvwaʀ] *vt* (*distinguer*) perceive, detect; (*taxe, impôt*) to collec (*revenu, indemnité*) to receive

perche [pɛʀʃ] *nf* (*bâton*) pole

percher [pɛʀʃe] *vt*, *vi* to perch; **se ~** *vi* perch; **perchoir** *nm* perch

perçois *etc* [pɛʀswa] *vb voir* **percevoir**

percolateur [pɛʀkɔlatœʀ] *nm* percolator

perçu, e [pɛʀsy] *pp de* **percevoir**

percussion [pɛʀkysjɔ̃] *nf* percussion

percuter [pɛʀkyte] *vt* to strike; (*suj: vé cule*) to crash into

perdant, e [pɛʀdɑ̃, ɑ̃t] *nm/f* loser

perdre [pɛʀdʀ] *vt* to lose; (*gaspiller: temp argent*) to waste; (*personne: moraleme etc*) to ruin ♦ *vi* to lose; (*sur une vente e* to lose out; **se ~** *vi* (*s'égarer*) to get lo lose one's way; (*denrées*) to go to waste

perdrix [pɛʀdʀi] *nf* partridge

perdu, e [pɛʀdy] *pp de* **perdre** ♦ *a* (*isolé*) out-of-the-way; (*COMM: emballag* non-returnable; (*malade*): **il est ~** ther no hope left for him; **à vos moments** in your spare time

père [pɛʀ] *nm* father; ~ **de famille** father; **le ~ Noël** Father Christmas

perfection [pɛʀfɛksjɔ̃] *nf* perfection; **à la ~** to perfection; **perfectionné, e** *adj* sophisticated; **perfectionner** *vt* to improve, perfect

perforatrice [pɛʀfɔʀatʀis] *nf* (*de bureau*) punch

perforer [pɛʀfɔʀe] *vt* (*poinçonner*) to punch

performant, e [pɛʀfɔʀmɑ̃, ɑ̃t] *adj*: **très ~** high-performance *cpd*

perfusion [pɛʀfyzjɔ̃] *nf*: **faire une ~ à qn** to put sb on a drip

péricliter [peʀiklite] *vi* to collapse

péril [peʀil] *nm* peril

périmé, e [peʀime] *adj* (*ADMIN*) out-of-date, expired

périmètre [peʀimɛtʀ] *nm* perimeter

période [peʀjɔd] *nf* period; **périodique** *adj* periodic ♦ *nm* periodical

péripéties [peʀipesi] *nfpl* events, episodes

périphérique [peʀifeʀik] *adj* (*quartiers*) outlying ♦ *nm* (*AUTO*) ring road

périple [peʀipl] *nm* journey

périr [peʀiʀ] *vi* to die, perish

périssable [peʀisabl] *adj* perishable

perle [pɛʀl] *nf* pearl; (*de plastique, métal, sueur*) bead

permanence [pɛʀmanɑ̃s] *nf* permanence; (*local*) (duty) office; **assurer une ~** (*service public, bureaux*) to operate *ou* maintain a basic service; **être de ~** to be on call *ou* duty; **en ~** continuously

permanent, e [pɛʀmanɑ̃, ɑ̃t] *adj* permanent; (*spectacle*) continuous; **permanente** *nf* perm

perméable [pɛʀmeabl] *adj* (*terrain*) permeable; **~ à** (*fig*) receptive *ou* open to

permettre [pɛʀmɛtʀ] *vt* to allow, permit; **~ à qn de faire/qch** to allow sb to do/ sth; **se ~ de faire** to take the liberty of doing

permis [pɛʀmi, iz] *nm* permit, licence; **~ de chasse** hunting permit; **~ (de conduire)** (driving) licence (*BRIT*), (driver's) license (*US*); **~ de construire** planning permission (*BRIT*), building permit (*US*); **~ de séjour** residence permit; **~ de travail** work permit

permission [pɛʀmisjɔ̃] *nf* permission; (*MIL*) leave; **avoir la ~ de faire** to have permission to do; **en ~** on leave

permuter [pɛʀmyte] *vt* to change around, permutate ♦ *vi* to change, swap

Pérou [peʀu] *nm* Peru

perpétuel, le [pɛʀpetɥɛl] *adj* perpetual; **perpétuité** *nf*: **à perpétuité** for life; **être condamné à perpétuité** to receive a life sentence

perplexe [pɛʀplɛks] *adj* perplexed, puzzled

perquisitionner [pɛʀkizisjɔne] *vi* to carry out a search

perron [pɛʀɔ̃] *nm* steps *pl* (*leading to entrance*)

perroquet [pɛʀɔkɛ] *nm* parrot

perruche [pɛʀyʃ] *nf* budgerigar (*BRIT*), budgie (*BRIT*), parakeet (*US*)

perruque [pɛʀyk] *nf* wig

persan, e [pɛʀsɑ̃, an] *adj* Persian

persécuter [pɛʀsekyte] *vt* to persecute

persévérer [pɛʀseveʀe] *vi* to persevere

persiennes [pɛʀsjɛn] *nfpl* shutters

persil [pɛʀsi] *nm* parsley

Persique [pɛʀsik] *adj*: **le golfe ~** the (Persian) Gulf

persistant, e [pɛʀsistɑ̃, ɑ̃t] *adj* persistent

persister [pɛʀsiste] *vi* to persist; **~ à faire qch** to persist in doing sth

personnage [pɛʀsɔnaʒ] *nm* (*individu*) character, individual; (*célébrité*) important person; (*de roman, film*) character; (*PEINTURE*) figure

personnalité [pɛʀsɔnalite] *nf* personality; (*personnage*) prominent figure

personne [pɛʀsɔn] *nf* person ♦ *pron* nobody, no one; (*avec négation en anglais*) anybody, anyone; **~s** *nfpl* (*gens*) people *pl*; **il n'y a ~** there's nobody there, there isn't anybody there; **~ âgée** elderly person; **personnel, le** *adj* personal; (*égoïste*) selfish ♦ *nm* staff, personnel; **personnel-**

lement *adv* personally

perspective [pɛʀspɛktiv] *nf* (*ART*) perspective; (*vue*) view; (*point de vue*) viewpoint, angle; (*chose envisagée*) prospect; **en ~** in prospect

perspicace [pɛʀspikas] *adj* clear-sighted, gifted with (*ou* showing) insight; **perspicacité** *nf* clear-sightedness

persuader [pɛʀsɥade] *vt*: **~ qn (de faire)** to persuade sb (to do)

persuasif, -ive [pɛʀsɥazif, iv] *adj* persuasive

perte [pɛʀt] *nf* loss; (*de temps*) waste; (*fig: morale*) ruin; **à ~ de vue** as far as the eye can (*ou* could) see; **~s blanches** (vaginal) discharge *sg*

pertinemment [pɛʀtinamɑ̃] *adv* (*savoir*) full well

pertinent, e [pɛʀtinɑ̃, ɑ̃t] *adj* apt, relevant

perturbation [pɛʀtyʀbasjɔ̃] *nf*: **~ (atmosphérique)** atmospheric disturbance

perturber [pɛʀtyʀbe] *vt* to disrupt; (*PSYCH*) to perturb, disturb

pervers, e [pɛʀvɛʀ, ɛʀs] *adj* perverted

pervertir [pɛʀvɛʀtiʀ] *vt* to pervert

pesant, e [pəzɑ̃, ɑ̃t] *adj* heavy; (*fig: présence*) burdensome

pèse-personne [pɛzpɛʀsɔn] *nm* (bathroom) scales *pl*

peser [pəze] *vt* to weigh ♦ *vi* to weigh; (*fig: avoir de l'importance*) to carry weight; **~ lourd** to be heavy

pessimisme [pesimism] *nm* pessimism

pessimiste [pesimist] *adj* pessimistic ♦ *nm/f* pessimist

peste [pɛst] *nf* plague

pester [peste] *vi*: **~ contre** to curse

pétale [petal] *nm* petal

pétanque [petɑ̃k] *nf* type of bowls

---

pétanque

i Pétanque, *which originated in the south of France, is a version of the game of* **boules** *played on a variety of hard surfaces. Standing with their feet to-*

gether, players throw steel bowls towards a wooden jack.

---

pétarader [petaʀade] *vi* to backfire

pétard [petaʀ] *nm* banger (*BRIT*), firecracker

péter [pete] *vi* (*fam: casser*) to bust; (*fam!*) to fart (!)

pétillant, e [petijɑ̃, ɑ̃t] *adj* sparkling

pétiller [petije] *vi* (*feu*) to crackle; (*champagne*) to bubble; (*yeux*) to sparkle

petit, e [p(ə)ti, it] *adj* small; (*avec nuance affective*) little; (*voyage*) short, little; (*bruit etc*) faint, slight; **~s** *nmpl* (*d'un animal*) young *pl*; **les tout-~s** the little ones, the tiny tots; **~ à ~** bit by bit, gradually; **~(e) ami(e)** boyfriend/girlfriend; **~ déjeuner** breakfast; **~ pain** (bread) roll; **les ~es annonces** the small ads; **~s pois** garden peas; **petite-fille** *nf* granddaughter; **petit-fils** *nm* grandson

pétition [petisjɔ̃] *nf* petition

petits-enfants [pətizɑ̃fɑ̃] *nmpl* grandchildren

petit-suisse [pətisɥis] (*pl* **~s-~s**) *nm* small individual pot of cream cheese

pétrin [petʀɛ̃] *nm* (*fig*): **dans le ~** (*fam*) in a jam *ou* fix

pétrir [petʀiʀ] *vt* to knead

pétrole [petʀɔl] *nm* oil; (*pour lampe, réchaud etc*) paraffin (oil); **pétrolier, -ière** *nm* oil tanker

---

MOT-CLÉ

---

peu [pø] *adv* **1** (*modifiant verbe, adjectif, adverbe*): **il boit peu** he doesn't drink (very) much; **il est peu bavard** he's not very talkative; **peu avant/après** shortly before/afterwards

2 (*modifiant nom*): **peu de**: **peu de gens/d'arbres** few *ou* not (very) many people/trees; **il a peu d'espoir** he hasn' (got) much hope, he has little hope; **pour peu de temps** for (only) a short while

3 peu à peu little by little; **à peu près** just about, more or less; **à peu près 1**

kg/10 F approximately 10 kg/10F
♦ nm 1: le peu de gens qui the few people who; le peu de sable qui what little sand, the little sand which
2: un peu a little; un petit peu a little bit; un peu d'espoir a little hope
♦ pron: peu le savent few know (it); avant ou sous peu shortly, before long; de peu (only) just

euple [pœpl] nm people; peupler vt (pays, région) to populate; (étang) to stock; (suj: hommes, poissons) to inhabit
euplier [pøplije] nm poplar (tree)
eur [pœr] nf fear; avoir ~ (de/de faire/que) to be frightened ou afraid (of/of doing/that); faire ~ à to frighten; de ~ de/que for fear of/that; peureux, -euse adj fearful, timorous
eut [pø] vb voir pouvoir
eut-être [pøtεtʀ] adv perhaps, maybe; ~-~ que perhaps, maybe; ~-~ bien qu'il fera/est he may well do/be
eux etc [pø] vb voir pouvoir
hare [faʀ] nm lighthouse; (de véhicule) headlight; ~s de recul reversing lights
harmacie [faʀmasi] nf (magasin) chemist's (BRIT), pharmacy; (de salle de bain) medicine cabinet; pharmacien, ne nm/f pharmacist, chemist (BRIT)
hénomène [fenɔmεn] nm phenomenon
hilatélie [filateli] nf philately, stamp collecting
hilosophe [filɔzɔf] nm/f philosopher
♦ adj philosophical
hilosophie [filɔzɔfi] nf philosophy
hobie [fɔbi] nf phobia
honétique [fɔnetik] nf phonetics sg
hoque [fɔk] nm seal
hosphorescent, e [fɔsfɔʀesɑ̃, ɑ̃t] adj luminous
hoto [fɔto] nf photo(graph); prendre en ~ to take a photo of; faire de la ~ to take photos; ~ d'identité passport photograph; photocopie nf photocopy; photocopier vt to photocopy; photoco-

pieuse nf photocopier; photographe nm/f photographer; photographie nf (technique) photography; (cliché) photograph; photographier vt to photograph
phrase [fʀaz] nf sentence
physicien, ne [fizisjɛ̃, jεn] nm/f physicist
physionomie [fizjɔnɔmi] nf face
physique [fizik] adj physical ♦ nm physique ♦ nf physics sg; au ~ physically; physiquement adv physically
piailler [pjaje] vi to squawk
pianiste [pjanist] nm/f pianist
piano [pjano] nm piano; pianoter vi to tinkle away (at the piano)
pic [pik] nm (instrument) pick(axe); (montagne) peak; (ZOOL) woodpecker; à ~ vertically; (fig: tomber, arriver) just at the right time
pichet [piʃε] nm jug
picorer [pikɔʀe] vt to peck
picoter [pikɔte] vt (suj: oiseau) to peck ♦ vi (irriter) to smart, prickle
pie [pi] nf magpie
pièce [pjεs] nf (d'un logement) room; (THÉÂTRE) play; (de machine) part; (de monnaie) coin; (document) document; (fragment, de collection) piece; dix francs ~ ten francs each; vendre à la ~ to sell separately; travailler à la ~ to do piecework; un maillot une ~ a one-piece swimsuit; un deux-~s cuisine a two-room(ed) flat (BRIT) ou apartment (US) with kitchen; ~ à conviction exhibit; ~ d'identité: avez-vous une ~ d'identité? have you got any (means of) identification?; ~ montée tiered cake; ~s détachées spares, (spare) parts; ~s justificatives supporting documents
pied [pje] nm foot; (de table) leg; (de lampe) base; à ~ on foot; au ~ de la lettre literally; avoir ~ to be able to touch the bottom, not to be out of one's depth; avoir le ~ marin to be a good sailor; sur ~ (debout, rétabli) up and about; mettre sur ~ (entreprise) to set up; c'est le ~ (fam) it's brilliant; mettre les ~s dans le

plat (*fam*) to put one's foot in it; **il se débrouille comme un ~** (*fam*) he's completely useless; **pied-noir** *nm* Algerian-born Frenchman

piège [pjɛʒ] *nm* trap; **prendre au ~** to trap; **piéger** *vt* (*avec une bombe*) to booby-trap; **lettre/voiture piégée** letter-/car-bomb

pierre [pjɛʀ] *nf* stone; **~ précieuse** precious stone, gem; **~ tombale** tombstone; **pierreries** *nfpl* gems, precious stones

piétiner [pjetine] *vi* (*trépigner*) to stamp (one's foot); (*fig*) to be at a standstill ♦ *vt* to trample on

piéton, ne [pjetɔ̃, ɔn] *nm/f* pedestrian; **piétonnier, -ière** *adj*: **rue** *ou* **zone piétonnière** pedestrian precinct

pieu, x [pjø] *nm* post; (*pointu*) stake

pieuvre [pjœvʀ] *nf* octopus

pieux, -euse [pjø, pjøz] *adj* pious

piffer [pife] (*fam*) *vt*: **je ne peux pas le ~** I can't stand him

pigeon [piʒɔ̃] *nm* pigeon

piger [piʒe] (*fam*) *vi, vt* to understand

pigiste [piʒist] *nm/f* freelance(r)

pignon [piɲɔ̃] *nm* (*de mur*) gable

pile [pil] *nf* (*tas*) pile; (*ÉLEC*) battery ♦ *adv* (*fam: s'arrêter etc*) dead; **à deux heures ~** at two on the dot; **jouer à ~ ou face** to toss up (for it); **~ ou face?** heads or tails?

piler [pile] *vt* to crush, pound

pilier [pilje] *nm* pillar

piller [pije] *vt* to pillage, plunder, loot

pilote [pilɔt] *nm* pilot; (*de voiture*) driver ♦ *adj* pilot *cpd*; **~ de course** racing driver; **~ de ligne/d'essai/de chasse** airline/test/fighter pilot; **piloter** *vt* (*avion*) to pilot, fly; (*voiture*) to drive

pilule [pilyl] *nf* pill; **prendre la ~** to be on the pill

piment [pimɑ̃] *nm* (*aussi:* **~ rouge**) chilli; (*fig*) spice, piquancy; **~ doux** pepper, capsicum; **pimenté, e** *adj* (*plat*) hot, spicy

pimpant, e [pɛ̃pɑ̃, ɑ̃t] *adj* spruce

pin [pɛ̃] *nm* pine

pinard [pinaʀ] (*fam*) *nm* (cheap) wine, plonk (*BRIT*)

pince [pɛ̃s] *nf* (*outil*) pliers *pl*; (*de homard, crabe*) pincer, claw; (*COUTURE: pli*) dart; **à épiler** tweezers *pl*; **~ à linge** clothes peg (*BRIT*) *ou* pin (*US*)

pincé, e [pɛ̃se] *adj* (*air*) stiff

pinceau, x [pɛ̃so] *nm* (paint)brush

pincée [pɛ̃se] *nf*: **une ~ de** a pinch of

pincer [pɛ̃se] *vt* to pinch; (*fam*) to nab

pinède [pined] *nf* pinewood, pine forest

pingouin [pɛ̃gwɛ̃] *nm* penguin

ping-pong ® [piŋpɔ̃g] *nm* table tennis

pingre [pɛ̃gʀ] *adj* niggardly

pinson [pɛ̃sɔ̃] *nm* chaffinch

pintade [pɛ̃tad] *nf* guinea-fowl

pioche [pjɔʃ] *nf* pickaxe; **piocher** *vt* t dig up (with a pickaxe); **piocher dans (** *tas, ses économies*) to dig into

pion [pjɔ̃] *nm* (*ÉCHECS*) pawn; (*DAME* piece; (*SCOL*) supervisor

pionnier [pjɔnje] *nm* pioneer

pipe [pip] *nf* pipe; **fumer la ~** to smoke pipe

pipeau, x [pipo] *nm* (reed-)pipe

piquant, e [pikɑ̃, ɑ̃t] *adj* (*barbe, rosier et* prickly; (*saveur, sauce*) hot, pungent; (*d* tail) titillating; (*froid*) biting ♦ *nm* (*épin* thorn, prickle; (*fig*) spiciness, spice

pique [pik] *nf* pike; (*fig*) cutting rema ♦ *nm* (*CARTES*) spades *pl*

pique-nique [piknik] *nm* picnic; **pique niquer** *vi* to have a picnic

piquer [pike] *vt* (*suj: guêpe, fumée, orties*) sting; (: *moustique*) to bite; (: *barbe*) prick; (: *froid*) to bite; (*MÉD*) to give a ja to; (: *chien, chat*) to put to sleep; (*intéré* to arouse; (*fam: voler*) to pinch ♦ (*avion*) to go into a dive; **se ~** (*avec u aiguille*) to prick o.s.; (*dans les orties*) get stung; (*suj: toxicomane*) to shoot up; **une colère** to fly into a rage

piquet [pikɛ] *nm* (*pieu*) post, stake; (tente) peg; **~ de grève** (strike-)picket

piqûre [pikyʀ] *nf* (*d'épingle*) prick; (*d'ort.* sting; (*de moustique*) bite; (*MÉD*) injectio shot (*US*); **faire une ~ à qn** to give sb * injection

pirate [piʀat] *nm, adj* pirate; **~ de l'air** hijacker

pire [piʀ] *adj* worse; *(superlatif)*: **le(la) ~ ...** the worst ... ♦ *nm*: **le ~ (de)** the worst (of); **au ~** at (the very) worst

pis [pi] *nm (de vache)* udder; *(pire)*: **le ~** the worst ♦ *adj, adv* worse; **de mal en ~** from bad to worse

piscine [pisin] *nf (swimming)* pool; **~ couverte** indoor (swimming) pool

pissenlit [pisɑ̃li] *nm* dandelion

pistache [pistaʃ] *nf* pistachio (nut)

piste [pist] *nf (d'un animal, sentier)* track, trail; *(indice)* lead; *(de stade)* track; *(de cirque)* ring; *(de danse)* floor; *(de patinage)* rink; *(de ski)* run; *(AVIAT)* runway; **~ cyclable** cycle track

pistolet [pistɔlɛ] *nm (arme)* pistol, gun; *(à peinture)* spray gun; **pistolet-mitrailleur** *nm* submachine gun

piston [pistɔ̃] *nm (TECH)* piston; **avoir du ~** *(fam)* to have friends in the right places; **pistonner** *vt (candidat)* to pull strings for

piteux, -euse [pitø, øz] *adj* pitiful, sorry *(avant le nom)*

pitié [pitje] *nf* pity; **il me fait ~** I feel sorry for him; **avoir ~ de** *(compassion)* to pity, feel sorry for; *(merci)* to have pity *ou* mercy on

pitoyable [pitwajabl] *adj* pitiful

pitre [pitʀ] *nm* clown; **pitrerie** *nf* tomfoolery *no pl*

pittoresque [pitɔʀɛsk] *adj* picturesque

pivot [pivo] *nm* pivot; **pivoter** *vi* to revolve; *(fauteuil)* to swivel

P.J. *sigle f (= police judiciaire)* ≃ CID *(BRIT)*, ≃ FBI *(US)*

placard [plakaʀ] *nm (armoire)* cupboard; *(affiche)* poster, notice

place [plas] *nf (emplacement, classement)* place; *(de ville, village)* square; *(espace libre)* room, space; *(de parking)* space; *(siège: de train, cinéma, voiture)* seat; *(emploi)* job; **en ~ (mettre)** in its place; **sur ~** on the spot; **faire ~ à** to give way to; **ça prend de la**

~ it takes up a lot of room *ou* space; **à la ~ de** in place of, instead of; **à ta ~ ...** if I were you ...; **se mettre à la ~ de qn** to put o.s. in sb's place *ou* in sb's shoes

placé, e [plase] *adj*: **être bien/mal ~** *(spectateur)* to have a good/a poor seat; *(concurrent)* to be in a good/bad position; **il est bien ~ pour le savoir** he is in a position to know

placement [plasmɑ̃] *nm (FINANCE)* investment; **bureau de ~** employment agency

placer [plase] *vt* to place; *(convive, spectateur)* to seat; *(argent)* to place, invest; **il n'a pas pu ~ un mot** he couldn't get a word in; **se ~ au premier rang** to go and stand *(ou* sit) in the first row

plafond [plafɔ̃] *nm* ceiling

plage [plaʒ] *nf* beach

plagiat [plaʒja] *nm* plagiarism

plaid [plɛd] *nm (tartan)* car rug

plaider [plede] *vi (avocat)* to plead ♦ *vt* to plead; **~ pour** *(fig)* to speak for; **plaidoyer** *nm (JUR)* speech for the defence; *(fig)* plea

plaie [plɛ] *nf* wound

plaignant, e [plɛɲɑ̃, ɑ̃t] *nm/f* plaintiff

plaindre [plɛ̃dʀ] *vt* to pity, feel sorry for; **se ~** *vi (gémir)* to moan; *(protester)*: **se ~ (à qn) (de)** to complain (to sb) (about); *(souffrir)*: **se ~ de** to complain of

plaine [plɛn] *nf* plain

plain-pied [plɛ̃pje] *adv*: **de ~-~ (avec)** on the same level (as)

plainte [plɛ̃t] *nf (gémissement)* moan, groan; *(doléance)* complaint; **porter ~** to lodge a complaint

plaire [plɛʀ] *vi* to be a success, be successful; **ça plaît beaucoup aux jeunes** it's very popular with young people; **~ à**: **cela me plaît** I like it; **se ~ quelque part** to like being somewhere *ou* like it somewhere; **j'irai si ça me plaît** I'll go if I feel like it; **s'il vous plaît** please

plaisance [plɛzɑ̃s] *nf (aussi: **navigation de ~**)* (pleasure) sailing, yachting

plaisant, e [plɛzɑ̃, ɑ̃t] *adj* pleasant; *(his-*

toire, anecdote) amusing

plaisanter [plezɑ̃te] *vi* to joke; **plaisanterie** *nf* joke

plaise *etc* [plɛz] *vb voir* **plaire**

plaisir [plezir] *nm* pleasure; **faire ~ à qn** *(délibérément)* to be nice to sb, please sb; **ça me fait ~** I like (doing) it; **j'espère que ça te fera ~** I hope you'll like it; **pour le ~** for pleasure

plaît [plɛ] *vb voir* **plaire**

plan, e [plɑ̃, an] *adj* flat ♦ *nm* plan; *(fig)* level, plane; *(CINÉMA)* shot; **au premier/ second ~** in the foreground/middle distance; **à l'arrière ~** in the background; **rester en ~** *(fam)* to be left stranded; **laisser en ~** *(fam: travail)* to drop, abandon; **~ d'eau** lake

planche [plɑ̃ʃ] *nf (pièce de bois)* plank, (wooden) board; *(illustration)* plate; **~ à repasser** ironing board; **~ à roulettes** skateboard; **~ à voile** *(sport)* windsurfing

plancher [plɑ̃ʃe] *nm* floor; floorboards *pl* ♦ *vi (fam)* to work hard

planer [plane] *vi* to glide; *(fam: rêveur)* to have one's head in the clouds; **~ sur** *(fig: danger)* to hang over

planète [planɛt] *nf* planet

planeur [planœr] *nm* glider

planification [planifikasjɔ̃] *nf* (economic) planning

planifier [planifje] *vt* to plan

planning [planiŋ] *nm* programme, schedule

planque [plɑ̃k] *(fam) nf (emploi peu fatigant)* cushy *(BRIT)* ou easy number; *(cachette)* hiding place

plant [plɑ̃] *nm* seedling, young plant

plante [plɑ̃t] *nf* plant; **~ d'appartement** house ou pot plant; **~ des pieds** sole (of the foot)

planter [plɑ̃te] *vt (plante)* to plant; *(enfoncer)* to hammer ou drive in; *(tente)* to put up, pitch; *(fam: personne)* to dump; **se ~** *(fam: se tromper)* to get it wrong

plantureux, -euse [plɑ̃tyrø, øz] *adj* copious, lavish; *(femme)* buxom

plaque [plak] *nf* plate; *(de verglas, d'eczéma)* patch; *(avec inscription)* plaque; **~ chauffante** hotplate; **~ de chocolat** ba of chocolate; **~ (minéralogique ou d'im matriculation)** number *(BRIT)* ou licens *(US)* plate; **~ tournante** *(fig)* centre

plaqué, e [plake] *adj*: **~ or/argent** gold- silver-plated

plaquer [plake] *vt (aplatir)*: **~ qch sur o** **contre** to make sth stick ou cling to *(RUGBY)* to bring down; *(fam: laisser tom* ber)* to drop

plaquette [plakɛt] *nf (de chocolat)* ba *(beurre)* pack(et); **~ de frein** brake pad

plastique [plastik] *adj, nm* plastic; **plasti quer** *vt* to blow up *(with a plastic bomb)*

plat, e [pla, -at] *adj* flat; *(cheveux)* straight *(style)* flat, dull ♦ *nm (récipient, CULIN* dish; *(d'un repas)* course; **à ~ ventre** fac down; **à ~** *(pneu, batterie)* flat; *(fam: pe sonne)* dead beat; **~ cuisiné** pre-cooke meal; **~ de résistance** main course; **~ d jour** dish of the day

platane [platan] *nm* plane tree

plateau, x [plato] *nm (support)* tray; *(GÉC* plateau; *(CINÉMA)* set; **~ de fromage** cheeseboard

plate-bande [platbɑ̃d] *nf* flower bed

plate-forme [platfɔrm] *nf* platform; **~- de forage/pétrolière** drilling/oil rig

platine [platin] *nm* platinum ♦ *nf (d'u tourne-disque)* turntable

plâtre [platr] *nm (matériau)* plaster; *(st tue)* plaster statue; *(MÉD)* (plaster) cas **avoir un bras dans le ~** to have an arr in plaster

plein, e [plɛ̃, plɛn] *adj* full ♦ *nm*: **faire le (d'essence)** to fill up (with petrol); **à ~e mains** *(ramasser)* in handfuls; **à ~ temp** full-time; **en ~ air** in the open air; **en soleil** in direct sunlight; **en ~e nuit/ru** in the middle of the night/street; **en jour** in broad daylight

pleurer [plœre] *vi* to cry; *(yeux)* to wate ♦ *vt* to mourn (for); **~ sur** to lamer (over), to bemoan

pleurnicher [plœʀniʃe] *vi* to snivel, whine

pleurs [plœʀ] *nmpl*: **en ~** in tears

pleut [plø] *vb voir* **pleuvoir**

pleuvoir [pløvwaʀ] *vb impers* to rain ♦ *vi* (*coups*) to rain down; (*critiques, invitations*) to shower down; **il pleut** it's raining

pli [pli] *nm* fold; (*de jupe*) pleat; (*de pantalon*) crease; **prendre le ~ de faire** to get into the habit of doing; **un mauvais ~** a bad habit

pliant, e [plijã, plijãt] *adj* folding

plier [plije] *vt* to fold; (*pour ranger*) to fold up; (*genou, bras*) to bend ♦ *vi* to bend; (*fig*) to yield; **se ~** *vi* to fold; **se ~ à** to submit to

plinthe [plɛ̃t] *nf* skirting board

plisser [plise] *vt* (*jupe*) to put pleats in; (*yeux*) to screw up; (*front*) to crease

plomb [plɔ̃] *nm* (*métal*) lead; (*d'une cartouche*) (lead) shot; (*PÊCHE*) sinker; (*ÉLEC*) fuse; **sans ~** (*essence etc*) unleaded

plombage [plɔ̃baʒ] *nm* (*de dent*) filling

plomberie [plɔ̃bʀi] *nf* plumbing

plombier [plɔ̃bje] *nm* plumber

plonge [plɔ̃ʒ] *nf* washing-up

plongeant, e [plɔ̃ʒã, ãt] *adj* (*vue*) from above; (*décolleté*) plunging

plongée [plɔ̃ʒe] *nf* (*SPORT*) diving *no pl*; (*sans scaphandre*) skin diving; **~ sous-marine** diving

plongeoir [plɔ̃ʒwaʀ] *nm* diving board

plongeon [plɔ̃ʒɔ̃] *nm* dive

plonger [plɔ̃ʒe] *vi* to dive ♦ *vt*: **~ qch dans** to plunge sth into; **se ~ dans** (*études, lecture*) to bury *ou* immerse o.s. in; **plongeur** *nm* diver

ployer [plwaje] *vt, vi* to bend

plu [ply] *pp de* **plaire; pleuvoir**

pluie [plɥi] *nf* rain

plume [plym] *nf* feather; (*pour écrire*) (pen) nib; (*fig*) pen

plupart [plypaʀ]: **la ~** *pron* the majority, most (of them); **la ~ des** most, the majority of; **la ~ du temps/d'entre nous** most of the time/of us; **pour la ~** for the most part, mostly

pluriel [plyʀjɛl] *nm* plural

plus¹ [ply] *vb voir* **plaire**

MOT-CLÉ

---

plus² [ply] *adv* **1** (*forme négative*): **ne ... plus** no more, no longer; **je n'ai plus d'argent** I've got no more money *ou* no money left; **il ne travaille plus** he's no longer working, he doesn't work any more

2 (*comparatif*) more, ...+er; (*superlatif*): **le plus** the most, the ...+est; **plus grand/ intelligent (que)** bigger/more intelligent (than); **le plus grand/intelligent** the biggest/most intelligent; **tout au plus** at the very most

3 (*davantage*) more; **il travaille plus (que)** he works more (than); **plus il travaille, plus il est heureux** the more he works, the happier he is; **plus de pain** more bread; **plus de 10 personnes** more than 10 people, over 10 people; **3 heures de plus que** 3 hours more than; **de plus** what's more, moreover; **3 kilos en plus** 3 kilos more; **en plus de** in addition to; **de plus en plus** more and more; **plus ou moins** more or less; **ni plus ni moins** no more, no less

♦ *prép*: **4 plus 2** 4 plus 2

---

plusieurs [plyzjœʀ] *dét, pron* several; **ils sont ~** there are several of them

plus-value [plyvaly] *nf* (*bénéfice*) surplus

plut [ply] *vb voir* **plaire**

plutôt [plyto] *adv* rather; **je préfère ~ celui-ci** I'd rather have this one; **~ que (de) faire** rather than *ou* instead of doing

pluvieux, -euse [plyvjø, jøz] *adj* rainy, wet

PME *sigle f* (= *petite(s) et moyenne(s) entreprise(s)*) small business(es)

PMU *sigle m* (= *Pari mutuel urbain*) system of betting on horses; (*café*) betting agency

PNB *sigle m* (= *produit national brut*) GNP

pneu [pnø] *nm* tyre (*BRIT*), tire (*US*)

pneumonie [pnømɔni] *nf* pneumonia

poche [pɔʃ] *nf* pocket; (*sous les yeux*) bag, pouch; **argent de ~** pocket money

pocher [pɔʃe] *vt* (*CULIN*) to poach

pochette [pɔʃɛt] *nf* (*d'aiguilles etc*) case; (*mouchoir*) breast pocket handkerchief; (*sac à main*) clutch bag; **~ de disque** record sleeve

poêle [pwal] *nm* stove ♦ *nf*: **~ (à frire)** frying pan

poème [pɔɛm] *nm* poem

poésie [pɔezi] *nf* (*poème*) poem; (*art*): **la ~** poetry

poète [pɔɛt] *nm* poet

poids [pwa] *nm* weight; (*SPORT*) shot; **vendre au ~** to sell by weight; **prendre du ~** to put on weight; **~ lourd** (*camion*) lorry (*BRIT*), truck (*US*)

poignant, e [pwaɲɑ̃, ɑ̃t] *adj* poignant

poignard [pwaɲaʀ] *nm* dagger; **poignarder ~** to stab, knife

poigne [pwaɲ] *nf* grip; **avoir de la ~** (*fig*) to rule with a firm hand

poignée [pwaɲe] *nf* (*de sel etc, fig*) handful; (*de couvercle, porte*) handle; **~ de main** handshake

poignet [pwaɲɛ] *nm* (*ANAT*) wrist; (*de chemise*) cuff

poil [pwal] *nm* (*ANAT*) hair; (*de pinceau, brosse*) bristle; (*de tapis*) strand; (*pelage*) coat; **à ~** (*fam*) starkers; **au ~** (*fam*) hunky-dory; **poilu, e** *adj* hairy

poinçon [pwɛ̃sɔ̃] *nm* (*marque*) hallmark; **poinçonner** [pwɛ̃sɔne] *vt* (*bijou*) to hallmark; (*billet*) to punch

poing [pwɛ̃] *nm* fist; **coup de ~** punch

point [pwɛ̃] *nm* (*lieu*) point; (*endroit*) spot; (*marque, signe*) dot; (: *de ponctuation*) full stop, period (*US*); (*COUTURE, TRICOT*) stitch ♦ *adv* = **pas²; faire le ~** (*fig*) to take stock (of the situation); **sur le ~ de faire** (just) about to do; **à tel ~ que** so much so that; **mettre au ~** (*procédé*) to develop; (*affaire*) to settle; **à ~** (*CULIN: viande*) medium; **à ~ (nommé)** just at the right time; **deux ~s** colon; **~ (de côté)** stitch (*pain*); **~ d'exclamation/d'interrogation**

exclamation/question mark; **~ de repère** landmark; (*dans le temps*) point of reference; **~ de suture** (*MÉD*) stitch; **~ de vente** retail outlet; **~ de vue** viewpoint; (*fig: opinion*) point of view; **~ d'honneur: mettre un ~ d'honneur à faire qch** to make it a point of honour to do sth; **~ faible/fort** weak/strong point; **~ noir** blackhead; **~s de suspension** suspension points

pointe [pwɛ̃t] *nf* point; (*clou*) tack; (*fig*): **une ~ de** a hint of; **être à la ~ de** (*fig*) to be in the forefront of; **sur la ~ des pieds** on tiptoe; **en ~** pointed, tapered; **de ~** (*technique etc*) leading; **heures de ~** peak hours

pointer [pwɛ̃te] *vt* (*diriger: canon, doigt*): **~ sur qch** to point at sth ♦ *vi* (*employé*) to clock in

pointillé [pwɛ̃tije] *nm* (*trait*) dotted line

pointilleux, -euse [pwɛ̃tijø, øz] *adj* particular, pernickety

pointu, e [pwɛ̃ty] *adj* pointed; (*voix*) shrill; (*analyse*) precise

pointure [pwɛ̃tyʀ] *nf* size

point-virgule [pwɛ̃viʀgyl] *nm* semi-colon

poire [pwaʀ] *nf* pear; (*fam: péj*) mug

poireau, x [pwaʀo] *nm* leek

poireauter [pwaʀote] *vi* (*fam*) to be left kicking one's heels

poirier [pwaʀje] *nm* pear tree

pois [pwa] *nm* (*BOT*) pea; (*sur une étoffe*) dot, spot; **~ chiche** chickpea; **à ~** (*cravate etc*) spotted, polka-dot *cpd*

poison [pwazɔ̃] *nm* poison

poisse [pwas] (*fam*) *nf* rotten luck

poisseux, -euse [pwasø, øz] *adj* sticky

poisson [pwasɔ̃] *nm* fish *gén inv*; **les P~** (*signe*) Pisces; **~ d'avril!** April fool!; **~ rouge** goldfish; **poissonnerie** *nf* fish-shop; **poissonnier, -ière** *nm/f* fishmonger (*BRIT*), fish merchant (*US*)

poitrine [pwatʀin] *nf* chest; (*seins*) bust, bosom; (*CULIN*) breast

poivre [pwavʀ] *nm* pepper

poivron [pwavʀɔ̃] *nm* pepper, capsicum

polaire [pɔlɛʀ] *adj* polar

polar [pɔlaʀ] (*fam*) *nm* detective novel

pôle [pol] *nm* (*GÉO, ÉLEC*) pole

poli, e [pɔli] *adj* polite; (*lisse*) smooth

police [pɔlis] *nf* police; **~ d'assurance** insurance policy; **~ judiciaire** ≃ Criminal Investigation Department (*BRIT*), ≃ Federal Bureau of Investigation (*US*); **~ secours** ≃ emergency services *pl* (*BRIT*), ≃ paramedics *pl* (*US*); **policier, -ière** *adj* police *cpd* ♦ *nm* policeman; (*aussi:* **roman policier**) detective novel

polio [pɔljo] *nf* polio

polir [pɔliʀ] *vt* to polish

polisson, ne [pɔlisɔ̃, ɔn] *nm/f* (*enfant*) (little) rascal

politesse [pɔlites] *nf* politeness

politicien, ne [pɔlitisjɛ̃, jɛn] (*péj*) *nm/f* politician

politique [pɔlitik] *adj* political ♦ *nf* politics *sg*; (*mesures, méthode*) policies *pl*

pollen [pɔlɛn] *nm* pollen

polluant, e [pɔlɥɑ̃, ɑ̃t] *adj* polluting; **produit ~** pollutant

polluer [pɔlɥe] *vt* to pollute; **pollution** *nf* pollution

polo [pɔlo] *nm* (*chemise*) polo shirt

Pologne [pɔlɔɲ] *nf*: **la ~** Poland; **polonais, e** *adj* Polish ♦ *nm/f*: **Polonais, e** Pole ♦ *nm* (*LING*) Polish

poltron, ne [pɔltʀɔ̃, ɔn] *adj* cowardly

polycopier [pɔlikɔpje] *vt* to duplicate

Polynésie [pɔlinezi] *nf*: **la ~** Polynesia

polyvalent, e [pɔlivalɑ̃, ɑ̃t] *adj* (*rôle*) varied; (*salle*) multi-purpose

pommade [pɔmad] *nf* ointment, cream

pomme [pɔm] *nf* apple; **tomber dans les ~s** (*fam*) to pass out; **~ d'Adam** Adam's apple; **~ de pin** pine *ou* fir cone; **~ de terre** potato

pommeau, x [pɔmo] *nm* (*boule*) knob; (*de selle*) pommel

pommette [pɔmet] *nf* cheekbone

pommier [pɔmje] *nm* apple tree

pompe [pɔ̃p] *nf* pump; (*faste*) pomp (and ceremony); **~ à essence** petrol pump; **~s funèbres** funeral parlour *sg*, undertaker's *sg*; **pomper** *vt* to pump; (*aspirer*) to pump up; (*absorber*) to soak up

pompeux, -euse [pɔ̃pø, øz] *adj* pompous

pompier [pɔ̃pje] *nm* fireman

pompiste [pɔ̃pist] *nm/f* petrol (*BRIT*) *ou* gas (*US*) pump attendant

poncer [pɔ̃se] *vt* to sand (down)

ponctuation [pɔ̃ktɥasjɔ̃] *nf* punctuation

ponctuel, le [pɔ̃ktɥel] *adj* punctual

pondéré, e [pɔ̃deʀe] *adj* level-headed, composed

pondre [pɔ̃dʀ] *vt* to lay

poney [pɔne] *nm* pony

pont [pɔ̃] *nm* bridge; (*NAVIG*) deck; **faire le ~** to take the extra day off; **~ suspendu** suspension bridge; **pont-levis** *nm* drawbridge

---

faire le pont

*❶ The expression "**faire le pont**" refers to the practice of taking a Monday or Friday off to make a long weekend if a public holiday falls on a Tuesday or Thursday. The French often do this at* l'Ascension, l'Assomption *and* le 14 juillet.

---

pop [pɔp] *adj inv* pop

populace [pɔpylas] (*péj*) *nf* rabble

populaire [pɔpylɛʀ] *adj* popular; (*manifestation*) mass *cpd*; (*milieux, quartier*) working-class; (*expression*) vernacular

popularité [pɔpylaʀite] *nf* popularity

population [pɔpylasjɔ̃] *nf* population; **~ active** working population

populeux, -euse [pɔpylø, øz] *adj* densely populated

porc [pɔʀ] *nm* pig; (*CULIN*) pork

porcelaine [pɔʀsəlɛn] *nf* porcelain, china; piece of china(ware)

porc-épic [pɔʀkepik] *nm* porcupine

porche [pɔʀʃ] *nm* porch

porcherie [pɔʀʃəʀi] *nf* pigsty

pore [pɔʀ] *nm* pore

porno [pɔʀno] *adj* porno ♦ *nm* porn

port [pɔʀ] *nm* harbour, port; (*ville*) port; (*de l'uniforme etc*) wearing; (*pour lettre*) postage; (*pour colis, aussi: posture*) carriage; **~ de pêche/de plaisance** fishing/sailing harbour

portable [pɔʀtabl] *nm* (*COMPUT*) laptop (computer)

portail [pɔʀtaj] *nm* gate

portant, e [pɔʀtɑ̃, ɑ̃t] *adj*: **bien/mal ~** in good/poor health

portatif, -ive [pɔʀtatif, iv] *adj* portable

porte [pɔʀt] *nf* door; (*de ville, jardin*) gate; **mettre à la ~** to throw out; **~ à ~** ♦ *nm* door-to-door selling; **~ d'entrée** front door; **porte-avions** *nm inv* aircraft carrier; **porte-bagages** *nm inv* luggage rack; **porte-bonheur** *nm inv* lucky charm; **porte-clefs** *nm inv* key ring; **porte-documents** *nm inv* attaché *ou* document case

porté, e [pɔʀte] *adj*: **être ~ à faire** to be inclined to do; **être ~ sur qch** to be keen on sth; **portée** *nf* (*d'une arme*) range; (*fig: effet*) impact, import; (*: capacité*) scope, capability; (*de chatte etc*) litter; (*MUS*) stave, staff; **à/hors de portée (de)** within/out of reach (of); **à portée de (la) main** within (arm's) reach; **à la portée de qn** (*fig*) at sb's level, within sb's capabilities

porte...: **porte-fenêtre** *nf* French window; **portefeuille** *nm* wallet; **portemanteau, x** *nm* (*cintre*) coat hanger; (*au mur*) coat rack; **porte-monnaie** *nm inv* purse; **porte-parole** *nm inv* spokesman

porter [pɔʀte] *vt* to carry; (*sur soi: vêtement, barbe, bague*) to wear; (*fig: responsabilité etc*) to bear, carry; (*inscription, nom, fruits*) to bear; (*coup*) to deal; (*attention*) to turn; (*apporter*): **~ qch à qn** to take sth to sb ♦ *vi* (*voix*) to carry; (*coup, argument*) to hit home; **se ~** *vi* (*se sentir*): **se ~ bien/mal** to be well/unwell; **~ sur** (*recherches*) to be concerned with; **se faire ~ malade** to report sick

porteur [pɔʀtœʀ, øz] *nm* (*de bagages*) porter; (*de chèque*) bearer

porte-voix [pɔʀtəvwa] *nm inv* megaphone

portier [pɔʀtje] *nm* doorman

portière [pɔʀtjɛʀ] *nf* door

portillon [pɔʀtijɔ̃] *nm* gate

portion [pɔʀsjɔ̃] *nf* (*part*) portion, share; (*partie*) portion, section

porto [pɔʀto] *nm* port (wine)

portrait [pɔʀtʀɛ] *nm* (*peinture*) portrait; (*photo*) photograph; **portrait-robot** *nm* Identikit ® *ou* photo-fit ® picture

portuaire [pɔʀtɥɛʀ] *adj* port *cpd*, harbour *cpd*

portugais, e [pɔʀtygɛ, ɛz] *adj* Portuguese ♦ *nm/f*: **P~, e** Portuguese ♦ *nm* (*LING*) Portuguese

Portugal [pɔʀtygal] *nm*: **le ~** Portugal

pose [poz] *nf* (*de moquette*) laying; (*attitude, d'un modèle*) pose; (*PHOTO*) exposure

posé, e [poze] *adj* serious

poser [poze] *vt* to put; (*installer: moquette, carrelage*) to lay; (*rideaux, papier peint*) to hang; (*question*) to ask; (*principe, conditions*) to lay *ou* set down; (*problème*) to formulate; (*difficulté*) to pose ♦ *vi* (*modèle*) to pose; **se ~** *vi* (*oiseau, avion*) to land; (*question*) to arise; **~ qch (sur)** (*déposer*) to put sth down (on); **~ qch sur/quelque part** (*placer*) to put sth on/somewhere; **~ sa candidature à un poste** to apply for a post

positif, -ive [pozitif, iv] *adj* positive

position [pozisjɔ̃] *nf* position; **prendre ~** (*fig*) to take a stand

posologie [pozɔlɔʒi] *nf* dosage

posséder [pɔsede] *vt* to own, possess; (*qualité, talent*) to have, possess; (*sexuellement*) to possess; **possession** *nf* ownership *no pl*, possession

possibilité [pɔsibilite] *nf* possibility; **~s** *nfpl* (*potentiel*) potential *sg*

possible [pɔsibl] *adj* possible; (*projet, entreprise*) feasible ♦ *nm*: **faire son ~** to do all one can, do one's utmost; **le plus/moins de livres ~** as many/few books as possible; **le plus vite ~** as quickly as pos sible; **dès que ~** as soon as possible

postal, e, -aux [pɔstal, o] *adj* postal

poste [pɔst] *nf (service)* post, postal service; *(administration, bureau)* post office ♦ *nm (fonction, MIL)* post; *(TÉL)* extension; *(de radio etc)* set; **mettre à la ~** to post; **~ (de police)** *nm* police station; **~ de secours** *nm* first-aid post; **~ restante** *nf* poste restante *(BRIT)*, general delivery *(US)*

poster¹ [pɔste] *vt* to post

poster² [pɔstɛʀ] *nm* poster

postérieur, e [pɔsteʀjœʀ] *adj (date)* later; *(partie)* back ♦ *nm (fam)* behind

posthume [pɔstym] *adj* posthumous

postulant, e [pɔstylɑ̃, ɑ̃t] *nm/f* applicant

postuler [pɔstyle] *vi*: **~ à** *ou* **pour un emploi** to apply for a job

posture [pɔstyʀ] *nf* position

pot [po] *nm (en verre)* jar; *(en terre)* pot; *(en plastique, carton)* carton; *(en métal)* tin; *(fam: chance)* luck; **avoir du ~** *(fam)* to be lucky; **boire** *ou* **prendre un ~** *(fam)* to have a drink; **petit ~ (pour bébé)** (jar of) baby food; **~ catalytique** catalytic converter; **~ d'échappement** exhaust pipe; **~ de fleurs** plant pot, flowerpot; *(plante)* pot plant

potable [pɔtabl] *adj*: **eau (non) ~** (non-) drinking water

potage [pɔtaʒ] *nm* soup; **potager, -ère** *adj*: **(jardin) potager** kitchen *ou* vegetable garden

pot-au-feu [pɔtofø] *nm inv* (beef) stew

pot-de-vin [podvɛ̃] *nm* bribe

pote [pɔt] *(fam) nm* pal

poteau, x [pɔto] *nm* post; **~ indicateur** signpost

potelé, e [pɔt(ə)le] *adj* plump, chubby

potence [pɔtɑ̃s] *nf* gallows *sg*

potentiel, le [pɔtɑ̃sjɛl] *adj, nm* potential

poterie [pɔtʀi] *nf* pottery; *(objet)* piece of pottery

potier, jer [pɔtje, jɛʀ] *nm* potter

potins [pɔtɛ̃] *(fam) nmpl* gossip *sg*

potiron [pɔtiʀɔ̃] *nm* pumpkin

pou, x [pu] *nm* louse

poubelle [pubɛl] *nf* (dust)bin

pouce [pus] *nm* thumb

poudre [pudʀ] *nf* powder; *(fard)* (face) powder; *(explosif)* gunpowder; **en ~: café en ~** instant coffee; **lait en ~** dried *ou* powdered milk; **poudreuse** *nf* powder snow; **poudrier** *nm* (powder) compact

pouffer [pufe] *vi*: **~ (de rire)** to burst out laughing

poulailler [pulaje] *nm* henhouse

poulain [pulɛ̃] *nm* foal; *(fig)* protégé

poule [pul] *nf* hen; *(CULIN)* (boiling) fowl

poulet [pulɛ] *nm* chicken; *(fam)* cop

poulie [puli] *nf* pulley

pouls [pu] *nm* pulse; **prendre le ~ de qn** to feel sb's pulse

poumon [pumɔ̃] *nm* lung

poupe [pup] *nf* stern; **en ~** astern

poupée [pupe] *nf* doll

pouponnière [pupɔnjɛʀ] *nf* crèche, day nursery

pour [puʀ] *prép* for ♦ *nm*: **le ~ et le contre** the pros and cons; **~ faire** (so as) to do, in order to do; **~ avoir fait** for having done; **~ que** so that, in order that; **~ 100 francs d'essence** 100 francs' worth of petrol; **~ cent** per cent; **~ ce qui est de** as for

pourboire [puʀbwaʀ] *nm* tip

pourcentage [puʀsɑ̃taʒ] *nm* percentage

pourchasser [puʀʃase] *vt* to pursue

pourparlers [puʀpaʀle] *nmpl* talks, negotiations

pourpre [puʀpʀ] *adj* crimson

pourquoi [puʀkwa] *adv, conj* why ♦ *nm inv*: **le ~ (de)** the reason (for)

pourrai *etc* [puʀe] *vb voir* **pouvoir**

pourri, e [puʀi] *adj* rotten

pourrir [puʀiʀ] *vi* to rot; *(fruit)* to go rotten *ou* bad ♦ *vt* to rot; *(fig)* to spoil thoroughly; **pourriture** *nf* rot

pourrons *etc* [puʀɔ̃] *vb voir* **pouvoir**

poursuite [puʀsɥit] *nf* pursuit, chase; **~s** *nfpl (JUR)* legal proceedings

poursuivre [puʀsɥivʀ] *vt* to pursue, chase (after); *(obséder)* to haunt; *(JUR)* to bring

proceedings against, prosecute; (: *au civil*)
to sue; (*but*) to strive towards; (*continuer:
études etc*) to carry on with, continue; **se
~** *vi* to go on, continue
pourtant [puʀtɑ̃] *adv* yet; **c'est ~ facile**
(and) yet it's easy
pourtour [puʀtuʀ] *nm* perimeter
pourvoir [puʀvwaʀ] *vt*: **~ qch/qn de** to
equip sth/sb with ♦ *vi*: **~ à** to provide for;
pourvoyeur *nm* supplier; **pourvu, e**
adj: **pourvu de** equipped with; **pourvu
que** (*si*) provided that, so long as; (*espér-
ons que*) let's hope (that)
pousse [pus] *nf* growth; (*bourgeon*) shoot
poussé, e [puse] *adj* (*enquête*) exhaustive;
(*études*) advanced; **poussée** *nf* thrust;
(*d'acné*) eruption; (*fig: prix*) upsurge
pousser [puse] *vt* to push; (*émettre: cri,
soupir*) to give; (*stimuler: élève*) to urge on;
(*poursuivre: études, discussion*) to carry on
(further) ♦ *vi* to push; (*croître*) to grow;
se ~ *vi* to move over; **~ qn à** (*inciter*) to
urge ou press sb to; (*acculer*) to drive sb
to; **faire ~** (*plante*) to grow
poussette [puset] *nf* push chair (*BRIT*),
stroller (*US*)
poussière [pusjɛʀ] *nf* dust; **poussié-
reux, -euse** *adj* dusty
poussin [pusɛ̃] *nm* chick
poutre [putʀ] *nf* beam

─── MOT-CLÉ ───

pouvoir [puvwaʀ] *nm* power; (*POL: diri-
geants*): **le pouvoir** those in power; **les
pouvoirs publics** the authorities; **pouvoir
d'achat** purchasing power
♦ *vb semi-aux* **1** (*être en état de*) can, be
able to; **je ne peux pas le réparer** I can't
ou I am not able to repair it; **déçu de ne
pas pouvoir le faire** disappointed not to
be able to do it
2 (*avoir la permission*) can, may, be allowed to; **vous pouvez aller au cinéma**
you can *ou* may go to the pictures
3 (*probabilité, hypothèse*) may, might,
could; **il a pu avoir un accident** he may

ou might *ou* could have had an accident,
il aurait pu le dire! he might *ou* could
have said (so)!
♦ *vb impers* may, might, could; **il peut arriver que** it may *ou* might *ou* could happen that
♦ *vt* can, be able to; **j'ai fait tout ce que
j'ai pu** I did all I could; **je n'en peux
plus** (*épuisé*) I'm exhausted; (*à bout*) I
can't take any more; **se pouvoir** *vi*: **il se
peut que** it may *ou* might be that; **cela
se pourrait** that's quite possible

prairie [pʀeʀi] *nf* meadow
praline [pʀalin] *nf* sugared almond
praticable [pʀatikabl] *adj* passable, prac-
ticable
pratiquant, e [pʀatikɑ̃, ɑ̃t] *nm/f* (regular)
churchgoer
pratique [pʀatik] *nf* practice ♦ *adj* practical; **pratiquement** *adv* (*pour ainsi dire*)
practically, virtually; **pratiquer** *vt* to practise; (*l'équitation, la pêche*) to go in for; (*le
golf, football*) to play; (*intervention, opération*) to carry out
pré [pʀe] *nm* meadow
préalable [pʀealabl] *adj* preliminary; **au ~**
beforehand
préambule [pʀeɑ̃byl] *nm* preamble; (*fig*)
prelude; **sans ~** straight away
préau [pʀeo] *nm* (*SCOL*) covered playground
préavis [pʀeavi] *nm* notice
précaution [pʀekosjɔ̃] *nf* precaution; **ave**
~ cautiously; **par ~** as a precaution
précédemment [pʀesedamɑ̃] *adv* before,
previously
précédent, e [pʀesedɑ̃, ɑ̃t] *adj* previou
♦ *nm* precedent
précéder [pʀesede] *vt* to precede
précepteur, -trice [pʀeseptœʀ, tʀi
nm/f (private) tutor
prêcher [pʀefe] *vt* to preach
précieux, -euse [pʀesjø, jøz] *adj* pre
cious; (*aide, conseil*) invaluable
précipice [pʀesipis] *nm* drop, chasm

précipitamment [pʀesipitamɑ̃] *adv* hurriedly, hastily

précipitation [pʀesipitasjɔ̃] *nf* (*hâte*) haste; **~s** *nfpl* (*pluie*) rain *sg*

précipité, e [pʀesipite] *adj* hurried, hasty

précipiter [pʀesipite] *vt* (*hâter: départ*) to hasten; (*faire tomber*): **~ qn/qch du haut de** to throw *ou* hurl sb/sth off *ou* from; **se ~** *vi* to speed up; **se ~ sur/vers** to rush at/towards

précis, e [pʀesi, iz] *adj* precise; (*mesures*) accurate, precise; **à 4 heures ~es** at 4 o'clock sharp; **précisément** *adv* precisely; **préciser** *vt* (*expliquer*) to be more specific about, clarify; (*spécifier*) to state, specify; **se préciser** *vi* to become clear(er); **précision** *nf* precision; (*détail*) point *ou* detail; **demander des précisions** to ask for further explanation

précoce [pʀekɔs] *adj* early; (*enfant*) precocious

préconçu, e [pʀekɔ̃sy] *adj* preconceived

préconiser [pʀekɔnize] *vt* to advocate

prédécesseur [pʀedesesœʀ] *nm* predecessor

prédilection [pʀedileksjɔ̃] *nf*: **avoir une ~ pour** to be partial to

prédire [pʀediʀ] *vt* to predict

prédominer [pʀedɔmine] *vi* to predominate

préface [pʀefas] *nf* preface

préfecture [pʀefektyʀ] *nf* prefecture; **~ de police** police headquarters *pl*

préférable [pʀefeʀabl] *adj* preferable

préféré, e [pʀefeʀe] *adj, nm/f* favourite

préférence [pʀefeʀɑ̃s] *nf* preference; **de ~** preferably

préférer [pʀefeʀe] *vt*: **~ qn/qch (à)** to prefer sb/sth (to), like sb/sth better (than); **~ faire** to prefer to do; **je ~ais du thé** I would rather have tea, I'd prefer tea

préfet [pʀefe] *nm* prefect

préhistorique [pʀeistɔʀik] *adj* prehistoric

préjudice [pʀeʒydis] *nm* (*matériel*) loss; (*moral*) harm *no pl*; **porter ~ à** to harm, be detrimental to; **au ~ de** at the expense of

préjugé [pʀeʒyʒe] *nm* prejudice; **avoir un ~ contre** to be prejudiced *ou* biased against

préjuger [pʀeʒyʒe]: **~ de** *vt* to prejudge

prélasser [pʀelase]: **se ~** *vi* to lounge

prélèvement [pʀelɛvmɑ̃] *nm* (*montant*) deduction; **faire un ~ de sang** to take a blood sample

prélever [pʀel(ə)ve] *vt* (*échantillon*) to take; **~ (sur)** (*montant*) to deduct (from); (*argent: sur son compte*) to withdraw (from)

prématuré, e [pʀematyʀe] *adj* premature ♦ *nm* premature baby

premier, -ière [pʀəmje, jɛʀ] *adj* first; (*rang*) front; (*fig: objectif*) basic; **le ~ venu** the first person to come along; **de ~ ordre** first-rate; **P~ Ministre** Prime Minister; **première** *nf* (*SCOL*) lower sixth form; (*THÉÂTRE*) first night; (*AUTO*) first (gear); (*AVIAT, RAIL etc*) first class; (*CINÉMA*) première; (*exploit*) first; **premièrement** *adv* firstly

prémonition [pʀemɔnisjɔ̃] *nf* premonition

prémunir [pʀemyniʀ]: **se ~** *vi*: **se ~ contre** to guard against

prenant, e [pʀənɑ̃, ɑ̃t] *adj* absorbing, engrossing

prénatal, e [pʀenatal] *adj* (*MÉD*) antenatal

prendre [pʀɑ̃dʀ] *vt* to take; (*repas*) to have; (*se procurer*) to get; (*malfaiteur, poisson*) to catch; (*passager*) to pick up; (*personnel*) to take on; (*traiter: personne*) to handle; (*voix, ton*) to put on; (*ôter*): **~ qch à** to take sth from; (*coincer*): **se ~ les doigts dans** to get one's fingers caught in ♦ *vi* (*liquide, ciment*) to set; (*greffe, vaccin*) to take; (*feu: foyer*) to go; (*se diriger*): **~ à gauche** to turn (to the) left; **~ froid** to catch cold; **se ~ pour** to think one is; **s'en ~ à** to attack; **se ~ d'amitié pour** to befriend; **s'y ~** (*procéder*) to set about it

preneur [pʀənœʀ, øz] *nm*: **être/trouver ~** to be willing to buy/find a buyer

preniez [pʀənje] *vb voir* **prendre**

prenne *etc* [pʀɛn] *vb voir* **prendre**

prénom [pʀenɔ̃] *nm* first *ou* Christian name

préoccupation [pʀeɔkypasjɔ̃] *nf* (*souci*) concern; (*idée fixe*) preoccupation

préoccuper [pʀeɔkype] *vt* (*inquiéter*) to worry; (*absorber*) to preoccupy; **se ~ de** to be concerned with

préparatifs [pʀepaʀatif] *nmpl* preparations

préparation [pʀepaʀasjɔ̃] *nf* preparation

préparer [pʀepaʀe] *vt* to prepare; (*café, thé*) to make; (*examen*) to prepare for; (*voyage, entreprise*) to plan; **se ~** *vi* (*orage, tragédie*) to brew, be in the air; **~ qch à qn** (*surprise etc*) to have sth in store for sb; **se ~ (à qch/faire)** to prepare (o.s.) *ou* get ready (for sth/to do)

prépondérant, e [pʀepɔ̃deʀɑ̃, ɑ̃t] *adj* major, dominating

préposé, e [pʀepoze] *nm/f* employee; (*facteur*) postman

préposition [pʀepozisjɔ̃] *nf* preposition

près [pʀɛ] *adv* near, close; **~ de** near (to), close to; (*environ*) nearly, almost; **de ~** closely; **à 5 kg ~** to within about 5 kg; **à cela ~ que** apart from the fact that; **il n'est pas à 10 minutes ~** he can spare 10 minutes

présage [pʀezaʒ] *nm* omen; **présager** *vt* to foresee

presbyte [pʀɛsbit] *adj* long-sighted

presbytère [pʀɛsbiteʀ] *nm* presbytery

prescription [pʀɛskʀipsjɔ̃] *nf* prescription

prescrire [pʀɛskʀiʀ] *vt* to prescribe

présence [pʀezɑ̃s] *nf* presence; (*au bureau, à l'école*) attendance

présent, e [pʀezɑ̃, ɑ̃t] *adj, nm* present; **à ~ (que)** now (that)

présentation [pʀezɑ̃tasjɔ̃] *nf* presentation; (*de nouveau venu*) introduction; (*allure*) appearance; **faire les ~s** to do the introductions

présenter [pʀezɑ̃te] *vt* to present; (*excuses, condoléances*) to offer; (*invité, conférencier*): **~ qn (à)** to introduce sb (to) ♦ *vi*: **~ bien** to have a pleasing appearance; **se**

~ *vi* (*occasion*) to arise; **se ~ à** (*examen*) to sit; (*élection*) to stand at, run for

préservatif [pʀezɛʀvatif, iv] *nm* sheath, condom

préserver [pʀezɛʀve] *vt*: **~ de** (*protéger*) to protect from

président [pʀezidɑ̃] *nm* (*POL*) president; (*d'une assemblée, COMM*) chairman; **~ directeur général** chairman and managing director; **présidentielles** *nfpl* presidential elections

présider [pʀezide] *vt* to preside over; (*dîner*) to be the guest of honour at

présomptueux, -euse [pʀezɔ̃ptɥø, øz] *adj* presumptuous

presque [pʀɛsk] *adv* almost, nearly; **~ personne** hardly anyone; **~ rien** hardly anything; **~ pas** hardly (at all); **~ pas (de)** hardly any

presqu'île [pʀɛskil] *nf* peninsula

pressant, e [pʀesɑ̃, ɑ̃t] *adj* urgent

presse [pʀɛs] *nf* press; (*affluence*): **heures de ~** busy times

pressé, e [pʀese] *adj* in a hurry; (*travail*) urgent; **orange ~e** freshly-squeezed orange juice

pressentiment [pʀesɑ̃timɑ̃] *nm* foreboding, premonition

pressentir [pʀesɑ̃tiʀ] *vt* to sense

presse-papiers [pʀɛspapje] *nm inv* paperweight

presser [pʀese] *vt* (*fruit, éponge*) to squeeze; (*bouton*) to press; (*allure*) to speed up; (*inciter*): **~ qn de faire** to urge *ou* press sb to do ♦ *vi* to be urgent; **se ~** *vi* (*se hâter*) to hurry (up); **se ~ contre qn** to squeeze up against sb; **rien ne presse** there's no hurry

pressing [pʀesiŋ] *nm* (*magasin*) dry cleaner's

pression [pʀesjɔ̃] *nf* pressure; (*bouton*) press stud; (*fam: bière*) draught beer; **faire ~ sur** to put pressure on; **~ artérielle** blood pressure

prestance [pʀɛstɑ̃s] *nf* presence, imposing bearing

restataire [prestatɛr] *nm/f* supplier

restation [prestasjɔ̃] *nf* (*allocation*) benefit; (*d'une entreprise*) service provided; (*d'un artiste*) performance

restidigitateur, -trice [prestidiʒitatœr, tris] *nm/f* conjurer

restige [prestiʒ] *nm* prestige; **prestigieux, -euse** *adj* prestigious

résumer [prezyme] *vt*: **~ que** to presume *ou* assume that

rêt, e [prɛ, prɛt] *adj* ready ♦ *nm* (*somme*) loan; **prêt-à-porter** *nm* ready-to-wear *ou* off-the-peg (*BRIT*) clothes *pl*

rétendre [pretɑ̃dr] *vt* (*affirmer*): **~ que** to claim that; (*avoir l'intention de*): **~ faire qch** to mean *ou* intend to do sth; **prétendu, e** *adj* (*supposé*) so-called

rétentieux, -euse [pretɑ̃sjø, jøz] *adj* pretentious

rétention [pretɑ̃sjɔ̃] *nf* claim; (*vanité*) pretentiousness; **~s** *nfpl* (*salaire*) expected salary

rêter [prete] *vt* (*livres, argent*): **~ qch (à)** to lend sth (to); (*supposer*): **~ à qn** (*caractère, propos*) to attribute to sb; **se ~ à** to lend o.s. (*ou* itself) to; (*manigances etc*) to go along with; **~ à** (*critique, commentaires etc*) to be open to, give rise to; **~ attention à** to pay attention to; **~ serment** to take the oath

rétexte [pretɛkst] *nm* pretext, excuse; **sous aucun ~** on no account; **prétexter** *vt* to give as a pretext *ou* an excuse

rêtre [prɛtr] *nm* priest

reuve [prœv] *nf* proof; (*indice*) proof, evidence *no pl*; **faire ~ de** to show; **faire ses ~s** to prove o.s. (*ou* itself)

révaloir [prevalwar] *vi* to prevail

révenant, e [prev(ə)nɑ̃, ɑ̃t] *adj* thoughtful, kind

révenir [prev(ə)nir] *vt* (*éviter: catastrophe etc*) to avoid, prevent; (*anticiper: désirs, besoins*) to anticipate; **~ qn (de)** (*avertir*) to warn sb (about); (*informer*) to tell *ou* inform sb (about)

'éventif, -ive [prevɑ̃tif, iv] *adj* preventive

prévention [prevɑ̃sjɔ̃] *nf* prevention; **~ routière** road safety

prévenu, e [prev(ə)ny] *nm/f* (*JUR*) defendant, accused

prévision [previzjɔ̃] *nf*: **~s** predictions; (*ÉCON*) forecast *sg*; **en ~ de** in anticipation of; **~s météorologiques** weather forecast *sg*

prévoir [prevwar] *vt* (*anticiper*) to foresee; (*s'attendre à*) to expect, reckon on; (*organiser: voyage etc*) to plan; (*envisager*) to allow; **comme prévu** as planned; **prévoyant, e** *adj* gifted with (*ou* showing) foresight; **prévu, e** *pp* de **prévoir**

prier [prije] *vi* to pray ♦ *vt* (*Dieu*) to pray to; (*implorer*) to beg; (*demander*): **~ qn de faire** to ask sb to do; **se faire ~** to need coaxing *ou* persuading; **je vous en prie** (*allez-y*) please do; (*de rien*) don't mention it; **prière** *nf* prayer; **"prière de ..."** "please ..."

primaire [primɛr] *adj* primary ♦ *nm* (*SCOL*) primary education

prime [prim] *nf* (*bonus*) bonus; (*subvention*) premium; (*COMM: cadeau*) free gift; (*ASSURANCES, BOURSE*) premium ♦ *adj*: **de ~ abord** at first glance; **primer** *vt* (*récompenser*) to award a prize to ♦ *vi* to dominate; to be most important

primeurs [primœr] *nfpl* early fruits and vegetables

primevère [primvɛr] *nf* primrose

primitif, -ive [primitif, iv] *adj* primitive; (*originel*) original

primordial, e, -iaux [primɔrdjal, jo] *adj* essential

prince [prɛ̃s] *nm* prince; **princesse** *nf* princess

principal, e, -aux [prɛ̃sipal, o] *adj* principal, main ♦ *nm* (*SCOL*) principal, head(master); (*essentiel*) main thing

principe [prɛ̃sip] *nm* principle; **par ~** on principle; **en ~** (*habituellement*) as a rule; (*théoriquement*) in principle

printemps [prɛ̃tɑ̃] *nm* spring

priorité [prijɔrite] *nf* priority; (*AUTO*) right of way; **~ à droite** right of way to vehicles coming from the right

pris, e [pri, priz] *pp de* **prendre** ♦ *adj* (*place*) taken; (*mains*) full; (*personne*) busy; **avoir le nez/la gorge ~(e)** to have a stuffy nose/a hoarse throat; **être ~ de panique** to be panic-stricken

prise [priz] *nf* (*d'une ville*) capture; (*PÊCHE, CHASSE*) catch; (*point d'appui ou pour empoigner*) hold; (*ÉLEC: fiche*) plug; (: *femelle*) socket; **être aux ~s avec** to be grappling with; **~ de conscience** awareness, realization; **~ de contact** (*rencontre*) initial meeting, first contact; **~ de courant** power point; **~ de sang** blood test; **~ de vue** (*photo*) shot; **~ multiple** adaptor

priser [prize] *vt* (*estimer*) to prize, value

prison [prizɔ̃] *nf* prison; **aller/être en ~** to go to/be in prison *ou* jail; **prisonnier, -ière** *nm/f* prisoner ♦ *adj* captive

prit [pri] *vb voir* **prendre**

privé, e [prive] *adj* private ♦ *nm* (*COMM*) private sector; **en ~** in private

priver [prive] *vt*: **~ qn de** to deprive sb of; **se ~ de** to go *ou* do without

privilège [privilɛʒ] *nm* privilege

prix [pri] *nm* price; (*récompense, SCOL*) prize; **hors de ~** exorbitantly priced; **à aucun ~** not at any price; **à tout ~** at all costs; **~ d'achat/de vente/de revient** purchasing/selling/cost price

probable [prɔbabl] *adj* likely, probable; **probablement** *adv* probably

probant, e [prɔbɑ̃, ɑ̃t] *adj* convincing

problème [prɔblɛm] *nm* problem

procédé [prɔsede] *nm* (*méthode*) process; (*comportement*) behaviour *no pl*

procéder [prɔsede] *vi* to proceed; (*moralement*) to behave; **~ à** to carry out

procès [prɔsɛ] *nm* trial; (*poursuites*) proceedings *pl*; **être en ~ avec** to be involved in a lawsuit with

processus [prɔsesys] *nm* process

procès-verbal, -aux [prɔsɛverbal, o] *nm* (*de réunion*) minutes *pl*; (*aussi*: **P.V.**) parking ticket

prochain, e [prɔʃɛ̃, ɛn] *adj* next; (*proche: départ, arrivée*) impending ♦ *nm* fellow man; **la ~e fois/semaine ~e** next time/week; **prochainement** *adv* soon, shortly

proche [prɔʃ] *adj* nearby; (*dans le temps*) imminent; (*parent, ami*) close; **~s** *nmp* (*parents*) close relatives; **être ~ (de)** to be near, be close (to); **le P~ Orient** the Middle East

proclamer [prɔklame] *vt* to proclaim

procuration [prɔkyrasjɔ̃] *nf* proxy

procurer [prɔkyre] *vt*: **~ qch à qn** (*fournir*) to obtain sth for sb; (*causer: plaisir etc*) to bring sb sth; **se ~** *vt* to get; **procureur** *nm* public prosecutor

prodige [prɔdiʒ] *nm* marvel, wonder; (*personne*) prodigy; **prodiguer** *vt* (*soins, attentions*): **prodiguer qch à qn** to give sb sth

producteur, -trice [prɔdyktœr, tris] *nm/f* producer

productif, -ive [prɔdyktif, iv] *adj* productive

production [prɔdyksjɔ̃] *nf* production; (*rendement*) output

productivité [prɔdyktivite] *nf* productivity

produire [prɔdɥir] *vt* to produce; **se ~** (*événement*) to happen, occur; (*acteur*) to perform, appear

produit [prɔdɥi] *nm* product; **~ chimique** chemical; **~ d'entretien** cleaning product; **~ national brut** gross national product; **~s alimentaires** foodstuffs

prof [prɔf] (*fam*) *nm* teacher

profane [prɔfan] *adj* (*REL*) secular ♦ *nm* layman(-woman)

proférer [prɔfere] *vt* to utter

professeur [prɔfesœr] *nm* teacher; (*de faculté*) (university) lecturer; (: *titulaire d'une chaire*) professor

profession [prɔfesjɔ̃] *nf* occupation; **~ libérale** (liberal) profession; **sans ~** unemployed; **professionnel, le** *adj, nm/f* professional

profil [prɔfil] *nm* profile; **de ~** in profile

profit [pʀɔfi] nm (avantage) benefit, advantage; (COMM, FINANCE) profit; **au ~ de** in aid of; **tirer ~ de** to profit from; **profitable** adj (utile) beneficial; (lucratif) profitable; **profiter** vi: **profiter de** (situation, occasion) to take advantage of; (vacances, jeunesse etc) to make the most of

profond, e [pʀɔfɔ̃, ɔ̃d] adj deep; (sentiment, intérêt) profound; **profondément** adv deeply; **il dort profondément** he is sound asleep; **profondeur** nf depth

progéniture [pʀɔʒenityʀ] nf offspring inv

programme [pʀɔgʀam] nm programme; (SCOL) syllabus, curriculum; (INFORM) program; **programmer** vt (émission) to schedule; (INFORM) to program; **programmeur, -euse** nm/f programmer

progrès [pʀɔgʀɛ] nm progress no pl; **faire des ~** to make progress; **progresser** vi to progress; **progressif, -ive** adj progressive

prohiber [pʀɔibe] vt to prohibit, ban

proie [pʀwa] nf prey no pl

projecteur [pʀɔʒɛktœʀ] nm (pour film) projector; (de théâtre, cirque) spotlight

projectile [pʀɔʒɛktil] nm missile

projection [pʀɔʒɛksjɔ̃] nf projection; (séance) showing

projet [pʀɔʒɛ] nm plan; (ébauche) draft; **~ de loi** bill; **projeter** vt (envisager) to plan; (film, photos) to project; (ombre, lueur) to throw, cast; (jeter) to throw up (ou off ou out)

prolétaire [pʀɔletɛʀ] adj, nmf proletarian

prolongement [pʀɔlɔ̃ʒmɑ̃] nm extension; **dans le ~ de** running on from

prolonger [pʀɔlɔ̃ʒe] vt (débat, séjour) to prolong; (délai, billet, rue) to extend; **se ~** vi to go on

promenade [pʀɔm(ə)nad] nf walk (ou drive ou ride); **faire une ~** to go for a walk; **une ~ en voiture/à vélo** a drive/(bicycle) ride

promener [pʀɔm(ə)ne] vt (chien) to take out for a walk; (doigts, regard): **~ qch sur** to run sth over; **se ~** vi to go for (ou be

out for) a walk

promesse [pʀɔmɛs] nf promise

promettre [pʀɔmɛtʀ] vt to promise ♦ vi to be ou look promising; **~ à qn de faire** to promise sb that one will do

promiscuité [pʀɔmiskɥite] nf (chambre) lack of privacy

promontoire [pʀɔmɔ̃twaʀ] nm headland

promoteur, -trice [pʀɔmɔtœʀ, tʀis] nm/f: **~ (immobilier)** property developer (BRIT), real estate promoter (US)

promotion [pʀɔmosjɔ̃] nf promotion; **en ~** on special offer

promouvoir [pʀɔmuvwaʀ] vt to promote

prompt, e [pʀɔ̃(pt), pʀɔ̃(p)t] adj swift, rapid

prôner [pʀone] vt (préconiser) to advocate

pronom [pʀɔnɔ̃] nm pronoun

prononcer [pʀɔnɔ̃se] vt to pronounce; (dire) to utter; (discours) to deliver; **se ~** vi to be pronounced; **se ~ (sur)** (se décider) to reach a decision (on ou about), give a verdict (on); **prononciation** nf pronunciation

pronostic [pʀɔnɔstik] nm (MÉD) prognosis; (fig: aussi: **~s**) forecast

propagande [pʀɔpagɑ̃d] nf propaganda

propager [pʀɔpaʒe] vt to spread; **se ~** vi to spread

prophète [pʀɔfɛt] nm prophet

prophétie [pʀɔfesi] nf prophecy

propice [pʀɔpis] adj favourable

proportion [pʀɔpɔʀsjɔ̃] nf proportion; **toute(s) ~(s) gardée(s)** making due allowance(s)

propos [pʀɔpo] nm (intention) intention, aim; (sujet): **à quel ~?** what about? ♦ nmpl (paroles) talk no pl, remarks; **à ~ de** about, regarding; **à tout ~** for the slightest thing ou reason; **à ~** by the way; (opportunément) at the right moment

proposer [pʀɔpoze] vt to propose; **~ qch (à qn)** (suggérer) to suggest sth (to sb), propose sth to sb); (offrir) to offer (sb) sth; **se ~** to offer one's services; **se ~ de faire** to intend ou propose to do; **propo-**

sition (*suggestion*) *nf* proposal, suggestion; (*LING*) clause

propre [pʀɔpʀ] *adj* clean; (*net*) neat, tidy; (*possessif*) own; (*sens*) literal; (*particulier*): ~ **à** peculiar to; (*approprié*): ~ **à** suitable for
♦ *nm*: **recopier au ~** to make a fair copy of; **proprement** *adv* (*avec propreté*) cleanly; **le village proprement dit** the village itself; **à proprement parler** strictly speaking; **propreté** *nf* cleanliness

propriétaire [pʀɔpʀijetɛʀ] *nm/f* owner; (*pour le locataire*) landlord(-lady)

propriété [pʀɔpʀijete] *nf* property; (*droit*) ownership

propulser [pʀɔpylse] *vt* to propel

proroger [pʀɔʀɔʒe] *vt* (*prolonger*) to extend

proscrire [pʀɔskʀiʀ] *vt* (*interdire*) to ban, prohibit

prose [pʀoz] *nf* (*style*) prose

prospecter [pʀɔspɛkte] *vt* to prospect; (*COMM*) to canvass

prospectus [pʀɔspɛktys] *nm* leaflet

prospère [pʀɔspɛʀ] *adj* prosperous; **prospérer** *vi* to prosper

prosterner [pʀɔstɛʀne]: **se ~** *vi* to bow low, prostrate o.s.

prostituée [pʀɔstitɥe] *nf* prostitute

prostitution [pʀɔstitysjɔ̃] *nf* prostitution

protecteur, -trice [pʀɔtɛktœʀ, tʀis] *adj* protective; (*air, ton*: *péj*) patronizing
♦ *nm/f* protector

protection [pʀɔtɛksjɔ̃] *nf* protection; (*d'un personnage influent*: *aide*) patronage

protéger [pʀɔteʒe] *vt* to protect; **se ~ de** *ou* **contre** to protect o.s. from

protéine [pʀɔtein] *nf* protein

protestant, e [pʀɔtɛstɑ̃, ɑ̃t] *adj, nm/f* Protestant

protestation [pʀɔtɛstasjɔ̃] *nf* (*plainte*) protest

protester [pʀɔtɛste] *vi*: ~ **(contre)** to protest (against *ou* about); ~ **de** (*son innocence*) to protest

prothèse [pʀɔtɛz] *nf*: ~ **dentaire** denture

protocole [pʀɔtɔkɔl] *nm* (*fig*) etiquette

proue [pʀu] *nf* bow(s *pl*), prow

prouesse [pʀuɛs] *nf* feat

prouver [pʀuve] *vt* to prove

provenance [pʀɔv(ə)nɑ̃s] *nf* origin; **avio** **en ~ de** plane (arriving) from

provenir [pʀɔv(ə)niʀ]: ~ **de** *vt* to com from

proverbe [pʀɔvɛʀb] *nm* proverb

province [pʀɔvɛ̃s] *nf* province

proviseur [pʀɔvizœʀ] *nm* ≃ head(teache (*BRIT*), ≃ principal (*US*)

provision [pʀɔvizjɔ̃] *nf* (*réserve*) stock, sup ply; **~s** *nfpl* (*vivres*) provisions, food *no pl*

provisoire [pʀɔvizwaʀ] *adj* temporary **provisoirement** *adv* temporarily

provocant, e [pʀɔvɔkɑ̃, ɑ̃t] *adj* provoca tive

provoquer [pʀɔvɔke] *vt* (*défier*) to pro voke; (*causer*) to cause, bring about; (*inc ter*): ~ **qn à** to incite sb to

proxénète [pʀɔksenɛt] *nm* procurer

proximité [pʀɔksimite] *nf* nearness, close ness; (*dans le temps*) imminence, close ness; **à ~** near *ou* close by; **à ~ de** nea (to), close to

prudemment [pʀydamɑ̃] *adv* carefully wisely, sensibly

prudence [pʀydɑ̃s] *nf* carefulness; **avec ~** carefully; **par ~** as a precaution

prudent, e [pʀydɑ̃, ɑ̃t] *adj* (*pas téméraire* careful; (: *en général*) safety-consciou (*sage, conseillé*) wise, sensible; **c'est plu** ~ it's wiser

prune [pʀyn] *nf* plum

pruneau, x [pʀyno] *nm* prune

prunelle [pʀynɛl] *nf* (*BOT*) sloe; **il y tie** **comme à la ~ de ses yeux** he treasure *ou* cherishes it

prunier [pʀynje] *nm* plum tree

PS *sigle m* = **parti socialiste**

psaume [psom] *nm* psalm

pseudonyme [psødɔnim] *nm* (*gén*) fic tious name; (*d'écrivain*) pseudonym, pe name

psychanalyse [psikanaliz] *nf* psych analysis

●**sychiatre** [psikjatʀ] *nm/f* psychiatrist; **psychiatrique** *adj* psychiatric

●**sychique** [psiʃik] *adj* psychological

●**sychologie** [psikɔlɔʒi] *nf* psychology; **psychologique** *adj* psychological; **psychologue** *nm/f* psychologist

●**.T.T.** *sigle fpl* = **Postes, Télécommunications et Télédiffusion**

●**u** [py] *pp de* **pouvoir**

uanteur [pɥɑ̃tœʀ] *nf* stink, stench

●**ub** [pyb] *nf* (*fam: annonce*) ad, advert; (*pratique*) advertising

●**ublic, -ique** [pyblik] *adj* public; (*école, instruction*) state *cpd* ♦ *nm* public; (*assistance*) audience; **en ~** in public

●**ublicitaire** [pyblisitɛʀ] *adj* advertising *cpd*; (*film*) publicity *cpd*

ublicité [pyblisite] *nf* (*méthode, profession*) advertising; (*annonce*) advertisement; (*révélations*) publicity

ublier [pyblije] *vt* to publish

ublique [pyblik] *adj voir* **public**

uce [pys] *nf* flea; (*INFORM*) chip; **carte à ~** smart card; **~s** *nfpl* (*marché*) flea market *sg*

udeur [pydœʀ] *nf* modesty

udique [pydik] *adj* (*chaste*) modest; (*discret*) discreet

uer [pɥe] (*péj*) *vi* to stink

uéricultrice [pɥeʀikyltʀis] *nf* p(a)ediatric nurse

uéril, e [pɥeʀil] *adj* childish

uis [pɥi] *vb voir* **pouvoir** ♦ *adv* then

uiser [pɥize] *vt*: **~ (dans)** to draw (from)

uisque [pɥisk] *conj* since

uissance [pɥisɑ̃s] *nf* power; **en ~** ♦ *adj* potential

uissant, e [pɥisɑ̃, ɑ̃t] *adj* powerful

uisse *etc* [pɥis] *vb voir* **pouvoir**

uits [pɥi] *nm* well

ull(-over) [pyl(ɔvɛʀ)] *nm* sweater

ulluler [pylyle] *vi* to swarm

ulpe [pylp] *nf* pulp

ulvérisateur [pylveʀizatœʀ] *nm* spray

ulvériser [pylveʀize] *vt* to pulverize; (*liquide*) to spray

punaise [pynɛz] *nf* (*ZOOL*) bug; (*clou*) drawing pin (*BRIT*), thumbtack (*US*)

punch¹ [pɔ̃ʃ] *nm* (*boisson*) punch

punch² [pœnʃ] *nm* (*BOXE, fig*) punch

punir [pyniʀ] *vt* to punish; **punition** *nf* punishment

pupille [pypij] *nf* (*ANAT*) pupil ♦ *nm/f* (*enfant*) ward

pupitre [pypitʀ] *nm* (*SCOL*) desk

pur, e [pyʀ] *adj* pure; (*vin*) undiluted; (*whisky*) neat; **en ~e perte** to no avail; **c'est de la folie ~e** it's sheer madness; **purement** *adv* purely

purée [pyʀe] *nf*: **~ (de pommes de terre)** mashed potatoes *pl*; **~ de marrons** chestnut purée

purgatoire [pyʀgatwaʀ] *nm* purgatory

purger [pyʀʒe] *vt* (*MÉD, POL*) to purge; (*JUR: peine*) to serve

purin [pyʀɛ̃] *nm* liquid manure

pur-sang [pyʀsɑ̃] *nm inv* thoroughbred

pus [py] *nm* pus

putain [pytɛ̃] (*fam!*) *nf* whore (*!*)

puzzle [pœzl] *nm* jigsaw (puzzle)

P.-V. *sigle m* = **procès-verbal**

pyjama [piʒama] *nm* pyjamas *pl* (*BRIT*), pajamas *pl* (*US*)

pyramide [piʀamid] *nf* pyramid

Pyrénées [piʀene] *nfpl*: **les ~** the Pyrenees

Q, q

QI *sigle m* (= *quotient intellectuel*) IQ

quadragénaire [k(w)adʀaʒenɛʀ] *nm/f* man/woman in his/her forties

quadriller [kadʀije] *vt* (*POLICE*) to keep under tight control

quadruple [k(w)adʀypl] *nm*: **le ~ de** four times as much as; **quadruplés, -ées** *nm/fpl* quadruplets, quads

quai [ke] *nm* (*de port*) quay; (*de gare*) platform; **être à ~** (*navire*) to be alongside

qualification [kalifikasjɔ̃] *nf* (*aptitude*)

qualification

qualifié, e [kalifje] *adj* qualified; *(main d'œuvre)* skilled

qualifier [kalifje] *vt* to qualify; **se ~** *vi* to qualify; **~ qch/qn de** to describe sth/sb as

qualité [kalite] *nf* quality

quand [kɑ̃] *conj, adv* when; **~ je serai riche** when I'm rich; **~ même** all the same; **~ même, il exagère!** really, he overdoes it!; **~ bien même** even though

quant [kɑ̃]: **~ à** *prép (pour ce qui est de)* as for, as to; *(au sujet de)* regarding; **quant-à-soi** *nm*: **rester sur son quant-à-soi** to remain aloof

quantité [kɑ̃tite] *nf* quantity, amount; *(grand nombre)*: **une** *ou* **des ~(s) de** a great deal of

quarantaine [karɑ̃tɛn] *nf* (*MÉD*) quarantine; **avoir la ~** *(âge)* to be around forty; **une ~ (de)** forty or so, about forty

quarante [karɑ̃t] *num* forty

quart [kar] *nm (fraction)* quarter; *(surveillance)* watch; **un ~ de vin** a quarter litre of wine; **le ~ de** a quarter of; **~ d'heure** quarter of an hour; **~s de finale** quarter finals

quartier [kartje] *nm (de ville)* district, area; *(de bœuf)* quarter; *(de fruit)* piece; **cinéma de ~** local cinema; **avoir ~ libre** *(fig)* to be free; **~ général** headquarters *pl*

quartz [kwarts] *nm* quartz

quasi [kazi] *adv* almost, nearly; **quasiment** *adv* almost, nearly; **quasiment jamais** hardly ever

quatorze [katɔrz] *num* fourteen

quatre [katr] *num* four; **à ~ pattes** on all fours; **se mettre en ~ pour qn** to go out of one's way for sb; **~ à ~** *(monter, descendre)* four at a time; **quatre-quarts** *nm inv* pound cake; **quatre-vingt-dix** *num* ninety; **quatre-vingts** *num* eighty; **quatre-vingt-un** *num* eighty-one; **quatrième** *num* fourth ♦ *nf (SCOL)* third form *ou* year

quatuor [kwatɥɔr] *nm* quartet(te)

┌─ *MOT-CLÉ* ─────────────────

que [kə] *conj* **1** *(introduisant complétive)* that; **il sait que tu es là** he knows (that) you're here; **je veux que tu acceptes** want you to accept; **il a dit que oui** h said he would *(ou* it was *etc)*

2 *(reprise d'autres conjonctions)*: **quand** rentrera et qu'il aura mangé when h gets back and (when) he has eaten; **s vous y allez ou que vous ...** if you g there or if you ...

3 *(en tête de phrase: hypothèse, souhait etc)*: **qu'il le veuille ou non** whether he likes or not; **qu'il fasse ce qu'il voudra!** le him do as he pleases!

4 *(après comparatif)* than, as; *voir aus* **plus; aussi; autant** *etc*

5 *(seulement)*: **ne ... que** only; **il ne bo que de l'eau** he only drinks water

♦ *adv (exclamation)*: **qu'il** *ou* **qu'est-c qu'il est bête/court vite!** he's so silly!/h runs so fast!; **que de livres!** what a lot c books!

♦ *pron* **1** *(relatif: personne)* whom; (: *chos* that, which; **l'homme que je vois** th man (whom) I see; **le livre que tu voi** the book (that *ou* which) you see; **u jour que j'étais ...** a day when I was ...

2 *(interrogatif)* what; **que fais-tu? qu'est-ce que tu fais?** what are yo doing?; **qu'est-ce que c'est?** what is it what's that?; **que faire?** what can or do?

└──────────────────────────

Québec [kebɛk] *n*: **le ~** Quebec; **québé cois, e** *adj* Quebec ♦ *nm/f*: **Québecoi e** Quebecker ♦ *nm (LING)* Quebec French

┌─ *MOT-CLÉ* ─────────────────

quel, quelle [kɛl] *adj* **1** *(interrogatif: pe sonne)* who; (: *chose)* what; which; **qu est cet homme?** who is this man?; **qu est ce livre?** what is this book?; **qu livre/homme?** what book/man?; *(par un certain choix)* which book/man?; **que**

acteurs préférez-vous? which actors do you prefer?; **dans quels pays êtes-vous allé?** which *ou* what countries did you go to?
2 (*exclamatif*): **quelle surprise!** what a surprise!
3: quel que soit le coupable whoever is guilty; **quel que soit votre avis** whatever your opinion

quelconque [kɛlkɔ̃k] *adj* (*indéfini*): **un ami/prétexte ~** some friend/pretext or other; (*médiocre: repas*) indifferent, poor; (*laid: personne*) plain-looking

---
MOT-CLÉ
---

quelque [kɛlk] *adj* **1** some; a few; (*tournure interrogative*) any; **quelque espoir** some hope; **il a quelques amis** he has a few *ou* some friends; **a-t-il quelques amis?** has he any friends?; **les quelques livres qui** the few books which; **20 kg et quelque(s)** a bit over 20 kg
2: quelque ... que: quelque livre qu'il choisisse whatever (*ou* whichever) book he chooses
3: quelque chose something; (*tournure interrogative*) anything; **quelque chose d'autre** something else; anything else; **quelque part** somewhere; anywhere; **en quelque sorte** as it were
♦ *adv* (*environ*): **quelque 100 mètres** some 100 metres
2: quelque peu rather, somewhat

---

quelquefois [kɛlkəfwa] *adv* sometimes
quelques-uns, -unes [kɛlkəzœ̃, yn] *pron* a few, some
quelqu'un [kɛlkœ̃] *pron* someone, somebody; (+*tournure interrogative*) anyone, anybody; **~ d'autre** someone *ou* somebody else; (+ *tournure interrogative*) anybody else
quémander [kemɑ̃de] *vt* to beg for
qu'en dira-t-on [kɑ̃diratɔ̃] *nm inv*: **le ~-~-~** gossip, what people say

querelle [kəʀɛl] *nf* quarrel; **quereller: se quereller** *vi* to quarrel
qu'est-ce que [kɛskə] *voir* **que**
qu'est-ce qui [kɛski] *voir* **qui**
question [kɛstjɔ̃] *nf* question; (*fig*) matter, issue; **il a été ~ de** we (*ou* they) spoke about; **de quoi est-il ~?** what is it about?; **il n'en est pas ~** there's no question of it; **hors de ~** out of the question; **remettre en ~** to question; **questionnaire** *nm* questionnaire; **questionner** *vt* to question
quête [kɛt] *nf* collection; (*recherche*) quest, search; **faire la ~** (*à l'église*) to take the collection; (*artiste*) to pass the hat round
quetsche [kwɛtʃ] *nf* kind of dark-red plum
queue [kø] *nf* tail; (*fig: du classement*) bottom; (: *de poêle*) handle; (: *de fruit, feuille*) stalk; (: *de train, colonne, file*) rear; **faire la ~** to queue (up) (*BRIT*), line up (*US*); **~ de cheval** ponytail; **~ de poisson** (*AUT*): **faire une ~ de poisson à qn** to cut in front of sb
qui [ki] *pron* (*personne*) who; (+*prép*) whom; (*chose, animal*) which; that; **qu'est-ce ~ est sur la table?** what is on the table?; **~ est-ce ~?** who?; **~ est-ce que?** who?; **à ~ est ce sac?** whose bag is this?; **à ~ parlais-tu?** who were you talking to?, to whom were you talking?; **amenez ~ vous voulez** bring who you like; **~ que ce soit** whoever it may be
quiconque [kikɔ̃k] *pron* (*celui qui*) whoever, anyone who; (*n'importe qui*) anyone, anybody
quiétude [kjetyd] *nf*: **en toute ~** in complete peace
quille [kij] *nf*: **(jeu de) ~s** skittles *sg* (*BRIT*), bowling (*US*)
quincaillerie [kɛ̃kajʀi] *nf* (*ustensiles*) hardware; (*magasin*) hardware shop; **quincaillier, -ière** *nm/f* hardware dealer
quinquagénaire [kɛ̃kaʒenɛʀ] *nm/f* man/woman in his/her fifties
quintal, -aux [kɛ̃tal, o] *nm* quintal (*100 kg*)

quinte [kɛ̃t] *nf*: ~ **(de toux)** coughing fit

quintuple [kɛ̃typl] *nm*: **le ~ de** five times as much as; **quintuplés, -ées** *nm/fpl* quintuplets, quins

quinzaine [kɛ̃zɛn] *nf*: **une ~ (de)** about fifteen, fifteen or so; **une ~ (de jours)** a fortnight (*BRIT*), two weeks

quinze [kɛ̃z] *num* fifteen; **dans ~ jours** in a fortnight('s time), in two weeks(' time)

quiproquo [kiprɔko] *nm* misunderstanding

quittance [kitɑ̃s] *nf* (*reçu*) receipt

quitte [kit] *adj*: **être ~ envers qn** to be no longer in sb's debt; (*fig*) to be quits with sb; **~ à faire** even if it means doing

quitter [kite] *vt* to leave; (*vêtement*) to take off; **se ~** *vi* (*couples, interlocuteurs*) to part; **ne quittez pas** (*au téléphone*) hold the line

qui-vive [kiviv] *nm*: **être sur le ~-~** to be on the alert

quoi [kwa] *pron* (*interrogatif*) what; **~ de neuf?** what's the news?; **as-tu de ~ écrire?** have you anything to write with?; **~ qu'il arrive** whatever happens; **~ qu'il en soit** be that as it may; **~ que ce soit** anything at all; **"il n'y a pas de ~"** "(please) don't mention it"; **il n'y a pas de ~ rire** there's nothing to laugh about; **à ~ bon?** what's the use?; **en ~ puis-je vous aider?** how can I help you?

quoique [kwak] *conj* (al)though

quote-part [kɔtpar] *nf* share

quotidien, ne [kɔtidjɛ̃, jɛn] *adj* daily; (*banal*) everyday ♦ *nm* (*journal*) daily (paper); **quotidiennement** *adv* daily

R, r

r. *abr* = **route**; **rue**

rab [rab] (*fam*) *nm* (*nourriture*) extra; **est-ce qu'il y a du ~?** is there any extra (left)?

rabâcher [rabaʃe] *vt* to keep on repeating

rabais [rabɛ] *nm* reduction, discount; **rabaisser** *vt* (*dénigrer*) to belittle; (*rabattre:*

prix) to reduce

rabat-joie [rabaʒwa] *nm inv* killjoy

rabattre [rabatr] *vt* (*couvercle, siège*) to pull down; (*déduire*) to reduce; **se ~** *vi* (*se refermer: couvercle*) to fall shut; (*véhicule, coureur*) to cut in; **se ~ sur** to fall back on

rabbin [rabɛ̃] *nm* rabbi

râblé, e [rable] *adj* stocky

rabot [rabo] *nm* plane

rabougri, e [rabugri] *adj* stunted

rabrouer [rabrue] *vt* to snub

racaille [rakaj] (*péj*) *nf* rabble, riffraff

raccommoder [rakɔmɔde] *vt* to mend, repair; **se ~** *vi* (*fam*) to make it up

raccompagner [rakɔ̃paɲe] *vt* to take *or* see back

raccord [rakɔr] *nm* link; (*retouche*) touch up; **raccorder** *vt* to join (up), link up; (*suj: pont etc*) to connect, link

raccourci [rakursi] *nm* short cut

raccourcir [rakursir] *vt* to shorten ♦ *vi* (*jours*) to grow shorter, draw in

raccrocher [rakrɔʃe] *vt* (*tableau*) to hang back up; (*récepteur*) to put down ♦ *vi* (*TÉL*) to hang up, ring off; **se ~ à** *vt* to cling to, hang on to

race [ras] *nf* race; (*d'animaux, fig*) breed; **de ~** purebred, pedigree

rachat [raʃa] *nm* buying; (*du même objet*) buying back

racheter [raʃ(ə)te] *vt* (*article perdu*) to buy another; (*après avoir vendu*) to buy back; (*d'occasion*) to buy; (*COMM: part, firme*) to buy up; (*davantage*): **~ du lait/3 œufs** to buy more milk/another 3 eggs *ou* 3 more eggs; **se ~** *vi* (*fig*) to make amends

racial, e, -aux [rasjal, jo] *adj* racial

racine [rasin] *nf* root; **~ carrée/cubique** square/cube root

raciste [rasist] *adj, nm/f* raci(al)ist

racket [raket] *nm* racketeering *no pl*

raclée [rakle] (*fam*) *nf* hiding, thrashing

racler [rakle] *vt* (*surface*) to scrape; **se ~ gorge** to clear one's throat

racoler [rakɔle] *vt* (*suj: prostituée*) to solicit;

(: *parti, marchand*) to tout for
acontars [Rakɔ̃tar] *nmpl* story, lie
aconter [Rakɔ̃te] *vt*: ~ **(à qn)** (*décrire*) to
relate (to sb), tell (sb) about; (*dire de mauvaise foi*) to tell (sb); ~ **une histoire** to tell
a story
acorni, e [Rakɔʀni] *adj* hard(ened)
adar [Radar] *nm* radar
ade [Rad] *nf* (*natural*) harbour; **rester en**
~ (*fig*) to be left stranded
adeau, x [Rado] *nm* raft
adiateur [Radjatœʀ] *nm* radiator, heater;
(*AUTO*) radiator; ~ **électrique/à gaz**
electric/gas heater *ou* fire
adiation [Radjasjɔ̃] *nf* (*PHYSIQUE*) radiation
adical, e, -aux [Radikal, o] *adj* radical
adier [Radje] *vt* to strike off
adieux, -euse [Radjø, jøz] *adj* radiant
adin, e [Radɛ̃, in] (*fam*) *adj* stingy
adio [Radjo] *nf* radio; (*MÉD*) X-ray ♦ *nm*
radio operator; **à la** ~ on the radio; **ra-
dioactif, -ive** *adj* radioactive; **radiocassette** *nm* cassette radio, radio cassette
player; **radiodiffuser** *vt* to broadcast;
radiographie *nf* radiography; (*photo*)
X-ray photograph; **radiophonique** *adj*
radio *cpd*; **radio-réveil** (*pl* **radios-
réveils**) *nm* radio alarm clock
adis [Radi] *nm* radish
adoter [Radɔte] *vi* to ramble on
adoucir [Radusir]: **se** ~ *vi* (*temps*) to become milder; (*se calmer*) to calm down
afale [Rafal] *nf* (*vent*) gust (of wind); (*tir*)
burst of gunfire
affermir [Rafɛrmir] *vt* to firm up; **se** ~
vi (*fig: autorité, prix*) to strengthen
affiner [Rafine] *vt* to refine; **raffinerie** *nf*
refinery
affoler [Rafɔle]: ~ **de** *vt* to be very keen
on
afistoler [Rafistɔle] (*fam*) *vt* to patch up
afle [Rafl] *nf* (*de police*) raid; **rafler** (*fam*)
vt to swipe, nick
afraîchir [Rafreʃir] *vt* (*atmosphère, température*) to cool (down); (*aussi:* **mettre à
~**) to chill; (*fig: rénover*) to brighten up; **se**

~ *vi* (*temps*) to grow cooler; (*en se lavant*)
to freshen up; (*en buvant*) to refresh o.s.;
rafraîchissant, e *adj* refreshing; **ra-
fraîchissement** *nm* (*boisson*) cool drink;
rafraîchissements *nmpl* (*boissons, fruits
etc*) refreshments
rage [Raʒ] *nf* (*MÉD*): **la** ~ rabies; (*fureur*)
rage, fury; **faire** ~ to rage; ~ **de dents**
(raging) toothache
ragot [Rago] (*fam*) *nm* malicious gossip *no
pl*
ragoût [Ragu] *nm* stew
raide [Rɛd] *adj* stiff; (*câble*) taut, tight; (*escarpé*) steep; (*droit: cheveux*) straight; (*fam:
sans argent*) flat broke; (*osé*) daring, bold
♦ *adv* (*en pente*) steeply; ~ **mort** stone
dead; **raidir** *vt* (*muscles*) to stiffen; **se raidir** *vi* (*tissu*) to stiffen; (*personne*) to tense
up; (: *se préparer moralement*) to brace
o.s.; (*fig: position*) to harden; **raideur** *nf*
(*rigidité*) stiffness; **avec raideur** (*répondre*)
stiffly, abruptly
raie [Rɛ] *nf* (*ZOOL*) skate, ray; (*rayure*)
stripe; (*des cheveux*) parting
raifort [Refɔr] *nm* horseradish
rail [Raj] *nm* rail; (*chemins de fer*) railways
pl; **par** ~ by rail
railler [Raje] *vt* to scoff at, jeer at
rainure [Renyr] *nf* groove
raisin [Rezɛ̃] *nm* (*aussi:* ~**s**) grapes *pl*; ~**s
secs** raisins
raison [Rezɔ̃] *nf* reason; **avoir** ~ to be
right; **donner** ~ **à qn** to agree with sb;
(*événement*) to prove sb right; **perdre la** ~
to become insane; ~ **de plus** all the
more reason; **à plus forte** ~ all the more
so; **en** ~ **de** because of; **à** ~ **de** at the
rate of; **sans** ~ for no reason; **raisonnable** *adj* reasonable, sensible
raisonnement [Rezɔnmɑ̃] *nm* (*façon de
réfléchir*) reasoning; (*argumentation*) argument
raisonner [Rezɔne] *vi* (*penser*) to reason;
(*argumenter, discuter*) to argue ♦ *vt* (*personne*) to reason with
rajeunir [Raʒœnir] *vt* (*suj: coiffure, robe*): ~

qn to make sb look younger; *(fig: personnel)* to inject new blood into ♦ *vi* to become *(ou* look) younger

rajouter [ʀaʒute] *vt* to add

rajuster [ʀaʒyste] *vt (vêtement)* to straighten, tidy; *(salaires)* to adjust

ralenti [ʀalɑ̃ti] *nm*: **au ~** *(fig)* at a slower pace; **tourner au ~** *(AUTO)* to tick over *(AUTO)*, idle

ralentir [ʀalɑ̃tiʀ] *vt* to slow down

râler [ʀɑle] *vi* to groan; *(fam)* to grouse, moan (and groan)

rallier [ʀalje] *vt (rejoindre)* to rejoin; *(gagner à sa cause)* to win over; **se ~ à** *(avis)* to come over *ou* round to

rallonge [ʀalɔ̃ʒ] *nf (de table)* (extra) leaf

rallonger [ʀalɔ̃ʒe] *vt* to lengthen

rallye [ʀali] *nm* rally; *(POL)* march

ramassage [ʀamasaʒ] *nm*: **~ scolaire** school bus service

ramassé, e [ʀamase] *adj (trapu)* squat

ramasser [ʀamase] *vt (objet tombé ou par terre, fam)* to pick up; *(recueillir: copies, ordures)* to collect; *(récolter)* to gather; **se ~** *vi (sur soi-même)* to huddle up; **ramassis** *(péj) nm (de voyous)* bunch; *(d'objets)* jumble

rambarde [ʀɑ̃baʀd] *nf* guardrail

rame [ʀam] *nf (aviron)* oar; *(de métro)* train; *(de papier)* ream

rameau, x [ʀamo] *nm* (small) branch; **les R~x** *(REL)* Palm Sunday *sg*

ramener [ʀam(ə)ne] *vt* to bring back; *(reconduire)* to take back; **~ qch à** *(réduire à)* to reduce sth to

ramer [ʀame] *vi* to row

ramollir [ʀamɔliʀ] *vt* to soften; **se ~** *vi* to go soft

ramoner [ʀamɔne] *vt* to sweep

rampe [ʀɑ̃p] *nf (d'escalier)* banister(s *pl*); *(dans un garage)* ramp; *(THÉÂTRE)*: **la ~** the footlights *pl*; **~ de lancement** launching pad

ramper [ʀɑ̃pe] *vi* to crawl

rancard [ʀɑ̃kaʀ] *(fam) nm (rendez-vous)* date

rancart [ʀɑ̃kaʀ] *nm*: **mettre au ~** *(fam)* to scrap

rance [ʀɑ̃s] *adj* rancid

rancœur [ʀɑ̃kœʀ] *nf* rancour

rançon [ʀɑ̃sɔ̃] *nf* ransom

rancune [ʀɑ̃kyn] *nf* grudge, rancour; **garder ~ à qn (de qch)** to bear sb a grudge (for sth); **sans ~!** no hard feelings!; **rancunier, -ière** *adj* vindictive, spiteful

randonnée [ʀɑ̃dɔne] *nf* ride; *(pédestre)* walk, ramble; *(: en montagne)* hike, hiking, *no pl*

rang [ʀɑ̃] *nm (rangée)* row; *(grade, classement)* rank; **~s** *nmpl (MIL)* ranks; **se mettre en ~s** to get into *ou* form rows; **au premier ~** in the first row; *(fig)* ranking first

rangé, e [ʀɑ̃ʒe] *adj (vie)* well-ordered; *(personne)* steady

rangée [ʀɑ̃ʒe] *nf* row

ranger [ʀɑ̃ʒe] *vt (mettre de l'ordre dans)* to tidy up; *(classer, grouper)* to order, arrange; *(mettre à sa place)* to put away; *(fig: classer)*: **~ qn/qch parmi** to rank sb/ sth among; **se ~** *vi (véhicule, conducteur)* to pull over *ou* in; *(piéton)* to step aside; *(s'assagir)* to settle down; **se ~ à** *(avis)* to come round to

ranimer [ʀanime] *vt (personne)* to bring round; *(douleur, souvenir)* to revive; *(feu)* to rekindle

rap [ʀap] *nm* rap (music)

rapace [ʀapas] *nm* bird of prey

râpe [ʀɑp] *nf (CULIN)* grater; **râper** *vt (CULIN)* to grate

rapetisser [ʀap(ə)tise] *vt* to shorten

rapide [ʀapid] *adj* fast; *(prompt: coup d'œil, mouvement)* quick ♦ *nm* express (train); *(de cours d'eau)* rapid; **rapidement** *adv* fast; quickly

rapiécer [ʀapjese] *vt* to patch

rappel [ʀapel] *nm (THÉÂTRE)* curtain call; *(MÉD: vaccination)* booster; *(deuxième avis)* reminder; **rappeler** *vt* to call back; *(ambassadeur, MIL)* to recall; *(faire se souvenir)*: **rappeler qch à qn** to remind sb of sth

se rappeler vt (*se souvenir de*) to remember, recall

rapport [ʀapɔʀ] nm (*lien, analogie*) connection; (*compte rendu*) report; (*profit*) yield, return; **~s** nmpl (*entre personnes, pays*) relations; **avoir ~ à** to have something to do with; **être/se mettre en ~ avec qn** to be/get in touch with sb; **par ~ à** in relation to; **~s (sexuels)** (sexual) intercourse sg

rapporter [ʀapɔʀte] vt (*rendre, ramener*) to bring back; (*bénéfice*) to yield, bring in; (*mentionner, répéter*) to report ♦ vi (*investissement*) to give a good return ou yield; (: *activité*) to be very profitable; **se ~ à** vt (*correspondre à*) to relate to; **rapporteur, -euse** nm/f (*péj*) telltale ♦ nm (*GÉOM*) protractor

rapprochement [ʀapʀɔʃmɑ̃] nm (*de nations*) reconciliation; (*rapport*) parallel

rapprocher [ʀapʀɔʃe] vt (*deux objets*) to bring closer together; (*fig: ennemis, partis etc*) to bring together; (*comparer*) to establish a parallel between; (*chaise d'une table*): **~ qch (de)** to bring sth closer (to); **se ~** vi to draw closer ou nearer; **se ~ de** to come closer to; (*présenter une analogie avec*) to be close to

rapt [ʀapt] nm abduction

raquette [ʀakɛt] nf (*de tennis*) racket; (*de ping-pong*) bat

rare [ʀaʀ] adj rare; **se faire ~** to become scarce; **rarement** adv rarely, seldom

ras, e [ʀɑ, ʀɑz] adj (*poil, herbe*) short; (*tête*) close-cropped ♦ adv short; **en ~e campagne** in open country; **à ~ bords** to the brim; **en avoir ~ le bol** (*fam*) to be fed up; **~ du cou** ♦ adj (*pull, robe*) crew-neck

rasade [ʀɑzad] nf glassful

raser [ʀɑze] vt (*barbe, cheveux*) to shave off; (*menton, personne*) to shave; (*fam: ennuyer*) to bore; (*démolir*) to raze (to the ground); (*frôler*) to graze, skim; **se ~** vi to shave; (*fam*) to be bored (to tears); **rasoir** nm razor

rassasier [ʀɑsazje] vt: **être rassasié** to have eaten one's fill

rassemblement [ʀasɑ̃bləmɑ̃] nm (*groupe*) gathering; (*POL*) union

rassembler [ʀasɑ̃ble] vt (*réunir*) to assemble, gather; (*documents, notes*) to gather together, collect; **se ~** vi to gather

rassis, e [ʀasi, iz] adj (*pain*) stale

rassurer [ʀasyʀe] vt to reassure; **se ~** vi to reassure o.s.; **rassure-toi** don't worry

rat [ʀa] nm rat

rate [ʀat] nf spleen

raté, e [ʀate] adj (*tentative*) unsuccessful, failed ♦ nm/f (*fam: personne*) failure

râteau, x [ʀɑto] nm rake

rater [ʀate] vi (*affaire, projet etc*) to go wrong, fail ♦ vt (*fam: cible, train, occasion*) to miss; (*plat*) to spoil; (*fam: examen*) to fail

ration [ʀasjɔ̃] nf ration

ratisser [ʀatise] vt (*allée*) to rake; (*feuilles*) to rake up; (*suj: armée, police*) to comb

RATP sigle f (= *Régie autonome des transports parisiens*) Paris transport authority

rattacher [ʀataʃe] vt (*animal, cheveux*) to tie up again; (*fig: relier*): **~ qch à** to link sth with

rattrapage [ʀatʀapaʒ] nm: **cours de ~** remedial class

rattraper [ʀatʀape] vt (*fugitif*) to recapture; (*empêcher de tomber*) to catch (hold of); (*atteindre, rejoindre*) to catch up with; (*réparer: erreur*) to make up for; **se ~** vi to make up for it; **se ~ (à)** (*se raccrocher*) to stop o.s. falling (by catching hold of)

rature [ʀatyʀ] nf deletion, erasure

rauque [ʀok] adj (*voix*) hoarse

ravages [ʀavaʒ] nmpl: **faire des ~** to wreak havoc

ravaler [ʀavale] vt (*mur, façade*) to restore; (*déprécier*) to lower

ravi, e [ʀavi] adj: **être ~ de/que** to be delighted with/that

ravigoter [ʀavigɔte] (*fam*) vt to buck up

ravin [ʀavɛ̃] nm gully, ravine

ravir [ʀaviʀ] vt (*enchanter*) to delight; **à ~** adv beautifully

raviser [ravize]: **se ~** *vi* to change one's mind

ravissant, e [ravisɑ̃, ɑ̃t] *adj* delightful

ravisseur, -euse [ravisœr, øz] *nm/f* abductor, kidnapper

ravitaillement [ravitajmɑ̃] *nm* (*réserves*) supplies *pl*

ravitailler [ravitaje] *vt* (*en vivres, ammunitions*) to provide with fresh supplies; (*avion*) to refuel; **se ~** *vi* to get fresh supplies; (*avion*) to refuel

raviver [ravive] *vt* (*feu, douleur*) to revive; (*couleurs*) to brighten up

rayé, e [reje] *adj* (*à rayures*) striped

rayer [reje] *vt* (*érafler*) to scratch; (*barrer*) to cross out; (*d'une liste*) to cross off

rayon [rejɔ̃] *nm* (*de soleil etc*) ray; (*GÉOM*) radius; (*de roue*) spoke; (*étagère*) shelf; (*de grand magasin*) department; **dans un ~ de** within a radius of; **~ de soleil** sunbeam; **~s X** X-rays

rayonnement [rejɔnmɑ̃] *nm* (*fig: d'une culture*) influence

rayonner [rejɔne] *vi* (*fig*) to shine forth; (*personne: de joie, de beauté*) to be radiant; (*touriste*) to go touring (*from one base*)

rayure [rejyr] *nf* (*motif*) stripe; (*éraflure*) scratch; **à ~s** striped

raz-de-marée [rɑdmare] *nm inv* tidal wave

ré [re] *nm* (*MUS*) D; (*en chantant la gamme*) re

réacteur [reaktœr] *nm* (*d'avion*) jet engine; (*nucléaire*) reactor

réaction [reaksjɔ̃] *nf* reaction

réadapter [readapte]: **se ~ (à)** *vi* to readjust (to)

réagir [reaʒir] *vi* to react

réalisateur, -trice [realizatœr, tris] *nm/f* (*TV, CINÉMA*) director

réalisation [realizasjɔ̃] *nf* realization; (*cinéma*) production; **en cours de ~** under way

réaliser [realize] *vt* (*projet, opération*) to carry out, realize; (*rêve, souhait*) to realize, fulfil; (*exploit*) to achieve; (*film*) to produce; (*se rendre compte de*) to realize; **se ~** *vi* to be realized

réaliste [realist] *adj* realistic

réalité [realite] *nf* reality; **en ~** in (actual) fact; **dans la ~** in reality

réanimation [reanimasjɔ̃] *nf* resuscitation; **service de ~** intensive care unit

rébarbatif, -ive [rebarbatif, iv] *adj* forbidding

rebattu, e [r(ə)baty] *adj* hackneyed

rebelle [rəbɛl] *nm/f* rebel ♦ *adj* (*troupes*) rebel; (*enfant*) rebellious; (*mèche etc*) unruly

rebeller [r(ə)bele]: **se ~** *vi* to rebel

rebondi, e [r(ə)bɔ̃di] *adj* (*joues*) chubby

rebondir [r(ə)bɔ̃dir] *vi* (*ballon: au sol*) to bounce; (: *contre un mur*) to rebound; (*fig*) to get moving again; **rebondissement** *nm* new development

rebord [r(ə)bɔr] *nm* edge; **le ~ de la fenêtre** the windowsill

rebours [r(ə)bur]: **à ~** *adv* the wrong way

rebrousser [r(ə)bruse] *vt*: **~ chemin** to turn back

rebut [rəby] *nm*: **mettre au ~** to scrap; **rebutant, e** *adj* off-putting; **rebuter** *vt* to put off

récalcitrant, e [rekalsitrɑ̃, ɑ̃t] *adj* refractory

recaler [r(ə)kale] *vt* (*SCOL*) to fail; **se faire ~** to fail

récapituler [rekapityle] *vt* to recapitulate, sum up

receler [r(ə)səle] *vt* (*produit d'un vol*) to receive; (*fig*) to conceal; **receleur, -euse** *nm/f* receiver

récemment [resamɑ̃] *adv* recently

recensement [r(ə)sɑ̃smɑ̃] *nm* (*population*) census

recenser [r(ə)sɑ̃se] *vt* (*population*) to take a census of; (*inventorier*) to list

récent, e [resɑ̃, ɑ̃t] *adj* recent

récépissé [resepise] *nm* receipt

récepteur [reseptœr, tris] *nm* receiver

réception [resɛpsjɔ̃] *nf* receiving *no p*

(*accueil*) reception, welcome; (*bureau*) reception desk; (*réunion mondaine*) reception, party; **réceptionniste** *nm/f* receptionist

recette [R(ə)sɛt] *nf* recipe; (*COMM*) takings *pl*; **~s** *nfpl* (*COMM: rentrées*) receipts

receveur, -euse [R(ə)səvœR, øz] *nm/f* (*des contributions*) tax collector; (*des postes*) postmaster(-mistress)

recevoir [R(ə)səvwaR] *vt* to receive; (*client, patient*) to see; **être reçu** (*à un examen*) to pass

rechange [R(ə)ʃɑ̃ʒ]: **de ~** *adj* (*pièces, roue*) spare; (*fig: solution*) alternative; **des vêtements de ~** a change of clothes

réchapper [Reʃape]: **~ de** *ou* **à** *vt* (*accident, maladie*) to come through

recharge [R(ə)ʃaRʒ] *nf* refill; **rechargeable** *adj* (*stylo etc*) refillable; **recharger** *vt* (*stylo*) to refill; (*batterie*) to recharge

réchaud [Reʃo] *nm* (portable) stove

réchauffer [Reʃofe] *vt* (*plat*) to reheat; (*mains, personne*) to warm; **se ~** *vi* (*température*) to get warmer; (*personne*) to warm o.s. (up)

rêche [Rɛʃ] *adj* rough

recherche [R(ə)ʃɛRʃ] *nf* (*action*) search; (*raffinement*) studied elegance; (*scientifique etc*): **la ~** research; **~s** *nfpl* (*de la police*) investigations; (*scientifiques*) research.*sg*; **la ~ de** the search for; **être à la ~ de qch** to be looking for sth

recherché, e [R(ə)ʃɛRʃe] *adj* (*rare, demandé*) much sought-after; (*raffiné: style*) mannered; (: *tenue*) elegant

rechercher [R(ə)ʃɛRʃe] *vt* (*objet égaré, personne*) to look for; (*causes, nouveau procédé*) to try to find; (*bonheur, compliments*) to seek

rechigner [R(ə)ʃiɲe] *vi*: **~ à faire qch** to balk *ou* jib at doing sth

rechute [R(ə)ʃyt] *nf* (*MÉD*) relapse

récidiver [Residive] *vi* to commit a subsequent offence; (*fig*) to do it again

récif [Resif] *nm* reef

récipient [Resipjɑ̃] *nm* container

réciproque [Resiprɔk] *adj* reciprocal

récit [Resi] *nm* story; **récital** *nm* recital; **réciter** *vt* to recite

réclamation [Reklamasjɔ̃] *nf* complaint; **~s** *nfpl* (*bureau*) complaints department *sg*

réclame [Reklam] *nf* ad, advert(isement); **en ~** on special offer; **réclamer** *vt* to ask for; (*revendiquer*) to claim, demand ♦ *vi* to complain

réclusion [Reklyzjɔ̃] *nf* imprisonment

recoin [Rəkwɛ̃] *nm* nook, corner

reçois *etc* [Rəswa] *vb voir* **recevoir**

récolte [Rekɔlt] *nf* harvesting, gathering; (*produits*) harvest, crop; **récolter** *vt* to harvest, gather (in); (*fig*) to collect

recommandé [R(ə)kɔmɑ̃de] *nm* (*POSTES*): **en ~** by registered mail

recommander [R(ə)kɔmɑ̃de] *vt* to recommend; (*POSTES*) to register

recommencer [R(ə)kɔmɑ̃se] *vt* (*reprendre: lutte, séance*) to resume, start again; (*refaire: travail, explications*) to start afresh, start (over) again ♦ *vi* to start again; (*récidiver*) to do it again

récompense [Rekɔ̃pɑ̃s] *nf* reward; (*prix*) award; **récompenser** *vt*: **récompenser qn (de** *ou* **pour)** to reward sb (for)

réconcilier [Rekɔ̃silje] *vt* to reconcile; **se ~ (avec)** to be reconciled (with)

reconduire [R(ə)kɔ̃dɥiR] *vt* (*raccompagner*) to take *ou* see back; (*renouveler*) to renew

réconfort [Rekɔ̃fɔR] *nm* comfort; **réconforter** *vt* (*consoler*) to comfort

reconnaissance [R(ə)kɔnɛsɑ̃s] *nf* (*gratitude*) gratitude, gratefulness; (*action de reconnaître*) recognition; (*MIL*) reconnaissance, recce; **reconnaissant, e** *adj* grateful

reconnaître [R(ə)kɔnɛtR] *vt* to recognize; (*MIL: lieu*) to reconnoitre; (*JUR: enfant, torts*) to acknowledge; **~ que** to admit *ou* acknowledge that; **reconnu, e** *adj* (*indiscuté, connu*) recognized

reconstituant, e [R(ə)kɔ̃stitɥɑ̃, ɑ̃t] *adj* (*aliment, régime*) strength-building

reconstituer [R(ə)kɔ̃stitɥe] *vt* (*événement, accident*) to reconstruct; (*fresque, vase brisé*) to piece together, reconstitute

reconstruction [R(ə)kɔ̃stryksjɔ̃] *nf* rebuilding

reconstruire [R(ə)kɔ̃strɥiʀ] *vt* to rebuild

reconvertir [R(ə)kɔ̃vɛʀtiʀ]: **se ~ dans** *vr* (*un métier, une branche*) to go into

record [R(ə)kɔʀ] *nm, adj* record

recoupement [R(ə)kupmɑ̃] *nm*: **par ~** by cross-checking

recouper [R(ə)kupe]: **se ~** *vi* (*témoignages*) to tie *ou* match up

recourber [R(ə)kuʀbe]: **se ~** *vi* to curve (up), bend (up)

recourir [R(ə)kuʀiʀ]: **~ à** *vt* (*ami, agence*) to turn *ou* appeal to; (*force, ruse, emprunt*) to resort to

recours [R(ə)kuʀ] *nm*: **avoir ~ à** = **recourir à**; **en dernier ~** as a last resort

recouvrer [R(ə)kuvʀe] *vt* (*vue, santé etc*) to recover, regain

recouvrir [R(ə)kuvʀiʀ] *vt* (*couvrir à nouveau*) to re-cover; (*couvrir entièrement, aussi fig*) to cover

récréation [ʀekʀeasjɔ̃] *nf* (*SCOL*) break

récrier [ʀekʀije]: **se ~** *vi* to exclaim

récriminations [ʀekʀiminasjɔ̃] *nfpl* remonstrations, complaints

recroqueviller [R(ə)kʀɔk(ə)vije]: **se ~** *vi* (*personne*) to huddle up

recrudescence [R(ə)kʀydesɑ̃s] *nf* fresh outbreak

recrue [ʀəkʀy] *nf* recruit

recruter [R(ə)kʀyte] *vt* to recruit

rectangle [ʀɛktɑ̃gl] *nm* rectangle; **rectangulaire** *adj* rectangular

rectificatif [ʀɛktifikatif, iv] *nm* correction

rectifier [ʀɛktifje] *vt* (*calcul, adresse, paroles*) to correct; (*erreur*) to rectify

rectiligne [ʀɛktiliɲ] *adj* straight

recto [ʀɛkto] *nm* front (of a page); **~ verso** on both sides (of the page)

reçu, e [R(ə)sy] *pp de* **recevoir** ♦ *adj* (*candidat*) successful; (*admis, consacré*) accepted ♦ *nm* (*COMM*) receipt

recueil [ʀəkœj] *nm* collection; **recueillir** *vt* to collect; (*voix, suffrages*) to win; (*accueillir: réfugiés, chat*) to take in; **se recueillir** *vi* to gather one's thoughts, meditate

recul [R(ə)kyl] *nm* (*éloignement*) distance; (*déclin*) decline; **être en ~** to be on the decline; **avec du ~** with hindsight; **avoir un mouvement de ~** to recoil; **prendre du ~** to stand back; **reculé, e** *adj* remote; **reculer** *vi* to move back, move away; (*AUTO*) to reverse, back (up); (*fig*) to (be on the) decline ♦ *vt* to move back; (*véhicule*) to reverse, back (up); (*date, décision*) to postpone; **reculons: à reculons** *adv* backwards

récupérer [ʀekypeʀe] *vt* to recover, get back; (*heures de travail*) to make up; (*déchets*) to salvage ♦ *vi* to recover

récurer [ʀekyʀe] *vt* to scour

récuser [ʀekyze] *vt* to challenge; **se ~** *vi* to decline to give an opinion

reçut [ʀəsy] *vb voir* **recevoir**

recycler [R(ə)sikle] *vt* (*TECH*) to recycle; **se ~** *vi* to retrain

rédacteur, -trice [ʀedaktœʀ, tʀis] *nm/f* (*journaliste*) writer; subeditor; (*d'ouvrage de référence*) editor, compiler; **~ en chef** chief editor

rédaction [ʀedaksjɔ̃] *nf* writing; (*rédacteurs*) editorial staff; (*SCOL: devoir*) essay, composition

redemander [ʀədmɑ̃de] *vt* (*une nouvelle fois*) to ask again for; (*davantage*) to ask for more of

redescendre [R(ə)desɑ̃dʀ] *vi* to go back down ♦ *vt* (*pente etc*) to go down

redevance [R(ə)dəvɑ̃s] *nf* (*TÉL*) rental charge; (*TV*) licence fee

rédiger [ʀediʒe] *vt* to write; (*contrat*) to draw up

redire [R(ə)diʀ] *vt* to repeat; **trouver à ~ à** to find fault with

redonner [R(ə)dɔne] *vt* (*rendre*) to give back; (*resservir: nourriture*) to give more

redoubler [R(ə)duble] *vi* (*tempête, violence*)

to intensify; (SCOL) to repeat a year; **~ de patience/prudence** to be doubly patient/careful

redoutable [R(ə)dutabl] adj formidable, fearsome

redouter [R(ə)dute] vt to dread

redressement [R(ə)dRɛsmɑ̃] nm (économique) recovery

redresser [R(ə)dRɛse] vt (relever) to set upright; (pièce tordue) to straighten out; (situation, économie) to put right; **se ~** vi (personne) to sit (ou stand) up (straight); (économie) to recover

réduction [Redyksjɔ̃] nf reduction

réduire [RedɥiR] vt to reduce; (prix, dépenses) to cut, reduce; **se ~ à** (revenir à) to boil down to; **réduit** nm (pièce) tiny room

rééducation [Reedykasjɔ̃] nf (d'un membre) re-education; (de délinquants, d'un blessé) rehabilitation

réel, le [Reɛl] adj real; **réellement** adv really

réexpédier [Reɛkspedje] vt (à l'envoyeur) to return, send back; (au destinataire) to send on, forward

refaire [R(ə)fɛR] vt to do again; (faire de nouveau: sport) to take up again; (réparer, restaurer) to do up

réfection [Refɛksjɔ̃] nf repair

réfectoire [RefɛktwaR] nm refectory

référence [RefeRɑ̃s] nf reference; **~s** nfpl (recommandations) reference sg

référer [RefeRe]: **se ~ à** vt to refer to

refermer [R(ə)fɛRme] vt to close ou shut again; **se ~** vi (porte) to close ou shut (again)

refiler [R(ə)file] vi (fam) to palm off

réfléchi, e [Refleʃi] adj (caractère) thoughtful; (action) well-thought-out; (LING) reflexive; **c'est tout ~** my mind's made up

réfléchir [RefleʃiR] vt to reflect ♦ vi to think; **~ à** to think about

reflet [R(ə)flɛ] nm reflection; (sur l'eau etc) sheen no pl, glint; **refléter** vt to reflect;

se refléter vi to be reflected

réflexe [Reflɛks] nm, adj reflex

réflexion [Reflɛksjɔ̃] nf (de la lumière etc) reflection; (fait de penser) thought; (remarque) remark; **~ faite, à la ~** on reflection

refluer [R(ə)flye] vi to flow back; (foule) to surge back

reflux [Rəfly] nm (de la mer) ebb

réforme [RefɔRm] nf reform; (REL): **la R~** the Reformation; **réformer** vt to reform; (MIL) to declare unfit for service

refouler [R(ə)fule] vt (envahisseurs) to drive back; (larmes) to force back; (désir, colère) to repress

refrain [R(ə)fRɛ̃] nm refrain, chorus

refréner [Rəfrene] vt, **réfréner** [Refrene] vt to curb, check

réfrigérateur [RefRiʒeRatœR] nm refrigerator, fridge

refroidir [R(ə)fRwadiR] vt to cool; (fig: personne) to put off ♦ vi to cool (down); **se ~** vi (temps) to get cooler ou colder; (fig: ardeur) to cool (off); **refroidissement** nm (grippe etc) chill

refuge [R(ə)fyʒ] nm refuge; **réfugié, e** adj, nm/f refugee; **réfugier: se réfugier** vi to take refuge

refus [R(ə)fy] nm refusal; **ce n'est pas de ~** I won't say no, it's welcome; **refuser** vt to refuse; (SCOL: candidat) to fail; **refuser qch à qn** to refuse sb sth; **se refuser à faire** to refuse to do

réfuter [Refyte] vt to refute

regagner [R(ə)gaɲe] vt (faveur) to win back; (lieu) to get back to

regain [Rəgɛ̃] nm (renouveau): **un ~ de** renewed +nom

régal [Regal] nm treat; **régaler: se régaler** vi to have a delicious meal; (fig) to enjoy o.s.

regard [R(ə)gaR] nm (coup d'œil) look, glance; (expression) look (in one's eye); **au ~ de** (loi, morale) from the point of view of; **en ~ de** in comparison with

regardant, e [R(ə)gaRdɑ̃, ɑ̃t] adj (économe) tight-fisted; **peu ~ (sur)** very free (about)

regarder [ʀ(ə)ɡaʀde] *vt* to look at; (*film, télévision, match*) to watch; (*concerner*) to concern ♦ *vi* to look; **ne pas ~ à la dépense** to spare no expense; **~ qn/qch comme** to regard sb/sth as

régie [ʀeʒi] *nf* (*COMM, INDUSTRIE*) state-owned company; (*THÉÂTRE, CINÉMA*) production; (*RADIO, TV*) control room

regimber [ʀ(ə)ʒɛ̃be] *vi* to balk, jib

régime [ʀeʒim] *nm* (*POL*) régime; (*MÉD*) diet; (*ADMIN: carcéral, fiscal etc*) system; (*de bananes, dattes*) bunch; **se mettre au/ suivre un ~** to go on/be on a diet

régiment [ʀeʒimɑ̃] *nm* regiment

région [ʀeʒjɔ̃] *nf* region; **régional, e, -aux** *adj* regional

régir [ʀeʒiʀ] *vt* to govern

régisseur [ʀeʒisœʀ] *nm* (*d'un domaine*) steward; (*CINÉMA, TV*) assistant director; (*THÉÂTRE*) stage manager

registre [ʀəʒistʀ] *nm* register

réglage [ʀeglaʒ] *nm* adjustment

règle [ʀɛɡl] *nf* (*instrument*) ruler; (*loi*) rule; **~s** *nfpl* (*menstruation*) period *sg*; **en ~** (*papiers d'identité*) in order; **en ~ générale** as a (general) rule

réglé, e [ʀegle] *adj* (*vie*) well-ordered; (*arrangé*) settled

règlement [ʀɛgləmɑ̃] *nm* (*paiement*) settlement; (*arrêté*) regulation; (*règles, statuts*) regulations *pl*, rules *pl*; **~ de compte(s)** settling of old scores; **réglementaire** *adj* conforming to the regulations; (*tenue*) regulation *cpd*; **réglementation** *nf* (*règles*) regulations; **réglementer** *vt* to regulate

régler [ʀegle] *vt* (*conflit, facture*) to settle; (*personne*) to settle up with; (*mécanisme, machine*) to regulate, adjust; (*thermostat etc*) to set, adjust

réglisse [ʀeglis] *nf* liquorice

règne [ʀɛɲ] *nm* (*d'un roi etc, fig*) reign; **régner** *vi* (*roi*) to rule, reign; (*fig*) to reign

regorger [ʀ(ə)gɔʀʒe] *vi*: **~ de** to overflow with, be bursting with

regret [ʀ(ə)gʀɛ] *nm* regret; **à ~** with re-

gret; **sans ~** with no regrets; **regrettable** *adj* regrettable; **regretter** *vt* to regret; (*personne*) to miss; **je regrette mais ...** I'm sorry but ...

regrouper [ʀ(ə)gʀupe] *vt* (*grouper*) to group together; (*contenir*) to include, comprise; **se ~** *vi* to gather (together)

régulier, -ière [ʀegylje, jɛʀ] *adj* (*gén*) regular; (*vitesse, qualité*) steady; (*égal: couche, ligne*) even, (*TRANSPORTS: ligne, service*), scheduled, regular; (*légal*) lawful, in order; (*honnête*) straight, on the level; **régulièrement** *adv* regularly; (*uniformément*) evenly

rehausser [ʀəose] *vt* (*relever*) to heighten, raise; (*fig: souligner*) to set off, enhance

rein [ʀɛ̃] *nm* kidney; **~s** *nmpl* (*dos*) back *sg*

reine [ʀɛn] *nf* queen

reine-claude [ʀɛnklod] *nf* greengage

réinsertion [ʀeɛ̃sɛʀsjɔ̃] *nf* (*de délinquant*) reintegration, rehabilitation

réintégrer [ʀeɛ̃tegʀe] *vt* (*lieu*) to return to; (*fonctionnaire*) to reinstate

rejaillir [ʀ(ə)ʒajiʀ] *vi* to splash up; **~ sur** (*fig: scandale*) to rebound on; (: *gloire*) to be reflected on

rejet [ʀəʒɛ] *nm* rejection; **rejeter** *vt* (*relancer*) to throw back; (*écarter*) to reject; (*déverser*) to throw out, discharge; (*vomir*) to bring *ou* throw up; **rejeter la responsabilité de qch sur qn** to lay the responsibility for sth at sb's door

rejoindre [ʀ(ə)ʒwɛ̃dʀ] *vt* (*famille, régiment*) to rejoin, return to; (*lieu*) to get (back) to; (*suj: route etc*) to meet, join; (*rattraper*) to catch up (with); **se ~** *vi* to meet; **je te rejoins à la gare** I'll see *ou* meet you at the station

réjouir [ʀeʒwiʀ] *vt* to delight; **se ~ (de)** *vi* to be delighted (about); **réjouissances** *nfpl* (*fête*) festivities

relâche [ʀəlɑʃ] *nm ou nf*: **sans ~** without respite *ou* a break; **relâché, e** *adj* loose, lax; **relâcher** *vt* (*libérer*) to release; (*desserrer*) to loosen; **se relâcher** *vi* (*discipline*) to become slack *ou* lax; (*élève etc*) to slacken off

relais [R(ə)lɛ] *nm* (*SPORT*): **(course de) ~** relay (race); **prendre le ~ (de)** to take over (from); **~ routier** ≃ transport café (*BRIT*), ≃ truck stop (*US*)

relancer [R(ə)lɑ̃se] *vt* (*balle*) to throw back; (*moteur*) to restart; (*fig*) to boost, revive; (*harceler*): **~ qn** to pester sb

relatif, -ive [R(ə)latif, iv] *adj* relative

relation [R(ə)lasjɔ̃] *nf* (*rapport*) relation(ship); (*connaissance*) acquaintance; **~s** *nfpl* (*rapports*) relations; (*connaissances*) connections; **être/entrer en ~(s) avec** to be/get in contact with

relaxe [Rəlaks] (*fam*) *adj* (*tenue*) informal; (*personne*) relaxed; **relaxer: se relaxer** *vi* to relax

relayer [R(ə)leje] *vt* (*collaborateur, coureur etc*) to relieve; **se ~** *vi* (*dans une activité*) to take it in turns

reléguer [R(ə)lege] *vt* to relegate

relent(s) [Rəlɑ̃] *nm(pl)* (foul) smell

relevé, e [Rəl(ə)ve] *adj* (*manches*) rolled-up; (*sauce*) highly-seasoned ♦ *nm* (*de compteur*) reading; (*bancaire*) statement

relève [Rəlɛv] *nf* (*personne*) relief; **prendre la ~** to take over

relever [Rəl(ə)ve] *vt* (*meuble*) to stand up again; (*personne tombée*) to help up; (*vitre, niveau de vie*) to raise; (*col*) to turn up; (*style*) to elevate; (*plat, sauce*) to season; (*sentinelle, équipe*) to relieve; (*fautes*) to pick out; (*défi*) to accept, take up; (*noter: adresse etc*) to take down, note; (*: plan*) to sketch; (*compteur*) to read; (*ramasser: cahiers*) to collect, take in; **se ~** *vi* (*se remettre debout*) to get up; **~ de** (*maladie*) to be recovering from; (*être du ressort de*) to be a matter for; (*fig*) to pertain to; **~ qn de** (*fonctions*) to relieve sb of

relief [Rəljɛf] *nm* relief; **mettre en ~** (*fig*) to bring out, highlight

relier [Rəlje] *vt* to link up; (*livre*) to bind; **~ qch à** to link sth to

religieuse [R(ə)liʒjøz] *nf* nun; (*gâteau*) cream bun

religieux, -euse [R(ə)liʒjø, jøz] *adj* religious ♦ *nm* monk

religion [R(ə)liʒjɔ̃] *nf* religion

relire [R(ə)liR] *vt* (*à nouveau*) to reread, read again; (*vérifier*) to read over

reliure [RəljyR] *nf* binding

reluire [R(ə)lɥiR] *vi* to gleam

remanier [R(ə)manje] *vt* to reshape, recast; (*POL*) to reshuffle

remarquable [R(ə)maRkabl] *adj* remarkable

remarque [R(ə)maRk] *nf* remark; (*écrite*) note

remarquer [R(ə)maRke] *vt* (*voir*) to notice; **se ~** *vi* to be noticeable; **faire ~ (à qn) que** to point out (to sb) that; **faire ~ qch (à qn)** to point sth out (to sb); **remarquez, ...** mind you ...; **se faire ~** to draw attention to o.s.

rembourrer [Rɑ̃buRe] *vt* to stuff

remboursement [Rɑ̃buRsəmɑ̃] *nm* (*de dette, d'emprunt*) repayment; (*de frais*) refund; **rembourser** *vt* to pay back, repay; (*frais, billet etc*) to refund; **se faire rembourser** to get a refund

remède [R(ə)mɛd] *nm* (*médicament*) medicine; (*traitement, fig*) remedy, cure

remémorer [R(ə)memɔRe]: **se ~** *vt* to recall, recollect

remerciements [RəmɛRsimɑ̃] *nmpl* thanks

remercier [R(ə)mɛRsje] *vt* to thank; (*congédier*) to dismiss; **~ qn de/d'avoir fait** to thank sb for/for having done

remettre [R(ə)mɛtR] *vt* (*replacer*) to put back; (*vêtement*) to put back on; (*ajouter*) to add; (*ajourner*): **~ qch (à)** to postpone sth (until); **se ~** *vi*: **se ~ (de)** to recover (from); **~ qch à qn** (*donner: lettre, clé etc*) to hand over sth to sb; (: *prix, décoration*) to present sb with sth; **se ~ à faire qch** to start doing sth again

remise [R(ə)miz] *nf* (*rabais*) discount; (*local*) shed; **~ de peine** reduction of sentence; **~ en jeu** (*FOOTBALL*) throw-in

remontant [R(ə)mɔ̃tɑ̃, ɑ̃t] *nm* tonic, pickme-up

remonte-pente [R(ə)mɔ̃tpɑ̃t] *nm* ski-lift
remonter [R(ə)mɔ̃te] *vi* to go back up;
(*prix, température*) to go up again ♦ *vt*
(*pente*) to go up; (*fleuve*) to sail (*ou* swim
etc) up; (*manches, pantalon*) to roll up;
(*col*) to turn up; (*niveau, limite*) to raise;
(*fig: personne*) to buck up; (*qch de démonté*) to put back together, reassemble;
(*montre*) to wind up; **~ le moral à qn** to
raise sb's spirits; **~ à** (*dater de*) to date *ou*
go back to
remontrance [R(ə)mɔ̃tRɑ̃s] *nf* reproof,
reprimand
remontrer [R(ə)mɔ̃tRe] *vt* (*fig*): **en ~ à** to
prove one's superiority over
remords [R(ə)mɔR] *nm* remorse *no pl*;
avoir des ~ to feel remorse
remorque [R(ə)mɔRk] *nf* trailer; **remorquer** *vt* to tow; **remorqueur** *nm*
tug(boat)
remous [Rəmu] *nm* (*d'un navire*)
(back)wash *no pl*; (*de rivière*) swirl, eddy
♦ *nmpl* (*fig*) stir *sg*
remparts [Rɑ̃paR] *nmpl* walls, ramparts
remplaçant, e [Rɑ̃plasɑ̃, ɑ̃t] *nm/f* replace-
ment, stand-in; (*SCOL*) supply teacher
remplacement [Rɑ̃plasmɑ̃] *nm* replace-
ment; **faire des ~s** (*professeur*) to do supply teaching; (*secrétaire*) to temp
remplacer [Rɑ̃plase] *vt* to replace; **~
qch/qn par** to replace sth/sb with
rempli, e [Rɑ̃pli] *adj* (*emploi du temps*) full,
busy; **~ de** full of, filled with
remplir [Rɑ̃pliR] *vt* to fill (up); (*questionnaire*) to fill out *ou* up; (*obligations, fonction, condition*) to fulfil; **se ~** *vi* to fill up
remporter [Rɑ̃pɔRte] *vt* (*marchandise*) to
take away; (*fig*) to win, achieve
remuant, e [Rəmɥɑ̃, ɑ̃t] *adj* restless
remue-ménage [R(ə)mymenaʒ] *nm inv*
commotion
remuer [Rəmɥe] *vt* to move; (*café, sauce*)
to stir ♦ *vi* to move; **se ~** *vi* to move;
(*fam: s'activer*) to get a move on
rémunérer [RemyneRe] *vt* to remunerate

renard [RənaR] *nm* fox
renchérir [Rɑ̃ʃeRiR] *vi* (*fig*): **~ (sur)** (*en paroles*) to add something (to)
rencontre [Rɑ̃kɔ̃tR] *nf* meeting; (*imprévue*)
encounter; **aller à la ~ de qn** to go and
meet sb; **rencontrer** *vt* to meet; (*mot,
expression*) to come across; (*difficultés*) to
meet with; **se rencontrer** *vi* to meet
rendement [Rɑ̃dmɑ̃] *nm* (*d'un travailleur,
d'une machine*) output; (*d'un champ*) yield
rendez-vous [Rɑ̃devu] *nm* appointment;
(*d'amoureux*) date; (*lieu*) meeting place;
donner ~-~ à qn to arrange to meet sb;
avoir/prendre ~-~ (avec) to have/make
an appointment (with)
rendre [Rɑ̃dR] *vt* (*restituer*) to give back,
return; (*invitation*) to return, repay; (*vomir*)
to bring up; (*exprimer, traduire*) to render;
(*faire devenir*): **~ qn célèbre/qch possible**
to make sb famous/sth possible; **se ~** *vi*
(*capituler*) to surrender, give o.s. up; (*aller*): **se ~ quelque part** to go somewhere;
~ la monnaie à qn to give sb his change;
se ~ compte de qch to realize sth
rênes [Ren] *nfpl* reins
renfermé, e [Rɑ̃feRme] *adj* (*fig*) with-
drawn ♦ *nm*: **sentir le ~** to smell stuffy
renfermer [Rɑ̃feRme] *vt* to contain
renflouer [Rɑ̃flue] *vt* to refloat; (*fig*) to set
back on its (*ou* his/her *etc*) feet
renfoncement [Rɑ̃fɔ̃smɑ̃] *nm* recess
renforcer [Rɑ̃fɔRse] *vt* to reinforce; **renfort: renforts** *nmpl* reinforcements; **à
grand renfort de** a great deal of
renfrogné, e [Rɑ̃fRɔɲe] *adj* sullen
rengaine [Rɑ̃gɛn] (*péj*) *nf* old tune
renier [Rənje] *vt* (*personne*) to disown, repudiate; (*foi*) to renounce
renifler [R(ə)nifle] *vi, vt* to sniff
renne [Ren] *nm* reindeer *inv*
renom [Rənɔ̃] *nm* reputation; (*célébrité*) renown; **renommé, e** *adj* celebrated, renowned; **renommée** *nf* fame
renoncer [R(ə)nɔ̃se]: **~ à** *vt* to give up; **~ à
faire** to give up the idea of doing
renouer [Rənwe] *vt*: **~ avec** (*habitude*) to

take up again

renouvelable [ʀ(ə)nuv(ə)labl] *adj* (*énergie etc*) renewable

renouveler [ʀ(ə)nuv(ə)le] *vt* to renew; (*exploit, méfait*) to repeat; **se ~** *vi* (*incident*) to recur, happen again; **renouvellement** *nm* (*remplacement*) renewal

rénover [ʀenɔve] *vt* (*immeuble*) to renovate, do up; (*quartier*) to redevelop

renseignement [ʀɑ̃sɛɲmɑ̃] *nm* information *no pl*, piece of information; **(bureau des) ~s** information office

renseigner [ʀɑ̃seɲe] *vt*: **~ qn (sur)** to give information to sb (about); **se ~** *vi* to ask for information, make inquiries

rentabilité [ʀɑ̃tabilite] *nf* profitability

rentable [ʀɑ̃tabl] *adj* profitable

rente [ʀɑ̃t] *nf* private income; (*pension*) pension

rentrée [ʀɑ̃tʀe] *nf*: **~ (d'argent)** cash *no pl* coming in; **la ~ (des classes)** the start of the new school year

---
rentrée (des classes)
---

❶ La rentrée (des classes) *in September marks an important point in the French year. Children and teachers return to school, and political and social life begin again after the long summer break.*

---

rentrer [ʀɑ̃tʀe] *vi* (*revenir chez soi*) to go (*ou* come) (back) home; (*entrer de nouveau*) to go (*ou* come) back in; (*entrer*) to go (*ou* come) in; (*air, clou: pénétrer*) to go in; (*revenu*) to come in ♦ *vt* to bring in; (*mettre à l'abri: animaux etc*) to bring in; (*: véhicule*) to put away; (*chemise dans pantalon etc*) to tuck in; (*griffes*) to draw in; **~ le ventre** to pull in one's stomach; **~ dans** (*heurter*) to crash into; **~ dans l'ordre** to be back to normal; **~ dans ses frais** to recover one's expenses

renverse [ʀɑ̃vɛʀs]: **à la ~** *adv* backwards

renverser [ʀɑ̃vɛʀse] *vt* (*faire tomber: chaise, verre*) to knock over, overturn; (*liquide, contenu*) to spill, upset; (*piéton*) to knock

down; (*retourner*) to turn upside down; (*: ordre des mots etc*) to reverse; (*fig: gouvernement etc*) to overthrow; (*fam: stupéfier*) to bowl over; **se ~** *vi* (*verre, vase*) to fall over; (*contenu*) to spill

renvoi [ʀɑ̃vwa] *nm* (*d'employé*) dismissal; (*d'élève*) expulsion; (*référence*) cross-reference; (*éructation*) belch; **renvoyer** *vt* to send back; (*congédier*) to dismiss; (*élève: définitivement*) to expel; (*lumière*) to reflect; (*ajourner*): **renvoyer qch (à)** to put sth off *ou* postpone sth (until)

repaire [ʀ(ə)pɛʀ] *nm* den

répandre [ʀepɑ̃dʀ] *vt* (*renverser*) to spill; (*étaler, diffuser*) to spread; (*odeur*) to give off; **se ~** *vi* to spill; (*se propager*) to spread; **répandu, e** *adj* (*opinion, usage*) widespread

réparation [ʀepaʀasjɔ̃] *nf* repair

réparer [ʀepaʀe] *vt* to repair; (*fig: offense*) to make up for, atone for; (*: oubli, erreur*) to put right

repartie [ʀepaʀti] *nf* retort; **avoir de la ~** to be quick at repartee

repartir [ʀ(ə)paʀtiʀ] *vi* to leave again; (*voyageur*) to set off again; (*fig*) to get going again; **~ à zéro** to start from scratch (again)

répartir [ʀepaʀtiʀ] *vt* (*pour attribuer*) to share out; (*pour disperser, disposer*) to divide up; (*poids*) to distribute; **se ~** *vt* (*travail, rôles*) to share out between themselves; **répartition** *nf* (*des richesses etc*) distribution

repas [ʀ(ə)pa] *nm* meal

repassage [ʀ(ə)pasaʒ] *nm* ironing

repasser [ʀ(ə)pase] *vi* to come (*ou* go) back ♦ *vt* (*vêtement, tissu*) to iron; (*examen*) to retake, resit; (*film*) to show again; (*leçon: revoir*) to go over (again)

repêcher [ʀ(ə)peʃe] *vt* to fish out; (*candidat*) to pass (*by inflating marks*)

repentir [ʀapɑ̃tiʀ] *nm* repentance; **se ~** *vi* to repent; **se ~ d'avoir fait qch** (*regretter*) to regret having done sth

répercussions [ʀepɛʀkysjɔ̃] *nfpl* (*fig*) re-

percussions
répercuter [ʀepɛʀkyte]: **se ~** *vi* (*bruit*) to reverberate; (*fig*): **se ~ sur** to have repercussions on
repère [ʀ(ə)pɛʀ] *nm* mark; (*monument, événement*) landmark
repérer [ʀ(ə)peʀe] *vt* (*fam: erreur, personne*) to spot; (: *endroit*) to locate; **se ~** *vi* to find one's way about
répertoire [ʀepɛʀtwaʀ] *nm* (*liste*) (alphabetical) list; (*carnet*) index notebook; (*INFORM*) folder, directory; (*d'un artiste*) repertoire
répéter [ʀepete] *vt* to repeat; (*préparer: leçon*) to learn, go over; (*THÉÂTRE*) to rehearse; **se ~** *vi* (*redire*) to repeat o.s.; (*se reproduire*) to be repeated, recur
répétition [ʀepetisjɔ̃] *nf* repetition; (*THÉÂTRE*) rehearsal
répit [ʀepi] *nm* respite
replier [ʀ(ə)plije] *vt* (*rabattre*) to fold down *ou* over; **se ~** *vi* (*troupes, armée*) to withdraw, fall back; (*sur soi-même*) to withdraw into o.s.
réplique [ʀeplik] *nf* (*repartie, fig*) reply; (*THÉÂTRE*) line; (*copie*) replica; **répliquer** *vi* to reply; (*riposter*) to retaliate
répondeur [ʀepɔ̃dœʀ, øz] *nm*: **~ automatique** (*TÉL*) answering machine
répondre [ʀepɔ̃dʀ] *vi* to answer, reply; (*freins*) to respond; **~ à** to reply to, answer; (*affection, salut*) to return; (*provocation*) to respond to; (*correspondre à: besoin*) to answer; (: *conditions*) to meet; (: *description*) to match; (*avec impertinence*): **~ à qn** to answer sb back; **~ de** to answer for
réponse [ʀepɔ̃s] *nf* answer, reply; **en ~ à** in reply to
reportage [ʀ(ə)pɔʀtaʒ] *nm* report; **~ en direct** (live) commentary
reporter[1] [ʀəpɔʀtɛʀ] *nm* reporter
reporter[2] [ʀəpɔʀte] *vt* (*ajourner*): **~ qch (à)** to postpone sth (until); (*transférer*): **~ qch sur** to transfer sth to; **se ~ à** (*époque*) to think back to; (*document*) to refer to
repos [ʀ(ə)po] *nm* rest; (*tranquillité*) peace (and quiet); (*MIL*): **~!** stand at ease!; **ce**

n'est pas de tout ~! it's no picnic!
reposant, e [ʀ(ə)pozã, ãt] *adj* restful
reposer [ʀ(ə)poze] *vt* (*verre, livre*) to put down; (*délasser*) to rest ♦ *vi*: **laisser ~** (*pâte*) to leave to stand; **se ~** *vi* to rest; **se ~ sur qn** to rely on sb; **~ sur** (*fig*) to rest on
repoussant, e [ʀ(ə)pusã, ãt] *adj* repulsive
repousser [ʀ(ə)puse] *vi* to grow again ♦ *vt* to repel, repulse; (*offre*) to turn down, reject; (*personne*) to push back; (*différer*) to put back
reprendre [ʀ(ə)pʀɑ̃dʀ] *vt* (*objet prêté, donné*) to take back; (*prisonnier, ville*) to recapture; (*firme, entreprise*) to take over; (*le travail*) to resume; (*emprunter: argument, idée*) to take up, use; (*refaire: article etc*) to go over again; (*vêtement*) to alter; (*réprimander*) to tell off; (*corriger*) to correct; (*chercher*): **je viendrai te ~ à 4 h** I'll come and fetch you at 4; (*se resservir de*): **~ du pain/un œuf** to take (*ou* eat) more bread/another egg ♦ *vi* (*classes, pluie*) to start (up) again; (*activités, travaux, combats*) to resume, start (up) again; (*affaires*) to pick up; (*dire*): **reprit-il** he went on; **se ~** *vi* (*se ressaisir*) to recover; **~ des forces** to recover one's strength; **~ courage** to take new heart; **~ la route** to set off again; **~ haleine** *ou* **son souffle** to get one's breath back
représailles [ʀ(ə)pʀezaj] *nfpl* reprisals
représentant, e [ʀ(ə)pʀezãtã, ãt] *nm/f* representative
représentation [ʀ(ə)pʀezãtasjɔ̃] *nf* (*symbole, image*) representation; (*spectacle*) performance
représenter [ʀ(ə)pʀezãte] *vt* to represent; (*donner: pièce, opéra*) to perform; **se ~** *vt* (*se figurer*) to imagine
répression [ʀepʀesjɔ̃] *nf* repression
réprimer [ʀepʀime] *vt* (*émotions*) to suppress; (*peuple etc*) to repress
repris [ʀ(ə)pʀi, iz] *nm*: **~ de justice** ex-prisoner, ex-convict
reprise [ʀ(ə)pʀiz] *nf* (*recommencement*) re-

sumption; (économique) recovery; (TV) repeat; (COMM) trade-in, part exchange; (raccommodage) mend; **à plusieurs ~s** on several occasions

repriser [R(ə)pRize] vt (chaussette, lainage) to darn; (tissu) to mend

reproche [R(ə)pRɔʃ] nm (remontrance) reproach; **faire des ~s à qn** to reproach sb; **sans ~(s)** beyond reproach; **reprocher** vt: **reprocher qch à qn** to reproach ou blame sb for sth; **reprocher qch à** (critiquer) to have sth against

reproduction [R(ə)pRɔdyksjɔ̃] nf reproduction

reproduire [R(ə)pRɔdɥiR] vt to reproduce; **se ~** vi (BIO) to reproduce; (recommencer) to recur, re-occur

reprouver [RepRuve] vt to reprove

reptile [Reptil] nm reptile

repu, e [Rəpy] adj satisfied, sated

république [Repyblik] nf republic

répugnant, e [Repyɲɑ̃, ɑ̃t] adj disgusting

répugner [Repyɲe] ~ **à** vt: ~ **à qn** to repel ou disgust sb; ~ **à faire** to be loath ou reluctant to do

réputation [Repytasjɔ̃] nf reputation; **réputé, e** adj renowned

requérir [RəkeRiR] vt (nécessiter) to require, call for

requête [Rəkɛt] nf request

requin [Rəkɛ̃] nm shark

requis, e [Rəki, iz] adj required

RER sigle m (= réseau express régional) Greater Paris high-speed train service

rescapé, e [Rɛskape] nm/f survivor

rescousse [Rɛskus] nf: **aller à la ~ de qn** to go to sb's aid ou rescue

réseau, x [Rezo] nm network

réservation [Rezɛrvasjɔ̃] nf booking, reservation

réserve [RezɛRv] nf (retenue) reserve; (entrepôt) storeroom; (restriction, d'Indiens) reservation; (de pêche, chasse) preserve; **de ~** (provisions etc) in reserve

réservé, e [RezɛRve] adj reserved; **chasse/pêche ~e** private hunting/fishing

réserver [RezɛRve] vt to reserve; (chambre, billet etc) to book, reserve; (fig: destiner) to have in store; (garder): ~ **qch pour/à** to keep ou save sth for

réservoir [RezɛRvwaR] nm tank

résidence [Rezidɑ̃s] nf residence; ~ **secondaire** second home; **résidentiel, le** adj residential; **résider** vi: **résider à/dans/en** to reside in; **résider dans** (fig) to lie in

résidu [Rezidy] nm residue no pl

résigner [Reziɲe]: **se ~** vi: **se ~ (à qch/à faire)** to resign o.s. (to sth/to doing)

résilier [Rezilje] vt to terminate

résistance [Rezistɑ̃s] nf resistance; (de ré chaud, bouilloire: fil) element

résistant, e [Rezistɑ̃, ɑ̃t] adj (personne) robust, tough; (matériau) strong, hardwearing

résister [Reziste] vi to resist; ~ **à** (assaut, tentation) to resist; (supporter: gel etc) to withstand; (désobéir à) to stand up to, oppose

résolu, e [Rezɔly] pp de **résoudre** ♦ adj: **être ~ à qch/faire** to be set upon sth/doing

résolution [Rezɔlysjɔ̃] nf (fermeté, décision) resolution; (d'un problème) solution

résolve etc [Rezɔlv] vb voir **résoudre**

résonner [Rezɔne] vi (cloche, pas) to reverberate, resound; (salle) to be resonant

résorber [RezɔRbe]: **se ~** vi (fig: chômage) to be reduced; (: déficit) to be absorbed

résoudre [RezudR] vt to solve; **se ~ à faire** to bring o.s. to do

respect [Rɛspɛ] nm respect; **tenir en ~** to keep at bay; **respecter** vt to respect; **respectueux, -euse** adj respectful

respiration [Rɛspirasjɔ̃] nf breathing no pl

respirer [Rɛspire] vi to breathe; (fig: se détendre) to get one's breath; (: se rassurer) to breathe again ♦ vt to breathe (in), inhale; (manifester: santé, calme etc) to exude

resplendir [RɛsplɑdiR] vi to shine; (fig): ~ **(de)** to be radiant (with)

responsabilité [Rɛspɔ̃sabilite] nf responsibility; (*légale*) liability

responsable [Rɛspɔ̃sabl] *adj* responsible
♦ *nm/f* (*coupable*) person responsible; (*personne compétente*) person in charge; (*de parti, syndicat*) official; **~ de** responsible for

resquiller [Rɛskije] (*fam*) *vi* to get in without paying; (*ne pas faire la queue*) to jump the queue

ressaisir [R(ə)sezir]: **se ~** *vi* to regain one's self-control

ressasser [R(ə)sase] *vt* to keep going over

ressemblance [R(ə)sãblãs] *nf* resemblance, similarity, likeness

ressemblant, e [R(ə)sãblã, ãt] *adj* (*portrait*) lifelike, true to life

ressembler [R(ə)sãble]: **~ à** *vt* to be like, resemble; (*visuellement*) to look like; **se ~** *vi* to be (*ou* look) alike

ressemeler [R(ə)səm(ə)le] *vt* to (re)sole

ressentiment [R(ə)sãtimã] *nm* resentment

ressentir [R(ə)sãtir] *vt* to feel

resserrer [R(ə)sere] *vt* (*nœud, boulon*) to tighten (up); (*fig: liens*) to strengthen

resservir [R(ə)servir] *vi* to do *ou* serve again; **se ~** *vi* to help o.s. again

ressort [Rəsɔr] *nm* (*pièce*) spring; (*énergie*) spirit; (*recours*): **en dernier ~** as a last resort; (*compétence*): **être du ~ de** to fall within the competence of

ressortir [Rəsɔrtir] *vi* to go (*ou* come) out (again); (*contraster*) to stand out; **~ de** to emerge from; **faire ~** (*fig: souligner*) to bring out

ressortissant, e [R(ə)sɔrtisã, ãt] *nm/f* national

ressources [R(ə)surs] *nfpl* (*moyens*) resources

ressusciter [Resysite] *vt* (*fig*) to revive, bring back ♦ *vi* to rise (from the dead)

restant, e [Rɛstã, ãt] *adj* remaining ♦ *nm*: **le ~ (de)** the remainder (of); **un ~ de** (*de trop*) some left-over

restaurant [Rɛstɔrã] *nm* restaurant

restauration [Rɛstɔrasjɔ̃] *nf* restoration; (*hôtellerie*) catering; **~ rapide** fast food

restaurer [Rɛstɔre] *vt* to restore; **se ~** to have something to eat

reste [Rɛst] *nm* (*restant*): **le ~ (de)** the re (of); (*de trop*): **un ~ (de)** some left-ove **~s** *nmpl* (*nourriture*) left-overs; (*d'une c etc, dépouille mortelle*) remains; **du ~, au** besides, moreover

rester [Rɛste] *vi* to stay, remain; (*subsiste* to remain, be left; (*durer*) to last, live o ♦ *vb impers*: **il reste du pain/2 œuf** there's some bread/there are 2 eggs le (over); **restons-en là** let's leave it at tha **il me reste assez de temps** I hav enough time left; **il ne me reste plu qu'à ...** I've just got to ...

restituer [Rɛstitɥe] *vt* (*objet, somme*): qch (à qn) to return sth (to sb)

restreindre [Rɛstrɛ̃dr] *vt* to restrict, limit

restriction [Rɛstriksjɔ̃] *nf* restriction

résultat [Rezylta] *nm* result; (*d'exame d'élection*) results *pl*

résulter [Rezylte]: **~ de** *vt* to result fro be the result of

résumé [Rezyme] *nm* summary, résumé

résumer [Rezyme] *vt* (*texte*) to summariz (*récapituler*) to sum up

résurrection [Rezyrɛksjɔ̃] *nf* resurrection

rétablir [Retablir] *vt* to restore, establish; **se ~** *vi* (*guérir*) to recover; (*lence, calme*) to return, be restored; **rét blissement** *nm* restoring; (*guérison*) covery

retaper [R(ə)tape] (*fam*) *vt* (*maison, voite etc*) to do up; (*revigorer*) to buck up

retard [R(ə)tar] *nm* (*d'une personne atte due*) lateness *no pl*; (*sur l'horaire, un p gramme*) delay; (*fig: scolaire, mental e* backwardness; **en ~ (de 2 heures)** hours) late; **avoir du ~** to be late; (*sur programme*) to be behind (schedul **prendre du ~** (*train, avion*) to be c layed; **sans ~** without delay

retardataire [R(ə)tardatɛr] *nmf* latecom

retardement [R(ə)tardəmã]: **à ~** *adj* c layed action *cpd*; **bombe à ~** time bom

retarder [R(ə)tarde] *vt* to delay; (*mont*

tó put back ♦ vi (montre) to be slow; ~ qn (d'une heure) (sur un horaire) to delay sb (an hour); ~ qch (de 2 jours) (départ, date) to put sth back (2 days)

etenir [Rət(ə)niʀ] vt (garder, retarder) to keep, detain; (maintenir: objet qui glisse, fig: colère, larmes) to hold back; (se rappeler) to retain; (réserver) to reserve; (accepter: proposition etc) to accept; (fig: empêcher d'agir): ~ qn (de faire) to hold sb back (from doing); (prélever): ~ qch (sur) to deduct sth (from); se ~ vi (se raccrocher): se ~ à to hold onto; (se contenir): se ~ de faire to restrain o.s. from doing; ~ son souffle to hold one's breath

etentir [R(ə)tātiʀ] vi to ring out; (salle): ~ de to ring ou resound with; **retentissant, e** adj resounding; **retentissement** nm repercussion

etenu, e [Rət(ə)ny] adj (place) reserved; (personne: empêché) held up; **retenue** nf (prélèvement) deduction; (SCOL) detention; (modération) (self-)restraint

eticence [Retisãs] nf hesitation, reluctance no pl; **réticent, e** adj hesitant, reluctant

etine [Retin] nf retina

etiré, e [R(ə)tiʀe] adj (vie) secluded; (lieu) remote

etirer [R(ə)tiʀe] vt (vêtement, lunettes) to take off, remove; (argent, plainte) to withdraw; (reprendre: bagages, billets) to collect, pick up; (extraire): ~ qch de to take sth out of, remove sth from

etombées [Rət5be] nfpl (radioactives) fallout sg; (fig: répercussions) effects

etomber [R(ə)t5be] vi (à nouveau) to fall again; (atterrir: après un saut etc) to land; (échoir): ~ sur qn to fall on sb

etorquer [Retɔʀke] vt: ~ (à qn) que to retort (to sb) that

etouche [R(ə)tuʃ] nf (sur vêtement) alteration; **retoucher** vt (photographie) to touch up; (texte, vêtement) to alter

etour [R(ə)tuʀ] nm return; **au ~** (en route) on the way back; **à mon ~** when I get/

got back; **être de ~ (de)** to be back (from); **par ~ du courrier** by return of post

retourner [R(ə)tuʀne] vt (dans l'autre sens: matelas, crêpe etc) to turn (over); (: sac, vêtement) to turn inside out; (fam: bouleverser) to shake; (renvoyer, restituer): ~ qch à qn to return sth to sb ♦ vi (aller, revenir): ~ quelque part/à to go back ou return somewhere/to; **se ~** vi (tourner la tête) to turn round; ~ **à** (état, activité) to return to, go back to; **se ~ contre** (fig) to turn against

retrait [R(ə)tʀɛ] nm (d'argent) withdrawal; **en ~** set back; ~ **du permis (de conduire)** disqualification from driving (BRIT), revocation of driver's license (US)

retraite [R(ə)tʀɛt] nf (d'un employé) retirement; (revenu) pension; (d'une armée, REL) retreat; **prendre sa ~** to retire; ~ **anticipée** early retirement; **retraité, e** adj retired ♦ nm/f pensioner

retrancher [R(ə)tʀɑ̃ʃe] vt (nombre, somme): ~ **qch de** to take ou deduct sth from; **se ~ derrière/dans** to take refuge behind/in

retransmettre [R(ə)tʀɑ̃smɛtʀ] vt (RADIO) to broadcast; (TV) to show

rétrécir [Retʀesiʀ] vt (vêtement) to take in ♦ vi to shrink

rétribution [Retʀibysjɔ̃] nf payment

rétro [Retʀo] adj inv: **la mode ~** the nostalgia vogue

rétrograde [Retʀɔgʀad] adj reactionary, backward-looking

rétroprojecteur [Retʀopʀɔʒɛktœʀ] nm overhead projector

rétrospective [Retʀɔspektiv] nf retrospective exhibition/season; **rétrospectivement** adv in retrospect

retrousser [R(ə)tʀuse] vt to roll up

retrouvailles [R(ə)tʀuvaj] nfpl reunion sg

retrouver [R(ə)tʀuve] vt (fugitif, objet perdu) to find; (calme, santé) to regain; (revoir) to see again; (rejoindre) to meet (again), join; **se ~** vi to meet; (s'orienter) to find one's way; **se ~ quelque part** to find o.s.

somewhere; **s'y ~** *(y voir clair)* to make sense of it; *(rentrer dans ses frais)* to break even

rétroviseur [retrɔvizœr] *nm* (rear-view) mirror

réunion [reynjɔ̃] *nf (séance)* meeting

réunir [reynir] *vt (rassembler)* to gather together; *(inviter: amis, famille)* to have round, have in; *(cumuler: qualités etc)* to combine; *(rapprocher: ennemis)* to bring together (again), reunite; *(rattacher: parties)* to join (together); **se ~** *vi (se rencontrer)* to meet

réussi, e [reysi] *adj* successful

réussir [reysir] *vi* to succeed, be successful; *(à un examen)* to pass ♦ *vt* to make a success of; **~ à faire** to succeed in doing; **~ à qn** *(être bénéfique à)* to agree with sb; **réussite** *nf* success; *(CARTES)* patience

revaloir [r(ə)valwar] *vt*: **je vous revaudrai cela** I'll repay you some day; *(en mal)* I'll pay you back for this

revanche [r(ə)vɑ̃ʃ] *nf* revenge; *(sport)* revenge match; **en ~** on the other hand

rêve [rɛv] *nm* dream; **de ~** dream *cpd*; **faire un ~** to have a dream

revêche [rəvɛʃ] *adj* surly, sour-tempered

réveil [revɛj] *nm* waking up *no pl*; *(fig)* awakening; *(pendule)* alarm (clock); **au ~** on waking (up); **réveille-matin** *nm inv* alarm clock; **réveiller** *vt (personne)* to wake up; *(fig)* to awaken, revive; **se réveiller** *vi* to wake up

réveillon [revɛjɔ̃] *nm* Christmas Eve; *(de la Saint-Sylvestre)* New Year's Eve; **réveillonner** *vi* to celebrate Christmas Eve *(ou* New Year's Eve)

révélateur, -trice [revelatœr, tris] *adj*: **~ (de qch)** revealing (sth)

révéler [revele] *vt* to reveal; **se ~** *vi* to be revealed, reveal itself ♦ *vb +attrib*: **se ~ difficile/aisé** to prove difficult/easy

revenant, e [r(ə)vənɑ̃, ɑ̃t] *nm/f* ghost

revendeur, -euse [r(ə)vɑ̃dœr, øz] *nm/f (détaillant)* retailer; *(de drogue)* (drug-) dealer

revendication [r(ə)vɑ̃dikasjɔ̃] *nf* claim demand

revendiquer [r(ə)vɑ̃dike] *vt* to claim, de mand; *(responsabilité)* to claim

revendre [r(ə)vɑ̃dr] *vt (d'occasion)* to re sell; *(détailler)* to sell; **à ~** *(en abondanc* to spare

revenir [rəv(ə)nir] *vi* to come bac *(coûter)*: **~ cher/à 100 F (à qn)** to co (sb) a lot/100 F; **~ à** *(reprendre: étude projet)* to return to, go back to; *(équivalo à)* to amount to; **~ à qn** *(part, honneur)* go to sb, be sb's; *(souvenir, nom)* to com back to sb; **~ sur** *(question, sujet)* to g back over; *(engagement)* to go back on; **à soi** to come round; **n'en pas ~**: **n'en reviens pas** I can't get over it; **sur ses pas** to retrace one's steps; **ce revient à dire que/au même** it amoun to saying that/the same thing; **faire** *(CULIN)* to brown

revenu [rəv(ə)ny] *nm* income; **~s** *nmpl* i come *sg*

rêver [reve] *vi, vt* to dream; **~ de/à** dream of

réverbère [reverber] *nm* street lamp c light; **réverbérer** *vt* to reflect

révérence [reverɑ̃s] *nf (salut)* bow; (: femme)* curtsey

rêverie [revri] *nf* daydreaming *no pl*, da dream

revers [r(ə)ver] *nm (de feuille, main)* bac *(d'étoffe)* wrong side; *(de pièce, médaill* back, reverse; *(TENNIS, PING-PONG)* bac hand; *(de veste)* lapel; *(fig: échec)* setback

revêtement [r(ə)vɛtmɑ̃] *nm (des so* flooring; *(de chaussée)* surface

revêtir [r(ə)vetir] *vt (habit)* to don, p on; *(prendre: importance, apparence)* to ta on; **~ qch de** to cover sth with

rêveur, -euse [revœr, øz] *adj* dream ♦ *nm/f* dreamer

revient [rəvjɛ̃] *vb voir* **revenir**

revigorer [r(ə)vigɔre] *vt (air frais)* to inv orate, brace up; *(repas, boisson)* to reviv buck up

revirement [R(ə)viRmã] nm change of mind; (d'une situation) reversal

reviser [Revize] vt to revise; (machine) to overhaul, service

revision [Revizjɔ̃] nf revision; (de voiture) servicing no pl

revivre [R(ə)vivR] vi (reprendre des forces) to come alive again ♦ vt (épreuve, moment) to relive

revoir [RəvwaR] vt to see again; (réviser) to revise ♦ nm: **au ~** goodbye

révoltant, e [Revɔltã, ãt] adj revolting, appalling

révolte [Revɔlt] nf rebellion, revolt

révolter [Revɔlte] vt to revolt; **se ~ (contre)** to rebel (against); **ça me révolte (de voir que ...)** I'm revolted ou appalled (to see that ...)

révolu, e [Revɔly] adj past; (ADMIN): **âgé de 18 ans ~s** over 18 years of age

révolution [Revɔlysjɔ̃] nf revolution; **révolutionnaire** adj, nm/f revolutionary

revolver [RevɔlvɛR] nm gun; (à barillet) revolver

révoquer [Revɔke] vt (fonctionnaire) to dismiss; (arrêt, contrat) to revoke

revue [R(ə)vy] nf review; (périodique) review, magazine; (de music-hall) variety show; **passer en ~** (mentalement) to go through

rez-de-chaussée [Red(ə)ʃose] nm inv ground floor

RF sigle f = République française

Rhin [Rɛ̃] nm Rhine

rhinocéros [RinɔseRɔs] nm rhinoceros

Rhône [Ron] nm Rhone

rhubarbe [RybaRb] nf rhubarb

rhum [Rɔm] nm rum

rhumatisme [Rymatism] nm rheumatism no pl

rhume [Rym] nm cold; **~ de cerveau** head cold; **le ~ des foins** hay fever

ri [Ri] pp de **rire**

riant, e [R(i)jã, R(i)jãt] adj smiling, cheerful

ricaner [Rikane] vi (avec méchanceté) to snigger; (bêtement) to giggle

riche [Riʃ] adj rich; (personne, pays) rich, wealthy; **~ en** rich in; **richesse** nf wealth; (fig: de sol, musée etc) richness; **richesses** nfpl (ressources, argent) wealth sg; (fig: trésors) treasures

ricochet [Rikɔʃe] nm: **faire des ~s** to skip stones; **par ~** (fig) as an indirect result

rictus [Riktys] nm grin

ride [Rid] nf wrinkle

rideau, x [Rido] nm curtain; **~ de fer** (boutique) metal shutter(s)

rider [Ride] vt to wrinkle; **se ~** vi to become wrinkled

ridicule [Ridikyl] adj ridiculous ♦ nm: **le ~** ridicule; **ridiculiser: se ridiculiser** vi to make a fool of o.s.

MOT-CLÉ

rien [Rjɛ̃] pron 1: **(ne) ... rien** nothing; tournure negative + anything; **qu'est-ce que vous avez? – rien** what have you got? – nothing; **il n'a rien dit/fait** he said/did nothing; he hasn't said/done anything; **il n'a rien** (n'est pas blessé) he's all right; **de rien!** not at all!

2 (quelque chose): **a-t-il jamais rien fait pour nous?** has he ever done anything for us?

3: **rien de: rien d'intéressant** nothing interesting; **rien d'autre** nothing else; **rien du tout** nothing at all

4: **rien que** just, only; nothing but; **rien que pour lui faire plaisir** only ou just to please him; **rien que la vérité** nothing but the truth; **rien que cela** that alone

♦ nm: **un petit rien** (cadeau) a little something; **des riens** trivia pl; **un rien de** a hint of; **en un rien de temps** in no time at all

---

rieur, -euse [R(i)jœR, R(i)jøz] adj cheerful

rigide [Riʒid] adj stiff; (fig) rigid; strict

rigole [Rigɔl] nf (conduit) channel

rigoler [Rigɔle] vi (fam: rire) to laugh; (s'amuser) to have (some) fun; (plaisanter) to be joking ou kidding; **rigolo, -ote**

(fam) adj funny ♦ nm/f comic; *(péj)* fraud, phoney

rigoureusement [Rigurøzmɑ̃] adv *(vrai)* absolutely; *(interdit)* strictly

rigoureux, -euse [RiguRø, øz] adj rigorous; *(hiver)* hard, harsh

rigueur [RigœR] nf rigour; **être de ~** to be the rule; **à la ~** at a pinch; **tenir ~ à qn de qch** to hold sth against sb

rillettes [Rijɛt] nfpl potted meat *(made from pork or goose)*

rime [Rim] nf rhyme

rinçage [Rɛ̃saʒ] nm rinsing (out); *(opération)* rinse

rincer [Rɛ̃se] vt to rinse; *(récipient)* to rinse out

ring [Riŋ] nm (boxing) ring

ringard, e [Rɛ̃gaR, aRd] *(fam)* adj old-fashioned

rions [Ri5] vb voir **rire**

riposter [Ripɔste] vi to retaliate ♦ vt: **~ que** to retort that

rire [RiR] vi to laugh; *(se divertir)* to have fun ♦ nm laugh; **le ~** laughter; **~ de** to laugh at; **pour ~** *(pas sérieusement)* for a joke ou a laugh

risée [Rize] nf: **être la ~ de** to be the laughing stock of

risible [Rizibl] adj laughable

risque [Risk] nm risk; **le ~** danger; **à ses ~s et périls** at his own risk; **risqué, e** adj risky; *(plaisanterie)* risqué, daring; **risquer** vt to risk; *(allusion, question)* to venture, hazard; **ça ne risque rien** it's quite safe; **risquer de: il risque de se tuer** he could get himself killed; **ce qui risque de se produire** what might ou could well happen; **il ne risque pas de recommencer** there's no chance of him doing that again; **se risquer à faire** *(tenter)* to venture ou dare to do

rissoler [Risɔle] vi, vt: **(faire) ~** to brown

ristourne [RistuRn] nf discount

rite [Rit] nm rite; *(fig)* ritual

rivage [Rivaʒ] nm shore

rival, e, -aux [Rival, o] adj, nm/f rival; **ri-**

valiser vi: **rivaliser avec** *(personne)* to rival, vie with; **rivalité** nf rivalry

rive [Riv] nf shore; *(de fleuve)* bank; **riverain, e** nm/f riverside *(ou lakeside)* resident; *(d'une route)* local resident

rivet [Rivɛ] nm rivet

rivière [RivjɛR] nf river

rixe [Riks] nf brawl, scuffle

riz [Ri] nm rice; **rizière** nf paddy-field, rice field

RMI sigle m *(= revenu minimum d'insertion)* ≈ income support *(BRIT)*, welfare *(US)*

RN sigle f = **route nationale**

robe [Rɔb] nf dress; *(de juge)* robe; *(pelage)* coat; **~ de chambre** dressing gown; **~ de soirée/de mariée** evening/wedding dress

robinet [Rɔbinɛ] nm tap

robot [Rɔbo] nm robot

robuste [Rɔbyst] adj robust, sturdy; **robustesse** nf robustness, sturdiness

roc [Rɔk] nm rock

rocade [Rɔkad] nf bypass

rocaille [Rɔkɑj] nf loose stones pl; *(jardin)* rockery, rock garden

roche [Rɔʃ] nf rock

rocher [Rɔʃe] nm rock

rocheux, -euse [Rɔʃø, øz] adj rocky

rodage [Rɔdaʒ] nm: **en ~** running in

roder [Rɔde] vt *(AUTO)* to run in

rôder [Rode] vi to roam about; *(de façon suspecte)* to lurk (about ou around); **rôdeur, -euse** nm/f prowler

rogne [Rɔɲ] *(fam)* nf: **être en ~** to be in a temper

rogner [Rɔɲe] vt to clip; **~ sur** *(fig)* to cut down ou back on

rognons [Rɔɲ5] nmpl *(CULIN)* kidneys

roi [Rwa] nm king; **la fête des R~s, les R~s** Twelfth Night

┌─────────────────┐
│ **fête des Rois** │
└─────────────────┘

i **La fête des Rois** *is celebrated on January 6. Figurines representing the magi are traditionally added to the Christmas crib and people eat* **la galette des**

Rois, a plain, flat cake in which a porcelain charm (la **fève**) is hidden. Whoever finds the charm is king or queen for the day and chooses a partner.

ôle [Rol] nm role, part

ollers [RɔlœR] mpl Rollerblades ®

omain, e [Rɔmɛ̃, ɛn] adj Roman ♦ nm/f: R~, e Roman

oman, e [Rɔmɑ̃, an] adj (ARCHIT) Romanesque ♦ nm novel; ~ **d'espionnage** spy novel ou story; ~ **policier** detective story

omance [Rɔmɑ̃s] nf ballad

omancer [Rɔmɑ̃se] vt (agrémenter) to romanticize; **romancier, -ière** nm/f novelist; **romanesque** adj (amours, aventures) storybook cpd; (sentimental) romantic

oman-feuilleton [Rɔmɑ̃fœjtɔ̃] nm serialized novel

omanichel, le [Rɔmaniʃɛl] (péj) nm/f gipsy

omantique [Rɔmɑ̃tik] adj romantic

omarin [RɔmaRɛ̃] nm rosemary

ompre [Rɔ̃pR] vt to break; (entretien, fiançailles) to break off ♦ vi (fiancés) to break it off; **se ~** vi to break; **rompu, e** adj (fourbu) exhausted

onces [Rɔ̃s] nfpl brambles

onchonner [Rɔ̃ʃɔne] (fam) vi to grouse, grouch

ond, e [Rɔ̃, Rɔ̃d] adj round; (joues, mollets) well-rounded; (fam: ivre) tight ♦ nm (cercle) ring; (fam: sou): **je n'ai plus un ~** I haven't a penny left; **en ~** (s'asseoir, danser) in a ring; **ronde** nf (gén: de surveillance) rounds pl, patrol; (danse) round (dance); (MUS) semibreve (BRIT), whole note (US); **à la ronde** (alentour): **à 10 km à la ronde** for 10 km round; **rondelet, te** adj plump

ondelle [Rɔ̃dɛl] nf (tranche) slice, round; (TECH) washer

ondement [Rɔ̃dmɑ̃] adv (efficacement) briskly

ondin [Rɔ̃dɛ̃] nm log

ond-point [Rɔ̃pwɛ̃] nm roundabout

ronflant, e [Rɔ̃flɑ̃, ɑ̃t] (péj) adj high-flown, grand

ronflement [Rɔ̃fləmɑ̃] nm snore, snoring

ronfler [Rɔ̃fle] vi to snore; (moteur, poêle) to hum

ronger [Rɔ̃ʒe] vt to gnaw (at); (suj: vers, rouille) to eat into; **se ~ les ongles** to bite one's nails; **se ~ les sangs** to worry o.s. sick; **rongeur** nm rodent

ronronner [Rɔ̃Rɔne] vi to purr

rosace [Rozas] nf (vitrail) rose window

rosbif [Rɔsbif] nm: **du ~** roasting beef; (cuit) roast beef

rose [Roz] nf rose ♦ adj pink

rosé, e [Roze] adj pinkish; (vin) ~ rosé

roseau, x [Rozo] nm reed

rosée [Roze] nf dew

rosette [Rozɛt] nf (nœud) bow

rosier [Rozje] nm rosebush, rose tree

rosse [Rɔs] (fam) adj nasty, vicious

rossignol [Rɔsiɲɔl] nm (ZOOL) nightingale

rot [Ro] nm belch; (de bébé) burp

rotatif, -ive [Rɔtatif, iv] adj rotary

rotation [Rɔtasjɔ̃] nf rotation

roter [Rɔte] (fam) vi to burp, belch

rôti [Roti] nm: **du ~** roasting meat; (cuit) roast meat; ~ **de bœuf/porc** joint of beef/pork

rotin [Rɔtɛ̃] nm rattan (cane); **fauteuil en ~** cane (arm)chair

rôtir [RotiR] vi, vt (aussi: **faire ~**) to roast; **rôtisserie** nf (restaurant) steakhouse; (traiteur) roast meat shop; **rôtissoire** nf (roasting) spit

rotule [Rɔtyl] nf kneecap

roturier, -ière [RɔtyRje, jɛR] nm/f commoner

rouage [Rwaʒ] nm cog(wheel), gearwheel; **les ~s de l'État** the wheels of State

roucouler [Rukule] vi to coo

roue [Ru] nf wheel; ~ **de secours** spare wheel

roué, e [Rwe] adj wily

rouer [Rwe] vt: ~ **qn de coups** to give sb a thrashing

rouge [Ruʒ] adj, nm/f red ♦ nm red; (vin)

~ red wine; **sur la liste** ~ ex-directory (*BRIT*), unlisted (*US*); **passer au** ~ (*signal*) to go red; (*automobiliste*) to go through a red light; ~ **(à lèvres)** lipstick; **rouge-gorge** *nm* robin (redbreast)

rougeole [ruʒɔl] *nf* measles *sg*

rougeoyer [ruʒwaje] *vi* to glow red

rouget [ruʒɛ] *nm* mullet

rougeur [ruʒœr] *nf* redness; (*MÉD: tache*) red blotch

rougir [ruʒir] *vi* to turn red; (*de honte, timidité*) to blush, flush; (*de plaisir, colère*) to flush

rouille [ruj] *nf* rust; **rouillé, e** *adj* rusty; **rouiller** *vt* to rust ♦ *vi* to rust, go rusty; **se rouiller** *vi* to rust

roulant, e [rulɑ̃, ɑ̃t] *adj* (*meuble*) on wheels; (*tapis etc*) moving; **escalier** ~ escalator

rouleau, x [rulo] *nm* roll; (*à mise en plis, à peinture, vague*) roller; ~ **à pâtisserie** rolling pin

roulement [rulmɑ̃] *nm* (*rotation*) rotation; (*bruit*) rumbling *no pl*, rumble; **travailler par** ~ to work on a rota (*BRIT*) *ou* rotation (*US*) basis; ~ **(à billes)** ball bearings *pl*; ~ **de tambour** drum roll

rouler [rule] *vt* to roll; (*papier, tapis*) to roll up; (*CULIN: pâte*) to roll out; (*fam: duper*) to do, con ♦ *vi* (*bille, boule*) to roll; (*voiture, train*) to go, run; (*automobiliste*) to drive; (*bateau*) to roll; **se** ~ **dans** (*boue*) to roll in; (*couverture*) to roll o.s. (up) in

roulette [rulɛt] *nf* (*de table, fauteuil*) castor; (*de dentiste*) drill; (*jeu*) roulette; **à ~s** on castors; **ça a marché comme sur des ~s** (*fam*) it went off very smoothly

roulis [ruli] *nm* roll(ing)

roulotte [rulɔt] *nf* caravan

roumain, e [rumɛ̃, ɛn] *adj* Rumanian ♦ *nm/f*: **R~, e** Rumanian

Roumanie [rumani] *nf* Rumania

rouquin, e [rukɛ̃, in] (*péj*) *nm/f* redhead

rouspéter [ruspete] (*fam*) *vi* to moan

rousse [rus] *adj voir* **roux**

roussir [rusir] *vt* to scorch ♦ *vi* (*CULIN*):

faire ~ to brown

route [rut] *nf* road; (*fig: chemin*) way; (*iti-néraire, parcours*) route; (*fig: voie*) road, path; **il y a 3h de** ~ it's a 3-hour ride o journey; **en** ~ on the way; **mettre en** ~ to start up; **se mettre en** ~ to set off; **nationale** ≃ A road (*BRIT*), ≃ state high way (*US*); **routier, -ière** *adj* road *cp* ♦ *nm* (*camionneur*) (long-distance) lorr (*BRIT*) *ou* truck (*US*) driver; (*restaurant*) ≃ transport café (*BRIT*), ≃ truck stop (*US*)

routine [rutin] *nf* routine; **routinier -ière** (*péj*) *adj* (*activité*) humdrum; (*per sonne*) addicted to routine

rouvrir [ruvrir] *vt, vi* to reopen, ope again; **se** ~ *vi* to reopen, open again

roux, rousse [ru, rus] *adj* red; (*personne* red-haired ♦ *nm/f* redhead

royal, e, -aux [rwajal, o] *adj* royal; (*ca deau etc*) fit for a king

royaume [rwajom] *nm* kingdom; (*fi realm*; **le R~-Uni** the United Kingdom

royauté [rwajote] *nf* (*régime*) monarchy

RPR *sigle m*: **Rassemblement pour la Ré publique** *French right-wing political party*

ruban [rybɑ̃] *nm* ribbon; ~ **adhésif** adh sive tape

rubéole [rybeɔl] *nf* German measles s rubella

rubis [rybi] *nm* ruby

rubrique [rybrik] *nf* (*titre, catégorie*) head ing; (*PRESSE: article*) column

ruche [ryʃ] *nf* hive

rude [ryd] *adj* (*au toucher*) rough; (*métie tâche*) hard, tough; (*climat*) severe, hars (*bourru*) harsh, rough; (*fruste: manière* rugged, tough; (*fam: fameux*) jolly goo **rudement** (*fam*) *adv* (*très*) terribly

rudimentaire [rydimɑ̃tɛr] *adj* rudime tary, basic

rudiments [rydimɑ̃] *nmpl*: **avoir des d'anglais** to have a smattering of Englis

rudoyer [rydwaje] *vt* to treat harshly

rue [ry] *nf* street

ruée [rɥe] *nf* rush

ruelle [rɥɛl] *nf* alley(-way)

uer [ʀɥe] vi (cheval) to kick out; **se ~** vi: **se ~ sur** to pounce on; **se ~ vers/ dans/hors de** to rush ou dash towards/ into/out of

ugby [ʀygbi] nm rugby (football)

ugir [ʀyʒiʀ] vi to roar

ugueux, -euse [ʀygø, øz] adj rough

uine [ʀɥin] nf ruin; **ruiner** vt to ruin; **ruineux, -euse** adj ruinous

uisseau, x [ʀɥiso] nm stream, brook

uisseler [ʀɥis(ə)le] vi to stream

umeur [ʀymœʀ] nf (nouvelle) rumour; (bruit confus) rumbling

uminer [ʀymine] vt (herbe) to ruminate; (fig) to ruminate on ou over, chew over

upture [ʀyptyʀ] nf (séparation, désunion) break-up, split; (de négociations etc) breakdown; (de contrat) breach; (dans continuité) break

ural, e, -aux [ʀyʀal, o] adj rural, country cpd

use [ʀyz] nf: **la ~** cunning, craftiness; (pour tromper) trickery; **une ~** a trick, a ruse; **rusé, e** adj cunning, crafty

usse [ʀys] adj Russian ♦ nm/f: **R~** Russian ♦ nm (LING) Russian

ussie [ʀysi] nf: **la ~** Russia

ustine ® [ʀystin] nf rubber repair patch (for bicycle tyre)

ustique [ʀystik] adj rustic

ustre [ʀystʀ] nm boor

utilant, e [ʀytilɑ̃, ɑ̃t] adj gleaming

ythme [ʀitm] nm rhythm; (vitesse) rate; (: de la vie) pace, tempo; **rythmé, e** adj rhythmic(al)

S, s

' [s] pron voir **se**

a [sa] adj voir **son**[1]

A sigle (= société anonyme) ≃ Ltd (BRIT), ≃ Inc. (US)

able [sabl] nm sand; **~s mouvants** quicksand(s)

ablé [sable] nm shortbread biscuit

sabler [sable] vt (contre le verglas) to grit; **~ le champagne** to drink champagne

sablier [sablije] nm hourglass; (de cuisine) egg timer

sablonneux, -euse [sablɔnø, øz] adj sandy

saborder [sabɔʀde] vt (navire) to scuttle; (fig: projet) to put paid to, scupper

sabot [sabo] nm clog; (de cheval) hoof; **~ de frein** brake shoe

saboter [sabɔte] vt to sabotage; (bâcler) to make a mess of, botch

sac [sak] nm bag; (à charbon etc) sack; **~ à dos** rucksack; **~ à main** handbag; **~ de couchage** sleeping bag; **~ de voyage** travelling bag; **~ poubelle** bin liner

saccadé, e [sakade] adj jerky; (respiration) spasmodic

saccager [sakaʒe] vt (piller) to sack; (dévaster) to create havoc in

saccharine [sakaʀin] nf saccharin

sacerdoce [sasɛʀdɔs] nm priesthood; (fig) calling, vocation

sache etc [saʃ] vb voir **savoir**

sachet [saʃɛ] nm (small) bag; (de sucre, café) sachet; **du potage en ~** packet soup; **~ de thé** tea bag

sacoche [sakɔʃ] nf (gén) bag; (de bicyclette) saddlebag

sacquer [sake] (fam) vt (employé) to fire; (détester): **je ne peux pas le ~** I can't stand him

sacre [sakʀ] nm (roi) coronation

sacré, e [sakʀe] adj sacred; (fam: satané) blasted; (: fameux): **un ~ toupet** a heck of a cheek

sacrement [sakʀəmɑ̃] nm sacrament

sacrifice [sakʀifis] nm sacrifice; **sacrifier** vt to sacrifice

sacristie [sakʀisti] nf (catholique) sacristy; (protestante) vestry

sadique [sadik] adj sadistic

safran [safʀɑ̃] nm saffron

sage [saʒ] adj wise; (enfant) good

sage-femme [saʒfam] nf midwife

sagesse [saʒɛs] nf wisdom

Sagittaire [saʒitɛʀ] *nm*: **le ~** Sagittarius

Sahara [saaʀa] *nm*: **le ~** the Sahara (desert)

saignant, e [sɛɲɑ̃, ɑ̃t] *adj* (*viande*) rare

saignée [seɲe] *nf* (*fig*) heavy losses *pl*

saigner [seɲe] *vi* to bleed ♦ *vt* to bleed; (*animal*) to. kill (by bleeding); **~ du nez** to have a nosebleed

saillie [saji] *nf* (*sur un mur etc*) projection

saillir [sajiʀ] *vi* to project, stick out; (*veine, muscle*) to bulge

sain, e [sɛ̃, sɛn] *adj* healthy; **~ d'esprit** sound in mind, sane; **~ et sauf** safe and sound, unharmed

saindoux [sɛ̃du] *nm* lard

saint, e [sɛ̃, sɛ̃t] *adj* holy ♦ *nm/f* saint; **le S~ Esprit** the Holy Spirit *ou* Ghost; **la S~e Vierge** the Blessed Virgin; **la S~-Sylvestre** New Year's Eve; **sainteté** *nf* holiness

sais *etc* [sɛ] *vb voir* **savoir**

saisi, e [sezi] *adj*: **~ de panique** panic-stricken; **être ~ (par le froid)** to be struck by the sudden cold

saisie *nf* seizure; **~e (de données)** (data) capture

saisir [seziʀ] *vt* to take hold of, grab; (*fig: occasion*) to seize; (*comprendre*) to grasp; (*entendre*) to get, catch; (*données*) to capture; (*CULIN*) to fry quickly; (*JUR: biens, publication*) to seize; **se ~ de** *vt* to seize; **saisissant, e** *adj* startling, striking

saison [sɛzɔ̃] *nf* season; **morte ~** slack season; **saisonnier, -ière** *adj* seasonal

sait [sɛ] *vb voir* **savoir**

salade [salad] *nf* (*BOT*) lettuce *etc*; (*CULIN*) (green) salad; (*fam: confusion*) tangle, muddle; **~ composée** mixed salad; **~ de fruits** fruit salad; **saladier** *nm* (salad) bowl

salaire [salɛʀ] *nm* (*annuel, mensuel*) salary; (*hebdomadaire, journalier*) pay, wages *pl*; **~ minimum interprofessionnel de croissance** index-linked guaranteed minimum wage

salarié, e [salaʀje] *nm/f* salaried employee; wage-earner

salaud [salo] (*fam!*) *nm* sod (*!*), bastard (*!*)

sale [sal] *adj* dirty, filthy; (*fam: mauvais*) nasty

salé, e [sale] *adj* (*mer, goût*) salty; (*CULIN: amandes, beurre etc*) salted; (: *gâteaux*) savoury; (*fam: grivois*) spicy; (: *facture*) steep

saler [sale] *vt* to salt

saleté [salte] *nf* (*état*) dirtiness; (*crasse*) dirt, filth; (*tache etc*) dirt *no pl*; (*fam: méchanceté*) dirty trick; (: *camelote*) rubbish *no pl*; (: *obscénité*) filthy thing (to say)

salière [saljɛʀ] *nf* saltcellar

salin, e [salɛ̃, in] *adj* saline

salir [saliʀ] *vt* to (make) dirty; (*fig: que qu'un*) to soil the reputation of; **se ~** to get dirty; **salissant, e** *adj* (*tissu*) which shows the dirt; (*travail*) dirty, messy

salle [sal] *nf* room; (*d'hôpital*) ward; (*a restaurant*) dining room; (*d'un cinéma*) auditorium; (: *public*) audience; **~ à manger** dining room; **~ d'attente** waiting room; **~ de bain(s)** bathroom; **~ de classe** classroom; **~ de concert** concert hall; **~ d'eau** shower-room; **~ d'embarquement** (*à l'aéroport*) departure lounge; **~ de jeux** (*pour enfants*) playroom; **~ d'opération** (*d'hôpital*) operating theatre; **~ de séjour** living room; **~ des ventes** saleroom

salon [salɔ̃] *nm* lounge, sitting room; (*mobilier*) lounge suite; (*exposition*) exhibition, show; **~ de coiffure** hairdressing salon; **de thé** tearoom

salope [salɔp] (*fam!*) *nf* bitch (*!*); **saloperie** (*fam!*) *nf* (*action*) dirty trick; (*chose san valeur*) rubbish *no pl*

salopette [salɔpɛt] *nf* dungarees *pl* (*d'ouvrier*) overall(s)

salsifis [salsifi] *nm* salsify

salubre [salybʀ] *adj* healthy, salubrious

saluer [salɥe] *vt* (*pour dire bonjour, fig*) to greet; (*pour dire au revoir*) to take one's leave; (*MIL*) to salute

salut [saly] *nm* (*geste*) wave; (*parole*) greeting; (*MIL*) salute; (*sauvegarde*) safety; (*REL*) salvation ♦ *excl* (*fam: bonjour*) hi (there)

(: au revoir) see you, bye

salutations [salytasjɔ̃] *nfpl* greetings; **Veuillez agréer, Monsieur, mes ~ distinguées** yours faithfully

samedi [samdi] *nm* Saturday

SAMU [samy] *sigle m* (= *service d'assistance médicale d'urgence*) ≈ ambulance (service) (*BRIT*), ≈ paramedics *pl* (*US*)

sanction [sɑ̃ksjɔ̃] *nf* sanction; **sanctionner** *vt* (*loi, usage*) to sanction; (*punir*) to punish

sandale [sɑ̃dal] *nf* sandal

sandwich [sɑ̃dwi(t)ʃ] *nm* sandwich

sang [sɑ̃] *nm* blood; **en ~** covered in blood; **se faire du mauvais ~** to fret, get in a state; **sang-froid** *nm* calm, sangfroid; **de sang-froid** in cold blood; **sanglant, e** *adj* bloody

sangle [sɑ̃gl] *nf* strap

sanglier [sɑ̃glije] *nm* (wild) boar

sanglot [sɑ̃glo] *nm* sob; **sangloter** *vi* to sob

sangsue [sɑ̃sy] *nf* leech

sanguin, e [sɑ̃gɛ̃, in] *adj* blood *cpd*; **sanguinaire** *adj* bloodthirsty

sanitaire [sanitɛʀ] *adj* health *cpd*; **~s** *nmpl* (*lieu*) bathroom *sg*

sans [sɑ̃] *prép* without; **un pull ~ manches** a sleeveless jumper; **~ faute** without fail; **~ arrêt** without a break; **~ ça** (*fam*) otherwise; **~ qu'il s'en aperçoive** without him *ou* his noticing; **sans-abri** *nmpl* homeless; **sans-emploi** *nm/f inv* unemployed person; **les sans-emploi** the unemployed; **sans-gêne** *adj inv* inconsiderate

santé [sɑ̃te] *nf* health; **en bonne ~** in good health; **boire à la ~ de qn** to drink (to) sb's health; **à ta/votre ~!** cheers!

saoudien, ne [saudjɛ̃, jɛn] *adj* Saudi Arabian ♦ *nm/f*: **S~, ne** Saudi Arabian

saoul, e [su, sul] *adj* = **soûl**

saper [sape] *vt* to undermine, sap

sapeur-pompier [sapœʀpɔ̃pje] *nm* fireman

saphir [safiʀ] *nm* sapphire

sapin [sapɛ̃] *nm* fir (tree); (*bois*) fir; **~ de Noël** Christmas tree

sarcastique [saʀkastik] *adj* sarcastic

sarcler [saʀkle] *vt* to weed

Sardaigne [saʀdɛɲ] *nf*: **la ~** Sardinia

sardine [saʀdin] *nf* sardine

sarrasin [saʀazɛ̃] *nm* buckwheat

SARL *sigle f* (= *société à responsabilité limitée*) ≈ plc (*BRIT*), ≈ Inc. (*US*)

sas [sɑs] *nm* (*de sous-marin, d'engin spatial*) airlock; (*d'écluse*) lock

satané, e [satane] (*fam*) *adj* confounded

satellite [satelit] *nm* satellite

satin [satɛ̃] *nm* satin

satire [satiʀ] *nf* satire; **satirique** *adj* satirical

satisfaction [satisfaksjɔ̃] *nf* satisfaction

satisfaire [satisfɛʀ] *vt* to satisfy; **~ à** (*conditions*) to meet; **satisfaisant, e** *adj* (*acceptable*) satisfactory; **satisfait, e** *adj* satisfied; **satisfait de** happy *ou* satisfied with

saturer [satyʀe] *vt* to saturate

sauce [sos] *nf* sauce; (*avec un rôti*) gravy; **saucière** *nf* sauceboat

saucisse [sosis] *nf* sausage

saucisson [sosisɔ̃] *nm* (slicing) sausage

sauf, sauve [sof, sov] *adj* unharmed, unhurt; (*fig: honneur*) intact, saved ♦ *prép* except; **laisser la vie sauve à qn** to spare sb's life; **~ si** (*à moins que*) unless; **~ erreur** if I'm not mistaken; **~ avis contraire** unless you hear to the contrary

sauge [soʒ] *nf* sage

saugrenu, e [sogʀəny] *adj* preposterous

saule [sol] *nm* willow (tree)

saumon [somɔ̃] *nm* salmon *inv*

saumure [somyʀ] *nf* brine

saupoudrer [supudʀe] *vt*: **~ qch de** to sprinkle sth with

saur [sɔʀ] *adj m*: **hareng ~** smoked *ou* red herring, kipper

saurai *etc* [sɔʀe] *vb voir* **savoir**

saut [so] *nm* jump; (*discipline sportive*) jumping; **faire un ~ chez qn** to pop over to sb's (place); **~ à l'élastique** bungee

jumping; ~ **à la perche** pole vaulting; ~
en hauteur/longueur high/long jump; ~
périlleux somersault

saute [sot] *nf*: ~ **d'humeur** sudden
change of mood

sauter [sote] *vi* to jump, leap; (*exploser*) to
blow up, explode; (: *fusibles*) to blow; (*se
détacher*) to pop out (*ou* off) ♦ *vt* to jump
(over), leap (over); (*fig: omettre*) to skip,
miss (out); **faire ~** to blow up; (*CULIN*) to
sauté; ~ **au cou de qn** to fly into sb's
arms; ~ **sur une occasion** to jump at an
opportunity; ~ **aux yeux** to be (quite) obvious

sauterelle [sotʀɛl] *nf* grasshopper

sautiller [sotije] *vi* (*oiseau*) to hop; (*enfant*)
to skip

sauvage [sovaʒ] *adj* (*gén*) wild; (*peuplade*)
savage; (*farouche: personne*) unsociable;
(*barbare*) wild, savage; (*non officiel*) unauthorized, unofficial; **faire du camping ~**
to camp in the wild ♦ *nm/f* savage; (*timide*) unsociable type

sauve [sov] *adj f voir* **sauf**

sauvegarde [sovgaʀd] *nf* safeguard; (*IN-
FORM*) backup; **sauvegarder** *vt* to safeguard; (*INFORM: enregistrer*) to save; (: *copier*) to back up

sauve-qui-peut [sovkipø] *excl* run for
your life!

sauver [sove] *vt* to save; (*porter secours à*)
to rescue; (*récupérer*) to salvage, rescue;
se ~ *vi* (*s'enfuir*) to run away; (*fam: partir*)
to be off; **sauvetage** *nm* rescue; **sauveteur** *nm* rescuer; **sauvette**: **à la sauvette** *adv* (*se marier etc*) hastily, hurriedly;
sauveur *nm* saviour (*BRIT*), savior (*US*)

savais *etc* [save] *vb voir* **savoir**

savamment [savamɑ̃] *adv* (*avec érudition*)
learnedly; (*habilement*) skilfully, cleverly

savant, e [savɑ̃, ɑ̃t] *adj* scholarly, learned
♦ *nm* scientist

saveur [savœʀ] *nf* flavour, (*fig*) savour

savoir [savwaʀ] *vt* to know; (*être capable
de*): **il sait nager** he can swim ♦ *nm*
knowledge; **se ~** *vi* (*être connu*) to be

known; **à ~** that is, namely; **faire ~ qch
à qn** to let sb know sth; **pas que je sache** not as far as I know

savon [savɔ̃] *nm* (*produit*) soap; (*morceau*)
bar of soap; (*fam*): **passer un ~ à qn** to
give sb a good dressing-down; **savonner**
vt to soap; **savonnette** *nf* bar of soap

savons [savɔ̃] *vb voir* **savoir**

savourer [savuʀe] *vt* to savour; **savou-
reux, -euse** *adj* tasty; (*fig: anecdote*)
spicy, juicy

saxo(phone) [saksɔ(fɔn)] *nm* sax(ophone)

scabreux, -euse [skabʀø, øz] *adj* risky;
(*indécent*) improper, shocking

scandale [skɑ̃dal] *nm* scandal; (*tapage*)
faire un ~ to make a scene, create a disturbance; **faire ~** to scandalize people;
scandaleux, -euse *adj* scandalous, outrageous

scandinave [skɑ̃dinav] *adj* Scandinavian
♦ *nm/f*: **S~** Scandinavian

Scandinavie [skɑ̃dinavi] *nf* Scandinavia

scaphandre [skafɑ̃dʀ] *nm* (*de plongeur*)
diving suit

scarabée [skaʀabe] *nm* beetle

scarlatine [skaʀlatin] *nf* scarlet fever

scarole [skaʀɔl] *nf* endive

sceau, x [so] *nm* seal

scélérat, e [selera, at] *nm/f* villain

sceller [sele] *vt* to seal

scénario [senaʀjo] *nm* scenario

scène [sɛn] *nf* (*gén*) scene; (*estrade, fig:
théâtre*) stage; **entrer en ~** to come on
stage; **mettre en ~** (*THÉÂTRE*) to stage;
(*CINÉMA*) to direct; ~ **de ménage** domestic scene

sceptique [septik] *adj* sceptical

schéma [ʃema] *nm* (*diagramme*) diagram,
sketch; **schématique** *adj* diagrammat-
ic(al), schematic; (*fig*) oversimplified

sciatique [sjatik] *nf* sciatica

scie [si] *nf* saw; ~ **à métaux** hacksaw

sciemment [sjamɑ̃] *adv* knowingly

science [sjɑ̃s] *nf* science; (*savoir*) knowledge; ~**s naturelles** (*SCOL*) natural science *sg*, biology *sg*; ~**s po** political sc

ence *ou* studies *pl*; **science-fiction** *nf* science fiction; **scientifique** *adj* scientific ♦ *nm/f* scientist; *(étudiant)* science student

scier [sje] *vt* to saw; *(retrancher)* to saw off; **scierie** *nf* sawmill

scinder [sɛ̃de] *vt* to split up; **se ~** *vi* to split up

scintiller [sɛ̃tije] *vi* to sparkle; *(étoile)* to twinkle

scission [sisjɔ̃] *nf* split

sciure [sjyʀ] *nf*: **~ (de bois)** sawdust

sclérose [skleʀoz] *nf*: **~ en plaques** multiple sclerosis

scolaire [skɔlɛʀ] *adj* school *cpd*; **scolariser** *vt* to provide with schooling/schools; **scolarité** *nf* schooling

scooter [skutœʀ] *nm* (motor) scooter

score [skɔʀ] *nm* score

scorpion [skɔʀpjɔ̃] *nm (signe)*: **le S~** Scorpio

Scotch ® [skɔtʃ] *nm* adhesive tape

scout, e [skut] *adj, nm* scout

script [skʀipt] *nm (écriture)* printing; *(CINÉMA)* (shooting) script

scrupule [skʀypyl] *nm* scruple

scruter [skʀyte] *vt* to scrutinize; *(l'obscurité)* to peer into

scrutin [skʀytɛ̃] *nm (vote)* ballot; *(ensemble des opérations)* poll

sculpter [skylte] *vt* to sculpt; *(bois)* to carve; **sculpteur** *nm* sculptor; **sculpture** *nf* sculpture; **sculpture sur bois** wood carving

SDF *sigle m* (= *sans domicile fixe*) homeless person; **les SDF** the homeless

---

MOT-CLÉ

se [sə], **s'** *pron* **1** *(emploi réfléchi)* oneself; *(: masc)* himself; *(: fém)* herself; *(: sujet non humain)* itself; *(: pl)* themselves; **se voir comme l'on est** to see o.s. as one is

2 *(réciproque)* one another, each other; **ils s'aiment** they love one another *ou* each other

3 *(passif)*: **cela se répare facilement** it is easily repaired

4 *(possessif)*: **se casser la jambe/laver les mains** to break one's leg/wash one's hands

---

séance [seɑ̃s] *nf (d'assemblée)* meeting, session; *(de tribunal)* sitting, session; *(musicale, CINÉMA, THÉÂTRE)* performance; **~ tenante** forthwith

seau, X [so] *nm* bucket, pail

sec, sèche [sɛk, sɛʃ] *adj* dry; *(raisins, figues)* dried; *(cœur: insensible)* hard, cold ♦ *nm*: **tenir au ~** to keep in a dry place ♦ *adv* hard; **je le bois ~** I drink it straight *ou* neat; **à ~** *(puits)* dried up

sécateur [sekatœʀ] *nm* secateurs *pl* (BRIT), shears *pl*

sèche [sɛʃ] *adj f voir* **sec**; **sèche-cheveux** *nm inv* hair-drier; **sèche-linge** *nm inv* tumble dryer; **sèchement** *adv* *(répondre)* drily

sécher [seʃe] *vt* to dry; *(dessécher: peau, blé)* to dry (out); *(: étang)* to dry up; *(fam: cours)* to skip ♦ *vi* to dry; to dry out; to dry up; *(fam: candidat)* to be stumped; **se ~** *(après le bain)* to dry o.s.; **sécheresse** *nf* dryness; *(absence de pluie)* drought; **séchoir** *nm* drier

second, e [s(ə)gɔ̃, ɔ̃d] *adj* second ♦ *nm (assistant)* second in command; *(NAVIG)* first mate; **voyager en ~e** to travel second-class; **secondaire** *adj* secondary; **seconde** *nf* second; **seconder** *vt* to assist

secouer [s(ə)kwe] *vt* to shake; *(passagers)* to rock; *(traumatiser)* to shake (up); **se ~** *vi* (fam: faire un effort) to shake o.s. up; *(: se dépêcher)* to get a move on

secourir [s(ə)kuʀiʀ] *vt (venir en aide à)* to assist, aid; **secourisme** *nm* first aid; **secouriste** *nmf* first-aid worker

secours [s(ə)kuʀ] *nm* help, aid, assistance ♦ *nmpl* aid *sg*; **au ~!** help!; **appeler au ~** to shout *ou* call for help; **porter ~ à qn** to give sb assistance, help sb; **les premiers ~** first aid *sg*

secousse [s(ə)kus] *nf* jolt, bump; *(électri-*

que) shock; (*fig: psychologique*) jolt, shock; **~ sismique** earth tremor

secret, -ète [sǝkRɛ, ɛt] *adj* secret; (*fig: renfermé*) reticent, reserved ♦ *nm* secret; (*discrétion absolue*): **le ~** secrecy

secrétaire [s(ǝ)kRetɛR] *nm/f* secretary ♦ *nm* (*meuble*) writing desk; **~ de direction** private *ou* personal secretary; **~ d'État** junior minister; **~ général** (*COMM*) company secretary; **secrétariat** *nm* (*profession*) secretarial work; (*bureau*) office; (*: d'organisation internationale*) secretariat

secteur [sɛktœR] *nm* sector; (*zone*) area; (*ÉLEC*): **branché sur ~** plugged into the mains (supply)

section [sɛksjɔ̃] *nf* section; (*de parcours d'autobus*) fare stage; (*MIL: unité*) platoon; **sectionner** *vt* to sever

Sécu [seky] *abr f* = **sécurité sociale**

séculaire [sekylɛR] *adj* (*très vieux*) age-old

sécuriser [sekyRize] *vt* to give (a feeling of) security to

sécurité [sekyRite] *nf* (*absence de danger*) safety; (*absence de troubles*) security; **système de ~** security system; **être en ~** to be safe; **la ~ routière** road safety; **la ~ sociale** ≃ (the) Social Security (*BRIT*), ≃ Welfare (*US*)

sédentaire [sedɑ̃tɛR] *adj* sedentary

séduction [sedyksjɔ̃] *nf* seduction; (*charme, attrait*) appeal, charm

séduire [sedɥiR] *vt* to charm; (*femme: abuser de*) to seduce; **séduisant, e** *adj* (*femme*) seductive; (*homme, offre*) very attractive

ségrégation [segRegasjɔ̃] *nf* segregation

seigle [sɛgl] *nm* rye

seigneur [sɛɲœR] *nm* lord

sein [sɛ̃] *nm* breast; (*entrailles*) womb; **au ~ de** (*équipe, institution*) within

séisme [seism] *nm* earthquake

seize [sɛz] *num* sixteen; **seizième** *num* sixteenth

séjour [seʒuR] *nm* stay; (*pièce*) living room; **séjourner** *vi* to stay

sel [sɛl] *nm* salt; (*fig: piquant*) spice

sélection [selɛksjɔ̃] *nf* selection; **sélectionner** *vt* to select

self-service [sɛlfsɛRvis] *adj, nm* self-service

selle [sɛl] *nf* saddle; **~s** *nfpl* (*MÉD*) stools; **seller** *vt* to saddle

sellette [sɛlɛt] *nf*: **être sur la ~** to be in the hot seat

selon [s(ǝ)lɔ̃] *prép* according to; (*en se conformant à*) in accordance with; **~ que** according to whether; **~ moi** as I see it

semaine [s(ǝ)mɛn] *nf* week; **en ~** during the week, on weekdays

semblable [sɑ̃blabl] *adj* similar; (*de ce genre*): **de ~s mésaventures** such mishaps ♦ *nm* fellow creature *ou* man; **~ à** similar to, like

semblant [sɑ̃blɑ̃] *nm*: **un ~ de ...** a semblance of ...; **faire ~ (de faire)** to pretend (to do)

sembler [sɑ̃ble] *vb +attrib* to seem ♦ *vb impers*: **il semble (bien) que/inutile de** it (really) seems *ou* appears that/useless to; **il me semble que** it seems to me that; **comme bon lui semble** as he sees fit

semelle [s(ǝ)mɛl] *nf* sole; (*intérieure*) in-sole, inner sole

semence [s(ǝ)mɑ̃s] *nf* (*graine*) seed

semer [s(ǝ)me] *vt* to sow; (*fig: éparpiller*) to scatter; (*: confusion*) to spread; (*fam: poursuivants*) to lose, shake off; **semé de** (*difficultés*) riddled with

semestre [s(ǝ)mɛstR] *nm* half-year; (*SCOL*) semester

séminaire [seminɛR] *nm* seminar

semi-remorque [sǝmiRǝmɔRk] *nm* articulated lorry (*BRIT*), semi(trailer) (*US*)

semoule [s(ǝ)mul] *nf* semolina

sempiternel, le [sɑ̃pitɛRnɛl] *adj* eternal, never-ending

sénat [sena] *nm* senate; **sénateur** *nm* senator

sens [sɑ̃s] *nm* (*PHYSIOL, instinct*) sense; (*signification*) meaning, sense; (*direction*) direction; **à mon ~** to my mind; **dans le ~ des aiguilles d'une montre** clockwise;

dessus dessous upside down; **~ interdit** one-way street; **~ unique** one-way street

sensation [sɑ̃sasjɔ̃] *nf* sensation; **à ~** (*péj*) sensational; **faire ~** to cause *ou* create a sensation; **sensationnel, le** *adj* (*fam*) fantastic, terrific

sensé, e [sɑ̃se] *adj* sensible

sensibiliser [sɑ̃sibilize] *vt*: **~ qn à** to make sb sensitive to

sensibilité [sɑ̃sibilite] *nf* sensitivity

sensible [sɑ̃sibl] *adj* sensitive; (*aux sens*) perceptible; (*appréciable: différence, progrès*) appreciable, noticeable; **sensiblement** *adv* (*à peu près*): **ils sont sensiblement du même âge** they are approximately the same age; **sensiblerie** *nf* sentimentality

sensuel, le [sɑ̃sɥɛl] *adj* (*personne*) sensual; (*musique*) sensuous

sentence [sɑ̃tɑ̃s] *nf* (*jugement*) sentence

sentier [sɑ̃tje] *nm* path

sentiment [sɑ̃timɑ̃] *nm* feeling; **sentimental, e, -aux** *adj* sentimental; (*vie, aventure*) love *cpd*

sentinelle [sɑ̃tinɛl] *nf* sentry

sentir [sɑ̃tiʀ] *vt* (*par l'odorat*) to smell; (*par le goût*) to taste; (*au toucher, fig*) to feel; (*répandre une odeur de*) to smell of; (: *ressemblance*) to smell like ♦ *vi* to smell; **~ mauvais** to smell bad; **se ~ bien** to feel good; **se ~ mal** (*être indisposé*) to feel unwell *ou* ill; **se ~ le courage/la force de faire** to feel brave/strong enough to do; **il ne peut pas le ~** (*fam*) he can't stand him

séparation [separasjɔ̃] *nf* separation; (*cloison*) division, partition

séparé, e [separe] *adj* (*distinct*) separate; (*époux*) separated; **séparément** *adv* separately

séparer [separe] *vt* to separate; (*désunir*) to drive apart; (*détacher*): **~ qch de** to pull sth (off) from; **se ~** *vi* (*époux, amis*) to separate, part; (*se diviser: route etc*) to divide; **se ~ de** (*époux*) to separate *ou* part from; (*employé, objet personnel*) to part with

sept [sɛt] *num* seven; **septante** (*BELGIQUE, SUISSE*) *adj inv* seventy

septembre [sɛptɑ̃bʀ] *nm* September

septennat [sɛptena] *nm* seven year term of office (of French President)

septentrional, e, -aux [sɛptɑ̃tʀijɔnal, o] *adj* northern

septicémie [sɛptisemi] *nf* blood poisoning, septicaemia

septième [sɛtjɛm] *num* seventh

septique [sɛptik] *adj*: **fosse ~** septic tank

sépulture [sepyltyʀ] *nf* (*tombeau*) burial place, grave

séquelles [sekɛl] *nfpl* after-effects; (*fig*) aftermath *sg*

séquestrer [sekɛstʀe] *vt* (*personne*) to confine illegally; (*biens*) to impound

serai *etc* [səʀe] *vb voir* **être**

serein, e [səʀɛ̃, ɛn] *adj* serene

serez [səʀe] *vb voir* **être**

sergent [sɛʀʒɑ̃] *nm* sergeant

série [seʀi] *nf* series *inv*; (*de clés, casseroles, outils*) set; (*catégorie: SPORT*) rank; **en ~** in quick succession; (*COMM*) mass *cpd*; **hors ~** (*COMM*) custom-built

sérieusement [seʀjøzmɑ̃] *adv* seriously

sérieux, -euse [seʀjø, jøz] *adj* serious; (*élève, employé*) reliable, responsible; (*client, maison*) reliable, dependable ♦ *nm* seriousness; (*d'une entreprise etc*) reliability; **garder son ~** to keep a straight face; **prendre qch/qn au ~** to take sth/sb seriously

serin [s(ə)ʀɛ̃] *nm* canary

seringue [s(ə)ʀɛ̃g] *nf* syringe

serions [səʀjɔ̃] *vb voir* **être**

serment [sɛʀmɑ̃] *nm* (*juré*) oath; (*promesse*) pledge, vow

sermon [sɛʀmɔ̃] *nm* sermon

séronégatif, -ive [seʀonegatif, iv] *adj* (*MÉD*) HIV negative

séropositif, -ive [seʀopozitif, iv] *adj* (*MÉD*) HIV positive

serpent [sɛʀpɑ̃] *nm* snake; **serpenter** *vi* to wind

serpillière [sɛʀpijɛʀ] *nf* floorcloth

serre [sɛʀ] *nf* (AGR) greenhouse; **~s** *nfpl* (*griffes*) claws, talons

serré, e [sɛʀe] *adj* (*habits*) tight; (*fig: lutte, match*) tight, close-fought; (*passagers etc*) (tightly) packed; (*réseau*) dense; **avoir le cœur ~** to have a heavy heart

serrer [sɛʀe] *vt* (*tenir*) to grip *ou* hold tight; (*comprimer, coincer*) to squeeze; (*poings, mâchoires*) to clench; (*suj: vêtement*) to be too tight for; (*ceinture, nœud, vis*) to tighten ♦ *vi*: **~ à droite** to keep *ou* get over to the right; **se ~** *vi* (*se rapprocher*) to squeeze up; **se ~ contre qn** to huddle up to sb; **~ la main à qn** to shake sb's hand; **~ qn dans ses bras** to hug sb, clasp sb in one's arms

serrure [sɛʀyʀ] *nf* lock; **serrurier** *nm* locksmith

sert *etc* [sɛʀ] *vb voir* **servir**

servante [sɛʀvɑ̃t] *nf* (maid)servant

serveur, -euse [sɛʀvœʀ, øz] *nm/f* waiter (waitress)

serviable [sɛʀvjabl] *adj* obliging, willing to help

service [sɛʀvis] *nm* service; (*assortiment de vaisselle*) set, service; (*bureau: de la vente etc*) department, section; (*travail*) duty; **premier ~** (*série de repas*) first sitting; **être de ~** to be on duty; **faire le ~** to serve; **rendre un ~ à qn** to do sb a favour; (*objet: s'avérer utile*) to come in useful *ou* handy for sb; **mettre en ~** to put into service *ou* operation; **~ compris/non compris** service included/not included; **hors ~** out of order; **~ après-vente** after-sales service; **~ d'ordre** police (*ou* stewards) in charge of maintaining order; **~ militaire** military service; **~s secrets** secret service *sg*

---

service militaire

> *French men over eighteen are required to do ten months'* **service militaire** *if pronounced fit. The call-up can be delayed if the conscript is in full-time higher education. Conscientious objectors are required*

to do two years' public service. Since 1970, women have been able to do military service, though few do.

---

serviette [sɛʀvjɛt] *nf* (*de table*) (table) napkin, serviette; (*de toilette*) towel; (*porte-documents*) briefcase; **~ hygiénique** sanitary towel

servir [sɛʀviʀ] *vt* to serve; (*au restaurant*) to wait on; (*au magasin*) to serve, attend to ♦ *vi* (TENNIS) to serve; (CARTES) to deal; **se ~** *vi* (*prendre d'un plat*) to help o.s.; **vous êtes servi?** are you being served?; **~ à qn** (*diplôme, livre*) to be of use to sb; **~ à qch/faire** (*outil etc*) to be used for sth doing; **ça ne sert à rien** it's no use; **~ (à) qn de** to serve as (for sb); **se ~ de** (*plat*) to help o.s. to; (*voiture, outil, relations*) to use

serviteur [sɛʀvitœʀ] *nm* servant

ses [se] *adj voir* **son**¹

set [sɛt] *nm*: **~ (de table)** tablemat, place mat

seuil [sœj] *nm* doorstep; (*fig*) threshold

seul, e [sœl] *adj* (*sans compagnie*) alone; (*unique*): **un ~ livre** only one book, a single book ♦ *adv* (*vivre*) alone, on one's own ♦ *nm, nf*: **il en reste un(e) ~(e)** there's only one left; **le ~ livre** the only book; **parler tout ~** to talk to oneself; **faire qch (tout) ~** to do sth (all) on one's own *ou* (all) by oneself; **à lui (tout) ~** single-handed, on his own; **se sentir ~** to feel lonely; **seulement** *adv* only; **non seulement ... mais aussi** *ou* **encore** not only ... but also

sève [sɛv] *nf* sap

sévère [sevɛʀ] *adj* severe

sévices [sevis] *nmpl* (physical) cruelty *sg*, ill treatment *sg*

sévir [seviʀ] *vi* (*punir*) to use harsh measures, crack down; (*suj: fléau*) to rage, be rampant

sevrer [səvʀe] *vt* (*enfant etc*) to wean

sexe [sɛks] *nm* sex; (*organes génitaux*) genitals, sex organs; **sexuel, le** *adj* sexual

seyant, e [sejɑ̃, ɑ̃t] *adj* becoming
shampooing [ʃɑ̃pwɛ̃] *nm* shampoo
short [ʃɔʀt] *nm* (pair of) shorts *pl*

```
MOT-CLÉ
```

si [si] *nm* (MUS) B; (*en chantant la gamme*) ti
♦ *adv* 1 (*oui*) yes
2 (*tellement*) so; **si gentil/rapidement** so
kind/fast; **(tant et) si bien que** so much
so that; **si rapide qu'il soit** however fast
he may be
♦ *conj* if; **si tu veux** if you want; **je me
demande si** I wonder if *ou* whether; **si
seulement** if only

Sicile [sisil] *nf*: **la ~** Sicily
SIDA [sida] *sigle m* (= *syndrome immuno-
déficitaire acquis*) AIDS *sg*
sidéré, e [sideʀe] *adj* staggered
sidérurgie [sideʀyʀʒi] *nf* steel industry
siècle [sjɛkl] *nm* century
siège [sjɛʒ] *nm* seat; (*d'entreprise*) head
office; (*d'organisation*) headquarters *pl*;
(MIL) siege; **~ social** registered office; **siéger** *vi* to sit
sien, ne [sjɛ̃, sjɛn] *pron*: **le(la) ~(ne), les
~(ne)s** (*homme*) his; (*femme*) hers; (*chose,
animal*) its; **les ~s** (*sa famille*) one's family;
faire des ~nes (*fam*) to be up to one's
(usual) tricks
sieste [sjɛst] *nf* (afternoon) snooze *ou* nap;
faire la ~ to have a snooze *ou* nap
sifflement [sifləmɑ̃] *nm*: **un ~** a whistle
siffler [sifle] *vi* (*gén*) to whistle; (*en respi-
rant*) to wheeze; (*serpent, vapeur*) to hiss ♦ *vt*
(*chanson*) to whistle; (*chien etc*) to whistle
for; (*fille*) to whistle at; (*pièce, orateur*) to hiss,
boo; (*fin du match, départ*) to blow one's
whistle for; (*fam: verre*) to guzzle
sifflet [siflɛ] *nm* whistle; **coup de ~** whistle
siffloter [siflɔte] *vi, vt* to whistle
sigle [sigl] *nm* acronym
signal, -aux [siɲal, o] *nm* signal; (*indice,
écriteau*) sign; **donner le ~ de** to give the
signal for; **~ d'alarme** alarm signal; **si-**

gnaux (lumineux) (AUTO) traffic signals;
signalement *nm* description, particulars
pl
signaler [siɲale] *vt* to indicate; (*personne:
faire un signe*) to signal; (*vol, perte*) to report; (*faire remarquer*): **~ qch à qn/(à qn)
que** to point out sth to sb/(to sb) that;
se ~ (par) to distinguish o.s. (by)
signature [siɲatyʀ] *nf* signature; (*action*)
signing
signe [siɲ] *nm* sign; (TYPO) mark; **faire un
~ de la main** to give a sign with one's
hand; **faire ~ à qn** (*fig: contacter*) to get
in touch with sb; **faire ~ à qn d'entrer** to
motion (to) sb to come in; **signer** *vt* to
sign; **se signer** *vi* to cross o.s.
significatif, -ive [siɲifikatif, iv] *adj* significant
signification [siɲifikasjɔ̃] *nf* meaning
signifier [siɲifje] *vt* (*vouloir dire*) to mean;
(*faire connaître*): **~ qch (à qn)** to make sth
known (to sb)
silence [silɑ̃s] *nm* silence; (MUS) rest; **garder le ~** to keep silent, say nothing; **silencieux, -euse** *adj* quiet, silent ♦ *nm*
silencer
silex [silɛks] *nm* flint
silhouette [silwɛt] *nf* outline, silhouette;
(*lignes, contour*) outline; (*allure*) figure
silicium [silisjɔm] *nm* silicon
sillage [sijaʒ] *nm* wake
sillon [sijɔ̃] *nm* furrow; (*de disque*) groove;
sillonner *vt* to criss-cross
simagrées [simagʀe] *nfpl* fuss *sg*
similaire [similɛʀ] *adj* similar; **similicuir**
nm imitation leather; **similitude** *nf* similarity
simple [sɛ̃pl] *adj* simple; (*non multiple*) single; **~ messieurs** *nm* (TENNIS) men's sin-
gles *sg*; **~ soldat** private
simplicité [sɛ̃plisite] *nf* simplicity
simplifier [sɛ̃plifje] *vt* to simplify
simulacre [simylakʀ] *nm* (*péj*): **un ~ de** a
pretence of
simuler [simyle] *vt* to sham, simulate
simultané, e [simyltane] *adj* simulta-

neous
sincère [sɛ̃sɛR] *adj* sincere; **sincèrement** *adv* sincerely; (*pour parler franchement*) honestly, really; **sincérité** *nf* sincerity
sine qua non [sinekwanɔn] *adj*: **condition ~** indispensable condition
singe [sɛ̃ʒ] *nm* monkey; (*de grande taille*) ape; **singer** *vt* to ape, mimic; **singeries** *nfpl* antics
singulariser [sɛ̃gylaRize]: **se ~** *vi* to call attention to o.s.
singularité [sɛ̃gylaRite] *nf* peculiarity
singulier, -ière [sɛ̃gylje, jɛR] *adj* remarkable, singular ♦ *nm* singular
sinistre [sinistR] *adj* sinister ♦ *nm* (*incendie*) blaze; (*catastrophe*) disaster; (*ASSURANCES*) damage (*giving rise to a claim*); **sinistré, e** *adj* disaster-stricken ♦ *nm/f* disaster victim
sinon [sinɔ̃] *conj* (*autrement, sans quoi*) otherwise, or else; (*sauf*) except, other than; (*si ce n'est*) if not
sinueux, -euse [sinɥø, øz] *adj* winding
sinus [sinys] *nm* (*ANAT*) sinus; (*GÉOM*) sine; **sinusite** *nf* sinusitis
siphon [sifɔ̃] *nm* (*tube, d'eau gazeuse*) siphon; (*d'évier etc*) U-bend
sirène [siRɛn] *nf* siren; **~ d'alarme** fire alarm; (*en temps de guerre*) air-raid siren
sirop [siRo] *nm* (*à diluer: de fruit etc*) syrup; (*pharmaceutique*) syrup, mixture; **~ pour la toux** cough mixture
siroter [siRɔte] *vt* to sip
sismique [sismik] *adj* seismic
site [sit] *nm* (*paysage, environnement*) setting; (*d'une ville etc: emplacement*) site; **~ (pittoresque)** beauty spot; **~s touristiques** places of interest; **~ Web** (*INFORM*) website
sitôt [sito] *adv*: **~ parti** as soon as he *etc* had left; **~ que** as soon as; **pas de ~** not for a long time
situation [sitɥasjɔ̃] *nf* situation; (*d'un édifice, d'une ville*) position, location; **~ de famille** marital status
situé, e [sitɥe] *adj* situated

situer [sitɥe] *vt* to site, situate; (*en pensée*) to set, place; **se ~** *vi* to be situated
six [sis] *num* six; **sixième** *num* sixth ♦ *nf* (*SCOL*) first form
Skaï ® [skaj] *nm* Leatherette ®
ski [ski] *nm* (*objet*) ski; (*sport*) skiing; **faire du ~** to ski; **~ de fond** cross-country skiing; **~ nautique** water-skiing; **~ de piste** downhill skiing; **~ de randonnée** cross-country skiing; **skier** *vi* to ski; **skieur -euse** *nm/f* skier
slip [slip] *nm* (*sous-vêtement*) pants *pl*, briefs *pl*; (*de bain: d'homme*) trunks *pl*; (*: du bikini*) (bikini) briefs *pl*
slogan [slɔgã] *nm* slogan
SMIC [smik] *sigle m* = **salaire minimum interprofessionnel de croissance**

SMIC

ⓘ *In France, the* **SMIC** *is the minimum legal hourly rate for workers over eighteen. It is index-linked and is raised each time the cost of living rises by 2%.*

---

smicard, e [smikaR, aRd] (*fam*) *nm/f* minimum wage earner
smoking [smokiŋ] *nm* dinner suit
SNCF *sigle f* (= *Société nationale des chemins de fer français*) French railways
snob [snɔb] *adj* snobbish ♦ *nm/f* snob; **snobisme** *nm* snobbery, snobbishness
sobre [sɔbR] *adj* (*personne*) temperate, abstemious; (*élégance, style*) sober
sobriquet [sɔbRikɛ] *nm* nickname
social, e, -aux [sɔsjal, jo] *adj* social
socialisme [sɔsjalism] *nm* socialism; **socialiste** *nm/f* socialist
société [sɔsjete] *nf* society; (*sportive*) club; (*COMM*) company; **la ~ de consommation** the consumer society; **~ anonyme** = limited (*BRIT*) *ou* incorporated (*US*) company
sociologie [sɔsjɔlɔʒi] *nf* sociology
socle [sɔkl] *nm* (*de colonne, statue*) plinth, pedestal; (*de lampe*) base
socquette [sɔkɛt] *nf* ankle sock

sœur [sœʀ] *nf* sister; (*religieuse*) nun, sister

soi [swa] *pron* oneself; **en ~** (*intrinsèquement*) in itself; **cela va de ~** that *ou* it goes without saying; **soi-disant** *adj inv* so-called ♦ *adv* supposedly

soie [swa] *nf* silk; **soierie** *nf* (*tissu*) silk

soif [swaf] *nf* thirst; **avoir ~** to be thirsty; **donner ~ à qn** to make sb thirsty

soigné, e [swaɲe] *adj* (*tenue*) well-groomed, neat; (*travail*) careful, meticulous

soigner [swaɲe] *vt* (*malade, maladie: suj: docteur*) to treat; (*suj: infirmière, mère*) to nurse, look after; (*travail, détails*) to take care over; (*jardin, invités*) to look after; **soigneux, -euse** *adj* (*propre*) tidy, neat; (*appliqué*) painstaking, careful

soi-même [swamɛm] *pron* oneself

soin [swɛ̃] *nm* (*application*) care; (*propreté, ordre*) tidiness, neatness; **~s** *nmpl* (*à un malade, blessé*) treatment *sg*, medical attention *sg*; (*hygiène*) care *sg*; **prendre ~ de** to take care of, look after; **prendre ~ de faire** to take care to do; **les premiers ~s** first aid *sg*

soir [swaʀ] *nm* evening; **ce ~** this evening, tonight; **demain ~** tomorrow evening, tomorrow night; **soirée** *nf* evening; (*réception*) party

soit [swa] *vb voir* **être** ♦ *conj* (*à savoir*) namely; (*ou*): **~ ... ~** either ... or ♦ *adv* so be it, very well; **~ que ... ~ que** *ou* **ou que** whether ... or whether

soixantaine [swasɑ̃tɛn] *nf*: **une ~ (de)** sixty *ou* so, about sixty; **avoir la ~** (*âge*) to be around sixty

soixante [swasɑ̃t] *num* sixty; **soixante-dix** *num* seventy

soja [sɔʒa] *nm* soya; (*graines*) soya beans *pl*; **germes de ~** beansprouts

sol [sɔl] *nm* ground; (*de logement*) floor; (*AGR*) soil; (*MUS*) G; (: *en chantant la gamme*) so(h)

solaire [sɔlɛʀ] *adj* (*énergie etc*) solar; (*crème etc*) sun *cpd*

soldat [sɔlda] *nm* soldier

solde [sɔld] *nf* pay ♦ *nm* (*COMM*) balance; **~s** *nm ou f pl* (*articles*) sale goods; (*vente*) sales; **en ~** at sale price; **solder** *vt* (*marchandise*) to sell at sale price, sell off; **se solder par** (*fig*) to end in; **article soldé (à) 10 F** item reduced to 10 F

sole [sɔl] *nf* sole *inv* (*fish*)

soleil [sɔlɛj] *nm* sun; (*lumière*) sun(light); (*temps ensoleillé*) sun(shine); **il fait du ~** it's sunny; **au ~** in the sun

solennel, le [sɔlanɛl] *adj* solemn

solfège [sɔlfɛʒ] *nm* musical theory

solidaire [sɔlidɛʀ] *adj*: **être ~s** to show solidarity, stand *ou* stick together; **être ~ de** (*collègues*) to stand by; **solidarité** *nf* solidarity; **par solidarité (avec)** in sympathy (with)

solide [sɔlid] *adj* solid; (*mur, maison, meuble*) solid, sturdy; (*connaissances, argument*) sound; (*personne, estomac*) robust, sturdy ♦ *nm* solid

soliste [sɔlist] *nm/f* soloist

solitaire [sɔlitɛʀ] *adj* (*sans compagnie*) solitary, lonely; (*lieu*) lonely ♦ *nm/f* (*ermite*) recluse; (*fig: ours*) loner

solitude [sɔlityd] *nf* loneliness; (*tranquillité*) solitude

solive [sɔliv] *nf* joist

solliciter [sɔlisite] *vt* (*personne*) to appeal to; (*emploi, faveur*) to seek

sollicitude [sɔlisityd] *nf* concern

soluble [sɔlybl] *adj* soluble

solution [sɔlysjɔ̃] *nf* solution; **~ de facilité** easy way out

solvable [sɔlvabl] *adj* solvent

sombre [sɔ̃bʀ] *adj* dark; (*fig*) gloomy; **sombrer** *vi* (*bateau*) to sink; **sombrer dans** (*misère, désespoir*) to sink into

sommaire [sɔmɛʀ] *adj* (*simple*) basic; (*expéditif*) summary ♦ *nm* summary

sommation [sɔmasjɔ̃] *nf* (*JUR*) summons *sg*; (*avant de faire feu*) warning

somme [sɔm] *nf* (*MATH*) sum; (*quantité*) amount; (*argent*) sum, amount ♦ *nm*: **faire un ~** to have a (short) nap; **en ~** all in all; **~ toute** all in all

sommeil [sɔmɛj] *nm* sleep; **avoir ~** to be sleepy; **sommeiller** *vi* to doze

sommer [sɔme] *vt*: **~ qn de faire** to command *ou* order sb to do

sommes [sɔm] *vb voir* **être**

sommet [sɔmɛ] *nm* top; (*d'une montagne*) summit, top; (*fig: de la perfection, gloire*) height

sommier [sɔmje] *nm* (bed) base

somnambule [sɔmnɑ̃byl] *nm/f* sleepwalker

somnifère [sɔmnifɛʀ] *nm* sleeping drug *no pl* (*ou* pill)

somnoler [sɔmnɔle] *vi* to doze

somptueux, -euse [sɔ̃ptɥø, øz] *adj* sumptuous

son¹, sa [sɔ̃, sa] (*pl* **ses**) *adj* (*antécédent humain: mâle*) his; (: *femelle*) her; (: *valeur indéfinie*) one's, his/her; (*antécédent non humain*) its

son² [sɔ̃] *nm* sound; (*de blé*) bran

sondage [sɔ̃daʒ] *nm*: **~ (d'opinion)** (opinion) poll

sonde [sɔ̃d] *nf* (*NAVIG*) lead *ou* sounding line; (*MÉD*) probe; (*TECH: de forage*) borer, driller

sonder [sɔ̃de] *vt* (*NAVIG*) to sound; (*TECH*) to bore, drill; (*fig: personne*) to sound out; **~ le terrain** (*fig*) to test the ground

songe [sɔ̃ʒ] *nm* dream; **songer** *vi*: **songer à** (*penser à*) to think over; (*envisager*) to consider, think of; **songer que** to think that; **songeur, -euse** *adj* pensive

sonnant, e [sɔnɑ̃, ɑ̃t] *adj*: **à 8 heures ~es** on the stroke of 8

sonné, e [sɔne] *adj* (*fam*) cracked; **il est midi ~** it's gone twelve

sonner [sɔne] *vi* to ring ♦ *vt* (*cloche*) to ring; (*glas, tocsin*) to sound; (*portier, infirmière*) to ring for; **~ faux** (*instrument*) to sound out of tune; (*rire*) to ring false

sonnerie [sɔnʀi] *nf* (*son*) ringing; (*sonnette*) bell; **~ d'alarme** alarm bell

sonnette [sɔnɛt] *nf* bell; **~ d'alarme** alarm bell

sono [sɔno] *abr f* = **sonorisation**

sonore [sɔnɔʀ] *adj* (*voix*) sonorous, ringing; (*salle*) resonant; (*film, signal*) sound *cpd*; **sonorisation** *nf* (*équipement: de salle de conférences*) public address system, P.A. system; (: *de discothèque*) sound system; **sonorité** *nf* (*de piano, violon*) tone; (*d'une salle*) acoustics *pl*

sont [sɔ̃] *vb voir* **être**

sophistiqué, e [sɔfistike] *adj* sophisticated

sorbet [sɔʀbɛ] *nm* water ice, sorbet

sorcellerie [sɔʀsɛlʀi] *nf* witchcraft *no pl*

sorcier [sɔʀsje] *nm* sorcerer; **sorcière** *nf* witch *ou* sorceress

sordide [sɔʀdid] *adj* (*lieu*) squalid; (*action*) sordid

sornettes [sɔʀnɛt] *nfpl* twaddle *sg*

sort [sɔʀ] *nm* (*destinée*) fate; (*condition*) lot; (*magique*) curse, spell; **tirer au ~** to draw lots

sorte [sɔʀt] *nf* sort, kind; **de la ~** in that way; **de (telle) ~ que** so that; **en quelque ~** in a way; **faire en ~ que** to see to it that

sortie [sɔʀti] *nf* (*issue*) way out, exit; (*remarque drôle*) sally; (*promenade*) outing; (*le soir: au restaurant etc*) night out; (*COMM d'un disque*) release; (: *d'un livre*) publication; (: *d'un modèle*) launching; **~s** *nfp* (*COMM: somme*) items of expenditure, outgoings; **~ de bain** (*vêtement*) bathrobe; **~ de secours** emergency exit

sortilège [sɔʀtilɛʒ] *nm* (magic) spell

sortir [sɔʀtiʀ] *vi* (*gén*) to come out; (*partir, se promener, aller au spectacle*) to go out; (*numéro gagnant*) to come up ♦ *vt* (*gén*) to take out; (*produit, modèle*) to bring out; (*fam: dire*) to come out with; **~ avec qn** to be going out with sb; **s'en ~** (*malade*) to pull through; (*d'une difficulté etc*) to get through; **~ de** (*endroit*) to go (*ou* come) out of, leave; (*provenir de*) to come from; (*compétence*) to be outside

sosie [sɔzi] *nm* double

sot, sotte [so, sɔt] *adj* silly, foolish ♦ *nm/f* fool; **sottise** *nf* (*caractère*) silliness, fool ishness; (*action*) silly *ou* foolish thing

sou [su] *nm*: **près de ses ~s** tight-fisted; **sans le ~** penniless

soubresaut [subʀəso] *nm* start; (*cahot*) jolt

souche [suʃ] *nf* (*d'arbre*) stump; (*de carnet*) counterfoil (*BRIT*), stub

souci [susi] *nm* (*inquiétude*) worry; (*préoccupation*) concern; (*BOT*) marigold; **se faire du ~** to worry; **soucier: se soucier de** *vt* to care about; **soucieux, -euse** *adj* concerned, worried

soucoupe [sukup] *nf* saucer; **~ volante** flying saucer

soudain, e [sudɛ̃, ɛn] *adj* (*douleur, mort*) sudden ♦ *adv* suddenly, all of a sudden

soude [sud] *nf* soda

souder [sude] *vt* (*avec fil à ~*) to solder; (*par soudure autogène*) to weld; (*fig*) to bind together

soudoyer [sudwaje] (*péj*) *vt* to bribe

soudure [sudyʀ] *nf* soldering; welding; (*joint*) soldered joint; weld

souffert, e [sufɛʀ, ɛʀt] *pp* de **souffrir**

souffle [sufl] *nm* (*en expirant*) breath; (*en soufflant*) puff, blow; (*respiration*) breathing; (*d'explosion, de ventilateur*) blast; (*du vent*) blowing; **être à bout de ~** to be out of breath; **un ~ d'air** a breath of air

soufflé, e [sufle] *adj* (*fam: stupéfié*) staggered ♦ *nm* (*CULIN*) soufflé

souffler [sufle] *vi* (*gén*) to blow; (*haleter*) to puff (and blow) ♦ *vt* (*feu, bougie*) to blow out; (*chasser: poussière etc*) to blow away; (*TECH: verre*) to blow; (*dire*): **~ qch à qn** to whisper sth to sb; **soufflet** *nm* (*instrument*) bellows *pl*; (*gifle*) slap (in the face); **souffleur** *nm* (*THÉÂTRE*) prompter

souffrance [sufʀɑ̃s] *nf* suffering; **en ~** (*affaire*) pending

souffrant, e [sufʀɑ̃, ɑ̃t] *adj* unwell

souffre-douleur [sufʀədulœʀ] *nm inv* butt, underdog

souffrir [sufʀiʀ] *vi* to suffer, be in pain ♦ *vt* to suffer, endure; (*supporter*) to bear, stand; **~ de** (*maladie, froid*) to suffer from;

elle ne peut pas le ~ she can't stand *ou* bear him

soufre [sufʀ] *nm* sulphur

souhait [swɛ] *nm* wish; **tous nos ~s de** good wishes *ou* our best wishes for; **à vos ~s!** bless you!; **souhaitable** *adj* desirable

souhaiter [swete] *vt* to wish for; **~ la bonne année à qn** to wish sb a happy New Year; **~ que** to hope that

souiller [suje] *vt* to dirty, soil; (*fig: réputation etc*) to sully, tarnish

soûl, e [su, sul] *adj* drunk ♦ *nm*: **tout son ~** to one's heart's content

soulagement [sulaʒmɑ̃] *nm* relief

soulager [sulaʒe] *vt* to relieve

soûler [sule] *vt*: **~ qn** to get sb drunk; (*suj: boisson*) to make sb drunk; (*fig*) to make sb's head spin *ou* reel; **se ~** *vi* to get drunk

soulever [sul(ə)ve] *vt* to lift; (*poussière*) to send up; (*enthousiasme*) to arouse; (*question, débat*) to raise; **se ~** *vi* (*peuple*) to rise up; (*personne couchée*) to lift o.s. up

soulier [sulje] *nm* shoe

souligner [suliɲe] *vt* to underline; (*fig*) to emphasize, stress

soumettre [sumɛtʀ] *vt* (*pays*) to subject, subjugate; (*rebelle*) to put down, subdue; **se ~ (à)** to submit (to); **~ qch à qn** (*projet etc*) to submit sth to sb

soumis, e [sumi, iz] *adj* submissive; **soumission** *nf* submission

soupape [supap] *nf* valve

soupçon [supsɔ̃] *nm* suspicion; (*petite quantité*): **un ~ de** a hint *ou* touch of; **soupçonner** *vt* to suspect; **soupçonneux, -euse** *adj* suspicious

soupe [sup] *nf* soup

souper [supe] *vi* to have supper ♦ *nm* supper

soupeser [supəze] *vt* to weigh in one's hand(s); (*fig*) to weigh up

soupière [supjɛʀ] *nf* (soup) tureen

soupir [supiʀ] *nm* sigh; **pousser un ~ de soulagement** to heave a sigh of relief

soupirail, -aux [supiʀaj, o] *nm* (small) basement window

soupirer [supiʀe] *vi* to sigh

souple [supl] *adj* supple; (*fig: règlement, caractère*) flexible; (: *démarche, taille*) lithe, supple; **souplesse** *nf* suppleness; (*de caractère*) flexibility

source [suʀs] *nf* (*point d'eau*) spring; (*d'un cours d'eau, fig*) source; **de bonne ~** on good authority

sourcil [suʀsi] *nm* (eye)brow; **sourciller** *vi:* **sans sourciller** without turning a hair *ou* batting an eyelid

sourd, e [suʀ, suʀd] *adj* deaf; (*bruit*) muffled; (*douleur*) dull ♦ *nm/f* deaf person; **faire la ~e oreille** to turn a deaf ear; **sourdine** *nf* (*MUS*) mute; **en sourdine** softly, quietly; **sourd-muet, sourde-muette** *adj* deaf-and-dumb ♦ *nm/f* deaf-mute

souriant, e [suʀjɑ̃, jɑ̃t] *adj* cheerful

souricière [suʀisjɛʀ] *nf* mousetrap; (*fig*) trap

sourire [suʀiʀ] *nm* smile ♦ *vi* to smile; **~ à qn** to smile at sb; (*fig: plaire à*) to appeal to sb; (*suj: chance*) to smile on sb; **garder le ~** to keep smiling

souris [suʀi] *nf* mouse

sournois, e [suʀnwa, waz] *adj* deceitful, underhand

sous [su] *prép* under; **~ la pluie** in the rain; **~ terre** underground; **~ peu** shortly, before long; **sous-bois** *nm inv* undergrowth

souscrire [suskʀiʀ]: **~ à** *vt* to subscribe to

sous...: **sous-directeur, -trice** *nm/f* assistant manager(-manageress); **sous-entendre** *vt* to imply, infer; **sous-entendu, e** *adj* implied ♦ *nm* innuendo, insinuation; **sous-estimer** *vt* to underestimate; **sous-jacent, e** *adj* underlying; **sous-louer** *vt* to sublet; **sous-marin, e** *adj* (*flore, faune*) submarine; (*pêche*) underwater ♦ *nm* submarine; **sous-officier** *nm* ≈ non-commissioned officer (N.C.O.);

sous-produit *nm* by-product; **sous-pull** *nm* thin poloneck jersey; **soussigné, e** *adj:* **je soussigné** I the undersigned; **sous-sol** *nm* basement; **sous-titre** *nm* subtitle

soustraction [sustʀaksjɔ̃] *nf* subtraction

soustraire [sustʀɛʀ] *vt* to subtract, take away; (*dérober*) **~ qch à qn** to remove sth from sb; **se ~ à** (*autorité etc*) to elude, escape from

sous...: **sous-traitant** *nm* subcontractor; **sous-traiter** *vt* to subcontract; **sous-vêtements** *nmpl* underwear *sg*

soutane [sutan] *nf* cassock, soutane

soute [sut] *nf* hold

soutenir [sut(ə)niʀ] *vt* to support; (*assaut, choc*) to stand up to, withstand; (*intérêt, effort*) to keep up; (*assurer*): **~ que** to maintain that; **soutenu, e** *adj* (*efforts*) sustained, unflagging; (*style*) elevated

souterrain, e [suteʀɛ̃, ɛn] *adj* underground ♦ *nm* underground passage

soutien [sutjɛ̃] *nm* support; **soutien-gorge** *nm* bra

soutirer [sutiʀe] *vt:* **~ qch à qn** to squeeze *ou* get sth out of sb

souvenir [suv(ə)niʀ] *nm* (*réminiscence*) memory; (*objet*) souvenir ♦ *vb:* **se ~ de** ♦ *vt* to remember; **se ~ que** to remember that; **en ~ de** in memory *ou* remembrance of

souvent [suvɑ̃] *adv* often; **peu ~** seldom, infrequently

souverain, e [suv(ə)ʀɛ̃, ɛn] *nm/f* sovereign, monarch

soyeux, -euse [swajø, øz] *adj* silky

soyons *etc* [swajɔ̃] *vb voir* **être**

spacieux, -euse [spasjø, jøz] *adj* spacious, roomy

spaghettis [spageti] *nmpl* spaghetti *sg*

sparadrap [spaʀadʀa] *nm* sticking plaster (*BRIT*), Bandaid ® (*US*)

spatial, e, -aux [spasjal, jo] *adj* (*AVIAT*) space *cpd*

speaker, ine [spikœʀ, kʀin] *nm/f* an

nouncer

spécial, e, -aux [spesjal, jo] *adj* special; *(bizarre)* peculiar; **spécialement** *adv* especially, particularly; *(tout exprès)* specially; **spécialiser: se spécialiser** *vi* to specialize; **spécialiste** *nm/f* specialist; **spécialité** *nf* speciality; *(branche)* special field

spécifier [spesifje] *vt* to specify, state

spécimen [spesimɛn] *nm* specimen

spectacle [spɛktakl] *nm* *(scène)* sight; *(représentation)* show; *(industrie)* show business; **spectaculaire** *adj* spectacular

spectateur, -trice [spɛktatœʀ, tʀis] *nm/f* *(CINÉMA etc)* member of the audience; *(SPORT)* spectator; *(d'un événement)* onlooker, witness

spéculer [spekyle] *vi* to speculate

spéléologie [speleɔlɔʒi] *nf* potholing

sperme [spɛʀm] *nm* semen, sperm

sphère [sfɛʀ] *nf* sphere

spirale [spiʀal] *nf* spiral

spirituel, le [spiʀitɥɛl] *adj* spiritual; *(fin, piquant)* witty

splendide [splɑ̃did] *adj* splendid

sponsoriser [spɔ̃sɔʀize] *vt* to sponsor

spontané, e [spɔ̃tane] *adj* spontaneous; **spontanéité** *nf* spontaneity

sport [spɔʀ] *nm* sport ♦ *adj inv* *(vêtement)* casual; **faire du ~** to do sport; **~s d'hiver** winter sports; **sportif, -ive** *adj* *(journal, association, épreuve)* sports *cpd*; *(allure, démarche)* athletic; *(attitude, esprit)* sporting

spot [spɔt] *nm* *(lampe)* spot(light); *(annonce)*: **~ (publicitaire)** commercial (break)

square [skwaʀ] *nm* public garden(s)

squelette [skəlɛt] *nm* skeleton; **squelettique** *adj* scrawny

stabiliser [stabilize] *vt* to stabilize

stable [stabl] *adj* stable, steady

stade [stad] *nm* *(SPORT)* stadium; *(phase, niveau)* stage

stage [staʒ] *nm* *(cours)* training course; **~ de formation (professionnelle)** voca-

tional *(training)* course; **~ de perfectionnement** advanced training course; **stagiaire** *nm/f, adj* trainee

stagner [stagne] *vi* to stagnate

stalle [stal] *nf* stall, box

stand [stɑ̃d] *nm* *(d'exposition)* stand; *(de foire)* stall; **~ de tir** *(à la foire, SPORT)* shooting range

standard [stɑ̃daʀ] *adj inv* standard ♦ *nm* switchboard; **standardiste** *nm/f* switchboard operator

standing [stɑ̃diŋ] *nm* standing; **de grand ~** luxury

starter [staʀtɛʀ] *nm* *(AUTO)* choke

station [stasjɔ̃] *nf* station; *(de bus)* stop; *(de villégiature)* resort; **~ balnéaire** seaside resort; **~ de ski** ski resort; **~ de taxis** taxi rank *(BRIT)* ou stand *(US)*; **stationnement** *nm* parking; **stationner** *vi* to park; **station-service** *nf* service station

statistique [statistik] *nf* *(science)* statistics *sg*; *(rapport, étude)* statistic ♦ *adj* statistical

statue [staty] *nf* statue

statu quo [statykwo] *nm* status quo

statut [staty] *nm* status; **~s** *nmpl* *(JUR, ADMIN)* statutes; **statutaire** *adj* statutory

Sté *abr* = **société**

steak [stɛk] *nm* steak; **~ haché** hamburger

sténo(dactylo) [steno(daktilo)] *nf* shorthand typist *(BRIT)*, stenographer *(US)*

sténo(graphie) [stenɔ(gʀafi)] *nf* shorthand

stéréo [steʀeo] *adj* stereo

stérile [steʀil] *adj* sterile

stérilet [steʀilɛ] *nm* coil, loop

stériliser [steʀilize] *vt* to sterilize

stigmates [stigmat] *nmpl* scars, marks

stimulant [stimylɑ̃] *nm* *(fig)* stimulus, incentive; *(physique)* stimulant

stimuler [stimyle] *vt* to stimulate

stipuler [stipyle] *vt* to stipulate

stock [stɔk] *nm* stock; **stocker** *vt* to stock

stop [stɔp] *nm* *(AUTO: écriteau)* stop sign; *(: feu arrière)* brake-light; **faire du ~** *(fam)* to hitch(hike); **stopper** *vt, vi* to stop, halt

store [stɔʀ] *nm* blind; *(de magasin)* shade,

awning

strabisme [stʀabism] *nm* squinting

strapontin [stʀapɔ̃tɛ̃] *nm* jump *ou* fold-away seat

stratégie [stʀateʒi] *nf* strategy; **stratégique** *adj* strategic

stress [stʀɛs] *nm* stress; **stressant, e** *adj* stressful; **stresser** *vt*: **stresser qn** to make sb (feel) tense

strict, e [stʀikt] *adj* strict; (*tenue, décor*) severe, plain; **le ~ nécessaire/minimum** the bare essentials/minimum

strident, e [stʀidɑ̃, ɑ̃t] *adj* shrill, strident

strophe [stʀɔf] *nf* verse, stanza

structure [stʀyktyʀ] *nf* structure

studieux, -euse [stydjø, jøz] *adj* studious

studio [stydjo] *nm* (*logement*) (one-roomed) flatlet (*BRIT*) *ou* apartment (*US*); (*d'artiste, TV etc*) studio

stupéfait, e [stypefɛ, ɛt] *adj* astonished

stupéfiant [stypefjɑ̃, jɑ̃t] *adj* (*étonnant*) stunning, astounding ♦ *nm* (*MÉD*) drug, narcotic

stupéfier [stypefje] *vt* (*étonner*) to stun, astonish

stupeur [stypœʀ] *nf* astonishment

stupide [stypid] *adj* stupid; **stupidité** *nf* stupidity; (*parole, acte*) stupid thing (to do *ou* say)

style [stil] *nm* style

stylé, e [stile] *adj* well-trained

styliste [stilist] *nm/f* designer

stylo [stilo] *nm*: **~ (à encre)** (fountain) pen; **~ (à) bille** ball-point pen; **~-feutre** felt-tip pen

su, e [sy] *pp de* **savoir** ♦ *nm*: **au ~ de** with the knowledge of

suave [sɥav] *adj* sweet

subalterne [sybaltɛʀn] *adj* (*employé, officier*) junior; (*rôle*) subordinate, subsidiary ♦ *nm/f* subordinate

subconscient [sypkɔ̃sjɑ̃] *nm* subconscious

sublr [sybiʀ] *vt* (*affront, dégâts*) to suffer; (*opération, châtiment*) to undergo

subit, e [sybi, it] *adj* sudden; **subitement** *adv* suddenly, all of a sudden

subjectif, -ive [sybʒɛktif, iv] *adj* subjective

subjonctif [sybʒɔ̃ktif] *nm* subjunctive

subjuguer [sybʒyge] *vt* to captivate

submerger [sybmɛʀʒe] *vt* to submerge; (*fig*) to overwhelm

subordonné, e [sybɔʀdɔne] *adj, nm/f* subordinate

subrepticement [sybʀɛptismɑ̃] *adv* surreptitiously

subside [sybzid] *nm* grant

subsidiaire [sybzidjɛʀ] *adj*: **question ~** deciding question

subsister [sybziste] *vi* (*rester*) to remain, subsist; (*survivre*) to live on

substance [sypstɑ̃s] *nf* substance

substituer [sypstitɥe] *vt*: **~ qn/qch à** to substitute sb/sth for; **se ~ à qn** (*évincer*) to substitute o.s. for sb

substitut [sypstity] *nm* (*succédané*) substitute

subterfuge [sybtɛʀfyʒ] *nm* subterfuge

subtil, e [syptil] *adj* subtle

subtiliser [syptilize] *vt*: **~ qch (à qn)** to spirit sth away (from sb)

subvenir [sybvəniʀ] : **~ à** *vt* to meet

subvention [sybvɑ̃sjɔ̃] *nf* subsidy, grant; **subventionner** *vt* to subsidize

suc [syk] *nm* (*BOT*) sap; (*de viande, fruit*) juice

succédané [syksedane] *nm* substitute

succéder [syksede]: **~ à** *vt* to succeed; **se ~** *vi* (*accidents, années*) to follow one another

succès [syksɛ] *nm* success; **avoir du ~** to be a success, be successful; **à ~** successful; **~ de librairie** bestseller; **~ (féminins)** conquests

successif, -ive [syksesif, iv] *adj* successive

successeur [syksesœʀ] *nm* successor

succession [syksesjɔ̃] *nf* (*série, POL*) succession; (*JUR: patrimoine*) estate, inheritance

succomber [sykɔ̃be] *vi* to die, succumb;

succulent → suivre

(*fig*): ~ **à** to succumb to

ucculent, e [sykylã, ãt] *adj* (*repas, mets*) delicious

uccursale [sykyʀsal] *nf* branch

ucer [syse] *vt* to suck; **sucette** *nf* (*bonbon*) lollipop; (*de bébé*) dummy (*BRIT*), pacifier (*US*)

ucre [sykʀ] *nm* (*substance*) sugar; (*morceau*) lump of sugar, sugar lump *ou* cube; ~ **d'orge** barley sugar; ~ **en morceaux/en poudre** lump/caster sugar; ~ **glace/roux** icing/brown sugar; **sucré, e** *adj* (*produit alimentaire*) sweetened; (*au goût*) sweet; **sucrer** *vt* (*thé, café*) to sweeten, put sugar in; **sucreries** *nfpl* (*bonbons*) sweets, sweet things; **sucrier** *nm* (*récipient*) sugar bowl

ud [syd] *nm*: **le ~** the south ♦ *adj inv* south; (*côte*) south, southern; **au ~** (*situation*) in the south; (*direction*) to the south; **au ~ de** (to the) south of; **sud-africain, e** *adj* South African ♦ *nm/f*: **Sud-Africain, e** South African; **sud-américain, e** *adj* South American ♦ *nm/f*: **Sud-Américain, e** South American; **sud-est** *nm, adj inv* south-east; **sud-ouest** *nm, adj inv* south-west

uède [syɛd] *nf*: **la ~** Sweden; **suédois, e** *adj* Swedish ♦ *nm/f*: **Suédois, e** Swede ♦ *nm* (*LING*) Swedish

uer [sye] *vi* to sweat; (*suinter*) to ooze; **sueur** *nf* sweat; **en sueur** sweating, in a sweat; **donner des sueurs froids à qn** to put sb in(to) a cold sweat

ffire [syfiʀ] *vi* (*être assez*): ~ **(à qn/pour qch/pour faire)** to be enough *ou* sufficient (for sb/for sth/to do); **il suffit d'une négligence ...** it only takes one act of carelessness ...; **il suffit qu'on oublie pour que ...** one only needs to forget for ...; **ça suffit!** that's enough!

ffisamment [syfizamã] *adv* sufficiently, enough; ~ **de** sufficient, enough

ffisant, e [syfizã, ãt] *adj* sufficient; (*résultats*) satisfactory; (*vaniteux*) self-important, bumptious

suffixe [syfiks] *nm* suffix

suffoquer [syfɔke] *vt* to choke, suffocate; (*stupéfier*) to stagger, astound ♦ *vi* to choke, suffocate

suffrage [syfʀaʒ] *nm* (*POL: voix*) vote

suggérer [sygʒeʀe] *vt* to suggest; **suggestion** *nf* suggestion

suicide [sɥisid] *nm* suicide; **suicider: se suicider** *vi* to commit suicide

suie [sɥi] *nf* soot

suinter [sɥɛte] *vi* to ooze

suis [sɥi] *vb voir* **être; suivre**

suisse [sɥis] *adj* Swiss ♦ *nm*: **S~** Swiss *pl inv* ♦ *nf*: **la S~** Switzerland; **la S~ romande/allemande** French-speaking/German-speaking Switzerland; **Suissesse** *nf* Swiss (woman *ou* girl)

suite [sɥit] *nf* (*continuation: d'énumération etc*) rest, remainder; (: *de feuilleton*) continuation; (: *film etc sur le même thème*) sequel; (*série*) series, succession; (*conséquence*) result; (*ordre, liaison logique*) coherence; (*appartement, MUS*) suite; (*escorte*) retinue, suite; ~**s** *nfpl* (*d'une maladie etc*) effects; **prendre la ~ de** (*directeur etc*) to succeed, take over from; **donner ~ à** (*requête, projet*) to follow up; **faire ~ à** to follow; **(faisant) ~ à votre lettre du ...** further to your letter of the ...; **de ~** (*d'affilée*) in succession; (*immédiatement*) at once; **par la ~** afterwards, subsequently; **à la ~** one after the other; **à la ~ de** (*derrière*) behind; (*en conséquence de*) following

suivant, e [sɥivã, ãt] *adj* next, following ♦ *prép* (*selon*) according to; **au ~!** next!

suivi, e [sɥivi] *adj* (*effort, qualité*) consistent; (*cohérent*) coherent; **très/peu ~** (*cours*) well-/poorly-attended

suivre [sɥivʀ] *vt* (*gén*) to follow; (*SCOL: cours*) to attend; (*comprendre*) to keep up with; (*COMM: article*) to continue to stock ♦ *vi* to follow; (*élève: assimiler*) to keep up; **se ~** *vi* (*accidents etc*) to follow one after the other; **faire ~** (*lettre*) to forward; **"à ~"** "to be continued"

sujet, te [syʒɛ, ɛt] *adj*: **être ~ à** (*vertige etc*) to be liable *ou* subject to ♦ *nm/f* (*d'un souverain*) subject ♦ *nm* subject; **au ~ de** about; **~ de conversation** topic *ou* subject of conversation; **~ d'examen** (*SCOL*) examination question

summum [sɔ(m)mɔm] *nm*: **le ~ de** the height of

super [sypɛʀ] (*fam*) *adj inv* terrific, great, fantastic, super

superbe [sypɛʀb] *adj* magnificent, superb

super(carburant) [sypɛʀ(kaʀbyʀɑ̃)] *nm* ≈ 4-star petrol (*BRIT*), ≈ high-octane gasoline (*US*)

supercherie [sypɛʀʃəʀi] *nf* trick

supérette [sypeʀɛt] *nf* (*COMM*) minimarket, superette (*US*)

superficie [sypɛʀfisi] *nf* (surface) area

superficiel, le [sypɛʀfisjɛl] *adj* superficial

superflu, e [sypɛʀfly] *adj* superfluous

supérieur, e [sypeʀjœʀ] *adj* (*lèvre, étages, classes*) upper; (*plus élevé: température, niveau, enseignement*): **~ (à)** higher (than); (*meilleur: qualité, produit*): **~ (à)** superior (to); (*excellent, hautain*) superior ♦ *nm, nf* superior; **supériorité** *nf* superiority

superlatif [sypɛʀlatif] *nm* superlative

supermarché [sypɛʀmaʀʃe] *nm* supermarket

superposer [sypɛʀpoze] *vt* (*faire chevaucher*) to superimpose; **lits superposés** bunk beds

superproduction [sypɛʀpʀɔdyksjɔ̃] *nf* (*film*) spectacular

superpuissance [sypɛʀpɥisɑ̃s] *nf* superpower

superstitieux, -euse [sypɛʀstisjø, jøz] *adj* superstitious

superviser [sypɛʀvize] *vt* to supervise

supplanter [syplɑ̃te] *vt* to supplant

suppléance [sypleɑ̃s] *nf*: **faire des ~s** (*professeur*) to do supply teaching; **suppléant, e** *adj* (*professeur*) supply *cpd*; (*juge, fonctionnaire*) deputy *cpd* ♦ *nm/f* (*professeur*) supply teacher

suppléer [syplee] *vt* (*ajouter: mot man-* *quant etc*) to supply, provide; (*compense*(*lacune*) to fill in; **~ à** to make up for

supplément [syplemɑ̃] *nm* supplemen (*de frites etc*) extra portion; **un ~ de tra vail** extra *ou* additional work; **payer un** to pay an additional charge; **le vin est e ~** wine is extra; **supplémentaire** *a⊂* additional, further; (*train, bus*) relief *cp⊂* extra

supplications [syplikasjɔ̃] *nfpl* pleas, er treaties

supplice [syplis] *nm* torture *no pl*

supplier [syplije] *vt* to implore, beseech

support [sypɔʀ] *nm* support; (*publicitaire* medium; (*audio-visuel*) aid

supportable [sypɔʀtabl] *adj* (*douleu* bearable

supporter¹ [sypɔʀtɛʀ] *nm* supporter, fa⊓

supporter² [sypɔʀte] *vt* (*conséquence* *épreuve*) to bear, endure; (*défauts, pe* *sonne*) to put up with; (*suj: chose: chale* *etc*) to withstand; (*: personne: chaleur, vi* to be able to take

supposer [sypoze] *vt* to suppose; (*imp* *quer*) to presuppose; **à ~ que** supposir (that)

suppositoire [sypozitwaʀ] *nm* supposito

suppression [sypʀesjɔ̃] *nf* (*voir supprime* cancellation; removal; deletion

supprimer [sypʀime] *vt* (*congés, serv.* *d'autobus etc*) to cancel; (*emplois, privilèg⊂* *témoin gênant*) to do away with; (*cloiso* *cause, anxiété*) to remove; (*clause, mot*) delete

suprême [sypʀɛm] *adj* supreme

MOT-CLÉ
---

sur [syʀ] *prép* 1 (*position*) on; (*par-dess⊂* over; (*au-dessus*) above; **pose-le sur la** **ble** put it on the table; **je n'ai pas d'a** **gent sur moi** I haven't any money on n

2 (*direction*) towards; **en allant sur Pa⊓** going towards Paris; **sur votre droite** *ou* to your right

3 (*à propos de*) on, about; **un livre/u⊓** **conférence sur Balzac** a book/lecture ⊂

ou about Balzac

4 (*proportion, mesures*) out of, by; **un sur 10** one in 10; (*SCOL*) one out of 10; **4 m sur 2** 4 m by 2

sur ce *adv* hereupon

---

sûr, e [syʀ] *adj* sure, certain; (*digne de confiance*) reliable; (*sans danger*) safe; (*diagnostic, goût*) reliable; **le plus ~ est de** the safest thing is to; **~ de soi** self-confident; **~ et certain** absolutely certain

surcharge [syʀʃaʀʒ] *nf* (*de passagers, marchandises*) excess load; **surcharger** *vt* to overload

surchoix [syʀʃwa] *adj inv* top-quality

surclasser [syʀklɑse] *vt* to outclass

surcroît [syʀkʀwa] *nm*: **un ~ de** additional (*nm*; **par** *ou* **de ~** moreover; **en ~** in addition

surdité [syʀdite] *nf* deafness

surélever [syʀel(ə)ve] *vt* to raise, heighten

sûrement [syʀmɑ] *adv* (*certainement*) certainly; (*sans risques*) safely

surenchère [syʀɑʃɛʀ] *nf* (*aux enchères*) higher bid; **surenchérir** *vi* to bid higher; (*fig*) to try and outbid each other

surent [syʀ] *vb voir* **savoir**

surestimer [syʀɛstime] *vt* to overestimate

sûreté [syʀte] *nf* (*sécurité*) safety; (*exactitude: de renseignements etc*) reliability; (*d'un geste*) steadiness; **mettre en ~** to put in a safe place; **pour plus de ~** as an extra precaution, to be on the safe side

surf [sœʀf] *nm* surfing

surface [syʀfas] *nf* surface; (*superficie*) surface area; **une grande ~** a supermarket; **faire ~** to surface; **en ~** near the surface; (*fig*) superficially

surfait, e [syʀfɛ, ɛt] *adj* overrated

surgelé, e [syʀʒəle] *adj* (deep-)frozen ♦ *nm*: **les ~s** (deep-)frozen food

surgir [syʀʒiʀ] *vi* to appear suddenly; (*fig: problème, conflit*) to arise

sur...: **surhumain, e** *adj* superhuman; **sur-le-champ** *adv* immediately; **surlendemain** *nm*: **le surlendemain (soir)** two

days later (in the evening); **le surlendemain de** two days after; **surmenage** *nm* overwork(ing); **surmener: se surmener** *vi* to overwork

surmonter [syʀmɔte] *vt* (*vaincre*) to overcome; (*être au-dessus de*) to top

surnaturel, le [syʀnatyʀɛl] *adj, nm* supernatural

surnom [syʀnɔ] *nm* nickname

surnombre [syʀnɔbʀ] *nm*: **être en ~** to be too many (*ou* one too many)

surpeuplé, e [syʀpœple] *adj* overpopulated

sur-place [syʀplas] *nm*: **faire du ~-~** to mark time

surplomber [syʀplɔbe] *vt, vi* to overhang

surplus [syʀply] *nm* (*COMM*) surplus; (*reste*): **~ de bois** wood left over

surprenant, e [syʀpʀənɑ, ɑt] *adj* amazing

surprendre [syʀpʀɑdʀ] *vt* (*étonner*) to surprise; (*tomber sur: intrus etc*) to catch; (*entendre*) to overhear

surpris, e [syʀpʀi, iz] *adj*: **~ (de/que)** surprised (at/that); **surprise** *nf* surprise; **faire une surprise à qn** to give sb a surprise; **surprise-partie** *nf* party

surréservation [syʀʀezɛʀvasjɔ] *nf* double booking, overbooking

sursaut [syʀso] *nm* start, jump; **~ de** (*énergie, indignation*) sudden fit *ou* burst of; **en ~** with a start; **sursauter** *vi* to (give a) start, jump

sursis [syʀsi] *nm* (*JUR: gén*) suspended sentence; (*fig*) reprieve

surtaxe [syʀtaks] *nf* surcharge

surtout [syʀtu] *adv* (*avant tout, d'abord*) above all; (*spécialement, particulièrement*) especially; **~, ne dites rien!** whatever you do don't say anything!; **~ pas!** certainly *ou* definitely not!; **~ que ...** especially as ...

surveillance [syʀvejɑs] *nf* watch; (*POLICE, MIL*) surveillance; **sous ~ médicale** under medical supervision

surveillant, e [syʀvejɑ, ɑt] *nm/f* (*de pri-*

son) warder; (*SCOL*) monitor

surveiller [syʀveje] *vt* (*enfant, élèves, bagages*) to watch, keep an eye on; (*prisonnier, suspect*) to keep (a) watch on; (*territoire, bâtiment*) to (keep) watch over; (*travaux, cuisson*) to supervise; (*SCOL: examen*) to invigilate; **~ son langage/sa ligne** to watch one's language/figure

survenir [syʀvaniʀ] *vi* (*incident, retards*) to occur, arise; (*événement*) to take place

survêt(ement) [syʀvɛt(mã)] *nm* tracksuit

survie [syʀvi] *nf* survival; **survivant, e** *nm/f* survivor; **survivre** *vi* to survive; **survivre à** (*accident etc*) to survive

survoler [syʀvɔle] *vt* to fly over; (*fig: livre*) to skim through

survolté, e [syʀvɔlte] *adj* (*fig*) worked up

sus [sy(s)]: **en ~ de** *prép* in addition to, over and above; **en ~** in addition

susceptible [sysɛptibl] *adj* touchy, sensitive; **~ de faire** (*hypothèse*) liable to do

susciter [sysite] *vt* (*admiration*) to arouse; (*ennuis*): **~ (à qn)** to create (for sb)

suspect, e [syspɛ(kt), ɛkt] *adj* suspicious; (*témoignage, opinions*) suspect ♦ *nm/f* suspect; **suspecter** *vt* to suspect; (*honnêteté de qn*) to question, have one's suspicions about

suspendre [syspãdʀ] *vt* (*accrocher: vêtement*): **~ qch (à)** to hang sth up (on); (*interrompre, démettre*) to suspend; **se ~ à** to hang from

suspendu, e [syspãdy] *adj* (*accroché*): **~ à** hanging on (*ou* from); (*perché*): **~ au-dessus de** suspended over

suspens [syspã]: **en ~** *adv* (*affaire*) in abeyance; **tenir en ~** to keep in suspense

suspense [syspɛns, syspãs] *nm* suspense

suspension [syspãsjɔ̃] *nf* suspension; (*lustre*) light fitting *ou* fitment

sut [sy] *vb voir* **savoir**

suture [sytyʀ] *nf* (*MÉD*): **point de ~** stitch

svelte [svɛlt] *adj* slender, svelte

SVP *abr* (= *s'il vous plaît*) please

sweat-shirt [switʃœʀt] (*pl* **~-~s**) *nm* sweatshirt

syllabe [si(l)lab] *nf* syllable

symbole [sɛ̃bɔl] *nm* symbol; **symboliqu** *adj* symbolic(al); (*geste, offrande*) toke *cpd*; **symboliser** *vt* to symbolize

symétrique [simetʀik] *adj* symmetrical

sympa [sɛ̃pa] (*fam*) *adj inv* nice; **sois ~ prête-le moi** be a pal and lend it to me

sympathie [sɛ̃pati] *nf* (*inclination*) likin (*affinité*) friendship; (*condoléances*) syn pathy; **j'ai beaucoup de ~ pour lui** I lik him a lot; **sympathique** *adj* nic friendly

sympathisant, e [sɛ̃patizã, ãt] *nm/f* syn pathizer

sympathiser [sɛ̃patize] *vi* (*voisins et s'entendre*) to get on *ou* along (*U* (well)

symphonie [sɛ̃fɔni] *nf* symphony

symptôme [sɛ̃ptom] *nm* symptom

synagogue [sinagɔg] *nf* synagogue

syncope [sɛ̃kɔp] *nf* (*MÉD*) blackout; **ton ber en ~** to faint, pass out

syndic [sɛ̃dik] *nm* (*d'immeuble*) managir agent

syndical, e, -aux [sɛ̃dikal, o] *adj* (trad union *cpd*; **syndicaliste** *nm/f* trade u ionist

syndicat [sɛ̃dika] *nm* (*d'ouvriers, employé* (trade) union; **~ d'initiative** tourist offic **syndiqué, e** *adj* belonging to a (trad union; **syndiquer: se syndiquer** *vi* form a trade union; (*adhérer*) to join trade union

synonyme [sinɔnim] *adj* synonymo ♦ *nm* synonym; **~ de** synonymous with

syntaxe [sɛ̃taks] *nf* syntax

synthèse [sɛ̃tez] *nf* synthesis

synthétique [sɛ̃tetik] *adj* synthetic

Syrie [siʀi] *nf*: **la ~** Syria

systématique [sistematik] *adj* systemati

système [sistɛm] *nm* system; **~ D** (*fam*) sourcefulness

T, t

t [t] *pron voir* **te**

ta [ta] *adj voir* **ton**[1]

tabac [taba] *nm* tobacco; (*magasin*) tobacconist's (shop); **~ blond/brun** light/dark tobacco

tabagisme [tabaʒism] *nm*: **~ passif** passive smoking

tabasser [tabase] (*fam*) *vt* to beat up

table [tabl] *nf* table; **à ~!** dinner *etc* is ready!; **se mettre à ~** to sit down to eat; **mettre la ~** to lay the table; **faire ~ rase de** to make a clean sweep of; **~ à repasser** ironing board; **~ de cuisson** (*à l'électricité*) hotplate; (*au gaz*) gas ring; **~ de nuit** *ou* **de chevet** bedside table; **~ des matières** (table of) contents *pl*; **~ d'orientation** viewpoint indicator; **~ roulante** trolley

tableau, x [tablo] *nm* (*peinture*) painting; (*reproduction, fig*) picture; (*panneau*) board; (*schéma*) table, chart; **~ d'affichage** notice board; **~ de bord** dashboard; (*AVIAT*) instrument panel; **~ noir** blackboard

tabler [table] *vi*: **~ sur** to bank on

tablette [tablet] *nf* (*planche*) shelf; **~ de chocolat** bar of chocolate

tableur [tablœr] *nm* spreadsheet

tablier [tablije] *nm* apron

tabou [tabu] *nm* taboo

tabouret [taburɛ] *nm* stool

tac [tak] *nm*: **il m'a répondu du ~ au ~** he answered me right back

tache [taʃ] *nf* (*saleté*) stain, mark; (*ART, de couleur, lumière*) spot; **~ de rousseur** freckle

tâche [taʃ] *nf* task

tacher [taʃe] *vt* to stain, mark

tâcher [taʃe] *vi*: **~ de faire** to try *ou* endeavour to do

tacheté, e [taʃte] *adj* spotted

tacot [tako] *nm* (*péj*) banger (*BRIT*), (old) heap

tact [takt] *nm* tact; **avoir du ~** to be tactful

tactique [taktik] *adj* tactical ♦ *nf* (*technique*) tactics *sg*; (*plan*) tactic

taie [tɛ] *nf*: **~ (d'oreiller)** pillowslip, pillowcase

taille [taj] *nf* cutting; (*d'arbre etc*) pruning; (*milieu du corps*) waist; (*hauteur*) height; (*grandeur*) size; **de ~ à faire** capable of doing; **de ~** sizeable; **taille-crayon(s)** *nm* pencil sharpener

tailler [taje] *vt* (*pierre, diamant*) to cut; (*arbre, plante*) to prune; (*vêtement*) to cut out; (*crayon*) to sharpen

tailleur [tajœr] *nm* (*couturier*) tailor; (*vêtement*) suit; **en ~** (*assis*) cross-legged

taillis [taji] *nm* copse

taire [tɛr] *vi*: **faire ~ qn** to make sb be quiet; **se ~** *vi* to be silent *ou* quiet

talc [talk] *nm* talc, talcum powder

talent [talɑ̃] *nm* talent

talkie-walkie [tokiwoki] *nm* walkie-talkie

taloche [talɔʃ] (*fam*) *nf* clout, cuff

talon [talɔ̃] *nm* heel; (*de chèque, billet*) stub, counterfoil (*BRIT*); **~s plats/aiguilles** flat/stiletto heels

talonner [talɔne] *vt* (*suivre*) to follow hot on the heels of; (*harceler*) to hound

talus [taly] *nm* embankment

tambour [tɑ̃bur] *nm* (*MUS, aussi*) drum; (*musicien*) drummer; (*porte*) revolving door(s *pl*); **tambourin** *nm* tambourine; **tambouriner** *vi* to drum; **tambouriner à/sur** to drum on

tamis [tami] *nm* sieve

Tamise [tamiz] *nf*: **la ~** the Thames

tamisé, e [tamize] *adj* (*fig*) subdued, soft

tampon [tɑ̃pɔ̃] *nm* (*de coton, d'ouate*) wad, pad; (*amortisseur*) buffer; (*bouchon*) plug, stopper; (*cachet, timbre*) stamp; **(mémoire) ~** (*INFORM*) buffer; **~ (hygiénique)** tampon; **tamponner** *vt* (*timbres*) to stamp; (*heurter*) to crash *ou* ram into; **tamponneuse** *adj f*: **autos tamponneuses** dodgems

tandem [tɑ̃dɛm] *nm* tandem

tandis [tɑ̃di]: ~ **que** *conj* while

tanguer [tɑ̃ge] *vi* to pitch (and toss)

tanière [tanjɛR] *nf* lair, den

tanné, e [tane] *adj* weather-beaten

tanner [tane] *vt* to tan; (*fam: harceler*) to badger

tant [tɑ̃] *adv* so much; ~ **de** (*sable, eau*) so much; (*gens, livres*) so many; ~ **que** as long as; (*autant que*) as much as; ~ **mieux** that's great; (*avec une certaine réserve*) so much the better; ~ **pis** too bad; (*conciliant*) never mind

tante [tɑ̃t] *nf* aunt

tantôt [tɑ̃to] *adv* (*parfois*): ~ ... ~ now ... now; (*cet après-midi*) this afternoon

taon [tɑ̃] *nm* horsefly

tapage [tapaʒ] *nm* uproar, din

tapageur, -euse [tapaʒœR, øz] *adj* noisy; (*voyant*) loud, flashy

tape [tap] *nf* slap

tape-à-l'œil [tapalœj] *adj inv* flashy, showy

taper [tape] *vt* (*porte*) to bang, slam; (*enfant*) to slap; (*dactylographier*) to type (out); (*fam: emprunter*): ~ **qn de 10 F** to touch sb for 10 F ♦ *vi* (*soleil*) to beat down; **se** ~ *vt* (*repas*) to put away; (*fam: corvée*) to get landed with; ~ **sur qn** to thump sb; (*fig*) to run sb down; ~ **sur un clou** to hit a nail; ~ **à** (*porte etc*) to knock on; ~ **dans** (*se servir*) to dig into; ~ **des mains/pieds** to clap one's hands/stamp one's feet; ~ **(à la machine)** to type; **se** ~ **un travail** (*fam*) to land o.s. a job

tapi, e [tapi] *adj* (*blotti*) crouching; (*caché*) hidden away

tapis [tapi] *nm* carpet; (*petit*) rug; **mettre sur le** ~ (*fig*) to bring up for discussion; ~ **de bain** bath mat; ~ **de sol** (*de tente*) groundsheet; ~ **de souris** mouse mat; ~ **roulant** (*pour piétons*) moving walkway; (*pour bagages*) carousel

tapisser [tapise] *vt* (*avec du papier peint*) to paper; (*recouvrir*): ~ **qch (de)** to cover sth (with); **tapisserie** *nf* (*tenture, broderie*) tapestry; (*papier peint*) wallpaper; **tapissier,**

-ière *nm/f*: **tapissier-décorateur** interio[r] decorator

tapoter [tapote] *vt* (*joue, main*) to pat; (*ob[jet]*) to tap

taquin, e [takɛ̃, in] *adj* teasing; **taquine[r]** *vt* to tease

tarabiscoté, e [tarabiskote] *adj* over[-] ornate, fussy

tard [taR] *adv* late; **plus** ~ later (on); **a[u] plus** ~ at the latest; **sur le** ~ late in life

tarder [taRde] *vi* (*chose*) to be a long tim[e] coming; (*personne*): ~ **à faire** to dela[y] doing; **il me tarde d'être** I am longing t[o] be; **sans (plus)** ~ without (further) delay

tardif, -ive [taRdif, iv] *adj* late

taré, e [taRe] *nm/f* cretin

tarif [taRif] *nm*: ~ **des consommation[s]** price list; **~s postaux/douaniers** posta[l] customs rates; ~ **des taxis** taxi fares; **plein/réduit** (*train*) full/reduced fare; (*télé[-] phone*) peak/off-peak rate

tarir [taRiR] *vi* to dry up, run dry

tarte [taRt] *nf* tart; ~ **aux fraises** straw[-] berry tart; ~ **Tatin** ≃ apple upside-dow[n] tart

tartine [taRtin] *nf* slice of bread; ~ **de mie[l]** slice of bread and honey; **tartiner** *vt* t[o] spread; **fromage à tartiner** cheese sprea[d]

tartre [taRtR] *nm* (*des dents*) tartar; (*d[e] bouilloire*) fur, scale

tas [ta] *nm* heap, pile; (*fig*): **un** ~ **de** hea[p] of, lots of; **en** ~ in a heap *ou* pile; **form[é] sur le** ~ trained on the job

tasse [tas] *nf* cup; ~ **à café** coffee cup

tassé, e [tase] *adj*: **bien** ~ (*café et[c]*) strong

tasser [tase] *vt* (*terre, neige*) to pack dow[n] (*entasser*): ~ **qch dans** to cram sth int[o] **se** ~ *vi* (*se serrer*) to squeeze u[p] (*s'affaisser*) to settle; (*fig*) to settle down

tata [tata] *nf* auntie

tâter [tate] *vt* to feel; (*fig*) to try out; **se** ~ (*hésiter*) to be in two minds; ~ **de** (*pris[on] etc*) to have a taste of

tatillon, ne [tatijɔ̃, ɔn] *adj* pernickety

tâtonnement [tatɔnmɑ̃] *nm*: **par ~s** (*fi[g]*

by trial and error

tâtonner [tɑtɔne] *vi* to grope one's way along

tâtons [tɑtɔ̃]: **à ~** *adv*: **chercher à ~** to grope around for

tatouage [tatwaʒ] *nm* tattoo

tatouer [tatwe] *vt* to tattoo

taudis [todi] *nm* hovel, slum

taule [tol] (*fam*) *nf* nick (*fam*), prison

taupe [top] *nf* mole

taureau, x [tɔʀo] *nm* bull; (*signe*): **le T~** Taurus

tauromachie [tɔʀɔmaʃi] *nf* bullfighting

taux [to] *nm* rate; (*d'alcool*) level; **~ de change** exchange rate; **~ d'intérêt** interest rate

taxe [taks] *nf* tax; (*douanière*) duty; **toutes ~s comprises** inclusive of tax; **la boutique hors ~s** the duty free shop; **~ à la valeur ajoutée** value added tax

taxer [takse] *vt* (*personne*) to tax; (*produit*) to put a tax on, tax

taxi [taksi] *nm*; (*fam*) taxi driver

Tchécoslovaquie [tʃekɔslɔvaki] *nf* Czechoslovakia; **tchèque** *adj* Czech ♦ *nm/f*: **Tchèque** Czech ♦ *nm* (*LING*) Czech; **la République tchèque** the Czech Republic

te, t' [tə] *pron* you; (*réfléchi*) yourself

technicien, ne [tɛknisjɛ̃, jɛn] *nm/f* technician

technico-commercial, e, -aux [tɛknikokɔmɛʀsjal, jo] *adj*: **agent ~-~** sales technician

technique [tɛknik] *adj* technical ♦ *nf* technique; **techniquement** *adv* technically

technologie [tɛknɔlɔʒi] *nf* technology; **technologique** *adj* technological

teck [tɛk] *nm* teak

tee-shirt [tiʃœʀt] *nm* T-shirt, tee-shirt

teignais *etc* [tɛɲɛ] *vb voir* **teindre**

teindre [tɛ̃dʀ] *vt* to dye; **se ~ les cheveux** to dye one's hair; **teint, e** *adj* dyed ♦ *nm* (*du visage*) complexion; (*momentané*) colour ♦ *nf* shade; **grand teint** colourfast

teinté, e [tɛ̃te] *adj*: **~ de** (*fig*) tinged with

teinter [tɛ̃te] *vt* (*verre, papier*) to tint; (*bois*) to stain

teinture [tɛ̃tyʀ] *nf* dye; **~ d'iode** tincture of iodine; **teinturerie** *nf* dry cleaner's; **teinturier** *nm* dry cleaner

tel, telle [tɛl] *adj* (*pareil*) such; (*comme*): **~ un/des ...** like a/like ...; (*indéfini*) such-and-such a; (*intensif*): **un ~/de tels ...** such (a)/such ...; **rien de ~** nothing like it; **~ que** like, such as; **~ quel** as it is *ou* stands (*ou* was *etc*); **venez ~ jour** come on such-and-such a day

télé [tele] (*fam*) *nf* TV

télé...: **télécabine** *nf* (*benne*) cable car; **télécarte** *nf* phonecard; **télécharger** *vt* to download; **télécommande** *nf* remote control; **télécopie** *nf* fax; **envoyer qch par télécopie** to fax sth; **télécopieur** *nm* fax machine; **télédistribution** *nf* cable TV; **téléférique** *nm* = **téléphérique**; **télégramme** *nm* telegram; **télégraphier** *vt* to telegraph, cable; **téléguider** *vt* to radio-control; **télématique** *nf* telematics *sg*; **téléobjectif** *nm* telephoto lens *sg*; **télépathie** *nf* telepathy; **téléphérique** *nm* cable car

téléphone [telefɔn] *nm* telephone; **avoir le ~** to be on the (tele)phone; **au ~** on the phone; **~ mobile** mobile phone; **~ rouge** hot line; **~ sans fil** cordless (tele)phone; **~ de voiture** car phone; **téléphoner** *vi* to make a phone call; **téléphoner à** to phone, call up; **téléphonique** *adj* (tele)phone *cpd*

télescope [telɛskɔp] *nm* telescope

télescoper [telɛskɔpe] *vt* to smash up; **se ~** (*véhicules*) to concertina

télé...: **téléscripteur** *nm* teleprinter; **télésiège** *nm* chairlift; **téléski** *nm* ski-tow; **téléspectateur, -trice** *nm/f* (television) viewer; **télévente** *nf* telesales; **téléviseur** *nm* television set; **télévision** *nf* television; **à la télévision** on television; **télévision numérique** digital TV

télex [telɛks] *nm* telex

telle [tɛl] *adj voir* **tel; tellement** *adv* (*tant*) so much; (*si*) so; **tellement de** (*sable, eau*) so much; (*gens, livres*) so many; **il s'est endormi tellement il était fatigué** he was so tired (that) he fell asleep; **pas tellement** not (all) that much; not (all) that +*adjectif*

téméraire [temeʀɛʀ] *adj* reckless, rash; **témérité** *nf* recklessness, rashness

témoignage [temwaɲaʒ] *nm* (*JUR: déclaration*) testimony *no pl*, evidence *no pl*; (*rapport, récit*) account; (*fig: d'affection etc: cadeau*) token, mark; (: *geste*) expression

témoigner [temwaɲe] *vt* (*intérêt, gratitude*) to show ♦ *vi* (*JUR*) to testify, give evidence; **~ de** to bear witness to, testify to

témoin [temwɛ̃] *nm* witness ♦ *adj*: **appartement ~** show flat (*BRIT*); **être ~ de** to witness; **~ oculaire** eyewitness

tempe [tɑ̃p] *nf* temple

tempérament [tɑ̃peʀamɑ̃] *nm* temperament, disposition; **à ~** (*vente*) on deferred (payment) terms; (*achat*) by instalments, hire purchase *cpd*

température [tɑ̃peʀatyʀ] *nf* temperature; **avoir** *ou* **faire de la ~** to be running *ou* have a temperature

tempéré, e [tɑ̃peʀe] *adj* temperate

tempête [tɑ̃pɛt] *nf* storm; **~ de sable/ neige** sand/snowstorm

temple [tɑ̃pl] *nm* temple; (*protestant*) church

temporaire [tɑ̃pɔʀɛʀ] *adj* temporary

temps [tɑ̃] *nm* (*atmosphérique*) weather; (*durée*) time; (*époque*) time, times *pl*; (*LING*) tense; (*MUS*) beat; (*TECH*) stroke; **un ~ de chien** (*fam*) rotten weather; **quel ~ fait-il?** what's the weather like?; **il fait beau/mauvais ~** the weather is fine/ bad; **avoir le ~/tout son ~** to have time/plenty of time; **en ~ de paix/guerre** in peacetime/wartime; **en ~ utile** *ou* **voulu** in due time *ou* course; **ces derniers ~** lately; **dans quelque ~** in a (little) while; **de ~ en ~, de ~ à autre** from time to time; **à ~** (*partir, arriver*) in time; **à ~**

complet, à plein ~ full-time; **à ~ partie[l]** part-time; **dans le ~** at one time; **~ d'ar[r]êt** pause, halt; **~ mort** (*COMM*) slack pe[riod]

tenable [t(ə)nabl] *adj* bearable

tenace [tənas] *adj* persistent

tenailler [tənaje] *vt* (*fig*) to torment

tenailles [tənaj] *nfpl* pincers

tenais *etc* [t(ə)nɛ] *vb voir* **tenir**

tenancier, -ière [tənɑ̃sje] *nm/[f]* manager/manageress

tenant, e [tənɑ̃, ɑ̃t] *nm/f* (*SPORT*): **~ du ti[tre** title-holder

tendance [tɑ̃dɑ̃s] *nf* tendency; (*opinions*) leanings *pl*, sympathies *pl*; (*évolution*) trend; **avoir ~ à** to have a tendency t[o] tend to

tendeur [tɑ̃dœʀ] *nm* (*attache*) elastic strap

tendre [tɑ̃dʀ] *adj* tender; (*bois, roche, cou[leur*) soft ♦ *vt* (*élastique, peau*) to stretch[, (*corde*) to tighten; (*muscle*) to tense; (*fig[: piège*) to set, lay; (*donner*): **~ qch à qn** t[o] hold sth out to sb; (*offrir*) to offer sb sth[; **se ~** *vi* (*corde*) to tighten; (*relations*) t[o] become strained; **~ à qch/à faire** to ten[d] towards sth/to do; **~ l'oreille** to prick u[p] one's ears; **~ la main/le bras** to hold ou[t] one's hand/stretch out one's arm; **ten[drement** *adv* tenderly; **tendresse** *[nf]* tenderness

tendu, e [tɑ̃dy] *pp de* **tendre** ♦ *adj* (*cord[e*) tight; (*muscles*) tensed; (*relations*) strained

ténèbres [tenɛbʀ] *nfpl* darkness *sg*

teneur [tənœʀ] *nf* content; (*d'une lettre*) terms *pl*, content

tenir [t(ə)niʀ] *vt* to hold; (*magasin, hôtel*) t[o] run; (*promesse*) to keep ♦ *vi* to hol[d] (*neige, gel*) to last; **se ~** *vi* (*avoir lieu*) [to] be held, take place; (*être: personne*) t[o] stand; **~ à** (*personne, objet*) to be a[t]tached to; (*réputation*) to care about; **~ [à] faire** to be determined to do; **~ de** (*re[sembler à*) to take after; **ça ne tient qu'[à] lui** it is entirely up to him; **~ qn pour** t[o] regard sb as; **~ qch de qn** (*histoire*) [to] have heard *ou* learnt sth from sb; (*qualit[é*) *défaut)* to have inherited *ou* got sth from sb; **~ dans** to fit into; **~ compte de qch** to take sth into account; **~ les comptes** to keep the books; **~ bon** to stand fast; **~ le coup** to hold out; **~ au chaud** to keep hot; **tiens/tenez, voilà le stylo** there's the pen!; **tiens, voilà Alain!** look, here's Alain!; **tiens?** *(surprise)* really?; **se ~ droit** to stand *(ou* sit) up straight; **bien se ~** to behave well; **se ~ à qch** to hold on to sth; **s'en ~ à qch** to confine o.s. to sth

ennis [tenis] *nm* tennis; *(court)* tennis court ♦ *nm ou f pl (aussi:* **chaussures de ~**) tennis *ou* gym shoes; **~ de table** table tennis; **tennisman** *nm* tennis player

ension [tɑ̃sjɔ̃] *nf* tension; *(MÉD)* blood pressure; **avoir de la ~** to have high blood pressure

entation [tɑ̃tasjɔ̃] *nf* temptation

entative [tɑ̃tativ] *nf* attempt

ente [tɑ̃t] *nf* tent

enter [tɑ̃te] *vt (éprouver, attirer)* to tempt; *(essayer)*: **~ qch/de faire** to attempt *ou* try sth/to do; **~ sa chance** to try one's luck

enture [tɑ̃tyʀ] *nf* hanging

enu, e [t(ə)ny] *pp de* **tenir** ♦ *adj (maison, comptes)*: **bien ~** well-kept; *(obligé)*: **~ de faire** obliged to do ♦ *nf (vêtements)* clothes *pl; (comportement)* (good) manners *pl,* good behaviour; *(d'une maison)* up-keep; **en petite ~e** scantily dressed *ou* clad; **~e de route** *(AUTO)* road-holding; **~e de soirée** evening dress

er [teʀ] *adj:* **16 ~ 16b** *ou* B

erébenthine [teʀebɑ̃tin] *nf:* **(essence de) ~** (oil of) turpentine

ergal ® [teʀgal] *nm* Terylene ®

erme [teʀm] *nm* term; *(fin)* end; **à court/long ~** ♦ *adj* short-/long-term ♦ *adv* in the short/long term; **avant ~** *(MÉD)* prematurely; **mettre un ~ à** to put an end *ou* a stop to; **en bons ~s** on good terms

erminaison [teʀminɛzɔ̃] *nf (LING)* ending

erminal [teʀminal, o] *nm* terminal; **termi-**

nale *nf (SCOL)* ≃ sixth form *ou* year *(BRIT),* ≃ twelfth grade *(US)*

terminer [teʀmine] *vt* to finish; **se ~** *vi* to end

terne [teʀn] *adj* dull

ternir [teʀniʀ] *vt* to dull; *(fig)* to sully, tarnish; **se ~** *vi* to become dull

terrain [teʀɛ̃] *nm (sol, fig)* ground; *(COMM: étendue de terre)* land *no pl; (parcelle)* plot (of land); *(à bâtir)* site; **sur le ~** *(fig)* on the field; **~ d'aviation** airfield; **~ de camping** campsite; **~ de football/rugby** football/rugby pitch *(BRIT) ou* field *(US);* **~ de golf** golf course; **~ de jeu** games field; *(pour les petits)* playground; **~ de sport** sports ground; **~ vague** waste ground *no pl*

terrasse [teʀas] *nf* terrace; **à la ~** *(café)* outside; **terrasser** *vt (adversaire)* to floor; *(suj: maladie etc)* to strike down

terre [teʀ] *nf (gén, aussi ÉLEC)* earth; *(substance)* soil, earth; *(opposé à mer)* land *no pl; (contrée)* land; **~s** *nfpl (terrains)* lands, land *sg;* **en ~** *(pipe, poterie)* clay *cpd;* **à ~** *ou* **par ~** *(mettre, être, s'asseoir)* on the ground *(ou* floor); *(jeter, tomber)* to the ground, down; **~ à ~** *adj inv* down-to-earth; **~ cuite** terracotta; **la ~ ferme** dry land; **~ glaise** clay

terreau [teʀo] *nm* compost

terre-plein [teʀplɛ̃] *nm* platform; *(sur chaussée)* central reservation

terrer [teʀe]: **se ~** *vi* to hide away

terrestre [teʀɛstʀ] *adj (surface)* earth's, of the earth; *(BOT, ZOOL, MIL)* land *cpd; (REL)* earthly

terreur [teʀœʀ] *nf* terror *no pl*

terrible [teʀibl] *adj* terrible, dreadful; *(fam)* terrific; **pas ~** nothing special

terrien, ne [teʀjɛ̃, jen] *adj:* **propriétaire ~** landowner ♦ *nm/f (non martien etc)* earthling

terrier [teʀje] *nm* burrow, hole; *(chien)* terrier

terrifier [teʀifje] *vt* to terrify

terrine [teʀin] *nf (récipient)* terrine; *(CULIN)*

pâté

territoire [teʀitwaʀ] *nm* territory

terroir [teʀwaʀ] *nm*: **accent du ~** country accent

terroriser [teʀɔʀize] *vt* to terrorize

terrorisme [teʀɔʀism] *nm* terrorism; **terroriste** *nm/f* terrorist

tertiaire [teʀsjɛʀ] *adj* tertiary ♦ *nm* (*ÉCON*) service industries *pl*

tertre [tɛʀtʀ] *nm* hillock, mound

tes [te] *dét voir* **ton**[1]

tesson [tesɔ̃] *nm*: **~ de bouteille** piece of broken bottle

test [tɛst] *nm* test

testament [testamɑ̃] *nm* (*JUR*) will; (*REL*) Testament; (*fig*) legacy

tester [teste] *vt* to test

testicule [tɛstikyl] *nm* testicle

tétanos [tetanos] *nm* tetanus

têtard [tetaʀ] *nm* tadpole

tête [tɛt] *nf* head; (*cheveux*) hair *no pl*; (*visage*) face; **de ~** *adj* (*wagon etc*) front *cpd* ♦ *adv* (*calculer*) in one's head, mentally; **tenir ~ à qn** to stand up to sb; **la ~ en bas** with one's head down; **la ~ la première** (*tomber*) headfirst; **faire une ~** (*FOOTBALL*) to head the ball; **faire la ~** (*fig*) to sulk; **en ~** at the front; (*SPORT*) in the lead; **à la ~ de** at the head of; **à ~ reposée** in a more leisurely moment; **n'en faire qu'à sa ~** to do as one pleases; **en avoir par-dessus la ~** to be fed up; **en ~ à ~** in private, alone together; **de la ~ aux pieds** from head to toe; **~ de lecture** (playback) head; **~ de liste** (*POL*) chief candidate; **~ de série** (*TENNIS*) seeded player, seed; **tête-à-queue** *nm inv*: **faire un tête-à-queue** to spin round

téter [tete] *vt*: **~ (sa mère)** to suck at one's mother's breast, feed

tétine [tetin] *nf* teat; (*sucette*) dummy (*BRIT*), pacifier (*US*)

têtu, e [tety] *adj* stubborn, pigheaded

texte [tɛkst] *nm* text; (*morceau choisi*) passage

textile [tɛkstil] *adj* textile *cpd* ♦ *nm* textile;

le ~ the textile industry

texto [tɛksto] (*fam*) *adj* word for word

texture [tɛkstyʀ] *nf* texture

thaïlandais, e [tajlɑ̃dɛ, ɛz] *adj* Th... ♦ *nm/f*: **T~, e** Thai

Thaïlande [tailɑ̃d] *nf* Thailand

TGV *sigle m* (= *train à grande vitesse*) high speed train

thé [te] *nm* tea; **~ au citron** lemon tea; **~ au lait** tea with milk; **prendre le ~** t... have tea; **faire le ~** to make the tea

théâtral, e, -aux [teatʀal, o] *adj* theatr... cal

théâtre [teatʀ] *nm* theatre; (*péj: simulation*) playacting; (*fig: lieu*): **le ~ de** the scene o... **faire du ~** to act

théière [tejɛʀ] *nf* teapot

thème [tɛm] *nm* theme; (*SCOL: traduction*) prose (composition)

théologie [teɔlɔʒi] *nf* theology

théorie [teɔʀi] *nf* theory; **théorique** *a...* theoretical

thérapie [teʀapi] *nf* therapy

thermal, e, -aux [tɛʀmal, o] *adj*: **statio... ~e** spa; **cure ~e** water cure

thermes [tɛʀm] *nmpl* thermal baths

thermomètre [tɛʀmɔmɛtʀ] *nm* therm... meter

thermos ® [tɛʀmos] *nm ou nf*: **(bouteille ~** vacuum *ou* Thermos ® flask

thermostat [tɛʀmɔsta] *nm* thermostat

thèse [tɛz] *nf* thesis

thon [tɔ̃] *nm* tuna (fish)

thym [tɛ̃] *nm* thyme

tibia [tibja] *nm* shinbone, tibia; (*partie ant... rieure de la jambe*) shin

tic [tik] *nm* tic, (nervous) twitch; (*de la... gage etc*) mannerism

ticket [tikɛ] *nm* ticket; **~ de caisse** receip... **~ de quai** platform ticket

tic-tac [tiktak] *nm* ticking; **faire ~-~** ... tick

tiède [tjɛd] *adj* lukewarm; (*vent, air*) mil... warm; **tiédir** *vi* to cool; (*se réchauffer*) ... grow warmer

tien, ne [tjɛ̃, tjɛn] *pron*: **le(la) ~(ne), le...**

~(ne)s yours; **à la ~ne!** cheers!

tiens [tjɛ̃] *vb, excl voir* **tenir**

tierce [tjɛʀs] *adj voir* **tiers**

tiercé [tjɛʀse] *nm system of forecast betting giving first 3 horses*

tiers, tierce [tjɛʀ, tjɛʀs] *adj* third ♦ *nm* (*JUR*) third party; (*fraction*) third; **le ~ monde** the Third World

tifs [tif] (*fam*) *nmpl* hair

tige [tiʒ] *nf* stem; (*baguette*) rod

tignasse [tiɲas] (*péj*) *nf* mop of hair

tigre [tigʀ] *nm* tiger; **tigresse** *nf* tigress; **tigré, e** *adj* (*rayé*) striped; (*tacheté*) spotted; (*chat*) tabby

tilleul [tijœl] *nm* lime (tree), linden (tree); (*boisson*) lime(-blossom) tea

timbale [tɛ̃bal] *nf* (metal) tumbler; **~s** *nfpl* (*MUS*) timpani, kettledrums

timbre [tɛ̃bʀ] *nm* (*tampon*) stamp; (*aussi:* **~-poste**) (postage) stamp; (*MUS: de voix, instrument*) timbre, tone

timbré, e [tɛ̃bʀe] (*fam*) *adj* cracked

timide [timid] *adj* shy; (*timoré*) timid; **timidement** *adv* shyly; timidly; **timidité** *nf* shyness; timidity

tins *etc* [tɛ̃] *vb voir* **tenir**

tintamarre [tɛ̃tamaʀ] *nm* din, uproar

tinter [tɛ̃te] *vi* to ring, chime; (*argent, clefs*) to jingle

tique [tik] *nf* (*parasite*) tick

tir [tiʀ] *nm* (*sport*) shooting; (*fait ou manière de ~er*) firing *no pl*; (*rafale*) fire; (*stand*) shooting gallery; **~ à l'arc** archery; **~ au pigeon** clay pigeon shooting

tirage [tiʀaʒ] *nm* (*action*) printing; (*PHOTO*) print; (*de journal*) circulation; (*de livre: nombre d'exemplaires*) (print) run; (*: édition*) edition; (*de loterie*) draw; **par ~ au sort** by drawing lots

tirailler [tiʀaje] *vt*: **être tiraillé entre** to be torn between

tire [tiʀ] *nf*: **vol à la ~** pickpocketing

tiré, e [tiʀe] *adj* (*traits*) drawn; **~ par les cheveux** far-fetched

tire-au-flanc [tiʀoflɑ̃] (*péj*) *nm inv* skiver

tire-bouchon [tiʀbuʃ3] *nm* corkscrew

tirelire [tiʀliʀ] *nf* moneybox

tirer [tiʀe] *vt* (*gén*) to pull; (*extraire*): **~ qch de** to take *ou* pull sth out of; (*trait, rideau, carte, conclusion, chèque*) to draw; (*langue*) to stick out; (*en faisant feu: balle, coup*) to fire; (*: animal*) to shoot; (*journal, livre, photo*) to print; (*FOOTBALL: corner etc*) to take ♦ *vi* (*faire feu*) to fire; (*faire du tir, FOOTBALL*) to shoot; **se ~** *vi* (*fam*) to push off; **s'en ~** (*éviter le pire*) to get off; (*survivre*) to pull through; (*se débrouiller*) to manage; **~ sur** (*corde*) to pull on *ou* at; (*faire feu sur*) to shoot *ou* fire at; (*pipe*) to draw on; (*approcher de: couleur*) to verge *ou* border on; **~ qn de** (*embarras etc*) to help *ou* get sb out of; **~ à l'arc/la carabine** to shoot with a bow and arrow/with a rifle; **~ à sa fin** to be drawing to a close; **~ qch au clair** to clear sth up; **~ au sort** to draw lots; **~ parti de** to take advantage of; **~ profit de** to profit from

tiret [tiʀe] *nm* dash

tireur [tiʀœʀ] *nm* gunman; **~ d'élite** marksman

tiroir [tiʀwaʀ] *nm* drawer; **tiroir-caisse** *nm* till

tisane [tizan] *nf* herb tea

tisonnier [tizɔnje] *nm* poker

tisser [tise] *vt* to weave; **tisserand** *nm* weaver

tissu [tisy] *nm* fabric, material, cloth *no pl*; (*ANAT, BIO*) tissue; **tissu-éponge** *nm* (terry) towelling *no pl*

titre [titʀ] *nm* (*gén*) title; (*de journal*) headline; (*diplôme*) qualification; (*COMM*) security; **en ~** (*champion*) official; **à juste ~** rightly; **à quel ~?** on what grounds?; **à aucun ~** on no account; **au même ~ (que)** in the same way (as); **à ~ d'information** for (your) information; **à ~ gracieux** free of charge; **à ~ d'essai** on a trial basis; **à ~ privé** in a private capacity; **~ de propriété** title deed; **~ de transport** ticket

tituber [titybe] *vi* to stagger (along)

titulaire [titylɛʀ] *adj* (*ADMIN*) with tenure ♦ *nm/f* (*de permis*) holder

toast [tost] *nm* slice *ou* piece of toast; (*de bienvenue*) (welcoming) toast; **porter un ~ à qn** to propose *ou* drink a toast to sb

toboggan [tɔbɔgɑ̃] *nm* slide; (*AUTO*) fly-over

toc [tɔk] *excl*: **~, ~** knock knock ♦ *nm*: **en ~** fake

tocsin [tɔksɛ̃] *nm* alarm (bell)

toge [tɔʒ] *nf* toga; (*de juge*) gown

tohu-bohu [tɔybɔy] *nm* hubbub

toi [twa] *pron* you

Toile [twal] *nf* Web

toile *nf* (*tableau*) canvas; **de** *ou* **en ~** (*pantalon*) cotton; (*sac*) canvas; **~ cirée** oilcloth; **~ d'araignée** cobweb; **~ de fond** (*fig*) backdrop

toilette [twalɛt] *nf* (*habits*) outfit; **~s** *nfpl* (*w.-c.*) toilet *sg*; **faire sa ~** to get washed; **articles de ~** toiletries

toi-même [twamɛm] *pron* yourself

toiser [twaze] *vt* to eye up and down

toison [twazɔ̃] *nf* (*de mouton*) fleece

toit [twa] *nm* roof; **~ ouvrant** sunroof

toiture [twatyʀ] *nf* roof

tôle [tol] *nf* (*plaque*) steel *ou* iron sheet; **~ ondulée** corrugated iron

tolérable [tɔleʀabl] *adj* tolerable

tolérant, e [tɔleʀɑ̃, ɑ̃t] *adj* tolerant

tolérer [tɔleʀe] *vt* to tolerate; (*ADMIN*: *hors taxe etc*) to allow

tollé [tɔ(l)le] *nm* outcry

tomate [tɔmat] *nf* tomato; **~s farcies** stuffed tomatoes

tombe [tɔ̃b] *nf* (*sépulture*) grave; (*avec monument*) tomb

tombeau, x [tɔ̃bo] *nm* tomb

tombée [tɔ̃be] *nf*: **à la ~ de la nuit** at nightfall

tomber [tɔ̃be] *vi* to fall; (*fièvre, vent*) to drop; **laisser ~** (*objet*) to drop; (*personne*) to let down; (*activité*) to give up; **laisse ~!** forget it!; **faire ~** to knock over; **~ sur** (*rencontrer*) to bump into; **~ de fatigue/sommeil** to drop from exhaustion/be falling asleep on one's feet; **ça tombe bien** that's come at the right time; **il est bien tombé** he's been lucky; **~ à l'eau** (*projet*) to fall through; **~ en panne** to break down

tombola [tɔ̃bɔla] *nf* raffle

tome [tɔm] *nm* volume

ton¹, ta [tɔ̃, ta] (*pl* **tes**) *adj* your

ton² [tɔ̃] *nm* (*gén*) tone; (*couleur*) shade tone; **de bon ~** in good taste

tonalité [tɔnalite] *nf* (*au téléphone*) dialling tone

tondeuse [tɔ̃døz] *nf* (*à gazon*) (lawn)mower; (*du coiffeur*) clippers *pl*; (*pour les moutons*) shears *pl*

tondre [tɔ̃dʀ] *vt* (*pelouse, herbe*) to mow; (*haie*) to cut, clip; (*mouton, toison*) to shear; (*cheveux*) to crop

tongs [tɔ̃g] *nfpl* flip-flops

tonifier [tɔnifje] *vt* (*peau, organisme*) to tone up

tonique [tɔnik] *adj* fortifying ♦ *nm* tonic

tonne [tɔn] *nf* metric ton, tonne

tonneau, x [tɔno] *nm* (*à vin, cidre*) barrel; **faire des ~x** (*voiture, avion*) to roll over

tonnelle [tɔnɛl] *nf* bower, arbour

tonner [tɔne] *vi* to thunder; **il tonne** it is thundering, there's some thunder

tonnerre [tɔnɛʀ] *nm* thunder

tonton [tɔ̃tɔ̃] *nm* uncle

tonus [tɔnys] *nm* energy

top [tɔp] *nm*: **au 3ème ~** at the 3rd stroke

topinambour [tɔpinɑ̃buʀ] *nm* Jerusalem artichoke

topo [tɔpo] (*fam*) *nm* rundown; **c'est le même ~** it's the same old story

toque [tɔk] *nf* (*de fourrure*) fur hat; **~ de cuisinier** chef's hat; **~ de jockey/juge** jockey's/judge's cap

toqué, e [tɔke] (*fam*) *adj* cracked

torche [tɔʀʃ] *nf* torch

torchon [tɔʀʃɔ̃] *nm* cloth; (*à vaisselle*) tea towel *ou* cloth

tordre [tɔʀdʀ] *vt* (*chiffon*) to wring; (*barre, fig*: *visage*) to twist; **se ~** *vi*: **se ~ le**

poignet/la cheville to twist one's wrist/ankle; **se ~ de douleur/rire** to be doubled up with pain/laughter; **tordu, e** *adj* bent; *(fig)* crazy

tornade [tɔrnad] *nf* tornado

torpille [tɔrpij] *nf* torpedo

torréfier [tɔrefje] *vt* to roast

torrent [tɔrɑ̃] *nm* mountain stream

torsade [tɔrsad] *nf*: **un pull à ~s** a cable sweater

torse [tɔrs] *nm* chest; *(ANAT, SCULPTURE)* torso; **~ nu** stripped to the waist

tort [tɔr] *nm* (*défaut*) fault; **~s** *nmpl* (*JUR*) fault *sg*; **avoir ~** to be wrong; **être dans son ~** to be in the wrong; **donner ~ à qn** to lay the blame on sb; **causer du ~ à** to harm; **à ~** wrongly; **à ~ et à travers** wildly

torticolis [tɔrtikɔli] *nm* stiff neck

tortiller [tɔrtije] *vt* to twist; (*moustache*) to twirl; **se ~** *vi* to wriggle; *(en dansant)* to wiggle

tortionnaire [tɔrsjɔnɛr] *nm* torturer

tortue [tɔrty] *nf* tortoise; *(d'eau douce)* terrapin; *(d'eau de mer)* turtle

tortueux, -euse [tɔrtɥø, øz] *adj (rue)* twisting; *(fig)* tortuous

torture [tɔrtyr] *nf* torture; **torturer** *vt* to torture; *(fig)* to torment

tôt [to] *adv* early; **~ ou tard** sooner or later; **si ~** so early; *(déjà)* so soon; **plus ~** earlier; **au plus ~** at the earliest; **il eut ~ fait de faire** he soon did

total, e, -aux [tɔtal, o] *adj, nm* total; **au ~** in total; *(fig)* on the whole; **faire le ~** to work out the total; **totalement** *adv* totally; **totaliser** *vt* to total; **totalitaire** *adj* totalitarian; **totalité** *nf*: **la totalité de** all (of); the whole +sg; **en totalité** entirely

toubib [tubib] *(fam) nm* doctor

touchant, e [tuʃɑ̃, ɑ̃t] *adj* touching

touche [tuʃ] *nf (de piano, de machine à écrire)* key; *(de téléphone)* button; *(PEINTURE etc)* stroke, touch; *(fig: de nostalgie)* touch; *(FOOTBALL: aussi:* **remise en ~**) throw-in; *(aussi:* **ligne de ~**) touch-line

toucher [tuʃe] *nm* touch ♦ *vt* to touch; *(palper)* to feel; *(atteindre: d'un coup de feu etc)* to hit; *(concerner)* to concern, affect; *(contacter)* to reach, contact; *(recevoir: récompense)* to receive, get; (: *salaire)* to draw, get; (: *chèque)* to cash; **se ~** *(être en contact)* to touch; **au ~** to the touch; **~ à** to touch; *(concerner)* to have to do with, concern; **je vais lui en ~ un mot** I'll have a word with him about it; **~ à sa fin** to be drawing to a close

touffe [tuf] *nf* tuft

touffu, e [tufy] *adj* thick, dense

toujours [tuʒur] *adv* always; *(encore)* still; *(constamment)* forever; **~ plus** more and more; **pour ~** forever; **~ est-il que** the fact remains that; **essaie ~** (you can) try anyway

toupet [tupɛ] *(fam) nm* cheek

toupie [tupi] *nf* (spinning) top

tour [tur] *nf* tower; *(immeuble)* high-rise block *(BRIT)* ou building *(US)*; *(ÉCHECS)* castle, rook ♦ *nm (excursion)* trip; *(à pied)* stroll, walk; *(en voiture)* run, ride; *(SPORT: aussi:* **~ de piste**) lap; *(d'être servi ou de jouer etc)* turn; *(de roue etc)* revolution; *(POL: aussi:* **~ de scrutin**) ballot; *(ruse, de prestidigitation)* trick; *(de potier)* wheel; *(à bois, métaux)* lathe; *(circonférence):* **de 3 m de ~** 3 m round, with a circumference ou girth of 3 m; **faire le ~ de** to go round; *(à pied)* to walk round; **c'est au ~ de Renée** it's Renée's turn; **à ~ de rôle, ~ à ~** in turn; **~ de chant** *nm* song recital; **~ de contrôle** *nf* control tower; **~ de garde** *nm* spell of duty; **~ d'horizon** *nm (fig)* general survey; **~ de taille/tête** *nm* waist/head measurement; **un 33 ~s** an LP; **un 45 ~s** a single

tourbe [turb] *nf* peat

tourbillon [turbijɔ̃] *nm* whirlwind; *(d'eau)* whirlpool; *(fig)* whirl, swirl; **tourbillonner** *vi* to whirl (round)

tourelle [turɛl] *nf* turret

tourisme [turism] *nm* tourism; **agence de ~** tourist agency; **faire du ~** to go touring; (*en ville*) to go sightseeing; **touriste** *nm/f* tourist; **touristique** *adj* tourist *cpd*; (*région*) touristic

tourment [tuʀmɑ̃] *nm* torment; **tourmenter** *vt* to torment; **se tourmenter** *vi* to fret, worry o.s.

tournage [tuʀnaʒ] *nm* (CINÉMA) shooting

tournant [tuʀnɑ̃] *nm* (*de route*) bend; (*fig*) turning point

tournebroche [tuʀnəbʀɔʃ] *nm* roasting spit

tourne-disque [tuʀnədisk] *nm* record player

tournée [tuʀne] *nf* (*du facteur etc*) round; (*d'artiste, politicien*) tour; (*au café*) round (of drinks)

tournemain [tuʀnəmɛ̃]: **en un ~** *adv* (as) quick as a flash

tourner [tuʀne] *vt* to turn; (*sauce, mélange*) to stir; (CINÉMA: *faire les prises de vues*) to shoot; (: *produire*) to make ♦ *vi* to turn; (*moteur*) to run; (*taximètre*) to tick away; (*lait etc*) to turn (sour); **se ~** *vi* to turn round; **mal ~** to go wrong; **~ autour de** to go round; (*péj*) to hang round; **~ à/en** to turn into; **~ à gauche/droite** to turn left/right; **~ le dos à** to turn one's back on; to have one's back to; **~ de l'œil** to pass out; **se ~ vers** to turn towards; (*fig*) to turn to

tournesol [tuʀnəsɔl] *nm* sunflower

tournevis [tuʀnəvis] *nm* screwdriver

tourniquet [tuʀnike] *nm* (*pour arroser*) sprinkler; (*portillon*) turnstile; (*présentoir*) revolving stand

tournoi [tuʀnwa] *nm* tournament

tournoyer [tuʀnwaje] *vi* to swirl (round)

tournure [tuʀnyʀ] *nf* (LING) turn of phrase; (*évolution*): **la ~ de qch** the way sth is developing; **~ d'esprit** turn *ou* cast of mind; **la ~ des événements** the turn of events

tourte [tuʀt] *nf* pie

tourterelle [tuʀtəʀɛl] *nf* turtledove

tous [tu] *adj, pron voir* **tout**

Toussaint [tusɛ̃] *nf*: **la ~** All Saints' Day

Toussaint

i **La Toussaint**, November 1, is a public holiday in France. People traditionally visit the graves of friends and relatives to lay wreaths of heather and chrysanthemums.

---

tousser [tuse] *vi* to cough

MOT-CLÉ

tout, e [tu, tut] (*mpl* **tous**, *fpl* **toutes**) *ad*
1 (*avec article singulier*) all; **tout le lait** al the milk; **toute la nuit** all night, the whole night; **tout le livre** the whole book; **tout un pain** a whole loaf; **tout le temps** all the time; the whole time; **c'es tout le contraire** it's quite the opposite
2 (*avec article pluriel*) every, all; **tous les li vres** all the books; **toutes les nuits** ever night; **toutes les fois** every time; **toutes les trois/deux semaines** every third *ou* second week, every three/two weeks; **tous les deux** both *ou* each of u (*ou* them *ou* you); **toutes les trois** a three of us (*ou* them *ou* you)
3 (*sans article*): **à tout âge** at any age **pour toute nourriture, il avait ...** his onl food was ...

♦ *pron* everything, all; **il a tout fait** he done everything; **je les vois tous** I ca see them all *ou* all of them; **nous y som mes tous allés** all of us went, we a went; **en tout** in all; **tout ce qu'il sait** a he knows

♦ *nm* whole; **le tout** all of it (*ou* them); **l tout est de ...** the main thing is to .. **pas du tout** not at all

♦ *adv* 1 (*très, complètement*) very; **tou près** very near; **le tout premier** the ver first; **tout seul** all alone; **le livre tout en tier** the whole book; **tout en haut** righ at the top; **tout droit** straight ahead
2: **tout en** while; **je vous vois tous en travaillan** while working, as he *etc* works
3: **tout d'abord** first of all; **tout à cou**

suddenly; **tout à fait** absolutely; **tout à l'heure** a short while ago; (*futur*) in a short while, shortly; **à tout à l'heure!** see you later!; **tout de même** all the same; **tout le monde** everybody; **tout de suite** immediately, straight away; **tout terrain** *ou* **tous terrains** all-terrain

toutefois [tutfwa] *adv* however

toutes [tut] *adj, pron voir* **tout**

toux [tu] *nf* cough

toxicomane [tɔksikɔman] *nm/f* drug addict

toxique [tɔksik] *adj* toxic

trac [tʀak] *nm* (*au théâtre, en public*) stage fright; (*aux examens*) nerves *pl*; **avoir le ~** (*au théâtre, en public*) to have stage fright; (*aux examens*) to be feeling nervous

tracasser [tʀakase] *vt* to worry, bother; **se ~** to worry

trace [tʀas] *nf* (*empreintes*) tracks *pl*; (*marques, aussi fig*) mark; (*quantité infime, indice, vestige*) trace; **~s de pas** footprints

tracé [tʀase] *nm* (*parcours*) line; (*plan*) layout

tracer [tʀase] *vt* to draw; (*piste*) to open up

tract [tʀakt] *nm* tract, pamphlet

tractations [tʀaktasjɔ̃] *nfpl* dealings, bargaining *sg*

tracteur [tʀaktœʀ] *nm* tractor

traction [tʀaksjɔ̃] *nf:* **~ avant/arrière** front-wheel/rear-wheel drive

tradition [tʀadisjɔ̃] *nf* tradition; **traditionnel, le** *adj* traditional

traducteur, -trice [tʀadyktœʀ, tʀis] *nm/f* translator

traduction [tʀadyksjɔ̃] *nf* translation

traduire [tʀadɥiʀ] *vt* to translate; (*exprimer*) to convey; **~ qn en justice** to bring sb before the courts

trafic [tʀafik] *nm* traffic; **~ d'armes** arms dealing; **trafiquant, e** *nm/f* trafficker; (*d'armes*) dealer; **trafiquer** (*péj*) *vt* (*vin*) to doctor; (*moteur, document*) to tamper with

tragédie [tʀaʒedi] *nf* tragedy; **tragique**

adj tragic

trahir [tʀaiʀ] *vt* to betray; **trahison** *nf* betrayal; (*JUR*) treason

train [tʀɛ̃] *nm* (*RAIL*) train; (*allure*) pace; **être en ~ de faire qch** to be doing sth; **mettre qn en ~** to put sb in good spirits; **se sentir en ~** to feel in good form; **~ d'atterrissage** undercarriage; **~ de vie** style of living; **~ électrique** (*jouet*) (electric) train set; **~-autos-couchettes** car-sleeper train

traîne [tʀɛn] *nf* (*de robe*) train; **être à la ~** to lag behind

traîneau, x [tʀɛno] *nm* sleigh, sledge

traînée [tʀɛne] *nf* trail; (*sur un mur, dans le ciel*) streak; (*péj*) slut

traîner [tʀɛne] *vt* (*remorque*) to pull; (*enfant, chien*) to drag *ou* trail along ♦ *vi* (*robe, manteau*) to trail; (*être en désordre*) to lie around; (*aller lentement*) to dawdle (along); (*vagabonder, agir lentement*) to hang about; (*durer*) to drag on; **se ~** *vi* to drag o.s. along; **~ les pieds** to drag one's feet

train-train [tʀɛ̃tʀɛ̃] *nm* humdrum routine

traire [tʀɛʀ] *vt* to milk

trait [tʀɛ] *nm* (*ligne*) line; (*de dessin*) stroke; (*caractéristique*) feature, trait; **~s** *nmpl* (*du visage*) features; **d'un ~** (*boire*) in one gulp; **de ~** (*animal*) draught; **avoir ~ à** to concern; **~ d'union** hyphen

traitant, e [tʀɛtɑ̃, ɑ̃t] *adj* (*shampooing*) medicated; **votre médecin ~** your usual *ou* family doctor

traite [tʀɛt] *nf* (*COMM*) draft; (*AGR*) milking; **d'une ~** without stopping; **la ~ des noirs** the slave trade

traité [tʀɛte] *nm* treaty

traitement [tʀɛtmɑ̃] *nm* treatment; (*salaire*) salary; **~ de données** data processing; **~ de texte** word processing; (*logiciel*) word processing package

traiter [tʀɛte] *vt* to treat; (*qualifier*): **~ qn d'idiot** to call sb a fool ♦ *vi* to deal; **~ de** to deal with

traiteur [tʀɛtœʀ] *nm* caterer

traître, -esse [tʀɛtʀ, tʀɛtʀɛs] *adj (dangereux)* ♦ *nm* traitor

trajectoire [tʀaʒɛktwaʀ] *nf* path

trajet [tʀaʒɛ] *nm (parcours, voyage)* journey; *(itinéraire)* route; *(distance à parcourir)* distance

trame [tʀam] *nf (de tissu)* weft; *(fig)* framework; **usé jusqu'à la ~** threadbare

tramer [tʀame] *vt:* **il se trame quelque chose** there's something brewing

trampoline [tʀɑ̃pɔlin] *nm* trampoline

tramway [tʀamwɛ] *nm* tram(way); *(voiture)* tram(car) *(BRIT)*, streetcar *(US)*

tranchant, e [tʀɑ̃ʃɑ̃, ɑ̃t] *adj* sharp; *(fig)* peremptory ♦ *nm (d'un couteau)* cutting edge; *(de la main)* edge; **à double ~** double-edged

tranche [tʀɑ̃ʃ] *nf (morceau)* slice; *(arête)* edge; **~ d'âge/de salaires** age/wage bracket

tranché, e [tʀɑ̃ʃe] *adj (couleurs)* distinct; *(opinions)* clear-cut; **tranchée** *nf* trench

trancher [tʀɑ̃ʃe] *vt* to cut, sever ♦ *vi* to take a decision; **~ avec** to contrast sharply with

tranquille [tʀɑ̃kil] *adj* quiet; *(rassuré)* easy in one's mind, with one's mind at rest; **se tenir ~** *(enfant)* to be quiet; **laisse-moi/laisse-ça ~** leave me/it alone; **avoir la conscience ~** to have a clear conscience; **tranquillisant** *nm* tranquillizer; **tranquillité** *nf* peace (and quiet); *(d'esprit)* peace of mind

transat [tʀɑ̃zat] *nm* deckchair

transborder [tʀɑ̃sbɔʀde] *vt* to tran(s)ship

transcription [tʀɑ̃skʀipsjɔ̃] *nf* transcription; *(copie)* transcript

transférer [tʀɑ̃sfeʀe] *vt* to transfer; **transfert** *nm* transfer

transformation [tʀɑ̃sfɔʀmasjɔ̃] *nf* change; transformation; alteration; *(RUGBY)* conversion

transformer [tʀɑ̃sfɔʀme] *vt* to change; *(radicalement)* to transform; *(vêtement)* to alter; *(matière première, appartement, RUGBY)* to convert; **(se) ~ en** to turn into

transfusion [tʀɑ̃sfyzjɔ̃] *nf:* **~ sanguine** blood transfusion

transgresser [tʀɑ̃sgʀese] *vt* to contravene

transi, e [tʀɑ̃zi] *adj* numb (with cold), chilled to the bone

transiger [tʀɑ̃ziʒe] *vi* to compromise

transit [tʀɑ̃zit] *nm* transit; **transiter** *vi* to pass in transit

transitif, -ive [tʀɑ̃zitif, iv] *adj* transitive

transition [tʀɑ̃zisjɔ̃] *nf* transition; **transitoire** *adj* transitional

translucide [tʀɑ̃slysid] *adj* translucent

transmettre [tʀɑ̃smɛtʀ] *vt (passer):* **~ qch à qn** to pass sth on to sb; *(TECH, TÉL, MÉD)* to transmit; *(TV, RADIO: retransmettre)* to broadcast; **transmission** *nf* transmission

transparent, e [tʀɑ̃spaʀɑ̃, ɑ̃t] *adj* transparent

transpercer [tʀɑ̃spɛʀse] *vt (froid, pluie)* to go through, pierce; *(balle)* to go through

transpiration [tʀɑ̃spiʀasjɔ̃] *nf* perspiration

transpirer [tʀɑ̃spiʀe] *vi* to perspire

transplanter [tʀɑ̃splɑ̃te] *vt (MÉD, BOT)* to transplant; **transplantation** *nf (MÉD)* transplant

transport [tʀɑ̃spɔʀ] *nm* transport; **~s en commun** public transport *sg*; **transporter** *vt* to carry, move; *(COMM)* to transport, convey; **transporteur** *nm* haulage contractor *(BRIT)*, trucker *(US)*

transvaser [tʀɑ̃svaze] *vt* to decant

transversal, e, -aux [tʀɑ̃svɛʀsal, o] *adj (rue)* which runs across; **coupe ~e** cross section

trapèze [tʀapɛz] *nm (au cirque)* trapeze

trappe [tʀap] *nf* trap door

trapu, e [tʀapy] *adj* squat, stocky

traquenard [tʀaknaʀ] *nm* trap

traquer [tʀake] *vt* to track down; *(harceler)* to hound

traumatiser [tʀomatize] *vt* to traumatize

travail, -aux [tʀavaj] *nm (gén)* work; *(tâche, métier)* work *no pl*, job; *(ÉCON, MÉD)* labour; **être sans ~** *(employé)* to be out of work *ou* unemployed; *voir aussi* **tra-**

vaux; ~ **(au) noir** moonlighting

travailler [tʀavaje] *vi* to work; (*bois*) to warp ♦ *vt* (*bois, métal*) to work; (*objet d'art, discipline*) to work on; **cela le travaille** it is on his mind; **travailleur, -euse** *adj* hard-working ♦ *nm/f* worker; **travailliste** *adj* ≈ Labour *cpd*

travaux [tʀavo] *nmpl* (*de réparation, agricoles etc*) work *sg*; (*sur route*) roadworks *pl*; (*de construction*) building (work); **travaux des champs** farmwork *sg*; **travaux dirigés** (*SCOL*) tutorial; **travaux forcés** hard labour *sg*; **travaux manuels** (*SCOL*) handicrafts; **travaux ménagers** housework *sg*; **travaux pratiques** (*SCOL*) practical work; (*en laboratoire*) lab work

travers [tʀavɛʀ] *nm* fault, failing; **en ~ (de)** across; **au ~ (de)/à ~** through; **de ~** (*nez, bouche*) crooked; (*chapeau*) askew; **comprendre de ~** to misunderstand; **regarder de ~** (*fig*) to look askance at

traverse [tʀavɛʀs] *nf* (*de voie ferrée*) sleeper; **chemin de ~** shortcut

traversée [tʀavɛʀse] *nf* crossing

traverser [tʀavɛʀse] *vt* (*gén*) to cross; (*ville, tunnel, aussi: percer, fig*) to go through; (*suj: ligne, trait*) to run across

traversin [tʀavɛʀsɛ̃] *nm* bolster

travesti [tʀavɛsti] *nm* transvestite

rébucher [tʀebyʃe] *vi*: ~ **(sur)** to stumble (over), trip (against)

trèfle [tʀɛfl] *nm* (*BOT*) clover; (*CARTES: couleur*) clubs *pl*; (: *carte*) club

treille [tʀɛj] *nf* vine arbour

treillis [tʀeji] *nm* (*métallique*) wire-mesh; (*MIL: tenue*) combat uniform; (*pantalon*) combat trousers *pl*

treize [tʀɛz] *num* thirteen; **treizième** *num* thirteenth

---
treizième mois
---

i **Le treizième mois** *is an end-of-year bonus roughly equal to one month's salary. For many employees it is a standard part of their salary package.*

tréma [tʀema] *nm* diaeresis

tremblement [tʀɑ̃bləmɑ̃] *nm*: ~ **de terre** earthquake

trembler [tʀɑ̃ble] *vi* to tremble, shake; ~ **de** (*froid, fièvre*) to shiver *ou* tremble with; (*peur*) to shake *ou* tremble with; ~ **pour qn** to fear for sb

trémousser [tʀemuse]: **se ~** *vi* to jig about, wriggle about

trempe [tʀɑ̃p] *nf* (*fig*): **de cette/sa ~** of this/his calibre

trempé, e [tʀɑ̃pe] *adj* soaking (wet), drenched; (*TECH*) tempered

tremper [tʀɑ̃pe] *vt* to soak, drench; (*aussi*: **faire ~, mettre à ~**) to soak; (*plonger*): ~ **qch dans** to dip sth in(to) ♦ *vi* to soak; (*fig*): ~ **dans** to be involved *ou* have a hand in; **se ~** *vi* to have a quick dip; **trempette** *nf*: **faire trempette** to go paddling

tremplin [tʀɑ̃plɛ̃] *nm* springboard; (*SKI*) ski-jump

trentaine [tʀɑ̃tɛn] *nf*: **une ~ (de)** thirty or so, about thirty; **avoir la ~** (*âge*) to be around thirty

trente [tʀɑ̃t] *num* thirty; **être sur son ~ et un** to be wearing one's Sunday best; **trentième** *num* thirtieth

trépidant, e [tʀepidɑ̃, ɑ̃t] *adj* (*fig: rythme*) pulsating; (: *vie*) hectic

trépied [tʀepje] *nm* tripod

trépigner [tʀepiɲe] *vi* to stamp (one's feet)

très [tʀɛ] *adv* very; much +*pp*, highly +*pp*

trésor [tʀezɔʀ] *nm* treasure; **T~ (public)** public revenue; **trésorerie** *nf* (*gestion*) accounts *pl*; (*bureaux*) accounts department; **difficultés de trésorerie** cash problems, shortage of cash *ou* funds; **trésorier, -ière** *nm/f* treasurer

tressaillir [tʀesajiʀ] *vi* to shiver, shudder

tressauter [tʀesote] *vi* to start, jump

tresse [tʀɛs] *nf* braid, plait; **tresser** *vt* (*cheveux*) to braid, plait; (*corbeille*) to weave

tréteau, x [tʀeto] *nm* trestle

treuil [tʀœj] *nm* winch

trêve [tʀɛv] *nf* (*MIL, POL*) truce; (*fig*) respite; **~ de ...** enough of this ...

tri [tʀi] *nm*: **faire le ~ (de)** to sort out; **le (bureau de) ~** (*POSTES*) the sorting office

triangle [tʀijɑ̃gl] *nm* triangle; **triangulaire** *adj* triangular

tribord [tʀibɔʀ] *nm*: **à ~** to starboard, on the starboard side

tribu [tʀiby] *nf* tribe

tribunal, -aux [tʀibynal, o] *nm* (*JUR*) court; (*MIL*) tribunal

tribune [tʀibyn] *nf* (*estrade*) platform, rostrum; (*débat*) forum; (*d'église, de tribunal*) gallery; (*de stade*) stand

tribut [tʀiby] *nm* tribute

tributaire [tʀibytɛʀ] *adj*: **être ~ de** to be dependent on

tricher [tʀiʃe] *vi* to cheat; **tricheur, -euse** *nm/f* cheat(er)

tricolore [tʀikɔlɔʀ] *adj* three-coloured; (*français*) red, white and blue

tricot [tʀiko] *nm* (*technique, ouvrage*) knitting *no pl*; (*vêtement*) jersey, sweater; **~ de peau** vest; **tricoter** *vt* to knit

trictrac [tʀiktʀak] *nm* backgammon

tricycle [tʀisikl] *nm* tricycle

triennal, e, -aux [tʀijenal, o] *adj* three-year

trier [tʀije] *vt* to sort out; (*POSTES, fruits*) to sort

trimestre [tʀimɛstʀ] *nm* (*SCOL*) term; (*COMM*) quarter; **trimestriel, le** *adj* quarterly; (*SCOL*) end-of-term

tringle [tʀɛ̃gl] *nf* rod

trinquer [tʀɛ̃ke] *vi* to clink glasses

triomphe [tʀijɔ̃f] *nm* triumph; **triompher** *vi* to triumph, win; **triompher de** to triumph over, overcome

tripes [tʀip] *nfpl* (*CULIN*) tripe *sg*

triple [tʀipl] *adj* triple ♦ *nm*: **le ~ (de)** (*comparaison*) three times as much (as); **en ~ exemplaire** in triplicate; **tripler** *vi, vt* to triple, treble

triplés, -ées [tʀiple] *nm/fpl* triplets

tripoter [tʀipɔte] *vt* to fiddle with

triste [tʀist] *adj* sad; (*couleur, temps, jour-*née) dreary; (*péj*): **~ personnage/affaire** sorry individual/affair; **tristesse** *nf* sadness

trivial, e, -aux [tʀivjal, jo] *adj* coarse, crude; (*commun*) mundane

troc [tʀɔk] *nm* barter

troène [tʀɔɛn] *nm* privet

trognon [tʀɔɲɔ̃] *nm* (*de fruit*) core; (*de légume*) stalk

trois [tʀwa] *num* three; **troisième** *num* third; **trois quarts** *nmpl*: **les trois quarts de** three-quarters of

trombe [tʀɔ̃b] *nf*: **des ~s d'eau** a downpour; **en ~** like a whirlwind

trombone [tʀɔ̃bɔn] *nm* (*MUS*) trombone; (*de bureau*) paper clip

trompe [tʀɔ̃p] *nf* (*d'éléphant*) trunk; (*MUS*) trumpet, horn

tromper [tʀɔ̃pe] *vt* to deceive; (*vigilance, poursuivants*) to elude; **se ~** *vi* to make a mistake, be mistaken; **se ~ de voiture/ jour** to take the wrong car/get the day wrong; **se ~ de 3 cm/20 F** to be out by 3 cm/20 F; **tromperie** *nf* deception, trickery *no pl*

trompette [tʀɔ̃pɛt] *nf* trumpet; **en ~** (*nez*) turned-up

trompeur, -euse [tʀɔ̃pœʀ, øz] *adj* deceptive

tronc [tʀɔ̃] *nm* (*BOT, ANAT*) trunk; (*d'église*) collection box

tronçon [tʀɔ̃sɔ̃] *nm* section; **tronçonner** *vt* to saw up

trône [tʀon] *nm* throne

trop [tʀo] *adv* (*+vb*) too much; (*+adjectif adverbe*) too; **~ (nombreux)** too many; **~ peu (nombreux)** too few; **~ (souvent)** too often; **~ (longtemps)** (for) too long; **~ de** (*nombre*) too many; (*quantité*) too much; **de ~, en ~**: **des livres en ~** a few books too many; **du lait en ~** too much milk; **3 livres/3 F de ~** 3 books too many/3 F too much

tropical, e, -aux [tʀɔpikal, o] *adj* tropical

tropique [tʀɔpik] *nm* tropic

trop-plein [tʀoplɛ̃] *nm* (*tuyau*) overflow *ou*

outlet (pipe); (*liquide*) overflow

troquer [tʀɔke] *vt*: ~ **qch contre** to barter *ou* trade sth for; (*fig*) to swap sth for

trot [tʀo] *nm* trot; **trotter** *vi* to trot

trotteuse [tʀɔtøz] *nf* (sweep) second hand

trottinette [tʀɔtinɛt] *nf* (child's) scooter

trottoir [tʀɔtwaʀ] *nm* pavement; **faire le ~** (*péj*) to walk the streets; **~ roulant** moving walkway, travellator

trou [tʀu] *nm* hole; (*fig*) gap; (*COMM*) deficit; **~ d'air** air pocket; **~ d'ozone** ozone hole; **le ~ de la serrure** the keyhole; **~ de mémoire** blank, lapse of memory

troublant, e [tʀublɑ̃, ɑ̃t] *adj* disturbing

trouble [tʀubl] *adj* (*liquide*) cloudy; (*image, photo*) blurred; (*affaire*) shady, murky ♦ *nm* agitation; **~s** *nmpl* (*POL*) disturbances, troubles, unrest *sg*; (*MÉD*) trouble *sg*, disorders; **trouble-fête** *nm* spoilsport

troubler [tʀuble] *vt* to disturb; (*liquide*) to make cloudy; (*intriguer*) to bother; **se ~** *vi* (*personne*) to become flustered *ou* confused

trouer [tʀue] *vt* to make a hole (*ou* holes) in

trouille [tʀuj] (*fam*) *nf*: **avoir la ~** to be scared to death

troupe [tʀup] *nf* troop; **~ (de théâtre)** (theatrical) company

troupeau, x [tʀupo] *nm* (*de moutons*) flock; (*de vaches*) herd

trousse [tʀus] *nf* case, kit; (*d'écolier*) pencil case; **aux ~s de** (*fig*) on the heels *ou* tail of; **~ à outils** toolkit; **~ de toilette** toilet bag

trousseau, x [tʀuso] *nm* (*de mariée*) trousseau; **~ de clefs** bunch of keys

trouvaille [tʀuvaj] *nf* find

trouver [tʀuve] *vt* to find; (*rendre visite*): **aller/venir ~ qn** to go/come and see sb; **se ~** *vi* (*être*) to be; **je trouve que** I find *ou* think that; **~ à boire/critiquer** to find something to drink/criticize; **se ~ bien** to feel well; **se ~ mal** to pass out

truand [tʀyɑ̃] *nm* gangster; **truander** *vt*: **se faire truander** to be swindled

truc [tʀyk] *nm* (*astuce*) way, trick; (*de cinéma, prestidigitateur*) trick, effect; (*chose*) thing, thingumajig; **avoir le ~** to have the knack

truelle [tʀyɛl] *nf* trowel

truffe [tʀyf] *nf* truffle; (*nez*) nose

truffé, e [tʀyfe] *adj*: **~ de** (*fig*) peppered with; (*fautes*) riddled with; (*pièges*) bristling with

truie [tʀɥi] *nf* sow

truite [tʀɥit] *nf* trout *inv*

truquage [tʀykaʒ] *nm* special effects

truquer [tʀyke] *vt* (*élections, serrure, dés*) to fix

TSVP *sigle* (= *tournez svp*) PTO

TTC *sigle* (= *toutes taxes comprises*) inclusive of tax

tu[1] [ty] *pron* you

tu[2], **e** [ty] *pp de* **taire**

tuba [tyba] *nm* (*MUS*) tuba; (*SPORT*) snorkel

tube [tyb] *nm* tube; (*chanson*) hit

tuberculose [tybɛʀkyloz] *nf* tuberculosis

tuer [tɥe] *vt* to kill; **se ~** *vi* to be killed; (*suicide*) to kill o.s.; **tuerie** *nf* slaughter *no pl*

tue-tête [tytɛt]: **à ~-~** *adv* at the top of one's voice

tueur [tɥœʀ] *nm* killer; **~ à gages** hired killer

tuile [tɥil] *nf* tile; (*fam*) spot of bad luck, blow

tulipe [tylip] *nf* tulip

tuméfié, e [tymefje] *adj* puffed-up, swollen

tumeur [tymœʀ] *nf* growth, tumour

tumulte [tymylt] *nm* commotion; **tumultueux, -euse** *adj* stormy, turbulent

tunique [tynik] *nf* tunic

Tunisie [tynizi] *nf*: **la ~** Tunisia; **tunisien, ne** *adj* Tunisian ♦ *nm/f*: **Tunisien, ne** Tunisian

tunnel [tynɛl] *nm* tunnel; **le ~ sous la Manche** the Channel Tunnel

turbulences [tyʀbylɑ̃s] *nfpl* (*AVIAT*) turbulence *sg*

turbulent, e [tyʀbylɑ̃, ɑ̃t] *adj* boisterous,

unruly

turc, turque [tyʀk] *adj* Turkish ♦ *nm/f*: **T~, -que** Turk/Turkish woman ♦ *nm* (*LING*) Turkish

turf [tyʀf] *nm* racing; **turfiste** *nm/f* race-goer

Turquie [tyʀki] *nf*: **la ~** Turkey

turquoise [tyʀkwaz] *nf* turquoise ♦ *adj inv* turquoise

tus *etc* [ty] *vb voir* **taire**

tutelle [tytɛl] *nf* (*JUR*) guardianship; (*POL*) trusteeship; **sous la ~ de** (*fig*) under the supervision of

tuteur [tytœʀ] *nm* (*JUR*) guardian; (*de plante*) stake, support

tutoyer [tytwaje] *vt*: **~ qn** to address sb as "tu"

tuyau, x [tɥijo] *nm* pipe; (*flexible*) tube; (*fam*) tip; **~ d'arrosage** hosepipe; **~ d'échappement** exhaust pipe; **tuyauterie** *nf* piping *no pl*

TVA *sigle f* (= taxe à la valeur ajoutée) VAT

tympan [tɛ̃pɑ̃] *nm* (*ANAT*) eardrum

type [tip] *nm* type; (*fam*) chap, guy ♦ *adj* typical, classic

typé, e [tipe] *adj* ethnic

typique [tipik] *adj* typical

tyran [tiʀɑ̃] *nm* tyrant; **tyrannique** *adj* tyrannical

tzigane [dzigan] *adj* gipsy, tzigane

U, u

UEM *sigle f* (= union économique et monétaire) EMU

ulcère [ylsɛʀ] *nm* ulcer; **ulcérer** *vt* (*fig*) to sicken, appal

ultérieur, e [ylteʀjœʀ] *adj* later, subsequent; **remis à une date ~e** postponed to a later date; **ultérieurement** *adv* later, subsequently

ultime [yltim] *adj* final

ultra... [yltʀa] *préfixe*: **~moderne/-rapide** ultra-modern/-fast

---

MOT-CLÉ

un, une [œ̃, yn] *art indéf* a; (*devant voyelle*) an; **un garçon/vieillard** a boy/an old man; **une fille** a girl

♦ *pron* one; **l'un des meilleurs** one of the best; **l'un ..., l'autre** (the) one ..., the other; **les uns ..., les autres** some ..., others; **l'un et l'autre** both (of them); **l'un ou l'autre** either (of them); **l'un l'autre, les uns les autres** each other, one another; **pas un seul** not a single one; **un par un** one by one

♦ *num* one; **une pomme seulement** one apple only

---

unanime [ynanim] *adj* unanimous; **unanimité** *nf*: **à l'unanimité** unanimously

uni, e [yni] *adj* (*ton, tissu*) plain; (*surface*) smooth, even; (*famille*) close(-knit); (*pays*) united

unifier [ynifje] *vt* to unite, unify

uniforme [ynifɔʀm] *adj* uniform; (*surface, ton*) even ♦ *nm* uniform; **uniformiser** *vt* (*systèmes*) to standardize

union [ynjɔ̃] *nf* union; **~ de consommateurs** consumers' association; **U~ européenne** European Union; **U~ soviétique** Soviet Union

unique [ynik] *adj* (*seul*) only; (*exceptionnel*) unique; (*le même*): **un prix/système ~** a single price/system; **fils/fille ~** only son/daughter, only child; **sens ~** one-way street; **uniquement** *adv* only, solely; (*juste*) only, merely

unir [yniʀ] *vt* (*nations*) to unite; (*en mariage*) to unite, join together; **s'~** *vi* to unite; (*en mariage*) to be joined together

unitaire [yniteʀ] *adj*: **prix ~** unit price

unité [ynite] *nf* unit; (*harmonie, cohésion*) unity

univers [yniveʀ] *nm* universe; **universel, le** *adj* universal

universitaire [yniveʀsitɛʀ] *adj* university *cpd*; (*diplôme, études*) academic, university *cpd* ♦ *nm/f* academic

université [yniveʀsite] *nf* university

urbain, e [yʀbɛ̃, ɛn] *adj* urban, city *cpd*, town *cpd*; **urbanisme** *nm* town planning

urgence [yʀʒɑ̃s] *nf* urgency; (*MÉD etc*) emergency; **d'~** *adj* emergency *cpd* ♦ *adv* as a matter of urgency; **(service des) ~s** casualty

urgent, e [yʀʒɑ̃, ɑ̃t] *adj* urgent

urine [yʀin] *nf* urine; **urinoir** *nm* (public) urinal

urne [yʀn] *nf* (*électorale*) ballot box; (*vase*) urn

urticaire [yʀtikɛʀ] *nf* nettle rash

us [ys] *nmpl*: **~ et coutumes** (habits and) customs

USA *sigle mpl*: **les USA** the USA

usage [yzaʒ] *nm* (*emploi, utilisation*) use; (*coutume*) custom; **à l'~** with use; **à l'~ de** (*pour*) (for use of); **hors d'~** out of service; **à ~ interne** (*MÉD*) to be taken; **à ~ externe** (*MÉD*) for external use only; **usagé, e** *adj* (*usé*) worn; **usager, -ère** *nm/f* user

usé, e [yze] *adj* worn; (*banal: argument etc*) hackneyed

user [yze] *vt* (*outil*) to wear down; (*vêtement*) to wear out; (*matière*) to wear away; (*consommer: charbon etc*) to use; **s'~** *vi* (*tissu, vêtement*) to wear out; **~ de** (*moyen, procédé*) to use, employ; (*droit*) to exercise

usine [yzin] *nf* factory

usité, e [yzite] *adj* common

ustensile [ystɑ̃sil] *nm* implement; **~ de cuisine** kitchen utensil

usuel, le [yzɥɛl] *adj* everyday, common

usure [yzyʀ] *nf* wear

utérus [yteʀys] *nm* uterus, womb

utile [ytil] *adj* useful

utilisation [ytilizasjɔ̃] *nf* use

utiliser [ytilize] *vt* to use

utilitaire [ytilitɛʀ] *adj* utilitarian

utilité [ytilite] *nf* usefulness *no pl*; **de peu d'~** of little use *ou* help

utopie [ytɔpi] *nf* utopia

V, v

va [va] *vb voir* **aller**

vacance [vakɑ̃s] *nf* (*ADMIN*) vacancy; **~s** *nfpl* holiday(s *pl*), vacation *sg*; **les grandes ~s** the summer holidays; **prendre des/ses ~s** to take a holiday/one's holiday(s); **aller en ~s** to go on holiday; **vacancier, -ière** *nm/f* holiday-maker

vacant, e [vakɑ̃, ɑ̃t] *adj* vacant

vacarme [vakaʀm] *nm* (*bruit*) racket

vaccin [vaksɛ̃] *nm* vaccine; (*opération*) vaccination; **vaccination** *nf* vaccination; **vacciner** *vt* to vaccinate; **être vacciné contre qch** (*fam*) to be cured of sth

vache [vaʃ] *nf* (*ZOOL*) cow; (*cuir*) cowhide ♦ *adj* (*fam*) rotten, mean; **vachement** (*fam*) *adv* (*très*) really; (*pleuvoir, travailler*) a hell of a lot; **vacherie** *nf* (*action*) dirty trick; (*remarque*) nasty remark

vaciller [vasije] *vi* to sway, wobble; (*bougie, lumière*) to flicker; (*fig*) to be failing, falter

va-et-vient [vaevjɛ̃] *nm inv* (*de personnes, véhicules*) comings and goings *pl*, to-ings and fro-ings *pl*

vagabond [vagabɔ̃] *nm* (*rôdeur*) tramp, vagrant; (*voyageur*) wanderer; **vagabonder** *vi* to roam, wander

vagin [vaʒɛ̃] *nm* vagina

vague [vag] *nf* wave ♦ *adj* vague; (*regard*) faraway; (*manteau, robe*) loose(-fitting); (*quelconque*): **un ~ bureau/cousin** some office/cousin or other; **~ de fond** ground swell; **~ de froid** cold spell

vaillant, e [vajɑ̃, ɑ̃t] *adj* (*courageux*) gallant; (*robuste*) hale and hearty

vaille [vaj] *vb voir* **valoir**

vain, e [vɛ̃, vɛn] *adj* vain; **en ~** in vain

vaincre [vɛ̃kʀ] *vt* to defeat; (*fig*) to conquer, overcome; **vaincu, e** *nm/f* defeated party; **vainqueur** *nm* victor; (*SPORT*) winner

vais [vɛ] *vb voir* **aller**

vaisseau, x [veso] *nm* (*ANAT*) vessel; (*NA-VIG*) ship, vessel; **~ spatial** spaceship

vaisselier [vesəlje] *nm* dresser

vaisselle [vesɛl] *nf* (*service*) crockery; (*plats etc à laver*) (dirty) dishes *pl*; **faire la ~** to do the washing-up (*BRIT*) *ou* the dishes

val [val, vo] (*pl* **vaux** *ou* **~s**) *nm* valley

valable [valabl] *adj* valid; (*acceptable*) decent, worthwhile

valent *etc* [val] *vb voir* **valoir**

valet [valɛ] *nm* manservant; (*CARTES*) jack

valeur [valœR] *nf* (*gén*) value; (*mérite*) worth, merit; (*COMM: titre*) security; **mettre en ~** (*détail*) to highlight; (*objet décoratif*) to show off to advantage; **avoir de la ~** to be valuable; **sans ~** worthless; **prendre de la ~** to go up *ou* gain in value

valide [valid] *adj* (*en bonne santé*) fit; (*valable*) valid; **valider** *vt* to validate

valions [valjɔ̃] *vb voir* **valoir**

valise [valiz] *nf* (suit)case; **faire ses ~s** to pack one's bags

vallée [vale] *nf* valley

vallon [valɔ̃] *nm* small valley; **vallonné, e** *adj* hilly

valoir [valwaR] *vi* (*être valable*) to hold, apply ♦ *vt* (*prix, valeur, effort*) to be worth; (*causer*): **~ qch à qn** to earn sb sth; **se ~** *vi* to be of equal merit; (*péj*) to be two of a kind; **faire ~** (*droits, prérogatives*) to assert; **faire ~ que** to point out that; **à ~ sur** to be deducted from; **vaille que vaille** somehow or other; **cela ne me dit rien qui vaille** I don't like the look of it at all; **ce climat ne me vaut rien** this climate doesn't suit me; **~ le coup** *ou* **la peine** to be worth the trouble *ou* worth it; **~ mieux: il vaut mieux se taire** it's better to say nothing; **ça ne vaut rien** it's worthless; **que vaut ce candidat?** how good is this applicant?

valse [vals] *nf* waltz

valu, e [valy] *pp de* **valoir**

vandalisme [vɑ̃dalism] *nm* vandalism

vanille [vanij] *nf* vanilla

vanité [vanite] *nf* vanity; **vaniteux, -euse** *adj* vain, conceited

vanne [van] *nf* gate; (*fig*) joke

vannerie [vanRi] *nf* basketwork

vantard, e [vɑ̃taR, aRd] *adj* boastful

vanter [vɑ̃te] *vt* to speak highly of, praise; **se ~** *vi* to boast, brag; **se ~ de** to pride o.s. on; (*péj*) to boast of

vapeur [vapœR] *nf* steam; (*émanation*) vapour, fumes *pl*; **~s** *nfpl* (*bouffées*) vapours; **à ~** steam-powered, steam *cpd*; **cuit à la ~** steamed; **vaporeux, -euse** *adj* (*flou*) hazy, misty; (*léger*) filmy; **vaporisateur** *nm* spray; **vaporiser** *vt* (*parfum etc*) to spray

varappe [vaRap] *nf* rock climbing

vareuse [vaRøz] *nf* (*blouson*) pea jacket; (*d'uniforme*) tunic

variable [vaRjabl] *adj* variable; (*temps, humeur*) changeable; (*divers: résultats*) varied, various

varice [vaRis] *nf* varicose vein

varicelle [vaRisɛl] *nf* chickenpox

varié, e [vaRje] *adj* varied; (*divers*) various

varier [vaRje] *vi* to vary; (*temps, humeur*) to change ♦ *vt* to vary; **variété** *nf* variety; **variétés** *nfpl*: **spectacle/émission de variétés** variety show

variole [vaRjɔl] *nf* smallpox

vas [va] *vb voir* **aller**

vase [vaz] *nm* vase ♦ *nf* silt, mud; **vaseux, -euse** *adj* silty, muddy; (*fig: confus*) woolly, hazy; (: *fatigué*) woozy

vasistas [vazistas] *nm* fanlight

vaste [vast] *adj* vast, immense

vaudrai *etc* [vodre] *vb voir* **valoir**

vaurien, ne [voRjɛ̃, jɛn] *nm/f* good-for-nothing

vaut [vo] *vb voir* **valoir**

vautour [votuR] *nm* vulture

vautrer [votRe] *vb*: **se ~ dans/sur** to wallow in/sprawl on

vaux [vo] *nmpl de* **val** ♦ *vb voir* **valoir**

va-vite [vavit]: **à la ~-~** *adv* in a rush *ou* hurry

VDQS

i **VDQS** *(vin délimité de qualité supérieure) is the second highest French wine classification after AOC, indicating high-quality wine from an approved regional vineyard. It is followed by vin de pays. Vin de table or vin ordinaire is table wine of unspecified origin, often blended.*

---

veau, x [vo] *nm* (ZOOL) calf; (CULIN) veal; *(peau)* calfskin

vécu, e [veky] *pp de* **vivre**

vedette [vədɛt] *nf (artiste etc)* star; *(canot)* motor boat; *(police)* launch

végétal, e, -aux [veʒetal, o] *adj* vegetable ♦ *nm* vegetable, plant; **végétalien, ne** *adj, nm/f* vegan

végétarien, ne [veʒetaʀjɛ̃, jɛn] *adj, nm/f* vegetarian

végétation [veʒetasjɔ̃] *nf* vegetation; **~s** *nfpl* (MÉD) adenoids

véhicule [veikyl] *nm* vehicle; **~ utilitaire** commercial vehicle

veille [vɛj] *nf (état)* wakefulness; *(jour):* **la ~ (de)** the day before; **la ~ au soir** the previous evening; **à la ~ de** on the eve of; **la ~ de Noël** Christmas Eve; **la ~ du jour de l'An** New Year's Eve

veillée [veje] *nf (soirée)* evening; *(réunion)* evening gathering; **~ (funèbre)** wake

veiller [veje] *vi* to stay up ♦ *vt (malade, mort)* to watch over, sit up with; **~ à** to attend to, see to; **~ à ce que** to make sure that; **~ sur** to watch over; **veilleur** *nm:* **veilleur de nuit** night watchman; **veilleuse** *nf (lampe)* night light; (AUTO) sidelight; *(flamme)* pilot light

veinard, e [vɛnaʀ, aʀd] *nm/f* lucky devil

veine [vɛn] *nf* (ANAT, *du bois etc)* vein; *(filon)* vein, seam; *(fam: chance):* **avoir de la ~** to be lucky

véliplanchiste [veliplɑ̃ʃist] *nm/f* windsurfer

vélo [velo] *nm* bike, cycle; **faire du ~** to go cycling; **~ tout-terrain** mountain bike; **vélomoteur** *nm* moped

velours [v(ə)luʀ] *nm* velvet; **~ côtelé** corduroy; **velouté, e** *adj* velvety ♦ *nm:* **velouté de tomates** cream of tomato soup

velu, e [vəly] *adj* hairy

venais *etc* [vənɛ] *vb voir* **venir**

venaison [vənɛzɔ̃] *nf* venison

vendange [vɑ̃dɑ̃ʒ] *nf (aussi:* **~s)** grape harvest; **vendanger** *vi* to harvest the grapes

vendeur, -euse [vɑ̃dœʀ, øz] *nm/f* shop assistant ♦ *nm* (JUR) vendor, seller; **~ de journaux** newspaper seller

vendre [vɑ̃dʀ] *vt* to sell; **~ qch à qn** to sell sb sth; **"à ~"** "for sale"

vendredi [vɑ̃dʀədi] *nm* Friday; **V~ saint** Good Friday

vénéneux, -euse [venenø, øz] *adj* poisonous

vénérien, ne [veneʀjɛ̃, jɛn] *adj* venereal

vengeance [vɑ̃ʒɑ̃s] *nf* vengeance *no pl*, revenge *no pl*

venger [vɑ̃ʒe] *vt* to avenge; **se ~** *vi* to avenge o.s.; **se ~ de qch** to avenge o.s. for sth, take one's revenge for sth; **se ~ de qn** to take revenge on sb; **se ~ sur** to take revenge on

venimeux, -euse [vənimø, øz] *adj* poisonous, venomous; *(fig: haineux)* venomous, vicious

venin [vənɛ̃] *nm* venom, poison

venir [v(ə)niʀ] *vi* to come; **~ de** to come from; **~ de faire: je viens d'y aller/de le voir** I've just been there/seen him; **s'il vient à pleuvoir** if it should rain; **j'en viens à croire que** I have come to believe that; **faire ~** *(docteur)* to call (out)

vent [vɑ̃] *nm* wind; **il y a du ~** it's windy; **c'est du ~** it's all hot air; **au ~** to windward; **sous le ~** to leeward; **avoir le ~ debout/arrière** to head into the wind/ have the wind astern; **dans le ~** *(fam)* trendy

vente [vɑ̃t] *nf* sale; **la ~** *(activité)* selling; *(secteur)* sales *pl*; **mettre en ~** *(produit)* to put on sale; (*maison, objet personnel*) to put up for sale; **~ aux enchères** auction sale; **~ de charité** jumble sale

venteux, -euse [vɑ̃tø, øz] *adj* windy

ventilateur [vɑ̃tilatœʀ] *nm* fan

ventiler [vɑ̃tile] *vt* to ventilate

ventouse [vɑ̃tuz] *nf* (*de caoutchouc*) suction pad

ventre [vɑ̃tʀ] *nm* (ANAT) stomach; (*légèrement péj*) belly; (*utérus*) womb; **avoir mal au ~** to have stomach ache (BRIT) *ou* a stomach ache (US)

ventriloque [vɑ̃tʀilɔk] *nm/f* ventriloquist

venu, e [v(ə)ny] *pp de* **venir** ♦ *adj*: **bien ~** timely; **mal ~** out of place; **être mal ~ à** *ou* **de faire** to have no grounds for doing, be in no position to do

ver [vɛʀ] *nm* worm; (*des fruits etc*) maggot; (*du bois*) woodworm *no pl*; *voir aussi* **vers**; **~ à soie** silkworm; **~ de terre** earthworm; **~ luisant** glow-worm; **~ solitaire** tapeworm

verbaliser [vɛʀbalize] *vi* (POLICE) to book *ou* report an offender

verbe [vɛʀb] *nm* verb

verdâtre [vɛʀdɑtʀ] *adj* greenish

verdict [vɛʀdik(t)] *nm* verdict

verdir [vɛʀdiʀ] *vi, vt* to turn green; **verdure** *nf* greenery

véreux, -euse [veʀø, øz] *adj* worm-eaten; (*malhonnête*) shady, corrupt

verge [vɛʀʒ] *nf* (ANAT) penis

verger [vɛʀʒe] *nm* orchard

verglacé, e [vɛʀɡlase] *adj* icy, iced-over

verglas [vɛʀɡla] *nm* (black) ice

vergogne [vɛʀɡɔɲ]: **sans ~** *adv* shamelessly

véridique [veʀidik] *adj* truthful

vérification [veʀifikasjɔ̃] *nf* (*action*) checking *no pl*; (*contrôle*) check

vérifier [veʀifje] *vt* to check; (*corroborer*) to confirm, bear out

véritable [veʀitabl] *adj* real; (*ami, amour*) true

vérité [veʀite] *nf* truth; **en ~** really, actually

vermeil, le [vɛʀmɛj] *adj* ruby red

vermine [vɛʀmin] *nf* vermin *pl*

vermoulu, e [vɛʀmuly] *adj* worm-eaten

verni, e [vɛʀni] *adj* (*fam*) lucky; **cuir ~** patent leather

vernir [vɛʀniʀ] *vt* (*bois, tableau, ongles*) to varnish; (*poterie*) to glaze

vernis *nm* (*enduit*) varnish; glaze; (*fig*) veneer; **~ à ongles** nail polish *ou* varnish; **vernissage** *nm* (*d'une exposition*) preview

vérole [veʀɔl] *nf* (*variole*) smallpox

verrai *etc* [veʀe] *vb voir* **voir**

verre [vɛʀ] *nm* glass; (*de lunettes*) lens *sg*, **boire** *ou* **prendre un ~** to have a drink; **~ dépoli** frosted glass; **~s de contact** contact lenses; **verrerie** *nf* (*fabrique*) glassworks *sg*; (*activité*) glass-making; (*objets*) glassware; **verrière** *nf* (*paroi vitrée*) glass wall; (*toit vitré*) glass roof

verrons *etc* [veʀɔ̃] *vb voir* **voir**

verrou [veʀu] *nm* (*targette*) bolt; **mettre qn sous les ~s** to put sb behind bars; **verrouillage** *nm* locking; **verrouillage centralisé** central locking; **verrouiller** *vt* (*porte*) to bolt; (*ordinateur*) to lock

verrue [veʀy] *nf* wart

vers [vɛʀ] *nm* line ♦ *nmpl* (*poésie*) verse *sg* ♦ *prép* (*en direction de*) toward(s); (*près de*) around (about); (*temporel*) about, around

versant [vɛʀsɑ̃] *nm* slopes *pl*, side

versatile [vɛʀsatil] *adj* fickle, changeable

verse [vɛʀs]: **à ~** *adv*: **il pleut à ~** it's pouring (with rain)

Verseau [vɛʀso] *nm*: **le ~** Aquarius

versement [vɛʀsəmɑ̃] *nm* payment; **en 3 ~s** in 3 instalments

verser [vɛʀse] *vt* (*liquide, grains*) to pour; (*larmes, sang*) to shed; (*argent*) to pay ♦ *vi* (*véhicule*) to overturn; (*fig*): **~ dans** to lapse into

verset [vɛʀse] *nm* verse

version [vɛʀsjɔ̃] *nf* version; (SCOL) translation (*into the mother tongue*); **film en originale** film in the original language

verso [vɛʀso] *nm* back; **voir au ~** see over(leaf)

vert, e [vɛʀ, vɛʀt] *adj* green; *(vin)* young; *(vigoureux)* sprightly ♦ *nm* green

vertèbre [vɛʀtɛbʀ] *nf* vertebra

vertement [vɛʀtəmɑ̃] *adv (réprimander)* sharply

vertical, e, -aux [vɛʀtikal, o] *adj* vertical; **verticale** *nf* vertical; **à la verticale** vertically; **verticalement** *adv* vertically

vertige [vɛʀtiʒ] *nm (peur du vide)* vertigo; *(étourdissement)* dizzy spell; *(fig)* fever; **vertigineux, -euse** *adj* breathtaking

vertu [vɛʀty] *nf* virtue; **en ~ de** in accordance with; **vertueux, -euse** *adj* virtuous

verve [vɛʀv] *nf* witty eloquence; **être en ~** to be in brilliant form

verveine [vɛʀvɛn] *nf (BOT)* verbena, vervain; *(infusion)* verbena tea

vésicule [vezikyl] *nf* vesicle; **~ biliaire** gall-bladder

vessie [vesi] *nf* bladder

veste [vɛst] *nf* jacket; **~ droite / croisée** single-/double-breasted jacket

vestiaire [vɛstjɛʀ] *nm (au théâtre etc)* cloakroom; *(de stade etc)* changing-room *(BRIT)*, locker-room *(US)*

vestibule [vɛstibyl] *nm* hall

vestige [vɛstiʒ] *nm* relic; *(fig)* vestige; **~s** *nmpl (de ville)* remains

vestimentaire [vɛstimɑ̃tɛʀ] *adj (détail)* of dress; *(élégance)* sartorial; **dépenses ~s** clothing expenses

veston [vɛstɔ̃] *nm* jacket

vêtement [vɛtmɑ̃] *nm* garment, item of clothing; **~s** *nmpl* clothes

vétérinaire [veteʀinɛʀ] *nm/f* vet, veterinary surgeon

vêtir [vetiʀ] *vt* to clothe, dress

veto [veto] *nm* veto; **opposer un ~ à** to veto

vêtu, e [vety] *pp de* **vêtir**

vétuste [vetyst] *adj* ancient, timeworn

veuf, veuve [vœf, vœv] *adj* widowed ♦ *nm* widower

veuille [vœj] *vb voir* **vouloir**

veuillez [vœje] *vb voir* **vouloir**

veule [vøl] *adj* spineless

veuve [vœv] *nf* widow

veux [vø] *vb voir* **vouloir**

vexant, e [vɛksɑ̃, ɑ̃t] *adj (contrariant)* annoying; *(blessant)* hurtful

vexation [vɛksasjɔ̃] *nf* humiliation

vexer [vɛkse] *vt*: **~ qn** to hurt sb's feelings; **se ~** *vi* to be offended

viable [vjabl] *adj* viable; *(économie, industrie etc)* sustainable

viaduc [vjadyk] *nm* viaduct

viager, -ère [vjaʒe, ɛʀ] *adj*: **rente viagère** life annuity

viande [vjɑ̃d] *nf* meat

vibrer [vibʀe] *vi* to vibrate; *(son, voix)* to be vibrant; *(fig)* to be stirred; **faire ~** to *(cause to)* vibrate; *(fig)* to stir, thrill

vice [vis] *nm* vice; *(défaut)* fault ♦ *préfixe*: **~...** vice-; **~ de forme** legal flaw *ou* irregularity

vichy [viʃi] *nm (toile)* gingham

vicié, e [visje] *adj (air)* polluted, tainted; *(JUR)* invalidated

vicieux, -euse [visjø, jøz] *adj (pervers)* lecherous; *(rétif)* unruly ♦ *nm/f* lecher

vicinal, e, -aux [visinal, o] *adj*: **chemin ~** by-road, byway

victime [viktim] *nf* victim; *(d'accident)* casualty

victoire [viktwaʀ] *nf* victory

victuailles [viktɥaj] *nfpl* provisions

vidange [vidɑ̃ʒ] *nf (d'un fossé, réservoir)* emptying; *(AUTO)* oil change; *(de lavabo: bonde)* waste outlet; **~s** *nfpl (matières)* sewage *sg*; **vidanger** *vt* to empty

vide [vid] *adj* empty ♦ *nm (PHYSIQUE)* vacuum; *(espace)* (empty) space, gap; *(futilité, néant)* void; **avoir peur du ~** to be afraid of heights; **emballé sous ~** vacuum packed; **à ~** *(sans occupants)* empty; *(sans charge)* unladen

vidéo [video] *nf* video ♦ *adj*: **cassette ~** video cassette; **jeu ~** video game; **vidéo-clip** *nm* music video; **vidéoclub** *nm* video shop

vide-ordures [vidɔʀdyʀ] *nm inv* (rubbish)

chute

vidéothèque [videɔtɛk] *nf* video library

vide-poches [vidpɔʃ] *nm inv* tidy; (*AUTO*) glove compartment

vider [vide] *vt* to empty; (*CULIN: volaille, poisson*) to gut, clean out; **se ~** *vi* to empty; **~ les lieux** to quit *ou* vacate the premises; **videur** *nm* (*de boîte de nuit*) bouncer

vie [vi] *nf* life; **être en ~** to be alive; **sans ~** lifeless; **à ~** for life

vieil [vjɛj] *adj m voir* **vieux**; **vieillard** *nm* old man; **les vieillards** old people, the elderly; **vieille** *adj, nf voir* **vieux**; **vieilleries** *nfpl* old things; **vieillesse** *nf* old age; **vieillir** *vi* (*prendre de l'âge*) to grow old; (*population, vin*) to age; (*doctrine, auteur*) to become dated ♦ *vt* to age; **vieillissement** *nm* growing old; ageing

Vienne [vjɛn] *nf* Vienna

viens [vjɛ̃] *vb voir* **venir**

vierge [vjɛʀʒ] *adj* virgin; (*page*) clean, blank ♦ *nf* virgin; (*signe*): **la V~** Virgo

Vietnam, Viet-Nam [vjɛtnam] *nm* Vietnam; **vietnamien, ne** *adj* Vietnamese ♦ *nm/f*: **Vietnamien, ne** Vietnamese

vieux (vieil), vieille [vjø, vjɛj] *adj* old ♦ *nm/f* old man (woman) ♦ *nmpl* old people; **mon ~/ma vieille** (*fam*) old man/girl; **prendre un coup de ~** to put years on; **vieille fille** spinster; **~ garçon** bachelor; **~ jeu** *adj inv* old-fashioned

vif, vive [vif, viv] *adj* (*animé*) lively; (*alerte, brusque, aigu*) sharp; (*lumière, couleur*) bright; (*air*) crisp; (*vent, émotion*) keen; (*fort: regret, déception*) great, deep; (*vivant*): **brûlé ~** burnt alive; **de vive voix** personally; **avoir l'esprit ~** to be quick-witted; **piquer qn au ~** to cut sb to the quick; **à ~** (*plaie*) open; **avoir les nerfs à ~** to be on edge

vigne [viɲ] *nf* (*plante*) vine; (*plantation*) vineyard; **vigneron** *nm* wine grower

vignette [viɲɛt] *nf* (*ADMIN*) ≈ (road) tax disc (*BRIT*), ≈ license plate sticker (*US*); (*de médicament*) price label (*used for reimburse-*

ment)

vignoble [viɲɔbl] *nm* (*plantation*) vineyard; (*vignes d'une région*) vineyards *pl*

vigoureux, -euse [viguʀø, øz] *adj* vigorous, robust

vigueur [vigœʀ] *nf* vigour; **entrer en ~** to come into force; **en ~** current

vil, e [vil] *adj* vile, base

vilain, e [vilɛ̃, ɛn] *adj* (*laid*) ugly; (*affaire, blessure*) nasty; (*pas sage: enfant*) naughty

villa [vila] *nf* (*detached*) house; **~ en multipropriété** time-share villa

village [vilaʒ] *nm* village; **villageois, e** *adj* village *cpd* ♦ *nm/f* villager

ville [vil] *nf* town; (*importante*) city; (*administration*): **la ~** ≈ the Corporation; ≈ the (town) council; **~ d'eaux** spa

villégiature [vi(l)leʒjatyʀ] *nf* holiday; (*lieu de*) **~** (holiday) resort

vin [vɛ̃] *nm* wine; **avoir le ~ gai** to get happy after a few drinks; **~ d'honneur** reception (*with wine and snacks*); **~ de pays** local wine; **~ ordinaire** table wine

vinaigre [vinɛgʀ] *nm* vinegar; **vinaigrette** *nf* vinaigrette, French dressing

vindicatif, -ive [vɛ̃dikatif, iv] *adj* vindictive

vineux, -euse [vinø, øz] *adj* win(e)y

vingt [vɛ̃] *num* twenty; **vingtaine** *nf*: **une vingtaine (de)** about twenty, twenty or so; **vingtième** *num* twentieth

vinicole [vinikɔl] *adj* wine *cpd*, winegrowing

vins *etc* [vɛ̃] *vb voir* **venir**

vinyle [vinil] *nm* vinyl

viol [vjɔl] *nm* (*d'une femme*) rape; (*d'un lieu sacré*) violation

violacé, e [vjɔlase] *adj* purplish, mauvish

violemment [vjɔlamɑ̃] *adv* violently

violence [vjɔlɑ̃s] *nf* violence

violent, e [vjɔlɑ̃, ɑ̃t] *adj* violent; (*remède*) drastic

violer [vjɔle] *vt* (*femme*) to rape; (*sépulture, loi, traité*) to violate

violet, te [vjɔlɛ, ɛt] *adj, nm* purple, mauve; **violette** *nf* (*fleur*) violet

violon [vjɔlɔ̃] *nm* violin; (*fam: prison*) lock-up; **~ d'Ingres** hobby; **violoncelle** *nm* cello; **violoniste** *nm/f* violinist

vipère [vipɛʀ] *nf* viper, adder

virage [viʀaʒ] *nm* (*d'un véhicule*) turn; (*d'une route, piste*) bend

virée [viʀe] *nf* trip; (*à pied*) walk; (*longue*) walking tour; (*dans les cafés*) tour

virement [viʀmɑ̃] *nm* (COMM) transfer

virent [viʀ] *vb voir* **voir**

virer [viʀe] *vt* (COMM): **~ qch (sur)** to transfer sth (into); (*fam: expulser*): **~ qn** to kick sb out ♦ *vi* to turn; (CHIMIE) to change colour; **~ de bord** to tack

virevolter [viʀvɔlte] *vi* to twirl around

virgule [viʀgyl] *nf* comma; (MATH) point

viril, e [viʀil] *adj* (*propre à l'homme*) masculine; (*énergique, courageux*) manly, virile

virtuel, le [viʀtɥɛl] *adj* potential; (*théorique*) virtual

virtuose [viʀtɥoz] *nm/f* (MUS) virtuoso; (*gén*) master

virus [viʀys] *nm* virus

vis[1] [vi] *vb voir* **voir**; **vivre**

vis[2] [vi] *nf* screw

visa [viza] *nm* (*sceau*) stamp; (*validation de passeport*) visa

visage [vizaʒ] *nm* face

vis-à-vis [vizavi] *prép*: **~-~-~ de qn** to(wards) sb; **en ~-~-~** facing each other

viscéral, e, -aux [viseʀal, o] *adj* (*fig*) deep-seated, deep-rooted

visées [vize] *nfpl* (*intentions*) designs

viser [vize] *vi* to aim ♦ *vt* to aim at; (*concerner*) to be aimed *ou* directed at; (*apposer un visa sur*) to stamp, visa; **~ à qch/faire** to aim at sth/at doing *ou* to do; **viseur** *nm* (*d'arme*) sights *pl*; (PHOTO) view-finder

visibilité [vizibilite] *nf* visibility

visible [vizibl] *adj* visible; (*disponible*): **est-il ~?** can he see me?, will he see visitors?

visière [vizjɛʀ] *nf* (*de casquette*) peak; (*qui s'attache*) eyeshade

vision [vizjɔ̃] *nf* vision; (*sens*) (eye)sight, vision; (*fait de voir*): **la ~ de** the sight of; **vi-sionneuse** *nf* viewer

visite [vizit] *nf* visit; **~ médicale** medical examination; **~ accompagnée** *ou* **guidée** guided tour; **faire une ~ à qn** to call on sb, pay sb a visit; **rendre ~ à qn** to visit sb, pay sb a visit; **être en ~ (chez qn)** to be visiting (sb); **avoir de la ~** to have visitors; **heures de ~** (*hôpital, prison*) visiting hours

visiter [vizite] *vt* to visit; **visiteur, -euse** *nm/f* visitor

vison [vizɔ̃] *nm* mink

visser [vise] *vt*: **~ qch** (*fixer, serrer*) to screw sth on

visuel, le [vizɥɛl] *adj* visual

vit [vi] *vb voir* **voir**; **vivre**

vital, e, -aux [vital, o] *adj* vital

vitamine [vitamin] *nf* vitamin

vite [vit] *adv* (*rapidement*) quickly, fast; (*sans délai*) quickly; (*sous peu*) soon; **~!** quick!; **faire ~** to be quick; **le temps passe ~** time flies

vitesse [vitɛs] *nf* speed; (AUTO: *dispositif*) gear; **prendre de la ~** to pick up *ou* gather speed; **à toute ~** at full *ou* top speed; **en ~** (*rapidement*) quickly; (*en hâte*) in a hurry

viticole [vitikɔl] *adj* wine *cpd*, wine-growing; **viticulteur** *nm* wine grower

vitrage [vitʀaʒ] *nm*: **double ~** double glazing

vitrail, -aux [vitʀaj, o] *nm* stained-glass window

vitre [vitʀ] *nf* (*window*) pane; (*de portière, voiture*) window; **vitré, e** *adj* glass *cpd*; **vitrer** *vt* to glaze; **vitreux, -euse** *adj* (*terne*) glassy

vitrine [vitʀin] *nf* (*shop*) window; (*petite armoire*) display cabinet; **en ~** in the window; **~ publicitaire** display case, show-case

vivable [vivabl] *adj* (*personne*) livable-with; (*maison*) fit to live in

vivace [vivas] *adj* (*arbre, plante*) hardy; (*fig*) indestructible, inveterate

vivacité [vivasite] *nf* liveliness, vivacity

vivant, e [vivã, ãt] *adj* (*qui vit*) living, alive; (*animé*) lively; (*preuve, exemple*) living ♦ *nm*: **du ~ de qn** in sb's lifetime; **les ~s** the living

vive [viv] *adj voir* **vif** ♦ *vb voir* **vivre** ♦ *excl*: **~ le roi!** long live the king!; **vivement** *adv* deeply ♦ *excl*: **vivement les vacances!** roll on the holidays!

vivier [vivje] *nm* (*étang*) fish tank; (*réservoir*) fishpond

vivifiant, e [vivifjã, jãt] *adj* invigorating

vivions [vivjõ] *vb voir* **vivre**

vivoter [vivɔte] *vi* (*personne*) to scrape a living, get by; (*fig: affaire etc*) to struggle along

vivre [vivʀ] *vi, vt* to live; (*période*) to live through; **~ de** to live on; **il vit encore** he is still alive; **se laisser ~** to take life as it comes; **ne plus ~** (*être anxieux*) to live on one's nerves; **il a vécu** (*eu une vie aventureuse*) he has seen life; **être facile à ~** to be easy to get on with; **faire ~ qn** (*pourvoir à sa subsistance*) to provide (a living) for sb; **vivres** *nmpl* provisions, food supplies

vlan [vlã] *excl* wham!, bang!

VO [veo] *nf*: **film en ~** film in the original version; **en ~ sous-titrée** in the original version with subtitles

vocable [vɔkabl] *nm* term

vocabulaire [vɔkabylɛʀ] *nm* vocabulary

vocation [vɔkasjõ] *nf* vocation, calling

vociférer [vɔsifeʀe] *vi, vt* to scream

vœu, x [vø] *nm* wish; (*promesse*) vow; **faire ~ de** to take a vow of; **tous nos ~x de bonne année, meilleurs ~x** best wishes for the New Year

vogue [vɔg] *nf* fashion, vogue

voguer [vɔge] *vi* to sail

voici [vwasi] *prép* (*pour introduire, désigner*) here is +*sg*, here are +*pl*; **et ~ que ...** and now it (*ou* he) ...; *voir aussi* **voilà**

voie [vwa] *nf* way; (*RAIL*) track, line; (*AUTO*) lane; **être en bonne ~** to be going well; **mettre qn sur la ~** to put sb on the right track; **pays en ~ de développe-**ment developing country; **être en ~ d'achèvement/de rénovation** to be nearing completion/in the process of renovation; **par ~ buccale** *ou* **orale** orally; **à ~ étroite** narrow-gauge; **~ d'eau** (*NAVIG*) leak; **~ de garage** (*RAIL*) siding; **~ ferrée** track; railway line; **la ~ publique** the public highway

voilà [vwala] *prép* (*en désignant*) there is +*sg*, there are +*pl*; **les ~** *ou* **voici** there they are; **en ~** *ou* **voici un** here's one, there's one; **voici mon frère et ~ ma sœur** this is my brother and that's my sister; **~** *ou* **voici deux ans** two years ago; **~** *ou* **voici deux ans que** it's two years since; **et ~!** there we are!; **~ tout** that's all; **~** *ou* **voici** (*en offrant etc*) there *ou* here you are; **tiens! ~ Paul** look! there's Paul

voile [vwal] *nm* veil; (*tissu léger*) net ♦ *nf* sail; (*sport*) sailing; **voiler** *vt* to veil; (*fausser: roue*) to buckle; (: *bois*) to warp; **se voiler** *vi* (*lune, regard*) to mist over; (*voix*) to become husky; (*roue, disque*) to buckle; (*planche*) to warp; **voilier** *nm* sailing ship; (*de plaisance*) sailing boat; **voilure** *nf* (*de voilier*) sails *pl*

voir [vwaʀ] *vi, vt* to see; **se ~** *vt* (*être visible*) to show; (*se fréquenter*) to see each other; (*se produire*) to happen; **se ~ critiquer/transformer** to be criticized/transformed; **cela se voit** (*c'est visible*) that's obvious, it shows; **faire ~ qch à qn** to show sb sth; **en faire ~ à qn** (*fig*) to give sb a hard time; **ne pas pouvoir ~ qn** not to be able to stand sb; **voyons!** let's see now; (*indignation etc*) come on!; **avoir quelque chose à ~ avec** to have something to do with

voire [vwaʀ] *adv* even

voisin, e [vwazɛ̃, in] *adj* (*proche*) neighbouring; (*contigu*) next; (*ressemblant*) connected ♦ *nm/f* neighbour; **voisinage** *nm* (*proximité*) proximity; (*environs*) vicinity; (*quartier, voisins*) neighbourhood

voiture [vwatyʀ] *nf* car; (*wagon*) coach,

carriage; **~ de course** racing car; **~ de sport** sports car

voix [vwa] *nf* voice; (*POL*) vote; **à haute ~** aloud; **à ~ basse** in a low voice; **à 2/4 ~** (*MUS*) in 2/4 parts; **avoir ~ au chapitre** to have a say in the matter

vol [vɔl] *nm* (*d'oiseau, d'avion*) flight; (*larcin*) theft; **~ régulier** scheduled flight; **à ~ d'oiseau** as the crow flies; **au ~: attraper qch au ~** to catch sth as it flies past; **en ~** in flight; **~ à main armée** armed robbery; **~ à voile** gliding; **~ libre** hang-gliding

volage [vɔlaʒ] *adj* fickle

volaille [vɔlaj] *nf* (*oiseaux*) poultry *pl*; (*viande*) poultry *no pl*; (*oiseau*) fowl

volant, e [vɔlã, ãt] *adj voir* **feuille** *etc*
♦ *nm* (*d'automobile*) (steering) wheel; (*de commande*) wheel; (*objet lancé*) shuttle-cock; (*bande de tissu*) flounce

volcan [vɔlkã] *nm* volcano

volée [vɔle] *nf* (*TENNIS*) volley; **à la ~: rattraper à la ~** to catch in mid-air; **à toute ~** (*sonner les cloches*) vigorously; (*lancer un projectile*) with full force; **~ de coups/de flèches** volley of blows/arrows

voler [vɔle] *vi* (*avion, oiseau, fig*) to fly; (*voleur*) to steal ♦ *vt* (*objet*) to steal; (*personne*) to rob; **~ qch à qn** to steal sth from sb; **il ne l'a pas volé!** he asked for it!

volet [vɔlɛ] *nm* (*de fenêtre*) shutter; (*de feuillet, document*) section

voleur, -euse [vɔlœʀ, øz] *nm/f* thief
♦ *adj* thieving; **"au ~!"** "stop thief!"

volière [vɔljɛʀ] *nf* aviary

volley [vɔlɛ] *nm* volleyball

volontaire [vɔlɔ̃tɛʀ] *adj* (*acte, enrôlement, prisonnier*) voluntary; (*oubli*) intentional; (*caractère, personne: décidé*) self-willed
♦ *nm/f* volunteer

volonté [vɔlɔ̃te] *nf* (*faculté de vouloir*) will; (*énergie, fermeté*) will(power); (*souhait, désir*) wish; **à ~** as much as one likes; **bonne ~** goodwill, willingness; **mauvaise ~** lack of goodwill, unwillingness

volontiers [vɔlɔ̃tje] *adv* (*avec plaisir*) willingly, gladly; (*habituellement, souvent*) readily, willingly; **voulez-vous boire quelque chose? - ~!** would you like something to drink? - yes, please!

volt [vɔlt] *nm* volt

volte-face [vɔltəfas] *nf inv*: **faire ~-~** to turn round

voltige [vɔltiʒ] *nf* (*ÉQUITATION*) trick riding; (*au cirque*) acrobatics *sg*; **voltiger** *vi* to flutter (about)

volubile [vɔlybil] *adj* voluble

volume [vɔlym] *nm* volume; (*GÉOM: solide*) solid; **volumineux, -euse** *adj* voluminous, bulky

volupté [vɔlypte] *nf* sensual delight *ou* pleasure

vomi [vɔmi] *nm* vomit; **vomir** *vi* to vomit, be sick ♦ *vt* to vomit, bring up; (*fig*) to belch forth, spew out; (*exécrer*) to loathe, abhor; **vomissements** *nmpl*: **être pris de vomissements** to (suddenly) start vomiting

vont [vɔ̃] *vb voir* **aller**

vorace [vɔʀas] *adj* voracious

vos [vo] *adj voir* **votre**

vote [vɔt] *nm* vote; **~ par correspondance/procuration** postal/proxy vote; **voter** *vi* to vote ♦ *vt* (*projet de loi*) to vote for; (*loi, réforme*) to pass

votre [vɔtʀ] (*pl* **vos**) *adj* your

vôtre [votʀ] *pron*: **le ~, la ~, les ~s** yours; **les ~s** (*fig*) your family *ou* folks; **à la ~** (*toast*) your (good) health!

voudrai *etc* [vudʀe] *vb voir* **vouloir**

voué, e [vwe] *adj*: **~ à** doomed to

vouer [vwe] *vt*: **~ qch à** (*Dieu, un saint*) to dedicate sth to; **~ sa vie à** (*étude, cause etc*) to devote one's life to; **~ une amitié éternelle à qn** to vow undying friendship to sb

---

MOT-CLÉ

vouloir [vulwaʀ] *nm*: **le bon vouloir de qn** sb's goodwill; sb's pleasure
♦ *vt* **1** (*exiger, désirer*) to want; **vouloir**

faire/que qn fasse to want to do/sb to do; **voulez-vous du thé?** would you like *ou* do you want some tea?; **que me veut-il?** what does he want with me?; **sans le vouloir** (*involontairement*) without meaning to, unintentionally; **je voudrais ceci/faire** I would *ou* I'd like this/to do **2** (*consentir*): **je veux bien** (*bonne volonté*) I'll be happy to; (*concession*) fair enough, that's fine; **oui, si on veut** (*en quelque sorte*) yes, if you like; **veuillez attendre** please wait; **veuillez agréer ...** (*formule épistolaire*) yours faithfully **3: en vouloir à qn** to bear sb a grudge; **s'en vouloir (de)** to be annoyed with o.s. (for); **il en veut à mon argent** he's after my money **4: vouloir de: l'entreprise ne veut plus de lui** the firm doesn't want him any more; **elle ne veut pas de son aide** she doesn't want his help **5: vouloir dire** to mean

voulu, e [vuly] *adj* (*requis*) required, requisite; (*délibéré*) deliberate, intentional; *voir aussi* **vouloir**

vous [vu] *pron* you; (*objet indirect*) (to) you; (*réfléchi*: *sg*) yourself; (: *pl*) yourselves; (*réciproque*) each other; **~-même** yourself; **~-mêmes** yourselves

voûte [vut] *nf* vault; **voûter: se voûter** *vi* (*dos, personne*) to become stooped

vouvoyer [vuvwaje] *vt*: **~ qn** to address sb as "vous"

voyage [vwajaʒ] *nm* journey, trip; (*fait de ~r*): **le ~** travel(ling); **partir/être en ~** to go off/be away on a journey *ou* trip; **faire bon ~** to have a good journey; **~ d'agrément/d'affaires** pleasure/business trip; **~ de noces** honeymoon; **~ organisé** package tour

voyager [vwajaʒe] *vi* to travel; **voyageur, -euse** *nm/f* traveller; (*passager*) passenger

voyant, e [vwajɑ̃, ɑ̃t] *adj* (*couleur*) loud, gaudy ♦ *nm* (*signal*) (warning) light; **voyante** *nf* clairvoyant

voyelle [vwajɛl] *nf* vowel

voyons *etc* [vwajɔ̃] *vb voir* **voir**

voyou [vwaju] *nm* hooligan

vrac [vʀak]: **en ~** *adv* (*au détail*) loose; (*en gros*) in bulk; (*en désordre*) in a jumble

vrai, e [vʀɛ] *adj* (*véridique*: *récit, faits*) true; (*non factice, authentique*) real; **à ~ dire** to tell the truth; **vraiment** *adv* really; **vraisemblable** *adj* likely; (*excuse*) convincing; **vraisemblablement** *adv* probably; **vraisemblance** *nf* likelihood; (*romanesque*) verisimilitude

vrille [vʀij] *nf* (*de plante*) tendril; (*outil*) gimlet; (*spirale*) spiral; (*AVIAT*) spin

vrombir [vʀɔ̃biʀ] *vi* to hum

VRP *sigle m* (= *voyageur, représentant, placier*) sales rep (*fam*)

VTT *sigle m* (= *vélo tout-terrain*) mountain bike

vu, e [vy] *pp de* **voir** ♦ *adj*: **bien/mal ~** (*fig*: *personne*) popular/unpopular; (: *chose*) approved/disapproved of ♦ *prép* (*en raison de*) in view of; **~ que** in view of the fact that

vue [vy] *nf* (*fait de voir*): **la ~ de** the sight of; (*sens, faculté*) (eye)sight; (*panorama, image, photo*) view; **~s** *nfpl* (*idées*) views; (*dessein*) designs; **hors de ~** out of sight; **avoir en ~** to have in mind; **tirer à ~** to shoot on sight; **à ~ d'œil** visibly; **de ~** by sight; **perdre de ~** to lose sight of; **en ~** (*visible*) in sight; (*célèbre*) in the public eye; **en ~ de faire** with a view to doing

vulgaire [vylgɛʀ] *adj* (*grossier*) vulgar, coarse; (*ordinaire*) commonplace, mundane; (*péj*: *quelconque*): **de ~s touristes** common tourists; (*BOT, ZOOL*: *non latin*) common; **vulgariser** *vt* to popularize

vulnérable [vylneʀabl] *adj* vulnerable

W, w

wagon [vagɔ̃] *nm* (*de voyageurs*) carriage; (*de marchandises*) truck, wagon; **wagon-lit** *nm* sleeper, sleeping car; **wagon-restaurant** *nm* restaurant *ou* dining car

wallon, ne [walɔ̃, ɔn] *adj* Walloon

waters [watɛR] *nmpl* toilet *sg*

watt [wat] *nm* watt

WC *sigle mpl* (= water-closet(s)) toilet

Web [wɛb] *nm inv*: **le ~** the (World Wide) Web

week-end [wikɛnd] *nm* weekend

western [wɛstɛRn] *nm* western

whisky [wiski] (*pl* **whiskies**) *nm* whisky

X, x

xénophobe [gzenɔfɔb] *adj* xenophobic ♦ *nm/f* xenophobe

xérès [gzeRɛs] *nm* sherry

xylophone [gzilɔfɔn] *nm* xylophone

Y, y

y [i] *adv* (*à cet endroit*) there; (*dessus*) on it (*ou* them); (*dedans*) in it (*ou* them) ♦ *pron* (about *ou* on *ou* of) it (*d'après le verbe employé*); **j'~ pense** I'm thinking about it; **ça ~ est!** that's it!; *voir aussi* **aller**; **avoir**

yacht [jɔt] *nm* yacht

yaourt [jauRt] *nm* yoghourt; **~ nature / aux fruits** plain/fruit yogurt

yeux [jø] *nmpl de* **œil**

yoga [jɔga] *nm* yoga

yoghourt [jɔguRt] *nm* = **yaourt**

yougoslave [jugɔslav] (*HISTOIRE*) *adj* Yugoslav(ian) ♦ *nm/f*: **Y~** Yugoslav

Yougoslavie [jugɔslavi] (*HISTOIRE*) *nf* Yugoslavia

Z, z

zapper [zape] *vi* to zap

zapping [zapiŋ] *nm*: **faire du ~** to flick through the channels

zèbre [zɛbR(ə)] *nm* (*ZOOL*) zebra; **zébré, e** *adj* striped, streaked

zèle [zɛl] *nm* zeal; **faire du ~** (*péj*) to be over-zealous; **zélé, e** *adj* zealous

zéro [zeRo] *nm* zero, nought (*BRIT*); **au-dessous de ~** below zero (Centigrade) *ou* freezing; **partir de ~** to start from scratch; **trois (buts) à ~** 3 (goals to) nil

zeste [zɛst] *nm* peel, zest

zézayer [zezeje] *vi* to have a lisp

zigzag [zigzag] *nm* zigzag; **zigzaguer** *vi* to zigzag

zinc [zɛ̃g] *nm* (*CHIMIE*) zinc

zizanie [zizani] *nf*: **semer la ~** to stir up ill-feeling

zizi [zizi] *nm* (*langage enfantin*) willy

zodiaque [zɔdjak] *nm* zodiac

zona [zona] *nm* shingles *sg*

zone [zon] *nf* zone, area; **~ bleue** ≃ restricted parking area; **~ industrielle** industrial estate

zoo [zo(o)] *nm* zoo

zoologie [zɔɔlɔʒi] *nf* zoology; **zoologique** *adj* zoological

zut [zyt] *excl* dash (it)! (*BRIT*), nuts! (*US*)

PUZZLES AND WORDGAMES

Introduction

We are delighted that you have decided to invest in this Collins French Dictionary! Whether you intend to use it in school, at home, on holiday or at work, we are sure that you will find it very useful.

In the pages which follow you will find explanations and wordgames (not too difficult!) designed to give you practice in exploring the dictionary's contents and in retrieving information for a variety of purposes. Answers are provided at the end. If you spend a little time on these pages you should be able to use your dictionary more efficiently and effectively. Have fun!

Supplement by
Roy Simon
reproduced by kind permission of
Tayside Region Education Department

WORDGAME 1

DICTIONARY ENTRIES

Complete the crossword below by looking up the English words in the list and finding the correct French translations. There is a slight catch, however! All the English words can be translated several ways into French, but only one translation will fit correctly into each part of the crossword.

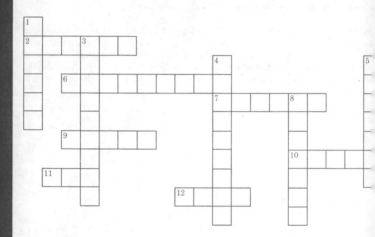

1. HORN   5. LEAN   9. TRACK

2. THROW   6. FORBID   10. STEEP

3. KNOW   7. CALF   11. HARD

4. MOVE   8. PLACE   12. PLACE

WORDGAME 2

SYNONYMS

Complete the crossword by supplying SYNONYMS of the words below. You will sometimes find the synonym you are looking for in italics and bracketed at the entries for the words listed below. Sometimes you will have to turn to the English-French section for help.

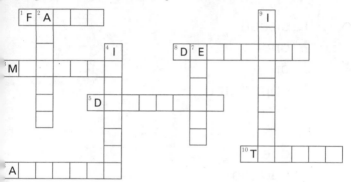

1. manière
2. se passer
3. récolte
4. feu
5. doubler

6. gentil
7. faute
8. haïr
9. défendre
10. essayer

WORDGAME 3

SPELLING

You will often use your dictionary to check spellings. The person who ha
compiled this list of ten French words has made <u>three</u> spelling mistakes
Find the three words which have been misspelt and write them out correctly

1. oiseau
2. ondée
3. ongel
4. opportun
5. orage
6. ortiel
7. ouest
8. ourigan
9. ouvreuse
10. oxygène

WORDGAME 4

ANTONYMS

Complete the crossword by supplying ANTONYMS (i.e. opposites) in French of the words below. Use your dictionary to help.

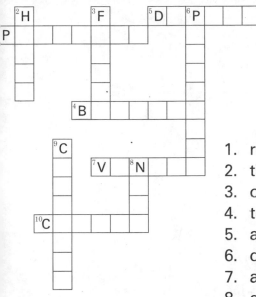

1. richesse
2. timide
3. ouvrir
4. tranquille
5. arrivée
6. défendre
7. acheter
8. avouer
9. innocent
10. révéler

WORDGAME 5

PHONETIC SPELLINGS

The phonetic transcriptions of ten French words are given below. If you study pages xiii to xiv near the front of your dictionary you should be able to work out what the words are.

1. ku

2. tɔmat

3. ʒœn

4. ɔ̃gl(ə)

5. kɛ̃z

6. mɛ̃

7. ʒy

8. ɛkskyze

9. ʀepɔ̃dʀ(ə)

10. vulwaʀ

WORDGAME 6

EXPRESSIONS IN WHICH THE HEADWORD APPEARS

f you look up the headword 'coup' in the French-English section of your dictionary you will find that the word has many meanings. Study the entry carefully and translate the following sentences into English.

1. L'automobiliste a donné un coup de frein en abordant le virage.

2. Il est resté trop longtemps sur la plage et a pris un coup de soleil.

3. Ils sont arrivés sur le coup de midi.

4. On va boire un coup?

5. Il a un œil au beurre noir — quelqu'un lui a donné un coup de poing.

6. Je vais donner un coup de téléphone à mon frère.

7. Il a jeté un coup d'œil sur la liste.

8. Je vais te donner un coup de main.

9. Un coup de vent a fait chavirer le voilier.

0. Les éclairs se sont suivis coup sur coup.

WORDGAME 7

RELATED WORDS

Fill in the blanks in the pairs of sentences below. The missing words are related to the headwords on the left. Choose the correct 'relative' each time. You will find it in your dictionary near the headwords provided.

HEADWORD	RELATED WORDS
permettre	1. Il a demandé la _____ de sortir.
	2 Il a son _____ de conduire.
emploi	3. Il est _____ de banque.
	4. Je vais _____ tous les moyens pour réussir.
faux	5. Le _____ a été condamné à trois ans de prison.
	6. Il dit qu'il a été _____ accusé de vol.
écarter	7. Le cycliste a dû faire un _____ pour éviter le poteau.
	8. Ils habitent un village _____.
étudiant	9. Il fait ses _____ à la Sorbonne.
	10. Le professeur a commencé à _____ le texte.
sifflement	11. Un coup de _____ a marqué le commencement du match.
	12. Il s'est fait _____ par l'agent au carrefour.

WORDGAME 8

'KEY' WORDS

Study carefully the entry **'faire'** in your dictionary and find translations for the following:

1. the weather is fine

2. to do law

3. I don't mind

4. it makes you sleep

5. to have one's eyes tested

6. it's not done

7. to do the washing

8. we must act quickly

9. to start up an engine

0. to make friends

WORDGAME 9

PARTS OF SPEECH

In each sentence below a word has been shaded. Put a tick in the appropriate box to indicate the **part of speech** each time. Remember, different parts of speech are indicated by lozenges within entries.

SENTENCE	Noun	Adj	Adv	Verb
1. Il étudie le droit à Paris.				
2. Il chante juste.				
3. Le lancer du poids est une épreuve d'athlétisme.				
4. Le dîner est prêt.				
5. Allez tout droit, puis prenez la première à gauche.				
6. Elle a le fou rire.				
7. Je vais mettre fin à cette stupidité!				
8. Nous allons dîner en ville.				
9. Il ne ferait pas de mal à une mouche.				
10. C'était un bon repas.				

WORDGAME 10

NOUNS

This list contains the feminine form of some French nouns. Use your dictionary to find the **masculine** form.

Use your dictionary to find the **plural** of the following nouns.

MASCULINE	FEMININE	SINGULAR	PLURAL
	paysanne	oiseau	
	chanteuse	pneu	
	directrice	genou	
	espionne	voix	
	domestique	bail	
	lycéenne	jeu	
	épicière	bijou	
	lectrice	œil	
	cadette	lave-vaisselle	
	contractuelle	journal	

xi

MEANING CHANGING WITH GENDER

Some French nouns change meaning according to their gender, i.e. according to whether they are masculine or feminine. Look at the pairs of sentences below and fill in the blanks with either **'un'**, **'une'**, **'le'** or **'la'**.

1. Il a acheté _____ livre de sucre.
   Sa sœur a acheté _____ livre de cuisine.

2. Pour faire une tarte il faut _____ moule.
   Elle a trouvé _____ moule sous le rocher.

3. On va faire _____ tour en voiture.
   Ils habitent dans _____ tour de seize étages.

4. Ce bateau a _____ voile jaune.
   La mariée portait _____ voile.

5. _____ mousse est un apprenti marin.
   Tu aimes _____ mousse au chocolat?

6. Il y avait _____ poêle à bois qui chauffait l cuisine.
   Elle prépare des crêpes dans _____ poêle.

7. Il a relevé _____ manche gauche de son pull-over.
   Il tenait le couteau par _____ manche.

8. Les femmes aiment suivre _____ mode.
   _____ mode d'emploi est assez facile.

WORDGAME 12

ADJECTIVES

Use your dictionary to find the **feminine singular** form of these adjectives.

MASCULINE	FEMININE
1. frais	
2. songeur	
3. épais	
4. public	
5. franc	
6. complet	
7. oisif	
8. pareil	
9. ancien	
10. mou	
11. favori	
12. doux	
13. artificiel	
14. flatteur	

WORDGAME 13

VERB TENSES

Use your dictionary to help you fill in the blanks in the table below. (Read pages 585, 586 at the back and pages ix to x at the front of your dictionary.)

INFINITIVE	PRESENT TENSE	IMPERFECT	FUTURE
venir		je	
maudire	je		
voir			je
savoir		je	
avoir			j'
partir	je		
être			je
vouloir		je	
devoir	je		
permettre	je		
dormir		je	
pouvoir			je

WORDGAME 14

PAST PARTICIPLES

Use the verb tables at the back of your dictionary to find the past participle of these verbs. Check that you have found the correct form by looking in the main text. Some of the verbs below have prefixes in front of them.

INFINITIVE	PAST PARTICIPLE
venir	
mourir	
couvrir	
vivre	
offrir	
servir	
connaître	
remettre	
surprendre	
pleuvoir	
renaître	
conduire	
plaire	
défaire	
sourire	

WORDGAME 15

IDENTIFYING INFINITIVES

In the sentences below you will see various French verbs shaded. Use you
dictionary to help you find the **infinitive** form of each verb.

1. Quand j'étais jeune je partageais une chambre avec mon
   frère.

2. Mes amis viennent à la discothèque.

3. Sa mère l'amène à l'école en voiture.

4. Je me lèverai à dix heures demain.

5. Ce week-end nous sortirons ensemble.

6. Ils avaient déjà vendu la maison.

7. Elle suit un régime.

8. Il est né en Espagne.

9. J'aimerais vivre aux États-Unis.

10. Ils feront une partie de tennis.

11. Il prenait un bain tous les soirs.

12. Il a repris le travail.

13. Nous voudrions visiter le château.

14. Les enfants avaient froid.

15. Quand j'essaie de réparer la voiture j'ai toujours les
    mains couvertes d'huile.

MORE ABOUT MEANING

this section we will consider some of the problems associated with using a
ilingual dictionary.

verdependence on your dictionary

hat the dictionary is an invaluable tool for the language learner is beyond
spute. Nevertheless, it is possible to become overdependent on your dic-
nary, turning to it in an almost automatic fashion every time you come up
ainst a new French word or phrase. Tackling an unfamiliar text in this way
ll turn reading in French into an extremely tedious activity. If you stop to
ok up every new word you may actually be *hindering* your ability to read in
ench — you are so concerned with the individual words that you pay no
tention to the text as a whole and to the context which gives them meaning.
is therefore important to develop appropriate reading skills — using clues
ch as titles, headlines, illustrations, etc., understanding relations within a
ntence, etc. — so as to predict or infer what a text is about.

detailed study of the development of reading skills is not within the scope
this supplement; we are concerned with knowing how to use a dictionary,
iich is only one of several important skills involved in reading. Neverthe-
s, it may be instructive to look at one example. Imagine that you see the
lowing text in a Swiss newspaper and are interested in working out what it
about.

ntextual clues here include the
rds in large type which you would
obably recognise as a French
me, something that looks like a
te in the middle, and the name
d address in the bottom right-
nd corner. The French words
nnoncer' and 'clinique' closely
semble the words 'announce' and
nic' in English, so you would not

> *Nous sommes très heureux
> d'annoncer la naissance de*
>
> ## Flavien, Christophe
>
> le 29 mars 1988
>
> *Claudine et Pierre LELOUP*
> *Clinique   88, chemin des Saules*
> *des Etoiles   1233 Genève*

ve to look them up in your dictionary. Other 'form' words such as 'nous',
mmes', 'très', 'la' and 'de' will be familiar to you from your general studies
French. Given that we are dealing with a newspaper, you will probably
ve worked out by now that this could be an announcement placed in the
rsonal Column'.

So you have used a series of cultural, contextual and word-formation clue[s] get you to the point where you have understood that Claudine and Pie[rre] Leloup have placed this notice in the 'Personal Column' of the newspa[per] and that something happened to Christophe on 29 March 1988, someth[ing] connected with a hospital. And you have reached this point *without* open[ing] your dictionary once. Common sense and your knowledge of newspaper c[on]tents in this country might suggest that this must be an announcemen[t of] someone's birth or death. Thus 'heureux' ('happy') and 'naissance' ('bir[th]') become the only words that you might have to look up in order to conf[irm] that this is indeed a birth announcement.

When learning French we are helped considerably by the fact that ma[ny] French and English words look and sound alike and have exactly the sa[me] meaning. Such words are called 'COGNATES'. Many words which l[ook] similar in French and English often come from a common Latin root. Ot[her] words are the same or nearly the same in both languages because the Fre[nch] language has borrowed a word from English or vice versa. The dictionary [will] often not be necessary where cognates are concerned — provided you k[now] the English word that the French word resembles!

Words with more than one meaning

The need to examine with care *all* the information contained in a diction[ary] entry must be stressed. This is particularly important with the many wo[rds] which have more than one meaning. For example, the French 'journal' [can] mean 'diary' as well as 'newspaper'. How you translated the word w[ould] depend on the context in which you found it.

Similarly, if you were trying to translate a phrase such as 'en plein visa[ge]' you would have to look through the whole entry for 'plein' to get the r[ight] translation. If you restricted your search to the first line of the entry and [saw] that the first meaning given is 'full', you might be tempted to assume that [the] phrase meant 'a full (i.e. fat) face'. But if you examined the entry closely [you] would see that 'en plein . . .' means 'right in the middle of . . .'. So 'en p[lein] visage' means 'right in the middle of the face', as in the sentence 'La boul[e de] neige l'a frappé en plein visage'.

The same need for care applies when you are using the English-French [sec]tion of your dictionary to translate a word from English into French. W[atch] out in particular for the lozenges indicating changes in parts of speech[.]

e noun 'sink' is 'évier', while the
-b is 'couler'. If you don't watch
at you are doing, you could end
with ridiculous non-French e.g.
le a mis la vaisselle dans le
ıler'!

ırasal verbs

other   potential   source   of
ficulty is English phrasal verbs.
ese consist of a common verb
)', 'make', etc.) plus an adverb
d/or a preposition to give English
pressions such as 'to make out',
take after', etc. Entries for such
-bs tend to be fairly full,
erefore close examination of the
itents is required. Note how
se verbs appear in colour within
: entry.

sink [sɪŋk] (*pt* **sank**, *pp* **sunk**) *n* évier *m*
♦ *vt* (*ship*) (faire) couler, faire sombrer;
(*foundations*) creuser ♦ *vi* couler, sombrer;
(*ground etc*) s'affaisser; (*also:* ~ **back**, ~
down) s'affaisser, se laisser retomber; **to** ~
sth into enfoncer qch dans; **my heart
sank** j'ai complètement perdu courage; ~
in *vi* (*fig*) pénétrer, être compris(e)

make [meɪk] (*pt, pp* **made**) *vt* faire; (*manufacture*) faire, fabriquer; (*earn*) gagner;
(*cause to be*): **to** ~ **sb sad** *etc* rendre qn
triste *etc*; (*force*): **to** ~ **sb do sth** obliger
qn à faire qch, faire faire qch à qn;
(*equal*): **2 and 2** ~ **4** 2 et 2 font 4 ♦ *n* fabrication *f*; (*brand*) marque *f*; **to** ~ **a fool
of sb** (*ridicule*) ridiculiser qn; (*trick*) avoir
or duper qn; **to** ~ **a profit** faire un *or* des
bénéfice(s); **to** ~ **a loss** essuyer une perte;
to ~ **it** (*arrive*) arriver; (*achieve sth*) parvenir à qch, réussir; **what time do you** ~ **it?**
quelle heure avez-vous?; **to** ~ **do with** se
contenter de; se débrouiller avec; ~ **for** *vt
fus* (*place*) se diriger vers; ~ **out** *vt* (*write*

ux amis

any French and English words have similar forms *and* meanings. Many
nch words, however, *look* like English words but have a completely
ferent meaning. For example, 'le store' means 'the (window) blind'; 'les
ps' means 'potato crisps'. This can easily lead to serious mistranslations.

metimes the meaning of the French word is **close** to the English. For
ımple, 'la monnaie' means 'loose change' rather than 'money'; 'le surnom'
ans 'nickname' not 'surname'. But some French words have two
anings, one the same as the English, the other completely different! 'La
ıre' can mean 'face' as well as 'figure'; 'la marche' can mean 'march/walk'
: also 'the step (on the stairs)'.

ch words are often referred to as 'FAUX AMIS' ('false friends'). You will
e to look at the context in which they appear to arrive at the correct
aning. If they seem to fit in with the sense of the passage as a whole, you
I probably not need to look them up. If they don't make sense, however,
I may be dealing with 'faux amis'.

WORDGAME 16

WORDS IN CONTEXT

Study the sentences below. Translations of the shaded words are given at the bottom. Match the number of the sentence and the letter of the translation correctly each time.

1. Les vagues déferlent sur la grève.
2. La grève des cheminots a commencé hier.
3. Elle a versé le café dans une grande tasse.
4. J'ai versé la somme de 500F à titre d'arrhes.
5. L'avion a touché terre.
6. Il touche un salaire mensuel de 10 000F.
7. Beaucoup de fleurs poussent dans leur jardin.
8. Il a dû pousser la brouette.
9. Il voudrait suivre une carrière dans le commerce.
10. Il a visité une carriére où des ouvriers extrayaient de pierres.
11. Il a acheté deux pellicules pour son appareil-photo.
12. Tu as les épaules saupoudrées de pellicules – tu dois te laver les cheveux.

a. poured	e. films	i. draws
b. quarry	f. shore	j. career
c. paid	g. push	k. strike
d. grow	h. dandruff	i. touched

WORDGAME 17

WORDS WITH MORE THAN ONE MEANING
UN PEU DE PUBLICITÉ

Look at the advertisements below. The words which have been shaded can have more than one meaning. Use your dictionary to help you work out the correct translation in the context.

1

PRÊT-À-PORTER

TRICOTS
LINGERIE
BAS
FOULARDS
BIJOUX

BENOIT

36, Rue Nationale
T O U R S
Tél. (47) 57 . 14 . 34

2

RESTAURANT 'AU PASSÉ SIMPLE'
vous accueille tous les jours sauf
dimanche midi et lundi (pendant la saison)
UNE GAMME DE 5 MENUS de 50F à 165F + carte
Fruits de mer - Poissons - Service jusqu'à 22h
21 bis, pl. Ch. de Gaulle AUTUN - Tél. 27.88.71.02

3

**CAISSE D'ÉPARGNE
DE CHAMPIGNY**

Le chéquier 'Girafe',
Complément idéal de votre livret

25, rue Maréchal-Foch   Tél. 42.38.53.55.

4

RESTAURANT **LE MARAIS**
Sa Cuisine du Marché, son Cadre
ses Spécialités Maison
10, rue Lesson - SEDAN
Tél 46.99.47.13

5

Le Château
PLACE DE LA GALISSONNIÈRE
VUE SUR LA PORTE DU SOLEIL
Le Self-Service pour toutes les bourses
A l'étage: le Restaurant gastronomique
LES JARDINS DU 'CHÂTEAU'
Carte de spécialités – Poissons et grillades

6

*Comment vous protég
contre le vol*
adressez-vous à

SECURITA
22, rue Levallois à Aveyron
Tél: 757.48.80

7

CHATEAUROUX D 40

l'Hostel du Roy **NN

JACQUES DE QUÉRÉ   **CUISINE SOIGNÉE**
Propriétaire   **PRIX MODÉRÉS**
                             CAVE RÉPUTÉE

8

Les produits frais...
chez HYPERFRAICHE

9

La roulotte:

Elle deviendra votre maison pendant votre
séjour. Elle est confortable et accueillante.
Prévue pour 4 personnes ou 2 adultes et 3
enfants, elle comprend:

– *Le nécessaire de couchage (draps,
   couvertures);*
– *Vaisselle pour 5 personnes;*
– *Batterie de cuisine;*
– *1 évier*

xxii

WORDGAME 18

FAUX AMIS

Look at the advertisements below. The words which have been shaded resemble English words but have different meanings here. Find a correct translation for each word in the context.

1
STAGES
INITIATION
PERFECTIONNEMENT

48, Avenue de Baisse   Plage des Demoiselles
Tél. 61.59.27.53

2
VOYAGES LEGRAND

Cinq Cars avec toilettes **TAXI**
Equipement lits pendant la saison d'hiver
Location de cars de 20 à 65 places assises

Voyages touristiques France et Etranger

3
**PRENEZ UN CHARIOT
POUR EFFECTUER VOS
ACHATS
        MERCI!**

4
Hôtel ** NN
de France
Parking important à proximité
Face à la Poste
55, rue du Docteur-Peltier
17300 BORDEAUX
Tél. : 66.89.34.00 et 66.89.33.23

WORDGAME 19

MOTS CODÉS

n the boxes below, the letters of eight French words have been replaced
y numbers. A number represents the same letter each time.

ry to crack the code and find the eight words. If you need help, use your dic-
onary.

ere is a clue: all the words you are looking for have something to do with
RANSPORT.

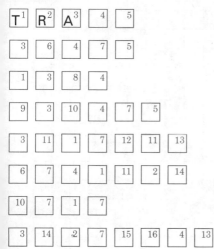

| T¹ | R² | A³ | 4 | 5 |

| 3 | 6 | 4 | 7 | 5 |

| 1 | 3 | 8 | 4 |

| 9 | 3 | 10 | 4 | 7 | 5 |

| 3 | 11 | 1 | 7 | 12 | 11 | 13 |

| 6 | 7 | 4 | 1 | 11 | 2 | 14 |

| 10 | 7 | 1 | 7 |

| 3 | 14 | 2 | 7 | 15 | 16 | 4 | 13 | 13 | 14 | 11 | 2 |

WORDGAME 20

MOTS CROISÉS

Complete this crossword by looking up the words listed below in the English French section of your dictionary. Remember to read through the entry care fully to find the word that will fit.

1 To dirty
2 (A piece of) news
3 Mood
4 Relationship
5 Meal
6 To record
7 Novelty
8 To fold
9 Ebony
10 Porthole
11 Heavily
12 Sad
13 To replace
14 To admire
15 To reassure
16 To start up
   (a car, machin
17 Tearful
18 Width
19 To withdraw

WORDGAME 21

MOTS COUPÉS

There are twelve French words hidden in the grid below. Each word is made up of five letters but has been split into two parts.

Find the French words. Each group of letters can only be used once.

Use your dictionary to help you.

fer	lge	at	ta	fou	re
can	ma	le	pr	su	rin
ise	bac	cre	ég	ine	por
te	ach	me	be	out	ot

WORDGAME 22

MOTS CUISINÉS

Here is a list of French words for things you will find in the kitchen. Unfortunately, they have all been jumbled up. Try to work out what each word is and put the word in the boxes on the right. You will see that there are six shaded boxes below. With the six letters in the shaded boxes make up <u>anothe</u> French word for an object you can find in the kitchen.

1 saset   Tu veux une ____ de café?   ☐☐☐▨☐

2 gfoir   Mets le beurre dans le ____ !   ☐☐▨☐☐

3 telab   À ____ ! On mange!   ☐▨☐☐☐

4 cpldraa   Mets les provisions dans le ____ !   ☐☐☐▨☐☐☐

5 éeèirth   Elle met le thé dans la ____   ☐▨☐☐☐☐☐

6 caleserso   Elle fait bouillir de l'eau dans une ____   ☐☐☐☐☐☐☐☐☐

The word you are looking for is:

☐☐☐☐☐☐

WORDGAME 23

MOTS EN CROIX

Take the four letters given each time and put them in the four empty boxes in the centre of each grid. Arrange them in such a way that you form four six letter words. Use your dictionary to check the words.

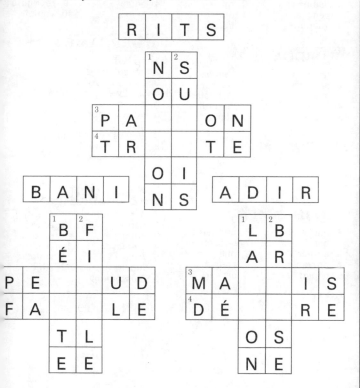

xxix

ANSWERS

WORDGAME 1

1	klaxon	7	mollet
2	lancer	8	endroit
3	connaître	9	piste
4	déménager	10	raide
5	pencher	11	dur
6	interdire	12	lieu

WORDGAME 2

1	façon	6	aimable
2	arriver	7	erreur
3	moisson	8	détester
4	incendie	9	interdire
5	dépasser	10	tenter

WORDGAME 3

1 ongle
2 orteil
3 ouragan

WORDGAME 4

1	pauvreté	6	permettre
2	hardi	7	vendre
3	fermer	8	nier
4	bruyant	9	coupable
5	départ	10	cacher

WORDGAME 5

1	cou	6	main
2	tomate	7	jus
3	jeune	8	excuser
4	ongle	9	répondre
5	quinze	10	vouloir

WORDGAME 6

1 braked
2 got sunburnt
3 on the stroke of
4 shall we have a drink?
5 punch
6 make a phone call
7 glanced
8 I'll give you a hand
9 a gust of wind
10 in quick succession

WORDGAME 7

1	permission	7	écart
2	permis	8	écarté
3	employé	9	études
4	employer	10	étudier
5	faux-monnayeur	11	sifflet
6	faussement	12	siffler

WORDGAME 9

1	n	6	n
2	adv	7	n
3	n	8	v
4	adj	9	n
5	adv	10	adj

WORDGAME 10

1	paysan	11	oiseaux
2	chanteur	12	pneus
3	directeur	13	genoux
4	espion	14	voix
5	domestique	15	baux
6	lycéen	16	jeux
7	épicier	17	bijoux
8	lecteur	18	yeux
9	cadet	19	lave-vaisselle
0	contractuel	20	journaux

WORDGAME 11

1	une un	5	Un la
2	un une	6	un une
3	un une	7	la le
4	une un	8	la Le

WORDGAME 12

1	fraîche	8	pareille
2	songeuse	9	ancienne
3	épaisse	10	molle
4	publique	11	favorite
5	franche	12	douce
6	complète	13	artificielle
7	oisive	14	flatteuse

WORDGAME 13

je venais	je serai
je maudis	je voulais
je verrai	je dois
je savais	je permets
j'aurai	je dormais
je pars	je pourrai

WORDGAME 14

1	venu	8	remis
2	mort	9	surpris
3	couvert	10	plu
4	vécu	11	rené
5	offert	12	conduit
6	servi	13	plu
7	connu	14	défait
		15	souri

WORDGAME 15

1	partager	9	aimer
2	venir	10	faire
3	amener	11	prendre
4	se lever	12	reprendre
5	sortir	13	vouloir
6	vendre	14	avoir
7	suivre	15	essayer
8	naître		

WORDGAME 16

1	f	5	l	9	j
2	k	6	i	10	b
3	a	7	d	11	e
4	c	8	g	12	h

WORDGAME 17

1 wear
2 except
3 bank
4 cooking; surroundings
5 purses
6 theft
7 prices
8 fresh
9 essentials; pots and pans

WORDGAME 18

1 training courses
2 coaches
3 trolley
4 large
5 cellars
6 wearing; briefs
7 accommodation
8 breeds
9 hire
10 facing; management

WORDGAME 19

1 train
2 avion
3 taxi
4 camion
5 autobus
6 voiture
7 moto
8 aéroglisseur

WORDGAME 20

1 salir
2 nouvelle
3 humeur
4 rapport
5 repas
6 enregistrer
7 nouveauté
8 plier
9 ébène
10 hublot
11 lourdement
12 triste
13 remplacer
14 admirer
15 rassurer
16 démarrer
17 larmoyant
18 largeur
19 retirer

WORDGAME 21

ferme	belge	sucre
canot	marin	foule
prise	tabac	égout
porte	achat	reine

WORDGAME 22

1 tasse
2 frigo
3 table
4 placard
5 théière
6 casserole

Missing word – **chaise**

WORDGAME 23

1 notion	1 bénite	1 lardon
2 sursis	2 fiable	2 braise
3 patron	3 penaud	3 marais
4 triste	4 faible	4 dédire

A, a

A [eɪ] *n* (*MUS*) la *m*

KEYWORD

a [eɪ, ə] (*before vowel or silent h: an*) *indef art*
1 un(e); **a book** un livre; **an apple** une
pomme; **she's a doctor** elle est médecin
2 (*instead of the number "one"*) un(e); **a
year ago** il y a un an; **a hundred/
thousand** *etc* **pounds** cent/mille *etc* livres
3 (*in expressing ratios, prices etc*): **3 a day/
week** 3 par jour/semaine; **10 km an hour**
10 km à l'heure; **30p a kilo** 30p le kilo

A.A. *n abbr* = **Alcoholics Anonymous**;
(*BRIT: Automobile Association*) ≈ TCF *m*
A.A.A. (*US*) *n abbr* (= *American Automobile
Association*) ≈ TCF *m*
aback [ə'bæk] *adv*: **to be taken ~** être
stupéfait(e), être décontenancé(e)
abandon [ə'bændən] *vt* abandonner
abate [ə'beɪt] *vi* s'apaiser, se calmer
abbey ['æbɪ] *n* abbaye *f*
abbot ['æbət] *n* père supérieur
abbreviation [əbriːvɪ'eɪʃən] *n* abréviation *f*
abdicate ['æbdɪkeɪt] *vt, vi* abdiquer
abdomen ['æbdəmen] *n* abdomen *m*
abduct [æb'dʌkt] *vt* enlever
aberration [æbə'reɪʃən] *n* anomalie *f*
abide [ə'baɪd] *vt*: **I can't ~ it/him** je ne
peux pas le souffrir *or* supporter; **~ by** *vt
fus* observer, respecter
ability [ə'bɪlɪtɪ] *n* compétence *f*; capacité *f*;
(*skill*) talent *m*
abject ['æbdʒekt] *adj* (*poverty*) sordide;
(*apology*) plat(e)
ablaze [ə'bleɪz] *adj* en feu, en flammes
able ['eɪbl] *adj* capable, compétent(e); **to
be ~ to do sth** être capable de faire qch,
pouvoir faire qch; **~-bodied** *adj* robuste;
ably *adv* avec compétence *or* talent, ha-

bilement
abnormal [æb'nɔːməl] *adj* anormal(e)
aboard [ə'bɔːd] *adv* à bord ♦ *prep* à bord
de
abode [ə'bəud] *n* (*LAW*): **of no fixed ~** sans
domicile fixe
abolish [ə'bɔlɪʃ] *vt* abolir
aborigine [æbə'rɪdʒɪnɪ] *n* aborigène *m/f*
abort [ə'bɔːt] *vt* faire avorter; **~ion** *n* avortement *m*; **to have an ~ion** se faire avorter; **~ive** [ə'bɔːtɪv] *adj* manqué(e)

KEYWORD

about [ə'baut] *adv* **1** (*approximately*) environ, à peu près; **about a hundred/
thousand** *etc* environ cent/mille *etc*, une
centaine/un millier *etc*; **it takes about 10
hours** ça prend environ *or* à peu près 10
heures; **at about 2 o'clock** vers 2 heures;
i've just about finished j'ai presque fini
2 (*referring to place*) çà et là, de côté et
d'autre; **to run about** courir çà et là; **to
walk about** se promener, aller et venir
3: **to be about to do sth** être sur le point
de faire qch
♦ *prep* **1** (*relating to*) au sujet de, à propos
de; **a book about London** un livre sur
Londres; **what is it about?** de quoi
s'agit-il?; **we talked about it** nous en
avons parlé; **what** *or* **how about doing
this?** et si nous faisions ceci?
2 (*referring to place*) dans; **to walk about
the town** se promener dans la ville

about-face [ə'baut'feɪs] *n* demi-tour *m*
about-turn [ə'baut'tɜːn] *n* (*MIL*) demi-tour
m; (*fig*) volte-face *f*
above [ə'bʌv] *adv* au-dessus ♦ *prep* au-
dessus de; (*more*) plus de; **mentioned ~**
mentionné ci-dessus; **~ all** par-dessus

tout, surtout; **~board** *adj* franc (franche); honnête

abrasive [əˈbreɪzɪv] *adj* abrasif(-ive); (*fig*) caustique, agressif(-ive)

abreast [əˈbrest] *adv* de front; **to keep ~ of** se tenir au courant de

abroad [əˈbrɔːd] *adv* à l'étranger

abrupt [əˈbrʌpt] *adj* (*steep, blunt*) abrupt(e); (*sudden, gruff*) brusque; **~ly** *adv* (*speak, end*) brusquement

abscess [ˈæbsɪs] *n* abcès *m*

absence [ˈæbsəns] *n* absence *f*

absent [ˈæbsənt] *adj* absent(e); **~ee** [æbsənˈtiː] *n* absent(e); (*habitual*) absentéiste *m/f*; **~-minded** *adj* distrait(e)

absolute [ˈæbsəluːt] *adj* absolu(e); **~ly** [æbsəˈluːtlɪ] *adv* absolument

absolve [əbˈzɔlv] *vt*: **to ~ sb (from)** (*blame, responsibility, sin*) absoudre qn (de)

absorb [əbˈzɔːb] *vt* absorber; **to be ~ed in a book** être plongé(e) dans un livre; **~ent cotton** (*US*) *n* coton *m* hydrophile

abstain [əbˈsteɪn] *vi*: **to ~ (from)** s'abstenir (de)

abstract [ˈæbstrækt] *adj* abstrait(e)

absurd [əbˈsəːd] *adj* absurde

abundant [əˈbʌndənt] *adj* abondant(e)

abuse [*n* əˈbjuːs, *vb* əˈbjuːz] *n* abus *m*; (*insults*) insultes *fpl*, injures *fpl* ♦ *vt* abuser de; (*insult*) insulter; **abusive** [əˈbjuːsɪv] *adj* grossier(-ère), injurieux(-euse)

abysmal [əˈbɪzməl] *adj* exécrable; (*ignorance etc*) sans bornes

abyss [əˈbɪs] *n* abîme *m*, gouffre *m*

AC *abbr* (= *alternating current*) courant alternatif

academic [ækəˈdemɪk] *adj* universitaire; (*person: scholarly*) intellectuel(le); (*pej: issue*) oiseux(-euse), purement théorique ♦ *n* universitaire *m/f*; **~ year** *n* année *f* universitaire

academy [əˈkædəmɪ] *n* (*learned body*) académie *f*; (*school*) collège *m*; **~ of music** conservatoire *m*

accelerate [ækˈseləreɪt] *vt, vi* accélérer; **accelerator** *n* accélérateur *m*

accent [ˈæksent] *n* accent *m*

accept [əkˈsept] *vt* accepter; **~able** *adj* acceptable; **~ance** *n* acceptation *f*

access [ˈækses] *n* accès *m*; (*LAW: in divorce*) droit *m* de visite; **~ible** [ækˈsesəbl] *adj* accessible

accessory [ækˈsesərɪ] *n* accessoire *m*

accident [ˈæksɪdənt] *n* accident *m*, (*chance*) hasard *m*; **by ~** accidentellement, par hasard; **~al** [æksɪˈdentl] *adj* accidentel(le); **~ally** [æksɪˈdentəlɪ] *adv* accidentellement; **~ insurance** *n* assurance *f* accident; **~-prone** *adj* sujet(te) aux accidents

acclaim [əˈkleɪm] *n* acclamations *fpl* ♦ *v* acclamer

accommodate [əˈkɔmədeɪt] *vt* loger, recevoir; (*oblige, help*) obliger; (*car etc*) contenir; **accommodating** *adj* obligeant(e), arrangeant(e); **accommodation** [əkɔməˈdeɪʃən] (*US* **accommodations**) *n* logement *m*

accompany [əˈkʌmpənɪ] *vt* accompagner

accomplice [əˈkʌmplɪs] *n* complice *m/f*

accomplish [əˈkʌmplɪʃ] *vt* accomplir; **~ment** *n* accomplissement *m*; réussite *f* (*skill: gen pl*) talent *m*

accord [əˈkɔːd] *n* accord *m* ♦ *vt* accorder **of his own ~** de son plein gré; **~ance** [əˈkɔːdəns] *n*: **in ~ance with** conformément à; **~ing: ~ing to** *prep* selon; **~ingl** *adv* en conséquence

accordion [əˈkɔːdɪən] *n* accordéon *m*

account [əˈkaunt] *n* (*COMM*) compte *m* (*report*) compte rendu; récit *m*; **~s** *n* (*COMM*) comptabilité *f*, comptes; **of no ~** sans importance; **on ~** en acompte; **no ~** en aucun cas; **on ~ of** à cause de **to take into ~, take ~ of** tenir compte de; **~ for** *vt fus* expliquer, rendre compte de; **~able** *adj*: **~able (to)** responsable (devant); **~ancy** *n* comptabilité *f*; **~ant** comptable *m/f*; **~ number** *n* (*at bank etc*) numéro *m* de compte

accrued interest [əˈkruːd-] *n* intérêt *m* cumulé

accumulate [əˈkjuːmjuleɪt] *vt* accumule amasser ♦ *vi* s'accumuler, s'amasser

accuracy [ˈækjurəsɪ] *n* exactitude *f*, présion f

accurate ['ækjurıt] adj exact(e), précis(e); **~ly** adv avec précision

accusation [ækjuːˈzeıʃən] n accusation f

accuse [əˈkjuːz] vt: **to ~ sb (of sth)** accuser qn (de qch); **the ~d** l'accusé(e)

accustom [əˈkʌstəm] vt accoutumer, habituer; **~ed** adj (usual) habituel(le); (in the habit): **~ed to** habitué(e) or accoutumé(e) à

ace [eıs] n as m

ache [eık] n mal m, douleur f ♦ vi (yearn): **to ~ to do sth** mourir d'envie de faire qch; **my head ~s** j'ai mal à la tête

achieve [əˈtʃiːv] vt (aim) atteindre; (victory, success) remporter, obtenir; **~ment** n exploit m, réussite f

acid ['æsıd] adj acide ♦ n acide m; **~ rain** n pluies fpl acides

acknowledge [əkˈnɔlıdʒ] vt (letter: also: **~ receipt of**) accuser réception de; (fact) reconnaître; **~ment** n (of letter) accusé m de réception

acne ['æknı] n acné f

acorn ['eıkɔːn] n gland m

acoustic [əˈkuːstık] adj acoustique; **~s** n, npl acoustique f

acquaint [əˈkweınt] vt: **to ~ sb with sth** mettre qn au courant de qch; **to be ~ed with** connaître; **~ance** n connaissance f

acquire [əˈkwaıər] vt acquérir

acquit [əˈkwıt] vt acquitter; **to ~ o.s. well** bien se comporter, s'en tirer très honorablement

acre ['eıkər] n acre f (= 4047 m2)

acrid ['ækrıd] adj âcre

acrobat ['ækrəbæt] n acrobate m/f

across [əˈkrɔs] prep (on the other side) de l'autre côté de; (crosswise) en travers de ♦ adv de l'autre côté; en travers; **to run/swim ~** traverser en courant/à la nage; **~ from** en face de

acrylic [əˈkrılık] adj acrylique

act [ækt] n acte m, action f; (of play) acte m; (in music-hall etc) numéro m; (LAW) loi f ♦ vi agir; (THEATRE) jouer; (pretend) jouer la comédie ♦ vt (part) jouer, tenir; **in the ~**

of en train de; **to ~ as** servir de; **~ing** adj suppléant(e), par intérim ♦ n (activity): **to do some ~ing** faire du théâtre (or du cinéma)

action ['ækʃən] n action f; (MIL) combat(s) m(pl); **out of ~** hors de combat; (machine) hors d'usage; **to take ~** agir, prendre des mesures; **~ replay** n (TV) ralenti m

activate ['æktıveıt] vt (mechanism) actionner, faire fonctionner

active ['æktıv] adj actif(-ive); (volcano) en activité; **~ly** adv activement; **activity** [ækˈtıvıtı] n activité f; **activity holiday** n vacances actives

actor ['æktər] n acteur m

actress ['æktrıs] n actrice f

actual ['æktjuəl] adj réel(le), véritable; **~ly** adv (really) réellement, véritablement; (in fact) en fait

acute [əˈkjuːt] adj aigu(ë); (mind, observer) pénétrant(e), perspicace

ad [æd] n abbr = **advertisement**

A.D. adv abbr (= anno Domini) ap. J.-C.

adamant ['ædəmənt] adj inflexible

adapt [əˈdæpt] vt adapter ♦ vi: **to ~ (to)** s'adapter (à); **~able** adj (device) adaptable; (person) qui s'adapte facilement; **~er**, **~or** n (ELEC) adaptateur m

add [æd] vt ajouter; (figures: also: **to ~ up**) additionner ♦ vi: **to ~ to** (increase) ajouter à, accroître

adder ['ædər] n vipère f

addict ['ædıkt] n intoxiqué(e); (fig) fanatique m/f; **~ed** [əˈdıktıd] adj: **to be ~ed to** (drugs, drink etc) être adonné(e) à; (fig: football etc) être un(e) fanatique de; **~ion** n (MED) dépendance f; **~ive** adj qui crée une dépendance

addition [əˈdıʃən] n addition f; (thing added) ajout m; **in ~** de plus; de surcroît; **in ~ to** en plus de; **~al** adj supplémentaire

additive ['ædıtıv] n additif m

address [əˈdrɛs] n adresse f; (talk) discours m, allocution f ♦ vt adresser; (speak to) s'adresser à; **to ~ (o.s. to) a problem** s'attaquer à un problème

adept ['ædɛpt] adj: **~ at** expert(e) à or en

adequate ['ædɪkwɪt] *adj* adéquat(e); suffisant(e)

adhere [əd'hɪər] *vi*: **to ~ to** adhérer à; (*fig: rule, decision*) se tenir à

adhesive [əd'hi:zɪv] *n* adhésif *m*; **~ tape** *n* (*BRIT*) ruban adhésif; (*US: MED*) sparadrap *m*

ad hoc [æd'hɔk] *adj* improvisé(e), ad hoc

adjacent [ə'dʒeɪsənt] *adj*: **~ (to)** adjacent (à)

adjective ['ædʒektɪv] *n* adjectif *m*

adjoining [ə'dʒɔɪnɪŋ] *adj* voisin(e), adjacent(e), attenant(e)

adjourn [ə'dʒə:n] *vt* ajourner ♦ *vi* suspendre la séance; clore la session

adjust [ə'dʒʌst] *vt* (*machine*) ajuster, régler; (*prices, wages*) rajuster ♦ *vi*: **to ~ (to)** s'adapter (à); **~able** *adj* réglable; **~ment** *n* (*PSYCH*) adaptation *f*; (*to machine*) ajustage *m*, réglage *m*; (*of prices, wages*) rajustement *m*

ad-lib [æd'lɪb] *vt, vi* improviser; **ad lib** *adv* à volonté, à loisir

administer [əd'mɪnɪstər] *vt* administrer; (*justice*) rendre; **administration** [ədmɪnɪs'treɪʃən] *n* administration *f*; **administrative** [əd'mɪnɪstrətɪv] *adj* administratif(-ive)

admiral ['ædmərəl] *n* amiral *m*; **A~ty** ['ædmərəltɪ] (*BRIT*) *n*: **the A~ty** ministère *m* de la Marine

admire [əd'maɪər] *vt* admirer

admission [əd'mɪʃən] *n* admission *f*; (*to exhibition, night club etc*) entrée *f*; (*confession*) aveu *m*; **~ charge** *n* droits *mpl* d'admission

admit [əd'mɪt] *vt* laisser entrer; admettre; (*agree*) reconnaître, admettre; **~ to** *vt fus* reconnaître, avouer; **~tance** *n* admission *f*, (droit *m* d')entrée *f*; **~tedly** *adv* il faut en convenir

ado [ə'du:] *n*: **without (any) more ~** sans plus de cérémonies

adolescence [ædəu'lɛsns] *n* adolescence *f*; **adolescent** *adj, n* adolescent(e)

adopt [ə'dɔpt] *vt* adopter; **~ed** *adj* adoptif(-ive), adopté(e); **~ion** *n* adoption *f*

adore [ə'dɔ:ʳ] *vt* adorer

adorn [ə'dɔ:n] *vt* orner

Adriatic (Sea) [eɪdrɪ'ætɪk-] *n* Adriatique *f*

adrift [ə'drɪft] *adv* à la dérive

adult ['ædʌlt] *n* adulte *m/f* ♦ *adj* adulte; (*literature, education*) pour adultes

adultery [ə'dʌltərɪ] *n* adultère *m*

advance [əd'vɑ:ns] *n* avance *f* ♦ *adj*: **~ booking** réservation *f* ♦ *vt* avancer ♦ *vi* avancer, s'avancer; **~ notice** avertissement *m*; **to make ~s (to sb)** faire des propositions (à qn); (*amorously*) faire des avances (à qn); **in ~** à l'avance, d'avance; **~d** *adj* avancé(e); (*SCOL: studies*) supérieur(e)

advantage [əd'vɑ:ntɪdʒ] *n* (*also TENNIS*) avantage *m*; **to take ~ of** (*person*) exploiter

advent ['ædvənt] *n* avènement *m*, venue *f*; **A~** Avent *m*

adventure [əd'ventʃər] *n* aventure *f*

adverb ['ædvə:b] *n* adverbe *m*

adverse ['ædvə:s] *adj* défavorable, contraire

advert ['ædvə:t] (*BRIT*) *n abbr* = **advertisement**

advertise ['ædvətaɪz] *vi, vt* faire de la publicité (pour); (*in classified ads etc*) mettre une annonce (pour vendre); **to ~ for** (*staff, accommodation*) faire paraître une annonce pour trouver; **~ment** [əd'və:tɪsmənt] *n* (*COMM*) réclame *f*, publicité *f*; (*in classified ads*) annonce *f*; **advertising** *n* publicité *f*

advice [əd'vaɪs] *n* conseils *mpl*; (*notification*) avis *m*; **piece of ~** conseil; **to take legal ~** consulter un avocat

advisable [əd'vaɪzəbl] *adj* conseillé(e), indiqué(e)

advise [əd'vaɪz] *vt* conseiller; **to ~ sb of sth** aviser *or* informer qn de qch; **to ~ against sth/doing sth** déconseiller qch, conseiller de ne pas faire qch; **~r, advisor** *n* conseiller(-ère); **advisory** *adj* consultatif(-ive)

advocate [*n* 'ædvəkɪt, *vb* 'ædvəkeɪt] *n* (*upholder*) défenseur *m*, avocat(e); (*LAW* avocat(e) ♦ *vt* recommander, prôner

Aegean (Sea) [iːˈdʒiːən-] *n* (mer *f*) Égée *f*

aerial [ˈɛərɪəl] *n* antenne *f* ♦ *adj* aérien(ne)

aerobics [ɛəˈrəubɪks] *n* aérobic *f*

aeroplane [ˈɛərəpleɪn] (*BRIT*) *n* avion *m*

aerosol [ˈɛərəsɔl] *n* aérosol *m*

aesthetic [iːsˈθetɪk] *adj* esthétique

afar [əˈfɑːr] *adv*: **from ~** de loin

affair [əˈfɛər] *n* affaire *f*; (*also:* **love ~**) liaison *f*; aventure *f*

affect [əˈfekt] *vt* affecter; (*disease*) atteindre; **~ed** *adj* affecté(e); **~ion** *n* affection *f*; **~ionate** *adj* affectueux(-euse)

affinity [əˈfɪnɪtɪ] *n* (*bond, rapport*): **to have an ~ with/for** avoir une affinité avec/pour

afflict [əˈflɪkt] *vt* affliger

affluence [ˈæfluəns] *n* abondance *f*, opulence *f*

affluent [ˈæfluənt] *adj* (*person, family, surroundings*) aisé(e), riche; **the ~ society** la société d'abondance

afford [əˈfɔːd] *vt* se permettre; (*provide*) fournir, procurer

afloat [əˈfləut] *adj, adv* à flot; **to stay ~** surnager

afoot [əˈfut] *adv*: **there is something ~** il se prépare quelque chose

afraid [əˈfreɪd] *adj* effrayé(e); **to be ~ of** or **to** avoir peur de; **I am ~ that ...** je suis désolé(e), mais ...; **I am ~ so/not** hélas oui/non

Africa [ˈæfrɪkə] *n* Afrique *f*; **~n** *adj* africain(e) ♦ *n* Africain(e)

after [ˈɑːftər] *prep, adv* après ♦ *conj* après que, après avoir or être +*pp*; **what/who are you ~?** que/qui cherchez-vous?; **~ he left/having done** après qu'il fut parti/après avoir fait; **ask ~ him** demandez de ses nouvelles; **to name sb ~ sb** donner à qn le nom de qn; **twenty ~ eight** (*US*) huit heures vingt; **~ all** après tout; **~ you!** après vous, Monsieur (or Madame *etc*); **~effects** *npl* (*of disaster, radiation, drink etc*) répercussions *fpl*; (*of illness*) séquelles *fpl*, suites *fpl*; **~math** *n* conséquences *fpl*, suites *fpl*; **~noon** *n* après-midi *m or f*; **~s**

(*inf*) *n* (*dessert*) dessert *m*; **~-sales service** (*BRIT*) *n* (*for car, washing machine etc*) service *m* après-vente; **~-shave (lotion)** *n* after-shave *m*; **~sun** *n* après-soleil *m inv*; **~thought** *n*: **I had an ~thought** il m'est venu une idée après coup; **~wards** (*US* **afterward**) *adv* après

again [əˈgen] *adv* de nouveau; encore (une fois); **to do sth ~** refaire qch; **not ... ~** ne ... plus; **~ and ~** à plusieurs reprises

against [əˈgenst] *prep* contre; (*compared to*) par rapport à

age [eɪdʒ] *n* âge *m* ♦ *vt, vi* vieillir; **it's been ~s since** ça fait une éternité que ne; **he is 20 years of ~** il a 20 ans; **to come of ~** atteindre sa majorité; **~d** [*adj* eɪdʒd, *npl* ˈeɪdʒɪd] *adj*: **~d 10** âgé(e) de 10 ans ♦ *npl*: **the ~d** les personnes âgées; **~ group** *n* tranche *f* d'âge; **~ limit** limite *f* d'âge

agency [ˈeɪdʒənsɪ] *n* agence *f*; (*government body*) organisme *m*, office *m*

agenda [əˈdʒɛndə] *n* ordre *m* du jour

agent [ˈeɪdʒənt] *n* agent *m*, représentant *m*; (*firm*) concessionnaire *m*

aggravate [ˈægrəveɪt] *vt* aggraver; (*annoy*) exaspérer

aggressive [əˈgresɪv] *adj* agressif(-ive)

agitate [ˈædʒɪteɪt] *vt* (*person*) agiter, émouvoir, troubler ♦ *vi*: **to ~ for/against** faire campagne pour/contre

AGM *n abbr* (= *annual general meeting*) AG *f*

ago [əˈgəu] *adv*: **2 days ~** il y a deux jours; **not long ~** il n'y a pas longtemps; **how long ~?** il y a combien de temps (de cela)?

agony [ˈægənɪ] *n* (*pain*) douleur *f* atroce; **to be in ~** souffrir le martyre

agree [əˈgriː] *vt* (*price*) convenir de ♦ *vi*: **to ~ with** (*person*) être d'accord avec; (*statements etc*) concorder avec; (*LING*) s'accorder avec; **to ~ to do** accepter de or consentir à faire; **to ~ to sth** consentir à qch; **to ~ that** (*admit*) convenir or reconnaître que; **garlic doesn't ~ with me** je ne supporte pas l'ail; **~able** *adj* agréable; (*willing*) consentant(e), d'accord; ~d *adj* (*time, place*) convenu(e); ~ment *n* accord *m*; in ~ment d'accord

agricultural [ægrɪˈkʌltʃərəl] *adj* agricole

agriculture [ˈægrɪkʌltʃəʳ] *n* agriculture *f*

aground [əˈgraʊnd] *adv*: to run ~ échouer, s'échouer

ahead [əˈhɛd] *adv* (*in front: of position, place*) devant; (: *at the head*) en avant; (*look, plan, think*) en avant; ~ of devant; (*fig: schedule etc*) en avance sur; ~ of time en avance; go right *or* straight ~ allez tout droit; go ~! (*fig: permission*) allez-y!

aid [eɪd] *n* aide *f*; (*device*) appareil *m* ♦ *vt* aider; in ~ of en faveur de; *see also* **hearing**

aide [eɪd] *n* (*person*) aide *mf*, assistant(e)

AIDS [eɪdz] *n abbr* (= *acquired immune deficiency syndrome*) SIDA *m*; AIDS-related *adj* associé(e) au sida

aim [eɪm] *vt*: to ~ sth (at) (*gun, camera*) braquer *or* pointer qch (sur); (*missile*) lancer qch (à *or* contre *or* en direction de); (*blow*) allonger qch (à); (*remark*) destiner *or* adresser qch (à) ♦ *vi* (*also*: to take ~) viser ♦ *n* but *m*; (*skill*): his ~ is bad il vise mal; to ~ at viser; (*fig*) viser (à); to ~ to do avoir l'intention de faire; ~less *adj* sans but

ain't [eɪnt] (*inf*) = **am not; aren't; isn't**

air [ɛəʳ] *n* air *m* ♦ *vt* (*room, bed, clothes*) aérer; (*grievances, views, ideas*) exposer, faire connaître ♦ *cpd* (*currents, attack etc*) aérien(ne); to throw sth into the ~ jeter qch en l'air; by ~ (*travel*) par avion; to be on the ~ (*RADIO, TV: programme*) être diffusé(e); (: *station*) diffuser; ~bed *n* matelas *m* pneumatique; ~-conditioned *adj* climatisé(e); ~ conditioning *n* climatisation *f*; ~craft *n inv* avion *m*; ~craft carrier *n* porte-avions *m inv*; ~field *n* terrain *m* d'aviation; A~ Force *n* armée *f* de l'air; ~ freshener *n* désodorisant *m*; ~gun *n* fusil *m* à air comprimé; ~hostess *n* (*BRIT*) hôtesse *f* de l'air; ~ letter *n* (*BRIT*) aérogramme *m*; ~lift *n* pont aérien; ~line *n* ligne aérienne, compagnie *f*

d'aviation; ~liner *n* avion *m* de ligne; ~mail *n*: by ~mail par avion; ~ mile *n* air mile *m*; ~plane *n* (*US*) avion *m*; ~port *n* aéroport *m*; ~ raid *n* attaque *or* raid aérien(ne); ~sick *adj*: to be ~sick avoir le mal de l'air; ~tight *adj* hermétique; ~traffic controller *n* aiguilleur *m* du ciel; ~y *adj* bien aéré(e); (*manners*) dégagé(e)

aisle [aɪl] *n* (*of church*) allée centrale; nef latérale; (*of theatre etc*) couloir *m*, passage *m*, allée; ~ seat *n* place *m* côté couloir

ajar [əˈdʒɑːʳ] *adj* entrouvert(e)

akin [əˈkɪn] *adj*: ~ to (*similar*) qui tient de *or* ressemble à

alarm [əˈlɑːm] *n* alarme *f* ♦ *vt* alarmer; ~ call *n* coup de fil *m* pour réveiller; ~ clock *n* réveille-matin *m inv*, réveil *m*

alas [əˈlæs] *excl* hélas!

album [ˈælbəm] *n* album *m*

alcohol [ˈælkəhɔl] *n* alcool *m*; ~-free *adj* sans alcool; ~ic [ælkəˈhɔlɪk] *adj* alcoolique ♦ *n* alcoolique *m/f*; A~ics Anonymous Alcooliques anonymes

ale [eɪl] *n* bière *f*

alert [əˈləːt] *adj* alerte, vif (vive); vigilant(e) ♦ *n* alerte *f* ♦ *vt* alerter; on the ~ sur le qui-vive; (*MIL*) en état d'alerte

algebra [ˈældʒɪbrə] *n* algèbre *m*

Algeria [ælˈdʒɪərɪə] *n* Algérie *f*

alias [ˈeɪlɪəs] *adv* alias ♦ *n* faux nom, nom d'emprunt; (*writer*) pseudonyme *m*

alibi [ˈælɪbaɪ] *n* alibi *m*

alien [ˈeɪlɪən] *n* étranger(-ère); (*from outer space*) extraterrestre *mf* ♦ *adj*: ~ (to) étranger(-ère) (à)

alight [əˈlaɪt] *adj, adv* en feu ♦ *vi* mettre pied à terre; (*passenger*) descendre

alike [əˈlaɪk] *adj* semblable, pareil(le) ♦ *adv* de même; to look ~ se ressembler

alimony [ˈælɪmənɪ] *n* (*payment*) pension alimentaire

alive [əˈlaɪv] *adj* vivant(e); (*lively*) plein(e) de vie

| KEYWORD |

all [ɔːl] *adj* (*singular*) tout(e); (*plural*) tou (toutes); **all day** toute la journée; **a**

night toute la nuit; **all men** tous les hommes; **all five** tous les cinq; **all the food** toute la nourriture; **all the books** tous les livres; **all the time** tout le temps; **all his life** toute sa vie
♦ *pron* 1 tout; **I ate it all, I ate all of it** j'ai tout mangé; **all of us went** nous y sommes tous allés; **all of the boys went** tous les garçons y sont allés
2 *(in phrases)*: **above all** surtout, par-dessus tout; **after all** après tout; **not at all** *(in answer to question)* pas du tout; *(in answer to thanks)* je vous en prie!; **I'm not at all tired** je ne suis pas du tout fatigué(e); **anything at all will do** n'importe quoi fera l'affaire; **all in all** tout bien considéré, en fin de compte
♦ *adv*: **all alone** tout(e) seul(e); **it's not as hard as all that** ce n'est pas si difficile que ça; **all the more/the better** d'autant plus/mieux; **all but** presque, pratiquement; **the score is 2 all** le score est de 2 partout

allege [əˈlɛdʒ] *vt* alléguer, prétendre; **~dly** [əˈlɛdʒɪdlɪ] *adv* à ce que l'on prétend, paraît-il
allegiance [əˈliːdʒəns] *n* allégeance *f*, fidélité *f*, obéissance *f*
allergic [əˈlɜːdʒɪk] *adj*: **~ to** allergique à
allergy [ˈælədʒɪ] *n* allergie *f*
alleviate [əˈliːvɪeɪt] *vt* soulager, adoucir
alley [ˈælɪ] *n* ruelle *f*
alliance [əˈlaɪəns] *n* alliance *f*
allied [ˈælaɪd] *adj* allié(e)
all-in [ˈɔːlɪn] *(BRIT) adj (also adv: charge)* tout compris
all-night [ˈɔːlˈnaɪt] *adj* ouvert(e) *or* qui dure toute la nuit
allocate [ˈæləkeɪt] *vt (share out)* répartir, distribuer; **to ~ sth to** *(duties)* assigner *or* attribuer qch à; *(sum, time)* allouer qch à
allot [əˈlɔt] *vt*: **to ~ (to)** *(money)* répartir (entre), distribuer (à); *(time)* allouer (à); **~ment** *n (share)* part *f*; *(garden)* lopin *m* de terre *(loué à la municipalité)*
all-out [ˈɔːlaut] *adj (effort etc)* total(e)

♦ *adv*: **all out** à fond
allow [əˈlau] *vt (practice, behaviour)* permettre, autoriser; *(sum to spend etc)* accorder, allouer; *(sum, time estimated)* compter, prévoir; *(claim, goal)* admettre; *(concede)*: **to ~ that** convenir que; **to ~ sb to do** permettre à qn de faire, autoriser qn à faire; **he is ~ed to ...** on lui permet de ...; **~ for** *vt fus* tenir compte de; **~ance** [əˈlauəns] *n (money received)* allocation *f*; subside *m*; indemnité *f*; *(TAX)* somme *f* déductible du revenu imposable, abattement *m*; **to make ~ances for** tenir compte de
alloy [ˈælɔɪ] *n* alliage *m*
all: **~ right** *adv (feel, work)* bien; *(as answer)* d'accord; **~-rounder** *n*: **to be a good ~-rounder** être doué(e) en tout; **~-time** *adj (record)* sans précédent, absolu(e)
ally [*n* ˈælaɪ, *vb* əˈlaɪ] *n* allié *m* ♦ *vt*: **to ~ o.s. with** s'allier avec
almighty [ɔːlˈmaɪtɪ] *adj* tout-puissant; *(tremendous)* énorme
almond [ˈɑːmənd] *n* amande *f*
almost [ˈɔːlməust] *adv* presque
alone [əˈləun] *adj, adv* seul(e); **to leave sb ~** laisser qn tranquille; **to leave sth ~** ne pas toucher à qch; **let ~ ...** sans parler de ...; encore moins ...
along [əˈlɔŋ] *prep* le long de ♦ *adv*: **is he coming ~ with us?** vient-il avec nous?; **he was hopping/limping ~** il avançait en sautillant/boitant; **~ with** *(together with: person)* en compagnie de; *(: thing)* avec, en plus de; **all ~** *(all the time)* depuis le début; **~side** *prep* le long de; à côté de
♦ *adv* bord à bord
aloof [əˈluːf] *adj* distant(e) ♦ *adv*: **to stand ~** se tenir à distance *or* à l'écart
aloud [əˈlaud] *adv* à haute voix
alphabet [ˈælfəbɛt] *n* alphabet *m*; **~ical** [ælfəˈbɛtɪkl] *adj* alphabétique
alpine [ˈælpaɪn] *adj* alpin(e), alpestre
Alps [ælps] *npl*: **the ~** les Alpes *fpl*
already [ɔːlˈrɛdɪ] *adv* déjà
alright [ˈɔːlˈraɪt] *(BRIT) adv* = **all right**

Alsatian [æl'seɪʃən] (*BRIT*) *n* (*dog*) berger allemand

also ['ɔːlsəʊ] *adv* aussi

altar ['ɔːltər] *n* autel *m*

alter ['ɔːltər] *vt, vi* changer

alternate [*adj* ɔlˈtəːnɪt, *vb* ˈɔltəːneɪt] *adj* alterné(e), alternant(e), alternatif(-ive) ♦ *vi* alterner; **on ~ days** un jour sur deux, tous les jours; **alternating current** *n* courant alternatif

alternative [ɔlˈtəːnətɪv] *adj* (*solutions*) possible, au choix; (*plan*) autre, de rechange; (*lifestyle etc*) parallèle ♦ *n* (*choice*) alternative *f*; (*other possibility*) autre possibilité *f*; **an ~ comedian** un nouveau comique; **~ medicine** médecines *fpl* parallèles *or* douces; **~ly** *adv*: **~ly one could** une autre *or* l'autre solution serait de, on pourrait aussi

alternator ['ɔltəːneɪtər] *n* (*AUT*) alternateur *m*

although [ɔːl'ðəʊ] *conj* bien que +*sub*

altitude ['æltɪtjuːd] *n* altitude *f*

alto ['æltəʊ] *n* (*female*) contralto *m*; (*male*) haute-contre *f*

altogether [ɔːltəˈgɛðər] *adv* entièrement, tout à fait; (*on the whole*) tout compte fait; (*in all*) en tout

aluminium [ælju'mɪnɪəm] (*BRIT*), **aluminum** [ə'luːmɪnəm] (*US*) *n* aluminium *m*

always ['ɔːlweɪz] *adv* toujours

Alzheimer's (disease) ['æltshaɪməz-] *n* maladie *f* d'Alzheimer

AM *n abbr* (= *Assembly Member*) député *m* au Parlement gallois

am [æm] *vb see* **be**

a.m. *adv abbr* (= *ante meridiem*) du matin

amalgamate [ə'mælgəmeɪt] *vt, vi* fusionner

amateur ['æmətər] *n* amateur *m*; **~ish** (*pej*) *adj* d'amateur

amaze [ə'meɪz] *vt* stupéfier; **to be ~d (at)** être stupéfait(e) (de); **~ment** *n* stupéfaction *f*, stupeur *f*; **amazing** *adj* étonnant(e); exceptionnel(le)

ambassador [æm'bæsədər] *n* ambassadeur *m*

amber ['æmbər] *n* ambre *m*; **at ~** (*BRIT*:

AUT) à l'orange

ambiguous [æm'bɪgjuəs] *adj* ambigu(ë)

ambition [æm'bɪʃən] *n* ambition *f*; **ambitious** *adj* ambitieux(-euse)

ambulance ['æmbjuləns] *n* ambulance *f*

ambush ['æmbuʃ] *n* embuscade *f* ♦ *vt* tendre une embuscade à

amenable [ə'miːnəbl] *adj*: **~ to** (*advice etc*) disposé(e) à écouter

amend [ə'mɛnd] *vt* (*law*) amender; (*text*) corriger; **to make ~s** réparer ses torts, faire amende honorable

amenities [ə'miːnɪtɪz] *npl* aménagements *mpl*, équipements *mpl*

America [ə'mɛrɪkə] *n* Amérique *f*; **~n** *adj* américain(e) ♦ *n* Américain(e)

amiable ['eɪmɪəbl] *adj* aimable, affable

amicable ['æmɪkəbl] *adj* amical(e); (*LAW*) à l'amiable

amid(st) [ə'mɪd(st)] *prep* parmi, au milieu de

amiss [ə'mɪs] *adj, adv*: **there's something ~** il y a quelque chose qui ne va pas *or* qui cloche; **to take sth ~** prendre qch mal *or* de travers

ammonia [ə'məʊnɪə] *n* (*gas*) ammoniac *m*; (*liquid*) ammoniaque *f*

ammunition [æmju'nɪʃən] *n* munitions *fpl*

amok [ə'mɔk] *adv*: **to run ~** être pris(e) d'un accès de folie furieuse

among(st) [ə'mʌŋ(st)] *prep* parmi, entre

amorous ['æmərəs] *adj* amoureux(-euse)

amount [ə'maʊnt] *n* (*sum*) somme *f*, montant *m*; (*quantity*) quantité *f*, nombre *m* ♦ *vi*: **to ~ to** (*total*) s'élever à; (*be same as*) équivaloir à, revenir à

amp(ere) ['æmp(ɛər)] *n* ampère *m*

ample ['æmpl] *adj* ample; spacieux(-euse); (*enough*): **this is ~** c'est largement suffisant; **to have ~ time/room** avoir bien assez de temps/place

amplifier ['æmplɪfaɪər] *n* amplificateur *m*

amuse [ə'mjuːz] *vt* amuser, divertir; **~ment** *n* amusement *m*; **~ment arcade** *n* salle *f* de jeu; **~ment park** *n* parc *m* d'attractions

an [æn, ən] *indef art see* **a**

anaemic [əˈniːmɪk] (*US* **anemic**) *adj* anémique

anaesthetic [ænɪsˈθetɪk] (*US* **anesthetic**) *n* anesthésique *m*

analog(ue) [ˈænəlɒg] *adj* (*watch, computer*) analogique

analyse [ˈænəlaɪz] (*US* **analyze**) *vt* analyser; **analysis** [əˈnæləsɪs] (*pl* **analyses**) *n* analyse *f*; **analyst** [ˈænəlɪst] *n* (*POL etc*) spécialiste *m/f*; (*US*) psychanalyste *m/f*

analyze [ˈænəlaɪz] (*US*) *vt* = **analyse**

anarchist [ˈænəkɪst] *n* anarchiste *m/f*

anarchy [ˈænəkɪ] *n* anarchie *f*

anatomy [əˈnætəmɪ] *n* anatomie *f*

ancestor [ˈænsɪstər] *n* ancêtre *m*, aïeul *m*

anchor [ˈæŋkər] *n* ancre *f* ♦ *vi* (*also:* **to drop ~**) jeter l'ancre, mouiller ♦ *vt* mettre à l'ancre; (*fig*): **to ~ sth to** fixer qch à

anchovy [ˈæntʃovɪ] *n* anchois *m*

ancient [ˈeɪnʃənt] *adj* ancien(ne), antique; (*person*) d'un âge vénérable; (*car*) antédiluvien(ne)

ancillary [ænˈsɪlərɪ] *adj* auxiliaire

and [ænd] *conj* et; **~ so on** et ainsi de suite; **try ~ come** tâchez de venir; **he talked ~ talked** il n'a pas arrêté de parler; **better ~ better** de mieux en mieux

anew [əˈnjuː] *adv* à nouveau

angel [ˈeɪndʒəl] *n* ange *m*

anger [ˈæŋgər] *n* colère *f*

angina [ænˈdʒaɪnə] *n* angine *f* de poitrine

angle [ˈæŋgl] *n* angle *m*; **from their ~** de leur point de vue

angler [ˈæŋglər] *n* pêcheur(-euse) à la ligne

Anglican [ˈæŋglɪkən] *adj, n* anglican(e)

angling [ˈæŋglɪŋ] *n* pêche *f* à la ligne

Anglo- [ˈæŋgləu] *prefix* anglo(-)

angrily [ˈæŋgrɪlɪ] *adv* avec colère

angry [ˈæŋgrɪ] *adj* en colère, furieux(-euse); (*wound*) enflammé(e); **to be ~ with sb/at sth** être furieux contre qn/de qch; **to get ~** se fâcher, se mettre en colère

anguish [ˈæŋgwɪʃ] *n* (*mental*) angoisse *f*

animal [ˈænɪməl] *n* animal *m* ♦ *adj* animal(e)

animate [*vb* ˈænɪmeɪt, *adj* ˈænɪmɪt] *vt* animer ♦ *adj* animé(e), vivant(e); **~d** *adj* animé(e)

mé(e)

aniseed [ˈænɪsiːd] *n* anis *m*

ankle [ˈæŋkl] *n* cheville *f*; **~ sock** *n* socquette *f*

annex [*n* ˈæneks, *vb* əˈneks] *n* (*BRIT*: ~e) annexe *f* ♦ *vt* annexer

anniversary [ænɪˈvɜːsərɪ] *n* anniversaire *m*

announce [əˈnauns] *vt* annoncer; (*birth, death*) faire part de; **~ment** *n* annonce *f*; (*for births etc: in newspaper*) avis *m* de faire-part; (: *letter, card*) faire-part *m*; **~r** *n* (*RADIO, TV: between programmes*) speaker(ine)

annoy [əˈnɔɪ] *vt* agacer, ennuyer, contrarier; **don't get ~ed!** ne vous fâchez pas!; **~ance** *n* mécontentement *m*, contrariété *f*; **~ing** *adj* agaçant(e), contrariant(e)

annual [ˈænjuəl] *adj* annuel(le) ♦ *n* (*BOT*) plante annuelle; (*children's book*) album *m*

annul [əˈnʌl] *vt* annuler

annum [ˈænəm] *n* see **per**

anonymous [əˈnɒnɪməs] *adj* anonyme

anorak [ˈænəræk] *n* anorak *m*

anorexia [ænəˈreksɪə] *n* (*also:* ~ **nervosa**) anorexie *f*

another [əˈnʌðər] *adj*: ~ **book** (*one more*) un autre livre, encore un livre, un livre de plus; (*a different one*) un autre livre ♦ *pron* un(e) autre, encore un(e), un(e) de plus; *see also* **one**

answer [ˈɑːnsər] *n* réponse *f*; (*to problem*) solution *f* ♦ *vi* répondre ♦ *vt* (*reply to*) répondre à; (*problem*) résoudre; (*prayer*) exaucer; **in ~ to your letter** en réponse à votre lettre; **to ~ the phone** répondre (au téléphone); **to ~ the bell** *or* **the door** aller *or* venir ouvrir (la porte); **~ back** *vi* répondre, répliquer; **~ for** *vt fus* (*person*) répondre de, se porter garant de; (*crime, one's actions*) être responsable de; **~ to** *vt fus* (*description*) répondre *or* correspondre à; **~able** *adj*: **~able (to sb/for sth)** responsable (devant qn/de qch); **~ing machine** *n* répondeur *m* automatique

ant [ænt] *n* fourmi *f*

antagonism [ænˈtægənɪzəm] *n* antagonisme *m*

antagonize → apart

298 ENGLISH-FRENCH

antagonize [ænˈtægənaɪz] vt éveiller l'hostilité de, contrarier
Antarctic [æntˈɑːktɪk] n: the ~ l'Antarctique m
antenatal [ˈæntɪˈneɪtl] adj prénatal(e); ~ clinic n service m de consultation prénatale
anthem [ˈænθəm] n: national ~ hymne national
anti: ~-aircraft adj (missile) anti-aérien(ne); ~biotic [ˈæntɪbaɪˈɔtɪk] n antibiotique m; ~body n anticorps m
anticipate [ænˈtɪsɪpeɪt] vt s'attendre à; prévoir; (wishes, request) aller au devant de, devancer
anticipation [æntɪsɪˈpeɪʃən] n attente f; in ~ par anticipation, à l'avance
anticlimax [ˈæntɪˈklaɪmæks] n déception f, douche froide (fam)
anticlockwise [ˈæntɪˈklɔkwaɪz] adj, adv dans le sens inverse des aiguilles d'une montre
antics [ˈæntɪks] npl singeries fpl
antidepressant [ˈæntɪdɪˈpresənt] n antidépresseur m
antifreeze [ˈæntɪfriːz] n antigel m
antihistamine [ˈæntɪˈhɪstəmɪn] n antihistaminique m
antiquated [ˈæntɪkweɪtɪd] adj vieilli(e), suranné(e), vieillot(te)
antique [ænˈtiːk] n objet m d'art ancien, meuble ancien or d'époque, antiquité f ♦ adj ancien(ne); ~ dealer n antiquaire m; ~ shop n magasin m d'antiquités
anti: ~-Semitism [ˈæntɪˈsemɪtɪzəm] n antisémitisme m; ~septic [ˈæntɪˈseptɪk] n antiseptique m; ~social [ˈæntɪˈsəuʃəl] adj peu liant(e), sauvage, insociable; (against society) antisocial(e)
antlers [ˈæntləz] npl bois mpl, ramure f
anvil [ˈænvɪl] n enclume f
anxiety [æŋˈzaɪətɪ] n anxiété f; (keenness): ~ to do grand désir or impatience f de faire
anxious [ˈæŋkʃəs] adj anxieux(-euse); (worrying: time, situation) inquiétant(e); (keen): ~ to do/that qui tient beaucoup à faire/à

ce que; impatient(e) de faire/que

KEYWORD

any [ˈenɪ] adj 1 (in questions etc: singular) du, de l', de la; (: plural) des; have you any butter/children/ink? avez-vous du beurre/des enfants/de l'encre?
2 (with negative) de, d'; I haven't any books je n'ai pas de livres
3 (no matter which) n'importe quel(le); choose any book you like vous pouvez choisir n'importe quel livre
4 (in phrases): in any case de toute façon; any day now d'un jour à l'autre; at any moment à tout moment, d'un instant à l'autre; at any rate en tout cas
♦ pron 1 (in questions etc) en; have you got any? est-ce que vous en avez?; can any of you sing? est-ce que parmi vous il y en a qui savent chanter?
2 (with negative) en; I haven't any (of them) je n'en ai pas, je n'en ai aucun
3 (no matter which one(s)) n'importe lequel (or laquelle); take any of those books (you like) vous pouvez prendre n'importe lequel de ces livres
♦ adv 1 (in questions etc): do you want any more soup/sandwiches? voulez-vous encore de la soupe/des sandwichs?; are you feeling any better? est-ce que vous vous sentez mieux?
2 (with negative): I can't hear him any more je ne l'entends plus; don't wait any longer n'attendez pas plus longtemps

any: ~body pron n'importe qui; (in interrogative sentences) quelqu'un; (in negative sentences): I don't see ~body je ne vois personne; ~how adv (at any rate) de toute façon, quand même; (haphazard) n'importe comment; ~one pron = anybody; ~thing pron n'importe quoi, quelque chose, ne ... rien; ~way adv de toute façon; ~where adv n'importe où, quelque part; I don't see him ~where je ne le vois nulle part
apart [əˈpɑːt] adv (to one side) à part; de

côté; à l'écart; (*separately*) séparément; **10 miles ~** à 10 miles l'un de l'autre; **to take ~** démonter; **~ from** à part, excepté
apartheid [ə'pɑ:teɪt] *n* apartheid *m*
apartment [ə'pɑ:tmənt] *n* (*US*) appartement *m*, logement *m*; (*room*) chambre *f*; **~ building** (*US*) *n* immeuble *m*; (*divided house*) maison divisée en appartements
ape [eɪp] *n* (grand) singe ♦ *vt* singer
apéritif [ə'peritif] *n* apéritif *m*
aperture ['æpətʃuər] *n* orifice *m*, ouverture *f*; (*PHOT*) ouverture (du diaphragme)
APEX ['eɪpeks] *n abbr* (*AVIAT*) (= *advance purchase excursion*) APEX *m*
apologetic [əpɔlə'dʒetɪk] *adj* (*tone, letter*) d'excuse; (*person*): **to be ~** s'excuser
apologize [ə'pɔlədʒaɪz] *vi*: **to ~ (for sth to sb)** s'excuser (de qch auprès de qn), présenter des excuses (à qn pour qch)
apology [ə'pɔlədʒɪ] *n* excuses *fpl*
apostle [ə'pɔsl] *n* apôtre *m*
apostrophe [ə'pɔstrəfɪ] *n* apostrophe *f*
appalling [ə'pɔ:lɪŋ] *adj* épouvantable; (*stupidity*) consternant(e)
apparatus [æpə'reɪtəs] *n* appareil *m*, dispositif *m*; (*in gymnasium*) agrès *mpl*; (*of government*) dispositif *m*
apparel [ə'pærəl] (*US*) *n* habillement *m*
apparent [ə'pærənt] *adj* apparent(e); **~ly** *adv* apparemment
appeal [ə'pi:l] *vi* (*LAW*) faire *or* interjeter appel ♦ *n* appel *m*; (*request*) prière *f*; appel *m*; (*charm*) attrait *m*, charme *m*; **to ~ for** lancer un appel pour; **to ~ to** (*beg*) faire appel à; (*be attractive*) plaire à; **it doesn't ~ to me** cela ne m'attire pas; **~ing** *adj* (*attractive*) attrayant(e)
appear [ə'pɪər] *vi* apparaître, se montrer; (*LAW*) comparaître; (*publication*) paraître, sortir, être publié(e); (*seem*) paraître, sembler; **it would ~ that** il semble que; **to ~ in Hamlet** jouer dans Hamlet; **to ~ on TV** passer à la télé; **~ance** *n* apparition *f*; parution *f*; (*look, aspect*) apparence *f*, aspect *m*
appease [ə'pi:z] *vt* apaiser, calmer
appendicitis [əpendɪ'saɪtɪs] *n* appendicite *f*
appendix [ə'pendɪks] (*pl* **appendices**) *n* appendice *m*
appetite ['æpɪtaɪt] *n* appétit *m*; **appetizer** *n* amuse-gueule *m*; (*drink*) apéritif *m*
applaud [ə'plɔ:d] *vt, vi* applaudir
applause [ə'plɔ:z] *n* applaudissements *mpl*
apple ['æpl] *n* pomme *f*; **~ tree** *n* pommier *m*
appliance [ə'plaɪəns] *n* appareil *m*
applicable [ə'plɪkəbl] *adj* (*relevant*): **to be ~ to** valoir pour
applicant ['æplɪkənt] *n*: **~ (for)** candidat(e) (à)
application [æplɪ'keɪʃən] *n* application *f*; (*for a job, a grant etc*) demande *f*; candidature *f*; **~ form** *n* formulaire *m* de demande
applied [ə'plaɪd] *adj* appliqué(e)
apply [ə'plaɪ] *vt*: **to ~ (to)** (*paint, ointment*) appliquer (sur); (*law etc*) appliquer (à) ♦ *vi*: **to ~ to** (*be suitable for, relevant to*) s'appliquer à; (*ask*) s'adresser à; **to ~ (for)** (*permit, grant*) faire une demande (en vue d'obtenir); (*job*) poser sa candidature (pour), faire une demande d'emploi (concernant); **to ~ o.s. to** s'appliquer à
appoint [ə'pɔɪnt] *vt* nommer, engager; **~ed** *adj*: **at the ~ed time** à l'heure dite; **~ment** *n* nomination *f*; (*meeting*) rendez-vous *m*; **to make an ~ment (with)** prendre rendez-vous (avec)
appraisal [ə'preɪzl] *n* évaluation *f*
appreciate [ə'pri:ʃɪeɪt] *vt* (*like*) apprécier; (*be grateful for*) être reconnaissant(e) de; (*understand*) comprendre; se rendre compte de ♦ *vi* (*FINANCE*) prendre de la valeur
appreciation [əpri:ʃɪ'eɪʃən] *n* appréciation *f*; (*gratitude*) reconnaissance *f*; (*COMM*) hausse *f*, valorisation *f*
appreciative [ə'pri:ʃɪətɪv] *adj* (*person*) sensible; (*comment*) élogieux(-euse)
apprehensive [æprɪ'hensɪv] *adj* inquiet(-ète), appréhensif(-ive)
apprentice [ə'prentɪs] *n* apprenti *m*; **~ship** *n* apprentissage *m*

approach [əˈprəʊtʃ] *vi* approcher ♦ *vt* (*come near*) approcher de; (*ask, apply to*) s'adresser à; (*situation, problem*) aborder ♦ *n* approche *f*; (*access*) accès *m*; **~able** *adj* accessible

appropriate [*adj* əˈprəʊprɪɪt, *vb* əˈprəʊprɪeɪt] *adj* (*moment, remark*) opportun(e); (*tool etc*) approprié(e) ♦ *vt* (*take*) s'approprier

approval [əˈpruːvəl] *n* approbation *f*; **on ~** (*COMM*) à l'examen

approve [əˈpruːv] *vt* approuver; **~ of** *vt fus* approuver

approximate [*adj* əˈprɒksɪmɪt, *vb* əˈprɒksɪmeɪt] *adj* approximatif(-ive) ♦ *vt* se rapprocher de, être proche de; **~ly** *adv* approximativement

apricot [ˈeɪprɪkɒt] *n* abricot *m*

April [ˈeɪprəl] *n* avril *m*; **~ Fool's Day** le premier avril

---
| April Fool's Day |

🅘 **April Fool's Day** *est le 1er avril, à l'occasion duquel on fait des farces de toutes sortes. Les victimes de ces farces sont les "April fools". Les médias britanniques se prennent aussi au jeu, diffusant de fausses nouvelles, comme la découverte d'îles de la taille de l'Irlande, ou faisant des reportages bidon, montrant par exemple la culture d'arbres à spaghettis en Italie.*

---

apron [ˈeɪprən] *n* tablier *m*

apt [æpt] *adj* (*suitable*) approprié(e); (*likely*): **~ to do** susceptible de faire; qui a tendance à faire

Aquarius [əˈkwɛərɪəs] *n* le Verseau

Arab [ˈærəb] *adj* arabe ♦ *n* Arabe *m/f*; **~ian** [əˈreɪbɪən] *adj* arabe; **~ic** *adj* arabe ♦ *n* arabe *m*

arbitrary [ˈɑːbɪtrərɪ] *adj* arbitraire

arbitration [ɑːbɪˈtreɪʃən] *n* arbitrage *m*

arcade [ɑːˈkeɪd] *n* arcade *f*; (*passage with shops*) passage *m*, galerie marchande; (*with video games*) salle *f* de jeu

arch [ɑːtʃ] *n* arc *m*; (*of foot*) cambrure *f*,

voûte *f* plantaire ♦ *vt* arquer, cambrer

archaeologist [ɑːkɪˈɒlədʒɪst] *n* archéologue *m/f*

archaeology [ɑːkɪˈɒlədʒɪ] *n* archéologie *f*

archbishop [ɑːtʃˈbɪʃəp] *n* archevêque *m*

archeology *etc* (*US*) [ɑːkɪˈɒlədʒɪ] = **archaeology** *etc*

archery [ˈɑːtʃərɪ] *n* tir *m* à l'arc

architect [ˈɑːkɪtɛkt] *n* architecte *m*; **~ure** *n* architecture *f*

archives [ˈɑːkaɪvz] *npl* archives *fpl*

Arctic [ˈɑːktɪk] *adj* arctique ♦ *n* Arctique *m*

ardent [ˈɑːdənt] *adj* fervent(e)

are [ɑːr] *vb see* **be**

area [ˈɛərɪə] *n* (*GEOM*) superficie *f*; (*zone*) région *f*; (*: smaller*) secteur *m*, partie *f*; (*in room*) coin *m*; (*knowledge, research*) domaine *m*; **~ code** (*US*) *n* (*TEL*) indicatif *m* téléphonique

aren't [ɑːnt] = **are not**

Argentina [ɑːdʒənˈtiːnə] *n* Argentine *f*; **Argentinian** [ɑːdʒənˈtɪnɪən] *adj* argentin(e) ♦ *n* Argentin(e)

arguably [ˈɑːɡjuəblɪ] *adv*: **it is ~ ...** on peut soutenir que c'est ...

argue [ˈɑːɡjuː] *vi* (*quarrel*) se disputer; (*reason*) argumenter; **to ~ that** objecter *or* alléguer que

argument [ˈɑːɡjumənt] *n* (*reasons*) argument *m*; (*quarrel*) dispute *f*; **~ative** [ɑːɡjuˈmɛntətɪv] *adj* ergoteur(-euse), raisonneur(-euse)

Aries [ˈɛərɪz] *n* le Bélier

arise [əˈraɪz] (*pt* **arose**, *pp* **arisen**) *vi* survenir, se présenter

aristocrat [ˈærɪstəkræt] *n* aristocrate *m/f*

arithmetic [əˈrɪθmətɪk] *n* arithmétique *f*

ark [ɑːk] *n*: **Noah's A~** l'Arche *f* de Noé

arm [ɑːm] *n* bras *m* ♦ *vt* armer; **~s** *npl* (*weapons, HERALDRY*) armes *fpl*; **~ in ~** bras dessus bras dessous

armaments [ˈɑːməmənts] *npl* armements *m*

armchair [ˈɑːmtʃɛər] *n* fauteuil *m*

armed [ɑːmd] *adj* armé(e); **~ robbery** *n* vol *m* à main armée

armour [ˈɑːmər] (*US* **armor**) *n* armure *f*

(*MIL: tanks*) blindés *mpl*; **~ed car** *n* véhicule blindé

armpit [ˈɑːmpɪt] *n* aisselle *f*

armrest [ˈɑːmrest] *n* accoudoir *m*

army [ˈɑːmɪ] *n* armée *f*

A road (*BRIT*) *n* (*AUT*) route nationale

aroma [əˈrəumə] *n* arôme *m*; **~therapy** *n* aromathérapie *f*

arose [əˈrəuz] *pt of* **arise**

around [əˈraund] *adv* autour; (*nearby*) dans les parages ♦ *prep* autour de; (*near*) près de; (*fig: about*) environ; (: *date, time*) vers

arouse [əˈrauz] *vt* (*sleeper*) éveiller; (*curiosity, passions*) éveiller, susciter; (*anger*) exciter

arrange [əˈreɪndʒ] *vt* arranger; **to ~ to do sth** prévoir de faire qch; **~ment** *n* arrangement *m*; **~ments** *npl* (*plans etc*) arrangements *mpl*, dispositions *fpl*

array [əˈreɪ] *n*: **~ of** déploiement *m or* étalage *m* de

arrears [əˈrɪəz] *npl* arriéré *m*; **to be in ~ with one's rent** devoir un arriéré de loyer

arrest [əˈrest] *vt* arrêter; (*sb's attention*) retenir, attirer ♦ *n* arrestation *f*; **under ~** en état d'arrestation

arrival [əˈraɪvl] *n* arrivée *f*; **new ~** nouveau venu, nouvelle venue; (*baby*) nouveau-né(e)

arrive [əˈraɪv] *vi* arriver

arrogant [ˈærəgənt] *adj* arrogant(e)

arrow [ˈærəu] *n* flèche *f*

arse [ɑːs] (*BRIT: infl*) *n* cul *m* (!)

arson [ˈɑːsn] *n* incendie criminel

art [ɑːt] *n* art *m*; **A~s** *npl* (*SCOL*) les lettres *fpl*

artery [ˈɑːtərɪ] *n* artère *f*

art gallery *n* musée *m* d'art; (*small and private*) galerie *f* de peinture

arthritis [ɑːˈθraɪtɪs] *n* arthrite *f*

artichoke [ˈɑːtɪtʃəuk] *n* (*also:* **globe ~**) artichaut *m*; (*also:* **Jerusalem ~**) topinambour *m*

article [ˈɑːtɪkl] *n* article *m*; **~s** *npl* (*BRIT: LAW: training*) ≈ stage *m*; **~ of clothing** vêtement *m*

articulate [*adj* ɑːˈtɪkjulɪt, *vb* ɑːˈtɪkjuleɪt] *adj*

(*person*) qui s'exprime bien; (*speech*) bien articulé(e), prononcé(e) clairement ♦ *vt* exprimer; **~d lorry** (*BRIT*) *n* (camion *m*) semi-remorque *m*

artificial [ɑːtɪˈfɪʃəl] *adj* artificiel(le); **~ respiration** *n* respiration artificielle

artist [ˈɑːtɪst] *n* artiste *m/f*; **~ic** [ɑːˈtɪstɪk] *adj* artistique; **~ry** *n* art *m*, talent *m*

art school *n* ≈ école *f* des beaux-arts

KEYWORD

as [æz, əz] *conj* **1** (*referring to time*) comme, alors que; à mesure que; **he came in as I was leaving** il est arrivé comme je partais; **as the years went by** à mesure que les années passaient; **as from tomorrow** à partir de demain

2 (*in comparisons*): **as big as** aussi grand que; **twice as big as** deux fois plus grand que; **as much** *or* **many as** autant que; **as much money/many books** autant d'argent/de livres que; **as soon as** dès que

3 (*since, because*) comme, puisque; **as he had to be home by 10 ...** comme il *or* puisqu'il devait être de retour avant 10 h ...

4 (*referring to manner, way*) comme; **do as you wish** faites comme vous voudrez

5 (*concerning*): **as for** *or* **to that** quant à cela, pour ce qui est de cela

6: as if *or* **though** comme si; **he looked as if he was ill** il avait l'air d'être malade; *see also* **long**; **such**; **well**

♦ *prep*: **he works as a driver** il travaille comme chauffeur; **as chairman of the company, he ...** en tant que président de la société, il ...; **dressed up as a cowboy** déguisé en cowboy; **he gave me it as a present** il me l'a offert, il m'en a fait cadeau

a.s.a.p. *abbr* (= *as soon as possible*) dès que possible

asbestos [æzˈbestəs] *n* amiante *f*

ascend [əˈsend] *vt* gravir; (*throne*) monter sur

ascertain [æsə'teɪn] *vt* vérifier

ash [æʃ] *n* (*dust*) cendre *f*; (*also:* ~ **tree**) frêne *m*

ashamed [ə'feɪmd]. *adj* honteux(-euse), confus(e); **to be ~ of** avoir honte de

ashore [ə'fɔːr] *adv* à terre

ashtray ['æʃtreɪ] *n* cendrier *m*

Ash Wednesday *n* mercredi *m* des cendres

Asia ['eɪʃə] *n* Asie *f*; ~**n** *n* Asiatique *m/f*
♦ *adj* asiatique

aside [ə'saɪd] *adv* de côté; à l'écart ♦ *n* aparté *m*

ask [ɑːsk] *vt* demander; (*invite*) inviter; **to ~ sb sth/to do sth** demander qch à qn/à qn de faire qch; **to ~ sb about sth** questionner qn sur qch; se renseigner auprès de qn sur qch; **to ~ (sb) a question** poser une question (à qn); **to ~ sb out to dinner** inviter qn au restaurant; ~ **after** *vt fus* demander des nouvelles de; ~ **for** *vt fus* demander; (*trouble*) chercher

asking price ['ɑːskɪŋ-] *n*: **the ~** le prix de départ

asleep [ə'sliːp] *adj* endormi(e); **to fall ~** s'endormir

asparagus [əs'pærəgəs] *n* asperges *fpl*

aspect ['æspɛkt] *n* aspect *m*; (*direction in which a building etc faces*) orientation *f*, exposition *f*

aspire [əs'paɪər] *vi*: **to ~ to** aspirer à

aspirin ['æsprɪn] *n* aspirine *f*

ass [æs] *n* âne *m*; (*inf*) imbécile *m/f*; (*US: inf!*) cul *m* (*!*)

assailant [ə'seɪlənt] *n* agresseur *m*; assaillant *m*

assassinate [ə'sæsɪneɪt] *vt* assassiner; **assassination** [əsæsɪ'neɪʃən] *n* assassinat *m*

assault [ə'sɔːlt] *n* (*MIL*) assaut *m*; (*gen: attack*) agression *f* ♦ *vt* attaquer; (*sexually*) violenter

assemble [ə'sɛmbl] *vt* assembler ♦ *vi* s'assembler, se rassembler; **assembly** *n* assemblée *f*, réunion *f*; (*institution*) assemblée; (*construction*) assemblage *m*; **assembly line** *n* chaîne *f* de montage

assent [ə'sɛnt] *n* assentiment *m*, consentement *m*

assert [ə'sɜːt] *vt* affirmer, déclarer; (*one's authority*) faire valoir; (*one's innocence*) protester de

assess [ə'sɛs] *vt* évaluer; (*tax, payment*) établir *or* fixer le montant de; (*property etc: for tax*) calculer la valeur imposable de; (*person*) juger la valeur de; ~**ment** *n* évaluation *f*, fixation *f*, calcul *m* de la valeur imposable de, jugement *m*; ~**or** *n* expert *m* (*impôt et assurance*)

asset ['æsɛt] *n* avantage *m*, atout *m*; ~**s** *npl* (*FINANCE*) capital *m*; avoir(s) *m(pl)*; actif *m*

assign [ə'saɪn] *vt* (*date*) fixer; (*task*) assigner à; (*resources*) affecter à; ~**ment** *n* tâche *f*, mission *f*

assist [ə'sɪst] *vt* aider, assister; ~**ance** *n* aide *f*, assistance *f*; ~**ant** *n* assistant(e), adjoint(e); (*BRIT: also:* **shop** ~**ant**) vendeur(-euse)

associate [*n, adj* ə'səʊʃɪɪt, *vb* ə'səʊʃɪeɪt] *adj, n* associé(e) ♦ *vt* associer ♦ *vi*: **to ~ with sb** fréquenter qn; **association** [əsəʊsɪ'eɪʃən] *n* association *f*

assorted [ə'sɔːtɪd] *adj* assorti(e)

assortment [ə'sɔːtmənt] *n* assortiment *m*

assume [ə'sjuːm] *vt* supposer, présumer; (*responsibilities etc*) assumer; (*attitude, name*) prendre, adopter; **assumption** [ə'sʌmpʃən] *n* supposition *f*, hypothèse *f*; (*of power*) assomption *f*, prise *f*

assurance [ə'ʃuərəns] *n* assurance *f*

assure [ə'ʃuər] *vt* assurer

asthma ['æsmə] *n* asthme *m*

astonish [ə'stɒnɪʃ] *vt* étonner, stupéfier; ~**ment** *n* étonnement *m*

astound [ə'staund] *vt* stupéfier, sidérer

astray [ə'streɪ] *adv*: **to go ~** s'égarer; (*fig*) quitter le droit chemin; **to lead ~** détourner du droit chemin

astride [ə'straɪd] *prep* à cheval sur

astrology [əs'trɒlədʒɪ] *n* astrologie *f*

astronaut ['æstrənɔːt] *n* astronaute *m/f*

astronomy [əs'trɒnəmɪ] *n* astronomie *f*

asylum [ə'saɪləm] *n* asile *m*

KEYWORD
---

at [æt] *prep* **1** (*referring to position, direction*) à; **at the top** au sommet; **at home/school** à la maison *or* chez soi/à l'école; **at the baker's** à la boulangerie, chez le boulanger; **to look at sth** regarder qch
2 (*referring to time*): **at 4 o'clock** à 4 heures; **at Christmas** à Noël; **at night** la nuit; **at times** par moments, parfois
3 (*referring to rates, speed etc*) à; **at £1 a kilo** une livre le kilo; **two at a time** deux à la fois; **at 50 km/h** à 50 km/h
4 (*referring to manner*): **at a stroke** d'un seul coup; **at peace** en paix
5 (*referring to activity*): **to be at work** être au travail, travailler; **to play at cowboys** jouer aux cowboys; **to be good at sth** être bon en qch
6 (*referring to cause*): **shocked/surprised/annoyed at sth** choqué par/étonné de/agacé par qch; **I went at his suggestion** j'y suis allé sur son conseil

ate [eɪt] *pt of* **eat**
atheist ['eɪθɪɪst] *n* athée *m/f*
Athens ['æθɪnz] *n* Athènes
athlete ['æθliːt] *n* athlète *m/f*; **athletic** [æθ'letɪk] *adj* athlétique; **athletics** *n* athlétisme *m*
Atlantic [ət'læntɪk] *adj* atlantique ♦ *n*: **the ~ (Ocean)** l'océan *m*) Atlantique *m*
atlas ['ætləs] *n* atlas *m*
ATM *n abbr* (= *automated telling machine*) guichet *m* automatique
atmosphere ['ætməsfɪə] *n* atmosphère *f*
atom ['ætəm] *n* atome *m*; **~ic** [ə'tɒmɪk] *adj* atomique; **~(ic) bomb** *n* bombe *f* atomique; **~izer** *n* atomiseur *m*
atone [ə'təun] *vi*: **to ~ for** expier, racheter
atrocious [ə'trəuʃəs] *adj* (*very bad*) atroce, exécrable
attach [ə'tætʃ] *vt* attacher; (*document, letter*) joindre; **to be ~ed to sb/sth** être attaché à qn/qch
attaché case [ə'tæʃeɪ] *n* mallette *f*, attaché-case *m*

attachment [ə'tætʃmənt] *n* (*tool*) accessoire *m*; (*love*): **~ (to)** affection *f* (pour), attachement *m* (à)
attack [ə'tæk] *vt* attaquer; (*task etc*) s'attaquer à ♦ *n* attaque *f*; (*also*: **heart ~**) crise *f* cardiaque
attain [ə'teɪn] *vt* (*also*: **to ~ to**) parvenir à, atteindre à; (: *knowledge*) acquérir
attempt [ə'tempt] *n* tentative *f* ♦ *vt* essayer, tenter; **to make an ~ on sb's life** attenter à la vie de qn; **~ed** *adj*: **~ed murder/suicide** tentative *f* de meurtre/suicide
attend [ə'tend] *vt* (*course*) suivre; (*meeting, talk*) assister à; (*school, church*) aller à, fréquenter; (*patient*) soigner, s'occuper de; **~ to** *vt fus* (*needs, affairs etc*) s'occuper de; (*customer, patient*) s'occuper de; **~ance** *n* (*being present*) présence *f*; (*people present*) assistance *f*; **~ant** *n* employé(e) ♦ *adj* (*dangers*) inhérent(e), concomitant(e)
attention [ə'tenʃən] *n* attention *f*; **~!** (*MIL*) garde-à-vous!; **for the ~ of** (*ADMIN*) à l'attention de
attentive [ə'tentɪv] *adj* attentif(-ive); (*kind*) prévenant(e)
attest [ə'test] *vi*: **to ~ to** (*demonstrate*) démontrer; (*confirm*) témoigner
attic ['ætɪk] *n* grenier *m*
attitude ['ætɪtjuːd] *n* attitude *f*; pose *f*, maintien *m*
attorney [ə'tɜːnɪ] *n* (*US*: *lawyer*) avoué *m*; **A~ General** *n* (*BRIT*) ≃ procureur général; (*US*) ≃ garde *m* des Sceaux, ministre *m* de la Justice
attract [ə'trækt] *vt* attirer; **~ion** *n* (*gen pl*: *pleasant things*) attraction *f*, attrait *m*; (*PHYSICS*) attraction *f*; (*fig: towards sb or sth*) attirance *f*; **~ive** *adj* attrayant(e); (*person*) séduisant(e)
attribute [*n* 'ætrɪbjuːt, *vb* ə'trɪbjuːt] *n* attribut *m* ♦ *vt*: **to ~ sth to** attribuer qch à
attrition [ə'trɪʃən] *n*: **war of ~** guerre *f* d'usure
aubergine ['əubəʒiːn] *n* aubergine *f*
auction ['ɔːkʃən] *n* (*also*: **sale by ~**) vente *f* aux enchères ♦ *vt* (*also*: **sell by ~**) ven-

dre aux enchères; (*also:* **put up for ~**) mettre aux enchères; **~eer** [ɔːkʃəˈnɪəʳ] *n* commissaire-priseur *m*

audience [ˈɔːdɪəns] *n* (*people*) assistance *f*; public *m*; spectateurs *mpl*; (*interview*) audience *f*

audiovisual [ˈɔːdɪəʊˈvɪzjuəl] *adj* audiovisuel(le); **~ aids** *npl* supports *or* moyens audiovisuels

audit [ˈɔːdɪt] *vt* vérifier

audition [ɔːˈdɪʃən] *n* audition *f*

auditor [ˈɔːdɪtəʳ] *n* vérificateur *m* des comptes

augur [ˈɔːgəʳ] *vi*: **it ~s well** c'est bon signe *or* de bon augure

August [ˈɔːgəst] *n* août *m*

aunt [ɑːnt] *n* tante *f*; **~ie, ~y** [ˈɑːntɪ] *n dimin of* **aunt**

au pair [ˈəʊˈpɛəʳ] *n* (*also:* **~ girl**) jeune fille *f* au pair

auspicious [ɔːsˈpɪʃəs] *adj* de bon augure, propice

Australia [ɔsˈtreɪlɪə] *n* Australie *f*; **~n** *adj* australien(ne) ♦ *n* Australien(ne)

Austria [ˈɔstrɪə] *n* Autriche *f*; **~n** *adj* autrichien(ne) ♦ *n* Autrichien(ne)

authentic [ɔːˈθɛntɪk] *adj* authentique

author [ˈɔːθəʳ] *n* auteur *m*

authoritarian [ɔːθɒrɪˈtɛərɪən] *adj* autoritaire

authoritative [ɔːˈθɒrɪtətɪv] *adj* (*account*) digne de foi; (*study, treatise*) qui fait autorité; (*person, manner*) autoritaire

authority [ɔːˈθɒrɪtɪ] *n* autorité *f*; (*permission*) autorisation (formelle); **the authorities** *npl* (*ruling body*) les autorités *fpl*, l'administration *f*

authorize [ˈɔːθəraɪz] *vt* autoriser

auto [ˈɔːtəʊ] (*US*) *n* auto *f*, voiture *f*

auto: **~biography** [ɔːtəbaɪˈɒgrəfɪ] *n* autobiographie *f*; **~graph** [ˈɔːtəgrɑːf] *n* autographe *m* ♦ *vt* signer, dédicacer; **~mated** [ˈɔːtəmeɪtɪd] *adj* automatisé(e), automatique; **~matic** [ɔːtəˈmætɪk] *adj* automatique ♦ *n* (*gun*) automatique *m*; (*washing machine*) machine *f* à laver automatique; (*BRIT: AUT*) voiture *f* à transmission auto-

matique; **~matically** *adv* automatiquement; **~mation** [ɔːtəˈmeɪʃən] *n* automatisation *f* (électronique); **~mobile** [ˈɔːtəməbiːl] (*US*) *n* automobile *f*; **~nomy** [ɔːˈtɒnəmɪ] *n* autonomie *f*

autumn [ˈɔːtəm] *n* automne *m*; **in ~** en automne

auxiliary [ɔːgˈzɪlɪərɪ] *adj* auxiliaire ♦ *n* auxiliaire *m/f*

avail [əˈveɪl] *vt*: **to ~ o.s. of** profiter de ♦ *n*: **to no ~** sans résultat, en vain, en pure perte

availability [əveɪləˈbɪlɪtɪ] *n* disponibilité *f*

available [əˈveɪləbl] *adj* disponible

avalanche [ˈævəlɑːnʃ] *n* avalanche *f*

Ave *abbr* = **avenue**

avenge [əˈvɛndʒ] *vt* venger

avenue [ˈævənjuː] *n* avenue *f*; (*fig*) moyen *m*

average [ˈævərɪdʒ] *n* moyenne *f*; (*fig*) moyen *m* ♦ *adj* moyen(ne) ♦ *vt* (*a certain figure*) atteindre *or* faire *etc* en moyenne; **on ~** en moyenne; **~ out** *vi*: **to ~ out at** représenter en moyenne, donner une moyenne de

averse [əˈvɜːs] *adj*: **to be ~ to sth/doing sth** éprouver une forte répugnance envers qch/à faire qch

avert [əˈvɜːt] *vt* (*danger*) prévenir, écarter; (*one's eyes*) détourner

aviary [ˈeɪvɪərɪ] *n* volière *f*

avocado [ævəˈkɑːdəʊ] *n* (*BRIT: ~ pear*) avocat *m*

avoid [əˈvɔɪd] *vt* éviter

await [əˈweɪt] *vt* attendre

awake [əˈweɪk] (*pt* **awoke**, *pp* **awoken**) *adj* éveillé(e) ♦ *vt* éveiller ♦ *vi* s'éveiller; **~ to** (*dangers, possibilities*) conscient(e) de; **to be ~** être réveillé(e); **he was still ~** il ne dormait pas encore; **~ning** *n* réveil *m*

award [əˈwɔːd] *n* récompense *f*, prix *m* (*LAW: damages*) dommages-intérêts *mp* ♦ *vt* (*prize*) décerner; (*LAW: damages*) accorder

aware [əˈwɛəʳ] *adj*: **~ (of)** (*conscious*) conscient(e) (de); (*informed*) au courant (de); **to become ~ of/that** prendre conscience de/que; se rendre compte de/que; **~ness** *n* conscience *f*, connaissance *f*

away [ə'weɪ] *adj, adv* (au) loin; absent(e); **two kilometres ~** à (une distance de) deux kilomètres, à deux kilomètres de distance; **two hours ~ by car** à deux heures de voiture *or* de route; **the holiday was two weeks ~** il restait deux semaines jusqu'aux vacances; **~ from** loin de; **he's ~ for a week** il est parti (pour) une semaine; **to pedal/work/laugh ~** être en train de pédaler/travailler/rire; **to fade ~** (*sound*) s'affaiblir; (*colour*) s'estomper; **to wither ~** (*plant*) se dessécher; **to take ~** emporter; (*subtract*) enlever; **~ game** *n* (*SPORT*) match *m* à l'extérieur

awe [ɔː] *n* respect mêlé de crainte; **~-inspiring** ['ɔːɪnspaɪərɪŋ] *adj* impressionnant(e)

awful ['ɔːfəl] *adj* affreux(-euse); **an ~ lot (of)** un nombre incroyable (de); **~ly** *adv* (*very*) terriblement, vraiment

awkward ['ɔːkwəd] *adj* (*clumsy*) gauche, maladroit(e); (*inconvenient*) peu pratique; (*embarrassing*) gênant(e), délicat(e)

awning ['ɔːnɪŋ] *n* (*of tent*) auvent *m*; (*of shop*) store *m*; (*of hotel etc*) marquise *f*

woke [ə'wəuk] *pt of* **awake**; **~n** [ə'wəukən] *pp of* **awake**

axe [æks] (*US* **ax**) *n* hache *f* ♦ *vt* (*project etc*) abandonner; (*jobs*) supprimer

axes¹ ['æksɪz] *npl of* **axe**

axes² ['æksiːz] *npl of* **axis**

axis ['æksɪs] (*pl* **axes**) *n* axe *m*

axle ['æksl] *n* (*also:* **~-tree:** *AUT*) essieu *m*

ay(e) [aɪ] *excl* (*yes*) oui

B, b

[biː] *n* (*MUS*) si *m*; **~ road** (*BRIT*) route départmentale

.A. *abbr* = **Bachelor of Arts**

abble ['bæbl] *vi* bredouiller; (*baby, stream*) gazouiller

aby ['beɪbɪ] *n* bébé *m*; (*US: inf: darling*):

come on, ~! viens ma belle/mon gars!; **~ carriage** (*US*) *n* voiture *f* d'enfant; **~ food** *n* aliments *mpl* pour bébé(s); **~-sit** *vi* garder les enfants; **~-sitter** *n* babysitter *m/f*; **~ wipe** *n* lingette *f* (*pour bébé*)

bachelor ['bætʃələr] *n* célibataire *m*; **B~ of Arts/Science** ≈ licencié(e) ès *or* en lettres/sciences

back [bæk] *n* (*of person, horse, book*) dos *m*; (*of hand*) dos, revers *m*; (*of house*) derrière *m*; (*of car, train*) arrière *m*; (*of chair*) dossier *m*; (*of page*) verso *m*; (*of room, audience*) fond *m*; (*SPORT*) arrière *m* ♦ *vt* (*candidate: also:* **~ up**) soutenir, appuyer; (*horse: at races*) parier *or* miser sur; (*car*) (*faire*) reculer ♦ *vi* (*also:* **~ up**) reculer; (*also:* **~ up:** *car etc*) faire marche arrière ♦ *adj* (*in compounds*) de derrière, à l'arrière ♦ *adv* (*not forward*) en arrière; (*returned*): **he's ~** il est rentré, il est de retour; (*restitution*): **throw the ball ~** renvoie la balle; (*again*): **he called ~** il a rappelé; **~ seat/wheels** (*AUT*) sièges *mpl*/roues *fpl* arrières; **~ payments/rent** arriéré *m* de paiements/loyer; **he ran ~** il est revenu en courant; **~ down** *vi* rabattre de ses prétentions; **~ out** *vi* (*of promise*) se dédire; **~ up** *vt* (*candidate etc*) soutenir, appuyer; (*COMPUT*) sauvegarder; **~ache** *n* mal *m* de dos; **~bencher** (*BRIT*) *n* membre du parlement sans portefeuille; **~bone** *n* colonne vertébrale, épine dorsale; **~date** *vt* (*letter*) antidater; **~dated pay rise** augmentation *f* avec effet rétroactif; **~fire** *vi* (*AUT*) pétarader; (*plans*) mal tourner; **~ground** *n* arrière-plan *m*; (*of events*) situation *f*, conjoncture *f*; (*basic knowledge*) éléments *mpl* de base; (*experience*) formation *f*; **family ~ground** milieu familial; **~hand** *n* (*TENNIS: also:* **~hand stroke**) revers *m*; **~hander** (*BRIT*) *n* (*bribe*) pot-de-vin *m*; **~ing** *n* (*fig*) soutien *m*, appui *m*; **~lash** *n* contre-coup *m*, répercussion *f*; **~log** *n*: **~log of work** travail *m* en retard; **~ number** *n* (*of magazine etc*) vieux numéro; **~pack** *n* sac *m* à dos; **~packer** *n* randonneur(-euse); **~ pain** *n* mal *m* de dos; **~ pay** *n* rappel *m* de salaire; **~side** (*inf*) *n* derrière *m*, postérieur *m*; **~stage** *adv* ♦ *n* derrière la scène, dans la coulisse; **~stroke** *n* dos crawlé; **~up** *adj* (*train, plane*) supplémentaire, de réserve; (COMPUT) de sauvegarde ♦ *n* (*support*) appui *m*, soutien *m*; (*also:* **~up disk/file**) sauvegarde *f*; **~ward** *adj* (*movement*) en arrière; (*person, country*) arriéré(e); attardé(e); **~wards** *adv* (*move, go*) en arrière; (*read a list*) à l'envers, à rebours; (*fall*) à la renverse; (*walk*) à reculons; **~water** *n* (*fig*) coin reculé; bled perdu (*péj*); **~yard** *n* arrière-cour *f*

bacon ['beɪkən] *n* bacon *m*, lard *m*

bacteria [bæk'tɪərɪə] *npl* bactéries *fpl*

bad [bæd] *adj* mauvais(e); (*child*) vilain(e); (*mistake, accident etc*) grave; (*meat, food*) gâté(e), avarié(e); **his ~ leg** sa jambe malade; **to go ~** (*meat, food*) se gâter

badge [bædʒ] *n* insigne *m*; (*of policeman*) plaque *f*

badger ['bædʒər] *n* blaireau *m*

badly ['bædlɪ] *adv* (*work, dress etc*) mal; **~ wounded** grièvement blessé; **he needs it ~** il en a absolument besoin; **~ off** *adj*, *adv* dans la gêne

badminton ['bædmɪntən] *n* badminton *m*

bad-tempered ['bæd'tempəd] *adj* (*person: by nature*) ayant mauvais caractère; (: *on one occasion*) de mauvaise humeur

baffle ['bæfl] *vt* (*puzzle*) déconcerter

bag [bæg] *n* sac *m* ♦ *vt* (*inf: take*) empocher; s'approprier; **~s of** (*inf: lots of*) des masses de; **~gage** *n* bagages *mpl*; **~gage allowance** *n* franchise *f* de bagages; **~gage reclaim** *n* livraison *f* de bagages; **~gy** *adj* avachi(e), qui fait des poches; **~pipes** *npl* cornemuse *f*

bail [beɪl] *n* (*payment*) caution *f*; (*release*) mise *f* en liberté sous caution ♦ *vt* (*prisoner: also:* **grant ~ to**) mettre en liberté sous caution; (*boat: also:* **~ out**) écoper; **on ~** (*prisoner*) sous caution; *see also* **bale**; **~ out** *vt* (*prisoner*) payer la caution de

bailiff ['beɪlɪf] *n* (BRIT) ≃ huissier *m*; (US) ≃

huissier-audiencier *m*

bait [beɪt] *n* appât *m* ♦ *vt* appâter; (*fig: tease*) tourmenter

bake [beɪk] *vt* (faire) cuire au four ♦ *v* (*bread etc*) cuire (au four); (*make cakes etc*) faire de la pâtisserie; **~d beans** *npl* haricots blancs à la sauce tomate; **~d potato** *n* pomme *f* de terre en robe des champs; **~r** *n* boulanger *m*; **~ry** *n* boulangerie *f*, boulangerie industrielle; **baking** *n* cuisson *f*; **baking powder** *n* levure *f* (chimique)

balance ['bæləns] *n* équilibre *m*; (COMM: *sum*) solde *m*; (*remainder*) reste *m*; (*scales*) balance *f* ♦ *vt* mettre *or* faire tenir en équilibre; (*pros and cons*) peser; (*budget*) équilibrer; (*account*) balancer; **~ of trade/payments** balance commerciale/de comptes *or* paiements; **~d** *adj* (*personality, diet*) équilibré(e); (*report*) objectif(-ive); **~ sheet** *n* bilan *m*

balcony ['bælkənɪ] *n* balcon *m*; (*in theatre*) deuxième balcon

bald [bɔːld] *adj* chauve; (*tyre*) lisse

bale [beɪl] *n* balle *f*, ballot *m*; **~ out** *vi* (*of a plane*) sauter en parachute

ball [bɔːl] *n* boule *f*; (*football*) ballon *m*; (*for tennis, golf*) balle *f*; (*of wool*) pelote *f*; (*of string*) bobine *f*; (*dance*) bal *m*; **to play (with sb)** (*fig*) coopérer (avec qn)

ballast ['bæləst] *n* lest *m*

ball bearings *npl* roulement *m* à billes

ballerina [bælə'riːnə] *n* ballerine *f*

ballet ['bæleɪ] *n* ballet *m*; (*art*) danse *f* (classique); **~ dancer** *n* danseur(-euse) *m/f* de ballet; **~ shoe** *n* chausson *m* de danse

balloon [bə'luːn] *n* ballon *m*; (*in comic strip*) bulle *f*

ballot ['bælət] *n* scrutin *m*; **~ paper** *n* bulletin *m* de vote

ballpoint (pen) ['bɔːlpɔɪnt(-)] *n* stylo *m* à bille

ballroom ['bɔːlrum] *n* salle *f* de bal

ban [bæn] *n* interdiction *f* ♦ *vt* interdire

banana [bə'nɑːnə] *n* banane *f*

band [bænd] *n* bande *f*; (*at a dance*) orchestre *m*; (MIL) musique *f*, fanfare *f*;

together vi se liguer

bandage ['bændɪdʒ] n bandage m, pansement m ♦ vt bander

Bandaid ® ['bændeɪd] (US) n pansement adhésif

bandit ['bændɪt] n bandit m

bandy-legged ['bændɪ'legɪd] adj aux jambes arquées

bang [bæŋ] n détonation f; (of door) claquement m; (blow) coup (violent) ♦ vt frapper (violemment); (door) claquer ♦ vi détoner; claquer ♦ excl pan!; ~s (US) npl (fringe) frange f

banish ['bænɪʃ] vt bannir

banister(s) ['bænɪstə(z)] n(pl) rampe f (d'escalier)

bank [bæŋk] n banque f; (of river, lake) bord m, rive f; (of earth) talus m, remblai m ♦ vi (AVIAT) virer sur l'aile; ~ on vt fus miser or tabler sur; ~ account n compte m en banque; ~ card n carte f d'identité bancaire; ~er n banquier m; ~er's card (BRIT) n = bank card; ~ holiday (BRIT) n jour férié (les banques sont fermées); ~ing n opérations fpl bancaires; profession f de banquier; ~note n billet m de banque; ~ rate n taux m de l'escompte

bank holiday

Un bank holiday en Grande-Bretagne est un lundi férié et donc l'occasion d'un week-end prolongé. La circulation sur les routes et le trafic dans les gares et les aéroports augmentent considérablement à ces périodes. Les principaux bank holidays, à part Pâques et Noël, ont lieu au mois de mai et fin août.

bankrupt ['bæŋkrʌpt] adj en faillite; to go ~ faire faillite; ~cy n faillite f

bank statement n relevé m de compte

banner ['bænər] n bannière f

bannister(s) ['bænɪstə(z)] n(pl) = banister(s)

baptism ['bæptɪzəm] n baptême m

bar [bɑːr] n (pub) bar m; (counter: in pub) comptoir m, bar; (rod: of metal etc) barre f; (on window etc) barreau m; (of chocolate) tablette f, plaque f; (fig) obstacle m; (prohibition) mesure f d'exclusion; (MUS) mesure f ♦ vt (road) barrer; (window) munir de barreaux; (person) exclure; (activity) interdire; ~ of soap savonnette f; the B~ (LAW) le barreau; behind ~s (prisoner) sous les verrous; ~ none sans exception

barbaric [bɑːˈbærɪk] adj barbare

barbecue ['bɑːbɪkjuː] n barbecue m

barbed wire ['bɑːbd-] n fil m de fer barbelé

barber ['bɑːbər] n coiffeur m (pour hommes)

bar code n (on goods) code m à barres

bare [beər] adj nu(e) ♦ vt mettre à nu, dénuder; (teeth) montrer; the ~ necessities le strict nécessaire; ~back adv à cru, sans selle; ~faced adj impudent(e), effronté(e); ~foot adj, adv nu-pieds, (les) pieds nus; ~ly adv à peine

bargain ['bɑːgɪn] n (transaction) marché m; (good buy) affaire f, occasion f ♦ vi (haggle) marchander; (negotiate): to ~ (with sb) négocier (avec qn), traiter (avec qn); into the ~ par-dessus le marché; ~ for vt fus: he got more than he ~ed for il ne s'attendait pas à un coup pareil

barge [bɑːdʒ] n péniche f; ~ in vi (walk in) faire irruption; (interrupt talk) intervenir mal à propos

bark [bɑːk] n (of tree) écorce f; (of dog) aboiement m ♦ vi aboyer

barley ['bɑːlɪ] n orge f; ~ sugar n sucre m d'orge

bar: ~maid n serveuse f de bar, barmaid f; ~man (irreg) n barman m; ~ meal n repas m de bistrot; to go for a ~ meal aller manger au bistrot

barn [bɑːn] n grange f

barometer [bəˈrɒmɪtər] n baromètre m

baron ['bærən] n baron m; ~ess ['bærənɪs] n baronne f

barracks ['bærəks] npl caserne f

barrage ['bærɑːʒ] n (MIL) tir m de barrage; (dam) barrage m; (fig) pluie f

barrel ['bærəl] n tonneau m; (of oil) baril

m; (*of gun*) canon *m*

barren ['bærən] *adj* stérile

barricade [bærɪ'keɪd] *n* barricade *f*

barrier ['bærɪər] *n* barrière *f*; (*fig: to progress etc*) obstacle *m*

barring ['bɑːrɪŋ] *prep* sauf

barrister ['bærɪstər] (*BRIT*) *n* avocat (plaidant)

barrow ['bærəu] *n* (*wheelbarrow*) charrette *f* à bras

bartender ['bɑːtendər] (*US*) *n* barman *m*

barter ['bɑːtər] *vt*: **to ~ sth for** échanger qch contre

base [beɪs] *n* base *f*; (*of tree, post*) pied *m*
♦ *vt*: **to ~ sth on** baser *or* fonder qch sur
♦ *adj* vil(e), bas(se)

baseball ['beɪsbɔːl] *n* base-ball *m*

basement ['beɪsmənt] *n* sous-sol *m*

bases[1] ['beɪsɪz] *npl of* **base**

bases[2] ['beɪsiːz] *npl of* **basis**

bash [bæʃ] (*inf*) *vt* frapper, cogner

bashful ['bæʃful] *adj* timide; modeste

basic ['beɪsɪk] *adj* fondamental(e), de base; (*minimal*) rudimentaire; **~ally** *adv* fondamentalement, à la base; (*in fact*) en fait, au fond; **~s** *npl*: **the ~s** l'essentiel *m*

basil ['bæzl] *n* basilic *m*

basin ['beɪsn] *n* (*vessel, also GEO*) cuvette *f*, bassin *m*; (*also:* **washbasin**) lavabo *m*

basis ['beɪsɪs] *n* (*pl* **bases**) base *f*; **on a trial ~** à titre d'essai; **on a part-time ~** à temps partiel

bask [bɑːsk] *vi*: **to ~ in the sun** se chauffer au soleil

basket ['bɑːskɪt] *n* corbeille *f*; (*with handle*) panier *m*; **~ball** *n* basket-ball *m*

bass [beɪs] *n* (*MUS*) basse *f*; **~ drum** *n* grosse caisse *f*

bassoon [bə'suːn] *n* (*MUS*) basson *m*

bastard ['bɑːstəd] *n* enfant naturel(le), bâtard(e); (*inf!*) salaud *m* (!)

bat [bæt] *n* chauve-souris *f*; (*for baseball etc*) batte *f*; (*BRIT: for table tennis*) raquette *f*
♦ *vt*: **he didn't ~ an eyelid** il n'a pas sourcillé *or* bronché

batch [bætʃ] *n* (*of bread*) fournée *f*; (*of papers*) liasse *f*

bated ['beɪtɪd] *adj*: **with ~ breath** en retenant son souffle

bath [bɑːθ] *n* bain *m*; (*~tub*) baignoire
♦ *vt* baigner, donner un bain à; **to have a ~** prendre un bain; *see also* **baths**

bathe [beɪð] *vi* se baigner ♦ *vt* (*wound*) laver; **bathing** *n* baignade *f*; **bathing costume, bathing suit** (*US*) *n* maillot *m* (de bain)

bath: **~robe** *n* peignoir *m* de bain;
~room *n* salle *f* de bains; **~s** *npl* (*also:* **swimming ~s**) piscine *f*; **~ towel** *n* serviette *f* de bain

baton ['bætən] *n* bâton *m*; (*MUS*) baguette *f*; (*club*) matraque *f*

batter ['bætər] *vt* battre ♦ *n* pâte *f* à frire;
~ed ['bætəd] *adj* (*hat, pan*) cabossé(e)

battery ['bætərɪ] *n* batterie *f*; (*of torch*) pile *f*; **~ farming** *n* élevage *f* en batterie

battle ['bætl] *n* bataille *f*, combat *m* ♦ *vi* se battre, lutter; **~field** *n* champ *m* de bataille; **~ship** *n* cuirassé *m*

Bavaria [bə'veərɪə] *n* Bavière *f*

bawl [bɔːl] *vi* hurler; (*child*) brailler

bay [beɪ] *n* (*of sea*) baie *f*; **to hold sb at ~** tenir qn à distance *or* en échec; **~ leaf** *n* laurier *m*; **~ window** *n* baie vitrée

bazaar [bə'zɑːr] *n* bazar *m*; vente *f* de charité

B & B *n abbr* = **bed and breakfast**

BBC *n abbr* (= *British Broadcasting Corporation*) office de la radiodiffusion et télévision britannique

B.C. *adv abbr* (= *before Christ*) av. J.-C.

KEYWORD

be [biː] (*pt* **was, were**, *pp* **been**) *aux vb*
1 (*with present participle: forming continuous tenses*): **what are you doing?** que faites vous?; **they're coming tomorrow** ils viennent demain; **I've been waiting for you for 2 hours** je t'attends depuis 2 heures
2 (*with pp: forming passives*) être; **to be killed** être tué(e); **he was nowhere to be seen** on ne le voyait nulle part
3 (*in tag questions*): **it was fun, wasn't it** c'était drôle, n'est-ce pas?; **she's back,**

she? elle est rentrée, n'est-ce pas *or* alors?
4 (+*to* +*infinitive*): **the house is to be sold** la maison doit être vendue; **he's not to open it** il ne doit pas l'ouvrir
♦ *vb* + *complement* 1 (*gen*) être; **I'm English** je suis anglais(e); **I'm tired** je suis fatigué(e); **I'm hot/cold** j'ai chaud/froid; **he's a doctor** il est médecin; **2 and 2 are 4** 2 et 2 font 4
2 (*of health*) aller; **how are you?** comment allez-vous?; **he's fine now** il va bien maintenant; **he's very ill** il est très malade
3 (*of age*) avoir; **how old are you?** quel âge avez-vous?; **I'm sixteen (years old)** j'ai seize ans
4 (*cost*) coûter; **how much was the meal?** combien a coûté le repas?; **that'll be £5, please** ça fera 5 livres, s'il vous plaît
♦ *vi* 1 (*exist, occur etc*) être, exister; **the prettiest girl that ever was** la fille la plus jolie qui ait jamais existé; **be that as it may** quoi qu'il en soit; **so be it** soit
2 (*referring to place*) être, se trouver; **I won't be here tomorrow** je ne serai pas là demain; **Edinburgh is in Scotland** Édimbourg est *or* se trouve en Écosse
3 (*referring to movement*) aller; **where have you been?** où êtes-vous allé(s)?
♦ *impers vb* 1 (*referring to time, distance*) être; **it's 5 o'clock** il est 5 heures; **it's the 28th of April** c'est le 28 avril; **it's 10 km to the village** le village est à 10 km
2 (*referring to the weather*) faire; **it's too hot/cold** il fait trop chaud/froid; **it's windy** il y a du vent
3 (*emphatic*): **it's me/the postman** c'est moi/le facteur

each [biːtʃ] *n* plage *f* ♦ *vt* échouer
acon ['biːkən] *n* (*lighthouse*) fanal *m*; (*marker*) balise *f*
ad [biːd] *n* perle *f*
ak [biːk] *n* bec *m*
aker ['biːkər] *n* gobelet *m*

beam [biːm] *n* poutre *f*; (*of light*) rayon *m* ♦ *vi* rayonner
bean [biːn] *n* haricot *m*; (*of coffee*) grain *m*; **runner ~** haricot *m* (à rames); **broad ~** fève *f*; **~sprouts** *npl* germes *mpl* de soja
bear [beər] (*pt* **bore**, *pp* **borne**) *n* ours *m* ♦ *vt* porter; (*endure*) supporter ♦ *vi*: **to ~ right/left** obliquer à droite/gauche, se diriger vers la droite/gauche; **~ out** *vt* corroborer, confirmer; **~ up** *vi* (*person*) tenir le coup
beard [biəd] *n* barbe *f*; **~ed** *adj* barbu(e)
bearer ['beərər] *n* porteur *m*; (*of passport*) titulaire *m/f*
bearing ['beərɪŋ] *n* maintien *m*, allure *f*; (*connection*) rapport *m*; **~s** *npl* (*also:* **ball ~s**) roulement *m* (à billes); **to take a ~** faire le point
beast [biːst] *n* bête *f*; (*inf: person*) brute *f*; **~ly** *adj* infect(e)
beat [biːt] (*pt* **beat**, *pp* **beaten**) *n* battement *m*; (*MUS*) temps *m*, mesure *f*; (*of policeman*) ronde *f* ♦ *vt, vi* battre; **off the ~en track** hors des chemins *or* sentiers battus; **~ it!** (*inf*) fiche(-moi) le camp!; **~ off** *vt* repousser; **~ up** *vt* (*inf: person*) tabasser; (*eggs*) battre; **~ing** *n* raclée *f*
beautiful ['bjuːtɪful] *adj* beau (belle); **~ly** *adv* admirablement
beauty ['bjuːtɪ] *n* beauté *f*; **~ salon** *n* institut *m* de beauté; **~ spot** (*BRIT*) *n* (*TOURISM*) site naturel (d'une grande beauté)
beaver ['biːvər] *n* castor *m*
because [bɪˈkɔz] *conj* parce que; **~ of** *prep* à cause de
beck [bek] *n*: **to be at sb's ~ and call** être à l'entière disposition de qn
beckon ['bekən] *vt* (*also:* **~ to**) faire signe (de venir) à
become [bɪˈkʌm] (*irreg: like* **come**) *vi* devenir; **to ~ fat/thin** grossir/maigrir; **becoming** *adj* (*behaviour*) convenable, bienséant(e); (*clothes*) seyant(e)
bed [bed] *n* lit *m*; (*of flowers*) parterre *m*; (*of coal, clay*) couche *f*; (*of sea*) fond *m*; **to go to ~** aller se coucher; **~ and breakfast** *n* (*terms*) chambre et petit déjeuner;

(*place*) ≃ chambre *f* d'hôte; **~clothes** *npl* couvertures *fpl* et draps *mpl*; **~ding** *n* literie *f*; **~ linen** *n* draps *mpl* de lit (et taies *fpl* d'oreillers), literie *f*

---

bed and breakfast

Un **bed and breakfast** *est une petite pension dans une maison particulière ou une ferme où l'on peut louer une chambre avec petit déjeuner compris pour un prix modique par rapport à ce que l'on paierait dans un hôtel. Ces établissements sont communément appelés B & B, et sont signalés par une pancarte dans le jardin ou au-dessus de la porte.*

---

bedraggled [bɪ'drægld] *adj* (*person, clothes*) débraillé(e); (*hair: wet*) trempé(e)
bed: **~ridden** *adj* cloué(e) au lit; **~room** *n* chambre *f* (à coucher); **~side** *n*: **at sb's ~side** au chevet de qn; **~sit(ter)** *n* (*BRIT*) chambre meublée, studio *m*; **~spread** *n* couvre-lit *m*, dessus-de-lit *m inv*; **~time** *n* heure *f* du coucher
bee [biː] *n* abeille *f*
beech [biːtʃ] *n* hêtre *m*
beef [biːf] *n* bœuf *m*; **roast ~** rosbif *m*; **~burger** *n* hamburger *m*; **~eater** *n* hallebardier de la Tour de Londres
bee: **~hive** *n* ruche *f*; **~line** *n*: **to make a ~line for** se diriger tout droit vers
been [biːn] *pp of* **be**
beer [bɪər] *n* bière *f*
beet [biːt] *n* (*vegetable*) betterave *f*; (*US: also:* **red ~**) betterave (potagère)
beetle [biːtl] *n* scarabée *m*
beetroot ['biːtruːt] (*BRIT*) *n* betterave *f*
before [bɪ'fɔːr] *prep* (*in time*) avant; (*in space*) devant ♦ *conj* avant que +*sub*; avant de ♦ *adv* avant; devant; **~ going** avant de partir; **~ she goes** avant qu'elle ne parte; **the week ~** la semaine précédente *or* d'avant; **I've seen it ~** je l'ai déjà vu; **~hand** *adv* au préalable, à l'avance
beg [beg] *vi* mendier ♦ *vt* mendier; (*forgiveness, mercy etc*) demander; (*entreat*) supplier; *see also* **pardon**

began [bɪ'gæn] *pt of* **begin**
beggar ['begər] *n* mendiant(e)
begin [bɪ'gɪn] (*pt* **began**, *pp* **begun**) *vt, v* commencer; **to ~ doing** *or* **to do st** commencer à *or* de faire qch; **~ner** *n* débutant(e); **~ning** *n* commencement *m* début *m*
behalf [bɪ'hɑːf] *n*: **on ~ of**, (*US*) **in ~ o** (*representing*) de la part de; (*for benefit o* pour le compte de; **on my/his ~** pou moi/lui
behave [bɪ'heɪv] *vi* se conduire, s comporter; (*well: also:* **~ o.s.**) se conduir bien *or* comme il faut; **behaviour** (*US* **be havior**) [bɪ'heɪvjər] *n* comportement *m* conduite *f*
behead [bɪ'hed] *vt* décapiter
behind [bɪ'haɪnd] *prep* derrière; (*time, pr gress*) en retard sur; (*work, studies*) en re tard dans ♦ *adv* derrière ♦ *n* derrière *m* **to be ~ (schedule)** avoir du retard; **~ th scenes** dans les coulisses
behold [bɪ'həʊld] (*irreg: like* **hold**) *vt* ape cevoir, voir
beige [beɪʒ] *adj* beige
Beijing ['beɪ'dʒɪŋ] *n* Bei-jing, Pékin
being ['biːɪŋ] *n* être *m*
Beirut [beɪ'ruːt] *n* Beyrouth
Belarus [belə'rus] *n* Bélarus *f*
belated [bɪ'leɪtɪd] *adj* tardif(-ive)
belch [beltʃ] *vi* avoir un renvoi, roter ♦ (*also:* **~ out:** *smoke etc*) vomir, cracher
Belgian ['beldʒən] *adj* belge, de Belgiqu ♦ *n* Belge *m/f*
Belgium ['beldʒəm] *n* Belgique *f*
belie [bɪ'laɪ] *vt* démentir
belief [bɪ'liːf] *n* (*opinion*) conviction (*trust, faith*) foi *f*
believe [bɪ'liːv] *vt, vi* croire; **to ~ in** (*Go* croire en; (*method, ghosts*) croire à; **~r** (*in idea, activity*): **~r in** partisan(e) de; (*R* croyant(e)
belittle [bɪ'lɪtl] *vt* déprécier, rabaisser
bell [bel] *n* cloche *f*; (*small*) clochette grelot *m*; (*on door*) sonnette *f*; (*electr* sonnerie *f*
belligerent [bɪ'lɪdʒərənt] *adj* (*person, c*

tude) agressif(-ive)

ellow ['beləu] vi (bull) meugler; (person) brailler

elly ['belɪ] n ventre m

elong [bɪ'lɔŋ] vi: **to ~ to** appartenir à; (club etc) faire partie de; **this book ~s here** ce livre va ici; **~ings** npl affaires fpl, possessions fpl

eloved [bɪ'lʌvɪd] adj (bien-)aimé(e)

elow [bɪ'ləu] prep sous, au-dessous de ♦ adv en dessous; **see ~** voir plus bas or plus loin or ci-dessous

elt [belt] n ceinture f; (of land) région f; (TECH) courroie f ♦ vt (thrash) donner une raclée à; **~way** (US) n (AUT) route f de ceinture; (: motorway) périphérique m

emused [bɪ'mju:zd] adj stupéfié(e)

ench [bentʃ] n (gen, also BRIT: POL) banc m; (in workshop) établi m; **the B~** (LAW: judge) le juge; (: judges collectively) la magistrature, la Cour

end [bend] (pt, pp bent) vt courber; (leg, arm) plier ♦ vi se courber ♦ n (BRIT: in road) virage m, tournant m; (in pipe, river) coude m; **~ down** vi se baisser; **~ over** vi se pencher

eneath [bɪ'ni:θ] prep sous, au-dessous de; (unworthy of) indigne de ♦ adv dessous, au-dessous, en bas

enefactor ['benɪfæktər] n bienfaiteur m

eneficial [benɪ'fɪʃəl] adj salutaire; avantageux(-euse); **~ to the health** bon(ne) pour la santé

enefit ['benɪfɪt] n avantage m, profit m; (allowance of money) allocation f ♦ vt faire du bien à, profiter à ♦ vi: **he'll ~ from it** cela lui fera du bien, il y gagnera or s'en trouvera bien

enelux ['benɪlʌks] n Bénélux m

enevolent [bɪ'nevələnt] adj bienveillant(e); (organization) bénévole

enign [bɪ'naɪn] adj (person, smile) bienveillant(e), affable; (MED) bénin(-igne)

ent [bent] pt, pp of **bend** ♦ n inclination f, penchant m; **to be ~ on** être résolu(e) à

quest [bɪ'kwest] n legs m

reaved [bɪ'ri:vd] n: **the ~** la famille du

disparu

beret ['bereɪ] n béret m

Berlin [bə:'lɪn] n Berlin

berm [bə:m] (US) n (AUT) accotement m

Bermuda [bə:'mju:də] n Bermudes fpl

berry ['berɪ] n baie f

berserk [bə'sə:k] adj: **to go ~** (madman, crowd) se déchaîner

berth [bə:θ] n (bed) couchette f; (for ship) poste m d'amarrage, mouillage m ♦ vi (in harbour) venir à quai; (at anchor) mouiller

beseech [bɪ'si:tʃ] (pt, pp besought) vt implorer, supplier

beset [bɪ'set] (pt, pp beset) vt assaillir

beside [bɪ'saɪd] prep à côté de; **to be ~ o.s. (with anger)** être hors de soi; **that's ~ the point** cela n'a rien à voir; **~s** adv en outre, de plus; (in any case) d'ailleurs ♦ prep (as well as) en plus de

besiege [bɪ'si:dʒ] vt (town) assiéger; (fig) assaillir

best [best] adj meilleur(e) ♦ adv le mieux; **the ~ part of** (quantity) le plus clair de, la plus grande partie de; **at ~** au mieux; **to make the ~ of sth** s'accommoder de qch (du mieux que l'on peut); **to do one's ~** faire de son mieux; **to the ~ of my knowledge** pour autant que je sache; **to the ~ of my ability** du mieux que je pourrai; **~ before date** n date f de limite d'utilisation or de consommation; **~ man** n garçon m d'honneur

bestow [bɪ'stəu] vt: **to ~ sth on sb** accorder qch à qn; (title) conférer qch à qn

bet [bet] (pt, pp bet or betted) n pari m ♦ vt, vi parier

betray [bɪ'treɪ] vt trahir

better ['betər] adj meilleur(e) ♦ adv mieux ♦ vt améliorer ♦ n: **to get the ~ of** triompher de, l'emporter sur; **you had ~ do it** vous feriez mieux de le faire; **he thought ~ of it** il s'est ravisé; **to get ~** aller mieux; s'améliorer; **~ off** adj plus à l'aise financièrement; (fig): **you'd be ~ off this way** vous vous en trouveriez mieux ainsi

betting ['betɪŋ] n paris mpl; **~ shop** (BRIT) n bureau m de paris

between [bɪˈtwiːn] *prep* entre ♦ *adv*: **(in) ~** au milieu; dans l'intervalle; (*in time*) dans l'intervalle

beverage [ˈbevərɪdʒ] *n* boisson *f* (*gén sans alcool*)

beware [bɪˈweəʳ] *vi*: **to ~ (of)** prendre garde (à); **"~ of the dog"** "(attention) chien méchant"

bewildered [bɪˈwɪldəd] *adj* dérouté(e), ahuri(e)

beyond [bɪˈjɔnd] *prep* (*in space, time*) au-delà de; (*exceeding*) au-dessus de ♦ *adv* au-delà; **~ doubt** hors de doute; **~ repair** irréparable

bias [ˈbaɪəs] *n* (*prejudice*) préjugé *m*, parti pris; **~(s)ed** *adj* partial(e), montrant un parti pris

bib [bɪb] *n* bavoir *m*, bavette *f*

Bible [ˈbaɪbl] *n* Bible *f*

bicarbonate of soda [baɪˈkɑːbənɪt-] *n* bicarbonate *m* de soude

bicker [ˈbɪkəʳ] *vi* se chamailler

bicycle [ˈbaɪsɪkl] *n* bicyclette *f*

bid [bɪd] (*pt* **bid** *or* **bade**, *pp* **bid(den)**) *n* offre *f*; (*at auction*) enchère *f*; (*attempt*) tentative *f* ♦ *vi* faire une enchère *or* offre ♦ *vt* faire une enchère *or* offre de; **to ~ sb good day** souhaiter le bonjour à qn; **~der** *n*: **the highest ~der** le plus offrant; **~ding** *n* enchères *fpl*

bide [baɪd] *vt*: **to ~ one's time** attendre son heure

bifocals [baɪˈfəuklz] *npl* verres *mpl* à double foyer, lunettes bifocales

big [bɪg] *adj* grand(e); gros(se); **~headed** *adj* prétentieux(-euse)

bigot [ˈbɪgət] *n* fanatique *m/f*, sectaire *m/f*; **~ed** *adj* fanatique, sectaire; **~ry** *n* fanatisme *m*, sectarisme *m*

big top *n* grand chapiteau

bike [baɪk] *n* vélo *m*, bécane *f*

bikini [bɪˈkiːnɪ] *n* bikini *m*

bilingual [baɪˈlɪŋgwəl] *adj* bilingue

bill [bɪl] *n* note *f*, facture *f*; (*POL*) projet *m* de loi; (*US: banknote*) billet *m* (de banque); (*of bird*) bec *m*; (*THEATRE*): **on the ~** à l'affiche; **"post no ~s"** "défense d'affi-

cher"; **to fit** *or* **fill the ~** (*fig*) faire l'affaire; **~board** *n* panneau *m* d'affichage

billet [ˈbɪlɪt] *n* cantonnement *m* (chez l'habitant)

billfold [ˈbɪlfəuld] (*US*) *n* portefeuille *m*

billiards [ˈbɪljədz] *n* (jeu *m* de) billard *m*

billion [ˈbɪljən] *n* (*BRIT*) billion *m* (*million of millions*); (*US*) milliard *m*

bimbo [ˈbɪmbəu] (*inf*) *n* ravissante idiote *f*, potiche *f*

bin [bɪn] *n* boîte *f*; (*also*: **dustbin**) poubelle *f*; (*for coal*) coffre *m*

bind [baɪnd] (*pt, pp* **bound**) *vt* attacher; (*book*) relier; (*oblige*) obliger, contraindre ♦ *n* (*inf: nuisance*) scie *f*; **~ing** *adj* (*contract*) constituant une obligation

binge [bɪndʒ] (*inf*) *n*: **to go on a/the ~** aller faire la bringue

bingo [ˈbɪŋgəu] *n* jeu *de loto pratiqué dans des établissements publics*

binoculars [bɪˈnɔkjuləz] *npl* jumelles *fpl*

bio *prefix*: **~chemistry** *n* biochimie *f*; **~degradable** *adj* biodégradable; **~graphy** *n* biographie *f*; **~logical** *adj* biologique; **~logy** *n* biologie *f*

birch [bəːtʃ] *n* bouleau *m*

bird [bəːd] *n* oiseau *m*; (*BRIT: inf: girl*) nana *f*; **~'s-eye view** *n* vue *f* à vol d'oiseau; (*fig*) vue d'ensemble *or* générale; **~ watcher** *n* ornithologue *m/f* amateur

Biro [ˈbaɪərəu] ® *n* stylo *m* à bille

birth [bəːθ] *n* naissance *f*; **to give ~ to** (*subj: woman*) donner naissance à; (: *animal*) mettre bas; **~ certificate** *n* acte *m* de naissance; **~ control** *n* (*policy*) limitation *f* des naissances; (*method*) méthode(s) contraceptive(s); **~day** *n* anniversaire *m* ♦ *cpd* d'anniversaire; **~place** *n* lieu *m* de naissance; (*fig*) berceau *m*; **~ rate** *n* (taux *m* de) natalité *f*

biscuit [ˈbɪskɪt] *n* (*BRIT*) biscuit *m*; (*US*) petit pain au lait

bisect [baɪˈsekt] *vt* couper *or* diviser en deux

bishop [ˈbɪʃəp] *n* évêque *m*; (*CHESS*) fou *m*

bit [bɪt] *pt of* **bite** ♦ *n* morceau *m*; (*of tool*) mèche *f*; (*of horse*) mors *m*; (*COMPUT*) élment *m* binaire; **a ~ of** un peu de; **a ~ mad** un peu fou; **~ by ~** petit à petit

bitch [bɪtʃ] *n* (*dog*) chienne *f*; (*inf!*) salope *f* (*!*), garce *f*

bite [baɪt] (*pt* **bit**, *pp* **bitten**) *vt, vi* mordre; (*insect*) piquer ♦ *n* (*insect ~*) piqûre *f*; (*mouthful*) bouchée *f*; **let's have a ~ (to eat)** (*inf*) mangeons un morceau; **to ~ one's nails** se ronger les ongles

bitter ['bɪtər] *adj* amer(-ère); (*weather, wind*) glacial(e); (*criticism*) cinglant(e); (*struggle*) acharné(e) ♦ *n* (BRIT: *beer*) bière *f* (forte); **~ness** *n* amertume *f*; (*taste*) goût amer

black [blæk] *adj* noir(e) ♦ *n* (*colour*) noir *m*; (*person*): **B~** noir(e) ♦ *vt* (BRIT: INDUSTRY) boycotter; **to give sb a ~ eye** pocher l'œil à qn, faire un œil au beurre noir à qn; **~ and blue** couvert(e) de bleus; **to be in the ~** (*in credit*) être créditeur(-trice); **~berry** *n* mûre *f*; **~bird** *n* merle *m*; **~board** *n* tableau noir; **~ coffee** *n* café noir; **~currant** *n* cassis *m*; **~en** *vt* noircir; **~ ice** *n* verglas *m*; **~leg** (BRIT) *n* briseur *m* de grève, jaune; **~list** *n* liste noire; **~mail** *n* chantage *m* ♦ *vt* faire chanter, soumettre au chantage; **~ market** *n* marché noir; **~out** *n* panne *f* d'électricité; (*TV etc*) interruption *f* d'émission; (*fainting*) syncope *f*; **~ pudding** *n* boudin (noir); **B~ Sea** *n*: **the B~ Sea** la mer Noire; **~ sheep** *n* brebis galeuse; **~smith** *n* forgeron *m*; **~ spot** (AUT) *n* point noir

bladder ['blædər] *n* vessie *f*

blade [bleɪd] *n* lame *f*; (*of propeller*) pale *f*; **~ of grass** brin *m* d'herbe

blame [bleɪm] *n* faute *f*, blâme *m* ♦ *vt*: **to ~ sb/sth for sth** attribuer à qn/qch la responsabilité de qch; reprocher qch à qn/qch; **who's to ~?** qui est le fautif *or* coupable *or* responsable?

bland [blænd] *adj* (*taste, food*) doux (douce), fade

blank [blæŋk] *adj* blanc (blanche); (*look*) sans expression, dénué(e) d'expression ♦ *n* espace *m* vide, blanc *m*; (*cartridge*) cartouche *f* à blanc; **his mind was a ~** il avait la tête vide; **~ cheque** chèque *m* en blanc

blanket ['blæŋkɪt] *n* couverture *f*; (*of snow, cloud*) couche *f*

blare [blɛər] *vi* beugler

blast [blɑːst] *n* souffle *m*; (*of explosive*) explosion *f* ♦ *vt* faire sauter *or* exploser; **~-off** *n* (SPACE) lancement *m*

blatant ['bleɪtənt] *adj* flagrant(e), criant(e)

blaze [bleɪz] *n* (*fire*) incendie *m*; (*fig*) flamboiement *m* ♦ *vi* (*fire*) flamber; (*fig: eyes*) flamboyer; (: *guns*) crépiter ♦ *vt*: **to ~ a trail** (*fig*) montrer la voie

blazer ['bleɪzər] *n* blazer *m*

bleach [bliːtʃ] *n* (*also*: **household ~**) eau *f* de Javel ♦ *vt* (*linen etc*) blanchir; **~ed** *adj* (*hair*) oxygéné(e), décoloré(e)

bleak [bliːk] *adj* morne; (*countryside*) désolé(e)

bleat [bliːt] *vi* bêler

bleed [bliːd] (*pt, pp* **bled**) *vt, vi* saigner; **my nose is ~ing** je saigne du nez

bleeper ['bliːpər] *n* (*device*) bip *m*

blemish ['blemɪʃ] *n* défaut *m*; (*on fruit, reputation*) tache *f*

blend [blend] *n* mélange *m* ♦ *vt* mélanger ♦ *vi* (*colours etc: also:* **~ in**) se mélanger, se fondre; **~er** *n* mixeur *m*

bless [bles] (*pt, pp* **blessed** *or* **blest**) *vt* bénir; **~ you!** (*after sneeze*) à vos souhaits!; **~ing** *n* bénédiction *f*; (*godsend*) bienfait *m*

blew [bluː] *pt of* **blow**

blight [blaɪt] *vt* (*hopes etc*) anéantir; (*life*) briser

blimey ['blaɪmɪ] (BRIT: *inf*) *excl* mince alors!

blind [blaɪnd] *adj* aveugle ♦ *n* (*for window*) store *m* ♦ *vt* aveugler; **~ alley** *n* impasse *f*; **~ corner** (BRIT) *n* virage *m* sans visibilité; **~fold** *n* bandeau *m* ♦ *adj, adv* les yeux bandés ♦ *vt* bander les yeux à; **~ly** *adv* aveuglément; **~ness** *n* cécité *f*; **~ spot** *n* (AUT *etc*) angle mort; **that is her ~ spot** (*fig*) elle refuse d'y voir clair sur ce point

blink [blɪŋk] *vi* cligner des yeux; (*light*) clignoter; **~ers** *npl* œillères *fpl*

bliss [blɪs] *n* félicité *f*, bonheur *m* sans mélange

blister ['blɪstə^r] *n* (*on skin*) ampoule *f*, cloque *f*; (*on paintwork, rubber*) boursouflure *f* ♦ *vi* (*paint*) se boursoufler, se cloquer

blizzard ['blɪzəd] *n* blizzard *m*, tempête *f* de neige

bloated ['bləʊtɪd] *adj* (*face*) bouffi(e); (*stomach, person*) gonflé(e)

blob [blɒb] *n* (*drop*) goutte *f*; (*stain, spot*) tache *f*

block [blɒk] *n* bloc *m*; (*in pipes*) obstruction *f*; (*toy*) cube *m*; (*of buildings*) pâté *m* (de maisons) ♦ *vt* bloquer; (*fig*) faire obstacle à; **~ of flats** (*BRIT*) immeuble (locatif); **mental ~** trou *m* de mémoire; **~ade** [blɒ'keɪd] *n* blocus *m*; **~age** *n* obstruction *f*; **~buster** *n* (*film, book*) grand succès; **~ letters** *npl* majuscules *fpl*

bloke [bləʊk] (*BRIT: inf*) *n* type *m*

blond(e) [blɒnd] *adj, n* blond(e)

blood [blʌd] *n* sang *m*; **~ donor** *n* donneur(-euse) de sang; **~ group** *n* groupe sanguin; **~hound** *n* limier *m*; **~ poisoning** *n* empoisonnement *m* du sang; **~ pressure** *n* tension *f* (artérielle); **~shed** *n* effusion *f* de sang, carnage *m*; **~ sports** *npl* sports *mpl* sanguinaires; **~shot** *adj*: **~shot eyes** yeux injectés de sang; **~stream** *n* sang *m*, système sanguin; **~ test** *n* prise *f* de sang; **~thirsty** *adj* sanguinaire; **~ vessel** *n* vaisseau sanguin; **~y** *adj* sanglant(e); (*nose*) en sang; (*BRIT: inf!*): **this ~y ...** ce foutu ... (*!*), ce putain de ... (*!*); **~y strong/good** vachement *or* sacrément fort/bon; **~y-minded** (*BRIT: inf*) *adj* contrariant(e), obstiné(e)

bloom [blu:m] *n* fleur *f* ♦ *vi* être en fleur

blossom ['blɒsəm] *n* fleur(s) *f(pl)* ♦ *vi* être en fleurs; (*fig*) s'épanouir; **to ~ into** devenir

blot [blɒt] *n* tache *f* ♦ *vt* tacher; **~ out** *vt* (*memories*) effacer; (*view*) cacher, masquer

blotchy ['blɒtʃɪ] *adj* (*complexion*) couvert(e) de marbrures

blotting paper ['blɒtɪŋ-] *n* buvard *m*

blouse [blaʊz] *n* chemisier *m*, corsage *m*

blow [bləʊ] (*pt* **blew**, *pp* **blown**) *n* coup *m* ♦ *vi* souffler ♦ *vt* souffler; (*fuse*) faire sauter; (*instrument*) jouer de; **to ~ one's nose** se moucher; **to ~ a whistle** siffler; **~ away** *vt* chasser, faire s'envoler; **~ down** *vt* faire tomber, renverser; **~ off** *vt* emporter; **~ out** *vi* (*fire, flame*) s'éteindre; **~ over** *vi* s'apaiser; **~ up** *vt* faire sauter; (*tyre*) gonfler; (*PHOT*) agrandir ♦ *vi* exploser, sauter; **~-dry** *n* brushing *m*; **~lamp** (*BRIT*) *n* chalumeau *m*; **~-out** *n* (*of tyre*) éclatement *m*; **~-torch** *n* = **blowlamp**

blue [blu:] *adj* bleu(e); (*fig*) triste; **~s** *n* (*MUS*): **the ~s** le blues; **~ film/joke** film *m*/histoire *f* pornographique; **to come out of the ~** (*fig*) être complètement inattendu; **~bell** *n* jacinthe *f* des bois; **~bottle** *n* mouche *f* à viande; **~print** *n* (*fig*) projet *m*, plan directeur

bluff [blʌf] *vi* bluffer ♦ *n* bluff *m*; **to call sb's ~** mettre qn au défi d'exécuter ses menaces

blunder ['blʌndə^r] *n* gaffe *f*, bévue *f* ♦ *vi* faire une gaffe *or* une bévue

blunt [blʌnt] *adj* (*person*) brusque, ne mâchant pas ses mots; (*knife*) émoussé(e), peu tranchant(e); (*pencil*) mal taillé

blur [blə:^r] *n* tache *or* masse floue *or* confuse ♦ *vt* brouiller

blush [blʌʃ] *vi* rougir ♦ *n* rougeur *f*

blustery ['blʌstərɪ] *adj* (*weather*) à bourrasques

boar [bɔ:^r] *n* sanglier *m*

board [bɔ:d] *n* planche *f*; (*on wall*) panneau *m*; (*for chess*) échiquier *m*; (*cardboard*) carton *m*; (*committee*) conseil *m*, comité *m*; (*in firm*) conseil d'administration; (*NAUT, AVIAT*): **on ~** à bord ♦ *vi* (*ship*) monter à bord de; (*train*) monter dans; **full ~** (*BRIT*) pension complète; **half ~** demi-pension *f*; **~ and lodging** chambre *f* avec pension; **which goes by the ~** (*fig*) qu'on laisse tomber, qu'on abandonne; **~ up** *vt* (*door, window*) boucher; **~er** *n* (*SCOL*) interne *m/f*, pensionnaire; **~ game** *n* jeu *m* de société; **~ing card** *n* = **boarding pass**; **~ing house** *n* pension *f*; **~ing pass** *n* (*AVIAT, NAUT*) carte *f* d'embarquement; **~ing school** *n* internat *m* pensionnat *m*; ~ **room** *n* salle *f* du conseil d'administration

boast [bəust] *vi*: **to ~ (about** *or* **of)** se vanter (de)

boat [bəut] *n* bateau *m*; (*small*) canot *m*; barque *f*; ~ **train** *n* train *m* (qui assue correspondance avec le ferry)

bob [bɔb] *vi* (*boat, cork on water: also:* ~ **up and down**) danser, se balancer

bobby ['bɔbɪ] (*BRIT: inf*) *n* ≃ agent *m* (de police)

bobsleigh ['bɔbsleɪ] *n* bob *m*

bode [bəud] *vi*: **to ~ well/ill (for)** être de bon/mauvais augure (pour)

bodily ['bɔdɪlɪ] *adj* corporel(le) ♦ *adv* dans ses bras

body ['bɔdɪ] *n* corps *m*; (*of car*) carrosserie *f*; (*of plane*) fuselage *m*; (*fig: society*) organe *m*, organisme *m*; (*: quantity*) ensemble *m*, masse *f*; (*of wine*) corps *m*; ~-**building** *n* culturisme *m*; ~**guard** *n* garde *m* du corps; ~**work** *n* carrosserie *f*

bog [bɔg] *n* tourbière *f* ♦ *vt*: **to get ~ged down** (*fig*) s'enliser

bog-standard (*inf*) *adj* tout à fait ordinaire

bogus ['bəugəs] *adj* bidon *inv*; fantôme

boil [bɔɪl] *vt* (faire) bouillir ♦ *vi* bouillir ♦ *n* (*MED*) furoncle *m*; **to come to the** (*BRIT*) ~ *or* **a** (*US*) ~ bouillir; ~ **down to** *vt fus* (*fig*) se réduire *or* ramener à; ~ **over** *vi* déborder; ~**ed egg** *n* œuf *m* à la coque; ~**ed potatoes** *npl* pommes *fpl* à l'anglaise *or* à l'eau; ~**er** *n* chaudière *f*; ~**ing point** *n* point *m* d'ébullition

boisterous ['bɔɪstərəs] *adj* bruyant(e), tapageur(-euse)

bold [bəuld] *adj* hardi(e), audacieux(-euse); (*pej*) effronté(e); (*outline, colour*) franc (franche), tranché(e), marqué(e); (*pattern*) grand(e)

bollard ['bɔləd] (*BRIT*) *n* (*AUT*) borne lumineuse *or* de signalisation

bolt [bəult] *n* (*lock*) verrou *m*; (*with nut*) boulon *m* ♦ *adv*: ~ **upright** droit(e) comme un piquet ♦ *vt* verrouiller; (*TECH: also:* ~ **on,** ~ **together**) boulonner; (*food*)

engloutir ♦ *vi* (*horse*) s'emballer

bomb [bɔm] *n* bombe *f* ♦ *vt* bombarder; ~**ing** *n* (*by terrorist*) attentat *m* à la bombe; ~ **disposal unit** *n* section *f* de déminage; ~**er** *n* (*AVIAT*) bombardier *m*; ~**shell** *n* (*fig*) bombe *f*

bond [bɔnd] *n* lien *m*; (*binding promise*) engagement *m*, obligation *f*; (*COMM*) obligation; **in ~** (*of goods*) en douane

bondage ['bɔndɪdʒ] *n* esclavage *m*

bone [bəun] *n* os *m*; (*of fish*) arête *f* ♦ *vt* désosser; ôter les arêtes de; ~ **dry** *adj* complètement sec (sèche); ~ **idle** *adj* fainéant(e); ~ **marrow** *n* moelle *f* osseuse

bonfire ['bɔnfaɪər] *n* feu *m* (de joie); (*for rubbish*) feu

bonnet ['bɔnɪt] *n* bonnet *m*; (*BRIT: of car*) capot *m*

bonus ['bəunəs] *n* prime *f*, gratification *f*

bony ['bəunɪ] *adj* (*arm, face, MED: tissue*) osseux(-euse); (*meat*) plein(e) d'os; (*fish*) plein d'arêtes

boo [bu:] *excl* hou!, peuh! ♦ *vt* huer

booby trap ['bu:bɪ-] *n* engin piégé

book [buk] *n* livre *m*; (*of stamps, tickets*) carnet *m* ♦ *vt* (*ticket*) prendre; (*seat, room*) réserver; (*driver*) dresser un procès-verbal à; (*football player*) prendre le nom de; ~**s** *npl* (*accounts*) comptes *mpl*, comptabilité *f*; ~**case** *n* bibliothèque *f* (*meuble*); ~**ing office** (*BRIT*) *n* bureau *m* de location; ~-**keeping** *n* comptabilité *f*; ~**let** *n* brochure *f*; ~**maker** *n* bookmaker *m*; ~**seller** *n* libraire *m/f*; ~**shelf** *n* (*single*) étagère *f* (à livres); ~**shop** *n* librairie *f*; ~**store** *n* librairie *f*

boom [bu:m] *n* (*noise*) grondement *m*; (*in prices, population*) forte augmentation ♦ *vi* gronder; prospérer

boon [bu:n] *n* bénédiction *f*, grand avantage

boost [bu:st] *n* stimulant *m*, remontant *m* ♦ *vt* stimuler; ~**er** *n* (*MED*) rappel *m*

boot [bu:t] *n* botte *f*; (*for hiking*) chaussure *f* (de marche); (*for football etc*) soulier *m*; (*BRIT: of car*) coffre *m* ♦ *vt* (*COMPUT*) amorcer, initialiser; **to ~** (*in addition*) par-dessus le marché

booth [buːð] *n* (*at fair*) baraque (foraine); (*telephone etc*) cabine *f*; (*also:* **voting ~**) isoloir *m*

booze [buːz] (*inf*) *n* boissons *fpl* alcooliques, alcool *m*

border ['bɔːdər] *n* bordure *f*; bord *m*; (*of a country*) frontière *f* ♦ *vt* border; (*also:* **~ on**: *country*) être limitrophe de; **B~s** *n* (*GEO*): **the B~s** *la région frontière entre l'Écosse et l'Angleterre*; **~ on** *vt fus* être voisin(e) de, toucher à; **~line** *n* (*fig*) ligne *f* de démarcation; **~line case** cas *m* limite

bore [bɔːr] *pt of* **bear** ♦ *vt* (*hole*) percer; (*oil well, tunnel*) creuser; (*person*) ennuyer, raser ♦ *n* raseur(-euse); (*of gun*) calibre *m*; **to be ~d** s'ennuyer; **~dom** *n* ennui *m*; **boring** *adj* ennuyeux(-euse)

born [bɔːn] *adj*: **to be ~** naître; **I was ~ in 1960** je suis né en 1960

borne [bɔːn] *pp of* **bear**

borough ['bʌrə] *n* municipalité *f*

borrow ['bɔrəu] *vt*: **to ~ sth (from sb)** emprunter qch (à qn)

Bosnia (and) Herzegovina ['bɔznɪə-(ənd)hɜːtsəgəu'viːnə] *n* Bosnie-Herzégovine *f*; **Bosnian** *adj* bosniaque, bosnien(ne) ♦ *n* Bosniaque *m/f*

bosom ['buzəm] *n* poitrine *f*; (*fig*) sein *m*

boss [bɔs] *n* patron(ne) ♦ *vt* (*also:* **~ around/about**) mener à la baguette; **~y** *adj* autoritaire

bosun ['bəusn] *n* maître *m* d'équipage

botany ['bɔtənɪ] *n* botanique *f*

botch [bɔtʃ] *vt* (*also:* **~ up**) saboter, bâcler

both [bəuθ] *adj* les deux, l'un(e) et l'autre ♦ *pron*: **~ (of them)** les deux, tous (toutes) (les) deux, l'un(e) et l'autre; **they sell ~ the fabric and the finished curtains** ils vendent (et) le tissu et les rideaux (finis), ils vendent à la fois le tissu et les rideaux (finis); **~ of us went, we ~ went** nous y sommes allés (tous) les deux

bother ['bɔðər] *vt* (*worry*) tracasser; (*disturb*) déranger ♦ *vi* (*also:* **~ o.s.**) se tracasser, se faire du souci ♦ *n*: **it is a ~ to have to do** c'est vraiment ennuyeux d'avoir à fai-

re; **it's no ~** aucun problème; **to ~ doing** prendre la peine de faire

bottle ['bɔtl] *n* bouteille *f*; (*baby's*) biberon *m* ♦ *vt* mettre en bouteille(s); **~d beer** bière *f* en canette; **~d water** eau minérale; **~ up** *vt* refouler, contenir; **~ bank** *n* conteneur *m* à verre; **~neck** *n* étranglement *m*; **~-opener** *n* ouvre-bouteille *m*

bottom ['bɔtəm] *n* (*of container, sea etc*) fond *m*; (*buttocks*) derrière *m*; (*of page, list*) bas *m* ♦ *adj* du fond; du bas; **the ~ of the class** le dernier de la classe

bough [bau] *n* branche *f*, rameau *m*

bought [bɔːt] *pt, pp of* **buy**

boulder ['bəuldər] *n* gros rocher

bounce [bauns] *vi* (*ball*) rebondir; (*cheque*) être refusé(e) (*étant sans provision*) ♦ *vt* faire rebondir ♦ *n* (*rebound*) rebond *m*; **~r** (*inf*) *n* (*at dance, club*) videur *m*

bound [baund] *pt, pp of* **bind** ♦ *n* (*gen pl*) limite *f*; (*leap*) bond *m* ♦ *vi* (*leap*) bondir ♦ *vt* (*limit*) borner ♦ *adj*: **to be ~ to do sth** (*obliged*) être obligé(e) *or* avoir obligation de faire qch; **he's ~ to fail** (*likely*) est sûr d'échouer, son échec est inévitable *or* assuré; **~ by** (*law, regulation*) engagé(e) par; **~ for** à destination de; **out of ~s** dont l'accès est interdit

boundary ['baundrɪ] *n* frontière *f*

bout [baut] *n* période *f*; (*of malaria etc*) accès *m*, crise *f*, attaque *f*; (*BOXING etc*) combat *m*, match *m*

bow¹ [bəu] *n* nœud *m*; (*weapon*) arc *m*; (*MUS*) archet *m*

bow² [bau] *n* (*with body*) révérence *f*, inclination *f* (*du buste or corps*); (*NAUT: also:* **~s**) proue *f* ♦ *vi* faire une révérence, s'incliner; (*yield*): **to ~ to** *or* **before** s'incliner devant, se soumettre à

bowels ['bauəlz] *npl* intestins *mpl*; (*fig*) entrailles *fpl*

bowl [bəul] *n* (*for eating*) bol *m*; (*ball*) boule *f* ♦ *vi* (*CRICKET, BASEBALL*) lancer (la balle)

bow-legged ['bəu'legɪd] *adj* aux jambes arquées

bowler ['bəulər] *n* (*CRICKET, BASEBALL*) lanceur *m* (de la balle); (*BRIT: also:* **~ ha-**

(chapeau *m*) melon *m*

owling ['bəʊlɪŋ] *n* (*game*) jeu *m* de boules; jeu *m* de quilles; **~ alley** *n* bowling *m*; **~ green** *n* terrain *m* de boules (*gazonné et carré*)

owls [bəʊlz] *n* (*game*) (jeu *m* de) boules *fpl*

ow tie [bəʊ-] *n* nœud *m* papillon

ox [bɔks] *n* boîte *f*; (*also:* **cardboard ~**) carton *m*; (*THEATRE*) loge *f* ♦ *vt* mettre en boîte; (*SPORT*) boxer avec ♦ *vi* boxer, faire de la boxe; **~er** *n* (*person*) boxeur *m*; **~er shorts** *npl* caleçon *msg*; **~ing** *n* (*SPORT*) boxe *f*; **B~ing Day** (*BRIT*) *n* le lendemain de Noël; **~ing gloves** *npl* gants *mpl* de boxe; **~ing ring** *n* ring *m*; **~ office** *n* bureau *m* de location; **~room** *n* débarras *m*; chambrette *f*

Boxing Day

i Boxing Day *est le lendemain de Noël, férié en Grande-Bretagne. Si Noël* *ombe un samedi, le jour férié est reculé* *usqu'au lundi suivant. Ce nom vient* *d'une coutume du XIXe siècle qui con-* *istait à donner des cadeaux de Noël (dans* *es boîtes) à ses employés etc le 26 dé-* *embre.*

oy [bɔɪ] *n* garçon *m*

oycott ['bɔɪkɔt] *n* boycottage *m* ♦ *vt* boycotter

oyfriend ['bɔɪfrɛnd] *n* (petit) ami

oyish ['bɔɪʃ] *adj* (*behaviour*) de garçon; (*girl*) garçonnier(-ière)

R *n abbr* = **British Rail**

ra [brɑː] *n* soutien-gorge *m*

ace [breɪs] *n* (*on teeth*) appareil *m* (dentaire); (*tool*) vilbrequin *m* ♦ *vt* (*knees, shoulders*) appuyer; **~s** *npl* (*BRIT: for trousers*) bretelles *fpl*; **to ~ o.s.** (*lit*) s'arc-bouter; (*fig*) se préparer mentalement

acelet ['breɪslɪt] *n* bracelet *m*

acing ['breɪsɪŋ] *adj* tonifiant(e), tonique

acket ['brækɪt] *n* (*TECH*) tasseau *m*, sup-port *m*; (*group*) classe *f*, tranche *f*; (*also:* **brace ~**) accolade *f*; (*also:* **round ~**) pa-

renthèse *f*; (*also:* **square ~**) crochet *m* ♦ *vt* mettre entre parenthèse(s); (*fig: also:* **~ together**) regrouper

brag [bræg] *vi* se vanter

braid [breɪd] *n* (*trimming*) galon *m*; (*of hair*) tresse *f*

brain [breɪn] *n* cerveau *m*; **~s** *npl* (*intellect, CULIN*) cervelle *f*; **he's got ~s** il est intelligent; **~wash** *vt* faire subir un lavage de cerveau à; **~wave** *n* idée géniale; **~y** *adj* intelligent(e), doué(e)

braise [breɪz] *vt* braiser

brake [breɪk] *n* (*on vehicle, also fig*) frein *m* ♦ *vi* freiner; **~ light** *n* feu *m* de stop

bran [bræn] *n* son *m*

branch [brɑːntʃ] *n* branche *f*; (*COMM*) succursale *f* ♦ *vi* bifurquer; **~ out** *vi* (*fig*): **to ~ out into** étendre ses activités à

brand [brænd] *n* marque (commerciale) ♦ *vt* (*cattle*) marquer (au fer rouge); **~new** *adj* tout(e) neuf (neuve), flambant neuf (neuve)

brandy ['brændɪ] *n* cognac *m*, fine *f*

brash [bræʃ] *adj* effronté(e)

brass [brɑːs] *n* cuivre *m* (jaune), laiton *m*; **the ~** (*MUS*) les cuivres; **~ band** *n* fanfare *f*

brat [bræt] *n* (*pej*) mioche *m/f*, môme *m/f*

brave [breɪv] *adj* courageux(-euse), brave ♦ *n* guerrier indien ♦ *vt* braver, affronter; **~ry** *n* bravoure *f*, courage *m*

brawl [brɔːl] *n* rixe *f*, bagarre *f*

brazen ['breɪzn] *adj* impudent(e), effronté(e) ♦ *vt*: **to ~ it out** payer d'effronterie, crâner

brazier ['breɪzɪər] *n* brasero *m*

Brazil [brə'zɪl] *n* Brésil *m*

breach [briːtʃ] *vt* ouvrir une brèche dans ♦ *n* (*gap*) brèche *f*; (*breaking*): **~ of contract** rupture *f* de contrat; **~ of the peace** attentat *m* à l'ordre public

bread [brɛd] *n* pain *m*; **~ and butter** *n* tartines (beurrées); (*fig*) subsistance *f*; **~bin** (*BRIT*) *n* boîte *f* à pain; (*bigger*) huche *f* à pain; **~crumbs** *npl* miettes *fpl* de pain; (*CULIN*) chapelure *f*, panure *f*; **~line** *n*: **to be on the ~line** être sans le sou *or* dans l'indigence

breadth [brɛtθ] n largeur f; (fig) ampleur f

breadwinner ['brɛdwɪnəʳ] n soutien m de famille

break [breɪk] (pt **broke**, pp **broken**) vt casser, briser; (promise) rompre; (law) violer ♦ vi (se) casser, se briser; (weather) tourner; (story, news) se répandre; (day) se lever ♦ n (gap) brèche f; (fracture) cassure f; (pause, interval) interruption f, arrêt m; (: short) pause f; (: at school) récréation f; (chance) chance f, occasion f favorable; **to ~ one's leg** etc se casser la jambe etc; **to ~ a record** battre un record; **to ~ the news to sb** annoncer la nouvelle à qn; **~ even** rentrer dans ses frais; **~ free** or **loose** se dégager, s'échapper; **~ open** (door etc) forcer, fracturer; **~ down** vt (figures, data) décomposer, analyser ♦ vi s'effondrer; (MED) faire une dépression (nerveuse); (AUT) tomber en panne; **~ in** vt (horse etc) dresser ♦ vi (burglar) entrer par effraction; (interrupt) interrompre; **~ into** vt fus (house) s'introduire or pénétrer par effraction dans; **~ off** vi (speaker) s'interrompre; (branch) se rompre; **~ out** vi éclater, se déclarer; (prisoner) s'évader; **to ~ out in spots** or **a rash** avoir une éruption de boutons; **~ up** vi (ship) se disloquer; (crowd, meeting) se disperser, se séparer; (marriage) se briser; (SCOL) entrer en vacances ♦ vt casser; (fight etc) interrompre, faire cesser; **~age** n casse f; **~down** n (AUT) panne f; (in communications, marriage) rupture f; (MED: also: **nervous ~down**) dépression (nerveuse); (of statistics) ventilation f; **~down van** (BRIT) n dépanneuse f; **~er** n brisant m

breakfast ['brɛkfəst] n petit déjeuner

break: **~-in** n cambriolage m; **~ing and entering** n (LAW) effraction f; **~through** n percée f; **~water** n brise-lames m inv, digue f

breast [brɛst] n (of woman) sein m; (chest, of meat) poitrine f; **~-feed** (irreg: like **feed**) vt, vi allaiter; **~stroke** n brasse f

breath [brɛθ] n haleine f; **out of ~** à bout de souffle, essoufflé(e); **B~alyser** ® ['brɛθəlaɪzəʳ] n Alcootest ® m

breathe [briːð] vt, vi respirer; **~ in** vt, vi aspirer, inspirer; **~ out** vt, vi expirer; **~r** n moment m de repos or de répit; **breathing** n respiration f

breathless ['brɛθlɪs] adj essoufflé(e), haletant(e)

breathtaking ['brɛθteɪkɪŋ] adj stupéfiant(e)

breed [briːd] (pt, pp **bred**) vt élever, faire l'élevage de ♦ vi se reproduire ♦ n race f, variété f; **~ing** n (upbringing) éducation f

breeze [briːz] n brise f; **breezy** adj frais (fraîche); aéré(e); (manner etc) désinvolte, jovial(e)

brevity ['brɛvɪtɪ] n brièveté f

brew [bruː] vt (tea) faire infuser; (beer) brasser ♦ vi (fig) se préparer, couver; **~ery** n brasserie f (fabrique)

bribe [braɪb] n pot-de-vin m ♦ vt acheter, soudoyer; **~ry** n corruption f

brick [brɪk] n brique f; **~layer** n maçon m

bridal ['braɪdl] adj nuptial(e)

bride [braɪd] n mariée f, épouse f; **~groom** n marié m, époux m; **~smaid** n demoiselle f d'honneur

bridge [brɪdʒ] n pont m; (NAUT) passerelle f (de commandement); (of nose) arête f; (CARDS, DENTISTRY) bridge m ♦ vt (fig: gap, gulf) combler

bridle ['braɪdl] n bride f; **~ path** n piste or allée cavalière

brief [briːf] adj bref (brève) ♦ n (LAW) dossier m, cause f; (gen) tâche f ♦ vt mettre au courant; **~s** npl (undergarment) slip m; **~case** n serviette f, porte-documents m inv; **~ly** adv brièvement

bright [braɪt] adj brillant(e); (room, weather) clair(e); (clever: person, idea) intelligent(e); (cheerful: colour, person) vif (vive)

brighten ['braɪtn] (also: **~ up**) vt (room) éclaircir, égayer; (event) égayer ♦ vi s'éclaircir; (person) retrouver un peu de sa gaieté; (face) s'éclairer; (prospects) s'améliorer

brilliance ['brɪljəns] n éclat m

brilliant ['brɪljənt] *adj* brillant(e); (*sunshine, light*) éclatant(e); (*inf: holiday etc*) super

brim [brɪm] *n* bord *m*

brine [braɪn] *n* (CULIN) saumure *f*

bring [brɪŋ] (*pt, pp* **brought**) *vt* apporter; (*person*) amener; ~ **about** *vt* provoquer, entraîner; ~ **back** *vt* rapporter; ramener; (*restore: hanging*) réinstaurer; ~ **down** *vt* (*price*) faire baisser; (*enemy plane*) descendre; (*government*) faire tomber; ~ **forward** *vt* avancer; ~ **off** *vt* (*task, plan*) réussir, mener à bien; ~ **out** *vt* (*meaning*) faire ressortir; (*book*) publier; (*object*) sortir; ~ **round** *vt* (*unconscious person*) ranimer; ~ **up** *vt* (*child*) élever; (*carry up*) monter; (*question*) soulever; (*food: vomit*) vomir, rendre

rink [brɪŋk] *n* bord *m*

risk [brɪsk] *adj* vif (vive)

ristle ['brɪsl] *n* poil *m* ♦ *vi* se hérisser

ritain ['brɪtən] *n* (*also:* **Great ~**) Grande-Bretagne *f*

ritish ['brɪtɪʃ] *adj* britannique ♦ *npl:* **the ~** les Britanniques *mpl;* ~ **Isles** *npl:* **the ~ Isles** les Îles *fpl* Britanniques; ~ **Rail** *n* compagnie ferroviaire britannique

riton ['brɪtən] *n* Britannique *m/f*

rittany ['brɪtənɪ] *n* Bretagne *f*

rittle ['brɪtl] *adj* cassant(e), fragile

roach [brəʊtʃ] *vt* (*subject*) aborder

road [brɔːd] *adj* large; (*general: outlines*) grand(e); (: *distinction*) général(e); (*accent*) prononcé(e); **in ~ daylight** en plein jour; ~**cast** (*pt, pp* **broadcast**) *n* émission *f* ♦ *vt* radiodiffuser; téléviser ♦ *vi* émettre; ~**en** *vt* élargir ♦ *vi* s'élargir; **to ~en one's mind** élargir ses horizons; ~**ly** *adv* en gros, généralement; ~**-minded** *adj* large d'esprit

roccoli ['brɒkəlɪ] *n* brocoli *m*

rochure ['brəʊʃjʊər] *n* prospectus *m*, dépliant *m*

roil [brɔɪl] *vt* griller

roke [brəʊk] *pt of* **break** ♦ *adj* (*inf*) fauché(e)

roken ['brəʊkn] *pp of* **break** ♦ *adj* cassé(e); (*machine: also:* ~ **down**) fichu(e); **in**

~ **English/French** dans un anglais/français approximatif *or* hésitant; ~ **leg** *etc* jambe *etc* cassée; ~**-hearted** *adj* (ayant) le cœur brisé

broker ['brəʊkər] *n* courtier *m*

brolly ['brɒlɪ] (BRIT: *inf*) *n* pépin *m*, parapluie *m*

bronchitis [brɒŋ'kaɪtɪs] *n* bronchite *f*

brooch [brəʊtʃ] *n* broche *f*

brood [bruːd] *n* couvée *f* ♦ *vi* (*person*) méditer (sombrement), ruminer

broom [brum] *n* balai *m;* (BOT) genêt *m;* ~**stick** *n* manche *m* à balai

Bros. *abbr* = **Brothers**

broth [brɒθ] *n* bouillon *m* de viande et de légumes

brothel ['brɒθl] *n* maison close, bordel *m*

brother ['brʌðər] *n* frère *m;* ~**-in-law** *n* beau-frère *m*

brought [brɔːt] *pt, pp of* **bring**

brow [braʊ] *n* front *m;* (*eyebrow*) sourcil *m;* (*of hill*) sommet *m*

brown [braʊn] *adj* brun(e), marron *inv;* (*hair*) châtain *inv*, brun; (*eyes*) marron *inv;* (*tanned*) bronzé(e) ♦ *n* (*colour*) brun *m* ♦ *vt* (CULIN) faire dorer; ~ **bread** *n* pain *m* bis; **B~ie** *n* (*also:* **B~ie Guide**) jeannette *f*, éclaireuse (cadette); ~**ie** (US) *n* (*cake*) gâteau *m* au chocolat et aux noix; ~ **paper** *n* papier *m* d'emballage; ~ **sugar** *n* cassonade *f*

browse [braʊz] *vi* (*among books*) bouquiner, feuilleter les livres; **to ~ through a book** feuilleter un livre; ~**r** *n* navigateur *m*

bruise [bruːz] *n* bleu *m*, contusion *f* ♦ *vt* contusionner, meurtrir

brunette [bruː'net] *n* (*femme*) brune

brunt [brʌnt] *n:* **the ~ of** (*attack, criticism etc*) le plus gros de

brush [brʌʃ] *n* brosse *f;* (*painting*) pinceau *m;* (*shaving*) blaireau *m;* (*quarrel*) accrochage *m*, prise *f* de bec ♦ *vt* brosser; (*also:* ~ **against**) effleurer, frôler; ~ **aside** *vt* écarter, balayer; ~ **up** *vt* (*knowledge*) rafraîchir, réviser; ~**wood** *n* broussailles *fpl*, taillis *m*

Brussels ['brʌslz] *n* Bruxelles; ~ **sprout** *n* chou *m* de Bruxelles
brutal ['bru:tl] *adj* brutal(e)
brute [bru:t] *n* brute *f* ♦ *adj*: **by ~ force** par la force
BSc *abbr* = **Bachelor of Science**
BSE *n abbr* (= *bovine spongiform encephalo-pathy*) ESB *f*, BSE *f*
bubble ['bʌbl] *n* bulle *f* ♦ *vi* bouillonner, faire des bulles; (*sparkle*) pétiller; ~ **bath** *n* bain moussant; ~ **gum** *n* bubblegum *m*
buck [bʌk] *n* mâle *m* (*d'un lapin, daim etc*); (*US: inf*) dollar *m* ♦ *vi* ruer, lancer une ruade; **to pass the ~ (to sb)** se décharger de la responsabilité (sur qn); ~ **up** *vi* (*cheer up*) reprendre du poil de la bête, se remonter
bucket ['bʌkɪt] *n* seau *m*

Buckingham Palace
---

i Buckingham Palace *est la résidence officielle londonienne du souverain britannique depuis 1762. Construit en 1703, il fut à l'origine le palais du duc de Buckingham. Il a été reconstruit au début du siècle.*

---

buckle ['bʌkl] *n* boucle *f* ♦ *vt* (*belt etc*) boucler, attacher ♦ *vi* (*warp*) tordre, gauchir; (: *wheel*) se voiler; se déformer
bud [bʌd] *n* bourgeon *m*; (*of flower*) bouton *m* ♦ *vi* bourgeonner; (*flower*) éclore
Buddhism ['budɪzəm] *n* bouddhisme *m*
Buddhist *adj* bouddhiste ♦ *n* Bouddhiste *m/f*
budding ['bʌdɪŋ] *adj* (*poet etc*) en herbe; (*passion etc*) naissant(e)
buddy ['bʌdɪ] (*US*) *n* copain *m*
budge [bʌdʒ] *vt* faire bouger; (*fig: person*) faire changer d'avis ♦ *vi* bouger; changer d'avis
budgerigar ['bʌdʒərɪgɑ:'] (*BRIT*) *n* perruche *f*
budget ['bʌdʒɪt] *n* budget *m* ♦ *vi*: **to ~ for sth** inscrire qch au budget
budgie ['bʌdʒɪ] (*BRIT*) *n* = **budgerigar**
buff [bʌf] *adj* (*couleur f*) chamois *m* ♦ *n*

(*inf: enthusiast*) mordu(e); **he's a ...** c'est un mordu de ...
buffalo ['bʌfələu] (*pl ~ or ~es*) *n* buffle *m* (*US*) bison *m*
buffer ['bʌfə'] *n* tampon *m*; (*COMPUT*) mé moire *f* tampon
buffet¹ ['bʌfɪt] *vt* secouer, ébranler
buffet² ['bufeɪ] *n* (*food, BRIT: bar*) buff *m*; ~ **car** (*BRIT*) *n* (*RAIL*) voiture-buffet *f*
bug [bʌg] *n* (*insect*) punaise *f*; (: *gen*) inse te *m*, bestiole *f*; (*fig: germ*) virus *m*, micro be *m*; (*COMPUT*) erreur *f*; (*fig: spy devic* dispositif *m* d'écoute (électronique) ♦ garnir de dispositifs d'écoute; (*inf: anno* embêter; ~**ged** *adj* sur écoute
bugle ['bju:gl] *n* clairon *m*
build [bɪld] (*pt, pp built*) *n* (*of person*) ca rure *f*, charpente *f* ♦ *vt* construire, bât ~ **up** *vt* accumuler, amasser; accroîtr ~**er** *n* entrepreneur *m*; ~**ing** *n* (*trad* construction *f*; (*house, structure*) bâtime *m*, construction; (*offices, flats*) immeub *m*; ~**ing society** (*BRIT*) *n* société *f* de cr dit immobilier

---
building society
---

i Une **building society** *est une mutue le dont les épargnants et emprunteurs sont les propriétaires. Ces mutuelles offre deux services principaux: on peut y avoir un compte d'épargne duquel on peut retir son argent sur demande ou moyennant u court préavis; et on peut également y fair des emprunts à long terme, par exemple pour acheter une maison.*

---

built [bɪlt] *pt, pp of* **build**; ~**-in** ['bɪlt'ɪn] *c* (*cupboard, oven*) encastré(e); (*device*) inc poré(e); intégré(e); ~**-up area** ['bɪltʌp-] zone urbanisée
bulb [bʌlb] *n* (*BOT*) bulbe *m*, oignon (*ELEC*) ampoule *f*
Bulgaria [bʌl'geərɪə] *n* Bulgarie *f*
bulge [bʌldʒ] *n* renflement *m*, gonfleme *m* ♦ *vi* (*pocket, file etc*) être plein(e) à c quer; (*cheeks*) être gonflé(e)
bulk [bʌlk] *n* masse *f*, volume *m*; (*of p*

son) corpulence f; **in ~** (COMM) en vrac; **the ~ of** la plus grande or grosse partie de; **~y** adj volumineux(-euse), encombrant(e)

bull [bʊl] n taureau m; (male elephant/ whale) mâle m; **~dog** n bouledogue m

bulldozer ['bʊldəʊzə⁺] n bulldozer m

bullet ['bʊlɪt] n balle f (de fusil etc)

bulletin ['bʊlɪtɪn] n bulletin m, communiqué m; (news ~) (bulletin d')informations fpl; **~ board** n (Internet) messagerie f électronique

bulletproof ['bʊlɪtpruːf] adj (car) blindé(e); (vest etc) pare-balles inv

bullfight ['bʊlfaɪt] n corrida f, course f de taureaux; **~er** n torero m; **~ing** n tauromachie f

bullion ['bʊljən] n or m ou argent m en lingots

bullock ['bʊlək] n bœuf m

bullring ['bʊlrɪŋ] n arènes fpl

bull's-eye ['bʊlzaɪ] n centre m (de la cible)

bully ['bʊlɪ] n brute f, tyran m ♦ vt tyranniser, rudoyer

bum [bʌm] n (inf: backside) derrière m; (esp US: tramp) vagabond(e), traîne-savates m/f inv

bumblebee ['bʌmblbiː] n bourdon m

bump [bʌmp] n (in car: minor accident) accrochage m; (jolt) cahot m; (on road etc, on head) bosse f ♦ vt heurter, cogner; **~ into** vt fus rentrer dans, tamponner; (meet) tomber sur; **~er** n pare-chocs m inv ♦ adj: **~er crop/harvest** récolte/ moisson exceptionnelle; **~er cars** (US) npl autos tamponneuses; **~y** adj cahoteux(-euse)

bun [bʌn] n petit pain au lait; (of hair) chignon m

bunch [bʌntʃ] n (of flowers) bouquet m; (of keys) trousseau m; (of bananas) régime m; (of people) groupe m; **~es** npl (in hair) couettes fpl; **~ of grapes** grappe f de raisin

bundle ['bʌndl] n paquet m ♦ vt (also: ~ **up**) faire un paquet de; (put): **to ~ sth/sb into** fourrer ou enfourner qch/qn dans

bungalow ['bʌŋgələʊ] n bungalow m

bungle ['bʌŋgl] vt bâcler, gâcher

bunion ['bʌnjən] n oignon m (au pied)

bunk [bʌŋk] n couchette f; **~ beds** npl lits superposés

bunker ['bʌŋkə⁺] n (coal store) soute f à charbon; (MIL, GOLF) bunker m

bunting ['bʌntɪŋ] n pavoisement m, drapeaux mpl

buoy [bɔɪ] n bouée f; **~ up** vt faire flotter; (fig) soutenir, épauler; **~ant** adj capable de flotter; (carefree) gai(e), plein(e) d'entrain; (economy) ferme, actif

burden ['bəːdn] n fardeau m ♦ vt (trouble) accabler, surcharger

bureau ['bjʊərəʊ] (pl **~x**) n (BRIT: writing desk) bureau m, secrétaire m; (US: chest of drawers) commode f; (office) bureau, office m; **~cracy** [bjʊəˈrɔkrəsɪ] n bureaucratie f

burglar ['bəːglə⁺] n cambrioleur m; **~ alarm** n sonnerie f d'alarme

Burgundy ['bəːgəndɪ] n Bourgogne f

burial ['bɛrɪəl] n enterrement m

burly ['bəːlɪ] adj de forte carrure, costaud(e)

Burma ['bəːmə] n Birmanie f

burn [bəːn] (pt, pp **burned** or **burnt**) vt, vi brûler ♦ n brûlure f; **~ down** vt incendier, détruire par le feu; **~er** n brûleur m; **~ing** adj brûlant(e); (house) en flammes; (ambition) dévorant(e)

burrow ['bʌrəʊ] n terrier m ♦ vt creuser

bursary ['bəːsərɪ] (BRIT) n bourse f (d'études)

burst [bəːst] (pt,pp **burst**) vt crever; faire éclater; (subj: river: banks etc) rompre ♦ vi éclater; (tyre) crever ♦ n (of gunfire) rafale f (de tir); (also: ~ **pipe**) rupture f; fuite f; **a ~ of enthusiasm/energy** un accès d'enthousiasme/d'énergie; **to ~ into flames** s'enflammer soudainement; **to ~ out laughing** éclater de rire; **to ~ into tears** fondre en larmes; **to be ~ing with** être plein (à craquer) de; (fig) être débordant(e) de; **~ into** vt fus (room etc) faire irruption dans

bury ['bɛrɪ] vt enterrer

bus [bʌs] (*pl* **~es**) *n* autobus *m*

bush [buʃ] *n* buisson *m*; (*scrubland*) brousse *f*; **to beat about the ~** tourner autour du pot; **~y** *adj* broussailleux(-euse), touffu(e)

busily ['bɪzɪlɪ] *adv* activement

business ['bɪznɪs] *n* (*matter, firm*) affaire *f*; (*trading*) affaires *fpl*; (*job, duty*) travail *m*; **to be away on ~** être en déplacement d'affaires; **it's none of my ~** cela ne me regarde pas, ce ne sont pas mes affaires; **he means ~** il ne plaisante pas, il est sérieux; **~like** *adj* (*firm*) sérieux(-euse); (*method*) efficace; **~man** (*irreg*) *n* homme *m* d'affaires; **~ trip** *n* voyage *m* d'affaires; **~woman** (*irreg*) *n* femme *f* d'affaires

busker ['bʌskər] (*BRIT*) *n* musicien ambulant

bus: **~ shelter** *n* abribus *m*; **~ station** *n* gare routière; **~ stop** *n* arrêt *m* d'autobus

bust [bʌst] *n* buste *m*; (*measurement*) tour *m* de poitrine ♦ *adj* (*inf: broken*) fichu(e), fini(e); **to go ~** faire faillite

bustle ['bʌsl] *n* remue-ménage *m*, affairement *m* ♦ *vi* s'affairer, se démener; **bustling** *adj* (*town*) bruyant(e), affairé(e)

busy ['bɪzɪ] *adj* occupé(e); (*shop, street*) très fréquenté(e) ♦ *vt*: **to ~ o.s.** s'occuper; **~body** *n* mouche *f* du coche, âme *f* charitable; **~ signal** (*US*) *n* (*TEL*) tonalité *f* occupé *inv*

but [bʌt] *conj* mais; **I'd love to come, but I'm busy** j'aimerais venir mais je suis occupé

♦ *prep* (*apart from, except*) sauf, excepté; **we've had nothing but trouble** nous n'avons eu que des ennuis; **no-one but him can do it** lui seul peut le faire; **but for you/your help** sans toi/ton aide; **anything but that** tout sauf *or* excepté ça, tout mais pas ça

♦ *adv* (*just, only*) ne ... que; **she's but a child** elle n'est qu'une enfant; **had I but known** si seulement j'avais su; **all but finished** pratiquement terminé

butcher ['butʃər] *n* boucher *m* ♦ *vt* massacrer; (*cattle etc for meat*) tuer; **~'s (shop)** *n* boucherie *f*

butler ['bʌtlər] *n* maître *m* d'hôtel

butt [bʌt] *n* (*large barrel*) gros tonneau; (*of gun*) crosse *f*; (*of cigarette*) mégot *m*; (*BRIT: fig: target*) cible *f* ♦ *vt* donner un coup de tête à; **~ in** *vi* (*interrupt*) s'immiscer dans la conversation

butter ['bʌtər] *n* beurre *m* ♦ *vt* beurrer; **~cup** *n* bouton *m* d'or

butterfly ['bʌtəflaɪ] *n* papillon *m*; (*SWIMMING: also:* **~ stroke**) brasse *f* papillon

buttocks ['bʌtəks] *npl* fesses *fpl*

button ['bʌtn] *n* bouton *m*; (*US: badge*) pin *m* ♦ *vt* (*also:* **~ up**) boutonner ♦ *vi* se boutonner

buttress ['bʌtrɪs] *n* contrefort *m*

buy [baɪ] (*pt, pp* **bought**) *vt* acheter ♦ *n* achat *m*; **to ~ sb sth/sth from sb** acheter qch à qn; **to ~ sb a drink** offrir un verre *or* à boire à qn; **~er** *n* acheteur(-euse)

buzz [bʌz] *n* bourdonnement *m*; (*inf: phone call*) **to give sb a ~** passer un coup *n* de fil à qn ♦ *vi* bourdonner; **~er** *n* timbre *m* électrique; **~ word** *n* (*inf*) mot *m* à la mode

by [baɪ] *prep* **1** (*referring to cause, agent*) par, de; **killed by lightning** tué par la foudre; **surrounded by a fence** entouré d'une barrière; **a painting by Picasso** un tableau de Picasso

2 (*referring to method, manner, means*): **by bus/car** en autobus/voiture; **by train** par le *or* en train; **to pay by cheque** payer par chèque; **by saving hard, he ...** à force d'économiser, il ...

3 (*via, through*) par; **we came by Dover** nous sommes venus par Douvres

4 (*close to, past*) à côté de; **the house by the school** la maison à côté de l'école; **holiday by the sea** des vacances au bord de la mer; **she sat by his bed** elle était assise à son chevet; **she went by me** elle

est passée à côté de moi; **I go by the post office every day** je passe devant la poste tous les jours
5 (*with time: not later than*) avant; (: *during*): **by daylight** à la lumière du jour; **by night** la nuit, de nuit; **by 4 o'clock** avant 4 heures; **by this time tomorrow** d'ici demain à la même heure; **by the time I get here it was too late** lorsque je suis arrivé il était déjà trop tard
6 (*amount*) à; **by the kilo/metre** au kilo/au mètre; **paid by the hour** payé à l'heure
7 (*MATH, measure*): **to divide/multiply by 3** diviser/multiplier par 3; **a room 3 metres by 4** une pièce de 3 mètres sur 4; **it's broader by a metre** c'est plus large d'un mètre; **one by one** un à un; **little by little** petit à petit, peu à peu
8 (*according to*) d'après, selon; **it's 3 o'clock by my watch** il est 3 heures à ma montre; **it's all right by me** je n'ai rien contre
9: (all) by oneself *etc* tout(e) seul(e)
10: by the way au fait, à propos
♦ *adv* **1** *see* **go; pass** *etc*
2: by and by un peu plus tard, bientôt; **by and large** dans l'ensemble

bye(-bye) ['baɪ('baɪ)] *excl* au revoir!, salut!
bye(e)-law ['baɪlɔ:] *n* arrêté municipal
by: **~-election** (*BRIT*) *n* élection (législative) partielle; **~gone** *adj* passé(e) ♦ *n*: **let ~gones be ~gones** passons l'éponge, oublions le passé; **~pass** *n* (route *f* de) contournement *m*; (*MED*) pontage *m* ♦ *vt* éviter; **~-product** *n* sous-produit *m*, dérivé *m*; (*fig*) conséquence *f* secondaire, retombée *f*; **~stander** *n* spectateur(-trice), badaud(e)
byte [baɪt] *n* (*COMPUT*) octet *m*
byword ['baɪwɔ:d] *n*: **to be a ~ for** être synonyme de (*fig*)

C, c

C [si:] *n* (*MUS*) do *m*
CA *abbr* = **chartered accountant**
cab [kæb] *n* taxi *m*; (*of train, truck*) cabine *f*
cabaret ['kæbəreɪ] *n* (*show*) spectacle *m* de cabaret
cabbage ['kæbɪdʒ] *n* chou *m*
cabin ['kæbɪn] *n* (*house*) cabane *f*, hutte *f*; (*on ship*) cabine *f*; (*on plane*) compartiment *m*; **~ crew** *n* (*AVIAT*) équipage *m*; **~ cruiser** *n* cruiser *m*
cabinet ['kæbɪnɪt] *n* (*POL*) cabinet *m*; (*furniture*) petit meuble à tiroirs et rayons; (*also:* **display ~**) vitrine *f*, petite armoire vitrée
cable ['keɪbl] *n* câble *m* ♦ *vt* câbler, télégraphier; **~-car** *n* téléphérique *m*; **~ television** *n* télévision *f* par câble
cache [kæʃ] *n* stock *m*
cackle ['kækl] *vi* caqueter
cactus ['kæktəs] (*pl* **cacti**) *n* cactus *m*
cadet [kə'dɛt] *n* (*MIL*) élève *m* officier
cadge [kædʒ] (*inf*) *vt*: **to ~ (from** *or* **off)** se faire donner (par)
Caesarian [sɪ'zɛərɪən] *n* (*also:* **~ section**) césarienne *f*
café ['kæfeɪ] *n* ≃ café(-restaurant) *m* (*sans alcool*)
cage [keɪdʒ] *n* cage *f*
cagey ['keɪdʒɪ] (*inf*) *adj* réticent(e); méfiant(e)
cagoule [kə'gu:l] *n* K-way ® *m*
Cairo ['kaɪərəu] *n* le Caire
cajole [kə'dʒəul] *vt* couvrir de flatteries *or* de gentillesses
cake [keɪk] *n* gâteau *m*; **~d** *adj*: **~d with** raidi(e) par, couvert(e) d'une croûte de
calculate ['kælkjuleɪt] *vt* calculer; (*estimate: chances, effect*) évaluer; **calculation** *n* calcul *m*; **calculator** *n* machine *f* à calculer, calculatrice *f*; (*pocket*) calculette *f*
calendar ['kæləndər] *n* calendrier *m*; **~ year** *n* année civile
calf [kɑ:f] (*pl* **calves**) *n* (*of cow*) veau *m*; (*of*

other animals) petit *m*; (*also:* **~skin**) veau *m*, vachette *f*; (*ANAT*) mollet *m*
calibre [ˈkælɪbəʳ] (*US* **caliber**) *n* calibre *m*
call [kɔːl] *vt* appeler; (*meeting*) convoquer ♦ *vi* appeler; (*visit: also:* **~ in**, **~ round**) passer ♦ *n* (*shout*) appel *m*, cri *m*; (*also:* **telephone ~**) coup *m* de téléphone; (*visit*) visite *f*; **she's ~ed Suzanne** elle s'appelle Suzanne; **to be on ~** être de permanence; **~ back** *vi* (*return*) repasser; (*TEL*) rappeler; **~ for** *vt fus* (*demand*) demander; (*fetch*) passer prendre; **~ off** *vt* annuler; **~ on** *vt fus* (*visit*) rendre visite à, passer voir; (*request*): **to ~ on sb to do** inviter qn à faire; **~ out** *vi* pousser un cri *or* des cris; **~ up** *vt* (*MIL*) appeler, mobiliser; (*TEL*) appeler; **~box** (*BRIT*) *n* (*TEL*) cabine *f* téléphonique; **~ centre** *n* centre *m* d'appels; **~er** *n* (*TEL*) personne *f* qui appelle; (*visitor*) visiteur *m*; **~ girl** *n* call-girl *f*; **~-in** (*US*) *n* (*RADIO, TV: phone-in*) programme *m* à ligne ouverte; **~ing** *n* vocation *f*; (*trade, occupation*) état *m*; **~ing card** (*US*) *n* carte *f* de visite
callous [ˈkæləs] *adj* dur(e), insensible
calm [kɑːm] *adj* calme ♦ *n* calme *m* ♦ *vt* calmer, apaiser; **~ down** *vi* se calmer ♦ *vt* calmer, apaiser
Calor gas ® [ˈkæləʳ-] *n* butane *m*, butagaz *m* ®
calorie [ˈkælərɪ] *n* calorie *f*
calves [kɑːvz] *npl of* **calf**
camber [ˈkæmbəʳ] *n* (*of road*) bombement *m*
Cambodia [kæmˈbəudɪə] *n* Cambodge *m*
camcorder [ˈkæmkɔːdəʳ] *n* caméscope *m*
came [keɪm] *pt of* **come**
camel [ˈkæməl] *n* chameau *m*
camera [ˈkæmərə] *n* (*PHOT*) appareil-photo *m*; (*also:* **cine-~**, **movie ~**) caméra *f*; **in ~** à huis clos; **~man** (*irreg*) *n* caméraman *m*
camouflage [ˈkæməflɑːʒ] *n* camouflage *m* ♦ *vt* camoufler
camp [kæmp] *n* camp *m* ♦ *vi* camper ♦ *adj* (*man*) efféminé(e)
campaign [kæmˈpeɪn] *n* (*MIL, POL etc*) campagne *f* ♦ *vi* faire campagne

camp: **~bed** (*BRIT*) *n* lit *m* de camp; **~er** *n* campeur(-euse); (*vehicle*) camping-car *m*; **~ing** *n* camping *m*; **to go ~ing** faire du camping; **~ing gas** ® *n* butane *m*; **~site** *n* campement *m*, (*terrain m de*) camping *m*
can[1] [kæn] *n* (*of milk, oil, water*) bidon *m*; (*tin*) boîte *f* de conserve ♦ *vt* mettre en conserve

KEYWORD

can[2] [kæn] (*negative* **cannot**, **can't**, *conditional and pt* **could**) *aux vb* **1** (*be able to*) pouvoir; **you can do it if you try** vous pouvez le faire si vous essayez; **I can't hear you** je ne t'entends pas
2 (*know how to*) savoir; **I can swim/play tennis/drive** je sais nager/jouer au tennis/conduire; **can you speak French?** parlez-vous français?
3 (*may*) pouvoir; **can I use your phone?** puis-je me servir de votre téléphone?
4 (*expressing disbelief, puzzlement etc*): **it can't be true!** ce n'est pas possible!; **what CAN he want?** qu'est-ce qu'il peut bien vouloir?
5 (*expressing possibility, suggestion etc*): **he could be in the library** il est peut-être dans la bibliothèque; **she could have been delayed** il se peut qu'elle ait été retardée

Canada [ˈkænədə] *n* Canada *m*; **Canadian** [kəˈneɪdɪən] *adj* canadien(ne) ♦ *n* Canadien(ne)
canal [kəˈnæl] *n* canal *m*
canapé [ˈkænəpeɪ] *n* canapé *m*
canary [kəˈnɛərɪ] *n* canari *m*, serin *m*
cancel [ˈkænsəl] *vt* annuler; (*train*) supprimer; (*party, appointment*) décommander; (*cross out*) barrer, rayer; **~lation** [kænsəˈleɪʃən] *n* annulation *f*; suppression *f*
cancer [ˈkænsəʳ] *n* (*MED*) cancer *m*; **C~** (*ASTROLOGY*) le Cancer
candid [ˈkændɪd] *adj* (*très*) franc (franche) sincère
candidate [ˈkændɪdeɪt] *n* candidat(e)

candle ['kændl] *n* bougie *f*; (*of tallow*) chandelle *f*; (*in church*) cierge *m*; **~light** *n*: **by ~light** à la lumière d'une bougie; (*dinner*) aux chandelles; **~stick** *n* (*also:* **~ holder**) bougeoir *m*; (*bigger, ornate*) chandelier *m*

candour ['kændər] (*US* **candor**) *n* (grande) franchise *or* sincérité

candy ['kændı] *n* sucre candi; (*US*) bonbon *m*; **~-floss** (*BRIT*) *n* barbe *f* à papa

cane [keın] *n* canne *f*; (*for furniture, baskets etc*) rotin *m* ♦ *vt* (*BRIT: SCOL*) administrer des coups de bâton à

canister ['kænıstər] *n* boîte *f*; (*of gas, pressurized substance*) bombe *f*

cannabis ['kænəbıs] *n* (*drug*) cannabis *m*

canned [kænd] *adj* (*food*) en boîte, en conserve

cannon ['kænən] (*pl* **~** *or* **~s**) *n* (*gun*) canon *m*

cannot ['kænɒt] = **can not**

canoe [kə'nu:] *n* pirogue *f*; (*SPORT*) canoë *m*; **~ing** *n*: **to go ~ing** faire du canoë

canon ['kænən] *n* (*clergyman*) chanoine *m*; (*standard*) canon *m*

can-opener ['kænəupnər] *n* ouvre-boîte *m*

canopy ['kænəpı] *n* baldaquin *m*; dais *m*

can't [kænt] = **cannot**

canteen [kæn'ti:n] *n* cantine *f*; (*BRIT: of cutlery*) ménagère *f*

canter ['kæntər] *vi* (*horse*) aller au petit galop

canvas ['kænvəs] *n* toile *f*

canvass ['kænvəs] *vi* (*POL*): **to ~ for** faire campagne pour ♦ *vt* (*investigate: opinions etc*) sonder

canyon ['kænjən] *n* cañon *m*, gorge (profonde)

cap [kæp] *n* casquette *f*; (*of pen*) capuchon *m*; (*of bottle*) capsule *f*; (*contraceptive: also:* **Dutch ~**) diaphragme *m*; (*for toy gun*) amorce *f* ♦ *vt* (*outdo*) surpasser; (*put limit on*) plafonner

capability [keɪpə'bɪlɪtɪ] *n* aptitude *f*, capacité *f*

capable ['keɪpəbl] *adj* capable

capacity [kə'pæsɪtɪ] *n* capacité *f*; (*capabili-*

ty) aptitude *f*; (*of factory*) rendement *m*

cape [keɪp] *n* (*garment*) cape *f*; (*GEO*) cap *m*

caper ['keɪpər] *n* (*CULIN: gen pl*) câpre *f*; (*prank*) farce *f*

capital ['kæpɪtl] *n* (*also:* **~ city**) capitale *f*; (*money*) capital *m*; (*also:* **~ letter**) majuscule *f*; **~ gains tax** *n* (*COMM*) impôt *m* sur les plus-values; **~ism** *n* capitalisme *m*; **~ist** *adj* capitaliste ♦ *n* capitaliste *m/f*; **~ize** ['kæpɪtəlaɪz] *vi*: **to ~ize on** tirer parti de; **~ punishment** *n* peine capitale

---
Capitol

i Le **Capitol** est le siège du **Congress**, à Washington. Il est situé sur Capitol Hill.

Capricorn ['kæprɪkɔːn] *n* le Capricorne

capsize [kæp'saɪz] *vt* faire chavirer ♦ *vi* chavirer

capsule ['kæpsjuːl] *n* capsule *f*

captain ['kæptɪn] *n* capitaine *m*

caption ['kæpʃən] *n* légende *f*

captive ['kæptɪv] *adj, n* captif(-ive)

capture ['kæptʃər] *vt* capturer, prendre; (*attention*) capter; (*COMPUT*) saisir ♦ *n* capture *f*; (*data ~*) saisie *f* de données

car [kɑːr] *n* voiture *f*, auto *f*; (*RAIL*) wagon *m*, voiture

caramel ['kærəməl] *n* caramel *m*

caravan ['kærəvæn] *n* caravane *f*; **~ning** *n*: **to go ~ning** faire du caravaning; **~ site** (*BRIT*) *n* camping *m* pour caravanes

carbohydrate [kɑːbəu'haɪdreɪt] *n* hydrate *m* de carbone; (*food*) féculent *m*

carbon ['kɑːbən] *n* carbone *m*; **~ dioxide** *n* gaz *m* carbonique; **~ monoxide** *n* oxyde *m* de carbone; **~ paper** *n* papier *m* carbone

car boot sale *n* marché aux puces où les particuliers vendent des objets entreposés dans le coffre de leur voiture

carburettor [kɑːbju'rɛtər] (*US* **carburetor**) *n* carburateur *m*

card [kɑːd] *n* carte *f*; (*material*) carton *m*; **~board** *n* carton *m*; **~ game** *n* jeu *m* de

cartes
cardiac [ˈkɑːdɪæk] *adj* cardiaque
cardigan [ˈkɑːdɪgən] *n* cardigan *m*
cardinal [ˈkɑːdɪnl] *adj* cardinal(e) ♦ *n* cardinal *m*
card index *n* fichier *m*
cardphone *n* téléphone *m* à carte
care [kɛəʳ] *n* soin *m*, attention *f*; (*worry*) souci *m*; (*charge*) charge *f*, garde *f* ♦ *vi*: **to ~ about** se soucier de, s'intéresser à; (*person*) être attaché(e) à; **~ of** chez, aux bons soins de; **in sb's ~** à la garde de qn, confié(e) à qn; **to take ~ (to do)** faire attention (à faire); **to take ~ of** s'occuper de; **I don't ~** ça m'est bien égal; **I couldn't ~ less** je m'en fiche complètement (*inf*); **~ for** *vt fus* s'occuper de; (*like*) aimer
career [kəˈrɪəʳ] *n* carrière *f* ♦ *vi* (*also:* **~ along**) aller à toute allure; **~ woman** (*irreg*) *n* femme ambitieuse
care: **~free** *adj* sans souci, insouciant(e); **~ful** *adj* (*thorough*) soigneux(-euse); (*cautious*) prudent(e); **(be) ~ful!** (fais) attention!; **~fully** *adv* avec soin, soigneusement; prudemment; **~less** *adj* négligent(e); (*heedless*) insouciant(e); **~r** *n* (*MED*) aide *f*
caress [kəˈrɛs] *n* caresse *f* ♦ *vt* caresser
caretaker [ˈkɛəteɪkəʳ] *n* gardien(ne), concierge *m/f*
car-ferry [ˈkɑːfɛrɪ] *n* (*on sea*) ferry(-boat) *m*
cargo [ˈkɑːgəʊ] (*pl* **~es**) *n* cargaison *f*, chargement *m*
car hire *n* location *f* de voitures
Caribbean [kærɪˈbiːən] *adj*: **the ~ (Sea)** la mer des Antilles *or* Caraïbes
caring [ˈkɛərɪŋ] *adj* (*person*) bienveillant(e); (*society, organization*) humanitaire
carnation [kɑːˈneɪʃən] *n* œillet *m*
carnival [ˈkɑːnɪvl] *n* (*public celebration*) carnaval *m*; (*US: funfair*) fête foraine
carol [ˈkærəl] *n*: **(Christmas) ~** chant *m* de Noël
carp [kɑːp] *n* (*fish*) carpe *f*
car park (*BRIT*) *n* parking *m*, parc *m* de stationnement

carpenter [ˈkɑːpɪntəʳ] *n* charpentier *m*; **carpentry** *n* menuiserie *f*
carpet [ˈkɑːpɪt] *n* tapis *m* ♦ *vt* recouvrir d'un tapis; **~ sweeper** *n* balai *m* mécanique
car phone *n* (*TEL*) téléphone *m* de voiture
car rental *n* location *f* de voitures
carriage [ˈkærɪdʒ] *n* voiture *f*; (*of goods*) transport *m*; (: *cost*) port *m*; **~way** (*BRIT*) *n* (*part of road*) chaussée *f*
carrier [ˈkærɪəʳ] *n* transporteur *m*, camionneur *m*; (*company*) entreprise *f* de transport; (*MED*) porteur(-euse); **~ bag** (*BRIT*) *n* sac *m* (en papier *or* en plastique)
carrot [ˈkærət] *n* carotte *f*
carry [ˈkærɪ] *vt* (*subj: person*) porter; (: *vehicle*) transporter; (*involve: responsibilities etc*) comporter, impliquer ♦ *vi* (*sound*) porter; **to get carried away** (*fig*) s'emballer, s'enthousiasmer; **~ on** *vi*: **to ~ on with sth/doing** continuer qch/de faire ♦ *vt* pour suivre; **~ out** *vt* (*orders*) exécuter; (*investigation*) mener; **~cot** (*BRIT*) *n* porte-bébé *m*; **~-on** (*inf*) *n* (*fuss*) histoires *fpl*
cart [kɑːt] *n* charrette *f* ♦ *vt* (*inf*) transporter, trimballer (*inf*)
carton [ˈkɑːtən] *n* (*box*) carton *m*; (*of yogurt*) pot *m*; (*of cigarettes*) cartouche *f*
cartoon [kɑːˈtuːn] *n* (*PRESS*) dessin *m* (humoristique), caricature *f*; (*BRIT: comic strip*) bande dessinée; (*CINEMA*) dessin animé
cartridge [ˈkɑːtrɪdʒ] *n* cartouche *f*
carve [kɑːv] *vt* (*meat*) découper; (*wood, stone*) tailler, sculpter; **~ up** *vt* découper; (*fig: country*) morceler; **carving** *n* sculpture *f*; **carving knife** *n* couteau *m* à découper
car wash *n* station *f* de lavage (de voitures)
case [keɪs] *n* cas *m*; (*LAW*) affaire *f*, procès *m*; (*box*) caisse *f*, boîte *f*, étui *m*; (*BRIT: also: suitcase*) valise *f*; **in ~ of** en cas de; **in ~ he ...** au cas où il ...; **just in ~** à tout hasard; **in any ~** en tout cas, de toute façon
cash [kæʃ] *n* argent *m*; (*COMM*) argent *m*

quide, espèces *fpl* ♦ *vt* encaisser; **to pay (in)** ~ payer comptant; ~ **on delivery** payable *or* paiement à la livraison; ~**book** *n* livre *m* de caisse; ~ **card** (*BRIT*) carte *f* de retrait; ~ **desk** (*BRIT*) *n* caisse *f*; ~ **dispenser** (*BRIT*) *n* distributeur *m* automatique de billets, billeterie *f*

cashew [kæ'ʃuː] *n* (*also:* ~ **nut**) noix *f* de cajou

cashier [kæ'ʃɪəʳ] *n* caissier(-ère)

cashmere [ˈkæʃmɪəʳ] *n* cachemire *m*

cash register *n* caisse (enregistreuse)

casing [ˈkeɪsɪŋ] *n* revêtement (protecteur), enveloppe (protectrice)

casino [kəˈsiːnəu] *n* casino *m*

casket [ˈkɑːskɪt] *n* coffret *m*; (*US: coffin*) cercueil *m*

casserole [ˈkæsərəul] *n* (*container*) cocotte *f*; (*food*) ragoût *m* (en cocotte)

cassette [kæ'set] *n* cassette *f*, musicassette *f*; ~ **player** *n* lecteur *m* de cassettes; ~ **recorder** *n* magnétophone *m* à cassettes

cast [kɑːst] (*pt, pp* **cast**) *vt* (*throw*) jeter; (*shed*) perdre; se dépouiller de; (*statue*) mouler; (*THEATRE*): **to ~ sb as Hamlet** attribuer à qn le rôle de Hamlet ♦ *n* (*THEATRE*) distribution *f*; (*also:* **plaster ~**) plâtre *m*; **to ~ one's vote** voter; ~ **off** *vi* (*NAUT*) larguer les amarres; (*KNITTING*) arrêter les mailles; ~ **on** *vi* (*KNITTING*) monter les mailles

castaway [ˈkɑːstəweɪ] *n* naufragé(e)

caster sugar [ˈkɑːstə-] (*BRIT*) *n* sucre *m* semoule

casting vote (*BRIT*) *n* voix prépondérante (*pour départager*)

cast iron *n* fonte *f*

castle [ˈkɑːsl] *n* château (fort); (*CHESS*) tour *f*

castor [ˈkɑːstəʳ] *n* (*wheel*) roulette *f*; ~ **oil** *n* huile *f* de ricin

castrate [kæsˈtreɪt] *vt* châtrer

casual [ˈkæʒjul] *adj* (*by chance*) de hasard, fait(e) au hasard, fortuit(e); (*irregular: work etc*) temporaire; (*unconcerned*) désinvolte; ~**ly** *adv* avec désinvolture, négligemment; (*dress*) de façon décontractée

casualty [ˈkæʒjulti] *n* accidenté(e), blessé(e); (*dead*) victime *f*, mort(e); (*MED: department*) urgences *fpl*

casual wear *n* vêtements *mpl* décontractés

cat [kæt] *n* chat *m*

catalogue [ˈkætəlɔg] (*US* **catalog**) *n* catalogue *m* ♦ *vt* cataloguer

catalyst [ˈkætəlɪst] *n* catalyseur *m*

catalytic converter [kætəˈlɪtɪk kənˈvɔːtəʳ] *n* pot *m* catalytique

catapult [ˈkætəpʌlt] (*BRIT*) *n* (*sling*) lance-pierres *m inv*, fronde *f*

catarrh [kəˈtɑːʳ] *n* rhume *m* chronique, catarrhe *m*

catastrophe [kəˈtæstrəfi] *n* catastrophe *f*

catch [kætʃ] (*pt, pp* **caught**) *vt* attraper; (*person: by surprise*) prendre, surprendre; (*understand, hear*) saisir ♦ *vi* (*fire*) prendre; (*become trapped*) se prendre, s'accrocher ♦ *n* prise *f*; (*trick*) attrape *f*; (*of lock*) loquet *m*; **to ~ sb's attention** *or* **eye** attirer l'attention de qn; **to ~ one's breath** retenir son souffle; **to ~ fire** prendre feu; **to ~ sight of** apercevoir; ~ **on** *vi* saisir; (*grow popular*) prendre; ~ **up** *vi* se rattraper, combler son retard ♦ *vt* (*also:* ~ **up with**) rattraper; ~**ing** *adj* (*MED*) contagieux(-euse); ~**ment area** [ˈkætʃmənt-] (*BRIT*) *n* (*SCOL*) secteur *m* de recrutement; (*of hospital*) circonscription hospitalière; ~ **phrase** *n* slogan *m*; expression *f* (à la mode); ~**y** *adj* (*tune*) facile à retenir

category [ˈkætɪgərɪ] *n* catégorie *f*

cater [ˈkeɪtəʳ] *vi* (*provide food*): **to ~ (for)** préparer des repas (pour), se charger de la restauration (pour); ~ **for** (*BRIT*) *vt fus* (*needs*) satisfaire, pourvoir à; (*readers, consumers*) s'adresser à, pourvoir aux besoins de; ~**er** *n* traiteur *m*; fournisseur *m*; ~**ing** *n* restauration *f*; approvisionnement *m*, ravitaillement *m*

caterpillar [ˈkætəpɪləʳ] *n* chenille *f*

cathedral [kəˈθiːdrəl] *n* cathédrale *f*

catholic [ˈkæθəlɪk] *adj* (*tastes*) éclectique, varié(e); **C~** *adj* catholique ♦ *n* catholique *m/f*

Catseye ® ['kæts'aɪ] (*BRIT*) *n* (*AUT*) cata-
dioptre *m*

cattle ['kætl] *npl* bétail *m*

catty ['kætɪ] *adj* méchant(e)

caucus ['kɔːkəs] *n* (*POL: group*) comité local
d'un parti politique; (*US: POL*) comité électoral (pour désigner des candidats)

caught [kɔːt] *pt*, *pp* of **catch**

cauliflower ['kɔlɪflauəʳ] *n* chou-fleur *m*

cause [kɔːz] *n* cause *f* ♦ *vt* causer

caution [ˈkɔːʃən] *n* prudence *f*; (*warning*)
avertissement *m* ♦ *vt* avertir, donner un
avertissement à; **cautious** *adj* prudent(e)

cavalry ['kævəlrɪ] *n* cavalerie *f*

cave [keɪv] *n* caverne *f*, grotte *f*; **~ in** *vi*
(*roof etc*) s'effondrer; **~man** ['keɪvmæn] (*irreg*) *n* homme *m* des cavernes

caviar(e) ['kævɪɑːʳ] *n* caviar *m*

CB *n abbr* (= *Citizens' Band (Radio)*) CB *f*

CBI *n abbr* (= *Confederation of British Industries*) groupement du patronat

cc *abbr* = **carbon copy**; **cubic centi-
metres**

CCTV *n abbr* (= *closed-circuit television*) télévision *f* en circuit fermé

CD *n abbr* (= *compact disc (player)*) CD *m*;
CDI *n abbr* (= *Compact Disk Interactive*)
CD-I *m*; **CD player** *n* platine *f* laser;
CD-ROM [siːdiːˈrɔm] *n abbr* (= *compact
disc read-only memory*) CD-Rom *m*

cease [siːs] *vt*, *vi* cesser; **~fire** *n* cessez-
le-feu *m*; **~less** *adj* incessant(e), conti-
nuel(le)

cedar ['siːdəʳ] *n* cèdre *m*

ceiling ['siːlɪŋ] *n* plafond *m*

celebrate ['selɪbreɪt] *vt*, *vi* célébrer; **~d** *adj*
célèbre; **celebration** [selɪˈbreɪʃən] *n* célé-
bration *f*; **celebrity** [sɪˈlebrɪtɪ] *n* célébrité *f*

celery ['selərɪ] *n* céleri *m* (à côtes)

cell [sel] *n* cellule *f*; (*ELEC*) élément *m* (de
pile)

cellar ['seləʳ] *n* cave *f*

cello ['tʃeləu] *n* violoncelle *m*

cellphone ['selfəun] *n* téléphone *m* cellu-
laire

Celt [kelt, selt] *n* Celte *m/f*; **~ic** *adj* celte

cement [səˈment] *n* ciment *m*

cemetery ['semɪtrɪ] *n* cimetière *m*

censor ['sensəʳ] *n* censeur *m* ♦ *vt* censurer;
~ship *n* censure *f*

censure ['senʃəʳ] *vt* blâmer, critiquer

census ['sensəs] *n* recensement *m*

cent [sent] *n* (*US etc: coin*) cent *m* (= *un
centième du dollar, de l'euro*); *see also* **per**

centenary [sen'tiːnərɪ] *n* centenaire *m*

center ['sentəʳ] (*US*) *n* = **centre**

centigrade ['sentɪɡreɪd] *adj* centigrade

centimetre ['sentɪmiːtəʳ] (*US* **centimeter**)
n centimètre *m*

centipede ['sentɪpiːd] *n* mille-pattes *m inv*

central ['sentrəl] *adj* central(e); **C~
America** *n* Amérique centrale; **~ heat-
ing** *n* chauffage central; **~ reservation**
(*BRIT*) *n* (*AUT*) terre-plein central

centre ['sentəʳ] (*US* **center**) *n* centre *m* ♦ *vt*
centrer; **~-forward** *n* (*SPORT*) avant-centre
m; **~-half** *n* (*SPORT*) demi-centre *m*

century ['sentjurɪ] *n* siècle *m*; **20th ~** XXe
siècle

ceramic [sɪˈræmɪk] *adj* céramique

cereal ['siːrɪəl] *n* céréale *f*

ceremony ['serɪmənɪ] *n* cérémonie *f*; **to
stand on ~** faire des façons

certain ['sɜːtən] *adj* certain(e); **for ~** certainement, sûrement; **~ly** *adv* certainement; **~ty** *n* certitude *f*

certificate [səˈtɪfɪkɪt] *n* certificat *m*

certified ['sɜːtɪfaɪd] *adj*: **by ~ mail** (*US*) en
recommandé, avec avis de réception; **~
public accountant** (*US*) expert-comptable
m

certify ['sɜːtɪfaɪ] *vt* certifier; (*award diploma
to*) conférer un diplôme *etc* à; (*declare insane*) déclarer malade mental(e)

cervical ['sɜːvɪkl] *adj*: **~ cancer** cancer *m*
du col de l'utérus; **~ smear** frottis vaginal

cervix ['sɜːvɪks] *n* col *m* de l'utérus

cf. *abbr* (= *compare*) cf., voir

CFC *n abbr* (= *chlorofluorocarbon*) CFC *m*

ch. *abbr* (= *chapter*) chap

chafe [tʃeɪf] *vt* irriter, frotter contre

chain [tʃeɪn] *n* chaîne *f* ♦ *vt* (*also:* **~ up**)
enchaîner, attacher (avec une chaîne); **~
reaction** *n* réaction *f* en chaîne; **~**

smoke vi fumer cigarette sur cigarette; ~ **store** n magasin m à succursales multiples

chair [tʃeəʳ] n chaise f; (armchair) fauteuil m; (of university) chaire f; (of meeting, committee) présidence f ♦ vt (meeting) présider; **~lift** n télésiège m; **~man** (irreg) n président m

chalet [ˈʃæleɪ] n chalet m

chalk [tʃɔːk] n craie f

challenge [ˈtʃælɪndʒ] n défi m ♦ vt défier; (statement, right) mettre en question, contester; **to ~ sb to do** mettre qn au défi de faire; **challenging** adj (tone, look) de défi, provocateur(-trice); (task, career) qui représente un défi or une gageure

chamber [ˈtʃeɪmbəʳ] n chambre f; **~ of commerce** chambre de commerce; **~maid** n femme f de chambre; **~ music** n musique f de chambre

champagne [ʃæmˈpeɪn] n champagne m

champion [ˈtʃæmpɪən] n champion(ne); **~ship** n championnat m

chance [tʃɑːns] n (opportunity) occasion f, possibilité f; (hope, likelihood) chance f; (risk) risque m ♦ vt: **to ~ it** risquer (le coup), essayer ♦ adj fortuit(e), de hasard; **to take a ~** prendre un risque; **by ~** par hasard

chancellor [ˈtʃɑːnsələʳ] n chancelier m; **C~ of the Exchequer** (BRIT) n chancelier m de l'Échiquier, ≈ ministre m des Finances

chandelier [ʃændəˈlɪəʳ] n lustre m

change [tʃeɪndʒ] vt (alter, replace, COMM: money) changer; (hands, trains, clothes, one's name) changer de; (transform): **to ~ sb into** changer or transformer qn en ♦ vi (gen) changer; (one's clothes) se changer; (be transformed): **to ~ into** se changer or transformer en ♦ n changement m; (money) monnaie f; **to ~ gear** (AUT) changer de vitesse; **to ~ one's mind** changer d'avis; **a ~ of clothes** des vêtements de rechange; **for a ~** pour changer; **~able** adj (weather) variable; **~ machine** n distributeur m de monnaie; **~over** n (to new

system) changement m, passage m; **changing** adj changeant(e); **changing room** (BRIT) n (in shop) salon m d'essayage; (SPORT) vestiaire m

channel [ˈtʃænl] n (TV) chaîne f; (navigable passage) chenal m; (irrigation) canal m ♦ vt canaliser; **the (English) C~** la Manche; **the C~ Islands** les îles de la Manche, les îles Anglo-Normandes; **the C~ Tunnel** le tunnel sous la Manche; **~-hopping** n (TV) zapping m

chant [tʃɑːnt] n chant m; (REL) psalmodie f ♦ vt chanter, scander

chaos [ˈkeɪɔs] n chaos m

chap [tʃæp] (BRIT: inf) n (man) type m

chapel [ˈtʃæpl] n chapelle f; (BRIT: nonconformist ~) église f

chaplain [ˈtʃæplɪn] n aumônier m

chapped [tʃæpt] adj (skin, lips) gercé(e)

chapter [ˈtʃæptəʳ] n chapitre m

char [tʃɑːʳ] vt (burn) carboniser

character [ˈkærɪktəʳ] n caractère m; (in novel, film) personnage m; (eccentric) numéro m, phénomène m; **~istic** [kærɪktəˈrɪstɪk] adj caractéristique ♦ n caractéristique f

charcoal [ˈtʃɑːkəul] n charbon m de bois; (for drawing) charbon m

charge [tʃɑːdʒ] n (cost) prix (demandé); (accusation) accusation f; (LAW) inculpation f ♦ vt: **to ~ sb (with)** inculper qn (de); (battery, enemy) charger; (customer, sum) faire payer ♦ vi foncer; **~s** npl (costs) frais mpl; **to reverse the ~s** (TEL) téléphoner en P.C.V.; **to take ~ of** se charger de; **to be in ~ of** être responsable de, s'occuper de; **how much do you ~?** combien prenez-vous?; **to ~ an expense (up) to sb** mettre une dépense sur le compte de qn; **~ card** n carte f de client

charity [ˈtʃærɪtɪ] n charité f; (organization) institution f charitable or de bienfaisance, œuvre f (de charité)

charm [tʃɑːm] n charme m; (on bracelet) breloque f ♦ vt charmer, enchanter; **~ing** adj charmant(e)

chart [tʃɑːt] n tableau m, diagramme m; graphique m; (map) carte marine ♦ vt dresser *or* établir la carte de; **~s** *npl* (*hit parade*) hit-parade *m*

charter ['tʃɑːtəʳ] *vt* (*plane*) affréter ♦ *n* (*document*) charte *f*; **~ed accountant** (*BRIT*) *n* expert-comptable *m*; **~ flight** *n* charter *m*

chase [tʃeɪs] *vt* poursuivre, pourchasser; (*also: ~ away*) chasser ♦ *n* poursuite *f*, chasse *f*

chasm ['kæzəm] *n* gouffre *m*, abîme *m*

chat [tʃæt] *vi* (*also: have a ~*) bavarder, causer ♦ *n* conversation *f*; **~ show** (*BRIT*) *n* causerie télévisée

chatter ['tʃætəʳ] *vi* (*person*) bavarder; (*animal*) jacasser ♦ *n* bavardage *m*; jacassement *m*; **my teeth are ~ing** je claque des dents; **~box** (*inf*) *n* moulin *m* à paroles

chatty ['tʃætɪ] *adj* (*style*) familier(-ère); (*person*) bavard(e)

chauffeur ['ʃəufəʳ] *n* chauffeur *m* (de maître)

chauvinist ['ʃəuvɪnɪst] *n* (*male ~*) phallocrate *m*; (*nationalist*) chauvin(e)

cheap [tʃiːp] *adj* bon marché *inv*, pas cher (chère), (*joke*) facile, d'un goût douteux; (*poor quality*) à bon marché, de qualité médiocre ♦ *adv* à bon marché, pour pas cher; **~ day return** billet *m* d'aller et retour réduit (*valable pour la journée*); **~er** *adj* moins cher (chère); **~ly** *adv* à bon marché, à bon compte

cheat [tʃiːt] *vi* tricher ♦ *vt* tromper, duper; (*rob*): **to ~ sb out of sth** escroquer qch à qn ♦ *n* tricheur(-euse); escroc *m*

check [tʃɛk] *vt* vérifier; (*passport, ticket*) contrôler; (*halt*) arrêter; (*restrain*) maîtriser ♦ *n* vérification *f*; contrôle *m*; (*curb*) frein *m*; (*US: bill*) addition *f*; (*pattern: gen pl*) carreaux *mpl*; (*US*) = **cheque** ♦ *adj* (*pattern, cloth*) à carreaux; **~ in** *vi* (*in hotel*) remplir sa fiche (d'hôtel); (*at airport*) se présenter à l'enregistrement ♦ *vt* (*luggage*) (faire) enregistrer; **~ out** *vi* (*in hotel*) régler sa note; **to ~ up** *vi* (**on sth**) vérifier (qch); **to ~ up on sb** se renseigner sur le compte de qn; **~ered** (*US*) *adj* = **chequered**; **~ers** (*US*) *npl* jeu *m* de dames; **~-in (desk)** *n* enregistrement *m*; **~ing account** (*US*) *n* (*current account*) compte courant; **~mate** *n* échec et mat *m*; **~out** *n* (*in shop*) caisse *f*; **~point** *n* contrôle *m*; **~room** (*US*) *n* (*left-luggage office*) consigne *f*; **~up** *n* (*MED*) examen médical, check-up *m*

cheek [tʃiːk] *n* joue *f*; (*impudence*) toupet *m*, culot *m*; **~bone** *n* pommette *f*; **~y** *adj* effronté(e), culotté(e)

cheep [tʃiːp] *vi* piauler

cheer [tʃɪəʳ] *vt* acclamer, applaudir; (*gladden*) réjouir, réconforter ♦ *vi* applaudir ♦ *n* (*gen pl*) acclamations *fpl*, applaudissements *mpl*; bravos *mpl*, hourras *mpl*; **~s!** à la vôtre!; **~ up** *vi* se dérider, reprendre courage ♦ *vt* remonter le moral à *or* de, dérider; **~ful** *adj* gai(e), joyeux(-euse)

cheerio [tʃɪərɪ'əu] (*BRIT*) *excl* salut!, au revoir!

cheese [tʃiːz] *n* fromage *m*; **~board** *n* plateau *m* de fromages

cheetah ['tʃiːtə] *n* guépard *m*

chef [ʃɛf] *n* chef (cuisinier)

chemical ['kɛmɪkl] *adj* chimique ♦ *n* produit *m* chimique

chemist ['kɛmɪst] *n* (*BRIT: pharmacist*) pharmacien(ne); (*scientist*) chimiste *m/f*; **~ry** *n* chimie *f*; **~'s (shop)** (*BRIT*) *n* pharmacie *f*

cheque [tʃɛk] (*BRIT*) *n* chèque *m*; **~book** *n* chéquier *m*, carnet *m* de chèques; **~ card** *n* carte *f* (d'identité) bancaire

chequered ['tʃɛkəd] (*US* **checkered**) *adj* (*fig*) varié(e)

cherish ['tʃɛrɪʃ] *vt* chérir

cherry ['tʃɛrɪ] *n* cerise *f*; (*also: ~ tree*) cerisier *m*

chess [tʃɛs] *n* échecs *mpl*; **~board** *n* échiquier *m*

chest [tʃɛst] *n* poitrine *f*; (*box*) coffre *m*, caisse *f*; **~ of drawers** *n* commode *f*

chestnut ['tʃɛsnʌt] *n* châtaigne *f*; (*also: ~ tree*) châtaignier *m*

chew [tʃuː] *vt* mâcher; **~ing gum** *n* chewing-gum *m*

chic [ʃiːk] *adj* chic *inv*, élégant(e)

chick [tʃɪk] *n* poussin *m*; (*inf*) nana *f*

chicken ['tʃɪkɪn] *n* poulet *m*; (*inf: coward*) poule mouillée; ~ **out** (*inf*) *vi* se dégonfler; **~pox** *n* varicelle *f*

chicory ['tʃɪkərɪ] *n* (*for coffee*) chicorée *f*; (*salad*) endive *f*

chief [tʃiːf] *n* chef *m* ♦ *adj* principal(e); ~ **executive** (*US* **chief executive officer**) *n* directeur(-trice) général(e); **~ly** *adv* principalement, surtout

chiffon ['ʃɪfɔn] *n* mousseline *f* de soie

chilblain ['tʃɪlbleɪn] *n* engelure *f*

child [tʃaɪld] (*pl* **~ren**) *n* enfant *m/f*; **~birth** *n* accouchement *m*; **~hood** *n* enfance *f*; **~ish** *adj* puéril(e), enfantin(e); **~like** *adj* d'enfant, innocent(e); ~ **minder** (*BRIT*) *n* garde *f* d'enfants; **~ren** ['tʃɪldrən] *npl of* **child**

Chile ['tʃɪlɪ] *n* Chili *m*

chill [tʃɪl] *n* (*of water*) froid *m*; (*of air*) fraîcheur *f*; (*MED*) refroidissement *m*, coup *m* de froid ♦ *vt* (*person*) faire frissonner; (*CULIN*) mettre au frais, rafraîchir

chil(l)i ['tʃɪlɪ] *n* piment *m* (rouge)

chilly ['tʃɪlɪ] *adj* froid(e), glacé(e); (*sensitive to cold*) frileux(-euse); **to feel** ~ avoir froid

chime [tʃaɪm] *n* carillon *m* ♦ *vi* carillonner, sonner

chimney ['tʃɪmnɪ] *n* cheminée *f*; ~ **sweep** *n* ramoneur *m*

chimpanzee [tʃɪmpæn'ziː] *n* chimpanzé *m*

chin [tʃɪn] *n* menton *m*

China ['tʃaɪnə] *n* Chine *f*

china ['tʃaɪnə] *n* porcelaine *f*; (*crockery*) (vaisselle *f* en) porcelaine

Chinese [tʃaɪ'niːz] *adj* chinois(e) ♦ *n inv* (*person*) Chinois(e); (*LING*) chinois *m*

chink [tʃɪŋk] *n* (*opening*) fente *f*, fissure *f*; (*noise*) tintement *m*

chip [tʃɪp] *n* (*gen pl: CULIN: BRIT*) frite *f*; (: *US: potato* ~) chip *m*; (*of wood*) copeau *m*; (*of glass, stone*) éclat *m*; (*also: microchip*) puce *f* ♦ *vt* (*cup, plate*) ébrécher

---

chip shop

i Un **chip shop**, que l'on appelle également un "*fish-and-chip shop*", est un magasin où l'on vend des plats à emporter. Les chip shops sont d'ailleurs à l'origine des **takeaways**. On y achète en particulier du poisson frit et des frites, mais on y trouve également des plats traditionnels britanniques (steak pies, saucisses, etc). Tous les plats étaient à l'origine emballés dans du papier journal. Dans certains de ces magasins, on peut s'asseoir pour consommer sur place.

---

chiropodist [kɪ'rɔpədɪst] (*BRIT*) *n* pédicure *m/f*

chirp [tʃɜːp] *vi* pépier, gazouiller

chisel ['tʃɪzl] *n* ciseau *m*

chit [tʃɪt] *n* mot *m*, note *f*

chitchat ['tʃɪttʃæt] *n* bavardage *m*

chivalry ['ʃɪvəlrɪ] *n* esprit *m* chevaleresque, galanterie *f*

chives [tʃaɪvz] *npl* ciboulette *f*, civette *f*

chock-a-block ['tʃɔkə'blɔk], **chock-full** [tʃɔk'ful] *adj* plein(e) à craquer

chocolate ['tʃɔklɪt] *n* chocolat *m*

choice [tʃɔɪs] *n* choix *m* ♦ *adj* de choix

choir ['kwaɪər] *n* chœur *m*, chorale *f*; **~boy** *n* jeune choriste *m*

choke [tʃəʊk] *vi* étouffer ♦ *vt* étrangler; étouffer ♦ *n* (*AUT*) starter *m*; **street ~d with traffic** rue engorgée *or* embouteillée

cholesterol [kə'lestərɔl] *n* cholestérol *m*

choose [tʃuːz] (*pt* **chose**, *pp* **chosen**) *vt* choisir; **to ~ to do** décider de faire, juger bon de faire; **choosy** *adj*: **(to be) choosy** (faire le/la) difficile

chop [tʃɔp] *vt* (*wood*) couper (à la hache); (*CULIN: also:* ~ **up**) couper (fin), émincer, hacher (en morceaux) ♦ *n* (*CULIN*) côtelette *f*; **~s** *npl* (*jaws*) mâchoires *fpl*

chopper ['tʃɔpər] *n* (*helicopter*) hélicoptère *m*, hélico *m*

choppy ['tʃɔpɪ] *adj* (*sea*) un peu agité(e)

chopsticks ['tʃɔpstɪks] *npl* baguettes *fpl*

chord [kɔːd] *n* (*MUS*) accord *m*

chore [tʃɔːᵣ] *n* travail *m* de routine; **household ~s** travaux *mpl* du ménage

chortle ['tʃɔːtl] *vi* glousser

chorus ['kɔːrəs] *n* chœur *m*; (*repeated part of song: also fig*) refrain *m*

chose [tʃəuz] *pt of* **choose**; **~n** *pp of* **choose**

chowder ['tʃaudəᵣ] *n* soupe *f* de poisson

Christ [kraist] *n* Christ *m*

christen ['krɪsn] *vt* baptiser

christening *n* baptême *m*

Christian ['krɪstɪən] *adj, n* chrétien(ne); **~ity** [krɪstɪ'ænɪtɪ] *n* christianisme *m*; **~ name** *n* prénom *m*

Christmas ['krɪsməs] *n* Noël *m or f*; **Happy or Merry ~!** joyeux Noël!; **~ card** *n* carte *f* de Noël; **~ Day** *n* le jour de Noël; **~ Eve** *n* la veille de Noël; la nuit de Noël; **~ tree** *n* arbre *m* de Noël

chrome [krəum] *n* chrome *m*

chromium ['krəumɪəm] *n* chrome *m*

chronic ['krɔnɪk] *adj* chronique

chronicle ['krɔnɪkl] *n* chronique *f*

chronological [krɔnə'lɔdʒɪkl] *adj* chronologique

chrysanthemum [krɪ'sænθəməm] *n* chrysanthème *m*

chubby ['tʃʌbɪ] *adj* potelé(e), rondelet(te)

chuck [tʃʌk] (*inf*) *vt* (*throw*) lancer, jeter; (*BRIT: person*) plaquer; (: *also:* **~ up**: *job*) lâcher; **~ out** *vt* flanquer dehors *or* à la porte; (*rubbish*) jeter

chuckle ['tʃʌkl] *vi* glousser

chug [tʃʌg] *vi* faire teuf-teuf; (*also:* **~ along**) avancer en faisant teuf-teuf

chum [tʃʌm] *n* copain (copine)

chunk [tʃʌŋk] *n* gros morceau

church [tʃəːtʃ] *n* église *f*; **~yard** *n* cimetière *m*

churn [tʃəːn] *n* (*for butter*) baratte *f*; (*also:* **milk ~**) (grand) bidon à lait; **~ out** *vt* débiter

chute [ʃuːt] *n* glissoire *f*; (*also:* **rubbish ~**) vide-ordures *m inv*

chutney ['tʃʌtnɪ] *n* condiment *m* à base de fruits au vinaigre

CIA *n abbr* (= *Central Intelligence Agency*)

CIA *f*

CID (*BRIT*) *n abbr* (= *Criminal Investigation Department*) P.J. *f*

cider ['saidəᵣ] *n* cidre *m*

cigar [sɪ'gaːᵣ] *n* cigare *m*

cigarette [sɪgə'ret] *n* cigarette *f*; **~ case** *n* étui *m* à cigarettes; **~ end** *n* mégot *m*

Cinderella [sɪndə'relə] *n* Cendrillon *f*

cinders ['sɪndəz] *npl* cendres *fpl*

cine-camera ['sɪnɪ'kæmərə] (*BRIT*) *n* caméra *f*

cinema ['sɪnəmə] *n* cinéma *m*

cinnamon ['sɪnəmən] *n* cannelle *f*

circle ['səːkl] *n* cercle *m*; (*in cinema, theatre*) balcon *m* ♦ *vi* faire *or* décrire des cercles ♦ *vt* (*move round*) faire le tour de, tourner autour de; (*surround*) entourer, encercler

circuit ['səːkɪt] *n* circuit *m*; **~ous** [səː'kjuɪtəs] *adj* indirect(e), qui fait un détour

circular ['səːkjuləᵣ] *adj* circulaire ♦ *n* circulaire *f*

circulate ['səːkjuleɪt] *vi* circuler ♦ *vt* faire circuler; **circulation** [səːkju'leɪʃən] *n* circulation *f*; (*of newspaper*) tirage *m*

circumflex ['səːkəmfleks] *n* (*also:* **~ accent**) accent *m* circonflexe

circumstances ['səːkəmstənsɪz] *npl* circonstances *fpl*; (*financial condition*) moyens *mpl*, situation financière

circus ['səːkəs] *n* cirque *m*

CIS *n abbr* (= *Commonwealth of Independent States*) CEI *f*

cistern ['sɪstən] *n* réservoir *m* (d'eau); (*in toilet*) réservoir de la chasse d'eau

citizen ['sɪtɪzn] *n* citoyen(ne); (*resident*): **the ~s of this town** les habitants de cette ville; **~ship** *n* citoyenneté *f*

citrus fruit ['sɪtrəs-] *n* agrume *m*

city ['sɪtɪ] *n* ville *f*, cité *f*; **the C~** la Cité de Londres (*centre des affaires*); **~ technology college** *n* établissement *m* d'enseignement technologique

civic ['sɪvɪk] *adj* civique; (*authorities*) municipal(e); **~ centre** (*BRIT*) *n* centre administratif (municipal)

civil ['sɪvɪl] *adj* civil(e); (*polite*) courtois(e); (*disobedience, defence*) passif(-ive); ~ **engineer** *n* ingénieur *m* des travaux publics; **~ian** [sɪ'vɪlɪən] *adj, n* civil(e)

civilization [sɪvɪlaɪ'zeɪʃən] *n* civilisation *f*

civilized ['sɪvɪlaɪzd] *adj* civilisé(e); (*fig*) où règnent les bonnes manières

civil: ~ **law** *n* code civil; (*study*) droit civil; ~ **servant** *n* fonctionnaire *m/f*; **C~ Service** *n* fonction publique, administration *f*; ~ **war** *n* guerre civile

clad [klæd] *adj*: ~ (**in**) habillé(e) (de)

claim [kleɪm] *vt* revendiquer; (*rights, inheritance*) demander, prétendre à; (*assert*) déclarer, prétendre ♦ *vi* (*for insurance*) faire une déclaration de sinistre ♦ *n* revendication *f*; demande *f*; prétention *f*, déclaration *f*; (*right*) droit *m*, titre *m*; **~ant** *n* (*ADMIN, LAW*) requérant(e)

clairvoyant [kleə'vɔɪənt] *n* voyant(e), extra-lucide *m/f*

clam [klæm] *n* palourde *f*

clamber ['klæmbər] *vi* grimper, se hisser

clammy ['klæmɪ] *adj* humide (et froid(e)), moite

clamour ['klæmər] (*US* **clamor**) *vi*: **to ~ for** réclamer à grands cris

clamp [klæmp] *n* agrafe *f*, crampon *m* ♦ *vt* serrer; (*sth to sth*) fixer; (*wheel*) mettre un sabot à; ~ **down on** *vt fus* sévir or prendre des mesures draconiennes contre

clan [klæn] *n* clan *m*

clang [klæŋ] *vi* émettre un bruit or fracas métallique

clap [klæp] *vi* applaudir; **~ping** *n* applaudissements *mpl*

claret ['klærət] *n* (vin *m* de) bordeaux *m* (rouge)

clarinet [klærɪ'nɛt] *n* clarinette *f*

clarity ['klærɪtɪ] *n* clarté *f*

clash [klæʃ] *n* choc *m*; (*fig*) conflit *m* ♦ *vi* se heurter; être or entrer en conflit; (*colours*) jurer; (*two events*) tomber en même temps

clasp [klɑːsp] *n* (*of necklace, bag*) fermoir *m*; (*hold, embrace*) étreinte *f* ♦ *vt* serrer, étreindre

class [klɑːs] *n* classe *f* ♦ *vt* classer, classifier

classic ['klæsɪk] *adj* classique ♦ *n* (*author, work*) classique *m*; **~al** *adj* classique

classified ['klæsɪfaɪd] *adj* (*information*) secret(-ète); ~ **advertisement** *n* petite annonce

classmate ['klɑːsmeɪt] *n* camarade *m/f* de classe

classroom ['klɑːsrum] *n* (salle *f* de) classe *f*

clatter ['klætər] *n* cliquetis *m* ♦ *vi* cliqueter

clause [klɔːz] *n* clause *f*; (*LING*) proposition *f*

claw [klɔː] *n* griffe *f*; (*of bird of prey*) serre *f*; (*of lobster*) pince *f*

clay [kleɪ] *n* argile *f*

clean [kliːn] *adj* propre; (*clear, smooth*) net(te); (*record, reputation*) sans tache; (*joke, story*) correct(e) ♦ *vt* nettoyer; ~ **out** *vt* nettoyer (à fond); ~ **up** *vt* nettoyer; (*fig*) remettre de l'ordre dans; **~-cut** *adj* (*person*) net(te), soigné(e); **~er** *n* (*person*) nettoyeur(-euse), femme *f* de ménage; (*product*) détachant *m*; **~er's** *n* (*also:* **dry ~er's**) teinturier *m*; **~ing** *n* nettoyage *m*; **~liness** ['klɛnlɪnɪs] *n* propreté *f*

cleanse [klɛnz] *vt* nettoyer; (*purify*) purifier; **~r** *n* (*for face*) démaquillant *m*

clean-shaven ['kliːn'ʃeɪvn] *adj* rasé(e) de près

cleansing department ['klɛnzɪŋ-] (*BRIT*) *n* service *m* de voirie

clear [klɪər] *adj* clair(e); (*glass, plastic*) transparent(e); (*road, way*) libre, dégagé(e); (*conscience*) net(te) ♦ *vt* (*room*) débarrasser; (*of people*) faire évacuer; (*cheque*) compenser; (*LAW: suspect*) innocenter; (*obstacle*) franchir or sauter sans heurter ♦ *vi* (*weather*) s'éclaircir; (*fog*) se dissiper ♦ *adv*: ~ **of** à distance de, à l'écart de; **to** ~ **the table** débarrasser la table, desservir; ~ **up** *vt* ranger, mettre en ordre; (*mystery*) éclaircir, résoudre; **~ance** *n* (*removal*) déblaiement *m*; (*permission*) autorisation *f*; **~-cut** *adj* clair(e), nettement défini(e); **~ing** *n* (*in forest*) clairière *f*; **~ing bank** (*BRIT*) *n* banque qui appartient à une *chambre de compensation*; ~**ly** *adv* clairement; (*evidently*) de toute évidence; ~**way** (*BRIT*) *n* route *f* à stationnement interdit

clef [klɛf] *n* (*MUS*) clé *f*

cleft [klɛft] *n* (*in rock*) crevasse *f*, fissure *f*

clementine ['klɛməntam] *n* clémentine *f*

clench [klɛntʃ] *vt* serrer

clergy ['klɜːdʒɪ] *n* clergé *m*; ~**man** (*irreg*) *n* ecclésiastique *m*

clerical ['klɛrɪkl] *adj* de bureau, d'employé de bureau; (*REL*) clérical(e), du clergé

clerk [klɑːk, (*US*) klɜːrk] *n* employé(e) de bureau; (*US*: *salesperson*) vendeur(-euse)

clever ['klɛvəʳ] *adj* (*mentally*) intelligent(e); (*crafty*) habile, adroit(e); (*device, arrangement*) ingénieux(-euse), astucieux(-euse)

click [klɪk] *vi* faire un bruit sec *or* un déclic; ~ **on** *vt* (*COMPUT*) cliquer sur

client ['klaɪənt] *n* client(e)

cliff [klɪf] *n* falaise *f*

climate ['klaɪmɪt] *n* climat *m*

climax ['klaɪmæks] *n* apogée *m*, point culminant; (*sexual*) orgasme *m*

climb [klaɪm] *vi* grimper, monter ♦ *vt* gravir, escalader, monter sur ♦ *n* montée *f*, escalade *f*; ~-**down** *n* reculade *f*; ~**er** *n* (*mountaineer*) grimpeur(-euse), varappeur(-euse); (*plant*) plante grimpante; ~**ing** *n* (*mountaineering*) escalade *f*, varappe *f*

clinch [klɪntʃ] *vt* (*deal*) conclure, sceller

cling [klɪŋ] (*pt, pp* **clung**) *vi*: **to ~ (to)** se cramponner (à), s'accrocher (à); (*of clothes*) coller (à)

clinic ['klɪnɪk] *n* centre médical; ~**al** *adj* clinique; (*attitude*) froid(e), détaché(e)

clink [klɪŋk] *vi* tinter, cliqueter

clip [klɪp] *n* (*for hair*) barrette *f*; (*also*: **paper ~**) trombone *m* ♦ *vt* (*fasten*) attacher; (*hair, nails*) couper; (*hedge*) tailler; ~**pers** *npl* (*for hedge*) sécateur *m*; (*also*: **nail ~pers**) coupe-ongles *m inv*; ~**ping** *n* (*from newspaper*) coupure *f* de journal

cloak [kləʊk] *n* grande cape ♦ *vt* (*fig*) masquer, cacher; ~**room** *n* (*for coats etc*) vestiaire *m*; (*BRIT*: *WC*) toilettes *fpl*

clock [klɒk] *n* (*large*) horloge *f*; (*small*) pendule *f*; ~ **in** (*BRIT*) *vi* pointer (en arrivant);

~ **off** (*BRIT*) *vi* pointer (en partant); ~ **on** (*BRIT*) *vi* = **clock in**; ~ **out** (*BRIT*) *vi* = **clock off**; ~**wise** *adv* dans le sens des aiguilles d'une montre; ~**work** *n* rouages *mpl*, mécanisme *m*; (*of clock*) mouvement *m* (d'horlogerie) ♦ *adj* mécanique

clog [klɒg] *n* sabot *m* ♦ *vt* boucher ♦ *vi* (*also*: ~ **up**) se boucher

cloister ['klɔɪstəʳ] *n* cloître *m*

clone [kləʊn] *n* clone *m* ♦ *vt* cloner

close¹ [kləʊs] *adj* (*near*) près, proche; (*contact, link*) étroit(e); (*contest*) très serré(e); (*watch*) étroit(e), strict(e); (*examination*) attentif(-ive), minutieux(-euse); (*weather*) lourd(e), étouffant(e) ♦ *adv* près, à proximité; ~ **to** près de, proche de; ~ **by** *adj* proche ♦ *adv* tout(e) près; ~ **at hand** = **close by**; **a ~ friend** un ami intime; **to have a ~ shave** (*fig*) l'échapper belle

close² [kləʊz] *vt* fermer ♦ *vi* (*shop etc*) fermer; (*lid, door etc*) se fermer; (*end*) se terminer, se conclure ♦ *n* (*end*) conclusion *f*, fin *f*; ~ **down** *vt, vi* fermer (*définitivement*); ~**d** *adj* fermé(e); ~**d shop** *n* organisation *f* qui n'admet que des travailleurs syndiqués

close-knit ['kləʊs'nɪt] *adj* (*family, community*) très uni(e)

closely ['kləʊslɪ] *adv* (*examine, watch*) de près

closet ['klɒzɪt] *n* (*cupboard*) placard *m*, réduit *m*

close-up ['kləʊsʌp] *n* gros plan

closure ['kləʊʒəʳ] *n* fermeture *f*

clot [klɒt] *n* (*gen*: *blood ~*) caillot *m*; (*inf*: *person*) ballot *m* ♦ *vi* (*blood*) se coaguler; ~**ted cream** crème fraîche très épaisse

cloth [klɒθ] *n* (*material*) tissu *m*, étoffe *f*; (*also*: **teacloth**) torchon *m*; lavette *f*

clothe [kləʊð] *vt* habiller, vêtir; ~**s** *npl* vêtements *mpl*, habits *mpl*; ~**s brush** *n* brosse *f* à habits; ~**s line** *n* corde *f* (à linge); ~**s peg** (*US* **clothes pin**) *n* pince *f* à linge; **clothing** *n* = **clothes**

cloud [klaʊd] *n* nuage *m*; ~**burst** *n* grosse averse; ~**y** *adj* nuageux(-euse), couvert(e); (*liquid*) trouble

ENGLISH-FRENCH 335

clout [klaʊt] *vt* flanquer une taloche à

clove [kləʊv] *n* (CULIN: *spice*) clou *m* de gi- rofle; **~ of garlic** gousse *f* d'ail

clover ['kləʊvəʳ] *n* trèfle *m*

clown [klaʊn] *n* clown *m* ♦ *vi* (*also*: **~ about, ~ around**) faire le clown

cloying ['klɔɪɪŋ] *adj* (*taste, smell*) écœu- rant(e)

club [klʌb] *n* (*society, place*: *also*: **golf ~**) club *m*; (*weapon*) massue *f*, matraque *f* ♦ *vt* matraquer ♦ *vi*: **to ~ together** s'asso- cier; **~s** *npl* (CARDS) trèfle *m*; **~ class** *n* (AVIAT) classe *f* club; **~house** *n* club *m*

cluck [klʌk] *vi* glousser

clue [kluː] *n* indice *m*; (*in crosswords*) défi- nition *f*; **I haven't a ~** je n'en ai pas la moindre idée

clump [klʌmp] *n*: **~ of trees** bouquet *m* d'arbres

clumsy ['klʌmzɪ] *adj* gauche, maladroit(e)

clung [klʌŋ] *pt, pp of* **cling**

cluster ['klʌstəʳ] *n* (*of people*) (petit) grou- pe; (*of flowers*) grappe *f*; (*of stars*) amas *m* ♦ *vi* se rassembler

clutch [klʌtʃ] *n* (*grip, grasp*) étreinte *f*, prise *f*; (AUT) embrayage *m* ♦ *vt* (*grasp*) agrip- per; (*hold tightly*) serrer fort; (*hold on to*) se cramponner à

clutter ['klʌtəʳ] *vt* (*also*: **~ up**) encombrer

CND *n abbr* (= *Campaign for Nuclear Dis- armament*) *mouvement pour le désarme- ment nucléaire*

Co. *abbr* = **county; company**

c/o *abbr* (= *care of*) c/o, aux bons soins de

coach [kəʊtʃ] *n* (*bus*) autocar *m*; (*horse- drawn*) diligence *f*; (*of train*) voiture *f*, wa- gon *m*; (SPORT: *trainer*) entraîneur(-euse) *f*; (SCOL: *tutor*) répétiteur(-trice) ♦ *vt* en- traîner; (*student*) faire travailler; **~ trip** *n* excursion *f* en car

coal [kəʊl] *n* charbon *m*; **~ face** *n* front *m* de taille; **~field** *n* bassin houiller

coalition [kəʊəˈlɪʃən] *n* coalition *f*

coalman (*irreg*) *n* charbonnier *m*, mar- chand *m* de charbon

coalmine *n* mine *f* de charbon

coarse [kɔːs] *adj* grossier(-ère), rude

coast [kəʊst] *n* côte *f* ♦ *vi* (*car, cycle etc*) descendre en roue libre; **~al** *adj* côtier(- ère); **~guard** *n* garde-côte *m*; (*service*) gendarmerie *f* maritime; **~line** *n* côte *f*, littoral *m*

coat [kəʊt] *n* manteau *m*; (*of animal*) pela- ge *m*, poil *m*; (*of paint*) couche *f* ♦ *vt* cou- vrir; **~ hanger** *n* cintre *m*; **~ing** *n* couche *f*, revêtement *m*; **~ of arms** *n* blason *m*, armoiries *fpl*

coax [kəʊks] *vt* persuader par des cajoleries

cobbler ['kɔbləʳ] *n* cordonnier *m*

cobbles ['kɔblz] (*also*: **~tones**) *npl* pavés (ronds)

cobweb ['kɔbweb] *n* toile *f* d'araignée

cocaine [kəˈkeɪn] *n* cocaïne *f*

cock [kɔk] *n* (*rooster*) coq *m*; (*male bird*) mâle *m* ♦ *vt* (*gun*) armer; **~erel** *n* jeune coq *m*

cockle ['kɔkl] *n* coque *f*

cockney ['kɔknɪ] *n* cockney *m*, habitant des quartiers populaires de l'East End de Londres, ≈ faubourien(ne)

cockpit ['kɔkpɪt] *n* (*in aircraft*) poste *m* de pilotage, cockpit *m*

cockroach ['kɔkrəʊtʃ] *n* cafard *m*

cocktail ['kɔkteɪl] *n* cocktail *m*; (*fruit ~ etc*) salade *f*; **~ cabinet** *n* (meuble-)bar *m*; **~ party** *n* cocktail *m*

cocoa ['kəʊkəʊ] *n* cacao *m*

coconut ['kəʊkənʌt] *n* noix *f* de coco

COD *abbr* = **cash on delivery**

cod [kɔd] *n* morue fraîche, cabillaud *m*

code [kəʊd] *n* code *m*

cod-liver oil *n* huile *f* de foie de morue

coercion [kəʊˈəːʃən] *n* contrainte *f*

coffee ['kɔfɪ] *n* café *m*; **~ bar** *n* (BRIT) café *m*; **~ bean** *n* grain *m* de café; **~ break** *n* pause-café *f*; **~pot** *n* cafetière *f*; **~ table** *n* (petite) table basse

coffin ['kɔfɪn] *n* cercueil *m*

cog [kɔg] *n* dent *f* (d'engrenage); (*wheel*) roue dentée

cogent ['kəʊdʒənt] *adj* puissant(e), convaincant(e)

coil [kɔɪl] *n* rouleau *m*, bobine *f*; (*contracep- tive*) stérilet *m* ♦ *vt* enrouler

coin [kɔɪn] *n* pièce *f* de monnaie ♦ *vt* (*word*) inventer; **~age** *n* monnaie *f*, système *m* monétaire; **~ box** (*BRIT*) *n* cabine *f* téléphonique

coincide [kəʊɪn'saɪd] *vi* coïncider; **~nce** [kəʊ'ɪnsɪdəns] *n* coïncidence *f*

Coke [kəʊk] ® *n* coca *m*

coke [kəʊk] *n* coke *m*

colander ['kɔləndəʳ] *n* passoire *f*

cold [kəʊld] *adj* froid(e) ♦ *n* froid *m*; (*MED*) rhume *m*; **it's ~** il fait froid; **to be** *or* **feel ~** (*person*) avoir froid; **to catch ~** prendre *or* attraper froid; **to catch a ~** attraper un rhume; **in ~ blood** de sang-froid; **~-shoulder** *vt* se montrer froid(e) envers, snober; **~ sore** *n* bouton *m* de fièvre

coleslaw ['kəʊlslɔː] *n* sorte de salade de chou cru

colic ['kɔlɪk] *n* colique(s) *f(pl)*

collapse [kə'læps] *vi* s'effondrer, s'écrouler ♦ *n* effondrement *m*, écroulement *m*; **collapsible** *adj* pliant(e); télescopique

collar ['kɔləʳ] *n* (*of coat, shirt*) col *m*; (*for animal*) collier *m*; **~bone** *n* clavicule *f*

collateral [kə'lætərl] *n* nantissement *m*

colleague ['kɔliːg] *n* collègue *m/f*

collect [kə'lɛkt] *vt* rassembler; ramasser; (*as a hobby*) collectionner; (*BRIT: call and pick up*) (passer) prendre; (*mail*) faire la levée de, ramasser; (*money owed*) encaisser; (*donations, subscriptions*) recueillir ♦ *vi* (*people*) se rassembler; (*things*) s'amasser; **to call ~** (*US: TEL*) téléphoner en P.C.V.; **~ion** *n* collection *f*; (*of mail*) levée *f*; (*for money*) collecte *f*, quête *f*; **~or** *n* collectionneur *m*

college ['kɔlɪdʒ] *n* collège *m*

collide [kə'laɪd] *vi* entrer en collision

colliery ['kɔlɪərɪ] (*BRIT*) *n* mine *f* de charbon, houillère *f*

collision [kə'lɪʒən] *n* collision *f*

colloquial [kə'ləʊkwɪəl] *adj* familier(-ère)

colon ['kəʊlən] *n* (*sign*) deux-points *m inv*; (*MED*) côlon *m*

colonel ['kɜːnl] *n* colonel *m*

colony ['kɔlənɪ] *n* colonie *f*

colour ['kʌləʳ] (*US* **color**) *n* couleur *f* ♦ *vt* (*paint*) peindre; (*dye*) teindre; (*news*) fausser, exagérer ♦ *vi* (*blush*) rougir; **~s** *npl* (*of party, club*) couleurs *fpl*; **~ in** *vt* colorier; **~ bar** *n* discrimination raciale (*dans un établissement*); **~-blind** *adj* daltonien(ne); **~ed** *adj* (*person*) de couleur; (*illustration*) en couleur; **~ film** *n* (*for camera*) pellicule *f* (en) couleur; **~ful** *adj* coloré(e), vif (vive); (*personality*) pittoresque, haut(e) en couleurs; **~ing** ['kʌlərɪŋ] *n* colorant *m*; (*complexion*) teint *m*; **~ scheme** *n* combinaison *f* de(s) couleurs; **~ television** *n* télévision *f* (en) couleur

colt [kəʊlt] *n* poulain *m*

column ['kɔləm] *n* colonne *f*; **~ist** ['kɔləmnɪst] *n* chroniqueur(-euse)

coma ['kəʊmə] *n* coma *m*

comb [kəʊm] *n* peigne *m* ♦ *vt* (*hair*) peigner; (*area*) ratisser, passer au peigne fin

combat ['kɔmbæt] *n* combat *m* ♦ *vt* combattre, lutter contre

combination [kɔmbɪ'neɪʃən] *n* combinaison *f*

combine [*vb* kəm'baɪn, *n* 'kɔmbaɪn] *vt*: **~ sth with sth** combiner qch avec qch; (*one quality with another*) joindre *or* allier qch à qch ♦ *vi* s'associer; (*CHEM*) se combiner ♦ *n* (*ECON*) trust *m*; **~ (harvester)** *n* moissonneuse-batteuse(-lieuse) *f*

come [kʌm] (*pt* **came**, *pp* **come**) *vi* venir, arriver; **to ~ to** (*decision etc*) parvenir *or* arriver à; **to ~ undone/loose** se défaire/desserrer; **~ about** se produire, arriver; **~ across** *vt fus* rencontrer par hasard, tomber sur; **~ along** *vi* = **come on**; **~ away** *vi* partir, s'en aller, se détacher; **~ back** *vi* revenir; **~ by** *vt fus* (*acquire*) obtenir, se procurer; **~ down** *vi* descendre; (*prices*) baisser; (*buildings*) s'écrouler, être démoli(e); **~ forward** *vi* s'avancer, se présenter, s'annoncer; **~ from** *vt fus* être originaire de, venir de; **~ in** *vi* entrer; **~ in for** *vt* (*criticism etc*) être l'objet de; **~ into** *vt fus* (*money*) hériter de; **~ off** *vt* (*button*) se détacher; (*stain*) s'enlever; (*attempt*) réussir; **~ on** *vi* (*pupil, work, project*) faire des progrès, s'avancer; (*lights, electri* city) s'allumer; (central heating) se mettre en marche; **~ on!** viens!, allons!, allez!; **~ out** vi sortir; (book) paraître; (strike) cesser le travail, se mettre en grève; **~ round** vi (after faint, operation) revenir à soi, reprendre connaissance; **~ to** vi revenir à soi; **~ up** vi monter; **~ up against** vt fus (resistance, difficulties) rencontrer; **~ up with** vt fus: **he came up with an idea** il a eu une idée, il a proposé quelque chose; **~ upon** vt fus tomber sur; **~back** n (THEATRE etc) rentrée f

:omedian [kə'mi:dɪən] n (in music hall etc) comique m; (THEATRE) comédien m

omedy ['kɒmɪdɪ] n comédie f

omeuppance [kʌm'ʌpəns] n: **to get one's ~** recevoir ce qu'on mérite

omfort ['kʌmfət] n confort m, bien-être m; (relief) soulagement m, réconfort m ♦ vt consoler, réconforter; **the ~s of home** les commodités fpl de la maison; **~able** adj confortable; (person) à l'aise; (patient) dont l'état est stationnaire; (walk etc) facile; **~ably** adv (sit) confortablement; (live) à l'aise; **~ station** (US) n toilettes fpl

omic ['kɒmɪk] adj (also: **~al**) comique ♦ n comique m; (BRIT: magazine) illustré m; **~ strip** n bande dessinée

oming ['kʌmɪŋ] n arrivée f ♦ adj prochain(e), à venir; **~(s) and going(s)** n(pl) va-et-vient m inv

omma ['kɒmə] n virgule f

ommand [kə'mɑːnd] n ordre m, commandement m; (MIL: authority) commandement; (mastery) maîtrise f ♦ vt (troops) commander; **to ~ sb to do** ordonner à qn de faire; **~eer** [kɒmən'dɪər] vt réquisitionner; **~er** n (MIL) commandant m

ommando [kə'mɑːndəu] n commando m; membre m d'un commando

ommemorate [kə'mɛmərent] vt commémorer

ommence [kə'mɛns] vt, vi commencer

ommend [kə'mɛnd] vt louer; (recommend) recommander

ommensurate [kə'mɛnʃərɪt] adj: **~ with**

or **to** en proportion de, proportionné(e) à

comment ['kɒmɛnt] n commentaire m ♦ vi: **to ~ (on)** faire des remarques (sur); **"no ~"** "je n'ai rien à dire"; **~ary** ['kɒməntərɪ] n commentaire m; (SPORT) reportage m (en direct); **~ator** ['kɒmənteɪtər] n commentateur m; reporter m

commerce ['kɒmə:s] n commerce m

commercial [kə'mə:ʃəl] adj commercial(e) ♦ n (TV, RADIO) annonce f publicitaire, spot m (publicitaire)

commiserate [kə'mɪzəreɪt] vi: **to ~ with sb** témoigner de la sympathie pour qn

commission [kə'mɪʃən] n (order for work) commande f; (committee, fee) commission f ♦ vt (work of art) commander, charger un artiste de l'exécution de; **out of ~** (not working) hors service; **~aire** [kəmɪʃə'nɛər] (BRIT) n (at shop, cinema etc) portier m (en uniforme); **~er** n (POLICE) préfet m (de police)

commit [kə'mɪt] vt (act) commettre; (resources) consacrer; (to sb's care) confier (à); **to ~ o.s. (to do)** s'engager (à faire); **to ~ suicide** se suicider; **~ment** n engagement m; (obligation) responsabilité(s) f(pl)

committee [kə'mɪtɪ] n comité m

commodity [kə'mɒdɪtɪ] n produit m, marchandise f, article m

common ['kɒmən] adj commun(e); (usual) courant(e) ♦ n terrain communal; **the C~s** (BRIT) npl la chambre des Communes; **in ~** en commun; **~er** n roturier(-ière); **~ law** n droit coutumier; **~ly** adv communément, généralement; couramment; **C~ Market** n Marché commun; **~place** adj banal(e), ordinaire; **~ room** n salle commune; **~ sense** n bon sens; **C~wealth** (BRIT) n Commonwealth m

commotion [kə'məuʃən] n désordre m, tumulte m

communal ['kɒmju:nl] adj (life) communautaire; (for common use) commun(e)

commune [n 'kɒmju:n, vb kə'mju:n] n (group) communauté f ♦ vi: **to ~ with** communier avec

communicate [kə'mju:nɪkeɪt] *vt, vi* communiquer; **communication** [kəmjuːnɪ'keɪʃən] *n* communication *f*; **communication cord** (*BRIT*) *n* sonnette *f* d'alarme

communion [kə'mju:nɪən] *n* (*also:* **Holy C~**) communion *f*

communism ['kɔmjunɪzəm] *n* communisme *m*; **communist** *adj* communiste ♦ *n* communiste *m/f*

community [kə'mju:nɪtɪ] *n* communauté *f*; ~ **centre** *n* centre *m* de loisirs; ~ **chest** (*US*) *n* fonds commun

commutation ticket [kɔmju'teɪʃən-] (*US*) *n* carte *f* d'abonnement

commute [kə'mju:t] *vi* faire un trajet journalier pour se rendre à son travail ♦ *vt* (*LAW*) commuer; ~**r** *n* banlieusard(e) (*qui fait un trajet journalier pour se rendre à son travail*)

compact [*adj* kəm'pækt, *n* 'kɔmpækt] *adj* compact(e) ♦ *n* (*also:* **powder ~**) poudrier *m*; ~ **disc** *n* disque compact; ~ **disc player** *n* lecteur *m* de disque compact

companion [kəm'pænjən] *n* compagnon (compagne); ~**ship** *n* camaraderie *f*

company ['kʌmpənɪ] *n* compagnie *f*; **to keep sb ~** tenir compagnie à qn; ~ **secretary** (*BRIT*) *n* (*COMM*) secrétaire général (*d'une société*)

comparative [kəm'pærətɪv] *adj* (*study*) comparatif(-ive); (*relative*) relatif(-ive); ~**ly** *adv* (*relatively*) relativement

compare [kəm'pɛər] *vt*: **to ~ sth/sb with/to** comparer qch/qn avec *or* et/à ♦ *vi*: **to ~ (with)** se comparer (à); être comparable (à); **comparison** [kəm'pærɪsn] *n* comparaison *f*

compartment [kəm'pɑ:tmənt] *n* compartiment *m*

compass ['kʌmpəs] *n* boussole *f*; ~**es** *npl* (*GEOM: also:* **pair of ~es**) compas *m*

compassion [kəm'pæʃən] *n* compassion *f*; ~**ate** *adj* compatissant(e)

compatible [kəm'pætɪbl] *adj* compatible

compel [kəm'pɛl] *vt* contraindre, obliger

compensate ['kɔmpənseɪt] *vt* indemniser,

dédommager ♦ *vi*: **to ~ for** compenser; **compensation** [kɔmpən'seɪʃən] *n* compensation *f*; (*money*) dédommagement *m*, indemnité *f*

compère ['kɔmpɛər] *n* (*TV*) animateur(-trice)

compete [kəm'pi:t] *vi*: **to ~ (with)** rivaliser (avec), faire concurrence (à)

competent ['kɔmpɪtənt] *adj* compétent(e), capable

competition [kɔmpɪ'tɪʃən] *n* (*contest*) compétition *f*, concours *m*; (*ECON*) concurrence *f*

competitive [kəm'petɪtɪv] *adj* (*ECON*) concurrentiel(le); (*sport*) de compétition; (*person*) qui a l'esprit de compétition; **competitor** *n* concurrent(e)

complacency [kəm'pleɪsnsɪ] *n* suffisance *f*, vaine complaisance

complain [kəm'pleɪn] *vi*: **to ~ (about)** se plaindre (de); (*in shop etc*) réclamer (au sujet de); **to ~ of** (*pain*) se plaindre de; ~**t** *n* plainte *f*; réclamation *f*; (*MED*) affection *f*

complement [*n* 'kɔmplɪmənt, *vb* 'kɔmplɪment] *n* complément *m*; (*especially of ship's crew etc*) effectif complet ♦ *vt* (*enhance*) compléter; ~**ary** [kɔmplɪ'mentərɪ] *adj* complémentaire

complete [kəm'pli:t] *adj* complet(-ète) ♦ *vt* achever, parachever; (*set, group*) compléter; (*a form*) remplir; ~**ly** *adv* complètement; **completion** *n* achèvement *m*; (*of contract*) exécution *f*

complex ['kɔmplɛks] *adj* complexe ♦ *n* complexe *m*

complexion [kəm'plɛkʃən] *n* (*of face*) teint *m*

compliance [kəm'plaɪəns] *n* (*submission*) docilité *f*; (*agreement*): ~ **with** le fait de se conformer à; **in ~ with** en accord avec

complicate ['kɔmplɪkeɪt] *vt* compliquer; ~**d** *adj* compliqué(e); **complication** [kɔmplɪ'keɪʃən] *n* complication *f*

compliment [*n* 'kɔmplɪmənt, *vb* 'kɔmplɪment] *n* compliment *m* ♦ *vt* complimenter; ~**s** *npl* (*respects*) comp[

ments *mpl*, hommages *mpl*; **to pay sb a ~** faire *or* adresser un compliment à qn; **~ary** [kɔmplɪ'mentərɪ] *adj* flatteur(-euse); (*free*) (offert(e)) à titre gracieux; **~ary ticket** *n* billet *m* de faveur

comply [kəm'plaɪ] *vi*: **to ~ with** se soumettre à, se conformer à

component [kəm'pəunənt] *n* composant *m*, élément *m*

compose [kəm'pəuz] *vt* composer; (*form*): **to be ~d of** se composer de; **to ~ o.s.** se calmer, se maîtriser; prendre une contenance; **~d** *adj* calme, posé(e); **~r** *n* (*MUS*) compositeur *m*; **composition** [kɔmpə'zɪʃən] *n* composition *f*; **composure** [kəm'pəuʒəʳ] *n* calme *m*, maîtrise *f* de soi

compound ['kɔmpaund] *n* composé *m*; (*enclosure*) enclos *m*, enceinte *f*; **~ fracture** *n* fracture compliquée; **~ interest** *n* intérêt composé

comprehend [kɔmprɪ'hend] *vt* comprendre; **comprehension** *n* compréhension *f*

comprehensive [kɔmprɪ'hensɪv] *adj* (très) complet(-ète); **~ policy** *n* (*INSURANCE*) assurance *f* tous risques; **~ (school)** (*BRIT*) *n* école secondaire polyvalente; ≈ C.E.S. *m*

compress [*vb* kəm'pres, *n* 'kɔmpres] *vt* comprimer; (*text, information*) condenser ♦ *n* (*MED*) compresse *f*

comprise [kəm'praɪz] *vt* (*also*: **be ~d of**) comprendre; (*constitute*) constituer, représenter

compromise ['kɔmprəmaɪz] *n* compromis *m* ♦ *vt* compromettre ♦ *vi* transiger, accepter un compromis

compulsion [kəm'pʌlʃən] *n* contrainte *f*, force *f*

compulsive [kəm'pʌlsɪv] *adj* (*PSYCH*) compulsif(-ive); (*book, film etc*) captivant(e)

compulsory [kəm'pʌlsərɪ] *adj* obligatoire

computer [kəm'pjuːtəʳ] *n* ordinateur *m*; **~ game** *n* jeu *m* vidéo; **~-generated** *adj* de synthèse; **~ize** *vt* informatiser; **~ programmer** *n* programmeur(-euse); **~ programming** *n* programmation *f*; **~ sci-**

ence *n* informatique *f*; **computing** *n* = **computer science**

comrade ['kɔmrɪd] *n* camarade *m/f*

con [kɔn] *vt* duper; (*cheat*) escroquer ♦ *n* escroquerie *f*

conceal [kən'siːl] *vt* cacher, dissimuler

conceit [kən'siːt] *n* vanité *f*, suffisance *f*, prétention *f*; **~ed** *adj* vaniteux(-euse), suffisant(e)

conceive [kən'siːv] *vt, vi* concevoir

concentrate ['kɔnsəntreɪt] *vi* se concentrer ♦ *vt* concentrer; **concentration** *n* concentration *f*; **concentration camp** *n* camp *m* de concentration

concept ['kɔnsept] *n* concept *m*

concern [kən'səːn] *n* affaire *f*; (*COMM*) entreprise *f*, firme *f*; (*anxiety*) inquiétude *f*, souci *m* ♦ *vt* concerner; **to be ~ed (about)** s'inquiéter (de), être inquiet(-ète) (au sujet de); **~ing** *prep* en ce qui concerne, à propos de

concert ['kɔnsət] *n* concert *m*; **~ed** [kən'səːtɪd] *adj* concerté(e); **~ hall** *n* salle *f* de concert

concerto [kən'tʃəːtəu] *n* concerto *m*

concession [kən'seʃən] *n* concession *f*; **tax ~** dégrèvement fiscal

conclude [kən'kluːd] *vt* conclure; **conclusion** [kən'kluːʒən] *n* conclusion *f*; **conclusive** [kən'kluːsɪv] *adj* concluant(e), définitif(-ive)

concoct [kən'kɔkt] *vt* confectionner, composer; (*fig*) inventer; **~ion** *n* mélange *m*

concourse ['kɔnkɔːs] *n* (*hall*) hall *m*, salle *f* des pas perdus

concrete ['kɔnkriːt] *n* béton *m* ♦ *adj* concret(-ète); (*floor etc*) en béton

concur [kən'kəːʳ] *vi* (*agree*) être d'accord

concurrently [kən'kʌrntlɪ] *adv* simultanément

concussion [kən'kʌʃən] *n* (*MED*) commotion (cérébrale)

condemn [kən'dem] *vt* condamner

condensation [kɔnden'seɪʃən] *n* condensation *f*

condense [kən'dens] *vi* se condenser ♦ *vt*

condenser; **~d milk** *n* lait concentré (sucré)

condition [kən'dɪʃən] *n* condition *f*; (*MED*) état *m* ♦ *vt* déterminer, conditionner; **on ~ that** à condition que +*sub*, à condition de; **~al** *adj* conditionnel(le); **~er** *n* (*for hair*) baume après-shampooing *m*; (*for fabrics*) assouplissant *m*

condolences [kən'dəʊlənsɪz] *npl* condoléances *fpl*

condom ['kɒndəm] *n* préservatif *m*

condominium [kɒndə'mɪnɪəm] (*US*) *n* (*building*) immeuble *m* (en copropriété)

condone [kən'dəʊn] *vt* fermer les yeux sur, approuver (tacitement)

conducive [kən'dju:sɪv] *adj*: **~ to** favorable à, qui contribue à

conduct [*n* 'kɒndʌkt, *vb* kən'dʌkt] *n* conduite *f* ♦ *vt* conduire; (*MUS*) diriger; **to ~ o.s.** se conduire, se comporter; **~ed tour** *n* voyage organisé; (*of building*) visite guidée; **~or** *n* (*of orchestra*) chef *m* d'orchestre; (*on bus*) receveur *m*; (*US: on train*) chef *m* de train; (*ELEC*) conducteur *m*; **~ress** *n* (*on bus*) receveuse *f*

cone [kəʊn] *n* cône *m*; (*for ice-cream*) cornet *m*; (*BOT*) pomme *f* de pin, cône

confectioner [kən'fekʃənər] *n* confiseur(-euse); **~'s (shop)** *n* confiserie *f*; **~y** *n* confiserie *f*

confer [kən'fə:r] *vt*: **to ~ sth on** conférer qch à ♦ *vi* conférer, s'entretenir

conference ['kɒnfərəns] *n* conférence *f*

confess [kən'fes] *vt* confesser, avouer ♦ *vi* se confesser; **~ion** *n* confession *f*

confetti [kən'fetɪ] *n* confettis *mpl*

confide [kən'faɪd] *vi*: **to ~ in** se confier à

confidence ['kɒnfɪdns] *n* confiance *f*; (*also:* **self-~**) assurance *f*, confiance en soi; (*secret*) confidence *f*; **in ~** (*speak, write*) en confidence, confidentiellement; **~ trick** *n* escroquerie *f*; **confident** *adj* sûr(e), assuré(e); **confidential** [kɒnfɪ'denʃəl] *adj* confidentiel(le)

confine [kən'faɪn] *vt* limiter, borner; (*shut up*) confiner, enfermer; **~d** *adj* (*space*) restreint(e), réduit(e); **~ment** *n* emprisonne-

ment *m*, détention *f*; **~s** ['kɒnfaɪnz] *np* confins *mpl*, bornes *fpl*

confirm [kən'fə:m] *vt* confirmer; (*appointment*) ratifier; **~ation** [kɒnfə'meɪʃən] *n* confirmation *f*; **~ed** *adj* invétéré(e), incorrigible

confiscate ['kɒnfɪskeɪt] *vt* confisquer

conflict [*n* 'kɒnflɪkt, *vb* kən'flɪkt] *n* conflit *m*, lutte *f* ♦ *vi* être *or* entrer en conflit (*opinions*) s'opposer, se heurter; **~ing** [kən'flɪktɪŋ] *adj* contradictoire

conform [kən'fɔ:m] *vi*: **to ~ (to)** se conformer (à)

confound [kən'faʊnd] *vt* confondre

confront [kən'frʌnt] *vt* confronter, mettr en présence; (*enemy, danger*) affronter, faire face à; **~ation** [kɒnfrən'teɪʃən] confrontation *f*

confuse [kən'fju:z] *vt* (*person*) troubler (*situation*) embrouiller; (*one thing with another*) confondre; **~d** *adj* (*person*) dérouté(e), désorienté(e); **confusing** *adj* peu clair(e), déroutant(e); **confusion** [kən'fju:ʒən] *n* confusion *f*

congeal [kən'dʒi:l] *vi* (*blood*) se coaguler (*oil etc*) se figer

congenial [kən'dʒi:nɪəl] *adj* sympathique agréable

congested [kən'dʒestɪd] *adj* (*MED*) congestionné(e); (*area*) surpeuplé(e); (*road*) blo qué(e); **congestion** *n* congestion *f*; (*fig* encombrement *m*

congratulate [kən'grætjuleɪt] *vt*: **to ~ s (on)** féliciter qn (de); **congratulation** [kəngrætju'leɪʃənz] *npl* félicitations *fpl*

congregate ['kɒŋgrɪgeɪt] *vi* se rassemble se réunir; **congregation** [kɒŋgrɪ'geɪʃən assemblée *f* (des fidèles)

congress ['kɒŋgres] *n* congrès *m*; **~ma** (*irreg*) (*US*) *n* membre *m* du Congrès

conjunction [kən'dʒʌŋkʃən] *n* (*LING* conjonction *f*

conjunctivitis [kəndʒʌŋktɪ'vaɪtɪs] conjonctivite *f*

conjure ['kʌndʒər] *vi* faire des tours d passe-passe; **~ up** *vt* (*ghost, spirit*) fai apparaître; (*memories*) évoquer; **~r** *n* pre tidigitateur *m*, illusionniste *m/f*

con man (*irreg*) *n* escroc *m*

connect [kə'nɛkt] *vt* joindre, relier; (*ELEC*) connecter; (*TEL: caller*) mettre en connection (*with* avec); (: *new subscriber*) brancher; (*fig*) établir un rapport entre, faire un rapprochement entre ♦ *vi* (*train*): **to ~ with** assurer la correspondance avec; **to be ~ed with** (*fig*) avoir un rapport avec, avoir des rapports avec, être en relation avec; **~ion** *n* relation *f*, lien *m*; (*ELEC*) connexion *f*; (*train, plane etc*) correspondance *f*; (*TEL*) branchement *m*, communication *f*

onnive [kə'naɪv] *vi*: **to ~ at** se faire le complice de

onquer ['kɒŋkə'] *vt* conquérir; (*feelings*) vaincre, surmonter; **conquest** ['kɒŋkwɛst] *n* conquête *f*

ons [kɒnz] *npl see* **convenience; pro**

onscience ['kɒnʃəns] *n* conscience *f*; **conscientious** [kɒnʃɪ'ɛnʃəs] *adj* consciencieux(-euse)

onscious ['kɒnʃəs] *adj* conscient(e); **~ness** *n* conscience *f*; (*MED*) connaissance *f*

onscript ['kɒnskrɪpt] *n* conscrit *m*

onsent [kən'sɛnt] *n* consentement *m* ♦ *vi*: **to ~ (to)** consentir (à)

onsequence ['kɒnsɪkwəns] *n* conséquence *f*, suites *fpl*; (*significance*) importance *f*; **consequently** *adv* par conséquent, donc

onservation [kɒnsə'veɪʃən] *n* préservation *f*, protection *f*

onservative [kən'sə:vətɪv] *adj* conservateur(-trice); **at a ~ estimate** au bas mot; **C~** (*BRIT*) *adj, n* (*POL*) conservateur(-trice)

onservatory [kən'sə:vətrɪ] *n* (*greenhouse*) serre *f*

onserve [kən'sə:v] *vt* conserver, préserver; (*supplies, energy*) économiser ♦ *n* confiture *f*

onsider [kən'sɪdə'] *vt* (*study*) considérer, réfléchir à; (*take into account*) penser à, prendre en considération; (*regard, judge*)

considérer, estimer; **to ~ doing sth** envisager de faire qch; **~able** *adj* considérable; **~ably** *adv* nettement; **~ate** *adj* prévenant(e), plein(e) d'égards; **~ation** [kənsɪdə'reɪʃən] *n* considération *f*; **~ing** *prep* étant donné

consign [kən'saɪn] *vt* expédier; (*to sb's care*) confier; (*fig*) livrer; **~ment** *n* arrivage *m*, envoi *m*

consist [kən'sɪst] *vi*: **to ~ of** consister en, se composer de

consistency [kən'sɪstənsɪ] *n* consistance *f*; (*fig*) cohérence *f*

consistent [kən'sɪstənt] *adj* logique, cohérent(e)

consolation [kɒnsə'leɪʃən] *n* consolation *f*

console[1] [kən'səul] *vt* consoler

console[2] ['kɒnsəul] *n* (*COMPUT*) console *f*

consonant ['kɒnsənənt] *n* consonne *f*

conspicuous [kən'spɪkjuəs] *adj* voyant(e), qui attire l'attention

conspiracy [kən'spɪrəsɪ] *n* conspiration *f*, complot *m*

constable ['kʌnstəbl] (*BRIT*) *n* ≃ agent *m* de police, gendarme *m*; **chief ~** ≃ préfet *m* de police; **constabulary** [kən'stæbjulərɪ] (*BRIT*) *n* ≃ police *f*, gendarmerie *f* .

constant ['kɒnstənt] *adj* constant(e); incessant(e); **~ly** *adv* constamment, sans cesse

constipated ['kɒnstɪpeɪtɪd] *adj* constipé(e); **constipation** [kɒnstɪ'peɪʃən] *n* constipation *f*

constituency [kən'stɪtjuənsɪ] *n* circonscription électorale

constituent [kən'stɪtjuənt] *n* (*POL*) électeur(-trice); (*part*) élément constitutif, composant *m*

constitution [kɒnstɪ'tju:ʃən] *n* constitution *f*; **~al** *adj* constitutionnel(le)

constraint [kən'streɪnt] *n* contrainte *f*

construct [kən'strʌkt] *vt* construire; **~ion** *n* construction *f*; **~ive** *adj* constructif(-ive); **~ive dismissal** démission forcée

consul ['kɒnsl] *n* consul *m*; **~ate** ['kɒnsjulɪt] *n* consulat *m*

consult [kən'sʌlt] *vt* consulter; **~ant** *n*

(*MED*) médecin consultant; (*other specialist*) consultant *m*, (expert-)conseil *m*; **~ing room** (*BRIT*) *n* cabinet *m* de consultation

consume [kən'sjuːm] *vt* consommer; **~r** *n* consommateur(-trice); **~r goods** *npl* biens *mpl* de consommation; **~r society** *n* société *f* de consommation

consummate ['kɒnsʌmeɪt] *vt* consommer

consumption [kən'sʌmpʃən] *n* consommation *f*

cont. *abbr* (= *continued*) suite

contact ['kɒntækt] *n* contact *m*; (*person*) connaissance *f*, relation *f* ♦ *vt* contacter, se mettre en contact *or* en rapport avec; **~ lenses** *npl* verres *mpl* de contact, lentilles *fpl*

contagious [kən'teɪdʒəs] *adj* contagieux(-euse)

contain [kən'teɪn] *vt* contenir; **to ~ o.s.** se contenir, se maîtriser; **~er** *n* récipient *m*; (*for shipping etc*) container *m*

contaminate [kən'tæmɪneɪt] *vt* contaminer

cont'd *abbr* (= *continued*) suite

contemplate ['kɒntəmpleɪt] *vt* contempler; (*consider*) envisager

contemporary [kən'tempərərɪ] *adj* contemporain(e); (*design, wallpaper*) moderne ♦ *n* contemporain(e)

contempt [kən'tempt] *n* mépris *m*, dédain *m*; **~ of court** (*LAW*) outrage *m* à l'autorité de la justice; **~uous** [kən'temptjuəs] *adj* dédaigneux(-euse), méprisant(e)

contend [kən'tend] *vt*: **to ~ that** soutenir *or* prétendre que ♦ *vi*: **to ~ with** (*compete*) rivaliser avec; (*struggle*) lutter avec; **~er** *n* concurrent(e); (*POL*) candidat(e)

content [*adj, vb* kən'tent, *n* 'kɒntent] *adj* content(e), satisfait(e) ♦ *vt* contenter, satisfaire ♦ *n* contenu *m*; (*of fat, moisture*) teneur *f*; **~s** *npl* (*of container etc*) contenu *m*; **(table of) ~s** table *f* des matières; **~ed** *adj* content(e), satisfait(e)

contention [kən'tenʃən] *n* dispute *f*, contestation *f*; (*argument*) assertion *f*, affirmation *f*

contest [*n* 'kɒntest, *vb* kən'test] *n* combat

m, lutte *f*; (*competition*) concours *m* ♦ *v*(?) (*decision, statement*) contester, discuter; (*compete for*) disputer; **~ant** [kən'testənt] *n*(?) concurrent(e); (*in fight*) adversaire *m/f*

context ['kɒntekst] *n* contexte *m*

continent ['kɒntɪnənt] *n* continent *m*; **the C~** (*BRIT*) l'Europe continentale; **~al** [kɒntɪ'nentl] *adj* continental(e); **~al breakfast** *n* petit déjeuner *m* à la française; **~al quilt** (*BRIT*) *n* couette *f*

contingency [kən'tɪndʒənsɪ] *n* éventualité *f*, événement imprévu

continual [kən'tɪnjuəl] *adj* continuel(le)

continuation [kəntɪnju'eɪʃən] *n* continuation *f*; (*after interruption*) reprise *f*; (*of story*) suite *f*

continue [kən'tɪnjuː] *vi, vt* continuer; (*after interruption*) reprendre, poursuivre

continuity [kɒntɪ'njuːɪtɪ] *n* continuité *f*; (*TV etc*) enchaînement *m*; **continuous** [kən'tɪnjuəs] *adj* continu(e); (*LING*) progressif(-ive)

contort [kən'tɔːt] *vt* tordre, crisper

contour ['kɒntuər] *n* contour *m*, profil *m*; (*on map: also*: **~ line**) courbe *f* de niveau

contraband ['kɒntrəbænd] *n* contrebande *f*

contraceptive [kɒntrə'septɪv] *ad*(?) contraceptif(-ive), anticonceptionnel(le) ♦ *n* contraceptif *m*

contract [*n* 'kɒntrækt, *vb* kən'trækt] *n* contrat *m* ♦ *vi* (*become smaller*) s(?) contracter, se resserrer; (*COMM*): **to ~ to do sth** s'engager (par contrat) à fai(?) qch; **~ion** [kən'trækʃən] *n* contraction(?) **~or** [kən'træktər] *n* entrepreneur *m*

contradict [kɒntrə'dɪkt] *vt* contredire

contraflow ['kɒntrəfləu] *n* (*AUT*): **~ lan(?)** voie *f* à contresens; **there's a ~ syster(?) in operation on ...** une voie a été mis(?) en sens inverse sur ...

contraption [kən'træpʃən] (*pej*) *n* machi(?) *m*, truc *m*

contrary[1] ['kɒntrərɪ] *adj* contraire, oppo(?) sé(e) ♦ *n* contraire *m*; **on the ~** a(?) contraire; **unless you hear to the ~** sa(?) avis contraire

contrary² [kən'treərɪ] *adj* (*perverse*) contrariant(e), entêté(e)

contrast [*n* 'kɒntrɑːst, *vb* kən'trɑːst] *n* contraste *m* ♦ *vt* mettre en contraste, contraster; **in ~ to** *or* **with** contrairement à

contravene [kɒntrə'viːn] *vt* enfreindre, violer, contrevenir à

contribute [kən'trɪbjuːt] *vi* contribuer ♦ *vt*: **to ~ £10/an article to** donner 10 livres/un article à; **to ~ to** contribuer à; (*newspaper*) collaborer à; **contribution** [kɒntrɪ'bjuːʃən] *n* contribution *f*; **contributor** [kən'trɪbjutəʳ] *n* (*to newspaper*) collaborateur(-trice)

contrive [kən'traɪv] *vi*: **to ~ to do** s'arranger pour faire, trouver le moyen de faire

control [kən'trəul] *vt* maîtriser, commander; (*check*) contrôler ♦ *n* contrôle *m*, autorité *f*; maîtrise *f*; **~s** *npl* (*of machine etc*) commandes *fpl*; (*on radio, TV*) boutons *mpl* de réglage; **~led substance** narcotique *m*; **everything is under ~** tout va bien, j'ai (*or* il a *etc*) la situation en main; **to be in ~ of** être maître de, maîtriser; **the car went out of ~** j'ai (*or* il a *etc*) perdu le contrôle du véhicule; **~ panel** *n* tableau *m* de commande; **~ room** *n* (*AVIAT*) salle *f* des commandes; **~ tower** *n* (*AVIAT*) tour *f* de contrôle

controversial [kɒntrə'vəːʃl] *adj* (*topic*) discutable, controversé(e); (*person*) qui fait beaucoup parler de lui; **controversy** ['kɒntrəvəːsɪ] *n* controverse *f*, polémique *f*

convalesce [kɒnvə'les] *vi* relever de maladie, se remettre (d'une maladie)

convector [kən'vektəʳ] *n* (*heater*) radiateur *m* (à convexion)

convene [kən'viːn] *vt* convoquer, assembler ♦ *vi* se réunir, s'assembler

convenience [kən'viːnɪəns] *n* commodité *f*; **at your ~** quand *or* comme cela vous convient; **all modern ~s**, (*BRIT*) **all mod cons** avec tout le confort moderne, tout confort

convenient [kən'viːnɪənt] *adj* commode

convent ['kɒnvənt] *n* couvent *m*; ~

school *n* couvent *m*

convention [kən'venʃən] *n* convention *f*; **~al** *adj* conventionnel(le)

conversant [kən'vəːsnt] *adj*: **to be ~ with** s'y connaître en; être au courant de

conversation [kɒnvə'seɪʃən] *n* conversation *f*

converse [*n* 'kɒnvəːs, *vb* kən'vəːs] *n* contraire *m*, inverse *m* ♦ *vi* s'entretenir; **~ly** [kɒn'vəːslɪ] *adv* inversement, réciproquement

convert [*vb* kən'vəːt, *n* 'kɒnvəːt] *vt* (*REL, COMM*) convertir; (*alter*) transformer; (*house*) aménager ♦ *n* converti(e); **~ible** [kən'vəːtəbl] *n* (*voiture f*) décapotable *f*

convey [kən'veɪ] *vt* transporter; (*thanks*) transmettre; (*idea*) communiquer; **~or belt** *n* convoyeur *m*, tapis roulant

convict [*vb* kən'vɪkt, *n* 'kɒnvɪkt] *vt* déclarer (*or* reconnaître) coupable ♦ *n* forçat *m*, détenu *m*; **~ion** [-ʃən] *n* (*LAW*) condamnation *f*; (*belief*) conviction *f*

convince [kən'vɪns] *vt* convaincre, persuader; **convincing** *adj* persuasif(-ive), convaincant(e)

convoluted ['kɒnvəluːtɪd] *adj* (*argument*) compliqué(e)

convulse [kən'vʌls] *vt*: **to be ~d with laughter/pain** se tordre de rire/douleur

cook [kuk] *vt* (faire) cuire ♦ *vi* cuire; (*person*) faire la cuisine ♦ *n* cuisinier(-ière); **~book** *n* livre *m* de cuisine; **~er** *n* cuisinière *f*; **~ery** *n* cuisine *f*; **~ery book** (*BRIT*) *n* = **cookbook**; **~ie** (*US*) *n* biscuit *m*, petit gâteau sec; **~ing** *n* cuisine *f*

cool [kuːl] *adj* frais (fraîche); (*calm, unemotional*) calme; (*unfriendly*) froid(e) ♦ *vt, vi* rafraîchir, refroidir

coop [kuːp] *n* poulailler *m*; (*for rabbits*) clapier *m* ♦ *vt*: **to ~ up** (*fig*) cloîtrer, enfermer

cooperate [kəu'ɒpəreɪt] *vi* coopérer, collaborer; **cooperation** [kəuɒpə'reɪʃən] *n* coopération *f*, collaboration *f*; **cooperative** [kəu'ɒpərətɪv] *adj* coopératif(-ive) ♦ *n* coopérative *f*

coordinate [*vb* kəu'ɔːdɪneɪt, *n* kəu'ɔːdɪneɪt]

vt· coordonner ♦ n (MATH) coordonnée f;
~s npl (clothes) ensemble m, coordonnés
mpl

co-ownership [kəu'əunəʃip] n co-propriété f

cop [kɔp] (inf) n flic m

cope [kəup] vi: **to ~ with** faire face à;
(solve) venir à bout de

copper ['kɔpər] n cuivre m; (BRIT: inf:
policeman) flic m; ~s npl (coins) petite
monnaie

copy ['kɔpɪ] n copie f; (of book etc) exemplaire m ♦ vt copier; ~**right** n droit m
d'auteur, copyright m

coral ['kɔrəl] n corail m

cord [kɔ:d] n corde f; (fabric) velours
côtelé; (ELEC) cordon m, fil m

cordial ['kɔ:dɪəl] adj cordial(e),
chaleureux(-euse) ♦ n cordial m

cordon ['kɔ:dn] n cordon m; ~ **off** vt boucler (par cordon de police)

corduroy ['kɔ:dərɔɪ] n velours côtelé

core [kɔ:r] n noyau m; (of fruit) trognon m,
cœur m; (of building, problem) cœur ♦ vt
enlever le trognon or le cœur de

cork [kɔ:k] n liège m; (of bottle) bouchon
m; ~**screw** n tire-bouchon m

corn [kɔ:n] n (BRIT: wheat) blé m; (US:
maize) maïs m; (on foot) cor m; ~ **on the
cob** (CULIN) épi m de maïs; ~**ed beef** n
corned-beef m

corner ['kɔ:nər] n coin m; (AUT) tournant
m, virage m; (FOOTBALL: also: ~ **kick**) corner m ♦ vt acculer, mettre au pied du
mur; coincer; (COMM: market) accaparer
♦ vi prendre un virage; ~**stone** n pierre f
angulaire

cornet ['kɔ:nɪt] n (MUS) cornet m à pis-
tons; (BRIT: of ice-cream) cornet (de glace)

cornflakes ['kɔ:nfleɪks] npl corn-flakes m

cornflour ['kɔ:nflauər] (BRIT), **cornstarch**
['kɔ:nstɑ:tʃ] (US) n farine f de maïs,
maïzena f ®

Cornwall ['kɔ:nwəl] n Cornouailles f

corny ['kɔ:nɪ] (inf) adj rebattu(e)

coronary ['kɔrənərɪ] n (also: ~ **thrombosis**) infarctus m (du myocarde), thrombo-

se f coronarienne

coronation [kɔrə'neɪʃən] n couronnemen
m

coroner ['kɔrənər] n officiel chargé de dé
terminer les causes d'un décès

corporal ['kɔ:pərl] n caporal m, brigadie
m ♦ adj: ~ **punishment** châtiment corpo
rel

corporate ['kɔ:pərɪt] adj en commun
collectif(-ive); (proper) de l'entreprise

corporation [kɔ:pə'reɪʃən] n (of town) mu
nicipalité f, conseil municipal; (COMM) so
ciété f

corps [kɔ:r] (pl ~) n corps m

corpse [kɔ:ps] n cadavre m

correct [kə'rɛkt] adj (accurate) correct(e)
exact(e); (proper) correct, convenable ♦ v
corriger; ~**ion** n correction f

correspond [kɔrɪs'pɔnd] vi correspondre
~**ence** n correspondance f; ~**enc**
course n cours m par correspondance
~**ent** n correspondant(e)

corridor ['kɔrɪdɔ:r] n couloir m, corridor m

corrode [kə'rəud] vt corroder, ronger ♦ v
se corroder

corrugated ['kɔrəgeɪtɪd] adj plissé(e); or
dulé(e); ~ **iron** n tôle ondulée

corrupt [kə'rʌpt] adj corrompu(e) ♦ vt co
rompre; ~**ion** n corruption f

Corsica ['kɔ:sɪkə] n Corse f

cosmetic [kɔz'mɛtɪk] n produit m d
beauté, cosmétique m

cost [kɔst] (pt, pp cost) n coût m ♦ v
coûter ♦ vt établir or calculer le prix o
revient de; ~**s** npl (COMM) frais mpl; (LAW
dépens mpl; **it ~s £5/too much** ce
coûte cinq livres/c'est trop cher; **at all ~**
coûte que coûte, à tout prix

co-star ['kəustɑ:r] n partenaire m/f

cost: ~**-effective** adj rentable; ~**ly** a
coûteux(-euse); ~**-of-living** adj: ~**-o**
living allowance indemnité f de v
chère; ~**-of-living index** index m du co
de la vie; ~ **price** (BRIT) n prix coûtant
de revient

costume ['kɔstjuːm] n costume m; (lad)
suit) tailleur m; (BRIT: also: **swimming**

maillot *m* (de bain); ~ **jewellery** *n* bijoux *mpl* fantaisie

cosy ['kəʊzɪ] (*US* **cozy**) *adj* douillet(te); (*person*) à l'aise, au chaud

cot [kɒt] *n* (*BRIT: child's*) lit *m* d'enfant, petit lit; (*US: campbed*) lit de camp

cottage ['kɒtɪdʒ] *n* petite maison (à la campagne), cottage *m*; ~ **cheese** *n* fromage blanc (*maigre*)

cotton ['kɒtn] *n* coton *m*; ~ **on** (*inf*) *vi*: **to ~ on to** piger; ~ **candy** (*US*) *n* barbe *f* à papa; ~ **wool** (*BRIT*) *n* ouate *f*, coton *m* hydrophile

couch [kaʊtʃ] *n* canapé *m*; divan *m*

couchette [kuːˈʃɛt] *n* couchette *f*

cough [kɒf] *vi* tousser ♦ *n* toux *f*; ~ **sweet** *n* pastille *f* pour or contre la toux

could [kʊd] *pt of* **can²**; ~**n't** = **could not**

council ['kaʊnsl] *n* conseil *m*; **city** or **town ~** conseil municipal; ~ **estate** (*BRIT*) *n* (zone *f* de) logements loués à/par la municipalité; ~ **house** (*BRIT*) *n* maison *f* (à loyer modéré) louée par la municipalité; ~**lor** *n* conseiller(-ère)

counsel ['kaʊnsl] *n* (*lawyer*) avocat(e); (*advice*) conseil *m*, consultation *f*; ~**lor** *n* conseiller(-ère); (*US: lawyer*) avocat(e)

count [kaʊnt] *vt*, *vi* compter ♦ *n* compte *m*; (*nobleman*) comte *m*; ~ **on** *vt fus* compter sur; ~**down** *n* compte *m* à rebours

countenance ['kaʊntɪnəns] *n* expression *f* ♦ *vt* approuver

counter ['kaʊntə*r*] *n* comptoir *m*; (*in post office, bank*) guichet *m*; (*in game*) jeton *m* ♦ *vt* aller à l'encontre de, opposer ♦ *adv*: ~ **to** contrairement à; ~**act** *vt* neutraliser, contrebalancer; ~**feit** *n* faux *m*, contrefaçon *f* ♦ *vt* contrefaire ♦ *adj* faux (fausse); ~**foil** *n* talon *m*, souche *f*; ~**part** *n* (*of person etc*) homologue *m/f*

countess ['kaʊntɪs] *n* comtesse *f*

countless ['kaʊntlɪs] *adj* innombrable

country ['kʌntrɪ] *n* pays *m*; (*native land*) patrie *f*; (*as opposed to town*) campagne *f*; (*region*) région *f*, pays; ~ **dancing** (*BRIT*) *n* danse *f* folklorique; ~ **house** *n* manoir *m*, (petit) château; ~**man** (*irreg*) *n* (*compatriot*) compatriote *m*; (*country dweller*) habitant *m* de la campagne, campagnard *m*; ~**side** *n* campagne *f*

county ['kaʊntɪ] *n* comté *m*

coup [kuː] (*pl* ~**s**) *n* beau coup; (*also:* ~ **d'état**) coup d'État

couple ['kʌpl] *n* couple *m*; **a ~ of** deux; (*a few*) quelques

coupon ['kuːpɒn] *n* coupon *m*, bon-prime *m*, bon-réclame *m*; (*COMM*) coupon *m*

courage ['kʌrɪdʒ] *n* courage *m*

courier ['kʊrɪə*r*] *n* messager *m*, courrier *m*; (*for tourists*) accompagnateur(-trice), guide *m/f*

course [kɔːs] *n* cours *m*; (*of ship*) route *f*; (*for golf*) terrain *m*; (*part of meal*) plat *m*; **first ~** entrée *f*; **of ~** bien sûr; ~ **of action** parti *m*, ligne *f* de conduite; ~ **of treatment** (*MED*) traitement *m*

court [kɔːt] *n* cour *f*; (*LAW*) cour, tribunal *m*; (*TENNIS*) court *m* ♦ *vt* (*woman*) courtiser, faire la cour à; **to take to ~** actionner or poursuivre en justice

courteous ['kɜːtɪəs] *adj* courtois(e), poli(e); **courtesy** ['kɜːtəsɪ] *n* courtoisie *f*, politesse *f*; **(by) courtesy of** avec l'aimable autorisation de; **courtesy bus** or **coach** *n* navette gratuite

court: ~**house** (*US*) *n* palais *m* de justice; ~**ier** *n* courtisan *m*, dame *f* de la cour; ~ **martial** (*pl* **courts martial**) *n* cour martiale, conseil *m* de guerre; ~**room** *n* salle *f* de tribunal; ~**yard** *n* cour *f*

cousin ['kʌzn] *n* cousin(e); **first ~** cousin(e) germain(e)

cove [kəʊv] *n* petite baie, anse *f*

covenant ['kʌvənənt] *n* engagement *m*

cover ['kʌvə*r*] *vt* couvrir ♦ *n* couverture *f*; (*of pan*) couvercle *m*; (*over furniture*) housse *f*; (*shelter*) abri *m*; **to take ~** se mettre à l'abri; **under ~** à l'abri; **under ~ of darkness** à la faveur de la nuit; **under separate ~** (*COMM*) sous pli séparé; **to ~ up for sb** couvrir qn; ~**age** *n* (*TV, PRESS*) reportage *m*; ~ **charge** *n* couvert *m* (*supplément à payer*); ~**ing** *n* couche *f*; ~**ing**

letter (*US* **cover letter**) *n* lettre explicative; ~ **note** *n* (*INSURANCE*) police *f* provisoire

covert ['kʌvət] *adj* (*threat*) voilé(e), caché(e); (*glance*) furtif(-ive)

cover-up ['kʌvərʌp] *n* tentative *f* pour étouffer une affaire

covet ['kʌvɪt] *vt* convoiter

cow [kau] *n* vache *f* ♦ *vt* effrayer, intimider

coward ['kauəd] *n* lâche *m/f*; **~ice** *n* lâcheté *f*; **~ly** *adj* lâche

cowboy ['kaubɔɪ] *n* cow-boy *m*

cower ['kauəʳ] *vi* se recroqueviller

coy [kɔɪ] *adj* faussement effarouché(e) *or* timide

cozy ['kəuzɪ] (*US*) *adj* = **cosy**

CPA (*US*) *n abbr* = **certified public accountant**

crab [kræb] *n* crabe *m*; ~ **apple** *n* pomme *f* sauvage

crack [kræk] *n* (*split*) fente *f*, fissure *f*; (*in cup, bone etc*) fêlure *f*; (*in wall*) lézarde *f*; (*noise*) craquement *m*, coup (sec); (*drug*) crack *m* ♦ *vt* fendre, fissurer; fêler; lézarder; (*whip*) faire claquer; (*nut*) casser; (*code*) déchiffrer; (*problem*) résoudre ♦ *adj* (*athlete*) de première classe, d'élite; ~ **down on** *vt fus* mettre un frein à; ~ **up** *vi* être au bout du rouleau, s'effondrer; **~ed** *adj* (*cup, bone*) fêlé(e); (*broken*) cassé(e); (*wall*) lézardé(e); (*surface*) craquelé(e); (*inf: mad*) cinglé(e); **~er** *n* (*Christmas cracker*) pétard *m*; (*biscuit*) biscuit (salé)

crackle ['krækl] *vi* crépiter, grésiller

cradle ['kreɪdl] *n* berceau *m*

craft [krɑːft] *n* métier (artisanal); (*pl inv: boat*) embarcation *f*, barque *f*; (: *plane*) appareil *m*; **~sman** (*irreg*) *n* artisan *m*, ouvrier (qualifié); **~smanship** *n* travail *m*; **~y** *adj* rusé(e), malin(-igne)

crag [kræg] *n* rocher escarpé

cram [kræm] *vt* (*fill*): **to ~ sth with** bourrer qch de; (*put*): **to ~ sth into** fourrer qch dans ♦ *vi* (*for exams*) bachoter

cramp [kræmp] *n* crampe *f* ♦ *vt* gêner, entraver; **~ed** *adj* à l'étroit, très serré(e)

cranberry ['krænbərɪ] *n* canneberge *f*

crane [kreɪn] *n* grue *f*

crank [kræŋk] *n* manivelle *f*; (*person*) excentrique *m/f*

cranny ['krænɪ] *n see* **nook**

crash [kræʃ] *n* fracas *m*; (*of car*) collision *f*; (*of plane*) accident *m* ♦ *vt* avoir un accident avec ♦ *vi* (*plane*) s'écraser; (*two cars*) se percuter, s'emboutir; (*COMM*) s'effondrer; **to ~ into** se jeter *or* se fracasser contre; ~ **course** *n* cours intensif; ~ **helmet** *n* casque (protecteur); ~ **landing** *n* atterrissage forcé *or* en catastrophe

crate [kreɪt] *n* cageot *m*; (*for bottles*) caisse *f*

cravat(e) [krə'væt] *n* foulard (noué autour du cou)

crave [kreɪv] *vt*, *vi*: **to ~ (for)** avoir une envie irrésistible de

crawl [krɔːl] *vi* ramper; (*vehicle*) avancer au pas ♦ *n* (*SWIMMING*) crawl *m*

crayfish ['kreɪfɪʃ] *n inv* (*freshwater*) écrevisse *f*; (*saltwater*) langoustine *f*

crayon ['kreɪən] *n* crayon *m* (de couleur)

craze [kreɪz] *n* engouement *m*

crazy ['kreɪzɪ] *adj* fou (folle)

creak [kriːk] *vi* grincer; craquer

cream [kriːm] *n* crème *f* ♦ *adj* (*colour*) crème *inv*; ~ **cake** *n* (petit) gâteau à la crème; ~ **cheese** *n* fromage *m* à la crème, fromage blanc; **~y** *adj* crémeux(-euse)

crease [kriːs] *n* pli *m* ♦ *vt* froisser, chiffonner ♦ *vi* se froisser, se chiffonner

create [kriː'eɪt] *vt* créer; **creation** *n* création *f*; **creative** *adj* (*artistic*) créatif(-ive); (*ingenious*) ingénieux(-euse)

creature ['kriːtʃəʳ] *n* créature *f*

crèche [krɛʃ] *n* garderie *f*, crèche *f*

credence ['kriːdns] *n*: **to lend** *or* **give ~ to** ajouter foi à

credentials [krɪ'dɛnʃlz] *npl* (*references*) références *fpl*; (*papers of identity*) pièce *f* d'identité

credit ['krɛdɪt] *n* crédit *m*; (*recognition*) honneur *m* ♦ *vt* (*COMM*) créditer; (*believe: also:* **give ~ to**) ajouter foi à, croire; **~s** *npl* (*CINEMA, TV*) générique *m*; **to be in ~**

(*person, bank account*) être créditeur(-trice); **to ~ sb with** (*fig*) prêter *or* attribuer à qn; **~ card** *n* carte *f* de crédit; **~or** *n* créancier(-ière)

creed [kriːd] *n* croyance *f*; credo *m*

creek [kriːk] *n* crique *f*, anse *f*; (*US: stream*) ruisseau *m*, petit cours d'eau

creep [kriːp] (*pt, pp* **crept**) *vi* ramper; **~er** *n* plante grimpante; **~y** *adj* (*frightening*) qui fait frissonner, qui donne la chair de poule

cremate [krɪˈmeɪt] *vt* incinérer; **crematorium** [kremaˈtɔːrɪəm] (*pl* **crematoria**) *n* four *m* crématoire

crêpe [kreɪp] *n* crêpe *m*; **~ bandage** (*BRIT*) *n* bande *f* Velpeau ®

crept [krept] *pt, pp of* **creep**

crescent [ˈkresnt] *n* croissant *m*; (*street*) rue *f* (*en arc de cercle*)

cress [kres] *n* cresson *m*

crest [krest] *n* crête *f*; **~fallen** *adj* déconfit(e), découragé(e)

Crete [kriːt] *n* Crète *f*

crevice [ˈkrevɪs] *n* fissure *f*, lézarde *f*, fente *f*

crew [kruː] *n* équipage *m*; (*CINEMA*) équipe *f*; **~-cut** *n*: **to have a ~-cut** avoir les cheveux en brosse; **~-neck** *n* col ras du cou

crib [krɪb] *n* lit *m* d'enfant; (*for baby*) berceau *m* ♦ *vt* (*inf*) copier

crick [krɪk] *n*: **~ in the neck** torticolis *m*; **~ in the back** tour *m* de reins

cricket [ˈkrɪkɪt] *n* (*insect*) grillon *m*, cri-cri *m inv*; (*game*) cricket *m*

crime [kraɪm] *n* crime *m*; **criminal** [ˈkrɪmɪnl] *adj*, *n* criminel(le)

crimson [ˈkrɪmzn] *adj* cramoisi(e)

cringe [krɪndʒ] *vi* avoir un mouvement de recul

crinkle [ˈkrɪŋkl] *vt* froisser, chiffonner

cripple [ˈkrɪpl] *n* boiteux(-euse), infirme *m/f* ♦ *vt* estropier

crisis [ˈkraɪsɪs] (*pl* **crises**) *n* crise *f*

crisp [krɪsp] *adj* croquant(e); (*weather*) vif (vive); (*manner etc*) brusque; **~s** (*BRIT*) *npl* (pommes) chips *fpl*

crisscross [ˈkrɪskrɒs] *adj* entrecroisé(e)

criterion [kraɪˈtɪərɪən] (*pl* **criteria**) *n* critère *m*

critic [ˈkrɪtɪk] *n* critique *m*; **~al** *adj* critique; **~ally** *adv* (*examine*) d'un œil critique; (*speak etc*) sévèrement; **~ally ill** gravement malade; **~ism** [ˈkrɪtɪsɪzəm] *n* critique *f*; **~ize** [ˈkrɪtɪsaɪz] *vt* critiquer

croak [krəʊk] *vi* (*frog*) coasser; (*raven*) croasser; (*person*) parler d'une voix rauque

Croatia [krəʊˈeɪʃə] *n* Croatie *f*

crochet [ˈkrəʊʃeɪ] *n* travail *m* au crochet

crockery [ˈkrɒkərɪ] *n* vaisselle *f*

crocodile [ˈkrɒkədaɪl] *n* crocodile *m*

crocus [ˈkrəʊkəs] *n* crocus *m*

croft [krɒft] (*BRIT*) *n* petite ferme

crony [ˈkrəʊnɪ] (*inf: pej*) *n* copain (copine)

crook [krʊk] *n* escroc *m*; (*of shepherd*) houlette *f*; **~ed** [ˈkrʊkɪd] *adj* courbé(e), tordu(e); (*action*) malhonnête

crop [krɒp] *n* (*produce*) culture *f*; (*amount produced*) récolte *f*; (*riding ~*) cravache *f* ♦ *vt* (*hair*) tondre; **~ up** *vi* surgir, se présenter, survenir

cross [krɒs] *n* croix *f*; (*BIO etc*) croisement *m* ♦ *vt* (*street etc*) traverser; (*arms, legs, BIO*) croiser; (*cheque*) barrer ♦ *adj* en colère, fâché(e); **~ out** *vt* barrer, biffer; **~ over** *vi* traverser; **~bar** *n* barre (transversale); **~-country (race)** *n* cross(-country) *m*; **~-examine** *vt* (*LAW*) faire subir un examen contradictoire à; **~-eyed** *adj* qui louche; **~fire** *n* feux croisés; **~ing** *n* (*sea passage*) traversée *f*; (*also*: **pedestrian ~ing**) passage clouté; **~ing guard** (*US*) *n contractuel qui fait traverser la rue aux enfants*; **~ purposes** *npl*: **to be at ~ purposes with sb** comprendre qn de travers; **~-reference** *n* renvoi *m*, référence *f*; **~roads** *n* carrefour *m*; **~ section** *n* (*of object*) coupe transversale; (*in population*) échantillon *m*; **~walk** (*US*) *n* passage clouté; **~wind** *n* vent *m* de travers; **~word** *n* mots *mpl* croisés

crotch [krɒtʃ] *n* (*ANAT, of garment*) entrejambes *m inv*

crouch [kraʊtʃ] *vi* s'accroupir; se tapir

crow [krəʊ] *n* (*bird*) corneille *f*; (*of cock*)

chant *m* du coq, cocorico *m* ♦ *vi* (*cock*) chanter

crowbar ['krəʊbɑːʳ] *n* levier *m*

crowd [kraʊd] *n* foule *f* ♦ *vt* remplir ♦ *vi* affluer, s'attrouper, s'entasser; **to ~ in** entrer en foule; **~ed** *adj* bondé(e), plein(e)

crown [kraʊn] *n* couronne *f*; (*of head*) sommet *m* de la tête; (*of hill*) sommet ♦ *vt* couronner; **~ jewels** *npl* joyaux *mpl* de la Couronne

crow's-feet ['krəʊzfiːt] *npl* pattes *fpl* d'oie

crucial ['kruːʃl] *adj* crucial(e), décisif(-ive)

crucifix ['kruːsɪfɪks] *n* (*REL*) crucifix *m*; **~ion** [kruːsɪ'fɪkʃən] *n* (*REL*) crucifixion *f*

crude [kruːd] *adj* (*materials*) brut(e); non raffiné(e); (*fig: basic*) rudimentaire, sommaire; (: *vulgar*) cru(e), grossier(-ère); **~ (oil)** *n* (pétrole) brut *m*

cruel ['kruəl] *adj* cruel(le); **~ty** *n* cruauté *f*

cruise [kruːz] *n* croisière *f* ♦ *vi* (*ship*) croiser; (*car*) rouler; **~r** *n* croiseur *m*; (*motorboat*) yacht *m* de croisière

crumb [krʌm] *n* miette *f*

crumble ['krʌmbl] *vt* émietter ♦ *vi* (*plaster etc*) s'effriter; (*land, earth*) s'ébouler; (*building*) s'écrouler, crouler; (*fig*) s'effondrer; **crumbly** *adj* friable

crumpet ['krʌmpɪt] *n* petite crêpe (épaisse)

crumple ['krʌmpl] *vt* froisser, friper

crunch [krʌntʃ] *vt* croquer; (*underfoot*) faire craquer *or* crisser, écraser ♦ *n* (*fig*) instant *m* *or* moment *m* critique, moment de vérité; **~y** *adj* croquant(e), croustillant(e)

crusade [kruː'seɪd] *n* croisade *f*

crush [krʌʃ] *n* foule *f*, cohue *f*; (*love*): **to have a ~ on sb** avoir le béguin pour qn (*inf*); (*drink*): **lemon ~** citron pressé ♦ *vt* écraser; (*crumple*) froisser; (*fig: hopes*) anéantir

crust [krʌst] *n* croûte *f*

crutch [krʌtʃ] *n* béquille *f*

crux [krʌks] *n* point crucial

cry [kraɪ] *vi* pleurer; (*shout: also: ~ out*) crier ♦ *n* cri *m*; **~ off** (*inf*) *vi* se dédire; se décommander

cryptic ['krɪptɪk] *adj* énigmatique

crystal ['krɪstl] *n* cristal *m*; **~-clear** *adj* clair(e) comme de l'eau de roche

CSA *n abbr* (= *Child Support Agency*) organisme pour la protection des enfants de parents séparés, qui contrôle le versement des pensions alimentaires

CTC *n abbr* = **city technology college**

cub [kʌb] *n* petit *m* (*d'un animal*); (*also:* **C~ scout**) louveteau *m*

Cuba ['kjuːbə] *n* Cuba *m*

cube [kjuːb] *n* cube *m* ♦ *vt* (*MATH*) élever au cube; **cubic** *adj* cubique; **cubic metre** *etc* mètre *m* *etc* cube; **cubic capacity** *n* cylindrée *f*

cubicle ['kjuːbɪkl] *n* (*in hospital*) box *m*; (*at pool*) cabine *f*

cuckoo ['kuku:] *n* coucou *m*; **~ clock** *n* (pendule *f* à) coucou *m*

cucumber ['kjuːkʌmbəʳ] *n* concombre *m*

cuddle ['kʌdl] *vt* câliner, caresser ♦ *vi* se blottir l'un contre l'autre

cue [kjuː] *n* (*snooker ~*) queue *f* de billard; (*THEATRE etc*) signal *m*

cuff [kʌf] *n* (*BRIT: of shirt, coat etc*) poignet *m*, manchette *f*; (*US: of trousers*) revers *m*; (*blow*) tape *f*; **off the ~** à l'improviste; **~ links** *npl* boutons *mpl* de manchette

cul-de-sac ['kʌldəsæk] *n* cul-de-sac *m*, impasse *f*

cull [kʌl] *vt* sélectionner ♦ *n* (*of animals*) massacre *m*

culminate ['kʌlmɪneɪt] *vi*: **to ~ in** finir *or* se terminer par; (*end in*) mener à; **culmination** [kʌlmɪ'neɪʃən] *n* point culminant

culottes [kjuː'lɒts] *npl* jupe-culotte *f*

culprit ['kʌlprɪt] *n* coupable *m/f*

cult [kʌlt] *n* culte *m*

cultivate ['kʌltɪveɪt] *vt* cultiver; **cultivation** [kʌltɪ'veɪʃən] *n* culture *f*

cultural ['kʌltʃərəl] *adj* culturel(le)

culture ['kʌltʃəʳ] *n* culture *f*; **~d** *adj* (*person*) cultivé(e)

cumbersome ['kʌmbəsəm] *adj* encombrant(e), embarrassant(e)

cunning ['kʌnɪŋ] *n* ruse *f*, astuce *f* ♦ *adj* rusé(e), malin(-igne); (*device, idea*) astucieux(-euse)

cup [kʌp] *n* tasse *f*; (*as prize*) coupe *f*; (*of bra*) bonnet *m*

cupboard ['kʌbəd] *n* armoire *f*; (*built-in*) placard *m*

cup tie (*BRIT*) *n* match *m* de coupe

curate ['kjuərıt] *n* vicaire *m*

curator [kjuə'reıtə'] *n* conservateur *m* (*d'un musée etc*)

curb [kə:b] *vt* refréner, mettre un frein à ♦ *n* (*fig*) frein *m*, restriction *f*; (*US: kerb*) bord *m* du trottoir

curdle ['kə:dl] *vi* se cailler

cure [kjuə'] *vt* guérir; (*CULIN: salt*) saler; (*: smoke*) fumer; (*: dry*) sécher ♦ *n* remède *m*

curfew ['kə:fju:] *n* couvre-feu *m*

curiosity [kjuərı'ɔsıtı] *n* curiosité *f*

curious ['kjuərıəs] *adj* curieux(-euse)

curl [kə:l] *n* boucle *f* (de cheveux) ♦ *vt, vi* boucler; (*tightly*) friser; **~ up** *vi* s'enrouler; se pelotonner; **~er** *n* bigoudi *m*, rouleau *m*; **~y** *adj* bouclé(e); frisé(e)

currant ['kʌrnt] *n* (*dried*) raisin *m* de Corinthe, raisin sec; (*bush*) groseiller *m*; (*fruit*) groseille *f*

currency ['kʌrnsı] *n* monnaie *f*; **to gain ~** (*fig*) s'accréditer

current ['kʌrnt] *n* courant *m* ♦ *adj* courant(e); **~ account** (*BRIT*) *n* compte courant; **~ affairs** *npl* (questions *fpl* d')actualité *f*; **~ly** *adv* actuellement

curriculum [kə'rıkjuləm] (*pl* **~s** *or* **curricula**) *n* programme *m* d'études; **~ vitae** *n* curriculum vitae *m*

curry ['kʌrı] *n* curry *m* ♦ *vt*: **to ~ favour with** chercher à s'attirer les bonnes grâces de

curse [kə:s] *vi* jurer, blasphémer ♦ *vt* maudire ♦ *n* (*spell*) malédiction *f*; (*problem, scourge*) fléau *m*; (*swearword*) juron *m*

cursor ['kə:sə'] *n* (*COMPUT*) curseur *m*

cursory ['kə:sərı] *adj* superficiel(le), hâtif(-ive)

curt [kə:t] *adj* brusque, sec (sèche)

curtail [kə:'teıl] *vt* (*visit etc*) écourter; (*expenses, freedom etc*) réduire

curtain ['kə:tn] *n* rideau *m*

curts(e)y ['kə:tsı] *vi* faire une révérence

curve [kə:v] *n* courbe *f*; (*in the road*) tournant *m*, virage *m* ♦ *vi* se courber; (*road*) faire une courbe

cushion ['kuʃən] *n* coussin *m* ♦ *vt* (*fall, shock*) amortir

custard ['kʌstəd] *n* (*for pouring*) crème anglaise

custody ['kʌstədı] *n* (*of child*) garde *f*; **to take sb into ~** (*suspect*) placer qn en détention préventive

custom ['kʌstəm] *n* coutume *f*, usage *m*; (*COMM*) clientèle *f*; **~ary** *adj* habituel(le)

customer ['kʌstəmə'] *n* client(e)

customized ['kʌstəmaızd] *adj* (*car etc*) construit(e) sur commande

custom-made ['kʌstəm'meıd] *adj* (*clothes*) fait(e) sur mesure; (*other goods*) hors série, fait(e) sur commande

customs ['kʌstəmz] *npl* douane *f*; **~ officer** *n* douanier(-ière)

cut [kʌt] (*pt, pp* **cut**) *vt* couper; (*meat*) découper; (*reduce*) réduire ♦ *vi* couper ♦ *n* coupure *f*; (*of clothes*) coupe *f*; (*in salary etc*) réduction *f*; (*of meat*) morceau *m*; **to ~ one's hand** se couper la main; **to ~ a tooth** percer une dent; **~ down** *vt fus* (*tree etc*) abattre; (*consumption*) réduire; **~ off** *vt* couper; (*fig*) isoler; **~ out** *vt* découper; (*stop*) arrêter; (*remove*) ôter; **~ up** *vt* (*meat*) découper; **~back** *n* réduction *f*

cute [kju:t] *adj* mignon(ne), adorable

cutlery ['kʌtlərı] *n* couverts *mpl*

cutlet ['kʌtlıt] *n* côtelette *f*

cut: ~out *n* (*switch*) coupe-circuit *m inv*; (*cardboard cutout*) découpage *m*; **~-price** (*US* **cut-rate**) *adj* au rabais, à prix réduit; **~-throat** *n* assassin *m* ♦ *adj* acharné(e); **~ting** *adj* tranchant(e), coupant(e); (*fig*) cinglant(e), mordant(e) ♦ *n* (*BRIT: from newspaper*) coupure *f* (de journal); (*from plant*) bouture *f*

CV *n abbr* = **curriculum vitae**

cwt *abbr* = **hundredweight(s)**

cyanide ['saıənaıd] *n* cyanure *m*

cybercafé ['saıbəkæfeı] *n* cybercafé *m*

cyberspace ['saıbəspeıs] *n* cyberspace *m*

cycle ['saikl] n cycle m; (bicycle) bicyclette f, vélo m ♦ vi faire de la bicyclette; ~ hire n location f de vélos; ~ lane or path n piste f cyclable; cycling n cyclisme m; cyclist ['saiklist] n cycliste m/f

cygnet ['signit] n jeune cygne m

cylinder ['silindəʳ] n cylindre m; ~-head gasket n joint m de culasse

cymbals ['simblz] npl cymbales fpl

cynic ['sinik] n cynique m/f; ~al adj cynique; ~ism ['sinisizəm] n cynisme m

Cypriot ['sipriət] adj cypriote, chypriote ♦ n Cypriote m/f, Chypriote m/f

Cyprus ['saiprəs] n Chypre f

cyst [sist] n kyste m

cystitis [sis'taitis] n cystite f

czar [zɑːʳ] n tsar m

Czech [tʃɛk] adj tchèque ♦ n Tchèque m/f; (LING) tchèque m

Czechoslovak [tʃɛkə'sləuvæk] adj tchécoslovaque ♦ n Tchécoslovaque m/f

Czechoslovakia [tʃɛkəslə'vækiə] n Tchécoslovaquie f

D, d

D [diː] n (MUS) ré m

dab [dæb] vt (eyes, wound) tamponner; (paint, cream) appliquer (par petites touches or rapidement)

dabble ['dæbl] vi: to ~ in faire or se mêler or s'occuper un peu de

dad [dæd] n, daddy ['dædi] n papa m

daffodil ['dæfədil] n jonquille f

daft [dɑːft] adj idiot(e), stupide

dagger ['dægəʳ] n poignard m

daily ['deili] adj quotidien(ne), journalier(-ère) ♦ n quotidien m ♦ adv tous les jours

dainty ['deinti] adj délicat(e), mignon(ne)

dairy ['dɛəri] n (BRIT: shop) crémerie f, laiterie f; (on farm) laiterie; ~ products npl produits laitiers; ~ store (US) n crémerie f, laiterie f

daisy ['deizi] n pâquerette f

dale [deil] n vallon m

dam [dæm] n barrage m ♦ vt endiguer

damage ['dæmidʒ] n dégâts mpl, dommages mpl; (fig) tort m ♦ vt endommager, abîmer; (fig) faire du tort à; ~s npl (LAW) dommages-intérêts mpl

damn [dæm] vt condamner; (curse) maudire ♦ n (inf): I don't give a ~ je m'en fous ♦ adj (inf: also: ~ed): this ~ ... ce sacré or foutu ...; ~ (it)! zut!; ~ing adj accablant(e)

damp [dæmp] adj humide ♦ n humidité f ♦ vt (also: ~en: cloth, rag) humecter; (: enthusiasm) refroidir

damson ['dæmzən] n prune f de Damas

dance [dɑːns] n danse f; (social event) bal m ♦ vi danser; ~ hall n salle f de bal, dancing m; ~r n danseur(-euse); dancing n danse f

dandelion ['dændilaiən] n pissenlit m

dandruff ['dændrəf] n pellicules fpl

•Dane [dein] n Danois(e)

danger ['deindʒəʳ] n danger m; there is a ~ of fire il y a (un) risque d'incendie; in ~ en danger; he was in ~ of falling il risquait de tomber; ~ous adj dangereux(-euse)

dangle ['dæŋgl] vt balancer ♦ vi pendre

Danish ['deiniʃ] adj danois(e) ♦ n (LING) danois m

dare [dɛəʳ] vt: to ~ sb to do défier qn de faire ♦ vi: to ~ (to) do sth oser faire qch; I ~ say (I suppose) il est probable (que); daring adj hardi(e), audacieux(-euse); (dress) osé(e) ♦ n audace f, hardiesse f

dark [dɑːk] adj (night, room) obscur(e), sombre; (colour, complexion) foncé(e), sombre ♦ n: in the ~ dans le noir; in the ~ about (fig) ignorant tout de; after ~ après la tombée de la nuit; ~en vt obscurcir, assombrir ♦ vi s'obscurcir, s'assombrir; ~ glasses npl lunettes noires; ~ness n obscurité f; ~room n chambre noire

darling ['dɑːliŋ] adj chéri(e) ♦ n chéri(e); (favourite): to be the ~ of être la coqueluche de

darn [dɑːn] vt repriser, raccommoder

dart [dɑːt] n fléchette f; (sewing) pince f

♦ vi: **to ~ towards** (also: **make a ~ towards**) se précipiter or s'élancer vers; **to ~ away/along** partir/passer comme une flèche; **~board** n cible f (de jeu de fléchettes); **~s** n (jeu m de) fléchettes fpl

dash [dæʃ] n (sign) tiret m; (small quantity) goutte f, larme f ♦ vt (missile) jeter or lancer violemment; (hopes) anéantir ♦ vi: **to ~ towards** (also: **make a ~ towards**) se précipiter or se ruer vers; **~ away** vi partir à toute allure, filer; **~ off** vi = **dash away**

dashboard ['dæʃbɔːd] n (AUT) tableau m de bord

dashing ['dæʃɪŋ] adj fringant(e)

data ['deɪtə] npl données fpl; **~base** n (COMPUT) base f de données; **~ processing** n traitement m de données

date [deɪt] n date f; (with sb) rendez-vous m; (fruit) datte f ♦ vt dater; (person) sortir avec; **~ of birth** date de naissance; **to ~** (until now) à ce jour; **out of ~** (passport) périmé(e); (theory etc) dépassé(e); (clothes etc) démodé(e); **up to ~** moderne; (news) très récent; **~d** ['deɪtɪd] adj démodé(e); **~ rape** n viol m (à l'issue d'un rendez-vous galant)

daub [dɔːb] vt barbouiller

daughter ['dɔːtər] n fille f; **~-in-law** n belle-fille f, bru f

daunting ['dɔːntɪŋ] adj décourageant(e)

dawdle ['dɔːdl] vi traîner, lambiner

dawn [dɔːn] n aube f, aurore f ♦ vi (day) se lever, poindre; (fig): **it ~ed on him that ...** il lui vint à l'esprit que ...

day [deɪ] n jour m; (as duration) journée f; (period of time, age) époque f, temps m; **the ~ before** la veille, le jour précédent; **the ~ after, the following ~** le lendemain, le jour suivant; **the ~ after tomorrow** après-demain; **the ~ before yesterday** avant-hier; **by ~** de jour; **~break** n point m du jour; **~dream** vi rêver (tout éveillé), **~light** n (lumière f du) jour m; **~ return** (BRIT) n billet m d'aller-retour (valable pour la journée); **~time** n jour m, journée f; **~-to-~** adj quotidien(ne);

(event) journalier(-ère)

daze [deɪz] vt (stun) étourdir ♦ n: **in a ~** étourdi(e), hébété(e)

dazzle ['dæzl] vt éblouir, aveugler

DC abbr (= direct current) courant continu

D-day ['diːdeɪ] n le jour J

dead [ded] adj mort(e); (numb) engourdi(e), insensible; (battery) à plat; (telephone): **the line is ~** la ligne est coupée ♦ adv absolument, complètement ♦ npl: **the ~** les morts; **he was shot ~** il a été tué d'un coup de revolver; **~ on time** à l'heure pile; **~ tired** éreinté(e), complètement fourbu(e); **to stop ~** s'arrêter pile or net; **~en** vt (blow, sound) amortir; (pain) calmer; **~ end** n impasse f; **~ heat** n (SPORT): **to finish in a ~ heat** terminer ex-æquo; **~line** n date f or heure f limite; **~lock** n (fig) impasse f; **~ loss** n: **to be a ~ loss** (inf: person) n'être bon(ne) à rien; **~ly** adj mortel(le); (weapon) meurtrier(-ère); (accuracy) extrême; **~pan** adj impassible; **D~ Sea** n: **the D~ Sea** la mer Morte

deaf [def] adj sourd(e); **~en** vt rendre sourd; **~ening** adj assourdissant(e); **~-mute** n sourd(e)-muet(te); **~ness** n surdité f

deal [diːl] n (pt, pp dealt) n affaire f, marché m ♦ vt (blow) porter; (cards) donner, distribuer; **a great ~ (of)** beaucoup (de); **~ in** vt fus faire le commerce de; **~ with** vt fus (person, problem) s'occuper or se charger de; (be about: book etc) traiter de; **~er** n marchand m; **~ings** npl (COMM) transactions fpl; (relations) relations fpl, rapports mpl

dean [diːn] n (REL, BRIT: SCOL) doyen m; (US: SCOL) conseiller(-ère) (principal(e)) d'éducation

dear [dɪər] adj cher (chère); (expensive) cher, coûteux(-euse) ♦ n: **my ~** mon cher/ma chère; **~ me!** mon Dieu!; **D~ Sir/Madam** (in letter) Monsieur/Madame; **D~ Mr/Mrs X** Cher Monsieur/Chère Madame; **~ly** adv (love) tendrement; (pay) cher

death [deθ] *n* mort *f*; (*fatality*) mort *m*; (*ADMIN*) décès *m*; ~ **certificate** *n* acte *m* de décès; ~**ly** *adj* de mort; ~ **penalty** *n* peine *f* de mort; ~ **rate** *n* (taux *m* de) mortalité *f*; ~ **toll** *n* nombre *m* de morts

debase [dɪ'beɪs] *vt* (*value*) déprécier, dévaloriser

debatable [dɪ'beɪtəbl] *adj* discutable

debate [dɪ'beɪt] *n* discussion *f*, débat *m* ♦ *vt* discuter, débattre

debit ['debɪt] *n* débit *m* ♦ *vt*: **to ~ a sum to sb** *or* **to sb's account** porter une somme au débit de qn, débiter qn d'une somme; *see also* **direct**

debt [det] *n* dette *f*; **to be in ~** avoir des dettes, être endetté(e); ~**or** *n* débiteur(-trice)

decade ['dekeɪd] *n* décennie *f*, décade *f*

decadence ['dekədəns] *n* décadence *f*

decaff ['di:kæf] (*inf*) *n* déca *m*

decaffeinated [dɪ'kæfɪneɪtɪd] *adj* décaféiné(e)

decanter [dɪ'kæntər] *n* carafe *f*

decay [dɪ'keɪ] *n* (*of building*) délabrement *m*; (*also:* **tooth ~**) carie *f* (dentaire) ♦ *vi* (*rot*) se décomposer, pourrir; (: *teeth*) se carier

deceased [dɪ'si:st] *n* défunt(e)

deceit [dɪ'si:t] *n* tromperie *f*, supercherie *f*; ~**ful** *adj* trompeur(-euse); **deceive** *vt* tromper

December [dɪ'sembər] *n* décembre *m*

decent ['di:sənt] *adj* décent(e), convenable

deception [dɪ'sepʃən] *n* tromperie *f*

deceptive [dɪ'septɪv] *adj* trompeur(-euse)

decide [dɪ'saɪd] *vt* (*person*) décider; (*question, argument*) trancher, régler ♦ *vi* se décider, décider; **to ~ to do/that** décider de faire/que; **to ~ on** décider, se décider pour; ~**d** *adj* (*resolute*) résolu(e), décidé(e); (*clear, definite*) net(te), marqué(e); ~**dly** *adv* résolument; (*distinctly*) incontestablement, nettement

deciduous [dɪ'sɪdjuəs] *adj* à feuilles caduques

decimal ['desɪməl] *adj* décimal(e) ♦ *n* décimale *f*; ~ **point** *n* ≃ virgule *f*

decipher [dɪ'saɪfər] *vt* déchiffrer

decision [dɪ'sɪʒən] *n* décision *f*

decisive [dɪ'saɪsɪv] *adj* décisif(-ive); (*person*) décidé(e)

deck [dek] *n* (*NAUT*) pont *m*; (*of bus*): **top ~** impériale *f*; (*of cards*) jeu *m*; (*record ~*) platine *f*; ~**chair** *n* chaise longue

declare [dɪ'kleər] *vt* déclarer

decline [dɪ'klaɪn] *n* (*decay*) déclin *m*; (*lessening*) baisse *f* ♦ *vt* refuser, décliner ♦ *vi* décliner; (*business*) baisser

decoder [di:'kəudər] *n* (*TV*) décodeur *m*

decorate ['dekəreɪt] *vt* (*adorn, give a medal to*) décorer; (*paint and paper*) peindre et tapisser; **decoration** [dekə'reɪʃən] *n* (*medal etc, adornment*) décoration *f*; **decorator** *n* peintre-décorateur *m*

decoy ['di:kɔɪ] *n* piège *m*; (*person*) compère *m*

decrease [*n* 'di:kri:s, *vb* di:'kri:s] *n*: ~ **(in)** diminution *f* (de) ♦ *vt, vi* diminuer

decree [dɪ'kri:] *n* (*POL, REL*) décret *m*; (*LAW*) arrêt *m*, jugement *m*; ~ **nisi** [-'naɪsaɪ] *n* jugement *m* provisoire de divorce

dedicate ['dedɪkeɪt] *vt* consacrer; (*book etc*) dédier; ~**d** *adj* (*person*) dévoué(e); (*COMPUT*) spécialisé(e), dédié(e); **dedication** [dedɪ'keɪʃən] *n* (*devotion*) dévouement *m*; (*in book*) dédicace *f*

deduce [dɪ'dju:s] *vt* déduire, conclure

deduct [dɪ'dʌkt] *vt*: **to ~ sth (from)** déduire qch (de), retrancher qch (de); ~**ion** *n* (*deducting, deducing*) déduction *f*; (*from wage etc*) prélèvement *m*, retenue *f*

deed [di:d] *n* action *f*, acte *m*; (*LAW*) acte notarié, contrat *m*

deep [di:p] *adj* profond(e); (*voice*) grave ♦ *adv*: **spectators stood 20 ~** il y avait 20 rangs de spectateurs; **4 metres ~** de 4 mètres de profondeur; ~ **end** (*of swimming pool*) grand bain; ~**en** *vt* approfondir ♦ *vi* (*fig*) s'épaissir; ~**freeze** *n* congélateur *m*; ~**fry** *vt* faire frire (en friteuse); ~**ly** *adv* profondément; (*interested*) vivement; ~**-sea diver** *n* sous-marin(e); ~**-sea diving** *n* plongée sous-marine; ~**-sea fishing** *n* grande pêche; ~**-seated** *adj* profond(e), profondément enraciné(e)

deer [dɪəʳ] *n inv*: **(red) ~** cerf *m*, biche *f*; **(fallow) ~** daim *m*; **(roe) ~** chevreuil *m*; **~skin** *n* daim

deface [dɪ'feɪs] *vt* dégrader; (*notice, poster*) barbouiller

default [dɪ'fɔ:lt] *n* (COMPUT: *also*: **~ value**) valeur *f* par défaut; **by ~** (LAW) par défaut, par contumace; (SPORT) par forfait

defeat [dɪ'fi:t] *n* défaite *f* ♦ *vt* (*team, opponents*) battre

defect [*n* 'di:fekt, *vb* dɪ'fekt] *n* défaut *m* ♦ *vi*: **to ~ to the enemy** passer à l'ennemi; **~ive** [dɪ'fektɪv] *adj* défectueux(-euse)

defence [dɪ'fens] (US **defense**) *n* défense *f*; **~less** *adj* sans défense

defend [dɪ'fend] *vt* défendre; **~ant** *n* défendeur(-deresse); (*in criminal case*) accusé(e), prévenu(e); **~er** *n* défenseur *m*

defer [dɪ'fə:ʳ] *vt* (*postpone*) différer, ajourner

defiance [dɪ'faɪəns] *n* défi *m*; **in ~ of** au mépris de; **defiant** *adj* provocant(e), de défi; (*person*) rebelle, intraitable

deficiency [dɪ'fɪʃənsɪ] *n* insuffisance *f*, déficience *f*; **deficient** *adj* (*inadequate*) insuffisant(e); **to be deficient in** manquer de

deficit ['defɪsɪt] *n* déficit *m*

define [dɪ'faɪn] *vt* définir

definite ['defɪnɪt] *adj* (*fixed*) défini(e), (bien) déterminé(e); (*clear, obvious*) net(te), manifeste; (*certain*) sûr(e); **he was ~ about it** il a été catégorique; **~ly** *adv* sans aucun doute

definition [defɪ'nɪʃən] *n* définition *f*; (*clearness*) netteté *f*

deflate [di:'fleɪt] *vt* dégonfler

deflect [dɪ'flekt] *vt* détourner, faire dévier

deformed [dɪ'fɔ:md] *adj* difforme

defraud [dɪ'frɔ:d] *vt* frauder; **to ~ sb of sth** escroquer qch à qn

defrost [di:'frɔst] *vt* dégivrer; (*food*) décongeler; **~er** (US) *n* (*demister*) dispositif *m* anti-buée *inv*

deft [deft] *adj* adroit(e), preste

defunct [dɪ'fʌŋkt] *adj* défunt(e)

defuse [di:'fju:z] *vt* désamorcer

defy [dɪ'faɪ] *vt* défier; (*efforts etc*) résister à

degenerate [*vb* dɪ'dʒenəreɪt, *adj* dɪ'dʒenərənt] *vi* dégénérer ♦ *adj* dégénéré(e)

degree [dɪ'gri:] *n* degré *m*; (SCOL) diplôme *m* (universitaire); **a (first) ~ in maths** une licence en maths; **by ~s** (*gradually*) par degrés; **to some ~, to a certain ~** jusqu'à un certain point, dans une certaine mesure

dehydrated [di:haɪ'dreɪtɪd] *adj* déshydraté(e); (*milk, eggs*) en poudre

de-ice ['di:'aɪs] *vt* (*windscreen*) dégivrer

deign [deɪn] *vi*: **to ~ to do** daigner faire

dejected [dɪ'dʒektɪd] *adj* abattu(e), déprimé(e)

delay [dɪ'leɪ] *vt* retarder ♦ *vi* s'attarder ♦ *n* délai *m*, retard *m*; **to be ~ed** être en retard

delectable [dɪ'lektəbl] *adj* délicieux(-euse)

delegate [*n* 'delɪgɪt, *vb* 'delɪgeɪt] *n* délégué(e) ♦ *vt* déléguer

delete [dɪ'li:t] *vt* rayer, supprimer

deliberate [*adj* dɪ'lɪbərɪt, *vb* dɪ'lɪbəreɪt] *adj* (*intentional*) délibéré(e); (*slow*) mesuré(e) ♦ *vi* délibérer, réfléchir; **~ly** [dɪ'lɪbərɪtlɪ] *adv* (*on purpose*) exprès, délibérément

delicacy ['delɪkəsɪ] *n* délicatesse *f*; (*food*) mets fin *or* délicat, friandise *f*

delicate ['delɪkɪt] *adj* délicat(e)

delicatessen [delɪkə'tesn] *n* épicerie fine

delicious [dɪ'lɪʃəs] *adj* délicieux(-euse)

delight [dɪ'laɪt] *n* (grande) joie, grand plaisir ♦ *vt* enchanter; **to take (a) ~ in** prendre grand plaisir à; **~ed** *adj*: **~ed (at** *or* **with/to do)** ravi(e) (de/de faire); **~ful** *adj* (*person*) adorable; (*meal, evening*) merveilleux(-euse)

delinquent [dɪ'lɪŋkwənt] *adj, n* délinquant(e)

delirious [dɪ'lɪrɪəs] *adj*: **to be ~** délirer

deliver [dɪ'lɪvəʳ] *vt* (*mail*) distribuer; (*goods*) livrer; (*message*) remettre; (*speech*) prononcer; (MED: *baby*) mettre au monde; **~y** *n* distribution *f*; livraison *f*; (*of speaker*) élocution *f*; (MED) accouchement *m*; **to take ~y of** prendre livraison de

delude [dɪ'luːd] *vt* tromper, leurrer; **delusion** *n* illusion *f*

demand [dɪ'mɑːnd] *vt* réclamer, exiger ♦ *n* exigence *f*; (*claim*) revendication *f*; (*ECON*) demande *f*; **in ~** demandé(e), recherché(e); **on ~** sur demande; **~ing** *adj* (*person*) exigeant(e); (*work*) astreignant(e)

demean [dɪ'miːn] *vt*: **to ~ o.s.** s'abaisser

demeanour [dɪ'miːnəʳ] (*US* **demeanor**) *n* comportement *m*; maintien *m*

demented [dɪ'mɛntɪd] *adj* dément(e), fou (folle)

demise [dɪ'maɪz] *n* mort *f*

demister [diː'mɪstəʳ] (*BRIT*) *n* (*AUT*) dispositif *m* anti-buée *inv*

demo ['dɛməu] (*inf*) *n* *abbr* (= *demonstration*) manif *f*

democracy [dɪ'mɒkrəsɪ] *n* démocratie *f*; **democrat** ['dɛməkræt] *n* démocrate *m/f*; **democratic** [dɛmə'krætɪk] *adj* démocratique

demolish [dɪ'mɒlɪʃ] *vt* démolir

demonstrate ['dɛmənstreɪt] *vt* démontrer, prouver; (*show*) faire une démonstration de ♦ *vi*: **to ~ (for/against)** manifester (en faveur de/contre); **demonstration** [dɛmən'streɪʃən] *n* démonstration *f*, manifestation *f*; **demonstrator** *n* (*POL*) manifestant(e)

demote [dɪ'məut] *vt* rétrograder

demure [dɪ'mjuəʳ] *adj* sage, réservé(e)

den [dɛn] *n* tanière *f*, antre *m*

denial [dɪ'naɪəl] *n* démenti *m*; (*refusal*) dénégation *f*

denim ['dɛnɪm] *n* jean *m*; **~s** *npl* (*jeans*) (blue-)jean(s) *m(pl)*

Denmark ['dɛnmɑːk] *n* Danemark *m*

denomination [dɪnɒmɪ'neɪʃən] *n* (*of money*) valeur *f*; (*REL*) confession *f*

denounce [dɪ'nauns] *vt* dénoncer

dense [dɛns] *adj* dense; (*stupid*) obtus(e), bouché(e); **~ly** *adv*: **~ly populated** à forte densité de population; **density** ['dɛnsɪtɪ] *n* densité *f*; **double/high-density diskette** disquette *f* double densité/haute densité

dent [dɛnt] *n* bosse *f* ♦ *vt* (*also*: **make a ~ in**) cabosser

dental ['dɛntl] *adj* dentaire; **~ surgeon** *n* (chirurgien(ne)) dentiste

dentist ['dɛntɪst] *n* dentiste *m/f*

dentures ['dɛntʃəz] *npl* dentier *m sg*

deny [dɪ'naɪ] *vt* nier; (*refuse*) refuser

deodorant [diː'əudərənt] *n* déodorant *m*, désodorisant *m*

depart [dɪ'pɑːt] *vi* partir; **to ~ from** (*fig: differ from*) s'écarter de

department [dɪ'pɑːtmənt] *n* (*COMM*) rayon *m*; (*SCOL*) section *f*; (*POL*) ministère *m*, département *m*; **~ store** *n* grand magasin

departure [dɪ'pɑːtʃəʳ] *n* départ *m*; **a new ~** une nouvelle voie; **~ lounge** *n* (*at airport*) salle *f* d'embarquement

depend [dɪ'pɛnd] *vi*: **to ~ on** dépendre de; (*rely on*) compter sur; **it ~s** cela dépend; **~ing on the result** selon le résultat; **~able** *adj* (*person*) sérieux(-euse), sûr(e); (*car, watch*) solide, fiable; **~ant** *n* personne *f* à charge; **~ent** *adj*: **to be ~ent (on)** dépendre (de) ♦ *n* = **dependant**

depict [dɪ'pɪkt] *vt* (*in picture*) représenter; (*in words*) (dé)peindre, décrire

depleted [dɪ'pliːtɪd] *adj* (considérablement) réduit(e) *or* diminué(e)

deport [dɪ'pɔːt] *vt* expulser

deposit [dɪ'pɒzɪt] *n* (*CHEM, COMM, GEO*) dépôt *m*; (*of ore, oil*) gisement *m*; (*part payment*) arrhes *fpl*, acompte *m*; (*on bottle etc*) consigne *f*; (*for hired goods etc*) cautionnement *m*, garantie *f* ♦ *vt* déposer; **~ account** *n* compte *m* sur livret

depot ['dɛpəu] *n* dépôt *m*; (*US: RAIL*) gare *f*

depress [dɪ'prɛs] *vt* déprimer; (*press down*) appuyer sur, abaisser; (*prices, wages*) faire baisser; **~ed** *adj* (*person*) déprimé(e); (*area*) en déclin, touché(e) par le sous-emploi; **~ing** *adj* déprimant(e); **~ion** *n* dépression *f*; (*hollow*) creux *m*

deprivation [dɛprɪ'veɪʃən] *n* privation *f*, (*loss*) perte *f*

deprive [dɪ'praɪv] *vt*: **to ~ sb of** priver qn de; **~d** *adj* déshérité(e)

depth [dɛpθ] *n* profondeur *f*; **in the ~s of despair** au plus profond du désespoir; **to be out of one's ~** avoir perdu pied, nager

deputize ['depjutaɪz] *vi*: **to ~ for** assurer l'intérim de

deputy ['depjutɪ] *adj* adjoint(e) ♦ *n* (*second in command*) adjoint(e); (*US: also:* **~ sheriff**) shérif adjoint; **~ head** directeur adjoint, sous-directeur *m*

derail [dɪ'reɪl] *vt*: **to be ~ed** dérailler

deranged [dɪ'reɪndʒd] *adj*: **to be (mentally) ~** avoir le cerveau dérangé

derby ['dɑːrbɪ] (*US*) *n* (*bowler hat*) (chapeau *m*) melon *m*

derelict ['derɪlɪkt] *adj* abandonné(e), à l'abandon

derisory [dɪ'raɪsərɪ] *adj* (*sum*) dérisoire; (*smile, person*) moqueur(-euse)

derive [dɪ'raɪv] *vt*: **to ~ sth from** tirer qch de; trouver qch dans ♦ *vi*: **~ from** provenir de, dériver de

derogatory [dɪ'rɒgətərɪ] *adj* désobligeant(e); péjoratif(-ive)

descend [dɪ'send] *vt, vi* descendre; **to ~ from** descendre de, être issu(e) de; **to ~ to (doing) sth** s'abaisser à (faire) qch; **descent** *n* descente *f*; (*origin*) origine *f*

describe [dɪs'kraɪb] *vt* décrire; **description** [dɪs'krɪpʃən] *n* description *f*; (*sort*) sorte *f*, espèce *f*

desecrate ['desɪkreɪt] *vt* profaner

desert [*n* 'dezət, *vb* dɪ'zɜːt] *n* désert *m* ♦ *vt* déserter, abandonner ♦ *vi* (*MIL*) déserter; **~s** *npl*: **to get one's just ~s** n'avoir que ce qu'on mérite; **~er** [dɪ'zɜːtər] *n* déserteur *m*; **~ion** [dɪ'zɜːʃən] *n* (*MIL*) désertion *f*; (*LAW: of spouse*) abandon *m* du domicile conjugal; **~ island** *n* île déserte

deserve [dɪ'zɜːv] *vt* mériter; **deserving** *adj* (*person*) méritant(e); (*action, cause*) méritoire

design [dɪ'zaɪn] *n* (*sketch*) plan *m*, dessin *m*; (*layout, shape*) conception *f*, ligne *f*; (*pattern*) dessin *m*, motif(s) *m(pl)*; (*COMM, art*) design *m*, stylisme *m*; (*intention*) dessein *m* ♦ *vt* dessiner; élaborer; **~er** *n* (*TECH*) concepteur-projeteur *m*; (*ART*) dessinateur(-trice), designer *m*; (*fashion*) styliste *m/f*

desire [dɪ'zaɪər] *n* désir *m* ♦ *vt* désirer

desk [desk] *n* (*in office*) bureau *m*; (*for pupil*) pupitre *m*; (*BRIT: in shop, restaurant*) caisse *f*; (*in hotel, at airport*) réception *f*; **~-top publishing** *n* publication assistée par ordinateur, PAO *f*

desolate ['desəlɪt] *adj* désolé(e); (*person*) affligé(e)

despair [dɪs'peər] *n* désespoir *m* ♦ *vi*: **to ~ of** désespérer de

despatch [dɪs'pætʃ] *n, vt* = **dispatch**

desperate ['despərɪt] *adj* désespéré(e); (*criminal*) prêt(e) à tout; **to be ~ for sth/ to do sth** avoir désespérément besoin de qch/de faire qch; **~ly** *adv* désespérément; (*very*) terriblement, extrêmement; **desperation** [despə'reɪʃən] *n* désespoir *m*; **in (sheer) desperation** en désespoir de cause

despicable [dɪs'pɪkəbl] *adj* méprisable

despise [dɪs'paɪz] *vt* mépriser

despite [dɪs'paɪt] *prep* malgré, en dépit de

despondent [dɪs'pɒndənt] *adj* découragé(e), abattu(e)

dessert [dɪ'zɜːt] *n* dessert *m*; **~spoon** *n* cuiller *f* à dessert

destination [destɪ'neɪʃən] *n* destination *f*

destined ['destɪnd] *adj*: **to be ~ to do/for sth** être destiné(e) à faire/à qch

destiny ['destɪnɪ] *n* destinée *f*, destin *m*

destitute ['destɪtjuːt] *adj* indigent(e)

destroy [dɪs'trɔɪ] *vt* détruire; (*injured horse*) abattre; (*dog*) faire piquer; **~er** *n* (*NAUT*) contre-torpilleur *m*

destruction [dɪs'trʌkʃən] *n* destruction *f*

detach [dɪ'tætʃ] *vt* détacher; **~ed** *adj* (*attitude, person*) détaché(e); **~ed house** *n* pavillon *m*, maison(nette) (individuelle); **~ment** *n* (*MIL*) détachement *m*; (*fig*) détachement, indifférence *f*

detail ['diːteɪl] *n* détail *m* ♦ *vt* raconter en détail, énumérer; **in ~** en détail; **~ed** *adj* détaillé(e)

detain [dɪ'teɪn] *vt* retenir; (*in captivity*) détenir; (*in hospital*) hospitaliser

detect [dɪ'tekt] *vt* déceler, percevoir; (*MED, POLICE*) dépister; (*MIL, RADAR, TECH*) détecter; **~ion** n découverte f; **~ive** n agent m de la sûreté, policier m; **private ~ive** détective privé; **~ive story** n roman policier

detention [dɪ'tɛnʃən] n détention f; (SCOL) retenue f, consigne f

deter [dɪ'təːʳ] vt dissuader

detergent [dɪ'təːdʒənt] n détergent m, détersif m

deteriorate [dɪ'tɪərɪəreɪt] vi se détériorer, se dégrader

determine [dɪ'təːmɪn] vt déterminer; **to ~ to do** résoudre de faire, se déterminer à faire; **~d** adj (person) déterminé(e), décidé(e)

deterrent [dɪ'tɛrənt] n effet m de dissuasion; force f de dissuasion

detest [dɪ'tɛst] vt détester, avoir horreur de

detonate ['dɛtəneɪt] vt faire détoner or exploser

detour ['diːtuəʳ] n détour m; (US: AUT: diversion) déviation f

detract [dɪ'trækt] vt: **to ~ from** (quality, pleasure) diminuer; (reputation) porter atteinte à

detriment ['dɛtrɪmənt] n: **to the ~ of** au détriment de, au préjudice de; **~al** [dɛtrɪ'mɛntl] adj: **~al to** préjudiciable or nuisible à

devaluation [dɪvæljuːˈeɪʃən] n dévaluation f

devastate ['dɛvəsteɪt] vt dévaster; **~d** adj (fig) anéanti(e); **devastating** adj dévastateur(-trice); (news) accablant(e)

develop [dɪ'vɛləp] vt (gen) développer; (disease) commencer à souffrir de; (resources) mettre en valeur, exploiter ♦ vi se développer; (situation, disease: evolve) évoluer; (facts, symptoms: appear) se manifester, se produire; **~ing country** pays m en voie de développement; **the machine has ~ed a fault** un problème s'est manifesté dans cette machine; **~er** [dɪ'vɛləpəʳ] n (also: **property ~er**) promoteur m; **~ment** [dɪ'vɛləpmənt] n développement m; (of affair, case) rebondissement m, fait(s) nouveau(x)

device [dɪ'vaɪs] n (apparatus) engin m, dispositif m

devil ['dɛvl] n diable m; démon m

devious ['diːvɪəs] adj (person) sournois(e), dissimulé(e)

devise [dɪ'vaɪz] vt imaginer, concevoir

devoid [dɪ'vɔɪd] adj: **~ of** dépourvu(e) de, dénué(e) de

devolution [diːvə'luːʃən] n (POL) décentralisation f

devote [dɪ'vəut] vt: **to ~ sth to** consacrer qch à; **~d** [dɪ'vəutɪd] adj dévoué(e); **to be ~d to** (book etc) être consacré(e) à; (person) être très attaché(e) à; **~e** [dɛvəu'tiː] n (REL) adepte m/f; (MUS, SPORT) fervent(e); **devotion** n dévouement m, attachement m; (REL) dévotion f, piété f

devour [dɪ'vauəʳ] vt dévorer

devout [dɪ'vaut] adj pieux(-euse), dévot(e)

dew [djuː] n rosée f

diabetes [daɪə'biːtiːz] n diabète m; **diabetic** [daɪə'bɛtɪk] adj diabétique ♦ n diabétique m/f

diabolical [daɪə'bɔlɪkl] (inf) adj (weather) atroce; (behaviour) infernal(e)

diagnosis [daɪəg'nəusɪs] (pl **diagnoses**) n diagnostic m

diagonal [daɪ'ægənl] adj diagonal(e) ♦ n diagonale f

diagram ['daɪəgræm] n diagramme m, schéma m

dial ['daɪəl] n cadran m ♦ vt (number) faire, composer

dialect ['daɪəlɛkt] n dialecte m

dialling code (BRIT) n indicatif m (téléphonique)

dialling tone (BRIT) n tonalité f

dialogue ['daɪəlɔg] n dialogue m

dial tone (US) n = **dialling tone**

diameter [daɪ'æmɪtəʳ] n diamètre m

diamond ['daɪəmənd] n diamant m; (shape) losange m; **~s** npl (CARDS) carreau m

diaper ['daɪəpəʳ] (US) n couche f

diaphragm ['daɪəfræm] n diaphragme m

diarrhoea [daɪə'riːə] (US **diarrhea**) n diarrhée f

diary ['daɪərɪ] n (daily account) journal m

(*book*) agenda *m*

dice [daɪs] *n inv* dé *m* ♦ *vt* (*CULIN*) couper en dés *or* en cubes

dictate [dɪk'teɪt] *vt* dicter; **dictation** *n* dictée *f*

dictator [dɪk'teɪtər] *n* dictateur *m*; **~ship** *n* dictature *f*

dictionary [ˈdɪkʃənrɪ] *n* dictionnaire *m*

did [dɪd] *pt of* **do**; **~n't = did not**

die [daɪ] *vi* mourir; **to be dying for sth** avoir une envie folle de qch; **to be dying to do sth** mourir d'envie de faire qch; **~ away** *vi* s'éteindre; **~ down** *vi* se calmer, s'apaiser; **~ out** *vi* disparaître

diesel [ˈdiːzl] *n* (*vehicle*) diesel *m*; (*also:* **~ oil**) carburant *m* diesel, gas-oil *m*; **~ engine** *n* moteur *m* diesel

diet [ˈdaɪət] *n* alimentation *f*; (*restricted food*) régime *m* ♦ *vi* (*also:* **be on a ~**) suivre un régime

differ [ˈdɪfər] *vi* (*be different*): **to ~ (from)** être différent (de); différer (de); (*disagree*): **to ~ (from sb over sth)** ne pas être d'accord (avec qn au sujet de qch); **~ence** *n* différence *f*; (*quarrel*) différend *m*, désaccord *m*; **~ent** *adj* différent(e); **~entiate** [dɪfəˈrenʃɪeɪt] *vi*: **to ~entiate (between)** faire une différence (entre)

difficult [ˈdɪfɪkəlt] *adj* difficile; **~y** *n* difficulté *f*

diffident [ˈdɪfɪdənt] *adj* qui manque de confiance *or* d'assurance

dig [dɪg] (*pt, pp* **dug**) *vt* (*hole*) creuser; (*garden*) bêcher ♦ *n* (*prod*) coup *m* de coude; (*fig*) coup *m* de griffe *or* de patte; (*archeological*) fouilles *fpl*; **~ in** *vi* (*MIL: also:* **~ o.s. in**) se retrancher; **~ into** *vt fus* (*savings*) puiser dans; **to ~ one's nails into sth** enfoncer ses ongles dans qch; **~ up** *vt* déterrer

digest [*vb* daɪˈdʒɛst, *n* ˈdaɪdʒɛst] *vt* digérer ♦ *n* sommaire *m*, résumé *m*; **~ion** [dɪˈdʒɛstʃən] *n* digestion *f*

digit [ˈdɪdʒɪt] *n* (*number*) chiffre *m*; (*finger*) doigt *m*; **~al** *adj* digital(e), à affichage numérique *or* digital; **~al camera** appareil *m* photo numérique; **~al computer** cal-

culateur *m* numérique; **~al TV** télévision *f* numérique; **~al watch** montre *f* à affichage numérique

dignified [ˈdɪgnɪfaɪd] *adj* digne

dignity [ˈdɪgnɪtɪ] *n* dignité *f*

digress [daɪˈgrɛs] *vi*: **to ~ from** s'écarter de, s'éloigner de

digs [dɪgz] (*BRIT: inf*) *npl* piaule *f*, chambre meublée

dilapidated [dɪˈlæpɪdeɪtɪd] *adj* délabré(e)

dilemma [daɪˈlɛmə] *n* dilemme *m*

diligent [ˈdɪlɪdʒənt] *adj* appliqué(e)

dilute [daɪˈluːt] *vt* diluer

dim [dɪm] *adj* (*light*) faible; (*memory, outline*) vague, indécis(e); (*room*) sombre; (*stupid*) borné(e), obtus(e) ♦ *vt* (*light*) réduire, baisser; (*US: AUT*) mettre en code

dime [daɪm] (*US*) *n* = **10 cents**

dimension [daɪˈmɛnʃən] *n* dimension *f*

diminish [dɪˈmɪnɪʃ] *vt, vi* diminuer

diminutive [dɪˈmɪnjutɪv] *adj* minuscule, tout(e) petit(e)

dimmers [ˈdɪməz] (*US*) *npl* (*AUT*) phares *mpl* code *inv*; feux *mpl* de position

dimple [ˈdɪmpl] *n* fossette *f*

din [dɪn] *n* vacarme *m*

dine [daɪn] *vi* dîner; **~r** *n* (*person*) dîneur(-euse); (*US: restaurant*) petit restaurant

dinghy [ˈdɪŋgɪ] *n* youyou *m*; (*also:* **rubber ~**) canot *m* pneumatique; (*also:* **sailing ~**) voilier *m*, dériveur *m*

dingy [ˈdɪndʒɪ] *adj* miteux(-euse), minable

dining car (*BRIT*) *n* wagon-restaurant *m*

dining room *n* salle *f* à manger

dinner [ˈdɪnər] *n* dîner *m*; (*lunch*) déjeuner *m*; (*public*) banquet *m*; **~ jacket** *n* smoking *m*; **~ party** *n* dîner *m*; **~ time** *n* heure *f* du dîner; (*midday*) heure du déjeuner

dinosaur [ˈdaɪnəsɔːr] *n* dinosaure *m*

dip [dɪp] *n* déclivité *f*; (*in sea*) baignade *f*, bain *m*; (*CULIN*) ≃ sauce *f* ♦ *vt* tremper, plonger; (*BRIT: AUT: lights*) mettre en code, baisser ♦ *vi* plonger

diploma [dɪˈpləʊmə] *n* diplôme *m*

diplomacy [dɪˈpləʊməsɪ] *n* diplomatie *f*

diplomat [ˈdɪpləmæt] *n* diplomate *m*; **~ic**

[dɪpləˈmætɪk] *adj* diplomatique
dipstick [ˈdɪpstɪk] *n* (AUT) jauge *f* de niveau d'huile
dipswitch [ˈdɪpswɪtʃ] (BRIT) *n* (AUT) interrupteur *m* de lumière réduite
dire [daɪəʳ] *adj* terrible, extrême, affreux(-euse)
direct [daɪˈrɛkt] *adj* direct(e) ♦ *vt* diriger, orienter; (*letter, remark*) adresser; (*film, programme*) réaliser; (*play*) mettre en scène; (*order*) : **to ~ sb to do sth** ordonner à qn de faire qch ♦ *adv* directement; **can you ~ me to ...?** pouvez-vous m'indiquer le chemin de ...?; **~ debit** (BRIT) *n* prélèvement *m* automatique
direction [dɪˈrɛkʃən] *n* direction *f*; **~s** *npl* (*advice*) indications *fpl*; **sense of ~** sens *m* de l'orientation; **~s for use** mode *m* d'emploi
directly [dɪˈrɛktlɪ] *adv* (*in a straight line*) directement, tout droit; (*at once*) tout de suite, immédiatement
director [dɪˈrɛktəʳ] *n* directeur *m*; (THEATRE) metteur *m* en scène; (CINEMA, TV) réalisateur(-trice)
directory [dɪˈrɛktərɪ] *n* annuaire *m*; (COMPUT) répertoire *m*; **~ enquiries** (US **directory assistance**) *n* renseignements *mpl*
dirt [dəːt] *n* saleté *f*; crasse *f*; (*earth*) terre *f*, boue *f*; **~-cheap** *adj* très bon marché *inv*; **~y** *adj* sale ♦ *vt* salir; **~y trick** coup tordu
disability [dɪsəˈbɪlɪtɪ] *n* invalidité *f*, infirmité *f*
disabled [dɪsˈeɪbld] *adj* infirme, invalide ♦ *npl*: **the ~** les handicapés
disadvantage [dɪsədˈvɑːntɪdʒ] *n* désavantage *m*, inconvénient *m*
disagree [dɪsəˈgriː] *vi* (*be different*) ne pas concorder; (*be against, think otherwise*): **to ~ (with)** ne pas être d'accord (avec); **~able** *adj* désagréable; **~ment** *n* désaccord *m*, différend *m*
disallow [dɪsəˈlau] *vt* rejeter
disappear [dɪsəˈpɪəʳ] *vi* disparaître; **~ance** *n* disparition *f*

disappoint [dɪsəˈpɔɪnt] *vt* décevoir; **~ed** *adj* déçu(e); **~ing** *adj* décevant(e); **~ment** *n* déception *f*
disapproval [dɪsəˈpruːvəl] *n* désapprobation *f*
disapprove [dɪsəˈpruːv] *vi*: **to ~ (of)** désapprouver
disarmament [dɪsˈɑːməmənt] *n* désarmement *m*
disarray [dɪsəˈreɪ] *n*: **in ~** (*army*) en déroute; (*organization*) en désarroi; (*hair, clothes*) en désordre
disaster [dɪˈzɑːstəʳ] *n* catastrophe *f*, désastre *m*; **disastrous** *adj* désastreux(-euse)
disband [dɪsˈbænd] *vt* démobiliser; disperser ♦ *vi* se séparer; se disperser
disbelief [ˈdɪsbəˈliːf] *n* incrédulité *f*
disc [dɪsk] *n* disque *m*; (COMPUT) = **disk**
discard [dɪsˈkɑːd] *vt* (*old things*) se débarrasser de; (*fig*) écarter, renoncer à
discern [dɪˈsəːn] *vt* discerner, distinguer; **~ing** *adj* perspicace
discharge [*vb* dɪsˈtʃɑːdʒ, *n* ˈdɪstʃɑːdʒ] *vt* décharger; (*duties*) s'acquitter de; (*patient*) renvoyer (chez lui); (*employee*) congédier, licencier; (*soldier*) rendre à la vie civile, réformer; (*defendant*) relaxer, élargir ♦ *n* décharge *f*; (*dismissal*) renvoi *m*; licenciement *m*; élargissement *m*; (MED) écoulement *m*
discipline [ˈdɪsɪplɪn] *n* discipline *f*
disc jockey *n* disc-jockey *m*
disclaim [dɪsˈkleɪm] *vt* nier
disclose [dɪsˈkləuz] *vt* révéler, divulguer; **disclosure** *n* révélation *f*
disco [ˈdɪskəu] *n abbr* = **discotheque**
discomfort [dɪsˈkʌmfət] *n* malaise *m*, gêne *f*; (*lack of comfort*) manque *m* de confort
disconcert [dɪskənˈsəːt] *vt* déconcerter
disconnect [dɪskəˈnɛkt] *vt* (ELEC, RADIO, *pipe*) débrancher; (TEL, *water*) couper
discontent [dɪskənˈtɛnt] *n* mécontentement *m*; **~ed** *adj* mécontent(e)
discontinue [dɪskənˈtɪnjuː] *vt* cesser, interrompre; **"~d"** (COMM) "fin de série"
discord [ˈdɪskɔːd] *n* discorde *f*, dissension

f; (MUS) dissonance f

discotheque ['dıskəutek] n discothèque f

discount [n 'dıskaunt, vb dıs'kaunt] n remise f, rabais m ♦ vt (sum) faire une remise de; (fig) ne pas tenir compte de

discourage [dıs'kʌrıdʒ] vt décourager

discover [dıs'kʌvər] vt découvrir; **~y** n découverte f

discredit [dıs'kredıt] vt (idea) mettre en doute; (person) discréditer

discreet [dıs'kri:t] adj discret(-ète)

discrepancy [dıs'krepənsı] n divergence f, contradiction f

discretion [dıs'kreʃən] n discrétion f; **use your own ~** à vous de juger

discriminate [dıs'krımıneıt] vi: **to ~ between** établir une distinction entre, faire la différence entre; **to ~ against** pratiquer une discrimination contre; **discriminating** adj qui a du discernement; **discrimination** [dıskrımı'neıʃən] n discrimination f; (judgment) discernement m

discuss [dıs'kʌs] vt discuter de; (debate) discuter; **~ion** n discussion f

disdain [dıs'deın] n dédain m

disease [dı'zi:z] n maladie f

disembark [dısım'ba:k] vi débarquer

disentangle [dısın'tæŋgl] vt (wool, wire) démêler, débrouiller; (from wreckage) dégager

disfigure [dıs'fıgər] vt défigurer

disgrace [dıs'greıs] n honte f; (disfavour) disgrâce f ♦ vt déshonorer, couvrir de honte; **~ful** adj scandaleux(-euse), honteux(-euse)

disgruntled [dıs'grʌntld] adj mécontent(e)

disguise [dıs'gaız] n déguisement m ♦ vt déguiser; **in ~** déguisé(e)

disgust [dıs'gʌst] n dégoût m, aversion f ♦ vt dégoûter, écœurer; **~ing** adj dégoûtant(e); révoltant(e)

dish [dıʃ] n plat m; **to do** or **wash the ~es** faire la vaisselle; **~ out** vt servir, distribuer; **~ up** vt servir; **~cloth** n (for washing) lavette f

dishearten [dıs'ha:tn] vt décourager

dishevelled [dı'ʃevəld] (US **disheveled**) adj ébouriffé(e); décoiffé(e); débraillé(e)

dishonest [dıs'ɔnıst] adj malhonnête

dishonour [dıs'ɔnər] (US **dishonor**) n déshonneur m; **~able** adj (behaviour) déshonorant(e); (person) peu honorable

dishtowel ['dıʃtauəl] (US) n torchon m

dishwasher ['dıʃwɔʃər] n lave-vaisselle m

disillusion [dısı'lu:ʒən] vt désabuser, désillusionner

disinfect [dısın'fekt] vt désinfecter; **~ant** n désinfectant m

disintegrate [dıs'ıntıgreıt] vi se désintégrer

disinterested [dıs'ıntrəstıd] adj désintéressé(e)

disjointed [dıs'dʒɔıntıd] adj décousu(e), incohérent(e)

disk [dısk] n (COMPUT) disque m; (: floppy ~) disquette f; **single-/double-sided ~** disquette simple/double face; **~ drive** n lecteur m de disquettes; **~ette** [dıs'ket] n disquette f, disque m souple

dislike [dıs'laık] n aversion f, antipathie f ♦ vt ne pas aimer

dislocate ['dıslakeıt] vt disloquer; déboîter

dislodge [dıs'lɔdʒ] vt déplacer, faire bouger

disloyal [dıs'lɔıəl] adj déloyal(e)

dismal ['dızml] adj lugubre, maussade

dismantle [dıs'mæntl] vt démonter

dismay [dıs'meı] n consternation f

dismiss [dıs'mıs] vt congédier, renvoyer; (soldiers) faire rompre les rangs à; (idea) écarter; (LAW): **to ~ a case** rendre une fin de non-recevoir; **~al** n renvoi m

dismount [dıs'maunt] vi mettre pied à terre, descendre

disobedient [dısə'bi:dıənt] adj désobéissant(e)

disobey [dısə'beı] vt désobéir à

disorder [dıs'ɔ:dər] n désordre m; (rioting) désordres mpl; (MED) troubles mpl; **~ly** adj en désordre; désordonné(e)

disorientated [dıs'ɔ:rıenteıtıd] adj désorienté(e)

disown [dıs'əun] vt renier

disparaging [dɪsˈpærɪdʒɪŋ] *adj* désobligeant(e)

dispassionate [dɪsˈpæʃənət] *adj* calme, froid(e); impartial(e), objectif(-ive)

dispatch [dɪsˈpætʃ] *vt* expédier, envoyer ♦ *n* envoi *m*, expédition *f*; (*MIL, PRESS*) dépêche *f*

dispel [dɪsˈpɛl] *vt* dissiper, chasser

dispense [dɪsˈpɛns] *vt* distribuer, administrer; ~ **with** *vt fus* se passer de; ~**r** *n* (*machine*) distributeur *m*; **dispensing chemist** (*BRIT*) *n* pharmacie *f*

disperse [dɪsˈpəːs] *vt* disperser ♦ *vi* se disperser

dispirited [dɪsˈpɪrɪtɪd] *adj* découragé(e), déprimé(e)

displace [dɪsˈpleɪs] *vt* déplacer

display [dɪsˈpleɪ] *n* étalage *m*; déploiement *m*; affichage *m*; (*screen*) écran *m*, visuel *m*; (*of feeling*) manifestation *f* ♦ *vt* montrer; (*goods*) mettre à l'étalage, exposer; (*results, departure times*) afficher; (*pej*) faire étalage de

displease [dɪsˈpliːz] *vt* mécontenter, contrarier; ~**d** *adj*: ~**d with** mécontent(e) de; **displeasure** [dɪsˈplɛʒəʳ] *n* mécontentement *m*

disposable [dɪsˈpəuzəbl] *adj* (*pack etc*) jetable, à jeter; (*income*) disponible; ~ **nappy** (*BRIT*) *n* couche *f* à jeter, couche-culotte *f*

disposal [dɪsˈpəuzl] *n* (*of goods for sale*) vente *f*; (*of property*) disposition *f*, cession *f*; (*of rubbish*) enlèvement *m*; destruction *f*; **at one's** ~ à sa disposition

dispose [dɪsˈpəuz] *vt* disposer; ~ **of** *vt fus* (*unwanted goods etc*) se débarrasser de, se défaire de; (*problem*) expédier; ~**d** *adj*: **to be** ~**d to do sth** être disposé(e) à faire qch; **disposition** [dɪspəˈzɪʃən] *n* disposition *f*; (*temperament*) naturel *m*

disprove [dɪsˈpruːv] *vt* réfuter

dispute [dɪsˈpjuːt] *n* discussion *f*; (*also:* **industrial** ~) conflit *m* ♦ *vt* contester; (*matter*) discuter; (*victory*) disputer

disqualify [dɪsˈkwɔlɪfaɪ] *vt* (*SPORT*) disqualifier; **to** ~ **sb for sth/from doing** rendre

qn inapte à qch/à faire

disquiet [dɪsˈkwaɪət] *n* inquiétude *f*, trouble *m*

disregard [dɪsrɪˈgɑːd] *vt* ne pas tenir compte de

disrepair [ˈdɪsrɪˈpɛəʳ] *n*: **to fall into** ~ (*building*) tomber en ruine

disreputable [dɪsˈrɛpjutəbl] *adj* (*person*) de mauvaise réputation; (*behaviour*) déshonorant(e)

disrespectful [dɪsrɪˈspɛktful] *adj* irrespectueux(-euse)

disrupt [dɪsˈrʌpt] *vt* (*plans*) déranger; (*conversation*) interrompre

dissatisfied [dɪsˈsætɪsfaɪd] *adj*: ~ **(with)** insatisfait(e) (de)

dissect [dɪˈsɛkt] *vt* disséquer

dissent [dɪˈsɛnt] *n* dissentiment *m*, différence *f* d'opinion

dissertation [dɪsəˈteɪʃən] *n* mémoire *m*

disservice [dɪsˈsəːvɪs] *n*: **to do sb a** ~ rendre un mauvais service à qn

dissimilar [dɪˈsɪmɪləʳ] *adj*: ~ **(to)** dissemblable (à), différent(e) (de)

dissipate [ˈdɪsɪpeɪt] *vt* dissiper; (*money, efforts*) disperser

dissolute [ˈdɪsəluːt] *adj* débauché(e), dissolu(e)

dissolve [dɪˈzɔlv] *vt* dissoudre ♦ *vi* se dissoudre, fondre; **to** ~ **in(to) tears** fondre en larmes

distance [ˈdɪstns] *n* distance *f*; **in the** ~ au loin

distant [ˈdɪstnt] *adj* lointain(e), éloigné(e); (*manner*) distant(e), froid(e)

distaste [dɪsˈteɪst] *n* dégoût *m*; ~**ful** *adj* déplaisant(e), désagréable

distended [dɪsˈtɛndɪd] *adj* (*stomach*) dilaté(e)

distil [dɪsˈtɪl] (*US* **distill**) *vt* distiller; ~**lery** *n* distillerie *f*

distinct [dɪsˈtɪŋkt] *adj* distinct(e); (*clear*) marqué(e); **as** ~ **from** par opposition à; ~**ion** *n* distinction *f*; (*in exam*) mention très bien; ~**ive** *adj* distinctif(-ive)

distinguish [dɪsˈtɪŋgwɪʃ] *vt* distinguer; ~**ed** *adj* (*eminent*) distingué(e); ~**ing** *ad* *(feature)* distinctif(-ive), caractéristique

distort [dɪsˈtɔːt] *vt* déformer

distract [dɪsˈtrækt] *vt* distraire, déranger; **~ed** *adj* distrait(e); *(anxious)* éperdu(e), égaré(e); **~ion** *n* distraction *f*; égarement *m*

distraught [dɪsˈtrɔːt] *adj* éperdu(e)

distress [dɪsˈtrɛs] *n* détresse *f* ♦ *vt* affliger; **~ing** *adj* douloureux(-euse), pénible

distribute [dɪsˈtrɪbjuːt] *vt* distribuer; **distribution** [dɪstrɪˈbjuːʃən] *n* distribution *f*; **distributor** *n* distributeur *m*

district [ˈdɪstrɪkt] *n (of country)* région *f*; *(of town)* quartier *m*; *(ADMIN)* district *m*; **~ attorney** *(US)* *n* ≃ procureur *m* de la République; **~ nurse** *(BRIT)* *n* infirmière visiteuse

distrust [dɪsˈtrʌst] *n* méfiance *f* ♦ *vt* se méfier de

disturb [dɪsˈtəːb] *vt* troubler; *(inconvenience)* déranger; **~ance** *n* dérangement *m*; *(violent event, political etc)* troubles *mpl*; **~ed** *adj* *(worried, upset)* agité(e), troublé(e); **to be emotionally ~ed** avoir des problèmes affectifs; **~ing** *adj* troublant(e), inquiétant(e)

disuse [dɪsˈjuːs] *n*: **to fall into ~** tomber en désuétude; **~d** [dɪsˈjuːzd] *adj* désaffecté(e)

ditch [dɪtʃ] *n* fossé *m*; *(irrigation)* rigole *f* ♦ *vt (inf)* abandonner; *(person)* plaquer

dither [ˈdɪðəʳ] *vi* hésiter

ditto [ˈdɪtəʊ] *adv* idem

dive [daɪv] *n* plongeon *m*; *(of submarine)* plongée *f* ♦ *vi* plonger; **to ~ into** *(bag, drawer etc)* plonger la main dans; *(shop, car etc)* se précipiter dans; **~r** *n* plongeur *m*

diversion [daɪˈvəːʃən] *n (BRIT: AUT)* déviation *f*; *(distraction, MIL)* diversion *f*

divert [daɪˈvəːt] *vt (funds, BRIT: traffic)* dévier; *(river, attention)* détourner

divide [dɪˈvaɪd] *vt* diviser; *(separate)* séparer ♦ *vi* se diviser; **~d highway** *(US)* *n* route *f* à quatre voies

dividend [ˈdɪvɪdɛnd] *n* dividende *m*

divine [dɪˈvaɪn] *adj* divin(e)

diving [ˈdaɪvɪŋ] *n* plongée (sous-marine); **~ board** *n* plongeoir *m*

divinity [dɪˈvɪnɪtɪ] *n* divinité *f*; *(SCOL)* théologie *f*

division [dɪˈvɪʒən] *n* division *f*

divorce [dɪˈvɔːs] *n* divorce *m* ♦ *vt* divorcer d'avec; *(dissociate)* séparer; **~d** *adj* divorcé(e); **~e** *n* divorcé(e)

D.I.Y. *(BRIT)* *n abbr* = **do-it-yourself**

dizzy [ˈdɪzɪ] *adj*: **to make sb ~** donner le vertige à qn; **to feel ~** avoir la tête qui tourne

DJ *n abbr* = **disc jockey**

DNA fingerprinting *n* technique *f* des empreintes génétiques

---

KEYWORD

---

do [duː] *(pt* **did**, *pp* **done)** *n (inf: party etc)* soirée *f*, fête *f*

♦ *vb* **1** *(in negative constructions)* non traduit; **I don't understand** je ne comprends pas

2 *(to form questions)* non traduit; **didn't you know?** vous ne le saviez pas?; **why didn't you come?** pourquoi n'êtes-vous pas venu?

3 *(for emphasis, in polite expressions)*: **she does seem rather late** je trouve qu'elle est bien en retard; **do sit down/help yourself** asseyez-vous/servez-vous je vous en prie

4 *(used to avoid repeating vb)*: **she swims better than I do** elle nage mieux que moi; **do you agree? - yes, I do/no, I don't** vous êtes d'accord? - oui/non; **she lives in Glasgow - so do I** elle habite Glasgow - moi aussi; **who broke it? - I did** qui l'a cassé? - c'est moi

5 *(in question tags)*: **he laughed, didn't he?** il a ri, n'est-ce pas?; **I don't know him, do I?** je ne crois pas le connaître

♦ *vt (gen: carry out, perform etc)* faire; **what are you doing tonight?** qu'est-ce que vous faites ce soir?; **to do the cooking/washing-up** faire la cuisine/la vaisselle; **to do one's teeth/hair/nails** se brosser les dents/se coiffer/se faire les ongles; **the**

car was doing 100 ≃ la voiture faisait du 160 (à l'heure)
♦ *vi* 1 (*act, behave*) faire; **do as I do** faites comme moi
2 (*get on, fare*) marcher; **the firm is doing well** l'entreprise marche bien; **how do you do?** comment allez-vous?; (*on being introduced*) enchanté(e)!
3 (*suit*) aller; **will it do?** est-ce que ça ira?
4 (*be sufficient*) suffire, aller; **will £10 do?** est-ce que 10 livres suffiront?; **that'll do** ça suffit, ça ira; **that'll do!** (*in annoyance*) ça va *or* suffit comme ça!; **to make do (with)** se contenter (de)
do away with *vt fus* supprimer
do up *vt* (*laces, dress*) attacher; (*buttons*) boutonner; (*zip*) fermer; (*renovate: room*) refaire; (: *house*) remettre à neuf
do with *vt fus* (*need*): **I could do with a drink/some help** quelque chose à boire/un peu d'aide ne serait pas de refus; (*be connected*): **that has nothing to do with you** cela ne vous concerne pas; **I won't have anything to do with it** je ne veux pas m'en mêler
do without *vi* s'en passer ♦ *vt fus* se passer de

dock [dɔk] *n* dock *m*; (*LAW*) banc *m* des accusés ♦ *vi* se mettre à quai; (*SPACE*) s'arrimer; **~er** *n* docker *m*; **~yard** *n* chantier *m* de construction navale
doctor ['dɔktəʳ] *n* médecin *m*, docteur *m*; (*PhD etc*) docteur ♦ *vt* (*drink*) frelater; **D~ of Philosophy** *n* (*degree*) doctorat *m*; (*person*) Docteur *m* en Droit *or* Lettres *etc*, titulaire *m/f* d'un doctorat
document ['dɔkjumənt] *n* document *m*; **~ary** [dɔkju'mɛntərɪ] *adj* documentaire ♦ *n* documentaire *m*
dodge [dɔdʒ] *n* truc *m*; combine *f* ♦ *vt* esquiver, éviter
dodgems ['dɔdʒəmz] (*BRIT*) *npl* autos tamponneuses
doe [dəu] *n* (*deer*) biche *f*; (*rabbit*) lapine *f*
does [dʌz] *vb see* do; **~n't** = **does not**
dog [dɔg] *n* chien(ne) ♦ *vt* suivre de près;

poursuivre, harceler; **~ collar** *n* collier *m* de chien; (*fig*) faux-col *m* d'ecclésiastique; **~-eared** *adj* corné(e); **~ged** ['dɔgɪd] *adj* obstiné(e), opiniâtre; **~sbody** *n* bonne *f* à tout faire, tâcheron *m*
doings ['duːɪŋz] *npl* activités *fpl*
do-it-yourself ['duːɪtjɔː'sɛlf] *n* bricolage *m*
doldrums ['dɔldrəmz] *npl*: **to be in the ~** avoir le cafard; (*business*) être dans le marasme
dole [dəul] *n* (*BRIT: payment*) allocation *f* de chômage; **on the ~** au chômage; **~ out** *vt* donner au compte-goutte
doll [dɔl] *n* poupée *f*
dollar ['dɔləʳ] *n* dollar *m*
dolled up (*inf*) *adj*: **(all) ~** sur son trente et un
dolphin ['dɔlfɪn] *n* dauphin *m*
dome [dəum] *n* dôme *m*
domestic [də'mɛstɪk] *adj* (*task, appliances*) ménager(-ère); (*of country: trade, situation etc*) intérieur(e); (*animal*) domestique; **~ated** *adj* (*animal*) domestiqué(e); (*husband*) pantouflard(e)
dominate ['dɔmɪneɪt] *vt* dominer
domineering [dɔmɪ'nɪərɪŋ] *adj* dominateur(-trice), autoritaire
dominion [də'mɪnɪən] *n* (*territory*) territoire *m*; **to have ~ over** contrôler
domino ['dɔmɪnəu] (*pl* **~es**) *n* domino *m*; **~es** *n* (*game*) dominos *mpl*
don [dɔn] (*BRIT*) *n* professeur *m* d'université
donate [də'neɪt] *vt* faire don de, donner
done [dʌn] *pp of* **do**
donkey ['dɔŋkɪ] *n* âne *m*
donor ['dəunəʳ] *n* (*of blood etc*) donneur(-euse); (*to charity*) donateur(-trice); **~ card** *n* carte *f* de don d'organes
don't [dəunt] *vb* = **do not**
donut ['dəunʌt] (*US*) *n* = **doughnut**
doodle ['duːdl] *vi* griffonner, gribouiller
doom [duːm] *n* destin *m* ♦ *vt*: **to be ~ed (to failure)** être voué(e) à l'échec
door [dɔːʳ] *n* porte *f*; (*RAIL, car*) portière *f*; **~bell** *n* sonnette *f*; **~handle** *n* poignée de la porte; (*car*) poignée de portière; **~man** (*irreg*) *n* (*in hotel*) portier *m*; **~ma**

n paillasson *m*; **~step** *n* pas *m* de (la) porte, seuil *m*; **~way** *n* (embrasure *f* de la) porte *f*

dope [dəup] *n* (*inf*: *drug*) drogue *f*; (: *person*) andouille *f* ♦ *vt* (*horse etc*) doper

dormant ['dɔːmənt] *adj* assoupi(e), en veilleuse

dormitory ['dɔːmɪtrɪ] *n* dortoir *m*; (*US*: *building*) résidence *f* universitaire

dormouse ['dɔːmaus] (*pl* **dormice**) *n* loir *m*

DOS [dɔs] *n abbr* (= *disk operating system*) DOS

dose [dəus] *n* dose *f*

dosh [dɔʃ] (*inf*) *n* fric *m*

doss house ['dɔs-] (*BRIT*) *n* asile *m* de nuit

dot [dɔt] *n* point *m*; (*on material*) pois *m* ♦ *vt*: **~ted with** parsemé(e) de; **on the ~** à l'heure tapante *or* pile; **~ted line** *n* pointillé(s) *m*(*pl*)

double ['dʌbl] *adj* double ♦ *adv* (*twice*): **to cost ~** (**sth**) coûter le double (de qch) *or* deux fois plus (que qch) ♦ *n* double *m* ♦ *vt* doubler; (*fold*) plier en deux ♦ *vi* doubler; **~s** *n* (*TENNIS*) double *m*; **on** *or* (*BRIT*) **at the ~** au pas de course; **~ bass** (*BRIT*) *n* contrebasse *f*; **~ bed** *n* grand lit; **~ bend** (*BRIT*) *n* virage *m* en S; **~-breasted** *adj* croisé(e); **~-click** *vi* (*COMPUT*) double-cliquer; **~-cross** *vt* doubler, trahir; **~-decker** *n* autobus *m* à impériale; **~ glazing** (*BRIT*) *n* double vitrage *m*; **~ room** *n* chambre *f* pour deux personnes; **doubly** *adv* doublement, deux fois plus

doubt [daut] *n* doute *m* ♦ *vt* douter de; **to ~ that** douter que; **~ful** *adj* douteux(-euse); (*person*) incertain(e); **~less** *adv* sans doute, sûrement

dough [dəu] *n* pâte *f*; **~nut** (*US* **donut**) *n* beignet *m*

dove [dʌv] *n* colombe *f*

Dover ['dəuvər] *n* Douvres

dovetail ['dʌvteɪl] *vi* (*fig*) concorder

dowdy ['daudɪ] *adj* démodé(e); mal fagoté(e) (*inf*)

down [daun] *n* (*soft feathers*) duvet *m*

♦ *adv* en bas, vers le bas; (*on the ground*) par terre ♦ *prep* en bas de ♦ *vt* (*inf*: *drink, food*) s'envoyer; **~ with X!** à bas X!; **~-and-out** *n* clochard(e); **~-at-heel** *adj* (*fig*) miteux(-euse); **~cast** *adj* démoralisé(e); **~fall** *n* chute *f*; ruine *f*; **~hearted** *adj* découragé(e); **~hill** *adv*: **to go ~hill** descendre; (*fig*) péricliter; **~load** *vt* (*COMPUT*) télécharger; **~ payment** *n* acompte *m*; **~pour** *n* pluie torrentielle, déluge *m*; **~right** *adj* (*lie etc*) effronté(e); (*refusal*) catégorique; **~size** *vt* (*ECON*) réduire ses effectifs

---

Downing Street

i **Downing Street** est une rue de Westminster (à Londres) où se trouve la résidence officielle du Premier minister (numéro 10) et celle du ministre des Finances (numéro 11). Le nom "Downing Street" est souvent utilisé pour désigner le gouvernement britannique.

Down's syndrome [daunz-] *n* (*MED*) trisomie *f*

down: **~stairs** *adv* au rez-de-chaussée; à l'étage inférieur; **~stream** *adv* en aval; **~-to-earth** *adj* terre à terre *inv*; **~town** *adv* en ville; **~ under** *adv* en Australie/Nouvelle-Zélande; **~ward** *adj*, *adv* vers le bas; **~wards** *adv* vers le bas

dowry ['dauri] *n* dot *f*

doz. *abbr* = **dozen**

doze [dəuz] *vi* sommeiller; **~ off** *vi* s'assoupir

dozen ['dʌzn] *n* douzaine *f*; **a ~ books** une douzaine de livres; **~s of** des centaines de

Dr. *abbr* = **doctor**; **drive**

drab [dræb] *adj* terne, morne

draft [drɑːft] *n* ébauche *f*; (*of letter, essay etc*) brouillon *m*; (*COMM*) traite *f*; (*US*: *call-up*) conscription *f* ♦ *vt* faire le brouillon *or* un projet de; (*MIL*: *send*) détacher; *see also* **draught**

draftsman ['drɑːftsmən] (*irreg*) (*US*) *n* = **draughtsman**

drag [dræg] *vt* traîner; (*river*) draguer ♦ *vi*

traîner ♦ *n* (*inf*) casse-pieds *m/f*; (*women's clothing*): **in ~** (en) travesti; **~ on** *vi* s'éterniser

dragon ['drægn] *n* dragon *m*

dragonfly ['drægənflaɪ] *n* libellule *f*

drain [dreɪn] *n* égout *m*, canalisation *f*; (*on resources*) saignée *f* ♦ *vt* (*land, marshes etc*) drainer, assécher; (*vegetables*) égoutter; (*glass*) vider ♦ *vi* (*water*) s'écouler; **~age** *n* drainage *m*; système *m* d'égouts *or* de canalisations; **~ing board** (*us* **drain board**) *n* égouttoir *m*; **~pipe** *n* tuyau *m* d'écoulement

drama ['drɑːmə] *n* (*art*) théâtre *m*, art *m* dramatique; (*play*) pièce *f* (de théâtre); (*event*) drame *m*; **~tic** [drə'mætɪk] *adj* dramatique; spectaculaire; **~tist** ['dræmətɪst] *n* auteur *m* dramatique; **~tize** ['dræmətaɪz] *vt* (*events*) dramatiser; (*adapt: for TV/cinema*) adapter pour la télévision/pour l'écran

drank [dræŋk] *pt of* **drink**

drape [dreɪp] *vt* draper; **~s** (*us*) *npl* rideaux *mpl*

drastic ['dræstɪk] *adj* sévère; énergique; (*change*) radical(e)

draught [drɑːft] (*us* **draft**) *n* courant *m* d'air; (*NAUT*) tirant *m* d'eau; **on ~** (*beer*) à la pression; **~board** (*BRIT*) *n* damier *m*; **~s** (*BRIT*) *n* (jeu de) dames *fpl*

draughtsman ['drɑːftsmən] (*irreg*) *n* dessinateur(-trice) (industriel(le))

draw [drɔː] (*pt* **drew**, *pp* **drawn**) *vt* tirer; (*tooth*) arracher, extraire; (*attract*) attirer; (*picture*) dessiner; (*line, circle*) tracer; (*money*) retirer; (*wages*) toucher ♦ *vi* (*SPORT*) faire match nul ♦ *n* match nul; (*lottery*) tirage *m* au sort; loterie *f*; **to ~ near** s'approcher; approcher; **~ out** *vi* (*lengthen*) s'allonger ♦ *vt* (*money*) retirer; **~ up** *vi* (*stop*) s'arrêter ♦ *vt* (*chair*) approcher; (*document*) établir, dresser; **~back** *n* inconvénient *m*, désavantage *m*; **~bridge** *n* pont-levis *m*

drawer [drɔː^r] *n* tiroir *m*

drawing ['drɔːɪŋ] *n* dessin *m*; **~ board** *n* planche *f* à dessin; **~ pin** (*BRIT*) *n* punaise

f; **~ room** *n* salon *m*

drawl [drɔːl] *n* accent traînant

drawn [drɔːn] *pp of* **draw**

dread [drɛd] *n* terreur *f*, effroi *m* ♦ *vt* redouter, appréhender; **~ful** *adj* affreux(-euse)

dream [driːm] (*pt, pp* **dreamed** *or* **dreamt**) *n* rêve *m* ♦ *vt, vi* rêver; **~y** *adj* rêveur(-euse); (*music*) langoureux(-euse)

dreary ['drɪərɪ] *adj* morne; monotone

dredge [drɛdʒ] *vt* draguer

dregs [drɛgz] *npl* lie *f*

drench [drɛntʃ] *vt* tremper

dress [drɛs] *n* robe *f*; (*no pl: clothing*) habillement *m*, tenue *f* ♦ *vi* s'habiller ♦ *vt* habiller; (*wound*) panser; **to get ~ed** s'habiller; **~ up** *vi* s'habiller; (*in fancy ~*) se déguiser; **~ circle** (*BRIT*) *n* (*THEATRE*) premier balcon; **~er** *n* (*furniture*) vaisselier *m*; (: *us*) coiffeuse *f*, commode *f*; **~ing** *n* (*MED*) pansement *m*; (*CULIN*) sauce *f*, assaisonnement *m*; **~ing gown** (*BRIT*) *n* robe *f* de chambre; **~ing room** *n* (*THEATRE*) loge *f*; (*SPORT*) vestiaire *m*; **~ing table** *n* coiffeuse *f*; **~maker** *n* couturière *f*; **~ rehearsal** *n* (répétition *f*) générale *f*

drew [druː] *pt of* **draw**

dribble ['drɪbl] *vi* (*baby*) baver ♦ *vt* (*ball*) dribbler

dried [draɪd] *adj* (*fruit, beans*) sec (sèche); (*eggs, milk*) en poudre

drier ['draɪə^r] *n* = **dryer**

drift [drɪft] *n* (*of current etc*) force *f*; direction *f*, mouvement *m*; (*of snow*) rafale *f*, (: *on ground*) congère *f*; (*general meaning*) sens (général) ♦ *vi* (*boat*) aller à la dérive, dériver; (*sand, snow*) s'amonceler, s'entasser; **~wood** *n* bois flotté

drill [drɪl] *n* perceuse *f*; (~ *bit*) foret *m* mèche *f*; (*of dentist*) roulette *f*, fraise *f*. (*MIL*) exercice *m* ♦ *vt* percer; (*troops*) entraîner ♦ *vi* (*for oil*) faire un *or* des forage(s)

drink [drɪŋk] (*pt* **drank**, *pp* **drunk**) *n* boisson *f*; (*alcoholic*) verre *m* ♦ *vt, vi* boire; **to have a ~** boire quelque chose, boire un verre; prendre l'apéritif; **a ~ of water** un verre d'eau; ~**er** n buveur(-euse); ~**ing water** n eau f potable

drip [drɪp] n goutte f; (MED) goutte-à-goutte m inv, perfusion f ♦ vi tomber goutte à goutte; (tap) goutter; ~-**dry** adj (shirt) sans repassage; ~**ping** n graisse f (de rôti)

drive [draɪv] (pt **drove**, pp **driven**) n promenade f or trajet m en voiture; (also: ~**way**) allée f; (energy) dynamisme m, énergie f; (push) effort (concerté), campagne f; (also: **disk** ~) lecteur m de disquettes ♦ vt conduire; (push) chasser, pousser; (TECH: motor, wheel) faire fonctionner; entraîner; (nail, stake etc): **to** ~ **sth into sth** enfoncer qch dans qch ♦ vi (AUT: at controls) conduire; (: travel) aller en voiture; **left-/right-hand** ~ conduite f à gauche/droite; **to** ~ **sb mad** rendre qn fou (folle); **to** ~ **sb home/to the airport** reconduire qn chez lui/conduire qn à l'aéroport; ~-**by shooting** n (tentative d'assassinat par coups de feu tirés d'un voiture

drivel ['drɪvl] (inf) n idioties fpl

driver ['draɪvəʳ] n conducteur(-trice); (of taxi, bus) chauffeur m; ~'**s license** (US) n permis m de conduire

driveway ['draɪvweɪ] n allée f

driving ['draɪvɪŋ] n conduite f; ~ **instructor** n moniteur m d'auto-école; ~ **lesson** n leçon f de conduite; ~ **licence** (BRIT) n permis m de conduire; ~ **school** n auto-école f; ~ **test** n examen m du permis de conduire

drizzle ['drɪzl] n bruine f, crachin m

drool [druːl] vi baver

droop [druːp] vi (shoulders) tomber; (head) pencher; (flower) pencher la tête

drop [drɔp] n goutte f; (fall) baisse f; (also: **parachute** ~) saut m ♦ vt laisser tomber; (voice, eyes, price) baisser; (set down from car) déposer ♦ vi tomber; ~**s** npl (MED) gouttes; ~ **off** vi (sleep) s'assoupir ♦ vt (passenger) déposer; ~ **out** vi (withdraw) se retirer; (student etc) abandonner, décrocher; ~**out** n marginal(e); ~**per** n

compte-gouttes m inv; ~**pings** npl crottes fpl

drought [draut] n sécheresse f

drove [drəuv] pt of **drive**

drown [draun] vt noyer ♦ vi se noyer

drowsy ['drauzɪ] adj somnolent(e)

drug [drʌg] n médicament m; (narcotic) drogue f ♦ vt droguer; **to be on** ~**s** se droguer; ~ **addict** n toxicomane m/f; ~**gist** (US) n pharmacien(ne)-droguiste; ~**store** (US) n pharmacie-droguerie f, drugstore m

drum [drʌm] n tambour m; (for oil, petrol) bidon m; ~**s** npl (kit) batterie f; ~**mer** n (joueur m de) tambour m

drunk [drʌŋk] pp of **drink** ♦ adj ivre, soûl(e) ♦ n (also: ~**ard**) ivrogne m/f; ~**en** adj (person) ivre, soûl(e); (rage, stupor) ivrogne, d'ivrogne

dry [draɪ] adj sec (sèche); (day) sans pluie; (humour) pince-sans-rire inv; (lake, riverbed, well) à sec ♦ vt sécher; (clothes) faire sécher ♦ vi sécher; ~ **up** vi tarir; ~-**cleaner's** n teinturerie f; ~**er** n séchoir m; (spin-dryer) essoreuse f; ~**ness** n sécheresse f; ~ **rot** n pourriture sèche (du bois)

DSS n abbr (= Department of Social Security) ≈ Sécurité sociale

DTP n abbr (= desk-top publishing) PAO f

dual ['djuəl] adj double; ~ **carriageway** (BRIT) n route f à quatre voies or à chaussées séparées; ~-**purpose** adj à double usage

dubbed [dʌbd] adj (CINEMA) doublé(e)

dubious ['djuːbɪəs] adj hésitant(e), incertain(e); (reputation, company) douteux(-euse)

duchess ['dʌtʃɪs] n duchesse f

duck [dʌk] n canard m ♦ vi se baisser vivement, baisser subitement la tête; ~**ling** ['dʌklɪŋ] n caneton m

duct [dʌkt] n conduite f, canalisation f; (ANAT) conduit m

dud [dʌd] n (object, tool): **it's a** ~ c'est de la camelote, ça ne marche pas ♦ adj: ~ **cheque** (BRIT) chèque sans provision

due [dju:] *adj* dû (due); (*expected*) attendu(e); (*fitting*) qui convient ♦ *n*: **to give sb his** (*or* **her**) **~** être juste envers qn ♦ *adv*: **~ north** droit vers le nord; **~s** *npl* (*for club, union*) cotisation *f*; **in ~ course** en temps utile *or* voulu; finalement; **~ to** dû (due) à; causé(e) par; **he's ~ to finish tomorrow** normalement il doit finir demain

duet [dju:'ɛt] *n* duo *m*

duffel bag ['dʌfl-] *n* sac *m* marin

duffel coat *n* duffel-coat *m*

dug [dʌg] *pt, pp of* **dig**

duke [dju:k] *n* duc *m*

dull [dʌl] *adj* terne, morne; (*boring*) ennuyeux(-euse); (*sound, pain*) sourd(e); (*weather, day*) gris(e), maussade ♦ *vt* (*pain, grief*) atténuer; (*mind, senses*) engourdir

duly ['dju:lɪ] *adv* (*on time*) en temps voulu; (*as expected*) comme il se doit

dumb [dʌm] *adj* muet(te); (*stupid*) bête; **~founded** *adj* sidéré(e)

dummy ['dʌmɪ] *n* (*tailor's model*) mannequin *m*; (*mock-up*) factice *m*, maquette *f*; (*BRIT: for baby*) tétine *f* ♦ *adj* faux (fausse), factice

dump [dʌmp] *n* (*also*: **rubbish ~**) décharge (publique); (*pej*) trou *m* ♦ *vt* (*put down*) déposer; déverser; (*get rid of*) se débarrasser de; (*COMPUT: data*) vider

dumpling ['dʌmplɪŋ] *n* boulette *f* (de pâte)

dumpy ['dʌmpɪ] *adj* boulot(te)

dunce [dʌns] *n* âne *m*, cancre *m*

dune [dju:n] *n* dune *f*

dung [dʌŋ] *n* fumier *m*

dungarees [dʌŋgə'ri:z] *npl* salopette *f*; bleu(s) *m(pl)*

dungeon ['dʌndʒən] *n* cachot *m*

duplex ['dju:plɛks] (*US*) *n* maison jumelée; (*apartment*) duplex *m*

duplicate [*n* 'dju:plɪkət, *vb* 'dju:plɪkeɪt] *n* double *m* ♦ *vt* faire un double de; (*on machine*) polycopier; photocopier; **in ~** en deux exemplaires

durable ['djuərəbl] *adj* durable; (*clothes, metal*) résistant(e), solide

duration [djuə'reɪʃən] *n* durée *f*

during ['djuərɪŋ] *prep* pendant, au cours de

dusk [dʌsk] *n* crépuscule *m*

dust [dʌst] *n* poussière *f* ♦ *vt* (*furniture*) épousseter, essuyer; (*cake etc*): **to ~ with** saupoudrer de; **~bin** (*BRIT*) *n* poubelle *f*; **~er** *n* chiffon *m*; **~man** (*BRIT*) (*irreg*) *n* boueux *m*, éboueur *m*; **~y** *adj* poussiéreux(-euse)

Dutch [dʌtʃ] *adj* hollandais(e), néerlandais(e) ♦ *n* (*LING*) hollandais *m* ♦ *adv* (*inf*): **to go ~** partager les frais; **the ~** *npl* (*people*) les Hollandais; **~man** (*irreg*) *n* Hollandais; **~woman** (*irreg*) *n* Hollandaise *f*

duty ['dju:tɪ] *n* devoir *m*; (*tax*) droit *m*, taxe *f*; **on ~** de service; (*at night etc*) de garde; **off ~** libre, pas de service *or* de garde; **~-free** *adj* exempté(e) de douane, hors taxe *inv*

duvet ['du:veɪ] (*BRIT*) *n* couette *f*

DVD *n abbr* (= *digital versatile disc*) DVD *m*

dwarf [dwɔ:f] (*pl* **dwarves**) *n* nain(e) ♦ *vt* écraser

dwell [dwɛl] (*pt, pp* **dwelt**) *vi* demeurer; **~ on** *vt fus* s'appesantir sur

dwindle ['dwɪndl] *vi* diminuer, décroître

dye [daɪ] *n* teinture *f* ♦ *vt* teindre

dying ['daɪɪŋ] *adj* mourant(e), agonisant(e)

dyke [daɪk] (*BRIT*) *n* digue *f*

dynamic [daɪ'næmɪk] *adj* dynamique

dynamite ['daɪnəmaɪt] *n* dynamite *f*

dynamo ['daɪnəməu] *n* dynamo *f*

dyslexia [dɪs'lɛksɪə] *n* dyslexie *f*

E, e

E [i:] *n* (*MUS*) mi *m*

each [i:tʃ] *adj* chaque ♦ *pron* chacun(e); **~ other** l'un(e) l'autre; **they hate ~ other** ils se détestent (mutuellement); **you are jealous of ~ other** vous êtes jaloux l'un de l'autre; **they have 2 books ~** ils ont 2 livres chacun

eager ['i:gə'] *adj* (*keen*) avide; **to be ~ to do sth** avoir très envie de faire qch; **to be**

~ **for** désirer vivement, être avide de

eagle ['iːgl] *n* aigle *m*

ear [ɪəʳ] *n* oreille *f*; (*of corn*) épi *m*; ~**ache** *n* mal *m* aux oreilles; ~**drum** *n* tympan *m*

earl [əːl] (*BRIT*) *n* comte *m*

earlier ['əːlɪəʳ] *adj* (*date etc*) plus rapproché(e); (*edition, fashion etc*) plus ancien(ne), antérieur(e) ♦ *adv* plus tôt

early ['əːlɪ] *adv* tôt, de bonne heure; (*ahead of time*) en avance; (*near the beginning*) au début ♦ *adj* qui se manifeste (*or* se fait*) tôt *or* de bonne heure; (*work*) de jeunesse; (*settler, Christian*) premier(-ère); (*reply*) rapide; (*death*) prématuré(e); **to have an ~ night** se coucher tôt *or* de bonne heure; **in the ~** *or* **~ in the spring/19th century** au début du printemps/19ème siècle; ~ **retirement** *n*: **to take ~ retirement** prendre sa retraite anticipée

earmark ['ɪəmɑːk] *vt*: **to ~ sth for** réserver *or* destiner qch à

earn [əːn] *vt* gagner; (*COMM: yield*) rapporter

earnest ['əːnɪst] *adj* sérieux(-euse); **in ~** ♦ *adv* sérieusement

earnings ['əːnɪŋz] *npl* salaire *m*; (*of company*) bénéfices *mpl*

ear: ~**phones** *npl* écouteurs *mpl*; ~**ring** *n* boucle *f* d'oreille; ~**shot** *n*: **within ~shot** à portée de voix

earth [əːθ] *n* (*gen, also BRIT: ELEC*) terre *f* ♦ *vt* relier à la terre; ~**enware** *n* poterie *f*; faïence *f*; ~**quake** *n* tremblement *m* de terre, séisme *m*; ~**y** *adj* (*vulgar: humour*) truculent(e)

ease [iːz] *n* facilité *f*, aisance *f*; (*comfort*) bien-être *m* ♦ *vt* (*soothe*) calmer; (*loosen*) relâcher, détendre; **to ~ sth in/out** faire pénétrer/sortir qch délicatement *or* avec douceur; faciliter la pénétration/la sortie de qch; **at ~!** (*MIL*) repos!; ~ **off** *or* **up** *vi* diminuer; (*slow down*) ralentir

easel ['iːzl] *n* chevalet *m*

easily ['iːzɪlɪ] *adv* facilement

east [iːst] *n* est *m* ♦ *adj* (*wind*) d'est; (*side*) est *inv* ♦ *adv* à l'est, vers l'est; **the E~**

l'Orient *m*; (*POL*) les pays *mpl* de l'Est

Easter ['iːstəʳ] *n* Pâques *fpl*; ~ **egg** *n* œuf *m* de Pâques

east: ~**erly** ['iːstəlɪ] *adj* (*wind*) d'est; (*direction*) est *inv*; (*point*) à l'est; ~**ern** ['iːstən] *adj* de l'est, oriental(e); ~**ward(s)** ['iːstwəd(z)] *adv* vers l'est, à l'est

easy ['iːzɪ] *adj* facile; (*manner*) aisé(e) ♦ *adv*: **to take it** *or* **things ~** ne pas se fatiguer; (*not worry*) ne pas (trop) s'en faire; ~ **chair** *n* fauteuil *m*; ~**-going** *adj* accommodant(e), facile à vivre

eat [iːt] (*pt* **ate**, *pp* **eaten**) *vt*, *vi* manger; ~ **away at**, ~ **into** *vt fus* ronger, attaquer; (*savings*) entamer

eaves [iːvz] *npl* avant-toit *m*

eavesdrop ['iːvzdrɔp] *vi*: **to ~ (on a conversation)** écouter (une conversation) de façon indiscrète

ebb [eb] *n* reflux *m* ♦ *vi* refluer; (*fig: also: ~ away*) décliner

ebony ['ebənɪ] *n* ébène *f*

EC *n abbr* (= *European Community*) C.E. *f*

ECB *n abbr* (= *European Central Bank*) BCE *f*

eccentric [ɪk'sɛntrɪk] *adj* excentrique

echo ['ekəu] (*pl* ~**es**) *n* écho *m* ♦ *vt* répéter ♦ *vi* résonner, faire écho

eclipse [ɪ'klɪps] *n* éclipse *f*

ecology [ɪ'kɔlədʒɪ] *n* écologie *f*

e-commerce ['iːkɔmɜːs] *n* commerce *m* électronique

economic [iːkə'nɔmɪk] *adj* économique; (*business etc*) rentable; **economical** *adj* économique; (*person*) économe

economics [iːkə'nɔmɪks] *n* économie *f* politique ♦ *npl* (*of project, situation*) aspect *m* financier

economize [ɪ'kɔnəmaɪz] *vi* économiser, faire des économies

economy [ɪ'kɔnəmɪ] *n* économie *f*; ~ **class** *n* classe *f* touriste; ~ **size** *n* format *m* économique

ecstasy ['ekstəsɪ] *n* extase *f* (*drogue aussi*); **ecstatic** [eks'tætɪk] *adj* extatique

ECU ['eɪkjuː] *n abbr* (= *European Currency Unit*) ECU *m*

eczema ['ɛksɪmə] *n* eczéma *m*

edge [ɛdʒ] *n* bord *m*; (*of knife etc*) tranchant *m*, fil *m* ♦ *vt* border; **on ~** (*fig*) crispé(e), tendu(e); **to ~ away from** s'éloigner furtivement de; **~ways** *adv*: **he couldn't get a word in ~ways** il ne pouvait pas placer un mot

edgy ['ɛdʒɪ] *adj* crispé(e), tendu(e)

edible ['ɛdɪbl] *adj* comestible

Edinburgh ['ɛdɪnbərə] *n* Édimbourg

edit ['ɛdɪt] *vt* (*text, book*) éditer; (*report*) préparer; (*film*) monter; (*broadcast*) réaliser; **~ion** [ɪ'dɪʃn] *n* édition *f*; **~or** *n* (*of column*) rédacteur(-trice); (*of newspaper*) rédacteur(-trice) en chef; (*of sb's work*) éditeur(-trice); **~orial** [ɛdɪ'tɔ:rɪəl] *adj* de la rédaction, éditorial(e) ♦ *n* éditorial *m*

educate ['ɛdjukeɪt] *vt* (*teach*) instruire; (*instruct*) éduquer; **~d** *adj* (*person*) cultivé(e); **education** [ɛdju'keɪʃən] *n* éducation *f*; (*studies*) études *fpl*; (*teaching*) enseignement *m*, instruction *f*; **educational** *adj* (*experience, toy*) pédagogique; (*institution*) scolaire; (*policy*) d'éducation

eel [i:l] *n* anguille *f*

eerie ['ɪərɪ] *adj* inquiétant(e)

effect [ɪ'fɛkt] *n* effet *m* ♦ *vt* effectuer; **to take ~** (*law*) entrer en vigueur, prendre effet; (*drug*) agir, faire son effet; **in ~** en fait; **~ive** [ɪ'fɛktɪv] *adj* efficace; (*actual*) véritable; **~ively** *adv* efficacement; (*in reality*) effectivement; **~iveness** *n* efficacité *f*

effeminate [ɪ'fɛmɪnɪt] *adj* efféminé(e)

effervescent [ɛfə'vɛsnt] *adj* (*drink*) gazeux(-euse)

efficiency [ɪ'fɪʃənsɪ] *n* efficacité *f*; (*of machine*) rendement *m*

efficient [ɪ'fɪʃənt] *adj* efficace; (*machine*) qui a un bon rendement

effort ['ɛfət] *n* effort *m*; **~less** *adj* (*style*) aisé(e); (*achievement*) facile

effusive [ɪ'fju:sɪv] *adj* chaleureux(-euse)

e.g. *adv abbr* (= *exempli gratia*) par exemple, p. ex.

egg [ɛg] *n* œuf *m*; **hard-boiled/soft-boiled ~** œuf dur/à la coque; **~ on** *vt* pousser; **~cup** *n* coquetier *m*; **~plant** *n*

(*esp US*) aubergine *f*; **~shell** *n* coquille *f* d'œuf

ego ['i:gəu] *n* (*self-esteem*) amour-propre *m*

egotism ['ɛgəutɪzəm] *n* égotisme *m*

egotist ['ɛgəutɪst] *n* égocentrique *m/f*

Egypt ['i:dʒɪpt] *n* Égypte *f*; **~ian** [ɪ'dʒɪpʃən] *adj* égyptien(ne) ♦ *n* Égyptien(ne)

eiderdown ['aɪdədaun] *n* édredon *m*

Eiffel Tower ['aɪfəl-] *n* tour *f* Eiffel

eight [eɪt] *num* huit; **~een** [eɪ'ti:n] *num* dix-huit; **~h** [eɪtθ] *num* huitième; **~y** ['eɪtɪ] *num* quatre-vingt(s)

Eire ['ɛərə] *n* République *f* d'Irlande

either ['aɪðə] *adj* l'un ou l'autre; (*both, each*) chaque ♦ *pron*: **~ (of them)** l'un ou l'autre ♦ *adv* non plus ♦ *conj*: **~ good or bad** ou bon ou mauvais, soit bon soit mauvais; **on ~ side** de chaque côté; **I don't like ~** je n'aime ni l'un ni l'autre; **no, I don't ~** moi non plus

eject [ɪ'dʒɛkt] *vt* (*tenant etc*) expulser; (*object*) éjecter

elaborate [*adj* ɪ'læbərɪt, *vb* ɪ'læbəreɪt] *adj* compliqué(e), recherché(e) ♦ *vt* élaborer ♦ *vi*: **to ~ (on)** entrer dans les détails (de)

elastic [ɪ'læstɪk] *adj* élastique ♦ *n* élastique *m*; **~ band** *n* élastique *m*

elated [ɪ'leɪtɪd] *adj* transporté(e) de joie

elation [ɪ'leɪʃən] *n* allégresse *f*

elbow ['ɛlbəu] *n* coude *m*

elder ['ɛldə] *adj* aîné(e) ♦ *n* (*tree*) sureau *m*; **one's ~s** ses aînés; **~ly** *adj* âgé(e) ♦ *npl*: **the ~ly** les personnes âgées

eldest ['ɛldɪst] *adj, n*: **the ~ (child)** l'aîné(e) (des enfants)

elect [ɪ'lɛkt] *vt* élire ♦ *adj*: **the president ~** le président désigné; **to ~ to do** choisir de faire; **~ion** *n* élection *f*; **~ioneering** [ɪlɛkʃə'nɪərɪŋ] *n* propagande électorale, manœuvres électorales; **~or** *n* électeur(-trice); **~orate** *n* électorat *m*

electric [ɪ'lɛktrɪk] *adj* électrique; **~al** *adj* électrique; **~ blanket** *n* couverture chauffante; **~ fire** (*BRIT*) *n* radiateur *m* électrique; **~ian** [ɪlɛk'trɪʃən] *n* électricien *m*; **~ity** [ɪlɛk'trɪsɪtɪ] *n* électricité *f*; **electrify** [ɪ'lɛktrɪfaɪ] *vt* (*RAIL, fence*) électrifier; (*audi* *ence*) électriser

electronic [ɪlek'trɒnɪk] *adj* électronique; ~ **mail** *n* courrier *m* électronique; ~**s** *n* électronique *f*

elegant ['elɪgənt] *adj* élégant(e)

element ['elɪmənt] *n* (*gen*) élément *m*; (*of heater, kettle etc*) résistance *f*; ~**ary** [elɪ'mentərɪ] *adj* élémentaire; (*school, education*) primaire

elephant ['elɪfənt] *n* éléphant *m*

elevation [elɪ'veɪʃən] *n* (*raising, promotion*) avancement *m*, promotion *f*; (*height*) hauteur *f*

elevator ['elɪveɪtər] *n* (*in warehouse etc*) élévateur *m*, monte-charge *m inv*; (*US: lift*) ascenseur *m*

eleven [ɪ'levn] *num* onze; ~**ses** [ɪ'levnzɪz] *npl* ≈ pause-café *f*; ~**th** *num* onzième

elicit [ɪ'lɪsɪt] *vt*: **to ~ (from)** obtenir (de), arracher (à)

eligible ['elɪdʒəbl] *adj*: **to be ~ for** remplir les conditions requises pour; **an ~ young man/woman** un beau parti

elm [elm] *n* orme *m*

elongated ['iːlɒŋgeɪtɪd] *adj* allongé(e)

elope [ɪ'ləup] *vi* (*lovers*) s'enfuir (ensemble)

eloquent ['eləkwənt] *adj* éloquent(e)

else [els] *adv* d'autre; **something ~** quelque chose d'autre, autre chose; **somewhere ~** ailleurs, autre part; **everywhere ~** partout ailleurs; **nobody ~** personne d'autre; **where ~?** à quel autre endroit?; **little ~** pas grand-chose d'autre; ~**where** *adv* ailleurs, autre part

elude [ɪ'luːd] *vt* échapper à

elusive [ɪ'luːsɪv] *adj* insaisissable

emaciated [ɪ'meɪsɪeɪtɪd] *adj* émacié(e), décharné(e)

e-mail ['iːmeɪl] *n* courrier *m* électronique ♦ *vt* (*person*) envoyer un message électronique à

emancipate [ɪ'mænsɪpeɪt] *vt* émanciper

embankment [ɪm'bæŋkmənt] *n* (*of road, railway*) remblai *m*, talus *m*; (*of river*) berge *f*, quai *m*

embark [ɪm'bɑːk] *vi* embarquer; **to ~ on** (*journey*) entreprendre; (*fig*) se lancer *or*

s'embarquer dans; ~**ation** [embɑː'keɪʃən] *n* embarquement *m*

embarrass [ɪm'bærəs] *vt* embarrasser, gêner; ~**ed** *adj* gêné(e); ~**ing** *adj* gênant(e), embarrassant(e); ~**ment** *n* embarras *m*, gêne *f*

embassy ['embəsɪ] *n* ambassade *f*

embedded [ɪm'bedɪd] *adj* enfoncé(e)

embellish [ɪm'belɪʃ] *vt* orner, décorer; (*fig: account*) enjoliver

embers ['embəz] *npl* braise *f*

embezzle [ɪm'bezl] *vt* détourner; ~**ment** *n* détournement *m* de fonds

embitter [ɪm'bɪtər] *vt* (*person*) aigrir; (*relations*) envenimer

embody [ɪm'bɒdɪ] *vt* (*features*) réunir, comprendre; (*ideas*) formuler, exprimer

embossed [ɪm'bɒst] *adj* (*metal*) estampé(e); (*leather*) frappé(e); ~ **wallpaper** papier gaufré

embrace [ɪm'breɪs] *vt* embrasser, étreindre; (*include*) embrasser ♦ *vi* s'étreindre, s'embrasser ♦ *n* étreinte *f*

embroider [ɪm'brɔɪdər] *vt* broder; ~**y** *n* broderie *f*

emerald ['emərəld] *n* émeraude *f*

emerge [ɪ'mɜːdʒ] *vi* apparaître; (*from room, car*) surgir; (*from sleep, imprisonment*) sortir

emergency [ɪ'mɜːdʒənsɪ] *n* urgence *f*; **in an ~** en cas d'urgence; ~ **cord** *n* sonnette *f* d'alarme; ~ **exit** *n* sortie *f* de secours; ~ **landing** *n* atterrissage forcé; ~ **services** *npl*: **the ~ services** (*fire, police, ambulance*) les services *mpl* d'urgence

emery board ['eməri-] *n* lime *f* à ongles (*en carton émerisé*)

emigrate ['emɪgreɪt] *vi* émigrer

eminent ['emɪnənt] *adj* éminent(e)

emissions [ɪ'mɪʃənz] *npl* émissions *fpl*

emit [ɪ'mɪt] *vt* émettre

emotion [ɪ'məuʃən] *n* émotion *f*; ~**al** *adj* (*person*) émotif(-ive), très sensible; (*needs, exhaustion*) affectif(-ive); (*scene*) émouvant(e); (*tone, speech*) qui fait appel aux sentiments; **emotive** *adj* chargé(e) d'émotion; (*subject*) sensible

emperor ['empərər] *n* empereur *m*

emphasis [ˈɛmfəsɪs] (*pl* **-ases**) *n* (*stress*) accent *m*; (*importance*) insistance *f*

emphasize [ˈɛmfəsaɪz] *vt* (*syllable, word, point*) appuyer *or* insister sur; (*feature*) souligner, accentuer

emphatic [ɛmˈfætɪk] *adj* (*strong*) énergique, vigoureux(-euse); (*unambiguous, clear*) catégorique

empire [ˈɛmpaɪəʳ] *n* empire *m*

employ [ɪmˈplɔɪ] *vt* employer; ~**ee** *n* employé(e); ~**er** *n* employeur(-euse); ~**ment** *n* emploi *m*; ~**ment agency** *n* agence *f or* bureau *m* de placement

empower [ɪmˈpauəʳ] *vt*: **to** ~ **sb to do** autoriser *or* habiliter qn à faire

empress [ˈɛmprɪs] *n* impératrice *f*

emptiness [ˈɛmptɪnɪs] *n* (*of area, region*) aspect *m* désertique; (*of life*) vide *m*, vacuité *f*

empty [ˈɛmptɪ] *adj* vide; (*threat, promise*) en l'air, vain(e) ♦ *vt* vider ♦ *vi* se vider; (*liquid*) s'écouler; ~**-handed** *adj* les mains vides

EMU *n abbr* (= *economic and monetary union*) UME *f*

emulate [ˈɛmjuleɪt] *vt* rivaliser avec, imiter

emulsion [ɪˈmʌlʃən] *n* émulsion *f*; (*also:* ~ **paint**) peinture mate

enable [ɪˈneɪbl] *vt*: **to** ~ **sb to do** permettre à qn de faire

enamel [ɪˈnæməl] *n* émail *m*; (*also:* ~ **paint**) peinture laquée

enchant [ɪnˈtʃɑːnt] *vt* enchanter; ~**ing** *adj* ravissant(e), enchanteur(-teresse)

encl. *abbr* = **enclosed**

enclose [ɪnˈkləʊz] *vt* (*land*) clôturer; (*space, object*) entourer; (*letter etc*): **to** ~ (**with**) joindre (à); **please find** ~**d** veuillez trouver ci-joint; **enclosure** *n* enceinte *f*

encompass [ɪnˈkʌmpəs] *vt* (*include*) contenir, inclure

encore [ɔŋˈkɔːʳ] *excl* bis ♦ *n* bis *m*

encounter [ɪnˈkauntəʳ] *n* rencontre *f* ♦ *vt* rencontrer

encourage [ɪnˈkʌrɪdʒ] *vt* encourager; ~**ment** *n* encouragement *m*

encroach [ɪnˈkrəʊtʃ] *vi*: **to** ~ (**up**)**on** empiéter sur

encyclop(a)edia [ɛnsaɪkləʊˈpiːdɪə] *n* encyclopédie *f*

end [ɛnd] *n* (*gen, also: aim*) fin *f*; (*of table, street, rope etc*) bout *m*, extrémité *f* ♦ *vt* terminer; (*also:* **bring to an** ~, **put an** ~ **to**) mettre fin à ♦ *vi* se terminer, finir; **in the** ~ finalement; **on** ~ (*object*) debout, dressé(e); **to stand on** ~ (*hair*) se dresser sur la tête; **for hours on** ~ pendant des heures et des heures; ~ **up** *vi*: **to** ~ **up in** (*condition*) finir *or* se terminer par; (*place*) finir *or* aboutir à

endanger [ɪnˈdeɪndʒəʳ] *vt* mettre en danger; **an** ~**ed species** une espèce en voie de disparition

endearing [ɪnˈdɪərɪŋ] *adj* attachant(e)

endeavour [ɪnˈdɛvəʳ] (*US* **endeavor**) *n* tentative *f*, effort *m* ♦ *vi*: **to** ~ **to do** tenter *or* s'efforcer de faire

ending [ˈɛndɪŋ] *n* dénouement *m*, fin *f*; (*LING*) terminaison *f*

endive [ˈɛndaɪv] *n* chicorée *f*; (*smooth*) endive *f*

endless [ˈɛndlɪs] *adj* sans fin, interminable

endorse [ɪnˈdɔːs] *vt* (*cheque*) endosser; (*approve*) appuyer, approuver, sanctionner; ~**ment** *n* (*approval*) appui *m*, aval *m*; (*BRIT: on driving licence*) contravention portée au permis de conduire

endure [ɪnˈdjuəʳ] *vt* supporter, endurer ♦ *vi* durer

enemy [ˈɛnəmɪ] *adj, n* ennemi(e)

energetic [ɛnəˈdʒɛtɪk] *adj* énergique; (*activity*) qui fait se dépenser (physiquement)

energy [ˈɛnədʒɪ] *n* énergie *f*

enforce [ɪnˈfɔːs] *vt* (*law*) appliquer, faire respecter

engage [ɪnˈgeɪdʒ] *vt* engager; (*attention etc*) retenir ♦ *vi* (*TECH*) s'enclencher, s'engrener; **to** ~ **in** se lancer dans; ~**d** *adj* (*BRIT: busy, in use*) occupé(e); (*betrothed*) fiancé(e); **to get** ~**d** se fiancer; ~**d tone** *n* (*TEL*) tonalité *f* occupé *inv or* pas libre; ~**ment** *n* obligation *f*, engagement *m*; rendez-vous *m inv*; (*to marry*) fiançailles *fpl*; ~**ment ring** *n* bague *f* de fiançailles

engaging *adj* engageant(e), attirant(e)

engine ['ɛndʒɪn] *n* (*AUT*) moteur *m*; (*RAIL*) locomotive *f*; ~ **driver** *n* mécanicien *m*

engineer [ɛndʒɪ'nɪər] *n* ingénieur *m*; (*BRIT: repairer*) dépanneur *m*; (*NAVY, US RAIL*) mécanicien *m*; ~**ing** *n* engineering *m*, ingénierie *f*; (*of bridges, ships*) génie *m*; (*of machine*) mécanique *f*

England ['ɪŋɡlənd] *n* Angleterre *f*; **English** *adj* anglais(e) ♦ *n* (*LING*) anglais *m*; **the English** *npl* (*people*) les Anglais; **the English Channel** la Manche; **Englishman** (*irreg*) *n* Anglais; **Englishwoman** (*irreg*) *n* Anglaise *f*

engraving [ɪn'ɡreɪvɪŋ] *n* gravure *f*

engrossed [ɪn'ɡrəust] *adj*: ~ **in** absorbé(e) par, plongé(e) dans

engulf [ɪn'ɡʌlf] *vt* engloutir

enhance [ɪn'hɑːns] *vt* rehausser, mettre en valeur

enjoy [ɪn'dʒɔɪ] *vt* aimer, prendre plaisir à; (*have: health, fortune*) jouir de; (: *success*) connaître; **to ~ o.s.** s'amuser; ~**able** *adj* agréable; ~**ment** *n* plaisir *m*

enlarge [ɪn'lɑːdʒ] *vt* accroître; (*PHOT*) agrandir ♦ *vi*: **to ~ on** (*subject*) s'étendre sur; ~**ment** [ɪn'lɑːdʒmənt] *n* (*PHOT*) agrandissement *m*

enlighten [ɪn'laɪtn] *vt* éclairer; ~**ed** *adj* éclairé(e); ~**ment** *n*: **the E~ment** (*HISTORY*) ≃ le Siècle des lumières

enlist [ɪn'lɪst] *vt* recruter; (*support*) s'assurer ♦ *vi* s'engager

enmity ['ɛnmɪtɪ] *n* inimitié *f*

enormous [ɪ'nɔːməs] *adj* énorme

enough [ɪ'nʌf] *adj, pron*: ~ **time/books** assez *or* suffisamment de temps/livres ♦ *adv*: **big** ~ assez *or* suffisamment grand; **have you got ~?** en avez-vous assez?; **he has not worked** ~ il n'a pas assez *or* suffisamment travaillé; ~ **to eat** assez à manger; ~**!** assez!, ça suffit!; **that's** ~, **thanks** cela suffit *or* c'est assez, merci; **I've had** ~ **of him** j'en ai assez de lui; **... which, funnily** *or* **oddly** ~ ... qui, chose curieuse

enquire [ɪn'kwaɪər] *vt, vi* = **inquire**

enrage [ɪn'reɪdʒ] *vt* mettre en fureur *or* en rage, rendre furieux(-euse)

enrol [ɪn'rəul] (*US* **enroll**) *vt* inscrire ♦ *vi* s'inscrire; ~**ment** (*US* **enrollment**) *n* inscription *f*

en suite ['ɒnswiːt] *adj*: **with ~ bathroom** avec salle de bains en attenante

ensure [ɪn'ʃuər] *vt* assurer; garantir; **to ~ that** s'assurer que

entail [ɪn'teɪl] *vt* entraîner, occasionner

entangled [ɪn'tæŋɡld] *adj*: **to become ~ (in)** s'empêtrer (dans)

enter ['ɛntər] *vt* (*room*) entrer dans, pénétrer dans; (*club, army*) entrer à; (*competition*) s'inscrire à *or* pour; (*sb for a competition*) (faire) inscrire; (*write down*) inscrire, noter; (*COMPUT*) entrer, introduire ♦ *vi* entrer; ~ **for** *vt fus* s'inscrire à, se présenter pour *or* à; ~ **into** *vt fus* (*explanation*) se lancer dans; (*discussion, negotiations*) entamer; (*agreement*) conclure

enterprise ['ɛntəpraɪz] *n* entreprise *f*; (*initiative*) (esprit *m* d')initiative *f*; **free ~** libre entreprise; **private ~** entreprise privée; **enterprising** *adj* entreprenant(e), dynamique; (*scheme*) audacieux(-euse)

entertain [ɛntə'teɪn] *vt* amuser, distraire; (*invite*) recevoir (à dîner); (*idea, plan*) envisager; ~**er** *n* artiste *m/f* de variétés; ~**ing** *adj* amusant(e), distrayant(e); ~**ment** *n* (*amusement*) divertissement *m*, amusement *m*; (*show*) spectacle *m*

enthralled [ɪn'θrɔːld] *adj* captivé(e)

enthusiasm [ɪn'θuːzɪæzəm] *n* enthousiasme *m*

enthusiast [ɪn'θuːzɪæst] *n* enthousiaste *m/f*; ~**ic** [ɪnθuːzɪ'æstɪk] *adj* enthousiaste; **to be ~ic about** être enthousiasmé(e) par

entire [ɪn'taɪər] *adj* (tout) entier(-ère); ~**ly** *adv* entièrement, complètement; ~**ty** [ɪn'taɪərətɪ] *n*: **in its ~ty** dans sa totalité

entitle [ɪn'taɪtl] *vt* (*book*) intituler; ~**d** *adj* (*book*) intitulé(e); **to be ~d to do** avoir le droit de *or* être habilité à faire

entrance [*n* 'ɛntrns, *vb* ɪn'trɑːns] *n* entrée *f* ♦ *vt* enchanter, ravir; **to gain ~ to** (*university etc*) être admis à; ~ **examination**

n examen *m* d'entrée; ~ **fee** *n* (*to museum etc*) prix *m* d'entrée; (*to join club etc*) droit *m* d'inscription; ~ **ramp** (*US*) (*AUT*) bretelle *f* d'accès; **entrant** *n* participant(e); concurrent(e); (*BRIT: in exam*) candidat(e)

entrenched [ɛn'trɛntʃt] *adj* retranché(e); (*ideas*) arrêté(e)

entrepreneur ['ɔntrəprə'nə:ʳ] *n* entrepreneur *m*

entrust [ɪn'trʌst] *vt*: **to ~ sth to** confier qch à

entry ['ɛntrɪ] *n* entrée *f*; (*in register*) inscription *f*; **no ~** défense d'entrer, entrée interdite; (*AUT*) sens interdit; ~ **form** feuille *f* d'inscription; ~ **phone** (*BRIT*) *n* interphone *m*

envelop [ɪn'vɛləp] *vt* envelopper

envelope ['ɛnvələup] *n* enveloppe *f*

envious ['ɛnvɪəs] *adj* envieux(-euse)

environment [ɪn'vaɪərnmənt] *n* environnement *m*; (*social, moral*) milieu *m*; ~**al** [ɪnvaɪərn'mɛntl] *adj* écologique; du milieu; ~-**friendly** *adj* écologique

envisage [ɪn'vɪzɪdʒ] *vt* (*foresee*) prévoir

envoy ['ɛnvɔɪ] *n* (*diplomat*) ministre *m* plénipotentiaire

envy ['ɛnvɪ] *n* envie *f* ♦ *vt* envier; **to ~ sb sth** envier qch à qn

epic ['ɛpɪk] *n* épopée *f* ♦ *adj* épique

epidemic [ɛpɪ'dɛmɪk] *n* épidémie *f*

epilepsy ['ɛpɪlɛpsɪ] *n* épilepsie *f*; **epileptic** *n* épileptique *m/f*

episode ['ɛpɪsəud] *n* épisode *m*

epitome [ɪ'pɪtəmɪ] *n* modèle *m*; **epitomize** *vt* incarner

equal ['i:kwl] *adj* égal(e) ♦ *n* égal(e) ♦ *vt* égaler; ~ **to** (*task*) à la hauteur de; ~**ity** [i:'kwɔlɪtɪ] *n* égalité *f*; ~**ize** *vi* (*SPORT*) égaliser; ~**ly** *adv* également; (*just as*) tout aussi

equanimity [ɛkwə'nɪmɪtɪ] *n* égalité *f* d'humeur

equate [ɪ'kweɪt] *vt*: **to ~ sth with** comparer qch à; assimiler qch à; **equation** *n* (*MATH*) équation *f*

equator [ɪ'kweɪtəʳ] *n* équateur *m*

equilibrium [i:kwɪ'lɪbrɪəm] *n* équilibre *m*

equip [ɪ'kwɪp] *vt*: **to ~ (with)** équiper (de); **to be well ~ped** être bien équipé(e); ~**ment** *n* équipement *m*; (*electrical etc*) appareillage *m*, installation *f*

equities ['ɛkwɪtɪz] (*BRIT*) *npl* (*COMM*) actions cotées en Bourse

equivalent [ɪ'kwɪvələnt] *adj*: ~ **(to)** équivalent(e) (à) ♦ *n* équivalent *m*

era ['ɪərə] *n* ère *f*, époque *f*

eradicate [ɪ'rædɪkeɪt] *vt* éliminer

erase [ɪ'reɪz] *vt* effacer; ~**r** *n* gomme *f*

erect [ɪ'rɛkt] *adj* droit(e) ♦ *vt* construire; (*monument*) ériger, élever; (*tent etc*) dresser; ~**ion** *n* érection *f*

ERM *n abbr* (= *Exchange Rate Mechanism*) MTC *m*

erode [ɪ'rəud] *vt* éroder; (*metal*) ronger

erotic [ɪ'rɔtɪk] *adj* érotique

errand ['ɛrənd] *n* course *f*, commission *f*

erratic [ɪ'rætɪk] *adj* irrégulier(-ère); inconstant(e)

error ['ɛrəʳ] *n* erreur *f*

erupt [ɪ'rʌpt] *vi* entrer en éruption; (*fig*) éclater; ~**ion** *n* éruption *f*

escalate ['ɛskəleɪt] *vi* s'intensifier

escalator ['ɛskəleɪtəʳ] *n* escalier roulant

escapade [ɛskə'peɪd] *n* (*misdeed*) fredaine *f*; (*adventure*) équipée *f*

escape [ɪs'keɪp] *n* fuite *f*; (*from prison*) évasion *f* ♦ *vi* s'échapper, fuir; (*from jail*) s'évader; (*fig*) s'en tirer; (*leak*) s'échapper ♦ *vt* échapper à; **to ~ from** (*person*) échapper à; (*place*) s'échapper de; (*fig*) fuir; **escapism** *n* (*fig*) évasion *f*

escort [*n* 'ɛskɔ:t, *vb* ɪs'kɔ:t] *n* escorte *f* ♦ *vt* escorter

Eskimo ['ɛskɪməu] *n* Esquimau(de)

especially [ɪs'pɛʃlɪ] *adv* (*particularly*) particulièrement; (*above all*) surtout

espionage ['ɛspɪənɑ:ʒ] *n* espionnage *m*

Esquire [ɪs'kwaɪəʳ] *n*: **J. Brown, ~** Monsieur J. Brown

essay ['ɛseɪ] *n* (*SCOL*) dissertation *f*; (*LITERATURE*) essai *m*

essence ['ɛsns] *n* essence *f*

essential [ɪ'sɛnʃl] *adj* essentiel(le); (*basic*) fondamental(e) ♦ *n*: ~**s** éléments essentiels; **~ly** *adv* essentiellement

establish [ɪs'tæblɪʃ] *vt* établir; (*business*) fonder, créer; (*one's power etc*) asseoir, affermir; **~ed** *adj* bien établi(e); **~ment** *n* établissement *m*; (*founding*) création *f*

estate [ɪs'teɪt] *n* (*land*) domaine *m*, propriété *f*; (*LAW*) biens *mpl*, succession *f*; (*BRIT: also:* **housing ~**) lotissement *m*, cité *f*; **~ agent** *n* agent immobilier; **~ car** (*BRIT*) *n* break *m*

esteem [ɪs'ti:m] *n* estime *f*

esthetic [ɪs'θetɪk] (*US*) *adj* = **aesthetic**

estimate [*n* 'estɪmət, *vb* 'estɪmeɪt] *n* estimation *f*; (*COMM*) devis *m* ♦ *vt* estimer; **estimation** [estɪ'meɪʃən] *n* opinion *f*; (*calculation*) estimation *f*

estranged [ɪs'treɪndʒd] *adj* séparé(e); dont on s'est séparé(e)

etc. *abbr* (= *et cetera*) etc

eternal [ɪ'tə:nl] *adj* éternel(le)

eternity [ɪ'tə:nɪtɪ] *n* éternité *f*

ethical ['eθɪkl] *adj* moral(e); **ethics** *n* éthique *f* ♦ *npl* moralité *f*

Ethiopia [i:θɪ'əʊpɪə] *n* Éthiopie *f*

ethnic ['eθnɪk] *adj* ethnique; (*music etc*) folklorique; **~ minority** *n* minorité *f* ethnique

ethos ['i:θɔs] *n* génie *m*

etiquette ['etɪket] *n* convenances *fpl*, étiquette *f*

EU *n abbr* (= *European Union*) UE *f*

euro ['juərəu] *n* (*currency*) euro *m*

Eurocheque ['juərəutʃek] *n* eurochèque *m*

Euroland ['juərəulænd] *n* Euroland *m*

Europe ['juərəp] *n* Europe *f*; **~an** [juərə'pi:ən] *adj* européen(ne) ♦ *n* Européen(ne); **~an Community** Communauté européenne

evacuate [ɪ'vækjueɪt] *vt* évacuer

evade [ɪ'veɪd] *vt* échapper à; (*question etc*) éluder; (*duties*) se dérober à; **to ~ tax** frauder le fisc

evaporate [ɪ'væpəreɪt] *vi* s'évaporer; **~d milk** *n* lait condensé non sucré

evasion [ɪ'veɪʒən] *n* dérobade *f*; **tax ~** fraude fiscale

eve [i:v] *n*: **on the ~ of** à la veille de

even ['i:vn] *adj* (*level, smooth*) régulier(-ère); (*equal*) égal(e); (*number*) pair(e) ♦ *adv* même; **~ if** même si +*indic*; **~ though** alors même que +*cond*; **~ more** encore plus; **~ so** quand même; **not ~** pas même; **to get ~ with sb** prendre sa revanche sur qn

evening ['i:vnɪŋ] *n* soir *m*; (*as duration, event*) soirée *f*; **in the ~** le soir; **~ class** *n* cours *m* du soir; **~ dress** *n* tenue *f* de soirée

event [ɪ'vent] *n* événement *m*; (*SPORT*) épreuve *f*; **in the ~ of** en cas de; **~ful** *adj* mouvementé(e)

eventual [ɪ'ventʃuəl] *adj* final(e); **~ity** [ɪventʃu'ælɪtɪ] *n* possibilité *f*, éventualité *f*; **~ly** *adv* finalement

ever ['evər] *adv* jamais; (*at all times*) toujours; **the best ~** le meilleur qu'on ait jamais vu; **have you ~ seen it?** l'as-tu déjà vu?, as-tu eu l'occasion *or* t'est-il arrivé de le voir?; **why ~ not?** mais enfin, pourquoi pas?; **~ since** *adv* depuis ♦ *conj* depuis que; **~green** *n* arbre *m* à feuilles persistantes; **~lasting** *adj* éternel(le)

every ['evrɪ] *adj* chaque; **~ day** tous les jours, chaque jour; **~ other/third day** tous les deux/trois jours; **~ other car** une voiture sur deux; **~ now and then** de temps en temps; **~body** *pron* tout le monde, tous *pl*; **~day** *adj* quotidien(ne), de tous les jours; **~one** *pron* = **everybody**; **~thing** *pron* tout; **~where** *adv* partout

evict [ɪ'vɪkt] *vt* expulser; **~ion** *n* expulsion *f*

evidence ['evɪdns] *n* (*proof*) preuve(s) *f(pl)*; (*of witness*) témoignage *m*; (*sign*): **to show ~ of** présenter des signes de; **to give ~** témoigner, déposer

evident ['evɪdnt] *adj* évident(e); **~ly** *adv* de toute évidence; (*apparently*) apparemment

evil ['i:vl] *adj* mauvais(e) ♦ *n* mal *m*

evoke [ɪ'vəuk] *vt* évoquer

evolution [i:və'lu:ʃən] *n* évolution *f*

evolve [ɪ'vɔlv] *vt* élaborer ♦ *vi* évoluer

ewe [ju:] n brebis f

ex- [ɛks] *prefix* ex-

exact [ɪgˈzækt] *adj* exact(e) ♦ *vt*: **to ~ sth (from)** extorquer qch (à); exiger qch (de); **~ing** *adj* exigeant(e); (*work*) astreignant(e); **~ly** *adv* exactement

exaggerate [ɪgˈzædʒəreɪt] *vt, vi* exagérer; **exaggeration** [ɪgzædʒəˈreɪʃən] *n* exagération *f*

exalted [ɪgˈzɔːltɪd] *adj* (*prominent*) élevé(e); (: *person*) haut placé(e)

exam [ɪgˈzæm] *n abbr* (SCOL) = **examination**

examination [ɪgzæmɪˈneɪʃən] *n* (SCOL, MED) examen *m*

examine [ɪgˈzæmɪn] *vt* (*gen*) examiner; (SCOL: *person*) interroger; **~r** *n* examinateur(-trice)

example [ɪgˈzɑːmpl] *n* exemple *m*; **for ~** par exemple

exasperate [ɪgˈzɑːspəreɪt] *vt* exaspérer; **exasperation** [ɪgzɑːspəˈreɪʃən] *n* exaspération *f*, irritation *f*

excavate [ˈɛkskəveɪt] *vt* excaver; **excavation** [ɛkskəˈveɪʃən] *n* fouilles *fpl*

exceed [ɪkˈsiːd] *vt* dépasser; (*one's powers*) outrepasser; **~ingly** *adv* extrêmement

excellent [ˈɛksələnt] *adj* excellent(e)

except [ɪkˈsɛpt] *prep* (*also*: **~ for, ~ing**) sauf, excepté ♦ *vt* excepter; **~ if/when** sauf si/quand; **~ that** sauf que, si ce n'est que; **~ion** *n* exception *f*; **to take ~ion to** s'offusquer de; **~ional** *adj* exceptionnel(le)

excerpt [ˈɛksəːpt] *n* extrait *m*

excess [ɪkˈsɛs] *n* excès *m*; **~ baggage** *n* excédent *m* de bagages; **~ fare** (BRIT) *n* supplément *m*; **~ive** *adj* excessif(-ive)

exchange [ɪksˈtʃeɪndʒ] *n* échange *m*; (*also*: **telephone ~**) central *m* ♦ *vt*: **to ~ (for)** échanger (contre); **~ rate** *n* taux *m* de change

Exchequer [ɪksˈtʃɛkəʳ] (BRIT) *n*: **the ~** l'Échiquier *m*, ≈ le ministère des Finances

excise [*n* ˈɛksaɪz, *vb* ɛkˈsaɪz] *n* taxe *f* ♦ *vt* exciser

excite [ɪkˈsaɪt] *vt* exciter; **to get ~d** s'exci-

ter; **~ment** *n* excitation *f*; **exciting** *adj* passionnant(e)

exclaim [ɪksˈkleɪm] *vi* s'exclamer; **exclamation** [ɛkskləˈmeɪʃən] *n* exclamation *f*; **exclamation mark** *n* point *m* d'exclamation

exclude [ɪksˈkluːd] *vt* exclure; **exclusion zone** *n* zone interdite; **exclusive** *adj* exclusif(-ive); (*club, district*) sélect(e); (*item of news*) en exclusivité; **exclusive of VAT** TVA non comprise; **mutually exclusive** qui s'excluent l'un(e) l'autre

excruciating [ɪksˈkruːʃɪeɪtɪŋ] *adj* atroce

excursion [ɪksˈkəːʃən] *n* excursion *f*

excuse [*n* ɪksˈkjuːs, *vb* ɪksˈkjuːz] *n* excuse *f* ♦ *vt* excuser; **to ~ sb from** (*activity*) dispenser qn de; **~ me!** excusez-moi!, pardon!; **now if you will ~ me, ...** maintenant, si vous (le) permettez ...

ex-directory [ˈɛksdɪˈrɛktərɪ] (BRIT) *adj* sur la liste rouge

execute [ˈɛksɪkjuːt] *vt* exécuter; **execution** *n* exécution *f*

executive [ɪgˈzɛkjutɪv] *n* (COMM) cadre *m*, (*of organization, political party*) bureau *m* ♦ *adj* exécutif(-ive)

exemplify [ɪgˈzɛmplɪfaɪ] *vt* illustrer; (*typify*) incarner

exempt [ɪgˈzɛmpt] *adj*: **~ from** exempté(e) or dispensé(e) de ♦ *vt*: **to ~ sb from** exempter or dispenser qn de

exercise [ˈɛksəsaɪz] *n* exercice *m* ♦ *v*, exercer; (*patience etc*) faire preuve de; (*dog*) promener ♦ *vi* prendre de l'exercice; **~ book** *n* cahier *m*

exert [ɪgˈzəːt] *vt* exercer, employer; **to ~ o.s.** se dépenser; **~ion** *n* effort *m*

exhale [ɛksˈheɪl] *vt* exhaler ♦ *vi* expirer

exhaust [ɪgˈzɔːst] *n* (*also*: **~ fumes**) gaz *mpl* d'échappement; (*also*: **~ pipe**) tuyau *m* d'échappement ♦ *vt* épuiser; **~ed** *ad* épuisé(e); **~ion** *n* épuisement *m*; **nervous ~ion** fatigue nerveuse; surmenage mental **~ive** *adj* très complet(-ète)

exhibit [ɪgˈzɪbɪt] *n* (ART) pièce exposée, objet exposé; (LAW) pièce à conviction ♦ *v* exposer; (*courage, skill*) faire preuve de

~ion [ɛksɪ'bɪʃən] n exposition f; (of ill-temper, talent etc) démonstration f

exhilarating [ɪg'zɪləreɪtɪŋ] adj grisant(e); stimulant(e)

ex-husband n ex-mari m

exile ['ɛksaɪl] n exil m; (person) exilé(e) ♦ vt exiler

exist [ɪg'zɪst] vi exister; **~ence** n existence f; **~ing** adj actuel(le)

exit ['ɛksɪt] n sortie f ♦ vi (COMPUT, THEATRE) sortir; **~ poll** n sondage m (fait à la sortie de l'isoloir); **~ ramp** n (AUT) bretelle f d'accès

exodus ['ɛksədəs] n exode m

exonerate [ɪg'zɔnəreɪt] vt: **to ~ from** disculper de

exotic [ɪg'zɔtɪk] adj exotique

expand [ɪks'pænd] vt agrandir; accroître ♦ vi (trade etc) se développer, s'accroître; (gas, metal) se dilater

expanse [ɪks'pæns] n étendue f

expansion [ɪks'pænʃən] n développement m, accroissement m

expect [ɪks'pɛkt] vt (anticipate) s'attendre à, s'attendre à ce que +sub; (count on) compter sur, escompter; (require) demander, exiger; (suppose) supposer; (await, also baby) attendre ♦ vi: **to be ~ing** être enceinte; **~ancy** n (anticipation) attente f; **life ~ancy** espérance f de vie; **~ant mother** n future maman; **~ation** [ɛkspɛk'teɪʃən] n attente f; espérance(s) f(pl)

expedient [ɪks'piːdɪənt] adj indiqué(e), opportun(e) ♦ n expédient m

expedition [ɛkspə'dɪʃən] n expédition f

expel [ɪks'pɛl] vt chasser, expulser; (SCOL) renvoyer

expend [ɪks'pɛnd] vt consacrer; (money) dépenser; **~iture** [ɪks'pɛndɪtʃəʳ] n dépense f; dépenses fpl

expense [ɪks'pɛns] n dépense f, frais mpl; (high cost) coût m; **~s** npl (COMM) frais mpl; **at the ~ of** aux dépens de; **~ account** n (note f de) frais mpl; **expensive** adj cher (chère), coûteux(-euse); **to be expensive** coûter cher

experience [ɪks'pɪərɪəns] n expérience f ♦ vt connaître, faire l'expérience de; (feeling) éprouver; **~d** adj expérimenté(e)

experiment [ɪks'pɛrɪmənt] n expérience f ♦ vi faire une expérience; **to ~ with** expérimenter

expert ['ɛkspəːt] adj expert(e) ♦ n expert m; **~ise** [ɛkspəː'tiːz] n (grande) compétence

expire [ɪks'paɪəʳ] vi expirer; **expiry** n expiration f

explain [ɪks'pleɪn] vt expliquer; **explanation** [ɛksplə'neɪʃən] n explication f; **explanatory** [ɪks'plænətrɪ] adj explicatif(-ive)

explicit [ɪks'plɪsɪt] adj explicite; (definite) formel(le)

explode [ɪks'pləud] vi exploser

exploit [n 'ɛksplɔɪt, vb ɪks'plɔɪt] n exploit m ♦ vt exploiter; **~ation** [ɛksplɔɪ'teɪʃən] n exploitation f

exploratory [ɪks'plɔrətrɪ] adj (expedition) d'exploration; (fig: talks) préliminaire

explore [ɪks'plɔːʳ] vt explorer; (possibilities) étudier, examiner; **~r** n explorateur(-trice)

explosion [ɪks'pləuʒən] n explosion f; **explosive** adj explosif(-ive) ♦ n explosif m

exponent [ɪks'pəunənt] n (of school of thought etc) interprète m, représentant m

export [vb ɛks'pɔːt, n 'ɛkspɔːt] vt exporter ♦ n exportation f ♦ cpd d'exportation; **~er** n exportateur m

expose [ɪks'pəuz] vt exposer; (unmask) démasquer, dévoiler; **~d** adj (position, house) exposé(e); **exposure** n exposition f; (publicity) couverture f; (PHOT) (temps m de) pose f; (: shot) pose; **to die from exposure** (MED) mourir de froid; **exposure meter** n posemètre m

express [ɪks'prɛs] adj (definite) formel(le), exprès(-esse); (BRIT: letter etc) exprès inv ♦ n (train) rapide m; (bus) car m express ♦ vt exprimer; **~ion** n expression f; **~ly** adv expressément, formellement; **~way** (US) n (urban motorway) voie f express (à plusieurs files)

exquisite [ɛks'kwɪzɪt] adj exquis(e)

extend [ɪks'tɛnd] vt (visit, street) prolonger;

(*building*) agrandir; (*offer*) présenter, offrir; (*hand, arm*) tendre ♦ *vi* s'étendre; **extension** *n* prolongation *f*; agrandissement *m*; (*building*) annexe *f*; (*to wire, table*) rallonge *f*; (*telephone: in offices*) poste *m*; (: *in private house*) téléphone *m* supplémentaire; **extensive** *adj* étendu(e), vaste; (*damage, alterations*) considérable; (*inquiries*) approfondi(e); **extensively** *adv*: **he's travelled extensively** il a beaucoup voyagé

extent [ɪks'tɛnt] *n* étendue *f*; **to some ~** dans une certaine mesure; **to what ~?** dans quelle mesure?, jusqu'à quel point?; **to the ~ of ...** au point de ...; **to such an ~ that ...** à tel point que ...

extenuating [ɪks'tɛnjʊeɪtɪŋ] *adj*: **~ circumstances** circonstances atténuantes

exterior [ɛks'tɪərɪər] *adj* extérieur(e) ♦ *n* extérieur *m*; dehors *m*

external [ɛks'tə:nl] *adj* externe

extinct [ɪks'tɪŋkt] *adj* éteint(e)

extinguish [ɪks'tɪŋgwɪʃ] *vt* éteindre

extort [ɪks'tɔ:t] *vt*: **to ~ sth (from)** extorquer qch (à); **~ionate** *adj* exorbitant(e)

extra [ˈɛkstrə] *adj* supplémentaire, de plus ♦ *adv* (*in addition*) en plus ♦ *n* supplément *m*; (*perk*) à-côté *m*; (*THEATRE*) figurant(e) ♦ *prefix* extra...

extract [*vb* ɪks'trækt, *n* ˈɛkstrækt] *vt* extraire; (*tooth*) arracher; (*money, promise*) soutirer ♦ *n* extrait *m*

extracurricular [ˈɛkstrəkəˈrɪkjʊlər] *adj* parascolaire

extradite [ˈɛkstrədaɪt] *vt* extrader

extra...: **~marital** [ˈɛkstrəˈmærɪtl] *adj* extra-conjugal(e); **~mural** [ˈɛkstrəˈmjuərl] *adj* hors faculté *inv*; (*lecture*) public(-que); **~ordinary** [ɪks'trɔ:dnrɪ] *adj* extraordinaire

extravagance [ɪks'trævəgəns] *n* prodigalités *fpl*; (*thing bought*) folie *f*, dépense excessive; **extravagant** *adj* extravagant(e); (*in spending: person*) prodigue, dépensier(-ère); (: *tastes*) dispendieux(-euse)

extreme [ɪks'tri:m] *adj* extrême ♦ *n* extrême *m*; **~ly** *adv* extrêmement; **extremist** *adj*, *n* extrémiste *m/f*

extricate [ˈɛkstrɪkeɪt] *vt*: **to ~ sth (from)**

dégager qch (de)

extrovert [ˈɛkstrəvə:t] *n* extraverti(e)

ex-wife *n* ex-femme *f*

eye [aɪ] *n* œil *m* (*pl* yeux); (*of needle*) trou *m*, chas *m* ♦ *vt* examiner; **to keep an ~ on** surveiller; **~brow** *n* sourcil *m*; **~drops** *npl* gouttes *fpl* pour les yeux; **~lash** *n* cil *m*; **~lid** *n* paupière *f*; **~liner** *n* eye-liner *m*; **~-opener** *n* révélation *f*; **~shadow** *n* ombre *f* à paupières; **~sight** *n* vue *f*; **~sore** *n* horreur *f*; **~ witness** *n* témoin *m* oculaire

F, f

F [ɛf] *n* (*MUS*) fa *m*

fable [ˈfeɪbl] *n* fable *f*

fabric [ˈfæbrɪk] *n* tissu *m*

fabulous [ˈfæbjʊləs] *adj* fabuleux(-euse); (*inf: super*) formidable

face [feɪs] *n* visage *m*, figure *f*; (*expression*) expression *f*; (*of clock*) cadran *m*; (*of cliff*) paroi *f*; (*of mountain*) face *f*; (*of building*) façade *f* ♦ *vt* faire face à; **~ down** (*person*) à plat ventre; (*card*) face en dessous; **to lose/save ~** perdre/sauver la face; **to make** *or* **pull a ~** faire une grimace; **in the ~ of** (*difficulties etc*) face à, devant; **on the ~ of it** à première vue; **~ to ~** face à face; **~ up to** *vt fus* faire face à, affronter; **~ cloth** (*BRIT*) *n* gant *m* de toilette; **~ cream** *n* crème *f* pour le visage; **~ lift** *n* lifting *m*; (*of building etc*) ravalement *m*, retapage *m*; **~ powder** *n* poudre *f* de riz; **~ value** *n* (*of coin*) valeur nominale; **to take sth at ~ value** (*fig*) prendre qch pour argent comptant

facilities [fəˈsɪlɪtɪz] *npl* installations *fpl*, équipement *m*; **credit ~** facilités *fpl* de paiement

facing [ˈfeɪsɪŋ] *prep* face à, en face de

facsimile [fækˈsɪmɪlɪ] *n* (*exact replica*) facsimilé *m*; (*fax*) télécopie *f*

fact [fækt] *n* fait *m*; **in ~** en fait

factor [ˈfæktər] *n* facteur *m*

factory [ˈfæktərɪ] *n* usine *f*, fabrique *f*

factual ['fæktjuəl] *adj* basé(e) sur les faits

faculty ['fækəltı] *n* faculté *f*; (US: *teaching staff*) corps enseignant

fad [fæd] *n* (*craze*) engouement *m*

fade [feɪd] *vi* se décolorer, passer; (*light, sound*) s'affaiblir; (*flower*) se faner

fag [fæg] (BRIT: *inf*) *n* (*cigarette*) sèche *f*

fail [feɪl] *vt* (*exam*) échouer à; (*candidate*) recaler; (*subj: courage, memory*) faire défaut à ♦ *vi* échouer; (*brakes*) lâcher; (*eyesight, health, light*) baisser, s'affaiblir; **to ~ to do sth** (*neglect*) négliger de faire qch; (*be unable*) ne pas arriver *or* parvenir à faire qch; **without ~** à coup sûr; sans faute; **~ing** *n* défaut *m* ♦ *prep* faute de; **~ure** *n* échec *m*; (*person*) raté(e); (*mechanical etc*) défaillance *f*

faint [feɪnt] *adj* faible; (*recollection*) vague; (*mark*) à peine visible ♦ *n* évanouissement *m* ♦ *vi* s'évanouir; **to feel ~** défaillir

fair [feər] *adj* équitable, juste, impartial(e); (*hair*) blond(e); (*skin, complexion*) pâle, blanc (blanche); (*weather*) beau (belle); (*good enough*) assez bon(ne); (*sizeable*) considérable ♦ *adv*: **to play ~** jouer franc-jeu ♦ *n* foire *f*; (BRIT: *funfair*) fête (foraine); **~ly** *adv* équitablement; (*quite*) assez; **~ness** *n* justice *f*, équité *f*, impartialité *f*

fairy ['fεərı] *n* fée *f*; **~ tale** *n* conte *m* de fées

faith [feɪθ] *n* foi *f*; (*trust*) confiance *f*; (*specific religion*) religion *f*; **~ful** *adj* fidèle; **~fully** *adv see* **yours**

fake [feɪk] *n* (*painting etc*) faux *m*; (*person*) imposteur *m* ♦ *adj* faux (fausse) ♦ *vt* simuler; (*painting*) faire un faux de

falcon ['fɔːlkən] *n* faucon *m*

fall [fɔːl] (*pt* **fell**, *pp* **fallen**) *n* chute *f*; (US: *autumn*) automne *m* ♦ *vi* tomber; (*price, temperature, dollar*) baisser; **~s** *npl* (*waterfall*) chute *f* d'eau, cascade *f*; **to ~ flat** (*on one's face*) tomber de tout son long, s'étaler; (*joke*) tomber à plat; (*plan*) échouer; **~ back** *vi* reculer, se retirer; **~ back on** *vt fus* se rabattre sur; **~ behind** *vi* prendre du retard; **~ down** *vi* (*person*) tomber;

(*building*) s'effondrer, s'écrouler; **~ for** *vt fus* (*trick, story etc*) se laisser prendre à; (*person*) tomber amoureux de; **~ in** *vi* s'effondrer; (MIL) se mettre en rangs; **~ off** *vi* tomber; (*diminish*) baisser, diminuer; **~ out** *vi* (*hair, teeth*) tomber; (MIL) rompre les rangs; (*friends etc*) se brouiller; **~ through** *vi* (*plan, project*) tomber à l'eau

fallacy ['fæləsı] *n* erreur *f*, illusion *f*

fallout ['fɔːlaut] *n* retombées (radioactives)

fallow ['fæləu] *adj* en jachère; en friche

false [fɔːls] *adj* faux (fausse); **~ alarm** *n* fausse alerte; **~ pretences** *npl*: **under ~ pretences** sous un faux prétexte; **~ teeth** (BRIT) *npl* fausses dents

falter ['fɔːltər] *vi* chanceler, vaciller

fame [feɪm] *n* renommée *f*, renom *m*

familiar [fə'mılıər] *adj* familier(-ère); **to be ~ with** (*subject*) connaître

family ['fæmılı] *n* famille *f* ♦ *cpd* (*business, doctor etc*) de famille; **has he any ~?** (*children*) a-t-il des enfants?

famine ['fæmın] *n* famine *f*

famished ['fæmıʃt] (*inf*) *adj* affamé(e)

famous ['feɪməs] *adj* célèbre; **~ly** *adv* (*get on*) fameusement, à merveille

fan [fæn] *n* (*folding*) éventail *m*; (ELEC) ventilateur *m*; (*of person*) fan *m*, admirateur(-trice); (*of team, sport etc*) supporter *m/f* ♦ *vt* éventer; (*fire, quarrel*) attiser

fanatic [fə'nætɪk] *n* fanatique *m/f*

fan belt *n* courroie *f* de ventilateur

fancy ['fænsı] *n* fantaisie *f*, envie *f*; imagination *f* ♦ *adj* (de) fantaisie *inv* ♦ *vt* (*feel like, want*) avoir envie de; (*imagine, think*) imaginer; **to take a ~ to** se prendre d'affection pour; s'enticher de; **he fancies her** (*inf*) elle lui plaît; **~ dress** *n* déguisement *m*, travesti *m*; **~-dress ball** *n* bal masqué *or* costumé

fang [fæŋ] *n* croc *m*; (*of snake*) crochet *m*

fantastic [fæn'tæstɪk] *adj* fantastique

fantasy ['fæntəsı] *n* imagination *f*, fantaisie *f*; (*dream*) chimère *f*

far [fɑːr] *adj* lointain(e), éloigné(e) ♦ *adv* loin; **~ away** *or* **off** au loin, dans le lointain; **at the ~ side/end** à l'autre côté/

bout; ~ **better** beaucoup mieux; ~ **from** loin de; **by** ~ de loin, de beaucoup; **go as** ~ **as the farm** allez jusqu'à la ferme; **as** ~ **as I know** pour autant que je sache; **how** ~ **is it to ...?** combien y a-t-il jusqu'à ...?; **how** ~ **have you got?** où en êtes-vous?; **~away** ['fɑːrəweɪ] *adj* lointain(e); *(look)* distrait(e)

farce [fɑːs] *n* farce *f*

fare [feəʳ] *n (on trains, buses)* prix *m* du billet; *(in taxi)* prix de la course; *(food)* table *f*, chère *f*; **half** ~ demi-tarif; **full** ~ plein tarif

Far East *n* Extrême-Orient *m*

farewell [feəˈwel] *excl* adieu ♦ *n* adieu *m*

farm [fɑːm] *n* ferme *f* ♦ *vt* cultiver; **~er** *n* fermier(-ère); cultivateur(-trice); **~hand** *n* ouvrier(-ère) agricole; **~house** *n* (maison *f* de) ferme *f*; **~ing** *n* agriculture *f*; *(of animals)* élevage *m*; **~land** *n* terres cultivées; ~ **worker** *n* = **farmhand**; **~yard** *n* cour *f* de ferme

far-reaching ['fɑːˈriːtʃɪŋ] *adj* d'une grande portée

fart [fɑːt] *(inf!)* *vi* péter

farther ['fɑːðəʳ] *adv* plus loin ♦ *adj* plus éloigné(e), plus lointain(e)

farthest ['fɑːðɪst] *superl* of **far**

fascinate ['fæsɪneɪt] *vt* fasciner; **fascinating** *adj* fascinant(e)

fascism ['fæʃɪzəm] *n* fascisme *m*

fashion ['fæʃən] *n* mode *f*; *(manner)* façon *f*, manière *f* ♦ *vt* façonner; **in** ~ à la mode; **out of** ~ démodé(e); **~able** *adj* à la mode; ~ **show** *n* défilé *m* de mannequins *or* de mode

fast [fɑːst] *adj* rapide; *(clock):* **to be** ~ avancer; *(dye, colour)* grand *or* bon teint *inv* ♦ *adv* vite, rapidement; *(stuck, held)* solidement ♦ *n* jeûne *m* ♦ *vi* jeûner; ~ **asleep** profondément endormi

fasten ['fɑːsn] *vt* attacher, fixer; *(coat)* attacher, fermer ♦ *vi* se fermer, s'attacher; **~er**, **~ing** *n* attache *f*

fast food *n* fast food *m*, restauration *f* rapide

fastidious [fæsˈtɪdɪəs] *adj* exigeant(e), difficile

fat [fæt] *adj* gros(se) ♦ *n* graisse *f*; *(on meat)* gras *m*; *(for cooking)* matière grasse

fatal ['feɪtl] *adj (injury etc)* mortel(le); *(mistake)* fatal(e); **~ity** [fəˈtælɪtɪ] *n (road death etc)* victime *f*, décès *m*

fate [feɪt] *n* destin *m*; *(of person)* sort *m*; **~ful** *adj* fatidique

father ['fɑːðəʳ] *n* père *m*; **~-in-law** *n* beau-père *m*; **~ly** *adj* paternel(le)

fathom ['fæðəm] *n* brasse *f* (= 1828 mm) ♦ *vt (mystery)* sonder, pénétrer

fatigue [fəˈtiːg] *n* fatigue *f*

fatten ['fætn] *vt, vi* engraisser

fatty ['fætɪ] *adj (food)* gras(se) ♦ *n (inf)* gros(se)

fatuous ['fætjuəs] *adj* stupide

faucet ['fɔːsɪt] *(US)* *n* robinet *m*

fault [fɔːlt] *n* faute *f*; *(defect)* défaut *m*; *(GEO)* faille *f* ♦ *vt* trouver des défauts à; **it's my** ~ c'est de ma faute; **to find** ~ **with** trouver à redire or à critiquer à; **at** ~ fautif(-ive), coupable; **~y** *adj* défectueux(-euse)

fauna ['fɔːnə] *n* faune *f*

favour ['feɪvəʳ] *(US* **favor***) n* faveur *f*; *(help)* service *m* ♦ *vt (proposition)* être en faveur de; *(pupil etc)* favoriser; *(team, horse)* donner gagnant; **to do sb a** ~ rendre un service à qn; **to find** ~ **with** trouver grâce aux yeux de; **in** ~ **of** en faveur de; **~able** *adj* favorable; **~ite** ['feɪvrɪt] *adj, n* favori(te)

fawn [fɔːn] *n* faon *m* ♦ *adj (colour)* fauve ♦ *vi:* **to** ~ **(up)on** flatter servilement

fax [fæks] *n (document)* télécopie *f*; *(machine)* télécopieur *m* ♦ *vt* envoyer par télécopie

FBI *n abbr (US: Federal Bureau of Investigation)* F.B.I. *m*

fear [fɪəʳ] *n* crainte *f*, peur *f* ♦ *vt* craindre; **for** ~ **of** de peur que +*sub*, de peur de +*infin*; **~ful** *adj* craintif(-ive); *(sight, noise)* affreux(-euse), épouvantable; **~less** *adj* intrépide

feasible ['fiːzəbl] *adj* faisable, réalisable

feast [fiːst] *n* festin *m*, banquet *m*; *(REL:*

also: **~ day**) fête *f* ♦ *vi* festoyer

feat [fiːt] *n* exploit *m*, prouesse *f*

feather [ˈfɛðər] *n* plume *f*

feature [ˈfiːtʃər] *n* caractéristique *f*; (*article*) chronique *f*, rubrique *f* ♦ *vt* (*subj: film*) avoir pour vedette(s) ♦ *vi*: **to ~ in** figurer (en bonne place) dans; (*in film*) jouer dans; **~s** *npl* (*of face*) traits *mpl*; **~ film** *n* long métrage

February [ˈfɛbruəri] *n* février *m*

fed [fɛd] *pt, pp of* **feed**

federal [ˈfɛdərəl] *adj* fédéral(e)

fed up *adj*: **to be ~** en avoir marre, en avoir plein le dos

fee [fiː] *n* rémunération *f*; (*of doctor, lawyer*) honoraires *mpl*; (*for examination*) droits *mpl*; **school ~s** frais *mpl* de scolarité

feeble [ˈfiːbl] *adj* faible; (*pathetic: attempt, excuse*) pauvre; (: *joke*) piteux(-euse)

feed [fiːd] (*pt, pp* **fed**) *n* (*of animal*) fourrage *m*; pâture *f*; (*on printer*) mécanisme *m* d'alimentation ♦ *vt* (*person*) nourrir; (*BRIT: baby*) allaiter; (: *with bottle*) donner le biberon à; (*horse etc*) donner à manger à; (*machine*) alimenter; (*data, information*): **to ~ sth into** fournir qch à; **~ on** *vt fus* se nourrir de; **~back** *n* feed-back *m inv*

feel [fiːl] (*pt, pp* **felt**) *n* sensation *f*; (*impression*) impression *f* ♦ *vt* toucher; (*explore*) tâter, palper; (*cold, pain*) sentir; (*grief, anger*) ressentir, éprouver; (*think, believe*) trouver; **to ~ hungry/cold** avoir faim/ froid; **to ~ lonely/better** se sentir seul/ mieux; **I don't ~ well** je ne me sens pas bien; **it ~s soft** c'est doux (douce) au toucher; **to ~ like** (*want*) avoir envie de; **~ about** *vi* fouiller, tâtonner; **~er** *n* (*of insect*) antenne *f*; **~ing** *n* (*physical*) sensation *f*; (*emotional*) sentiment *m*

feet [fiːt] *npl of* **foot**

feign [feɪn] *vt* feindre, simuler

fell [fɛl] *pt of* **fall** ♦ *vt* (*tree, person*) abattre

fellow [ˈfɛləu] *n* type *m*; (*comrade*) compagnon *m*; (*of learned society*) membre *m* ♦ *cpd*: **their ~ prisoners/students** leurs camarades prisonniers/d'étude; **~ citizen** *n* concitoyen(ne) *m/f*; **~ countryman** (*ir-*

reg) *n* compatriote *m*; **~ men** *npl* semblables *mpl*; **~ship** *n* (*society*) association *f*; (*comradeship*) amitié *f*, camaraderie *f*; (*grant*) *sorte de bourse universitaire*

felony [ˈfɛləni] *n* crime *m*, forfait *m*

felt [fɛlt] *pt, pp of* **feel** ♦ *n* feutre *m*; **~-tip pen** *n* stylo-feutre *m*

female [ˈfiːmeɪl] *n* (*ZOOL*) femelle *f*; (*pej: woman*) bonne femme ♦ *adj* (*BIO*) femelle; (*sex, character*) féminin(e); (*vote etc*) des femmes

feminine [ˈfɛmɪnɪn] *adj* féminin(e)

feminist [ˈfɛmɪnɪst] *n* féministe *m/f*

fence [fɛns] *n* barrière *f* ♦ *vt* (*also:* **~ in**) clôturer ♦ *vi* faire de l'escrime; **fencing** *n* escrime *m*

fend [fɛnd] *vi*: **to ~ for o.s.** se débrouiller (tout seul); **~ off** *vt* (*attack etc*) parer

fender [ˈfɛndər] *n* garde-feu *m inv*; (*on boat*) défense *f*; (*US: of car*) aile *f*

ferment [*vb* fəˈmɛnt, *n* ˈfəːmɛnt] *vi* fermenter ♦ *n* agitation *f*, effervescence *f*

fern [fəːn] *n* fougère *f*

ferocious [fəˈrəuʃəs] *adj* féroce

ferret [ˈfɛrɪt] *n* furet *m*

ferry [ˈfɛri] *n* (*small*) bac *m*; (*large: also:* **~boat**) ferry(-boat) *m* ♦ *vt* transporter

fertile [ˈfəːtaɪl] *adj* fertile; (*BIO*) fécond(e); **fertilizer** [ˈfəːtɪlaɪzər] *n* engrais *m*

fester [ˈfɛstər] *vi* suppurer

festival [ˈfɛstɪvəl] *n* (*REL*) fête *f*; (*ART, MUS*) festival *m*

festive [ˈfɛstɪv] *adj* de fête; **the ~ season** (*BRIT: Christmas*) la période des fêtes; **festivities** *npl* réjouissances *fpl*

festoon [fɛsˈtuːn] *vt*: **to ~ with** orner de

fetch [fɛtʃ] *vt* aller chercher; (*sell for*) se vendre

fête [feɪt] *n* fête *f*, kermesse *f*

feud [fjuːd] *n* dispute *f*, dissension *f*

fever [ˈfiːvər] *n* fièvre *f*; **~ish** *adj* fiévreux(- euse), fébrile

few [fjuː] *adj* (*not many*) peu de; **a ~** ♦ *adj* quelques ♦ *pron* quelques-uns(-unes); **~er** [ˈfjuːər] *adj* moins de; moins (nombreux); **~est** [ˈfjuːɪst] *adj* le moins (de)

fiancé, e [fɪˈɑ̃ːŋseɪ] *n* fiancé(e) *m/f*

fib [fɪb] *n* bobard *m*

fibre ['faɪbə'] (*US* **fiber**) *n* fibre *f*; **~glass** ['faɪbəglɑ:s] (*US* **Fiberglass** ®) *n* fibre de verre

fickle ['fɪkl] *adj* inconstant(e), volage, capricieux(-euse)

fiction ['fɪkʃən] *n* romans *mpl*, littérature *f* romanesque; (*invention*) fiction *f*; **~al** *adj* fictif(-ive)

fictitious *adj* fictif(-ive), imaginaire

fiddle ['fɪdl] *n* (*MUS*) violon *m*; (*cheating*) combine *f*; escroquerie *f* ♦ *vt* (*BRIT: accounts*) falsifier, maquiller; **~ with** *vt fus* tripoter

fidget ['fɪdʒɪt] *vi* se trémousser, remuer

field [fi:ld] *n* champ *m*; (*fig*) domaine *m*, champ; (*SPORT: ground*) terrain *m*; **~work** *n* travaux *mpl* pratiques (sur le terrain)

fiend [fi:nd] *n* démon *m*

fierce [fɪəs] *adj* (*look, animal*) féroce, sauvage; (*wind, attack, person*) (très) violent(e); (*fighting, enemy*) acharné(e)

fiery ['faɪəri] *adj* ardent(e), brûlant(e); (*temperament*) fougueux(-euse)

fifteen [fɪf'ti:n] *num* quinze

fifth [fɪfθ] *num* cinquième

fifty ['fɪftɪ] *num* cinquante; **~-fifty** *adj*: **a ~-fifty chance** *etc* une chance *etc* sur deux ♦ *adv* moitié-moitié

fig [fɪg] *n* figue *f*

fight [faɪt] (*pt, pp* **fought**) *n* (*MIL*) combat *m*; (*between persons*) bagarre *f*; (*against cancer etc*) lutte *f* ♦ *vt* se battre contre; (*cancer, alcoholism, emotion*) combattre, lutter contre; (*election*) se présenter à ♦ *vi* se battre; **~er** *n* (*fig*) lutteur *m*; (*plane*) chasseur *m*; **~ing** *n* combats *mpl*; (*brawl*) bagarres *fpl*

figment ['fɪgmənt] *n*: **a ~ of the imagination** une invention

figurative ['fɪgjurətɪv] *adj* figuré(e)

figure ['fɪgə'] *n* figure *f*; (*number, cipher*) chiffre *m*; (*body, outline*) silhouette *f*; (*shape*) ligne *f*, formes *fpl* ♦ *vt* (*think: esp US*) supposer ♦ *vi* (*appear*) figurer; **~ out** *vt* (*work out*) calculer; **~head** *n* (*NAUT*) figure *f* de proue; (*pej*) prête-nom *m*; **~**

of speech *n* figure *f* de rhétorique

file [faɪl] *n* (*dossier*) dossier *m*; (*folder*) dossier, chemise *f*; (: *with hinges*) classeur *m*; (*COMPUT*) fichier *m*; (*row*) file *f*; (*tool*) lime *f* ♦ *vt* (*nails, wood*) limer; (*papers*) classer; (*LAW: claim*) faire enregistrer; déposer ♦ *vi*: **to ~ in/out** entrer/sortir l'un derrière l'autre; **to ~ for divorce** faire une demande en divorce; **filing cabinet** *n* classeur *m* (*meuble*)

fill [fɪl] *vt* remplir; (*need*) répondre à ♦ *n*: **to eat one's ~** manger à sa faim; **to ~ with** remplir de; **~ in** *vt* (*hole*) boucher; (*form*) remplir; **~ up** *vt* remplir; **~ it up, please** (*AUT*) le plein, s'il vous plaît

fillet ['fɪlɪt] *n* filet *m*; **~ steak** *n* filet *m* de bœuf, tournedos *m*

filling ['fɪlɪŋ] *n* (*CULIN*) garniture *f*, farce *f*; (*for tooth*) plombage *m*; **~ station** *n* station-service *f*

film [fɪlm] *n* film *m*; (*PHOT*) pellicule *f*, film *m*; (*of powder, liquid*) couche *f*, pellicule ♦ *vt* (*scene*) filmer ♦ *vi* tourner; **~ star** *n* vedette *f* de cinéma

filter ['fɪltə'] *n* filtre *m* ♦ *vt* filtrer; **~ lane** *n* (*AUT*) voie *f* de sortie; **~-tipped** *adj* à bout filtre

filth [fɪlθ] *n* saleté *f*; **~y** *adj* sale, dégoûtant(e); (*language*) ordurier(-ère)

fin [fɪn] *n* (*of fish*) nageoire *f*

final ['faɪnl] *adj* final(e); (*definitive*) définitif(-ive) ♦ *n* (*SPORT*) finale *f*; **~s** *npl* (*SCOL*) examens *mpl* de dernière année; **~e** [fɪ'nɑ:lɪ] *n* finale *m*; **~ist** *n* finaliste *m/f*; **~ize** *vt* mettre au point; **~ly** *adv* (*eventually*) enfin, finalement; (*lastly*) en dernier lieu

finance [faɪ'næns] *n* finance *f* ♦ *vt* financer; **~s** *npl* (*financial position*) finances *fpl*; **financial** [faɪ'nænʃəl] *adj* financier(-ère)

find [faɪnd] (*pt, pp* **found**) *vt* trouver; (*lost object*) retrouver ♦ *n* trouvaille *f*, découverte *f*; **to ~ sb guilty** (*LAW*) déclarer qn coupable; **~ out** *vt* (*truth, secret*) découvrir; (*person*) démasquer ♦ *vi*: **to ~ out about** (*make enquiries*) se renseigner; (*by chance*) apprendre; **~ings** *npl* (*LAW*) conclusions *fpl*, verdict *m*; (*of report*) conclusions

fine [faɪn] *adj* (*excellent*) excellent(e); (*thin, not coarse, subtle*) fin(e); (*weather*) beau (belle) ♦ *adv* (*well*) très bien ♦ *n* (LAW) amende *f*; contravention *f* ♦ *vt* (LAW) condamner à une amende; donner une contravention à; **to be ~** (*person*) aller bien; (*weather*) être beau; **~ arts** *npl* beaux-arts *mpl*; **~ry** *n* parure *f*

finger ['fɪŋɡəʳ] *n* doigt *m* ♦ *vt* palper, toucher; **little ~** auriculaire *m*, petit doigt; **index ~** index *m*; **~nail** *n* ongle *m* (de la main); **~print** *n* empreinte digitale; **~tip** *n* bout *m* du doigt

finish ['fɪnɪʃ] *n* fin *f*; (SPORT) arrivée *f*; (*polish etc*) finition *f* ♦ *vt* finir, terminer ♦ *vi* finir, se terminer; **to ~ doing sth** finir de faire qch; **to ~ third** arriver *or* terminer troisième; **~ off** *vt* finir, terminer; (*kill*) achever; **~ up** *vi*, *vt* finir; **~ing line** *n* ligne *f* d'arrivée

finite ['faɪnaɪt] *adj* fini(e); (*verb*) conjugué(e)

Finland ['fɪnlənd] *n* Finlande *f*; **Finn** [fɪn] *n* Finlandais(e); **Finnish** *adj* finlandais(e) ♦ *n* (LING) finnois *m*

fir [fəːʳ] *n* sapin *m*

fire ['faɪəʳ] *n* feu *m*; (*accidental*) incendie *m*; (*heater*) radiateur *m* ♦ *vt* (*fig*) enflammer, animer; (*inf: dismiss*) mettre à la porte, renvoyer; (*discharge*): **to ~ a gun** tirer un coup de feu ♦ *vi* (*shoot*) tirer, faire feu; **on ~** en feu; **~ alarm** *n* avertisseur *m* d'incendie; **~arm** *n* arme *f* à feu; **~ brigade** *n* (sapeurs-)pompiers *mpl*; **~ department** (US) *n* = **fire brigade**; **~ engine** *n* (*vehicle*) voiture *f* des pompiers; **~ escape** *n* escalier *m* de secours; **~ extinguisher** *n* extincteur *m*; **~man** *n* pompier *m*; **~place** *n* cheminée *f*; **~side** *n* foyer *m*, coin *m* du feu; **~ station** *n* caserne *f* de pompiers; **~wood** *n* bois *m* de chauffage; **~works** *npl* feux *mpl* d'artifice; (*display*) feu(x) d'artifice

firing squad ['faɪərɪŋ-] *n* peloton *m* d'exécution

firm [fəːm] *adj* ferme ♦ *n* compagnie *f*, firme *f*

first [fəːst] *adj* premier(-ère) ♦ *adv* (*before all others*) le premier, la première; (*before all other things*) en premier, d'abord; (*when listing reasons etc*) en premier lieu, premièrement ♦ *n* (*person: in race*) premier(-ère); (BRIT: SCOL) mention *f* très bien; (AUT) première *f*; **at ~** au commencement, au début; **~ of all** tout d'abord, pour commencer; **~ aid** *n* premiers secours *or* soins; **~-aid kit** *n* trousse *f* à pharmacie; **~-class** *adj* de première classe; (*excellent*) excellent(e), exceptionnel(le); **~-hand** *adj* de première main; **~ lady** (US) *n* femme *f* du président; **~ly** *adv* premièrement, en premier lieu; **~ name** *n* prénom *m*; **~-rate** *adj* excellent(e)

fish [fɪʃ] *n inv* poisson *m* ♦ *vt*, *vi* pêcher; **to go ~ing** aller à la pêche; **~erman** *n* pêcheur *m*; **~ farm** *n* établissement *m* piscicole; **~ fingers** (BRIT) *npl* bâtonnets de poisson (congelés); **~ing boat** *n* barque *f* *or* bateau *m* de pêche; **~ing line** *n* ligne *f* (de pêche); **~ing rod** *n* canne *f* à pêche; **~ing tackle** *n* attirail *m* de pêche; **~monger's (shop)** *n* poissonnerie *f*; **~ slice** *n* pelle *f* à poisson; **~ sticks** (US) *npl* = **fish fingers**; **~y** (*inf*) *adj* suspect(e), louche

fist [fɪst] *n* poing *m*

fit [fɪt] *adj* (*healthy*) en (bonne) forme; (*proper*) convenable; approprié(e) ♦ *vt* (*subj: clothes*) aller à; (*put in, attach*) installer, poser; adapter; (*equip*) équiper, garnir, munir; (*suit*) convenir à ♦ *vi* (*clothes*) aller; (*parts*) s'adapter; (*in space, gap*) entrer, s'adapter ♦ *n* (MED) accès *m*, crise *f*; (*of anger*) accès; (*of hysterics, jealousy*) crise; **~ to** en état de; **~ for** digne de; apte à; **~ of coughing** quinte *f* de toux; **a ~ of giggles** le fou rire; **this dress is a good ~** cette robe (me) va très bien; **by ~s and starts** par à-coups; **~ in** *vi* s'accorder; s'adapter; **~ful** *adj* (*sleep*) agité(e); **~ment** *n* meuble encastré, élément *m*; **~ness** *n*

five → flesh

(MED) forme f physique; **~ted carpet** n moquette f; **~ted kitchen** (BRIT) n cuisine équipée; **~ter** n monteur m; **~ting** adj approprié(e) ♦ n (of dress) essayage m; (of piece of equipment) pose f, installation f; **~tings** npl (in building) installations fpl; **~ting room** n cabine f d'essayage

five [faɪv] num cinq; **~r** (inf) n (BRIT) billet m de cinq livres; (US) billet m de cinq dollars

fix [fɪks] vt (date, amount etc) fixer; (organize) arranger; (mend) réparer; (meal, drink) préparer ♦ n: **to be in a ~** être dans le pétrin; **~ up** vt (meeting) arranger; **to ~ sb up with sth** faire avoir qch à qn; **~ation** [fɪk'seɪʃən] n (PSYCH) fixation f; (fig) obsession f; **~ed** adj (prices etc) fixe; (smile) figé(e); **~ture** n installation f (fixe); (SPORT) rencontre f (au programme)

fizzy ['fɪzɪ] adj pétillant(e); gazeux(-euse)

flabbergasted ['flæbəgɑːstɪd] adj sidéré(e), ahuri(e)

flabby ['flæbɪ] adj mou (molle)

flag [flæg] n drapeau m; (also: **~stone**) dalle f ♦ vi faiblir; fléchir; **~ down** vt héler, faire signe (de s'arrêter) à; **~pole** n mât m; **~ship** n vaisseau m amiral; (fig) produit m vedette

flair [flɛəʳ] n flair m

flak [flæk] n (MIL) tir antiaérien; (inf: criticism) critiques fpl

flake [fleɪk] n (of rust, paint) écaille f; (of snow, soap powder) flocon m ♦ vi (also: **~ off**) s'écailler

flamboyant [flæm'bɔɪənt] adj flamboyant(e), éclatant(e); (person) haut(e) en couleur

flame [fleɪm] n flamme f

flamingo [flə'mɪŋɡəʊ] n flamant m (rose)

flammable ['flæməbl] adj inflammable

flan [flæn] (BRIT) n tarte f

flank [flæŋk] n flanc m ♦ vt flanquer

flannel ['flænl] n (fabric) flanelle f; (BRIT: also: **face ~**) gant m de toilette

flap [flæp] n (of pocket, envelope) rabat m ♦ vt (wings) battre (de) ♦ vi (sail, flag) claquer; (inf: also: **be in a ~**) paniquer

flare [flɛəʳ] n (signal) signal lumineux; (in

skirt etc) évasement m; **~ up** vi s'embraser; (fig: person) se mettre en colère, s'emporter; (: revolt etc) éclater

flash [flæʃ] n éclair m; (also: **news ~**) flash m (d'information); (PHOT) flash ♦ vt (light) projeter; (send: message) câbler; (look) jeter; (smile) lancer ♦ vi (light) clignoter; **a ~ of lightning** un éclair; **in a ~** en un clin d'œil; **to ~ one's headlights** faire un appel de phares; **to ~ by** ou **past** (person) passer (devant) comme un éclair; **~bulb** n ampoule f de flash; **~cube** n cube-flash m; **~light** n lampe f de poche; **~y** (pej) adj tape-à-l'œil inv, tapageur(-euse)

flask [flɑːsk] n flacon m, bouteille f; (also: **vacuum ~**) thermos ® m or f

flat [flæt] adj plat(e); (tyre) dégonflé(e), à plat; (beer) éventé(e); (denial) catégorique; (MUS) bémol inv; (: voice) faux (fausse); (fee, rate) fixe ♦ n (BRIT: apartment) appartement m; (AUT) crevaison f; (MUS) bémol m; **to work ~ out** travailler d'arrache-pied; **~ly** adv catégoriquement; **~ten** vt (also: **~ten out**) aplatir; (crop) coucher; (building(s)) raser

flatter ['flætəʳ] vt flatter; **~ing** adj flatteur(-euse); **~y** n flatterie f

flaunt [flɔːnt] vt faire étalage de

flavour ['fleɪvəʳ] (US **flavor**) n goût m, saveur f; (of ice cream etc) parfum m ♦ vt parfumer; **vanilla-~ed** à l'arôme de vanille, à la vanille; **~ing** n arôme m

flaw [flɔː] n défaut m; **~less** adj sans défaut

flax [flæks] n lin m

flea [fliː] n puce f

fleck [flek] n tacheture f; moucheture f

flee [fliː] (pt, pp **fled**) vt fuir ♦ vi fuir, s'enfuir

fleece [fliːs] n toison f ♦ vt (inf) voler, filouter

fleet [fliːt] n flotte f; (of lorries etc) parc m; convoi m

fleeting ['fliːtɪŋ] adj fugace, fugitif(-ive); (visit) très bref (brève)

Flemish ['flemɪʃ] adj flamand(e)

flesh [fleʃ] n chair f; **~ wound** n blessure

superficielle

flew [flu:] *pt of* **fly**

flex [fleks] *n* fil *m or* câble *m* électrique ♦ *vt* (*knee*) fléchir; (*muscles*) tendre; **~ible** *adj* flexible

flick [flɪk] *n* petite tape; chiquenaude *f*; (*of duster*) petit coup ♦ *vt* donner un petit coup à; (*switch*) appuyer sur; **~ through** *vt fus* feuilleter

flicker ['flɪkə'] *vi* (*light*) vaciller; **his eyelids ~ed** il a cillé

flier ['flaɪə'] *n* aviateur *m*

flight [flaɪt] *n* vol *m*; (*escape*) fuite *f*; (*also:* **~ of steps**) escalier *m*; **~ attendant** (*US*) *n* steward *m*, hôtesse *f* de l'air; **~ deck** *n* (*AVIAT*) poste *m* de pilotage; (*NAUT*) pont *m* d'envol

flimsy ['flɪmzɪ] *adj* peu solide; (*clothes*) trop léger(-ère); (*excuse*) pauvre, mince

flinch [flɪntʃ] *vi* tressaillir; **to ~ from** se dérober à, reculer devant

fling [flɪŋ] (*pt, pp* flung) *vt* jeter, lancer

flint [flɪnt] *n* silex *m*; (*in lighter*) pierre *f* (à briquet)

flip [flɪp] *vt* (*throw*) lancer (d'une chiquenaude); **to ~ sth over** retourner qch

flippant ['flɪpənt] *adj* désinvolte, irrévérencieux(-euse)

flipper ['flɪpə'] *n* (*of seal etc*) nageoire *f*; (*for swimming*) palme *f*

flirt [flə:t] *vi* flirter ♦ *n* flirteur(-euse) *m/f*

float [fləʊt] *n* flotteur *m*; (*in procession*) char *m*; (*money*) réserve *f* ♦ *vi* flotter

flock [flɔk] *n* troupeau *m*; (*of birds*) vol *m*; (*REL*) ouailles *fpl* ♦ *vi*: **to ~ to** se rendre en masse à

flog [flɔg] *vt* fouetter

flood [flʌd] *n* inondation *f*; (*of letters, refugees etc*) flot *m* ♦ *vt* inonder ♦ *vi* (*people*): **to ~ into** envahir; **~ing** *n* inondation *f*; **~light** *n* projecteur *m*

floor [flɔː'] *n* sol *m*; (*storey*) étage *m*; (*of sea, valley*) fond *m* ♦ *vt* (*subj: question*) décontenancer; (*: blow*) terrasser; **on the ~** par terre; **ground ~**, (*US*) **first ~** rez-de-chaussée *m inv*; **first ~**, (*US*) **second ~** premier étage; **~board** *n* planche *f* (du

plancher); **~ show** *n* spectacle *m* de variétés

flop [flɔp] *n* fiasco *m* ♦ *vi* être un fiasco; (*fall: into chair*) s'affaler, s'effondrer; **~py** *adj* lâche, flottant(e) ♦ *n* (*COMPUT: also:* **~py disk**) disquette *f*

flora ['flɔːrə] *n* flore *f*

floral ['flɔːrl] *adj* (*dress*) à fleurs

florid ['flɔrɪd] *adj* (*complexion*) coloré(e); (*style*) plein(e) de fioritures

florist ['flɔrɪst] *n* fleuriste *m/f*; **~'s (shop)** *n* magasin *m or* boutique *f* de fleuriste

flounder ['flaʊndə'] *vi* patauger ♦ *n* (*ZOOL*) flet *m*

flour ['flaʊə'] *n* farine *f*

flourish ['flʌrɪʃ] *vi* prospérer ♦ *n* (*gesture*) moulinet *m*

flout [flaʊt] *vt* se moquer de, faire fi de

flow [fləʊ] *n* (*ELEC, of river*) courant *m*; (*of blood in veins*) circulation *f*; (*of tide*) flux *m*; (*of orders, data*) flot *m* ♦ *vi* couler; (*traffic*) s'écouler; (*robes, hair*) flotter; **the ~ of traffic** l'écoulement *m* de la circulation; **~ chart** *n* organigramme *m*

flower ['flaʊə'] *n* fleur *f* ♦ *vi* fleurir; **~ bed** *n* plate-bande *f*; **~pot** *n* pot *m* (de fleurs); **~y** *adj* fleuri(e)

flown [fləʊn] *pp of* **fly**

flu [flu:] *n* grippe *f*

fluctuate ['flʌktjʊeɪt] *vi* varier, fluctuer

fluent ['fluːənt] *adj* (*speech*) coulant(e), aisé(e); **he speaks ~ French, he's ~ in French** il parle couramment le français

fluff [flʌf] *n* duvet *m*; (*on jacket, carpet*) peluche *f*; **~y** *adj* duveteux(-euse); (*toy*) en peluche

fluid ['fluːɪd] *adj* fluide ♦ *n* fluide *m*

fluke [fluːk] (*inf*) *n* (*luck*) coup *m* de veine

flung [flʌŋ] *pt, pp of* **fling**

fluoride ['fluərɑɪd] *n* fluorure *f*; **~ toothpaste** dentifrice *m* au fluor

flurry ['flʌrɪ] *n* (*of snow*) rafale *f*, bourrasque *f*; **~ of activity/excitement** affairement *m*/excitation *f* soudain(e)

flush [flʌʃ] *n* (*on face*) rougeur *f*; (*fig: of youth, beauty etc*) éclat *m* ♦ *vt* nettoyer à grande eau ♦ *vi* rougir ♦ *adj*: **~ with** au ras de, de niveau avec; **to ~ the toilet** tirer la chasse (d'eau); **~ed** adj (tout(e)) rouge

flustered ['flʌstəd] adj énervé(e)

flute [fluːt] n flûte f

flutter ['flʌtər] n (of panic, excitement) agitation f; (of wings) battement m ♦ vi (bird) battre des ailes, voleter

flux [flʌks] n: **in a state of ~** fluctuant sans cesse

fly [flaɪ] (pt **flew**, pp **flown**) n (insect) mouche f; (on trousers: also: **flies**) braguette f ♦ vt piloter; (passengers, cargo) transporter (par avion); (distances) parcourir ♦ vi voler; (passengers) aller en avion; (escape) s'enfuir, fuir; (flag) se déployer; **~ away** vi (bird, insect) s'envoler; **~ off** vi = **fly away**; **~-drive** n formule f avion plus voiture; **~ing** n (activity) aviation f; (action) vol m ♦ adj: **a ~ing visit** une visite éclair; **with ~ing colours** haut la main; **~ing saucer** n soucoupe volante; **~ing start** n: **to get off to a ~ing start** prendre un excellent départ; **~over** (BRIT) n (bridge) saut-de-mouton m; **~sheet** n (for tent) double toit m

foal [fəʊl] n poulain m

foam [fəʊm] n écume f; (on beer) mousse f; (also: ~ **rubber**) caoutchouc mousse m ♦ vi (liquid) écumer; (soapy water) mousser

fob [fɒb] vt: **to ~ sb off** se débarrasser de qn

focal point ['fəʊkl-] n (fig) point central

focus ['fəʊkəs] (pl **~es**) n foyer m; (of interest) centre m ♦ vt (camera etc) mettre au point ♦ vi: **to ~ (on)** (with camera) régler la mise au point (sur); (person) fixer son regard (sur); **out of/in ~** (picture) flou(e)/net(te); (camera) pas au point

fodder ['fɒdər] n fourrage m

foe [fəʊ] n ennemi m

fog [fɒɡ] n brouillard m; **~gy** adj: **it's ~gy** il y a du brouillard; **~ lamp** (US **fog light**) n (AUT) phare m antibrouillard

foil [fɔɪl] vt déjouer, contrecarrer ♦ n feuille f de métal; (kitchen ~) papier m alu(minium); (complement) repoussoir m

fold [fəʊld] n (bend, crease) pli m; (AGR) parc m à moutons; (fig) bercail m ♦ vt plier; (arms) croiser; **~ up** vi (map, table etc) se plier; (business) fermer boutique ♦ vt (map, clothes) plier; **~er** n (for papers) chemise f; (: with hinges) classeur m; (COMPUT) répertoire m; **~ing** adj (chair, bed) pliant(e)

foliage ['fəʊlɪɪdʒ] n feuillage m

folk [fəʊk] npl gens mpl ♦ cpd folklorique; **~s** (inf) npl (parents) parents mpl; **~lore** ['fəʊkbːr] n folklore m; **~ song** n chanson f folklorique

follow ['fɒləʊ] vt suivre ♦ vi suivre; (result) s'ensuivre; **to ~ suit** (fig) faire de même; **~ up** vt (letter, offer) donner suite à; (case) suivre; **~er** n disciple m/f, partisan(e); **~ing** adj suivant(e) ♦ n partisans mpl, disciples mpl

folly ['fɒlɪ] n inconscience f; folie f

fond [fɒnd] adj (memory, look) tendre; (hopes, dreams) un peu fou (folle); **to be ~ of** aimer beaucoup

fondle ['fɒndl] vt caresser

font [fɒnt] n (in church: for baptism) fonts baptismaux; (TYP) fonte f

food [fuːd] n nourriture f; **~ mixer** n mixer m; **~ poisoning** n intoxication f alimentaire; **~ processor** n robot m de cuisine; **~stuffs** npl denrées fpl alimentaires

fool [fuːl] n idiot(e); (CULIN) mousse f de fruits ♦ vt berner, duper ♦ vi faire l'idiot or l'imbécile; **~hardy** adj téméraire, imprudent(e); **~ish** adj idiot(e), stupide; (rash) imprudent(e); insensé(e); **~proof** adj (plan etc) infaillible

foot [fut] (pl **feet**) n pied m; (of animal) patte f; (measure) pied (= 30,48 cm; 12 inches) ♦ vt (bill) payer; **on ~** à pied; **~age** n (CINEMA: length) ≃ métrage m; (: material) séquences fpl; **~ball** n ballon m (de football); (sport: BRIT) football m, foot m; (: US) football américain; **~ball player** (BRIT) n (also: **~baller**) joueur m de football; **~brake** n frein m à pédale; **~bridge** n passerelle f; **~hills** npl contreforts mpl; **~hold** n prise f (de pied); **~ing**

n (*fig*) position *f*; **to lose one's ~ing** perdre pied; **~lights** *npl* rampe *f*; **~note** *n* note *f* (en bas de page); **~path** *n* sentier *m*; (*in street*) trottoir *m*; **~print** *n* trace *f* (de pas); **~step** *n* pas *m*; **~wear** *n* chaussure(s) *f(pl)*

---

football pools

i Les **football pools** - *ou plus familièrement les "pools"* - consistent à parier sur les résultats des matches de football qui se jouent tous les samedis. L'expression consacrée en anglais est "to do the pools". Les parieurs envoient à l'avance les fiches qu'ils ont complétées à l'organisme qui gère les paris et ils attendent 17 h le samedi que les résultats soient annoncés. Les sommes gagnées se comptent parfois en milliers (ou même en millions) de livres sterling.

---

for [fɔːʳ] *prep* **1** (*indicating destination, intention, purpose*) pour; **the train for London** le train pour *or* (à destination) de Londres; **he went for the paper** il est allé chercher le journal; **it's time for lunch** c'est l'heure du déjeuner; **what's it for?** ça sert à quoi?; **what for?** (*why*) pourquoi?

2 (*on behalf of, representing*) pour; **the MP for Hove** le député de Hove; **to work for sb/sth** travailler pour qn/qch; **G for George** G comme Georges

3 (*because of*) pour; **for this reason** pour cette raison; **for fear of being criticized** de peur d'être critiqué

4 (*with regard to*) pour; **it's cold for July** il fait froid pour juillet; **a gift for languages** un don pour les langues

5 (*in exchange for*): **I sold it for £5** je l'ai vendu 5 livres; **to pay 50 pence for a ticket** payer un billet 50 pence

6 (*in favour of*) pour; **are you for or against us?** êtes-vous pour ou contre nous?

7 (*referring to distance*) pendant, sur; **there are roadworks for 5 km** il y a des travaux sur 5 km; **we walked for miles** nous avons marché pendant des kilomètres

8 (*referring to time*) pendant; depuis; pour; **he was away for 2 years** il a été absent pendant 2 ans; **she will be away for a month** elle sera absente (pendant) un mois; **I have known her for years** je la connais depuis des années; **can you do it for tomorrow?** est-ce que tu peux le faire pour demain?

9 (*with infinitive clauses*): **it is not for me to decide** ce n'est pas à moi de décider; **it would be best for you to leave** le mieux serait que vous partiez; **there is still time for you to do it** vous avez encore le temps de le faire; **for this to be possible ...** pour que cela soit possible ...

10 (*in spite of*): **for all his work/efforts** malgré tout son travail/tous ses efforts; **for all his complaints, he's very fond of her** il a beau se plaindre, il l'aime beaucoup

♦ *conj* (*since, as: rather formal*) car

forage [ˈfɒrɪdʒ] *vi* fourrager
foray [ˈfɒreɪ] *n* incursion *f*
forbid [fəˈbɪd] (*pt* **forbad(e)**, *pp* **forbidden**) *vt* défendre, interdire; **to ~ sb to do** défendre *or* interdire à qn de faire; **~ding** *adj* sévère, sombre
force [fɔːs] *n* force *f* ♦ *vt* forcer; (*push*) pousser (de force); **the F~s** *npl* (MIL) l'armée *f*; **in ~** en vigueur; **~-feed** *vt* nourrir de force; **~ful** *adj* énergique, volontaire; **forcibly** *adv* par la force, de force; (*express*) énergiquement
ford [fɔːd] *n* gué *m*
fore [fɔːʳ] *n*: **to come to the ~** se faire remarquer; **~arm** *n* avant-bras *m inv*; **~boding** *n* pressentiment *m* (néfaste); **~cast** (*irreg: like* **cast**) *n* prévision *f* ♦ *vt* prévoir; **~court** *n* (*of garage*) devant *m*; **~finger** *n* index *m*; **~front** *n*: **in the ~front of** au premier rang *or* plan de

foregone ['fɔːgɔn] *adj*: **it's a ~ conclusion** c'est couru d'avance

foreground ['fɔːgraund] *n* premier plan

forehead ['fɔrɪd] *n* front *m*

foreign ['fɔrɪn] *adj* étranger(-ère); (*trade*) extérieur(-e); **~er** *n* étranger(-e); **~ exchange** *n* change *m*; **F~ Office** (*BRIT*) *n* ministère *m* des affaires étrangères; **F~ Secretary** (*BRIT*) *n* ministre *m* des affaires étrangères

fore: **~leg** *n* (*of cat, dog*) patte *f* de devant; (*of horse*) jambe antérieure; **~man** (*irreg*) *n* (*of factory, building site*) contremaître *m*, chef *m* d'équipe; **~most** *adj* le (la) plus en vue; premier(-ère) ♦ *adv*: **first and ~most** avant tout, tout d'abord

forensic [fə'rensɪk] *adj*: **~ medicine** médecine légale; **~ scientist** médecin *m* légiste

fore: **~runner** *n* précurseur *m*; **~see** (*irreg: like* **see**) *vt* prévoir; **~seeable** *adj* prévisible; **~shadow** *vt* présager, annoncer, laisser prévoir; **~sight** *n* prévoyance *f*

forest ['fɔrɪst] *n* forêt *f*; **~ry** *n* sylviculture *f*

foretaste ['fɔːteɪst] *n* avant-goût *m*

foretell [fɔː'tel] (*irreg: like* **tell**) *vt* prédire

forever [fə'revə*] *adv* pour toujours; (*fig*) continuellement

foreword ['fɔːwəːd] *n* avant-propos *m inv*

forfeit ['fɔːfɪt] *vt* (*lose*) perdre

forgave [fə'geɪv] *pt of* **forgive**

forge [fɔːdʒ] *n* forge *f* ♦ *vt* (*signature*) contrefaire; (*wrought iron*) forger; **to ~ money** fabriquer de la fausse monnaie; **~ ahead** *vi* pousser de l'avant, prendre de l'avance; **~d** *adj* faux (fausse); **~r** *n* faussaire *m*; **~ry** *n* faux *m*, contrefaçon *f*

forget [fə'get] (*pt* **forgot**, *pp* **forgotten**) *vt*, *vi* oublier; **~ful** *adj* distrait(e), étourdi(e); **~-me-not** *n* myosotis *m*

forgive [fə'gɪv] (*pt* **forgave**, *pp* **forgiven**) *vt* pardonner; **to ~ sb for sth/for doing sth** pardonner qch à qn/à qn de faire qch; **~ness** *n* pardon *m*

forgo [fɔː'gəu] (*pt* **forwent**, *pp* **forgone**) *vt* renoncer à

fork [fɔːk] *n* (*for eating*) fourchette *f*; (*for gardening*) fourche *f*; (*of roads*) bifurcation *f*; (*of railways*) embranchement *m* ♦ *vi* (*road*) bifurquer; **~ out** *vt* (*inf*) allonger; **~-lift truck** *n* chariot élévateur

forlorn [fə'lɔːn] *adj* (*deserted*) abandonné(e); (*attempt, hope*) désespéré(e)

form [fɔːm] *n* forme *f*; (*SCOL*) classe *f*; (*questionnaire*) formulaire *m* ♦ *vt* former; (*habit*) contracter; **in top ~** en pleine forme

formal ['fɔːməl] *adj* (*offer, receipt*) en bonne et due forme; (*person*) cérémonieux(-euse); (*dinner*) officiel(le); (*clothes*) de soirée; (*garden*) à la française; (*education*) à proprement parler; **~ly** *adv* officiellement; cérémonieusement

format ['fɔːmæt] *n* format *m* ♦ *vt* (*COMPUT*) formater

formation [fɔː'meɪʃən] *n* formation *f*

formative ['fɔːmətɪv] *adj*: **~ years** années *fpl* d'apprentissage *or* de formation

former ['fɔːmə*] *adj* ancien(ne) (*before n*), précédent(e); **the ~ ... the latter** le premier ... le second, celui-là ... celui-ci; **~ly** *adv* autrefois

formidable ['fɔːmɪdəbl] *adj* redoutable

formula ['fɔːmjulə] (*pl* **~s** *or* **~e**) *n* formule *f*

forsake [fə'seɪk] (*pt* **forsook**, *pp* **forsaken**) *vt* abandonner

fort [fɔːt] *n* fort *m*

forte ['fɔːtɪ] *n* (*point*) fort *m*

forth [fɔːθ] *adv* en avant; **to go back and ~** aller et venir; **and so ~** et ainsi de suite; **~coming** *adj* (*event*) qui va avoir lieu prochainement; (*character*) ouvert(e), communicatif(-ive); (*available*) disponible; **~right** *adj* franc (franche), direct(e); **~with** *adv* sur-le-champ

fortify ['fɔːtɪfaɪ] *vt* fortifier

fortitude ['fɔːtɪtjuːd] *n* courage *m*

fortnight ['fɔːtnaɪt] (*BRIT*) *n* quinzaine *f*, quinze jours *mpl*; **~ly** (*BRIT*) *adj* bimensuel(le) ♦ *adv* tous les quinze jours

fortunate ['fɔːtʃənɪt] *adj* heureux(-euse); (*person*) chanceux(-euse); **it is ~ that** c'est une chance que; **~ly** *adv* heureusement

fortune ['fɔ:tʃən] n chance f; (wealth) fortune f; **~-teller** n diseuse f de bonne aventure

forty ['fɔ:tɪ] num quarante

forward ['fɔ:wəd] adj (ahead of schedule) en avance; (movement, position) en avant, vers l'avant; (not shy) direct(e); effronté(e) ♦ n (SPORT) avant m ♦ vt (letter) faire suivre; (parcel, goods) expédier; (fig) promouvoir, favoriser; **~(s)** adv en avant; **to move ~** avancer

fossil ['fɒsl] n fossile m

foster ['fɒstər] vt encourager, favoriser; (child) élever (sans obligation d'adopter); **~ child** n enfant adoptif(-ive)

fought [fɔ:t] pt, pp of **fight**

foul [faul] adj (weather, smell, food) infect(e); (language) ordurier(-ère) ♦ n (SPORT) faute f ♦ vt (dirty) salir, encrasser; **he's got a ~ temper** il a un caractère de chien; **~ play** n (LAW) acte criminel

found [faund] pt, pp of **find** ♦ vt (establish) fonder; **~ation** [faun'deɪʃən] n (act) fondation f; (base) fondement m; (also: **~ation cream**) fond m de teint; **~ations** npl (of building) fondations fpl

founder ['faundər] n fondateur m ♦ vi couler, sombrer

foundry ['faundrɪ] n fonderie f

fountain ['fauntɪn] n fontaine f; **~ pen** n stylo m (à encre)

four [fɔːr] num quatre; **on all ~s** à quatre pattes; **~-poster** n (also: **~-poster bed**) lit m à baldaquin; **~teen** num quatorze; **~th** num quatrième

fowl [faul] n volaille f

fox [fɒks] n renard m ♦ vt mystifier

foyer ['fɔɪeɪ] n (hotel) hall m; (THEATRE) foyer m

fraction ['frækʃən] n fraction f

fracture ['fræktʃər] n fracture f

fragile ['frædʒaɪl] adj fragile

fragment ['frægmənt] n fragment m

fragrant ['freɪɡrənt] adj parfumé(e), odorant(e)

frail [freɪl] adj fragile, délicat(e)

frame [freɪm] n charpente f; (of picture, bicycle) cadre m; (of door, window) encadrement m, chambranle m; (of spectacles: also: **~s**) monture f ♦ vt encadrer; **~ of mind** disposition f d'esprit; **~work** n structure f

France [frɑːns] n France f

franchise ['fræntʃaɪz] n (POL) droit m de vote; (COMM) franchise f

frank [fræŋk] adj franc (franche) ♦ vt (letter) affranchir; **~ly** adv franchement

frantic ['fræntɪk] adj (hectic) frénétique; (distraught) hors de soi

fraternity [frə'tə:nɪtɪ] n (spirit) fraternité f; (club) communauté f, confrérie f

fraud [frɔ:d] n supercherie f, fraude f, tromperie f; (person) imposteur m

fraught [frɔ:t] adj: **~ with** chargé(e) de, plein(e) de

fray [freɪ] vi s'effilocher

freak [fri:k] n (also cpd) phénomène m, créature ou événement exceptionnel par sa rareté

freckle ['frekl] n tache f de rousseur

free [fri:] adj libre; (gratis) gratuit(e) ♦ vt (prisoner etc) libérer; (jammed object or person) dégager; **~ (of charge), for ~** gratuitement; **~dom** n liberté f; **F~fone** ® n numéro vert; **~-for-all** n mêlée générale; **~ gift** n prime f; **~hold** n propriété foncière libre; **~ kick** n coup franc; **~lance** adj indépendant(e); **~ly** adv librement; (liberally) libéralement; **F~mason** n franc-maçon m; **F~post** ® n port payé; **~-range** adj (hen, eggs) de ferme; **~ trade** n libre-échange m; **~way** n (US) n autoroute f; **~ will** n libre arbitre m; **of one's own ~ will** de son plein gré

freeze [fri:z] (pt **froze**, pp **frozen**) vi geler ♦ vt geler; (food) congeler; (prices, salaries) bloquer, geler ♦ n gel m; (fig) blocage m; **~-dried** adj lyophilisé(e); **~r** n congélateur m; **freezing** adj: **freezing (cold)** (weather, water) glacial(e) ♦ n: **3 degrees below freezing** 3 degrés au-dessous de zéro; **freezing point** n point m de congélation

freight [freɪt] n (goods) fret m, cargaison f;

(*money charged*) fret, prix *m* du transport; **~ train** *n* train *m* de marchandises

French [frentʃ] *adj* français(e) ♦ *n* (*LING*) français *m*; **the ~** *npl* (*people*) les Français; **~ bean** *n* haricot vert; **~ fried potatoes** (*US* **~ fries**) *npl* (pommes de terre *fpl*) frites *fpl*; **~ horn** *n* (*MUS*) cor *m* (d'harmonie); **~ kiss** *n* baiser profond; **~ loaf** *n* baguette *f*; **~man** (*irreg*) *n* Français *m*; **~ window** *n* porte-fenêtre *f*; **~woman** (*irreg*) *n* Française *f*

frenzy ['frenzɪ] *n* frénésie *f*

frequency ['friːkwənsɪ] *n* fréquence *f*

frequent [*adj* 'friːkwənt, *vb* frɪ'kwent] *adj* fréquent(e) ♦ *vt* fréquenter; **~ly** *adv* fréquemment

fresh [freʃ] *adj* frais (fraîche); (*new*) nouveau (nouvelle); (*cheeky*) familier(-ère), culotté(e); **~en** *vi* (*wind, air*) fraîchir; **~en up** *vi* faire un brin de toilette; **~er** (*BRIT: inf*) *n* (*SCOL*) bizuth *m*, étudiant(e) de 1ère année; **~ly** *adv* nouvellement, récemment; **~man** (*US*) (*irreg*) *n* = **fresher**; **~ness** *n* fraîcheur *f*; **~water** *adj* (*fish*) d'eau douce

fret [fret] *vi* s'agiter, se tracasser

friar ['fraɪə'] *n* moine *m*, frère *m*

friction ['frɪkʃən] *n* friction *f*

Friday ['fraɪdɪ] *n* vendredi *m*

fridge [frɪdʒ] (*BRIT*) *n* frigo *m*, frigidaire ® *m*

fried [fraɪd] *adj* frit(e); **~ egg** œuf *m* sur le plat

friend [frend] *n* ami(e); **~ly** *adj* amical(e); gentil(le); (*place*) accueillant(e); **they were killed by ~ly fire** ils sont morts sous les tirs de leur propre camp; **~ship** *n* amitié *f*

frieze [friːz] *n* frise *f*

fright [fraɪt] *n* peur *f*, effroi *m*; **to take ~** prendre peur, s'effrayer; **~en** *vt* effrayer, faire peur à; **~ened** *adj*: **to be ~ened (of)** avoir peur (de); **~ening** *adj* effrayant(e); **~ful** *adj* affreux(-euse)

frigid ['frɪdʒɪd] *adj* frigide

frill [frɪl] *n* (*on dress*) volant *m*; (*on shirt*) jabot *m*

fringe [frɪndʒ] *n* (*BRIT: of hair*) frange *f*; (*edge: of forest etc*) bordure *f*; **~ benefits** *npl* avantages sociaux *or* en nature

Frisbee ® ['frɪzbɪ] *n* Frisbee ® *m*

frisk [frɪsk] *vt* fouiller

fritter ['frɪtə'] *n* beignet *m*; **~ away** *vt* gaspiller

frivolous ['frɪvələs] *adj* frivole

frizzy ['frɪzɪ] *adj* crépu(e)

fro [frəu] *adv*: **to go to and ~** aller et venir

frock [frɔk] *n* robe *f*

frog [frɔg] *n* grenouille *f*; **~man** *n* homme-grenouille *m*

frolic ['frɔlɪk] *vi* folâtrer, batifoler

─── **KEYWORD** ───

from [frɔm] *prep* **1** (*indicating starting place, origin etc*) de; **where do you come from?, where are you from?** d'où venez-vous?; **from London to Paris** de Londres à Paris; **a letter from my sister** une lettre de ma sœur; **to drink from the bottle** boire à (même) la bouteille

2 (*indicating time*) (à partir) de; **from one o'clock to** *or* **until** *or* **till two** d'une heure à deux heures; **from January (on)** à partir de janvier

3 (*indicating distance*) de; **the hotel is one kilometre from the beach** l'hôtel est à un kilomètre de la plage

4 (*indicating price, number etc*) de; **the interest rate was increased from 9% to 10%** le taux d'intérêt est passé de 9 à 10%

5 (*indicating difference*) de; **he can't tell red from green** il ne peut pas distinguer le rouge du vert

6 (*because of, on the basis of*): **from what he says** d'après ce qu'il dit; **weak from hunger** affaibli par la faim

─────────────

front [frʌnt] *n* (*of house, dress*) devant *m*, (*of coach, train*) avant *m*; (*promenade: also*: **sea ~**) bord *m* de mer; (*MIL, METEOROLOGY*) front *m*; (*fig: appearances*) contenance *f*, façade *f* ♦ *adj* de devant; (*seat*) avant *inv*; **in ~ (of)** devant; **~age** *n* (*of building*) façade f; **~ door** n porte f d'entrée; (of car) portière f avant; **~ier** ['frʌntɪə'] n frontière f; **~ page** n première page; **~ room** (BRIT) n pièce f de devant, salon m; **~-wheel drive** n traction f avant

frost [frɒst] n gel m, gelée f; (also: **hoarfrost**) givre m; **~bite** n gelures fpl; **~ed** adj (glass) dépoli(e); **~y** adj (weather, welcome) glacial(e)

froth [frɒθ] n mousse f; écume f

frown [fraun] vi froncer les sourcils

froze [frəuz] pt of **freeze**

frozen ['frəuzn] pp of **freeze**

fruit [fruːt] n inv fruit m; **~erer** n fruitier m, marchand(e) de fruits; **~ful** adj (fig) fructueux(-euse); **~ion** [fruː'ɪʃən] n: **to come to ~ion** se réaliser; **~ juice** n jus m de fruit; **~ machine** (BRIT) n machine f à sous; **~ salad** n salade f de fruits

frustrate [frʌs'treɪt] vt frustrer

fry [fraɪ] (pt, pp **fried**) vt (faire) frire; see also **small**; **~ing pan** n poêle f (à frire)

ft. abbr = **foot; feet**

fudge [fʌdʒ] n (CULIN) caramel m

fuel ['fjuəl] n (for heating) combustible m; (for propelling) carburant m; **~ oil** n mazout m; **~ tank** n (in vehicle) réservoir m

fugitive ['fjuːdʒɪtɪv] n fugitif(-ive)

fulfil [ful'fɪl] (US **fulfill**) vt (function, condition) remplir; (order) exécuter; (wish, desire) satisfaire, réaliser; **~ment** (US **fulfillment**) n (of wishes etc) réalisation f; (feeling) contentement m

full [ful] adj plein(e); (details, information) complet(-ète); (skirt) ample, large ♦ adv: **to know ~ well that** savoir fort bien que; **I'm ~ (up)** j'ai bien mangé; **a ~ two hours** deux bonnes heures; **at ~ speed** à toute vitesse; **in ~** (reproduce, quote) intégralement; (write) en toutes lettres; **~ employment** plein emploi; **to pay in ~** tout payer; **~-length** adj (film) long métrage; (portrait, mirror) en pied; (coat) long(ue); **~ moon** n pleine lune; **~-scale** adj (attack, war) complet(-ète), total(e); (model) grandeur nature inv; **~ stop** n point m; **~-time** adj, adv (work) à plein temps; **~y**

adv entièrement, complètement; (at least) au moins; **~y licensed** (hotel, restaurant) autorisé(e) à vendre des boissons alcoolisées; **~y-fledged** adj (barrister etc) diplômé(e); (citizen, member) à part entière

fumble ['fʌmbl] vi: **~ with** tripoter

fume [fjuːm] vi rager; **~s** npl vapeurs fpl, émanations fpl, gaz mpl

fun [fʌn] n amusement m, divertissement m; **to have ~** s'amuser; **for ~** pour rire; **to make ~ of** se moquer de

function ['fʌŋkʃən] n fonction f; (social occasion) cérémonie f, soirée officielle ♦ vi fonctionner; **~al** adj fonctionnel(le)

fund [fʌnd] n caisse f, fonds m; (source, store) source f, mine f; **~s** npl (money) fonds mpl

fundamental [fʌndə'mentl] adj fondamental(e)

funeral ['fjuːnərəl] n enterrement m, obsèques fpl; **~ parlour** n entreprise f de pompes funèbres; **~ service** n service m funèbre

funfair ['fʌnfeə'] (BRIT) n fête (foraine)

fungi ['fʌŋgaɪ] npl of **fungus**

fungus ['fʌŋgəs] (pl **fungi**) n champignon m; (mould) moisissure f

funnel ['fʌnl] n entonnoir m; (of ship) cheminée f

funny ['fʌnɪ] adj amusant(e), drôle; (strange) curieux(-euse), bizarre

fur [fəː'] n fourrure f; (BRIT: in kettle etc) (dépôt m de) tartre m

furious ['fjuərɪəs] adj furieux(-euse); (effort) acharné(e)

furlong ['fəːlɒŋ] n = 201,17 m

furnace ['fəːnɪs] n fourneau m

furnish ['fəːnɪʃ] vt meubler; (supply): **to ~ sb with sth** fournir qch à qn; **~ings** npl mobilier m, ameublement m

furniture ['fəːnɪtʃə'] n meubles mpl, mobilier m; **piece of ~** meuble m

furrow ['fʌrəu] n sillon m

furry ['fəːrɪ] adj (animal) à fourrure; (toy) en peluche

further ['fəːðə'] adj (additional) supplémentaire, autre; nouveau (nouvelle) ♦ adv plus loin; *(more)* davantage; *(moreover)* de plus ♦ *vt* faire avancer *or* progresser, promouvoir; ~ **education** *n* enseignement *m* postscolaire; ~**more** *adv* de plus, en outre

furthest ['fəːðɪst] *superl of* **far**

fury ['fjuərɪ] *n* fureur *f*

fuse [fjuːz] *(US* **fuze**) *n* fusible *m*; *(for bomb etc)* amorce *f*, détonateur *m* ♦ *vt, vi (metal)* fondre; **to ~ the lights** *(BRIT)* faire sauter les plombs; ~ **box** *n* boîte *f* à fusibles

fuss [fʌs] *n (excitement)* agitation *f*; *(complaining)* histoire(s) *f(pl)*; **to make a ~** faire des histoires; **to make a ~ of sb** être aux petits soins pour qn; ~**y** *adj (person)* tatillon(ne), difficile; *(dress, style)* tarabiscoté(e)

future ['fjuːtʃəʳ] *adj* futur(e) ♦ *n* avenir *m*; *(LING)* futur *m*; **in ~** à l'avenir

fuze [fjuːz] *(US) n, vt, vi* = **fuse**

fuzzy ['fʌzɪ] *adj (PHOT)* flou(e); *(hair)* crépu(e)

G, g

G [dʒiː] *n (MUS)* sol *m*

G7 *n abbr (= Group of 7)* le groupe des 7

gabble ['gæbl] *vi* bredouiller

gable ['geɪbl] *n* pignon *m*

gadget ['gædʒɪt] *n* gadget *m*

Gaelic ['geɪlɪk] *adj* gaélique ♦ *n (LING)* gaélique *m*

gag [gæg] *n (on mouth)* bâillon *m*; *(joke)* gag *m* ♦ *vt* bâillonner

gaiety ['geɪtɪ] *n* gaieté *f*

gain [geɪn] *n (improvement)* gain *m*; *(profit)* gain, profit *m*; *(increase):* ~ **(in)** augmentation *f* (de) ♦ *vt* gagner ♦ *vi (watch)* avancer; **to ~ 3 lbs (in weight)** prendre 3 livres; **to ~ on sb** *(catch up)* rattraper qn; **to ~ from/by** gagner de/à

gal. *abbr* = **gallon**

gale [geɪl] *n* coup *m* de vent

gallant ['gælənt] *adj* vaillant(e), brave; *(towards ladies)* galant

gall bladder ['gɔːl-] *n* vésicule *f* biliaire

gallery ['gælərɪ] *n* galerie *f*; *(also:* **art ~**) musée *m*; *(: private)* galerie

gallon ['gæln] *n* gallon *m* *(BRIT = 4,5 l; US = 3,8 l)*

gallop ['gæləp] *n* galop *m* ♦ *vi* galoper

gallows ['gæləuz] *n* potence *f*

gallstone ['gɔːlstəun] *n* calcul *m* biliaire

galore [gə'lɔːʳ] *adv* en abondance, à gogo

Gambia ['gæmbɪə] *n:* **(The) ~** la Gambie

gambit ['gæmbɪt] *n (fig):* **(opening) ~** manœuvre *f* stratégique

gamble ['gæmbl] *n* pari *m*, risque calculé ♦ *vt, vi* jouer; **to ~ on** *(fig)* miser sur; ~**r** *n* joueur *m*; **gambling** *n* jeu *m*

game [geɪm] *n* jeu *m*; *(match)* match *m*; *(strategy, scheme)* plan *m*; projet *m*; *(HUNTING)* gibier *m* ♦ *adj (willing):* **to be ~ (for)** être prêt(e) (à *or* pour); **big ~** gros gibier; ~**keeper** *n* garde-chasse *m*

gammon ['gæmən] *n (bacon)* quartier *m* de lard fumé; *(ham)* jambon fumé

gamut ['gæmət] *n* gamme *f*

gang [gæŋ] *n* bande *f*; *(of workmen)* équipe *f*; ~ **up** *vi:* **to ~ up on sb** se liguer contre qn; ~**ster** *n* gangster *m*; ~**way** ['gæŋweɪ] *n* passerelle *f*; *(BRIT: of bus, plane)* couloir central; *(: in cinema)* allée centrale

gaol [dʒeɪl] *(BRIT) n* = **jail**

gap [gæp] *n* trou *m*; *(in time)* intervalle *m*; *(difference):* ~ **between** écart *m* entre

gape [geɪp] *vi (person)* être *or* rester bouche bée; *(hole, shirt)* être ouvert(e); **gaping** *adj (hole)* béant(e)

garage ['gærɑːʒ] *n* garage *m*

garbage ['gɑːbɪdʒ] *n (US: rubbish)* ordures *fpl*, détritus *mpl*; *(inf: nonsense)* foutaises *fpl*; ~ **can** *(US) n* poubelle *f*, boîte *f* à ordures

garbled ['gɑːbld] *adj (account, message)* embrouillé(e)

garden ['gɑːdn] *n* jardin *m*; ~**s** *npl* jardin public; ~**er** *n* jardinier *m*; ~**ing** *n* jardinage *m*

gargle ['gɑːgl] *vi* se gargariser

garish ['gɛərɪʃ] *adj* criard(e), voyant(e); *(light)* cru(e)

garland ['gɑːlənd] *n* guirlande *f*; couronne

f

garlic ['gɑːlɪk] *n* ail *m*

garment ['gɑːmənt] *n* vêtement *m*

garrison ['gærɪsn] *n* garnison *f*

garter ['gɑːtəʳ] *n* jarretière *f*; (*US*) jarretelle *f*

gas [gæs] *n* gaz *m*; (*US: gasoline*) essence *f* ♦ *vt* asphyxier; ~ **cooker** (*BRIT*) *n* cuisinière *f* à gaz; ~ **cylinder** *n* bouteille *f* de gaz; ~ **fire** (*BRIT*) *n* radiateur *m* à gaz

gash [gæʃ] *n* entaille *f*; (*on face*) balafre *f*

gasket ['gæskɪt] *n* (*AUT*) joint *m* de culasse

gas mask *n* masque *m* à gaz

gas meter *n* compteur *m* à gaz

gasoline ['gæsəliːn] (*US*) *n* essence *f*

gasp [gɑːsp] *vi* haleter

gas: ~ **ring** *n* brûleur *m*; ~ **station** (*US*) *n* station-service *f*; ~ **tap** *n* bouton *m* de (cuisinière à gaz); (*on pipe*) robinet *m* à gaz

gastric ['gæstrɪk] *adj* gastrique; ~ **flu** grippe *f* intestinale

gate [geɪt] *n* (*of garden*) portail *m*; (*of field*) barrière *f*; (*of building, at airport*) porte *f*

gateau ['gætəu] *n* (*pl* ~**x**) (gros) gâteau *m* à la crème

gatecrash *vt* s'introduire sans invitation dans

gateway *n* porte *f*

gather ['gæðəʳ] *vt* (*flowers, fruit*) cueillir; (*pick up*) ramasser; (*assemble*) rassembler, réunir, recueillir; (*understand*) comprendre; (*SEWING*) froncer ♦ *vi* (*assemble*) se rassembler; **to** ~ **speed** prendre de la vitesse; ~**ing** *n* rassemblement *m*

gaudy ['gɔːdɪ] *adj* voyant(e)

gauge [geɪdʒ] *n* (*instrument*) jauge *f* ♦ *vt* jauger

gaunt [gɔːnt] *adj* (*thin*) décharné(e); (*grim, desolate*) désolé(e)

gauntlet ['gɔːntlɪt] *n* (*glove*) gant *m*

gauze [gɔːz] *n* gaze *f*

gave [geɪv] *pt of* **give**

gay [geɪ] *adj* (*homosexual*) homosexuel(le); (*cheerful*) gai(e), réjoui(e); (*colour etc*) gai, vif (vive)

gaze [geɪz] *n* regard *m* fixe ♦ *vi*: **to** ~ **at** fixer du regard

gazump [gə'zʌmp] (*BRIT*) *vi* revenir sur une promesse de vente (*pour accepter une offre plus intéressante*)

GB *abbr* = **Great Britain**

GCE *n abbr* (*BRIT*) = **General Certificate of Education**

GCSE *n abbr* (*BRIT*) = **General Certificate of Secondary Education**

gear [gɪəʳ] *n* matériel *m*, équipement *m*; attirail *m*; (*TECH*) engrenage *m*; (*AUT*) vitesse *f* ♦ *vt* (*fig: adapt*): **to** ~ **sth to** adapter qch à; **top** *or* (*US*) **high** ~ quatrième (*or* cinquième) vitesse; **low** ~ première vitesse; **in** ~ en prise; ~ **box** *n* boîte *f* de vitesses; ~ **lever** (*US* **gear shift**) *n* levier *m* de vitesse

geese [giːs] *npl of* **goose**

gel [dʒɛl] *n* gel *m*

gem [dʒɛm] *n* pierre précieuse

Gemini ['dʒɛmɪnaɪ] *n* les Gémeaux *mpl*

gender ['dʒɛndəʳ] *n* genre *m*

gene [dʒiːn] *n* gène *m*

general ['dʒɛnərl] *n* général *m* ♦ *adj* général(e); **in** ~ en général; ~ **delivery** *n* poste restante; ~ **election** *n* élection(s) législative(s); ~ **knowledge** *n* connaissances générales; ~**ly** *adv* généralement; ~ **practitioner** *n* généraliste *m/f*

generate ['dʒɛnəreɪt] *vt* engendrer; (*electricity etc*) produire; **generation** *n* génération *f*; (*of electricity etc*) production *f*; **generator** *n* générateur *m*

generosity [dʒɛnə'rɒsɪtɪ] *n* générosité *f*

generous ['dʒɛnərəs] *adj* généreux(-euse); (*copious*) copieux(-euse)

genetic [dʒɪ'nɛtɪk] *adj*: ~ **engineering** ingénierie *f* génétique; ~ **fingerprinting** système *m* d'empreinte génétique

genetics [dʒɪ'nɛtɪks] *n* génétique *f*

Geneva [dʒɪ'niːvə] *n* Genève *m*

genial ['dʒiːnɪəl] *adj* cordial(e), chaleureux(-euse)

genitals ['dʒɛnɪtlz] *npl* organes génitaux

genius ['dʒiːnɪəs] *n* génie *m*

genteel [dʒɛn'tiːl] *adj* de bon ton, distingué(e)

gentle ['dʒɛntl] *adj* doux (douce)

gentleman ['dʒɛntlmən] *n* monsieur *m*; (*well-bred man*) gentleman *m*

gently ['dʒɛntlɪ] *adv* doucement

gentry ['dʒɛntrɪ] *n inv*: **the ~** la petite noblesse

gents [dʒɛnts] *n* W.-C. *mpl* (pour hommes)

genuine ['dʒɛnjuɪn] *adj* véritable, authentique; (*person*) sincère

geographical [dʒɪə'græfɪkl] *adj* géographique

geography [dʒɪ'ɔgrəfɪ] *n* géographie *f*

geology [dʒɪ'ɔlədʒɪ] *n* géologie *f*

geometric(al) [dʒɪə'mɛtrɪk(l)] *adj* géométrique

geometry [dʒɪ'ɔmətrɪ] *n* géométrie *f*

geranium [dʒɪ'reɪnɪəm] *n* géranium *m*

geriatric [dʒɛrɪ'ætrɪk] *adj* gériatrique

germ [dʒəːm] *n* (*MED*) microbe *m*

German ['dʒəːmən] *adj* allemand(e) ♦ *n* Allemand(e); (*LING*) allemand *m*; ~ **measles** (*BRIT*) *n* rubéole *f*

Germany ['dʒəːmənɪ] *n* Allemagne *f*

gesture ['dʒɛstjər] *n* geste *m*

KEYWORD

---

get [gɛt] (*pt, pp* **got**, *pp* **gotten** (*US*)) *vi* **1** (*become, be*) devenir; **to get old/tired** devenir vieux/fatigué, vieillir/se fatiguer; **to get drunk** s'enivrer; **to get killed** se faire tuer; **when do I get paid?** quand est-ce que je serai payé?; **it's getting late** il se fait tard

2 (*go*): **to get to/from** aller à/de; **to get home** rentrer chez soi; **how did you get here?** comment es-tu arrivé ici?

3 (*begin*) commencer *or* se mettre à; **I'm getting to like him** je commence à l'apprécier; **let's get going** *or* **started** allons-y

4 (*modal aux vb*): **you've got to do it** il faut que vous le fassiez; **I've got to tell the police** je dois le dire à la police

♦ *vt* **1**: **to get sth done** (*do*) faire qch; (*have done*) faire faire qch; **to get one's hair cut** se faire couper les cheveux; **to**

get sb to do sth faire faire qch à qn; **to get sb drunk** enivrer qn

2 (*obtain: money, permission, results*) obtenir, avoir; (*find: job, flat*) trouver; (*fetch: person, doctor, object*) aller chercher; **to get sth for sb** procurer qch à qn; **get me Mr Jones, please** (*on phone*) passez-moi Mr Jones, s'il vous plaît; **can I get you a drink?** est-ce que je peux vous servir à boire?

3 (*receive: present, letter*) recevoir, avoir; (*acquire: reputation*) avoir; (*: prize*) obtenir; **what did you get for your birthday?** qu'est-ce que tu as eu pour ton anniversaire?

4 (*catch*) prendre, saisir, attraper; (*hit: target etc*) atteindre; **to get sb by the arm/throat** prendre *or* saisir *or* attraper qn par le bras/à la gorge; **get him!** arrête-le!

5 (*take, move*) faire parvenir; **do you think we'll get it through the door?** est-ce qu'on arrivera à le faire passer par la porte?; **I'll get you there somehow** je me débrouillerai pour t'y emmener

6 (*catch, take: plane, bus etc*) prendre

7 (*understand*) comprendre, saisir; (*hear*) entendre; **I've got it!** j'ai compris!, je saisis!; **I didn't get your name** je n'ai pas entendu votre nom

8 (*have, possess*): **to have got** avoir; **how many have you got?** vous en avez combien?

get about *vi* se déplacer; (*news*) se répandre

get along *vi* (*agree*) s'entendre; (*depart*) s'en aller; (*manage*) = **get by**

get at *vt fus* (*attack*) s'en prendre à; (*reach*) attraper, atteindre

get away *vi* partir, s'en aller; (*escape*) s'échapper

get away with *vt fus* en être quitte pour; se faire passer *or* pardonner

get back *vi* (*return*) rentrer ♦ *vt* récupérer, recouvrer

get by *vi* (*pass*) passer; (*manage*) se débrouiller

get down *vi, vt fus* descendre ♦ *vt* descendre; (*depress*) déprimer

get down to *vt fus* (*work*) se mettre à (faire)

get in *vi* rentrer; (*train*) arriver

get into *vt fus* entrer dans; (*car, train etc*) monter dans; (*clothes*) mettre, enfiler, endosser; **to get into bed/a rage** se mettre au lit/en colère

get off *vi* (*from train etc*) descendre; (*depart: person, car*) s'en aller; (*escape*) s'en tirer ♦ *vt* (*remove: clothes, stain*) enlever ♦ *vt fus* (*train, bus*) descendre de

get on *vi* (*at exam etc*) se débrouiller; (*agree*): **to get on (with)** s'entendre (avec) ♦ *vt fus* monter dans; (*horse*) monter sur

get out *vi* sortir; (*of vehicle*) descendre ♦ *vt* sortir

get out of *vt fus* sortir de; (*duty etc*) échapper à, se soustraire à

get over *vt fus* (*illness*) se remettre de

get round *vt fus* contourner; (*fig: person*) entortiller

get through *vi* (*TEL*) avoir la communication; **to get through to sb** atteindre qn

get together *vi* se réunir ♦ *vt* assembler

get up *vi* (*rise*) se lever ♦ *vt fus* monter

get up to *vt fus* (*reach*) arriver à; (*prank etc*) faire

getaway ['gɛtəweɪ] *n*: **to make one's ~** filer

geyser ['gi:zər] *n* (*GEO*) geyser *m*; (*BRIT: water heater*) chauffe-eau *m inv*

Ghana ['gɑ:nə] *n* Ghana *m*

ghastly ['gɑ:stlɪ] *adj* atroce, horrible; (*pale*) livide, blême

gherkin ['gə:kɪn] *n* cornichon *m*

ghetto blaster ['gɛtəu'blɑ:stər] *n* stéréo *f* portable

ghost [gəust] *n* fantôme *m*, revenant *m*

giant ['dʒaɪənt] *n* géant(e) ♦ *adj* géant(e), énorme

gibberish ['dʒɪbərɪʃ] *n* charabia *m*

giblets ['dʒɪblɪts] *npl* abats *mpl*

Gibraltar [dʒɪ'brɔ:ltər] *n* Gibraltar *m*

giddy ['gɪdɪ] *adj* (*dizzy*): **to be** or **feel ~** avoir le vertige

gift [gɪft] *n* cadeau *m*; (*donation, ability*) don *m*; **~ed** *adj* doué(e); **~ shop** *n* boutique *f* de cadeaux; **~ token** *n* chèque-cadeau *m*

gigantic [dʒaɪ'gæntɪk] *adj* gigantesque

giggle ['gɪgl] *vi* pouffer (de rire), rire sottement

gill [dʒɪl] *n* (*measure*) = 0.25 pints (*BRIT* = 0.15 l, *US* = 0.12 l)

gills [gɪlz] *npl* (*of fish*) ouïes *fpl*, branchies *fpl*

gilt [gɪlt] *adj* doré(e) ♦ *n* dorure *f*; **~-edged** *adj* (*COMM*) de premier ordre

gimmick ['gɪmɪk] *n* truc *m*

gin [dʒɪn] *n* (*liquor*) gin *m*

ginger ['dʒɪndʒər] *n* gingembre *m*; **~ ale, ~ beer** *n* boisson gazeuse *au gingembre*; **~bread** *n* pain *m* d'épices

gingerly ['dʒɪndʒəlɪ] *adv* avec précaution

gipsy ['dʒɪpsɪ] *n* = **gypsy**

giraffe [dʒɪ'rɑ:f] *n* girafe *f*

girder ['gə:dər] *n* poutrelle *f*

girl [gə:l] *n* fille *f*, fillette *f*; (*young unmarried woman*) jeune fille; (*daughter*) fille; **an English ~** une jeune Anglaise; **~friend** *n* (*of girl*) amie *f*; (*of boy*) petite amie; **~ish** *adj* de petite *or* de jeune fille; (*for a boy*) efféminé(e)

giro ['dʒaɪrəu] *n* (*bank ~*) virement *m* bancaire; (*post office ~*) mandat *m*; (*BRIT: welfare cheque*) mandat *m* d'allocation chômage

gist [dʒɪst] *n* essentiel *m*

give [gɪv] (*pt* **gave**, *pp* **given**) *vt* donner ♦ *vi* (*break*) céder; (*stretch: fabric*) se prêter; **to ~ sb sth, ~ sth to sb** donner qch à qn; **to ~ a cry/sigh** pousser un cri/un soupir; **~ away** *vt* donner; (*~ free*) faire cadeau de; (*betray*) donner, trahir; (*disclose*) révéler; (*bride*) conduire à l'autel; **~ back** *vt* rendre; **~ in** *vi* céder ♦ *vt* donner; **~ off** *vt* dégager; **~ out** *vt* distribuer; annoncer; **~ up** *vi* renoncer ♦ *vt* renoncer à; **to ~ up smoking** arrêter de fumer; **to ~ o.s. up** se rendre; **~ way** (*BRIT*) *vi* céder; (*AUT*) céder la priorité

glacier ['glæsɪər] *n* glacier *m*

glad [glæd] *adj* content(e); **~ly** *adv* volontiers

glamorous ['glæmərəs] *adj* (*person*) séduisant(e); (*job*) prestigieux(-euse)

glamour ['glæmə^r] *n* éclat *m*, prestige *m*

glance [glɑːns] *n* coup *m* d'œil ♦ *vi*: **to ~ at** jeter un coup d'œil à; **glancing** *adj* (*blow*) oblique

gland *n* glande *f*

glare [glɛə^r] *n* (*of anger*) regard furieux; (*of light*) lumière éblouissante; (*of publicity*) feux *mpl* ♦ *vi* briller d'un éclat aveuglant; **to ~ at** lancer un regard furieux à; **glaring** *adj* (*mistake*) criant(e), qui saute aux yeux

glass [glɑːs] *n* verre *m*; **~es** *npl* (*spectacles*) lunettes *fpl*; **~house** (*BRIT*) *n* (*for plants*) serre *f*; **~ware** *n* verrerie *f*

glaze [gleɪz] *vt* (*door, window*) vitrer; (*pottery*) vernir ♦ *n* (*on pottery*) vernis *m*; **~d** *adj* (*pottery*) verni(e); (*eyes*) vitreux(-euse)

glazier ['gleɪzɪə^r] *n* vitrier *m*

gleam [gliːm] *vi* luire, briller

glean [gliːn] *vt* (*information*) glaner

glee [gliː] *n* joie *f*

glib [glɪb] *adj* (*person*) qui a du bagou; (*response*) désinvolte, facile

glide [glaɪd] *vi* glisser; (*AVIAT, birds*) planer; **~r** *n* (*AVIAT*) planeur *m*; **gliding** *n* (*SPORT*) vol *m* à voile

glimmer ['glɪmə^r] *n* lueur *f*

glimpse [glɪmps] *n* vision passagère, aperçu *m* ♦ *vt* entrevoir, apercevoir

glint [glɪnt] *vi* étinceler

glisten ['glɪsn] *vi* briller, luire

glitter ['glɪtə^r] *vi* scintiller, briller

gloat [gləut] *vi*: **to ~ (over)** jubiler (à propos de)

global ['gləubl] *adj* mondial(e); **~ warming** réchauffement *m* de la planète

globe [gləub] *n* globe *m*

gloom [gluːm] *n* obscurité *f*; (*sadness*) tristesse *f*, mélancolie *f*; **~y** *adj* sombre, triste, lugubre

glorious ['glɔːrɪəs] *adj* glorieux(-euse); splendide

glory ['glɔːrɪ] *n* gloire *f*; splendeur *f*

gloss [glɔs] *n* (*shine*) brillant *m*, vernis *m*; **~ over** *vt fus* glisser sur

glossary ['glɔsərɪ] *n* glossaire *m*

glossy ['glɔsɪ] *adj* brillant(e); **~ magazine** magazine *m* de luxe

glove [glʌv] *n* gant *m*; **~ compartment** *n* (*AUT*) boîte *f* à gants, vide-poches *m inv*

glow [gləu] *vi* rougeoyer; (*face*) rayonner; (*eyes*) briller

glower ['glauə^r] *vi*: **to ~ (at)** lancer des regards mauvais (à)

glucose ['gluːkəus] *n* glucose *m*

glue [gluː] *n* colle *f* ♦ *vt* coller

glum [glʌm] *adj* sombre, morne

glut [glʌt] *n* surabondance *f*

glutton ['glʌtn] *n* glouton(ne); **a ~ for work** un bourreau de travail; **a ~ for punishment** un masochiste (*fig*)

GM *abbr* (= *genetically modified*) génétiquement modifié(e)

gnat [næt] *n* moucheron *m*

gnaw [nɔː] *vt* ronger

go [gəu] (*pt* **went**, *pp* **gone**, *pl* **~es**) *vi* aller; (*depart*) partir, s'en aller; (*work*) marcher; (*break etc*) céder; (*be sold*): **to ~ for £10** se vendre 10 livres; (*fit, suit*): **to ~ with** aller avec; (*become*): **to ~ pale/mouldy** pâlir/moisir ♦ *n*: **to have a ~ (at)** essayer (de faire); **to be on the ~** être en mouvement; **whose ~ is it?** à qui est-ce de jouer?; **he's ~ing to do** il va faire, il est sur le point de faire; **to ~ for a walk** aller se promener; **to ~ dancing** aller danser; **how did it ~?** comment est-ce que ça s'est passé?; **to ~ round the back/by the shop** passer par derrière/devant le magasin; **~ about** *vi* (*rumour*) se répandre ♦ *vt fus*: **how do I ~ about this?** comment dois-je m'y prendre (pour faire ceci)?; **~ after** *vt fus* (*pursue*) poursuivre, courir après; (*job, record etc*) essayer d'obtenir; **~ ahead** *vi* (*make progress*) avancer; (*get ~ing*) y aller; **~ along** *vi* aller, avancer ♦ *vt fus* longer, parcourir; **~ away** *vi* partir, s'en aller; **~ back** *vi* rentrer; revenir; (*~ again*) retourner; **~ back on** *vt fus* (*promise*) revenir sur; **~ by** *vi* (*years, time*) passer, s'écouler ♦ *vt fus* s'en tenir à; en croire; ~ **down** *vi* descendre; *(ship)* couler; *(sun)* se coucher ♦ *vt fus* descendre; ~ **for** *vt fus (fetch)* aller chercher; *(like)* aimer; *(attack)* s'en prendre à, attaquer; ~ **in** *vi* entrer; ~ **in for** *vt fus (competition)* se présenter à; *(like)* aimer; ~ **into** *vt fus* entrer dans; *(investigate)* étudier, examiner; *(embark on)* se lancer dans; ~ **off** *vi* partir, s'en aller; *(food)* se gâter; *(explode)* sauter; *(event)* se dérouler ♦ *vt fus* ne plus aimer; **the gun went off** le coup est parti; ~ **on** *vi* continuer; *(happen)* se passer; **to ~ on doing** continuer à faire; ~ **out** *vi* sortir; *(fire, light)* s'éteindre; ~ **over** *vt fus (check)* revoir, vérifier; ~ **past** *vt fus:* **to ~ past sth** passer devant qch; ~ **round** *vi (circulate: news, rumour)* circuler; *(revolve)* tourner; *(suffice)* suffire (pour tout le monde); **to ~ round to sb's** *(visit)* passer chez qn; **to ~ round (by)** *(make a detour)* faire un détour (par); ~ **through** *vt fus (town etc)* traverser; ~ **up** *vi* monter; *(price)* augmenter ♦ *vt fus* gravir; ~ **with** *vt fus (suit)* aller avec; ~ **without** *vt fus* se passer de

goad [gəud] *vt* aiguillonner

go-ahead *adj* dynamique, entreprenant(e) ♦ *n* feu vert

goal [gəul] *n* but *m*; ~**keeper** *n* gardien *m* de but; ~**post** *n* poteau *m* de but

goat [gəut] *n* chèvre *f*

gobble [ˈgɔbl] *vt (also:* ~ **down,** ~ **up)** engloutir

go-between [ˈgəubɪtwiːn] *n* intermédiaire *m/f*

god [gɔd] *n* dieu *m*; G~ *n* Dieu *m*; ~**child** *n* filleul(e); ~**daughter** *n* filleule *f*; ~**dess** *n* déesse *f*; ~**father** *n* parrain *m*; ~-**forsaken** *adj* maudit(e); ~**mother** *n* marraine *f*; ~**send** *n* aubaine *f*; ~**son** *n* filleul *m*

goggles [ˈgɔglz] *npl (for skiing etc)* lunettes protectrices

going [ˈgəuɪŋ] *n (conditions)* état *m* du terrain ♦ *adj:* **the ~ rate** le tarif (en vigueur)

gold [gəuld] *n* or *m* ♦ *adj* en or; *(reserves)* d'or; ~**en** *adj (made of gold)* en or; *(gold*

in colour) doré(e); ~**fish** *n* poisson *m* rouge; ~-**plated** *adj* plaqué(e) or *inv*; ~**smith** *n* orfèvre *m*

golf [gɔlf] *n* golf *m*; ~ **ball** *n* balle *f* de golf; *(on typewriter)* boule *f*; ~ **club** *n* club *m* de golf; *(stick)* club *m*, crosse *f* de golf; ~ **course** *n* (terrain *m* de) golf *m*; ~**er** *n* joueur(-euse) de golf

gone [gɔn] *pp of* **go**

gong [gɔŋ] *n* gong *m*

good [gud] *adj* bon(ne); *(kind)* gentil(le); *(child)* sage ♦ *n* bien *m*; ~**s** *npl (COMM)* marchandises *fpl*, articles *mpl*; ~! bon!, très bien!; **to be ~ at** être bon en; **to be ~ for** être bon pour; **would you be ~ enough to ...?** auriez-vous la bonté *or* l'amabilité de ...?; **a ~ deal (of)** beaucoup (de); **a ~ many** beaucoup (de); **to make ~** *vi (succeed)* faire son chemin, réussir ♦ *vt (deficit)* combler; *(losses)* compenser; **it's no ~ complaining** cela ne sert à rien de se plaindre; **for ~** pour de bon, une fois pour toutes; ~ **morning/afternoon!** bonjour!; ~ **evening!** bonsoir!; ~ **night!** bonsoir!; *(on going to bed)* bonne nuit!; ~**bye** *excl* au revoir!; G~ **Friday** *n* Vendredi saint; ~-**looking** *adj* beau (belle), bien *inv*; ~-**natured** *adj (person)* qui a un bon naturel; ~**ness** *n (of person)* bonté *f*; **for ~ness sake!** je vous en prie!; ~**ness gracious!** mon Dieu!; ~**s train** *(BRIT)* *n* train *m* de marchandises; ~**will** *n* bonne volonté

goose [guːs] *n (pl* **geese)** oie *f*

gooseberry [ˈguzbəri] *n* groseille *f* à maquereau; **to play ~** *(BRIT)* tenir la chandelle

gooseflesh [ˈguːsfleʃ] *n,* **goose pimples** *npl* chair *f* de poule

gore [gɔːʳ] *vt* encorner ♦ *n* sang *m*

gorge [gɔːdʒ] *n* gorge *f* ♦ *vt:* **to ~ o.s. (on)** se gorger (de)

gorgeous [ˈgɔːdʒəs] *adj* splendide, superbe

gorilla [gəˈrɪlə] *n* gorille *m*

gorse [gɔːs] *n* ajoncs *mpl*

gory [ˈgɔːrɪ] *adj* sanglant(e); *(details)* horrible

go-slow ['gəʊ'sləʊ] (BRIT) n grève perlée

gospel ['gɔspl] n évangile m

gossip ['gɔsɪp] n (chat) bavardages mpl; commérage m, cancans mpl; (person) commère f ♦ vi bavarder; (maliciously) cancaner, faire des commérages

got [gɔt] pt, pp de **get**; ~**ten** (US) pp de **get**

gout [gaʊt] n goutte f

govern ['gʌvən] vt gouverner; ~**ess** n gouvernante f; ~**ment** n gouvernement m; (BRIT: ministers) ministère m; ~**or** n (of state, bank) gouverneur m; (of school, hospital) ≃ membre m/f du conseil d'établissement; (BRIT: of prison) directeur(-trice)

gown [gaʊn] n robe f; (of teacher, BRIT: of judge) toge f

GP n abbr = **general practitioner**

grab [græb] vt saisir, empoigner ♦ vi: **to ~ at** essayer de saisir

grace [greɪs] n grâce f ♦ vt honorer; (adorn) orner; **5 days' ~** cinq jours de répit; ~**ful** adj gracieux(-euse), élégant(e); **gracious** ['greɪʃəs] adj bienveillant(e)

grade [greɪd] n (COMM) qualité f; (in hierarchy) catégorie f, grade m, échelon m; (SCOL) note f; (US: school class) classe f ♦ vt classer; ~ **crossing** (US) n passage m à niveau; ~ **school** (US) n école f primaire

gradient ['greɪdɪənt] n inclinaison f, pente f

gradual ['grædjʊəl] adj graduel(le), progressif(-ive); ~**ly** adv peu à peu, graduellement

graduate [n 'grædjʊɪt, vb 'grædjʊeɪt] n diplômé(e), licencié(e); (US: of high school) bachelier(-ère) ♦ vi obtenir son diplôme; (US) obtenir son baccalauréat; **graduation** [grædjʊ'eɪʃən] n (cérémonie f de) remise f des diplômes

graffiti [grə'fiːtɪ] npl graffiti mpl

graft [grɑːft] n (AGR, MED) greffe f; (bribery) corruption f ♦ vt greffer; **hard ~** (BRIT: inf) boulot acharné

grain [greɪn] n grain m

gram [græm] n gramme m

grammar ['græmər] n grammaire f; ~

school (BRIT) n ≃ lycée m; **grammatical** [grə'mætɪkl] adj grammatical(e)

gramme [græm] n = **gram**

grand [grænd] adj magnifique, splendide; (gesture etc) noble; ~**children** npl petits-enfants mpl; ~**dad** (inf) n grand-papa m; ~**daughter** n petite-fille f; ~**father** n grand-père m; ~**ma** (inf) n grand-maman f; ~**mother** n grand-mère f; ~**pa** (inf) n = **granddad**; ~**parents** npl grands-parents mpl; ~ **piano** n piano m à queue; ~**son** n petit-fils m; ~**stand** n (SPORT) tribune f

granite ['grænɪt] n granit m

granny ['grænɪ] (inf) n grand-maman f

grant [grɑːnt] vt accorder; (a request) accéder à; (admit) concéder ♦ n (SCOL) bourse f; (ADMIN) subside m, subvention f; **to take it for ~ed that** trouver tout naturel que +sub; **to take sb for ~ed** considérer qn comme faisant partie du décor

granulated sugar ['grænjʊleɪtɪd-] n sucre m en poudre

grape [greɪp] n raisin m

grapefruit ['greɪpfruːt] n pamplemousse m

graph [grɑːf] n graphique m; ~**ic** ['græfɪk] adj graphique; (account, description) vivant(e); ~**ics** n arts mpl graphiques; graphisme m ♦ npl représentations fpl graphiques

grapple ['græpl] vi: **to ~ with** être aux prises avec

grasp [grɑːsp] vt saisir ♦ n (grip) prise f; (understanding) compréhension f, connaissance f; ~**ing** adj cupide

grass [grɑːs] n herbe f; (lawn) gazon m; ~**hopper** n sauterelle f; ~-**roots** adj de la base, du peuple

grate [greɪt] n grille f de cheminée ♦ vi grincer ♦ vt (CULIN) râper

grateful ['greɪtful] adj reconnaissant(e)

grater ['greɪtər] n râpe f

gratifying ['grætɪfaɪɪŋ] adj agréable

grating ['greɪtɪŋ] n (iron bars) grille f ♦ adj (noise) grinçant(e)

gratitude ['grætɪtjuːd] n gratitude f

gratuity [grə'tjuːɪtɪ] n pourboire m

grave [greɪv] n tombe f ♦ adj grave,

sérieux(-euse)

gravel ['grævl] n gravier m

gravestone ['greɪvstəun] n pierre tombale

graveyard ['greɪvjɑːd] n cimetière m

gravity ['grævɪtɪ] n (PHYSICS) gravité f; pesanteur f; (seriousness) gravité

gravy ['greɪvɪ] n jus m (de viande); sauce f

gray [greɪ] (US) adj = **grey**

graze [greɪz] vi paître, brouter ♦ vt (touch lightly) frôler, effleurer; (scrape) écorcher ♦ n écorchure f

grease [griːs] n (fat) graisse f; (lubricant) lubrifiant m ♦ vt graisser; lubrifier; ~**proof paper** (BRIT) n papier sulfurisé; **greasy** adj gras(se), graisseux(-euse)

great [greɪt] adj grand(e); (inf) formidable; G~ **Britain** n Grande-Bretagne f; ~**grandfather** n arrière-grand-père m; ~**grandmother** n arrière-grand-mère f; ~**ly** adv très, grandement; (with verbs) beaucoup; ~**ness** n grandeur f

Greece [griːs] n Grèce f

greed [griːd] n (also: ~**iness**) avidité f; (for food) gourmandise f, gloutonnerie f; ~**y** adj avide; gourmand(e), glouton(ne)

Greek [griːk] adj grec (grecque) ♦ n Grec (Grecque); (LING) grec m

green [griːn] adj vert(e); (inexperienced) (bien) jeune, naïf (naïve); (POL) vert(e), écologiste; (ecological) écologique ♦ n vert m; (stretch of grass) pelouse f; ~**s** npl (vegetables) légumes verts; (POL): **the G~s** les Verts mpl; **the G~ Party** (BRIT: POL) le parti écologiste; ~ **belt** n (round town) ceinture verte; ~ **card** n (AUT) carte verte; (US) permis m de travail; ~**ery** n verdure f; ~**grocer's** (BRIT) n marchand m de fruits et légumes; ~**house** n serre f; ~**house effect** n effet m de serre; ~**house gas** n gas m à effet de serre; ~**ish** adj verdâtre

Greenland ['griːnlənd] n Groenland m

greet [griːt] vt accueillir; ~**ing** n salutation f; ~**ing(s) card** n carte f de vœux

gregarious [grə'gɛərɪəs] adj (person) sociable

grenade [grə'neɪd] n grenade f

grew [gruː] pt of **grow**

grey [greɪ] (US **gray**) adj gris(e); (dismal) sombre; ~-**haired** adj grisonnant(e); ~**hound** n lévrier m

grid [grɪd] n grille f; (ELEC) réseau m; ~**lock** n (traffic jam) embouteillage m; ~**locked** adj: **to be ~locked** (roads) être bloqué par un embouteillage; (talks etc) être suspendu

grief [griːf] n chagrin m, douleur f

grievance ['griːvəns] n doléance f, grief m

grieve [griːv] vi avoir du chagrin; se désoler ♦ vt faire de la peine à, affliger; **to ~ for sb** (dead person) pleurer qn; **grievous** adj (LAW): **grievous bodily harm** coups mpl et blessures fpl

grill [grɪl] n (on cooker) gril m; (food: also mixed ~) grillade(s) f(pl) ♦ vt (BRIT) griller; (inf: question) cuisiner

grille [grɪl] n grille f, grillage m; (AUT) calandre f

grim [grɪm] adj sinistre, lugubre; (serious, stern) sévère

grimace [grɪ'meɪs] n grimace f ♦ vi grimacer, faire une grimace

grime [graɪm] n crasse f, saleté f

grin [grɪn] n large sourire m ♦ vi sourire

grind [graɪnd] (pt, pp **ground**) vt écraser; (coffee, pepper etc) moudre; (US: meat) hacher; (make sharp) aiguiser ♦ n (work) corvée f

grip [grɪp] n (hold) prise f, étreinte f; (control) emprise f; (grasp) connaissance f; (handle) poignée f; (holdall) sac m de voyage ♦ vt saisir, empoigner; **to come to ~s with** en venir aux prises avec; ~**ping** adj prenant(e), palpitant(e)

grisly ['grɪzlɪ] adj sinistre, macabre

gristle ['grɪsl] n cartilage m

grit [grɪt] n gravillon m; (courage) cran m ♦ vt (road) sabler; **to ~ one's teeth** serrer les dents

groan [grəun] n (of pain) gémissement m ♦ vi gémir

grocer ['grəusər] n épicier m; ~**ies** npl provisions fpl; ~**'s (shop)** n épicerie f

groin [grɔɪn] n aine f

groom [gruːm] n palefrenier m; (also:

bridegroom) marié *m* ♦ *vt* (*horse*) panser; (*fig*): **to ~ sb for** former qn pour; **well-~ed** très soigné(e)

groove [gru:v] *n* rainure *f*

grope [grəup] *vi*: **to ~ for** chercher à tâtons

gross [grəus] *adj* grossier(-ère); (*COMM*) brut(e); **~ly** *adv* (*greatly*) très, grandement

grotto ['grɔtəu] *n* grotte *f*

grotty ['grɔtɪ] (*inf*) *adj* minable, affreux(-euse)

ground [graund] *pt, pp of* **grind** ♦ *n* sol *m*, terre *f*; (*land*) terrain *m*, terres *fpl*; (*SPORT*) terrain; (*US: also:* **~ wire**) terre; (*reason: gen pl*) raison *f* ♦ *vt* (*plane*) empêcher de décoller, retenir au sol; (*US: ELEC*) équiper d'une prise de terre; **~s** *npl* (*of coffee etc*) marc *m*; (*gardens etc*) parc *m*, domaine *m*; **on the ~, to the ~** par terre; **to gain/lose ~** gagner/perdre du terrain; **~ cloth** (*US*) *n* = **groundsheet**; **~ing** *n* (*in education*) connaissances *fpl* de base; **~less** *adj* sans fondement; **~sheet** (*BRIT*) *n* tapis *m* de sol; **~ staff** *n* personnel *m* au sol; **~work** *n* préparation *f*

group [gru:p] *n* groupe *m* ♦ *vt* (*also:* **~ together**) grouper ♦ *vi* se grouper

grouse [graus] *n inv* (*bird*) grouse *f* ♦ *vi* (*complain*) rouspéter, râler

grove [grəuv] *n* bosquet *m*

grovel ['grɔvl] *vi* (*fig*) ramper

grow [grəu] (*pt* **grew**, *pp* **grown**) *vi* pousser, croître; (*person*) grandir; (*increase*) augmenter, se développer; (*become*): **to ~ rich/weak** s'enrichir/s'affaiblir; (*develop*): **he's ~n out of his jacket** sa veste est (devenue) trop petite pour lui ♦ *vt* cultiver, faire pousser; (*beard*) laisser pousser; **he'll ~ out of it!** ça lui passera!; **~ up** *vi* grandir; **~er** *n* producteur *m*; **~ing** *adj* (*fear, amount*) croissant(e), grandissant(e)

growl [graul] *vi* grogner

grown [grəun] *pp of* **grow**; **~-up** *n* adulte *m/f*, grande personne

growth [grəuθ] *n* croissance *f*, développement *m*; (*what has grown*) pousse *f*; pous-

sée *f*; (*MED*) grosseur *f*, tumeur *f*

grub [grʌb] *n* larve *f*; (*inf: food*) bouffe *f*

grubby ['grʌbɪ] *adj* crasseux(-euse)

grudge [grʌdʒ] *n* rancune *f* ♦ *vt*: **to ~ sb sth** (*in giving*) donner qch à qn à contre-cœur; (*resent*) reprocher qch à qn; **to bear sb a ~ (for)** garder rancune *or* en vouloir à qn (de)

gruelling ['gruəlɪŋ] (*US* **grueling**) *adj* exténuant(e)

gruesome ['gru:səm] *adj* horrible

gruff [grʌf] *adj* bourru(e)

grumble ['grʌmbl] *vi* rouspéter, ronchonner

grumpy ['grʌmpɪ] *adj* grincheux(-euse)

grunt [grʌnt] *vi* grogner

G-string ['dʒi:strɪŋ] *n* (*garment*) cache-sexe *m inv*

guarantee [gærən'ti:] *n* garantie *f* ♦ *vt* garantir

guard [gɑ:d] *n* garde *f*; (*one man*) garde *m*; (*BRIT: RAIL*) chef *m* de train; (*on machine*) dispositif *m* de sûreté; (*also:* **fire-guard**) garde-feu *m* ♦ *vt* garder, surveiller; (*protect*): **to ~ (against** *or* **from**) protéger (contre); **~ against** *vt* (*prevent*) empêcher, se protéger de; **~ed** *adj* (*fig*) prudent(e); **~ian** *n* gardien(ne); (*of minor*) tuteur(-trice); **~'s van** (*BRIT*) *n* (*RAIL*) fourgon *m*

guerrilla [gə'rɪlə] *n* guérillero *m*

guess [gɛs] *vt* deviner; (*estimate*) évaluer; (*US*) croire, penser ♦ *vi* deviner ♦ *n* supposition *f*, hypothèse *f*; **to take** *or* **have a ~** essayer de deviner; **~work** *n* hypothèse *f*

guest [gɛst] *n* invité(e); (*in hotel*) client(e); **~-house** *n* pension *f*; **~ room** *n* chambre *f* d'amis

guffaw [gʌ'fɔ:] *vi* pouffer de rire

guidance ['gaɪdəns] *n* conseils *mpl*

guide [gaɪd] *n* (*person, book etc*) guide *m*; (*BRIT: also:* **girl ~**) guide *f* ♦ *vt* guider; **~book** *n* guide *m*; **~ dog** *n* chien *m* d'aveugle; **~lines** *npl* (*fig*) instructions (*générales*), conseils *mpl*

guild [gɪld] *n* corporation *f*; cercle *m*, association *f*

guillotine ['gɪlətiːn] *n* guillotine *f*

guilt [gɪlt] *n* culpabilité *f*; **~y** *adj* coupable

guinea pig ['gɪnɪ-] *n* cobaye *m*

guise [gaɪz] *n* aspect *m*, apparence *f*

guitar [gɪ'tɑːʳ] *n* guitare *f*

gulf [gʌlf] *n* golfe *m*; (*abyss*) gouffre *m*

gull [gʌl] *n* mouette *f*; (*larger*) goéland *m*

gullible ['gʌlɪbl] *adj* crédule

gully ['gʌlɪ] *n* ravin *m*; ravine *f*; couloir *m*

gulp [gʌlp] *vi* avaler sa salive ♦ *vt* (*also:* ~ **down**) avaler

gum [gʌm] *n* (ANAT) gencive *f*; (*glue*) colle *f*; (*sweet: also* ~drop) boule *f* de gomme; (*also:* **chewing** ~) chewing-gum *m* ♦ *vt* coller; **~boots** (BRIT) *npl* bottes *fpl* en caoutchouc

gun [gʌn] *n* (*small*) revolver *m*, pistolet *m*; (*rifle*) fusil *m*, carabine *f*; (*cannon*) canon *m*; **~boat** *n* canonnière *f*; **~fire** *n* fusillade *f*; **~man** *n* bandit armé; **~point** *n*: **at ~point** sous la menace du pistolet (*or* fusil); **~powder** *n* poudre *f* à canon; **~shot** *n* coup *m* de feu

gurgle ['gəːgl] *vi* gargouiller; (*baby*) gazouiller

gush [gʌʃ] *vi* jaillir; (*fig*) se répandre en effusions

gust [gʌst] *n* (*of wind*) rafale *f*; (*of smoke*) bouffée *f*

gusto ['gʌstəu] *n* enthousiasme *m*

gut [gʌt] *n* intestin *m*, boyau *m*; **~s** *npl* (*inf: courage*) cran *m*

gutter ['gʌtəʳ] *n* (*in street*) caniveau *m*; (*of roof*) gouttière *f*

guy [gaɪ] *n* (*inf: man*) type *m*; (*also:* ~**rope**) corde *f*; (BRIT: *figure*) effigie de Guy Fawkes (*brûlée en plein air le 5 novembre*)

Guy Fawkes' Night

i **Guy Fawkes' Night**, *que l'on appelle également "bonfire night", commémore l'échec du complot (le "Gunpowder Plot") contre James Ist et son parlement le 5 no-*

vembre 1605. L'un des conspirateurs, Guy Fawkes, avait été surpris dans les caves du parlement alors qu'il s'apprêtait à y mettre le feu. Chaque année pour le 5 novembre, les enfants préparent à l'avance une effigie de Guy Fawkes et ils demandent aux passants "un penny pour le guy" avec lequel ils pourront s'acheter des fusées de feu d'artifice. Beaucoup de gens font encore un feu dans leur jardin sur lequel ils brûlent le "guy".

---

guzzle ['gʌzl] *vt* avaler gloutonnement

gym [dʒɪm] *n* (*also:* **~nasium**) gymnase *m*; (*also:* **~nastics**) gym *f*; **~nast** *n* gymnaste *m/f*; **~nastics** [dʒɪm'næstɪks] *n, npl* gymnastique *f*; ~ **shoes** *npl* chaussures *fpl* de gym; **~slip** (BRIT) *n* tunique *f* (d'écolière)

gynaecologist [gaɪnɪ'kɔlədʒɪst] (US **gynecologist**) *n* gynécologue *m/f*

gypsy ['dʒɪpsɪ] *n* gitan(e), bohémien(ne)

H, h

haberdashery [hæbə'dæʃərɪ] (BRIT) *n* mercerie *f*

habit ['hæbɪt] *n* habitude *f*; (REL: *costume*) habit *m*; **~ual** *adj* habituel(le); (*drinker, liar*) invétéré(e)

hack [hæk] *vt* hacher, tailler ♦ *n* (*pej: writer*) nègre *m*; **~er** *n* (COMPUT) pirate *m* (informatique); (: *enthusiast*) passionné(e) *m/f* des ordinateurs

hackneyed ['hæknɪd] *adj* usé(e), rebattu(e)

had [hæd] *pt, pp of* **have**

haddock ['hædək] (*pl* ~ *or* **~s**) *n* églefin *m*; **smoked** ~ haddock *m*

hadn't ['hædnt] = **had not**

haemorrhage ['hemərɪdʒ] (US **hemorrhage**) *n* hémorragie *f*

haemorrhoids ['hemərɔɪdz] (US **hemorrhoids**) *npl* hémorroïdes *fpl*

haggle ['hægl] *vi* marchander

Hague [heɪg] *n*: **The** ~ La Haye

hail [heɪl] *n* grêle *f* ♦ *vt* (*call*) héler; (*acclaim*) acclamer ♦ *vi* grêler; ~**stone** *n* grêlon *m*

hair [hɛəʳ] *n* cheveux *mpl*; (*of animal*) pelage *m*; (*single ~: on head*) cheveu *m*; (*: on body; of animal*) poil *m*; **to do one's ~** se coiffer; ~**brush** *n* brosse *f* à cheveux; ~**cut** *n* coupe *f* (de cheveux); ~**do** *n* coiffure *f*; ~**dresser** *n* coiffeur(-euse); ~**dresser's** *n* salon *m* de coiffure, coiffeur *m*; ~ **dryer** *n* sèche-cheveux *m*; ~ **gel** *n* gel *m* pour cheveux; ~**grip** *n* pince *f* à cheveux; ~**net** *n* filet *m* à cheveux; ~**piece** *n* perruque *f*; ~**pin** *n* épingle *f* à cheveux; ~**pin bend** (*US* **hairpin curve**) *n* virage *m* en épingle à cheveux; ~-**raising** *adj* à (vous) faire dresser les cheveux sur la tête; ~ **removing cream** *n* crème *f* dépilatoire; ~ **spray** *n* laque *f* (pour les cheveux); ~**style** *n* coiffure *f*; ~**y** *adj* poilu(e); (*inf: fig*) effrayant(e)

hake [heɪk] (*pl* ~ *or* ~**s**) *n* colin *m*, merlu *m*

half [hɑːf] (*pl* **halves**) *n* moitié *f*; (*of beer: also:* ~ **pint**) ≈ demi *m*; (*RAIL, bus: also:* ~ **fare**) demi-tarif *m* ♦ *adj* demi(e) ♦ *adv* (à) moitié, à demi; ~ **a dozen** une demi-douzaine; ~ **a pound** une demi-livre, ≈ 250 g; **two and a** ~ deux et demi; **to cut sth in** ~ couper qch en deux; ~-**caste** ['hɑːfkɑːst] *n* métis(se); ~-**hearted** *adj* tiède, sans enthousiasme; ~-**hour** *n* demi-heure *f*; ~-**mast:** **at** ~-**mast** *adv* (*flag*) en berne; ~**penny** (*BRIT*) *n* demi-penny *m*; ~-**price** *adj*, *adv*: (**at**) ~-**price** à moitié prix; ~ **term** (*BRIT*) *n* (*SCOL*) congé *m* de demi-trimestre; ~-**time** *n* mi-temps *f*; ~**way** *adv* à mi-chemin

hall [hɔːl] *n* salle *f*; (*entrance way*) hall *m*, entrée *f*

hallmark ['hɔːlmɑːk] *n* poinçon *m*; (*fig*) marque *f*

hallo [həˈləu] *excl* = **hello**

hall of residence (*BRIT*) (*pl* **halls of residence**) *n* résidence *f* universitaire

Hallowe'en ['hæləuˈiːn] *n* veille *f* de la Toussaint

hallucination [həluːsɪˈneɪʃən] *n* hallucination *f*

hallway ['hɔːlweɪ] *n* vestibule *m*

halo ['heɪləu] *n* (*of saint etc*) auréole *f*

halt [hɔːlt] *n* halte *f*, arrêt *m* ♦ *vt* (*progress etc*) interrompre ♦ *vi* faire halte, s'arrêter

halve [hɑːv] *vt* (*apple etc*) partager *or* diviser en deux; (*expense*) réduire de moitié; ~**s** *npl* of **half**

ham [hæm] *n* jambon *m*

hamburger ['hæmbəːgəʳ] *n* hamburger *m*

hamlet ['hæmlɪt] *n* hameau *m*

hammer ['hæməʳ] *n* marteau *m* ♦ *vt* (*nail*) enfoncer; (*fig*) démolir ♦ *vi* (*on door*) frapper à coups redoublés; **to ~ an idea into sb** faire entrer de force une idée dans la tête de qn

hammock ['hæmək] *n* hamac *m*

hamper ['hæmpəʳ] *vt* gêner ♦ *n* panier *m* (d'osier)

hamster ['hæmstəʳ] *n* hamster *m*

hand [hænd] *n* main *f*; (*of clock*) aiguille *f*; (~*writing*) écriture *f*; (*worker*) ouvrier(-ère); (*at cards*) jeu *m* ♦ *vt* passer, donner; **to give** *or* **lend sb a** ~ donner un coup de main à qn; **at** ~ à portée de la main; **in** ~ (*time*) à disposition; (*job, situation*) en main; **to be on** ~ (*person*) être disponible; (*emergency services*) se tenir prêt(e) (à intervenir); **to** ~ (*information etc*) sous la main, à portée de la main; **on the one** ~ ..., **on the other** ~ d'une part ..., d'autre part; ~ **in** *vt* remettre; ~ **out** *vt* distribuer; ~ **over** *vt* transmettre; céder; ~**bag** *n* sac *m* à main; ~**book** *n* manuel *m*; ~**brake** *n* frein *m* à main; ~**cuffs** *npl* menottes *fpl*;

~ful *n* poignée *f*

handicap ['hændıkæp] *n* handicap *m* ♦ *vt* handicaper; **mentally/physically ~ped** handicapé(e) mentalement/physiquement

handicraft ['hændıkrɑ:ft] *n* (*travail m* d')artisanat *m*, technique artisanale; (*object*) objet artisanal

handiwork ['hændıwə:k] *n* ouvrage *m*

handkerchief ['hæŋkətʃıf] *n* mouchoir *m*

handle ['hændl] *n* (*of door etc*) poignée *f*; (*of cup etc*) anse *f*; (*of knife etc*) manche *m*; (*of saucepan*) queue *f*; (*for winding*) manivelle *f* ♦ *vt* toucher, manier; (*deal with*) s'occuper de; (*treat: people*) prendre; **"~ with care"** "fragile"; **to fly off the ~** s'énerver; ~**bar(s)** *n(pl)* guidon *m*

hand: ~**luggage** *n* bagages *mpl* à main; ~**made** *adj* fait(e) à la main; ~**out** *n* (*from government, parents*) aide *f*, don *m*; (*leaflet*) documentation *f*, prospectus *m*; (*summary of lecture*) polycopié *m*; ~**rail** *n* rampe *f*, main courante; ~**set** *n* (TEL) combiné *m*; **please replace the ~set** raccrochez s'il vous plaît; ~**shake** *n* poignée *f* de main

handsome ['hænsəm] *adj* beau (belle); (*profit, return*) considérable

handwriting ['hændraıtıŋ] *n* écriture *f*

handy ['hændı] *adj* (*person*) adroit(e); (*close at hand*) sous la main; (*convenient*) pratique

hang [hæŋ] (*pt, pp* **hung**) *vt* accrocher; (*criminal: pt, pp:* ~ed) pendre ♦ *vi* pendre; (*hair, drapery*) tomber; **to get the ~ of (doing) sth** (*inf*) attraper le coup pour faire qch; ~ **about** *vi* traîner; ~ **around** *vi* = **hang about**; ~ **on** *vi* (*wait*) attendre; ~ **up** *vi* (TEL): **to ~ up (on sb)** raccrocher (au nez de qn) ♦ *vt* (*coat, painting etc*) accrocher, suspendre

hangar ['hæŋər] *n* hangar *m*

hanger ['hæŋər] *n* cintre *m*, portemanteau *m*; ~**on** *n* parasite *m*

hang: ~**gliding** *n* deltaplane *m*, vol *m* libre; ~**over** *n* (*after drinking*) gueule *f* de bois; ~**up** *n* complexe *m*

hanker ['hæŋkər] *vi*: **to ~ after** avoir envie de

hankie, hanky ['hæŋkı] *n abbr* = **handkerchief**

haphazard [hæp'hæzəd] *adj* fait(e) au hasard, fait(e) au petit bonheur

happen ['hæpən] *vi* arriver; se passer, se produire; **it so ~s that** il se trouve que; **as it ~s** justement; ~**ing** *n* événement *m*

happily ['hæpılı] *adv* heureusement; (*cheerfully*) joyeusement

happiness ['hæpınıs] *n* bonheur *m*

happy ['hæpı] *adj* heureux(-euse); ~ **with** (*arrangements etc*) satisfait(e) de; **to be ~ to do** faire volontiers; ~ **birthday!** bon anniversaire!; ~-**go-lucky** *adj* insouciant(e); ~ **hour** *n heure pendant laquelle les consommations sont à prix réduit*

harass ['hærəs] *vt* accabler, tourmenter; ~**ment** *n* tracasseries *fpl*

harbour ['hɑ:bər] (US **harbor**) *n* port *m* ♦ *vt* héberger, abriter; (*hope, fear etc*) entretenir

hard [hɑ:d] *adj* dur(e); (*question, problem*) difficile, dur(e); (*facts, evidence*) concret(-ète) ♦ *adv* (*work*) dur; (*think, try*) sérieusement; **to look ~ at** regarder fixement; (*thing*) regarder de près; **no ~ feelings!** sans rancune!; **to be ~ of hearing** être dur(e) d'oreille; **to be ~ done by** être traité(e) injustement; ~**back** *n* livre relié; ~ **cash** *n* espèces *fpl*; ~ **disk** *n* (COMPUT) disque dur; ~**en** *vt* durcir; (*fig*) endurcir ♦ *vi* durcir; ~-**headed** *adj* réaliste, décidé(e); ~ **labour** *n* travaux forcés

hardly ['hɑ:dlı] *adv* (*scarcely, no sooner*) à peine; ~ **anywhere/ever** presque nulle part/jamais

hard: ~**ship** *n* épreuves *fpl*; ~ **shoulder** (BRIT) *n* (AUT) accotement stabilisé; ~ **up** (*inf*) *adj* fauché(e); ~**ware** *n* quincaillerie *f*; (COMPUT, MIL) matériel *m*; ~**ware shop** *n* quincaillerie *f*; ~-**wearing** *adj* solide; ~-**working** *adj* travailleur(-euse)

hardy ['hɑ:dı] *adj* robuste; (*plant*) résistant(e) au gel

hare [heər] *n* lièvre *m*; ~-**brained** *adj* farfelu(e)

harm [hɑːm] *n* mal *m*; (*wrong*) tort *m* ♦ *vt* (*person*) faire du mal *or* du tort à; (*thing*) endommager; **out of ~'s way** à l'abri du danger, en lieu sûr; **~ful** *adj* nuisible; **~less** *adj* inoffensif(-ive); sans méchanceté

harmony ['hɑːmənɪ] *n* harmonie *f*

harness ['hɑːnɪs] *n* harnais *m*; (*safety* ~) harnais de sécurité ♦ *vt* (*horse*) harnacher; (*resources*) exploiter

harp [hɑːp] *n* harpe *f* ♦ *vi*: **to ~ on about** rabâcher

harrowing ['hærəʊɪŋ] *adj* déchirant(e), très pénible

harsh [hɑːʃ] *adj* (*hard*) dur(e); (*severe*) sévère; (*unpleasant*: *sound*) discordant(e); (: *light*) cru(e)

harvest ['hɑːvɪst] *n* (*of corn*) moisson *f*; (*of fruit*) récolte *f*; (*of grapes*) vendange *f* ♦ *vt* moissonner; récolter; vendanger

has [hæz] *vb see* **have**

hash [hæʃ] *n* (*CULIN*) hachis *m*; (*fig*: *mess*) gâchis *m*

hasn't ['hæznt] = **has not**

hassle ['hæsl] *n* (*inf*: *bother*) histoires *fpl*, tracas *mpl*

haste [heɪst] *n* hâte *f*; précipitation *f*; **~n** ['heɪsn] *vt* hâter, accélérer ♦ *vi* se hâter, s'empresser; **hastily** *adv* à la hâte; précipitamment; **hasty** *adj* hâtif(-ive); précipité(e)

hat [hæt] *n* chapeau *m*

hatch [hætʃ] *n* (*NAUT*: *also*: **~way**) écoutille *f*; (*also*: **service ~**) passe-plats *m inv* ♦ *vi* éclore; **~back** *n* (*AUT*) modèle *m* avec hayon arrière

hatchet ['hætʃɪt] *n* hachette *f*

hate [heɪt] *vt* haïr, détester ♦ *n* haine *f*; **~ful** *adj* odieux(-euse), détestable; **hatred** ['heɪtrɪd] *n* haine *f*

haughty ['hɔːtɪ] *adj* hautain(e), arrogant(e)

haul [hɔːl] *vt* traîner, tirer ♦ *n* (*of fish*) prise *f*; (*of stolen goods etc*) butin *m*; **~age** *n* transport routier; (*costs*) frais *mpl* de transport

haulier ['hɔːlɪər] (*US* **hauler**) *n* (*company*) transporteur (routier); (*driver*) camionneur

m

haunch [hɔːntʃ] *n* hanche *f*; (*of meat*) cuissot *m*

haunt [hɔːnt] *vt* (*subj*: *ghost*, *fear*) hanter; (: *person*) fréquenter ♦ *n* repaire *m*

| KEYWORD |
---

have [hæv] (*pt*, *pp* **had**) *aux vb* **1** (*gen*) avoir; être; **to have arrived/gone** être arrivé(e)/allé(e); **to have eaten/slept** avoir mangé/dormi; **he has been promoted** il a eu une promotion

2 (*in tag questions*): **you've done it, haven't you?** vous l'avez fait, n'est-ce pas?

3 (*in short answers and questions*): **no I haven't/yes we have!** mais non!/mais si!; **so I have!** ah oui!, oui c'est vrai!; **I've been there before, have you?** j'y suis déjà allé, et vous?

♦ *modal aux vb* (*be obliged*): **to have (got) to do sth** devoir faire qch; être obligé(e) de faire qch; **she has (got) to do it** elle doit le faire, il faut qu'elle le fasse; **you haven't to tell her** vous ne devez pas le lui dire

♦ *vt* **1** (*possess*, *obtain*) avoir; **he has (got) blue eyes/dark hair** il a les yeux bleus/les cheveux bruns; **may I have your address?** puis-je avoir votre adresse?

2 (+*noun*: *take*, *hold etc*): **to have breakfast/a bath/a shower** prendre le petit déjeuner/un bain/une douche; **to have dinner/lunch** dîner/déjeuner; **to have a swim** nager; **to have a meeting** se réunir; **to have a party** organiser une fête

3: **to have sth done** faire faire qch; **to have one's hair cut** se faire couper les cheveux; **to have sb do sth** faire faire qch à qn

4 (*experience*, *suffer*) avoir; **to have a cold/flu** avoir un rhume/la grippe; **to have an operation** se faire opérer

5 (*inf*: *dupe*) avoir; **he's been had** il s'est fait avoir *or* rouler

have out *vt*: **to have it out with sb** (*se*

tle a problem etc) s'expliquer (franchement) avec qn

haven ['heɪvn] *n* port *m*; (*fig*) havre *m*

haven't ['hævnt] = **have not**

havoc ['hævək] *n* ravages *mpl*

hawk [hɔːk] *n* faucon *m*

hay [heɪ] *n* foin *m*; ~ **fever** *n* rhume *m* des foins; ~**stack** *n* meule *f* de foin

haywire (*inf*) *adj*: **to go** ~ (*machine*) se détraquer; (*plans*) mal tourner

hazard ['hæzəd] *n* danger *m*, risque *m* ♦ *vt* risquer, hasarder; ~ **(warning) lights** *npl* (*AUT*) feux *mpl* de détresse

haze [heɪz] *n* brume *f*

hazelnut ['heɪzlnʌt] *n* noisette *f*

hazy ['heɪzɪ] *adj* brumeux(-euse); (*idea*) vague

he [hiː] *pron* il; **it is ~ who ...** c'est lui qui ...

head [hed] *n* tête *f*; (*leader*) chef *m*; (*of school*) directeur(-trice) ♦ *vt* (*list*) être en tête de; (*group*) être à la tête de; ~**s (or tails)** pile (ou face); ~ **first** la tête la première; ~ **over heels in love** follement *or* éperdument amoureux(-euse); **to ~ a ball** faire une tête; ~ **for** *vt fus* se diriger vers; ~**ache** *n* mal *m* de tête; ~**dress** (*BRIT*) *n* (*of Red Indian etc*) coiffure *f*; ~**ing** *n* titre *m*; ~**lamp** (*BRIT*) *n* = **headlight**; ~**land** *n* promontoire *m*, cap *m*; ~**light** *n* phare *m*; ~**line** *n* titre *m*; ~**long** *adv* (*fall*) la tête la première; (*rush*) tête baissée; ~**master** *n* directeur *m*; ~**mistress** *n* directrice *f*; ~ **office** *n* bureau central, siège *m*; ~**-on** *adj* (*collision*) de plein fouet; (*confrontation*) en face à face; ~**phones** *npl* casque *m* (à écouteurs); ~**quarters** *npl* bureau *or* siège central; (*MIL*) quartier général; ~**rest** *n* appui-tête *m*; ~**room** *n* (*in car*) hauteur *f* de plafond; (*under bridge*) hauteur limite; ~**scarf** *n* foulard *m*; ~**strong** *adj* têtu(e), entêté(e); ~ **teacher** *n* directeur(-trice); (*of secondary school*) proviseur *m*; ~ **waiter** *n* maître *m* d'hôtel; ~**way** *n*: **to make ~way** avancer, faire des progrès; ~**wind** *n* vent *m* contraire; (*NAUT*) vent debout; ~**y**

adj capiteux(-euse); enivrant(e); (*experience*) grisant(e)

heal [hiːl] *vt*, *vi* guérir

health [helθ] *n* santé *f*; ~ **food** *n* aliment(s) naturel(s); ~ **food shop** *n* magasin *m* diététique; **H~ Service** (*BRIT*) *n*: **the H~ Service** ≈ la Sécurité sociale; ~**y** *adj* (*person*) en bonne santé; (*climate, food, attitude etc*) sain(e), bon(ne) pour la santé

heap [hiːp] *n* tas *m* ♦ *vt*: **to ~ (up)** entasser, amonceler; **she ~ed her plate with cakes** elle a chargé son assiette de gâteaux

hear [hɪəʳ] (*pt*, *pp* **heard**) *vt* entendre; (*news*) apprendre ♦ *vi* entendre; **to ~ about** entendre parler de; avoir des nouvelles de; **to ~ from sb** recevoir *or* avoir des nouvelles de qn; ~**ing** *n* (*sense*) ouïe *f*; (*of witnesses*) audition *f*; (*of a case*) audience *f*; ~**ing aid** *n* appareil *m* acoustique; ~**say**: **by ~say** *adv* par ouï-dire *m*

hearse [hɜːs] *n* corbillard *m*

heart [hɑːt] *n* cœur *m*; ~**s** *npl* (*CARDS*) cœur; **to lose/take ~** perdre/prendre courage; **at ~** au fond; **by ~** (*learn, know*) par cœur; ~ **attack** *n* crise *f* cardiaque; ~**beat** *n* battement *m* du cœur; ~**breaking** *adj* déchirant(e), qui fend le cœur, ~**broken** *adj*: **to be ~broken** avoir beaucoup de chagrin *or* le cœur brisé; ~**burn** *n* brûlures *fpl* d'estomac; ~ **failure** *n* arrêt *m* du cœur; ~**felt** *adj* sincère

hearth [hɑːθ] *n* foyer *m*, cheminée *f*

heartily ['hɑːtɪlɪ] *adv* chaleureusement; (*laugh*) de bon cœur; (*eat*) de bon appétit; **to agree ~** être entièrement d'accord

hearty ['hɑːtɪ] *adj* chaleureux(-euse); (*appetite*) robuste; (*dislike*) cordial(e)

heat [hiːt] *n* chaleur *f*; (*fig*) feu *m*, agitation *f*; (*SPORT: also*: **qualifying ~**) éliminatoire *f* ♦ *vt* chauffer; ~ **up** *vi* (*water*) chauffer; (*room*) se réchauffer ♦ *vt* réchauffer; ~**ed** *adj* chauffé(e); (*fig*) passionné(e), échauffé(e); ~**er** *n* appareil *m* de chauffage; radiateur *m*; (*in car*) chauffage *m*; (*water heater*) chauffe-eau *m*

heath [hiːθ] (*BRIT*) *n* lande *f*

heather ['hɛðəʳ] *n* bruyère *f*

heating ['hiːtɪŋ] *n* chauffage *m*

heatstroke ['hiːtstrəuk] *n* (*MED*) coup *m* de chaleur

heat wave *n* vague *f* de chaleur

heave [hiːv] *vt* soulever (avec effort); (*drag*) traîner ♦ *vi* se soulever; (*retch*) avoir un haut-le-cœur; **to ~ a sigh** pousser un soupir

heaven ['hɛvn] *n* ciel *m*, paradis *m*; (*fig*) paradis; **~ly** *adj* céleste, divin(e)

heavily ['hɛvɪlɪ] *adv* lourdement; (*drink, smoke*) beaucoup; (*sleep, sigh*) profondément

heavy ['hɛvɪ] *adj* lourd(e); (*work, sea, rain, eater*) gros(se); (*snow*) beaucoup de; (*drinker, smoker*) grand(e); (*breathing*) bruyant(e); (*schedule, week*) chargé(e); **~ goods vehicle** *n* poids lourd; **~weight** *n* (*SPORT*) poids lourd

Hebrew ['hiːbruː] *adj* hébraïque ♦ *n* (*LING*) hébreu *m*

Hebrides ['hɛbrɪdiːz] *npl*: **the ~** les Hébrides *fpl*

heckle ['hɛkl] *vt* interpeller (*un orateur*)

hectic ['hɛktɪk] *adj* agité(e), trépidant(e)

he'd [hiːd] = **he would**; **he had**

hedge [hɛdʒ] *n* haie *f* ♦ *vi* se dérober; **to ~ one's bets** (*fig*) se couvrir

hedgehog ['hɛdʒhɔg] *n* hérisson *m*

heed [hiːd] *vt* (*also:* **take ~ of**) tenir compte de; **~less** *adj* insouciant(e)

heel [hiːl] *n* talon *m* ♦ *vt* retalonner

hefty ['hɛftɪ] *adj* (*person*) costaud(e); (*parcel*) lourd(e); (*profit*) gros(se)

heifer ['hɛfəʳ] *n* génisse *f*

height [haɪt] *n* (*of person*) taille *f*, grandeur *f*; (*of object*) hauteur *f*; (*of plane, mountain*) altitude *f*; (*high ground*) hauteur, éminence *f*; (*fig: of glory*) sommet *m*; (: *of luxury, stupidity*) comble *m*; **~en** *vt* (*fig*) augmenter

heir [ɛəʳ] *n* héritier *m*; **~ess** *n* héritière *f*; **~loom** *n* héritage *m*, meuble *m* (*or* bijou *m or* tableau *m*) de famille

held [hɛld] *pt, pp of* **hold**

helicopter ['hɛlɪkɔptəʳ] *n* hélicoptère *m*

hell [hɛl] *n* enfer *m*; **~!** (*inf!*) merde!

he'll [hiːl] = **he will**; **he shall**

hellish ['hɛlɪʃ] (*inf*) *adj* infernal(e)

hello [hə'ləu] *excl* bonjour!; (*to attract attention*) hé!; (*surprise*) tiens!

helm [hɛlm] *n* (*NAUT*) barre *f*

helmet ['hɛlmɪt] *n* casque *m*

help [hɛlp] *n* aide *f*; (*charwoman*) femme *f* de ménage ♦ *vt* aider; **~!** au secours!; **~ yourself** servez-vous; **he can't ~ it** il ne peut pas s'en empêcher; **~er** *n* aide *m/f*, assistant(e); **~ful** *adj* serviable, obligeant(e); (*useful*) utile; **~ing** *n* portion *f*, **~less** *adj* impuissant(e); (*defenceless*) faible

hem [hɛm] *n* ourlet *m* ♦ *vt* ourler; **~ in** *vt* cerner

hemorrhage ['hɛmərɪdʒ] (*US*) *n* = **haemorrhage**

hemorrhoids ['hɛmərɔɪdz] (*US*) *npl* = **haemorrhoids**

hen [hɛn] *n* poule *f*

hence [hɛns] *adv* (*therefore*) d'où, de là; **2 years ~** d'ici 2 ans, dans 2 ans; **~forth** *adv* dorénavant

her [həːʳ] *pron* (*direct*) la, l'; (*indirect*) lui, (*stressed, after prep*) elle ♦ *adj* son (sa), ses *pl*; *see also* **me**; **my**

herald ['hɛrəld] *n* héraut *m* ♦ *vt* annoncer; **~ry** *n* (*study*) héraldique *f*; (*coat of arms*) blason *m*

herb [həːb] *n* herbe *f*

herd [həːd] *n* troupeau *m*

here [hɪəʳ] *adv* ici; (*time*) alors ♦ *excl* tiens!, tenez!; **~!** présent!; **~ is, ~ are** voici; **~ he/she is!** le/la voici!; **~after** *adv* après, plus tard; **~by** *adv* (*formal: in letter*) par la présente

hereditary [hɪ'rɛdɪtrɪ] *adj* héréditaire

heresy ['hɛrəsɪ] *n* hérésie *f*

heritage ['hɛrɪtɪdʒ] *n* (*of country*) patrimoine *m*

hermit ['həːmɪt] *n* ermite *m*

hernia ['həːnɪə] *n* hernie *f*

hero ['hɪərəu] (*pl* **~es**) *n* héros *m*

heroin ['hɛrəuɪn] *n* héroïne *f*

heroine ['hɛrəuɪn] *n* héroïne *f*

heron ['herən] n héron m

herring ['herɪŋ] n hareng m

hers [hɜːz] pron le (la) sien(ne), les siens (siennes); see also **mine**[1]

herself [hɜːˈsɛlf] pron (reflexive) se; (emphatic) elle-même; (after prep) elle; see also **oneself**

he's [hiːz] = **he is; he has**

hesitant ['hɛzɪtənt] adj hésitant(e), indécis(e)

hesitate ['hɛzɪteɪt] vi hésiter; **hesitation** [hɛzɪˈteɪʃən] n hésitation f

heterosexual ['hɛtərəuˈsɛksjuəl] adj, n hétérosexuel(le)

heyday ['heɪdeɪ] n: **the ~ of** l'âge m d'or de, les beaux jours de

HGV n abbr = **heavy goods vehicle**

hi [haɪ] excl salut!; (to attract attention) hé!

hiatus [haɪˈeɪtəs] n (gap) lacune f; (interruption) pause f

hibernate ['haɪbəneɪt] vi hiberner

hiccough, hiccup ['hɪkʌp] vi hoqueter; **~s** npl hoquet m

hide [haɪd] (pt **hid**, pp **hidden**) n (skin) peau f ♦ vt cacher ♦ vi: **to ~ (from sb)** se cacher (de qn); **~-and-seek** n cache-cache m

hideous ['hɪdɪəs] adj hideux(-euse)

hiding ['haɪdɪŋ] n (beating) correction f, volée f de coups; **to be in ~** (concealed) se tenir caché(e)

hierarchy ['haɪərɑːkɪ] n hiérarchie f

hi-fi ['haɪfaɪ] n hi-fi f inv ♦ adj hi-fi inv

high [haɪ] adj haut(e); (speed, respect, number) grand(e); (price) élevé(e); (wind) fort(e), violent(e); (voice) aigu (aiguë) ♦ adv haut; **20 m ~** haut(e) de 20 m; **~brow** adj, n intellectuel(le); **~chair** n (child's) chaise haute; **~er education** n études supérieures; **~-handed** adj autoritaire; très cavalier(-ère); **~-heeled** adj à hauts talons; **~ jump** n (SPORT) saut m en hauteur; **~lands** npl Highlands mpl; **~light** n (fig: of event) point culminant ♦ vt faire ressortir, souligner; **~lights** npl (in hair) reflets mpl; **~ly** adv très, fort, hautement; **to speak/think ~ly of sb** dire/penser beaucoup de bien de qn; **~ly paid** adj très bien payé(e); **~ly strung** adj nerveux(-euse), toujours tendu(e); **~ness** n: **Her (or His) H~ness** Son Altesse f; **~-pitched** adj aigu (aiguë); **~-rise** adj: **~-rise block, ~-rise flats** tour f (d'habitation); **~ school** n lycée m; (US) établissement m d'enseignement supérieur; **~ season** (BRIT) n haute saison; **~ street** (BRIT) n grand-rue f; **~way** n route nationale; **H~way Code** (BRIT) n code m de la route

hijack ['haɪdʒæk] vt (plane) détourner; **~er** n pirate m de l'air

hike [haɪk] vi aller or faire des excursions à pied ♦ n excursion f à pied, randonnée f; **~r** n promeneur(-euse), excursionniste m/f; **hiking** n excursions fpl à pied

hilarious [hɪˈlɛərɪəs] adj (account, event) désopilant(e)

hill [hɪl] n colline f; (fairly high) montagne f; (on road) côte f; **~side** n (flanc m de) coteau m; **~-walking** n randonnée f de basse montagne; **~y** adj vallonné(e); montagneux(-euse)

hilt [hɪlt] n (of sword) garde f; **to the ~** (fig: support) à fond

him [hɪm] pron (direct) le, l'; (stressed, indirect, after prep) lui; see also **me**; **~self** pron (reflexive) se; (emphatic) lui-même; (after prep) lui; see also **oneself**

hinder ['hɪndər] vt gêner; (delay) retarder; **hindrance** n gêne f, obstacle m

hindsight ['haɪndsaɪt] n: **with ~** avec du recul, rétrospectivement

Hindu ['hɪnduː] adj hindou(e)

hinge [hɪndʒ] n charnière f ♦ vi (fig): **to ~ on** dépendre de

hint [hɪnt] n allusion f; (advice) conseil m ♦ vt: **to ~ that** insinuer que ♦ vi: **to ~ at** faire une allusion à

hip [hɪp] n hanche f

hippie ['hɪpɪ] n hippie m/f

hippo ['hɪpəu] (pl **~s**), **hippopotamus** [hɪpəˈpɒtəməs] (pl **~potamuses** or **~potami**) n hippopotame m

hire ['haɪər] vt (BRIT: car, equipment) louer;

(*worker*) embaucher, engager ♦ *n* location *f*; **for ~** à louer; (*taxi*) libre; **~(d) car** *n* voiture *f* de location; **~ purchase** (BRIT) *n* achat *m* (*or* vente *f*) à tempérament *or* crédit

his [hɪz] *pron* le (la) sien(ne), les siens (siennes) ♦ *adj* son (sa), ses *pl*; *see also* **my; mine**[1]

hiss [hɪs] *vi* siffler

historic [hɪ'stɔrɪk] *adj* historique; **~al** *adj* historique

history ['hɪstərɪ] *n* histoire *f*

hit [hɪt] (*pt, pp* hit) *vt* frapper; (*reach: target*) atteindre, toucher; (*collide with: car*) entrer en collision avec, heurter; (*fig: affect*) toucher ♦ *n* coup *m*; (*success*) succès *m*; (*: song*) tube *m*; **to ~ it off with sb** bien s'entendre avec qn; **~-and-run driver** *n* chauffard *m* (coupable du délit de fuite)

hitch [hɪtʃ] *vt* (*fasten*) accrocher, attacher; (*also:* **~ up**) remonter d'une saccade ♦ *n* (*difficulty*) anicroche *f*, contretemps *m*; **to ~ a lift** faire du stop; **~hike** *vi* faire de l'auto-stop; **~hiker** *n* auto-stoppeur(-euse)

hi-tech ['haɪ'tek] *adj* de pointe

hitherto [hɪðə'tuː] *adv* jusqu'ici

hit man *n* tueur *m* à gages

HIV *n*: **~-negative/-positive** *adj* séronégatif(-ive)/-positif(-ive)

hive [haɪv] *n* ruche *f*

HMS *abbr* = **Her/His Majesty's Ship**

hoard [hɔːd] *n* (*of food*) provisions *fpl*, réserves *fpl*; (*of money*) trésor *m* ♦ *vt* amasser; **~ing** (BRIT) *n* (*for posters*) panneau *m* d'affichage *or* publicitaire

hoarse [hɔːs] *adj* enroué(e)

hoax [həʊks] *n* canular *m*

hob [hɔb] *n* plaque (chauffante)

hobble ['hɔbl] *vi* boitiller

hobby ['hɔbɪ] *n* passe-temps favori

hobo ['həʊbəʊ] (US) *n* vagabond *m*

hockey ['hɔkɪ] *n* hockey *m*

hog [hɔg] *n* porc (châtré) ♦ *vt* (*fig*) accaparer; **to go the whole ~** aller jusqu'au bout

hoist [hɔɪst] *n* (*apparatus*) palan *m* ♦ *vt* hisser

hold [həʊld] (*pt, pp* held) *vt* tenir; (*contain*) contenir; (*believe*) considérer; (*possess*) avoir; (*detain*) détenir ♦ *vi* (*withstand pressure*) tenir (bon); (*be valid*) valoir ♦ *n* (*also fig*) prise *f*; (NAUT) cale *f*; **~ the line!** (TEL) ne quittez pas!; **to ~ one's own** (*fig*) (bien) se défendre; **to catch** *or* **get (a) ~ of** saisir; **to get ~ of** (*fig*) trouver; **~ back** *vt* retenir; (*secret*) taire; **~ down** *vt* (*person*) maintenir à terre; (*job*) occuper; **~ off** *vt* tenir à distance; **~ on** *vi* tenir bon; (*wait*) attendre; **~ on!** (TEL) ne quittez pas!; **~ on to** *vt fus* se cramponner à; (*keep*) conserver, garder; **~ out** *vt* offrir ♦ *vi* (*resist*) tenir bon; **~ up** *vt* (*raise*) lever; (*support*) soutenir; (*delay*) retarder; (*rob*) braquer; **~all** (BRIT) *n* fourre-tout *m inv*; **~er** *n* (*of ticket, record*) détenteur(-trice); (*of office, title etc*) titulaire *m/f*; (*container*) support *m*; **~ing** *n* (*share*) intérêts *mpl*; (*farm*) ferme *f*; **~-up** *n* (*robbery*) hold-up *m*; (*delay*) retard *m*; (BRIT: *in traffic*) bouchon *m*

hole [həʊl] *n* trou *m*; **~-in-the-wall** *n* (*cash dispenser*) distributeur *m* de billets

holiday ['hɔlɪdeɪ] *n* vacances *fpl*; (*day off*) jour *m* de congé; (*public*) jour férié; **on ~** en congé; **~ camp** *n* (*also:* **~ centre**) camp *m* de vacances; **~-maker** (BRIT) *n* vacancier(-ère); **~ resort** *n* centre *m* de villégiature *or* de vacances

Holland ['hɔlənd] *n* Hollande *f*

hollow ['hɔləʊ] *adj* creux(-euse) ♦ *n* creux *m* ♦ *vt*: **to ~ out** creuser, évider

holly ['hɔlɪ] *n* houx *m*

holocaust ['hɔləkɔːst] *n* holocauste *m*

holster ['həʊlstər] *n* étui *m* de revolver

holy ['həʊlɪ] *adj* saint(e); (*bread, water*) bénit(e); (*ground*) sacré(e); **H~ Ghost** *n* Saint-Esprit *m*

homage ['hɔmɪdʒ] *n* hommage *m*; **to pay ~ to** rendre hommage à

home [həʊm] *n* foyer *m*, maison *f*; (*country*) pays natal, patrie *f*; (*institution*) maison ♦ *adj* de famille; (ECON, POL) natio nal(e), intérieur(e); (SPORT: *game*) sur leur (*or* notre) terrain; (*team*) qui reçoit ♦ *adv* chez soi, à la maison; au pays natal; (*right in: nail etc*) à fond; **at ~** chez soi, à la maison; **make yourself at ~** faites comme chez vous; **~ address** qui exerce à domicile permanent; **~land** *n* patrie *f*; **~less** *adj* sans foyer; sans abri; **~ly** *adj* (*plain*) simple, sans prétention; **~-made** *adj* fait(e) à la maison; **~ match** *n* match *m* à domicile; **H~ Office** (BRIT) *n* ministère *m* de l'Intérieur; **~ page** *n* (COMPUT) page *f* d'accueil; **~ rule** *n* autonomie *f*; **H~ Secretary** (BRIT) *n* ministre *m* de l'Intérieur; **~sick** *adj*: **to be ~sick** avoir le mal du pays; s'ennuyer de sa famille; **~ town** *n* ville natale; **~ward** *adj* (*journey*) du retour; **~work** *n* devoirs *mpl*

homoeopathic [həumiəu'pæθɪk] (US **homeopathic**) *adj* (*medicine, methods*) homéopathique; (*doctor*) homéopathe

homogeneous [hɔməu'dʒiːnɪəs] *adj* homogène

homosexual [hɔməu'sɛksjuəl] *adj, n* homosexuel(le)

honest ['ɔnɪst] *adj* honnête; (*sincere*) franc (franche); **~ly** *adv* honnêtement; franchement; **~y** *n* honnêteté *f*

honey ['hʌnɪ] *n* miel *m*; **~comb** *n* rayon *m* de miel; **~moon** *n* lune *f* de miel, voyage *m* de noces; **~suckle** (BOT) *n* chèvrefeuille *m*

honk [hɔŋk] *vi* (AUT) klaxonner

honorary ['ɔnərərɪ] *adj* honoraire; (*duty, title*) honorifique

honour ['ɔnər] (US **honor**) *vt* honorer ♦ *n* honneur *m*; **hono(u)rable** *adj* honorable; **hono(u)rs degree** *n* (SCOL) licence *avec mention*

hood [hud] *n* capuchon *m*; (*of cooker*) hotte *f*; (AUT: BRIT) capote *f*; (: US) capot *m*

hoof [huːf] (*pl* **hooves**) *n* sabot *m*

hook [huk] *n* crochet *m*; (*on dress*) agrafe *f*; (*for fishing*) hameçon *m* ♦ *vt* accrocher; (*fish*) prendre

hooligan ['huːlɪgən] *n* voyou *m*

hoop [huːp] *n* cerceau *m*

hooray [huːˈreɪ] *excl* hourra

hoot [huːt] *vi* (AUT) klaxonner; (*siren*) mugir; (*owl*) hululer; **~er** *n* (BRIT: AUT) klaxon *m*; (NAUT, *factory*) sirène *f*

Hoover ® ['huːvər] (BRIT) *n* aspirateur *m* ♦ *vt*: **h~** passer l'aspirateur dans *or* sur

hooves [huːvz] *npl of* **hoof**

hop [hɔp] *vi* (*on one foot*) sauter à cloche-pied; (*bird*) sautiller

hope [həup] *vt, vi* espérer ♦ *n* espoir *m*; **I ~ so** je l'espère; **I ~ not** j'espère que non; **~ful** *adj* (*person*) plein(e) d'espoir; (*situation*) prometteur(-euse), encourageant(e); **~fully** *adv* (*expectantly*) avec espoir, avec optimisme; **~less** *adj* désespéré(e); (*useless*) nul(le)

hops [hɔps] *npl* houblon *m*

horizon [hə'raɪzn] *n* horizon *m*; **~tal** [hɔrɪ'zɔntl] *adj* horizontal(e)

horn [hɔːn] *n* corne *f*; (MUS: *also:* **French ~**) cor *m*; (AUT) klaxon *m*

hornet ['hɔːnɪt] *n* frelon *m*

horoscope ['hɔrəskəup] *n* horoscope *m*

horrendous [hə'rendəs] *adj* horrible, affreux(-euse)

horrible ['hɔrɪbl] *adj* horrible, affreux(-euse)

horrid ['hɔrɪd] *adj* épouvantable

horrify ['hɔrɪfaɪ] *vt* horrifier

horror ['hɔrər] *n* horreur *f*; **~ film** *n* film *m* d'épouvante

hors d'oeuvre [ɔː'dəːvrə] *n* (CULIN) hors-d'œuvre *m inv*

horse [hɔːs] *n* cheval *m*; **~back** *n*: **on ~back** à cheval; **~ chestnut** *n* marron *m* (d'Inde); **~man** (*irreg*) *n* cavalier *m*; **~power** *n* puissance *f* (en chevaux); **~racing** *n* courses *fpl* de chevaux; **~radish** *n* raifort *m*; **~shoe** *n* fer *m* à cheval

hose [həuz] *n* (*also:* **~pipe**) tuyau *m*; (*also:* **garden ~**) tuyau d'arrosage

hospitable ['hɔspɪtəbl] *adj* hospitalier(-ère)

hospital ['hɔspɪtl] *n* hôpital *m*; **in ~** à l'hôpital

hospitality [hɔspɪ'tælɪtɪ] *n* hospitalité *f*

host [həust] *n* hôte *m*; (TV, RADIO)

animateur(-trice); (*REL*) hostie *f*; (*large number*): **a ~ of** une foule de

hostage ['hɔstɪdʒ] *n* otage *m*

hostel ['hɔstl] *n* foyer *m*; (*also:* **youth ~**) auberge *f* de jeunesse

hostess ['həustɪs] *n* hôtesse *f*; (*TV, RADIO*) animatrice *f*

hostile ['hɔstaɪl] *adj* hostile; **hostility** [hɔ'stɪlɪtɪ] *n* hostilité *f*

hot [hɔt] *adj* chaud(e); (*as opposed to only warm*) très chaud(e); (*spicy*) fort(e); (*fig*) acharné(e); (*temper*) passionné(e); **to be ~** (*person*) avoir chaud; (*object*) être (très) chaud; (*weather*) faire chaud; **~bed** *n* (*fig*) foyer *m*, pépinière *f*; **~ dog** *n* hot-dog *m*

hotel [həu'tel] *n* hôtel *m*

hot: **~house** *n* serre (chaude); **~line** *n* (*POL*) téléphone *m* rouge, ligne directe; **~ly** *adv* passionnément, violemment; **~plate** *n* (*on cooker*) plaque chauffante; **~pot** *n* (*BRIT*) ragoût *m*; **~-water bottle** *n* bouillotte *f*

hound [haund] *vt* poursuivre avec acharnement ♦ *n* chien courant

hour ['auər] *n* heure *f*; **~ly** *adj, adv* toutes les heures; (*rate*) horaire

house [*n* haus, *vb* hauz] *n* maison *f*; (*POL*) chambre *f*; (*THEATRE*) salle *f*; auditoire *m* ♦ *vt* (*person*) loger, héberger; (*objects*) abriter; **on the ~** (*fig*) aux frais de la maison; **~ arrest** *n* assignation *f* à résidence; **~boat** *n* bateau *m* (aménagé en habitation); **~bound** *adj* confiné(e) chez soi; **~breaking** *n* cambriolage *m* (avec effraction); **~hold** *n* (*persons*) famille *f*, maisonnée *f*; (*ADMIN etc*) ménage *m*; **~keeper** *n* gouvernante *f*; **~keeping** *n* (*work*) ménage *m*; **~keeping (money)** *n* argent *m* du ménage; **~-warming (party)** *n* pendaison *f* de crémaillère; **~wife** (*irreg*) *n* ménagère *f*; femme *f* au foyer; **~work** *n* (travaux *mpl* du) ménage *m*

housing ['hauzɪŋ] *n* logement *m*; **~ development, ~ estate** *n* lotissement *m*

hovel ['hɔvl] *n* taudis *m*

hover ['hɔvər] *vi* planer; **~craft** *n* aéroglisseur *m*

how [hau] *adv* comment; **~ are you?** comment allez-vous?; **~ do you do?** bonjour; enchanté(e); **~ far is it to?** combien y a-t-il jusqu'à ...?; **~ long have you been here?** depuis combien de temps êtes-vous là?; **~ lovely!** que *or* comme c'est joli!; **~ many/much?** combien?; **~ many people/much milk?** combien de gens/lait?; **~ old are you?** quel âge avez-vous?

however [hau'ɛvər] *adv* de quelque façon *or* manière que +*subj*; (+*adj*) quelque *or* si ... que +*subj*; (*in questions*) comment ♦ *conj* pourtant, cependant

howl [haul] *vi* hurler

H.P. *abbr* = **hire purchase**

h.p. *abbr* = **horsepower**

HQ *abbr* = **headquarters**

HTML *n abbr* (= *Hypertext Mark-up Language*) HTML

hub [hʌb] *n* (*of wheel*) moyeu *m*; (*fig*) centre *m*, foyer *m*; **~cap** *n* enjoliveur *m*

huddle ['hʌdl] *vi*: **to ~ together** se blottir les uns contre les autres

hue [hju:] *n* teinte *f*, nuance *f*

huff [hʌf] *n*: **in a ~** fâché(e)

hug [hʌg] *vt* serrer dans ses bras; (*shore, kerb*) serrer

huge [hju:dʒ] *adj* énorme, immense

hulk [hʌlk] *n* (*ship*) épave *f*; (*car, building*) carcasse *f*; (*person*) mastodonte *m*

hull [hʌl] *n* coque *f*

hullo [hə'ləu] *excl* = **hello**

hum [hʌm] *vt* (*tune*) fredonner ♦ *vi* fredonner; (*insect*) bourdonner; (*plane, tool*) vrombir

human ['hju:mən] *adj* humain(e) ♦ *n*: **~ being** être humain; **~e** [hju:'meɪn] *adj* humain(e), humanitaire; **~itarian** [hju:mænɪ'teərɪən] *adj* humanitaire; **~ity** [hju:'mænɪtɪ] *n* humanité *f*

humble ['hʌmbl] *adj* humble, modeste ♦ *vt* humilier

humdrum ['hʌmdrʌm] *adj* monotone

humid ['hju:mɪd] *adj* humide

humiliate [hju:'mɪlɪeɪt] *vt* humilier; **humiliation** [hju:mɪlɪ'eɪʃən] *n* humiliation *f*

humorous ['hju:mərəs] *adj* humoristique

(person) plein(e) d'humour

humour ['hju:mər] (*US* **humor**) *n* humour *m*; (*mood*) humeur *f* ♦ *vt* (*person*) faire plaisir à; se prêter aux caprices de

hump [hʌmp] *n* bosse *f*

hunch [hʌntʃ] *n* (*premonition*) intuition *f*; ~**back** *n* bossu(e); ~**ed** *adj* voûté(e)

hundred ['hʌndrəd] *num* cent; ~**s of** des centaines de; ~**weight** *n* (*BRIT*) *50.8 kg, 112 lb*; (*US*) *45.3 kg, 100 lb*

hung [hʌŋ] *pt, pp of* **hang**

Hungary ['hʌŋgərɪ] *n* Hongrie *f*

hunger ['hʌŋgər] *n* faim *f* ♦ *vi*: **to ~ for** avoir faim de, désirer ardemment

hungry ['hʌŋgrɪ] *adj* affamé(e); (*keen*): ~ **for** avide de; **to be ~** avoir faim

hunk [hʌŋk] *n* (*of bread etc*) gros morceau

hunt [hʌnt] *vt* chasser; (*criminal*) pourchasser ♦ *vi* chasser; (*search*): **to ~ for** chercher (partout) ♦ *n* chasse *f*; ~**er** *n* chasseur *m*; ~**ing** *n* chasse *f*

hurdle ['hə:dl] *n* (*SPORT*) haie *f*; (*fig*) obstacle *m*

hurl [hə:l] *vt* lancer (avec violence); (*abuse, insults*) lancer

hurrah [hu'rɑ:] *excl* = **hooray**

hurray [hu'reɪ] *excl* = **hooray**

hurricane ['hʌrɪkən] *n* ouragan *m*

hurried ['hʌrɪd] *adj* pressé(e), précipité(e); (*work*) fait(e) à la hâte; ~**ly** *adv* précipitamment, à la hâte

hurry ['hʌrɪ] (*vb: also*: ~ **up**) *n* hâte *f*, précipitation *f* ♦ *vi* se presser, se dépêcher ♦ *vt* (*person*) faire presser, faire se dépêcher; (*work*) presser; **to be in a ~** être pressé(e); **to do sth in a ~** faire qch en vitesse; **to ~ in/out** entrer/sortir précipitamment

hurt [hə:t] (*pt, pp* **hurt**) *vt* (*cause pain to*) faire mal à; (*injure, fig*) blesser ♦ *vi* faire mal ♦ *adj* blessé(e); ~**ful** *adj* (*remark*) blessant(e)

hurtle ['hə:tl] *vi*: **to ~ past** passer en trombe; **to ~ down** dégringoler

husband ['hʌzbənd] *n* mari *m*

hush [hʌʃ] *n* calme *m*, silence *m* ♦ *vt* faire taire; ~**!** chut!; ~ **up** *vt* (*scandal*) étouffer

husk [hʌsk] *n* (*of wheat*) balle *f*; (*of rice,*

maize) enveloppe *f*

husky ['hʌskɪ] *adj* rauque ♦ *n* chien *m* esquimau *or* de traîneau

hustle ['hʌsl] *vt* pousser, bousculer ♦ *n*: ~ **and bustle** tourbillon *m* (d'activité)

hut [hʌt] *n* hutte *f*; (*shed*) cabane *f*

hutch [hʌtʃ] *n* clapier *m*

hyacinth ['haɪəsɪnθ] *n* jacinthe *f*

hydrant ['haɪdrənt] *n* (*also*: **fire ~**) bouche *f* d'incendie

hydraulic [haɪ'drɔːlɪk] *adj* hydraulique

hydroelectric [haɪdrəʊ'lektrɪk] *adj* hydro-électrique

hydrofoil ['haɪdrəfɔɪl] *n* hydrofoil *m*

hydrogen ['haɪdrədʒən] *n* hydrogène *m*

hyena [haɪ'iːnə] *n* hyène *f*

hygiene ['haɪdʒiːn] *n* hygiène *f*; **hygienic** *adj* hygiénique

hymn [hɪm] *n* hymne *m*; cantique *m*

hype [haɪp] (*inf*) *n* battage *m* publicitaire

hypermarket ['haɪpəmɑːkɪt] (*BRIT*) *n* hypermarché *m*

hypertext ['haɪpətekst] *n* (*COMPUT*) hypertexte *m*

hyphen ['haɪfn] *n* trait *m* d'union

hypnotize ['hɪpnətaɪz] *vt* hypnotiser

hypocrisy [hɪ'pɔkrɪsɪ] *n* hypocrisie *f*; **hypocrite** ['hɪpəkrɪt] *n* hypocrite *m/f*; **hypocritical** *adj* hypocrite

hypothesis [haɪ'pɔθɪsɪs] (*pl* **hypotheses**) *n* hypothèse *f*

hysterical [hɪ'sterɪkl] *adj* hystérique; (*funny*) hilarant(e); ~ **laughter** fou rire *m*

hysterics [hɪ'sterɪks] *npl*: **to be in/have ~** (*anger, panic*) avoir une crise de nerfs; (*laughter*) attraper un fou rire

I, i

I [aɪ] *pron* je; (*before vowel*) j'; (*stressed*) moi

ice [aɪs] *n* glace *f*; (*on road*) verglas *m* ♦ *vt* (*cake*) glacer ♦ *vi* (*also*: ~ **over**, ~ **up**) geler; (*window*) se givrer; ~**berg** *n* iceberg *m*; ~**box** *n* (*US*) réfrigérateur *m*; (*BRIT*) compartiment *m* à glace; (*insulated box*) glacière *f*; ~ **cream** *n* glace *f*; ~ **cube** *n* glaçon m; **~d** adj glacé(e); **~ hockey** n hockey m sur glace; **Iceland** n Islande f; **~ lolly** n (BRIT) esquimau m (glace); **~ rink** n patinoire f; **~-skating** n patinage m (sur glace)

icicle ['aɪsɪkl] n glaçon m (naturel)

icing ['aɪsɪŋ] n (CULIN) glace f; **~ sugar** (BRIT) n sucre m glace

icon ['aɪkɔn] n (COMPUT) icône f

icy ['aɪsɪ] adj glacé(e); (road) verglacé(e); (weather, temperature) glacial(e)

I'd [aɪd] = I would; I had

idea [aɪ'dɪə] n idée f

ideal [aɪ'dɪəl] n idéal m ♦ adj idéal(e)

identical [aɪ'dɛntɪkl] adj identique

identification [aɪdɛntɪfɪ'keɪʃən] n identification f; **means of ~** pièce f d'identité

identify [aɪ'dɛntɪfaɪ] vt identifier

Identikit picture ® [aɪ'dɛntɪkɪt-] n portrait-robot m

identity [aɪ'dɛntɪtɪ] n identité f; **~ card** n carte f d'identité

ideology [aɪdɪ'ɔlədʒɪ] n idéologie f

idiom ['ɪdɪəm] n expression f idiomatique; (style) style m

idiosyncrasy [ɪdɪəu'sɪŋkrəsɪ] n (of person) particularité f, petite manie

idiot ['ɪdɪət] n idiot(e), imbécile m/f; **~ic** [ɪdɪ'ɔtɪk] adj idiot(e), bête, stupide

idle ['aɪdl] adj sans occupation, désœuvré(e); (lazy) oisif(-ive), paresseux(-euse); (unemployed) au chômage; (question, pleasures) vain(e), futile ♦ vi (engine) tourner au ralenti; **to lie ~** être arrêté(e), ne pas fonctionner

idol ['aɪdl] n idole f; **~ize** vt idolâtrer, adorer

i.e. adv abbr (= id est) c'est-à-dire

if [ɪf] conj si; **~ so** si c'est le cas; **~ not** sinon; **~ only** si seulement

ignite [ɪg'naɪt] vt mettre le feu à, enflammer ♦ vi s'enflammer; **ignition** n (AUT) allumage m; **to switch on/off the ignition** mettre/couper le contact; **ignition key** n clé f de contact

ignorant ['ɪgnərənt] adj ignorant(e); **to be ~ of** (subject) ne rien connaître à; (events) ne pas être au courant de

ignore [ɪg'nɔːr] vt ne tenir aucun compte de; (person) faire semblant de ne pas reconnaître, ignorer; (fact) méconnaître

ill [ɪl] adj (sick) malade; (bad) mauvais(e) ♦ n mal m ♦ adv: **to speak/think ~ of** dire/penser du mal de; **~s** npl (misfortunes) maux mpl, malheurs mpl; **to be taken ~** tomber malade; **~-advised** adj (decision) peu judicieux(-euse); (person) malavisé(e); **~-at-ease** adj mal à l'aise

I'll [aɪl] = I will; I shall

illegal [ɪ'liːgl] adj illégal(e)

illegible [ɪ'lɛdʒɪbl] adj illisible

illegitimate [ɪlɪ'dʒɪtɪmət] adj illégitime

ill-fated [ɪl'feɪtɪd] adj malheureux(-euse); (day) néfaste

ill feeling n ressentiment m, rancune f

illiterate [ɪ'lɪtərət] adj illettré(e)

ill: ~-mannered adj (child) mal élevé(e); **~ness** n maladie f; **~-treat** vt maltraiter

illuminate [ɪ'luːmɪneɪt] vt (room, street) éclairer; (for special effect) illuminer; **illumination** [ɪluːmɪ'neɪʃən] n éclairage m; illumination f

illusion [ɪ'luːʒən] n illusion f

illustrate ['ɪləstreɪt] vt illustrer; **illustration** [ɪlə'streɪʃən] n illustration f

ill will n malveillance f

I'm [aɪm] = I am

image ['ɪmɪdʒ] n image f; (public face) image de marque; **~ry** n images fpl

imaginary [ɪ'mædʒɪnərɪ] adj imaginaire

imagination [ɪmædʒɪ'neɪʃən] n imagination f

imaginative [ɪ'mædʒɪnətɪv] adj imaginatif(-ive); (person) plein(e) d'imagination

imagine [ɪ'mædʒɪn] vt imaginer, s'imaginer; (suppose) imaginer, supposer

imbalance [ɪm'bæləns] n déséquilibre m

imitate ['ɪmɪteɪt] vt imiter; **imitation** [ɪmɪ'teɪʃən] n imitation f

immaculate [ɪ'mækjulət] adj impeccable; (REL) immaculé(e)

immaterial [ɪmə'tɪərɪəl] adj sans importance, insignifiant(e)

immature [ɪmə'tjuər] adj (fruit) (qui n'est)

pas mûr(e); (*person*) qui manque de maturité

immediate [ɪ'miːdɪət] *adj* immédiat(e); **~ly** *adv* (*at once*) immédiatement; **~ly next to** juste à côté de

immense [ɪ'mɛns] *adj* immense; énorme

immerse [ɪ'mɜːs] *vt* immerger, plonger; **immersion heater** (*BRIT*) *n* chauffe-eau *m* électrique

immigrant ['ɪmɪgrənt] *n* immigrant(e); immigré(e); **immigration** [ɪmɪ'greɪʃən] *n* immigration *f*

imminent ['ɪmɪnənt] *adj* imminent(e)

immoral [ɪ'mɒrl] *adj* immoral(e)

immortal [ɪ'mɔːtl] *adj, n* immortel(le)

immune [ɪ'mjuːn] *adj*: **~ (to)** immunisé(e) (contre); (*fig*) à l'abri de; **immunity** *n* immunité *f*

impact ['ɪmpækt] *n* choc *m*, impact *m*; (*fig*) impact

impair [ɪm'pɛər] *vt* détériorer, diminuer

impart [ɪm'pɑːt] *vt* communiquer, transmettre; (*flavour*) donner

impartial [ɪm'pɑːʃl] *adj* impartial(e)

impassable [ɪm'pɑːsəbl] *adj* infranchissable; (*road*) impraticable

impassive [ɪm'pæsɪv] *adj* impassible

impatience [ɪm'peɪʃəns] *n* impatience *f*

impatient [ɪm'peɪʃənt] *adj* impatient(e); **to get** *or* **grow ~** s'impatienter; **~ly** *adv* avec impatience

impeccable [ɪm'pɛkəbl] *adj* impeccable, parfait(e)

impede [ɪm'piːd] *vt* gêner; **impediment** *n* obstacle *m*; (*also*: **speech impediment**) défaut *m* d'élocution

impending [ɪm'pɛndɪŋ] *adj* imminent(e)

imperative [ɪm'pɛrətɪv] *adj* (*need*) urgent(e), pressant(e); (*tone*) impérieux(-euse) ♦ *n* (*LING*) impératif *m*

imperfect [ɪm'pɜːfɪkt] *adj* imparfait(e); (*goods etc*) défectueux(-euse)

imperial [ɪm'pɪərɪəl] *adj* impérial(e); (*BRIT*: *measure*) légal(e)

impersonal [ɪm'pɜːsənl] *adj* impersonnel(le)

impersonate [ɪm'pɜːsəneɪt] *vt* se faire

passer pour; (*THEATRE*) imiter

impertinent [ɪm'pɜːtɪnənt] *adj* impertinent(e), insolent(e)

impervious [ɪm'pɜːvɪəs] *adj* (*fig*): **~ to** insensible à

impetuous [ɪm'pɛtjuəs] *adj* impétueux(-euse), fougueux(-euse)

impetus ['ɪmpətəs] *n* impulsion *f*; (*of runner*) élan *m*

impinge [ɪm'pɪndʒ]: **to ~ on** *vt fus* (*person*) affecter, toucher; (*rights*) empiéter sur

implement [*n* 'ɪmplɪmənt, *vb* 'ɪmplɪment] *n* outil *m*, instrument *m*; (*for cooking*) ustensile *m* ♦ *vt* exécuter

implicit [ɪm'plɪsɪt] *adj* implicite; (*complete*) absolu(e), sans réserve

imply [ɪm'plaɪ] *vt* suggérer, laisser entendre; indiquer, supposer

impolite [ɪmpə'laɪt] *adj* impoli(e)

import [*vb* ɪm'pɔːt, *n* 'ɪmpɔːt] *vt* importer ♦ *n* (*COMM*) importation *f*

importance [ɪm'pɔːtns] *n* importance *f*

important [ɪm'pɔːtənt] *adj* important(e)

importer [ɪm'pɔːtər] *n* importateur(-trice)

impose [ɪm'pəuz] *vt* imposer ♦ *vi*: **to ~ on sb** abuser de la gentillesse de qn; **imposing** *adj* imposant(e), impressionnant(e); **imposition** [ɪmpə'zɪʃən] *n* (*of tax etc*) imposition *f*; **to be an imposition on** (*person*) abuser de la gentillesse *or* la bonté de

impossible [ɪm'pɒsɪbl] *adj* impossible

impotent ['ɪmpətnt] *adj* impuissant(e)

impound [ɪm'paund] *vt* confisquer, saisir

impoverished [ɪm'pɒvərɪʃt] *adj* appauvri(e), pauvre

impractical [ɪm'præktɪkl] *adj* pas pratique; (*person*) qui manque d'esprit pratique

impregnable [ɪm'prɛgnəbl] *adj* (*fortress*) imprenable

impress [ɪm'prɛs] *vt* impressionner, faire impression sur; (*mark*) imprimer, marquer; **to ~ sth on sb** faire bien comprendre qch à qn; **~ed** *adj* impressionné(e)

impression [ɪm'prɛʃən] *n* impression *f*; (*of stamp, seal*) empreinte *f*; (*imitation*) imitation *f*; **to be under the ~ that** avoir l'impression que; ~**ist** *n* (*ART*) impressioniste *m/f*; (*entertainer*) imitateur(-trice) *m/f*

impressive [ɪmˈprɛsɪv] *adj* impressionnant(e)

imprint [ˈɪmprɪnt] *n* (*outline*) marque *f*, empreinte *f*

imprison [ɪmˈprɪzn] *vt* emprisonner, mettre en prison

improbable [ɪmˈprɔbəbl] *adj* improbable; (*excuse*) peu plausible

improper [ɪmˈprɔpəʳ] *adj* (*unsuitable*) déplacé(e), de mauvais goût; indécent(e); (*dishonest*) malhonnête

improve [ɪmˈpruːv] *vt* améliorer ♦ *vi* s'améliorer; (*pupil etc*) faire des progrès; ~**ment** *n* amélioration *f* (*in* de); progrès *m*

improvise [ˈɪmprəvaɪz] *vt, vi* improviser

impudent [ˈɪmpjudnt] *adj* impudent(e)

impulse [ˈɪmpʌls] *n* impulsion *f*; **on ~** impulsivement, sur un coup de tête; **impulsive** *adj* impulsif(-ive)

KEYWORD

in [ɪn] *prep* **1** (*indicating place, position*) dans; **in the house/the fridge** dans la maison/ le frigo; **in the garden** dans le *or* au jardin; **in town** en ville; **in the country** à la campagne; **in school** à l'école; **in here/ there** ici/là

2 (*with place names: of town, region, country*): **in London** à Londres; **in England** en Angleterre; **in Japan** au Japon; **in the United States** aux États-Unis

3 (*indicating time: during*): **in spring** au printemps; **in summer** en été; **in May/ 1992** en mai/1992; **in the afternoon** (*dans*) l'après-midi; **at 4 o'clock in the afternoon** à 4 heures de l'après-midi

4 (*indicating time: in the space of*) en; (*: future*) dans; **I did it in 3 hours/days** je l'ai fait en 3 heures/jours; **I'll see you in 2 weeks** *or* **in 2 weeks' time** je te verrai dans 2 semaines

5 (*indicating manner etc*) à; **in a loud/soft voice** à voix haute/basse; **in pencil** au crayon; **in French** en français; **the boy in the blue shirt** le garçon à *or* avec la chemise bleue

6 (*indicating circumstances*): **in the sun** au soleil; **in the shade** à l'ombre; **in the rain** sous la pluie

7 (*indicating mood, state*): **in tears** en larmes; **in anger** sous le coup de la colère; **in despair** au désespoir; **in good condition** en bon état; **to live in luxury** vivre dans le luxe

8 (*with ratios, numbers*): **1 in 10 (households), 1 (household) in 10** 1 (ménage) sur 10; **20 pence in the pound** 20 pence par livre sterling; **they lined up in twos** ils se mirent en rangs (deux) par deux; **in hundreds** par centaines

9 (*referring to people, works*) chez; **the disease is common in children** c'est une maladie courante chez les enfants; **in (the works of) Dickens** chez Dickens, dans (l'œuvre de) Dickens

10 (*indicating profession etc*) dans; **to be in teaching** être dans l'enseignement

11 (*after superlative*) de; **the best pupil in the class** le meilleur élève de la classe

12 (*with present participle*): **in saying this** en disant ceci

♦ *adv*: **to be in** (*person: at home, work*) être là; (*train, ship, plane*) être arrivé(e); (*in fashion*) être à la mode; **to ask sb in** inviter qn à entrer; **to run/limp** *etc* **in** entrer en courant/boitant *etc*

♦ *n*: **the ins and outs (of)** (*of proposal, situation etc*) les tenants et aboutissants (de)

---

in. *abbr* = **inch**

inability [ɪnəˈbɪlɪtɪ] *n* incapacité *f*

inaccurate [ɪnˈækjurət] *adj* inexact(e); (*person*) qui manque de précision

inadequate [ɪnˈædɪkwət] *adj* insuffisant(e), inadéquat(e)

inadvertently [ɪnədˈvəːtntlɪ] *adv* par mégarde

inadvisable [ɪnədˈvaɪzəbl] *adj* (*action*) à déconseiller

inane [ɪˈneɪn] *adj* inepte, stupide

inanimate [ɪnˈænɪmət] *adj* inanimé(e)

inappropriate [ɪnəˈprəuprɪət] *adj* inopportun(e), mal à propos; (*word, expression*) impropre

inarticulate [ɪnɑːˈtɪkjulət] *adj* (*person*) qui s'exprime mal; (*speech*) indistinct(e)

inasmuch [ɪnəzˈmʌtʃ] *adv* (*insofar as*) dans la mesure où; (*seeing that*) attendu que

inauguration [ɪnɔːgjuˈreɪʃən] *n* inauguration *f*; (*of president*) investiture *f*

inborn [ɪnˈbɔːn] *adj* (*quality*) inné(e)

inbred [ɪnˈbred] *adj* inné(e), naturel(le); (*family*) consanguin(e)

Inc. *abbr* = **incorporated**

incapable [ɪnˈkeɪpəbl] *adj* incapable

incapacitate [ɪnkəˈpæsɪteɪt] *vt*: **to ~ sb from doing** rendre qn incapable de faire

incense [*n* ˈɪnsens, *vb* ɪnˈsens] *n* encens *m* ♦ *vt* (*anger*) mettre en colère

incentive [ɪnˈsentɪv] *n* encouragement *m*, raison *f* de se donner de la peine

incessant [ɪnˈsesnt] *adj* incessant(e); **~ly** *adv* sans cesse, constamment

inch [ɪntʃ] *n* pouce *m* (= 25 mm; 12 in a foot); **within an ~ of** à deux doigts de; **he didn't give an ~** (*fig*) il n'a pas voulu céder d'un pouce

incident [ˈɪnsɪdnt] *n* incident *m*; **~al** [ɪnsɪˈdentl] *adj* (*additional*) accessoire; **~al to** qui accompagne; **~ally** *adv* (*by the way*) à propos

inclination [ɪnklɪˈneɪʃən] *n* (*fig*) inclination *f*

incline [*n* ˈɪnklaɪn, *vb* ɪnˈklaɪn] *n* pente *f* ♦ *vt* incliner ♦ *vi* (*surface*) s'incliner; **to be ~d to do** avoir tendance à faire

include [ɪnˈkluːd] *vt* inclure, comprendre; **including** *prep* y compris; **inclusive** *adj* inclus(e), compris(e); **inclusive of tax** *etc* taxes *etc* comprises

income [ˈɪnkʌm] *n* revenu *m*; **~ tax** *n* impôt *m* sur le revenu

incoming [ˈɪnkʌmɪŋ] *adj* qui arrive; (*president*) entrant(e); **~ mail** courrier *m* du jour; **~ tide** marée montante

incompetent [ɪnˈkɔmpɪtnt] *adj* incompétent(e), incapable

incomplete [ɪnkəmˈpliːt] *adj* incomplet(-ète)

incongruous [ɪnˈkɔŋgruəs] *adj* incongru(e)

inconsiderate [ɪnkənˈsɪdərət] *adj* (*person*) qui manque d'égards; (*action*) inconsidéré(e)

inconsistency [ɪnkənˈsɪstənsɪ] *n* (*of actions etc*) inconséquence *f*; (*of work*) irrégularité *f*; (*of statement etc*) incohérence *f*

inconsistent [ɪnkənˈsɪstnt] *adj* inconséquent(e); irrégulier(-ère); peu cohérent(e); **~ with** incompatible avec

inconspicuous [ɪnkənˈspɪkjuəs] *adj* qui passe inaperçu(e); (*colour, dress*) discret(-ète)

inconvenience [ɪnkənˈviːnjəns] *n* inconvénient *m*; (*trouble*) dérangement *m* ♦ *vt* déranger

inconvenient [ɪnkənˈviːnjənt] *adj* (*house*) malcommode; (*time, place*) mal choisi(e), qui ne convient pas; (*visitor*) importun(e)

incorporate [ɪnˈkɔːpəreɪt] *vt* incorporer; (*contain*) contenir; **~d company** (*US*) *n* ≃ société *f* anonyme

incorrect [ɪnkəˈrekt] *adj* incorrect(e)

increase [*n* ˈɪnkriːs, *vb* ɪnˈkriːs] *n* augmentation *f* ♦ *vi, vt* augmenter; **increasing** *adj* (*number*) croissant(e); **increasingly** *adv* de plus en plus

incredible [ɪnˈkredɪbl] *adj* incroyable

incubator [ˈɪnkjubeɪtər] *n* (*for babies*) couveuse *f*

incumbent [ɪnˈkʌmbənt] *n* (*president*) président *m* en exercice; (*REL*) titulaire *m/f* ♦ *adj*: **it is ~ on him to ...** il lui incombe or appartient de ...

incur [ɪnˈkɜːr] *vt* (*expenses*) encourir; (*anger, risk*) s'exposer à; (*debt*) contracter; (*loss*) subir

indebted [ɪnˈdetɪd] *adj*: **to be ~ to sb (for)** être redevable à qn (de)

indecent [ɪnˈdiːsnt] *adj* indécent(e), inconvenant(e); **~ assault** (*BRIT*) *n* attentat *m* à la pudeur; **~ exposure** *n* outrage *m* (public) à la pudeur

indecisive [ɪndɪˈsaɪsɪv] *adj* (*person*) indécis(e)

indeed [ɪnˈdiːd] adv vraiment; en effet; (*furthermore*) d'ailleurs; **yes ~!** certainement!

indefinitely [ɪnˈdɛfɪnɪtlɪ] adv (*wait*) indéfiniment

indemnity [ɪnˈdɛmnɪtɪ] n (*safeguard*) assurance f, garantie f; (*compensation*) indemnité f

independence [ɪndɪˈpɛndns] n indépendance f

Independence Day

L'Independence Day est la fête nationale aux États-Unis, le 4 juillet. Il commémore l'adoption de la déclaration d'Indépendance, en 1776, écrite par Thomas Jefferson et proclamant la séparation des 13 colonies américaines de la Grande-Bretagne.

independent [ɪndɪˈpɛndnt] adj indépendant(e); (*school*) privé(e); (*radio*) libre

index [ˈɪndɛks] n (pl: ~es: in book) index m; (: in library etc) catalogue m; (pl: indices: ratio, sign) indice m; **~ card** n fiche f; **~ finger** n index m; **~-linked** adj indexé(e) (sur le coût de la vie etc)

India [ˈɪndɪə] n Inde f; **~n** adj indien(ne) ♦ n Indien(ne); (**American**) **~n** Indien(ne) (d'Amérique); **~n Ocean** n océan Indien

indicate [ˈɪndɪkeɪt] vt indiquer; **indication** [ɪndɪˈkeɪʃən] n indication f, signe m; **indicative** [ɪnˈdɪkətɪv] adj: **indicative of** symptomatique de ♦ n (*LING*) indicatif m; **indicator** n (*sign*) indicateur m; (*AUT*) clignotant m

indices [ˈɪndɪsiːz] npl of **index**

indictment [ɪnˈdaɪtmənt] n accusation f

indifferent [ɪnˈdɪfrənt] adj indifférent(e); (*poor*) médiocre, quelconque

indigenous [ɪnˈdɪdʒɪnəs] adj indigène

indigestion [ɪndɪˈdʒɛstʃən] n indigestion f, mauvaise digestion

indignant [ɪnˈdɪgnənt] adj: **~ (at sth / with sb)** indigné(e) (de qch/contre qn)

indignity [ɪnˈdɪgnɪtɪ] n indignité f, affront

indirect [ɪndɪˈrɛkt] adj indirect(e)

indiscreet [ɪndɪsˈkriːt] adj indiscret(-ète); (*rash*) imprudent(e)

indiscriminate [ɪndɪsˈkrɪmɪnət] adj (*person*) qui manque de discernement; (*killings*) commis(e) au hasard

indisputable [ɪndɪsˈpjuːtəbl] adj incontestable, indiscutable

individual [ɪndɪˈvɪdjuəl] n individu m ♦ adj individuel(le); (*characteristic*) particulier(-ère), original(e)

indoctrination [ɪndɔktrɪˈneɪʃən] n endoctrinement m

Indonesia [ɪndəˈniːzɪə] n Indonésie f

indoor [ˈɪndɔːʳ] adj (*plant*) d'appartement; (*swimming pool*) couvert(e); (*sport, games*) pratiqué(e) en salle; **~s** adv à l'intérieur

induce [ɪnˈdjuːs] vt (*persuade*) persuader; (*bring about*) provoquer; **~ment** n (*incentive*) récompense f; (*pej: bribe*) pot-de-vin m

indulge [ɪnˈdʌldʒ] vt (*whim*) céder à, satisfaire; (*child*) gâter ♦ vi: **to ~ in sth** (*luxury*) se permettre qch; (*fantasies etc*) se livrer à qch; **~nce** n fantaisie f (que l'on s'offre); (*leniency*) indulgence f; **~nt** adj indulgent(e)

industrial [ɪnˈdʌstrɪəl] adj industriel(le); (*injury*) du travail; **~ action** n action revendicative; **~ estate** (*BRIT*) n zone industrielle; **~ist** n industriel m; **~ park** (*US*) n = **industrial estate**

industrious [ɪnˈdʌstrɪəs] adj travailleur(-euse)

industry [ˈɪndəstrɪ] n industrie f; (*diligence*) zèle m, application f

inebriated [ɪˈniːbrɪeɪtɪd] adj ivre

inedible [ɪnˈɛdɪbl] adj immangeable; (*plant etc*) non comestible

ineffective [ɪnɪˈfɛktɪv], **ineffectual** [ɪnɪˈfɛktʃuəl] adj inefficace

inefficient [ɪnɪˈfɪʃənt] adj inefficace

inequality [ɪnɪˈkwɔlɪtɪ] n inégalité f

inescapable [ɪnɪsˈkeɪpəbl] adj inéluctable, inévitable

inevitable [ɪnˈɛvɪtəbl] adj inévitable; **inevitably** adv inévitablement

inexpensive [ɪnɪk'spɛnsɪv] *adj* bon marché *inv*

inexperienced [ɪnɪk'spɪərɪənst] *adj* inexpérimenté(e)

infallible [ɪn'fælɪbl] *adj* infaillible

infamous ['ɪnfəməs] *adj* infâme, abominable

infancy ['ɪnfənsɪ] *n* petite enfance, bas âge

infant ['ɪnfənt] *n* (*baby*) nourrisson *m*; (*young child*) petit(e) enfant; ~ **school** (*BRIT*) *n* classes *fpl* préparatoires (*entre 5 et 7 ans*)

infatuated [ɪn'fætjueɪtɪd] *adj*: ~ **with** entiché(e) de; **infatuation** [ɪnfætju'eɪʃən] *n* engouement *m*

infect [ɪn'fɛkt] *vt* infecter, contaminer; **~ion** *n* infection *f*; (*contagion*) contagion *f*; **~ious** *adj* infectieux(-euse); (*also fig*) contagieux(-euse)

infer [ɪn'fəːʳ] *vt* conclure, déduire

inferior [ɪn'fɪərɪəʳ] *adj* inférieur(e); (*goods*) de qualité inférieure ♦ *n* inférieur(e); (*in rank*) subalterne *m/f*; **~ity** [ɪnfɪərɪ'ɔrətɪ] *n* infériorité *f*

infertile [ɪn'fəːtaɪl] *adj* stérile

infighting ['ɪnfaɪtɪŋ] *n* querelles *fpl* internes

infinite ['ɪnfɪnɪt] *adj* infini(e)

infinitive [ɪn'fɪnɪtɪv] *n* infinitif *m*

infinity [ɪn'fɪnɪtɪ] *n* infinité *f*; (*also MATH*) infini *m*

infirmary [ɪn'fəːmərɪ] *n* (*hospital*) hôpital *m*

inflamed [ɪn'fleɪmd] *adj* enflammé(e)

inflammable [ɪn'flæməbl] (*BRIT*) *adj* inflammable

inflammation [ɪnflə'meɪʃən] *n* inflammation *f*

inflatable [ɪn'fleɪtəbl] *adj* gonflable

inflate [ɪn'fleɪt] *vt* (*tyre, balloon*) gonfler; (*price*) faire monter; **inflation** *n* (*ECON*) inflation *f*; **inflationary** *adj* inflationniste

inflict [ɪn'flɪkt] *vt*: **to ~ on** infliger à

influence ['ɪnfluəns] *n* influence *f* ♦ *vt* influencer; **under the ~ of alcohol** en état d'ébriété; **influential** [ɪnflu'ɛnʃl] *adj* influent(e)

influenza [ɪnflu'ɛnzə] *n* grippe *f*

influx ['ɪnflʌks] *n* afflux *m*

infomercial ['ɪnfəuməːʃl] (*US*) *n* (*for product*) publi-information *f*; (*POL*) émission où un candidat présente son programme électoral

inform [ɪn'fɔːm] *vt*: **to ~ sb (of)** informer *or* avertir qn (de) ♦ *vi*: **to ~ on sb** dénoncer qn

informal [ɪn'fɔːml] *adj* (*person, manner, party*) simple; (*visit, discussion*) dénué(e) de formalités; (*announcement, invitation*) non officiel(le); (*colloquial*) familier(-ère); **~ity** [ɪnfɔː'mælɪtɪ] *n* simplicité *f*, absence *f* de cérémonie; caractère non officiel

informant [ɪn'fɔːmənt] *n* informateur(-trice)

information [ɪnfə'meɪʃən] *n* information *f*; renseignements *mpl*; (*knowledge*) connaissances *fpl*; **a piece of ~** un renseignement; **~ desk** *n* accueil *m*; **~ office** *n* bureau *m* de renseignements

informative [ɪn'fɔːmətɪv] *adj* instructif(-ive)

informer [ɪn'fɔːməʳ] *n* (*also*: **police ~**) indicateur(-trice)

infringe [ɪn'frɪndʒ] *vt* enfreindre ♦ *vi*: **to ~ on** empiéter sur; **~ment** *n*: **~ment (of)** infraction *f* (à)

infuriating [ɪn'fjuərɪeɪtɪŋ] *adj* exaspérant(e)

ingenious [ɪn'dʒiːnjəs] *adj* ingénieux(-euse); **ingenuity** [ɪndʒɪ'njuːɪtɪ] *n* ingéniosité *f*

ingenuous [ɪn'dʒɛnjuəs] *adj* naïf (naïve), ingénu(e)

ingot ['ɪŋgət] *n* lingot *m*

ingrained [ɪn'greɪnd] *adj* enraciné(e)

ingratiate [ɪn'greɪʃɪeɪt] *vt*: **to ~ o.s. with** s'insinuer dans les bonnes grâces de, se faire bien voir de

ingredient [ɪn'griːdɪənt] *n* ingrédient *m*; (*fig*) élément *m*

inhabit [ɪn'hæbɪt] *vt* habiter; **~ant** *n* habitant(e)

inhale [ɪn'heɪl] *vt* respirer; (*smoke*) avaler ♦ *vi* aspirer; (*in smoking*) avaler la fumée

inherent [ɪn'hɪərənt] *adj*: ~ **(in** *or* **to)** inhérent(e) (à)

inherit [ɪn'herɪt] *vt* hériter (de); **~ance** *n* héritage *m*

inhibit [ɪn'hɪbɪt] *vt* (*PSYCH*) inhiber; (*growth*) freiner; **~ion** [ɪnhɪ'bɪʃən] *n* inhibition *f*

inhuman [ɪn'hju:mən] *adj* inhumain(e)

initial [ɪ'nɪʃl] *adj* initial(e) ♦ *n* initiale *f* ♦ *vt* parafer; **~s** *npl* (*letters*) initiales *fpl*; (*as signature*) parafe *m*; **~ly** *adv* initialement, au début

initiate [ɪ'nɪʃɪeɪt] *vt* (*start*) entreprendre, amorcer; (*entreprise*) lancer; (*person*) initier; **to ~ proceedings against sb** intenter une action à qn; **initiative** *n* initiative *f*

inject [ɪn'dʒekt] *vt* injecter; (*person*): **to ~ sb with sth** faire une piqûre de qch à qn; **~ion** *n* injection *f*, piqûre *f*

injure ['ɪndʒəʳ] *vt* blesser; (*reputation etc*) compromettre; **~d** *adj* blessé(e); **injury** *n* blessure *f*; **~ time** *n* (*SPORT*) arrêts *mpl* de jeu

injustice [ɪn'dʒʌstɪs] *n* injustice *f*

ink [ɪŋk] *n* encre *f*

inkling ['ɪŋklɪŋ] *n*: **to have an/no ~ of** avoir une (vague) idée de/n'avoir aucune idée de

inlaid ['ɪnleɪd] *adj* incrusté(e); (*table etc*) marqueté(e)

inland [*adj* 'ɪnlənd, *adv* ɪn'lænd] *adj* intérieur(e) ♦ *adv* à l'intérieur, dans les terres; **Inland Revenue** (*BRIT*) *n* fisc *m*

in-laws ['ɪnlɔ:z] *npl* beaux-parents *mpl*; belle famille

inlet ['ɪnlet] *n* (*GEO*) crique *f*

inmate ['ɪnmeɪt] *n* (*in prison*) détenu(e); (*in asylum*) interné(e)

inn [ɪn] *n* auberge *f*

innate [ɪ'neɪt] *adj* inné(e)

inner ['ɪnəʳ] *adj* intérieur(e); **~ city** *n* centre *m* de zone urbaine; **~ tube** *n* (*of tyre*) chambre *f* à air

innings ['ɪnɪŋz] *n* (*CRICKET*) tour *m* de batte

innocent ['ɪnəsnt] *adj* innocent(e)

innocuous [ɪ'nɔkjuəs] *adj* inoffensif(-ive)

innuendo [ɪnju'endəu] (*pl* **~es**) *n* insinuation *f*, allusion (malveillante)

innumerable [ɪ'nju:mrəbl] *adj* innombra-

ble

inpatient ['ɪnpeɪʃənt] *n* malade hospitalisé(e)

input ['ɪnput] *n* (*resources*) ressources *fpl*; (*COMPUT*) entrée *f* (de données); (: *data*) données *fpl*

inquest ['ɪnkwest] *n* enquête *f*; **(coroner's) ~** enquête judiciaire

inquire [ɪn'kwaɪəʳ] *vi* demander ♦ *vt* demander; **to ~ about** se renseigner sur; **~ into** *vt fus* faire une enquête sur; **inquiry** *n* demande *f* de renseignements; (*investigation*) enquête *f*, investigation *f*; **inquiries** *npl*: **the inquiries** (*RAIL etc*) les renseignements; **inquiry** *or* **inquiries office** (*BRIT*) *n* bureau *m* des renseignements

inquisitive [ɪn'kwɪzɪtɪv] *adj* curieux(-euse)

ins *abbr* = **inches**

insane [ɪn'seɪn] *adj* fou (folle); (*MED*) aliéné(e); **insanity** [ɪn'sænɪtɪ] *n* folie *f*; (*MED*) aliénation (mentale)

inscription [ɪn'skrɪpʃən] *n* inscription *f*; (*in book*) dédicace *f*

inscrutable [ɪn'skru:təbl] *adj* impénétrable; (*comment*) obscur(e)

insect ['ɪnsekt] *n* insecte *m*; **~icide** [ɪn'sektɪsaɪd] *n* insecticide *m*; **~ repellent** *n* crème *f* anti-insecte

insecure [ɪnsɪ'kjuəʳ] *adj* peu solide; peu sûr(e); (*person*) anxieux(-euse)

insensitive [ɪn'sensɪtɪv] *adj* insensible

insert [ɪn'sə:t] *vt* insérer; **~ion** *n* insertion *f*

in-service [ɪn'sə:vɪs] *adj* (*training*) continu(e), en cours d'emploi; (*course*) de perfectionnement; de recyclage

inshore [ɪn'ʃɔ:ʳ] *adj* côtier(-ère) ♦ *adv* près de la côte; (*move*) vers la côte

inside ['ɪn'saɪd] *n* intérieur *m* ♦ *adj* intérieur(e) ♦ *adv* à l'intérieur, dedans ♦ *prep* à l'intérieur de; (*of time*): **~ 10 minutes** en moins de 10 minutes; **~s** *npl* (*inf*) intestins *mpl*; **~ information** *n* renseignements obtenus à la source; **~ lane** *n* (*AUT: in Britain*) voie *f* de gauche; (: *in US, Europe etc*) voie de droite; **~ out** *adv* à l'envers; (*know*) à fond; **~r dealing**, **~r trading** *n* (*St Ex*) délit *m* d'initié

insight ['ɪnsaɪt] *n* perspicacité *f;* (*glimpse, idea*) aperçu *m*

insignificant [ɪnsɪg'nɪfɪknt] *adj* insignifiant(e)

insincere [ɪnsɪn'sɪəʳ] *adj* hypocrite

insinuate [ɪn'sɪnjʊeɪt] *vt* insinuer

insist [ɪn'sɪst] *vi* insister; **to ~ on doing** insister pour faire; **to ~ on sth** exiger qch; **to ~ that** insister pour que; (*claim*) maintenir *or* soutenir que; **~ent** *adj* insistant(e), pressant(e); (*noise, action*) ininterrompu(e)

insole ['ɪnsəʊl] *n* (*removable*) semelle intérieure

insolent ['ɪnsələnt] *adj* insolent(e)

insolvent [ɪn'sɔlvənt] *adj* insolvable

insomnia [ɪn'sɔmnɪə] *n* insomnie *f*

inspect [ɪn'spɛkt] *vt* inspecter; (*ticket*) contrôler; **~ion** *n* inspection *f;* contrôle *m;* **~or** *n* inspecteur(-trice); (*BRIT: on buses, trains*) contrôleur(-euse)

inspire [ɪn'spaɪəʳ] *vt* inspirer

install [ɪn'stɔːl] *vt* installer; **~ation** [ɪnstə'leɪʃən] *n* installation *f*

instalment [ɪn'stɔːlmənt] (*US* **installment**) *n* acompte *m,* versement partiel; (*of TV serial etc*) épisode *m;* **in ~s** (*pay*) à tempérament; (*receive*) en plusieurs fois

instance ['ɪnstəns] *n* exemple *m;* **for ~** par exemple; **in the first ~** tout d'abord, en premier lieu

instant ['ɪnstənt] *n* instant *m* ♦ *adj* immédiat(e); (*coffee, food*) instantané(e), en poudre; **~ly** *adv* immédiatement, tout de suite

instead [ɪn'stɛd] *adv* au lieu de cela; **~ of** au lieu de; **~ of sb** à la place de qn

instep ['ɪnstɛp] *n* cou-de-pied *m;* (*of shoe*) cambrure *f*

instigate ['ɪnstɪgeɪt] *vt* (*rebellion*) fomenter, provoquer; (*talks etc*) promouvoir

instil [ɪn'stɪl] *vt:* **to ~ (into)** inculquer (à); (*courage*) insuffler (à)

instinct ['ɪnstɪŋkt] *n* instinct *m*

institute ['ɪnstɪtjuːt] *n* institut *m* ♦ *vt* instituer, établir; (*inquiry*) ouvrir; (*proceedings*) entamer

institution [ɪnstɪ'tjuːʃən] *n* institution *f;* (*educational*) établissement *m* (scolaire); (*mental home*) établissement (psychiatrique)

instruct [ɪn'strʌkt] *vt:* **to ~ sb in sth** enseigner qch à qn; **to ~ sb to do** charger qn *or* ordonner à qn de faire; **~ion** *n* instruction *f;* **~ions** *npl* (*orders*) directives *fpl;* **~ions (for use)** mode *m* d'emploi; **~or** *n* professeur *m;* (*for skiing, driving*) moniteur *m*

instrument ['ɪnstrʊmənt] *n* instrument *m;* **~al** [ɪnstrʊ'mɛntl] *adj:* **to be ~al in** contribuer à; **~ panel** *n* tableau *m* de bord

insufficient [ɪnsə'fɪʃənt] *adj* insuffisant(e)

insular ['ɪnsjʊləʳ] *adj* (*outlook*) borné(e); (*person*) aux vues étroites

insulate ['ɪnsjʊleɪt] *vt* isoler; (*against sound*) insonoriser; **insulation** [ɪnsjʊ'leɪʃən] *n* isolation *f;* insonorisation *f*

insulin ['ɪnsjʊlɪn] *n* insuline *f*

insult [*n* 'ɪnsʌlt, *vb* ɪn'sʌlt] *n* insulte *f,* affront *m* ♦ *vt* insulter, faire affront à

insurance [ɪn'ʃʊərəns] *n* assurance *f;* **fire/life ~** assurance-incendie/-vie; **~ policy** *n* police *f* d'assurance

insure [ɪn'ʃʊəʳ] *vt* assurer; **to ~ (o.s.) against** (*fig*) parer à

intact [ɪn'tækt] *adj* intact(e)

intake ['ɪnteɪk] *n* (*of food, oxygen*) consommation *f;* (*BRIT: SCOL*) **an ~ of 200 a year** 200 admissions *fpl* par an

integral ['ɪntɪgrəl] *adj* (*part*) intégrant(e)

integrate ['ɪntɪgreɪt] *vt* intégrer ♦ *vi* s'intégrer

intellect ['ɪntəlɛkt] *n* intelligence *f;* **~ual** [ɪntə'lɛktjʊəl] *adj, n* intellectuel(le)

intelligence [ɪn'tɛlɪdʒəns] *n* intelligence *f;* (*MIL etc*) informations *fpl,* renseignements *mpl;* **~ service** *n* services secrets; **intelligent** *adj* intelligent(e)

intend [ɪn'tɛnd] *vt* (*gift etc*): **to ~ sth for** destiner qch à; **to ~ to do** avoir l'intention de faire

intense [ɪn'tɛns] *adj* intense; (*person*) véhément(e); **~ly** *adv* intensément; profondément

intensive [ɪnˈtɛnsɪv] *adj* intensif(-ive); ~ **care unit** *n* service *m* de réanimation

intent [ɪnˈtɛnt] *n* intention *f* ♦ *adj* attentif(-ive); **to all ~s and purposes** en fait, pratiquement; **to be ~ on doing sth** être (bien) décidé à faire qch; **~ion** *n* intention *f*; **~ional** *adj* intentionnel(le), délibéré(e); **~ly** *adv* attentivement

interact [ɪntərˈækt] *vi* avoir une action réciproque; (*people*) communiquer; **~ive** *adj* (*COMPUT*) interactif(-ive)

interchange [*n* ˈɪntətʃeɪndʒ, *vb* ɪntəˈtʃeɪndʒ] *n* (*exchange*) échange *m*; (*on motorway*) échangeur *m*; **~able** *adj* interchangeable

intercom [ˈɪntəkɔm] *n* interphone *m*

intercourse [ˈɪntəkɔ:s] *n* (*sexual*) rapports *mpl*

interest [ˈɪntrɪst] *n* intérêt *m*; (*pastime*): **my main ~** ce qui m'intéresse le plus; (*COMM*) intérêts *mpl* ♦ *vt* intéresser; **to be ~ed in sth** s'intéresser à qch; **I am ~ed in going** ça m'intéresse d'y aller; **~ing** *adj* intéressant(e); **~ rate** *n* taux *m* d'intérêt

interface [ˈɪntəfeɪs] *n* (*COMPUT*) interface *f*

interfere [ɪntəˈfɪə*] *vi*: **to ~ in** (*quarrel*) s'immiscer dans; (*other people's business*) se mêler de; **to ~ with** (*object*) toucher à; (*plans*) contrecarrer; (*duty*) être en conflit avec; **~nce** *n* (*in affairs*) ingérance *f*; (*RADIO, TV*) parasites *mpl*

interim [ˈɪntərɪm] *adj* provisoire ♦ *n*: **in the ~** dans l'intérim, entre-temps

interior [ɪnˈtɪərɪə*] *n* intérieur *m* ♦ *adj* intérieur(e); (*minister, department*) de l'Intérieur; **~ designer** *n* styliste *m/f*, designer *m/f*

interjection [ɪntəˈdʒɛkʃən] *n* (*interruption*) interruption *f*; (*LING*) interjection *f*

interlock [ɪntəˈlɔk] *vi* s'enclencher

interlude [ˈɪntəlu:d] *n* intervalle *m*; (*THEATRE*) intermède *m*

intermediate [ɪntəˈmi:dɪət] *adj* intermédiaire; (*SCOL: course, level*) moyen(ne)

intermission [ɪntəˈmɪʃən] *n* pause *f*; (*THEATRE, CINEMA*) entracte *m*

intern [*vb* ɪnˈtə:n, *n* ˈɪntə:n] *vt* interner ♦ *n* (*US*) interne *m/f*

internal [ɪnˈtə:nl] *adj* interne; (*politics*) intérieur(e); **~ly** *adv*: **"not to be taken ~ly"** "pour usage externe"; **I~ Revenue Service** (*US*) *n* fisc *m*

international [ɪntəˈnæʃənl] *adj* international(e)

Internet [ˈɪntənɛt] *n* Internet *m*; **~ café** *n* cybercafé *m*; **~ service provider** *n* fournisseur *m* d'accès à Internet

interplay [ˈɪntəpleɪ] *n* effet *m* réciproque, interaction *f*

interpret [ɪnˈtə:prɪt] *vt* interpréter ♦ *vi* servir d'interprète; **~er** *n* interprète *m/f*

interrelated [ɪntərɪˈleɪtɪd] *adj* en corrélation, en rapport étroit

interrogate [ɪnˈtɛrəʊgeɪt] *vt* interroger; (*suspect etc*) soumettre à un interrogatoire; **interrogation** [ɪntɛrəʊˈgeɪʃən] *n* interrogation *f*; interrogatoire *m*

interrupt [ɪntəˈrʌpt] *vt, vi* interrompre

intersect [ɪntəˈsɛkt] *vi* (*roads*) se croiser, se couper; **~ion** *n* (*of roads*) croisement *m*

intersperse [ɪntəˈspə:s] *vt*: **to ~ with** parsemer de

intertwine [ɪntəˈtwaɪn] *vi* s'entrelacer

interval [ˈɪntəvl] *n* intervalle *m*; (*BRIT: THEATRE*) entracte *m*; (: *SPORT*) mi-temps *f*; **at ~s** par intervalles

intervene [ɪntəˈvi:n] *vi* (*person*) intervenir; (*event*) survenir; (*time*) s'écouler (entre-temps); **intervention** *n* intervention *f*

interview [ˈɪntəvju:] *n* (*RADIO, TV etc*) interview *f*; (*for job*) entrevue *f* ♦ *vt* interviewer; avoir une entrevue avec; **~er** *n* (*RADIO, TV*) interviewer *m*

intestine [ɪnˈtɛstɪn] *n* intestin *m*

intimacy [ˈɪntɪməsɪ] *n* intimité *f*

intimate [*adj* ˈɪntɪmət, *vb* ˈɪntɪmeɪt] *adj* intime; (*friendship*) profond(e); (*knowledge*) approfondi(e) ♦ *vt* (*hint*) suggérer, laisser entendre

into [ˈɪntu] *prep* dans; **~ pieces/French** en morceaux/français

intolerant [ɪnˈtɔlərnt] *adj*: **~ (of)** intolérant(e) (de)

intoxicated [ɪnˈtɔksɪkeɪtɪd] *adj* (*drunk*) ivre

intractable [ɪn'træktəbl] *adj* (*child*) indocile, insoumis(e); (*problem*) insoluble

intranet ['ɪntrənet] *n* intranet *m*

intransitive [ɪn'trænsɪtɪv] *adj* intransitif(-ive)

intravenous [ɪntrə'viːnəs] *adj* intraveineux(-euse)

in-tray ['ɪntreɪ] *n* courrier *m* "arrivée"

intricate ['ɪntrɪkət] *adj* complexe, compliqué(e)

intrigue [ɪn'triːg] *n* intrigue *f* ♦ *vt* intriguer; **intriguing** *adj* fascinant(e)

intrinsic [ɪn'trɪnsɪk] *adj* intrinsèque

introduce [ɪntrə'djuːs] *vt* introduire; (*TV show, people to each other*) présenter; **to ~ sb to** (*pastime, technique*) initier qn à; **introduction** *n* introduction *f*; (*of person*) présentation *f*; (*to new experience*) initiation *f*; **introductory** *adj* préliminaire, d'introduction; **introductory offer** *n* (*COMM*) offre *f* de lancement

intrude [ɪn'truːd] *vi* (*person*) être importun(e); **to ~ on** (*conversation etc*) s'immiscer dans; **~r** *n* intrus(e)

intuition [ɪntjuː'ɪʃən] *n* intuition *f*

inundate ['ɪnʌndeɪt] *vt*: **to ~ with** inonder de

invade [ɪn'veɪd] *vt* envahir

invalid [*n* 'ɪnvəlɪd, *adj* ɪn'vælɪd] *n* malade *m/f*; (*with disability*) invalide *m/f* ♦ *adj* (*not valid*) non valide *or* valable

invaluable [ɪn'væljuəbl] *adj* inestimable, inappréciable

invariably [ɪn'veəriəbli] *adv* invariablement; toujours

invent [ɪn'vent] *vt* inventer; **~ion** *n* invention *f*; **~ive** *adj* inventif(-ive); **~or** *n* inventeur(-trice)

inventory ['ɪnvəntri] *n* inventaire *m*

invert [ɪn'vɜːt] *vt* intervertir; (*cup, object*) retourner; **~ed commas** (*BRIT*) *npl* guillemets *mpl*

invest [ɪn'vest] *vt* investir ♦ *vi*: **to ~ in sth** placer son argent dans qch; (*fig*) s'offrir qch

investigate [ɪn'vestɪgeɪt] *vt* (*crime etc*) faire une enquête sur; **investigation**

[ɪnvestɪ'geɪʃən] *n* (*of crime*) enquête *f*

investment [ɪn'vestmənt] *n* investissement *m*, placement *m*

investor [ɪn'vestər] *n* investisseur *m*; actionnaire *m/f*

invigilator [ɪn'vɪdʒɪleɪtər] *n* surveillant(e)

invigorating [ɪn'vɪgəreɪtɪŋ] *adj* vivifiant(e); (*fig*) stimulant(e)

invisible [ɪn'vɪzɪbl] *adj* invisible

invitation [ɪnvɪ'teɪʃən] *n* invitation *f*

invite [ɪn'vaɪt] *vt* inviter; (*opinions etc*) demander; **inviting** *adj* engageant(e), attrayant(e)

invoice ['ɪnvɔɪs] *n* facture *f*

involuntary [ɪn'vɒləntri] *adj* involontaire

involve [ɪn'vɒlv] *vt* (*entail*) entraîner, nécessiter; (*concern*) concerner; (*associate*): **to ~ sb (in)** impliquer qn (dans), mêler qn (à); faire participer qn (à); **~d** *adj* (*complicated*) complexe; **to be ~d in** participer à; **~ment** *n*: **~ment (in)** participation *f* (à); rôle *m* (dans); (*enthusiasm*) enthousiasme *m* (pour)

inward ['ɪnwəd] *adj* (*thought, feeling*) profond(e), intime; (*movement*) vers l'intérieur; **~(s)** *adv* vers l'intérieur

I/O *abbr* (*COMPUT*: = *input/output*) E/S

iodine ['aɪəudiːn] *n* iode *m*

iota [aɪ'əutə] *n* (*fig*) brin *m*, grain *m*

IOU *n abbr* (= *I owe you*) reconnaissance *f* de dette

IQ *n abbr* (= *intelligence quotient*) Q.I. *m*

IRA *n abbr* (= *Irish Republican Army*) IRA *m*

Iran [ɪ'rɑːn] *n* Iran *m*

Iraq [ɪ'rɑːk] *n* Irak *m*

irate [aɪ'reɪt] *adj* courroucé(e)

Ireland ['aɪələnd] *n* Irlande *f*

iris ['aɪrɪs] (*pl* **~es**) *n* iris *m*

Irish ['aɪrɪʃ] *adj* irlandais(e) ♦ *npl*: **the ~** les Irlandais; **~man** (*irreg*) *n* Irlandais *m*; **~ Sea** *n* mer *f* d'Irlande; **~woman** (*irreg*) *n* Irlandaise *f*

iron ['aɪən] *n* fer *m*; (*for clothes*) fer *m* à repasser ♦ *cpd* de *or* en fer; (*fig*) de fer ♦ *vt* (*clothes*) repasser; **~ out** *vt* (*fig*) aplanir; faire disparaître

ironic(al) [aɪ'rɒnɪk(l)] *adj* ironique

ironing [ˈaɪənɪŋ] *n* repassage *m*; **~ board** *n* planche *f* à repasser

ironmonger's (shop) [ˈaɪənmʌŋgəz-] *n* quincaillerie *f*

irony [ˈaɪrənɪ] *n* ironie *f*

irrational [ɪˈræʃənl] *adj* irrationnel(le)

irregular [ɪˈregjələʳ] *adj* irrégulier(-ère); (*surface*) inégal(e)

irrelevant [ɪˈreləvənt] *adj* sans rapport, hors de propos

irresistible [ɪrɪˈzɪstɪbl] *adj* irrésistible

irrespective [ɪrɪˈspektɪv]: **~ of** *prep* sans tenir compte de

irresponsible [ɪrɪˈspɔnsɪbl] *adj* (*act*) irréfléchi(e); (*person*) irresponsable, inconscient(e)

irrigate [ˈɪrɪgeɪt] *vt* irriguer; **irrigation** [ɪrɪˈgeɪʃən] *n* irrigation *f*

irritate [ˈɪrɪteɪt] *vt* irriter

irritating *adj* irritant(e); **irritation** [ɪrɪˈteɪʃən] *n* irritation *f*

IRS (*US*) *n abbr* = **Internal Revenue Service**

is [ɪz] *vb see* **be**

Islam [ˈɪzlɑːm] *n* Islam *m*; **~ic** *adj* islamique; **~ic fundamentalists** intégristes *mpl* musulmans

island [ˈaɪlənd] *n* île *f*; **~er** *n* habitant(e) d'une île, insulaire *m/f*

isle [aɪl] *n* île *f*

isn't [ˈɪznt] = **is not**

isolate [ˈaɪsəleɪt] *vt* isoler; **~d** *adj* isolé(e); **isolation** [aɪsəˈleɪʃən] *n* isolation *f*

ISP *n abbr* = **Internet Service Provider**

Israel [ˈɪzreɪl] *n* Israël *m*; **~i** [ɪzˈreɪlɪ] *adj* israélien(ne) ♦ *n* Israélien(ne)

issue [ˈɪʃuː] *n* question *f*, problème *m*; (*of book*) publication *f*, parution *f*; (*of bank-notes etc*) émission *f*; (*of newspaper etc*) numéro *m* ♦ *vt* (*rations, equipment*) distribuer; (*statement*) publier, faire; (*banknotes etc*) émettre, mettre en circulation; **at ~** en jeu, en cause; **to take ~ with sb (over)** exprimer son désaccord avec qn (sur); **to make an ~ of sth** faire une montagne de qch

---

it [ɪt] *pron* **1** (*specific: subject*) il (elle); (*: direct object*) le (la, l'); (*: indirect object*) lui; **it's on the table** c'est *or* il (*or* elle) est sur la table; **about/from/of it** en; **I spoke to him about it** je lui en ai parlé; **what did you learn from it?** qu'est-ce que vous en avez retiré?; **I'm proud of it** j'en suis fier; **in/to it** y; **put the book in it** mettez-y le livre; **he agreed to it** il y a consenti; **did you go to it?** (*party, concert etc*) est-ce que vous y êtes allé(s)?
2 (*impersonal*) il; ce; **it's raining** il pleut; **it's Friday tomorrow** demain c'est vendredi *or* nous sommes vendredi; **it's 6 o'clock** il est 6 heures; **who is it? - it's me** qui est-ce? - c'est moi

---

Italian [ɪˈtæljən] *adj* italien(ne) ♦ *n* Italien(ne); (*LING*) italien *m*

italics [ɪˈtælɪks] *npl* italiques *fpl*

Italy [ˈɪtəlɪ] *n* Italie *f*

itch [ɪtʃ] *n* démangeaison *f* ♦ *vi* (*person*) éprouver des démangeaisons; (*part of body*) démanger; **I'm ~ing to do** l'envie me démange de faire; **~y** *adj* qui démange; **to be ~y** avoir des démangeaisons

it'd [ˈɪtd] = **it would**; **it had**

item [ˈaɪtəm] *n* article *m*; (*on agenda*) question *f*, point *m*; (*also: news ~*) nouvelle *f*; **~ize** *vt* détailler, faire une liste de

itinerary [aɪˈtɪnərərɪ] *n* itinéraire *m*

it'll [ˈɪtl] = **it will**; **it shall**

its [ɪts] *adj* son (sa), ses *pl*

it's [ɪts] = **it is**; **it has**

itself [ɪtˈself] *pron* (*reflexive*) se; (*emphatic*) lui-même (elle-même)

ITV *n abbr* (*BRIT: Independent Television*) chaîne privée

IUD *n abbr* (= *intra-uterine device*) DIU *m*, stérilet *m*

I've [aɪv] = **I have**

ivory [ˈaɪvərɪ] *n* ivoire *m*

ivy [ˈaɪvɪ] *n* lierre *m*

J, j

jab [dʒæb] *vt*: **to ~ sth into** enfoncer *or* planter qch dans ♦ *n* (*inf*: *injection*) piqûre *f*

jack [dʒæk] *n* (*AUT*) cric *m*; (*CARDS*) valet *m*; **~ up** *vt* soulever (au cric)

jackal ['dʒækl] *n* chacal *m*

jacket ['dʒækɪt] *n* veste *f*, veston *m*; (*of book*) jaquette *f*, couverture *f*; **~ potato** *n* pomme *f* de terre en robe des champs

jack: **~knife** *vi*: **the lorry ~knifed** la remorque (du camion) s'est mise en travers; **~ plug** *n* (*ELEC*) prise jack mâle *f*; **~pot** *n* gros lot

jaded ['dʒeɪdɪd] *adj* éreinté(e), fatigué(e)

jagged ['dʒægɪd] *adj* dentelé(e)

jail [dʒeɪl] *n* prison *f* ♦ *vt* emprisonner, mettre en prison

jam [dʒæm] *n* confiture *f*; (*also:* **traffic ~**) embouteillage *m* ♦ *vt* (*passage etc*) encombrer, obstruer; (*mechanism, drawer etc*) bloquer, coincer; (*RADIO*) brouiller ♦ *vi* se coincer, se bloquer; (*gun*) s'enrayer; **to be in a ~** (*inf*) être dans le pétrin; **to ~ sth into** entasser qch dans; enfoncer qch dans

Jamaica [dʒə'meɪkə] *n* Jamaïque *f*

jam: **~ jar** *n* pot *m* à confiture; **~med** *adj* (*window etc*) coincé(e); **~-packed** *adj*: **~-packed (with)** bourré(e) (de)

jangle ['dʒæŋgl] *vi* cliqueter

janitor ['dʒænɪtər] *n* concierge *m*

January ['dʒænjuərɪ] *n* janvier *m*

Japan [dʒə'pæn] *n* Japon *m*; **~ese** [dʒæpə'niːz] *adj* japonais(e) ♦ *n inv* Japonais(e); (*LING*) japonais *m*

jar [dʒɑːr] *n* (*stone, earthenware*) pot *m*; (*glass*) bocal *m* ♦ *vi* (*sound discordant*) produire un son grinçant *or* discordant; (*colours etc*) jurer

jargon ['dʒɑːgən] *n* jargon *m*

jaundice ['dʒɔːndɪs] *n* jaunisse *f*

javelin ['dʒævlɪn] *n* javelot *m*

jaw [dʒɔː] *n* mâchoire *f*

jay [dʒeɪ] *n* geai *m*; **~walker** *n* piéton indiscipliné

jazz [dʒæz] *n* jazz *m*; **~ up** *vt* animer, égayer

jealous ['dʒeləs] *adj* jaloux(-ouse); **~y** *n* jalousie *f*

jeans [dʒiːnz] *npl* jean *m*

jeer [dʒɪər] *vi*: **to ~ (at)** se moquer cruellement (de), railler

Jehovah's Witness [dʒɪ'həuvəz-] *n* témoin *m* de Jéhovah

jelly ['dʒelɪ] *n* gelée *f*; **~fish** ['dʒelɪfɪʃ] *n* méduse *f*

jeopardy ['dʒepədɪ] *n*: **to be in ~** être en danger *or* péril

jerk [dʒəːk] *n* secousse *f*; saccade *f*; sursaut *m*, spasme *m*; (*inf*: *idiot*) pauvre type *m* ♦ *vt* (*pull*) tirer brusquement ♦ *vi* (*vehicles*) cahoter

jersey ['dʒəːzɪ] *n* (*pullover*) tricot *m*; (*fabric*) jersey *m*

Jesus ['dʒiːzəs] *n* Jésus

jet [dʒet] *n* (*gas, liquid*) jet *m*; (*AVIAT*) avion *m* à réaction, jet *m*; **~-black** *adj* (d'un noir) de jais; **~ engine** *n* moteur *m* à réaction; **~ lag** *n* (fatigue due au) décalage *m* horaire

jettison ['dʒetɪsn] *vt* jeter par-dessus bord

jetty ['dʒetɪ] *n* jetée *f*, digue *f*

Jew [dʒuː] *n* Juif *m*

jewel ['dʒuːəl] *n* bijou *m*, joyau *m*; (*in watch*) rubis *m*; **~ler** (*US* **jeweler**) *n* bijoutier(-ère), joaillier *m*; **~ler's (shop)** *n* bijouterie *f*, joaillerie *f*; **~lery** (*US* **jewelry**) *n* bijoux *mpl*

Jewess ['dʒuːɪs] *n* Juive *f*

Jewish ['dʒuːɪʃ] *adj* juif (juive)

jibe [dʒaɪb] *n* sarcasme *m*

jiffy ['dʒɪfɪ] (*inf*) *n*: **in a ~** en un clin d'œil

jigsaw ['dʒɪgsɔː] *n* (*also:* **~ puzzle**) puzzle *m*

jilt [dʒɪlt] *vt* laisser tomber, plaquer

jingle ['dʒɪŋgl] *n* (*for advert*) couplet *m* publicitaire ♦ *vi* cliqueter, tinter

jinx [dʒɪŋks] (*inf*) *n* (mauvais) sort *m*

jitters ['dʒɪtəz] (*inf*) *npl*: **to get the ~** (*inf*) avoir la trouille *or* la frousse

job [dʒɔb] *n* (*chore, task*) travail *m*, tâche *f*; (*employment*) emploi *m*, poste *m*, place *f*; **it's a good ~ that ...** c'est heureux *or* c'est une chance que ...; **just the ~!** (c'est) juste *or* exactement ce qu'il faut!; **~ centre** (*BRIT*) *n* agence *f* pour l'emploi; **~less** *adj* sans travail, au chômage

jockey ['dʒɔkɪ] *n* jockey *m* ♦ *vi*: **to ~ for position** manœuvrer pour être bien placé

jog [dʒɔg] *vt* secouer ♦ *vi* (*SPORT*) faire du jogging; **to ~ sb's memory** rafraîchir la mémoire de qn; **~ along** *vi* cheminer, trotter; **~ging** *n* jogging *m*

join [dʒɔɪn] *vt* (*put together*) unir, assembler; (*become member of*) s'inscrire à; (*meet*) rejoindre, retrouver; (*queue*) se joindre à ♦ *vi* (*roads, rivers*) se rejoindre, se rencontrer ♦ *n* raccord *m*; **~ in** *vi* se mettre de la partie, participer ♦ *vt fus* participer à, se mêler à; **~ up** *vi* (*meet*) se rejoindre; (*MIL*) s'engager

joiner ['dʒɔɪnə'] (*BRIT*) *n* menuisier *m*

joint [dʒɔɪnt] *n* (*TECH*) jointure *f*; joint *m*; (*ANAT*) articulation *f*, jointure; (*BRIT*: *CULIN*) rôti *m*; (*inf: place*) boîte *f*; (: *of cannabis*) joint *m* ♦ *adj* commun(e); **~ account** *n* (*with bank etc*) compte joint

joke [dʒəuk] *n* plaisanterie *f*; (*also*: **practical ~**) farce *f* ♦ *vi* plaisanter; **to play a ~ on** jouer un tour à, faire une farce à; **~r** *n* (*CARDS*) joker *m*

jolly ['dʒɔlɪ] *adj* gai(e), enjoué(e); (*enjoyable*) amusant(e), plaisant(e) ♦ *adv* (*BRIT*: *inf*) rudement, drôlement

jolt [dʒəult] *n* cahot *m*, secousse *f*; (*shock*) choc *m* ♦ *vt* cahoter, secouer

Jordan ['dʒɔːdən] *n* (*country*) Jordanie *f*

jostle ['dʒɔsl] *vt* bousculer, pousser

jot [dʒɔt] *n*: **not one ~** pas un brin; **~ down** *vt* noter; **~ter** (*BRIT*) *n* cahier *m* (de brouillon); (*pad*) bloc-notes *m*

journal ['dʒəːnl] *n* journal *m*; **~ism** *n* journalisme *m*; **~ist** *n* journaliste *m/f*

journey ['dʒəːnɪ] *n* voyage *m*; (*distance covered*) trajet *m*

joy [dʒɔɪ] *n* joie *f*; **~ful** *adj* joyeux(-euse); **~rider** *n* personne qui fait une virée dans

une voiture volée; **~stick** *n* (*AVIAT*, *COMPUT*) manche *m* à balai

JP *n abbr* = **Justice of the Peace**

Jr *abbr* = **junior**

jubilant ['dʒuːbɪlnt] *adj* triomphant(e); réjoui(e)

judge [dʒʌdʒ] *n* juge *m* ♦ *vt* juger; **judg(e)ment** *n* jugement *m*

judicial [dʒuːˈdɪʃl] *adj* judiciaire; **judiciary** *n* (pouvoir *m*) judiciaire *m*

judo ['dʒuːdəu] *n* judo *m*

jug [dʒʌg] *n* pot *m*, cruche *f*

juggernaut ['dʒʌgənɔːt] (*BRIT*) *n* (*huge truck*) énorme poids lourd

juggle ['dʒʌgl] *vi* jongler; **~r** *n* jongleur *m*

juice [dʒuːs] *n* jus *m*; **juicy** *adj* juteux(-euse)

jukebox ['dʒuːkbɔks] *n* juke-box *m*

July [dʒuːˈlaɪ] *n* juillet *m*

jumble ['dʒʌmbl] *n* fouillis *m* ♦ *vt* (*also*: **~ up**) mélanger, brouiller; **~ sale** (*BRIT*) *n* vente *f* de charité

---

jumble sale

ⓘ Les **jumble sales** ont lieu dans les églises, salles de fêtes ou halls d'écoles, et l'on y vend des articles de toutes sortes, en général bon marché et surtout d'occasion, pour collecter des fonds pour une œuvre de charité, une école ou encore une église.

---

jumbo (jet) ['dʒʌmbəu-] *n* jumbo-jet *m*, gros porteur

jump [dʒʌmp] *vi* sauter, bondir; (*start*) sursauter; (*increase*) monter en flèche ♦ *vt* sauter, franchir ♦ *n* saut *m*, bond *m*; sursaut *m*; **to ~ the queue** (*BRIT*) passer avant son tour

jumper ['dʒʌmpə'] *n* (*BRIT*: *pullover*) pullover *m*; (*US*: *dress*) robe-chasuble *f*

jumper cables (*US*), **jump leads** (*BRIT*) *npl* câbles *mpl* de démarrage

jumpy ['dʒʌmpɪ] *adj* nerveux(-euse), agité(e)

Jun. *abbr* = **junior**

junction ['dʒʌŋkʃən] (*BRIT*) *n* (*of roads*) carrefour *m*; (*of rails*) embranchement *m*

juncture ['dʒʌŋktʃəʳ] *n*: **at this ~** à ce moment-là, sur ces entrefaites

June [dʒuːn] *n* juin *m*

jungle ['dʒʌŋgl] *n* jungle *f*

junior ['dʒuːnɪəʳ] *adj*, *n*: **he's ~ to me (by 2 years); he's my ~ (by 2 years)** il est mon cadet (de 2 ans), il est plus jeune que moi (de 2 ans); **he's ~ to me** (*seniority*) il est en dessous de moi (dans la hiérarchie), j'ai plus d'ancienneté que lui; **~ school** (*BRIT*) *n* ≃ école *f* primaire

junk [dʒʌŋk] *n* (*rubbish*) camelote *f*; (*cheap goods*) bric-à-brac *m inv*; **~ food** *n* aliments *mpl* sans grande valeur nutritive; **~ mail** *n* prospectus *mpl* (non sollicités); **~ shop** *n* (boutique *f* de) brocanteur *m*

Junr *abbr* = **junior**

juror ['dʒuərəʳ] *n* juré *m*

jury ['dʒuərɪ] *n* jury *m*

just [dʒʌst] *adj* juste ♦ *adv*: **he's ~ done it/left** il vient de le faire/partir; **~ right/ two o'clock** exactement *or* juste ce qu'il faut/deux heures; **she's ~ as clever as you** elle est tout aussi intelligente que vous; **it's ~ as well (that) ...** heureusement que *or* ...; **~ as he was leaving** au moment *or* à l'instant précis où il partait; **~ before/enough/here** juste avant/ assez/ici; **it's ~ me/a mistake** ce n'est que moi/(rien) qu'une erreur; **~ missed/ caught** manqué/attrapé de justesse; **~ listen to this!** écoutez un peu ça!

justice ['dʒʌstɪs] *n* justice *f*; (*US: judge*) juge *m* de la Cour suprême; **J~ of the Peace** *n* juge *m* de paix

justify ['dʒʌstɪfaɪ] *vt* justifier

jut [dʒʌt] *vi* (*also*: **~ out**) dépasser, faire saillie

juvenile ['dʒuːvənaɪl] *adj* juvénile; (*court, books*) pour enfants ♦ *n* adolescent(e)

K, k

K *abbr* (= *one thousand*) K; (= *kilobyte*) Ko

kangaroo [kæŋgəˈruː] *n* kangourou *m*

karate [kəˈrɑːtɪ] *n* karaté *m*

kebab [kəˈbæb] *n* kébab *m*

keel [kiːl] *n* quille *f*; **on an even ~** (*fig*) à flot

keen [kiːn] *adj* (*eager*) plein(e) d'enthousiasme; (*interest, desire, competition*) vif (vive); (*eye, intelligence*) pénétrant(e); (*edge*) effilé(e); **to be ~ to do** *or* **on doing sth** désirer vivement faire qch, tenir beaucoup à faire qch; **to be ~ on sth/sb** aimer beaucoup qch/qn

keep [kiːp] (*pt, pp* **kept**) *vt* (*retain, preserve*) garder; (*detain*) retenir; (*shop, accounts, diary, promise*) tenir; (*house*) avoir; (*support*) entretenir; (*chickens, bees etc*) élever ♦ *vi* (*remain*) rester; (*food*) se conserver ♦ *n* (*of castle*) donjon *m*; (*food etc*): **enough for his ~** assez pour (assurer) sa subsistance; (*inf*): **for ~s** pour de bon, pour toujours; **to ~ doing sth** ne pas arrêter de faire qch; **to ~ sb from doing** empêcher qn de faire *or* que qn ne fasse; **to ~ sb happy/a place tidy** faire que qn soit content/ qu'un endroit reste propre; **to ~ sth to o.s.** garder qch pour soi, tenir qch secret; **to ~ sth (back) from sb** cacher qch à qn; **to ~ time** (*clock*) être à l'heure, ne pas retarder; **well kept** bien entretenu(e); **~ on** *vi*: **to ~ on doing** continuer à faire; **don't ~ on about it!** arrête (d'en parler)!; **~ out** *vt* empêcher d'entrer; **"~ out"** "défense d'entrer"; **~ up** *vt* continuer, maintenir ♦ *vi*: **to ~ up with sb** (*in race etc*) aller aussi vite que qn; (*in work etc*) se maintenir au niveau de qn; **~er** *n* gardien(ne); **~-fit** *n* gymnastique *f* d'entretien; **~ing** *n* (*care*) garde *f*; **in ~ing with** en accord avec; **~sake** *n* souvenir *m*

kennel ['kɛnl] *n* niche *f*; **~s** *npl* (*boarding ~s*) chenil *m*

kerb [kəːb] (*BRIT*) *n* bordure *f* du trottoir

kernel ['kɔ:nl] n (of nut) amande f; (fig) noyau m

kettle ['ketl] n bouilloire f; ~**drum** n timbale f

key [ki:] n (gen , MUS) clé f; (of piano, typewriter) touche f ♦ cpd clé ♦ vt (also: ~ **in**) introduire (au clavier), saisir; ~**board** n clavier m; ~**ed up** adj (person) surexcité(e); ~**hole** n trou m de la serrure; ~**hole surgery** n chirurgie très minutieuse où l'incision est minimale; ~**note** n (of speech) note dominante; (MUS) tonique f; ~ **ring** n porte-clés m

khaki ['kɑ:kɪ] n kaki m

kick [kɪk] vt donner un coup de pied à ♦ vi (horse) ruer ♦ n coup m de pied; (thrill): **he does it for ~s** il le fait parce que ça l'excite, il le fait pour le plaisir; **to ~ the habit** (inf) arrêter; ~ **off** vi (SPORT) donner le coup d'envoi

kid [kɪd] n (inf: child) gamin(e), gosse m/f; (animal, leather) chevreau m ♦ vi (inf) plaisanter, blaguer

kidnap ['kɪdnæp] vt enlever, kidnapper; ~**per** n ravisseur(-euse); ~**ping** n enlèvement m

kidney ['kɪdnɪ] n (ANAT) rein m; (CULIN) rognon m

kill [kɪl] vt tuer ♦ n mise f à mort; ~**er** n tueur(-euse); meurtrier(-ère); ~**ing** n meurtre m; (of group of people) tuerie f, massacre m; **to make a ~ing** (inf) réussir un beau coup (de filet); ~**joy** n rabat-joie m/f

kiln [kɪln] n four m

kilo ['ki:ləu] n kilo m; ~**byte** n (COMPUT) kilo-octet m; ~**gram(me)** n kilogramme m; ~**metre** (US **kilometer**) n kilomètre m; ~**watt** n kilowatt m

kilt [kɪlt] n kilt m

kin [kɪn] n see **next**

kind [kaɪnd] adj gentil(le), aimable ♦ n sorte f, espèce f, genre m; **to be two of a ~** se ressembler; **in ~** (COMM) en nature

kindergarten ['kɪndəgɑ:tn] n jardin m d'enfants

kind-hearted [kaɪnd'hɑ:tɪd] adj bon (bonne)

kindle ['kɪndl] vt allumer, enflammer

kindly ['kaɪndlɪ] adj bienveillant(e), plein(e) de gentillesse ♦ adv avec bonté; **will you ~ ...!** auriez-vous la bonté or l'obligeance de ...?

kindness ['kaɪndnɪs] n bonté f, gentillesse f

king [kɪŋ] n roi m; ~**dom** n royaume m; ~**fisher** n martin-pêcheur m; ~**-size bed** n grand lit (de 1,95 m de large); ~**-size(d)** adj format géant inv; (cigarettes) long (longue)

kiosk ['ki:ɔsk] n kiosque m; (BRIT: TEL) cabine f (téléphonique)

kipper ['kɪpər] n hareng fumé et salé

kiss [kɪs] n baiser m ♦ vt embrasser; **to ~ (each other)** s'embrasser; ~ **of life** (BRIT) n bouche à bouche m

kit [kɪt] n équipement m, matériel m; (set of tools etc) trousse f; (for assembly) kit m

kitchen ['kɪtʃɪn] n cuisine f; ~ **sink** n évier m

kite [kaɪt] n (toy) cerf-volant m

kitten ['kɪtn] n chaton m, petit chat

kitty ['kɪtɪ] n (money) cagnotte f

km abbr = **kilometre**

knack [næk] n: **to have the ~ of doing** avoir le coup pour faire

knapsack ['næpsæk] n musette f

knead [ni:d] vt pétrir

knee [ni:] n genou m; ~**cap** n rotule f

kneel [ni:l] (pt, pp **knelt**) vi (also: ~ **down**) s'agenouiller

knew [nju:] pt of **know**

knickers ['nɪkəz] (BRIT) npl culotte f (de femme)

knife [naɪf] (pl **knives**) n couteau m ♦ vt poignarder, frapper d'un coup de couteau

knight [naɪt] n chevalier m; (CHESS) cavalier m; ~**hood** (BRIT) n (title): **to get a ~hood** être fait chevalier

knit [nɪt] vt tricoter ♦ vi tricoter; (broken bones) se ressouder; **to ~ one's brows** froncer les sourcils; ~**ting** n tricot m; ~**ting needle** n aiguille f à tricoter; ~**wear** n tricots mpl, lainages mpl

knives [naɪvz] *npl of* **knife**

knob [nɔb] *n* bouton *m*

knock [nɔk] *vt* frapper; *(bump into)* heurter; *(inf)* dénigrer ♦ *vi (at door etc)*: **to ~ at** *or* **on** frapper à ♦ *n* coup *m*; ~ **down** *vt* renverser; ~ **off** *vi (inf: finish)* s'arrêter (de travailler) ♦ *vt (from price)* faire un rabais de; *(inf: steal)* piquer; ~ **out** *vt* assommer; *(BOXING)* mettre k.-o.; *(defeat)* éliminer; ~ **over** *vt* renverser, faire tomber; ~**er** *n (on door)* heurtoir *m*; ~**out** *n (BOXING)* knock-out *m*, K.-O. *m*; ~**out competition** compétition *f* avec épreuves éliminatoires

knot [nɔt] *n (gen)* nœud *m* ♦ *vt* nouer

know [nəu] *(pt* **knew**, *pp* **known**) *vt* savoir; *(person, place)* connaître; **to ~ how to do** savoir (comment) faire; **to ~ how to swim** savoir nager; **to ~ about** *or* **of sth** être au courant de qch; **to ~ about** *or* **of sb** avoir entendu parler de qn; ~**-all** *(pej)* *n* je-sais-tout *m/f*; ~**-how** *n* savoir-faire *m*; ~**ing** *adj (look etc)* entendu(e); ~**ingly** *adv* sciemment; *(smile, look)* d'un air entendu

knowledge ['nɔlɪdʒ] *n* connaissance *f*; *(learning)* connaissances, savoir *m*; ~**able** *adj* bien informé(e)

knuckle ['nʌkl] *n* articulation *f* (des doigts), jointure *f*

Koran [kɔ'rɑːn] *n* Coran *m*

Korea [kə'rɪə] *n* Corée *f*

kosher ['kəuʃər] *adj* kascher *inv*

Kosovo ['kɔsəvəu] *n* Kosovo *m*

L, l

L *abbr* (= *lake, large*) L; (= *left*) g; *(BRIT: AUT: learner)* signale un conducteur débutant

lab [læb] *n abbr* (= *laboratory*) labo *m*

label ['leɪbl] *n* étiquette *f* ♦ *vt* étiqueter

labor *etc* ['leɪbər] *(US)* = **labour** *etc*

laboratory [lə'bɔrətəri] *n* laboratoire *m*

labour ['leɪbər] *(US* **labor**) *n (work)* travail *m*; *(workforce)* main-d'œuvre *f* ♦ *vi*: **to ~ (at)** travailler dur (à), peiner (sur) ♦ *vt*: **to ~ a point** insister sur un point; **in ~** *(MED)* en travail, en train d'accoucher; **L~, the**

L~ party *(BRIT)* le parti travailliste, les travaillistes *mpl*; ~**ed** ['leɪbəd] *adj (breathing)* pénible, difficile; ~**er** *n* manœuvre *m*; **farm ~er** ouvrier *m* agricole

lace [leɪs] *n* dentelle *f*; *(of shoe etc)* lacet *m* ♦ *vt (shoe: also: ~ up)* lacer

lack [læk] *n* manque *m* ♦ *vt* manquer de; **through** *or* **for ~ of** faute de, par manque de; **to be ~ing** manquer, faire défaut; **to be ~ing in** manquer de

lacquer ['lækər] *n* laque *f*

lad [læd] *n* garçon *m*, gars *m*

ladder ['lædər] *n* échelle *f*; *(BRIT: in tights)* maille filée

laden ['leɪdn] *adj*: ~ **(with)** chargé(e) (de)

ladle ['leɪdl] *n* louche *f*

lady ['leɪdɪ] *n* dame *f*; *(in address)*: **ladies and gentlemen** Mesdames (et) Messieurs; **young ~** jeune fille *f*; *(married)* jeune femme *f*; **the ladies' (room)** les toilettes *fpl* (pour dames); ~**bird** *(US* **ladybug**) *n* coccinelle *f*; ~**like** *adj* distingué(e); ~**ship** *n*: **your ~ship** Madame la comtesse/la baronne *etc*

lag [læg] *n* retard *m* ♦ *vi (also:* ~ **behind)** rester en arrière, traîner; *(fig)* rester en traîne ♦ *vt (pipes)* calorifuger

lager ['lɑːgər] *n* bière blonde

lagoon [lə'guːn] *n* lagune *f*

laid [leɪd] *pt, pp of* **lay**; ~**-back** *(inf)* *adj* relaxe, décontracté(e); ~ **up** *adj* alité(e)

lain [leɪn] *pp of* **lie**

lake [leɪk] *n* lac *m*

lamb [læm] *n* agneau *m*; ~ **chop** *n* côtelette *f* d'agneau

lame [leɪm] *adj* boiteux(-euse)

lament [lə'ment] *n* lamentation *f* ♦ *vt* pleurer, se lamenter sur

laminated ['læmɪneɪtɪd] *adj* laminé(e); *(windscreen)* (en verre) feuilleté

lamp [læmp] *n* lampe *f*; ~**post** *(BRIT)* *n* réverbère *m*; ~**shade** *n* abat-jour *m inv*

land [lænd] *n (as opposed to sea)* terre *f* *(ferme)*; *(soil)* terre; terrain *m*; *(estate)* terre(s), domaine(s) *m(pl)*; *(country)* pays *m* ♦ *vi (AVIAT)* atterrir; *(fig)* (re)tomber ♦ *vt (passengers, goods)* débarquer; **to ~ sb**

with sth (*inf*) coller qch à qn; **~ up** *vi* atterrir, (finir par) se retrouver; **~fill site** *n* décharge *f*; **~ing** *n* (*AVIAT*) atterrissage *m*; (*of staircase*) palier *m*; (*of troops*) débarquement *m*; **~ing strip** *n* piste *f* d'atterrissage; **~lady** *n* propriétaire *f*, logeuse *f*; (*of pub*) patronne *f*; **~locked** *adj* sans littoral; **~lord** *n* propriétaire *m*, logeur *m*; (*of pub etc*) patron *m*; **~mark** *n* (point *m* de) repère *m*; **to be a ~mark** (*fig*) faire date *or* époque; **~owner** *n* propriétaire foncier *or* terrien; **~scape** *n* paysage *m*; **~scape gardener** *n* jardinier(-ère) paysagiste; **~slide** *n* (*GEO*) glissement *m* (de terrain); (*fig*: *POL*) raz-de-marée (électoral)

lane [leɪn] *n* (*in country*) chemin *m*; (*AUT*) voie *f*; file *f*; (*in race*) couloir *m*; **"get in ~"** (*AUT*) "mettez-vous dans *or* sur la bonne file"

language [ˈlæŋɡwɪdʒ] *n* langue *f*; (*way one speaks*) langage *m*; **bad ~** grossièretés *fpl*, langage grossier; **~ laboratory** *n* laboratoire *m* de langues

lank [læŋk] *adj* (*hair*) raide et terne

lanky [ˈlæŋkɪ] *adj* grand(e) et maigre, efflanqué(e)

lantern [ˈlæntən] *n* lanterne *f*

lap [læp] *n* (*of track*) tour *m* (de piste); (*of body*): **in** *or* **on one's ~** sur les genoux ♦ *vt* (*also*: **~ up**) laper ♦ *vi* (*waves*) clapoter; **~ up** *vt* (*fig*) accepter béatement, gober

lapel [ləˈpɛl] *n* revers *m*

Lapland [ˈlæplænd] *n* Laponie *f*

lapse [læps] *n* défaillance *f*; (*in behaviour*) écart *m* de conduite ♦ *vi* (*LAW*) cesser d'être en vigueur; (*contract*) expirer; **to ~ into bad habits** prendre de mauvaises habitudes; **~ of time** laps *m* de temps, intervalle *m*

laptop (computer) [ˈlæptɔp(-)] *n* portable *m*

larceny [ˈlɑːsənɪ] *n* vol *m*

larch [lɑːtʃ] *n* mélèze *m*

lard [lɑːd] *n* saindoux *m*

larder [ˈlɑːdəʳ] *n* garde-manger *m inv*

large [lɑːdʒ] *adj* grand(e); (*person, animal*) gros(se); **at ~** (*free*) en liberté; (*generally*) en général; *see also* **by**; **~ly** *adv* en grande partie; (*principally*) surtout; **~-scale** *adj* (*action*) d'envergure; (*map*) à grande échelle

lark [lɑːk] *n* (*bird*) alouette *f*; (*joke*) blague *f*, farce *f*

laryngitis [lærɪnˈdʒaɪtɪs] *n* laryngite *f*

laser [ˈleɪzəʳ] *n* laser *m*; **~ printer** *n* imprimante *f* laser

lash [læʃ] *n* coup *m* de fouet; (*also*: **eyelash**) cil *m* ♦ *vt* fouetter; (*tie*) attacher; **~ out** *vi*: **to ~ out at** *or* **against** attaquer violemment

lass [læs] (*BRIT*) *n* (jeune) fille *f*

lasso [læˈsuː] *n* lasso *m*

last [lɑːst] *adj* dernier(-ère) ♦ *adv* en dernier; (*finally*) finalement ♦ *vi* durer; **~ week** la semaine dernière; **~ night** (*evening*) hier soir; (*night*) la nuit dernière; **at ~** enfin; **~ but one** avant-dernier(-ère); **~-ditch** *adj* (*attempt*) ultime, désespéré(e); **~ing** *adj* durable; **~ly** *adv* en dernier lieu, pour finir; **~-minute** *adj* de dernière minute

latch [lætʃ] *n* loquet *m*

late [leɪt] *adj* (*not on time*) en retard; (*far on in day etc*) tardif(-ive); (*edition, delivery*) dernier(-ère); (*former*) ancien(ne) ♦ *adv* tard; (*behind time, schedule*) en retard; **of ~** dernièrement; **in ~ May** vers la fin (du mois) de mai, fin mai; **the ~ Mr X** feu M. X; **~comer** *n* retardataire *m/f*; **~ly** *adv* récemment; **~r** *adj* (*date etc*) ultérieur(e); (*version etc*) plus récent(e) ♦ *adv* plus tard; **~r on** plus tard; **~st** *adj* tout(e) dernier(-ère); **at the ~st** au plus tard

lathe [leɪð] *n* tour *m*

lather [ˈlɑːðəʳ] *n* mousse *f* (de savon) ♦ *vt* savonner

Latin [ˈlætɪn] *n* latin *m* ♦ *adj* latin(e); **~ America** *n* Amérique latine; **~ American** *adj* latino-américain(e)

latitude [ˈlætɪtjuːd] *n* latitude *f*

latter [ˈlætəʳ] *adj* deuxième, dernier(-ère) ♦ *n*: **the ~** ce dernier, celui-ci; **~ly** *adv* dernièrement, récemment

laudable [ˈlɔːdəbl] *adj* louable

laugh [lɑːf] *n* rire *m* ♦ *vi* rire; ~ **at** *vt fus* se moquer de; rire de; ~ **off** *vt* écarter par une plaisanterie *or* par une boutade; **~able** *adj* risible, ridicule; **~ing stock** *n*: **the ~ing stock of** la risée de; **~ter** *n* rire *m*; rires *mpl*

launch [lɔːntʃ] *n* lancement *m*; (*motorboat*) vedette *f* ♦ *vt* lancer; ~ **into** *vt fus* se lancer dans

Launderette ® [lɔːnˈdrɛt] (*BRIT*), **Laundromat** ® [ˈlɔːndrəmæt] (*US*) *n* laverie *f* (automatique)

laundry [ˈlɔːndrɪ] *n* (*clothes*) linge *m*; (*business*) blanchisserie *f*; (*room*) buanderie *f*

laurel [ˈlɔrl] *n* laurier *m*

lava [ˈlɑːvə] *n* lave *f*

lavatory [ˈlævətərɪ] *n* toilettes *fpl*

lavender [ˈlævəndəʳ] *n* lavande *f*

lavish [ˈlævɪʃ] *adj* (*amount*) copieux(-euse); (*person*): ~ **with** prodigue de ♦ *vt*: **to ~ sth on sb** prodiguer qch à qn; (*money*) dépenser qch sans compter pour qn/qch

law [lɔː] *n* loi *f*; (*science*) droit *m*; **~-abiding** *adj* respectueux(-euse) des lois; ~ **and order** *n* l'ordre public; **~ court** *n* tribunal *m*, cour *f* de justice; **~ful** *adj* légal(e); **~less** *adj* (*action*) illégal(e)

lawn [lɔːn] *n* pelouse *f*; **~mower** *n* tondeuse *f* à gazon; **~ tennis** *n* tennis *m*

law school (*US*) *n* faculté *f* de droit

lawsuit [ˈlɔːsuːt] *n* procès *m*

lawyer [ˈlɔːjəʳ] *n* (*consultant, with company*) juriste *m*; (*for sales, wills etc*) notaire *m*; (*partner, in court*) avocat *m*

lax [læks] *adj* relâché(e)

laxative [ˈlæksətɪv] *n* laxatif *m*

lay [leɪ] (*pt, pp* **laid**) *pt of* **lie** ♦ *adj* laïque; (*not expert*) profane ♦ *vt* poser, mettre; (*eggs*) pondre; **to ~ the table** mettre la table; ~ **aside** *vt* mettre de côté; ~ **by** *vt* = **lay aside**; ~ **down** *vt* poser; **to ~ down the law** faire la loi; **to ~ down one's life** sacrifier sa vie; ~ **off** *vt* (*workers*) licencier; ~ **on** *vt* (*provide*) fournir; ~ **out** *vt* (*display*) disposer, étaler; **~about** (*inf*) *n* fainéant(e); **~-by** (*BRIT*) *n* aire *f* de stationnement (sur le bas-côté)

layer [ˈleɪəʳ] *n* couche *f*

layman [ˈleɪmən] (*irreg*) *n* profane *m*

layout [ˈleɪaʊt] *n* disposition *f*, plan *m*, agencement *m*; (*PRESS*) mise *f* en page

laze [leɪz] *vi* (*also*: ~ **about**) paresser

lazy [ˈleɪzɪ] *adj* paresseux(-euse)

lb *abbr* = **pound** (*weight*)

lead¹ [liːd] *n* (*distance, time ahead*) avance *f*; (*clue*) piste *f*; (*THEATRE*) rôle principal; (*ELEC*) fil *m*; (*for dog*) laisse *f* ♦ *vt* mener, conduire; (*be ~er of*) être à la tête de ♦ *vi* (*street etc*) mener, conduire; (*SPORT*) mener, être en tête; **in the ~** en tête; **to ~ the way** montrer le chemin; ~ **away** *vt* emmener; ~ **back** *vt*: **to ~ back to** ramener à; ~ **on** *vt* (*tease*) faire marcher; ~ **to** *vt fus* mener à; conduire à; ~ **up to** *vt fus* conduire à

lead² [lɛd] *n* (*metal*) plomb *m*; (*in pencil*) mine *f*; **~ed petrol** *n* essence *f* au plomb; **~en** *adj* (*sky, sea*) de plomb

leader [ˈliːdəʳ] *n* chef *m*; dirigeant(e), leader *m*; (*SPORT: in league*) leader; (*: in race*) coureur *m* de tête; **~ship** *n* direction *f*; (*quality*) qualités *fpl* de chef

lead-free [ˈlɛdfriː] *adj* (*petrol*) sans plomb

leading [ˈliːdɪŋ] *adj* principal(e); de premier plan; (*in race*) de tête; ~ **lady** *n* (*THEATRE*) vedette (féminine); ~ **light** *n* (*person*) vedette *f*, sommité *f*; ~ **man** (*irreg*) *n* vedette (masculine)

lead singer [liːd-] *n* (*in pop group*) (chanteur *m*) vedette *f*

leaf [liːf] (*pl* **leaves**) *n* feuille *f* ♦ *vi*: **to ~ through** feuilleter; **to turn over a new ~** changer de conduite *or* d'existence

leaflet [ˈliːflɪt] *n* prospectus *m*, brochure *f*; (*POL, REL*) tract *m*

league [liːg] *n* ligue *f*; (*FOOTBALL*) championnat *m*; **to be in ~ with** avoir partie liée avec, être de mèche avec

leak [liːk] *n* fuite *f* ♦ *vi* (*pipe, liquid etc*) fuir; (*shoes*) prendre l'eau; (*ship*) faire eau ♦ *vt* (*information*) divulguer

lean [liːn] (*pt, pp* **leaned** *or* **leant**) *adj* maigre ♦ *vt*: **to ~ sth on sth** appuyer qch sur qch ♦ *vi* (*slope*) pencher; (*rest*): **to ~**

against s'appuyer contre; être appuyé(e) contre; **to ~ on** s'appuyer sur; **to ~ back/forward** se pencher en arrière/ avant; **~ out** *vi* se pencher au dehors; **~ over** *vi* se pencher; **~ing** *n*: **~ing (towards)** tendance *f* (à), penchant *m* (pour); **~t** [lɛnt] *pt, pp of* **lean**

leap [li:p] (*pt, pp* **leaped** *or* **leapt**) *n* bond *m*, saut *m* ♦ *vi* bondir, sauter; **~frog** *n* saute-mouton *m*; **~t** [lɛpt] *pt, pp of* **leap**; **~ year** année *f* bissextile

learn [lə:n] (*pt, pp* **learned** *or* **learnt**) *vt, vi* apprendre; **to ~ to do sth** apprendre à faire qch; **to ~ about** *or* **of sth** (*hear, read*) apprendre qch; **~ed** ['lə:nɪd] *adj* érudit(e), savant(e); **~er** (*BRIT*) *n* (*also:* **~er driver**) (conducteur(-trice)) débutant(e); **~ing** *n* (*knowledge*) savoir *m*; **~t** *pt, pp of* **learn**

lease [li:s] *n* bail *m* ♦ *vt* louer à bail

leash [li:ʃ] *n* laisse *f*

least [li:st] *adj:* **the ~** (*+noun*) le (la) plus petit(e), le (la) moindre; (: *smallest amount of*) le moins de ♦ *adv* (*+verb*) le moins; (*+adj*): **the ~** le (la) moins; **at ~** au moins; (*or rather*) du moins; **not in the ~** pas le moins du monde

leather ['lɛðə^r] *n* cuir *m*

leave [li:v] (*pt, pp* **left**) *vt* laisser; (*go away from*) quitter; (*forget*) oublier ♦ *vi* partir, s'en aller ♦ *n* (*time off*) congé *m*; (*MIL also: consent*) permission *f*; **to be left** rester; **there's some milk left over** il reste du lait; **on ~** en permission; **~ behind** *vt* (*person, object*) laisser; (*forget*) oublier; **~ out** *vt* oublier, omettre; **~ of absence** *n* congé exceptionnel; (*MIL*) permission spéciale

leaves [li:vz] *npl of* **leaf**

Lebanon ['lɛbənən] *n* Liban *m*

lecherous ['lɛtʃərəs] (*pej*) *adj* lubrique

lecture ['lɛktʃə^r] *n* conférence *f*; (*SCOL*) cours *m* ♦ *vi* donner des cours; enseigner ♦ *vt* (*scold*) sermonner, réprimander; **to give a ~ on** faire une conférence sur; donner un cours sur; **~r** (*BRIT*) *n* (*at university*) professeur *m* (d'université)

led [lɛd] *pt, pp of* **lead**¹

ledge [lɛdʒ] *n* (*of window, on wall*) rebord *m*; (*of mountain*) saillie *f*, corniche *f*

ledger ['lɛdʒə^r] *n* (*COMM*) registre *m*, grand livre

leech [li:tʃ] *n* (*also fig*) sangsue *f*

leek [li:k] *n* poireau *m*

leer [lɪə^r] *vi:* **to ~ at sb** regarder qn d'un air mauvais *or* concupiscent

leeway ['li:weɪ] *n* (*fig*): **to have some ~** avoir une certaine liberté d'action

left [lɛft] *pt, pp of* **leave** ♦ *adj* (*not right*) gauche ♦ *n* gauche *f* ♦ *adv* à gauche; **on the ~, to the ~** à gauche; **the L~** (*POL*) la gauche; **~-handed** *adj* gaucher(-ère); **~-hand side** *n* gauche *f*; **~-luggage locker** *n* (casier *m* à) consigne *f* automatique; **~-luggage (office)** (*BRIT*) *n* consigne *f*; **~overs** *npl* restes *mpl*; **~-wing** *adj* (*POL*) de gauche

leg [lɛg] *n* jambe *f*; (*of animal*) patte *f*; (*of furniture*) pied *m*; (*CULIN: of chicken, pork*) cuisse *f*; (: *of lamb*) gigot *m*; (*of journey*) étape *f*; **1st/2nd ~** (*SPORT*) match *m* aller/retour

legacy ['lɛgəsɪ] *n* héritage *m*, legs *m*

legal ['li:gl] *adj* légal(e); **~ holiday** (*US*) *n* jour férié; **~ tender** *n* monnaie légale

legend ['lɛdʒənd] *n* légende *f*

leggings ['lɛgɪnz] *npl* caleçon *m*

legible ['lɛdʒəbl] *adj* lisible

legislation [lɛdʒɪs'leɪʃən] *n* législation *f*; **legislature** ['lɛdʒɪslətʃə^r] *n* (corps *m*) législatif *m*

legitimate [lɪ'dʒɪtɪmət] *adj* légitime

leg-room ['lɛgru:m] *n* place *f* pour les jambes

leisure ['lɛʒə^r] *n* loisir *m*, temps *m* libre; loisirs *mpl*; **at ~** (tout) à loisir; à tête reposée; **~ centre** *n* centre *m* de loisirs; **~ly** *adj* tranquille; fait(e) sans se presser

lemon ['lɛmən] *n* citron *m*; **~ade** [lɛmə'neɪd] *n* limonade *f*; **~ tea** *n* thé *m* au citron

lend [lɛnd] (*pt, pp* **lent**) *vt:* **to ~ sth (to sb)** prêter qch (à qn)

length [lɛnθ] *n* longueur *f*; (*section: of road, pipe etc*) morceau *m*, bout *m*; (*of time*) durée *f*; **at ~** (*at last*) enfin, à la fin; (*~ily*) longuement; **~en** *vt* allonger, prolonger ♦ *vi* s'allonger; **~ways** *adv* dans le sens de la longueur, en long; **~y** *adj* (très) long (longue)

lenient ['liːnɪənt] *adj* indulgent(e), clément(e)

lens [lɛnz] *n* lentille *f*; (*of spectacles*) verre *m*; (*of camera*) objectif *m*

Lent [lɛnt] *n* carême *m*

lent [lɛnt] *pt, pp of* **lend**

lentil ['lɛntɪl] *n* lentille *f*

Leo ['liːəʊ] *n* le Lion

leotard ['liːətɑːd] *n* maillot *m* (*de danseur etc*), collant *m*

leprosy ['lɛprəsɪ] *n* lèpre *f*

lesbian ['lɛzbɪən] *n* lesbienne *f*

less [lɛs] *adj* moins de ♦ *pron, adv* moins ♦ *prep* moins; **~ than that / you** moins que cela/vous; **~ than half** moins de la moitié; **~ than ever** moins que jamais; **~ and ~** de moins en moins; **the ~ he works ...** moins il travaille ...; **~en** *vi* diminuer, s'atténuer ♦ *vt* diminuer, réduire, atténuer; **~er** *adj* moindre; **to a ~er extent** à un degré moindre

lesson ['lɛsn] *n* leçon *f*; **to teach sb a ~** (*fig*) donner une bonne leçon à qn

let [lɛt] (*pt, pp* **let**) *vt* laisser; (*BRIT: lease*) louer; **to ~ sb do sth** laisser qn faire qch; **to ~ sb know sth** faire savoir qch à qn, prévenir qn de qch; **~'s go** allons-y; **~ him come** qu'il vienne; **"to ~"** "à louer"; **~ down** *vt* (*tyre*) dégonfler; (*person*) décevoir, faire faux bond à; **~ go** *vi* lâcher prise ♦ *vt* lâcher; **~ in** *vt* laisser entrer; (*visitor etc*) faire entrer; **~ off** *vt* (*culprit*) ne pas punir; (*firework etc*) faire partir; **~ on** (*inf*) *vi* dire; **~ out** *vt* laisser sortir; (*scream*) laisser échapper; **~ up** *vi* diminuer; (*cease*) s'arrêter

lethal ['liːθl] *adj* mortel(le), fatal(e)

letter ['lɛtə'] *n* lettre *f*; **~ bomb** *n* lettre piégée; **~box** (*BRIT*) *n* boîte *f* aux or à lettres; **~ing** *n* lettres *fpl*; caractères *mpl*

lettuce ['lɛtɪs] *n* laitue *f*, salade *f*

let-up ['lɛtʌp] *n* répit *m*, arrêt *m*

leukaemia [luːˈkiːmɪə] (*US* **leukemia**) *n* leucémie *f*

level ['lɛvl] *adj* plat(e), plan(e), uni(e); horizontal(e) ♦ *n* niveau *m* ♦ *vt* niveler, aplanir; **to be ~ with** être au même niveau que; **to draw ~ with** (*person, vehicle*) arriver à la hauteur de; **"A" ~s** (*BRIT*) ≃ baccalauréat *m*; **"O" ~s** (*BRIT*) ≃ B.E.P.C.; **on the ~** (*fig: honest*) régulier(-ère); **~ off** *vi* (*prices etc*) se stabiliser; **~ out** *vi* = **level off**; **~ crossing** (*BRIT*) *n* passage *m* à niveau; **~-headed** *adj* équilibré(e)

lever ['liːvə'] *n* levier *m*; **~age** *n:* **~age (on** *or* **with)** prise *f* (sur)

levy ['lɛvɪ] *n* taxe *f*, impôt *m* ♦ *vt* prélever, imposer; percevoir

lewd [luːd] *adj* obscène, lubrique

liability [laɪəˈbɪlətɪ] *n* responsabilité *f*; (*handicap*) handicap *m*; **liabilities** *npl* (*on balance sheet*) passif *m*

liable ['laɪəbl] *adj* (*subject*): **~ to** sujet(te) à; passible de; (*responsible*): **~ (for)** responsable (de); (*likely*): **~ to do** susceptible de faire

liaise [liːˈeɪz] *vi:* **to ~ (with)** assurer la liaison avec; **liaison** *n* liaison *f*

liar ['laɪə'] *n* menteur(-euse)

libel ['laɪbl] *n* diffamation *f*; (*document*) écrit *m* diffamatoire ♦ *vt* diffamer

liberal ['lɪbərl] *adj* libéral(e); (*generous*): **~ with** prodigue de, généreux(-euse) avec; **the L~ Democrats** (*BRIT*) le parti libéral-démocrate

liberation [lɪbəˈreɪʃən] *n* libération *f*

liberty ['lɪbətɪ] *n* liberté *f*; **to be at ~ to do** être libre de faire

Libra ['liːbrə] *n* la Balance

librarian [laɪˈbrɛərɪən] *n* bibliothécaire *m/f*

library ['laɪbrərɪ] *n* bibliothèque *f*

libretto [lɪˈbrɛtəʊ] *n* livret *m*

Libya ['lɪbɪə] *n* Libye *f*

lice [laɪs] *npl of* **louse**

licence ['laɪsns] (*US* **license**) *n* autorisation *f*, permis *m*; (*RADIO, TV*) redevance *f*; **driving ~**, (*US*) **driver's license** permis *m* (de conduire); **~ number** *n* numéro *m* d'immatriculation; **~ plate** *n* plaque *f* minéralogique

license ['laɪsns] *n* (*US*) = **licence** ♦ *vt* donner une licence à; **~d** *adj* (*car*) muni(e) de la vignette; (*to sell alcohol*) patenté(e) pour la vente des spiritueux, qui a une licence de débit de boissons

lick [lɪk] *vt* lécher; (*inf: defeat*) écraser; **to ~ one's lips** (*fig*) se frotter les mains

licorice ['lɪkərɪs] (*US*) *n* = **liquorice**

lid [lɪd] *n* couvercle *m*; (*eyelid*) paupière *f*

lie [laɪ] (*pt* **lay**, *pp* **lain**) *vi* (*rest*) être étendu(e) *or* allongé(e) *or* couché(e); (*in grave*) être enterré(e), reposer; (*be situated*) se trouver, être; (*be untruthful: pt, pp* ~d) mentir ♦ *n* mensonge *m*; **to ~ low** (*fig*) se cacher; **~ about** *vi* traîner; **~ around** *vi* = **lie about**; **~-down** (*BRIT*) *n*: **to have a ~-down** s'allonger, se reposer; **~-in** (*BRIT*) *n*: **to have a ~-in** faire la grasse matinée

lieutenant [lef'tenənt, (*US*) luː'tenənt] *n* lieutenant *m*

life [laɪf] (*pl* **lives**) *n* vie *f*; **to come to ~** (*fig*) s'animer; **~ assurance** (*BRIT*) *n* = **life insurance**; **~belt** (*BRIT*) *n* bouée *f* de sauvetage; **~boat** *n* canot *m* *or* chaloupe *f* de sauvetage; **~buoy** *n* bouée *f* de sauvetage; **~guard** *n* surveillant *m* de baignade; **~ insurance** *n* assurance-vie *f*; **~ jacket** *n* gilet *m* *or* ceinture *f* de sauvetage; **~less** *adj* sans vie, inanimé(e); (*dull*) qui manque de vie *or* de vigueur; **~like** *adj* qui semble vrai(e) *or* vivant(e); (*painting*) réaliste; **~long** *adj* de toute une vie, de toujours; **~ preserver** (*US*) *n* = **life-belt**; **life jacket**; **~-saving** *n* sauvetage *m*; **~ sentence** *n* condamnation *f* à perpétuité; **~-size(d)** *adj* grandeur nature *inv*; **~ span** *n* (*durée f de*) vie *f*; **~style** *n* style *m* *or* mode *m* de vie; **~-support system** *n* (*MED*) respirateur artificiel; **~time** *n* vie *f*; **in his ~time** de son vivant

lift [lɪft] *vt* soulever, lever; (*end*) supprimer, lever ♦ *vi* (*fog*) se lever ♦ *n* (*BRIT: elevator*) ascenseur *m*; **to give sb a ~** (*BRIT: AUT*) emmener *or* prendre qn en voiture; **~-off** *n* décollage *m*

light [laɪt] (*pt, pp* **lit**) *n* lumière *f*; (*lamp*)

lampe *f*; (*AUT: rear ~*) feu *m*; (*: headlight*) phare *m*; (*for cigarette etc*): **have you got a ~?** avez-vous du feu? ♦ *vt* (*candle, cigarette, fire*) allumer; (*room*) éclairer ♦ *adj* (*room, colour*) clair(e); (*not heavy*) léger(-ère); (*not strenuous*) peu fatigant(e); **~s** *npl* (*AUT: traffic ~s*) feux *mpl*; **to come to ~** être dévoilé(e) *or* découvert(e); **~ up** *vi* (*face*) s'éclairer ♦ *vt* (*illuminate*) éclairer, illuminer; **~ bulb** *n* ampoule *f*; **~en** *vt* (*make less heavy*) alléger; **~er** *n* (*also:* **cigarette ~er**) briquet *m*; **~-headed** *adj* étourdi(e); (*excited*) grisé(e); **~-hearted** *adj* gai(e), joyeux(-euse), enjoué(e); **~house** *n* phare *m*; **~ing** *n* (*on road*) éclairage *m*; (*in theatre*) éclairages *mpl*; **~ly** *adv* légèrement; **to get off ~ly** s'en tirer à bon compte; **~ness** *n* (*in weight*) légèreté *f*

lightning ['laɪtnɪŋ] *n* éclair *m*, foudre *f*; **~ conductor** (*US* **lightning rod**) *n* paratonnerre *m*

light pen *n* crayon *m* optique

lightweight ['laɪtweɪt] *adj* (*suit*) léger(-ère) ♦ *n* (*BOXING*) poids léger

like [laɪk] *vt* aimer (bien) ♦ *prep* comme ♦ *adj* semblable, pareil(le) ♦ *n*: **and the ~** et d'autres du même genre; **his ~s and dislikes** ses goûts *mpl* *or* préférences *fpl*; **I would ~, I'd ~** je voudrais, j'aimerais; **would you ~ a coffee?** voulez-vous du café?; **to be/look ~ sb/sth** ressembler à qn/qch; **what does it look ~?** de quoi est-ce que ça a l'air?; **what does it taste ~?** quel goût est-ce que ça a?; **that's just ~ him** c'est bien de lui, ça lui ressemble; **do it ~ this** fais-le comme ceci; **it's nothing ~ ...** ce n'est pas du tout comme ...; **~able** *adj* sympathique, agréable

likelihood ['laɪklɪhud] *n* probabilité *f*

likely ['laɪklɪ] *adj* probable; plausible; **he's ~ to leave** il va sûrement partir, il risque fort de partir; **not ~!** (*inf*) pas de danger!

likeness ['laɪknɪs] *n* ressemblance *f*; **that's a good ~** c'est très ressemblant

likewise ['laɪkwaɪz] *adv* de même, pareillement

liking ['laɪkɪŋ] n (for person) affection f; (for thing) penchant m, goût m

lilac ['laɪlək] n lilas m

lily ['lɪlɪ] n lis m; ~ **of the valley** n muguet m

limb [lɪm] n membre m

limber up ['lɪmbər-] vi se dégourdir, faire des exercices d'assouplissement

limbo ['lɪmbəu] n: **to be in ~** (fig) être tombé(e) dans l'oubli

lime [laɪm] n (tree) tilleul m; (fruit) lime f, citron vert; (GEO) chaux f

limelight ['laɪmlaɪt] n: **in the ~** (fig) en vedette, au premier plan

limerick ['lɪmərɪk] n poème m humoristique (de 5 vers)

limestone ['laɪmstəun] n pierre f à chaux; (GEO) calcaire m

limit ['lɪmɪt] n limite f ♦ vt limiter; ~**ed** adj limité(e), restreint(e); **to be ~ed to** se limiter à, ne concerner que; ~**ed (liability) company** (BRIT) n ≈ société f anonyme

limousine ['lɪməzi:n] n limousine f

limp [lɪmp] n: **to have a ~** boiter ♦ vi boiter ♦ adj mou (molle)

limpet ['lɪmpɪt] n patelle f

line [laɪn] n ligne f; (stroke) trait m; (wrinkle) ride f; (rope) corde f; (wire) fil m; (of poem) vers m; (row, series) rangée f; (of people) file f, queue f; (railway track) voie f; (COMM: series of goods) article(s) m(pl); (work) métier m, type m d'activité; (attitude, policy) position f ♦ vt (subj: trees, crowd) border; **in a ~** aligné(e); **in his ~ of business** dans sa partie, dans son rayon; **in ~ with** en accord avec; **to ~ (with)** (clothes) doubler (de); (box) garnir or tapisser (de); ~ **up** vi s'aligner, se mettre en rang(s) ♦ vt aligner; (event) prévoir, préparer; ~**d** adj (face) ridé(e), marqué(e); (paper) réglé(e)

linen ['lɪnɪn] n linge m (de maison); (cloth) lin m

liner ['laɪnər] n paquebot m (de ligne); (for bin) sac m à poubelle

linesman ['laɪnzmən] (irreg) n juge m de

touche; (TENNIS) juge m de ligne

line-up ['laɪnʌp] n (US: queue) file f; (SPORT) composition f de l'équipe f

linger ['lɪŋgər] vi s'attarder; traîner; (smell, tradition) persister

linguist ['lɪŋgwɪst] n: **to be a good ~** être doué(e) par les langues; ~**ics** [lɪŋ'gwɪstɪks] n linguistique f

lining ['laɪnɪŋ] n doublure f

link [lɪŋk] n lien m, rapport m; (of a chain) maillon m ♦ vt relier, lier, unir; ~**s** npl (GOLF) (terrain m de) golf m; ~ **up** vt relier ♦ vi se rejoindre; s'associer

lino ['laɪnəu] n = **linoleum**

linoleum [lɪ'nəuliəm] n linoléum m

lion ['laɪən] n lion m; ~**ess** n lionne f

lip [lɪp] n lèvre f

liposuction ['lɪpəusʌkʃən] n liposuccion f

lip: ~-**read** vi lire sur les lèvres; ~ **salve** n pommade f rosat or pour les lèvres; ~ **service** n: **to pay ~ service to sth** ne reconnaître le mérite de qch que pour la forme; ~**stick** n rouge m à lèvres

liqueur [lɪ'kjuər] n liqueur f

liquid ['lɪkwɪd] adj liquide ♦ n liquide m; ~**ize** vt (CULIN) passer au mixer; ~**izer** n mixer m

liquor ['lɪkər] (US) n spiritueux m, alcool m

liquorice ['lɪkərɪs] (BRIT) n réglisse f

liquor store (US) n magasin m de vins et spiritueux

lisp [lɪsp] vi zézayer

list [lɪst] n liste f ♦ vt (write down) faire une or la liste de; (mention) énumérer; ~**ed building** (BRIT) n monument classé

listen ['lɪsn] vi écouter; **to ~ to** écouter; ~**er** n auditeur(-trice)

listless ['lɪstlɪs] adj indolent(e), apathique

lit [lɪt] pt, pp of **light**

liter ['li:tər] (US) n = **litre**

literacy ['lɪtərəsɪ] n degré m d'alphabétisation, fait m de savoir lire et écrire

literal ['lɪtərəl] adj littéral(e); ~**ly** adv littéralement; (really) réellement

literary ['lɪtərərɪ] adj littéraire

literate ['lɪtərət] adj qui sait lire et écrire, instruit(e)

literature [ˈlɪtrɪtʃəʳ] *n* littérature *f*; (*brochures etc*) documentation *f*

lithe [laɪð] *adj* agile, souple

litigation [lɪtɪˈgeɪʃən] *n* litige *m*; contentieux *m*

litre [ˈliːtəʳ] (*US* **liter**) *n* litre *m*

litter [ˈlɪtəʳ] *n* (*rubbish*) détritus *mpl*, ordures *fpl*; (*young animals*) portée *f*; ~ **bin** (*BRIT*) *n* boîte *f* à ordures, poubelle *f*; ~**ed** *adj*: ~**ed with** jonché(e) de, couvert(e) de

little [ˈlɪtl] *adj* (*small*) petit(e) ♦ *adv* peu; ~ **milk/time** peu de lait/temps; **a** ~ un peu (de); **a** ~ **bit** un peu; ~ **by** ~ petit à petit, peu à peu

live¹ [laɪv] *adj* (*animal*) vivant(e), en vie; (*wire*) sous tension; (*bullet, bomb*) non explosé(e); (*broadcast*) en direct; (*performance*) en public

live² [lɪv] *vi* vivre; (*reside*) vivre, habiter; ~ **down** *vt* faire oublier (avec le temps); ~ **on** *vt fus* (*food, salary*) vivre de; ~ **together** *vi* vivre ensemble, cohabiter; ~ **up to** *vt fus* se montrer à la hauteur de

livelihood [ˈlaɪvlɪhud] *n* moyens *mpl* d'existence

lively [ˈlaɪvlɪ] *adj* vif (vive), plein(e) d'entrain; (*place, book*) vivant(e)

liven up [ˈlaɪvn-] *vt* animer ♦ *vi* s'animer

liver [ˈlɪvəʳ] *n* foie *m*

lives [laɪvz] *npl of* **life**

livestock [ˈlaɪvstɔk] *n* bétail *m*, cheptel *m*

livid [ˈlɪvɪd] *adj* livide, blafard(e); (*inf: furious*) furieux(-euse), furibond(e)

living [ˈlɪvɪŋ] *adj* vivant(e), en vie ♦ *n*: **to earn** *or* **make a** ~ gagner sa vie; ~ **conditions** *npl* conditions *fpl* de vie; ~ **room** *n* salle *f* de séjour; ~ **standards** *npl* niveau *m* de vie; ~ **wage** *n* salaire *m* permettant de vivre (décemment)

lizard [ˈlɪzəd] *n* lézard *m*

load [ləud] *n* (*weight*) poids *m*; (*thing carried*) chargement *m*, charge *f* ♦ *vt* (*also:* ~ **up**): **to** ~ **(with)** charger (de); (*gun, camera*) charger (avec); (*COMPUT*) charger; **a** ~ **of**, ~**s of** (*fig*) un *or* des tas de, des masses de; **to talk a** ~ **of rubbish** dire des bêtises; ~**ed** *adj* (*question*) insidieux(-

euse); (*inf: rich*) bourré(e) de fric

loaf [ləuf] (*pl* **loaves**) *n* pain *m*, miche *f*

loan [ləun] *n* prêt *m* ♦ *vt* prêter; **on** ~ prêté(e), en prêt

loath [ləuθ] *adj*: **to be** ~ **to do** répugner à faire

loathe [ləuð] *vt* détester, avoir en horreur

loaves [ləuvz] *npl of* **loaf**

lobby [ˈlɔbɪ] *n* hall *m*, entrée *f*; (*POL*) groupe *m* de pression, lobby *m* ♦ *vt* faire pression sur

lobster [ˈlɔbstəʳ] *n* homard *m*

local [ˈləukl] *adj* local(e) ♦ *n* (*BRIT: pub*) pub *m or* café *m* du coin; **the** ~**s** *npl* (*inhabitants*) les gens *mpl* du pays *or* du coin; ~ **anaesthetic** *n* anesthésie locale; ~ **authority** *n* collectivité locale, municipalité *f*; ~ **call** *n* communication urbaine; ~ **government** *n* administration locale *or* municipale; ~**ity** [ləuˈkælɪtɪ] *n* région *f*, environs *mpl*; (*position*) lieu *m*

locate [ləuˈkeɪt] *vt* (*find*) trouver, repérer; (*situate*): **to be** ~**d in** être situé(e) à *or* en; **location** *n* emplacement *m*; **on location** (*CINEMA*) en extérieur

loch [lɔx] *n* lac *m*, loch *m*

lock [lɔk] *n* (*of door, box*) serrure *f*; (*of canal*) écluse *f*; (*of hair*) mèche *f*, boucle *f* ♦ *vt* (*with key*) fermer à clé ♦ *vi* (*door etc*) fermer à clé; (*wheels*) se bloquer; ~ **in** *vt* enfermer; ~ **out** *vt* enfermer dehors; (*deliberately*) mettre à la porte; ~ **up** *vt* (*person*) enfermer; (*house*) fermer à clé ♦ *vi* tout fermer (à clé)

locker [ˈlɔkəʳ] *n* casier *m*; (*in station*) consigne *f* automatique

locket [ˈlɔkɪt] *n* médaillon *m*

locksmith [ˈlɔksmɪθ] *n* serrurier *m*

lockup [ˈlɔkʌp] *n* (*prison*) prison *f*

locum [ˈləukəm] *n* (*MED*) suppléant(e) (de médecin)

lodge [lɔdʒ] *n* pavillon *m* (de gardien); (*hunting* ~) pavillon de chasse ♦ *vi* (*person*): **to** ~ **(with)** être logé(e) (chez), être en pension (chez); (*bullet*) se loger ♦ *vt*: **to** ~ **a complaint** porter plainte; ~**r** *n* locataire *m/f*; (*with meals*) pensionnaire *m/f*;

lodgings *npl* chambre *f*; meublé *m*

loft [lɔft] *n* grenier *m*

lofty ['lɔftɪ] *adj* (*noble*) noble, élevé(e); (*haughty*) hautain(e)

log [lɔg] *n* (*of wood*) bûche *f*; (*book*) = **logbook** ♦ *vt* (*record*) noter; **~book** *n* (NAUT) livre *m* or journal *m* de bord; (AVIAT) carnet *m* de vol; (*of car*) ≃ carte grise

loggerheads ['lɔgəhedz] *npl*: **at ~ (with)** à couteaux tirés (avec)

logic ['lɔdʒɪk] *n* logique *f*; **~al** *adj* logique

log on *vi* (COMPUT) se connecter

log off *or* **out** *vi* (COMPUT) se déconnecter

loin [lɔɪn] *n* (CULIN) filet *m*, longe *f*

loiter ['lɔɪtə*r*] *vi* traîner

loll [lɔl] *vi* (*also:* **~ about**) se prélasser, fainéanter

lollipop ['lɔlɪpɔp] *n* sucette *f*; **~ man / lady** *n* (BRIT) voir encadré

---

lollipop men / ladies

Les **lollipop men/ladies** *sont employés pour aider les enfants à traverser la rue à proximité des écoles à l'heure où ils entrent en classe et à la sortie. On les repère facilement à cause de leur long ciré blanc et ils portent une pancarte ronde pour faire signe aux automobilistes de s'arrêter. On les appelle ainsi car la forme circulaire de cette pancarte rappelle une sucette.*

---

lolly ['lɔlɪ] (*inf*) *n* (*lollipop*) sucette *f*; (*money*) fric *m*

London ['lʌndən] *n* Londres *m*; **~er** *n* Londonien(ne)

lone [ləun] *adj* solitaire

loneliness ['ləunlɪnɪs] *n* solitude *f*, isolement *m*

lonely ['ləunlɪ] *adj* seul(e); solitaire, isolé(e)

long [lɔŋ] *adj* long (longue) ♦ *adv* longtemps ♦ *vi*: **to ~ for sth** avoir très envie de qch; attendre qch avec impatience; **so** *or* **as ~ as** pourvu que; **don't be ~!** dépêchez-vous!; **how ~ is this river/course?** quelle est la longueur de ce fleuve/la durée de ce cours?; **6 metres ~**

(long) de 6 mètres; **6 months ~** qui dure 6 mois, de 6 mois; **all night ~** toute la nuit; **he no ~er comes** il ne vient plus; **I can't stand it any ~er** je ne peux plus le supporter; **~ before/after** longtemps avant/après; **before ~** (*+future*) avant peu, dans peu de temps; (*+past*) peu de temps après; **at ~ last** enfin; **~-distance** *adj* (*call*) interurbain(e); **~er** ['lɔŋgə*r*] *adv* *see* **long**; **~hand** *n* écriture normale *or* courante; **~ing** *n* désir *m*, envie *f*, nostalgie *f*

longitude ['lɔŋgɪtjuːd] *n* longitude *f*

long: **~ jump** *n* saut *m* en longueur; **~-life** *adj* (*batteries etc*) longue durée *inv*; (*milk*) longue conservation; **~-lost** *adj* (*person*) perdu(e) de vue depuis longtemps; **~-range** *adj* à longue portée; **~-sighted** *adj* (MED) presbyte; **~-standing** *adj* de longue date; **~-suffering** *adj* empreint(e) d'une patience résignée; extrêmement patient(e); **~-term** *adj* à long terme; **~ wave** *n* grandes ondes; **~-winded** *adj* intarissable, interminable

loo [luː] (BRIT: *inf*) *n* W.-C. *mpl*, petit coin

look [luk] *vi* regarder; (*seem*) sembler, paraître, avoir l'air; (*building etc*): **to ~ south/(out) onto the sea** donner au sud/sur la mer ♦ *n* regard *m*; (*appearance*) air *m*, allure *f*, aspect *m*; **~s** *npl* (*good ~s*) physique *m*, beauté *f*; **to have a ~** regarder; **~!** regardez!; **~ (here)!** (*annoyance*) écoutez!; **~ after** *vt fus* (*take care of, deal with*) s'occuper de; **~ at** *vt fus* regarder; (*problem etc*) examiner; **~ back** *vi*: **to ~ back on** (*event etc*) évoquer, repenser à; **~ down on** *vt fus* (*fig*) regarder de haut, dédaigner; **~ for** *vt fus* chercher; **~ forward to** *vt fus* attendre avec impatience; **we ~ forward to hearing from you** (*in letter*) dans l'attente de vous lire; **~ into** *vt fus* examiner, étudier; **~ on** *vi* regarder (en spectateur); **~ out** *vi* (*beware*): **to ~ out (for)** prendre garde (à), faire attention (à); **~ out for** *vt fus* être à la recherche de; guetter; **~ round** *vi* regarder derrière soi, se retourner; **~ to** *vt fus* (*rely on*) compter sur; **~ up** *vi* lever les yeux; (*improve*) s'améliorer ♦ *vt* (*word, name*) chercher; **~ up to** *vt fus* avoir du respect pour ♦ *n* poste *m* de guet; (*person*) guetteur *m*; **to be on the ~ out (for)** guetter

loom [luːm] *vi* (*also*: **~ up**) surgir; (*approach: event etc*) être imminent(e); (*threaten*) menacer ♦ *n* (*for weaving*) métier *m* à tisser

loony ['luːnɪ] (*inf*) *adj, n* timbré(e), cinglé(e)

loop [luːp] *n* boucle *f*; **~hole** *n* (*fig*) porte *f* de sortie; échappatoire *f*

loose [luːs] *adj* (*knot, screw*) desserré(e); (*clothes*) ample, lâche; (*hair*) dénoué(e), épars(e); (*not firmly fixed*) pas solide; (*morals, discipline*) relâché(e) ♦ *n*: **on the ~** en liberté; **~ change** *n* petite monnaie; **~ chippings** *npl* (*on road*) gravillons *mpl*; **~ end** *n*: **to be at a ~ end** or (*US*) **at ~ ends** ne pas trop savoir quoi faire; **~ly** *adv* sans serrer; (*imprecisely*) approximativement; **~n** *vt* desserrer

loot [luːt] *n* (*inf: money*) pognon *m*, fric *m* ♦ *vt* piller

lopsided ['lɔpˈsaɪdɪd] *adj* de travers, asymétrique

lord [lɔːd] *n* seigneur *m*; **L~ Smith** lord Smith; **the L~** le Seigneur; **good L~!** mon Dieu!; **the (House of) L~s** (*BRIT*) la Chambre des lords; **my L~** = **your Lordship**; **L~ship** *n*: **your L~ship** Monsieur le comte/le baron/le juge; (*to bishop*) Monseigneur

lore [lɔːʳ] *n* tradition(s) *f(pl)*

lorry ['lɔrɪ] (*BRIT*) *n* camion *m*; **~ driver** (*BRIT*) *n* camionneur *m*, routier *m*

lose [luːz] (*pt, pp* **lost**) *vt, vi* perdre; **to ~ (time)** (*clock*) retarder; **to get lost** ♦ *vi* se perdre; **~r** *n* perdant(e)

loss [lɔs] *n* perte *f*; **to be at a ~** être perplexe or embarrassé(e)

lost [lɔst] *pt, pp of* **lose** ♦ *adj* perdu(e); **~ and found** (*US*), **~ property** *n* objets trouvés

lot [lɔt] *n* (*set*) lot *m*; **the ~** le tout; **a ~ (of)** beaucoup (de); **~s of** des tas de; **to**

draw ~s (for sth) tirer (qch) au sort

lotion ['ləʊʃən] *n* lotion *f*

lottery ['lɔtərɪ] *n* loterie *f*

loud [laʊd] *adj* bruyant(e), sonore; (*voice*) fort(e); (*support, condemnation*) vigoureux(-euse); (*gaudy*) voyant(e), tapageur(-euse) ♦ *adv* (*speak etc*) fort; **out ~** tout haut; **~-hailer** (*BRIT*) *n* porte-voix *m inv*; **~ly** *adv* fort, bruyamment; **~speaker** *n* haut-parleur *m*

lounge [laʊndʒ] *n* salon *m*; (*at airport*) salle *f*; (*BRIT: also*: **~ bar**) (salle de) café *m* or bar *m* ♦ *vi* (*also*: **~ about** or **around**) se prélasser, paresser; **~ suit** (*BRIT*) *n* complet *m*; (*on invitation*) "tenue de ville"

louse [laʊs] (*pl* **lice**) *n* pou *m*

lousy ['laʊzɪ] (*inf*) *adj* infect(e), moche; **I feel ~** je suis mal fichu(e)

lout [laʊt] *n* rustre *m*, butor *m*

lovable ['lʌvəbl] *adj* adorable; très sympathique

love [lʌv] *n* amour *m* ♦ *vt* aimer; (*caringly, kindly*) aimer beaucoup; **"~ (from) Anne"** "affectueusement, Anne"; **I ~ chocolate** j'adore le chocolat; **to be/fall in ~ with** être/tomber amoureux(-euse) de; **to make ~** faire l'amour; **"15 ~"** (*TENNIS*) "15 à rien *or* zéro"; **~ affair** *n* liaison (amoureuse); **~ life** *n* vie sentimentale

lovely ['lʌvlɪ] *adj* (très) joli(e), ravissant(e); (*delightful: person*) charmant(e); (*holiday etc*) (très) agréable

lover ['lʌvəʳ] *n* amant *m*; (*person in love*) amoureux(-euse); (*amateur*): **a ~ of** un amateur de; un(e) amoureux(-euse) de

loving ['lʌvɪŋ] *adj* affectueux(-euse), tendre

low [ləʊ] *adj* bas (basse); (*quality*) mauvais(e), inférieur(e); (*person: depressed*) déprimé(e); (: *ill*) bas (basse), affaibli(e) ♦ *adv* bas (*in METEOROLOGY*); **to be ~ on** être à court de; **to feel ~** se sentir déprimé(e); **to reach an all-time ~** être au plus bas; **~-alcohol** *adj* peu alcoolisé(e); **~-calorie** *adj* hypocalorique; **~-cut** *adj* (*dress*) décolleté(e); **~er** *adj* inférieur(e) ♦ *vt* abaisser, baisser; **~er sixth** (*BRIT*) *n* (*SCOL*) première *f*; **~-fat** *adj* maigre; **~lands** *npl* (*GEO*) plaines *fpl*; **~ly** *adj* humble, modeste

loyal [ˈlɔɪəl] *adj* loyal(e), fidèle; **~ty** *n* loyauté *f*, fidélité *f*; **~ty card** *n* carte *f* de fidélité

lozenge [ˈlɔzɪndʒ] *n* (*MED*) pastille *f*

LP *n abbr* = **long-playing record**

L-plates [ˈelpleɪts] (*BRIT*) *npl* plaques *fpl* d'apprenti conducteur

L-plates

ⓘ Les **L-plates** sont des carrés blancs portant un "L" rouge que l'on met à l'avant et à l'arrière de sa voiture pour montrer qu'on n'a pas encore son permis de conduire. Jusqu'à l'obtention du permis, l'apprenti conducteur a un permis provisoire et n'a le droit de conduire que si un conducteur qualifié est assis à côté de lui. Il est interdit aux apprentis conducteurs de circuler sur les autoroutes, même s'ils sont accompagnés.

Ltd *abbr* (= **limited**) ≈ S.A.

lubricant [ˈluːbrɪkənt] *n* lubrifiant *m*

lubricate [ˈluːbrɪkeɪt] *vt* lubrifier, graisser

luck [lʌk] *n* chance *f*; **bad ~** malchance *f*, malheur *m*; **bad** or **hard** or **tough ~!** pas de chance!; **good ~!** bonne chance!; **~ily** *adv* heureusement, par bonheur; **~y** *adj* (*person*) qui a de la chance; (*coincidence, event*) heureux(-euse); (*object*) porte-bonheur *inv*

ludicrous [ˈluːdɪkrəs] *adj* ridicule, absurde

lug [lʌg] (*inf*) *vt* traîner, tirer

luggage [ˈlʌgɪdʒ] *n* bagages *mpl*; **~ rack** *n* (*on car*) galerie *f*

lukewarm [ˈluːkwɔːm] *adj* tiède

lull [lʌl] *n* accalmie *f*; (*in conversation*) pause *f* ♦ *vt*: **to ~ sb to sleep** bercer qn pour qu'il s'endorme; **to be ~ed into a false sense of security** s'endormir dans une fausse sécurité

lullaby [ˈlʌləbaɪ] *n* berceuse *f*

lumbago [lʌmˈbeɪgəu] *n* lumbago *m*

lumber [ˈlʌmbəʳ] *n* (*wood*) bois *m* de charpente; (*junk*) bric-à-brac *m inv*; **~jack** *n*

bûcheron *m*

luminous [ˈluːmɪnəs] *adj* lumineux(-euse)

lump [lʌmp] *n* morceau *m*; (*swelling*) grosseur *f* ♦ *vt*: **to ~ together** réunir, mettre en tas; **~ sum** *n* somme globale or forfaitaire; **~y** *adj* (*sauce*) avec des grumeaux; (*bed*) défoncé(e), peu confortable

lunar [ˈluːnəʳ] *adj* lunaire

lunatic [ˈluːnətɪk] *adj* fou (folle), cinglé(e) (*inf*)

lunch [lʌntʃ] *n* déjeuner *m*

luncheon [ˈlʌntʃən] *n* déjeuner *m* (chic); **~ meat** *n* sorte de mortadelle; **~ voucher** (*BRIT*) *n* chèque-repas *m*

lung [lʌŋ] *n* poumon *m*

lunge [lʌndʒ] *vi* (*also:* **~ forward**) faire un mouvement brusque en avant; **to ~ at** envoyer or assener un coup à

lurch [ləːtʃ] *vi* vaciller, tituber ♦ *n* écart *m* brusque; **to leave sb in the ~** laisser qn se débrouiller or se dépêtrer tout(e) seul(e)

lure [luəʳ] *n* (*attraction*) attrait *m*, charme *m* ♦ *vt* attirer or persuader par la ruse

lurid [ˈluərɪd] *adj* affreux(-euse), atroce; (*pej: colour, dress*) criard(e)

lurk [ləːk] *vi* se tapir, se cacher

luscious [ˈlʌʃəs] *adj* succulent(e); appétissant(e)

lush [lʌʃ] *adj* luxuriant(e)

lust [lʌst] *n* (*sexual*) désir *m*; (*fig*): **~ for** soif *f* de; **~y** *adj* vigoureux(-euse), robuste

Luxembourg [ˈlʌksəmbəːg] *n* Luxembourg *m*

luxurious [lʌgˈzjuərɪəs] *adj* luxueux(-euse)

luxury [ˈlʌkʃərɪ] *n* luxe *m* ♦ *cpd* de luxe

lying [ˈlaɪɪŋ] *n* mensonge(s) *m(pl)* ♦ *vb see* **lie**

lyrical [ˈlɪrɪkl] *adj* lyrique

lyrics [ˈlɪrɪks] *npl* (*of song*) paroles *fpl*

M, m

m. *abbr* = **metre; mile; million**

M.A. *abbr* = **Master of Arts**

mac [mæk] (*BRIT*) *n* imper(méable) *m*

macaroni [mækə'rəunɪ] *n* macaroni *mpl*

machine [mə'ʃiːn] *n* machine *f* ♦ *vt* (*TECH*) façonner à la machine; (*dress etc*) coudre à la machine; ~ **gun** *n* mitrailleuse *f*; ~ **language** *n* (*COMPUT*) langage-machine *m*; ~**ry** *n* machinerie *f*, machines *fpl*; (*fig*) mécanisme(s) *m(pl)*

mackerel ['mækrl] *n inv* maquereau *m*

mackintosh ['mækɪntɔʃ] (*BRIT*) *n* imperméable *m*

mad [mæd] *adj* fou (folle); (*foolish*) insensé(e); (*angry*) furieux(-euse); (*keen*): **to be ~ about** être fou (folle) de

madam ['mædəm] *n* madame *f*

madden ['mædn] *vt* exaspérer

made [meɪd] *pt, pp of* **make**

Madeira [mə'dɪərə] *n* (*GEO*) Madère *f*; (*wine*) madère *m*

made-to-measure ['meɪdtə'meʒəʳ] (*BRIT*) *adj* fait(e) sur mesure

madly ['mædlɪ] *adv* follement; ~ **in love** éperdument amoureux(-euse)

madman ['mædmən] (*irreg*) *n* fou *m*

madness ['mædnɪs] *n* folie *f*

magazine [mægə'ziːn] *n* (*PRESS*) magazine *m*, revue *f*; (*RADIO, TV*: *also*: ~ **programme**) magazine

maggot ['mægət] *n* ver *m*, asticot *m*

magic ['mædʒɪk] *n* magie *f* ♦ *adj* magique; ~**al** *adj* magique; (*experience, evening*) merveilleux(-euse); ~**ian** [mə'dʒɪʃən] *n* magicien(ne); (*conjurer*) prestidigitateur *m*

magistrate ['mædʒɪstreɪt] *n* magistrat *m*; juge *m*

magnet ['mægnɪt] *n* aimant *m*; ~**ic** [mæg'netɪk] *adj* magnétique

magnificent [mæg'nɪfɪsnt] *adj* superbe, magnifique; (*splendid: robe, building*) somptueux(-euse), magnifique

magnify ['mægnɪfaɪ] *vt* grossir; (*sound*) amplifier; ~**ing glass** *n* loupe *f*

magnitude ['mægnɪtjuːd] *n* ampleur *f*

magpie ['mægpaɪ] *n* pie *f*

mahogany [mə'hɔgənɪ] *n* acajou *m*

maid [meɪd] *n* bonne *f*; **old ~** (*pej*) vieille fille

maiden ['meɪdn] *n* jeune fille *f* ♦ *adj* (*aunt etc*) non mariée; (*speech, voyage*) inaugural(e); ~ **name** *n* nom *m* de jeune fille

mail [meɪl] *n* poste *f*; (*letters*) courrier *m* ♦ *vt* envoyer (par la poste); ~**box** (*US*) *n* boîte *f* aux lettres; ~**ing list** *n* liste *f* d'adresses; ~-**order** *n* vente *f* or achat *m* par correspondance

maim [meɪm] *vt* mutiler

main [meɪn] *adj* principal(e) ♦ *n*: **the ~(s)** ♦ *n(pl)* (*gas, water*) conduite principale, canalisation *f*; **the ~s** *npl* (*ELEC*) le secteur; **the ~ thing** l'essentiel; **in the ~** dans l'ensemble; ~**frame** *n* (*COMPUT*) (gros) ordinateur, unité centrale; ~**land** *n* continent *m*; ~**ly** *adv* principalement, surtout; ~ **road** *n* grand-route *f*; ~**stay** *n* (*fig*) pilier *m*; ~**stream** *n* courant principal

maintain [meɪn'teɪn] *vt* entretenir; (*continue*) maintenir; (*affirm*) soutenir; **maintenance** ['meɪntənəns] *n* entretien *m*; (*alimony*) pension *f* alimentaire

maize [meɪz] *n* maïs *m*

majestic [mə'dʒestɪk] *adj* majestueux(-euse)

majesty ['mædʒɪstɪ] *n* majesté *f*

major ['meɪdʒəʳ] *n* (*MIL*) commandant *m* ♦ *adj* (*important*) important(e); (*most important*) principal(e); (*MUS*) majeur(e)

Majorca [mə'jɔːkə] *n* Majorque *f*

majority [mə'dʒɔrɪtɪ] *n* majorité *f*

make [meɪk] (*pt, pp* **made**) *vt* faire; (*manufacture*) faire, fabriquer; (*earn*) gagner; (*cause to be*): **to ~ sb sad** *etc* rendre qn triste *etc*; (*force*): **to ~ sb do sth** obliger qn à faire qch, faire faire qch à qn; (*equal*): **2 and 2 ~ 4** 2 et 2 font 4 ♦ *n* fabrication *f*; (*brand*) marque *f*; **to ~ a fool of sb** (*ridicule*) ridiculiser qn; (*trick*) avoir *or* duper qn; **to ~ a profit** faire un *or* des bénéfice(s); **to ~ a loss** essuyer une perte;

to ~ it (*arrive*) arriver; (*achieve sth*) parvenir à qch, réussir; **what time do you ~ it?** quelle heure avez-vous?; **to ~ do with** se contenter de; se débrouiller avec; **~ for** vt fus (*place*) se diriger vers; **~ out** vt (*write out: cheque*) faire; (*decipher*) déchiffrer; (*understand*) comprendre; (*see*) distinguer; **~ up** vt (*constitute*) constituer; (*invent*) inventer, imaginer; (*parcel, bed*) faire ♦ vi se réconcilier; (*with cosmetics*) se maquiller; **~ up for** vt fus compenser; **~-believe** n: **it's just ~-believe** (*game*) c'est pour faire semblant; (*invention*) c'est de l'invention pure; **~r** n fabricant m; **~shift** adj provisoire, improvisé(e); **~-up** n maquillage m

making ['meɪkɪŋ] n (*fig*): **in the ~** en formation or gestation; **to have the ~s of** (*actor, athlete etc*) avoir l'étoffe de

malaria [mə'lɛərɪə] n malaria f

Malaysia [mə'leɪzɪə] n Malaisie f

male [meɪl] n (*BIO*) mâle m ♦ adj mâle; (*sex, attitude*) masculin(e); (*child etc*) du sexe masculin

malevolent [mə'lɛvələnt] adj malveillant(e)

malfunction [mæl'fʌŋkʃən] n fonctionnement défectueux

malice ['mælɪs] n méchanceté f, malveillance f; **malicious** [mə'lɪʃəs] adj méchant(e), malveillant(e)

malignant [mə'lɪgnənt] adj (*MED*) malin(-igne)

mall [mɔːl] n (*also:* **shopping ~**) centre commercial

mallet ['mælɪt] n maillet m

malpractice [mæl'præktɪs] n faute professionnelle; négligence f

malt [mɔːlt] n malt m ♦ cpd (*also:* **~ whisky**) pur malt

Malta ['mɔːltə] n Malte f

mammal ['mæml] n mammifère m

mammoth ['mæməθ] n mammouth m ♦ adj géant(e), monstre

man [mæn] (*pl* **men**) n homme m ♦ vt (*NAUT: ship*) garnir d'hommes; (*MIL: gun*) servir; (*: post*) être de service à; (*machine*) assurer le fonctionnement de; **an old ~**

un vieillard; **~ and wife** mari et femme

manage ['mænɪdʒ] vi se débrouiller ♦ vt (*be in charge of*) s'occuper de; (*: business etc*) gérer; (*control: ship*) manier, manœuvrer; (*: person*) savoir s'y prendre avec; **to ~ to do** réussir à faire; **~able** adj (*task*) faisable; (*number*) raisonnable; **~ment** n gestion f, administration f, direction f; **~r** n directeur m; administrateur m; (*SPORT*) manager m; (*of artist*) impresario m; **~ress** [mænɪdʒə'rɛs] n directrice f; gérante f; **~rial** [mænɪ'dʒɪərɪəl] adj directorial(e); (*skills*) de cadre, de gestion; **managing director** n directeur général

mandarin ['mændərɪn] n (*also:* **~ orange**) mandarine f; (*person*) mandarin m

mandatory ['mændətərɪ] adj obligatoire

mane [meɪn] n crinière f

maneuver [mə'nuːvər] (*US*) vt, vi, n = **manoeuvre**

manfully ['mænfəlɪ] adv vaillamment

mangle ['mæŋgl] vt déchiqueter; mutiler

mango ['mæŋgəu] (*pl* **~es**) n mangue f

mangy ['meɪndʒɪ] adj galeux(-euse)

man: **~handle** vt malmener; **~hole** n trou m d'homme; **~hood** n âge m d'homme; virilité f; **~-hour** n heure f de main-d'œuvre; **~hunt** n (*POLICE*) chasse f à l'homme

mania ['meɪnɪə] n manie f; **~c** ['meɪnɪæk] n maniaque m/f; (*fig*) fou (folle) m/f; **manic** ['mænɪk] adj maniaque

manicure ['mænɪkjuər] n manucure f

manifest ['mænɪfɛst] vt manifester ♦ adj manifeste, évident(e); **~o** [mænɪ'fɛstəu] n manifeste m

manipulate [mə'nɪpjuleɪt] vt manipuler; (*system, situation*) exploiter

man: **~kind** [mæn'kaɪnd] n humanité f, genre humain; **~ly** adj viril(e); **~-made** adj artificiel(le); (*fibre*) synthétique

manner ['mænər] n manière f, façon f; (*behaviour*) attitude f, comportement m; (*sort*): **all ~ of** toutes sortes de; **~s** npl (*behaviour*) manières f; **~ism** n particularité f de langage (or de comportement), tic m

manoeuvre [mə'nuːvər] (*US* **maneuver**) vt

(*move*) manœuvrer; (*manipulate*: *person*) manipuler; (: *situation*) exploiter ♦ *vi* manœuvrer ♦ *n* manœuvre *f*

manor ['mænə^r] *n* (*also*: **~ house**) manoir *m*

manpower ['mænpauə^r] *n* main-d'œuvre *f*

mansion ['mænʃən] *n* château *m*, manoir *m*

manslaughter ['mænslɔːtə^r] *n* homicide *m* involontaire

mantelpiece ['mæntlpiːs] *n* cheminée *f*

manual ['mænjuəl] *adj* manuel(le) ♦ *n* manuel *m*

manufacture [mænju'fæktʃə^r] *vt* fabriquer ♦ *n* fabrication *f*; **~r** *n* fabricant *m*

manure [mə'njuə^r] *n* fumier *m*

manuscript ['mænjuskrɪpt] *n* manuscrit *m*

many ['menɪ] *adj* beaucoup de, de nombreux(-euses) ♦ *pron* beaucoup, un grand nombre; **a great ~** un grand nombre (de); **~ a ...** bien des ..., plus d'un(e) ...

map [mæp] *n* carte *f*; (*of town*) plan *m*; **~ out** *vt* tracer; (*task*) planifier

maple ['meɪpl] *n* érable *m*

mar [mɑː^r] *vt* gâcher, gâter

marathon ['mærəθən] *n* marathon *m*

marble ['mɑːbl] *n* marbre *m*; (*toy*) bille *f*

March [mɑːtʃ] *n* mars *m*

march [mɑːtʃ] *vi* marcher au pas; (*fig*: *protesters*) défiler ♦ *n* marche *f*; (*demonstration*) manifestation *f*

mare [mɛə^r] *n* jument *f*

margarine [mɑːdʒə'riːn] *n* margarine *f*

margin ['mɑːdʒɪn] *n* marge *f*; **~al** (*seat*) *n* (*POL*) siège disputé

marigold ['mærɪɡəuld] *n* souci *m*

marijuana [mærɪ'wɑːnə] *n* marijuana *f*

marina [mə'riːnə] *n* (*harbour*) marina *f*

marine [mə'riːn] *adj* marin(e) ♦ *n* fusilier marin; (*US*) marine *m*

marital ['mærɪtl] *adj* matrimonial(e); **~ status** situation *f* de famille

marjoram ['mɑːdʒərəm] *n* marjolaine *f*

mark [mɑːk] *n* marque *f*; (*of skid etc*) trace *f*; (*BRIT*: *SCOL*) note *f*; (*currency*) mark *m* ♦ *vt* marquer; (*stain*) tacher; (*BRIT*: *SCOL*) no-

ter; corriger; **to ~ time** marquer le pas; **~er** *n* (*sign*) jalon *m*; (*bookmark*) signet *m*

market ['mɑːkɪt] *n* marché *m* ♦ *vt* (*COMM*) commercialiser; **~ garden** (*BRIT*) *n* jardin maraîcher; **~ing** *n* marketing *m*; **~place** *n* place *f* du marché; (*COMM*) marché *m*; **~ research** *n* étude *f* de marché

marksman ['mɑːksmən] (*irreg*) *n* tireur *m* d'élite

marmalade ['mɑːməleɪd] *n* confiture *f* d'oranges

maroon [mə'ruːn] *vt*: **to be ~ed** être abandonné(e); (*fig*) être bloqué(e) ♦ *adj* bordeaux *inv*

marquee [mɑː'kiː] *n* chapiteau *m*

marriage ['mærɪdʒ] *n* mariage *m*; **~ certificate** *n* extrait *m* d'acte de mariage

married ['mærɪd] *adj* marié(e); (*life, love*) conjugal(e)

marrow ['mærəu] *n* moelle *f*; (*vegetable*) courge *f*

marry ['mærɪ] *vt* épouser, se marier avec (*subj*: *father, priest etc*) marier ♦ *vi* (*also*: **get married**) se marier

Mars [mɑːz] *n* (*planet*) Mars *f*

marsh [mɑːʃ] *n* marais *m*, marécage *m*

marshal ['mɑːʃl] *n* maréchal *m*; (*US*: *fire police*) ≈ capitaine *m*; (*SPORT*) membre *m* du service d'ordre ♦ *vt* rassembler

marshy ['mɑːʃɪ] *adj* marécageux(-euse)

martyr ['mɑːtə^r] *n* martyr(e); **~dom** *n* martyre *m*

marvel ['mɑːvl] *n* merveille *f* ♦ *vi*: **to ~ (at)** s'émerveiller (de); **~lous** (*US* **marvelous**) *adj* merveilleux(-euse)

Marxist ['mɑːksɪst] *adj* marxiste ♦ *n* marxiste *m/f*

marzipan ['mɑːzɪpæn] *n* pâte *f* d'amandes

mascara [mæs'kɑːrə] *n* mascara *m*

masculine ['mæskjulɪn] *adj* masculin(e)

mash [mæʃ] *vt* écraser, réduire en purée **~ed potatoes** *npl* purée *f* de pomme de terre

mask [mɑːsk] *n* masque *m* ♦ *vt* masquer

mason ['meɪsn] *n* (*also*: **stonemason**) maçon *m*; (*also*: **freemason**) franc-maçon *m*; **~ry** *n* maçonnerie *f*

masquerade [mæskəˈreɪd] *vi*: **to ~ as** se faire passer pour

mass [mæs] *n* multitude *f*, masse *f*; (*PHYSICS*) masse; (*REL*) messe *f* ♦ *cpd* (*communication*) de masse; (*unemployment*) massif(-ive) ♦ *vi* se masser; **the ~es** les masses; **~es of** des tas de

massacre [ˈmæsəkəʳ] *n* massacre *m*

massage [ˈmæsɑːʒ] *n* massage *m* ♦ *vt* masser

massive [ˈmæsɪv] *adj* énorme, massif(-ive)

mass media *n inv* mass-media *mpl*

mass production *n* fabrication *f* en série

mast [mɑːst] *n* mât *m*; (*RADIO*) pylône *m*

master [ˈmɑːstəʳ] *n* maître *m*; (*in secondary school*) professeur *m*; (*title for boys*): **M~ X** Monsieur X ♦ *vt* maîtriser; (*learn*) apprendre à fond; **~ly** *adj* magistral(e); **~mind** *n* esprit supérieur ♦ *vt* diriger, être le cerveau de; **M~ of Arts/Science** *n* ≃ maîtrise *f* (en lettres/sciences); **~piece** *n* chef-d'œuvre *m*; **~plan** *n* stratégie *f* d'ensemble; **~y** *n* maîtrise *f*; connaissance parfaite

mat [mæt] *n* petit tapis; (*also*: **doormat**) paillasson *m*; (*also*: **tablemat**) napperon *m* ♦ *adj* = **matt**

match [mætʃ] *n* allumette *f*; (*game*) match *m*, partie *f*; (*fig*) égal(e) ♦ *vt* (*also*: **~ up**) assortir; (*go well with*) aller bien avec, s'assortir à; (*equal*) égaler, valoir ♦ *vi* être assorti(e); **to be a good ~** être bien assorti(e); **~box** *n* boîte *f* d'allumettes; **~ing** *adj* assorti(e)

mate [meɪt] *n* (*inf*) copain (copine); (*animal*) partenaire *m/f*, mâle/femelle; (*in merchant navy*) second *m* ♦ *vi* s'accoupler

material [məˈtɪərɪəl] *n* (*substance*) matière *f*, matériau *m*; (*cloth*) tissu *m*, étoffe *f*; (*information, data*) données *fpl* ♦ *adj* matériel(le); (*relevant*): **evidence** pertinent(e); **~s** *npl* (*equipment*) matériaux *mpl*

maternal [məˈtɜːnl] *adj* maternel(le)

maternity [məˈtɜːnɪtɪ] *n* maternité *f*; **~ dress** *n* robe *f* de grossesse; **~ hospital** *n* maternité *f*

mathematical [mæθəˈmætɪkl] *adj* mathématique

mathematics [mæθəˈmætɪks] *n* mathématiques *fpl*

maths [mæθs] (*US* **math**) *n* math(s) *fpl*

matinée [ˈmætɪneɪ] *n* matinée *f*

mating call *n* appel *m* du mâle

matrices [ˈmeɪtrɪsiːz] *npl of* **matrix**

matriculation [mətrɪkjuˈleɪʃən] *n* inscription *f*

matrimonial [mætrɪˈməʊnɪəl] *adj* matrimonial(e), conjugal(e)

matrimony [ˈmætrɪmənɪ] *n* mariage *m*

matrix [ˈmeɪtrɪks] (*pl* **matrices**) *n* matrice *f*

matron [ˈmeɪtrən] *n* (*in hospital*) infirmière-chef *f*; (*in school*) infirmière

matt(t) [mæt] *adj* mat(e)

matted [ˈmætɪd] *adj* emmêlé(e)

matter [ˈmætəʳ] *n* question *f*; (*PHYSICS*) matière *f*; (*content*) contenu *m*, fond *m*; (*MED: pus*) pus *m* ♦ *vi* importer; **~s** *npl* (*affairs, situation*) la situation; **it doesn't ~** cela n'a pas d'importance; (*I don't mind*) cela ne fait rien; **what's the ~?** qu'est-ce qu'il y a?, qu'est-ce qui ne va pas?; **no ~ what** quoiqu'il arrive; **as a ~ of course** tout naturellement; **as a ~ of fact** en fait; **~-of-fact** *adj* terre à terre; (*voice*) neutre

mattress [ˈmætrɪs] *n* matelas *m*

mature [məˈtjuəʳ] *adj* mûr(e); (*cheese*) fait(e); (*wine*) arrivé(e) à maturité ♦ *vi* (*person*) mûrir; (*wine, cheese*) se faire

maul [mɔːl] *vt* lacérer

mauve [məʊv] *adj* mauve

maximum [ˈmæksɪməm] (*pl* **maxima**) *adj* maximum ♦ *n* maximum *m*

May [meɪ] *n* mai *m*; **~ Day** *n* le Premier Mai; *see also* **mayday**

may [meɪ] (*conditional* **might**) *vi* (*indicating possibility*): **he ~ come** il se peut qu'il vienne; (*be allowed to*): **~ I smoke?** puis-je fumer?; (*wishes*): **~ God bless you!** (que) Dieu vous bénisse!; **you ~ as well go** à votre place, je partirais

maybe [ˈmeɪbiː] *adv* peut-être; **~ he'll ...** peut-être qu'il ...

mayday [ˈmeɪdeɪ] *n* SOS *m*

mayhem [ˈmeɪhem] n grabuge m

mayonnaise [meɪəˈneɪz] n mayonnaise f

mayor [mɛəʳ] n maire m; **~ess** n épouse f du maire

maze [meɪz] n labyrinthe m, dédale m

M.D. n abbr (= Doctor of Medicine) titre universitaire; = **managing director**

me [miː] pron me, m' +vowel; (stressed, after prep) moi; **he heard ~** il m'a entendu(e); **give ~ a book** donnez-moi un livre; **after ~** après moi

meadow [ˈmedəʊ] n prairie f, pré m

meagre [ˈmiːɡəʳ] (US **meager**) adj maigre

meal [miːl] n repas m; (flour) farine f; **~time** n l'heure f du repas

mean [miːn] (pt, pp **meant**) adj (with money) avare, radin(e); (unkind) méchant(e); (shabby) misérable; (average) moyen(ne) ♦ vt signifier, vouloir dire; (refer to) faire allusion à, parler de; (intend): **to ~ to do** avoir l'intention de faire ♦ n moyenne f; **~s** npl (way, money) moyens mpl; **by ~s of** par l'intermédiaire de; au moyen de; **by all ~s!** je vous en prie!; **to be ~t for sb/sth** être destiné(e) à qn/qch; **do you ~ it?** vous êtes sérieux?; **what do you ~?** que voulez-vous dire?

meander [mɪˈændəʳ] vi faire des méandres

meaning [ˈmiːnɪŋ] n signification f, sens m; **~ful** adj significatif(-ive); (relationship, occasion) important(e); **~less** adj dénué(e) de sens

meanness [ˈmiːnnɪs] n (with money) avarice f; (unkindness) méchanceté f; (shabbiness) médiocrité f

meant [ment] pt, pp of **mean**

meantime [ˈmiːntaɪm] adv (also: **in the ~**) pendant ce temps

meanwhile [ˈmiːnwaɪl] adv = **meantime**

measles [ˈmiːzlz] n rougeole f

measure [ˈmeʒəʳ] vt, vi mesurer ♦ n mesure f; (ruler) règle (graduée); **~ments** npl mesures fpl; **chest/hip ~ment(s)** tour m de poitrine/hanches

meat [miːt] n viande f; **~ball** n boulette f de viande

Mecca [ˈmekə] n La Mecque

mechanic [mɪˈkænɪk] n mécanicien m; **~al** adj mécanique; **~s** n (PHYSICS) mécanique f ♦ npl (of reading, government etc) mécanisme m

mechanism [ˈmekənɪzəm] n mécanisme m

medal [ˈmedl] n médaille f; **~lion** [mɪˈdælɪən] n médaillon m; **~list** (US **medalist**) n (SPORT) médaillé(e)

meddle [ˈmedl] vi: **to ~ in** se mêler de, s'occuper de; **to ~ with** toucher à

media [ˈmiːdɪə] npl media mpl

mediaeval [medɪˈiːvl] adj = **medieval**

median [ˈmiːdɪən] (US) n (also: **~ strip**) bande médiane

mediate [ˈmiːdɪeɪt] vi servir d'intermédiaire

Medicaid ® [ˈmedɪkeɪd] (US) n assistance médicale aux indigents

medical [ˈmedɪkl] adj médical(e) ♦ n visite médicale

Medicare ® [ˈmedɪkeəʳ] (US) n assistance médicale aux personnes âgées

medication [medɪˈkeɪʃən] n (drugs) médicaments mpl

medicine [ˈmedsɪn] n médecine f; (drug) médicament m

medieval [medɪˈiːvl] adj médiéval(e)

mediocre [miːdɪˈəʊkəʳ] adj médiocre

meditate [ˈmedɪteɪt] vi méditer

Mediterranean [medɪtəˈreɪnɪən] adj méditerranéen(ne); **the ~ (Sea)** la (mer) Méditerranée

medium [ˈmiːdɪəm] (pl **media**) adj moyen(ne) ♦ n (means) moyen m; (pl **~s**: person) médium m; **the happy ~** le juste milieu; **~-sized** adj de taille moyenne; **~ wave** n ondes moyennes

medley [ˈmedlɪ] n mélange m; (MUS) pot-pourri m

meek [miːk] adj doux (douce), humble

meet [miːt] (pt, pp **met**) vt rencontrer; (by arrangement) retrouver, rejoindre; (for the first time) faire la connaissance de; (go and fetch): **I'll ~ you at the station** j'irai te chercher à la gare; (opponent, danger) faire face à; (obligations) satisfaire à ♦ vi (friends) se rencontrer, se retrouver; (in

session) se réunir; (join: lines, roads) se rejoindre; ~ **with** vt rencontrer; **~ing** n
rencontre f; (session: of club etc) réunion f;
(POL) meeting m; **she's at a ~ing** (COMM)
elle est en conférence

mega ['mɛgə] (inf) adv: **he's ~ rich** il est
hyper-riche; **~byte** n (COMPUT) méga-
octet m; **~phone** n porte-voix m inv

melancholy ['mɛlənkəlɪ] n mélancolie f
♦ adj mélancolique

mellow ['mɛləʊ] adj velouté(e); doux
(douce); (sound) mélodieux(-euse) ♦ vi
(person) s'adoucir

melody ['mɛlədɪ] n mélodie f

melon ['mɛlən] n melon m

melt [mɛlt] vi fondre ♦ vt faire fondre;
(metal) fondre; **~ away** vi fondre
complètement; **~ down** vt fondre;
~down n fusion f (du cœur d'un réacteur
nucléaire); **~ing pot** n (fig) creuset m

member ['mɛmbə'] n membre m; **M~ of
Parliament** (BRIT) député m; **M~ of the
European Parliament** Eurodéputé m;
~ship n adhésion f; statut m de membre;
(members) membres mpl, adhérents mpl;
~ship card n carte f de membre

memento [mə'mɛntəʊ] n souvenir m

memo ['mɛməʊ] n note f (de service)

memoirs ['mɛmwɑːz] npl mémoires mpl

memorandum [mɛmə'rændəm] (pl **memoranda**) n note f (de service)

memorial [mɪ'mɔːrɪəl] n mémorial m ♦ adj
commémoratif(-ive)

memorize ['mɛməraɪz] vt apprendre par
cœur; retenir

memory ['mɛmərɪ] n mémoire f; (recollection) souvenir m

men [mɛn] npl of **man**

menace ['mɛnɪs] n menace f; (nuisance)
plaie f ♦ vt menacer; **menacing** adj me-
naçant(e)

mend [mɛnd] vt réparer; (darn) raccommoder, repriser ♦ n: **on the ~** en voie de
guérison; **to ~ one's ways** s'amender;
~ing n réparation f; (clothes) raccommodage m

menial ['miːnɪəl] adj subalterne

meningitis [mɛnɪn'dʒaɪtɪs] n méningite f

menopause ['mɛnəʊpɔːz] n ménopause f

menstruation [mɛnstru'eɪʃən] n menstruation f

mental ['mɛntl] adj mental(e); **~ity**
[mɛn'tælɪtɪ] n mentalité f

mention ['mɛnʃən] n mention f ♦ vt mentionner, faire mention de; **don't ~ it!** je
vous en prie, il n'y a pas de quoi!

menu ['mɛnjuː] n (set ~, COMPUT) menu m;
(list of dishes) carte f

MEP n abbr = **Member of the European
Parliament**

mercenary ['məːsɪnərɪ] adj intéressé(e),
mercenaire ♦ n mercenaire m

merchandise ['məːtʃəndaɪz] n marchandises fpl

merchant ['məːtʃənt] n négociant m, marchand m; **~ bank** (BRIT) n banque f d'affaires; **~ navy** (US **merchant marine**) n
marine marchande

merciful ['məːsɪful] adj miséricordieux(-
euse), clément(e); **a ~ release** une délivrance

merciless ['məːsɪlɪs] adj impitoyable, sans
pitié

mercury ['məːkjurɪ] n mercure m

mercy ['məːsɪ] n pitié f, indulgence f; (REL)
miséricorde f; **at the ~ of** à la merci de

mere [mɪə'] adj simple; (chance) pur(e); **a
~ two hours** seulement deux heures; **~ly**
adv simplement, purement

merge [məːdʒ] vt unir ♦ vi (colours, shapes,
sounds) se mêler; (roads) se joindre;
(COMM) fusionner; **~r** n (COMM) fusion f

meringue [mə'ræŋ] n meringue f

merit ['mɛrɪt] n mérite m, valeur f

mermaid ['məːmeɪd] n sirène f

merry ['mɛrɪ] adj gai(e); **M~ Christmas!**
Joyeux Noël!; **~-go-round** n manège m

mesh [mɛʃ] n maille f

mesmerize ['mɛzməraɪz] vt hypnotiser;
fasciner

mess [mɛs] n désordre m, fouillis m, pagaille f; (muddle: of situation) gâchis m;
(dirt) saleté f; (MIL) mess m, cantine f; **~
about** (inf) vi perdre son temps; **~ about**

with (*inf*) *vt fus* tripoter; **~ around** (*inf*) *vi* = **mess about**; **~ around with** *vt fus* = **mess about with**; **~ up** *vt* (*dirty*) salir; (*spoil*) gâcher

message ['mɛsɪdʒ] *n* message *m*; **messenger** ['mɛsɪndʒəʳ] *n* messager *m*

Messrs ['mɛsəz] *abbr* (*on letters*) MM

messy ['mɛsɪ] *adj* sale; en désordre

met [mɛt] *pt*, *pp* *of* **meet**

metal ['mɛtl] *n* métal *m*; **~lic** [mɪ'tælɪk] *adj* métallique

meteorology [miːtɪə'rɔlədʒɪ] *n* météorologie *f*

meter ['miːtəʳ] *n* (*instrument*) compteur *m*; (*also*: **parking ~**) parcomètre *m*; (*US: unit*) = **metre**

method ['mɛθəd] *n* méthode *f*; **~ical** [mɪ'θɔdɪkl] *adj* méthodique; **M~ist** *n* méthodiste *m/f*

meths [mɛθs] (*BRIT*), **methylated spirit** ['mɛθɪleɪtɪd-] (*BRIT*) *n* alcool *m* à brûler

metre ['miːtəʳ] (*US* **meter**) *n* mètre *m*; **metric** ['mɛtrɪk] *adj* métrique

metropolitan [mɛtrə'pɔlɪtn] *adj* métropolitain(e); **the M~ Police** (*BRIT*) la police londonienne

mettle ['mɛtl] *n*: **to be on one's ~** être d'attaque

mew [mjuː] *vi* (*cat*) miauler

mews [mjuːz] (*BRIT*) *n*: **~ cottage** cottage aménagé dans une ancienne écurie

Mexico ['mɛksɪkəu] *n* Mexique *m*

miaow [miː'au] *vi* miauler

mice [maɪs] *npl of* **mouse**

micro ['maɪkrəu] *n* (*also*: **~computer**) micro-ordinateur *m*; **~chip** *n* puce *f*; **~phone** *n* microphone *m*; **~scope** *n* microscope *m*; **~wave** *n* (*also*: **~wave oven**) four *m* à micro-ondes

mid [mɪd] *adj*: **in ~ May** à la mi-mai; **~ afternoon** le milieu de l'après-midi; **in ~ air** en plein ciel; **~day** *n* midi *m*

middle ['mɪdl] *n* milieu *m*; (*waist*) taille *f* ♦ *adj* du milieu; (*average*) moyen(ne); **in the ~ of the night** au milieu de la nuit; **~-aged** *adj* d'un certain âge; **M~ Ages** *npl*: **the M~ Ages** le moyen âge; **~-class**

adj ≃ bourgeois(e); **~ class(es)** *n(pl)*: **the ~ class(es)** ≃ les classes moyennes; **M~ East** *n* Proche-Orient *m*, Moyen-Orient *m*; **~man** (*irreg*) *n* intermédiaire *m*; **~ name** *n* deuxième nom *m*; **~-of-the-road** *adj* (*politician*) modéré(e); (*music*) neutre; **~weight** *n* (*BOXING*) poids moyen; **middling** *adj* moyen(ne)

midge [mɪdʒ] *n* moucheron *m*

midget ['mɪdʒɪt] *n* nain(e)

Midlands ['mɪdləndz] *npl* comtés du centre de l'Angleterre

midnight ['mɪdnaɪt] *n* minuit *m*

midriff ['mɪdrɪf] *n* estomac *m*, taille *f*

midst [mɪdst] *n*: **in the ~ of** au milieu de

midsummer [mɪd'sʌməʳ] *n* milieu *m* de l'été

midway [mɪd'weɪ] *adj*, *adv*: **~ (between)** à mi-chemin (entre); **~ through ...** au milieu de ..., en plein(e) ...

midweek [mɪd'wiːk] *adj* au milieu de la semaine

midwife ['mɪdwaɪf] (*pl* **midwives**) *n* sage-femme *f*

might [maɪt] *vb see* **may** ♦ *n* puissance *f*, force *f*; **~y** *adj* puissant(e)

migraine ['miːgreɪn] *n* migraine *f*

migrant ['maɪgrənt] *adj* (*bird*) migrateur(-trice); (*worker*) saisonnier(-ère)

migrate [maɪ'greɪt] *vi* émigrer

mike [maɪk] *n abbr* (= *microphone*) micro *m*

mild [maɪld] *adj* doux (douce); (*reproach, infection*) léger(-ère); (*illness*) bénin(-igne); (*interest*) modéré(e); (*taste*) peu relevé(e) ♦ *n* (*beer*) bière légère; **~ly** *adv* doucement; légèrement; **to put it ~ly** c'est le moins qu'on puisse dire

mile [maɪl] *n* mi(l)le *m* (= *1609 m*); **~age** *n* distance *f* en milles; ≃ kilométrage *m*; **~ometer** [maɪ'lɔmɪtəʳ] *n* compteur *m* (kilométrique); **~stone** *n* borne *f*; (*fig*) jalon *m*

militant ['mɪlɪtnt] *adj* militant(e)

military ['mɪlɪtərɪ] *adj* militaire

militia [mɪ'lɪʃə] *n* milice(s) *f(pl)*

milk [mɪlk] *n* lait *m* ♦ *vt* (*cow*) traire; (*fig: person*) dépouiller, plumer; (: *situation*) exploiter à fond; ~ **chocolate** *n* chocolat *m* au lait; **~man** (*irreg*) *n* laitier *m*; **~ shake** *n* milk-shake *m*; **~y** *adj* (*drink*) au lait; (*colour*) laiteux(-euse); **M~y Way** *n* voie lactée

mill [mɪl] *n* moulin *m*; (*steel ~*) aciérie *f*; (*spinning ~*) filature *f*; (*flour ~*) minoterie *f* ♦ *vt* moudre, broyer ♦ *vi* (*also:* **~ about**) grouiller; **~er** *n* meunier *m*

millennium bug [mɪ'lenɪəm-] *n* bogue *m* or bug *m* de l'an 2000

milligram(me) ['mɪlɪgræm] *n* milligramme *m*

millimetre ['mɪlɪmiːtər] (*US* **millimeter**) *n* millimètre *m*

million ['mɪljən] *n* million *m*

milometer [maɪ'lɒmɪtər] *n* ≈ compteur *m* kilométrique

mime [maɪm] *n* mime *m* ♦ *vt, vi* mimer; **mimic** ['mɪmɪk] *n* imitateur(-trice) ♦ *vt* imiter, contrefaire

min. *abbr* = **minute(s)**; **minimum**

mince [mɪns] *vt* hacher ♦ *n* (*BRIT: CULIN*) viande hachée, hachis *m*; **~meat** *n* (*fruit*) *hachis de fruits secs utilisé en pâtisserie*; (*US: meat*) viande hachée, hachis; **~ pie** *n* (*sweet*) *sorte de tarte aux fruits secs*; **~r** *n* hachoir *m*

mind [maɪnd] *n* esprit *m* ♦ *vt* (*attend to, look after*) s'occuper de; (*be careful*) faire attention à; (*object to*): **I don't ~ the noise** le bruit ne me dérange pas; **I don't ~** cela ne me dérange pas; **it is on my ~** cela me préoccupe; **to my ~** à mon avis *or* sens; **to be out of one's ~** ne plus avoir toute sa raison; **to keep** *or* **bear sth in ~** tenir compte de qch; **to make up one's ~** se décider; **you, ...** remarquez ...; **never ~** ça ne fait rien; (*don't worry*) ne vous en faites pas; **"~ the step"** "attention à la marche"; **~er** *n* (*child-minder*) gardienne *f*; (*inf: bodyguard*) ange gardien (*fig*); **~ful** *adj*: **~ful of** attentif(-ive) à, soucieux(-euse) de; **~less** *adj* irréfléchi(e); (*boring: job*) idiot(e)

mine¹ [maɪn] *pron* le (la) mien(ne), les miens (miennes) ♦ *adj*: **this book is ~** ce livre est à moi

mine² [maɪn] *n* mine *f* ♦ *vt* (*coal*) extraire; (*ship*) miner; **~field** *n* champ *m* de mines; (*fig*) situation (très délicate); **~r** *n* mineur *m*

mineral ['mɪnərəl] *adj* minéral(e) ♦ *n* minéral *m*; **~s** *npl* (*BRIT: soft drinks*) boissons gazeuses; **~ water** *n* eau minérale

mingle ['mɪŋgl] *vi*: **to ~ with** se mêler à

miniature ['mɪnətʃər] *adj* (en) miniature ♦ *n* miniature *f*

minibus ['mɪnɪbʌs] *n* minibus *m*

Minidisc ® ['mɪnɪdɪsk] *n* minidisque *m*, Minidisc ® *m*

minimal ['mɪnɪml] *adj* minime

minimize ['mɪnɪmaɪz] *vt* (*reduce*) réduire au minimum; (*play down*) minimiser

minimum ['mɪnɪməm] (*pl* **minima**) *adj, n* minimum *m*

mining ['maɪnɪŋ] *n* exploitation minière

minister ['mɪnɪstər] *n* (*BRIT: POL*) ministre *m*; (*REL*) pasteur *m* ♦ *vi*: **to ~ to sb('s needs)** pourvoir aux besoins de qn; **~ial** [mɪnɪs'tɪərɪəl] (*BRIT*) *adj* (*POL*) ministériel(le); **ministry** *n* (*BRIT: POL*) ministère *m*; (*REL*): **to go into the ministry** devenir pasteur

mink [mɪŋk] *n* vison *m*

minor ['maɪnər] *adj* petit(e), de peu d'importance; (*MUS, poet, problem*) mineur(e) ♦ *n* (*LAW*) mineur(e)

minority [maɪ'nɒrɪtɪ] *n* minorité *f*

mint [mɪnt] *n* (*plant*) menthe *f*; (*sweet*) bonbon *m* à la menthe ♦ *vt* (*coins*) battre; **the (Royal) M~**, (*US*) **the (US) M~** ≈ l'Hôtel *m* de la Monnaie; **in ~ condition** à l'état de neuf

minus ['maɪnəs] *n* (*also:* **~ sign**) signe *m* moins ♦ *prep* moins

minute¹ [maɪ'njuːt] *adj* minuscule; (*detail, search*) minutieux(-euse)

minute² ['mɪnɪt] *n* minute *f*; **~s** *npl* (*official record*) procès-verbal, compte rendu

miracle ['mɪrəkl] *n* miracle *m*

mirror ['mɪrər] *n* miroir *m*, glace *f*; (*in car*) rétroviseur *m*

mirth [mɜːθ] *n* gaieté *f*

misadventure [mɪsəd'ventʃər] *n* mésaventure *f*

misapprehension [ˈmɪsæprɪˈhɛnʃən] *n* malentendu *m*, méprise *f*

misappropriate [mɪsəˈprəuprɪeɪt] *vt* détourner

misbehave [mɪsbɪˈheɪv] *vi* mal se conduire

miscalculate [mɪsˈkælkjuleɪt] *vt* mal calculer

miscarriage [ˈmɪskærɪdʒ] *n* (*MED*) fausse couche; **~ of justice** erreur *f* judiciaire

miscellaneous [mɪsɪˈleɪnɪəs] *adj* (*items*) divers(es); (*selection*) varié(e)

mischief [ˈmɪstʃɪf] *n* (*naughtiness*) sottises *fpl*; (*fun*) farce *f*; (*playfulness*) espièglerie *f*; (*maliciousness*) méchanceté *f*; **mischievous** [ˈmɪstʃɪvəs] *adj* (*playful, naughty*) coquin(e), espiègle

misconception [ˈmɪskənˈsɛpʃən] *n* idée fausse

misconduct [mɪsˈkɔndʌkt] *n* inconduite *f*; **professional ~** faute professionnelle

misdemeanour [mɪsdɪˈmiːnəʳ] (*US* **misdemeanor**) *n* écart *m* de conduite; infraction *f*

miser [ˈmaɪzəʳ] *n* avare *m/f*

miserable [ˈmɪzərəbl] *adj* (*person, expression*) malheureux(-euse); (*conditions*) misérable; (*weather*) maussade; (*offer, donation*) minable; (*failure*) pitoyable

miserly [ˈmaɪzəlɪ] *adj* avare

misery [ˈmɪzərɪ] *n* (*unhappiness*) tristesse *f*; (*pain*) souffrances *fpl*; (*wretchedness*) misère *f*

misfire [mɪsˈfaɪəʳ] *vi* rater

misfit [ˈmɪsfɪt] *n* (*person*) inadapté(e)

misfortune [mɪsˈfɔːtʃən] *n* malchance *f*, malheur *m*

misgiving [mɪsˈgɪvɪŋ] *n* (*apprehension*) craintes *fpl*; **to have ~s about** avoir des doutes quant à

misguided [mɪsˈgaɪdɪd] *adj* malavisé(e)

mishandle [mɪsˈhændl] *vt* (*mismanage*) mal s'y prendre pour faire *or* résoudre *etc*

mishap [ˈmɪshæp] *n* mésaventure *f*

misinform [mɪsɪnˈfɔːm] *vt* mal renseigner

misinterpret [mɪsɪnˈtəːprɪt] *vt* mal interpréter

misjudge [mɪsˈdʒʌdʒ] *vt* méjuger

mislay [mɪsˈleɪ] (*irreg: like* **lay**) *vt* égarer

mislead [mɪsˈliːd] (*irreg: like* **lead**) *vt* induire en erreur; **~ing** *adj* trompeur(-euse)

mismanage [mɪsˈmænɪdʒ] *vt* mal gérer

misplace [mɪsˈpleɪs] *vt* égarer

misprint [ˈmɪsprɪnt] *n* faute *f* d'impression

Miss [mɪs] *n* Mademoiselle

miss [mɪs] *vt* (*fail to get, attend or see*) manquer, rater; (*regret the absence of: person*) **I ~ him/it** il/cela me manque ♦ *vi* manquer ♦ *n* (*shot*) coup manqué; **~ out** (*BRIT*) *vt* oublier

misshapen [mɪsˈʃeɪpən] *adj* difforme

missile [ˈmɪsaɪl] *n* (*MIL*) missile *m*; (*object thrown*) projectile *m*

missing [ˈmɪsɪŋ] *adj* manquant(e); (*after escape, disaster: person*) disparu(e); **to go ~** disparaître; **to be ~** avoir disparu

mission [ˈmɪʃən] *n* mission *f*; **~ary** [ˈmɪʃənrɪ] *n* missionnaire *m/f*; **~ statement** *n* déclaration *f* d'intention

mist [mɪst] *n* brume *f* ♦ *vi* (*also:* **~ over**: *eyes*) s'embuer; **~ over** *vi* (*windows etc*) s'embuer; **~ up** *vi* = **mist over**

mistake [mɪsˈteɪk] (*irreg: like* **take**) *n* erreur *f*, faute *f* ♦ *vt* (*meaning, remark*) mal comprendre; se méprendre sur; **to make a ~** se tromper, faire une erreur; **by ~** par erreur, par inadvertance; **to ~ for** prendre pour; **~n** *pp of* **mistake** ♦ *adj* (*idea etc*) erroné(e); **to be ~n** faire erreur, se tromper

mister [ˈmɪstəʳ] (*inf*) *n* Monsieur *m*; *see also* **Mr**

mistletoe [ˈmɪsltəu] *n* gui *m*

mistook [mɪsˈtuk] *pt of* **mistake**

mistress [ˈmɪstrɪs] *n* maîtresse *f*; (*BRIT: in primary school*) institutrice *f*; (: *in secondary school*) professeur *m*

mistrust [mɪsˈtrʌst] *vt* se méfier de

misty [ˈmɪstɪ] *adj* brumeux(-euse); (*glasses, window*) embué(e)

misunderstand [mɪsʌndəˈstænd] (*irreg*) *vt, vi* mal comprendre; **~ing** *n* méprise *f*, malentendu *m*

misuse [*n* mɪsˈjuːs, *vb* mɪsˈjuːz] *n* mauvais

emploi; (*of power*) abus *m* ♦ *vt* mal employer; abuser de; **~ of funds** détournement *m* de fonds

mitigate ['mɪtɪgeɪt] *vt* atténuer

mitt(en) ['mɪt(n)] *n* mitaine *f*; moufle *f*

mix [mɪks] *vt* mélanger; (*sauce, drink etc*) préparer ♦ *vi* se mélanger; (*socialize*): **he doesn't ~ well** il est peu sociable ♦ *n* mélange *m*; **to ~ with** (*people*) fréquenter; **~ up** *vt* mélanger; (*confuse*) confondre; **~ed** *adj* (*feelings, reactions*) contradictoire; (*salad*) mélangé(e); (*school, marriage*) mixte; **~ed grill** *n* assortiment de grillades; **~ed-up** *adj* (*confused*) désorienté(e), embrouillé(e); **~er** *n* (*for food*) batteur *m*, mixer *m*; (*person*): **he is a good ~er** il est très liant; **~ture** *n* assortiment *m*, mélange *m*; (*MED*) préparation *f*; **~-up** *n* confusion *f*

mm *abbr* (= *millimetre*) mm

moan [məʊn] *n* gémissement *m* ♦ *vi* gémir; (*inf: complain*): **to ~ (about)** se plaindre (de)

moat [məʊt] *n* fossé *m*, douves *fpl*

mob [mɒb] *n* foule *f*; (*disorderly*) cohue *f* ♦ *vt* assaillir

mobile ['məʊbaɪl] *adj* mobile ♦ *n* mobile *m*; **~ home** *n* (grande) caravane; **~ phone** *n* téléphone portatif

mock [mɒk] *vt* ridiculiser; (*laugh at*) se moquer de ♦ *adj* faux (fausse); **~ exam** examen blanc; **~ery** *n* moquerie *f*, raillerie *f*; **to make a ~ery of** tourner en dérision; **~-up** *n* maquette *f*

mod [mɒd] *adj see* **convenience**

mode [məʊd] *n* mode *m*

model ['mɒdl] *n* modèle *m*; (*person: for fashion*) mannequin *m*; (*: for artist*) modèle ♦ *vt* (*with clay etc*) modeler ♦ *vi* travailler comme mannequin ♦ *adj* (*railway: toy*) modèle réduit *inv*; (*child, factory*) modèle; **to ~ clothes** présenter des vêtements; **to ~ o.s. on** imiter

modem ['məʊdem] (*COMPUT*) *n* modem *m*

moderate [*adj* 'mɒdərət, *vb* 'mɒdəreɪt] *adj* modéré(e); (*amount, change*) peu important(e) ♦ *vi* se calmer ♦ *vt* modérer

modern ['mɒdən] *adj* moderne; **~ize** *vt* moderniser

modest ['mɒdɪst] *adj* modeste; **~y** *n* modestie *f*

modify ['mɒdɪfaɪ] *vt* modifier

mogul ['məʊgl] *n* (*fig*) nabab *m*

mohair ['məʊhɛəʳ] *n* mohair *m*

moist [mɔɪst] *adj* humide, moite; **~en** *vt* humecter, mouiller légèrement; **~ure** *n* humidité *f*; **~urizer** *n* produit hydratant

molar ['məʊləʳ] *n* molaire *f*

molasses [mə'læsɪz] *n* mélasse *f*

mold [məʊld] (*US*) *n, vt* = **mould**

mole [məʊl] *n* (*animal, fig: spy*) taupe *f*; (*spot*) grain *m* de beauté

molest [mə'lest] *vt* (*harass*) molester; (*LAW: sexually*) attenter à la pudeur de

mollycoddle ['mɒlɪkɒdl] *vt* chouchouter, couver

molt [məʊlt] (*US*) *vi* = **moult**

molten ['məʊltən] *adj* fondu(e); (*rock*) en fusion

mom [mɒm] (*US*) *n* = **mum**

moment ['məʊmənt] *n* moment *m*, instant *m*; **at the ~** en ce moment; **at that ~** à ce moment-là; **~ary** *adj* momentané(e), passager(-ère); **~ous** [məʊ'mentəs] *adj* important(e), capital(e)

momentum [məʊ'mentəm] *n* élan *m*, vitesse acquise; (*fig*) dynamique *f*; **to gather ~** prendre de la vitesse

mommy ['mɒmɪ] (*US*) *n* maman *f*

Monaco ['mɒnəkəʊ] *n* Monaco *m*

monarch ['mɒnək] *n* monarque *m*; **~y** *n* monarchie *f*

monastery ['mɒnəstərɪ] *n* monastère *m*

Monday ['mʌndɪ] *n* lundi *m*

monetary ['mʌnɪtərɪ] *adj* monétaire

money ['mʌnɪ] *n* argent *m*; **to make ~** gagner de l'argent; **~ belt** *n* ceinture-portefeuille *f*; **~ order** *n* mandat *m*; **~-spinner** (*inf*) *n* mine *f* d'or (*fig*)

mongrel ['mʌŋgrəl] *n* (*dog*) bâtard *m*

monitor ['mɒnɪtəʳ] *n* (*TV, COMPUT*) moniteur *m* ♦ *vt* contrôler; (*broadcast*) être à l'écoute de; (*progress*) suivre (de près)

monk [mʌŋk] *n* moine *m*

monkey ['mʌŋkɪ] *n* singe *m*; ~ **nut** (*BRIT*) *n* cacahuète *f*

monopoly [mə'nɔpəlɪ] *n* monopole *m*

monotone ['mɔnətəʊn] *n* ton *m* (*or* voix *f*) monocorde; **monotonous** [mə'nɔtənəs] *adj* monotone

monsoon [mɔn'suːn] *n* mousson *f*

monster ['mɔnstəʳ] *n* monstre *m*; **monstrous** ['mɔnstrəs] *adj* monstrueux(-euse); (*huge*) gigantesque

month [mʌnθ] *n* mois *m*; **~ly** *adj* mensuel(le) ♦ *adv* mensuellement

monument ['mɔnjumənt] *n* monument *m*

moo [muː] *vi* meugler, beugler

mood [muːd] *n* humeur *f*, disposition *f*; **to be in a good/bad ~** être de bonne/ mauvaise humeur; **~y** *adj* (*variable*) d'humeur changeante, lunatique; (*sullen*) morose, maussade

moon [muːn] *n* lune *f*; **~light** *n* clair *m* de lune; **~lighting** *n* travail *m* au noir; **~lit** *adj*: **a ~lit night** une nuit de lune

moor [mʊəʳ] *n* lande *f* ♦ *vt* (*ship*) amarrer ♦ *vi* mouiller; **~land** *n* lande *f*

moose [muːs] *n* *inv* élan *m*

mop [mɔp] *n* balai *m* à laver; (*for dishes*) lavette *f* (à vaisselle) ♦ *vt* essuyer; **~ of hair** tignasse *f*; **~ up** *vt* éponger

mope [məʊp] *vi* avoir le cafard, se morfondre

moped ['məʊpɛd] *n* cyclomoteur *m*

moral ['mɔrl] *adj* moral(e) ♦ *n* morale *f*; **~s** *npl* (*attitude, behaviour*) moralité *f*

morale [mɔ'rɑːl] *n* moral *m*

morality [mə'rælɪtɪ] *n* moralité *f*

morass [mə'ræs] *n* marais *m*, marécage *m*

───── KEYWORD ─────

more [mɔːʳ] *adj* **1** (*greater in number etc*) plus (de), davantage; **more people/work (than)** plus de gens/de travail (que)
2 (*additional*) encore (de); **do you want (some) more tea?** voulez-vous encore du thé?; **I have no** *or* **I don't have any more money** je n'ai plus d'argent; **it'll take a few more weeks** ça prendra encore quelques semaines

♦ *pron* plus, davantage; **more than 10** plus de 10; **it cost more than we expected** cela a coûté plus que prévu; **I want more** j'en veux plus *or* davantage; **is there any more?** est-ce qu'il en reste?; **there's no more** il n'y en a plus; **a little more** un peu plus; **many/much more** beaucoup plus, bien davantage

♦ *adv*: **more dangerous/easily (than)** plus dangereux/facilement (que); **more and more expensive** de plus en plus cher; **more or less** plus ou moins; **more than ever** plus que jamais

─────────────

moreover [mɔː'rəʊvəʳ] *adv* de plus

morning ['mɔːnɪŋ] *n* matin *m*; matinée *f* ♦ *cpd* matinal(e); (*paper*) du matin; **in the ~** le matin; **7 o'clock in the ~** 7 heures du matin; **~ sickness** *n* nausées matinales

Morocco [mə'rɔkəʊ] *n* Maroc *m*

moron ['mɔːrɔn] (*inf*) *n* idiot(e)

Morse [mɔːs] *n*: **~ code** morse *m*

morsel ['mɔːsl] *n* bouchée *f*

mortar ['mɔːtəʳ] *n* mortier *m*

mortgage ['mɔːgɪdʒ] *n* hypothèque *f*; (*loan*) prêt *m* (*or* crédit *m*) hypothécaire ♦ *vt* hypothéquer; **~ company** (*US*) *n* société *f* de crédit immobilier

mortuary ['mɔːtjuərɪ] *n* morgue *f*

mosaic [məʊ'zeɪk] *n* mosaïque *f*

Moscow ['mɔskəʊ] *n* Moscou

Moslem ['mɔzləm] *adj*, *n* = **Muslim**

mosque [mɔsk] *n* mosquée *f*

mosquito [mɔs'kiːtəʊ] (*pl* **~es**) *n* moustique *m*

moss [mɔs] *n* mousse *f*

most [məʊst] *adj* la plupart de; le plus de ♦ *pron* la plupart ♦ *adv* le plus; (*very*) très, extrêmement; **the ~** (*also:* + *adjective*) le plus; **~ of** la plus grande partie de; **~ of them** la plupart d'entre eux; **I saw (the) ~** j'en ai vu la plupart; c'est moi qui en ai vu le plus; **at the (very) ~** au plus; **to make the ~ of** profiter au maximum de; **~ly** *adv* (*chiefly*) surtout; (*usually*) généralement

MOT *n abbr* (*BRIT*: *Ministry of Transport*)

the MOT (test) *la visite technique (annuelle) obligatoire des véhicules à moteur*
motel [mǝʊ'tɛl] *n* motel *m*
moth [mɔθ] *n* papillon *m* de nuit; (*in clothes*) mite *f*
mother ['mʌðǝ'] *n* mère *f* ♦ *vt* (*act as ~ to*) servir de mère à; (*pamper, protect*) materner; ~ **country** mère patrie; **~hood** *n* maternité *f*; **~-in-law** *n* belle-mère *f*; **~ly** *adj* maternel(le); **~-of-pearl** *n* nacre *f*; **M~'s Day** *n* fête *f* des Mères; **~-to-be** *n* future maman; ~ **tongue** *n* langue maternelle
motion ['mǝʊʃǝn] *n* mouvement *m*; (*gesture*) geste *m*; (*at meeting*) motion *f* ♦ *vt, vi:* **to ~ (to) sb to do** faire signe à qn de faire; **~less** *adj* immobile, sans mouvement; ~ **picture** *n* film *m*
motivated ['mǝʊtɪveɪtɪd] *adj* motivé(e); **motivation** [mǝʊtɪ'veɪʃǝn] *n* motivation *f*
motive ['mǝʊtɪv] *n* motif *m*, mobile *m*
motley ['mɔtlɪ] *adj* hétéroclite
motor ['mǝʊtǝ'] *n* moteur *m*; (*BRIT: inf: vehicle*) auto *f* ♦ *cpd* (*industry, vehicle*) automobile; **~bike** *n* moto *f*; **~boat** *n* bateau *m* à moteur; **~car** (*BRIT*) *n* automobile *f*; **~cycle** *n* vélomoteur *m*; **~cycle racing** *n* course *f* de motos; **~cyclist** *n* motocycliste *m/f*; **~ing** (*BRIT*) *n* tourisme *m* automobile; **~ist** *n* automobiliste *m/f*; ~ **mechanic** *n* mécanicien *m* garagiste; ~ **racing** (*BRIT*) *n* course *f* automobile; **~way** (*BRIT*) *n* autoroute *f*
mottled ['mɔtld] *adj* tacheté(e), marbré(e)
motto ['mɔtǝʊ] (*pl* **~es**) *n* devise *f*
mould [mǝʊld] (*US* **mold**) *n* moule *m*; (*mildew*) moisissure *f* ♦ *vt* mouler, modeler; (*fig*) façonner; **mo(u)ldy** *adj* moisi(e); (*smell*) de moisi
moult [mǝʊlt] (*US* **molt**) *vi* muer
mound [maʊnd] *n* monticule *m*, tertre *m*; (*heap*) monceau *m*, tas *m*
mount [maʊnt] *n* mont *m*, montagne *f* ♦ *vt* monter ♦ *vi* (*inflation, tension*) augmenter; (*also:* ~ **up:** *problems etc*) s'accumuler; ~ **up** *vi* (*bills, costs, savings*) s'accumuler
mountain ['maʊntɪn] *n* montagne *f* ♦ *cpd* de montagne; ~ **bike** *n* VTT *m*, vélo

tout-terrain; **~eer** [maʊntɪ'nɪǝ'] *n* alpiniste *m/f*; **~eering** *n* alpinisme *m*; **~ous** *adj* montagneux(-euse); ~ **rescue team** *n* équipe *f* de secours en montagne; **~side** *n* flanc *m* or versant *m* de la montagne
mourn [mɔːn] *vt* pleurer ♦ *vi:* **to ~ (for)** (*person*) pleurer (la mort de); **~er** *n* parent(e) *or* ami(e) du défunt; personne *f* en deuil; **~ing** *n* deuil *m*; **in ~ing** en deuil
mouse [maʊs] (*pl* **mice**) *n* (*also COMPUT*) souris *f*; ~ **mat**, ~ **pad** *n* (*COMPUT*) tapis *m* de souris; **~trap** *n* souricière *f*
mousse [muːs] *n* mousse *f*
moustache [mǝs'taːʃ] (*US* **mustache**) *n* moustache(s) *f(pl)*
mousy ['maʊsɪ] *adj* (*hair*) d'un châtain terne
mouth [maʊθ] (*pl* **~s**) *n* bouche *f*; (*of dog, cat*) gueule *f*; (*of river*) embouchure *f*; (*of hole, cave*) ouverture *f*; **~ful** *n* bouchée *f*; ~ **organ** *n* harmonica *m*; **~piece** *n* (*of musical instrument*) embouchure *f*; (*spokesman*) porte-parole *m inv*; **~wash** *n* eau *f* dentifrice; **~-watering** *adj* qui met l'eau à la bouche
movable ['muːvǝbl] *adj* mobile
move [muːv] *n* (*~ment*) mouvement *m*; (*in game*) coup *m*; (: *turn to play*) tour *m*; (*change: of house*) déménagement *m*; (: *of job*) changement *m* d'emploi ♦ *vt* déplacer, bouger; (*emotionally*) émouvoir; (*POL: resolution etc*) proposer; (*in game*) jouer ♦ *vi* (*gen*) bouger, remuer; (*traffic*) circuler; (*also:* ~ **house**) déménager; (*situation*) progresser; **that was a good ~** bien joué!; **to get a ~ on** se dépêcher, se remuer; **to ~ sb to do sth** pousser or inciter qn à faire qch; ~ **about** *vi* (*fidget*) remuer; (*travel*) voyager, se déplacer; (*change residence, job*) ne pas rester au même endroit; ~ **along** *vi* se pousser; ~ **around** *vi* = **move about;** ~ **away** *vi* s'en aller; ~ **back** *vi* revenir, retourner; ~ **forward** *vi* avancer; ~ **in** *vi* (*to a house*) emménager; (*police, soldiers*) intervenir; ~ **on** *vi* se remettre en route; ~ **out** *vi* (*of house*) déménager; ~ **over** *vi* se pousser,

se déplacer; ~ **up** *vi* (*pupil*) passer dans la classe supérieure; (*employee*) avoir de l'avancement; ~**able** *adj* = **movable**

movement ['mu:vmənt] *n* mouvement *m*

movie ['mu:vɪ] *n* film *m*; **the ~s** le cinéma

moving ['mu:vɪŋ] *adj* en mouvement; (*emotional*) émouvant(e)

mow [məʊ] (*pt* **mowed**, *pp* **mowed** or **mown**) *vt* faucher; (*lawn*) tondre; ~ **down** *vt* faucher; ~**er** *n* (*also*: **lawn-mower**) tondeuse *f* à gazon

MP *n abbr* = **Member of Parliament**

mph *abbr* = **miles per hour**

Mr ['mɪstəʳ] *n*: ~ **Smith** Monsieur Smith, M. Smith

Mrs ['mɪsɪz] *n*: ~ **Smith** Madame Smith, Mme Smith

Ms [mɪz] *n* (= *Miss or Mrs*): ~ **Smith** Madame Smith, Mme Smith

MSc *abbr* = **Master of Science**

MSP *n abbr* = (*Member of the Scottish Parliament*) député *m* au Parlement écossais

much [mʌtʃ] *adj* beaucoup de ♦ *adv, n, pron* beaucoup; **how ~ is it?** combien est-ce que ça coûte?; **too ~** trop (de); **as ~ as** autant de

muck [mʌk] *n* (*dirt*) saleté *f*; ~ **about** or **around** (*inf*) *vi* faire l'imbécile; ~ **up** (*inf*) *vt* (*exam, interview*) se planter à (*fam*); ~**y** *adj* (*très*) sale

mud [mʌd] *n* boue *f*

muddle ['mʌdl] *n* (*mess*) pagaille *f*, désordre *m*; (*mix-up*) confusion *f* ♦ *vt* (*also*: ~ **up**) embrouiller; ~ **through** *vi* se débrouiller

muddy ['mʌdɪ] *adj* boueux(-euse)

mudguard ['mʌdgɑ:d] *n* garde-boue *m inv*

muesli ['mju:zlɪ] *n* muesli *m*

muffle ['mʌfl] *vt* (*sound*) assourdir, étouffer; (*against cold*) emmitoufler; ~**d** *adj* (*sound*) étouffé(e); ~**r** (*US*) *n* (*AUT*) silencieux *m*

mug [mʌg] *n* (*cup*) grande tasse (*sans soucoupe*); (: *for beer*) chope *f*; (*inf*: *face*) bouille *f*; (: *fool*) poire *f* ♦ *vt* (*assault*) agresser; ~**ger** *n* agresseur *m*; ~**ging** *n*

agression *f*

muggy ['mʌgɪ] *adj* lourd(e), moite

multi-level ['mʌltɪlevl] (*US*) *adj* = **multi-storey**

multiple ['mʌltɪpl] *adj* multiple ♦ *n* multiple *m*; ~ **sclerosis** [-sklɪ'rəʊsɪs] *n* sclérose *f* en plaques

multiplex cinema ['mʌltɪpleks-] *n* cinéma *m* multisalles

multiplication [mʌltɪplɪ'keɪʃən] *n* multiplication *f*; **multiply** ['mʌltɪplaɪ] *vt* multiplier ♦ *vi* se multiplier

multistorey ['mʌltɪ'stɔːrɪ] (*BRIT*) *adj* (*building*) à étages; (*car park*) à étages or niveaux multiples ♦ *n* (*car park*) parking *m* à plusieurs étages

mum [mʌm] (*BRIT*: *inf*) *n* maman *f* ♦ *adj*: **to keep ~** ne pas souffler mot

mumble ['mʌmbl] *vt, vi* marmotter, marmonner

mummy ['mʌmɪ] *n* (*BRIT*: *mother*) maman *f*; (*embalmed*) momie *f*

mumps [mʌmps] *n* oreillons *mpl*

munch [mʌntʃ] *vt, vi* mâcher

mundane [mʌn'deɪn] *adj* banal(e), terre à terre *inv*

municipal [mju:'nɪsɪpl] *adj* municipal(e)

murder ['mə:dəʳ] *n* meurtre *m*, assassinat *m* ♦ *vt* assassiner; ~**er** *n* meurtrier *m*, assassin *m*; ~**ous** ['mə:dərəs] *adj* meurtrier(-ère)

murky ['mə:kɪ] *adj* sombre, ténébreux(-euse); (*water*) trouble

murmur ['mə:məʳ] *n* murmure *m* ♦ *vt, vi* murmurer

muscle ['mʌsl] *n* muscle *m*; (*fig*) force *f*; ~ **in** *vi* (*on territory*) envahir; (*on success*) exploiter; **muscular** ['mʌskjʊləʳ] *adj* musculaire; (*person, arm*) musclé(e)

muse [mju:z] *vi* méditer, songer

museum [mju:'zɪəm] *n* musée *m*

mushroom ['mʌʃrʊm] *n* champignon *m* ♦ *vi* pousser comme un champignon

music ['mju:zɪk] *n* musique *f*; ~**al** *adj* musical(e); (*person*) musicien(ne) ♦ *n* (*show*) comédie musicale; ~**al instrument** *n* instrument *m* de musique; ~ **centre** *n* chaîne compacte; **~ian** [mjuː'zɪʃən] n musicien(ne)

Muslim ['mʌzlɪm] adj, n musulman(e)

muslin ['mʌzlɪn] n mousseline f

mussel ['mʌsl] n moule f

must [mʌst] aux vb (obligation): **I ~ do it** je dois le faire, il faut que je le fasse; (probability): **he ~ be there by now** il doit y être maintenant, il y est probablement maintenant; (suggestion, invitation): **you ~ come and see me** il faut que vous veniez me voir; (indicating sth unwelcome): **why ~ he behave so badly?** qu'est-ce qui le pousse à se conduire si mal? ♦ n nécessité f, impératif m; **it's a ~** c'est indispensable

mustache ['mʌstæʃ] (US) n = **moustache**

mustard ['mʌstəd] n moutarde f

muster ['mʌstəʳ] vt rassembler

mustn't ['mʌsnt] = **must not**

mute [mjuːt] adj muet(te); **~d** adj (colour) sourd(e); (reaction) voilé(e)

mutiny ['mjuːtɪnɪ] n mutinerie f ♦ vi se mutiner

mutter ['mʌtəʳ] vt, vi marmonner, marmotter

mutton ['mʌtn] n mouton m

mutual ['mjuːtʃuəl] adj mutuel(le), réciproque; (benefit, interest) commun(e); **~ly** adv mutuellement

muzzle ['mʌzl] n museau m; (protective device) muselière f; (of gun) gueule f ♦ vt museler

my [maɪ] adj mon (ma), mes pl; **~ house/car/gloves** ma maison/mon auto/mes gants; **I've washed ~ hair/cut ~ finger** je me suis lavé les cheveux/coupé le doigt; **~self** [maɪ'self] pron (reflexive) me; (emphatic) moi-même; (after prep) moi; see also **oneself**

mysterious [mɪs'tɪərɪəs] adj mystérieux(-euse)

mystery ['mɪstərɪ] n mystère m

mystify ['mɪstɪfaɪ] vt mystifier; (puzzle) ébahir

myth [mɪθ] n mythe m; **~ology** [mɪ'θɒlədʒɪ] n mythologie f

N, n

n/a abbr = **not applicable**

naff [næf] (BRIT: inf) adj nul(le)

nag [næg] vt (scold) être toujours après, reprendre sans arrêt; **~ging** adj (doubt, pain) persistant(e)

nail [neɪl] n (human) ongle m; (metal) clou m ♦ vt clouer; **to ~ sb down to a date/price** contraindre qn à accepter or donner une date/un prix; **~brush** n brosse f à ongles; **~file** n lime f à ongles; **~ polish** n vernis m à ongles; **~ polish remover** n dissolvant m, **~ scissors** npl ciseaux mpl à ongles; **~ varnish** (BRIT) n = **nail polish**

naïve [naɪ'iːv] adj naïf(-ïve)

naked ['neɪkɪd] adj nu(e)

name [neɪm] n nom m; (reputation) réputation f ♦ vt nommer; (identify: accomplice etc) citer; (price, date) fixer, donner; **by ~** par son nom; **in the ~ of** au nom de; **what's your ~?** comment vous appelez-vous?; **~less** adj sans nom; (witness, contributor) anonyme; **~ly** adv à savoir; **~sake** n homonyme m

nanny ['nænɪ] n bonne f d'enfants

nap [næp] n (sleep) (petit) somme ♦ vi: **to be caught ~ping** être pris à l'improviste or en défaut

nape [neɪp] n: **~ of the neck** nuque f

napkin ['næpkɪn] n serviette f (de table)

nappy ['næpɪ] (BRIT) n couche f (gen pl); **~ rash** n: **to have ~ rash** avoir les fesses rouges

narcissus [naː'sɪsəs] (pl **narcissi**) n narcisse m

narcotic [naː'kɒtɪk] n (drug) stupéfiant m; (MED) narcotique m

narrative ['nærətɪv] n récit m

narrow ['nærəu] adj étroit(e); (fig) restreint(e), limité(e) ♦ vi (road) devenir plus étroit, se rétrécir; (gap, difference) se réduire; **to have a ~ escape** l'échapper belle; **to ~ sth down to** réduire qch à; **~ly** adv:

he **~ly missed** *injury/the tree* il a failli se blesser/rentrer dans l'arbre; **~-minded** *adj* à l'esprit étroit, borné(e); *(attitude)* borné

nasty ['nɑːstɪ] *adj* *(person: malicious)* méchant(e); (: *rude*) très désagréable; *(smell)* dégoûtant(e); *(wound, situation, disease)* mauvais(e)

nation ['neɪʃən] *n* nation *f*

national ['næʃənl] *adj* national(e) ♦ *n* *(abroad)* ressortissant(e); *(when home)* national(e); **~ anthem** *n* hymne national; **~ dress** *n* costume national; **N~ Health Service** *(BRIT)* *n* service national de santé; ≈ Sécurité Sociale; **N~ Insurance** *(BRIT)* *n* ≈ Sécurité Sociale; **~ism** *n* nationalisme *m*; **~ist** *adj* nationaliste ♦ *n* nationaliste *m/f*; **~ity** [næʃə'nælɪtɪ] *n* nationalité *f*; **~ize** *vt* nationaliser; **~ly** *adv* *(as a nation)* du point de vue national; *(nationwide)* dans le pays entier; **~ park** *n* parc national

National Trust

🛈 Le **National Trust** *est un organisme indépendant, à but non lucratif, dont la mission est de protéger et de mettre en valeur les monuments et les sites britanniques en raison de leur intérêt historique ou de leur beauté naturelle.*

nationwide ['neɪʃənwaɪd] *adj* s'étendant à l'ensemble du pays, *(problem)* à l'échelle du pays entier ♦ *adv* à travers *or* dans tout le pays

native ['neɪtɪv] *n* autochtone *m/f*, habitant(e) du pays ♦ *adj* du pays, indigène; *(country)* natal(e); *(ability)* inné(e); **a ~ of Russia** une personne originaire de Russie; **a ~ speaker of French** une personne de langue maternelle française; **N~ American** *n* Indien(ne) d'Amérique; **~ language** *n* langue maternelle

NATO ['neɪtəʊ] *n abbr* (= *North Atlantic Treaty Organization*) OTAN *f*

natural ['nætʃrəl] *adj* naturel(le); **~ gas** *n* gaz naturel; **~ist** *n* naturaliste *m/f*; **~ly** *adv* naturellement

nature ['neɪtʃə*ʳ*] *n* nature *f*; **by ~** par tempérament, de nature

naught [nɔːt] *n* = **nought**

naughty ['nɔːtɪ] *adj* *(child)* vilain(e), pas sage

nausea ['nɔːsɪə] *n* nausée *f*

naval ['neɪvl] *adj* naval(e); **~ officer** *n* officier *m* de marine

nave [neɪv] *n* nef *f*

navel ['neɪvl] *n* nombril *m*

navigate ['nævɪgeɪt] *vt* *(steer)* diriger; *(plot course)* naviguer ♦ *vi* naviguer; **navigation** [nævɪ'geɪʃən] *n* navigation *f*

navvy ['nævɪ] *(BRIT)* *n* terrassier *m*

navy ['neɪvɪ] *n* marine *f*; **~(-blue)** *adj* bleu marine *inv*

Nazi ['nɑːtsɪ] *n* Nazi(e)

NB *abbr* (= *nota bene*) NB

near [nɪə*ʳ*] *adj* proche ♦ *adv* près ♦ *prep* (*also:* **~ to**) près de ♦ *vt* approcher de; **~by** [nɪə'baɪ] *adj* proche ♦ *adv* tout près, à proximité; **~ly** *adv* presque; **I ~ly fell** j'ai failli tomber; **~ miss** *n* *(AVIAT)* quasi-collision *f*; **that was a ~ miss** *(gen)* il s'en est fallu de peu; *(of shot)* c'est passé très près; **~side** *n* *(AUT: in Britain)* côté *m* gauche; (: *in US, Europe etc)* côté droit; **~-sighted** *adj* myope

neat [niːt] *adj* *(person, work)* soigné(e); *(room etc)* bien tenu(e) *or* rangé(e); *(skilful)* habile; *(spirits)* pur(e); **~ly** *adv* avec soin *or* ordre; habilement

necessarily ['nesɪsrɪlɪ] *adv* nécessairement

necessary ['nesɪsrɪ] *adj* nécessaire; **necessity** [nɪ'sesɪtɪ] *n* nécessité *f*; *(thing needed)* chose nécessaire *or* essentielle; **necessities** *npl* nécessaire *m*

neck [nɛk] *n* cou *m*; *(of animal, garment)* encolure *f*; *(of bottle)* goulot *m* ♦ *vi* (inf) se peloter; **~ and ~** à égalité; **~lace** *n* collier *m*; **~line** *n* encolure *f*; **~tie** *n* cravate *f*

need [niːd] *n* besoin *m* ♦ *vt* avoir besoin de; **to ~ to do** devoir faire; avoir besoin de faire; **you don't ~ to go** vous n'avez pas besoin *or* vous n'êtes pas obligé de partir

needle ['niːdl] *n* aiguille *f* ♦ *vt* asticoter, tourmenter

needless ['niːdlɪs] *adj* inutile

needlework ['niːdlwəːk] *n* (*activity*) travaux *mpl* d'aiguille; (*object(s)*) ouvrage *m*

needn't ['niːdnt] = **need not**

needy ['niːdɪ] *adj* nécessiteux(-euse)

negative ['nɛgətɪv] *n* (PHOT, ELEC) négatif *m*; (LING) terme *m* de négation ♦ *adj* négatif(-ive); **~ equity** situation dans laquelle la valeur d'une maison est inférieure à celle de l'emprunt-logement contracté pour la payer

neglect [nɪ'glɛkt] *vt* négliger ♦ *n* (*of person, duty, garden*) le fait de négliger; (*state of* ~) abandon *m*; **~ed** *adj* négligé(e), à l'abandon

negligee ['nɛglɪʒeɪ] *n* déshabillé *m*

negotiate [nɪ'gəuʃɪeɪt] *vi, vt* négocier; **negotiation** [nɪgəuʃɪ'eɪʃən] *n* négociation *f*, pourparlers *mpl*

neigh [neɪ] *vi* hennir

neighbour ['neɪbəʳ] (*US* **neighbor**) *n* voisin(e); **~hood** *n* (*place*) quartier *m*; (*people*) voisinage *m*; **~ing** *adj* voisin(e), avoisinant(e); **~ly** *adj* obligeant(e); (*action etc*) amical(e)

neither ['naɪðəʳ] *adj, pron* aucun(e) (des deux), ni l'un(e) ni l'autre ♦ *conj*: **I didn't move and ~ did Claude** je n'ai pas bougé, (et) Claude non plus ♦ *adv*: **~ good nor bad** ni bon ni mauvais; **..., ~ did I refuse ...**, (et *or* mais) je n'ai pas non plus refusé

neon ['niːɔn] *n* néon *m*; **~ light** *n* lampe *f* au néon

nephew ['nɛvjuː] *n* neveu *m*

nerve [nəːv] *n* nerf *m*; (*fig: courage*) sang-froid *m*, courage *m*; (: *impudence*) aplomb *m*, toupet *m*; **to have a fit of ~s** avoir le trac; **~-racking** *adj* angoissant(e)

nervous ['nəːvəs] *adj* nerveux(-euse); (*anxious*) inquiet(-ète), plein(e) d'appréhension; (*timid*) intimidé(e); **~ breakdown** *n* dépression nerveuse

nest [nɛst] *n* nid *m* ♦ *vi* (se) nicher, faire

son nid; **~ egg** *n* (*fig*) bas *m* de laine, magot *m*

nestle ['nɛsl] *vi* se blottir

net [nɛt] *n* filet *m*; **the Net** (INTERNET) le Net ♦ *adj* net(te) ♦ *vt* (*fish etc*) prendre au filet; (*profit*) rapporter; **~ball** *n* netball *m*

Netherlands ['nɛðələndz] *npl*: **the ~** les Pays-Bas *mpl*

nett [nɛt] *adj* = **net**

netting ['nɛtɪŋ] *n* (*for fence etc*) treillis *m*, grillage *m*

nettle ['nɛtl] *n* ortie *f*

network ['nɛtwəːk] *n* réseau *m*

neurotic [njuə'rɔtɪk] *adj* névrosé(e)

neuter ['njuːtəʳ] *adj* neutre ♦ *vt* (*cat etc*) châtrer, couper

neutral ['njuːtrəl] *adj* neutre ♦ *n* (AUT) point mort; **~ize** *vt* neutraliser

never ['nɛvəʳ] *adv* (ne ...) jamais; **~ again** plus jamais; **~ in my life** jamais de ma vie; *see also* **mind**; **~-ending** *adj* interminable; **~theless** *adv* néanmoins, malgré tout

new [njuː] *adj* nouveau (nouvelle); (*brand* ~) neuf (neuve); **N~ Age** *n* New Age *m*; **~born** *adj* nouveau-né(e); **~comer** *n* nouveau venu/nouvelle venue; **~-fangled** ['njuː'fæŋgld] (*pej*) *adj* ultramoderne (et farfelu(e)); **~-found** *adj* (*enthusiasm*) de fraîche date; (*friend*) nouveau (nouvelle); **~ly** *adv* nouvellement, récemment; **~lyweds** *npl* jeunes mariés *mpl*

news [njuːz] *n* nouvelle(s) *f(pl)*; (RADIO, TV) informations *fpl*, actualités *fpl*; **a piece of ~** une nouvelle; **~ agency** *n* agence *f* de presse; **~agent** (BRIT) *n* marchand *m* de journaux; **~caster** *n* présentateur(-trice); **~ flash** *n* flash *m* d'information; **~letter** *n* bulletin *m*; **~paper** *n* journal *m*; **~print** *n* papier *m* (de) journal; **~reader** *n* = **newscaster**; **~reel** *n* actualités (filmées); **~ stand** *n* kiosque *m* à journaux

newt [njuːt] *n* triton *m*

New Year *n* Nouvel An; **~'s Day** *n* le jour de l'An; **~'s Eve** *n* la Saint-Sylvestre

New Zealand [-'ziːlənd] *n* la Nouvelle-Zélande; **~er** *n* Néo-zélandais(e)

next [nɛkst] *adj* (*seat, room*) voisin(e), d'à côté; (*meeting, bus stop*) suivant(e); (*in time*) prochain(e) ♦ *adv* (*place*) à côté; (*time*) la fois suivante, la prochaine fois; (*afterwards*) ensuite; **the ~ day** le lendemain, le jour suivant or d'après; **~ year** l'année prochaine; **~ time** la prochaine fois; **~ to** à côté de; **~ to nothing** presque rien; **~, please!** (*at doctor's etc*) au suivant!; **~ door** *adv* à côté ♦ *adj* d'à côté; **~-of-kin** *n* parent *m* le plus proche

NHS *n abbr* = **National Health Service**

nib [nɪb] *n* (bec *m* de) plume *f*

nibble ['nɪbl] *vt* grignoter

nice [naɪs] *adj* (*pleasant, likeable*) agréable; (*pretty*) joli(e); (*kind*) gentil(le); **~ly** *adv* agréablement; joliment; gentiment

niceties ['naɪsɪtɪz] *npl* subtilités *fpl*

nick [nɪk] *n* (*indentation*) encoche *f*; (*wound*) entaille *f* ♦ *vt* (BRIT: *inf*) faucher, piquer; **in the ~ of time** juste à temps

nickel ['nɪkl] *n* nickel *m*; (US) pièce *f* de 5 cents

nickname ['nɪkneɪm] *n* surnom *m* ♦ *vt* surnommer

nicotine patch ['nɪkəti:n-] *n* timbre *m* anti-tabac, patch *m*

niece [ni:s] *n* nièce *f*

Nigeria [naɪ'dʒɪərɪə] *n* Nigéria *m or f*

niggling ['nɪglɪŋ] *adj* (*person*) tatillon(ne); (*detail*) insignifiant(e); (*doubts, injury*) persistant(e)

night [naɪt] *n* nuit *f*; (*evening*) soir *m*; **at ~** la nuit; **by ~** de nuit; **the ~ before last** avant-hier soir; **~cap** *n boisson prise avant le coucher*; **~ club** *n* boîte *f* de nuit; **~dress** *n* chemise *f* de nuit; **~fall** *n* tombée *f* de la nuit; **~gown** *n* chemise *f* de nuit; **~ie** ['naɪtɪ] *n* chemise *f* de nuit; **~ingale** ['naɪtɪŋgeɪl] *n* rossignol *m*; **~life** *n* vie *f* nocturne; **~ly** *adj* de chaque nuit or soir; (*by night*) nocturne ♦ *adv* chaque nuit or soir; **~mare** *n* cauchemar *m*; **~ porter** *n* gardien *m* de nuit, concierge *m* de service la nuit; **~ school** *n* cours *mpl* du soir; **~ shift** *n* équipe *f* de nuit; **~time** *n* nuit *f*; **~ watchman** *n* veilleur *m*

or gardien *m* de nuit

nil [nɪl] *n* rien *m*; (BRIT: SPORT) zéro *m*

Nile [naɪl] *n*: **the ~** le Nil

nimble ['nɪmbl] *adj* agile

nine [naɪn] *num* neuf; **~teen** ['naɪn'ti:n] *num* dix-neuf; **~ty** ['naɪntɪ] *num* quatre-vingt-dix; **ninth** [naɪnθ] *num* neuvième

nip [nɪp] *vt* pincer

nipple ['nɪpl] *n* (ANAT) mamelon *m*, bout *m* du sein

nitrogen ['naɪtrədʒən] *n* azote *m*

┌─────────────┐
│ *KEYWORD* │
└─────────────┘

no [nəu] (*pl* **noes**) *adv* (*opposite of "yes"*) non; **are you coming? - no (I'm not)** est-ce que vous venez? - non; **would you like some more? - no thank you** vous en voulez encore? - non merci

♦ *adj* (*not any*) pas de, aucun(e) (*used with "ne"*); **I have no money/books** je n'ai pas d'argent/de livres; **no student would have done it** aucun étudiant ne l'aurait fait; **"no smoking"** "défense de fumer"; **"no dogs"** "les chiens ne sont pas admis"

♦ *n* non *m*

nobility [nəu'bɪlɪtɪ] *n* noblesse *f*

noble ['nəubl] *adj* noble

nobody ['nəubədɪ] *pron* personne

nod [nɔd] *vi* faire un signe de tête (*affirmatif ou amical*); (*sleep*) somnoler ♦ *vt*: **to ~ one's head** faire un signe de (la) tête; (*in agreement*) faire signe que oui ♦ *n* signe *m* de (la) tête; **~ off** *vi* s'assoupir

noise [nɔɪz] *n* bruit *m*; **noisy** *adj* bruyant(e)

nominal ['nɔmɪnl] *adj* symbolique

nominate ['nɔmɪneɪt] *vt* (*propose*) proposer; (*appoint*) nommer; **nominee** [nɔmɪ'ni:] *n* candidat agréé; personne nommée

non... [nɔn] *prefix* non-; **~alcoholic** *adj* non-alcoolisé(e); **~committal** *adj* évasif(-ive); **~descript** *adj* quelconque, indéfinissable

none [nʌn] *pron* aucun(e); **~ of you** aucun

d'entre vous, personne parmi vous; **I've ~ left** je n'en ai plus; **he's ~ the worse for it** il ne s'en porte pas plus mal

nonentity [nɔ'nentɪtɪ] *n* personne insignifiante

nonetheless ['nʌnðə'lɛs] *adv* néanmoins

non-existent [nɔnɪg'zɪstənt] *adj* inexistant(e)

non-fiction [nɔn'fɪkʃən] *n* littérature *f* non-romanesque

nonplussed [nɔn'plʌst] *adj* perplexe

nonsense ['nɔnsəns] *n* absurdités *fpl*, idioties *fpl*; ~**!** ne dites pas d'idioties!

non: ~-**smoker** *n* non-fumeur *m*; ~-**smoking** *adj* non-fumeur; ~-**stick** *adj* qui n'attache pas; ~-**stop** *adj* direct(e), sans arrêt (*or* escale) ♦ *adv* sans arrêt

noodles ['nu:dlz] *npl* nouilles *fpl*

nook [nuk] *n:* ~**s and crannies** recoins *mpl*

noon [nu:n] *n* midi *m*

no one ['nəuwʌn] *pron* = **nobody**

noose [nu:s] *n* nœud coulant; (*hangman's*) corde *f*

nor [nɔːr] *conj* = **neither** ♦ *adv see* **neither**

norm [nɔːm] *n* norme *f*

normal *adj* normal(e); ~**ly** ['nɔːməlɪ] *adv* normalement

Normandy ['nɔːməndɪ] *n* Normandie *f*

north [nɔːθ] *n* nord *m* ♦ *adj* du nord, nord *inv* ♦ *adv* au *or* vers le nord; **N~ America** *n* Amérique *f* du Nord; ~-**east** *n* nord-est *m*; ~**erly** ['nɔːðəlɪ] *adj* du nord; ~**ern** ['nɔːðən] *adj* du nord, septentrional(e); **N~ern Ireland** *n* Irlande *f* du Nord; **N~ Pole** *n* pôle *m* Nord; **N~ Sea** *n* mer *f* du Nord; ~**ward(s)** *adv* vers le nord; ~-**west** *n* nord-ouest *m*

Norway ['nɔːweɪ] *n* Norvège *f*; **Norwegian** [nɔː'wiːdʒən] *adj* norvégien(ne) ♦ *n* Norvégien(ne); (*LING*) norvégien *m*

nose [nəuz] *n* nez *m*; ~ **about, around** *vi* fouiner *or* fureter (partout); ~**bleed** *n* saignement *m* du nez; ~-**dive** *n* (descente *f* en) piqué *m*; ~**y** (*inf*) *adj* = **nosy**

nostalgia [nɔs'tældʒɪə] *n* nostalgie *f*

nostril ['nɔstrɪl] *n* narine *f*; (*of horse*) naseau *m*

nosy ['nəuzɪ] (*inf*) *adj* curieux(-euse)

not [nɔt] *adv* (ne ...) pas; **he is ~** *or* **isn't here** il n'est pas ici; **you must ~** *or* **you mustn't do that** tu ne dois pas faire ça; **it's too late, isn't it** *or* **is it ~?** c'est trop tard, n'est-ce pas?; ~ **yet/now** pas encore/maintenant; ~ **at all** pas du tout; *see also* **all**; **only**

notably ['nəutəblɪ] *adv* (*particularly*) en particulier; (*markedly*) spécialement

notary ['nəutərɪ] *n* notaire *m*

notch [nɔtʃ] *n* encoche *f*

note [nəut] *n* note *f*; (*letter*) mot *m*; (*banknote*) billet *m* ♦ *vt* (*also*: ~ **down**) noter; (*observe*) constater; ~**book** *n* carnet *m*; ~**d** *adj* réputé(e); ~**pad** *n* bloc-notes *m*; ~**paper** *n* papier *m* à lettres

nothing ['nʌθɪŋ] *n* rien *m*; **he does ~** il ne fait rien; ~ **new** rien de nouveau; **for ~** pour rien

notice ['nəutɪs] *n* (*announcement, warning*) avis *m*; (*period of time*) délai *m*; (*resignation*) démission *f*; (*dismissal*) congé *m* ♦ *vt* remarquer, s'apercevoir de; **to take ~ of** prêter attention à; **to bring sth to sb's ~** porter qch à la connaissance de qn; **at short ~** dans un délai très court; **until further ~** jusqu'à nouvel ordre; **to hand in one's ~** donner sa démission, démissionner; ~**able** *adj* visible; ~ **board** (*BRIT*) *n* panneau *m* d'affichage

notify ['nəutɪfaɪ] *vt:* **to ~ sth to sb** notifier qch à qn; **to ~ sb (of sth)** avertir qn (de qch)

notion ['nəuʃən] *n* idée *f*; (*concept*) notion *f*

notorious [nəu'tɔːrɪəs] *adj* notoire (*souvent en mal*)

nought [nɔːt] *n* zéro *m*

noun [naun] *n* nom *m*

nourish ['nʌrɪʃ] *vt* nourrir; ~**ing** *adj* nourrissant(e); ~**ment** *n* nourriture *f*

novel ['nɔvl] *n* roman *m* ♦ *adj* nouveau (nouvelle), original(e); ~**ist** *n* romancier *m*; ~**ty** *n* nouveauté *f*

November [nəu'vembər] *n* novembre *m*

now [nau] *adv* maintenant ♦ *conj:* ~ **(that)**

maintenant que; **right ~** tout de suite; **by ~** à l'heure qu'il est; **just ~: that's the fashion just ~** c'est la mode en ce moment; **~ and then, ~ and again** de temps en temps; **from ~ on** dorénavant; **~adays** *adv* de nos jours

nowhere ['nəuwɛəʳ] *adv* nulle part

nozzle ['nɔzl] *n* (*of hose etc*) ajutage *m*; (*of vacuum cleaner*) suceur *m*

nuclear ['nju:klɪəʳ] *adj* nucléaire

nucleus ['nju:klɪəs] (*pl* **nuclei**) *n* noyau *m*

nude [nju:d] *adj* nu(e) ♦ *n* nu *m*; **in the ~** (tout(e)) nu(e)

nudge [nʌdʒ] *vt* donner un (petit) coup de coude à

nudist ['nju:dɪst] *n* nudiste *m/f*

nuisance ['nju:sns] *n*: **it's a ~** c'est (très) embêtant; **he's a ~** il est assommant *or* casse-pieds; **what a ~!** quelle barbe!

null [nʌl] *adj*: **~ and void** nul(le) et non avenu(e)

numb [nʌm] *adj* engourdi(e); (*with fear*) paralysé(e)

number ['nʌmbəʳ] *n* nombre *m*; (*numeral*) chiffre *m*; (*of house, bank account etc*) numéro *m* ♦ *vt* numéroter; (*amount to*) compter; **a ~ of** un certain nombre de; **they were seven in ~** ils étaient (au nombre de) sept; **to be ~ed among** compter parmi; **~ plate** *n* (*AUT*) plaque *f* minéralogique *or* d'immatriculation

numeral ['nju:mərəl] *n* chiffre *m*

numerate ['nju:mərɪt] (*BRIT*) *adj*: **to be ~** avoir des notions d'arithmétique

numerical [nju:'merɪkl] *adj* numérique

numerous ['nju:mərəs] *adj* nombreux(-euse)

nun [nʌn] *n* religieuse *f*, sœur *f*

nurse [nə:s] *n* infirmière *f* ♦ *vt* (*patient, cold*) soigner

nursery ['nə:sərɪ] *n* (*room*) nursery *f*; (*institution*) crèche *f*; (*for plants*) pépinière *f*; **~ rhyme** *n* comptine *f*, chansonnette *f* pour enfants; **~ school** *n* école maternelle; **~ slope** *n* (*SKI*) piste *f* pour débutants

nursing ['nə:sɪŋ] *n* (*profession*) profession *f* d'infirmière; (*care*) soins *mpl*; **~ home** *n*

clinique *f*; maison *f* de convalescence

nut [nʌt] *n* (*of metal*) écrou *m*; (*fruit*) noix *f*; noisette *f*; cacahuète *f*; **~crackers** *npl* casse-noix *m inv*, casse-noisette(s) *m*

nutmeg ['nʌtmeg] *n* (noix *f*) muscade *f*

nutritious [nju:'trɪʃəs] *adj* nutritif(-ive), nourrissant(e)

nuts [nʌts] (*inf*) *adj* dingue

nutshell ['nʌtʃel] *n*: **in a ~** en un mot

nutter ['nʌtəʳ] (*BRIT*: *inf*) *n*: **he's a complete ~** il est complètement cinglé

nylon ['naɪlɔn] *n* nylon *m* ♦ *adj* de *or* en nylon

O, o

oak [əuk] *n* chêne *m* ♦ *adj* de *or* en (bois de) chêne

OAP (*BRIT*) *n abbr* = **old-age pensioner**

oar [ɔ:ʳ] *n* aviron *m*, rame *f*

oasis [əu'eɪsɪs] (*pl* **oases**) *n* oasis *f*

oath [əuθ] *n* serment *m*; (*swear word*) juron *m*; **under ~,** (*BRIT*) **on ~** sous serment

oatmeal ['əutmi:l] *n* flocons *mpl* d'avoine

oats [əuts] *n* avoine *f*

obedience [ə'bi:dɪəns] *n* obéissance *f*; **obedient** *adj* obéissant(e)

obey [ə'beɪ] *vt* obéir à; (*instructions*) se conformer à

obituary [ə'bɪtjuərɪ] *n* nécrologie *f*

object [*n* 'ɔbdʒɪkt, *vb* əb'dʒekt] *n* objet *m*; (*purpose*) but *m*, objet; (*LING*) complément *m* d'objet ♦ *vi*: **to ~ to** (*attitude*) désapprouver; (*proposal*) protester contre; **expense is no ~** l'argent n'est pas un problème; **he ~ed that ...** il a fait valoir *or* a objecté que ...; **I ~!** je proteste!; **~ion** [əb'dʒekʃən] *n* objection *f*; **~ionable** *adj* très désagréable; (*language*) choquant(e); **~ive** *n* objectif *m* ♦ *adj* objectif(-ive)

obligation [ɔblɪ'geɪʃən] *n* obligation *f*, devoir *m*; **without ~** sans engagement; **obligatory** [ə'blɪgətərɪ] *adj* obligatoire

oblige [ə'blaɪdʒ] *vt* (*force*): **to ~ sb to do** obliger *or* forcer qn à faire; (*do a favour*) rendre service à, obliger; **to be ~d to sb**

for sth être obligé(e) à qn de qch; **obliging** adj obligeant(e), serviable

oblique [əˈbliːk] adj oblique; (allusion) indi-
rect(e)

obliterate [əˈblitəreit] vt effacer

oblivion [əˈbliviən] n oubli m; **oblivious**
adj: **oblivious of** oublieux(-euse) de

oblong [ˈɒblɒŋ] adj oblong (oblongue) ♦ n
rectangle m

obnoxious [əbˈnɒkʃəs] adj odieux(-euse);
(smell) nauséabond(e)

oboe [ˈəubəu] n hautbois m

obscene [əbˈsiːn] adj obscène

obscure [əbˈskjuəʳ] adj obscur(e) ♦ vt obscurcir; (hide: sun) cacher

observant [əbˈzəːvənt] adj observateur(-
trice)

observation [ɒbzəˈveiʃən] n (remark) observation f; (watching) surveillance f

observatory [əbˈzəːvətri] n observatoire m

observe [əbˈzəːv] vt observer; (remark) faire observer or remarquer; **~r** n
observateur(-trice)

obsess [əbˈses] vt obséder; **~ive** adj obsé-
dant(e)

obsolete [ˈɒbsəliːt] adj dépassé(e); démo-
dé(e)

obstacle [ˈɒbstəkl] n obstacle m; **~ race** n
course f d'obstacles

obstinate [ˈɒbstinit] adj obstiné(e)

obstruct [əbˈstrʌkt] vt (block) boucher,
obstruer; (hinder) entraver

obtain [əbˈtein] vt obtenir

obvious [ˈɒbviəs] adj évident(e), manifeste;
~ly adv manifestement; **~ly not!** bien sûr
que non!

occasion [əˈkeiʒən] n occasion f; (event)
événement m; **~al** adj pris(e) or fait(e) etc
de temps en temps; occasionnel(le); **~ally**
adv de temps en temps, quelquefois

occupation [ɒkjuˈpeiʃən] n occupation f;
(job) métier m, profession f; **~al hazard**
n risque m du métier

occupier [ˈɒkjupaiəʳ] n occupant(e)

occupy [ˈɒkjupai] vt occuper; **to ~ o.s. in**
or **with doing** s'occuper à faire

occur [əˈkəːʳ] vi (event) se produire; (phe-

nomenon, error) se rencontrer; **to ~ to sb**
venir à l'esprit de qn; **~rence** n (existence) présence f, existence f; (event) cas
m, fait m

ocean [ˈəuʃən] n océan m

o'clock [əˈklɒk] adv: **it is 5 ~** il est 5 heures

OCR n abbr = **optical character reader**;
optical character recognition

October [ɒkˈtəubəʳ] n octobre m

octopus [ˈɒktəpəs] n pieuvre f

odd [ɒd] adj (strange) bizarre, curieux(-
euse); (number) impair(e); (not of a set)
dépareillé(e); **60-~** 60 et quelques; **at ~
times** de temps en temps; **the ~ one out**
l'exception f; **~ity** n (person) excentrique
m/f; (thing) curiosité f; **~-job man** n
homme m à tout faire; **~ jobs** npl petits
travaux divers; **~ly** adv bizarrement,
curieusement; **~ments** npl (COMM) fins
fpl de série; **~s** npl (in betting) cote f; **it
makes no ~s** cela n'a pas d'importance;
at ~s en désaccord; **~s and ends** de petites choses

odour [ˈəudəʳ] (US **odor**) n odeur f

KEYWORD

of [ɒv, əv] prep **1** (gen) de; **a friend of ours**
un de nos amis; **a boy of 10** un garçon
de 10 ans; **that was kind of you** c'était
gentil de votre part

2 (expressing quantity, amount, dates etc)
de; **a kilo of flour** un kilo de farine; **how
much of this do you need?** combien
vous en faut-il?; **there were 3 of them**
(people) ils étaient 3; (objects) il y en avait
3; **3 of us went** 3 d'entre nous y sont al-
lé(e)s; **the 5th of July** le 5 juillet

3 (from, out of) en, de; **a statue of marble** une statue de or en marbre; **made of
wood** (fait) en bois

off [ɒf] adj, adv (engine) coupé(e); (tap) fer-
mé(e); (BRIT: food: bad) mauvais(e); (: milk:
bad) tourné(e); (absent) absent(e); (cancelled) annulé(e) ♦ prep de; sur; **to be ~**
(to leave) partir, s'en aller; **to be ~ sick**

être absent pour cause de maladie; **a day ~** un jour de congé; **to have an ~ day** n'être pas en forme; **he had his coat ~** il avait enlevé son manteau; **10% ~** (COMM) 10% de rabais; **~ the coast** au large de la côte; **I'm ~ meat** je ne mange plus de viande, je n'aime plus la viande; **on the ~ chance** à tout hasard

offal ['ɔfl] *n* (CULIN) abats *mpl*

off-colour ['ɔf'kʌlər] (BRIT) *adj* (*ill*) malade, mal fichu(e)

offence [ə'fɛns] (US **offense**) *n* (*crime*) délit *m*, infraction *f*; **to take ~ at** se vexer de, s'offenser de

offend [ə'fɛnd] *vt* (*person*) offenser, blesser; **~er** *n* délinquant(e)

offense [ə'fɛns] (US) *n* = **offence**

offensive [ə'fɛnsɪv] *adj* offensant(e), choquant(e); (*smell etc*) très déplaisant(e); (*weapon*) offensif(-ive) ♦ *n* (MIL) offensive *f*

offer ['ɔfər] *n* offre *f*, proposition *f* ♦ *vt* offrir, proposer; **"on ~"** (COMM) "en promotion"; **~ing** *n* offrande *f*

offhand [ɔf'hænd] *adj* désinvolte ♦ *adv* spontanément

office ['ɔfɪs] *n* (*place, room*) bureau *m*; (*position*) charge *f*, fonction *f*; **doctor's ~** (US) cabinet (médical); **to take ~** entrer en fonctions; **~ automation** *n* bureautique *f*; **~ block** (US **office building**) *n* immeuble *m* de bureaux; **~ hours** *npl* heures *fpl* de bureau; (US: MED) heures de consultation

officer ['ɔfɪsər] *n* (MIL etc) officier *m*; (*also:* **police ~**) agent *m* (de police); (*of organization*) membre *m* du bureau directeur

office worker *n* employé(e) de bureau

official [ə'fɪʃl] *adj* officiel(le) ♦ *n* officiel *m*; (*civil servant*) fonctionnaire *m/f*; employé(e)

officiate [ə'fɪʃɪeɪt] *vi* (REL) officier; **to ~ at a marriage** célébrer un mariage

officious [ə'fɪʃəs] *adj* trop empressé(e)

offing ['ɔfɪŋ] *n*: **in the ~** (*fig*) en perspective

off: **~-licence** (BRIT) *n* (*shop*) débit *m* de vins et de spiritueux; **~-line** *adj*, *adv* (COMPUT) (en mode) autonome; (: switched off) non connecté(e); **~-peak** *adj* aux heures creuses; (*electricity, heating, ticket*) au tarif heures creuses; **~-putting** (BRIT) *adj* (*remark*) rébarbatif(-ive); (*person*) rebutant(e), peu engageant(e); **~-road vehicle** *n* véhicule *m* tout-terrain; **~-season** *adj*, *adv* hors-saison *inv*; **~set** (*irreg*) *vt* (*counteract*) contrebalancer, compenser; **~shoot** *n* (*fig*) ramification *f*, antenne *f*; **~shore** *adj* (*breeze*) de terre; (*fishing*) côtier(-ère); **~side** *adj* (SPORT) hors jeu; (AUT: *in Britain*) de droite; (: *in US, Europe*) de gauche; **~spring** *n inv* progéniture *f*; **~stage** *adv* dans les coulisses; **~-the-peg** (US **off-the-rack**) *adv* en prêt-à-porter; **~-white** *adj* blanc cassé *inv*

---

off-licence

i Un **off-licence** *est un magasin où l'on vend de l'alcool (à emporter) aux heures où les pubs sont fermés. On peut également y acheter des boissons non alcoolisées, des cigarettes, des chips, des bonbons, des chocolats etc.*

Oftel ['ɔftɛl] *n organisme qui supervise les télécommunications*

often ['ɔfn] *adv* souvent; **how ~ do you go?** vous y allez tous les combien?; **how ~ have you gone there?** vous y êtes allé combien de fois?

Ofwat ['ɔfwɔt] *n organisme qui surveille les activités des compagnies des eaux*

oh [əu] *excl* ô!, oh!, ah!

oil [ɔɪl] *n* huile *f*; (*petroleum*) pétrole *m*; (*for central heating*) mazout *m* ♦ *vt* (*machine*) graisser; **~can** *n* burette *f* de graissage; (*for storing*) bidon *m* à huile; **~field** *n* gisement *m* de pétrole; **~ filter** *n* (AUT) filtre *m* à huile; **~ painting** *n* peinture *f* à l'huile; **~ refinery** *n* raffinerie *f*; **~ rig** *n* derrick *m*; (*at sea*) plate-forme pétrolière; **~ slick** *n* nappe *f* de mazout; **~ tanker** *n* (*ship*) pétrolier *m*; (*truck*) camion-citerne *m*; **~ well** *n* puits *m* de pétrole; **~y** *adj* huileux(-euse); (*food*) gras(se)

ointment [ˈɔɪntmənt] *n* onguent *m*

O.K., okay [ˈəuˈkeɪ] *excl* d'accord! ♦ *adj* (*average*) pas mal ♦ *vt* approuver, donner son accord à; **is it ~?, are you ~?** ça va?

old [əuld] *adj* vieux (vieille); (*person*) vieux, âgé(e); (*former*) ancien(ne), vieux; **how ~ are you?** quel âge avez-vous?; **he's 10 years ~** il a 10 ans, il est âgé de 10 ans; **~er brother/sister** frère/sœur aîné(e); **~ age** *n* vieillesse *f*; **~ age pensioner** (*BRIT*) *n* retraité(e); **~-fashioned** *adj* démodé(e); (*person*) vieux jeu *inv*

olive [ˈɔlɪv] *n* (*fruit*) olive *f*; (*tree*) olivier *m* ♦ *adj* (*also:* **~-green**) (vert) olive *inv*; **~ oil** *n* huile *f* d'olive

Olympic [əuˈlɪmpɪk] *adj* olympique; **the ~ Games, the ~s** les Jeux *mpl* olympiques

omelet(te) [ˈɔmlɪt] *n* omelette *f*

omen [ˈəumen] *n* présage *m*

ominous [ˈɔmɪnəs] *adj* menaçant(e), inquiétant(e); (*event*) de mauvais augure

omit [əuˈmɪt] *vt* omettre; **to ~ to do** omettre de faire

KEYWORD

on [ɔn] *prep* 1 (*indicating position*) sur; **on the table** sur la table; **on the wall** sur le *or* au mur; **on the left** à gauche

2 (*indicating means, method, condition etc*): **on foot** à pied; **on the train/plane** (*be*) dans le train/l'avion; (*go*) en train/avion; **on the telephone/radio/television** au téléphone/à la radio/à la télévision; **to be on drugs** se droguer; **on holiday** en vacances

3 (*referring to time*): **on Friday** vendredi; **on Fridays** le vendredi; **on June 20th** le 20 juin; **a week on Friday** vendredi en huit; **on arrival** à l'arrivée; **on seeing this** en voyant cela

4 (*about, concerning*) sur, de; **a book on Balzac/physics** un livre sur Balzac/de physique

♦ *adv* 1 (*referring to dress, covering*): **to have one's coat on** avoir (mis) son manteau; **to put one's coat on** mettre son manteau; **what's she got on?** qu'est-ce

qu'elle porte?; **screw the lid on tightly** vissez bien le couvercle

2 (*further, continuously*): **to walk** *etc* **on** continuer à marcher *etc*; **on and off** de temps à autre

♦ *adj* 1 (*in operation: machine*) en marche; (: *radio, TV, light*) allumé(e); (: *tap, gas*) ouvert(e); (: *brakes*) mis(e); **is the meeting still on?** (*not cancelled*) est-ce que la réunion a bien lieu?; (*in progress*) la réunion dure-t-elle encore?; **when is this film on?** quand passe ce film?

2 (*inf*): **that's not on!** (*not acceptable*) cela ne se fait pas!; (*not possible*) pas question!

---

once [wʌns] *adv* une fois; (*formerly*) autrefois ♦ *conj* une fois que; **~ he had left/it was done** une fois qu'il fut parti/que ce fut terminé; **at ~** tout de suite, immédiatement; (*simultaneously*) à la fois; **~ a week** une fois par semaine; **~ more** encore une fois; **~ and for all** une fois pour toutes; **~ upon a time** il y avait une fois, il était une fois

oncoming [ˈɔnkʌmɪŋ] *adj* (*traffic*) venant en sens inverse

KEYWORD

one [wʌn] *num* un(e); **one hundred and fifty** cent cinquante; **one day** un jour

♦ *adj* 1 (*sole*) seul(e), unique; **the one book** l'unique *or* le seul livre qui; **the one man who** le seul (homme) qui

2 (*same*) même; **they came in the one car** ils sont venus dans la même voiture

♦ *pron* 1: **this one** celui-ci (celle-ci); **that one** celui-là (celle-là); **I've already got one/a red one** j'en ai déjà un(e)/un(e) rouge; **one by one** un(e) à *or* par un(e)

2: **one another** l'un(e) l'autre; **to look at one another** se regarder

3 (*impersonal*) on; **one never knows** on ne sait jamais; **to cut one's finger** se couper le doigt

---

one: ~-day excursion (*US*) *n* billet *m* d'aller-retour (valable pour la journée);

~-man *adj* (*business*) dirigé(e) *etc* par un seul homme; **~-man band** *n* homme-orchestre *m*; **~-off** (BRIT: *inf*) *n* exemplaire *m* unique

oneself [wʌn'sɛlf] *pron* (*reflexive*) se; (*after prep*) soi(-même); (*emphatic*) soi-même; **to hurt ~** se faire mal; **to keep sth for ~** garder qch pour soi; **to talk to ~** se parler à soi-même

one: **~-sided** *adj* (*argument*) unilatéral; **~-to-~** *adj* (*relationship*) univoque; **~-way** *adj* (*street, traffic*) à sens unique

ongoing ['ɔngəʊɪŋ] *adj* en cours; (*relationship*) suivi(e)

onion ['ʌnjən] *n* oignon *m*

on-line ['ɔnlaɪn] *adj, adv* (COMPUT) en ligne; (: *switched on*) connecté(e)

onlooker ['ɔnlʊkəʳ] *n* spectateur(-trice)

only ['əʊnlɪ] *adv* seulement ♦ *adj* seul(e), unique ♦ *conj* seulement, mais; **an ~ child** un enfant unique; **not ~ ... but also** non seulement ... mais aussi

onset ['ɔnsɛt] *n* début *m*; (*of winter, old age*) approche *f*

onshore ['ɔnʃɔːʳ] *adj* (*wind*) du large

onslaught ['ɔnslɔːt] *n* attaque *f*, assaut *m*

onto ['ɔntu] *prep* = **on to**

onward(s) ['ɔnwəd(z)] *adv* (*move*) en avant; **from that time ~** à partir de ce moment

ooze [uːz] *vi* suinter

opaque [əʊ'peɪk] *adj* opaque

OPEC ['əʊpɛk] *n abbr* (= *Organization of Petroleum-Exporting Countries*) O.P.E.P. *f*

open ['əʊpn] *adj* ouvert(e); (*car*) découvert(e); (*road, view*) dégagé(e); (*meeting*) public(-ique); (*admiration*) manifeste ♦ *vt* ouvrir ♦ *vi* (*flower, eyes, door, debate*) s'ouvrir; (*shop, bank, museum*) ouvrir; (*book etc*: *commence*) commencer, débuter; **in the ~ (air)** en plein air; **~ on to** *vt fus* (*subj: room, door*) donner sur; **~ up** *vt* ouvrir; (*blocked road*) dégager ♦ *vi* s'ouvrir; **~ing** *n* ouverture *f*; (*opportunity*) occasion *f* ♦ *adj* (*remarks*) préliminaire; **~ing hours** *npl* heures *fpl* d'ouverture; **~ly** *adv* ouvertement; **~-minded** *adj* à l'esprit ouvert;

~-necked *adj* à col ouvert; **~-plan** *adj* sans cloisons

Open University

i L'**Open University** a été fondée en 1969. Ce type d'enseignement comprend des cours (certaines plages horaires sont réservées à cet effet à la télévision et à la radio), des devoirs qui sont envoyés par l'étudiant à son directeur ou sa directrice d'études, et un séjour obligatoire en université d'été. Il faut couvrir un certain nombre d'unités de valeur pendant une période de temps déterminée et obtenir la moyenne à un certain nombre d'entre elles pour recevoir le diplôme visé.

---

opera ['ɔpərə] *n* opéra *m*; **~ singer** *n* chanteur(-euse) d'opéra

operate ['ɔpəreɪt] *vt* (*machine*) faire marcher, faire fonctionner ♦ *vi* fonctionner; (MED): **to ~ (on sb)** opérer (qn)

operatic [ɔpə'rætɪk] *adj* d'opéra

operating table *n* table *f* d'opération

operating theatre *n* salle *f* d'opération

operation [ɔpə'reɪʃən] *n* opération *f*; (*of machine*) fonctionnement *m*; **to be in ~** (*system, law*) être en vigueur; **to have an ~** (MED) se faire opérer

operative ['ɔpərətɪv] *adj* (*measure*) en vigueur

operator ['ɔpəreɪtəʳ] *n* (*of machine*) opérateur(-trice); (TEL) téléphoniste *m/f*

opinion [ə'pɪnjən] *n* opinion *f*, avis *m*; **in my ~** à mon avis; **~ated** *adj* aux idées bien arrêtées; **~ poll** *n* sondage *m* (d'opinion)

opponent [ə'pəʊnənt] *n* adversaire *m/f*

opportunity [ɔpə'tjuːnɪtɪ] *n* occasion *f*; **to take the ~ of doing** profiter de l'occasion pour faire; en profiter pour faire

oppose [ə'pəʊz] *vt* s'opposer à; **~d to** opposé(e) à; **as ~d to** par opposition à; **opposing** *adj* (*side*) opposé(e)

opposite ['ɔpəzɪt] *adj* opposé(e); (*house etc*) d'en face ♦ *adv* en face ♦ *prep* en face de ♦ *n* opposé *m*, contraire *m*; **the ~**

sex l'autre sexe, le sexe opposé; **opposition** [ɔpə'zɪʃən] n opposition f

oppressive [ə'presɪv] adj (political regime) oppressif(-ive); (weather) lourd(e); (heat) accablant(e)

opt [ɔpt] vi: **to ~ for** opter pour; **to ~ to do** choisir de faire; **~ out** vi: **to ~ out of** choisir de ne pas participer à or de ne pas faire

optical ['ɔptɪkl] adj optique; (instrument) d'optique; **~ character recognition/reader** n lecture f/lecteur m optique

optician [ɔp'tɪʃən] n opticien(ne)

optimist ['ɔptɪmɪst] n optimiste m/f; **~ic** [ɔptɪ'mɪstɪk] adj optimiste

option ['ɔpʃən] n choix m, option f; (SCOL) matière f à option; (COMM) option; **~al** adj facultatif(-ive); (COMM) en option

or [ɔːr] conj ou; (with negative): **he hasn't seen ~ heard anything** il n'a rien vu ni entendu; **~ else** sinon; ou bien

oral ['ɔːrəl] adj oral(e) ♦ n oral m

orange ['ɔrɪndʒ] n (fruit) orange f ♦ adj orange inv

orbit ['ɔːbɪt] n orbite f ♦ vt graviter autour de; **~al (motorway)** n périphérique m

orchard ['ɔːtʃəd] n verger m

orchestra ['ɔːkɪstrə] n orchestre m; (US: seating) (fauteuils mpl d')orchestre

orchid ['ɔːkɪd] n orchidée f

ordain [ɔː'deɪn] vt (REL) ordonner

ordeal [ɔː'diːl] n épreuve f

order ['ɔːdər] n ordre m; (COMM) commande f ♦ vt ordonner; (COMM) commander; **in ~** en ordre; (document) en règle; **in (working) ~** en état de marche; **out of ~** (not in correct ~) en désordre; (not working) en dérangement; **in ~ to do/that** pour faire/que +sub; **on ~** (COMM) en commande; **to ~ sb to do** ordonner à qn de faire; **~ form** n bon m de commande; **~ly** n (MIL) ordonnance f; (MED) garçon m de salle ♦ adj (room) en ordre; (person) qui a de l'ordre

ordinary ['ɔːdnrɪ] adj ordinaire, normal(e); (pej) ordinaire, quelconque; **out of the ~** exceptionnel(le)

Ordnance Survey map ['ɔːdnəns-] n ≈ carte f d'Etat-Major

ore [ɔːr] n minerai m

organ ['ɔːgən] n organe m; (MUS) orgue m, orgues fpl; **~ic** [ɔː'gænɪk] adj organique; (food) biologique

organization [ɔːgənaɪ'zeɪʃən] n organisation f

organize ['ɔːgənaɪz] vt organiser; **~r** n organisateur(-trice)

orgasm ['ɔːgæzəm] n orgasme m

Orient ['ɔːrɪənt] n: **the ~** l'Orient m; **o~al** [ɔːrɪ'entl] adj oriental(e)

origin ['ɔrɪdʒɪn] n origine f

original [ə'rɪdʒɪnl] adj original(e); (earliest) originel(le) ♦ n original m; **~ly** adv (at first) à l'origine

originate [ə'rɪdʒɪneɪt] vi: **to ~ from** (person) être originaire de; (suggestion) provenir de; **to ~ in** prendre naissance dans; avoir son origine dans

Orkney ['ɔːknɪ] n (also: **the ~ Islands**) les Orcades fpl

ornament ['ɔːnəmənt] n ornement m; (trinket) bibelot m; **~al** [ɔːnə'mentl] adj décoratif(-ive); (garden) d'agrément

ornate [ɔː'neɪt] adj très orné(e)

orphan ['ɔːfn] n orphelin(e)

orthopaedic [ɔːθə'piːdɪk] (US **orthopedic**) adj orthopédique

ostensibly [ɔs'tensɪblɪ] adv en apparence

ostentatious [ɔsten'teɪʃəs] adj prétentieux(-euse)

ostracize ['ɔstrəsaɪz] vt frapper d'ostracisme

ostrich ['ɔstrɪtʃ] n autruche f

other ['ʌðər] adj autre ♦ pron: **the ~ (one)** l'autre; **~s** (~ people) d'autres; **~ than** autrement que; à part; **~wise** adv, conj autrement

otter ['ɔtər] n loutre f

ouch [autʃ] excl aïe!

ought [ɔːt] (pt **ought**) aux vb: **I ~ to do it** je devrais le faire, il faudrait que je le fasse; **this ~ to have been corrected** cela aurait dû être corrigé; **he ~ to win** il devrait gagner

ounce [auns] *n* once *f* (= *28.35g; 16 in a pound*)

our [ˈauər] *adj* notre, nos *pl; see also* **my**; **~s** *pron* le (la) nôtre, les nôtres; *see also* **mine¹**; **~selves** [auəˈsɛlvz] *pron pl* (*reflexive, after preposition*) nous; (*emphatic*) nous-mêmes; *see also* **oneself**

oust [aust] *vt* évincer

out [aut] *adv* dehors; (*published, not at home etc*) sorti(e); (*light, fire*) éteint(e); **~ here** ici; **~ there** là-bas; **he's ~** (*absent*) il est sorti; (*unconscious*) il est sans connaissance; **to be ~ in one's calculations** s'être trompé dans ses calculs; **to run/back etc ~** sortir en courant/en reculant *etc*; **~ loud** à haute voix; **~ of** (*~side*) en dehors de; (*because of: anger etc*) par; (*from among*): **~ of 10** sur 10; (*without*): **~ of petrol** sans essence, à court d'essence; **~ of order** (*machine*) en panne; (*TEL: line*) en dérangement; **~-and-~** *adj* (*liar, thief etc*) véritable; **~back** *n* (*in Australia*): **the ~back** l'intérieur *m*; **~board** *n* (*also:* **~board motor**) (moteur *m*) hors-bord *m*; **~break** *n* (*of war, disease*) début *m*; (*of violence*) éruption *f*; **~burst** *n* explosion *f*, accès *m*; **~cast** *n* exilé(e); (*socially*) paria *m*; **~come** *n* issue *f*, résultat *m*; **~crop** *n* (*of rock*) affleurement *m*; **~cry** *n* tollé (général); **~dated** *adj* démodé(e); **~do** (*irreg*) *vt* surpasser; **~door** *adj* de *or* en plein air; **~doors** *adv* dehors; au grand air

outer [ˈautər] *adj* extérieur(e); **~ space** *n* espace *m* cosmique

outfit [ˈautfɪt] *n* (*clothes*) tenue *f*

out: **~going** *adj* (*character*) ouvert(e), extraverti(e); (*departing*) sortant(e); **~goings** (*BRIT*) *npl* (*expenses*) dépenses *fpl*; **~grow** (*irreg*) *vt* (*clothes*) devenir trop grand(e) pour; **~house** *n* appentis *m*, remise *f*

outing [ˈautɪŋ] *n* sortie *f*; excursion *f*

out: **~law** *n* hors-la-loi *m inv* ♦ *vt* mettre hors-la-loi; **~lay** *n* dépenses *fpl*; (*investment*) mise *f* de fonds; **~let** *n* (*for liquid etc*) issue *f*, sortie *f*; (*US: ELEC*) prise *f* de courant; (*also:* **retail ~let**) point *m* de vente; **~line** *n* (*shape*) contour *m*; (*summary*) esquisse *f*, grandes lignes ♦ *vt* (*fig: theory, plan*) exposer à grands traits; **~live** *vt* survivre à; **~look** *n* perspective *f*; **~lying** *adj* écarté(e); **~moded** *adj* démodé(e); dépassé(e); **~number** *vt* surpasser en nombre; **~-of-date** *adj* (*passport*) périmé(e); (*theory etc*) dépassé(e); (*clothes etc*) démodé(e); **~-of-the-way** *adj* (*place*) loin de tout; **~patient** *n* malade *m/f* en consultation externe; **~post** *n* avant-poste *m*; **~put** *n* rendement *m*, production *f*; (*COMPUT*) sortie *f*

outrage [ˈautreɪdʒ] *n* (*anger*) indignation *f*; (*violent act*) atrocité *f*; (*scandal*) scandale *m* ♦ *vt* outrager; **~ous** [autˈreɪdʒəs] *adj* atroce; scandaleux(-euse)

outright [*adv* autˈraɪt, *adj* ˈautraɪt] *adv* complètement; (*deny, refuse*) catégoriquement; (*ask*) carrément; (*kill*) sur le coup ♦ *adj* complet(-ète); catégorique

outset [ˈautsɛt] *n* début *m*

outside [autˈsaɪd] *n* extérieur *m* ♦ *adj* extérieur(e) ♦ *adv* (au) dehors, à l'extérieur ♦ *prep* hors de, à l'extérieur de; **at the ~** (*fig*) au plus *or* maximum; **~ lane** *n* (*AUT: in Britain*) voie *f* de droite; (: *in US, Europe*) voie de gauche; **~ line** *n* (*TEL*) ligne extérieure; **~r** *n* (*stranger*) étranger(-ère)

out: **~size** [ˈautsaɪz] *adj* énorme; (*clothes*) grande taille *inv*; **~skirts** *npl* faubourgs *mpl*; **~spoken** *adj* très franc (franche); **~standing** *adj* remarquable, exceptionnel(le); (*unfinished*) en suspens; (*debt*) impayé(e); (*problem*) non réglé(e); **~stay** *vt*: **to ~stay one's welcome** abuser de l'hospitalité de son hôte; **~stretched** [autˈstrɛtʃt] *adj* (*hand*) tendu(e); **~strip** [autˈstrɪp] *vt* (*competitors, demand*) dépasser; **~ tray** *n* courrier *m* "départ"

outward [ˈautwəd] *adj* (*sign, appearances*) extérieur(e); (*journey*) (d')aller

outweigh [autˈweɪ] *vt* l'emporter sur

outwit [autˈwɪt] *vt* se montrer plus malin que

oval [ˈəuvl] *adj* ovale ♦ *n* ovale *m*

Oval Office

i L'**Oval Office** *est le bureau personnel du président des États-Unis à la Maison-Blanche, ainsi appelé du fait de sa forme ovale. Par extension, ce terme désigne la présidence elle-même.*

---

ovary ['əʊvəri] *n* ovaire *m*

oven ['ʌvn] *n* four *m*; **~proof** *adj* allant au four

over ['əʊvə'] *adv* (par-)dessus ♦ *adj* (*finished*) fini(e), terminé(e); (*too much*) en plus ♦ *prep* sur; par-dessus; (*above*) au-dessus de; (*on the other side of*) de l'autre côté de; (*more than*) plus de; (*during*) pendant; **~ here** ici; **~ there** là-bas; **all ~** (*everywhere*) partout, fini(e); **~ and ~ (again)** à plusieurs reprises; **~ and above** en plus de; **to ask sb ~** inviter qn (à passer)

overall [*adj, n* 'əʊvərɔːl, *adv* əʊvər'ɔːl] *adj* (*length, cost etc*) total(e); (*study*) d'ensemble ♦ *n* (BRIT) blouse *f* ♦ *adv* dans l'ensemble, en général; **~s** *npl* bleus *mpl* (de travail)

over: **~awe** *vt* impressionner; **~balance** *vi* basculer; **~board** *adv* (NAUT) par-dessus bord; **~book** *vt* faire du surbooking; **~cast** *adj* couvert(e)

overcharge [əʊvə'tʃɑːdʒ] *vt*: **to ~ sb for sth** faire payer qch trop cher à qn

overcoat ['əʊvəkəʊt] *n* pardessus *m*

overcome [əʊvə'kʌm] (*irreg*) *vt* (*defeat*) triompher de; (*difficulty*) surmonter

over: **~crowded** *adj* bondé(e); **~do** (*irreg*) *vt* exagérer; (*overcook*) trop cuire; **to ~do it** (*work etc*) se surmener; **~dose** *n* dose excessive; **~draft** *n* découvert *m*; **~drawn** *adj* (*account*) à découvert; (*person*) dont le compte est à découvert; **~due** *adj* en retard; (*change, reform*) qui tarde; **~estimate** *vt* surestimer

overflow [əʊvə'fləʊ] *vi* déborder ♦ *n* (*also*: **~ pipe**) tuyau *m* d'écoulement, trop-plein *m*

overgrown [əʊvə'grəʊn] *adj* (*garden*) envahi(e) par la végétation

overhaul [*vb* əʊvə'hɔːl, *n* 'əʊvəhɔːl] *vt* réviser ♦ *n* révision *f*

overhead [*adv* əʊvə'hɛd, *adj, n* 'əʊvəhɛd] *adv* au-dessus ♦ *adj* aérien(ne); (*lighting*) vertical(e) ♦ *n* (US) = **overheads**; **~s** *npl* (*expenses*) frais généraux; **~ projector** *n* rétroprojecteur *m*

over: **~hear** (*irreg*) *vt* entendre (par hasard); **~heat** *vi* (*engine*) chauffer; **~joyed** *adj*: **~joyed (at)** ravi(e) (de), enchanté(e) (de)

overland ['əʊvəlænd] *adj, adv* par voie de terre

overlap [əʊvə'læp] *vi* se chevaucher

over: **~leaf** *adv* au verso; **~load** *vt* surcharger; **~look** *vt* (*have view of*) donner sur; (*miss: by mistake*) oublier; (*forgive*) fermer les yeux sur

overnight [*adv* əʊvə'naɪt, *adj* 'əʊvənaɪt] *adv* (*happen*) durant la nuit; (*fig*) soudain ♦ *adj* d'une (*or* de) nuit; **he stayed there ~** il y a passé la nuit

overpass ['əʊvəpɑːs] *n* pont autoroutier

overpower [əʊvə'paʊə'] *vt* vaincre; (*fig*) accabler; **~ing** *adj* (*heat, stench*) suffocant(e)

over: **~rate** *vt* surestimer; **~ride** (*irreg: like ride*) *vt* (*order, objection*) passer outre à; **~riding** *adj* prépondérant(e); **~rule** *vt* (*decision*) annuler; (*claim*) rejeter; (*person*) rejeter l'avis de; **~run** (*irreg: like run*) *vt* (*country*) occuper; (*time limit*) dépasser

overseas [əʊvə'siːz] *adv* outre-mer; (*abroad*) à l'étranger ♦ *adj* (*trade*) extérieur(e); (*visitor*) étranger(-ère)

overshadow [əʊvə'ʃædəʊ] *vt* (*fig*) éclipser

oversight ['əʊvəsaɪt] *n* omission *f*, oubli *m*

oversleep [əʊvə'sliːp] (*irreg*) *vi* se réveiller (trop) tard

overstep [əʊvə'stɛp] *vt*: **to ~ the mark** dépasser la mesure

overt [əʊ'vəːt] *adj* non dissimulé(e)

overtake [əʊvə'teɪk] (*irreg*) *vt* (AUT) dépasser, doubler

over: **~throw** (*irreg*) *vt* (*government*) renverser; **~time** *n* heures *fpl* supplémentaires; **~tone** *n* (*also*: **~tones**) note *f*, sous-entendus *mpl*

overture ['əʊvətʃuəʳ] *n* (*MUS*, *fig*) ouverture *f*

over: **~turn** *vt* renverser ♦ *vi* se retourner; **~weight** *adj* (*person*) trop gros(se); **~whelm** *vt* (*subj: emotion*) accabler; (*enemy, opponent*) écraser; **~whelming** *adj* (*victory, defeat*) écrasant(e); (*desire*) irrésistible

overwrought [əʊvə'rɔːt] *adj* excédé(e)

owe [əʊ] *vt*: **to ~ sb sth, to ~ sth to sb** devoir qch à qn; **owing to** *prep* à cause de, en raison de

owl [aʊl] *n* hibou *m*

own [əʊn] *vt* posséder ♦ *adj* propre; **a room of my ~** une chambre à moi, ma propre chambre; **to get one's ~ back** prendre sa revanche; **on one's ~** tout(e) seul(e); **~ up** *vi* avouer; **~er** *n* propriétaire *m/f*; **~ership** *n* possession *f*

ox [ɔks] (*pl* **~en**) *n* bœuf *m*; **~tail** *n*: **~tail soup** soupe *f* à la queue de bœuf

oxygen ['ɔksɪdʒən] *n* oxygène *m*

oyster ['ɔɪstəʳ] *n* huître *f*

oz. *abbr* = **ounce(s)**

ozone ['əʊzəʊn] *n*: **~-friendly** *adj* qui n'attaque pas *or* qui préserve la couche d'ozone; **~ hole** *n* trou *m* d'ozone; **~ layer** *n* couche *f* d'ozone

P, p

p *abbr* = **penny**; **pence**

PA *n abbr* = **personal assistant**; **public address system**

pa [pɑː] (*inf*) *n* papa *m*

p.a. *abbr* = **per annum**

pace [peɪs] *n* pas *m*; (*speed*) allure *f*; vitesse *f* ♦ *vi*: **to ~ up and down** faire les cent pas; **to keep ~ with** aller à la même vitesse que; **~maker** *n* (*MED*) stimulateur *m* cardiaque; (*SPORT: also:* **~setter**) meneur(-euse) de train

Pacific [pə'sɪfɪk] *n*: **the ~ (Ocean)** le Pacifique, l'océan *m* Pacifique

pack [pæk] *n* (~*et, US: of cigarettes*) paquet *m*; (*of hounds*) meute *f*; (*of thieves etc*) bande *f*; (*back* ~) sac *m* à dos; (*of cards*) jeu *m* ♦ *vt* (*goods*) empaqueter, emballer; (*box*) remplir; (*cram*) entasser; **to ~ one's suitcase** faire sa valise; **to ~ (one's bags)** faire ses bagages; **to ~ sb off** expédier qn à; **~ it in!** laisse tomber!, écrase!

package ['pækɪdʒ] *n* paquet *m*; (*also:* **~ deal**) forfait *m*; **~ tour** (*BRIT*) *n* voyage organisé

packed *adj* (*crowded*) bondé(e); **~ lunch** (*BRIT*) *n* repas froid

packet ['pækɪt] *n* paquet *m*

packing ['pækɪŋ] *n* emballage *m*; **~ case** *n* caisse *f* (d'emballage)

pact [pækt] *n* pacte *m*; traité *m*

pad [pæd] *n* bloc(-notes) *m*; (*to prevent friction*) tampon *m*; (*inf: home*) piaule *f* ♦ *vt* rembourrer; **~ding** *n* rembourrage *m*

paddle ['pædl] *n* (*oar*) pagaie *f*; (*US: for table tennis*) raquette *f* de ping-pong ♦ *vt*: **to ~ a canoe** *etc* pagayer ♦ *vi* barboter, faire trempette; **paddling pool** (*BRIT*) *n* petit bassin

paddock ['pædək] *n* enclos *m*; (*RACING*) paddock *m*

padlock ['pædlɔk] *n* cadenas *m*

paediatrics [piːdɪ'ætrɪks] (*US* **pediatrics**) *n* pédiatrie *f*

pagan ['peɪgən] *adj*, *n* païen(ne)

page [peɪdʒ] *n* (*of book*) page *f*; (*also:* **~ boy**) groom *m*, chasseur *m*; (*at wedding*) garçon *m* d'honneur ♦ *vt* (*in hotel etc*) (faire) appeler

pageant ['pædʒənt] *n* spectacle *m* historique; **~ry** *n* apparat *m*, pompe *f*

pager ['peɪdʒəʳ], **paging device** *n* (*TEL*) récepteur *m* d'appels

paid [peɪd] *pt*, *pp* *of* **pay** ♦ *adj* (*work, official*) rémunéré(e); (*holiday*) payé(e); **to put ~ to** (*BRIT*) mettre fin à, régler

pail [peɪl] *n* seau *m*

pain [peɪn] *n* douleur *f*; **to be in ~** souffrir, avoir mal; **to take ~s to do** se donner du mal pour faire; **~ed** *adj* peiné(e), chagrin(e); **~ful** *adj* douloureux(-euse); (*fig*) difficile, pénible; **~fully** *adv* (*fig: very*) terriblement; **~killer** n analgésique m; **~less** adj indolore; **~staking** ['peɪnzteɪkɪŋ] adj (person) soigneux(-euse); (work) soigné(e)

paint [peɪnt] n peinture f ♦ vt peindre; **to ~ the door blue** peindre la porte en bleu; **~brush** n pinceau m; **~er** n peintre m; **~ing** n peinture f; (picture) tableau m; **~work** n peinture f

pair [peəʳ] n (of shoes, gloves etc) paire f; (of people) couple m; **~ of scissors** (paire de) ciseaux mpl; **~ of trousers** pantalon m

pajamas [pə'dʒɑ:məz] (US) npl pyjama(s) m(pl)

Pakistan [pɑ:kɪ'stɑ:n] n Pakistan m; **~i** adj pakistanais(e) ♦ n Pakistanais(e)

pal [pæl] (inf) n copain (copine)

palace ['pæləs] n palais m

palatable ['pælɪtəbl] adj bon (bonne), agréable au goût

palate ['pælɪt] n palais m (ANAT)

pale [peɪl] adj pâle ♦ n: **beyond the ~** (behaviour) inacceptable; **to grow ~** pâlir

Palestine ['pælɪstaɪn] n Palestine f; **Palestinian** [pælɪs'tɪnɪən] adj palestinien(ne) ♦ n Palestinien(ne)

palette ['pælɪt] n palette f

pall [pɔ:l] n (of smoke) voile m ♦ vi devenir lassant(e)

pallet ['pælɪt] n (for goods) palette f

pallid ['pælɪd] adj blême

palm [pɑ:m] n (of hand) paume f; (also: **~ tree**) palmier m ♦ vt: **to ~ sth off on sb** (inf) refiler qch à qn; **P~ Sunday** n le dimanche des Rameaux

paltry ['pɔ:ltrɪ] adj dérisoire

pamper ['pæmpəʳ] vt gâter, dorloter

pamphlet ['pæmflət] n brochure f

pan [pæn] n (also: **saucepan**) casserole f; (also: **frying ~**) poêle f; **~cake** n crêpe f

panda ['pændə] n panda m

pandemonium [pændɪ'məunɪəm] n tohu-bohu m

pander ['pændəʳ] vi: **to ~ to** flatter bassement; obéir servilement à

pane [peɪn] n carreau m, vitre f

panel ['pænl] n (of wood, cloth etc) panneau m; (RADIO, TV) experts mpl; (for interview, exams) jury m; **~ling** (US **paneling**) n boiseries fpl

pang [pæŋ] n: **~s of remorse/jealousy** âffres mpl du remords/de la jalousie; **~s of hunger/conscience** tiraillements mpl d'estomac/de la conscience

panic ['pænɪk] n panique f, affolement m ♦ vi s'affoler, paniquer; **~ky** adj (person) qui panique or s'affole facilement; **~-stricken** adj affolé(e)

pansy ['pænzɪ] n (BOT) pensée f; (inf: pej) tapette f, pédé m

pant [pænt] vi haleter

panther ['pænθəʳ] n panthère f

panties ['pæntɪz] npl slip m

pantomime ['pæntəmaɪm] (BRIT) n spectacle m de Noël

---
pantomime

ℹ️ Une **pantomime**, que l'on appelle également de façon familière "panto", est un genre de farce où le personnage principal est souvent un jeune garçon et où il y a toujours une dame, c'est-à-dire une vieille femme jouée par un homme, et un méchant. La plupart du temps, l'histoire est basée sur un conte de fées comme Cendrillon ou Le Chat botté, et le public est encouragé à participer en prévenant le héros d'un danger imminent. Ce genre de spectacle, qui s'adresse surtout aux enfants, vise également un public d'adultes au travers des nombreuses plaisanteries faisant allusion à des faits d'actualité.

pantry ['pæntrɪ] n garde-manger m inv

pants [pænts] npl (BRIT: woman's) slip m; (: man's) slip m, caleçon m; (US: trousers) pantalon m

pantyhose ['pæntɪhəuz] (US) npl collant m

paper ['peɪpəʳ] n papier m; (also: **wallpaper**) papier peint; (also: **newspaper**) journal m; (academic essay) article m; (exam) épreuve écrite ♦ adj en or de papier ♦ vt tapisser (de papier peint); **~s** npl (also: **identity ~s**) papiers (d'identité);

~back n livre m de poche; livre broché or non relié; **~ bag** n sac m en papier; **~ clip** n trombone m; **~ hankie** n mouchoir m en papier; **~weight** n presse-papiers m inv; **~work** n papiers mpl; (pej) paperasserie f

par [pɑː] n pair m; (GOLF) normale f du parcours; **on a ~ with** à égalité avec, au même niveau que

parachute [ˈpærəʃuːt] n parachute m

parade [pəˈreɪd] n défilé m ♦ vt (fig) faire étalage de ♦ vi défiler

paradise [ˈpærədaɪs] n paradis m

paradox [ˈpærədɒks] n paradoxe m; **~ically** [pærəˈdɒksɪklɪ] adv paradoxalement

paraffin [ˈpærəfɪn] (BRIT) n (also: **~ oil**) pétrole (lampant)

paragon [ˈpærəgən] n modèle m

paragraph [ˈpærəgrɑːf] n paragraphe m

parallel [ˈpærəlɛl] adj parallèle; (fig) semblable ♦ n (line) parallèle f; (fig, GEO) parallèle m

paralyse [ˈpærəlaɪz] (BRIT) vt paralyser; **paralysis** [pəˈrælɪsɪs] n paralysie f; **paralyze** (US) vt = **paralyse**

paramount [ˈpærəmaʊnt] adj: **of ~ importance** de la plus haute or grande importance

paranoid [ˈpærənɔɪd] adj (PSYCH) paranoïaque

paraphernalia [pærəfəˈneɪlɪə] n attirail m

parasol [ˈpærəsɔl] n ombrelle f; (over table) parasol m

paratrooper [ˈpærətruːpər] n parachutiste m (soldat)

parcel [ˈpɑːsl] n paquet m, colis m ♦ vt (also: **~ up**) empaqueter

parchment [ˈpɑːtʃmənt] n parchemin m

pardon [ˈpɑːdn] n pardon m; grâce f ♦ vt pardonner à; **~ me!, I beg your ~!** pardon!, je suis désolé!; **(I beg your) ~?, (US) ~ me?** pardon?

parent [ˈpɛərənt] n père m or mère f; **~s** npl parents mpl

Paris [ˈpærɪs] n Paris

parish [ˈpærɪʃ] n paroisse f; (BRIT: civil) ≃ commune f

Parisian [pəˈrɪzɪən] adj parisien(ne) ♦ n Parisien(ne)

park [pɑːk] n parc m, jardin public ♦ vt garer ♦ vi se garer

parking [ˈpɑːkɪŋ] n stationnement m; **"no ~"** "stationnement interdit"; **~ lot** (US) n parking m, parc m de stationnement; **~ meter** n parcomètre m; **~ ticket** n P.V. m

parliament [ˈpɑːləmənt] n parlement m; **~ary** [pɑːləˈmɛntərɪ] adj parlementaire

parlour [ˈpɑːlər] (US **parlor**) n salon m

parochial [pəˈrəʊkɪəl] (pej) adj à l'esprit de clocher

parole [pəˈrəʊl] n: **on ~** en liberté conditionnelle

parrot [ˈpærət] n perroquet m

parry [ˈpærɪ] vt (blow) esquiver

parsley [ˈpɑːslɪ] n persil m

parsnip [ˈpɑːsnɪp] n panais m

parson [ˈpɑːsn] n ecclésiastique m; (Church of England) pasteur m

part [pɑːt] n partie f; (of machine) pièce f; (THEATRE etc) rôle m; (of serial) épisode m; (US: in hair) raie f ♦ adv = **partly** ♦ vt séparer ♦ vi (people) se séparer; (crowd) s'ouvrir; **to take ~ in** participer à, prendre part à; **to take sth in good ~** prendre qch du bon côté; **to take sb's ~** prendre le parti de qn, prendre parti pour qn; **for my ~** en ce qui me concerne; **for the most ~** dans la plupart des cas; **~ with** vt fus se séparer de; **~ exchange** (BRIT) n: **in ~ exchange** en reprise

partial [ˈpɑːʃl] adj (not complete) partiel(le); **to be ~ to** avoir un faible pour

participate [pɑːˈtɪsɪpeɪt] vi: **to ~ (in)** participer (à), prendre part (à); **participation** [pɑːtɪsɪˈpeɪʃən] n participation f

participle [ˈpɑːtɪsɪpl] n participe m

particle [ˈpɑːtɪkl] n particule f

particular [pəˈtɪkjʊlər] adj particulier(-ère); (special) spécial(e); (fussy) difficile; méticuleux(-euse); **~s** npl (details) détails mpl; (personal) nom, adresse etc; **in ~** en particulier; **~ly** adv particulièrement

parting [ˈpɑːtɪŋ] n séparation f; (BRIT: in

hair) raie *f* ♦ *adj* d'adieu

partisan [pɑːˈtɪˈzæn] *n* partisan(e) ♦ *adj* partisan(e); de parti

partition [pɑːˈtɪʃən] *n* (*wall*) cloison *f*; (*POL*) partition *f*, division *f*

partly [ˈpɑːtlɪ] *adv* en partie, partiellement

partner [ˈpɑːtnər] *n* partenaire *m/f*; (*in marriage*) conjoint(e); (*boyfriend, girlfriend*) ami(e); (*COMM*) associé(e); (*at dance*) cavalier(-ère); **~ship** *n* association *f*

partridge [ˈpɑːtrɪdʒ] *n* perdrix *f*

part-time [ˈpɑːttaɪm] *adj, adv* à mi-temps, à temps partiel

party [ˈpɑːtɪ] *n* (*POL*) parti *m*; (*group*) groupe *m*; (*LAW*) partie *f*; (*celebration*) réception *f*; soirée *f*; fête *f* ♦ *cpd* (*POL*) de *or* du parti; **~ dress** *n* robe habillée

pass [pɑːs] *vt* passer; (*place*) passer devant; (*friend*) croiser; (*overtake*) dépasser; (*exam*) être reçu(e) à, réussir; (*approve*) approuver, accepter ♦ *vi* passer; (*SCOL*) être reçu(e) *or* admis(e), réussir ♦ *n* (*permit*) laissez-passer *m inv*; carte *f* d'accès *or* d'abonnement; (*in mountains*) col *m*; (*SPORT*) passe *f*; (*SCOL: also:* **~ mark**): **to get a ~** être reçu(e) (sans mention); **to make a ~ at sb** (*inf*) faire des avances à qn; **~ away** *vi* mourir; **~ by** *vi* passer ♦ *vt* négliger; **~ on** *vt* (*news, object*) transmettre; (*illness*) passer; **~ out** *vi* s'évanouir; **~ up** *vt* (*opportunity*) laisser passer; **~able** *adj* (*road*) praticable; (*work*) acceptable

passage [ˈpæsɪdʒ] *n* (*also:* **~way**) couloir *m*; (*gen, in book*) passage *m*; (*by boat*) traversée *f*

passbook [ˈpɑːsbuk] *n* livret *m*

passenger [ˈpæsɪndʒər] *n* passager(-ère)

passer-by [pɑːsəˈbaɪ] (*pl* **~s-~**) *n* passant(e)

passing [ˈpɑːsɪŋ] *adj* (*fig*) passager(-ère); **in ~** en passant; **~ place** *n* (*AUT*) aire *f* de croisement

passion [ˈpæʃən] *n* passion *f*; **~ate** *adj* passionné(e)

passive [ˈpæsɪv] *adj* (*also LING*) passif(-ive); **~ smoking** *n* tabagisme *m* passif

Passover [ˈpɑːsəuvər] *n* Pâque *f* (*juive*)

passport [ˈpɑːspɔːt] *n* passeport *m*; **~ control** *n* contrôle *m* des passeports; **~ office** *n* bureau *m* de délivrance des passeports

password [ˈpɑːswəːd] *n* mot *m* de passe

past [pɑːst] *prep* (*in front of*) devant; (*further than*) au delà de, plus loin que; après; (*later than*) après ♦ *adj* passé(e); (*president etc*) ancien(ne) ♦ *n* passé *m*; **he's ~ forty** il a dépassé la quarantaine, il a plus de *or* passé quarante ans; **for the ~ few/3 days** depuis quelques/3 jours; ces derniers/3 derniers jours; **ten/quarter ~ eight** huit heures dix/un *or* et quart

pasta [ˈpæstə] *n* pâtes *fpl*

paste [peɪst] *n* pâte *f*; (*meat ~*) pâté *m* (à tartiner); (*tomato ~*) purée *f*, concentré *m*; (*glue*) colle *f* (de pâte) ♦ *vt* coller

pasteurized [ˈpæstʃəraɪzd] *adj* pasteurisé(e)

pastille [ˈpæstɪl] *n* pastille *f*

pastime [ˈpɑːstaɪm] *n* passe-temps *m inv*

pastry [ˈpeɪstrɪ] *n* pâte *f*; (*cake*) pâtisserie *f*

pasture [ˈpɑːstʃər] *n* pâturage *m*

pasty [*n* ˈpæstɪ, *adj* ˈpeɪstɪ] *n* petit pâté (en croûte) ♦ *adj* (*complexion*) terreux(-euse)

pat [pæt] *vt* tapoter; (*dog*) caresser

patch [pætʃ] *n* (*of material*) pièce *f*; (*eye ~*) cache *m*; (*spot*) tache *f*; (*on tyre*) rustine *f* ♦ *vt* (*clothes*) rapiécer; **(to go through) a bad ~** (passer par) une période difficile; **~ up** *vt* réparer (grossièrement); **to ~ up a quarrel** se raccommoder; **~y** *adj* inégal(e); (*incomplete*) fragmentaire

pâté [ˈpæteɪ] *n* pâté *m*, terrine *f*

patent [ˈpeɪtnt] *n* brevet *m* (d'invention) ♦ *vt* faire breveter ♦ *adj* patent(e), manifeste; **~ leather** *n* cuir verni

paternal [pəˈtəːnl] *adj* paternel(le)

path [pɑːθ] *n* chemin *m*, sentier *m*; (*in garden*) allée *f*; (*trajectory*) trajectoire *f*

pathetic [pəˈθetɪk] *adj* (*pitiful*) pitoyable; (*very bad*) lamentable, minable

pathological [pæθəˈlɔdʒɪkl] *adj* pathologique

pathway [ˈpɑːθweɪ] *n* sentier *m*, passage

m

patience ['peɪʃns] *n* patience *f*; (*BRIT: CARDS*) réussite *f*

patient ['peɪʃnt] *n* malade *m/f*; (*of dentist etc*) patient(e) ♦ *adj* patient(e)

patio ['pætɪəʊ] *n* patio *m*

patriotic [pætrɪ'ɔtɪk] *adj* patriotique; (*person*) patriote

patrol [pə'trəʊl] *n* patrouille *f* ♦ *vt* patrouiller dans; ~ **car** *n* voiture *f* de police; ~**man** (*irreg*) (*US*) *n* agent *m* de police

patron ['peɪtrən] *n* (*in shop*) client(e); (*of charity*) patron(ne); ~ **of the arts** mécène *m*; ~**ize** ['pætrənaɪz] *vt* (*pej*) traiter avec condescendance; (*shop, club*) être (un) client *or* un habitué de

patter ['pætər] *n* crépitement *m*, tapotement *m*; (*sales talk*) boniment *m*

pattern ['pætən] *n* (*design*) motif *m*; (*SEWING*) patron *m*

pauper ['pɔːpər] *n* indigent(e)

pause [pɔːz] *n* pause *f*, arrêt *m* ♦ *vi* faire une pause, s'arrêter

pave [peɪv] *vt* paver, daller; **to ~ the way for** ouvrir la voie à

pavement ['peɪvmənt] (*BRIT*) *n* trottoir *m*

pavilion [pə'vɪliən] *n* pavillon *m*; tente *f*

paving ['peɪvɪŋ] *n* (*material*) pavé *m*, dalle *f*; ~ **stone** *n* mont-de-pavé *m*

paw [pɔː] *n* patte *f*

pawn [pɔːn] *n* (*CHESS, also fig*) pion *m* ♦ *vt* mettre en gage; ~**broker** *n* prêteur *m* sur gages; ~**shop** *n* mont-de-piété *m*

pay [peɪ] (*pt, pp* **paid**) *n* salaire *m*; paie *f* ♦ *vt* payer ♦ *vi* payer; (*be profitable*) être rentable; **to ~ attention (to)** prêter attention (à); **to ~ sb a visit** rendre visite à qn; **to ~ one's respects to sb** présenter ses respects à qn; ~ **back** *vt* rembourser; ~ **for** *vt fus* payer; ~ **in** *vt* verser; ~ **off** *vt* régler, acquitter; (*person*) rembourser ♦ *vi* (*scheme, decision*) se révéler payant(e); ~ **up** *vt* (*money*) payer; ~**able** *adj*: ~**able to sb** (*cheque*) à l'ordre de qn; ~**ee** [peɪ'iː] *n* bénéficiaire *m/f*; ~ **envelope** (*US*) *n* = **pay packet**; ~**ment** *n* paiement *m*; règlement *m*; **monthly ~ment** mensualité

f; ~ **packet** (*BRIT*) *n* paie *f*; ~ **phone** *n* cabine *f* téléphonique, téléphone public; ~**roll** *n* registre *m* du personnel; ~ **slip** (*BRIT*) *n* bulletin *m* de paie; ~ **television** *n* chaînes *fpl* payantes

PC *n abbr* = **personal computer**

p.c. *abbr* = **per cent**

pea [piː] *n* (petit) pois

peace [piːs] *n* paix *f*; (*calm*) calme *m*, tranquillité *f*; ~**ful** *adj* paisible, calme

peach [piːtʃ] *n* pêche *f*

peacock ['piːkɔk] *n* paon *m*

peak [piːk] *n* (*mountain*) pic *m*, cime *f*; (*of cap*) visière *f*; (*fig: highest level*) maximum *m*; (*: of career, fame*) apogée *m*; ~ **hours** *npl* heures *fpl* de pointe

peal [piːl] *n* (*of bells*) carillon *m*; ~ **of laughter** éclat *m* de rire

peanut ['piːnʌt] *n* arachide *f*, cacahuète *f*; ~ **butter** *n* beurre *m* de cacahuète

pear [pɛər] *n* poire *f*

pearl [pɜːl] *n* perle *f*

peasant ['peznt] *n* paysan(ne)

peat [piːt] *n* tourbe *f*

pebble ['pebl] *n* caillou *m*, galet *m*

peck [pek] *vt* (*also*: ~ **at**) donner un coup de bec à ♦ *n* coup *m* de bec; (*kiss*) bise *f*; ~**ing order** *n* ordre *m* des préséances; ~**ish** (*BRIT: inf*) *adj*: **I feel ~ish** je mangerais bien quelque chose

peculiar [pɪ'kjuːlɪər] *adj* étrange, bizarre, curieux(-euse); ~ **to** particulier(-ère) à

pedal ['pedl] *n* pédale *f* ♦ *vi* pédaler

pedantic [pɪ'dæntɪk] *adj* pédant(e)

peddler ['pedlər] *n* (*of drugs*) revendeur(-euse)

pedestal ['pedəstl] *n* piédestal *m*

pedestrian [pɪ'destrɪən] *n* piéton *m*; ~ **crossing** (*BRIT*) *n* passage clouté; ~**ized** *adj*: **a ~ized street** une rue piétonne

pediatrics [piːdɪ'ætrɪks] (*US*) *n* = **paediatrics**

pedigree ['pedɪgriː] *n* ascendance *f*; (*of animal*) pedigree *m* ♦ *cpd* (*animal*) de race

pee [piː] (*inf*) *vi* faire pipi, pisser

peek [piːk] *vi* jeter un coup d'œil (furtif)

peel [piːl] *n* pelure *f*, épluchure *f*; (*of or-*

ange, lemon) écorce f ♦ *vt* peler, éplucher ♦ *vi (paint etc)* s'écailler; *(wallpaper)* se décoller; *(skin)* peler

peep [piːp] *n (BRIT: look)* coup d'œil furtif; *(sound)* pépiement *m* ♦ *vi (BRIT)* jeter un coup d'œil (furtif); ~ **out** *vi (BRIT)* se montrer (furtivement); ~**hole** *n* judas *m*

peer [pɪəʳ] *vi:* **to ~ at** regarder attentivement, scruter ♦ *n (noble)* pair *m*; *(equal)* pair, égal(e); ~**age** ['pɪərɪdʒ] *n* pairie *f*

peeved [piːvd] *adj* irrité(e), fâché(e)

peg [pɛg] *n (for coat etc)* patère f; *(BRIT: also:* **clothes ~**) pince f à linge

Pekin(g)ese [piːkɪˈniːz] *n (dog)* pékinois *m*

pelican ['pɛlɪkən] *n* pélican *m*; ~ **crossing** *(BRIT) n (AUT)* feu *m* à commande manuelle

pellet ['pɛlɪt] *n* boulette f; *(of lead)* plomb *m*

pelt [pɛlt] *vt:* **to ~ sb (with)** bombarder qn (de) ♦ *vi (rain)* tomber à seaux; *(inf: run)* courir à toutes jambes ♦ *n* peau f

pelvis ['pɛlvɪs] *n* bassin *m*

pen [pɛn] *n (for writing)* stylo *m*; *(for sheep)* parc *m*

penal ['piːnl] *adj* pénal(e); *(system, colony)* pénitentiaire; ~**ize** ['piːnəlaɪz] *vt* pénaliser

penalty ['pɛnltɪ] *n* pénalité f; sanction f; *(fine)* amende f; *(SPORT)* pénalisation f; *(FOOTBALL)* penalty *m*; *(RUGBY)* pénalité f

penance ['pɛnəns] *n* pénitence f

pence [pɛns] *(BRIT) npl of* **penny**

pencil ['pɛnsl] *n* crayon *m*; ~ **case** *n* trousse f (d'écolier); ~ **sharpener** *n* taille-crayon(s) *m inv*

pendant ['pɛndnt] *n* pendentif *m*

pending ['pɛndɪŋ] *prep* en attendant ♦ *adj* en suspens

pendulum ['pɛndjuləm] *n (of clock)* balancier *m*

penetrate ['pɛnɪtreɪt] *vt* pénétrer dans; pénétrer

penfriend ['pɛnfrɛnd] *(BRIT) n* correspondant(e)

penguin ['pɛŋgwɪn] *n* pingouin *m*

penicillin [pɛnɪˈsɪlɪn] *n* pénicilline f

peninsula [pəˈnɪnsjulə] *n* péninsule f

penis ['piːnɪs] *n* pénis *m*, verge f

penitentiary [pɛnɪˈtɛnʃərɪ] *n* prison f

penknife ['pɛnnaɪf] *n* canif *m*

pen name *n* nom *m* de plume, pseudonyme *m*

penniless ['pɛnɪlɪs] *adj* sans le sou

penny ['pɛnɪ] *(pl* **pennies** *or (BRIT)* **pence**) *n* penny *m*

penpal ['pɛnpæl] *n* correspondant(e)

pension ['pɛnʃən] *n* pension f; *(from company)* retraite f; ~**er** *(BRIT) n* retraité(e); ~ **fund** *n* caisse f de pension; ~ **plan** *n* plan *m* de retraite

---

Pentagon

> *i* Le **Pentagon** est le nom donné aux bureaux du ministère de la Défense américain, situés à Arlington en Virginie, à cause de la forme pentagonale du bâtiment dans lequel ils se trouvent. Par extension, ce terme est également utilisé en parlant du ministère lui-même.

---

pentathlon [pɛnˈtæθlən] *n* pentathlon *m*

Pentecost ['pɛntɪkɔst] *n* Pentecôte f

penthouse ['pɛnthaus] *n* appartement *m* (de luxe) (en attique)

pent-up ['pɛntʌp] *adj (feelings)* refoulé(e)

penultimate [pɛˈnʌltɪmət] *adj* avant-dernier(-ère)

people ['piːpl] *npl* gens *mpl*; personnes *fpl*; *(inhabitants)* population f; *(POL)* peuple *m* ♦ *n (nation, race)* peuple *m*; **several ~ came** plusieurs personnes sont venues; ~ **say that ...** on dit que ...

pep up ['pɛp-] *(inf) vt* remonter

pepper ['pɛpəʳ] *n* poivre *m*; *(vegetable)* poivron *m* ♦ *vt (fig):* **to ~ with** bombarder de; ~**mill** *n* moulin *m* à poivre; ~**mint** *n (sweet)* pastille f de menthe

peptalk ['pɛptɔːk] *(inf) n* (petit) discours d'encouragement

per [pəːʳ] *prep* par; ~ **hour** *(miles etc)* à l'heure; *(fee)* (de) l'heure; ~ **kilo** *etc* le kilo *etc*; ~ **annum** par an; ~ **capita** par personne, par habitant

perceive [pə'si:v] *vt* percevoir; (*notice*) remarquer, s'apercevoir *f*

per cent *adv* pour cent; **percentage** *n* pourcentage *m*

perception [pə'sɛpʃən] *n* perception *f*; (*insight*) perspicacité *f*

perceptive [pə'sɛptɪv] *adj* pénétrant(e); (*person*) perspicace

perch [pə:tʃ] *n* (*fish*) perche *f*; (*for bird*) perchoir *m* ♦ *vi*: **to ~ on** se percher sur

percolator ['pə:kəleɪtər] *n* cafetière *f* (électrique)

percussion [pə'kʌʃən] *n* percussion *f*

perennial [pə'rɛnɪəl] *adj* perpétuel(le); (*BOT*) vivace

perfect [*adj, n* 'pə:fɪkt, *vb* pə'fɛkt] *adj* parfait(e) ♦ *n* (*also:* ~ **tense**) parfait *m* ♦ *vt* parfaire; mettre au point; ~**ly** *adv* parfaitement

perforate ['pə:fəreɪt] *vt* perforer, percer; **perforation** [pə:fə'reɪʃən] *n* perforation *f*

perform [pə'fɔ:m] *vt* (*carry out*) exécuter; (*concert etc*) jouer, donner ♦ *vi* jouer; ~**ance** *n* représentation *f*, spectacle *m*; (*of an artist*) interprétation *f*; (*SPORT*) performance *f*; (*of car, engine*) fonctionnement *m*; (*of company, economy*) résultats *mpl*; ~**er** *n* artiste *m/f*, interprète *m/f*

perfume ['pə:fju:m] *n* parfum *m*

perhaps [pə'hæps] *adv* peut-être

peril ['pɛrɪl] *n* péril *m*

perimeter [pə'rɪmɪtər] *n* périmètre *m*

period ['pɪərɪəd] *n* période *f*; (*of history*) époque *f*; (*SCOL*) cours *m*; (*full stop*) point *m*; (*MED*) règles *fpl* ♦ *adj* (*costume, furniture*) d'époque; ~**ic(al)** [pɪərɪ'ɔdɪk(l)] *adj* périodique; ~**ical** [pɪərɪ'ɔdɪkl] *n* périodique *m*

peripheral [pə'rɪfərəl] *adj* périphérique ♦ *n* (*COMPUT*) périphérique *m*

perish ['pɛrɪʃ] *vi* périr; (*decay*) se détériorer; ~**able** *adj* périssable

perjury ['pə:dʒərɪ] *n* parjure *m*, faux serment *m*

perk [pə:k] *n* avantage *m* accessoire, à-côté *m*; ~ **up** *vi* (*cheer up*) se ragaillardir; ~**y** *adj* (*cheerful*) guilleret(te)

perm [pə:m] *n* (*for hair*) permanente *f*

permanent ['pə:mənənt] *adj* permanent(e)

permeate ['pə:mɪeɪt] *vi* s'infiltrer ♦ *vt* s'infiltrer dans; pénétrer

permissible [pə'mɪsɪbl] *adj* permis(e), acceptable

permission [pə'mɪʃən] *n* permission *f*, autorisation *f*

permissive [pə'mɪsɪv] *adj* tolérant(e), permissif(-ive)

permit [*n* 'pə:mɪt, *vb* pə'mɪt] *n* permis *m* ♦ *vt* permettre

perpendicular [pə:pən'dɪkjulər] *adj* perpendiculaire

perplex [pə'plɛks] *vt* rendre perplexe

persecute ['pə:sɪkju:t] *vt* persécuter

persevere [pə:sɪ'vɪər] *vi* persévérer

Persian ['pə:ʃən] *adj* persan(e) ♦ *n* (*LING*) persan *m*; **the ~ Gulf** le golfe Persique

persist [pə'sɪst] *vi*: **to ~ (in doing)** persister *or* s'obstiner (à faire); ~**ent** [pə'sɪstənt] *adj* persistant(e), tenace; ~**ent vegetative state** état *m* végétatif persistant

person ['pə:sn] *n* personne *f*; **in ~** en personne; ~**al** *adj* personnel(le); ~**al assistant** *n* secrétaire privé(e); ~**al column** *n* annonces personnelles; ~**al computer** *n* ordinateur personnel; ~**ality** [pə:sə'nælɪtɪ] *n* personnalité *f*; ~**ally** *adv* personnellement; **to take sth ~ally** se sentir visé(e) (par qch); ~**al organizer** *n* filofax ® *m*; ~**al stereo** *n* Walkman ® *m*, baladeur *m*

personnel [pə:sə'nɛl] *n* personnel *m*

perspective [pə'spɛktɪv] *n* perspective *f*; **to get things into ~** faire la part des choses

Perspex ® ['pə:spɛks] *n* plexiglas ® *m*

perspiration [pə:spɪ'reɪʃən] *n* transpiration *f*

persuade [pə'sweɪd] *vt*: **to ~ sb to do sth** persuader qn de faire qch; **persuasion** [pə'sweɪʒən] *n* persuasion *f*; (*creed*) religion *f*

perverse [pə'və:s] *adj* pervers(e); (*contrary*) contrariant(e); **pervert** [*n* 'pə:və:t, *vb* pə'və:t] *n* perverti(e) ♦ *vt* pervertir; (*words*) déformer

pessimist ['pɛsɪmɪst] n pessimiste m/f; **~ic** [pɛsɪ'mɪstɪk] adj pessimiste

pest [pɛst] n animal m (or insecte m) nuisible; (fig) fléau m

pester ['pɛstər] vt importuner, harceler

pet [pɛt] n animal familier ♦ cpd (favourite) favori(te) ♦ vt (stroke) caresser, câliner; **teacher's ~** chouchou m du professeur; **~ hate** bête noire

petal ['pɛtl] n pétale m

peter out ['piːtə-] vi (stream, conversation) tarir; (meeting) tourner court; (road) se perdre

petite [pə'tiːt] adj menu(e)

petition [pə'tɪʃən] n pétition f

petrified ['pɛtrɪfaɪd] adj (fig) mort(e) de peur

petrol ['pɛtrəl] (BRIT) n essence f; **four-star ~** super m; **~ can** n bidon m à essence

petroleum [pə'trəulɪəm] n pétrole m

petrol: **~ pump** (BRIT) n pompe f à essence; **~ station** (BRIT) n station-service f; **~ tank** (BRIT) n réservoir m d'essence

petticoat ['pɛtɪkəut] n combinaison f

petty ['pɛtɪ] adj (mean) mesquin(e); (unimportant) insignifiant(e), sans importance; **~ cash** n caisse f des dépenses courantes; **~ officer** n second-maître m

petulant ['pɛtjulənt] adj boudeur(-euse), irritable

pew [pjuː] n banc m (d'église)

pewter ['pjuːtər] n étain m

phantom ['fæntəm] n fantôme m

pharmacy ['fɑːməsɪ] n pharmacie f

phase [feɪz] n phase f ♦ vt: **to ~ sth in / out** introduire/supprimer qch progressivement

PhD abbr = **Doctor of Philosophy** ♦ n abbr (title) ≈ docteur m (en droit or lettres etc), ≈ doctorat m; (person) titulaire m/f d'un doctorat

pheasant ['fɛznt] n faisan m

phenomenon [fə'nɔmɪnən] (pl **phenomena**) n phénomène m

philosophical [fɪlə'sɔfɪkl] adj philosophique

philosophy [fɪ'lɔsəfɪ] n philosophie f

phobia ['fəubjə] n phobie f

phone [fəun] n téléphone m ♦ vt téléphoner; **to be on the ~** avoir le téléphone; (be calling) être au téléphone; **~ back** vt, vi rappeler; **~ up** vt téléphoner à ♦ vi téléphoner; **~ bill** n facture f de téléphone; **~ book** n annuaire m; **~ booth**, **~ box** (BRIT) n cabine f téléphonique; **~ call** n coup m de fil or de téléphone; **~card** n carte f de téléphone; **~-in** (BRIT) n (RADIO, TV) programme m à ligne ouverte; **~ number** n numéro m de téléphone

phonetics [fə'nɛtɪks] n phonétique f

phoney ['fəunɪ] adj faux (fausse), factice; (person) pas franc (franche), poseur(-euse)

photo ['fəutəu] n photo f; **~copier** n photocopieuse f; **~copy** n photocopie f ♦ vt photocopier; **~graph** n photographie f ♦ vt photographier; **~grapher** [fə'tɔgrəfər] n photographe m/f; **~graphy** [fə'tɔgrəfɪ] n photographie f

phrase [freɪz] n expression f; (LING) locution f ♦ vt exprimer; **~ book** n recueil m d'expressions (pour touristes)

physical ['fɪzɪkl] adj physique; **~ education** n éducation f physique; **~ly** adv physiquement

physician [fɪ'zɪʃən] n médecin m

physicist ['fɪzɪsɪst] n physicien(ne)

physics ['fɪzɪks] n physique f

physiotherapist [fɪzɪəu'θɛrəpɪst] n kinésithérapeute m/f

physiotherapy [fɪzɪəu'θɛrəpɪ] n kinésithérapie f

physique [fɪ'ziːk] n physique m; constitution f

pianist ['piːənɪst] n pianiste m/f

piano [pɪ'ænəu] n piano m

pick [pɪk] n (tool: also: **~axe**) pic m, pioche f ♦ vt choisir; (fruit etc) cueillir; (remove) prendre; (lock) forcer; **take your ~** faites votre choix; **the ~ of** le (la) meilleur(e) de; **to ~ one's nose** se mettre les doigts dans le nez; **to ~ one's teeth** se curer les dents; **to ~ a quarrel with sb** chercher noise à qn; **~ at** vt fus: **to ~ at one's**

food manger du bout des dents, chipoter; **~ on** vt fus (person) harceler; **~ out** vt choisir; (distinguish) distinguer; **~ up** vi (improve) s'améliorer ♦ vt ramasser; (collect) passer prendre; (AUT: give lift to) prendre, emmener; (learn) apprendre; (RADIO) capter; **to ~ up speed** prendre de la vitesse; **to ~ o.s. up** se relever

picket ['pɪkɪt] n (in strike) piquet m de grève ♦ vt mettre un piquet de grève devant

pickle ['pɪkl] n (also: **~s**: as condiment) pickles mpl; petits légumes macérés dans du vinaigre ♦ vt conserver dans du vinaigre or dans de la saumure; **to be in a ~** (mess) être dans le pétrin

pickpocket ['pɪkpɔkɪt] n pickpocket m

pick-up ['pɪkʌp] n (small truck) pick-up m inv

picnic ['pɪknɪk] n pique-nique m

picture ['pɪktʃər] n image f; (painting) peinture f, tableau m; (etching) gravure f; (photograph) photo(graphie) f; (drawing) dessin m; (film) film m; (fig) description f; tableau m ♦ vt se représenter; **the ~s** (BRIT: inf) le cinéma; **~ book** n livre m d'images

picturesque [pɪktʃə'resk] adj pittoresque

pie [paɪ] n tourte f; (of fruit) tarte f; (of meat) pâté m en croûte

piece [pi:s] n morceau m; (item): **a ~ of furniture/advice** un meuble/conseil ♦ vt: **to ~ together** rassembler; **to take to ~s** démonter; **~meal** adv (irregularly) au coup par coup; (bit by bit) par bouts; **~work** n travail m aux pièces

pie chart n graphique m circulaire, camembert m

pier [pɪər] n jetée f

pierce [pɪəs] vt percer, transpercer; **~d** adj (ears etc) percé(e)

pig [pɪg] n cochon m, porc m

pigeon ['pɪdʒən] n pigeon m; **~hole** n casier m

piggy bank ['pɪgɪ-] n tirelire f

pig: ~headed adj entêté(e), têtu(e); **~let** n porcelet m, petit cochon m; **~skin** n peau

m de porc; **~sty** n porcherie f; **~tail** n natte f, tresse f

pike [paɪk] n (fish) brochet m

pilchard ['pɪltʃəd] n pilchard m (sorte de sardine)

pile [paɪl] n (pillar, of books) pile f; (heap) tas m; (of carpet) poils mpl ♦ vt (also: **~ up**) empiler, entasser ♦ vi (also: **~ up**) s'entasser, s'accumuler; **to ~ into** (car) s'entasser dans; **~s** npl hémorroïdes fpl; **~-up** n (AUT) télescopage m, collision f en série

pilfering ['pɪlfərɪŋ] n chapardage m

pilgrim ['pɪlgrɪm] n pèlerin m

pill [pɪl] n pilule f

pillage ['pɪlɪdʒ] vt piller

pillar ['pɪlər] n pilier m; **~ box** (BRIT) n boîte f aux lettres (publique)

pillion ['pɪljən] n: **to ride ~** (on motorcycle) monter derrière

pillow ['pɪləu] n oreiller m; **~case** n taie f d'oreiller

pilot ['paɪlət] n pilote m ♦ cpd (scheme etc) pilote, expérimental(e) ♦ vt piloter; **~ light** n veilleuse f

pimp [pɪmp] n souteneur m, maquereau m

pimple ['pɪmpl] n bouton m

pin [pɪn] n épingle f; (TECH) cheville f ♦ vt épingler; **~s and needles** fourmis fpl; **to ~ sb down** (fig) obliger qn à répondre; **to ~ sth on sb** (fig) mettre qch sur le dos de qn

PIN [pɪn] n abbr (= personal identification number) numéro m d'identification personnel

pinafore ['pɪnəfɔ:r] n tablier m

pinball ['pɪnbɔ:l] n flipper m

pincers ['pɪnsəz] npl tenailles fpl; (of crab etc) pinces fpl

pinch [pɪntʃ] n (of salt etc) pincée f ♦ vt pincer; (inf: steal) piquer, chiper; **at a ~** à la rigueur

pincushion ['pɪnkuʃən] n pelote f à épingles

pine [paɪn] n (also: **~ tree**) pin m ♦ vi: **to ~ for** s'ennuyer de, désirer ardemment; **~ away** vi dépérir

pineapple ['paɪnæpl] *n* ananas *m*

ping [pɪŋ] *n* (*noise*) tintement *m*; **~-pong** ® *n* ping-pong ® *m*

pink [pɪŋk] *adj* rose ♦ *n* (*colour*) rose *m*; (*BOT*) œillet *m*, mignardise *f*

PIN (number) ['pɪn(-)] *n* code *m* confidentiel

pinpoint ['pɪnpɔɪnt] *vt* indiquer *or* localiser (avec précision); (*problem*) mettre le doigt sur

pint [paɪnt] *n* pinte *f* (*BRIT* = 0.57l; *US* = 0.47l); (*BRIT*: *inf*) ≈ demi *m*

pioneer [paɪə'nɪər] *n* pionnier *m*

pious ['paɪəs] *adj* pieux(-euse)

pip [pɪp] *n* (*seed*) pépin *m*; **the ~s** *npl* (*BRIT*: *time signal on radio*) le(s) top(s) sonore(s)

pipe [paɪp] *n* tuyau *m*, conduite *f*; (*for smoking*) pipe *f* ♦ *vt* amener par tuyau; **~s** *npl* (*also*: **bagpipes**) cornemuse *f*; **~ cleaner** *n* cure-pipe *m*; **~ dream** *n* chimère *f*, château *m* en Espagne; **~line** *n* pipe-line *m*; **~r** *n* joueur(-euse) de cornemuse

piping ['paɪpɪŋ] *adv*: **~ hot** très chaud(e)

pique ['piːk] *n* dépit *m*

pirate ['paɪərət] *n* pirate *m*; **~d** *adj* pirate

Pisces ['paɪsiːz] *n* les Poissons *mpl*

piss [pɪs] (*inf!*) *vi* pisser; **~ed** (*inf!*) *adj* (*drunk*) bourré(e)

pistol ['pɪstl] *n* pistolet *m*

piston ['pɪstən] *n* piston *m*

pit [pɪt] *n* trou *m*, fosse *f*; (*also*: **coal ~**) puits *m* de mine; (*quarry*) carrière *f* ♦ *vt*: **to ~ one's wits against sb** se mesurer à qn; **~s** *npl* (*AUT*) aire *f* de service

pitch [pɪtʃ] *n* (*MUS*) ton *m*; (*BRIT*: *SPORT*) terrain *m*; (*tar*) poix *f*; (*fig*) degré *m*; point *m* ♦ *vt* (*throw*) lancer ♦ *vi* (*fall*) tomber; **to ~ a tent** dresser une tente; **~-black** *adj* noir(e) (comme du cirage); **~ed battle** *n* bataille rangée

pitfall ['pɪtfɔːl] *n* piège *m*

pith [pɪθ] *n* (*of orange etc*) intérieur *m* de l'écorce; **~y** *adj* piquant(e)

pitiful ['pɪtɪful] *adj* (*touching*) pitoyable

pitiless ['pɪtɪlɪs] *adj* impitoyable

pittance ['pɪtns] *n* salaire *m* de misère

pity ['pɪtɪ] *n* pitié *f* ♦ *vt* plaindre; **what a ~!** quel dommage!

pizza ['piːtsə] *n* pizza *f*

placard ['plækɑːd] *n* affiche *f*; (*in march*) pancarte *f*

placate [plə'keɪt] *vt* apaiser, calmer

place [pleɪs] *n* endroit *m*, lieu *m*; (*proper position, job, rank, seat*) place *f*; (*home*): **at/to his ~** chez lui ♦ *vt* (*object*) placer, mettre; (*identify*) situer; reconnaître; **to take ~** avoir lieu; **out of ~** (*not suitable*) déplacé(e), inopportun(e); **to change ~s with sb** changer de place avec qn; **in the first ~** d'abord, en premier

plague [pleɪg] *n* fléau *m*; (*MED*) peste *f* ♦ *vt* (*fig*) tourmenter

plaice [pleɪs] *n inv* carrelet *m*

plaid [plæd] *n* tissu écossais

plain [pleɪn] *adj* (*in one colour*) uni(e); (*simple*) simple; (*clear*) clair(e), évident(e); (*not handsome*) quelconque, ordinaire ♦ *adv* franchement, carrément ♦ *n* plaine *f*; **~ chocolate** *n* chocolat *m* à croquer; **~ clothes** *adj* (*police officer*) en civil; **~ly** *adv* clairement; (*frankly*) carrément, sans détours

plaintiff ['pleɪntɪf] *n* plaignant(e)

plait [plæt] *n* tresse *f*, natte *f*

plan [plæn] *n* plan *m*; (*scheme*) projet *m* ♦ *vt* (*think in advance*) projeter; (*prepare*) organiser; (*house*) dresser les plans de, concevoir ♦ *vi* faire des projets; **to ~ to do** prévoir de faire

plane [pleɪn] *n* (*AVIAT*) avion *m*; (*ART*, *MATH etc*) plan *m*; (*fig*) niveau *m*, plan; (*tool*) rabot *m*; (*also*: **~ tree**) platane *m* ♦ *vt* raboter

planet ['plænɪt] *n* planète *f*

plank [plæŋk] *n* planche *f*

planner ['plænər] *n* planificateur(-trice); (*town ~*) urbaniste *m/f*

planning ['plænɪŋ] *n* planification *f*; **family ~** planning familial; **~ permission** *n* permis *m* de construire

plant [plɑːnt] *n* plante *f*; (*machinery*) matériel *m*; (*factory*) usine *f* ♦ *vt* planter; (*bomb*) poser; (*microphone, incriminating evidence*) cacher

plaster ['plɑ:stər] *n* plâtre *m*; (*also:* ~ **of Paris**) plâtre à mouler; (*BRIT: also:* **sticking** ~) pansement adhésif ♦ *vt* plâtrer; (*cover*): **to** ~ **with** couvrir de; **~ed** (*inf*) *adj* soûl(e)

plastic ['plæstɪk] *n* plastique *m* ♦ *adj* (*made of* ~) en plastique; ~ **bag** *n* sac *m* en plastique

Plasticine ® ['plæstɪsi:n] *n* pâte *f* à modeler

plastic surgery *n* chirurgie *f* esthétique

plate [pleɪt] *n* (*dish*) assiette *f*; (*in book*) gravure *f*, planche *f*; (*dental* ~) dentier *m*

plateau ['plætəʊ] (*pl* ~**s** *or* ~**x**) *n* plateau *m*

plate glass *n* verre *m* (de vitrine)

platform ['plætfɔ:m] *n* plate-forme *f*; (*at meeting*) tribune *f*; (*stage*) estrade *f*; (*RAIL*) quai *m*

platinum ['plætɪnəm] *n* platine *m*

platter ['plætər] *n* plat *m*

plausible ['plɔ:zɪbl] *adj* plausible; (*person*) convaincant(e)

play [pleɪ] *n* (*THEATRE*) pièce *f* (de théâtre) ♦ *vt* (*game*) jouer à; (*team, opponent*) jouer contre; (*instrument*) jouer de; (*part, piece of music, note*) jouer; (*record etc*) passer ♦ *vi* jouer; **to** ~ **safe** ne prendre aucun risque; ~ **down** *vt* minimiser; ~ **up** *vi* (*cause trouble*) faire des siennes; ~**boy** *n* playboy *m*; ~**er** *n* joueur(-euse); (*THEATRE*) acteur(-trice); (*MUS*) musicien(ne); ~**ful** *adj* enjoué(e); ~**ground** *n* cour *f* de récréation; (*in park*) aire *f* de jeux; ~**group** *n* garderie *f*; ~**ing card** *n* carte *f* à jouer; ~**ing field** *n* terrain *m* de sport; ~**mate** *n* camarade *m/f*, copain (copine); ~**-off** *n* (*SPORT*) belle *f*; ~**pen** *n* parc *m* (pour bébé); ~**thing** *n* jouet *m*; ~**time** *n* récréation *f*; ~**wright** *n* dramaturge *m*

plc *abbr* (= public limited company) SARL *f*

plea [pli:] *n* (*request*) appel *m*; (*LAW*) défense *f*

plead [pli:d] *vt* plaider; (*give as excuse*) invoquer ♦ *vi* (*LAW*) plaider; (*beg*): **to** ~ **with sb** implorer qn

pleasant ['plɛznt] *adj* agréable; ~**ries** *npl* (*polite remarks*) civilités *fpl*

please [pli:z] *excl* s'il te (*or* vous) plaît ♦ *vt* plaire à ♦ *vi* plaire; (*think fit*): **do as you** ~ faites comme il vous plaira; ~ **yourself!** à ta (*or* votre) guise!; ~**d** *adj*: ~**d (with)** content(e) (de); ~**d to meet you** enchanté (de faire votre connaissance); **pleasing** *adj* plaisant(e), qui fait plaisir

pleasure ['plɛʒər] *n* plaisir *m*; **"it's a** ~**"** "je vous en prie"

pleat [pli:t] *n* pli *m*

pledge [plɛdʒ] *n* (*promise*) promesse *f* ♦ *vt* engager; promettre

plentiful ['plɛntɪful] *adj* abondant(e), copieux(-euse)

plenty ['plɛntɪ] *n*: ~ **of** beaucoup de; (bien) assez de

pliable ['plaɪəbl] *adj* flexible; (*person*) malléable

pliers ['plaɪəz] *npl* pinces *fpl*

plight [plaɪt] *n* situation *f* critique

plimsolls ['plɪmsəlz] (*BRIT*) *npl* chaussures *fpl* de tennis, tennis *mpl*

plinth [plɪnθ] *n* (*of statue*) socle *m*

P.L.O. *n abbr* (= Palestine Liberation Organization) OLP *f*

plod [plɒd] *vi* avancer péniblement; (*fig*) peiner

plonk [plɒŋk] (*inf*) *n* (*BRIT: wine*) pinard *m*, piquette *f* ♦ *vt*: **to** ~ **sth down** poser brusquement qch

plot [plɒt] *n* complot *m*, conspiration *f*; (*of story, play*) intrigue *f*; (*of land*) lot *m* de terrain, lopin *m* ♦ *vt* (*sb's downfall*) comploter; (*mark out*) pointer; relever, déterminer ♦ *vi* comploter

plough [plaʊ] (*US* **plow**) *n* charrue *f* ♦ *vt* (*earth*) labourer; **to** ~ **money into** investir dans; ~ **through** *vt fus* (*snow etc*) avancer péniblement dans; ~**man's lunch** (*BRIT*) *n* assiette froide avec du pain, du fromage et des pickles

ploy [plɔɪ] *n* stratagème *m*

pluck [plʌk] *vt* (*fruit*) cueillir; (*musical instrument*) pincer; (*bird*) plumer; (*eyebrow*) épiler ♦ *n* courage *m*, cran *m*; **to** ~ **up courage** prendre son courage à deux mains

plug [plʌg] n (ELEC) prise f de courant; (stopper) bouchon m, bonde f; (AUT: also: **spark(ing) ~**) bougie f ♦ vt (hole) boucher; (inf: advertise) faire du battage pour; **~ in** vt (ELEC) brancher

plum [plʌm] n (fruit) prune f ♦ cpd: **~ job** (inf) travail m en or

plumb [plʌm] vt: **to ~ the depths** (fig) toucher le fond (du désespoir)

plumber ['plʌmər] n plombier m

plumbing ['plʌmɪŋ] n (trade) plomberie f; (piping) tuyauterie f

plummet ['plʌmɪt] vi: **to ~ (down)** plonger, dégringoler

plump [plʌmp] adj rondelet(te), dodu(e), bien en chair ♦ vi: **to ~ for** (inf: choose) se décider pour

plunder ['plʌndər] n pillage m; (loot) butin m ♦ vt piller

plunge [plʌndʒ] n plongeon m; (fig) chute f ♦ vt plonger ♦ vi (dive) plonger; (fall) tomber, dégringoler; **to take the ~** se jeter à l'eau; **plunging** ['plʌndʒɪŋ] adj: **plunging neckline** décolleté plongeant

pluperfect [pluː'pɜːfɪkt] n plus-que-parfait m

plural ['plʊərl] adj pluriel(le) ♦ n pluriel m

plus [plʌs] n (also: **~ sign**) signe m plus ♦ prep plus; **ten/twenty ~** plus de dix/vingt

plush [plʌʃ] adj somptueux(-euse)

ply [plaɪ] vt (a trade) exercer ♦ vi (ship) faire la navette ♦ n (of wool, rope) fil m, brin m; **to ~ sb with drink** donner continuellement à boire à qn; **to ~ sb with questions** presser qn de questions; **~wood** n contre-plaqué m

PM abbr = **Prime Minister**

p.m. adv abbr (= post meridiem) de l'après-midi

pneumatic drill [njuː'mætɪk-] n marteau-piqueur m

pneumonia [njuː'məʊnɪə] n pneumonie f

poach [pəʊtʃ] vt (cook) pocher; (steal) pêcher (or chasser) sans permis ♦ vi braconner; **~ed egg** n œuf poché; **~er** n braconnier m

P.O. box n abbr = **post office box**

pocket ['pɔkɪt] n poche f ♦ vt empocher; **to be out of ~** (BRIT) en être de sa poche; **~book** (US) n (wallet) portefeuille m; **~ calculator** n calculette f; **~ knife** n canif m; **~ money** n argent m de poche

pod [pɔd] n cosse f

podgy ['pɔdʒɪ] adj rondelet(te)

podiatrist [pɔ'diːətrɪst] (US) n pédicure m/f, podologue m/f

poem ['pəʊɪm] n poème m

poet ['pəʊɪt] n poète m; **~ic** [pəʊ'etɪk] adj poétique; **~ry** ['pəʊɪtrɪ] n poésie f

poignant ['pɔɪnjənt] adj poignant(e); (sharp) vif (vive)

point [pɔɪnt] n point m; (tip) pointe f; (in time) moment m; (in space) endroit m; (subject, idea) point, sujet m; (purpose) sens m; (ELEC) prise f; (also: **decimal ~**): **2 ~ 3 (2.3)** 2 virgule 3 (2,3) ♦ vt (show) indiquer; (gun etc): **to ~ sth at** braquer or diriger qch sur ♦ vi: **to ~ at** montrer du doigt; **~s** npl (AUT) vis platinées; (RAIL) aiguillage m; **to be on the ~ of doing sth** être sur le point de faire qch; **to make a ~ of doing** ne pas manquer de faire; **to get the ~** comprendre, saisir; **to miss the ~** ne pas comprendre; **to come to the ~** en venir au fait; **there's no ~ (in doing)** cela ne sert à rien (de faire); **~ out** vt faire remarquer, souligner; **~ to** vt fus (fig) indiquer; **~-blank** adv (fig) catégoriquement; (also: **at ~-blank range**) à bout portant; **~ed** adj (shape) pointu(e); (remark) plein(e) de sous-entendus; **~er** n (needle) aiguille f; (piece of advice) conseil m; (clue) indice m; **~less** adj inutile, vain(e); **~ of view** n point m de vue

poise [pɔɪz] n (composure) calme m

poison ['pɔɪzn] n poison m ♦ vt empoisonner; **~ous** adj (snake) venimeux(-euse); (plant) vénéneux(-euse); (fumes etc) toxique

poke [pəʊk] vt (fire) tisonner; (jab with finger, stick etc) piquer; (pousser du doigt; (put): **to ~ sth in(to)** fourrer or enfoncer qch dans; **~ about** vi fureter; **~r** n tisonnier *m*; (*CARDS*) poker *m*

poky ['pəʊkɪ] *adj* exigu(ë)

Poland ['pəʊlənd] *n* Pologne *f*

polar ['pəʊləʳ] *adj* polaire; ~ **bear** *n* ours blanc

Pole [pəʊl] *n* Polonais(e)

pole [pəʊl] *n* poteau *m*; (*of wood*) mât *m*, perche *f*; (*GEO*) pôle *m*; ~ **bean** (*US*) *n* haricot *m* (à rames); ~ **vault** *n* saut *m* à la perche

police [pə'liːs] *npl* police *f* ♦ *vt* maintenir l'ordre dans; ~ **car** *n* voiture *f* de police; ~**man** (*irreg*) *n* agent *m* de police, policier *m*; ~ **station** *n* commissariat *m* de police; ~**woman** (*irreg*) *n* femme-agent *f*

policy ['pɒlɪsɪ] *n* politique *f*; (*also:* **insurance** ~) police *f* (d'assurance)

polio ['pəʊlɪəʊ] *n* polio *f*

Polish ['pəʊlɪʃ] *adj* polonais(e) ♦ *n* (*LING*) polonais *m*

polish ['pɒlɪʃ] *n* (*for shoes*) cirage *m*; (*for floor*) cire *f*, encaustique *f*; (*shine*) éclat *m*, poli *m*; (*fig: refinement*) raffinement *m* ♦ *vt* (*put ~ on shoes, wood*) cirer; (*make shiny*) astiquer, faire briller; ~ **off** (*inf*) *vt* (*food*) liquider; ~**ed** *adj* (*fig*) raffiné(e)

polite [pə'laɪt] *adj* poli(e); **in ~ society** dans la bonne société; ~**ly** *adv* poliment; ~**ness** *n* politesse *f*

political [pə'lɪtɪkl] *adj* politique; ~**ly correct** *adj* politiquement correct(e)

politician [pɒlɪ'tɪʃən] *n* homme *m*/femme *f* politique

politics ['pɒlɪtɪks] *npl* politique *f*

poll [pəʊl] *n* scrutin *m*, vote *m*; (*also:* **opinion** ~) sondage *m* (d'opinion) ♦ *vt* obtenir

pollen ['pɒlən] *n* pollen *m*

polling day ['pəʊlɪŋ-] (*BRIT*) *n* jour *m* des élections

polling station (*BRIT*) *n* bureau *m* de vote

pollute [pə'luːt] *vt* polluer; **pollution** *n* pollution *f*

polo ['pəʊləʊ] *n* polo *m*; ~-**necked** *adj* à col roulé; ~ **shirt** *n* polo *m*

polyester [pɒlɪ'estəʳ] *n* polyester *m*

polystyrene [pɒlɪ'staɪriːn] *n* polystyrène *m*

polythene ['pɒlɪθiːn] *n* polyéthylène *m*; ~ **bag** *n* sac *m* en plastique

pomegranate ['pɒmɪgrænɪt] *n* grenade *f*

pomp [pɒmp] *n* pompe *f*, faste *f*, apparat *m*; ~**ous** *adj* pompeux(-euse)

pond [pɒnd] *n* étang *m*; mare *f*

ponder ['pɒndəʳ] *vt* considérer, peser; ~**ous** *adj* pesant(e), lourd(e)

pong [pɒŋ] (*BRIT: inf*) *n* puanteur *f*

pony ['pəʊnɪ] *n* poney *m*; ~**tail** *n* queue *f* de cheval; ~ **trekking** (*BRIT*) *n* randonnée *f* à cheval

poodle ['puːdl] *n* caniche *m*

pool [puːl] *n* (*of rain*) flaque *f*; (*pond*) mare *f*; (*also:* **swimming** ~) piscine *f*; (*billiards*) poule *f* ♦ *vt* mettre en commun; ~**s** *npl* (*football* ~*s*) ≈ loto sportif

poor [pʊəʳ] *adj* pauvre; (*mediocre*) médiocre, faible, mauvais(e) ♦ *npl*: **the** ~ les pauvres *mpl*; ~**ly** *adj* souffrant(e), malade ♦ *adv* mal; médiocrement

pop [pɒp] *n* (*MUS*) musique *f* pop; (*drink*) boisson gazeuse; (*US: inf: father*) papa *m*; (*noise*) bruit sec ♦ *vt* (*put*) mettre (rapidement) ♦ *vi* éclater; (*cork*) sauter; ~ **in** *vi* entrer en passant; ~ **out** *vi* sortir (brièvement); ~ **up** *vi* apparaître, surgir; ~**corn** *n* pop-corn *m*

pope [pəʊp] *n* pape *m*

poplar ['pɒpləʳ] *n* peuplier *m*

popper ['pɒpəʳ] (*BRIT: inf*) *n* bouton-pression *m*

poppy ['pɒpɪ] *n* coquelicot *m*; pavot *m*

Popsicle ® ['pɒpsɪkl] (*US*) *n* esquimau *m* (*glace*)

popular ['pɒpjʊləʳ] *adj* populaire; (*fashionable*) à la mode

population [pɒpjʊ'leɪʃən] *n* population *f*

porcelain ['pɔːslɪn] *n* porcelaine *f*

porch [pɔːtʃ] *n* porche *m*; (*US*) véranda *f*

porcupine ['pɔːkjʊpaɪn] *n* porc-épic *m*

pore [pɔːʳ] *n* pore *m* ♦ *vi*: **to ~ over** s'absorber dans, être plongé(e) dans

pork [pɔːk] *n* porc *m*

porn [pɔːn] (*inf*) *adj*, *n* porno *m*

pornographic [pɔːnə'græfɪk] *adj* pornographique

pornography [pɔː'nɔɡrəfi] *n* pornographie *f*

porpoise ['pɔːpəs] *n* marsouin *m*

porridge ['pɔrɪdʒ] *n* porridge *m*

port [pɔːt] *n* (*harbour*) port *m*; (*NAUT: left side*) bâbord *m*; (*wine*) porto *m*; ~ **of call** escale *f*

portable ['pɔːtəbl] *adj* portatif(-ive)

porter ['pɔːtə'] *n* (*for luggage*) porteur *m*; (*doorkeeper*) gardien(ne); portier *m*

portfolio [pɔːt'fəuliəu] *n* portefeuille *m*; (*of artist*) portfolio *m*

porthole ['pɔːthəul] *n* hublot *m*

portion ['pɔːʃən] *n* portion *f*, part *f*

portrait ['pɔːtreɪt] *n* portrait *m*

portray [pɔː'treɪ] *vt* faire le portrait de; (*in writing*) dépeindre, représenter; (*subj: actor*) jouer

Portugal ['pɔːtjuɡl] *n* Portugal *m*; **Portuguese** [pɔːtju'ɡiːz] *adj* portugais(e) ♦ *n inv* Portugais(e); (*LING*) portugais *m*

pose [pəuz] *n* pose *f* ♦ *vi* (*pretend*): **to ~ as** se poser en ♦ *vt* poser; (*problem*) créer

posh [pɔʃ] (*inf*) *adj* chic *inv*

position [pə'zɪʃən] *n* position *f*; (*job*) situation *f* ♦ *vt* placer

positive ['pɔzɪtɪv] *adj* positif(-ive); (*certain*) sûr(e), certain(e); (*definite*) formel(le), catégorique

possess [pə'zɛs] *vt* posséder; **~ion** *n* possession *f*

possibility [pɔsɪ'bɪlɪtɪ] *n* possibilité *f*; éventualité *f*

possible ['pɔsɪbl] *adj* possible; **as big as ~** aussi gros que possible; **possibly** *adv* (*perhaps*) peut-être; **if you possibly can** si cela vous est possible; **I cannot possibly come** il m'est impossible de venir

post [pəust] *n* poste *f*; (*BRIT: letters, delivery*) courrier *m*; (*job, situation, MIL*) poste *m*; (*pole*) poteau *m* ♦ *vt* (*BRIT: send by ~*) poster; (*: appoint*): **to ~ to** affecter à; **~age** *n* tarifs *mpl* d'affranchissement; **~al order** *n* mandat(-poste) *m*; **~box** (*BRIT*) *n* boîte *f* aux lettres; **~card** *n* carte postale; **~code** (*BRIT*) *n* code postal

poster ['pəustə'] *n* affiche *f*

poste restante [pəust'rɛstɑ̃ːnt] (*BRIT*) *n* poste restante

postgraduate ['pəust'ɡrædjuət] *n* ≈ étudiant(e) de troisième cycle

posthumous ['pɔstjuməs] *adj* posthume

postman ['pəustmən] (*irreg*) *n* facteur *m*

postmark ['pəustmɑːk] *n* cachet *m* (de la poste)

postmortem [pəust'mɔːtəm] *n* autopsie *f*

post office *n* (*building*) poste *f*; (*organization*): **the P~ O~** les Postes; ~ ~ **box** *n* boîte postale

postpone [pəus'pəun] *vt* remettre (à plus tard)

posture ['pɔstjə'] *n* posture *f*; (*fig*) attitude *f*

postwar [pəust'wɔː'] *adj* d'après-guerre

postwoman *n* factrice *f*

posy ['pəuzɪ] *n* petit bouquet

pot [pɔt] *n* pot *m*; (*for cooking*) marmite *f*; casserole *f*; (*teapot*) théière *f*; (*coffeepot*) cafetière *f*; (*inf: marijuana*) herbe *f* ♦ *vt* (*plant*) mettre en pot; **to go to ~** (*inf: work, performance*) aller à vau-l'eau

potato [pə'teɪtəu] (*pl* **~es**) *n* pomme *f* de terre; ~ **peeler** *n* épluche-légumes *m inv*

potent ['pəutnt] *adj* puissant(e); (*drink*) fort(e), très alcoolisé(e); (*man*) viril

potential [pə'tɛnʃl] *adj* potentiel(le) ♦ *n* potentiel *m*

pothole ['pɔthəul] *n* (*in road*) nid *m* de poule; (*BRIT: underground*) gouffre *m*, caverne *f*; **potholing** (*BRIT*) *n*: **to go potholing** faire de la spéléologie

potluck [pɔt'lʌk] *n*: **to take ~** tenter sa chance

pot plant *n* plante *f* d'appartement

potted ['pɔtɪd] *adj* (*food*) en conserve; (*plant*) en pot; (*abbreviated*) abrégé(e)

potter ['pɔtə'] *n* potier *m* ♦ *vi*: **to ~ around, ~ about** (*BRIT*) bricoler; **~y** *n* poterie *f*

potty ['pɔtɪ] *adj* (*inf: mad*) dingue ♦ *n* (*child's*) pot *m*

pouch [pautʃ] *n* (*ZOOL*) poche *f*; (*for tobacco*) blague *f*; (*for money*) bourse *f*

poultry ['pəultrı] *n* volaille *f*

pounce [pauns] *vi:* **to ~ (on)** bondir (sur), sauter (sur)

pound [paund] *n* (*unit of money*) livre *f*; (*unit of weight*) livre ♦ *vt* (*beat*) bourrer de coups, marteler; (*crush*) piler, pulvériser ♦ *vi* (*heart*) battre violemment, taper

pour [pɔ:ʳ] *vt* verser ♦ *vi* couler à flots; **to ~ (with rain)** pleuvoir à verse; **to ~ sb a drink** verser *or* servir à boire à qn; **~ away** *vt* vider; **~ in** *vi* (*people*) affluer, se précipiter; (*news, letters etc*) arriver en masse; **~ off** *vt* = **pour away**; **~ out** *vi* (*people*) sortir en masse ♦ *vt* vider; (*fig*) déverser; (*serve: a drink*) verser; **~ing** ['pɔ:rɪŋ] *adj:* **~ing rain** pluie torrentielle

pout [paut] *vi* faire la moue

poverty ['pɔvətı] *n* pauvreté *f*, misère *f*; **~-stricken** *adj* pauvre, déshérité(e)

powder ['paudəʳ] *n* poudre *f* ♦ *vt:* **to ~ one's face** se poudrer; **~ compact** *n* poudrier *m*; **~ed milk** *n* lait *m* en poudre; **~ room** *n* toilettes *fpl* (pour dames)

power ['pauəʳ] *n* (*strength*) puissance *f*, force *f*; (*ability, authority*) pouvoir *m*; (*of speech, thought*) faculté *f*; (*ELEC*) courant *m*; **to be in ~** (*POL etc*) être au pouvoir; **~ cut** (*BRIT*) *n* coupure *f* de courant; **~ed** *adj:* **~ed by** actionné(e) par, fonctionnant à; **~ failure** *n* panne *f* de courant; **~ful** *adj* puissant(e); **~less** *adj* impuissant(e); **~ point** (*BRIT*) *n* prise *f* de courant; **~ station** *n* centrale *f* électrique; **~ struggle** *n* lutte *f* pour le pouvoir

p.p. *abbr* (= *per procurationem*): **p.p. J. Smith** pour M. J. Smith

PR *n abbr* = **public relations**

practical ['præktɪkl] *adj* pratique; **~ity** [præktɪˈkælɪtɪ] (*no pl*) *n* (*of person*) sens *m* pratique; **~ities** *npl* (*of situation*) aspect *m* pratique; **~ joke** *n* farce *f*; **~ly** *adv* (*almost*) pratiquement

practice ['præktɪs] *n* pratique *f*; (*of profession*) exercice *m*; (*at football etc*) entraînement *m*; (*business*) cabinet *m* ♦ *vt*, *vi* (*US*) = **practise**; **in ~** (*in reality*) en pratique; **out of ~** rouillé(e)

practise ['præktɪs] (*US* **practice**) *vt* (*musical instrument*) travailler; (*train for: sport*) s'entraîner à; (*a sport, religion*) pratiquer; (*profession*) exercer ♦ *vi* s'exercer, travailler; (*train*) s'entraîner; (*lawyer, doctor*) exercer; **practising** *adj* (*Christian etc*) pratiquant(e); (*lawyer*) en exercice

practitioner [prækˈtɪʃənəʳ] *n* praticien(ne)

prairie ['preərɪ] *n* steppe *f*, prairie *f*

praise [preɪz] *n* éloge(s) *m(pl)*, louange(s) *f(pl)* ♦ *vt* louer, faire l'éloge de; **~worthy** *adj* digne d'éloges

pram [præm] (*BRIT*) *n* landau *m*, voiture *f* d'enfant

prance [prɑ:ns] *vi* (*also: ~ about: person*) se pavaner

prank [præŋk] *n* farce *f*

prawn [prɔ:n] *n* crevette *f* (rose); **~ cocktail** *n* cocktail *m* de crevettes

pray [preɪ] *vi* prier; **~er** [preəʳ] *n* prière *f*

preach [pri:tʃ] *vt, vi* prêcher

precaution [prɪˈkɔ:ʃən] *n* précaution *f*

precede [prɪˈsi:d] *vt* précéder

precedent ['presɪdənt] *n* précédent *m*

preceding *adj* qui précède/précédait *etc*

precinct ['pri:sɪŋkt] *n* (*US*) circonscription *f*, arrondissement *m*; **~s** *npl* (*neighbourhood*) alentours *mpl*, environs *mpl*; **pedestrian ~** (*BRIT*) zone piétonnière *or* piétonne; **shopping ~** (*BRIT*) centre commercial

precious ['preʃəs] *adj* précieux(-euse)

precipitate [prɪˈsɪpɪteɪt] *vt* précipiter

precise [prɪˈsaɪs] *adj* précis(e); **~ly** *adv* précisément

precocious [prɪˈkəuʃəs] *adj* précoce

precondition ['pri:kənˈdɪʃən] *n* condition *f* nécessaire

predecessor ['pri:dɪsesəʳ] *n* prédécesseur *m*

predicament [prɪˈdɪkəmənt] *n* situation *f* difficile

predict [prɪˈdɪkt] *vt* prédire; **~able** *adj* prévisible

predominantly [prɪˈdɔmɪnəntlɪ] *adv* en majeure partie; surtout

pre-empt [pri:ˈemt] *vt* anticiper, devancer

preen [pri:n] *vt*: **to ~ itself** (*bird*) se lisser les plumes; **to ~ o.s.** s'admirer

prefab ['pri:fæb] *n* bâtiment préfabriqué

preface ['prɛfəs] *n* préface *f*

prefect ['pri:fɛkt] (*BRIT*) *n* (*in school*) élève chargé(e) de certaines fonctions de discipline

prefer [prɪ'fə:ʳ] *vt* préférer; **~ably** ['prɛfrəblɪ] *adv* de préférence; **~ence** ['prɛfrəns] *n* préférence *f*; **~ential** [prɛfə'rɛnʃəl] *adj*: **~ential treatment** traitement *m* de faveur *or* préférentiel

prefix ['pri:fɪks] *n* préfixe *m*

pregnancy ['prɛgnənsɪ] *n* grossesse *f*

pregnant ['prɛgnənt] *adj* enceinte; (*animal*) pleine

prehistoric ['pri:hɪs'tɔrɪk] *adj* préhistorique

prejudice ['prɛdʒudɪs] *n* préjugé *m*; **~d** *adj* (*person*) plein(e) de préjugés; (*in a matter*) partial(e)

premarital ['pri:'mærɪtl] *adj* avant le mariage

premature ['prɛmətʃuəʳ] *adj* prématuré(e)

premenstrual syndrome [pri:'mɛn-struəl-] *n* syndrome prémenstruel

premier ['prɛmɪəʳ] *adj* premier(-ère), principal(e) ♦ *n* (*POL*) Premier ministre

première ['prɛmɪɛəʳ] *n* première *f*

Premier League *n* première division

premise ['prɛmɪs] *n* prémisse *f*; **~s** *npl* (*building*) locaux *mpl*; **on the ~s** sur les lieux; sur place

premium ['pri:mɪəm] *n* prime *f*; **to be at a ~** faire prime; **~ bond** (*BRIT*) *n* bon *m* à lot, obligation *f* à prime

premonition [prɛmə'nɪʃən] *n* prémonition *f*

preoccupied [pri:'ɔkjupaɪd] *adj* préoccupé(e)

prep [prɛp] *n* (*SCOL*) étude *f*

prepaid [pri:'peɪd] *adj* payé(e) d'avance

preparation [prɛpə'reɪʃən] *n* préparation *f*; **~s** *npl* (*for trip, war*) préparatifs *mpl*

preparatory [prɪ'pærətərɪ] *adj* préliminaire; **~ school** (*BRIT*) *n* école primaire privée

prepare [prɪ'pɛəʳ] *vt* préparer ♦ *vi*: **to ~ for** se préparer à; **~d to** prêt(e) à

preposition [prɛpə'zɪʃən] *n* préposition *f*

preposterous [prɪ'pɔstərəs] *adj* absurde

prep school *n* = **preparatory school**

prerequisite [pri:'rɛkwɪzɪt] *n* condition *f* préalable

Presbyterian [prɛzbɪ'tɪərɪən] *adj*, *n* presbytérien(ne) *m/f*

prescribe [prɪ'skraɪb] *vt* prescrire; **prescription** [prɪ'skrɪpʃən] *n* (*MED*) ordonnance *f*; (: *medicine*) médicament (obtenu sur ordonnance)

presence ['prɛzns] *n* présence *f*; **~ of mind** présence d'esprit

present [*adj*, *n* 'prɛznt, *vb* prɪ'zɛnt] *adj* présent(e) ♦ *n* (*gift*) cadeau *m*; (*actuality*) présent *m* ♦ *vt* présenter; (*prize, medal*) remettre; (*give*): **to ~ sb with sth** *or* **sth to sb** offrir qch à qn; **to give sb a ~** offrir un cadeau à qn; **at ~** en ce moment; **~ation** [prɛzn'teɪʃən] *n* présentation *f*; (*ceremony*) remise *f* du cadeau (*or* de la médaille *etc*); **~-day** *adj* contemporain(e), actuel(le); **~er** *n* (*RADIO*, *TV*) présentateur(-trice); **~ly** *adv* (*with verb in past*) peu après; (*soon*) tout à l'heure, bientôt; (*at present*) en ce moment

preservative [prɪ'zə:vətɪv] *n* agent *m* de conservation

preserve [prɪ'zə:v] *vt* (*keep safe*) préserver, protéger; (*maintain*) conserver, garder; (*food*) mettre en conserve ♦ *n* (*often pl*: *jam*) confiture *f*

president ['prɛzɪdənt] *n* président(e); **~ial** [prɛzɪ'dɛnʃl] *adj* présidentiel(le)

press [prɛs] *n* presse *f*; (*for wine*) pressoir *m* ♦ *vt* (*squeeze*) presser, serrer; (*push*) appuyer sur; (*clothes: iron*) repasser; (*put pressure on*) faire pression sur; (*insist*): **to ~ sth on sb** presser qn d'accepter qch ♦ *vi* appuyer, peser; **to ~ for sth** faire pression pour obtenir qch; **we are ~ed for time/money** le temps/l'argent nous manque; **~ on** *vi* continuer; **~ conference** *n* conférence *f* de presse; **~ing** *adj* urgent(e), pressant(e); **~ stud** (*BRIT*) *n* bouton-pression *m*; **~-up** (*BRIT*) *n* traction *f*

pressure ['preʃəʳ] *n* pression *f*; (*stress*) tension *f*; **to put ~ on sb (to do)** faire pression sur qn (pour qu'il/elle fasse); **~ cooker** *n* cocotte-minute *f*; **~ gauge** *n* manomètre *m*; **~ group** *n* groupe *m* de pression

prestige [pres'tiːʒ] *n* prestige *m*; **prestigious** [pres'tɪdʒəs] *adj* prestigieux(-euse)

presumably [prɪ'zjuːməblɪ] *adv* vraisemblablement

presume [prɪ'zjuːm] *vt* présumer, supposer

pretence [prɪ'tens] (*US* **pretense**) *n* (*claim*) prétention *f*; **under false ~s** sous des prétextes fallacieux

pretend [prɪ'tend] *vt* (*feign*) feindre, simuler ♦ *vi* faire semblant

pretext ['priːtekst] *n* prétexte *m*

pretty ['prɪtɪ] *adj* joli(e) ♦ *adv* assez

prevail [prɪ'veɪl] *vi* (*be usual*) avoir cours; (*win*) l'emporter, prévaloir; **~ing** *adj* dominant(e); **prevalent** ['prevələnt] *adj* répandu(e), courant(e)

prevent [prɪ'vent] *vt*: **to ~ (from doing)** empêcher (de faire); **~ative** [prɪ'ventətɪv], **~ive** [prɪ'ventɪv] *adj* préventif(-ive)

preview ['priːvjuː] *n* (*of film etc*) avant-première *f*

previous ['priːvɪəs] *adj* précédent(e); antérieur(e); **~ly** *adv* précédemment, auparavant

prewar [priː'wɔːʳ] *adj* d'avant-guerre

prey [preɪ] *n* proie *f* ♦ *vi*: **to ~ on** s'attaquer à; **it was ~ing on his mind** cela le travaillait

price [praɪs] *n* prix *m* ♦ *vt* (*goods*) fixer le prix de; **~less** *adj* sans prix, inestimable; **~ list** *n* liste *f* des prix, tarif *m*

prick [prɪk] *n* piqûre *f* ♦ *vt* piquer; **to ~ up one's ears** dresser *or* tendre l'oreille

prickle ['prɪkl] *n* (*of plant*) épine *f*; (*sensation*) picotement *m*; **prickly** *adj* piquant(e), épineux(-euse); **prickly heat** *n* fièvre *f* miliaire

pride [praɪd] *n* orgueil *m*; fierté *f* ♦ *vt*: **to ~ o.s. on** se flatter de; s'enorgueillir de

priest [priːst] *n* prêtre *m*; **~hood** *n* prêtrise *f*, sacerdoce *m*

prim [prɪm] *adj* collet monté *inv*, guindé(e)

primarily ['praɪmərɪlɪ] *adv* principalement, essentiellement

primary ['praɪmərɪ] *adj* (*first in importance*) premier(-ère), primordial(e), principal(e) ♦ *n* (*US: election*) (élection *f*) primaire *f*; **~ school** (*BRIT*) *n* école primaire *f*

prime [praɪm] *adj* primordial(e), fondamental(e); (*excellent*) excellent(e) ♦ *n*: **in the ~ of life** dans la fleur de l'âge ♦ *vt* (*wood*) apprêter; (*fig*) mettre au courant; **P~ Minister** *n* Premier ministre *m*

primeval [praɪ'miːvəl] *adj* primitif(-ive); **~ forest** forêt *f* vierge

primitive ['prɪmɪtɪv] *adj* primitif(-ive)

primrose ['prɪmrəuz] *n* primevère *f*

primus (stove) ® ['praɪməs-] (*BRIT*) *n* réchaud *m* de camping

prince [prɪns] *n* prince *m*

princess [prɪn'ses] *n* princesse *f*

principal ['prɪnsɪpl] *adj* principal(e) ♦ *n* (*headmaster*) directeur(-trice), principal *m*

principle ['prɪnsɪpl] *n* principe *m*; **in/on ~** en/par principe

print [prɪnt] *n* (*mark*) empreinte *f*; (*letters*) caractères *mpl*; (*ART*) gravure *f*, estampe *f*; (: *photograph*) photo *f* ♦ *vt* imprimer; (*publish*) publier; (*write in block letters*) écrire en caractères d'imprimerie; **out of ~** épuisé(e); **~ed matter** *n* imprimé(s) *m(pl)*; **~er** *n* imprimeur *m*; (*machine*) imprimante *f*; **~ing** *n* impression *f*; **~-out** *n* copie *f* papier

prior ['praɪəʳ] *adj* antérieur(e), précédent(e); (*more important*) prioritaire ♦ *adv*: **~ to doing** avant de faire; **~ity** [praɪ'ɔrɪtɪ] *n* priorité *f*

prise [praɪz] *vt*: **to ~ open** forcer

prison ['prɪzn] *n* prison *f* ♦ *cpd* pénitentiaire; **~er** *n* prisonnier(-ère)

pristine ['prɪstiːn] *adj* parfait(e)

privacy ['prɪvəsɪ] *n* intimité *f*, solitude *f*

private ['praɪvɪt] *adj* privé(e); (*personal*) personnel(le); (*house, lesson*) particulier(-ère); (*quiet: place*) tranquille; (*reserved: per-*

son) secret(-ète) ♦ *n* soldat *m* de deuxième classe; **"~"** (*on envelope*) "personnelle"; **in ~** en privé; **~ detective** *n* détective privé; **~ enterprise** *n* l'entreprise privée; **~ property** *n* propriété privée; **privatize** *vt* privatiser

privet ['prɪvɪt] *n* troène *m*

privilege ['prɪvɪlɪdʒ] *n* privilège *m*

privy ['prɪvɪ] *adj*: **to be ~ to** être au courant de

prize [praɪz] *n* prix *m* ♦ *adj* (*example, idiot*) parfait(e); (*bull, novel*) primé(e) ♦ *vt* priser, faire grand cas de; **~-giving** *n* distribution *f* des prix; **~winner** *n* gagnant(e)

pro [prəʊ] *n* (*SPORT*) professionnel(le); **the ~s and cons** le pour et le contre

probability [prɒbə'bɪlɪtɪ] *n* probabilité *f*

probable ['prɒbəbl] *adj* probable; **probably** *adv* probablement

probation [prə'beɪʃən] *n*: **on ~** (*LAW*) en liberté surveillée, en sursis; (*employee*) à l'essai

probe [prəʊb] *n* (*MED, SPACE*) sonde *f*; (*enquiry*) enquête *f*, investigation *f* ♦ *vt* sonder, explorer

problem ['prɒbləm] *n* problème *m*

procedure [prə'siːdʒər] *n* (*ADMIN, LAW*) procédure *f*; (*method*) marche *f* à suivre, façon *f* de procéder

proceed [prə'siːd] *vi* continuer; (*go forward*) avancer; **to ~ (with)** continuer, poursuivre; **to ~ to do** se mettre à faire; **~ings** *npl* (*LAW*) poursuites *fpl*; (*meeting*) réunion *f*, séance *f*; **~s** ['prəʊsiːdz] *npl* produit *m*, recette *f*

process ['prəʊses] *n* processus *m*; (*method*) procédé *m* ♦ *vt* traiter; **~ing** *n* (*PHOT*) développement *m*; **~ion** [prə'seʃən] *n* défilé *m*, cortège *m*; (*REL*) procession *f*; **funeral ~ion** (*on foot*) cortège *m* funèbre; (*in cars*) convoi *m* mortuaire

proclaim [prə'kleɪm] *vt* déclarer, proclamer

procrastinate [prəʊ'kræstɪneɪt] *vi* faire traîner les choses, vouloir tout remettre au lendemain

procure [prə'kjʊər] *vt* obtenir

prod [prɒd] *vt* pousser

prodigal ['prɒdɪgl] *adj* prodigue

prodigy ['prɒdɪdʒɪ] *n* prodige *m*

produce [*n* 'prɒdjuːs, *vb* prə'djuːs] *n* (*AGR*) produits *mpl* ♦ *vt* produire; (*to show*) présenter; (*cause*) provoquer, causer; (*THEATRE*) monter, mettre en scène; **~r** *n* producteur *m*; (*THEATRE*) metteur *m* en scène

product ['prɒdʌkt] *n* produit *m*

production [prə'dʌkʃən] *n* production *f*; (*THEATRE*) mise *f* en scène; **~ line** *n* chaîne *f* (de fabrication)

productivity [prɒdʌk'tɪvɪtɪ] *n* productivité *f*

profession [prə'feʃən] *n* profession *f*; **~al** *n* professionnel(le) ♦ *adj* professionnel(le); (*work*) de professionnel; **~ally** *adv* professionnellement; (*SPORT: play*) en professionnel; **she sings ~ally** c'est une chanteuse professionnelle; **I only know him ~ally** je n'ai avec lui que des relations de travail

professor [prə'fesər] *n* professeur *m* (*titulaire d'une chaire*)

proficiency [prə'fɪʃənsɪ] *n* compétence *f*, aptitude *f*

profile ['prəʊfaɪl] *n* profil *m*

profit ['prɒfɪt] *n* bénéfice *m*; profit *m* ♦ *vi*: **to ~ (by** *or* **from)** profiter (de); **~able** *adj* lucratif(-ive), rentable

profound [prə'faʊnd] *adj* profond(e)

profusely [prə'fjuːslɪ] *adv* abondamment; avec effusion

prognosis [prɒg'nəʊsɪs] (*pl* **prognoses**) *n* pronostic *m*

programme ['prəʊgræm] (*US* **program**) *n* programme *m*; (*RADIO, TV*) émission *f* ♦ *vt* programmer; **~r** (*US* **programer**) *n* programmeur(-euse); **programming** (*US* **programing**) *n* programmation *f*

progress [*n* 'prəʊgres, *vb* prə'gres] *n* progrès *m(pl)* ♦ *vi* progresser, avancer; **in ~** en cours; **~ive** [prə'gresɪv] *adj* progressif(-ive); (*person*) progressiste

prohibit [prə'hɪbɪt] *vt* interdire, défendre

project [*n* 'prɒdʒekt, *vb* prə'dʒekt] *n* (*plan*) projet *m*, plan *m*; (*venture*) opération *f*, entreprise *f*; (*research*) étude *f*, dossier *m*

♦ *vt* projeter ♦ *vi* faire saillie, s'avancer; **~ion** *n* projection *f*; *(overhang)* saillie *f*; **~or** *n* projecteur *m*

prolong [prə'lɔŋ] *vt* prolonger

prom [prɔm] *n abbr* = **promenade**; *(US: ball)* bal *m* d'étudiants

promenade [prɔmə'nɑːd] *n (by sea)* esplanade *f*, promenade *f*; **~ concert** *(BRIT)* *n* concert *m* populaire (de musique classique)

┌─────────────────────────┐
│ **promenade concert** │
└─────────────────────────┘

i *En Grande-Bretagne, un* **promenade concert** *(ou* **prom)** *est un concert de musique classique, ainsi appelé car, à l'origine, le public restait debout et se promenait au lieu de rester assis. De nos jours, une partie du public reste debout, mais il y a également des places assises (plus chères). Les Proms les plus connus sont les Proms londoniens. La dernière séance (the Last Night of the Proms) est un grand événement médiatique où se jouent des airs traditionnels et patriotiques. Aux États-Unis et au Canada, le* **prom** *ou* **promenade** *est un bal organisé par le lycée.*

prominent ['prɔmɪnənt] *adj (standing out)* proéminent(e); *(important)* important(e)

promiscuous [prə'mɪskjuəs] *adj (sexually)* de mœurs légères

promise ['prɔmɪs] *n* promesse *f* ♦ *vt, vi* promettre; **promising** *adj* prometteur(-euse)

promote [prə'məut] *vt* promouvoir; *(new product)* faire la promotion de; **~r** *n (of event)* organisateur(-trice); *(of cause, idea)* promoteur(-trice); **promotion** *n* promotion *f*

prompt [prɔmpt] *adj* rapide ♦ *adv (punctually)* à l'heure ♦ *n (COMPUT)* message *m* (de guidage) ♦ *vt* provoquer; *(person)* inciter, pousser; *(THEATRE)* souffler (son rôle *or* ses répliques) à; **~ly** *adv* rapidement, sans délai; ponctuellement

prone [prəun] *adj (lying)* couché(e) (face contre terre); **~ to** enclin(e) à

prong [prɔŋ] *n (of fork)* dent *f*

pronoun ['prəunaun] *n* pronom *m*

pronounce [prə'nauns] *vt* prononcer; **pronunciation** [prənʌnsɪ'eɪʃən] *n* prononciation *f*

proof [pruːf] *n* preuve *f*; *(TYP)* épreuve *f* ♦ *adj*: **~ against** à l'épreuve de

prop [prɔp] *n* support *m*, étai *m*; *(fig)* soutien *m* ♦ *vt (also:* **~ up)** étayer, soutenir; *(lean)*: **to ~ sth against** appuyer qch contre *or* à

propaganda [prɔpə'gændə] *n* propagande *f*

propel [prə'pel] *vt* propulser, faire avancer; **~ler** *n* hélice *f*

propensity [prə'pensɪti] *n*: **a ~ for** *or* **to/ to do** une propension à/à faire

proper ['prɔpəʳ] *adj (suited, right)* approprié(e), bon (bonne); *(seemly)* correct(e), convenable; *(authentic)* vrai(e), véritable; *(referring to place)*: **the village ~** le village proprement dit; **~ly** *adv* correctement, convenablement; **~ noun** *n* nom *m* propre

property ['prɔpətɪ] *n* propriété *f*; *(things owned)* biens *mpl*; propriété(s) *f(pl)*; *(land)* terres *fpl*

prophecy ['prɔfɪsɪ] *n* prophétie *f*

prophesy ['prɔfɪsaɪ] *vt* prédire

prophet ['prɔfɪt] *n* prophète *m*

proportion [prə'pɔːʃən] *n* proportion *f*; *(share)* part *f*; partie *f*; **~al**, **~ate** *adj* proportionnel(le)

proposal [prə'pəuzl] *n* proposition *f*, offre *f*; *(plan)* projet *m*; *(of marriage)* demande *f* en mariage

propose [prə'pəuz] *vt* proposer, suggérer ♦ *vi* faire sa demande en mariage; **to ~ to do** avoir l'intention de faire; **proposition** [prɔpə'zɪʃən] *n* proposition *f*

proprietor [prə'praɪətəʳ] *n* propriétaire *m/f*

propriety [prə'praɪətɪ] *n (seemliness)* bienséance *f*, convenance *f*

prose [prəuz] *n (not poetry)* prose *f*

prosecute ['prɔsɪkjuːt] *vt* poursuivre; **prosecution** [prɔsɪ'kjuːʃən] *n* poursuites *fpl* judiciaires; *(accusing side)* partie plai-

gnante; **prosecutor** n (US: *plaintiff*) plai-
gnant(e); (*also:* **public prosecutor**) procureur m, ministère public
prospect [n 'prɒspɛkt, vb prə'spɛkt] n perspective f ♦ vt, vi prospecter; **~s** npl (*for
work etc*) possibilités fpl d'avenir, débou-
chés mpl; **~ing** n (*for gold, oil etc*) pros-
pection f; **~ive** adj (*possible*) éventuel(le);
(*future*) futur(e)
prospectus [prə'spɛktəs] n prospectus m
prosperity [prɒ'spɛrɪtɪ] n prospérité f
prostitute ['prɒstɪtjuːt] n prostitué(e)
protect [prə'tɛkt] vt protéger; **~ion** n protection f; **~ive** adj protecteur(-trice);
(*clothing*) de protection
protein ['prəutiːn] n protéine f
protest [n 'prəutɛst, vb prə'tɛst] n protestation f ♦ vi, vt: **to ~ (that)** protester (que)
Protestant ['prɒtɪstənt] adj, n protes-
tant(e)
protester [prə'tɛstəʳ] n manifestant(e)
protracted [prə'træktɪd] adj prolongé(e)
protrude [prə'truːd] vi avancer, dépasser
proud [praud] adj fier(-ère); (*pej*)
orgueilleux(-euse)
prove [pruːv] vt prouver, démontrer ♦ vi:
to ~ (to be) correct etc s'avérer juste etc;
to ~ o.s. montrer ce dont on est capable
proverb ['prɒvɜːb] n proverbe m
provide [prə'vaɪd] vt fournir; **to ~ sb with
sth** fournir qch à qn; **~ for** vt fus (*person*)
subvenir aux besoins de; (*future event*)
prévoir; **~d (that)** conj à condition que
+sub; **providing** conj: **providing (that)** à
condition que +sub
province ['prɒvɪns] n province f; (*fig*) domaine m; **provincial** [prə'vɪnʃəl] adj pro-
vincial(e)
provision [prə'vɪʒən] n (*supplying*) fourniture f; approvisionnement m; (*stipulation*)
disposition f; **~s** npl (*food*) provisions fpl;
~al adj provisoire
proviso [prə'vaɪzəu] n condition f
provocative [prə'vɒkətɪv] adj provo-
cateur(-trice), provocant(e)
provoke [prə'vəuk] vt provoquer
prowess ['prauɪs] n prouesse f

prowl [praul] vi (*also:* **~ about, ~ around**)
rôder ♦ n: **on the ~** à l'affût; **~er** n
rôdeur(-euse)
proxy ['prɒksɪ] n procuration f
prudent ['pruːdnt] adj prudent(e)
prune [pruːn] n pruneau m ♦ vt élaguer
pry [praɪ] vi: **to ~ into** fourrer son nez dans
PS n abbr (= *postscript*) p.s.
psalm [sɑːm] n psaume m
pseudonym ['sjuːdənɪm] n pseudonyme
m
psyche ['saɪkɪ] n psychisme m
psychiatrist [saɪ'kaɪətrɪst] n psychiatre m/f
psychic ['saɪkɪk] adj (*also:* **~al**) (mé-
ta)psychique; (*person*) doué(e) d'un
sixième sens
psychoanalyst [saɪkəu'ænəlɪst] n psychanalyste m/f
psychological [saɪkə'lɒdʒɪkl] adj psychologique
psychologist [saɪ'kɒlədʒɪst] n psychologue
m/f
psychology [saɪ'kɒlədʒɪ] n psychologie f
PTO abbr (= *please turn over*) T.S.V.P.
pub [pʌb] n (*public house*) pub m

pub

i Un **pub** comprend en général deux salles: l'une ("the lounge") est plutôt confortable, avec des fauteuils et des bancs
capitonnés, tandis que l'autre ("the public
bar") est simplement un bar où les consommations sont en général moins chères.
Cette dernière est souvent aussi une salle
de jeux, les jeux les plus courants étant les
fléchettes, les dominos et le billard. Il y a
parfois aussi une petite arrière-salle
douillette appelée "the snug". Beaucoup de
pubs servent maintenant des repas, surtout
à l'heure du déjeuner, et c'est alors le seul
moment où les enfants sont acceptés, à
condition d'être accompagnés. Les pubs
sont en général ouverts de 11 h à 23 h,
mais cela peut varier selon leur licence;
certains pubs ferment l'après-midi.

public ['pʌblɪk] adj public(-ique) ♦ n public

m; **in ~** en public; **to make ~** rendre public; **~ address system** *n* (système *m* de) sonorisation *f*; hauts-parleurs *mpl*

publican ['pʌblɪkən] *n* patron *m* de pub

public: **~ company** *n* société *f* anonyme (cotée en Bourse); **~ convenience** (BRIT) *n* toilettes *fpl*; **~ holiday** *n* jour férié; **~ house** (BRIT) *n* pub *m*

publicity [pʌb'lɪsɪtɪ] *n* publicité *f*

publicize ['pʌblɪsaɪz] *vt* faire connaître, rendre public(-ique)

public: **~ opinion** *n* opinion publique; **~ relations** *n* relations publiques; **~ school** *n* (BRIT) école (secondaire) privée; (US) école publique; **~-spirited** *adj* qui fait preuve de civisme; **~ transport** *n* transports *mpl* en commun

publish ['pʌblɪʃ] *vt* publier; **~er** *n* éditeur *m*; **~ing** *n* édition *f*

pub lunch *n* repas *m* de bistrot

pucker ['pʌkər] *vt* plisser

pudding ['pudɪŋ] *n* pudding *m*; (BRIT: sweet) dessert *m*, entremets *m*; **black ~,** (US) **blood ~** boudin (noir)

puddle ['pʌdl] *n* flaque *f* (d'eau)

puff [pʌf] *n* bouffée *f* ♦ *vt*: **to ~ one's pipe** tirer sur sa pipe ♦ *vi* (pant) haleter; **~ out** *vt* (fill with air) gonfler; **~ pastry** (US **puff paste**) *n* pâte feuilletée; **~y** *adj* bouffi(e), boursouflé(e)

pull [pul] *n* (tug): **to give sth a ~** tirer sur qch ♦ *vt* tirer; (trigger) presser ♦ *vi* tirer; **to ~ to pieces** mettre en morceaux; **to ~ one's punches** ménager son adversaire; **to ~ one's weight** faire sa part (du travail); **to ~ o.s. together** se ressaisir; **to ~ sb's leg** (fig) faire marcher qn; **~ apart** *vt* (break) mettre en pièces, démantibuler; **~ down** *vt* (house) démolir; **~ in** *vi* (AUT) entrer; (RAIL) entrer en gare; **~ off** *vt* enlever, ôter; (deal etc) mener à bien, conclure; **~ out** *vi* démarrer, partir ♦ *vt* sortir; arracher; **~ over** *vi* (AUT) se ranger; **~ through** *vi* s'en sortir; **~ up** *vi* (stop) s'arrêter ♦ *vt* remonter; (uproot) déraciner, arracher

pulley ['pulɪ] *n* poulie *f*

pullover ['puləuvər] *n* pull(-over) *m*, tricot *m*

pulp [pʌlp] *n* (of fruit) pulpe *f*

pulpit ['pulpɪt] *n* chaire *f*

pulsate [pʌl'seɪt] *vi* battre, palpiter; (music) vibrer

pulse [pʌls] *n* (of blood) pouls *m*; (of heart) battement *m*; (of music, engine) vibrations *fpl*; (BOT, CULIN) légume sec

pump [pʌmp] *n* pompe *f*; (shoe) escarpin *m* ♦ *vt* pomper; **~ up** *vt* gonfler

pumpkin ['pʌmpkɪn] *n* potiron *m*, citrouille *f*

pun [pʌn] *n* jeu *m* de mots, calembour *m*

punch [pʌntʃ] *n* (blow) coup *m* de poing; (tool) poinçon *m*; (drink) punch *m* ♦ *vt* (hit): **to ~ sb/sth** donner un coup de poing à qn/sur qch; **~line** *n* (of joke) conclusion *f*; **~-up** (BRIT: inf) *n* bagarre *f*

punctual ['pʌŋktjuəl] *adj* ponctuel(le)

punctuation [pʌŋktju'eɪʃən] *n* ponctuation *f*

puncture ['pʌŋktʃər] *n* crevaison *f*

pundit ['pʌndɪt] *n* individu *m* qui pontifie, pontife *m*

pungent ['pʌndʒənt] *adj* piquant(e), âcre

punish ['pʌnɪʃ] *vt* punir; **~ment** *n* punition *f*, châtiment *m*

punk [pʌŋk] *n* (also: **~ rocker**) punk *m/f*; (also: **~ rock**) le punk rock; (US: inf: hoodlum) voyou *m*

punt [pʌnt] *n* (boat) bachot *m*

punter ['pʌntər] (BRIT) *n* (gambler) parieur(-euse); (inf): **the ~s** le public

puny ['pju:nɪ] *adj* chétif(-ive); (effort) piteux(-euse)

pup [pʌp] *n* chiot *m*

pupil ['pju:pl] *n* (SCOL) élève *m/f*; (of eye) pupille *f*

puppet ['pʌpɪt] *n* marionnette *f*, pantin *m*

puppy ['pʌpɪ] *n* chiot *m*, jeune chien(ne)

purchase ['pə:tʃɪs] *n* achat *m* ♦ *vt* acheter; **~r** *n* acheteur(-euse)

pure [pjuər] *adj* pur(e); **~ly** *adv* purement

purge [pə:dʒ] *n* purge *f* ♦ *vt* purger

purple ['pə:pl] *adj* violet(te); (face) cramoisi(e)

purpose ['pə:pəs] *n* intention *f*, but *m*; **on ~** exprès; **~ful** *adj* déterminé(e), résolu(e)

purr [pə:ʳ] *vi* ronronner

purse [pə:s] *n* (*BRIT: for money*) porte-monnaie *m inv*; (*US: handbag*) sac *m* à main ♦ *vt* serrer, pincer

purser *n* (*NAUT*) commissaire *m* du bord

pursue [pə'sju:] *vt* poursuivre; **pursuit** [pə'sju:t] *n* poursuite *f*; (*occupation*) occupation *f*, activité *f*

push [puʃ] *n* poussée *f* ♦ *vt* pousser; (*button*) appuyer sur; (*product*) faire de la publicité pour; (*thrust*): **to ~ sth (into)** enfoncer qch (dans) ♦ *vi* pousser; (*demand*): **to ~ for** exiger, demander avec insistance; **~ aside** *vt* écarter; **~ off** (*inf*) *vi* filer, ficher le camp; **~ on** *vi* (*continue*) continuer; **~ through** *vi* se frayer un chemin ♦ *vt* (*measure*) faire accepter; **~ up** *vt* (*total, prices*) faire monter; **~chair** (*BRIT*) *n* poussette *f*; **~er** *n* (*drug pusher*) revendeur(-euse) (de drogue), ravitailleur(-euse) (en drogue); **~over** (*inf*) *n*: **it's a ~over** c'est un jeu d'enfant; **~up** (*US*) *n* traction *f*; **~y** (*pej*) *adj* arriviste

puss [pus], **pussy (cat)** ['pusi(kæt)] (*inf*) *n* minet *m*

put [put] (*pt, pp* put) *vt* mettre, poser, placer; (*say*) dire, exprimer; (*a question*) poser; (*case, view*) exposer, présenter; (*estimate*) estimer; **~ about** *vt* (*rumour*) faire courir; **~ across** *vt* (*ideas etc*) communiquer; **~ away** *vt* (*store*) ranger; **~ back** *vt* (*replace*) remettre, replacer; (*postpone*) remettre; (*delay*) retarder; **~ by** *vt* (*money*) mettre de côté, économiser; **~ down** *vt* (*parcel etc*) poser, déposer; (*in writing*) mettre par écrit, inscrire; (*suppress: revolt etc*) réprimer, faire cesser; (*animal*) abattre; (*dog, cat*) faire piquer; (*attribute*) attribuer; **~ forward** *vt* (*ideas*) avancer; **~ in** *vt* (*gas, electricity*) installer; (*application, complaint*) soumettre; (*time, effort*) consacrer; **~ off** *vt* (*light etc*) éteindre; (*postpone*) remettre à plus tard, ajourner; (*discourage*) dissuader; **~ on** *vt* (*clothes, lipstick, record*) mettre; (*light etc*) allumer; (*play etc*) monter; (*food: cook*) mettre à cuire *or* à chauffer; (*gain*): **to ~ on weight** prendre du poids, grossir; **to ~ the brakes on** freiner; **to ~ the kettle on** mettre l'eau à chauffer; **~ out** *vt* (*take out*) mettre dehors; (*one's hand*) tendre; (*light etc*) éteindre; (*person: inconvenience*) déranger, gêner; **~ through** *vt* (*TEL: call*) passer; (: *person*) mettre en communication; (*plan*) faire accepter; **~ up** *vt* (*raise*) lever, relever, remonter; (*pin up*) afficher; (*hang*) accrocher; (*build*) construire, ériger; (*tent*) monter; (*umbrella*) ouvrir; (*increase*) augmenter; (*accommodate*) loger; **~ up with** *vt fus* supporter

putt [pʌt] *n* coup roulé; **~ing green** *n* green *m*

putty ['pʌti] *n* mastic *m*

put-up ['putʌp] (*BRIT*) *adj*: **~-~ job** coup monté

puzzle ['pʌzl] *n* énigme *f*, mystère *m*; (*jigsaw*) puzzle *m* ♦ *vt* intriguer, rendre perplexe ♦ *vi* se creuser la tête; **~d** *adj* perplexe; **puzzling** *adj* déconcertant(e)

pyjamas [pə'dʒɑːməz] (*BRIT*) *npl* pyjama(s) *m(pl)*

pylon ['pailən] *n* pylône *m*

pyramid ['pirəmid] *n* pyramide *f*

Pyrenees [pirə'niːz] *npl*: **the ~** les Pyrénées *fpl*

Q, q

quack [kwæk] *n* (*of duck*) coin-coin *m inv*; (*pej: doctor*) charlatan *m*

quad [kwɔd] *n abbr* = **quadrangle**; **quadruplet**

quadrangle ['kwɔdræŋgl] *n* (*courtyard*) cour *f*

quadruple [kwɔ'druːpl] *vt, vi* quadrupler; **~ts** *npl* quadruplés

quail [kweil] *n* (*ZOOL*) caille *f* ♦ *vi*: **to ~ at** *or* **before** reculer devant

quaint [kweint] *adj* bizarre; (*house, village*) au charme vieillot, pittoresque

quake [kweik] *vi* trembler

qualification → quiet

484   *ENGLISH-FRENCH*

qualification [ˌkwɔlɪfɪˈkeɪʃən] *n* (*often pl*: *degree etc*) diplôme *m*; (*training*) qualification(s) *f(pl)*, expérience *f*; (*ability*) compétence(s) *f(pl)*; (*limitation*) réserve *f*, restriction *f*

qualified [ˈkwɔlɪfaɪd] *adj* (*trained*) qualifié(e); (*professionally*) diplômé(e); (*fit, competent*) compétent(e), qualifié(e); (*limited*) conditionnel(le)

qualify [ˈkwɔlɪfaɪ] *vt* qualifier; (*modify*) atténuer, nuancer ♦ *vi*: **to ~ (as)** obtenir son diplôme (de); **to ~ (for)** remplir les conditions requises (pour); (*SPORT*) se qualifier (pour)

quality [ˈkwɔlɪtɪ] *n* qualité *f*; **~ time** *n* moments privilégiés

quality (news)papers

🛈 Les **quality (news)papers** (*ou la* **quality press**) *englobent les journaux sérieux, quotidiens ou hebdomadaires, par opposition aux journaux populaires* (**tabloid press**). *Ces journaux visent un public qui souhaite des informations détaillées sur un éventail très vaste de sujets et qui est prêt à consacrer beaucoup de temps à leur lecture. Les* **quality newspapers** *sont en général de grand format.*

qualm [kwɑːm] *n* doute *m*; scrupule *m*
quandary [ˈkwɔndrɪ] *n*: **in a ~** devant un dilemme, dans l'embarras
quantity [ˈkwɔntɪtɪ] *n* quantité *f*; **~ surveyor** *n* métreur *m* vérificateur
quarantine [ˈkwɔrəntiːn] *n* quarantaine *f*
quarrel [ˈkwɔrəl] *n* querelle *f*, dispute *f* ♦ *vi* se disputer, se quereller
quarry [ˈkwɔrɪ] *n* (*for stone*) carrière *f*; (*animal*) proie *f*, gibier *m*
quart [kwɔːt] *n* ≃ litre *m*
quarter [ˈkwɔːtər] *n* quart *m*; (*US: coin: 25 cents*) quart de dollar; (*of year*) trimestre *m*; (*district*) quartier *m* ♦ *vt* (*divide*) partager en quartiers ou en quatre; **~s** *npl* (*living* ~) logement *m*; (*MIL*) quartiers *mpl*, cantonnement *m*; **a ~ of an hour** un quart d'heure; **~ final** *n* quart *m* de fina-

le; **~ly** *adj* trimestriel(le) ♦ *adv* tous les trois mois
quartet(te) [kwɔːˈtɛt] *n* quatuor *m*; (*jazz players*) quartette *m*
quartz [kwɔːts] *n* quartz *m*
quash [kwɔʃ] *vt* (*verdict*) annuler
quaver [ˈkweɪvər] *vi* trembler
quay [kiː] *n* (*also:* **~side**) quai *m*
queasy [ˈkwiːzɪ] *adj*: **to feel ~** avoir mal au cœur
queen [kwiːn] *n* reine *f*; (*CARDS etc*) dame *f*; **~ mother** *n* reine mère *f*
queer [kwɪər] *adj* étrange, curieux(-euse); (*suspicious*) louche ♦ *n* (*inf!*) homosexuel *m*
quell [kwɛl] *vt* réprimer, étouffer
quench [kwɛntʃ] *vt*: **to ~ one's thirst** se désaltérer
query [ˈkwɪərɪ] *n* question *f* ♦ *vt* remettre en question, mettre en doute
quest [kwɛst] *n* recherche *f*, quête *f*
question [ˈkwɛstʃən] *n* question *f* ♦ *vt* (*person*) interroger; (*plan, idea*) remettre en question, mettre en doute; **beyond ~** sans aucun doute; **out of the ~** hors de question; **~able** *adj* discutable; **~ mark** *n* point *m* d'interrogation; **~naire** [kwɛstʃəˈnɛər] *n* questionnaire *m*
queue [kjuː] (*BRIT*) *n* queue *f*, file *f* ♦ *vi* (*also:* **~ up**) faire la queue
quibble [ˈkwɪbl] *vi*: **~ (about sth)** *or* **(over sth)** *or* **(with sth)** ergoter (sur qch)
quick [kwɪk] *adj* rapide; (*agile*) agile, vif (vive) ♦ *n*: **cut to the ~** (*fig*) touché(e) au vif; **be ~!** dépêche-toi!; **~en** *vt* accélérer, presser ♦ *vi* s'accélérer, devenir plus rapide; **~ly** *adv* vite, rapidement; **~sand** *n* sables mouvants; **~-witted** *adj* à l'esprit vif
quid [kwɪd] (*BRIT: inf*) *n, pl inv* livre *f*
quiet [ˈkwaɪət] *adj* tranquille, calme; (*voice*) bas(se); (*ceremony, colour*) discret(-ète) ♦ *n* tranquillité *f*, calme *m*; (*silence*) silence *m* ♦ *vt, vi* (*US*) = **quieten; keep ~!** tais-toi!; **~en** *vi* (*also:* **~en down**) se calmer, s'apaiser ♦ *vt* calmer, apaiser; **~ly** *adv* tranquillement, calmement; (*silently*) silen-

cieusement; ~**ness** n tranquillité f, calme m; (silence) silence m

quilt [kwɪlt] n édredon m; (continental ~) couette f

quin [kwɪn] n abbr = **quintuplet**

quintuplets [kwɪnˈtjuːplɪts] npl quintuplé(e)s

quip [kwɪp] n remarque piquante or spirituelle, pointe f

quirk [kwəːk] n bizarrerie f

quit [kwɪt] (pt, pp **quit** or **quitted**) vt quitter; (smoking, grumbling) arrêter de ♦ vi (give up) abandonner, renoncer; (resign) démissionner

quite [kwaɪt] adv (rather) assez, plutôt; (entirely) complètement, tout à fait; (following a negative = almost): **that's not ~ big enough** ce n'est pas tout à fait assez grand; **I ~ understand** je comprends très bien; **~ a few of them** un assez grand nombre d'entre eux; **~ (so)!** exactement!

quits [kwɪts] adj: **~ (with)** quitte (envers); **let's call it ~** restons-en là

quiver [ˈkwɪvəʳ] vi trembler, frémir

quiz [kwɪz] n (game) jeu-concours m ♦ vt interroger; **~zical** adj narquois(e)

quota [ˈkwəʊtə] n quota m

quotation [kwəʊˈteɪʃən] n citation f; (estimate) devis m; **~ marks** npl guillemets mpl

quote [kwəʊt] n citation f; (estimate) devis m ♦ vt citer; (price) indiquer; **~s** npl guillemets mpl

R, r

rabbi [ˈræbaɪ] n rabbin m

rabbit [ˈræbɪt] n lapin m; **~ hutch** n clapier m

rabble [ˈræbl] (pej) n populace f

rabies [ˈreɪbiːz] n rage f

RAC n abbr (BRIT) = **Royal Automobile Club**

rac(c)oon [rəˈkuːn] n raton laveur

race [reɪs] n (species) race f; (competition, rush) course f ♦ vt (horse) faire courir ♦ vi (compete) faire la course, courir; (hurry) al-

ler à toute vitesse, courir; (engine) s'emballer; (pulse) augmenter; **~ car** (US) n = **racing car**; **~ car driver** n (US) = **racing driver**; **~course** n champ m de courses; **~horse** n cheval m de course; **~r** n (bike) vélo m de course; **~track** n piste f

racial [ˈreɪʃl] adj racial(e)

racing [ˈreɪsɪŋ] n courses fpl; **~ car** (BRIT) n voiture f de course; **~ driver** (BRIT) n pilote m de course

racism [ˈreɪsɪzəm] n racisme m; **racist** adj raciste ♦ n raciste m/f

rack [ræk] n (for guns, tools) râtelier m; (also: **luggage ~**) porte-bagages m inv, filet m à bagages; (also: **roof ~**) galerie f; (dish ~) égouttoir m ♦ vt tourmenter; **to ~ one's brains** se creuser la cervelle

racket [ˈrækɪt] n (for tennis) raquette f; (noise) tapage m; vacarme m; (swindle) escroquerie f

racquet [ˈrækɪt] n raquette f

racy [ˈreɪsɪ] adj plein(e) de verve; (slightly indecent) osé(e)

radar [ˈreɪdɑːʳ] n radar m

radial [ˈreɪdɪəl] adj (also: **~-ply**) à carcasse radiale

radiant [ˈreɪdɪənt] adj rayonnant(e)

radiate [ˈreɪdɪeɪt] vt (heat) émettre, dégager; (emotion) rayonner de ♦ vi (lines) rayonner; **radiation** [reɪdɪˈeɪʃən] n rayonnement m; (radioactive) radiation f; **radiator** [ˈreɪdɪeɪtəʳ] n radiateur m

radical [ˈrædɪkl] adj radical(e)

radii [ˈreɪdɪaɪ] npl of **radius**

radio [ˈreɪdɪəʊ] n radio f ♦ vt appeler par radio; **on the ~** à la radio; **~active** [ˈreɪdɪəʊˈæktɪv] adj radioactif(-ive); **~ cassette** n radiocassette m; **~-controlled** adj téléguidé(e); **~ station** n station f de radio

radish [ˈrædɪʃ] n radis m

radius [ˈreɪdɪəs] n (pl **radii**) n rayon m

RAF n abbr = **Royal Air Force**

raffle [ˈræfl] n tombola f

raft [rɑːft] n (craft; also: **life ~**) radeau m

rafter [ˈrɑːftəʳ] n chevron m

rag [ræg] n chiffon m; (pej: newspaper) feuille f de chou, torchon m; (*student ~*) attractions *organisées au profit d'œuvres de charité*; **~s** npl (*torn clothes etc*) haillons mpl; **~ doll** n poupée f de chiffon

rage [reɪdʒ] n (*fury*) rage f, fureur f ♦ vi (*person*) être fou (folle) de rage; (*storm*) faire rage, être déchaîné(e); **it's all the ~** cela fait fureur

ragged [ˈrægɪd] adj (*edge*) inégal(e); (*clothes*) en loques; (*appearance*) déguenillé(e)

raid [reɪd] n (*attack, also:* MIL) raid m; (*criminal*) hold-up m inv; (*by police*) descente f, rafle f ♦ vt faire un raid sur *or* un hold-up *or* une descente dans

rail [reɪl] n (*on stairs*) rampe f; (*on bridge, balcony*) balustrade f; (*of ship*) bastingage m; **~s** npl (*track*) rails mpl, voie ferrée; **by ~** par chemin de fer, en train; **~ing(s)** n(pl) grille f; **~road** (US), **~way** (BRIT) n (*track*) voie ferrée; (*company*) chemin m de fer; **~way line** (BRIT) n ligne f de chemin de fer; **~wayman** (BRIT) (*irreg*) n cheminot m; **~way station** (BRIT) n gare f

rain [reɪn] n pluie f ♦ vi pleuvoir; **in the ~** sous la pluie; **it's ~ing** il pleut; **~bow** n arc-en-ciel m; **~coat** n imperméable m; **~drop** n goutte f de pluie; **~fall** n chute f de pluie; (*measurement*) hauteur f des précipitations; **~forest** n forêt f tropicale humide; **~y** adj pluvieux(-euse)

raise [reɪz] n augmentation f ♦ vt (*lift*) lever, hausser; (*increase*) augmenter; (*morale*) remonter; (*standards*) améliorer; (*question, doubt*) provoquer, soulever; (*cattle, family*) élever; (*crop*) faire pousser; (*funds*) rassembler; (*loan*) obtenir; (*army*) lever; **to ~ one's voice** élever la voix

raisin [ˈreɪzn] n raisin sec

rake [reɪk] n (*tool*) râteau m ♦ vt ratisser

rally [ˈrælɪ] n (POL etc) meeting m, rassemblement m; (AUT) rallye m; (TENNIS) échange m ♦ vt (*support*) gagner ♦ vi (*sick person*) aller mieux; (*Stock Exchange*) reprendre; **~ round** vt fus venir en aide à

RAM [ræm] n abbr (= *random access memory*) mémoire vive

ram [ræm] n bélier m ♦ vt enfoncer; (*crash into*) emboutir; percuter

ramble [ˈræmbl] n randonnée f ♦ vi (*walk*) se promener, faire une randonnée; (*talk: also:* **~ on**) discourir, pérorer; **~r** n promeneur(-euse), randonneur(-euse); (BOT) rosier grimpant; **rambling** adj (*speech*) décousu(e); (*house*) plein(e) de coins et de recoins; (BOT) grimpant(e)

ramp [ræmp] n (*incline*) rampe f; dénivellation f; **on ~, off ~** (US: AUT) bretelle f d'accès

rampage [ræmˈpeɪdʒ] n: **to be on the ~** se déchaîner

rampant [ˈræmpənt] adj (*disease etc*) qui sévit

ram raiding [-reɪdɪŋ] n pillage d'un magasin en enfonçant la vitrine avec une voiture

ramshackle [ˈræmʃækl] adj (*house*) délabré(e); (*car etc*) déglingué(e)

ran [ræn] pt of **run**

ranch [rɑːntʃ] n ranch m; **~er** n propriétaire m de ranch

rancid [ˈrænsɪd] adj rance

rancour [ˈræŋkəʳ] (US **rancor**) n rancune f

random [ˈrændəm] adj fait(e) *or* établi(e) au hasard; (MATH) aléatoire ♦ n: **at ~** au hasard; **~ access** n (COMPUT) accès sélectif

randy [ˈrændɪ] (BRIT: inf) adj excité(e); lubrique

rang [ræŋ] pt of **ring**

range [reɪndʒ] n (*of mountains*) chaîne f; (*of missile, voice*) portée f; (*of products*) choix m, gamme f; (MIL: also: **shooting ~**) champ m de tir; (*indoor*) stand m de tir; (*also:* **kitchen ~**) fourneau m (de cuisine) ♦ vt (*place in a line*) mettre en rang, ranger ♦ vi: **to ~ over** (*extend*) couvrir; **to ~ from ... to** aller de ... à; **a ~ of** (*series: of proposals etc*) divers(es)

ranger [ˈreɪndʒəʳ] n garde forestier

rank [ræŋk] n rang m; (MIL) grade m; (BRIT: also: **taxi ~**) station f de taxis ♦ vi: **to ~ among** compter *or* se classer parmi ♦ adj (*stinking*) fétide, puant(e); **the ~ and file** (*fig*) la masse, la base

ransack ['rænsæk] *vt* fouiller (à fond); (*plunder*) piller

ransom ['rænsəm] *n* rançon *f*; **to hold to ~** (*fig*) exercer un chantage sur

rant [rænt] *vi* fulminer

rap [ræp] *vt* frapper sur *or* à; taper sur ♦ *n*: **~ music** rap *m*

rape [reɪp] *n* viol *m*; (*BOT*) colza *m* ♦ *vt* violer; **~(seed) oil** *n* huile *f* de colza

rapid ['ræpɪd] *adj* rapide; **~s** *npl* (*GEO*) rapides *mpl*

rapist ['reɪpɪst] *n* violeur *m*

rapport [ræ'pɔːʳ] *n* entente *f*

rapturous ['ræptʃərəs] *adj* enthousiaste, frénétique

rare [reəʳ] *adj* rare; (*CULIN: steak*) saignant(e)

raring ['reərɪŋ] *adj*: **~ to go** (*inf*) très impatient(e) de commencer

rascal ['rɑːskl] *n* vaurien *m*

rash [ræʃ] *adj* imprudent(e), irréfléchi(e) ♦ *n* (*MED*) rougeur *f*, éruption *f*; (*spate: of events*) série (noire)

rasher ['ræʃəʳ] *n* fine tranche (de lard)

raspberry ['rɑːzbərɪ] *n* framboise *f*; **~ bush** *n* framboisier *m*

rasping ['rɑːspɪŋ] *adj*: **~ noise** grincement *m*

rat [ræt] *n* rat *m*

rate [reɪt] *n* taux *m*; (*speed*) vitesse *f*, rythme *m*; (*price*) tarif *m* ♦ *vt* classer; évaluer; **~s** *npl* (*BRIT: tax*) impôts locaux; (*fees*) tarifs *mpl*; **to ~ sb/sth as** considérer qn/qch comme; **~able value** (*BRIT*) *n* valeur locative imposable; **~payer** ['reɪtpeɪəʳ] (*BRIT*) *n* contribuable *m/f* (*payant les impôts locaux*)

rather ['rɑːðəʳ] *adv* plutôt; **it's ~ expensive** c'est assez cher; (*too much*) c'est un peu cher; **there's ~ a lot** il y en a beaucoup; **I would ~** *or* **I'd ~ go** j'aimerais mieux *or* je préférerais partir

rating ['reɪtɪŋ] *n* (*assessment*) évaluation *f*; (*score*) classement *m*; **~s** *npl* (*RADIO, TV*) indice *m* d'écoute

ratio ['reɪʃɪəu] *n* proportion *f*

ration ['ræʃən] *n* (*gen pl*) ration(s) *f(pl)*

rational ['ræʃənl] *adj* raisonnable, sensé(e); (*solution, reasoning*) logique; **~e** [ræʃə'nɑːl] *n* raisonnement *m*; **~ize** *vt* rationaliser; (*conduct*) essayer d'expliquer *or* de motiver

rat race *n* foire *f* d'empoigne

rattle ['rætl] *n* (*of door, window*) battement *m*; (*of coins, chain*) cliquetis *m*; (*of train, engine*) bruit *m* de ferraille; (*object: for baby*) hochet *m* ♦ *vi* cliqueter; (*car, bus*): **to ~ along** rouler dans un bruit de ferraille ♦ *vt* agiter (bruyamment); (*unnerve*) décontenancer; **~snake** *n* serpent *m* à sonnettes

raucous ['rɔːkəs] *adj* rauque; (*noisy*) bruyant(e), tapageur(-euse)

rave [reɪv] *vi* (*in anger*) s'emporter; (*with enthusiasm*) s'extasier; (*MED*) délirer ♦ *n* (*BRIT: inf: party*) rave *f*, soirée *f* techno

raven ['reɪvən] *n* corbeau *m*

ravenous ['rævənəs] *adj* affamé(e)

ravine [rə'viːn] *n* ravin *m*

raving ['reɪvɪŋ] *adj*: **~ lunatic** ♦ *n* fou (folle) furieux(-euse)

ravishing ['rævɪʃɪŋ] *adj* enchanteur(-eresse)

raw [rɔː] *adj* (*uncooked*) cru(e); (*not processed*) brut(e); (*sore*) à vif, irrité(e); (*inexperienced*) inexpérimenté(e); (*weather, day*) froid(e) et humide; **~ deal** (*inf*) *n* sale coup *m*; **~ material** *n* matière première

ray [reɪ] *n* rayon *m*; **~ of hope** lueur *f* d'espoir

raze [reɪz] *vt* (*also: ~ to the ground*) raser, détruire

razor ['reɪzəʳ] *n* rasoir *m*; **~ blade** *n* lame *f* de rasoir

Rd *abbr* = **road**

RE *n abbr* = **religious education**

re [riː] *prep* concernant

reach [riːtʃ] *n* portée *f*, atteinte *f*; (*of river etc*) étendue *f* ♦ *vt* atteindre; (*conclusion, decision*) parvenir à ♦ *vi* s'étendre, étendre le bras; **out of/within ~** hors de/à portée; **within ~ of the shops** pas trop loin des *or* à proximité des magasins; **~ out** *vt* tendre ♦ *vi*: **to ~ out (for)** allonger le bras (pour prendre)

react [riː'ækt] *vi* réagir; **~ion** *n* réaction *f*

reactor [riː'æktəʳ] *n* réacteur *m*

read [riːd, *pt, pp* rɛd] (*pt, pp* **read**) *vi* lire ♦ *vt* lire; (*understand*) comprendre, interpréter; (*study*) étudier; (*meter*) relever; **~ out** *vt* lire à haute voix; **~able** *adj* facile *or* agréable à lire; (*writing*) lisible; **~er** *n* lecteur(-trice); (*BRIT: at university*) chargé(e) d'enseignement; **~ership** *n* (*of paper etc*) (nombre *m* de) lecteurs *mpl*

readily ['rɛdɪlɪ] *adv* volontiers, avec empressement; (*easily*) facilement

readiness ['rɛdɪnɪs] *n* empressement *m*; **in ~** (*prepared*) prêt(e)

reading ['riːdɪŋ] *n* lecture *f*; (*understanding*) interprétation *f*; (*on instrument*) indications *fpl*

ready ['rɛdɪ] *adj* prêt(e); (*willing*) prêt, disposé(e); (*available*) disponible ♦ *n*: **at the ~** (*MIL*) prêt à faire feu; **to get ~** se préparer ♦ *vt* préparer; **~-made** *adj* tout(e) fait(e); **~-to-wear** *adj* prêt(e) à porter

real [rɪəl] *adj* véritable; réel(le); **in ~ terms** dans la réalité; **~ estate** *n* biens fonciers *or* immobiliers; **~istic** [rɪə'lɪstɪk] *adj* réaliste; **~ity** [riː'ælɪtɪ] *n* réalité *f*

realization [rɪəlaɪ'zeɪʃən] *n* (*awareness*) prise *f* de conscience; (*fulfilment; also: of asset*) réalisation *f*

realize ['rɪəlaɪz] *vt* (*understand*) se rendre compte de; (*a project, COMM: asset*) réaliser

really ['rɪəlɪ] *adv* vraiment; **~?** vraiment?, c'est vrai?

realm [rɛlm] *n* royaume *m*; (*fig*) domaine *m*

realtor ® ['rɪəltɔːʳ] (*US*) *n* agent immobilier

reap [riːp] *vt* moissonner; (*fig*) récolter

reappear [riːə'pɪəʳ] *vi* réapparaître, reparaître

rear [rɪəʳ] *adj* de derrière, arrière *inv*; (*AUT: wheel etc*) arrière ♦ *n* arrière *m* ♦ *vt* (*cattle, family*) élever ♦ *vi* (*also:* **~ up:** *animal*) se cabrer; **~guard** *n* (*MIL*) arrière-garde *f*; **~-view mirror** *n* (*AUT*) rétroviseur *m*

reason ['riːzn] *n* raison *f* ♦ *vi*: **to ~ with**

sb raisonner qn, faire entendre raison à qn; **to have ~ to think** avoir lieu de penser; **it stands to ~ that** il va sans dire que; **~able** *adj* raisonnable; (*not bad*) acceptable; **~ably** *adv* raisonnablement; **~ing** *n* raisonnement *m*

reassurance [riːə'ʃuərəns] *n* réconfort *m*; (*factual*) assurance *f*, garantie *f*

reassure [riːə'ʃuəʳ] *vt* rassurer

rebate ['riːbeɪt] *n* (*on tax etc*) dégrèvement *m*

rebel [*n* 'rɛbl, *vb* rɪ'bɛl] *n* rebelle *m/f* ♦ *vi* se rebeller, se révolter; **~lious** [rɪ'bɛljəs] *adj* rebelle

rebound [*vb* rɪ'baund, *n* 'riːbaund] *vi* (*ball*) rebondir ♦ *n* rebond *m*; **to marry on the ~** se marier immédiatement après une déception amoureuse

rebuff [rɪ'bʌf] *n* rebuffade *f*

rebuke [rɪ'bjuːk] *vt* réprimander

rebut [rɪ'bʌt] *vt* réfuter

recall [*vb* rɪ'kɔːl, *n* 'riːkɔːl] *vt* rappeler; (*remember*) se rappeler, se souvenir de ♦ *n* rappel *m*; (*ability to remember*) mémoire *f*

recant [rɪ'kænt] *vi* se rétracter; (*REL*) abjurer

recap ['riːkæp], **recapitulate** [riːkə'pɪtjuleɪt] *vt, vi* récapituler

rec'd *abbr* = **received**

recede [rɪ'siːd] *vi* (*tide*) descendre; (*disappear*) disparaître peu à peu; (*memory, hope*) s'estomper; **receding** *adj* (*chin*) fuyant(e); **receding hairline** front dégarni

receipt [rɪ'siːt] *n* (*document*) reçu *m*; (*for parcel etc*) accusé *m* de réception; (*act of receiving*) réception *f*; **~s** *npl* (*COMM*) recettes *fpl*

receive [rɪ'siːv] *vt* recevoir; **~r** *n* (*TEL*) récepteur *m*, combiné *m*; (*RADIO*) récepteur *m*; (*of stolen goods*) receleur *m*; (*LAW*) administrateur *m* judiciaire

recent ['riːsnt] *adj* récent(e); **~ly** *adv* récemment

receptacle [rɪ'sɛptɪkl] *n* récipient *m*

reception [rɪ'sɛpʃən] *n* réception *f*; (*welcome*) accueil *m*, réception; **~ desk** *n* réception *f*; **~ist** *n* réceptionniste *m/f*

recess [rɪ'sɛs] n (in room) renfoncement m, alcôve f; (secret place) recoin m; (POL etc: holiday) vacances fpl

recession [rɪ'sɛʃən] n récession f

recipe ['rɛsɪpɪ] n recette f

recipient [rɪ'sɪpɪənt] n (of payment) bénéficiaire m/f; (of letter) destinataire m/f

recital [rɪ'saɪtl] n récital m

recite [rɪ'saɪt] vt (poem) réciter

reckless ['rɛkləs] adj (driver etc) imprudent(e)

reckon ['rɛkən] vt (count) calculer, compter; (think): **I ~ that ...** je pense que ...; **~ on** vt fus compter sur, s'attendre à; **~ing** n compte m, calcul m; estimation f

reclaim [rɪ'kleɪm] vt (demand back) réclamer (le remboursement or la restitution de); (land: from sea) assécher; (waste materials) récupérer

recline [rɪ'klaɪn] vi être allongé(e) or étendu(e); **reclining** adj (seat) à dossier réglable

recluse [rɪ'kluːs] n reclus(e), ermite m

recognition [rɛkəg'nɪʃən] n reconnaissance f; **to gain ~** être reconnu(e); **transformed beyond ~** méconnaissable

recognizable ['rɛkəgnaɪzəbl] adj: **~ (by)** reconnaissable (à)

recognize ['rɛkəgnaɪz] vt: **to ~ (by/as)** reconnaître (à/comme étant)

recoil [vb rɪ'kɔɪl, n 'riːkɔɪl] vi (person): **to ~ (from sth/doing sth)** reculer (devant qch/l'idée de faire qch) ♦ n (of gun) recul m

recollect [rɛkə'lɛkt] vt se rappeler, se souvenir de; **~ion** n souvenir m

recommend [rɛkə'mɛnd] vt recommander

reconcile ['rɛkənsaɪl] vt (two people) réconcilier; (two facts) concilier, accorder; **to ~ o.s. to** se résigner à

recondition [riːkən'dɪʃən] vt remettre à neuf; réviser entièrement

reconnoitre [rɛkə'nɔɪtər] (US **reconnoiter**) vt (MIL) reconnaître

reconsider [riːkən'sɪdər] vt reconsidérer

reconstruct [riːkən'strʌkt] vt (building) reconstruire; (crime, policy, system) reconstituer

record [n 'rɛkɔːd, vb rɪ'kɔːd] n rapport m, récit m; (of meeting etc) procès-verbal m; (register) registre m; (file) dossier m; (also: **criminal ~**) casier m judiciaire; (MUS: disc) disque m; (SPORT) record m; (COMPUT) article m ♦ vt (set down) noter; (MUS: song etc) enregistrer; **in ~ time** en un temps record inv; **off the ~** ♦ adj officieux(-euse) ♦ adv officieusement; **~ card** n (in file) fiche f; **~ed delivery** n (BRIT: POST): **~ed delivery letter** etc lettre etc recommandée; **~er** n (MUS) flûte f à bec; **~ holder** n (SPORT) détenteur(-trice) du record; **~ing** n (MUS) enregistrement m; **~ player** n tourne-disque m

recount [rɪ'kaunt] vt raconter

re-count ['riːkaunt] n (POL: of votes) deuxième compte m

recoup [rɪ'kuːp] vt: **to ~ one's losses** récupérer ce qu'on a perdu, se refaire

recourse [rɪ'kɔːs] n: **to have ~ to** avoir recours à

recover [rɪ'kʌvər] vt récupérer ♦ vi: **to ~ (from)** (illness) se rétablir (de); (from shock) se remettre (de); **~y** n récupération f; rétablissement m; (ÉCON) redressement m

recreation [rɛkrɪ'eɪʃən] n récréation f, détente f; **~al** adj pour la détente, récréatif(-ive)

recruit [rɪ'kruːt] n recrue f ♦ vt recruter

rectangle ['rɛktæŋgl] n rectangle m; **rectangular** [rɛk'tæŋgjulər] adj rectangulaire

rectify ['rɛktɪfaɪ] vt (error) rectifier, corriger

rector ['rɛktər] n (REL) pasteur m

recuperate [rɪ'kjuːpəreɪt] vi récupérer; (from illness) se rétablir

recur [rɪ'kəːr] vi se reproduire; (symptoms) réapparaître; **~rence** n répétition f; réapparition f; **~rent** adj périodique, fréquent(e)

recycle [riː'saɪkl] vt recycler; **recycling** n recyclage m

red [rɛd] n rouge m; (POL: pej) rouge m/f ♦ adj rouge; (hair) roux (rousse); **in the ~** (account) à découvert; (business) en déficit; **~ carpet treatment** n réception f en grande pompe; **R~ Cross** *n* Croix-Rouge *f*; **~currant** *n* groseille *f* (rouge); **~den** *vt, vi* rougir

redecorate [riːˈdekəreɪt] *vi* (with wallpaper) retapisser; (with paint) refaire les peintures

redeem [rɪˈdiːm] *vt* (debt) rembourser; (sth in pawn) dégager; (fig, also REL) racheter; **~ing** *adj* (feature) qui sauve, qui rachète (le reste)

redeploy [riːdɪˈplɔɪ] *vt* (resources) réorganiser

red: **~-haired** *adj* roux (rousse); **~-handed** *adj*: **to be caught ~-handed** être pris(e) en flagrant délit *or* la main dans le sac; **~head** *n* roux (rousse); **~ herring** *n* (fig) diversion *f*, fausse piste; **~-hot** *adj* chauffé(e) au rouge, brûlant(e)

redirect [riːdaɪˈrekt] *vt* (mail) faire suivre

red light *n*: **to go through a ~** (AUT) brûler un feu rouge; **red-light district** *n* quartier *m* des prostituées

redo [riːˈduː] (irreg) *vt* refaire

redress [rɪˈdres] *n* réparation *f* ♦ *vt* redresser

red: **R~ Sea** *n* mer Rouge *f*; **~skin** *n* Peau-Rouge *m/f*; **~ tape** *n* (fig) paperasserie (administrative)

reduce [rɪˈdjuːs] *vt* réduire; (lower) abaisser; **"~ speed now"** (AUT) "ralentir"; **reduction** [rɪˈdʌkʃən] *n* réduction *f*; (discount) rabais *m*

redundancy [rɪˈdʌndənsɪ] (BRIT) *n* licenciement *m*, mise *f* au chômage

redundant [rɪˈdʌndnt] *adj* (BRIT: worker) mis(e) au chômage, licencié(e); (detail, object) superflu(e); **to be made ~** être licencié(e), être mis(e) au chômage

reed [riːd] *n* (BOT) roseau *m*; (MUS: of clarinet etc) hanche *f*

reef [riːf] *n* (at sea) récif *m*, écueil *m*

reek [riːk] *vi*: **to ~ (of)** puer, empester

reel [riːl] *n* bobine *f*; (FISHING) moulinet *m*; (CINEMA) bande *f*; (dance) quadrille écossais ♦ *vi* (sway) chanceler; **~ in** *vt* (fish, line) ramener

ref [ref] (inf) *n abbr* (= referee) arbitre *m*

refectory [rɪˈfektərɪ] *n* réfectoire *m*

refer [rɪˈfəːr] *vt*: **to ~ sb to** (inquirer: for information, patient: to specialist) adresser qn à; (reader: to text) renvoyer qn à; (dispute, decision): **to ~ sth to** soumettre qch à ♦ *vi*: **~ to** (allude to) parler de, faire allusion à; (consult) se reporter à

referee [refəˈriː] *n* arbitre *m*; (BRIT: for job application) répondant(e)

reference [ˈrefrəns] *n* référence *f*, renvoi *m*; (mention) allusion *f*, mention *f*; (for job application: letter) références, lettre *f* de recommandation; **with ~ to** (COMM: in letter) me référant à, suite à; **~ book** *n* ouvrage *m* de référence

refill [vb riːˈfɪl, *n* ˈriːfɪl] *vt* remplir à nouveau; (pen, lighter etc) recharger ♦ *n* (for pen etc) recharge *f*

refine [rɪˈfaɪn] *vt* (sugar, oil) raffiner; (taste) affiner; (theory, idea) fignoler (inf); **~d** *adj* (person, taste) raffiné(e); **~ry** *n* raffinerie *f*

reflect [rɪˈflekt] *vt* (light, image) réfléchir, refléter; (fig) refléter ♦ *vi* (think) réfléchir, méditer; **it ~s badly on him** cela le discrédite; **it ~s well on him** c'est tout à son honneur; **~ion** *n* réflexion *f*; (image) reflet *m*; (criticism): **~ion on** critique *f* de; atteinte *f* à; **on ~ion** réflexion faite

reflex [ˈriːfleks] *adj* réflexe ♦ *n* réflexe *m*; **~ive** [rɪˈfleksɪv] *adj* (LING) réfléchi(e)

reform [rɪˈfɔːm] *n* réforme *f* ♦ *vt* réformer; **~atory** [rɪˈfɔːmətərɪ] (US) *n* ≈ centre *m* d'éducation surveillée

refrain [rɪˈfreɪn] *vi*: **to ~ from doing** s'abstenir de faire ♦ *n* refrain *m*

refresh [rɪˈfreʃ] *vt* rafraîchir; (subj: sleep) reposer; **~er course** (BRIT) *n* cours *m* de recyclage; **~ing** *adj* (drink) rafraîchissant(e); (sleep) réparateur(-trice); **~ments** *npl* rafraîchissements *mpl*

refrigerator [rɪˈfrɪdʒəreɪtər] *n* réfrigérateur *m*, frigidaire ® *m*

refuel [riːˈfjuəl] *vi* se ravitailler en carburant

refuge [ˈrefjuːdʒ] *n* refuge *m*; **to take ~ in** se réfugier dans; **~e** [refjuˈdʒiː] *n* réfugié(e)

refund [*n* ˈriːfʌnd, *vb* rɪˈfʌnd] *n* remboursement *m* ♦ *vt* rembourser

refurbish [riː'fɜːbɪʃ] *vt* remettre à neuf

refusal [rɪ'fjuːzəl] *n* refus *m*; **to have first ~ on** avoir droit de préemption sur

refuse[1] [rɪ'fjuːz] *vt, vi* refuser

refuse[2] ['refjuːs] *n* ordures *fpl*, détritus *mpl*; **~ collection** *n* ramassage *m* d'ordures

regain [rɪ'geɪn] *vt* regagner; retrouver

regal ['riːgl] *adj* royal(e)

regard [rɪ'gɑːd] *n* respect *m*, estime *f*, considération *f* ♦ *vt* considérer; **to give one's ~s to** faire ses amitiés à; **"with kindest ~s"** "bien amicalement"; **as ~s, with ~ to = regarding**; **~ing** *prep* en ce qui concerne; **~less** *adv* quand même; **~less of** sans se soucier de

régime [reɪ'ʒiːm] *n* régime *m*

regiment ['redʒɪmənt] *n* régiment *m*; **~al** [redʒɪ'mentl] *adj* d'un *or* du régiment

region ['riːdʒən] *n* région *f*; **in the ~ of** (*fig*) aux alentours de; **~al** *adj* régional(e)

register ['redʒɪstə*r] *n* registre *m*; (*also*: **electoral ~**) liste électorale ♦ *vt* enregistrer; (*birth, death*) déclarer; (*vehicle*) immatriculer; (*POST: letter*) envoyer en recommandé; (*subj: instrument*) marquer ♦ *vi* s'inscrire; (*at hotel*) signer le registre; (*make impression*) être (bien) compris(e); **~ed** *adj* (*letter, parcel*) recommandé(e); **~ed trademark** *n* marque déposée; **registrar** ['redʒɪstrɑː*r] *n* officier *m* de l'état civil; **registration** [redʒɪs'treɪʃən] *n* enregistrement *m*; (*BRIT: AUT: also*: **registration number**) numéro *m* d'immatriculation

registry ['redʒɪstrɪ] *n* bureau *m* de l'enregistrement; **~ office** (*BRIT*) *n* bureau *m* de l'état civil; **to get married in a ~ office** ≈ se marier à la mairie

regret [rɪ'gret] *n* regret *m* ♦ *vt* regretter; **~fully** *adv* à *or* avec regret

regular ['regjulə*r] *adj* régulier(-ère); (*usual*) habituel(le); (*soldier*) de métier ♦ *n* (*client etc*) habitué(e); **~ly** *adv* régulièrement

regulate ['regjuleɪt] *vt* régler; **regulation** [regju'leɪʃən] *n* (*rule*) règlement *m*; (*adjust-*

ment) réglage *m*

rehabilitation [riː'əbɪlɪ'teɪʃən] *n* (*of offender*) réinsertion *f*; (*of addict*) réadaptation *f*

rehearsal [rɪ'hɜːsəl] *n* répétition *f*

rehearse [rɪ'hɜːs] *vt* répéter

reign [reɪn] *n* règne *m* ♦ *vi* régner

reimburse [riːɪm'bɜːs] *vt* rembourser

rein [reɪn] *n* (*for horse*) rêne *f*

reindeer ['reɪndɪə*r] *n, pl inv* renne *m*

reinforce [riːɪn'fɔːs] *vt* renforcer; **~d concrete** *n* béton armé; **~ments** *npl* (*MIL*) renfort(s) *m(pl)*

reinstate [riːɪn'steɪt] *vt* rétablir, réintégrer

reject [*n* 'riːdʒekt, *vb* rɪ'dʒekt] *n* (*COMM*) article *m* de rebut ♦ *vt* refuser; (*idea*) rejeter; **~ion** *n* rejet *m*, refus *m*

rejoice [rɪ'dʒɔɪs] *vi*: **to ~ (at or over)** se réjouir de

rejuvenate [rɪ'dʒuːvəneɪt] *vt* rajeunir

relapse [rɪ'læps] *n* (*MED*) rechute *f*

relate [rɪ'leɪt] *vt* (*tell*) raconter; (*connect*) établir un rapport entre ♦ *vi*: **this ~s to** cela se rapporte à; **to ~ to sb** entretenir des rapports avec qn; **~d** *adj* apparenté(e); **relating to** *prep* concernant

relation [rɪ'leɪʃən] *n* (*person*) parent(e); (*link*) rapport *m*, lien *m*; **~ship** *n* rapport *m*, lien *m*; (*personal ties*) relations *fpl*, rapports; (*also*: **family ~ship**) lien de parenté

relative ['relətɪv] *n* parent(e) ♦ *adj* relatif(-ive); **all her ~s** toute sa famille; **~ly** *adv* relativement

relax [rɪ'læks] *vi* (*muscle*) se relâcher; (*person: unwind*) se détendre ♦ *vt* relâcher; (*mind, person*) détendre; **~ation** [riːlæk'seɪʃən] *n* relâchement *m*; (*of mind*) détente *f*, relaxation *f*; (*recreation*) détente, délassement *m*; **~ed** *adj* détendu(e); **~ing** *adj* délassant(e)

relay [*n* 'riːleɪ, *vb* rɪ'leɪ] *n* (*SPORT*) course *f* de relais ♦ *vt* (*message*) retransmettre, relayer

release [rɪ'liːs] *n* (*from prison, obligation*) libération *f*; (*of gas etc*) émission *f*; (*of film etc*) sortie *f*; (*new recording*) disque *m* ♦ *vt* (*prisoner*) libérer; (*gas etc*) émettre, dégager; (*free: from wreckage etc*) dégager;

(*TECH*: *catch, spring etc*) faire jouer; (*book, film*) sortir; (*report, news*) rendre public, publier

relegate ['rɛləgeɪt] *vt* reléguer; (*BRIT*: *SPORT*): **to be ~d** descendre dans une division inférieure

relent [rɪ'lɛnt] *vi* se laisser fléchir; **~less** *adj* implacable; (*unceasing*) continuel(le)

relevant ['rɛləvənt] *adj* (*question*) pertinent(e); (*fact*) significatif(-ive); (*information*) utile; **~ to** ayant rapport à, approprié à

reliable [rɪ'laɪəbl] *adj* (*person, firm*) sérieux(-euse), fiable; (*method, machine*) fiable; (*news, information*) sûr(e); **reliably** *adv*: **to be reliably informed** savoir de source sûre

reliance [rɪ'laɪəns] *n*: **~ (on)** (*person*) confiance *f* (en); (*drugs, promises*) besoin *m* (de), dépendance *f* (de)

relic ['rɛlɪk] *n* (*REL*) relique *f*; (*of the past*) vestige *m*

relief [rɪ'liːf] *n* (*from pain, anxiety etc*) soulagement *m*; (*help, supplies*) secours *m(pl)*; (*ART, GEO*) relief *m*

relieve [rɪ'liːv] *vt* (*pain, patient*) soulager; (*fear, worry*) dissiper; (*bring help*) secourir; (*take over from: gen*) relayer; (: *guàrd*) relever; **to ~ sb of sth** débarrasser qn de qch; **to ~ o.s.** se soulager

religion [rɪ'lɪdʒən] *n* religion *f*; **religious** *adj* religieux(-euse); (*book*) de piété

relinquish [rɪ'lɪŋkwɪʃ] *vt* abandonner; (*plan, habit*) renoncer à

relish ['rɛlɪʃ] *n* (*CULIN*) condiment *m*; (*enjoyment*) délectation *f* ♦ *vt* (*food etc*) savourer; **to ~ doing** se délecter à faire

relocate [riː'ləuˈkeɪt] *vt* installer ailleurs ♦ *vi* déménager, s'installer ailleurs

reluctance [rɪ'lʌktəns] *n* répugnance *f*

reluctant [rɪ'lʌktənt] *adj* peu disposé(e), qui hésite; **~ly** *adv* à contrecœur

rely on [rɪ'laɪ-] *vt fus* (*be dependent*) dépendre de; (*trust*) compter sur

remain [rɪ'meɪn] *vi* rester; **~der** *n* reste *m*; **~ing** *adj* qui reste; **~s** *npl* restes *mpl*

remake ['riːmeɪk] *n* (*CINEMA*) remake *m*

remand [rɪ'mɑːnd] *n*: **on ~** en détention préventive ♦ *vt*: **to be ~ed in custody** être placé(e) en détention préventive

remark [rɪ'mɑːk] *n* remarque *f*, observation *f* ♦ *vt* (faire) remarquer, dire; **~able** *adj* remarquable; **~ably** *adv* remarquablement

remarry [riː'mærɪ] *vi* se remarier

remedial [rɪ'miːdɪəl] *adj* (*tuition, classes*) de rattrapage; **~ exercises** gymnastique corrective

remedy ['rɛmədɪ] *n*: **~ (for)** remède *m* (contre *or* à) ♦ *vt* remédier à

remember [rɪ'mɛmbər] *vt* se rappeler, se souvenir de; (*send greetings*): **~ me to him** saluez-le de ma part; **remembrance** *n* souvenir *m*; mémoire *f*; **Remembrance Day** *n* le jour de l'Armistice

┌─────────────────────────────┐
│ **Remembrance Sunday** │
└─────────────────────────────┘

ⓘ **Remembrance Sunday** *ou* **Remembrance Day** *est le dimanche le plus proche du 11 novembre, jour où la Première Guerre mondiale a officiellement pris fin, et rend hommage aux victimes des deux guerres mondiales. À cette occasion, un silence de deux minutes est observé à 11 h, heure de la signature de l'armistice avec l'Allemagne en 1918; certains membres de la famille royale et du gouvernement déposent des gerbes de coquelicots au cénotaphe de Whitehall, et des couronnes sont placées sur les monuments aux morts dans toute la Grande-Bretagne; par ailleurs, les gens portent des coquelicots artificiels fabriqués et vendus par des membres de la légion britannique blessés au combat, au profit des blessés de guerre et de leur famille.*

remind [rɪ'maɪnd] *vt*: **to ~ sb of** rappeler à qn; **to ~ sb to do** faire penser à qn à faire, rappeler à qn qu'il doit faire; **~er** *n* (*souvenir*) souvenir *m*; (*letter*) rappel *m*

reminisce [rɛmɪ'nɪs] *vi*: **to ~ (about)** évoquer ses souvenirs (de); **~nt** *adj*: **to be ~nt of** rappeler, faire penser à

remiss [rɪ'mɪs] *adj* négligent(e); **~ion** *n* (*of illness, sins*) rémission *f*; (*of debt, prison sentence*) remise *f*

remit [rɪ'mɪt] *vt* (*send: money*) envoyer; **~tance** *n* paiement *m*

remnant ['rɛmnənt] *n* reste *m*, restant *m*; (*of cloth*) coupon *m*; **~s** *npl* (COMM) fins *fpl* de série

remorse [rɪ'mɔːs] *n* remords *m*; **~ful** *adj* plein(e) de remords; **~less** *adj* (*fig*) impitoyable

remote [rɪ'məʊt] *adj* éloigné(e), lointain(e); (*person*) distant(e); (*possibility*) vague; **~ control** *n* télécommande *f*; **~ly** *adv* au loin; (*slightly*) très vaguement

remould ['riːməʊld] (BRIT) *n* (*tyre*) pneu rechapé

removable [rɪ'muːvəbl] *adj* (*detachable*) amovible

removal [rɪ'muːvəl] *n* (*taking away*) enlèvement *m*; suppression *f*; (BRIT: *from house*) déménagement *m*; (*from office: dismissal*) renvoi *m*; (*of stain*) nettoyage *m*; (MED) ablation *f*; **~ van** (BRIT) *n* camion *m* de déménagement

remove [rɪ'muːv] *vt* enlever, retirer; (*employee*) renvoyer; (*stain*) faire partir; (*abuse*) supprimer; (*doubt*) chasser

render ['rɛndə*r] *vt* rendre; **~ing** *n* (MUS *etc*) interprétation *f*

rendezvous ['rɒndɪvuː] *n* rendez-vous *m* *inv*

renew [rɪ'njuː] *vt* renouveler; (*negotiations*) reprendre; (*acquaintance*) renouer; **~able** *adj* (*energy*) renouvelable; **~al** *n* renouvellement *m*; reprise *f*

renounce [rɪ'naʊns] *vt* renoncer à

renovate ['rɛnəveɪt] *vt* rénover; (*art work*) restaurer

renown [rɪ'naʊn] *n* renommée *f*; **~ed** *adj* renommé(e)

rent [rɛnt] *n* loyer *m* ♦ *vt* louer; **~al** *n* (*for television, car*) (prix *m* de) location *f*

reorganize [riː'ɔːgənaɪz] *vt* réorganiser

rep [rɛp] *n abbr* = **representative; repertory**

repair [rɪ'pɛə*r] *n* réparation *f* ♦ *vt* réparer;

in good/bad ~ en bon/mauvais état; **~ kit** *n* trousse *f* de réparation

repatriate [riː'pætrɪeɪt] *vt* rapatrier

repay [riː'peɪ] (*irreg*) *vt* (*money, creditor*) rembourser; (*sb's efforts*) récompenser; **~ment** *n* remboursement *m*

repeal [rɪ'piːl] *n* (*of law*) abrogation *f* ♦ *vt* (*law*) abroger

repeat [rɪ'piːt] *n* (RADIO, TV) reprise *f* ♦ *vt* répéter; (COMM: *order*) renouveler; (SCOL: *a class*) redoubler ♦ *vi* répéter; **~edly** *adv* souvent, à plusieurs reprises

repel [rɪ'pɛl] *vt* repousser; **~lent** *adj* repoussant(e) ♦ *n*: **insect ~lent** insectifuge *m*

repent [rɪ'pɛnt] *vi*: **to ~ (of)** se repentir (de); **~ance** *n* repentir *m*

repertory ['rɛpətərɪ] *n* (*also:* **~ theatre**) théâtre *m* de répertoire

repetition [rɛpɪ'tɪʃən] *n* répétition *f*

repetitive [rɪ'pɛtɪtɪv] *adj* (*movement, work*) répétitif(-ive); (*speech*) plein(e) de redites

replace [rɪ'pleɪs] *vt* (*put back*) remettre, replacer; (*take the place of*) remplacer; **~ment** *n* (*substitution*) remplacement *m*; (*person*) remplaçant(e)

replay ['riːpleɪ] *n* (*of match*) match rejoué; (*of tape, film*) répétition *f*

replenish [rɪ'plɛnɪʃ] *vt* (*glass*) remplir (de nouveau); (*stock etc*) réapprovisionner

replica ['rɛplɪkə] *n* réplique *f*, copie exacte

reply [rɪ'plaɪ] *n* réponse *f* ♦ *vi* répondre

report [rɪ'pɔːt] *n* rapport *m*; (PRESS *etc*) reportage *m*; (BRIT: *also:* **school ~**) bulletin *m* (scolaire); (*of gun*) détonation *f* ♦ *vt* rapporter, faire un compte rendu de; (PRESS *etc*) faire un reportage sur; (*bring to notice: occurrence*) signaler ♦ *vi* (*make a ~*) faire un rapport (*or* un reportage); (*present o.s.*): **to ~ (to sb)** se présenter (chez qn); (*be responsible to*): **to ~ to sb** être sous les ordres de qn; **~ card** (US, SCOTTISH) *n* bulletin *m* scolaire; **~edly** *adv*: **she is ~edly living in ...** elle habiterait ...; **he ~edly told them to ...** il leur aurait ordonné de ...; **~er** *n* reporter *m*

repose [rɪ'pəʊz] *n*: **in ~** en *or* au repos

represent [rɛprɪ'zɛnt] *vt* représenter; (*view, belief*) présenter, expliquer; (*describe*): **to ~ sth as** présenter *or* décrire qch comme; **~ation** [rɛprɪzɛn'teɪʃən] *n* représentation *f*; **~ations** *npl* (*protest*) démarche *f*; **~ative** [rɛprɪ'zɛntətɪv] *n* représentant(e); (*US: POL*) député *m* ♦ *adj* représentatif(-ive), caractéristique

repress [rɪ'prɛs] *vt* réprimer; **~ion** *n* répression *f*

reprieve [rɪ'priːv] *n* (*LAW*) grâce *f*; (*fig*) sursis *m*, délai *m*

reprisal [rɪ'praɪzl] *n*: **~s** ♦ *npl* représailles *fpl*

reproach [rɪ'prəutʃ] *vt*: **to ~ sb with sth** reprocher qch à qn; **~ful** *adj* de reproche

reproduce [riːprə'djuːs] *vt* reproduire ♦ *vi* se reproduire; **reproduction** [riːprə'dʌkʃən] *n* reproduction *f*

reproof [rɪ'pruːf] *n* reproche *m*

reptile ['rɛptaɪl] *n* reptile *m*

republic [rɪ'pʌblɪk] *n* république *f*; **~an** *adj* républicain(e)

repudiate [rɪ'pjuːdɪeɪt] *vt* répudier, rejeter

repulsive [rɪ'pʌlsɪv] *adj* repoussant(e), répulsif(-ive)

reputable ['rɛpjutəbl] *adj* de bonne réputation; (*occupation*) honorable

reputation [rɛpju'teɪʃən] *n* réputation *f*

reputed [rɪ'pjuːtɪd] *adj* (*supposed*) supposé(e); **~ly** *adv* d'après ce qu'on dit

request [rɪ'kwɛst] *n* demande *f*; (*formal*) requête *f* ♦ *vt*: **to ~** (*of or from sb*) demander (à qn); **~ stop** (*BRIT*) *n* (*for bus*) arrêt facultatif

require [rɪ'kwaɪər] *vt* (*need: subj: person*) avoir besoin de; (*: thing, situation*) demander; (*want*) exiger; (*order*): **to ~ sb to do sth/sth of sb** exiger que qn fasse qch/ qch de qn; **~ment** *n* exigence *f*; besoin *m*; condition requise

requisition [rɛkwɪ'zɪʃən] *n*: **~ (for)** demande *f* (de) ♦ *vt* (*MIL*) réquisitionner

rescue ['rɛskjuː] *n* (*from accident*) sauvetage *m*; (*help*) secours *mpl* ♦ *vt* sauver; **~ party** *n* équipe *f* de sauvetage; **~r** *n* sauveteur *m*

research [rɪ'səːtʃ] *n* recherche(s) *f(pl)* ♦ *vt* faire des recherches sur

resemblance [rɪ'zɛmbləns] *n* ressemblance *f*

resemble [rɪ'zɛmbl] *vt* ressembler à

resent [rɪ'zɛnt] *vt* être contrarié(e) par; **~ful** *adj* irrité(e), plein(e) de ressentiment; **~ment** *n* ressentiment *m*

reservation [rɛzə'veɪʃən] *n* (*booking*) réservation *f*; (*doubt*) réserve *f*; (*for tribe*) réserve; **to make a ~ (in a hotel/a restaurant/on a plane)** réserver *or* retenir une chambre/une table/une place

reserve [rɪ'zəːv] *n* réserve *f*; (*SPORT*) remplaçant(e) ♦ *vt* (*seats etc*) réserver, retenir; **~s** *npl* (*MIL*) réservistes *mpl*; **in ~** en réserve; **~d** *adj* réservé(e)

reshuffle [riː'ʃʌfl] *n*: **Cabinet ~** (*POL*) remaniement ministériel

residence ['rɛzɪdəns] *n* résidence *f*; **~ permit** (*BRIT*) *n* permis *m* de séjour

resident ['rɛzɪdənt] *n* résident(e) ♦ *adj* résidant(e); **~ial** [rɛzɪ'dɛnʃəl] *adj* résidentiel(le); (*course*) avec hébergement sur place; **~ial school** *n* internat *m*

residue ['rɛzɪdjuː] *n* reste *m*; (*CHEM, PHYSICS*) résidu *m*

resign [rɪ'zaɪn] *vt* (*one's post*) démissionner de ♦ *vi* démissionner; **to ~ o.s. to** se résigner à; **~ation** [rɛzɪg'neɪʃən] *n* (*of post*) démission *f*; (*state of mind*) résignation *f*; **~ed** *adj* résigné(e)

resilient [rɪ'zɪlɪənt] *adj* (*material*) élastique; (*person*) qui réagit, qui a du ressort

resist [rɪ'zɪst] *vt* résister à; **~ance** *n* résistance *f*

resit [riː'sɪt] *vt* (*exam*) repasser ♦ *n* deuxième session *f* (*d'un examen*)

resolution [rɛzə'luːʃən] *n* résolution *f*

resolve [rɪ'zɔlv] *vt* (*problem*) résoudre ♦ *vi*: **to ~ to do** résoudre *or* décider de faire

resort [rɪ'zɔːt] *n* (*seaside town*) station *f* balnéaire; (*ski ~*) station de ski; (*recourse*) recours *m* ♦ *vi*: **to ~ to** avoir recours à; **in the last ~** en dernier ressort

resounding [rɪ'zaundɪŋ] *adj* retentissant(e)

resource [rɪ'sɔːs] *n* ressource *f*; **~s** *npl* (*supplies, wealth etc*) ressources; **~ful** *adj* ingénieux(-euse), débrouillard(e)

respect [rɪs'pekt] *n* respect *m* ♦ *vt* respecter; **~s** *npl* (*compliments*) respects, hommages *mpl*; **with ~ to** en ce qui concerne; **in this ~** à cet égard; **~able** *adj* respectable; **~ful** *adj* respectueux(-euse); **~ively** *adv* respectivement

respite ['respaɪt] *n* répit *m*

respond [rɪs'pɔnd] *vi* répondre; (*react*) réagir; **response** *n* réponse *f*; réaction *f*

responsibility [rɪspɔnsɪ'bɪlɪtɪ] *n* responsabilité *f*

responsible [rɪs'pɔnsɪbl] *adj* (*liable*): **~ (for)** responsable (de); (*person*) digne de confiance; (*job*) qui comporte des responsabilités

responsive [rɪs'pɔnsɪv] *adj* qui réagit; (*person*) qui n'est pas réservé(e) *or* indifférent(e)

rest [rest] *n* repos *m*; (*stop*) arrêt *m*, pause *f*; (*MUS*) silence *m*; (*support*) support *m*, appui *m*; (*remainder*) reste *m*, restant *m* ♦ *vi* se reposer; (*be supported*): **to ~ on** appuyer *or* reposer sur; (*remain*) rester ♦ *vt* (*lean*): **to ~ sth on/against** appuyer qch sur/contre; **the ~ of them** les autres; **it ~s with him to ...** c'est à lui de ...

restaurant ['restərɔŋ] *n* restaurant *m*; **~ car** (*BRIT*) *n* wagon-restaurant *m*

restful ['restful] *adj* reposant(e)

restive ['restɪv] *adj* agité(e), impatient(e); (*horse*) rétif(-ive)

restless ['restlɪs] *adj* agité(e)

restoration [restə'reɪʃən] *n* restauration *f*; restitution *f*; rétablissement *m*

restore [rɪ'stɔːʳ] *vt* (*building*) restaurer; (*sth stolen*) restituer; (*peace, health*) rétablir; **to ~ to** (*former state*) ramener à

restrain [rɪs'treɪn] *vt* contenir; (*person*): **to ~ (from doing)** retenir (de faire); **~ed** *adj* (*style*) sobre; (*manner*) mesuré(e); **~t** *n* (*restriction*) contrainte *f*; (*moderation*) retenue *f*

restrict [rɪs'trɪkt] *vt* restreindre, limiter; **~ion** *n* restriction *f*, limitation *f*

rest room (*US*) *n* toilettes *fpl*

result [rɪ'zʌlt] *n* résultat *m* ♦ *vi*: **to ~ in** aboutir à, se terminer par; **as a ~ of** à la suite de

resume [rɪ'zjuːm] *vt, vi* (*work, journey*) reprendre

résumé ['reɪzjuːmeɪ] *n* résumé *m*; (*US*) curriculum vitae *m*

resumption [rɪ'zʌmpʃən] *n* reprise *f*

resurgence [rɪ'səːdʒəns] *n* (*of energy, activity*) regain *m*

resurrection [rezə'rekʃən] *n* résurrection *f*

resuscitate [rɪ'sʌsɪteɪt] *vt* (*MED*) réanimer

retail ['riːteɪl] *adj* de or au détail ♦ *adv* au détail; **~er** *n* détaillant(e); **~ price** *n* prix *m* de détail

retain [rɪ'teɪn] *vt* (*keep*) garder, conserver; **~er** *n* (*fee*) acompte *m*, provision *f*

retaliate [rɪ'tælɪeɪt] *vi*: **to ~ (against)** se venger (de); **retaliation** [rɪtælɪ'eɪʃən] *n* représailles *fpl*, vengeance *f*

retarded [rɪ'tɑːdɪd] *adj* retardé(e)

retch [retʃ] *vi* avoir des haut-le-cœur

retentive [rɪ'tentɪv] *adj*: **~ memory** excellente mémoire

retina ['retɪnə] *n* rétine *f*

retire [rɪ'taɪəʳ] *vi* (*give up work*) prendre sa retraite; (*withdraw*) se retirer, partir; (*go to bed*) (aller) se coucher; **~d** *adj* (*person*) retraité(e); **~ment** *n* retraite *f*; **retiring** *adj* (*shy*) réservé(e); (*leaving*) sortant(e)

retort [rɪ'tɔːt] *vi* riposter

retrace [riː'treɪs] *vt*: **to ~ one's steps** revenir sur ses pas

retract [rɪ'trækt] *vt* (*statement, claws*) rétracter; (*undercarriage, aerial*) rentrer, escamoter

retrain [riː'treɪn] *vt* (*worker*) recycler

retread ['riːtred] *n* (*tyre*) pneu rechapé

retreat [rɪ'triːt] *n* retraite *f* ♦ *vi* battre en retraite

retribution [retrɪ'bjuːʃən] *n* châtiment *m*

retrieval [rɪ'triːvəl] *n* (*see vb*) récupération *f*; réparation *f*

retrieve [rɪ'triːv] *vt* (*sth lost*) récupérer; (*situation, honour*) sauver; (*error, loss*) réparer; **~r** *n* chien *m* d'arrêt

retrospect ['retrəspekt] *n*: **in ~** rétrospectivement, après coup; **~ive** [retrə'spektɪv] *adj* rétrospectif(-ive); (*law*) rétroactif(-ive)

return [rɪ'tə:n] *n* (*going or coming back*) retour *m*; (*of sth stolen etc*) restitution *f*; (*FINANCE: from land, shares*) rendement *m*, rapport *m* ♦ *cpd* (*journey*) de retour; (*BRIT: ticket*) aller et retour; (*match*) retour ♦ *vi* (*come back*) revenir; (*go back*) retourner ♦ *vt* rendre; (*bring back*) rapporter; (*send back; also: ball*) renvoyer; (*put back*) remettre; (*POL: candidate*) élire; **~s** *npl* (*COMM*) recettes *fpl*; (*FINANCE*) bénéfices *mpl*; **in ~ (for)** en échange (de); **by ~ (of post)** par retour (du courrier); **many happy ~s (of the day)!** bon anniversaire!

reunion [ri:'ju:nɪən] *n* réunion *f*

reunite [ri:ju:'naɪt] *vt* réunir

reuse [ri:'ju:z] *vt* réutiliser

rev [rev] *n abbr* (*AUT: = revolution*) tour *m* ♦ *vt* (*also: rev up*) emballer

revamp [ri:'væmp] *vt* (*firm, system etc*) réorganiser

reveal [rɪ'vi:l] *vt* (*make known*) révéler; (*display*) laisser voir; **~ing** *adj* révélateur(-trice); (*dress*) au décolleté généreux *or* suggestif

revel ['revl] *vi*: **to ~ in sth/in doing** se délecter de qch/à faire

revenge [rɪ'vendʒ] *n* vengeance *f*; **to take ~ on** (*enemy*) se venger sur

revenue ['revənju:] *n* revenu *m*

reverberate [rɪ'və:bəreɪt] *vi* (*sound*) retentir, se répercuter; (*fig: shock etc*) se propager

reverence ['revərəns] *n* vénération *f*, révérence *f*

Reverend ['revərənd] *adj* (*in titles*): **the ~ John Smith** (*Anglican*) le révérend John Smith; (*Catholic*) l'abbé (John) Smith; (*Protestant*) le pasteur (John) Smith

reversal [rɪ'və:sl] *n* (*of opinion*) revirement *m*; (*of order*) renversement *m*; (*of direction*) changement *m*

reverse [rɪ'və:s] *n* contraire *m*, opposé *m*; (*back*) dos *m*, envers *m*; (*of paper*) verso *m*; (*of coin; also: setback*) revers *m*; (*AUT: also:* **~ gear**) marche *f* arrière ♦ *adj* (*order, direction*) opposé(e), inverse ♦ *vt* (*order, position*) changer, inverser; (*direction, policy*) changer complètement de; (*decision*) annuler; (*roles*) renverser; (*car*) faire marche arrière avec ♦ *vi* (*BRIT: AUT*) faire marche arrière; **he ~d (the car) into a wall** il a embouti un mur en marche arrière; **~d charge call** (*BRIT*) *n* (*TEL*) communication *f* en PCV; **reversing lights** (*BRIT*) *npl* (*AUT*) feux *mpl* de marche arrière *or* de recul

revert [rɪ'və:t] *vi*: **to ~ to** revenir à, retourner à

review [rɪ'vju:] *n* revue *f*; (*of book, film*) critique *f*, compte rendu; (*of situation, policy*) examen *m*, bilan *m* ♦ *vt* passer en revue; faire la critique de; examiner; **~er** *n* critique *m*

revise [rɪ'vaɪz] *vt* réviser, modifier; (*manuscript*) revoir, corriger ♦ *vi* (*study*) réviser; **revision** [rɪ'vɪʒən] *n* révision *f*

revival [rɪ'vaɪvəl] *n* reprise *f*; (*recovery*) rétablissement *m*; (*of faith*) renouveau *m*

revive [rɪ'vaɪv] *vt* (*person*) ranimer; (*custom*) rétablir; (*economy*) relancer; (*hope, courage*) raviver, faire renaître; (*play*) reprendre ♦ *vi* (*person*) reprendre connaissance; (: *from ill health*) se rétablir; (*hope etc*) renaître; (*activity*) reprendre

revoke [rɪ'vəuk] *vt* révoquer; (*law*) abroger

revolt [rɪ'vəult] *n* révolte *f* ♦ *vi* se révolter, se rebeller ♦ *vt* révolter, dégoûter; **~ing** *adj* dégoûtant(e)

revolution [revə'lu:ʃən] *n* révolution *f*; (*of wheel etc*) tour *m*, révolution; **~ary** *adj* révolutionnaire ♦ *n* révolutionnaire *m/f*

revolve [rɪ'vɔlv] *vi* tourner

revolver [rɪ'vɔlvə] *n* revolver *m*

revolving [rɪ'vɔlvɪŋ] *adj* tournant(e); (*chair*) pivotant(e); **~ door** *n* (porte *f* à) tambour *m*

revulsion [rɪ'vʌlʃən] *n* dégoût *m*, répugnance *f*

reward [rɪ'wɔ:d] *n* récompense *f* ♦ *vt*: **to ~ (for)** récompenser (de); **~ing** *adj* (*fig*) qui (en) vaut la peine, gratifiant(e)

rewind [ri:'waɪnd] (*irreg*) *vt* (*tape*) rembobiner

rewire [ri:'waɪəʳ] *vt* (*house*) refaire l'installation électrique de

rheumatism ['ru:mətɪzəm] *n* rhumatisme *m*

Rhine [raɪn] *n* Rhin *m*

rhinoceros [raɪ'nɔsərəs] *n* rhinocéros *m*

Rhone [rəun] *n* Rhône *m*

rhubarb ['ru:bɑ:b] *n* rhubarbe *f*

rhyme [raɪm] *n* rime *f*; (*verse*) vers *mpl*

rhythm ['rɪðm] *n* rythme *m*

rib [rɪb] *n* (*ANAT*) côte *f*

ribbon ['rɪbən] *n* ruban *m*; **in ~s** (*torn*) en lambeaux

rice [raɪs] *n* riz *m*; **~ pudding** *n* riz au lait

rich [rɪtʃ] *adj* riche; (*gift, clothes*) somptueux(-euse) ♦ *npl*: **the ~** les riches *mpl*; **~es** *npl* richesses *fpl*; **~ly** *adv* richement; (*deserved, earned*) largement

rickets ['rɪkɪts] *n* rachitisme *m*

rid [rɪd] (*pt, pp* **rid**) *vt*: **to ~ sb of** débarrasser qn de; **to get ~ of** se débarrasser de

riddle ['rɪdl] *n* (*puzzle*) énigme *f* ♦ *vt*: **to be ~d with** être criblé(e) de; (*fig: guilt, corruption, doubts*) être en proie à

ride [raɪd] (*pt* **rode**, *pp* **ridden**) *n* promenade *f*, tour *m*; (*distance covered*) trajet *m* ♦ *vi* (*as sport*) monter (à cheval), faire du cheval; (*go somewhere: on horse, bicycle*) aller (à cheval ou bicyclette *etc*); (*journey: on bicycle, motorcycle, bus*) rouler ♦ *vt* (*a certain horse*) monter; (*distance*) parcourir, faire; **to take sb for a ~** (*fig*) faire marcher qn; **to ~ a horse/bicycle** monter à cheval/à bicyclette; **~r** *n* cavalier(-ère); (*in race*) jockey *m*; (*on bicycle*) cycliste *m/f*; (*on motorcycle*) motocycliste *m/f*

ridge [rɪdʒ] *n* (*of roof, mountain*) arête *f*; (*of hill*) faîte *m*; (*on object*) strie *f*

ridicule ['rɪdɪkju:l] *n* ridicule *m*; dérision *f*

ridiculous [rɪ'dɪkjuləs] *adj* ridicule

riding ['raɪdɪŋ] *n* équitation *f*; **~ school** *n* manège *m*, école *f* d'équitation

rife [raɪf] *adj* répandu(e); **~ with** abondant(e) en, plein(e) de

riffraff ['rɪfræf] *n* racaille *f*

rifle ['raɪfl] *n* fusil *m* (à canon rayé) ♦ *vt* vider, dévaliser; **~ through** *vt* (*belongings*) fouiller; (*papers*) feuilleter; **~ range** *n* champ *m* de tir; (*at fair*) stand *m* de tir

rift [rɪft] *n* fente *f*, fissure *f*; (*fig: disagreement*) désaccord *m*

rig [rɪg] *n* (*also:* **oil ~**: *at sea*) plate-forme pétrolière ♦ *vt* (*election etc*) truquer; **~ out** (*BRIT*) *vt*: **to ~ out as/in** habiller en/de; **~ up** *vt* arranger, faire avec des moyens de fortune; **~ging** *n* (*NAUT*) gréement *m*

right [raɪt] *adj* (*correctly chosen: answer, road etc*) bon (bonne); (*true*) juste, exact(e); (*suitable*) approprié(e), convenable; (*just*) juste, équitable; (*morally good*) bien *inv*; (*not left*) droit(e) ♦ *n* (*what is morally ~*) bien *m*; (*title, claim*) droit *m*; (*not left*) droite *f* ♦ *adv* (*answer*) correctement, juste; (*treat*) bien, comme il faut; (*not on the left*) à droite ♦ *vt* redresser ♦ *excl* bon!; **to be ~** (*person*) avoir raison; (*answer*) être juste *or* correct(e); (*clock*) à l'heure (juste); **by ~s** en toute justice; **on the ~** à droite; **to be in the ~** avoir raison; **~ now** en ce moment même; tout de suite; **~ in the middle** en plein milieu; **~ away** immédiatement; **~ angle** *n* (*MATH*) angle droit; **~eous** ['raɪtʃəs] *adj* droit(e), vertueux(-euse); (*anger*) justifié(e); **~ful** *adj* légitime; **~-handed** *adj* (*person*) droitier(-ère); **~-hand man** *n* bras droit (*fig*); **~-hand side** *n* la droite; **~ly** *adv* (*with reason*) à juste titre; **~ of way** *n* droit *m* de passage; (*AUT*) priorité *f*; **~-wing** *adj* (*POL*) de droite

rigid ['rɪdʒɪd] *adj* rigide; (*principle, control*) strict(e)

rigmarole ['rɪgmərəul] *n* comédie *f*

rigorous ['rɪgərəs] *adj* rigoureux(-euse)

rile [raɪl] *vt* agacer

rim [rɪm] *n* bord *m*; (*of spectacles*) monture *f*; (*of wheel*) jante *f*

rind [raɪnd] *n* (*of bacon*) couenne *f*; (*of lemon etc*) écorce *f*, zeste *m*; (*of cheese*) croûte *f*

ring [rɪŋ] (*pt* **rang**, *pp* **rung**) *n* anneau *m*;

(*on finger*) bague f; (*also:* **wedding ~**) alliance f; (*of people, objects*) cercle m; (*of spies*) réseau m; (*of smoke etc*) rond m; (*arena*) piste f, arène f; (*for boxing*) ring m; (*sound of bell*) sonnerie f ♦ vi (*telephone, bell*) sonner; (*person: by telephone*) téléphoner; (*also:* **~ out:** *voice, words*) retentir; (*ears*) bourdonner ♦ vt (BRIT: TEL: *also:* **~ up**) téléphoner à, appeler; (*bell*) faire sonner; **to ~ the bell** sonner; **to give sb a ~** (BRIT: TEL) appeler qn; **~ back** (BRIT) vt, vi (TEL) rappeler; **~ off** (BRIT) vi (TEL) raccrocher; **~ up** (BRIT) vt (TEL) appeler; **~ binder** n classeur m à anneaux; **~ing** [ˈrɪŋɪŋ] n (*of telephone*) sonnerie f; (*of bell*) tintement m; (*in ears*) bourdonnement m; **~ing tone** (BRIT) n (TEL) sonnerie f; **~leader** n (*of gang*) chef m, meneur m; **~lets** npl anglaises fpl; **~ road** (BRIT) n route f de ceinture; (*motorway*) périphérique m

rink [rɪŋk] n (*also:* **ice ~**) patinoire f

rinse [rɪns] vt rincer

riot [ˈraɪət] n émeute f; (*of flowers, colour*) profusion f ♦ vi faire une émeute, manifester avec violence; **to run ~** se déchaîner; **~ous** adj (*mob, assembly*) séditieux(-euse), déchaîné(e); (*living, behaviour*) débauché(e); (*party*) très animé(e); (*welcome*) délirant(e)

rip [rɪp] n déchirure f ♦ vt déchirer ♦ vi se déchirer; **~cord** n poignée f d'ouverture

ripe [raɪp] adj (*fruit*) mûr(e); (*cheese*) fait(e); **~n** vt mûrir ♦ vi mûrir

rip-off (inf) n: **it's a ~-~!** c'est de l'arnaque!

ripple [ˈrɪpl] n ondulation f; (*of applause, laughter*) cascade f ♦ vi onduler

rise [raɪz] (pt **rose**, pp **risen**) n (*slope*) côte f, pente f; (*hill*) hauteur f; (*increase: in wages:* BRIT) augmentation f; (: *in prices, temperature*) hausse f, augmentation f; (*fig: to power etc*) ascension f ♦ vi s'élever, monter; (*prices, numbers*) augmenter; (*waters*) monter; (*sun; person: from chair, bed*) se lever; (*also:* **~ up**: *tower, building*) s'élever; (: *rebel*) se révolter; se rebeller; (*in rank*)

s'élever; **to give ~ to** donner lieu à; **to ~ to the occasion** se montrer à la hauteur; **~r** n: **to be an early ~r** être matinal(e); **rising** adj (*number, prices*) en hausse; (*tide*) montant(e); (*sun, moon*) levant(e)

risk [rɪsk] n risque m ♦ vt risquer; **at ~** en danger; **at one's own ~** à ses risques et périls; **~y** adj risqué(e)

rissole [ˈrɪsəʊl] n croquette f

rite [raɪt] n rite m; **last ~s** derniers sacrements

ritual [ˈrɪtjʊəl] adj rituel(le) ♦ n rituel m

rival [ˈraɪvl] adj, n rival(e); (*in business*) concurrent(e) ♦ vt (*match*) égaler; **~ry** [ˈraɪvlrɪ] n rivalité f, concurrence f

river [ˈrɪvəʳ] n rivière f; (*major, also fig*) fleuve m ♦ cpd (*port, traffic*) fluvial(e); **up/down ~** en amont/aval; **~bank** n rive f, berge f; **~bed** n lit m (de rivière/fleuve)

rivet [ˈrɪvɪt] n rivet m ♦ vt (*fig*) river, fixer

Riviera [rɪvɪˈɛərə] n: **the (French) ~** la Côte d'Azur; **the Italian ~** la Riviera (italienne)

road [rəʊd] n route f; (*in town*) rue f; (*fig*) chemin, voie f; **major/minor ~** route principale *or* à priorité/voie secondaire; **~ accident** n accident m de la circulation; **~block** n barrage routier; **~hog** n chauffard m; **~ map** n carte routière; **~ rage** n comportement très agressif de certains usagers de la route; **~ safety** n sécurité routière; **~side** n bord m de la route, bas-côté m; **~ sign** n panneau m de signalisation; **~way** n chaussée f; **~ works** npl travaux mpl (de réfection des routes); **~worthy** adj en bon état de marche

roam [rəʊm] vi errer, vagabonder

roar [rɔːʳ] n rugissement m; (*of crowd*) hurlements mpl; (*of vehicle, thunder, storm*) grondement m ♦ vi rugir; hurler; gronder; **to ~ with laughter** éclater de rire; **to do a ~ing trade** faire des affaires d'or

roast [rəʊst] n rôti m ♦ vt (faire) rôtir; (*coffee*) griller, torréfier; **~ beef** n rôti m de bœuf, rosbif m

rob [rɒb] vt (*person*) voler; (*bank*) dévaliser; **to ~ sb of sth** voler *or* dérober qch à qn;

(fig: deprive) priver qn de qch; **~ber** *n* bandit *m*, voleur *m*; **~bery** *n* vol *m*

robe [rəʊb] *n (for ceremony etc)* robe *f*; *(also:* **bathrobe***)* peignoir *m*; *(US)* couverture *f*

robin [ˈrɔbɪn] *n* rouge-gorge *m*

robot [ˈrəʊbɔt] *n* robot *m*

robust [rəʊˈbʌst] *adj* robuste; *(material, appetite)* solide

rock [rɔk] *n (substance)* roche *f*, roc *m*; *(boulder)* rocher *m*; *(US: small stone)* caillou *m*; *(BRIT: sweet)* ≃ sucre *m* d'orge ♦ *vt (swing gently: cradle)* balancer; *(: child)* bercer; *(shake)* ébranler, secouer ♦ *vi (se)* balancer; être ébranlé(e) *or* secoué(e); **on the ~s** *(drink)* avec des glaçons; *(marriage etc)* en train de craquer; **~ and roll** *n* rock *(and roll)* *n*, rock'n'roll *m*; **~-bottom** *adj (fig: prices)* sacrifié(e); **~ery** *n* (jardin *m* de) rocaille *f*

rocket [ˈrɔkɪt] *n* fusée *f*; *(MIL)* fusée, roquette *f*

rocking chair *n* fauteuil *m* à bascule

rocking horse *n* cheval *m* à bascule

rocky [ˈrɔkɪ] *adj (hill)* rocheux(-euse); *(path)* rocailleux(-euse)

rod [rɔd] *n (wooden)* baguette *f*; *(metallic)* tringle *f*; *(TECH)* tige *f*; *(also:* **fishing ~***)* canne *f* à pêche

rode [rəʊd] *pt of* ride

rodent [ˈrəʊdnt] *n* rongeur *m*

rodeo [ˈrəʊdɪəʊ] *(US) n* rodéo *m*

roe [rəʊ] *n (species: also:* **~ deer***)* chevreuil *m*; *(of fish: also:* **hard ~***)* œufs *mpl* de poisson; **soft ~** laitance *f*

rogue [rəʊg] *n* coquin(e)

role [rəʊl] *n* rôle *m*; **~ play** *n* jeu *m* de rôle

roll [rəʊl] *n* rouleau *m*; *(of banknotes)* liasse *f*; *(also:* **bread ~***)* petit pain; *(register)* liste *f*; *(sound: of drums etc)* roulement *m* ♦ *vt* rouler; *(also:* **~ up***: string)* enrouler; *(: sleeves)* retrousser; *(also:* **~ out***: pastry)* étendre au rouleau, abaisser ♦ *vi* rouler; **~ about** *vi* rouler ça et là; *(person)* se rouler par terre; **~ around** *vi* = roll about; **~ by** *vi (time)* s'écouler, passer; **~ over** *vi* se

retourner; **~ up** *vi (inf: arrive)* arriver, s'amener ♦ *vt* rouler; **~ call** *n* appel *m*; **~er** *n* rouleau *m*; *(wheel)* roulette *f*; *(for road)* rouleau compresseur; **~er blade** *n* patin *m* en ligne; **~er coaster** *n* montagnes *fpl* russes; **~er skates** *npl* patins *mpl* à roulettes; **~er skating** *n* patin *m* à roulettes; **~ing** *adj (landscape)* onduleux(-euse); **~ing pin** *n* rouleau *m* à pâtisserie; **~ing stock** *n (RAIL)* matériel roulant

ROM [rɔm] *n abbr (= read only memory)* mémoire morte

Roman [ˈrəʊmən] *adj* romain(e); **~ Catholic** *adj, n* catholique *m/f*

romance [rəˈmæns] *n (love affair)* idylle *f*; *(charm)* poésie *f*; *(novel)* roman *m* à l'eau de rose

Romania [rəʊˈmeɪnɪə] *n* Roumanie *f*; **~n** *adj* roumain(e) ♦ *n* Roumain(e); *(LING)* roumain *m*

Roman numeral *n* chiffre romain

romantic [rəˈmæntɪk] *adj* romantique; sentimental(e)

Rome [rəʊm] *n* Rome

romp [rɔmp] *n* jeux bruyants ♦ *vi (also:* **~ about***)* s'ébattre, jouer bruyamment; **~ers** *npl* barboteuse *f*

roof [ruːf] *(pl* **~s***) n* toit *m* ♦ *vt* couvrir *(d'un toit)*; **the ~ of the mouth** la voûte du palais; **~ing** *n* toiture *f*; **~ rack** *n (AUT)* galerie *f*

rook [rʊk] *n (bird)* freux *m*; *(CHESS)* tour *f*

room [ruːm] *n (in house)* pièce *f*; *(also:* **bedroom***)* chambre *f (à coucher)*; *(in school etc)* salle *f*; *(space)* place *f*; **~s** *npl (lodging)* meublé *m*; **"~s to let"** *or* **"~s for rent"** *(US)* "chambres à louer"; **single/double ~** chambre pour une personne/deux personnes; **there is ~ for improvement** cela laisse à désirer; **~ing house** *(US) n* maison *f or* immeuble *m* de rapport; **~mate** *n* camarade *m/f* de chambre; **~ service** *n* service *m* des chambres *(dans un hôtel)*; **~y** *adj* spacieux(-euse); *(garment)* ample

roost [ruːst] *vi* se jucher

rooster [ˈruːstəʳ] *n (esp US)* coq *m*

root [ruːt] *n* (*BOT, MATH*) racine *f*; (*fig: of problem*) origine *f*, fond *m* ♦ *vi* (*plant*) s'enraciner; ~ **about** *vi* (*fig*) fouiller; ~ **for** *vt fus* encourager, applaudir; ~ **out** *vt* (*find*) dénicher

rope [rəup] *n* corde *f*; (*NAUT*) cordage *m* ♦ *vt* (*tie up or together*) attacher; (*climbers: also:* ~ **together**) encorder; (*area:* ~ **off**) interdire l'accès de; (*: divide off*) séparer; **to know the ~s** (*fig*) être au courant, connaître les ficelles; ~ **in** *vt* (*fig: person*) embringuer

rosary [ˈrəuzərɪ] *n* chapelet *m*

rose [rəuz] *pt of* **rise** ♦ *n* rose *f*; (*also:* ~**bush**) rosier *m*; (*on watering can*) pomme *f*

rosé [ˈrəuzeɪ] *n* rosé *m*

rosebud [ˈrəuzbʌd] *n* bouton *m* de rose

rosemary [ˈrəuzmərɪ] *n* romarin *m*

roster [ˈrɒstəʳ] *n*: **duty ~** tableau *m* de service

rostrum [ˈrɒstrəm] *n* tribune *f* (*pour un orateur etc*)

rosy [ˈrəuzɪ] *adj* rose; **a ~ future** un bel avenir

rot [rɒt] *n* (*decay*) pourriture *f*; (*fig: pej*) idioties *fpl* ♦ *vt, vi* pourrir

rota [ˈrəutə] *n* liste *f*, tableau *m* de service; **on a ~ basis** par roulement

rotary [ˈrəutərɪ] *adj* rotatif(-ive)

rotate [rəuˈteɪt] *vt* (*revolve*) faire tourner; (*change round: jobs*) faire à tour de rôle ♦ *vi* (*revolve*) tourner; **rotating** *adj* (*movement*) tournant(e)

rotten [ˈrɒtn] *adj* (*decayed*) pourri(e); (*dishonest*) corrompu(e); (*inf: bad*) mauvais(e), moche; **to feel ~** (*ill*) être mal fichu(e);

rotund [rəuˈtʌnd] *adj* (*person*) rondelet(te)

rough [rʌf] *adj* (*cloth, skin*) rêche, rugueux(-euse); (*terrain*) accidenté(e); (*path*) rocailleux(-euse); (*voice*) rauque, rude; (*person, manner: coarse*) rude, fruste; (*: violent*) brutal(e); (*district, weather*) mauvais(e); (*sea*) houleux(-euse); (*plan etc*) ébauché(e); (*guess*) approximatif(-ive) ♦ *n* (*GOLF*) rough *m* ♦ *vt*: **to ~ it** vivre à la dure; **to sleep ~** (*BRIT*) coucher à la dure;

~**age** *n* fibres *fpl* alimentaires; ~-**and-ready** *adj* rudimentaire; ~ **copy**, ~ **draft** *n* brouillon *m*; ~**ly** *adv* (*handle*) rudement, brutalement; (*speak*) avec brusquerie; (*make*) grossièrement; (*approximately*) à peu près, en gros

roulette [ruːˈlet] *n* roulette *f*

Roumania [ruːˈmeɪnɪə] *n* = **Romania**

round [raund] *adj* rond(e) ♦ *n* (*BRIT: of toast*) tranche *f*; (*duty: of policeman, milkman etc*) tournée *f*; (*: of doctor*) visites *fpl*; (*game: of cards, in competition*) partie *f*; (*BOXING*) round *m*; (*of talks*) série *f* ♦ *vt* (*corner*) tourner ♦ *prep* autour de ♦ *adv*: **all ~** tout autour; **the long way ~** (par) le chemin le plus long; **all the year ~** toute l'année; **it's just ~ the corner** (*fig*) c'est tout près; ~ **the clock** 24 heures sur 24; **to go ~ to sb's (house)** aller chez qn; **go ~ the back** passez par derrière; **enough to go ~** assez pour tout le monde; ~ **of ammunition** cartouche *f*; ~ **of applause** ban *m*, applaudissements *mpl*; ~ **of drinks** tournée *f*; ~ **of sandwiches** sandwich *m*; ~ **off** *vt* (*speech etc*) terminer; ~ **up** *vt* rassembler; (*criminals*) effectuer une rafle de; (*price, figure*) arrondir (au chiffre supérieur); ~**about** *n* (*BRIT: AUT*) rond-point *m* (à sens giratoire); (*: at fair*) manège *m* (de chevaux de bois) ♦ *adj* (*route, means*) détourné(e); ~**ers** *n* (*game*) sorte de baseball; ~**ly** *adv* (*fig*) tout net, carrément; ~ **trip** *n* (*voyage m*) aller et retour *m*; ~**up** *n* rassemblement *m*; (*of criminals*) rafle *f*

rouse [rauz] *vt* (*wake up*) réveiller; (*stir up*) susciter; provoquer; éveiller; **rousing** *adj* (*welcome*) enthousiaste

route [ruːt] *n* itinéraire *m*; (*of bus*) parcours *m*; (*of trade, shipping*) route *f*

routine [ruːˈtiːn] *adj* (*work*) ordinaire, courant(e); (*procedure*) d'usage ♦ *n* (*habits*) habitudes *fpl*; (*pej*) train-train *m*; (*THEATRE*) numéro *m*

rove [rəuv] *vt* (*area, streets*) errer dans

row¹ [rəu] *n* (*line*) rangée *f*; (*of people, seats, KNITTING*) rang *m*; (*behind one an-*

other: of cars, people) file f ♦ vi (in boat) ramer; (as sport) faire de l'aviron ♦ vt (boat) faire aller à la rame or à l'aviron; **in a ~** (fig) d'affilée

row² [rau] n (noise) vacarme m; (dispute) dispute f, querelle f; (scolding) réprimande f, savon m ♦ vi se disputer, se quereller

rowboat ['rəubəut] (US) n canot m (à rames)

rowdy ['raudɪ] adj chahuteur(-euse); (occasion) tapageur(-euse)

rowing ['rəuɪŋ] n canotage m; (as sport) aviron m; **~ boat** (BRIT) n canot m (à rames)

royal ['rɔɪəl] adj royal(e); **R~ Air Force** (BRIT) n armée de l'air britannique; **~ty** n (royal persons) (membres mpl de la) famille royale; (payment: to author) droits mpl d'auteur; (: to inventor) royalties fpl

rpm abbr (AUT) (= revolutions per minute) tr/mn

RSVP abbr (= répondez s'il vous plaît) R.S.V.P.

Rt Hon. abbr (BRIT: Right Honourable) titre donné aux députés de la Chambre des communes

rub [rʌb] vt frotter; frictionner; (hands) se frotter ♦ n (with cloth) coup m chiffon or de torchon; **to give sth a ~** donner un coup de chiffon or de torchon à; **to ~ sb up** (BRIT) or **to ~ sb** (US) **the wrong way** prendre qn à rebrousse-poil; **~ off** vi partir; **~ off on** vt fus déteindre sur; **~ out** vt effacer

rubber ['rʌbər] n caoutchouc m; (BRIT: eraser) gomme f (à effacer); **~ band** n élastique m; **~ plant** n caoutchouc m (plante verte)

rubbish ['rʌbɪʃ] n (from household) ordures fpl; (fig: pej) camelote f; (: nonsense) bêtises fpl, idioties fpl; **~ bin** (BRIT) n poubelle f; **~ dump** n décharge publique, dépotoir m

rubble ['rʌbl] n décombres mpl; (smaller) gravats mpl; (CONSTR) blocage m

ruby ['ru:bɪ] n rubis m

rucksack ['rʌksæk] n sac m à dos

rudder ['rʌdər] n gouvernail m

ruddy ['rʌdɪ] adj (face) coloré(e); (inf: damned) sacré(e), fichu(e)

rude [ru:d] adj (impolite) impoli(e); (coarse) grossier(-ère); (shocking) indécent(e), inconvenant(e)

ruffle ['rʌfl] vt (hair) ébouriffer; (clothes) chiffonner; (fig: person): **to get ~d** s'énerver

rug [rʌg] n petit tapis; (BRIT: blanket) couverture f

rugby ['rʌgbɪ] n (also: ~ **football**) rugby m

rugged ['rʌgɪd] adj (landscape) accidenté(e); (features, character) rude

ruin ['ru:ɪn] n ruine f ♦ vt ruiner; (spoil, clothes) abîmer; (event) gâcher; **~s** npl (of building) ruine(s)

rule [ru:l] n règle f; (regulation) règlement m; (government) autorité f, gouvernement m ♦ vt (country) gouverner; (person) dominer ♦ vi commander; (LAW) statuer; **as a ~** normalement, en règle générale; **~ out** vt exclure; **~d** adj (paper) réglé(e); **~r** n (sovereign) souverain(e); (for measuring) règle f; **ruling** adj (party) au pouvoir; (class) dirigeant(e) ♦ n (LAW) décision f

rum [rʌm] n rhum m

Rumania [ruː'meɪnɪə] n = Romania

rumble ['rʌmbl] vi gronder; (stomach, pipe) gargouiller

rummage ['rʌmɪdʒ] vi fouiller

rumour ['ru:mər] (US **rumor**) n rumeur f, bruit m (qui court) ♦ vt: **it is ~ed that** le bruit court que

rump [rʌmp] n (of animal) croupe f; (inf: of person) postérieur m; **~ steak** n rumsteck m

rumpus ['rʌmpəs] (inf) n tapage m, chahut m

run [rʌn] (pt ran, pp run) n (fast pace) (pas m de) course f; (outing) tour m or promenade f (en voiture); (distance travelled) parcours m, trajet m; (series) suite f, série f; (THEATRE) série de représentations; (SKI) piste f; (CRICKET, BASEBALL) point m; (in tights, stockings) maille filée, échelle f ♦ vt (operate: business) diriger; (: competition, *course*) organiser; (: *hotel, house*) tenir; (*race*) participer à; (*COMPUT*) exécuter; (*to pass: hand, finger*) passer; (*water, bath*) faire couler; (*PRESS: feature*) publier ♦ *vi* courir; (*flee*) s'enfuir; (*work: machine, factory*) marcher; (*bus, train*) circuler; (*continue: play*) se jouer; (: *contract*) être valide; (*flow: river, bath; nose*) couler; (*colours, washing*) déteindre; (*in election*) être candidat, se présenter; **to go for a ~** faire un peu de course à pied; **there was a ~ on ...** (*meat, tickets*) les gens se sont rués sur ...; **in the long ~** à longue échéance; à la longue; **on the ~** en fuite; **I'll ~ you to the station** je vais vous emmener *or* conduire à la gare; **to ~ a risk** courir un risque; **~ about** *vi* (*children*) courir çà et là; **~ across** *vt fus* (*find*) trouver par hasard; **~ around** *vi* = **run about**; **~ away** *vi* s'enfuir; **~ down** *vt* (*production*) réduire progressivement; (*factory*) réduire progressivement la production de; (*AUT*) renverser; (*criticize*) critiquer, dénigrer; **to be ~ down** (*person: tired*) être fatigué(e) *or* à plat; **~ in** (*BRIT*) *vt* (*car*) roder; **~ into** *vt fus* (*meet: person*) rencontrer par hasard; (*trouble*) se heurter à; (*collide with*) heurter; **~ off** *vi* s'enfuir ♦ *vt* (*water*) laisser s'écouler; (*copies*) tirer; **~ out** *vi* (*person*) sortir en courant; (*liquid*) couler; (*lease*) expirer; (*money*) être épuisé(e); **~ out of** *vt fus* se trouver à court de; **~ over** *vt* (*AUT*) écraser ♦ *vt fus* (*revise*) revoir, reprendre; **~ through** *vt fus* (*recapitulate*) reprendre; (*play*) répéter; **~ up** *vt*: **to ~ up against** (*difficulties*) se heurter à; **to ~ up a debt** s'endetter; **~away** *adj* (*horse*) emballé(e); (*truck*) fou (folle); (*person*) fugitif(-ive); (*teenager*) fugueur(-euse)

rung [rʌŋ] *pp of* **ring** ♦ *n* (*of ladder*) barreau *m*

runner ['rʌnər] *n* (*in race: person*) coureur(-euse); (: *horse*) partant *m*; (*on sledge*) patin *m*; (*for drawer etc*) coulisseau *m*; **~ bean** (*BRIT*) haricot *m* (à rames); **~-up** *n* second(e)

running ['rʌnɪŋ] *n* course *f*; (*of business, organization*) gestion *f*, direction *f* ♦ *adj* (*water*) courant(e); **to be in/out of the ~ for sth** être/ne pas être sur les rangs pour qch; **6 days ~** 6 jours de suite; **~ commentary** *n* commentaire détaillé; **~ costs** *npl* frais *mpl* d'exploitation

runny ['rʌnɪ] *adj* qui coule

run-of-the-mill ['rʌnəvðə'mɪl] *adj* ordinaire, banal(e)

runt [rʌnt] *n* avorton *m*

run-up ['rʌnʌp] *n*: **~-~ to sth** (*election etc*) période *f* précédant qch

runway ['rʌnweɪ] *n* (*AVIAT*) piste *f*

rupture ['rʌptʃər] *n* (*MED*) hernie *f*

rural ['rʊərl] *adj* rural(e)

rush [rʌʃ] *n* (*hurry*) hâte *f*, précipitation *f*; (*of crowd, COMM: sudden demand*) ruée *f*; (*current*) flot *m*; (*of emotion*) vague *f*; (*BOT*) jonc *m* ♦ *vt* (*hurry*) transporter *or* envoyer d'urgence ♦ *vi* se précipiter; **~ hour** *n* heures *fpl* de pointe

rusk [rʌsk] *n* biscotte *f*

Russia ['rʌʃə] *n* Russie *f*; **~n** *adj* russe ♦ *n* Russe *m/f*; (*LING*) russe *m*

rust [rʌst] *n* rouille *f* ♦ *vi* rouiller

rustic ['rʌstɪk] *adj* rustique

rustle ['rʌsl] *vi* bruire, produire un bruissement ♦ *vt* froisser

rustproof ['rʌstpruːf] *adj* inoxydable

rusty ['rʌstɪ] *adj* rouillé(e)

rut [rʌt] *n* ornière *f*; (*ZOOL*) rut *m*; **to be in a ~** suivre l'ornière, s'encroûter

ruthless ['ruːθlɪs] *adj* sans pitié, impitoyable

rye [raɪ] *n* seigle *m*

S, s

Sabbath ['sæbəθ] *n* (*Jewish*) sabbat *m*; (*Christian*) dimanche *m*

sabotage ['sæbətɑːʒ] *n* sabotage *m* ♦ *vt* saboter

saccharin(e) ['sækərɪn] *n* saccharine *f*

sachet ['sæʃeɪ] *n* sachet *m*

sack [sæk] *n* (*bag*) sac *m* ♦ *vt* (*dismiss*) renvoyer, mettre à la porte; (*plunder*) piller, mettre à sac; **to get the ~** être renvoyé(e), être mis(e) à la porte; **~ing** *n* (*material*) toile *f* à sac; (*dismissal*) renvoi *m*

sacrament ['sækrəmənt] *n* sacrement *m*

sacred ['seɪkrɪd] *adj* sacré(e)

sacrifice ['sækrɪfaɪs] *n* sacrifice *m* ♦ *vt* sacrifier

sad [sæd] *adj* triste; (*deplorable*) triste, fâcheux(-euse)

saddle ['sædl] *n* selle *f* ♦ *vt* (*horse*) seller; **to be ~d with sth** (*inf*) avoir qch sur les bras; **~bag** *n* sacoche *f*

sadistic [sə'dɪstɪk] *adj* sadique

sadly ['sædlɪ] *adv* tristement; (*unfortunately*) malheureusement; (*seriously*) fort

sadness ['sædnɪs] *n* tristesse *f*

s.a.e. *n abbr* = **stamped addressed envelope**

safe [seɪf] *adj* (*out of danger*) hors de danger, en sécurité; (*not dangerous*) sans danger; (*cautious*) prudent(e); (*sure: bet etc*) assuré(e) ♦ *n* coffre-fort *m*; **~ from** à l'abri de; **~ and sound** sain(e) et sauf (sauve); **(just) to be on the ~ side** pour plus de sûreté, par précaution; **~ journey!** bon voyage!; **~-conduct** *n* sauf-conduit *m*; **~-deposit** *n* (*vault*) dépôt *m* de coffres-forts; (*box*) coffre-fort *m*; **~guard** *n* sauvegarde *f*, protection *f* ♦ *vt* sauvegarder, protéger; **~keeping** *n* bonne garde; **~ly** *adv* (*assume, say*) sans risque d'erreur; (*drive, arrive*) sans accident; **~ sex** *n* rapports *mpl* sexuels sans risque

safety ['seɪftɪ] *n* sécurité *f*; **~ belt** *n* ceinture *f* de sécurité; **~ pin** *n* épingle *f* de sûreté *or* de nourrice; **~ valve** *n* soupape *f* de sûreté

sag [sæg] *vi* s'affaisser; (*hem, breasts*) pendre

sage [seɪdʒ] *n* (*herb*) sauge *f*; (*person*) sage *m*

Sagittarius [sædʒɪ'tɛərɪəs] *n* le Sagittaire

Sahara [sə'hɑːrə] *n*: **the ~ (Desert)** le (désert du) Sahara

said [sed] *pt, pp of* **say**

sail [seɪl] *n* (*on boat*) voile *f*; (*trip*): **to go for a ~** faire un tour en bateau ♦ *vt* (*boat*) manœuvrer, piloter ♦ *vi* (*travel: ship*) avancer, naviguer; (*set off*) partir, prendre la mer; (*SPORT*) faire de la voile; **they ~ed into Le Havre** ils sont entrés dans le port du Havre; **~ through** *vi, vt fus* (*fig*) réussir haut la main; **~boat** (*US*) *n* bateau *m* à voiles, voilier *m*; **~ing** *n* (*SPORT*) voile *f*; **to go ~ing** faire de la voile; **~ing boat** *n* bateau *m* à voiles, voilier *m*; **~ing ship** *n* grand voilier; **~or** *n* marin *m*, matelot *m*

saint [seɪnt] *n* saint(e)

sake [seɪk] *n*: **for the ~ of** pour (l'amour de), dans l'intérêt de; par égard pour

salad ['sæləd] *n* salade *f*; **~ bowl** *n* saladier *m*; **~ cream** (*BRIT*) *n* (sorte *f* de) mayonnaise *f*; **~ dressing** *n* vinaigrette *f*

salami [sə'lɑːmɪ] *n* salami *m*

salary ['sælərɪ] *n* salaire *m*

sale [seɪl] *n* vente *f*; (*at reduced prices*) soldes *mpl*; **"for ~"** "à vendre"; **on ~** en vente; **on ~ or return** vendu(e) avec faculté de retour; **~room** *n* salle *f* des ventes; **~s assistant** (*US* **sales clerk**) *n* vendeur(-euse); **~sman** (*irreg*) *n* vendeur *m*; (*representative*) représentant *m*; **~s rep** *n* (*COMM*) représentant(e) *m/f*; **~swoman** (*irreg*) *n* vendeuse *f*; (*representative*) représentante *f*

salmon ['sæmən] *n inv* saumon *m*

salon ['sælɔn] *n* salon *m*

saloon [sə'luːn] *n* (*US*) bar *m*; (*BRIT: AUT*) berline *f*; (*ship's lounge*) salon *m*

salt [sɔːlt] *n* sel *m* ♦ *vt* saler; **~ cellar** *n* salière *f*; **~water** *adj* de mer; **~y** *adj* salé(e)

salute [sə'luːt] *n* salut *m* ♦ *vt* saluer

salvage ['sælvɪdʒ] *n* (*saving*) sauvetage *m*; (*things saved*) biens sauvés *or* récupérés ♦ *vt* sauver, récupérer

salvation [sæl'veɪʃən] *n* salut *m*; **S~ Army** *n* armée *f* du Salut

same [seɪm] *adj* même ♦ *pron*: **the ~** le (la) même, les mêmes; **the ~ book as** le même livre que; **at the ~ time** en même temps; **all** *or* **just the ~** tout de même, quand même; **to do the ~** faire de même, en faire autant; **to do the ~ as sb** faire comme qn; **the ~ to you!** à vous de même!; *(after insult)* toi-même!

sample ['sɑ:mpl] *n* échantillon *m*; *(blood)* prélèvement *m* ♦ *vt (food, wine)* goûter

sanction ['sæŋkʃən] *n* approbation *f*, sanction *f*

sanctity ['sæŋktɪtɪ] *n* sainteté *f*, caractère sacré

sanctuary ['sæŋktjuərɪ] *n (holy place)* sanctuaire *m*; *(refuge)* asile *m*; *(for wild life)* réserve *f*

sand [sænd] *n* sable *m* ♦ *vt (furniture: also:* **~ down)** poncer

sandal ['sændl] *n* sandale *f*

sand: ~box *(US) n* tas *m* de sable; **~castle** *n* château *m* de sable; **~paper** *n* papier *m* de verre; **~pit** *(BRIT) n (for children)* tas *m* de sable; **~stone** *n* grès *m*

sandwich ['sændwɪtʃ] *n* sandwich *m*; **cheese/ham ~** sandwich au fromage/jambon; **~ course** *(BRIT) n* cours *m* de formation professionnelle

sandy ['sændɪ] *adj* sablonneux(-euse); *(colour)* sable *inv*, blond roux *inv*

sane [seɪn] *adj (person)* sain(e) d'esprit; *(outlook)* sensé(e), sain(e)

sang [sæŋ] *pt of* **sing**

sanitary ['sænɪtərɪ] *adj (system, arrangements)* sanitaire; *(clean)* hygiénique; **~ towel** *(US* **sanitary napkin**) *n* serviette *f* hygiénique

sanitation [sænɪ'teɪʃən] *n (in house)* installations *fpl* sanitaires; *(in town)* système *m* sanitaire; **~ department** *(US) n* service *m* de voirie

sanity ['sænɪtɪ] *n* santé mentale; *(common sense)* bon sens

sank [sæŋk] *pt of* **sink**

Santa Claus [sæntə'klɔ:z] *n* le père Noël

sap [sæp] *n (of plants)* sève *f* ♦ *vt (strength)* saper, miner

sapling ['sæplɪŋ] *n* jeune arbre *m*

sapphire ['sæfaɪər] *n* saphir *m*

sarcasm ['sɑ:kæzm] *n* sarcasme *m*, raillerie *f*; **sarcastic** [sɑ:'kæstɪk] *adj* sarcastique

sardine [sɑ:'di:n] *n* sardine *f*

Sardinia [sɑ:'dɪnɪə] *n* Sardaigne *f*

sash [sæʃ] *n* écharpe *f*

sat [sæt] *pt, pp of* **sit**

satchel ['sætʃl] *n* cartable *m*

satellite ['sætəlaɪt] *n* satellite *m*; **~ dish** *n* antenne *f* parabolique; **~ television** *n* télévision *f* par câble

satin ['sætɪn] *n* satin *m* ♦ *adj* en *or* de satin, satiné(e)

satire ['sætaɪər] *n* satire *f*

satisfaction [sætɪs'fækʃən] *n* satisfaction *f*

satisfactory [sætɪs'fæktərɪ] *adj* satisfaisant(e)

satisfied ['sætɪsfaɪd] *adj* satisfait(e)

satisfy ['sætɪsfaɪ] *vt* satisfaire, contenter; *(convince)* convaincre, persuader; **~ing** *adj* satisfaisant(e)

Saturday ['sætədɪ] *n* samedi *m*

sauce [sɔ:s] *n* sauce *f*; **~pan** *n* casserole *f*

saucer ['sɔ:sər] *n* soucoupe *f*

Saudi ['saudɪ]: **~ Arabia** *n* Arabie Saoudite; **~ (Arabian)** *adj* saoudien(ne)

sauna ['sɔ:nə] *n* sauna *m*

saunter ['sɔ:ntər] *vi:* **to ~ along/in/out** *etc* marcher/entrer/sortir *etc* d'un pas nonchalant

sausage ['sɔsɪdʒ] *n* saucisse *f*; *(cold meat)* saucisson *m*; **~ roll** *n* ≈ friand *m*

savage ['sævɪdʒ] *adj (cruel, fierce)* brutal(e), féroce; *(primitive)* primitif(-ive), sauvage ♦ *n* sauvage *m/f*

save [seɪv] *vt (person, belongings)* sauver; *(money)* mettre de côté, économiser; *(time)* (faire) gagner; *(keep)* garder; *(COMPUT)* sauvegarder; *(SPORT: stop)* arrêter; *(avoid: trouble)* éviter ♦ *vi (also:* **~ up)** mettre de l'argent de côté ♦ *n (SPORT)* arrêt *m* (du ballon) ♦ *prep* sauf, à l'exception de

saving ['seɪvɪŋ] *n* économie *f* ♦ *adj:* **the ~ grace of sth** ce qui rachète qch; **~s** *npl (money saved)* économies *fpl*; **~s account** *n* compte *m* d'épargne; **~s bank** *n* caisse *f* d'épargne

saviour ['seɪvjər] *(US* **savior**) *n* sauveur *m*

savour ['seɪvər] *(US* **savor**) *vt* savourer; **~y** *(US* **savory**) *adj (dish: not sweet)* salé(e)

saw [sɔ:] (*pt* **sawed**, *pp* **sawed** *or* **sawn**) *vt* scier ♦ *n* (*tool*) scie *f* ♦ *pt of* **see**; **~dust** *n* sciure *f*; **~mill** *n* scierie *f*; **~n-off** *adj*: **~n-off shotgun** carabine *f* à canon scié

sax [sæks] (*inf*) *n* saxo *m*

saxophone ['sæksəfəun] *n* saxophone *m*

say [seɪ] (*pt, pp* **said**) *vt*: **to have one's ~** dire ce qu'on a à dire ♦ *vt* dire; **to have a** *or* **some ~ in sth** avoir voix au chapitre; **could you ~ that again?** pourriez-vous répéter ce que vous venez de dire?; **that goes without ~ing** cela va sans dire, cela va de soi; **~ing** *n* dicton *m*, proverbe *m*

scab [skæb] *n* croûte *f*; (*pej*) jaune *m*

scaffold ['skæfəld] *n* échafaud *m*; **~ing** *n* échafaudage *m*

scald [skɔ:ld] *n* brûlure *f* ♦ *vt* ébouillanter

scale [skeɪl] *n* (*of fish*) écaille *f*; (*MUS*) gamme *f*; (*of ruler, thermometer etc*) graduation *f*, échelle (graduée); (*of salaries, fees etc*) barème *m*; (*of map, also size, extent*) échelle *f* ♦ *vt* (*mountain*) escalader; **~s** *npl* (*for weighing*) balance *f*; (*also:* **bathroom ~**) pèse-personne *m inv*; **on a large ~** sur une grande échelle, en grand; **~ of charges** tableau *m* des tarifs; **~ down** *vt* réduire

scallop ['skɔləp] *n* coquille *f* Saint-Jacques; (*SEWING*) feston *m*

scalp [skælp] *n* cuir chevelu ♦ *vt* scalper

scampi ['skæmpɪ] *npl* langoustines (frites), scampi *mpl*

scan [skæn] *vt* scruter, examiner; (*glance at quickly*) parcourir; (*TV, RADAR*) balayer ♦ *n* (*MED*) scanographie *f*

scandal ['skændl] *n* scandale *m*; (*gossip*) ragots *mpl*

Scandinavia [skændɪ'neɪvɪə] *n* Scandinavie *f*; **~n** *adj* scandinave

scant [skænt] *adj* insuffisant(e); **~y** ['skæntɪ] *adj* peu abondant(e), insuffisant(e); (*underwear*) minuscule

scapegoat ['skeɪpgəut] *n* bouc *m* émissaire

scar [skɑ:] *n* cicatrice *f* ♦ *vt* marquer (d'une cicatrice)

scarce [skeəs] *adj* rare, peu abondant(e);

to make o.s. ~ (*inf*) se sauver; **~ly** *adv* à peine; **scarcity** *n* manque *m*, pénurie *f*

scare [skeər] *n* peur *f*, panique *f* ♦ *vt* effrayer, faire peur à; **to ~ sb stiff** faire une peur bleue à qn; **bomb ~** alerte *f* à la bombe; **~ away** *vt* faire fuir; **~ off** *vt* = **scare away**; **~crow** *n* épouvantail *m*; **~d** *adj*: **to be ~d** avoir peur

scarf [skɑ:f] (*pl* **~s** *or* **scarves**) *n* (*long*) écharpe *f*; (*square*) foulard *m*

scarlet ['skɑ:lɪt] *adj* écarlate; **~ fever** *n* scarlatine *f*

scary ['skeərɪ] (*inf*) *adj* effrayant(e)

scathing ['skeɪðɪŋ] *adj* cinglant(e), acerbe

scatter ['skætər] *vt* éparpiller, répandre; (*crowd*) disperser ♦ *vi* se disperser; **~brained** *adj* écervelé(e), étourdi(e)

scavenger ['skævəndʒər] *n* (*person: in bins etc*) pilleur *m* de poubelles

scene [si:n] *n* scène *f*; (*of crime, accident*) lieu(x) *m(pl)*; (*sight, view*) spectacle *m*, vue *f*; **~ry** [si:nəri] *n* (*THEATRE*) décor(s) *m(pl)*; (*landscape*) paysage *m*; **scenic** *adj* (*picturesque*) offrant de beaux paysages *or* panoramas

scent [sent] *n* parfum *m*, odeur *f*; (*track*) piste *f*

sceptical ['skeptɪkl] (*US* **skeptical**) *adj* sceptique

schedule ['ʃedju:l, (*US*) 'skedju:l] *n* programme *m*, plan *m*; (*of trains*) horaire *m*; (*of prices etc*) barème *m*, tarif *m* ♦ *vt* prévoir; **on ~** à l'heure (prévue); **to be ahead of/behind ~** avoir de l'avance/du retard; **~d flight** *n* vol régulier

scheme [ski:m] *n* plan *m*, projet *m*; (*dishonest plan, plot*) complot *m*, combine *f*; (*arrangement*) arrangement *m*, classification *f*; (*pension ~ etc*) régime *m* ♦ *vi* comploter, manigancer; **scheming** *adj* rusé(e), intrigant(e) ♦ *n* manigances *fpl*, intrigues *fpl*

scholar ['skɔlər] *n* érudit(e); (*pupil*) boursier(-ère); **~ship** *n* (*knowledge*) érudition *f*; (*grant*) bourse *f* (d'études)

school [sku:l] *n* école *f*; (*secondary ~*) collège *m*, lycée *m*; (*us: university*) université *f*; (*in university*) faculté *f* ♦ *cpd* scolaire; **~book** *n* livre *m* scolaire *or* de classe; **~boy** *n* écolier *m*; collégien *m*, lycéen *m*; **~children** *npl* écoliers *mpl*; collégiens *mpl*, lycéens *mpl*; **~girl** *n* écolière *f*; collégienne *f*, lycéenne *f*; **~ing** *n* instruction *f*, études *fpl*; **~master** *n* professeur *m*; **~mistress** *n* professeur *m*; **~teacher** *n* instituteur(-trice); professeur *m*

science ['saɪəns] *n* science *f*; **~ fiction** *n* science-fiction *f*; **scientific** [saɪən'tɪfɪk] *adj* scientifique; **scientist** *n* scientifique *m/f*; (*eminent*) savant *m*

scissors ['sɪzəz] *npl* ciseaux *mpl*

scoff [skɒf] *vt* (*BRIT: inf: eat*) avaler, bouffer ♦ *vi*: **to ~ (at)** (*mock*) se moquer (de)

scold [skəʊld] *vt* gronder

scone [skɒn] *n* sorte de petit pain rond au lait

scoop [sku:p] *n* pelle *f* (à main); (*for ice cream*) boule *f* à glace; (*PRESS*) scoop *m*; **~ out** *vt* évider, creuser; **~ up** *vt* ramasser

scooter ['sku:tə^r] *n* (*also*: **motor ~**) scooter *m*; (*toy*) trottinette *f*

scope [skəʊp] *n* (*capacity: of plan, undertaking*) portée *f*, envergure *f*; (: *of person*) compétence *f*, capacités *fpl*; (*opportunity*) possibilités *fpl*; **within the ~ of** dans les limites de

scorch [skɔ:tʃ] *vt* (*clothes*) brûler (légèrement), roussir; (*earth, grass*) dessécher, brûler

score [skɔ:^r] *n* score *m*, décompte *m* des points; (*MUS*) partition *f*; (*twenty*) vingt ♦ *vt* (*goal, point*) marquer; (*success*) remporter ♦ *vi* marquer des points; (*FOOTBALL*) marquer un but; (*keep ~*) compter les points; **~s of** (*very many*) beaucoup de, un tas de (*fam*); **on that ~** sur ce chapitre, à cet égard; **to ~ 6 out of 10** obtenir 6 sur 10; **~ out** *vt* rayer, barrer, biffer; **~board** *n* tableau *m*

scorn [skɔ:n] *n* mépris *m*, dédain *m*

Scorpio ['skɔ:pɪəʊ] *n* le Scorpion

Scot [skɒt] *n* Écossais(e)

Scotch [skɒtʃ] *n* whisky *m*, scotch *m*

scot-free ['skɒt'fri:] *adv*: **to get off ~-~** s'en tirer sans être puni(e)

Scotland ['skɒtlənd] *n* Écosse *f*; **Scots** *adj* écossais(e); **Scotsman** (*irreg*) *n* Écossais *m*; **Scotswoman** (*irreg*) *n* Écossaise *f*; **Scottish** *adj* écossais(e); **Scottish Parliament** *n* Parlement *m* écossais

scoundrel ['skaʊndrl] *n* vaurien *m*

scour ['skaʊə^r] *vt* (*search*) battre, parcourir

scout [skaʊt] *n* (*MIL*) éclaireur *m*; (*also*: **boy ~**) scout *m*; **girl ~** (*US*) guide *f*; **~ around** *vi* explorer, chercher

scowl [skaʊl] *vi* se renfrogner, avoir l'air maussade; **to ~ at** regarder de travers

scrabble ['skræbl] *vi* (*also*: **~ around**: *search*) chercher à tâtons; (*claw*): **to ~ (at)** gratter ♦ *n*: **S~** ® Scrabble ® *m*

scram [skræm] (*inf*) *vi* ficher le camp

scramble ['skræmbl] *n* (*rush*) bousculade *f*, ruée *f* ♦ *vi*: **to ~ up/down** grimper/descendre tant bien que mal; **to ~ out** sortir *or* descendre à toute vitesse; **to ~ through** se frayer un passage (à travers); **to ~ for** se bousculer *or* se disputer pour (avoir); **~d eggs** *npl* œufs brouillés

scrap [skræp] *n* bout *m*, morceau *m*; (*fight*) bagarre *f*; (*also*: **~ iron**) ferraille *f* ♦ *vt* jeter, mettre au rebut; (*fig*) abandonner, laisser tomber ♦ *vi* (*fight*) se bagarrer; **~s** *npl* (*waste*) déchets *mpl*; **~book** *n* album *m*; **~ dealer** *n* marchand *m* de ferraille

scrape [skreɪp] *vt, vi* gratter, racler ♦ *n*: **to get into a ~** s'attirer des ennuis; **to ~ through** réussir de justesse; **~ together** *vt* (*money*) racler ses fonds de tiroir pour réunir

scrap: **~ heap** *n*: **on the ~ heap** (*fig*) au rancart *or* rebut; **~ merchant** (*BRIT*) *n* marchand *m* de ferraille; **~ paper** *n* papier *m* brouillon

scratch [skrætʃ] *n* égratignure *f*, rayure *f*; éraflure *f*; (*from claw*) coup *m* de griffe ♦ *cpd*: **~ team** équipe de fortune *or* improvisée ♦ *vt* (*rub*) (se) gratter; (*record*) rayer; (*paint etc*) érafler; (*with claw, nail*) griffer

♦ *vi* (se) gratter; **to start from ~** partir de zéro; **to be up to ~** être à la hauteur

scrawl [skrɔ:l] *vi* gribouiller

scrawny [ˈskrɔ:nɪ] *adj* décharné(e)

scream [skri:m] *n* cri perçant, hurlement *m* ♦ *vi* crier, hurler

screech [skri:tʃ] *vi* hurler; (*tyres*) crisser; (*brakes*) grincer

screen [skri:n] *n* écran *m*; (*in room*) paravent *m*; (*fig*) écran, rideau *m* ♦ *vt* (*conceal*) masquer, cacher; (*from the wind etc*) abriter, protéger; (*film*) projeter; (*candidates etc*) filtrer; **~ing** *n* (*MED*) test *m* (*or* tests) de dépistage; **~play** *n* scénario *m*

screw [skru:] *n* vis *f* ♦ *vt* visser; **~ up** *vt* (*paper etc*) froisser; **to ~ up one's eyes** plisser les yeux; **~driver** *n* tournevis *m*

scribble [ˈskrɪbl] *vt, vi* gribouiller, griffonner

script [skrɪpt] *n* (*CINEMA etc*) scénario *m*, texte *m*; (*system of writing*) (écriture *f*) script *m*

Scripture(s) [ˈskrɪptʃə(r)(-əz)] *n(pl)* (*Christian*) Écriture sainte; (*other religions*) écritures saintes

scroll [skrəul] *n* rouleau *m*

scrounge [skraundʒ] (*inf*) *vt*: **to ~ sth off** *or* **from sb** taper qn de qch; **~r** (*inf*) *n* parasite *m*

scrub [skrʌb] *n* (*land*) broussailles *fpl* ♦ *vt* (*floor*) nettoyer à la brosse; (*pan*) récurer; (*washing*) frotter; (*inf: cancel*) annuler

scruff [skrʌf] *n*: **by the ~ of the neck** par la peau du cou

scruffy [ˈskrʌfɪ] *adj* débraillé(e)

scrum(mage) [ˈskrʌm(ɪdʒ)] *n* (*RUGBY*) mêlée *f*

scruple [ˈskru:pl] *n* scrupule *m*

scrutiny [ˈskru:tɪnɪ] *n* examen minutieux

scuff [skʌf] *vt* érafler

scuffle [ˈskʌfl] *n* échauffourée *f*, rixe *f*

sculptor [ˈskʌlptə(r)] *n* sculpteur *m*

sculpture [ˈskʌlptʃə(r)] *n* sculpture *f*

scum [skʌm] *n* écume *f*, mousse *f*; (*pej: people*) rebut *m*, lie *f*

scurry [ˈskʌrɪ] *vi* filer à toute allure; **to ~ off** détaler, se sauver

scuttle [ˈskʌtl] *n* (*also:* **coal ~**) seau *m* (à charbon) ♦ *vt* (*ship*) saborder ♦ *vi* (*scamper*): **to ~ away** *or* **off** détaler

scythe [saɪð] *n* faux *f*

SDP *n abbr* = **Social Democratic Party**

sea [si:] *n* mer *f* ♦ *cpd* marin(e), de (la) mer; **by ~** (*travel*) par mer, en bateau; **on the ~** (*boat*) en mer; (*town*) au bord de la mer; **to be all at ~** (*fig*) nager complètement; **out to ~** au large; (*out*) **at ~** en mer; **~board** *n* côte *f*; **~food** *n* fruits *mpl* de mer; **~front** *n* bord *m* de mer; **~going** *adj* (*ship*) de mer; **~gull** *n* mouette *f*

seal [si:l] *n* (*animal*) phoque *m*; (*stamp*) sceau *m*, cachet *m* ♦ *vt* sceller; (*envelope*) coller; (: *with* ~) cacheter; **~ off** *vt* (*forbid entry to*) interdire l'accès de

sea level *n* niveau *m* de la mer

sea lion *n* otarie *f*

seam [si:m] *n* couture *f*; (*of coal*) veine *f*, filon *m*

seaman [ˈsi:mən] (*irreg*) *n* marin *m*

seance [ˈseɪɔns] *n* séance *f* de spiritisme

seaplane [ˈsi:pleɪn] *n* hydravion *m*

search [sə:tʃ] *n* (*for person, thing, COMPUT*) recherche(s) *f(pl)*; (*LAW: at sb's home*) perquisition *f* ♦ *vt* fouiller; (*examine*) examiner minutieusement; scruter ♦ *vi*: **to ~ for** chercher; **in ~ of** à la recherche de; **~ through** *vt fus* fouiller; **~ engine** *n* (*COMPUT*) moteur *m* de recherche; **~ing** *adj* pénétrant(e); **~light** *n* projecteur *m*; **~ party** *n* expédition *f* de secours; **~ warrant** *n* mandat *m* de perquisition

sea: **~shore** *n* rivage *m*, plage *f*, bord *m* de (la) mer; **~sick** *adj*: **to be ~sick** avoir le mal de mer; **~side** *n* bord *m* de la mer; **~side resort** *n* station *f* balnéaire

season [ˈsi:zn] *n* saison *f* ♦ *vt* assaisonner, relever; **to be in/out of ~** être/ne pas être de saison; **~al** *adj* (*work*) saisonnier(-ère); **~ed** *adj* (*fig*) expérimenté(e); **~ ticket** *n* carte *f* d'abonnement

seat [si:t] *n* siège *m*; (*in bus, train: place*) place *f*; (*buttocks*) postérieur *m*; (*of trousers*) fond *m* ♦ *vt* faire asseoir, placer;

(*have room for*) avoir des places assises pour, pouvoir accueillir; **~ belt** *n* ceinture *f* de sécurité

sea: **~ water** *n* eau *f* de mer; **~weed** *n* algues *fpl*; **~worthy** *adj* en état de naviguer

sec. *abbr* = **second(s)**

secluded [sɪ'klu:dɪd] *adj* retiré(e), à l'écart

seclusion [sɪ'klu:ʒən] *n* solitude *f*

second¹ [sɪ'kɒnd] (*BRIT*) *vt* (*employee*) affecter provisoirement

second² ['sekənd] *adj* deuxième, second(e) ♦ *adv* (*in race etc*) en seconde position ♦ *n* (*unit of time*) seconde *f*; (*AUT*: *~ gear*) seconde; (*COMM*: *imperfect*) article *m* de second choix; (*BRIT*: *UNIV*) licence *f* avec mention ♦ *vt* (*motion*) appuyer; **~ary** *adj* secondaire; **~ary school** *n* collège *m*, lycée *m*; **~-class** *adj* de deuxième classe; (*RAIL*) de seconde (classe); (*POST*) au tarif réduit; (*pej*) de qualité inférieure ♦ *adv* (*RAIL*) en seconde; (*POST*) au tarif réduit; **~hand** *adj* d'occasion; de seconde main; **~ hand** *n* (*on clock*) trotteuse *f*; **~ly** *adv* deuxièmement; **~ment** [sɪ'kɒndmənt] (*BRIT*) *n* détachement *m*; **~-rate** *adj* de deuxième ordre, de qualité inférieure; **~ thoughts** *npl* doutes *mpl*; **on ~ thoughts** *or* (*US*) **thought** à la réflexion

secrecy ['si:krəsɪ] *n* secret *m*

secret ['si:krɪt] *adj* secret(-ète) ♦ *n* secret *m*; **in ~** en secret, secrètement, en cachette

secretary ['sekrətərɪ] *n* secrétaire *m/f*; (*COMM*) secrétaire général; **S~ of State (for)** (*BRIT*: *POL*) ministre *m* (de)

secretive ['si:krətɪv] *adj* dissimulé(e)

secretly ['si:krɪtlɪ] *adv* en secret, secrètement

sectarian [sek'teərɪən] *adj* sectaire

section ['sekʃən] *n* section *f*; (*of document*) section, article *m*, paragraphe *m*; (*cut*) coupe *f*

sector ['sektər] *n* secteur *m*

secular ['sekjulər] *adj* profane, laïque, séculier(-ère)

secure [sɪ'kjuər] *adj* (*free from anxiety*) sans

inquiétude, sécurisé(e); (*firmly fixed*) solide, bien attaché(e) (*or* fermé(e) *etc*); (*in safe place*) en lieu sûr, en sûreté ♦ *vt* (*fix*) fixer, attacher; (*get*) obtenir, se procurer

security [sɪ'kjuərɪtɪ] *n* sécurité *f*, mesures *fpl* de sécurité; (*for loan*) caution *f*, garantie *f*; **~ guard** *n* garde chargé de la sécurité; (*when transporting money*) convoyeur *m* de fonds

sedate [sɪ'deɪt] *adj* calme; posé(e) ♦ *vt* (*MED*) donner des sédatifs à

sedative ['sedɪtɪv] *n* calmant *m*, sédatif *m*

seduce [sɪ'dju:s] *vt* séduire; **seduction** [sɪ'dʌkʃən] *n* séduction *f*; **seductive** *adj* séduisant(e); (*smile*) séducteur(-trice); (*fig: offer*) alléchant(e)

see [si:] (*pt* **saw**, *pp* **seen**) *vt* voir; (*accompany*): **to ~ sb to the door** reconduire *or* raccompagner qn jusqu'à la porte ♦ *vi* voir ♦ *n* évêché *m*; **to ~ that** (*ensure*) veiller à ce que +*sub*, faire en sorte que +*sub*, s'assurer que; **~ you soon!** à bientôt!; **~ about** *vt fus* s'occuper de; **~ off** *vt* accompagner (à la gare *or* à l'aéroport *etc*); **~ through** *vt* mener à bonne fin ♦ *vt fus* voir clair dans; **~ to** *vt fus* s'occuper de, se charger de

seed [si:d] *n* graine *f*; (*sperm*) semence *f*; (*fig*) germe *m*; (*TENNIS etc*) tête *f* de série; **to go to ~** monter en graine; (*fig*) se laisser aller; **~ling** *n* jeune plant *m*, semis *m*; **~y** *adj* (*shabby*) minable, miteux(-euse)

seeing ['si:ɪŋ] *conj*: **~ (that)** vu que, étant donné que

seek [si:k] (*pt*, *pp* **sought**) *vt* chercher, rechercher

seem [si:m] *vi* sembler, paraître; **there ~s to be ...** il semble qu'il y a ...; on dirait qu'il y a ...; **~ingly** *adv* apparemment

seen [si:n] *pp of* **see**

seep [si:p] *vi* suinter, filtrer

seesaw ['si:sɔ:] *n* (jeu *m* de) bascule *f*

seethe [si:ð] *vi* être en effervescence; **to ~ with anger** bouillir de colère

see-through ['si:θru:] *adj* transparent(e)

segment ['segmənt] *n* segment *m*; (*of orange*) quartier *m*

segregate ['sɛgrɪgeɪt] vt séparer, isoler

seize [siːz] vt saisir, attraper; (*take possession of*) s'emparer de; (*opportunity*) saisir; ~ **up** vi (*TECH*) se gripper; ~ **(up)on** vt fus saisir, sauter sur

seizure ['siːʒəʳ] n (*MED*) crise f, attaque f; (*of power*) prise f

seldom ['sɛldəm] adv rarement

select [sɪ'lɛkt] adj choisi(e), d'élite ♦ vt sélectionner, choisir; ~**ion** n sélection f, choix m

self [sɛlf] (pl **selves**) n: **the ~** le moi inv ♦ prefix auto-; ~**-assured** adj sûr(e) de soi; ~**-catering** (*BRIT*) adj avec cuisine, où l'on peut faire sa cuisine; ~**-centred** (*US* **self-centered**) adj égocentrique; ~**-confidence** n confiance f en soi; ~**-conscious** adj timide, qui manque d'assurance; ~**-contained** (*BRIT*) adj (*flat*) avec entrée particulière, indépendant(e); ~**-control** n maîtrise f de soi; ~**-defence** (*US* **self-defense**) n autodéfense f; (*LAW*) légitime défense f; ~**-discipline** n discipline personnelle; ~**-employed** adj qui travaille à son compte; ~**-evident** adj: **to be ~-evident** être évident(e), aller de soi; ~**-governing** adj autonome; ~**-indulgent** adj qui ne se refuse rien; ~**-interest** n intérêt personnel; ~**-ish** adj égoïste; ~**-ishness** n égoïsme m; ~**-less** adj désintéressé(e); ~**-pity** n apitoiement m sur soi-même; ~**-possessed** adj assuré(e); ~**-preservation** n instinct m de conservation; ~**-respect** n respect m de soi, amour-propre m; ~**-righteous** adj suffisant(e); ~**-sacrifice** n abnégation f; ~**-satisfied** adj content(e) de soi, suffisant(e); ~**-service** adj libre-service, self-service; ~**-sufficient** adj autosuffisant(e); (*person: independent*) indépendant(e); ~**-taught** adj (*artist, pianist*) qui a appris par lui-même

sell [sɛl] (pt, pp **sold**) vt vendre ♦ vi se vendre; **to ~ at** or **for 10 F** se vendre 10 F; ~ **off** vt liquider; ~ **out** vi: **to ~ out (of sth)** (*use up stock*) vendre tout son stock (de qch); **the tickets are all sold out** il

ne reste plus de billets; ~**-by date** n date f limite de vente; ~**er** n vendeur(-euse), marchand(e); ~**ing price** n prix m de vente

Sellotape ® ['sɛləuteɪp] (*BRIT*) n papier m collant, scotch ® m

selves [sɛlvz] npl of **self**

semblance ['sɛmblns] n semblant m

semen ['siːmən] n sperme m

semester [sɪ'mɛstəʳ] (*esp US*) n semestre m

semi ['sɛmɪ] prefix semi-, demi-; à demi, à moitié; ~**circle** n demi-cercle m; ~**colon** n point-virgule m; ~**detached (house)** (*BRIT*) n maison jumelée or jumelle; ~**final** n demi-finale f

seminar ['sɛmɪnɑːʳ] n séminaire m; ~**y** n (*REL: for priests*) séminaire m

semiskilled [sɛmɪ'skɪld] adj: ~ **worker** ouvrier(-ère) spécialisé(e)

semi-skimmed milk [sɛmɪ'skɪmd-] n lait m demi-écrémé

senate ['sɛnɪt] n sénat m; **senator** n sénateur m

send [sɛnd] (pt, pp **sent**) vt envoyer; ~ **away** vt (*letter, goods*) envoyer, expédier; (*unwelcome visitor*) renvoyer; ~ **away for** vt fus commander par correspondance, se faire envoyer; ~ **back** vt renvoyer; ~ **for** vt fus envoyer chercher; faire venir; ~ **off** vt (*goods*) envoyer, expédier; (*BRIT: SPORT: player*) expulser or renvoyer du terrain; ~ **out** vt (*invitation*) envoyer (par la poste); (*light, heat, signal*) émettre; ~ **up** vt faire monter; (*BRIT: parody*) mettre en boîte, parodier; ~**er** n expéditeur(-trice); ~**-off** n: **a good ~-off** des adieux chaleureux

senior ['siːnɪəʳ] adj (*high-ranking*) de haut niveau; (*of higher rank*): **to be ~ to sb** être le supérieur de qn ♦ n (*older*): **she is 15 years his ~** elle est son aînée de 15 ans, elle est plus âgée que lui de 15 ans; ~ **citizen** n personne âgée; ~**ity** [siːnɪ'ɔrɪtɪ] n (*in service*) ancienneté f

sensation [sɛn'seɪʃən] n sensation f; ~**al** adj qui fait sensation; (*marvellous*) sensationnel(le)

sense [sɛns] n sens m; (*feeling*) sentiment

m; (*meaning*) sens, signification *f*; (*wisdom*) bon sens ♦ *vt* sentir, pressentir; **it makes ~** c'est logique; **~less** *adj* insensé(e), stupide; (*unconscious*) sans connaissance

sensible ['sɛnsɪbl] *adj* sensé(e), raisonnable; sage

sensitive ['sɛnsɪtɪv] *adj* sensible

sensual ['sɛnsjuəl] *adj* sensuel(le)

sensuous ['sɛnsjuəs] *adj* voluptueux(-euse), sensuel(le)

sent [sɛnt] *pt, pp of* **send**

sentence ['sɛntns] *n* (*LING*) phrase *f*; (*LAW: judgment*) condamnation *f*, sentence *f*; (: *punishment*) peine *f* ♦ *vt*: **to ~ sb to death/to 5 years in prison** condamner qn à mort/à 5 ans de prison

sentiment ['sɛntɪmənt] *n* sentiment *m*; (*opinion*) opinion *f*, avis *m*; **~al** [sɛntɪ'mɛntl] *adj* sentimental(e)

sentry ['sɛntrɪ] *n* sentinelle *f*

separate [*adj* 'sɛprɪt, *vb* 'sɛpəreɪt] *adj* séparé(e), indépendant(e), différent(e) ♦ *vt* séparer; (*make a distinction between*) distinguer ♦ *vi* se séparer; **~ly** *adv* séparément; **~s** *npl* (*clothes*) coordonnés *mpl*; **separation** [sɛpə'reɪʃən] *n* séparation *f*

September [sɛp'tɛmbəʳ] *n* septembre *m*

septic ['sɛptɪk] *adj* (*wound*) infecté(e); **~ tank** *n* fosse *f* septique

sequel ['siːkwl] *n* conséquence *f*; séquelles *fpl*; (*of story*) suite *f*

sequence ['siːkwəns] *n* ordre *m*, suite *f*; (*film* ~) séquence *f*; (*dance* ~) numéro *m*

sequin ['siːkwɪn] *n* paillette *f*

Serbia ['sɜːbɪə] *n* Serbie *f*

serene [sɪ'riːn] *adj* serein(e), calme, paisible

sergeant ['sɑːdʒənt] *n* sergent *m*; (*POLICE*) brigadier *m*

serial ['sɪərɪəl] *n* feuilleton *m*; **~ killer** *n* meurtrier *m* tuant en série; **~ number** *n* numéro *m* de série

series ['sɪərɪz] *n inv* série *f*; (*PUBLISHING*) collection *f*

serious ['sɪərɪəs] *adj* sérieux(-euse); (*illness*) grave; **~ly** *adv* sérieusement; (*hurt*) gravement

sermon ['sɜːmən] *n* sermon *m*

serrated [sɪ'reɪtɪd] *adj* en dents de scie

servant ['sɜːvənt] *n* domestique *m/f*; (*fig*) serviteur/servante

serve [sɜːv] *vt* (*employer etc*) servir, être au service de; (*purpose*) servir à; (*customer, food, meal*) servir; (*subj: train*) desservir; (*apprenticeship*) faire, accomplir; (*prison term*) purger ♦ *vi* servir; (*be useful*): **to ~ as/for/to do** servir de/à/à faire ♦ *n* (*TENNIS*) service *m*; **it ~s him right** c'est bien fait pour lui; **~ out**, **~ up** *vt* (*food*) servir

service ['sɜːvɪs] *n* service *m*; (*AUT: maintenance*) révision *f* ♦ *vt* (*car, washing machine*) réviser; **the S~s** les forces armées; **to be of ~ to sb** rendre service à qn; **15% ~ included** service 15% compris; **~ not included** service non compris; **~able** *adj* pratique, commode; **~ area** *n* (*on motorway*) aire *f* de services; **~ charge** (*BRIT*) *n* service *m*; **~man** (*irreg*) *n* militaire *m*; **~ station** *n* station-service *f*

serviette [sɜːvɪ'ɛt] (*BRIT*) *n* serviette *f* (de table)

session ['sɛʃən] *n* séance *f*

set [sɛt] (*pt, pp* **set**) *n* série *f*, assortiment *m*; (*of tools etc*) jeu *m*; (*RADIO, TV*) poste *m*; (*TENNIS*) set *m*; (*group of people*) cercle *m*, milieu *m*; (*THEATRE: stage*) scène *f*; (: *scenery*) décor *m*; (*MATH*) ensemble *m*; (*HAIRDRESSING*) mise *f* en plis ♦ *adj* (*fixed*) fixe, déterminé(e); (*ready*) prêt(e) ♦ *vt* (*place*) poser, placer; (*fix, establish*) fixer; (: *record*) établir; (*adjust*) régler; (*decide: rules etc*) fixer, choisir; (*task*) donner; (*exam*) composer ♦ *vi* (*sun*) se coucher; (*jam, jelly, concrete*) prendre; (*bone*) se ressouder; **to be ~ on doing** être résolu à faire; **to ~ the table** mettre la table; **to ~ (to music)** mettre en musique; **to ~ on fire** mettre le feu à; **to ~ free** libérer; **to ~ sth going** déclencher qch; **to ~ sail** prendre la mer; **~ about** *vt fus* (*task*) entreprendre, se mettre à; **~ aside** *vt* mettre de côté; (*time*) garder; **~ back** *vt* (*in time*): **to ~ back (by)** retarder (de); (*cost*): **to ~ sb back £5** coûter 5 livres à qn; **~ off** *vi* se mettre en route, partir ♦ vt (*bomb*) faire exploser; (*cause to start*) déclencher; (*show up well*) mettre en valeur, faire valoir; ~ **out** vi se mettre en route, partir ♦ vt (*arrange*) disposer; (*arguments*) présenter, exposer; **to ~ out to do** entreprendre de faire, avoir pour but *or* intention de faire; ~ **up** vt (*organization*) fonder, créer; ~**back** n (*hitch*) revers m, contretemps m; ~ **menu** n menu m

settee [se'ti:] n canapé m

setting ['sɛtɪŋ] n cadre m; (*of jewel*) monture f; (*position: of controls*) réglage m

settle ['sɛtl] vt (*argument, matter, account*) régler; (*problem*) résoudre; (*MED: calm*) calmer ♦ vi (*bird, dust etc*) se poser; (*also:* ~ **down**) s'installer, se fixer; (*calm down*) se calmer; **to ~ for sth** accepter qch, se contenter de qch; **to ~ on sth** opter *or* se décider pour qch; ~ **in** vi s'installer; ~ **up** vi: **to ~ up with sb** régler (ce que l'on doit à) qn; ~**ment** n (*payment*) règlement m; (*agreement*) accord m; (*village etc*) établissement m; hameau m; ~**r** n colon m

setup ['sɛtʌp] n (*arrangement*) manière f dont les choses sont organisées; (*situation*) situation f

seven ['sɛvn] num sept; ~**teen** num dix-sept; ~**th** num septième; ~**ty** num soixante-dix

sever ['sɛvər] vt couper, trancher; (*relations*) rompre

several ['sɛvərl] adj, pron plusieurs m/fpl; ~ **of us** plusieurs d'entre nous

severance ['sɛvərəns] n (*of relations*) rupture f; ~ **pay** n indemnité f de licenciement

severe [sɪ'vɪər] adj (*stern*) sévère, strict(e); (*serious*) grave, sérieux(-euse); (*plain*) sévère, austère; **severity** [sɪ'vɛrɪtɪ] n sévérité f; gravité f; rigueur f

sew [səu] (*pt* sewed, *pp* sewn) vt, vi coudre; ~ **up** vt (re)coudre

sewage ['su:ɪdʒ] n vidange(s) f(pl)

sewer ['su:ər] n égout m

sewing ['səuɪŋ] n couture f; (*item(s)*) ouvrage m; ~ **machine** n machine f à coudre

sewn [səun] pp of **sew**

sex [sɛks] n sexe m; **to have ~ with** avoir des rapports (sexuels) avec; ~**ism** n sexisme m; ~**ist** adj sexiste; ~**ual** ['sɛksjuəl] adj sexuel(le); ~**uality** [sɛksjuˈælɪtɪ] n sexualité f; ~**y** adj sexy inv

shabby ['ʃæbɪ] adj miteux(-euse); (*behaviour*) mesquin(e), méprisable

shack [ʃæk] n cabane f, hutte f

shackles ['ʃæklz] npl chaînes fpl, entraves fpl

shade [ʃeɪd] n ombre f; (*for lamp*) abat-jour m inv; (*of colour*) nuance f, ton m ♦ vt abriter du soleil, ombrager; **in the ~** à l'ombre; **a ~ too large/more** un tout petit peu trop grand(e)/plus

shadow [ʃædəu] n ombre f ♦ vt (*follow*) filer; ~ **cabinet** (*BRIT*) n (*POL*) cabinet parallèle formé par l'Opposition; ~**y** adj ombragé(e); (*dim*) vague, indistinct(e)

shady ['ʃeɪdɪ] adj ombragé(e); (*fig: dishonest*) louche, véreux(-euse)

shaft [ʃɑ:ft] n (*of arrow, spear*) hampe f; (*AUT, TECH*) arbre m; (*of mine*) puits m; (*of lift*) cage f; (*of light*) rayon m, trait m

shaggy ['ʃægɪ] adj hirsute; en broussaille

shake [ʃeɪk] (*pt* shook, *pp* shaken) vt secouer; (*bottle, cocktail*) agiter; (*house, confidence*) ébranler ♦ vi trembler; **to ~ one's head** (*in refusal*) dire *or* faire non de la tête; (*in dismay*) secouer la tête; **to ~ hands with sb** serrer la main à qn; ~ **off** vt secouer; (*pursuer*) se débarrasser de; ~ **up** vt secouer; ~**n** pp of **shake**; **shaky** adj (*hand, voice*) tremblant(e); (*building*) branlant(e), peu solide

shall [ʃæl] aux vb: **I ~ go** j'irai; ~ **I open the door?** j'ouvre la porte?; **I'll get the coffee, ~ I?** je vais chercher le café, d'accord?

shallow ['ʃæləu] adj peu profond(e); (*fig*) superficiel(le)

sham [ʃæm] n frime f ♦ vt simuler

shambles ['ʃæmblz] n (*muddle*) confusion f, pagaïe f, fouillis m

shame [ʃeɪm] n honte f ♦ vt faire honte à;

it is a ~ **(that/to do)** c'est dommage (que +*sub*/de faire); **what a ~!** quel dommage!; **~ful** *adj* honteux(-euse), scandaleux(-euse); **~less** *adj* éhonté(e), effronté(e)

shampoo [ʃæm'puː] *n* shampooing *m* ♦ *vt* faire un shampooing à; **~ and set** *n* shampooing *m* (et) mise *f* en plis

shamrock ['ʃæmrɔk] *n* trèfle *m* (*emblème de l'Irlande*)

shandy ['ʃændɪ] *n* bière panachée

shan't [ʃɑːnt] = **shall not**

shanty town ['ʃæntɪ-] *n* bidonville *m*

shape [ʃeɪp] *n* forme *f* ♦ *vt* façonner, modeler; (*sb's ideas*) former; (*sb's life*) déterminer ♦ *vi* (*also*: ~ **up**: *events*) prendre tournure; (: *person*) faire des progrès, s'en sortir; **to take ~** prendre forme *or* tournure; **~d** *suffix*: **heart-~d** en forme de cœur; **~less** *adj* informe, sans forme; **~ly** *adj* bien proportionné(e), beau (belle)

share [ʃeər] *n* part *f*; (*COMM*) action *f* ♦ *vt* partager; (*have in common*) avoir en commun; ~ **out** *vi* partager; **~holder** *n* actionnaire *m/f*

shark [ʃɑːk] *n* requin *m*

sharp [ʃɑːp] *adj* (*razor, knife*) tranchant(e), bien aiguisé(e); (*point, voice*) aigu(-guë); (*nose, chin*) pointu(e); (*outline, increase*) net(te); (*cold, pain*) vif (vive); (*taste*) piquant(e), âcre; (*MUS*) dièse; (*person: quick-witted*) vif (vive), éveillé(e); (: *unscrupulous*) malhonnête ♦ *n* (*MUS*) dièse *m* ♦ *adv* (*precisely*): **at 2 o'clock ~** à 2 heures pile *or* précises; **~en** *vt* aiguiser; (*pencil*) tailler; **~ener** *n* (*also*: **pencil ~ener**) taille-crayon(s) *m inv*; **~-eyed** *adj* à qui rien n'échappe; **~ly** *adv* (*turn, stop*) brusquement; (*stand out*) nettement; (*criticize, retort*) sèchement, vertement

shatter ['ʃætər] *vt* briser; (*fig: upset*) bouleverser; (: *ruin*) briser, ruiner ♦ *vi* voler en éclats, se briser

shave [ʃeɪv] *vt* raser ♦ *vi* se raser ♦ *n*: **to have a ~** se raser; **~r** *n* (*also*: **electric ~r**) rasoir *m* électrique

shaving ['ʃeɪvɪŋ] (*action*) rasage *m*; **~s** *npl*

(*of wood etc*) copeaux *mpl*; ~ **brush** *n* blaireau *m*; ~ **cream** *n* crème *f* à raser; ~ **foam** *n* mousse *f* à raser

shawl [ʃɔːl] *n* châle *m*

she [ʃiː] *pron* elle ♦ *prefix*: **~-cat** chatte *f*; **~-elephant** éléphant *m* femelle

sheaf [ʃiːf] (*pl* **sheaves**) *n* gerbe *f*; (*of papers*) liasse *f*

shear [ʃɪər] (*pt* **sheared**, *pp* **shorn**) *vt* (*sheep*) tondre; **~s** *npl* (*for hedge*) cisaille(s) *f(pl)*

sheath [ʃiːθ] *n* gaine *f*, fourreau *m*, étui *m*; (*contraceptive*) préservatif *m*

shed [ʃed] (*pt*, *pp* **shed**) *n* remise *f*, resserre *f* ♦ *vt* perdre; (*tears*) verser, répandre; (*workers*) congédier

she'd [ʃiːd] = **she had**; **she would**

sheen [ʃiːn] *n* lustre *m*

sheep [ʃiːp] *n inv* mouton *m*; **~dog** *n* chien *m* de berger; **~skin** *n* peau *f* de mouton

sheer [ʃɪər] *adj* (*utter*) pur(e), pur et simple; (*steep*) à pic, abrupt(e); (*almost transparent*) extrêmement fin(e) ♦ *adv* à pic, abruptement

sheet [ʃiːt] *n* (*on bed*) drap *m*; (*of paper*) feuille *f*; (*of glass, metal etc*) feuille, plaque *f*

sheik(h) [ʃeɪk] *n* cheik *m*

shelf [ʃelf] (*pl* **shelves**) *n* étagère *f*, rayon *m*

shell [ʃel] *n* (*on beach*) coquillage *m*; (*of egg, nut etc*) coquille *f*; (*explosive*) obus *m*; (*of building*) carcasse *f* ♦ *vt* (*peas*) écosser; (*MIL*) bombarder (d'obus)

she'll [ʃiːl] = **she will**; **she shall**

shellfish ['ʃelfɪʃ] *n inv* (*crab etc*) crustacé *m*; (*scallop etc*) coquillage *m* ♦ *npl* (*as food*) fruits *mpl* de mer

shell suit *n* survêtement *m* (*en synthétique froissé*)

shelter ['ʃeltər] *n* abri *m*, refuge *m* ♦ *vt* abriter, protéger; (*give lodging to*) donner asile à ♦ *vi* s'abriter, se mettre à l'abri; **~ed housing** *n* foyers *mpl* (*pour personnes âgées ou handicapées*)

shelve [ʃelv] *vt* (*fig*) mettre en suspens *or*

en sommeil; **~s** npl of **shelf**

shepherd ['ʃɛpəd] n berger m ♦ vt (guide) guider, escorter; **~'s pie** (BRIT) n ≃ hachis m Parmentier

sheriff ['ʃɛrɪf] (US) n shérif m

sherry ['ʃɛrɪ] n xérès m, sherry m

she's [ʃiːz] = **she is**; **she has**

Shetland ['ʃɛtlənd] n (also: **the ~ Islands**) les îles fpl Shetland

shield [ʃiːld] n bouclier m; (protection) écran m de protection ♦ vt: **to ~ (from)** protéger (de or contre)

shift [ʃɪft] n (change) changement m; (work period) période f de travail; (of workers) équipe f, poste m ♦ vt déplacer, changer de place; (remove) enlever ♦ vi changer de place, bouger; **~ work** n travail m en équipe or par relais or par roulement; **~y** adj sournois(e); (eyes) fuyant(e)

shimmer ['ʃɪmə'] vi miroiter, chatoyer

shin [ʃɪn] n tibia m

shine [ʃaɪn] (pt, pp **shone**) n éclat m, brillant m ♦ vi briller ♦ vt (torch etc): **to ~ on** braquer sur; (polish: pt, pp ~d) faire briller or reluire

shingle ['ʃɪŋɡl] n (on beach) galets mpl; **~s** n (MED) zona m

shiny ['ʃaɪnɪ] adj brillant(e)

ship [ʃɪp] n bateau m; (large) navire m ♦ vt transporter (par mer); (send) expédier (par mer); **~building** n construction navale; **~ment** n cargaison f; **~ping** n (ships) navires mpl; (the industry) industrie navale; (transport) transport m; **~wreck** n (ship) épave f; (event) naufrage m ♦ vt: **to be ~wrecked** faire naufrage; **~yard** n chantier naval

shire ['ʃaɪə'] (BRIT) n comté m

shirt [ʃɜːt] n (man's) chemise f; (woman's) chemisier m; **in (one's) ~ sleeves** en bras de chemise

shit [ʃɪt] (inf!) n, excl merde f (!)

shiver ['ʃɪvə'] n frisson m ♦ vi frissonner

shoal [ʃəʊl] n (of fish) banc m; (fig: also: **~s**) masse f, foule f

shock [ʃɔk] n choc m; (ELEC) secousse f; (MED) commotion f, choc ♦ vt (offend)

choquer, scandaliser; (upset) bouleverser; **~ absorber** n amortisseur m; **~ing** adj (scandalizing) choquant(e), scandaleux(-euse); (appalling) épouvantable

shoddy ['ʃɔdɪ] adj de mauvaise qualité, mal fait(e)

shoe [ʃuː] (pt, pp **shod**) n chaussure f, soulier m; (also: **horseshoe**) fer m à cheval ♦ vt (horse) ferrer; **~lace** n lacet m (de soulier); **~ polish** n cirage m; **~ shop** n magasin m de chaussures; **~string** n (fig): **on a ~string** avec un budget dérisoire

shone [ʃɔn] pt, pp of **shine**

shook [ʃuk] pt of **shake**

shoot [ʃuːt] (pt, pp **shot**) n (on branch, seedling) pousse f ♦ vt (game) chasser; tirer; abattre; (person) blesser (or tuer) d'un coup de fusil (or de revolver); (execute) fusiller; (arrow) tirer; (gun) tirer un coup de; (film) tourner ♦ vi (with gun, bow): **to ~ (at)** tirer (sur); (FOOTBALL) shooter, tirer; **~ down** vt (plane) abattre; **~ in** vi entrer comme une flèche; **~ out** vi sortir comme une flèche; **~ up** vi (fig) monter en flèche; **~ing** n (shots) coups mpl de feu, fusillade f; (HUNTING) chasse f; **~ing star** n étoile filante

shop [ʃɔp] n magasin m; (workshop) atelier m ♦ vi (also: **go ~ping**) faire ses courses or ses achats; **~ assistant** (BRIT) n vendeur(-euse); **~ floor** (BRIT) n (INDUSTRY: fig) ouvriers mpl; **~keeper** n commerçant(e); **~lifting** n vol m à l'étalage; **~per** n personne f qui fait ses courses, acheteur(-euse); **~ping** n (goods) achats mpl, provisions fpl; **~ping bag** n sac m (à provisions); **~ping centre** (US **shopping center**) n centre commercial; **~-soiled** adj défraîchi(e), qui a fait la vitrine; **~ steward** (BRIT) n (INDUSTRY) délégué(e) syndical(e); **~ window** n vitrine f

shore [ʃɔː'] n (of sea, lake) rivage m, rive f ♦ vt: **to ~ (up)** étayer; **on ~** à terre

shorn [ʃɔːn] pp of **shear**

short [ʃɔːt] adj (not long) court(e); (soon finished) court, bref (brève); (person, step) petit(e); (*curt*) brusque, sec (sèche); (*insufficient*) insuffisant(e); **to be/run ~ of sth** être à court de *or* manquer de qch; **in ~** bref; en bref; **~ of doing ...** à moins de faire ...; **everything ~ of** tout sauf; **it is ~ for** c'est l'abréviation *or* le diminutif de; **to cut ~** (*speech, visit*) abréger, écourter; **to fall ~ of** ne pas être à la hauteur de; **to run ~ of** arriver à court de, venir à manquer de; **to stop ~** s'arrêter net; **to stop ~ of** ne pas aller jusqu'à; **~age** *n* manque *m*, pénurie *f*; **~bread** *n* ≈ sablé *m*; **~change** *vt* ne pas rendre assez à; **~circuit** *n* court-circuit *m*; **~coming** *n* défaut *m*; **~(crust) pastry** (BRIT) *n* pâte brisée; **~cut** *n* raccourci *m*; **~en** *vt* raccourcir; (*text, visit*) abréger **♦** *vi* déficit *m*; **~fall** *n* déficit *m*; **~hand** (BRIT) *n* sténo(graphie) *f*; **~hand typist** (BRIT) *n* sténodactylo *m/f*; **~list** (BRIT) *n* (*for job*) liste *f* des candidats sélectionnés; **~ly** *adv* bientôt, sous peu; **~ notice** *n*: **at ~ notice** au dernier moment; **~s** *npl*: **(a pair of) ~s** un short; **~-sighted** *adj* (BRIT) myope; (*fig*) qui manque de clairvoyance; **~-staffed** *adj* à court de personnel; **~-stay** *adj* (*car park*) de courte durée; **~ story** *n* nouvelle *f*; **~-tempered** *adj* qui s'emporte facilement; **~-term** *adj* (*effect*) à court terme; **~ wave** *n* (RADIO) ondes courtes

shot [ʃɔt] *pt, pp* of **shoot ♦** *n* coup *m* (de feu); (*try*) coup, essai *m*; (*injection*) piqûre *f*; (PHOT) photo *f*; **he's a good/poor ~** il tire bien/mal; **like a ~** comme une flèche; (*very readily*) sans hésiter; **~gun** *n* fusil *m* de chasse

should [ʃud] *aux vb*: **I ~ go now** je devrais partir maintenant; **he ~ be there now** il devrait être arrivé maintenant; **I ~ go if I were you** si j'étais vous, j'irais; **I ~ like to** j'aimerais bien, volontiers

shoulder [ˈʃəuldəᵊ] *n* épaule *f* **♦** *vt* (*fig*) endosser, se charger de; **~ bag** *n* sac *m* à bandoulière; **~ blade** *n* omoplate *f*

shouldn't [ˈʃudnt] = **should not**

shout [ʃaut] *n* cri *m* **♦** *vt* crier **♦** *vi* (*also: ~ out*) crier, pousser des cris; **~ down** *vt*

huer; **~ing** *n* cris *mpl*

shove [ʃʌv] *vt* pousser; (*inf: put*): **to ~ sth in** fourrer *or* ficher qch dans; **~ off** (*inf*) *vi* ficher le camp

shovel [ˈʃʌvl] *n* pelle *f*

show [ʃəu] (*pt* **showed**, *pp* **shown**) *n* (*of emotion*) manifestation *f*, démonstration *f*; (*semblance*) semblant *m*, apparence *f*; (*exhibition*) exposition *f*, salon *m*; (THEATRE, TV) spectacle *m* **♦** *vt* montrer; (*film*) donner; (*courage etc*) faire preuve de, manifester; (*exhibit*) exposer **♦** *vi* se voir, être visible; **for ~** pour l'effet; **on ~** (*exhibits etc*) exposé(e); **~ in** *vt* (*person*) faire entrer; **~ off** *vi* (*pej*) crâner **♦** *vt* (*display*) faire valoir; **~ out** *vt* (*person*) reconduire (jusqu'à la porte); **~ up** *vi* (*stand out*) ressortir; (*inf: turn up*) se montrer **♦** *vt* (*flaw*) faire ressortir; **~ business** *n* le monde du spectacle; **~down** *n* épreuve *f* de force

shower [ˈʃauəᵊ] *n* (*rain*) averse *f*; (*of stones etc*) pluie *f*, grêle *f*; (*~bath*) douche *f* **♦** *vi* prendre une douche, se doucher **♦** *vt*: **to ~ sb with** (*gifts etc*) combler qn de; **to have** *or* **take a ~** prendre une douche; **~proof** *adj* imperméabilisé(e)

showing [ˈʃəuɪŋ] *n* (*of film*) projection *f*

show jumping *n* concours *m* hippique

shown [ʃəun] *pp* of **show**

show: **~-off** (*inf*) *n* (*person*) crâneur(-euse), m'as-tu-vu(e); **~piece** *n* (*of exhibition*) trésor *m*; **~room** *n* magasin *m* *or* salle *f* d'exposition

shrank [ʃræŋk] *pt* of **shrink**

shrapnel [ˈʃræpnl] *n* éclats *mpl* d'obus

shred [ʃrɛd] *n* (*gen pl*) lambeau *m*, petit morceau *m* **♦** *vt* mettre en lambeaux, déchirer; (CULIN: *grate*) râper; (: *lettuce etc*) couper en lanières; **~der** *n* (*for vegetables*) râpeur *m*; (*for documents*) déchiqueteuse *f*

shrewd [ʃruːd] *adj* astucieux(-euse), perspicace; (*businessman*) habile

shriek [ʃriːk] *vi* hurler, crier

shrill [ʃrɪl] *adj* perçant(e), aigu(-guë), strident(e)

shrimp [ʃrɪmp] *n* crevette *f*

shrine [ʃraɪn] *n* (*place*) lieu *m* de

pèlerinage

shrink [ʃrɪŋk] (*pt* **shrank**, *pp* **shrunk**) *vi* rétrécir; (*fig*) se réduire, diminuer; (*move: also:* ~ **away**) reculer ♦ *vt* (*wool*) (faire) rétrécir ♦ *n* (*inf: pej*) psychiatre *m/f*, psy *m/f*; **to ~ from (doing) sth** reculer devant (la pensée de faire) qch; **~wrap** *vt* emballer sous film plastique

shrivel ['ʃrɪvl] *vt* (*also:* ~ **up**) ratatiner, flétrir ♦ *vi* se ratatiner, se flétrir

shroud [ʃraud] *n* linceul *m* ♦ *vt*: **~ed in mystery** enveloppé(e) de mystère

Shrove Tuesday ['ʃrəuv-] *n* (le) Mardi gras

shrub *n* arbuste *m*; **~bery** *n* massif *m* d'arbustes

shrug [ʃrʌg] *vt*, *vi*: **to ~ (one's shoulders)** hausser les épaules; ~ **off** *vt* faire fi de

shrunk [ʃrʌŋk] *pp of* **shrink**

shudder ['ʃʌdər] *vi* frissonner, frémir

shuffle ['ʃʌfl] *vt* (*cards*) battre; **to ~ (one's feet)** traîner les pieds

shun [ʃʌn] *vt* éviter, fuir

shunt [ʃʌnt] *vt* (*RAIL*) aiguiller

shut [ʃʌt] (*pt*, *pp* **shut**) *vt* fermer ♦ *vi* (se) fermer; ~ **down** *vt*, *vi* fermer définitivement; ~ **off** *vt* couper, arrêter; ~ **up** *vi* (*inf: keep quiet*) se taire ♦ *vt* (*close*) fermer; (*silence*) faire taire; **~ter** *n* volet *m*; (*PHOT*) obturateur *m*

shuttle ['ʃʌtl] *n* navette *f*; (*also:* ~ **service**) (service *m* de) navette *f*; **~cock** *n* volant *m* (de badminton); ~ **diplomacy** *n* navettes *fpl* diplomatiques

shy [ʃaɪ] *adj* timide

Siberia [saɪ'bɪərɪə] *n* Sibérie *f*

Sicily ['sɪsɪlɪ] *n* Sicile *f*

sick [sɪk] *adj* (*ill*) malade; (*vomiting*): **to be ~** vomir; (*humour*) noir(e), macabre; **to feel ~** avoir envie de vomir, avoir mal au cœur; **to be ~ of** (*fig*) en avoir assez de; ~ **bay** *n* infirmerie *f*; **~en** *vt* écœurer; **~ening** *adj* (*fig*) écœurant(e), dégoûtant(e)

sickle ['sɪkl] *n* faucille *f*

sick: ~ **leave** *n* congé *m* de maladie; **~ly** *adj* maladif(-ive), souffreteux(-euse); (*causing nausea*) écœurant(e); **~ness** *n* mala-

die *f*; (*vomiting*) vomissement(s) *m(pl)*; ~ **note** *n* (*from parents*) mot *m* d'absence; (*from doctor*) certificat médical; ~ **pay** *n* indemnité *f* de maladie

side [saɪd] *n* côté *m*; (*of lake, road*) bord *m*; (*team*) camp *m*, équipe *f* ♦ *adj* (*door, entrance*) latéral(e) ♦ *vi*: **to ~ with sb** prendre le parti de qn, se ranger du côté de qn; **by the ~ of** au bord de; ~ **by ~** côte à côte; **from ~ to ~** d'un côté à l'autre; **to take ~s (with)** prendre parti (pour); **~board** *n* buffet *m*; **~boards** (*BRIT*), **~burns** *npl* (*whiskers*) pattes *fpl*; ~ **drum** *n* tambour plat; ~ **effect** *n* effet *m* secondaire; **~light** *n* (*AUT*) veilleuse *f*; **~line** *n* (*SPORT*) (ligne *f* de) touche *f*; (*fig*) travail *m* secondaire; **~long** *adj* oblique; **~show** *n* attraction *f*; **~step** *vt* (*fig*) éluder; éviter; ~ **street** *n* (petite) rue transversale; **~track** *vt* (*fig*) faire dévier de son sujet; **~walk** (*US*) *n* trottoir *m*; **~ways** *adv* de côté

siding ['saɪdɪŋ] *n* (*RAIL*) voie *f* de garage

siege [siːdʒ] *n* siège *m*

sieve [sɪv] *n* tamis *m*, passoire *f*

sift [sɪft] *vt* (*fig: also:* ~ **through**) passer en revue; (*lit: flour etc*) passer au tamis

sigh [saɪ] *n* soupir *m* ♦ *vi* soupirer, pousser un soupir

sight [saɪt] *n* (*faculty*) vue *f*; (*spectacle*) spectacle *m*; (*on gun*) mire *f* ♦ *vt* apercevoir; **in ~** visible; **out of ~** hors de vue; **~seeing** *n* tourisme *m*; **to go ~seeing** faire du tourisme

sign [saɪn] *n* signe *m*; (*with hand etc*) signe, geste *m*; (*notice*) panneau *m*, écriteau *m* ♦ *vt* signer; ~ **on** *vi* (*as unemployed*) s'inscrire au chômage; (*for course*) s'inscrire ♦ *vt* (*employee*) embaucher; ~ **over** *vt*: **to ~ sth over to sb** céder qch par écrit à qn; ~ **up** *vi* (*MIL*) s'engager ♦ *vt* (*MIL*) s'engager; (*for course*) s'inscrire

signal ['sɪgnl] *n* signal *m* ♦ *vi* (*AUT*) mettre son clignotant à; (*message*) communiquer par signaux; **~man** (*irreg*) *n* (*RAIL*) aiguilleur *m*

signature ['sɪgnətʃər] *n* signature *f*; ~

tune *n* indicatif musical

signet ring ['signət-] *n* chevalière *f*

significance [sig'nifikəns] *n* signification *f*; importance *f*

significant [sig'nifikənt] *adj* significatif(-ive); (*important*) important(e), considérable

sign language *n* langage *m* per signes

signpost *n* poteau indicateur

silence ['sailəns] *n* silence *m* ♦ *vt* faire taire, réduire au silence; **~r** *n* (*on gun, BRIT: AUT*) silencieux *m*

silent ['sailənt] *adj* silencieux(-euse); (*film*) muet(te); **to remain ~** garder le silence, ne rien dire; **~ partner** *n* (*COMM*) bailleur *m* de fonds, commanditaire *m*

silhouette [silu:'et] *n* silhouette *f*

silicon chip ['silikən-] *n* puce *f* électronique

silk [silk] *n* soie *f* ♦ *cpd* de or en soie; **~y** *adj* soyeux(-euse)

silly ['sili] *adj* stupide, sot(te), bête

silt [silt] *n* vase *f*; limon *m*

silver ['silvər] *n* argent *m*; (*money*) monnaie *f* (en pièces d'argent); (*also:* **~ware**) argenterie *f* ♦ *adj* d'argent, en argent; **~ paper** (*BRIT*) *n* papier *m* d'argent *or* d'étain; **~-plated** *adj* plaqué(e) argent *inv*; **~smith** *n* orfèvre *m/f*; **~y** *adj* argenté(e)

similar ['similər] *adj*: **~ (to)** semblable (à); **~ly** *adv* de la même façon, de même

simmer ['simər] *vi* cuire à feu doux, mijoter

simple ['simpl] *adj* simple; **simplicity** [sim'plisiti] *n* simplicité *f*; **simply** *adv* (*without fuss*) avec simplicité

simultaneous [siməl'teiniəs] *adj* simultané(e)

sin [sin] *n* péché *m* ♦ *vi* pécher

since [sins] *adv, prep* depuis ♦ *conj* (*time*) depuis que; (*because*) puisque, étant donné que, comme; **~ then, ever ~** depuis ce moment-là

sincere [sin'siər] *adj* sincère; **~ly** *adv see* **yours**; **sincerity** [sin'seriti] *n* sincérité *f*

sinew ['sinju:] *n* tendon *m*

sing [siŋ] (*pt* **sang**, *pp* **sung**) *vt, vi* chanter

Singapore [siŋgə'pɔːr] *n* Singapour *m*

singe [sindʒ] *vt* brûler légèrement; (*clothes*) roussir

singer ['siŋər] *n* chanteur(-euse)

singing ['siŋiŋ] *n* chant *m*

single ['siŋgl] *adj* seul(e), unique; (*unmarried*) célibataire; (*not double*) simple ♦ *n* (*BRIT: also:* **~ ticket**) aller *m* (simple); (*record*) 45 tours *m*; **~ out** *vt* choisir; (*distinguish*) distinguer; **~ bed** *n* lit *m* d'une personne; **~-breasted** *adj* droit(e); **~ file** *n*: **in ~ file** en file indienne; **~-handed** *adv* tout(e) seul(e), sans (aucune) aide; **~-minded** *adj* résolu(e), tenace; **~ parent** *n* parent *m* unique; **~ room** *n* chambre *f* à un lit *or* pour une personne; **~s** *n* (*TENNIS*) simple *m*; **~-track road** *n* route *f* à voie unique; **singly** *adv* séparément

singular ['siŋgjulər] *adj* singulier(-ère), étrange; (*outstanding*) remarquable; (*LING*) (au) singulier, du singulier ♦ *n* singulier *m*

sinister ['sinistər] *adj* sinistre

sink [siŋk] (*pt* **sank**, *pp* **sunk**) *n* évier *m* ♦ *vt* (*ship*) (faire) couler, faire sombrer; (*foundations*) creuser ♦ *vi* couler, sombrer; (*ground etc*) s'affaisser; (*also:* **~ back, ~ down**) s'affaisser, se laisser retomber; **to ~ sth into** enfoncer qch dans; **my heart sank** j'ai complètement perdu courage; **~ in** *vi* (*fig*) pénétrer, être compris(e)

sinner ['sinər] *n* pécheur(-eresse)

sinus ['sainəs] *n* sinus *m inv*

sip [sip] *n* gorgée *f* ♦ *vt* boire à petites gorgées

siphon ['saifən] *n* siphon *m*; **~ off** *vt* siphonner; (*money: illegally*) détourner

sir [sər] *n* monsieur *m*; **S~ John Smith** sir John Smith; **yes ~** oui, Monsieur

siren ['saiərn] *n* sirène *f*

sirloin ['sə:lɔin] *n* (*also:* **~ steak**) aloyau *m*

sissy ['sisi] (*inf*) *n* (*coward*) poule mouillée

sister ['sistər] *n* sœur *f*; (*nun*) religieuse *f*, sœur; (*BRIT: nurse*) infirmière *f* en chef; **~-in-law** *n* belle-sœur *f*

sit [sit] (*pt, pp* **sat**) *vi* s'asseoir; (*be ~ting*) être assis(e); (*assembly*) être en séance, siéger; (*for painter*) poser ♦ *vt* (*exam*) passer, se présenter à; **~ down** *vi* s'asseoir; **~ in on** *vt fus* assister à; **~ up** *vi* s'asseoir; (*straight*) se redresser; (*not go to bed*) rester debout, ne pas se coucher

sitcom ['sɪtkɔm] *n abbr* (= *situation comedy*) comédie *f* de situation

site [saɪt] *n* emplacement *m*, site *m*; (*also:* **building ~**) chantier *m* ♦ *vt* placer

sit-in ['sɪtɪn] *n* (*demonstration*) sit-in *m inv*, occupation *f* (de locaux)

sitting ['sɪtɪŋ] *n* (*of assembly etc*) séance *f*; (*in canteen*) service *m*; **~ room** *n* salon *m*

situated ['sɪtjueɪtɪd] *adj* situé(e)

situation [sɪtju'eɪʃən] *n* situation *f*; **"~s vacant"** (*BRIT*) "offres d'emploi"

six [sɪks] *num* six; **~teen** *num* seize; **~th** *num* sixième; **~ty** *num* soixante

size [saɪz] *n* taille *f*; dimensions *fpl*; (*of clothing*) taille; (*of shoes*) pointure *f*; (*fig*) ampleur *f*; (*glue*) colle *f*; **~ up** *vt* juger, jauger; **~able** *adj* assez grand(e); assez important(e)

sizzle ['sɪzl] *vi* grésiller

skate [skeɪt] *n* patin *m*; (*fish: pl inv*) raie *f* ♦ *vi* patiner; **~board** *n* skateboard *m*, planche *f* à roulettes; **~boarding** *n* skateboard *m*; **~r** *n* patineur(-euse); **skating** *n* patinage *m*; **skating rink** *n* patinoire *f*

skeleton ['skɛlɪtn] *n* squelette *m*; (*outline*) schéma *m*; **~ staff** *n* effectifs réduits

skeptical ['skɛptɪkl] (*US*) *adj* = **sceptical**

sketch [skɛtʃ] *n* (*drawing*) croquis *m*, esquisse *f*; (*THEATRE*) sketch *m*, saynète *f* ♦ *vt* esquisser, faire un croquis *or* une esquisse de; **~ book** *n* carnet *m* à dessin; **~y** *adj* incomplet(-ète), fragmentaire

skewer ['skju:əʳ] *n* brochette *f*

ski [ski:] *n* ski *m* ♦ *vi* skier, faire du ski; **~ boot** *n* chaussure *f* de ski

skid [skɪd] *vi* déraper

ski: ~er *n* skieur(-euse); **~ing** *n* ski *m*; **~ jump** *n* saut *m* à skis

skilful ['skɪlful] (*US* **skillful**) *adj* habile, adroit(e)

ski lift *n* remonte-pente *m inv*

skill [skɪl] *n* habileté *f*, adresse *f*, talent *m*;

(*requiring training: gen pl*) compétences *fpl*; **~ed** *adj* habile, adroit(e); (*worker*) qualifié(e)

skim [skɪm] *vt* (*milk*) écrémer; (*glide over*) raser, effleurer ♦ *vi*: **to ~ through** (*fig*) parcourir; **~med milk** *n* lait écrémé

skimp [skɪmp] *vt* (*also:* **~ on:** *work*) bâcler, faire à la va-vite; (: *cloth etc*) lésiner sur; **~y** *adj* (*skirt*) étriqué(e)

skin [skɪn] *n* peau *f* ♦ *vt* (*fruit etc*) éplucher; (*animal*) écorcher; **~ cancer** *n* cancer *m* de la peau; **~-deep** *adj* superficiel(le); **~-diving** *n* plongée sous-marine; **~head** *n* skinhead *m/f*; **~ny** *adj* maigre, maigrichon(ne); **~tight** *adj* (*jeans etc*) moulant(e), ajusté(e)

skip [skɪp] *n* petit bond *or* saut *m*; (*BRIT: container*) benne *f* ♦ *vi* gambader, sautiller; (*with rope*) sauter à la corde ♦ *vt* sauter

ski pass *n* forfait-skieur(s) *m*

ski pole *n* bâton *m* de ski

skipper ['skɪpəʳ] *n* capitaine *m*; (*in race*) skipper *m*

skipping rope ['skɪpɪŋ-] (*BRIT*) *n* corde *f* à sauter

skirmish ['skə:mɪʃ] *n* escarmouche *f*, accrochage *m*

skirt [skə:t] *n* jupe *f* ♦ *vt* longer, contourner; **~ing board** (*BRIT*) *n* plinthe *f*

ski: ~ slope *n* piste *f* de ski; **~ suit** *n* combinaison *f* (de ski); **~ tow** *n* remonte-pente *m inv*

skittle ['skɪtl] *n* quille *f*; **~s** *n* (*game*) (jeu *m* de) quilles *fpl*

skive [skaɪv] (*BRIT: inf*) *vi* tirer au flanc

skull [skʌl] *n* crâne *m*

skunk [skʌŋk] *n* mouffette *f*

sky [skaɪ] *n* ciel *m*; **~light** *n* lucarne *f*; **~scraper** *n* gratte-ciel *m inv*

slab [slæb] *n* (*of stone*) dalle *f*; (*of food*) grosse tranche

slack [slæk] *adj* (*loose*) lâche, desserré(e); (*slow*) stagnant(e); (*careless*) négligent(e), peu sérieux(-euse) *or* consciencieux(-euse); **~s** *npl* (*trousers*) pantalon *m*; **~en** *vi* ralentir, diminuer ♦ *vt* (*speed*) réduire; (*grip*) relâcher; (*clothing*) desserrer

slag heap [slæg-] *n* crassier *m*

slag off (*BRIT: inf*) *vt* dire du mal de

slam [slæm] *vt* (*door*) (faire) claquer; (*throw*) jeter violemment, flanquer (*fam*); (*criticize*) démolir ♦ *vi* claquer

slander ['slɑːndəʳ] *n* calomnie *f*; diffamation *f*

slang [slæŋ] *n* argot *m*

slant [slɑːnt] *n* inclinaison *f*; (*fig*) angle *m*, point *m* de vue; **~ed** *adj* = **slanting**; **~ing** *adj* en pente, incliné(e); **~ing eyes** yeux bridés

slap [slæp] *n* claque *f*, gifle *f*; tape *f* ♦ *vt* donner une claque or une gifle or une tape à; (*paint*) appliquer rapidement ♦ *adv* (*directly*) tout droit, en plein; **~dash** *adj* fait(e) sans soin or à la va-vite; (*person*) insouciant(e), négligent(e); **~stick** *n* (*comedy*) grosse farce, style *m* tarte à la crème; **~-up** (*BRIT*) *adj*: **a ~-up meal** un repas extra or fameux

slash [slæʃ] *vt* entailler, taillader; (*fig: prices*) casser

slat [slæt] *n* latte *f*, lame *f*

slate [sleɪt] *n* ardoise *f* ♦ *vt* (*fig: criticize*) éreinter, démolir

slaughter ['slɔːtəʳ] *n* carnage *m*, massacre *m* ♦ *vt* (*animal*) abattre; (*people*) massacrer; **~house** *n* abattoir *m*

slave [sleɪv] *n* esclave *m/f* ♦ *vi* (*also: ~ away*) trimer, travailler comme un forçat; **~ry** *n* esclavage *m*

slay [sleɪ] (*pt* **slew**, *pp* **slain**) *vt* tuer

sleazy ['sliːzɪ] *adj* miteux(-euse), minable

sledge [slɛdʒ] *n* luge *f* ♦ *vi*: **to go sledging** faire de la luge

sledgehammer *n* marteau *m* de forgeron

sleek [sliːk] *adj* (*hair, fur etc*) brillant(e), lisse; (*car, boat etc*) aux lignes pures or élégantes

sleep [sliːp] (*pt, pp* **slept**) *n* sommeil *m* ♦ *vi* dormir; (*spend night*) dormir, coucher; **to go to ~** s'endormir; **~ around** *vi* coucher à droite et à gauche; **~ in** *vi* (*oversleep*) se réveiller trop tard; **~er** (*BRIT*) *n*

(*RAIL: train*) train-couchettes *m*; (*: berth*) couchette *f*; **~ing bag** *n* sac *m* de couchage; **~ing car** *n* (*RAIL*) wagon-lit *m*, voiture-lit *f*; **~ing partner** (*BRIT*) *n* = **silent partner**; **~ing pill** *n* somnifère *m*; **~less** *adj*: **a ~less night** une nuit blanche; **~walker** *n* somnambule *m/f*; **~y** *adj* qui a sommeil; (*fig*) endormi(e)

sleet [sliːt] *n* neige fondue

sleeve [sliːv] *n* manche *f*; (*of record*) pochette *f*

sleigh [sleɪ] *n* traîneau *m*

sleight [slaɪt] *n*: **~ of hand** tour *m* de passe-passe

slender ['slɛndəʳ] *adj* svelte, mince; (*fig*) faible, ténu(e)

slept [slɛpt] *pt, pp of* **sleep**

slew [sluː] *vi* (*also: ~ around*) virer, pivoter ♦ *pt of* **slay**

slice [slaɪs] *n* tranche *f*; (*round*) rondelle *f*; (*utensil*) spatule *f*, truelle *f* ♦ *vt* couper en tranches (*or en rondelles*)

slick [slɪk] *adj* (*skilful*) brillant(e) (en apparence); (*salesman*) qui a du bagout ♦ *n* (*also:* **oil ~**) nappe *f* de pétrole, marée noire

slide [slaɪd] (*pt, pp* **slid**) *n* (*in playground*) toboggan *m*; (*PHOT*) diapositive *f*; (*BRIT: also:* **hair ~**) barrette *f*; (*in prices*) chute *f*, baisse *f* ♦ *vt* (faire) glisser ♦ *vi* glisser; **sliding** *adj* (*door*) coulissant(e); **sliding scale** *n* échelle *f* mobile

slight [slaɪt] *adj* (*slim*) mince, menu(e); (*frail*) frêle; (*trivial*) faible, insignifiant(e); (*small*) petit(e), léger(-ère) (*before n*) ♦ *n* offense *f*, affront *m*; **not in the ~est** pas le moins du monde, pas du tout; **~ly** *adv* légèrement, un peu

slim [slɪm] *adj* mince ♦ *vi* maigrir; (*diet*) suivre un régime amaigrissant

slime [slaɪm] *n* (*mud*) vase *f*; (*other substance*) substance visqueuse

slimming ['slɪmɪŋ] *adj* (*diet, pills*) amaigrissant(e); (*foodstuff*) qui ne fait pas grossir

sling [slɪŋ] (*pt, pp* **slung**) *n* (*MED*) écharpe *f*; (*for baby*) porte-bébé *m*; (*weapon*) fronde *f*, lance-pierre *m* ♦ *vt* lancer, jeter

slip [slɪp] *n* faux pas; *(mistake)* erreur *f*; étourderie *f*; bévue *f*; *(underskirt)* combinaison *f*; *(of paper)* petite feuille, fiche *f* ♦ *vt (slide)* glisser ♦ *vi* glisser; *(decline)* baisser; *(move smoothly)*: **to ~ into/out of** se glisser *or* se faufiler dans/hors de; **to ~ sth on/off** enfiler/enlever qch; **to give sb the ~** fausser compagnie à qn; **a ~ of the tongue** un lapsus; **~ away** *vi* s'esquiver; **~ in** *vt* glisser ♦ *vi (errors)* s'y glisser; **~ out** *vi* sortir; **~ up** *vi* faire une erreur, gaffer; **~ped disc** *n* déplacement *m* de vertèbre

slipper [ˈslɪpəʳ] *n* pantoufle *f*

slippery [ˈslɪpərɪ] *adj* glissant(e)

slip: **~ road** *(BRIT) n (to motorway)* bretelle *f* d'accès; **~-up** *n* bévue *f*; **~way** *n* cale *f* (de construction *or* de lancement)

slit [slɪt] *(pt, pp* slit*) n* fente *f*; *(cut)* incision *f* ♦ *vt* fendre; couper; inciser

slither [ˈslɪðəʳ] *vi* glisser; *(snake)* onduler

sliver [ˈslɪvəʳ] *n (of glass, wood)* éclat *m*; *(of cheese etc)* petit morceau, fine tranche

slob [slɔb] *(inf) n* rustaud(e)

slog [slɔg] *(BRIT) vi* travailler très dur ♦ *n* gros effort; tâche fastidieuse

slogan [ˈsləugən] *n* slogan *m*

slope [sləup] *n* pente *f*, côte *f*; *(side of mountain)* versant *m*; *(slant)* inclinaison *f* ♦ *vi*: **to ~ down** être *or* descendre en pente; **to ~ up** monter; **sloping** *adj* en pente; *(writing)* penché(e)

sloppy [ˈslɔpɪ] *adj (work)* peu soigné(e), bâclé(e); *(appearance)* négligé(e), débraillé(e)

slot [slɔt] *n* fente *f* ♦ *vt*: **to ~ sth into** encastrer *or* insérer qch dans

sloth [sləuθ] *n (laziness)* paresse *f*

slouch [slautʃ] *vi* avoir le dos rond, être voûté(e)

slovenly [ˈslʌvənlɪ] *adj* sale, débraillé(e); *(work)* négligé(e)

slow [sləu] *adj* lent(e); *(watch)*: **to be ~** retarder ♦ *adv* lentement ♦ *vt, vi (also:* **~ down**, **~ up**) ralentir; **"~"** *(road sign)* "ralentir"; **~ly** *adv* lentement; **~ motion** *n*: **in ~ motion** au ralenti

sludge [slʌdʒ] *n* boue *f*

slug [slʌg] *n* limace *f*; *(bullet)* balle *f*

sluggish [ˈslʌgɪʃ] *adj (person)* mou (molle), lent(e); *(stream, engine, trading)* lent

sluice [slu:s] *n (also:* **~ gate)** vanne *f*

slum [slʌm] *n (house)* taudis *m*

slump [slʌmp] *n* baisse soudaine, effondrement *m*; *(ECON)* crise *f* ♦ *vi* s'effondrer, s'affaisser

slung [slʌŋ] *pt, pp of* **sling**

slur [slə:ʳ] *n (fig: smear):* **~ (on)** atteinte *f* (à); insinuation *f* (contre) ♦ *vt* mal articuler

slush [slʌʃ] *n* neige fondue

slut [slʌt] *(pej) n* souillon *f*

sly [slaɪ] *adj (person)* rusé(e); *(smile, expression, remark)* sournois(e)

smack [smæk] *n (slap)* tape *f*; *(on face)* gifle *f* ♦ *vt* donner une tape à; *(on face)* gifler; *(on bottom)* donner la fessée à ♦ *vi*: **to ~ of** avoir des relents de, sentir

small [smɔ:l] *adj* petit(e); **~ ads** *(BRIT) npl* petites annonces; **~ change** *n* petite *or* menue monnaie; **~holder** *(BRIT) n* petit cultivateur; **~ hours** *npl*: **in the ~ hours** au petit matin; **~pox** *n* variole *f*; **~ talk** *n* menus propos

smart [smɑ:t] *adj (neat, fashionable)* élégant(e), chic *inv*; *(clever)* intelligent(e), astucieux(-euse), futé(e); *(quick)* rapide, vif (vive), prompt(e) ♦ *vi* faire mal, brûler; *(fig)* être piqué(e) au vif; **~ card** *n* carte *f* à puce; **~en up** *vi* devenir plus élégant(e), se faire beau (belle) ♦ *vt* rendre plus élégant(e)

smash [smæʃ] *n (also:* **~-up)** collision *f*, accident *m*; *(also:* **~ hit)** succès foudroyant ♦ *vt* casser, briser, fracasser; *(opponent)* écraser; *(SPORT: record)* pulvériser ♦ *vi* se briser, se fracasser; s'écraser; **~ing** *(inf) adj* formidable

smattering [ˈsmætərɪŋ] *n*: **a ~ of** quelques notions de

smear [smɪəʳ] *n* tache *f*, salissure *f*; trace *f*; *(MED)* frottis *m* ♦ *vt* enduire; *(make dirty)* salir; **~ campaign** *n* campagne *f* de diffamation

smell [smɛl] (*pt, pp* **smelt** *or* **smelled**) *n* odeur *f*; (*sense*) odorat *m* ♦ *vt* sentir ♦ *vi* (*food etc*): **to ~ (of)** sentir (de); (*pej*) sentir mauvais; **~y** *adj* qui sent mauvais, malodorant(e)

smile [smaɪl] *n* sourire *m* ♦ *vi* sourire

smirk [smɔːk] *n* petit sourire suffisant *or* affecté

smock [smɔk] *n* blouse *f*

smog [smɔg] *n* brouillard mêlé de fumée, smog *m*

smoke [smɔuk] *n* fumée *f* ♦ *vt, vi* fumer; **~d** *adj* (*bacon, glass*) fumé(e); **~r** *n* (*person*) fumeur(-euse); (*RAIL*) wagon *m* fumeurs; **~ screen** *n* rideau *m* or écran *m* de fumée; (*fig*) paravent *m*; **smoking** *n* tabagisme *m*; **"no smoking"** (*sign*) "défense de fumer"; **to give up smoking** arrêter de fumer; **smoking compartment** (*US* **smoking car**) *n* wagon *m* fumeurs; **smoky** *adj* enfumé(e); (*taste*) fumé(e)

smolder ['smɔuldər] (*US*) *vi* = **smoulder**

smooth [smuːð] *adj* lisse; (*sauce*) onctueux(-euse); (*flavour, whisky*) moelleux(-euse); (*movement*) régulier(-ère), sans à-coups *or* heurts; (*pej: person*) doucereux(-euse), mielleux(-euse) ♦ *vt* (*also: ~ out: skirt, paper*) lisser, défroisser; (*: creases, difficulties*) faire disparaître

smother ['smʌðər] *vt* étouffer

smoulder ['smɔuldər] (*US* **smolder**) *vi* couver

smudge [smʌdʒ] *n* tache *f*, bavure *f* ♦ *vt* salir, maculer

smug [smʌg] *adj* suffisant(e)

smuggle ['smʌgl] *vt* passer en contrebande *or* en fraude; **~r** *n* contrebandier(-ère); **smuggling** *n* contrebande *f*

smutty ['smʌtɪ] *adj* (*fig*) grossier(-ère), obscène

snack [snæk] *n* casse-croûte *m inv*; **~ bar** *n* snack(-bar) *m*

snag [snæg] *n* inconvénient *m*, difficulté *f*

snail [sneɪl] *n* escargot *m*

snake [sneɪk] *n* serpent *m*

snap [snæp] *n* (*sound*) claquement *m*, bruit sec; (*photograph*) photo *f*, instantané *m* ♦ *adj* subit(e); fait(e) sans réflexion ♦ *vt* (*break*) casser net; (*fingers*) faire claquer ♦ *vi* se casser net or avec un bruit sec; (*speak sharply*) parler d'un ton brusque; **to ~ shut** se refermer brusquement; **~ at** *vt fus* (*subj: dog*) essayer de mordre; **~ off** *vi* (*break*) casser net; **~ up** *vt* sauter sur, saisir; **~py** (*inf*) *adj* prompt(e); (*slogan*) qui a du punch; **make it ~py!** grouille-toi!, et que ça saute!; **~shot** *n* photo *f*, instantané *m*

snare [snɛər] *n* piège *m*

snarl [snɑːl] *vi* gronder

snatch [snætʃ] *n* (*small amount*): **~es of** des fragments *mpl* or bribes *fpl* de ♦ *vt* saisir (*d'un geste vif*); (*steal*) voler

sneak [sniːk] *vi*: **to ~ in/out** entrer/sortir furtivement *or* à la dérobée ♦ *n* (*inf: pej: informer*) faux jeton; **to ~ up on sb** s'approcher de qn sans faire de bruit; **~ers** *npl* tennis *mpl*, baskets *mpl*

sneer [snɪər] *vi* ricaner; **to ~ at** traiter avec mépris

sneeze [sniːz] *vi* éternuer

sniff [snɪf] *vi* renifler ♦ *vt* renifler, flairer; (*glue, drugs*) sniffer, respirer

snigger ['snɪgər] *vi* ricaner; pouffer de rire

snip [snɪp] *n* (*cut*) petit coup; (*BRIT: inf: bargain*) (bonne) occasion *or* affaire *f* ♦ *vt* couper

sniper ['snaɪpər] *n* tireur embusqué

snippet ['snɪpɪt] *n* bribe(s) *f(pl)*

snob [snɔb] *n* snob *m/f*; **~bish** *adj* snob *inv*

snooker ['snuːkər] *n* sorte de jeu de billard

snoop [snuːp] *vi*: **to ~ about** fureter

snooze [snuːz] *n* petit somme ♦ *vi* faire un petit somme

snore [snɔːr] *vi* ronfler

snorkel ['snɔːkl] *n* (*of swimmer*) tuba *m*

snort [snɔːt] *vi* grogner; (*horse*) renâcler

snout [snaut] *n* museau *m*

snow [snɔu] *n* neige *f* ♦ *vi* neiger; **~ball** *n* boule *f* de neige; **~bound** *adj* enneigé(e), bloqué(e) par la neige; **~drift** *n* congère *f*; **~drop** *n* perce-neige *m or f*; **~fall** *n* chute *f* de neige; **~flake** *n* flocon *m* de neige; **~man** (*irreg*) *n* bonhomme *m* de neige; **~plough** (*US* **snowplow**) *n* chasse-neige *m inv*; **~shoe** *n* raquette *f* (*pour la neige*); **~storm** *n* tempête *f* de neige

snub [snʌb] *vt* repousser, snober ♦ *n* rebuffade *f*; **~-nosed** *adj* au nez retroussé

snuff [snʌf] *n* tabac *m* à priser

snug [snʌg] *adj* douillet(te), confortable; (*person*) bien au chaud

snuggle ['snʌgl] *vi*: **to ~ up to sb** se serrer *or* se blottir contre qn

---
| KEYWORD |
---

so [səu] *adv* **1** (*thus, likewise*) ainsi; **if so** si oui; **so do** *or* **have I** moi aussi; **it's 5 o'clock – so it is!** il est 5 heures – en effet! *or* c'est vrai!; **I hope/think so** je l'espère/le crois; **so far** jusqu'ici, jusqu'à maintenant; (*in past*) jusque-là

2 (*in comparisons etc: to such a degree*) si, tellement; **so big (that)** si *or* tellement grand (que); **she's not so clever as her brother** elle n'est pas aussi intelligente que son frère

3: so much
♦ *adj, adv* tant (de); **I've got so much work** j'ai tant de travail; **I love you so much** je vous aime tant; **so many** tant (de)

4 (*phrases*): **10 or so** à peu près *or* environ 10; **so long!** (*inf: goodbye*) au revoir!, à un de ces jours!
♦ *conj* **1** (*expressing purpose*): **so as to do** pour faire, afin de faire; **so (that)** pour que *or* afin que +*sub*

2 (*expressing result*) donc, par conséquent; **so that** si bien que, de (telle) sorte que

---

soak [səuk] *vt* faire tremper; (*drench*) tremper ♦ *vi* tremper; **~ in** *vi* être absorbé(e); **~ up** *vt* absorber; **~ing** *adj* trempé(e)

soap [səup] *n* savon *m*; **~flakes** *npl* paillettes *fpl* de savon; **~ opera** *n* feuilleton télévisé; **~ powder** *n* lessive *f*; **~y** *adj* savonneux(-euse)

soar [sɔː^r] *vi* monter (en flèche), s'élancer;

(*building*) s'élancer

sob [sɔb] *n* sanglot *m* ♦ *vi* sangloter

sober ['səubə^r] *adj* qui n'est pas (*or* plus) ivre; (*serious*) sérieux(-euse), sensé(e); (*colour, style*) sobre, discret(-ète); **~ up** *vt* dessoûler (*inf*) ♦ *vi* dessoûler (*inf*)

so-called ['səu'kɔːld] *adj* soi-disant *inv*

soccer ['sɔkə^r] *n* football *m*

social ['səuʃl] *adj* social(e); (*sociable*) sociable ♦ *n* (*petite*) fête; **~ club** *n* amicale *f*, foyer *m*; **~ism** *n* socialisme *m*; **~ist** *adj* socialiste ♦ *n* socialiste *m/f*; **~ize** *vi*: **to ~ize (with)** lier connaissance (avec); parler (avec); **~ security** (*BRIT*) *n* aide sociale; **~ work** *n* assistance sociale, travail social; **~ worker** *n* assistant(e) social(e)

society [sə'saɪətɪ] *n* société *f*; (*club*) société, association *f*; (*also:* **high ~**) (haute) société, grand monde

sociology [səusɪ'ɔlədʒɪ] *n* sociologie *f*

sock [sɔk] *n* chaussette *f*

socket ['sɔkɪt] *n* cavité *f*; (*BRIT: ELEC: also:* **wall ~**) prise *f* de courant

sod [sɔd] *n* (*of earth*) motte *f*; (*BRIT: inf!*) con *m* (!); salaud *m* (!)

soda ['səudə] *n* (*CHEM*) soude *f*; (*also:* **~ water**) eau *f* de Seltz; (*US: also:* **~ pop**) soda *m*

sofa ['səufə] *n* sofa *m*, canapé *m*

soft [sɔft] *adj* (*not rough*) doux (douce); (*not hard*) doux; mou (molle); (*not loud*) doux, léger(-ère); (*kind*) doux, gentil(le); **~ drink** *n* boisson non alcoolisée; **~en** *vt* (r)amollir; (*fig*) adoucir; atténuer ♦ *vi* se ramollir; s'adoucir; s'atténuer; **~ly** *adv* doucement; gentiment; **~ness** *n* douceur *f*; **~ware** *n* (*COMPUT*) logiciel *m*, software *m*

soggy ['sɔgɪ] *adj* trempé(e); détrempé(e)

soil [sɔɪl] *n* (*earth*) sol *m*, terre *f* ♦ *vt* salir; (*fig*) souiller

solar ['səulə^r] *adj* solaire; **~ panel** *n* panneau *m* solaire; **~ power** *n* énergie solaire

sold [səuld] *pt, pp* of **sell**

solder ['səuldə^r] *vt* souder (*au fil à souder*) ♦ *n* soudure *f*

soldier [ˈsəʊldʒəʳ] *n* soldat *m*, militaire *m*

sole [səʊl] *n* (*of foot*) plante *f*; (*of shoe*) semelle *f*; (*fish: pl inv*) sole *f* ♦ *adj* seul(e), unique

solemn [ˈsɔləm] *adj* solennel(le); (*person*) sérieux(-euse), grave

sole trader *n* (COMM) chef *m* d'entreprise individuelle

solicit [səˈlɪsɪt] *vt* (*request*) solliciter ♦ *vi* (*prostitute*) racoler

solicitor [səˈlɪsɪtəʳ] *n* (*for wills etc*) ≃ notaire *m*; (*in court*) ≃ avocat *m*

solid [ˈsɔlɪd] *adj* solide; (*not hollow*) plein(e), compact(e), massif(-ive); (*entire*): **3 ~ hours** 3 heures entières ♦ *n* solide *m*

solidarity [sɔlɪˈdærɪtɪ] *n* solidarité *f*

solitary [ˈsɔlɪtərɪ] *adj* solitaire; **~ confinement** *n* (LAW) isolement *m*

solo [ˈsəʊləʊ] *n* solo *m* ♦ *adv* (*fly*) en solitaire; **~ist** *n* soliste *m/f*

soluble [ˈsɔljʊbl] *adj* soluble

solution [səˈluːʃən] *n* solution *f*

solve [sɔlv] *vt* résoudre

solvent [ˈsɔlvənt] *adj* (COMM) solvable ♦ *n* (CHEM) (dis)solvant *m*

KEYWORD

some [sʌm] *adj* **1** (*a certain amount or number of*): **some tea/water/ice cream** du thé/de l'eau/de la glace; **some children/apples** des enfants/pommes

2 (*certain: in contrasts*): **some people say that ...** il y a des gens qui disent que ...; **some films were excellent, but most ...** certains films étaient excellents, mais la plupart ...

3 (*unspecified*): **some woman was asking for you** il y avait une dame qui vous demandait; **he was asking for some book (or other)** il demandait un livre quelconque; **some day** un de ces jours; **some day next week** un jour la semaine prochaine

♦ *pron* **1** (*a certain number*) quelques-un(e)s, certain(e)s; **I've got some** (*books etc*) j'en ai (quelques-uns); **some (of them) have been sold** certains ont été vendus

2 (*a certain amount*) un peu; **I've got some** (*money, milk*) j'en ai (un peu)

♦ *adv*: **some 10 people** quelque 10 personnes, 10 personnes environ

---

some: **~body** [ˈsʌmbədɪ] *pron* = **someone**; **~how** *adv* d'une façon ou d'une autre; (*for some reason*) pour une raison ou une autre; **~one** *pron* quelqu'un; **~place** (*US*) *adv* = **somewhere**

somersault [ˈsʌməsɔːlt] *n* culbute *f*, saut périlleux ♦ *vi* faire la culbute *or* un saut périlleux; (*car*) faire un tonneau

some: **~thing** *pron* quelque chose; **~thing interesting** quelque chose d'intéressant; **~time** *adv* (*in future*) un de ces jours, un jour ou l'autre; (*in past*): **~time last month** au cours du mois dernier; **~times** *adv* quelquefois, parfois; **~what** *adv* quelque peu, un peu; **~where** *adv* quelque part

son [sʌn] *n* fils *m*

song [sɔŋ] *n* chanson *f*; (*of bird*) chant *m*

son-in-law [ˈsʌnɪnlɔː] *n* gendre *m*, beau-fils *m*

soon [suːn] *adv* bientôt; (*early*) tôt; **~ afterwards** peu après; *see also* **as**; **~er** *adv* (*time*) plus tôt; (*preference*): **I would ~er do** j'aimerais autant *or* je préférerais faire; **~er or later** tôt ou tard

soot [sʊt] *n* suie *f*

soothe [suːð] *vt* calmer, apaiser

sophisticated [səˈfɪstɪkeɪtɪd] *adj* raffiné(e); sophistiqué(e); (*machinery*) hautement perfectionné(e), très complexe

sophomore [ˈsɔfəmɔːʳ] (*US*) *n* étudiant(e) de seconde année

sopping [ˈsɔpɪŋ] *adj* (*also:* **~ wet**) complètement trempé(e)

soppy [ˈsɔpɪ] (*pej*) *adj* sentimental(e)

soprano [səˈprɑːnəʊ] *n* (*singer*) soprano *m/f*

sorcerer [ˈsɔːsərəʳ] *n* sorcier *m*

sore [sɔːʳ] *adj* (*painful*) douloureux(-euse), sensible ♦ *n* plaie *f*; **~ly** [ˈsɔːlɪ] *adv* (*tempted*) fortement

sorrow [ˈsɔrəʊ] *n* peine *f*, chagrin *m*

sorry ['sɔrɪ] *adj* désolé(e); (*condition, excuse*) triste, déplorable; **~!** pardon!, excusez-moi!; **~?** pardon?; **to feel ~ for sb** plaindre qn

sort [sɔːt] *n* genre *m*, espèce *f*, sorte *f* ♦ *vt* (*also:* **~ out**) trier; classer; ranger; (: *problems*) résoudre, régler; **~ing office** ['sɔːtɪŋ-] *n* bureau *m* de tri

SOS *n* S.O.S. *m*

so-so ['səʊsəʊ] *adv* comme ci comme ça

sought [sɔːt] *pt, pp of* **seek**

soul [səʊl] *n* âme *f*; **~ful** ['səʊlful] *adj* sentimental(e); (*eyes*) expressif(-ive)

sound [saʊnd] *adj* (*healthy*) en bonne santé, sain(e); (*safe, not damaged*) solide, en bon état; (*reliable, not superficial*) sérieux(-euse), solide; (*sensible*) sensé(e) ♦ *adv*: **~ asleep** profondément endormi(e) ♦ *n* son *m*; bruit *m*; (GEO) détroit *m*, bras *m* de mer ♦ *vt* (*alarm*) sonner ♦ *vi* sonner, retentir; (*fig: seem*) sembler (être); **to ~ like** ressembler à; **~ out** *vt* sonder; **~ barrier** *n* mur *m* du son; **~ bite** *n* phrase *f* toute faite (*pour être citée dans les médias*); **~ effects** *npl* bruitage *m*; **~ly** *adv* (*sleep*) profondément; (*beat*) complètement, à plate couture; **~proof** *adj* insonorisé(e); **~track** *n* (*of film*) bande *f* sonore

soup [suːp] *n* soupe *f*, potage *m*; **~ plate** *n* assiette creuse *or* à soupe; **~spoon** *n* cuiller *f* à soupe

sour ['saʊər] *adj* aigre; **it's ~ grapes** (*fig*) c'est du dépit

source [sɔːs] *n* source *f*

south [saʊθ] *n* sud *m* ♦ *adj* sud *inv*, du sud ♦ *adv* au sud, vers le sud; **S~ Africa** *n* Afrique *f* du Sud; **S~ African** *adj* sud-africain(e) ♦ *n* Sud-Africain(e); **S~ America** *n* Amérique *f* du Sud; **S~ American** *adj* sud-américain(e) ♦ *n* Sud-Américain(e); **~-east** *n* sud-est *m*; **~erly** ['sʌðəlɪ] *adj* du sud; au sud; **~ern** ['sʌðən] *adj* (du) sud; méridional(e); **S~ Pole** *n* Pôle *m* Sud; **S~ Wales** *n* sud *m* du Pays de Galles; **~ward(s)** *adv* vers le sud; **~-west** *n* sud-ouest *m*

souvenir [suːvə'nɪər] *n* (*objet*) souvenir *m*

sovereign ['sɔvrɪn] *n* souverain(e)

soviet ['səʊvɪət] *adj* soviétique; **the S~ Union** l'Union *f* soviétique

sow[1] [saʊ] *n* truie *f*

sow[2] [səʊ] (*pt* **sowed**, *pp* **sown**) *vt* semer

sown [səʊn] *pp of* **sow**[2]

soya ['sɔɪə] (US **soy**) *n*: **~ bean** graine *f* de soja; **soy(a) sauce** sauce *f* au soja

spa [spɑː] *n* (*town*) station thermale; (US: *also:* **health ~**) établissement *m* de cure de rajeunissement *etc*

space [speɪs] *n* espace *m*; (*room*) place *f*; espace; (*length of time*) laps *m* de temps ♦ *cpd* spatial(e) ♦ *vt* (*also:* **~ out**) espacer; **~craft** *n* engin spatial; **~man** (*irreg*) *n* astronaute *m*, cosmonaute *m*; **~ship** *n* = **spacecraft**; **spacing** *n* espacement *m*; **spacious** ['speɪʃəs] *adj* spacieux(-euse), grand(e)

spade [speɪd] *n* (*tool*) bêche *f*, pelle *f*; (*child's*) pelle; **~s** *npl* (CARDS) pique *m*

Spain [speɪn] *n* Espagne *f*

span [spæn] *n* (*of bird, plane*) envergure *f*; (*of arch*) portée *f*; (*in time*) espace *m* de temps, durée *f* ♦ *vt* enjamber, franchir; (*fig*) couvrir, embrasser

Spaniard ['spænjəd] *n* Espagnol(e)

spaniel ['spænjəl] *n* épagneul *m*

Spanish ['spænɪʃ] *adj* espagnol(e) ♦ *n* (LING) espagnol *m*; **the ~** *npl* les Espagnols *mpl*

spank [spæŋk] *vt* donner une fessée à

spanner ['spænər] (BRIT) *n* clé *f* (de mécanicien)

spare [speər] *adj* de réserve, de rechange; (*surplus*) *de* or *en* trop, de reste ♦ *n* (*part*) pièce *f* de rechange, pièce détachée ♦ *vt* (*do without*) se passer de; (*afford to give*) donner, accorder; (*refrain from hurting*) épargner; **to ~** (*surplus*) en surplus, de trop; **~ part** *n* pièce *f* de rechange, pièce détachée; **~ time** *n* moments *mpl* de loisir, temps *m* libre; **~ wheel** *n* (AUT) roue *f* de secours; **sparingly** *adv* avec modération

spark [spɑːk] *n* étincelle *f*; **~(ing) plug** *n* bougie *f*

sparkle ['spɑːkl] *n* scintillement *m*, éclat *m* ♦ *vi* étinceler, scintiller; **sparkling** *adj* (*wine*) mousseux(-euse), pétillant(e); (*water*) pétillant(e); (*fig: conversation, performance*) étincelant(e), pétillant(e)

sparrow ['spærəu] *n* moineau *m*

sparse [spɑːs] *adj* clairsemé(e)

spartan ['spɑːtən] *adj* (*fig*) spartiate

spasm ['spæzəm] *n* (*MED*) spasme *m*; **~odic** [spæz'mɔdɪk] *adj* (*fig*) intermittent(e)

spastic ['spæstɪk] *n* handicapé(e) moteur

spat [spæt] *pt, pp of* spit

spate [speɪt] *n* (*fig*): **a ~ of** une avalanche *or* un torrent de

spawn [spɔːn] *vi* frayer ♦ *n* frai *m*

speak [spiːk] (*pt* spoke, *pp* spoken) *vt* parler; (*truth*) dire ♦ *vi* parler; (*make a speech*) prendre la parole; **to ~ to sb/of** *or* **about sth** parler à qn/de qch; **~ up!** parle plus fort!; **~er** *n* (*in public*) orateur *m*; (*also:* **loudspeaker**) haut-parleur *m*; **the S~er** (*BRIT: POL*) le président de la chambre des Communes; (*US: POL*) le président de la chambre des Représentants

spear [spɪər] *n* lance *f* ♦ *vt* transpercer; **~head** *vt* (*attack etc*) mener

spec [spɛk] (*inf*) *n*: **on ~** à tout hasard

special ['spɛʃl] *adj* spécial(e); **~ist** *n* spécialiste *m/f*; **~ity** [spɛʃɪ'ælɪtɪ] *n* spécialité *f*; **~ize** *vi*: **to ~ize (in)** se spécialiser (dans); **~ly** *adv* spécialement, particulièrement; **~ty** (*esp US*) *n* = **speciality**

species ['spiːʃiːz] *n inv* espèce *f*

specific [spə'sɪfɪk] *adj* précis(e); particulier(-ère); (*BOT, CHEM etc*) spécifique; **~ally** *adv* expressément, explicitement; **~ation** [spɛsɪfɪ'keɪʃən] *n* (*TECH*) spécification *f*; (*requirement*) stipulation *f*

specimen ['spesɪmən] *n* spécimen *m*, échantillon *m*; (*of blood*) prélèvement *m*

speck [spɛk] *n* petite tache, petit point; (*particle*) grain *m*

speckled ['spɛkld] *adj* tacheté(e), moucheté(e)

specs [spɛks] (*inf*) *npl* lunettes *fpl*

spectacle ['spɛktəkl] *n* spectacle *m*; **~s** *npl* (*glasses*) lunettes *fpl*; **spectacular** [spɛk'tækjulər] *adj* spectaculaire

spectator [spɛk'teɪtər] *n* spectateur(-trice)

spectrum ['spɛktrəm] (*pl* spectra) *n* spectre *m*

speculation [spɛkju'leɪʃən] *n* spéculation *f*

speech [spiːtʃ] *n* (*faculty*) parole *f*; (*talk*) discours *m*, allocution *f*; (*manner of speaking*) façon *f* de parler, langage *m*; (*enunciation*) élocution *f*; **~less** *adj* muet(te)

speed [spiːd] *n* vitesse *f*; (*promptness*) rapidité *f* ♦ *vi*: **to ~ along/past** *etc* aller/ passer *etc* à toute vitesse *or* allure; **at full** *or* **top ~** à toute vitesse *or* allure; **~ up** *vi* aller plus vite, accélérer ♦ *vt* accélérer; **~boat** *n* vedette *f*, hors-bord *m inv*; **~ily** *adv* rapidement, promptement; **~ing** *n* (*AUT*) excès *m* de vitesse; **~ limit** *n* limitation *f* de vitesse, vitesse maximale permise; **~ometer** [spɪ'dɔmɪtər] *n* compteur *m* (de vitesse); **~way** *n* (*SPORT: also:* **~way racing**) épreuve(s) *f(pl)* de vitesse de motos; **~y** *adj* rapide, prompt(e)

spell [spɛl] (*pt, pp* spelt *or* spelled) *n* (*also:* **magic ~**) sortilège *m*, charme *m*; (*period of time*) (courte) période ♦ *vt* (*in writing*) écrire, orthographier; (*aloud*) épeler; (*fig*) signifier; **to cast a ~ on sb** jeter un sort à qn; **he can't ~** il fait des fautes d'orthographe; **~bound** *adj* envoûté(e), subjugué(e); **~ing** *n* orthographe *f*

spend [spɛnd] (*pt, pp* spent) *vt* (*money*) dépenser; (*time, life*) passer; consacrer; **~thrift** *n* dépensier(-ère)

sperm [spɑːm] *n* sperme *m*

sphere [sfɪər] *n* sphère *f*

spice [spaɪs] *n* épice *f*; **spicy** *adj* épicé(e), relevé(e); (*fig*) piquant(e)

spider ['spaɪdər] *n* araignée *f*

spike [spaɪk] *n* pointe *f*; (*BOT*) épi *m*

spill [spɪl] (*pt, pp* spilt *or* spilled) *vt* renverser; répandre ♦ *vi* se répandre; **~ over** *vi* déborder

spin [spɪn] (*pt* spun *or* span, *pp* spun) *n* (*revolution of wheel*) tour *m*; (*AVIAT*) (chute *f* en) vrille *f*; (*trip in car*) petit tour, balade *f* ♦ *vt* (*wool etc*) filer; (*wheel*) faire tourner

♦ *vi* filer; (*turn*) tourner, tournoyer

spinach ['spɪnɪtʃ] *n* épinard *m*; (*as food*) épinards

spinal ['spaɪnl] *adj* vertébral(e), spinal(e); **~ cord** *n* moelle épinière

spin doctor *n personne employée pour présenter un parti politique sous un jour favorable*

spin-dryer [spɪn'draɪər] (*BRIT*) *n* essoreuse *f*

spine [spaɪn] *n* colonne vertébrale; (*thorn*) épine *f*; **~less** *adj* (*fig*) mou (molle)

spinning ['spɪnɪŋ] *n* (*of thread*) filature *f*; **~ top** *n* toupie *f*

spin-off ['spɪnɔf] *n* avantage inattendu; sous-produit *m*

spinster ['spɪnstər] *n* célibataire *f*; vieille fille (*péj*)

spiral ['spaɪərl] *n* spirale *f* ♦ *vi* (*fig*) monter en flèche; **~ staircase** *n* escalier *m* en colimaçon

spire ['spaɪər] *n* flèche *f*, aiguille *f*

spirit ['spɪrɪt] *n* esprit *m*; (*mood*) état *m* d'esprit; (*courage*) courage *m*, énergie *f*; **~s** *npl* (*drink*) spiritueux *mpl*, alcool *m*; **in good ~s** de bonne humeur; **~ed** *adj* vif (vive), fougueux(-euse), plein(e) d'allant; **~ual** *adj* spirituel(le); (*religious*) religieux(-euse)

spit [spɪt] (*pt, pp* **spat**) *n* (*for roasting*) broche *f*; (*saliva*) salive *f* ♦ *vi* cracher; (*sound*) crépiter

spite [spaɪt] *n* rancune *f*, dépit *m* ♦ *vt* contrarier, vexer; **in ~ of** en dépit de, malgré; **~ful** *adj* méchant(e), malveillant(e)

spittle ['spɪtl] *n* salive *f*; (*of animal*) bave *f*; (*spat out*) crachat *m*

splash [splæʃ] *n* (*sound*) plouf *m*; (*of colour*) tache *f* ♦ *vt* éclabousser ♦ *vi* (*also: ~ about*) barboter, patauger

spleen [spli:n] *n* (*ANAT*) rate *f*

splendid ['splɛndɪd] *adj* splendide, superbe, magnifique

splint [splɪnt] *n* attelle *f*, éclisse *f*

splinter ['splɪntər] *n* (*wood*) écharde *f*; (*glass*) éclat *m* ♦ *vi* se briser, se fendre

split [splɪt] (*pt, pp* **split**) *n* fente *f*, déchiru-

re *f*; (*fig: POL*) scission *f* ♦ *vt* diviser; (*work, profits*) partager, répartir ♦ *vi* (*divide*) se diviser; **~ up** *vi* (*couple*) se séparer, rompre; (*meeting*) se disperser

spoil [spɔɪl] (*pt, pp* **spoilt** *or* **spoiled**) *vt* (*damage*) abîmer; (*mar*) gâcher; (*child*) gâter; **~s** *npl* butin *m*; (*fig: profits*) bénéfices *npl*; **~sport** *n* trouble-fête *m*, rabat-joie *m*

spoke [spəuk] *pt of* **speak** ♦ *n* (*of wheel*) rayon *m*

spoken ['spəukn] *pp of* **speak**

spokesman ['spəuksmən], **spokeswoman** ['spəukswumən] (*irreg*) *n* porte-parole *m inv*

sponge [spʌndʒ] *n* éponge *f*; (*also: ~ cake*) ≈ biscuit *m* de Savoie ♦ *vt* éponger ♦ *vi*: **to ~ off** *or* **on** vivre aux crochets de; **~ bag** (*BRIT*) *n* trousse *f* de toilette

sponsor ['spɔnsər] *n* (*RADIO, TV, SPORT*) sponsor *m*; (*for application*) parrain *m*, marraine *f*; (*BRIT: for fund-raising event*) donateur(-trice) ♦ *vt* sponsoriser; parrainer; faire un don à; **~ship** *n* sponsoring *m*; parrainage *m*; dons *mpl*

spontaneous [spɔn'teɪnɪəs] *adj* spontané(e)

spooky ['spu:kɪ] (*inf*) *adj* qui donne la chair de poule

spool [spu:l] *n* bobine *f*

spoon [spu:n] *n* cuiller *f*; **~-feed** *vt* nourrir à la cuiller; (*fig*) mâcher le travail à; **~ful** *n* cuillerée *f*

sport [spɔ:t] *n* sport *m*; (*person*) chic type (*fille*) ♦ *vt* arborer; **~ing** *adj* sportif(-ive); **to give sb a ~ing chance** donner sa chance à qn; **~ jacket** (*US*) *n* = **sports jacket**; **~s car** *n* voiture *f* de sport; **~s jacket** (*BRIT*) *n* veste *f* de sport; **~sman** (*irreg*) *n* sportif *m*; **~smanship** *n* esprit sportif, sportivité *f*; **~swear** *n* vêtements *mpl* de sport; **~swoman** (*irreg*) *n* sportive *f*; **~y** *adj* sportif(-ive)

spot [spɔt] *n* tache *f*; (*dot: on pattern*) pois *m*; (*pimple*) bouton *m*; (*place*) endroit *m*, coin *m*; (*RADIO, TV: in programme: for person*) numéro *m*; (: *for activity*) rubrique *f*;

(*small amount*): **a ~ of** un peu de ♦ vt (*notice*) apercevoir, repérer; **on the ~** sur place, sur les lieux; (*immediately*) sur-le-champ; (*in difficulty*) dans l'embarras; **~ check** n sondage m, vérification ponctuelle; **~less** adj immaculé(e); **~light** n projecteur m; **~ted** adj (*fabric*) à pois; **~ty** adj (*face, person*) boutonneux(-euse)

spouse [spaus] n époux (épouse)

spout [spaut] n (*of jug*) bec m; (*of pipe*) orifice m ♦ vi jaillir

sprain [sprein] n entorse f, foulure f ♦ vt: **to ~ one's ankle** etc se fouler or se tordre la cheville etc

sprang [spræŋ] pt of **spring**

sprawl [sprɔːl] vi s'étaler

spray [sprei] n jet m (en fines gouttelettes); (*from sea*) embruns mpl, vaporisateur m; (*for garden*) pulvérisateur m; (*aerosol*) bombe f; (*of flowers*) petit bouquet ♦ vt vaporiser, pulvériser; (*crops*) traiter

spread [spred] (*pt, pp* **spread**) n (*distribution*) répartition f; (*CULIN*) pâte f à tartiner; (*inf: meal*) festin m ♦ vt étendre, étaler; répandre; (*wealth, workload*) distribuer ♦ vi (*disease, news*) se propager; (*also: ~ out: stain*) s'étaler; **~ out** vi (*people*) se disperser; **~-eagled** adj étendu(e) bras et jambes écartés; **~sheet** n (*COMPUT*) tableur m

spree [spriː] n: **to go on a ~** faire la fête

sprightly ['spraitli] adj alerte

spring [spriŋ] (*pt* **sprang**, *pp* **sprung**) n (*leap*) bond m, saut m; (*coiled metal*) ressort m; (*season*) printemps m; (*of water*) source f ♦ vi (*leap*) bondir, sauter; **in ~** au printemps; **to ~ from** provenir de; **~ up** vi (*problem*) se présenter, surgir; (*plant, buildings*) surgir de terre; **~board** n tremplin m; **~-clean(ing)** n grand nettoyage de printemps; **~time** n printemps m

sprinkle ['spriŋkl] vt: **to ~ water** etc **on, ~ with water** etc asperger d'eau etc; **to ~ sugar** etc **on, ~ with sugar** etc saupoudrer de sucre etc; **~r** n (*for lawn*) arroseur m; (*to put out fire*) diffuseur m d'extincteur automatique d'incendie

sprint [sprint] n sprint m ♦ vi courir à toute vitesse; (*SPORT*) sprinter; **~er** n sprinteur(-euse)

sprout [spraut] vi germer, pousser; **~s** npl (*also:* **Brussels ~s**) choux mpl de Bruxelles

spruce [spruːs] n inv épicéa m ♦ adj net(te), pimpant(e)

sprung [sprʌŋ] pp of **spring**

spun [spʌn] pt, pp of **spin**

spur [spəːr] n éperon m; (*fig*) aiguillon m ♦ vt (*also:* **~ on**) éperonner; aiguillonner; **on the ~ of the moment** sous l'impulsion du moment

spurious ['spjuəriəs] adj faux (fausse)

spurn [spəːn] vt repousser avec mépris

spurt [spəːt] n (*of blood*) jaillissement m; (*of energy*) regain m, sursaut m ♦ vi jaillir, gicler

spy [spai] n espion(ne) ♦ vi: **to ~ on** espionner, épier; (*see*) apercevoir; **~ing** n espionnage m

sq. abbr = **square**

squabble ['skwɔbl] vi se chamailler

squad [skwɔd] n (*MIL, POLICE*) escouade f, groupe m; (*FOOTBALL*) contingent m

squadron ['skwɔdrn] n (*MIL*) escadron m; (*AVIAT, NAUT*) escadrille f

squalid ['skwɔlid] adj sordide

squall [skwɔːl] n rafale f, bourrasque f

squalor ['skwɔlər] n conditions fpl sordides

squander ['skwɔndər] vt gaspiller, dilapider

square [skwɛər] n carré m; (*in town*) place f ♦ adj carré(e); (*inf: ideas, tastes*) vieux jeu inv ♦ vt (*arrange*) régler; arranger; (*MATH*) élever au carré ♦ vi (*reconcile*) concilier; **all ~** quitte; à égalité; **a ~ meal** un repas convenable; **2 metres ~** (de) 2 mètres sur 2; **2 ~ metres** 2 mètres carrés; **~ly** adv carrément

squash [skwɔʃ] n (*BRIT: drink*): **lemon/orange ~** citronnade f/orangeade f; (*US: marrow*) courge f; (*SPORT*) squash m ♦ vt écraser

squat [skwɔt] adj petit(e) et épais(se), ramassé(e) ♦ vi (*also:* **~ down**) s'accroupir;

~ter n squatter m

squeak [skwi:k] vi grincer, crier; (mouse) pousser un petit cri

squeal [skwi:l] vi pousser un or des cri(s) aigu(s) or perçant(s); (brakes) grincer

squeamish ['skwi:mɪʃ] adj facilement dégoûté(e)

squeeze [skwi:z] n pression f; (ECON) restrictions fpl de crédit ♦ vt presser; (hand, arm) serrer; **~ out** vt exprimer

squelch [skweltʃ] vi faire un bruit de succion

squid [skwɪd] n calmar m

squiggle ['skwɪɡl] n gribouillis m

squint [skwɪnt] vi loucher ♦ n: **he has a ~** il louche, il souffre de strabisme

squirm [skwə:m] vi se tortiller

squirrel ['skwɪrəl] n écureuil m

squirt [skwə:t] vi jaillir, gicler

Sr abbr = **senior**

St abbr = **saint**; **street**

stab [stæb] n (with knife etc) coup m (de couteau etc); (of pain) lancée f; (inf: try): **to have a ~ at (doing) sth** s'essayer à (faire) qch ♦ vt poignarder

stable ['steɪbl] n écurie f ♦ adj stable

stack [stæk] n tas m, pile f ♦ vt (also: ~ up) empiler, entasser

stadium ['steɪdɪəm] (pl stadia or ~s) n stade m

staff [stɑ:f] n (workforce) personnel m; (BRIT: SCOL) professeurs mpl ♦ vt pourvoir en personnel

stag [stæɡ] n cerf m

stage [steɪdʒ] n scène f; (platform) estrade f ♦ n (point) étape f, stade m; (profession): **the ~** le théâtre ♦ vt (play) monter, mettre en scène; (demonstration) organiser; **in ~s** par étapes, par degrés; **~coach** n diligence f; **~ manager** n régisseur m

stagger ['stæɡər] vi chanceler, tituber ♦ vt (person: amaze) stupéfier; (hours, holidays) étaler, échelonner; **~ing** adj (amazing) stupéfiant(e), renversant(e)

stagnate [stæɡ'neɪt] vi stagner, croupir

stag party n enterrement m de vie de garçon

staid [steɪd] adj posé(e), rassis(e)

stain [steɪn] n tache f; (colouring) colorant m ♦ vt tacher; (wood) teindre; **~ed glass window** n vitrail m; **~less steel** n acier m inoxydable, inox m; **~ remover** n détachant m

stair [steər] n (step) marche f; **~s** npl (flight of steps) escalier m; **~case**, **~way** n escalier m

stake [steɪk] n pieu m, poteau m; (BETTING) enjeu m; (COMM: interest) intérêts mpl ♦ vt risquer, jouer; **to be at ~** être en jeu; **to ~ one's claim (to)** revendiquer

stale [steɪl] adj (bread) rassis(e); (food) pas frais (fraîche); (beer) éventé(e); (smell) de renfermé; (air) confiné(e)

stalemate ['steɪlmeɪt] n (CHESS) pat m; (fig) impasse f

stalk [stɔ:k] n tige f ♦ vt traquer ♦ vi: **to ~ out/off** sortir/partir d'un air digne

stall [stɔ:l] n (BRIT: in street, market etc) éventaire m, étal m; (in stable) stalle f ♦ vt (AUT) caler; (delay) retarder ♦ vi (AUT) caler; (fig) essayer de gagner du temps; **~s** npl (BRIT: in cinema, theatre) orchestre m

stallion ['stæljən] n étalon m (cheval)

stamina ['stæmɪnə] n résistance f, endurance f

stammer ['stæmər] n bégaiement m ♦ vi bégayer

stamp [stæmp] n timbre m; (rubber ~) tampon m; (mark, also fig) empreinte f ♦ vi (also: **~ one's foot**) taper du pied ♦ vt (letter) timbrer; (with rubber ~) tamponner; **~ album** n album m de timbres(-poste); **~ collecting** n philatélie f

stampede [stæm'pi:d] n ruée f

stance [stæns] n position f

stand [stænd] (pt, pp **stood**) n (position) position f; (for taxis) station f (de taxis); (music ~) pupitre m à musique; (COMM) étalage m, stand m; (SPORT: also: **~s**) tribune f ♦ vi être or se tenir (debout); (rise) se lever, se mettre debout; (be placed) se trouver; (remain: offer etc) rester valable; (BRIT: in election) être candidat(e), se présenter ♦ vt (place) mettre, poser; (tolerate, *withstand*) supporter; (*treat, invite to*) offrir, payer; **to make** *or* **take a ~** prendre position; **to ~ at** (*score, value etc*) être de; **to ~ for parliament** (*BRIT*) se présenter aux élections législatives; **~ by** *vi* (*be ready*) se tenir prêt(e) ♦ *vt fus* (*opinion*) s'en tenir à; (*person*) ne pas abandonner, soutenir; **down** *vi* (*withdraw*) se retirer; **~ for** *vt fus* (*signify*) représenter, signifier; (*tolerate*) supporter, tolérer; **~ in for** *vt fus* remplacer; **~ out** *vi* (*be prominent*) ressortir; **up** *vi* (*rise*) se lever, se mettre debout; **~ up for** *vt fus* défendre; **~ up to** *vt fus* tenir tête à, résister à

standard ['stændəd] *n* (*level*) niveau (voulu); (*norm*) norme *f*, étalon *m*; (*criterion*) critère *m*; (*flag*) étendard *m* ♦ *adj* (*size etc*) ordinaire, normal(e); courant(e); (*text*) de base; **~s** *npl* (*morals*) morale *f*, principes *mpl*; **~ lamp** (*BRIT*) *n* lampadaire *m*; **~ of living** *n* niveau *m* de vie

stand-by ['stændbaɪ] *n* remplaçant(e); **to be on ~-~** se tenir prêt(e) (à intervenir); être de garde; **~-~ ticket** *n* (*AVIAT*) billet *m* stand-by

stand-in ['stændɪn] *n* remplaçant(e)

standing ['stændɪŋ] *adj* debout *inv*; (*permanent*) permanent(e) ♦ *n* réputation *f*, rang *m*, standing *m*; **of many years'** ~ qui dure *or* existe depuis longtemps; **~ joke** *n* vieux sujet de plaisanterie; **~ order** (*BRIT*) *n* (*at bank*) virement *m* automatique, prélèvement *m* bancaire; **~ room** *n* places *fpl* debout

standpoint ['stændpɔɪnt] *n* point *m* de vue

standstill ['stændstɪl] *n*: **at a ~** paralysé(e); **to come to a ~** s'immobiliser, s'arrêter

stank [stæŋk] *pt of* **stink**

staple ['steɪpl] *n* (*for papers*) agrafe *f* ♦ *adj* (*food etc*) de base ♦ *vt* agrafer; **~r** *n* agrafeuse *f*

star [stɑːʳ] *n* étoile *f*; (*celebrity*) vedette *f* ♦ *vi*: **to ~ (in)** être la vedette (de) ♦ *vt* (*CINEMA etc*) avoir pour vedette; **the ~s** *npl* l'horoscope *m*

starboard ['stɑːbɔːd] *n* tribord *m*

starch [stɑːtʃ] *n* amidon *m*; (*in food*) fécule *f*

stardom ['stɑːdəm] *n* célébrité *f*

stare [steəʳ] *n* regard *m* fixe ♦ *vi*: **to ~ at** regarder fixement

starfish ['stɑːfɪʃ] *n* étoile *f* de mer

stark [stɑːk] *adj* (*bleak*) désolé(e), morne ♦ *adv*: **~ naked** complètement nu(e)

starling ['stɑːlɪŋ] *n* étourneau *m*

starry ['stɑːrɪ] *adj* étoilé(e); **~-eyed** *adj* (*innocent*) ingénu(e)

start [stɑːt] *n* commencement *m*, début *m*; (*of race*) départ *m*; (*sudden movement*) sursaut *m*; (*advantage*) avance *f*, avantage *m* ♦ *vt* commencer; (*found*) créer; (*engine*) mettre en marche ♦ *vi* partir, se mettre en route; (*jump*) sursauter; **to ~ doing** *or* **to do sth** se mettre à faire qch; **~ off** *vi* commencer; (*leave*) partir; **~ up** *vi* commencer; (*car*) démarrer ♦ *vt* (*business*) créer; (*car*) mettre en marche; **~er** *n* (*AUT*) démarreur *m*; (*SPORT: official*) starter *m*; (*BRIT: CULIN*) entrée *f*; **~ing point** *n* point *m* de départ

startle ['stɑːtl] *vt* faire sursauter; donner un choc à; **startling** *adj* (*news*) surprenant(e)

starvation [stɑːˈveɪʃən] *n* faim *f*, famine *f*

starve [stɑːv] *vi* mourir de faim; être affamé(e) ♦ *vt* affamer

state [steɪt] *n* état *m*; (*POL*) État ♦ *vt* déclarer, affirmer; **the S~s** *npl* (*America*) les États-Unis *mpl*; **to be in a ~** être dans tous ses états; **~ly** *adj* majestueux(-euse), imposant(e); **~ly home** *n* château *m*; **~ment** *n* déclaration *f*; **~sman** (*irreg*) *n* homme *m* d'État

static ['stætɪk] *n* (*RADIO, TV*) parasites *mpl* ♦ *adj* statique

station ['steɪʃən] *n* gare *f*; (*police ~*) poste *m* de police ♦ *vt* placer, poster

stationary ['steɪʃnərɪ] *adj* à l'arrêt, immobile

stationer ['steɪʃənəʳ] *n* papetier(-ère); **~'s (shop)** *n* papeterie *f*; **~y** *n* papier *m* à lettres, petit matériel de bureau

stationmaster ['steɪʃənmɑːstəʳ] n (RAIL) chef m de gare
station wagon (US) n break m
statistic n statistique f; **~s** [stə'tɪstɪks] n (science) statistique f
statue ['stætjuː] n statue f
status ['steɪtəs] n position f, situation f; (official) statut m; (prestige) prestige m; **~ symbol** n signe extérieur de richesse
statute ['stætjuːt] n loi f, statut m; **statutory** adj statutaire, prévu(e) par un article de loi
staunch [stɔːntʃ] adj sûr(e), loyal(e)
stay [steɪ] n (period of time) séjour m ♦ vi rester; (reside) loger; (spend some time) séjourner; **to ~ put** ne pas bouger; **to ~ with friends** loger chez des amis; **to ~ the night** passer la nuit; **~ behind** vi rester en arrière; **~ in** vi (at home) rester à la maison; **~ on** vi rester; **~ out** vi (of house) ne pas rentrer; **~ up** vi (at night) ne pas se coucher; **~ing power** n endurance f
stead [stɛd] n: **in sb's ~** à la place de qn, **to stand sb in good ~** être très utile à qn
steadfast ['stɛdfɑːst] adj ferme, résolu(e)
steadily ['stɛdɪlɪ] adv (regularly) progressivement; (firmly) fermement; (: walk) d'un pas ferme; (fixedly: look) sans détourner les yeux
steady ['stɛdɪ] adj stable, solide, ferme; (regular) constant(e), régulier(-ère); (person) calme, pondéré(e) ♦ vt stabiliser; (nerves) calmer; **a ~ boyfriend** un petit ami
steak [steɪk] n (beef) bifteck m, steak m; (fish, pork) tranche f
steal [stiːl] (pt **stole**, pp **stolen**) vt voler ♦ vi voler; (move secretly) se faufiler, se déplacer furtivement
stealth [stɛlθ] n: **by ~** furtivement
steam [stiːm] n vapeur f ♦ vt (CULIN) cuire à la vapeur ♦ vi fumer; **~ engine** n locomotive f à vapeur; **~er** n (bateau m à) vapeur m; **~ship** n = **steamer**; **~y** adj embué(e), humide
steel [stiːl] n acier m ♦ adj d'acier;

~works n aciérie f
steep [stiːp] adj raide, escarpé(e); (price) excessif(-ive)
steeple ['stiːpl] n clocher m
steer [stɪəʳ] vt diriger; (boat) gouverner; (person) guider, conduire ♦ vi tenir le gouvernail; **~ing** n (AUT) conduite f; **~ing wheel** n volant m
stem [stɛm] n (of plant) tige f; (of glass) pied m ♦ vt contenir, endiguer, juguler; **~ from** vt fus provenir de, découler de
stench [stɛntʃ] n puanteur f
stencil ['stɛnsl] n stencil m; (pattern used) pochoir m ♦ vt polycopier
stenographer [stɛ'nɔɡrəfəʳ] (US) n sténographe m/f
step [stɛp] n pas m; (stair) marche f; (action) mesure f, disposition f ♦ vi: **to ~ forward/back** faire un pas en avant/ arrière, avancer/reculer; **~s** npl (BRIT) = **stepladder**; **to be in/out of ~ (with)** (fig) aller dans le sens (de)/être déphasé(e) (par rapport à); **~ down** vi (fig) se retirer, se désister; **~ up** vt augmenter; intensifier; **~brother** n demi-frère m; **~daughter** n belle-fille f; **~father** n beau-père m; **~ladder** (BRIT) n escabeau m; **~mother** n belle-mère f; **~ping stone** n pierre f de gué; (fig) tremplin m; **~sister** n demi-sœur f; **~son** n beau-fils m
stereo ['stɛrɪəu] n (sound) stéréo f; (hi-fi) chaîne f stéréo inv ♦ adj (also: **~phonic**) stéréo(phonique)
sterile ['stɛraɪl] adj stérile; **sterilize** ['stɛrɪlaɪz] vt stériliser
sterling ['stɜːlɪŋ] adj (silver) de bon aloi, fin(e) ♦ n (ECON) livres fpl sterling inv; **a pound ~** une livre sterling
stern [stɜːn] adj sévère ♦ n (NAUT) arrière m, poupe f
stew [stjuː] n ragoût m ♦ vt, vi cuire (à la casserole)
steward ['stjuːəd] n (on ship, plane, train) steward m; **~ess** n hôtesse f (de l'air)
stick [stɪk] (pt, pp **stuck**) n bâton m; (walking ~) canne f ♦ vt (glue) coller; (inf: put) mettre, fourrer; (: tolerate) supporter;

(*thrust*): **to ~ sth into** planter *or* enfoncer qch dans ♦ *vi* (*become attached*) rester collé(e) *or* fixé(e); (*be unmoveable: wheels etc*) se bloquer; (*remain*) rester; **~ out** *vi* dépasser, sortir; **~ up** *vi* = **stick out**; **~ up for** *vt fus* défendre; **~er** *n* auto-collant *m*; **~ing plaster** *n* sparadrap *m*, pansement adhésif

stick-up ['stɪkʌp] (*inf*) *n* braquage *m*, hold-up *m inv*

sticky ['stɪkɪ] *adj* poisseux(-euse); (*label*) adhésif(-ive); (*situation*) délicat(e)

stiff [stɪf] *adj* raide; rigide; dur(e); (*difficult*) difficile, ardu(e); (*cold*) froid(e), distant(e); (*strong, high*) fort(e), élevé(e) ♦ *adv*: **to be bored/scared/frozen ~** s'ennuyer à mort/être mort(e) de peur/froid; **~en** *vi* se raidir; **~ neck** *n* torticolis *m*

stifle ['staɪfl] *vt* étouffer, réprimer

stigma ['stɪgmə] *n* stigmate *m*

stile [staɪl] *n* échalier *m*

stiletto [stɪ'letəʊ] (*BRIT*) *n* (*also: ~ heel*) talon *m* aiguille

still [stɪl] *adj* immobile ♦ *adv* (*up to this time*) encore, toujours; (*even*) encore; (*nonetheless*) quand même, tout de même; **~born** *adj* mort-né(e); **~ life** *n* nature morte

stilt [stɪlt] *n* (*for walking on*) échasse *f*; (*pile*) pilotis *m*

stilted ['stɪltɪd] *adj* guindé(e), emprunté(e)

stimulate ['stɪmjʊleɪt] *vt* stimuler

stimuli ['stɪmjʊlaɪ] *npl of* **stimulus**

stimulus ['stɪmjʊləs] (*pl* **stimuli**) *n* stimulant *m*; (*BIOL, PSYCH*) stimulus *m*

sting [stɪŋ] (*pt, pp* **stung**) *n* piqûre *f*; (*organ*) dard *m* ♦ *vt, vi* piquer

stingy ['stɪndʒɪ] *adj* avare, pingre

stink [stɪŋk] (*pt* **stank**, *pp* **stunk**) *n* puanteur *f* ♦ *vi* puer, empester; **~ing** (*inf*) *adj* (*fig*) infect(e), vache; **a ~ing ...** un(e) foutu(e) ...

stint [stɪnt] *n* part *f* de travail ♦ *vi*: **to ~ on** lésiner sur, être chiche de

stir [stɜ:ʳ] *n* agitation *f*, sensation *f* ♦ *vt* remuer ♦ *vi* remuer, bouger; **~ up** *vt* (*trouble*) fomenter, provoquer

stirrup ['stɪrəp] *n* étrier *m*

stitch [stɪtʃ] *n* (*SEWING*) point *m*; (*KNITTING*) maille *f*; (*MED*) point de suture; (*pain*) point de côté ♦ *vt* coudre, piquer; (*MED*) suturer

stoat [stəʊt] *n* hermine *f* (*avec son pelage d'été*)

stock [stɒk] *n* réserve *f*, provision *f*; (*COMM*) stock *m*; (*AGR*) cheptel *m*, bétail *m*; (*CULIN*) bouillon *m*; (*descent, origin*) souche *f*; (*FINANCE*) valeurs *fpl*, titres *mpl* ♦ *adj* (*fig: reply etc*) classique ♦ *vt* (*have in ~*) avoir, vendre; **~s and shares** valeurs (mobilières), titres; **in/out of ~** en stock *or* en magasin/épuisé(e); **to take ~ of** (*fig*) faire le point de; **~ up** *vi*: **to ~ up (with)** s'approvisionner (en); **~broker** *n* agent *m* de change; **~ cube** *n* bouillon-cube *m*; **~ exchange** *n* Bourse *f*

stocking ['stɒkɪŋ] *n* bas *m*

stock: **~ market** *n* Bourse *f*, marché financier; **~pile** *n* stock *m*, réserve *f* ♦ *vt* stocker, accumuler; **~taking** (*BRIT*) *n* (*COMM*) inventaire *m*

stocky ['stɒkɪ] *adj* trapu(e), râblé(e)

stodgy ['stɒdʒɪ] *adj* bourratif(-ive), lourd(e)

stoke [stəʊk] *vt* (*fire*) garnir, entretenir; (*boiler*) chauffer

stole [stəʊl] *pt of* **steal** ♦ *n* étole *f*

stolen ['stəʊln] *pp of* **steal**

stomach ['stʌmək] *n* estomac *m*; (*abdomen*) ventre *m* ♦ *vt* digérer, supporter; **~ache** *n* mal *m* à l'estomac *or* au ventre

stone [stəʊn] *n* pierre *f*; (*pebble*) caillou *m*, galet *m*; (*in fruit*) noyau *m*; (*MED*) calcul *m*; (*BRIT: weight*) **6,348 kg** ♦ *adj* de *or* en pierre ♦ *vt* (*person*) lancer des pierres sur, lapider; **~-cold** *adj* complètement froid(e); **~-deaf** *adj* sourd(e) comme un pot; **~work** *n* maçonnerie *f*

stood [stʊd] *pt, pp of* **stand**

stool [stu:l] *n* tabouret *m*

stoop [stu:p] *vi* (*also: have a ~*) être voûté(e); (*also: ~ down: bend*) se baisser

stop [stɒp] *n* arrêt *m*; halte *f*; (*in punctuation: also: full ~*) point *m* ♦ *vt* arrêter, bloquer; (*break off*) interrompre; (*also: put a*

~ to) mettre fin à ♦ *vi* s'arrêter; (*rain, noise etc*) cesser, s'arrêter; **to ~ doing sth** cesser *or* arrêter de faire qch; **~ dead** *vi* s'arrêter net; **~ off** *vi* faire une courte halte; **~ up** *vt* (*hole*) boucher; **~gap** *n* (*person*) bouche-trou *m*; (*measure*) mesure *f* intérimaire; **~over** *n* halte *f*; (AVIAT) escale *f*; **~page** *n* (*strike*) arrêt de travail; (*blockage*) obstruction *f*; **~per** *n* bouchon *m*; **~ press** *n* nouvelles *fpl* de dernière heure; **~watch** *n* chronomètre *m*

storage ['stɔ:rɪdʒ] *n* entreposage *m*; **~ heater** *n* radiateur *m* électrique par accumulation

store [stɔ:ʳ] *n* (*stock*) provision *f*, réserve *f*; (*depot*) entrepôt *m*; (BRIT: *large shop*) grand magasin; (US) magasin *m* ♦ *vt* emmagasiner; (*information*) enregistrer; **~s** *npl* (*food*) provisions *fpl*; **in ~** en réserve; **~ up** *vt* mettre en réserve; accumuler; **~room** *n* réserve *f*, magasin *m*

storey ['stɔ:rɪ] (US **story**) *n* étage *m*

stork [stɔ:k] *n* cigogne *f*

storm [stɔ:m] *n* tempête *f*; (*thunderstorm*) orage *m* ♦ *vi* (*fig*) fulminer ♦ *vt* prendre d'assaut; **~y** *adj* orageux(euse)

story ['stɔ:rɪ] *n* histoire *f*; récit *m*; (US) = **storey**; **~book** *n* livre *m* d'histoires *or* de contes

stout [staut] *adj* solide; (*fat*) gros(se), corpulent(e) ♦ *n* bière brune

stove [stəuv] *n* (*for cooking*) fourneau *m*; (: *small*) réchaud *m*; (*for heating*) poêle *m*

stow [stəu] *vt* (*also*: **~ away**) ranger; **~away** *n* passager(-ère) clandestin(e)

straddle ['strædl] *vt* enjamber, être à cheval sur

straggle ['strægl] *vi* être (*or* marcher) en désordre

straight [streit] *adj* droit(e); (*hair*) raide; (*frank*) honnête, franc (franche); (*simple*) simple ♦ *adv* (tout) droit; (*drink*) sec, sans eau; **to put** *or* **get ~** (*fig*) mettre au clair; **~ away**, **~ off** (*at once*) tout de suite; **~en** *vt* ajuster; (*bed*) arranger; **~en out** *vt* (*fig*) débrouiller; **~-faced** *adj* impassible; **~forward** *adj* simple; (*honest*) direct(e)

strain [streɪn] *n* tension *f*; pression *f*; (*physical*) effort *m*; (*mental*) tension (nerveuse); (*breed*) race *f* ♦ *vt* (*stretch: resources etc*) mettre à rude épreuve, grever; (*hurt: back etc*) se faire mal à; (*vegetables*) égoutter; **~s** *npl* (MUS) accords *mpl*, accents *mpl*; **back ~** tour *m* de rein; **~ed** *adj* (*muscle*) froissé(e); (*laugh etc*) forcé(e), contraint(e); (*relations*) tendu(e); **~er** *n* passoire *f*

strait [streɪt] *n* (GEO) détroit *m*; **~s** *npl*: **to be in dire ~s** avoir de sérieux ennuis (d'argent); **~jacket** *n* camisole *f* de force; **~-laced** [streɪt'leɪst] *adj* collet monté *inv*

strand [strænd] *n* (*of thread*) fil *m*, brin *m*; (*of rope*) toron *m*; (*of hair*) mèche *f*; **~ed** *adj* en rade, en plan

strange [streɪndʒ] *adj* (*not known*) inconnu(e); (*odd*) étrange, bizarre; **~ly** *adv* étrangement, bizarrement; *see also* **enough**; **~r** *n* inconnu(e); (*from another area*) étranger(-ère)

strangle ['stræŋgl] *vt* étrangler; **~hold** *n* (*fig*) emprise totale, mainmise *f*

strap [stræp] *n* lanière *f*, courroie *f*, sangle *f*; (*of slip, dress*) bretelle *f*; **~py** *adj* (*dress*) à bretelles; (*sandals*) à lanières

strategic [strə'ti:dʒɪk] *adj* stratégique; **strategy** ['strætɪdʒɪ] *n* stratégie *f*

straw [strɔ:] *n* paille *f*; **that's the last ~!** ça, c'est le comble!

strawberry ['strɔ:bərɪ] *n* fraise *f*

stray [streɪ] *adj* (*animal*) perdu(e), errant(e); (*scattered*) isolé(e) ♦ *vi* s'égarer; **~ bullet** *n* balle perdue

streak [stri:k] *n* bande *f*, filet *m*; (*in hair*) raie *f* ♦ *vt* zébrer, strier ♦ *vi*: **to ~ past** passer à toute allure

stream [stri:m] *n* (*brook*) ruisseau *m*; (*current*) courant *m*, flot *m*; (*of people*) défilé *m* ininterrompu, flot ♦ *vt* (SCOL) répartir par niveau ♦ *vi* ruisseler; **to ~ in/out** entrer/sortir à flots

streamer ['stri:məʳ] *n* serpentin *m*; (*banner*) banderole *f*

streamlined ['stri:mlaɪnd] *adj* aérodynamique; (*fig*) rationalisé(e)

street [stri:t] *n* rue *f*; **~car** (US) *n* tramway

m; **~ lamp** *n* réverbère *m*; **~ plan** *n* plan *m* (des rues); **~wise** (*inf*) *adj* futé(e), réaliste

strength [strɛŋθ] *n* force *f*; (*of girder, knot etc*) solidité *f*; **~en** *vt* (*muscle etc*) fortifier; (*nation, case etc*) renforcer; (*building, ECON*) consolider

strenuous ['strɛnjuəs] *adj* vigoureux(-euse), énergique

stress [strɛs] *n* (*force, pressure*) pression *f*; (*mental strain*) tension (nerveuse), stress *m*; (*accent*) accent *m* ♦ *vt* insister sur, souligner

stretch [strɛtʃ] *n* (*of sand etc*) étendue *f* ♦ *vi* s'étirer; (*extend*): **to ~ to** *or* **as far as** s'étendre jusqu'à ♦ *vt* tendre, étirer; (*fig*) pousser (au maximum); **~ out** *vi* s'étendre ♦ *vt* (*arm etc*) allonger, tendre; (*spread*) étendre

stretcher ['strɛtʃər] *n* brancard *m*, civière *f*

stretchy ['strɛtʃi] *adj* élastique

strewn [struːn] *adj*: **~ with** jonché(e) de

stricken ['strɪkən] *adj* (*person*) très éprouvé(e); (*city, industry etc*) dévasté(e); **~ with** (*disease etc*) frappé(e) *or* atteint(e) de

strict [strɪkt] *adj* strict(e)

stride [straɪd] (*pt* **strode**, *pp* **stridden**) *n* grand pas *m*, enjambée *f* ♦ *vi* marcher à grands pas

strife [straɪf] *n* conflit *m*, dissensions *fpl*

strike [straɪk] (*pt, pp* **struck**) *n* grève *f*; (*of oil etc*) découverte *f*; (*attack*) raid *m* ♦ *vt* frapper; (*oil etc*) trouver, découvrir; (*deal*) conclure ♦ *vi* faire grève; (*attack*) attaquer; (*clock*) sonner; **on ~** (*workers*) en grève; **to ~ a match** frotter une allumette; **~ down** *vt* terrasser; **~ up** *vt* (*MUS*) se mettre à jouer; **to ~ up a friendship with** se lier d'amitié avec; **to ~ up a conversation (with)** engager une conversation (avec); **~r** *n* gréviste *m/f*; (*SPORT*) buteur *m*; **striking** *adj* frappant(e), saisissant(e); (*attractive*) éblouissant(e)

string [strɪŋ] (*pt, pp* **strung**) *n* ficelle *f*; (*row: of beads*) rang *m*; (: *of onions*) chapelet *m*; (*MUS*) corde *f* ♦ *vt*: **to ~ out** échelonner; **the ~s** *npl* (*MUS*) les instruments

mpl à cordes; **to ~ together** enchaîner; **to pull ~s** (*fig*) faire jouer le piston; **~(ed) instrument** *n* (*MUS*) instrument *m* à cordes

stringent ['strɪndʒənt] *adj* rigoureux(-euse)

strip [strɪp] *n* bande *f* ♦ *vt* (*undress*) déshabiller; (*paint*) décaper; (*also*: **~ down**: *machine*) démonter ♦ *vi* se déshabiller; **~ cartoon** *n* bande dessinée

stripe [straɪp] *n* raie *f*, rayure *f*; (*MIL*) galon *m*; **~d** *adj* rayé(e), à rayures

strip: ~ lighting (*BRIT*) *n* éclairage *m* au néon *or* fluorescent; **~per** *n* stripteaseur(-euse) *f*; **~ search** *n* fouille corporelle (*en faisant se déshabiller la personne*) ♦ *vt*: **he was ~ searched** on l'a fait déshabiller et soumis à une fouille corporelle

stripy ['straɪpɪ] *adj* rayé(e)

strive [straɪv] (*pt* **strove**, *pp* **striven**) *vi*: **to ~ to do/for sth** s'efforcer de faire/ d'obtenir qch

strode [strəʊd] *pt of* **stride**

stroke [strəʊk] *n* coup *m*; (*SWIMMING*) nage *f*; (*MED*) attaque *f* ♦ *vt* caresser; **at a ~** d'un (seul) coup

stroll [strəʊl] *n* petite promenade ♦ *vi* flâner, se promener nonchalamment; **~er** (*US*) *n* (*pushchair*) poussette *f*

strong [strɒŋ] *adj* fort(e); vigoureux(-euse); (*heart, nerves*) solide; **they are 50 ~** ils sont au nombre de 50; **~hold** *n* bastion *m*; **~ly** *adv* fortement, avec force; vigoureusement; solidement; **~room** *n* chambre forte

strove [strəʊv] *pt of* **strive**

struck [strʌk] *pt, pp of* **strike**

structural ['strʌktʃrəl] *adj* structural(e); (*CONSTR: defect*) de construction; (*damage*) affectant les parties portantes

structure ['strʌktʃər] *n* structure *f*; (*building*) construction *f*

struggle ['strʌgl] *n* lutte *f* ♦ *vi* lutter, se battre

strum [strʌm] *vt* (*guitar*) jouer (en sourdine) de

strung [strʌŋ] *pt, pp of* **string**

strut [strʌt] n étai m, support m ♦ vi se pavaner

stub [stʌb] n (of cigarette) bout m, mégot m; (of cheque etc) talon m ♦ vt: **to ~ one's toe** se cogner le doigt de pied; **~ out** vt écraser

stubble ['stʌbl] n chaume m; (on chin) barbe f de plusieurs jours

stubborn ['stʌbən] adj têtu(e), obstiné(e), opiniâtre

stuck [stʌk] pt, pp of **stick** ♦ adj (jammed) bloqué(e), coincé(e); **~-up** (inf) adj prétentieux(-euse)

stud [stʌd] n (on boots etc) clou m; (on collar) bouton m de col; (earring) petite boucle d'oreille; (of horses: also: ~ **farm**) écurie f, haras m; (also: ~ **horse**) étalon m ♦ vt (fig): **~ded with** parsemé(e) or criblé(e) de

student ['stju:dənt] n étudiant(e) ♦ adj estudiantin(e); d'étudiant; ~ **driver** (US) n (conducteur(-trice)) débutant(e)

studio ['stju:dɪəu] n studio m, atelier m; (TV etc) studio

studious ['stju:dɪəs] adj studieux(-euse), appliqué(e); (attention) soutenu(e); **~ly** adv (carefully) soigneusement

study ['stʌdɪ] n étude f; (room) bureau m ♦ vt étudier; (examine) examiner ♦ vi étudier, faire ses études

stuff [stʌf] n chose(s) f(pl); affaires fpl, trucs mpl; (substance) substance f ♦ vt rembourrer; (CULIN) farcir; (inf: push) fourrer; **~ing** n bourre f, rembourrage m; (CULIN) farce f; **~y** adj (room) mal ventilé(e) or aéré(e); (ideas) vieux jeu inv

stumble ['stʌmbl] vi trébucher; **to ~ across** or **on** (fig) tomber sur; **stumbling block** n pierre f d'achoppement

stump [stʌmp] n souche f; (of limb) moignon m ♦ vt: **to be ~ed** sécher, ne pas savoir que répondre

stun [stʌn] vt étourdir; (fig) abasourdir

stung [stʌŋ] pt, pp of **sting**

stunk [stʌŋk] pp of **stink**

stunned [stʌnd] adj sidéré(e)

stunning ['stʌnɪŋ] adj (news etc) stupé-

fiant(e); (girl etc) éblouissant(e)

stunt [stʌnt] n (in film) cascade f, acrobatie f; (publicity ~) truc m publicitaire ♦ vt retarder, arrêter; **~man** ['stʌntmæn] (irreg) n cascadeur m

stupendous [stju:'pɛndəs] adj prodigieux(-euse), fantastique

stupid ['stju:pɪd] adj stupide, bête; **~ity** [stju:'pɪdɪtɪ] n stupidité f, bêtise f

sturdy ['stə:dɪ] adj robuste; solide

stutter ['stʌtəʳ] vi bégayer

sty [staɪ] n (for pigs) porcherie f

stye [staɪ] n (MED) orgelet m

style [staɪl] n style m; (distinction) allure f, cachet m, style; **stylish** adj élégant(e), chic inv

stylus ['staɪləs] (pl **styli** or **~es**) n (of record player) pointe f de lecture

suave [swɑ:v] adj doucereux(-euse), onctueux(-euse)

sub... [sʌb] prefix sub..., sous-; **~conscious** adj subconscient(e); **~contract** vt sous-traiter

subdue [səb'dju:] vt subjuguer, soumettre; **~d** adj (light) tamisé(e); (person) qui a perdu de son entrain

subject [n 'sʌbdʒɪkt, vb səb'dʒɛkt] n sujet m; (SCOL) matière f ♦ vt: **to ~ to** soumettre à; exposer à, **to be ~ to** (law) être soumis(e) à; (disease) être sujet(te) à; **~ive** [səb'dʒɛktɪv] adj subjectif(-ive); **~ matter** n (content) contenu m

sublet [sʌb'lɛt] vt sous-louer

submarine [sʌbmə'ri:n] n sous-marin m

submerge [səb'mə:dʒ] vt submerger ♦ vi plonger

submission [səb'mɪʃən] n soumission f; **submissive** adj soumis(e)

submit [səb'mɪt] vt soumettre ♦ vi se soumettre

subnormal [sʌb'nɔ:ml] adj au-dessous de la normale

subordinate [sə'bɔ:dɪnət] adj subalterne ♦ n subordonné(e)

subpoena [səb'pi:nə] n (LAW) citation f, assignation f

subscribe [səb'skraɪb] vi cotiser; **to ~ to**

(opinion, fund) souscrire à; (newspaper) s'abonner à; être abonné(e) à; **~r** n (to periodical, telephone) abonné(e); **subscription** [səb'skrɪpʃən] n (to magazine etc) abonnement m

subsequent ['sʌbsɪkwənt] adj ultérieur(e), suivant(e); consécutif(-ive); **~ly** adv par la suite

subside [səb'saɪd] vi (flood) baisser; (wind, feelings) tomber; **~nce** [səb'saɪdns] n affaissement m

subsidiary [səb'sɪdɪərɪ] adj subsidiaire; accessoire ♦ n filiale f

subsidize ['sʌbsɪdaɪz] vt subventionner; **subsidy** ['sʌbsɪdɪ] n subvention f

substance ['sʌbstəns] n substance f

substantial [səb'stænʃl] adj substantiel(le); (fig) important(e); **~ly** adv considérablement; (in essence) en grande partie

substantiate [səb'stænʃɪeɪt] vt étayer, fournir des preuves à l'appui de

substitute ['sʌbstɪtjuːt] n (person) remplaçant(e); (thing) succédané m ♦ vt: **to ~ sth/sb for** substituer qch/qn à, remplacer par qch/qn

subterranean [sʌbtə'reɪnɪən] adj souterrain(e)

subtitle ['sʌbtaɪtl] n (CINEMA, TV) sous-titre m; **~d** adj sous-titré(e)

subtle ['sʌtl] adj subtil(e)

subtotal [sʌb'təutl] n total partiel

subtract [səb'trækt] vt soustraire, retrancher; **~ion** n soustraction f

suburb ['sʌbəːb] n faubourg m; **the ~s** npl la banlieue; **~an** [sə'bəːbən] adj de banlieue, suburbain(e); **~ia** [sə'bəːbɪə] n la banlieue

subway ['sʌbweɪ] n (US: railway) métro m; (BRIT: underpass) passage souterrain

succeed [sək'siːd] vi réussir ♦ vt succéder à; **to ~ in doing** réussir à faire; **~ing** adj (following) suivant(e)

success [sək'ses] n succès m; réussite f; **~ful** adj (venture) couronné(e) de succès; **to be ~ful (in doing)** réussir (à faire); **~fully** adv avec succès

succession [sək'seʃən] n succession f; **3 days in ~** 3 jours de suite

successive [sək'sesɪv] adj successif(-ive); consécutif(-ive)

such [sʌtʃ] adj tel (telle); (of that kind): **~ a book** un livre de ce genre, un livre pareil, un tel livre; (so much): **~ courage** un tel courage ♦ adv si; **~ books** des livres de ce genre, des livres pareils, de tels livres; **~ a long trip** un si long voyage; **~ a lot of** tellement or tant de; **~ as** (like) tel que, comme; **as ~** en tant que tel, à proprement parler; **~-and-~** adj tel ou tel

suck [sʌk] vt sucer; (breast, bottle) téter; **~er** n ventouse f; (inf) poire f

suction ['sʌkʃən] n succion f

sudden ['sʌdn] adj soudain(e), subit(e); **all of a ~** soudain, tout à coup; **~ly** adv brusquement, tout à coup, soudain

suds [sʌdz] npl eau savonneuse

sue [suː] vt poursuivre en justice, intenter un procès à

suede [sweɪd] n daim m

suet ['suɪt] n graisse f de rognon

suffer ['sʌfər] vt souffrir, subir; (bear) tolérer, supporter ♦ vi souffrir; **~er** n (MED) malade m/f; (in) n souffrance(s) f(pl)

sufficient [sə'fɪʃənt] adj suffisant(e); **~ money** suffisamment d'argent; **~ly** adv suffisamment, assez

suffocate ['sʌfəkeɪt] vi suffoquer; étouffer

sugar ['ʃugər] n sucre m ♦ vt sucrer; **~ beet** n betterave sucrière; **~ cane** n canne f à sucre

suggest [sə'dʒest] vt suggérer, proposer; (indicate) dénoter; **~ion** n suggestion f

suicide ['suɪsaɪd] n suicide m; see also **commit**

suit [suːt] n (man's) costume m, complet m; (woman's) tailleur m, ensemble m; (LAW) poursuite(s) f(pl), procès m; (CARDS) couleur f ♦ vt aller à; convenir à; (adapt): **to ~ sth to** adapter or approprier qch à; **well ~ed** (well matched) faits l'un pour l'autre, très bien assortis; **~able** adj qui convient; approprié(e); **~ably** adv comme il se doit (or se devait etc), convenablement

suitcase ['suːtkeɪs] *n* valise *f*

suite [swiːt] *n* (*of rooms, also* MUS) suite *f*; (*furniture*): **bedroom/dining room ~** (ensemble *m* de) chambre *f* à coucher/salle *f* à manger

suitor ['suːtəʳ] *n* soupirant *m*, prétendant *m*

sulfur ['sʌlfəʳ] (*US*) *n* = **sulphur**

sulk [sʌlk] *vi* bouder; **~y** *adj* boudeur(-euse), maussade

sullen ['sʌlən] *adj* renfrogné(e), maussade

sulphur ['sʌlfəʳ] (*US* **sulfur**) *n* soufre *m*

sultana [sʌl'tɑːnə] *n* (CULIN) raisin (sec) de Smyrne

sultry ['sʌltrɪ] *adj* étouffant(e)

sum [sʌm] *n* somme *f*; (SCOL *etc*) calcul *m*; **~ up** *vt*, *vi* résumer

summarize ['sʌməraɪz] *vt* résumer

summary ['sʌmərɪ] *n* résumé *m*

summer ['sʌməʳ] *n* été *m* ♦ *adj* d'été, estival(e); **~house** *n* (*in garden*) pavillon *m*; **~time** *n* été *m*; **~ time** *n* (*by clock*) heure *f* d'été

summit ['sʌmɪt] *n* sommet *m*

summon ['sʌmən] *vt* appeler, convoquer; **~ up** *vt* rassembler, faire appel à; **~s** *n* citation *f*, assignation *f*

sun [sʌn] *n* soleil *m*; **in the ~** au soleil; **~bathe** *vi* prendre un bain de soleil; **~block** *n* écran *m* total; **~burn** *n* coup *m* de soleil; **~burned**, **~burnt** *adj* (*tanned*) bronzé(e)

Sunday ['sʌndɪ] *n* dimanche *m*; **~ school** *n* ≈ catéchisme *m*

sundial ['sʌndaɪəl] *n* cadran *m* solaire

sundown ['sʌndaun] *n* coucher *m* du (*or* de) soleil

sundries ['sʌndrɪz] *npl* articles divers

sundry ['sʌndrɪ] *adj* divers(e), différent(e) ♦ *n*: **all and ~** tout le monde, n'importe qui

sunflower ['sʌnflauəʳ] *n* tournesol *m*

sung [sʌŋ] *pp of* **sing**

sunglasses ['sʌnɡlɑːsɪz] *npl* lunettes *fpl* de soleil

sunk [sʌŋk] *pp of* **sink**

sun: ~light *n* (lumière *f* du) soleil *m*; **~lit**

adj ensoleillé(e); **~ny** *adj* ensoleillé(e); **~rise** *n* lever *m* du (*or* de) soleil; **~ roof** *n* (AUT) toit ouvrant; **~screen** *n* crème *f* solaire; **~set** *n* coucher *m* du (*or* de) soleil; **~shade** *n* (*over table*) parasol *m*; **~shine** *n* (lumière *f* du) soleil *m*; **~stroke** *n* insolation *f*; **~tan** *n* bronzage *m*; **~tan lotion** *n* lotion *f* *or* lait *m* solaire; **~tan oil** *n* huile *f* solaire

super ['suːpəʳ] (*inf*) *adj* formidable

superannuation [suːpərænjʊ'eɪʃən] *n* (*contribution*) cotisations *fpl* pour la pension

superb [suː'pəːb] *adj* superbe, magnifique

supercilious [suːpə'sɪlɪəs] *adj* hautain(e), dédaigneux(-euse)

superficial [suːpə'fɪʃəl] *adj* superficiel(le)

superimpose ['suːpərɪm'pəuz] *vt* superposer

superintendent [suːpərɪn'tendənt] *n* directeur(-trice); (POLICE) ≈ commissaire *m*

superior [suː'pɪərɪəʳ] *adj*, *n* supérieur(e); **~ity** [supɪərɪ'ɔrɪtɪ] *n* supériorité *f*

superlative [suː'pəːlətɪv] *n* (LING) superlatif *m*

superman ['suːpəmæn] (*irreg*) *n* surhomme *m*

supermarket ['suːpəmɑːkɪt] *n* supermarché *m*

supernatural [suːpə'nætʃərəl] *adj* surnaturel(le)

superpower ['suːpəpauəʳ] *n* (POL) superpuissance *f*

supersede [suːpə'siːd] *vt* remplacer, supplanter

superstitious [suːpə'stɪʃəs] *adj* superstitieux(-euse)

supervise ['suːpəvaɪz] *vt* surveiller; diriger; **supervision** [suːpə'vɪʒən] *n* surveillance *f*; contrôle *m*; **supervisor** *n* surveillant(e); (*in shop*) chef *m* de rayon

supper ['sʌpəʳ] *n* dîner *m*; (*late*) souper *m*

supple ['sʌpl] *adj* souple

supplement [*n* 'sʌplɪmənt, *vb* sʌplɪ'mənt] *n* supplément *m* ♦ *vt* compléter; **~ary** [sʌplɪ'mentərɪ] *adj* supplémentaire; **~ary benefit** (BRIT) *n* allocation *f* (supplémentaire) d'aide sociale

supplier [sə'plaɪə⁽ʳ⁾] *n* fournisseur *m*

supply [sə'plaɪ] *vt* (*provide*) fournir; (*equip*):
to ~ (with) approvisionner *or* ravitailler
(en); fournir (en) ♦ *n* provision *f*, réserve
f; (~*ing*) approvisionnement *m*; **supplies**
npl (*food*) vivres *mpl*; (*MIL*) subsistances
fpl; ~ **teacher** (*BRIT*) *n* suppléant(e)

support [sə'pɔːt] *n* (*moral, financial etc*)
soutien *m*, appui *m*; (*TECH*) support *m*,
soutien ♦ *vt* soutenir, supporter; (*financial-
ly*) subvenir aux besoins de; (*uphold*) être
pour, être partisan de, appuyer; ~**er** *n*
(*POL etc*) partisan(e); (*SPORT*) supporter *m*

suppose [sə'pəuz] *vt* supposer; imaginer;
to be ~d to do être censé(e) faire; ~**dly**
[sə'pəuzɪdlɪ] *adv* soi-disant; **supposing**
conj si, à supposer que +*sub*

suppress [sə'pres] *vt* (*revolt*) réprimer; (*information*) supprimer; (*yawn*) étouffer; (*feelings*) refouler

supreme [su'priːm] *adj* suprême

surcharge ['sɜːtʃɑːdʒ] *n* surcharge *f*

sure [ʃuə⁽ʳ⁾] *adj* sûr(e); (*definite, convinced*)
sûr, certain(e); ~**!** (*of course*) bien sûr!; ~
enough effectivement; **to make ~ of sth**
s'assurer de *or* vérifier qch; **to make ~
that** s'assurer *or* vérifier que; ~**ly** *adv*
sûrement; certainement

surf [sɜːf] *n* (*waves*) ressac *m*

surface ['sɜːfɪs] *n* surface *f* ♦ *vt* (*road*) poser un revêtement sur ♦ *vi* remonter à la
surface; faire surface; ~ **mail** *n* courrier *m*
par voie de terre (*or* maritime)

surfboard ['sɜːfbɔːd] *n* planche *f* de surf

surfeit ['sɜːfɪt] *n*: **a ~ of** un excès de; une
indigestion de

surfing ['sɜːfɪŋ] *n* surf *m*

surge [sɜːdʒ] *n* vague *f*, montée *f* ♦ *vi* déferler

surgeon ['sɜːdʒən] *n* chirurgien *m*

surgery ['sɜːdʒərɪ] *n* chirurgie *f*; (*BRIT:
room*) cabinet *m* (de consultation); (*: also:
~ hours*) heures *fpl* de consultation

surgical ['sɜːdʒɪkl] *adj* chirurgical(e); ~
spirit (*BRIT*) *n* alcool *m* à 90⁰

surname ['sɜːneɪm] *n* nom *m* de famille

surplus ['sɜːpləs] *n* surplus *m*, excédent *m*
♦ *adj* en surplus, de trop; (*COMM*) excé-
dentaire

surprise [sə'praɪz] *n* surprise *f*; (*astonishment*) étonnement *m* ♦ *vt* surprendre; (*astonish*) étonner; **surprising** *adj* surpre-
nant(e), étonnant(e); **surprisingly** *adv*
(*easy, helpful*) étonnamment

surrender [sə'rendə⁽ʳ⁾] *n* reddition *f*, capitu-
lation *f* ♦ *vi* se rendre, capituler

surreptitious [sʌrəp'tɪʃəs] *adj* subreptice,
furtif(-ive)

surrogate ['sʌrəgɪt] *n* substitut *m*; ~
mother *n* mère porteuse *or* de substitution

surround [sə'raund] *vt* entourer; (*MIL etc*)
encercler; ~**ing** *adj* environnant(e); ~**ings**
npl environs *mpl*, alentours *mpl*

surveillance [sɜː'veɪləns] *n* surveillance *f*

survey [*n* 'sɜːveɪ, *vb* sɜː'veɪ] *n* enquête *f*,
étude *f*; (*in housebuying etc*) inspection *f*,
(rapport *m* d')expertise *f*; (*of land*) levé *m*
♦ *vt* enquêter sur; inspecter; (*look at*) embrasser du regard; ~**or** *n* (*of house*) expert
m; (*of land*) (arpenteur *m*) géomètre *m*

survival [sə'vaɪvl] *n* survie *f*; (*relic*) vestige
m

survive [sə'vaɪv] *vi* survivre; (*custom etc*)
subsister ♦ *vt* survivre à; **survivor** *n* survi-
vant(e); (*fig*) battant(e)

susceptible [sə'septəbl] *adj*: ~ **(to)** sensible (à); (*disease*) prédisposé(e) (à)

suspect [*adj, n* 'sʌspɛkt, *vb* səs'pɛkt] *adj, n*
suspect(e) ♦ *vt* soupçonner, suspecter

suspend [səs'pend] *vt* suspendre; ~**ed
sentence** *n* condamnation *f* avec sursis;
~**er belt** *n* porte-jarretelles *m inv*; ~**ers**
npl (*BRIT*) jarretelles *fpl*; (*US*) bretelles *fpl*

suspense [səs'pens] *n* attente *f*, incertitude *f*; (*in film etc*) suspense *m*

suspension [səs'penʃən] *n* suspension *f*;
(*of driving licence*) retrait *m* provisoire; ~
bridge *n* pont suspendu

suspicion [səs'pɪʃən] *n* soupçon(s) *m(pl)*;
suspicious *adj* (*suspecting*)
soupçonneux(-euse), méfiant(e); (*causing
suspicion*) suspect(e)

sustain [səs'teɪn] *vt* soutenir; (*food etc*) nourrir, donner des forces à; (*suffer*) subir; recevoir; **~able** *adj* (*development, growth etc*) viable; **~ed** *adj* (*effort*) soutenu(e), prolongé(e); **sustenance** ['sʌstɪnəns] *n* nourriture *f*; (*money*) moyens *mpl* de subsistance

swab [swɔb] *n* (*MED*) tampon *m*

swagger ['swægə'] *vi* plastronner

swallow ['swɔləu] *n* (*bird*) hirondelle *f* ♦ *vt* avaler; **~ up** *vt* engloutir

swam [swæm] *pt of* **swim**

swamp [swɔmp] *n* marais *m*, marécage *m* ♦ *vt* submerger

swan [swɔn] *n* cygne *m*

swap [swɔp] *vt*: **to ~ (for)** échanger (contre), troquer (contre)

swarm [swɔːm] *n* essaim *m* ♦ *vi* fourmiller, grouiller

swastika ['swɔstɪkə] *n* croix gammée

swat [swɔt] *vt* écraser

sway [sweɪ] *vi* se balancer, osciller ♦ *vt* (*influence*) influencer

swear [sweə'] (*pt* **swore**, *pp* **sworn**) *vt*, *vi* jurer; **~word** *n* juron *m*, gros mot

sweat [swɛt] *n* sueur *f*, transpiration *f* ♦ *vi* suer

sweater ['swɛtə'] *n* tricot *m*, pull *m*

sweaty ['swɛtɪ] *adj* en sueur, moite *or* mouillé(e) de sueur

Swede [swiːd] *n* Suédois(e)

swede [swiːd] (*BRIT*) *n* rutabaga *m*

Sweden ['swiːdn] *n* Suède *f*; **Swedish** *adj* suédois(e) ♦ *n* (*LING*) suédois *m*

sweep [swiːp] (*pt, pp* **swept**) *n* (*also:* **chimney ~**) ramoneur *m* ♦ *vt* balayer; (*subj: current*) emporter; **~ away** *vt* balayer; entraîner; emporter; **~ past** *vi* passer majestueusement *or* rapidement; **~ up** *vt, vi* balayer; **~ing** *adj* (*gesture*) large; circulaire; **a ~ing statement** une généralisation hâtive

sweet [swiːt] *n* (*candy*) bonbon *m*; (*BRIT: pudding*) dessert *m* ♦ *adj* doux (douce); (*not savoury*) sucré(e); (*fig: kind*) gentil(le); (*baby*) mignon(ne); **~corn** ['swiːtkɔːn] *n* maïs *m*; **~en** *vt* adoucir; (*with sugar*) su-

crer; **~heart** *n* amoureux(-euse); **~ness** *n* goût sucré; douceur *f*; **~ pea** *n* pois *m* de senteur

swell [swɛl] (*pt* **swelled**, *pp* **swollen** *or* **swelled**) *n* (*of sea*) houle *f* ♦ *adj* (*US: inf: excellent*) chouette ♦ *vi* grossir, augmenter; (*sound*) s'enfler; (*MED*) enfler; **~ing** *n* (*MED*) enflure *f*; (*lump*) grosseur *f*

sweltering ['swɛltərɪŋ] *adj* étouffant(e), oppressant(e)

swept [swɛpt] *pt, pp of* **sweep**

swerve [swɜːv] *vi* faire une embardée *or* un écart; dévier

swift [swɪft] *n* (*bird*) martinet *m* ♦ *adj* rapide, prompt(e)

swig [swɪg] (*inf*) *n* (*drink*) lampée *f*

swill [swɪl] *vt* (*also:* **~ out**, **~ down**) laver à grande eau

swim [swɪm] (*pt* **swam**, *pp* **swum**) *n*: **to go for a ~** aller nager *or* se baigner ♦ *vi* nager; (*SPORT*) faire de la natation; (*head, room*) tourner ♦ *vt* traverser (à la nage); (*a length*) faire (à la nage); **~mer** *n* nageur(-euse); **~ming** *n* natation *f*; **~ming cap** *n* bonnet *m* de bain; **~ming costume** (*BRIT*) *n* maillot *m* (de bain); **~ming pool** *n* piscine *f*; **~ming trunks** *npl* caleçon *m* *or* slip *m* de bain; **~suit** *n* maillot *m* (de bain)

swindle ['swɪndl] *n* escroquerie *f*

swine [swaɪn] (*inf!*) *n inv* salaud *m* (!)

swing [swɪŋ] (*pt, pp* **swung**) *n* balançoire *f*; (*movement*) balancement *m*, oscillations *fpl*; (*change: in opinion etc*) revirement *m* ♦ *vt* balancer, faire osciller; (*also:* **~ round**) tourner, faire virer ♦ *vi* se balancer, osciller; (*also:* **~ round**) virer, tourner; **to be in full ~** battre son plein; **~ bridge** *n* pont tournant; **~ door** (*US* **swinging door**) *n* porte battante

swingeing ['swɪndʒɪŋ] (*BRIT*) *adj* écrasant(e); (*cuts etc*) considérable

swipe [swaɪp] (*inf*) *vt* (*steal*) piquer

swirl [swɜːl] *vi* tourbillonner, tournoyer

Swiss [swɪs] *adj* suisse ♦ *n inv* Suisse *m/f*

switch [swɪtʃ] *n* (*for light, radio etc*) bouton *m*; (*change*) changement *m*, revirement *m*

♦ *vt* changer; **~ off** *vt* éteindre; (*engine*) arrêter; **~ on** *vt* allumer; (*engine, machine*) mettre en marche; **~board** *n* (*TEL*) standard *m*

Switzerland ['swɪtsələnd] *n* Suisse *f*

swivel ['swɪvl] *vi* (*also:* **~ round**) pivoter, tourner

swollen ['swəulən] *pp of* **swell**

swoon [swu:n] *vi* se pâmer

swoop [swu:p] *n* (*by police*) descente *f* ♦ *vi* (*also:* **~ down**) descendre en piqué, piquer

swop [swɔp] *vt* = **swap**

sword [sɔ:d] *n* épée *f*; **~fish** *n* espadon *m*

swore [swɔ:ʳ] *pt of* **swear**

sworn [swɔ:n] *pp of* **swear** ♦ *adj* (*statement, evidence*) donné(e) sous serment

swot [swɔt] *vi* bûcher, potasser

swum [swʌm] *pp of* **swim**

swung [swʌŋ] *pt, pp of* **swing**

syllable ['sɪləbl] *n* syllabe *f*

syllabus ['sɪləbəs] *n* programme *m*

symbol ['sɪmbl] *n* symbole *m*

symmetry ['sɪmɪtrɪ] *n* symétrie *f*

sympathetic [sɪmpə'θɛtɪk] *adj* compatissant(e); bienveillant(e), compréhensif(-ive); (*likeable*) sympathique; **~ towards** bien disposé(e) envers

sympathize ['sɪmpəθaɪz] *vi*: **to ~ with sb** plaindre qn; (*in grief*) s'associer à la douleur de qn; **to ~ with sth** comprendre qch; **~r** *n* (*POL*) sympathisant(e)

sympathy ['sɪmpəθɪ] *n* (*pity*) compassion *f*; **sympathies** *npl* (*support*) soutien *m*; **left-wing etc sympathies** penchants *mpl* à gauche *etc*; **in ~ with** (*strike*) en or par solidarité avec; **with our deepest ~** en vous priant d'accepter nos sincères condoléances

symphony ['sɪmfənɪ] *n* symphonie *f*

symptom ['sɪmptəm] *n* symptôme *m*; indice *m*

syndicate ['sɪndɪkɪt] *n* syndicat *m*, coopérative *f*

synopsis [sɪ'nɔpsɪs] (*pl* **synopses**) *n* résumé *m*

synthetic [sɪn'θɛtɪk] *adj* synthétique

syphon ['saɪfən] *n*, *vb* = **siphon**

Syria ['sɪrɪə] *n* Syrie *f*

syringe [sɪ'rɪndʒ] *n* seringue *f*

syrup ['sɪrəp] *n* sirop *m*; (*also:* **golden ~**) mélasse raffinée

system ['sɪstəm] *n* système *m*; (*ANAT*) organisme *m*; **~atic** [sɪstə'mætɪk] *adj* systématique; méthodique; **~ disk** *n* (*COMPUT*) disque *m* système; **~s analyst** *n* analyste fonctionnel(le)

T, t

ta [tɑ:] (*BRIT: inf*) *excl* merci!

tab [tæb] *n* (*label*) étiquette *f*; (*on drinks can etc*) languette *f*; **to keep ~s on** (*fig*) surveiller

tabby ['tæbɪ] *n* (*also:* **~ cat**) chat(te) tigré(e)

table ['teɪbl] *n* table *f* ♦ *vt* (*BRIT: motion etc*) présenter; **to lay** *or* **set the ~** mettre le couvert *or* la table; **~cloth** *n* nappe *f*; **~ d'hôte** [tɑ:bl'dəut] *adj* (*meal*) à prix fixe; **~ lamp** *n* lampe *f* de table; **~mat** *n* (*for plate*) napperon *m*, set *m*; (*for hot dish*) dessous-de-plat *m inv*; **~ of contents** *n* table *f* des matières; **~spoon** *n* cuiller *f* de service; (*also:* **~spoonful**: *as measurement*) cuillerée *f* à soupe

tablet ['tæblɪt] *n* (*MED*) comprimé *m*

table tennis *n* ping-pong ® *m*, tennis *m* de table

table wine *n* vin *m* de table

tabloid ['tæblɔɪd] *n* quotidien *m* populaire

---
tabloid press
---

i *Le terme* **tabloid press** *désigne les journaux populaires de demi-format où l'on trouve beaucoup de photos et qui adoptent un style très concis. Ce type de journaux vise des lecteurs s'intéressant aux faits divers ayant un parfum de scandale; voir* **quality (news)papers.**

---

tack [tæk] *n* (*nail*) petit clou ♦ *vt* clouer; (*fig*) direction *f*; (*BRIT: stitch*) faufiler ♦ *vi* tirer un *or* des bord(s)

tackle ['tækl] *n* matériel *m*, équipement *m*; (*for lifting*) appareil *m* de levage; (*RUGBY*) plaquage *m* ♦ *vt* (*difficulty, animal, burglar etc*) s'attaquer à; (*person: challenge*) s'expliquer avec; (*RUGBY*) plaquer

tacky ['tæki] *adj* collant(e); (*pej: of poor quality*) miteux(-euse)

tact [tækt] *n* tact *m*; **~ful** *adj* plein(e) de tact

tactical ['tæktɪkl] *adj* tactique

tactics ['tæktɪks] *npl* tactique *f*

tactless ['tæktlɪs] *adj* qui manque de tact

tadpole ['tædpəul] *n* têtard *m*

tag [tæg] *n* étiquette *f*; **~ along** *vi* suivre

tail [teɪl] *n* queue *f*; (*of shirt*) pan *m* ♦ *vt* (*follow*) suivre, filer; **~s** *npl* habit *m*; **~ away, ~ off** *vi* (*in size, quality etc*) baisser peu à peu; **~back** (*BRIT*) *n* (*AUT*) bouchon *m*; **~ end** *n* bout *m*, fin *f*; **~gate** *n* (*AUT*) hayon *m* arrière

tailor ['teɪlə*r*] *n* tailleur *m*; **~ing** *n* (*cut*) coupe *f*; **~-made** *adj* fait(e) sur mesure; (*fig*) conçu(e) spécialement

tailwind ['teɪlwɪnd] *n* vent *m* arrière *inv*

tainted ['teɪntɪd] *adj* (*food*) gâté(e); (*water, air*) infecté(e); (*fig*) souillé(e)

take [teɪk] (*pt* **took**, *pp* **taken**) *vt* prendre; (*gain: prize*) remporter; (*require: effort, courage*) demander; (*tolerate*) accepter, supporter; (*hold: passengers etc*) contenir; (*accompany*) emmener, accompagner; (*bring, carry*) apporter, emporter; (*exam*) passer, se présenter à; **to ~ sth from** (*drawer etc*) prendre qch dans; (*person*) prendre qch à; **I ~ it that ...** je suppose que ...; **~ after** *vt fus* ressembler à; **~ apart** *vt* démonter; **~ away** *vt* enlever; (*carry off*) emporter; **~ back** *vt* (*return*) rendre, rapporter; (*one's words*) retirer; **~ down** *vt* (*building*) démolir; (*letter etc*) prendre, écrire; **~ in** *vt* (*deceive*) tromper, rouler; (*understand*) comprendre, saisir; (*include*) comprendre, inclure; (*lodger*) prendre; **~ off** *vi* (*AVIAT*) décoller ♦ *vt* (*go away*) s'en aller; (*remove*) enlever; **~ on** *vt* (*work*) accepter, se charger de; (*employee*) prendre, embaucher;

(*opponent*) accepter de se battre contre; **~ out** *vt* (*invite*) emmener, sortir; (*remove*) enlever; **to ~ sth out of sth** (*drawer, pocket etc*) prendre qch dans qch; **~ over** *vt* (*business*) reprendre ♦ *vi*: **to ~ over from sb** prendre la relève de qn; **~ to** *vt fus* (*person*) se prendre d'amitié pour; (*thing*) prendre goût à; **~ up** *vt* (*activity*) se mettre à; (*dress*) raccourcir; (*occupy: time, space*) prendre, occuper; **to ~ sb up on an offer** accepter la proposition de qn; **~away** (*BRIT*) *adj* (*food*) à emporter ♦ *n* (*shop, restaurant*) café *m* qui vend de plats à emporter; **~off** *n* (*AVIAT*) décollage *m*; **~over** *n* (*COMM*) rachat *m*; **takings** *npl* (*COMM*) recette *f*

talc [tælk] *n* (*also:* **~um powder**) talc *m*

tale [teɪl] *n* (*story*) conte *m*, histoire *f*; (*account*) récit *m*; **to tell ~s** (*fig*) rapporter

talent ['tælnt] *n* talent *m*, don *m*; **~ed** *adj* doué(e), plein(e) de talent

talk [tɔːk] *n* (*a speech*) causerie *f*, exposé *m*; (*conversation*) discussion *f*, entretien *m*; (*gossip*) racontars *mpl* ♦ *vi* parler; **~s** *npl* (*POL etc*) entretiens *mpl*; **to ~ about** parler de; **to ~ sb into/out of doing** persuader qn de faire/ne pas faire; **to ~ shop** parler métier *or* affaires; **~ over** *vt* discuter (de); **~ative** *adj* bavard(e); **~ show** *n* causerie (télévisée *or* radiodiffusée)

tall [tɔːl] *adj* (*person*) grand(e); (*building, tree*) haut(e); **to be 6 feet ~** ≈ mesurer 1 mètre 80; **~ story** *n* histoire *f* invraisemblable

tally ['tælɪ] *n* compte *m* ♦ *vi*: **to ~ (with)** correspondre (à)

talon ['tælən] *n* griffe *f*; (*of eagle*) serre *f*

tame [teɪm] *adj* apprivoisé(e); (*fig: story, style*) insipide

tamper ['tæmpə*r*] *vi*: **to ~ with** toucher à

tampon ['tæmpɔn] *n* tampon *m* (hygiénique *or* périodique)

tan [tæn] *n* (*also:* **suntan**) bronzage *m* ♦ *vt, vi* bronzer ♦ *adj* (*colour*) brun roux *inv*

tang [tæŋ] *n* odeur (*or* saveur) piquante

tangent ['tændʒənt] *n* (*MATH*) tangente *f*; **to go off at a ~** (*fig*) changer de sujet

tangerine [tændʒə'riːn] _n_ mandarine _f_

tangle ['tæŋgl] _n_ enchevêtrement _m_; **to get in(to) a ~** s'embrouiller

tank [tæŋk] _n_ (_water ~_) réservoir _m_; (_for fish_) aquarium _m_; (MIL) char _m_ d'assaut, tank _m_

tanker ['tæŋkə'] _n_ (_ship_) pétrolier _m_, tanker _m_; (_truck_) camion-citerne _m_

tantalizing ['tæntəlaɪzɪŋ] _adj_ (_smell_) extrêmement appétissant(e); (_offer_) terriblement tentant(e)

tantamount ['tæntəmaunt] _adj_: **~ to** qui équivaut à

tantrum ['tæntrəm] _n_ accès _m_ de colère

tap [tæp] _n_ (_on sink etc_) robinet _m_; (_gentle blow_) petite tape ♦ _vt_ frapper _or_ taper légèrement; (_resources_) exploiter, utiliser; (_telephone_) mettre sur écoute; **on ~** (_fig_: _resources_) disponible; **~-dancing** _n_ claquettes _fpl_

tape [teɪp] _n_ ruban _m_; (_also_: **magnetic ~**) bande _f_ (magnétique); (_cassette_) cassette _f_; (_sticky_) scotch _m_ ♦ _vt_ (_record_) enregistrer; (_stick with ~_) coller avec du scotch; **~ deck** _n_ platine _f_ d'enregistrement; **~ measure** _n_ mètre _m_ à ruban

taper ['teɪpə'] _vi_ s'effiler

tape recorder _n_ magnétophone _m_

tapestry ['tæpɪstrɪ] _n_ tapisserie _f_

tar [tɑː] _n_ goudron _m_

target ['tɑːgɪt] _n_ cible _f_; (_fig_) objectif _m_

tariff ['tærɪf] _n_ (COMM) tarif _m_; (_taxes_) tarif douanier

tarmac ['tɑːmæk] _n_ (BRIT: _on road_) macadam _m_; (AVIAT) piste _f_

tarnish ['tɑːnɪʃ] _vt_ ternir

tarpaulin [tɑː'pɔːlɪn] _n_ bâche (goudronnée)

tarragon ['tærəgən] _n_ estragon _m_

tart [tɑːt] _n_ (CULIN) tarte _f_; (BRIT: _inf_: _prostitute_) putain _f_ ♦ _adj_ (_flavour_) âpre, aigrelet(te); **~ up** (BRIT: _inf_) _vt_ (_object_) retaper; **to ~ o.s. up** se faire beau (belle), s'attifer (_pej_)

tartan ['tɑːtn] _n_ tartan _m_ ♦ _adj_ écossais(e)

tartar ['tɑːtə'] _n_ (_on teeth_) tartre _m_; **~(e) sauce** _n_ sauce _f_ tartare

task [tɑːsk] _n_ tâche _f_; **to take sb to ~** prendre qn à partie; **~ force** _n_ (MIL, POLICE) détachement spécial

tassel ['tæsl] _n_ gland _m_; pompon _m_

taste [teɪst] _n_ goût _m_; (_fig_: _glimpse_, _idea_) idée _f_, aperçu _m_ ♦ _vt_ goûter ♦ _vi_: **to ~ of** _or_ **like** (_fish etc_) avoir le _or_ un goût de; **you can ~ the garlic (in it)** on sent bien l'ail; **can I have a ~ of this wine?** puis-je goûter un peu de ce vin?; **in good/bad ~** de bon/mauvais goût; **~ful** _adj_ de bon goût; **~less** _adj_ (_food_) fade; (_remark_) de mauvais goût; **tasty** _adj_ savoureux(-euse), délicieux(-euse)

tatters ['tætəz] _npl_: **in ~** en lambeaux

tattoo [tə'tuː] _n_ tatouage _m_; (_spectacle_) parade _f_ militaire ♦ _vt_ tatouer

tatty ['tætɪ] (BRIT: _inf_) _adj_ (_clothes_) frippé(e); (_shop_, _area_) délabré(e)

taught [tɔːt] _pt_, _pp_ of **teach**

taunt [tɔːnt] _n_ raillerie _f_ ♦ _vt_ railler

Taurus ['tɔːrəs] _n_ le Taureau

taut [tɔːt] _adj_ tendu(e)

tax [tæks] _n_ (_on goods etc_) taxe _f_; (_on income_) impôts _mpl_, contributions _fpl_ ♦ _vt_ taxer; imposer; (_fig_: _patience etc_) mettre à l'épreuve; **~able** _adj_ (_income_) imposable; **~ation** [tæk'seɪʃən] _n_ taxation _f_; impôts _mpl_, contributions _fpl_; **~ avoidance** _n_ dégrèvement fiscal; **~ disc** (BRIT) _n_ (AUT) vignette _f_ (automobile); **~ evasion** _n_ fraude fiscale; **~-free** _adj_ exempt(e) d'impôts

taxi ['tæksɪ] _n_ taxi _m_ ♦ _vi_ (AVIAT) rouler (lentement) au sol; **~ driver** _n_ chauffeur _m_ de taxi; **~ rank** (BRIT) _n_ station _f_ de taxis; **~ stand** _n_ = **taxi rank**

tax: **~ payer** _n_ contribuable _m/f_; **~ relief** _n_ dégrèvement fiscal; **~ return** _n_ déclaration _f_ d'impôts _or_ de revenus

TB _n abbr_ = **tuberculosis**

tea [tiː] _n_ thé _m_; (BRIT: _snack_: _for children_) goûter _m_; **high ~** _collation combinant goûter et dîner_; **~ bag** _n_ sachet _m_ de thé; **~ break** (BRIT) _n_ pause-thé _f_

teach [tiːtʃ] (_pt_, _pp_ **taught**) _vt_: **to ~ sb sth**, **~ sth to sb** apprendre qch à qn; (_in_ *school etc*) enseigner qch à qn ♦ *vi* enseigner; **~er** *n* (*in secondary school*) professeur *m*; (*in primary school*) instituteur(-trice); **~ing** *n* enseignement *m*

tea: **~ cloth** *n* torchon *m*; **~ cosy** *n* cloche *f* à thé; **~cup** *n* tasse *f* à thé

teak [tiːk] *n* teck *m*

tea leaves *npl* feuilles *fpl* de thé

team [tiːm] *n* équipe *f*; (*of animals*) attelage *m*; **~work** *n* travail *m* d'équipe

teapot ['tiːpɔt] *n* théière *f*

tear¹ [tɛəʳ] (*pt* **tore**, *pp* **torn**) *n* déchirure *f* ♦ *vt* déchirer ♦ *vi* se déchirer; **~ along** *vi* (*rush*) aller à toute vitesse; **~ up** *vt* (*sheet of paper etc*) déchirer, mettre en morceaux *or* pièces

tear² [tɪəʳ] *n* larme *f*; **in ~s** en larmes; **~ful** *adj* larmoyant(e); **~ gas** *n* gaz *m* lacrymogène

tearoom ['tiːruːm] *n* salon *m* de thé

tease [tiːz] *vt* taquiner; (*unkindly*) tourmenter

tea set *n* service *m* à thé

teaspoon ['tiːspuːn] *n* petite cuiller; (*also*: **~ful**: *as measurement*) ≈ cuillerée *f* à café

teat [tiːt] *n* tétine *f*

teatime ['tiːtaɪm] *n* l'heure *f* du thé

tea towel (*BRIT*) *n* torchon *m* (à vaisselle)

technical ['tɛknɪkl] *adj* technique; **~ity** [tɛknɪ'kælɪtɪ] *n* (*detail*) détail *m* technique; (*point of law*) vice *m* de forme; **~ly** *adv* techniquement; (*strictly speaking*) en théorie

technician [tɛk'nɪʃən] *n* technicien(ne)

technique [tɛk'niːk] *n* technique *f*

techno ['tɛknəu] *n* (*music*) techno *f*

technological [tɛknə'lɔdʒɪkl] *adj* technologique

technology [tɛk'nɔlədʒɪ] *n* technologie *f*

teddy (bear) ['tɛdɪ(-)] *n* ours *m* en peluche

tedious ['tiːdɪəs] *adj* fastidieux(-euse)

teem [tiːm] *vi*: **to ~ (with)** grouiller (de); **it is ~ing (with rain)** il pleut à torrents

teenage ['tiːneɪdʒ] *adj* (*fashions etc*) pour jeunes, pour adolescents; (*children*) adolescent(e); **~r** *n* adolescent(e)

teens [tiːnz] *npl*: **to be in one's ~** être adolescent(e)

tee-shirt ['tiːʃəːt] *n* = **T-shirt**

teeter ['tiːtəʳ] *vi* chanceler, vaciller

teeth [tiːθ] *npl of* **tooth**

teethe [tiːð] *vi* percer ses dents

teething troubles *npl* (*fig*) difficultés initiales

teetotal ['tiː'təutl] *adj* (*person*) qui ne boit jamais d'alcool

tele: **~communications** *npl* télécommunications *fpl*; **~conferencing** *n* téléconférence(s) *f(pl)*; **~gram** *n* télégramme *m*; **~graph** *n* télégraphe *m*; **~graph pole** *n* poteau *m* télégraphique

telephone ['tɛlɪfəun] *n* téléphone *m* ♦ *vt* (*person*) téléphoner à; (*message*) téléphoner; **on the ~** au téléphone; **to be on the ~** (*BRIT: have a ~*) avoir le téléphone; **~ booth**, **~ box** (*BRIT*) *n* cabine *f* téléphonique; **~ call** *n* coup *m* de téléphone, appel *m* téléphonique; **~ directory** *n* annuaire *m* (du téléphone); **~ number** *n* numéro *m* de téléphone; **telephonist** [tə'lɛfənɪst] (*BRIT*) *n* téléphoniste *m/f*

telesales ['tɛlɪseɪlz] *n* télévente *f*

telescope ['tɛlɪskəup] *n* télescope *m*

television ['tɛlɪvɪʒən] *n* télévision *f*; **on ~** à la télévision; **~ set** *n* (poste *f* de) télévision *m*

telex ['tɛlɛks] *n* télex *m*

tell [tɛl] (*pt, pp* **told**) *vt* dire; (*relate: story*) raconter; (*distinguish*): **to ~ sth from** distinguer qch de ♦ *vi* (*talk*): **to ~ (of)** parler (de); (*have effect*) se faire sentir, se voir; **to ~ sb to do** dire à qn de faire; **~ off** *vt* réprimander, gronder; **~er** *n* (*in bank*) caissier(-ère); **~ing** *adj* (*remark, detail*) révélateur(-trice); **~tale** *adj* (*sign*) éloquent(e), révélateur(-trice)

telly ['tɛlɪ] (*BRIT: inf*) *n abbr* (= television) télé *f*

temp [tɛmp] *n abbr* (= temporary) (secrétaire *f*) intérimaire *f*

temper ['tɛmpəʳ] *n* (*nature*) caractère *m*; (*mood*) humeur *f*; (*fit of anger*) colère *f* ♦ *vt* (*moderate*) tempérer, adoucir; **to be**

in a ~ être en colère; **to lose one's ~** se mettre en colère

temperament ['tempрəmənt] *n* (*nature*) tempérament *m*; **~al** [tempрə'mentl] *adj* capricieux(-euse)

temperate ['tempрət] *adj* (*climate, country*) tempéré(e)

temperature ['tempрətʃə^r] *n* température *f*; **to have** *or* **run a ~** avoir de la fièvre

temple ['templ] *n* (*building*) temple *m*; (*ANAT*) tempe *f*

temporary ['tempрərɪ] *adj* temporaire, provisoire; (*job, worker*) temporaire

tempt [tempt] *vt* tenter; **to ~ sb into doing** persuader qn de faire; **~ation** [temp'teɪʃən] *n* tentation *f*; **~ing** *adj* tentant(e)

ten [ten] *num* dix

tenacity [tə'næsɪtɪ] *n* ténacité *f*

tenancy ['tenənsɪ] *n* location *f*; état *m* de locataire

tenant ['tenənt] *n* locataire *m/f*

tend [tend] *vt* s'occuper de ♦ *vi*: **to ~ to do** avoir tendance à faire; **~ency** ['tendənsɪ] *n* tendance *f*

tender ['tendə^r] *adj* tendre; (*delicate*) délicat(e); (*sore*) sensible ♦ *n* (*COMM: offer*) soumission *f* ♦ *vt* offrir

tenement ['tenəmənt] *n* immeuble *m*

tennis ['tenɪs] *n* tennis *m*; **~ ball** *n* balle *f* de tennis; **~ court** *n* (court *m* de) tennis; **~ player** *n* joueur(-euse) de tennis; **~ racket** *n* raquette *f* de tennis; **~ shoes** *npl* (chaussures *fpl* de) tennis *mpl*

tenor ['tenə^r] *n* (*MUS*) ténor *m*

tenpin bowling ['tenpɪn-] (*BRIT*) *n* bowling *m* (à dix quilles)

tense [tens] *adj* tendu(e) ♦ *n* (*LING*) temps *m*

tension ['tenʃən] *n* tension *f*

tent [tent] *n* tente *f*

tentative ['tentətɪv] *adj* timide, hésitant(e); (*conclusion*) provisoire

tenterhooks ['tentəhʊks] *npl*: **on ~** sur des charbons ardents

tenth [tenθ] *num* dixième

tent peg *n* piquet *m* de tente

tent pole *n* montant *m* de tente

tenuous ['tenjuəs] *adj* ténu(e)

tenure ['tenjuə^r] *n* (*of property*) bail *m*; (*of job*) période *f* de jouissance

tepid ['tepɪd] *adj* tiède

term [tɜːm] *n* terme *m*; (*SCOL*) trimestre *m* ♦ *vt* appeler; **~s** *npl* (*conditions*) conditions *fpl*; (*COMM*) tarif *m*; **in the short/long ~** à court/long terme; **to come to ~s with** (*problem*) faire face à

terminal ['tɜːmɪnl] *adj* (*disease*) dans sa phase terminale; (*patient*) incurable ♦ *n* (*ELEC*) borne *f*; (*for oil, ore etc, COMPUT*) terminal *m*; (*also:* **air ~**) aérogare *f*; (*BRIT: also:* **coach ~**) gare routière; **~ly** *adv*: **to be ~ly ill** être condamné(e)

terminate ['tɜːmɪneɪt] *vt* mettre fin à; (*pregnancy*) interrompre

termini ['tɜːmɪnaɪ] *npl of* **terminus**

terminus ['tɜːmɪnəs] (*pl* **termini**) *n* terminus *m inv*

terrace ['terəs] *n* terrasse *f*; (*BRIT: row of houses*) rangée *f* de maisons (*attenantes*); **the ~s** *npl* (*BRIT: SPORT*) les gradins *mpl*; **~d** *adj* (*garden*) en terrasses

terracotta ['terə'kɔtə] *n* terre cuite

terrain [te'reɪn] *n* terrain *m* (*sol*)

terrible ['terɪbl] *adj* terrible, atroce; (*weather, conditions*) affreux(-euse), épouvantable; **terribly** *adv* terriblement; (*very badly*) affreusement mal

terrier ['terɪə^r] *n* terrier *m* (*chien*)

terrific [tə'rɪfɪk] *adj* fantastique, incroyable, terrible; (*wonderful*) formidable, sensationnel(le)

terrify ['terɪfaɪ] *vt* terrifier

territory ['terɪtərɪ] *n* territoire *m*

terror ['terə^r] *n* terreur *f*; **~ism** *n* terrorisme *m*; **~ist** *n* terroriste *m/f*

test [test] *n* (*trial, check*) essai *m*; (*of courage etc*) épreuve *f*; (*MED*) examen *m*; (*CHEM*) analyse *f*; (*SCOL*) interrogation *f*; (*also:* **driving ~**) (examen du) permis *m* de conduire ♦ *vt* essayer; mettre à l'épreuve; examiner; analyser; faire subir une interrogation à

testament ['testəmənt] *n* testament *m*;

the **Old/New T~** l'Ancien/le Nouveau Testament

testicle ['tɛstɪkl] *n* testicule *m*

testify ['tɛstɪfaɪ] *vi* (*LAW*) témoigner, déposer; **to ~ to sth** attester qch

testimony ['tɛstɪmənɪ] *n* témoignage *m*; (*clear proof*): **to be (a) ~** être la preuve de

test match *n* (*CRICKET, RUGBY*) match international

test tube *n* éprouvette *f*

tetanus ['tɛtənəs] *n* tétanos *m*

tether ['tɛðər] *vt* attacher ♦ *n*: **at the end of one's ~** à bout (de patience)

text [tɛkst] *n* texte *m*; **~book** *n* manuel *m*

textile ['tɛkstaɪl] *n* textile *m*

texture ['tɛkstʃər] *n* texture *f*; (*of skin, paper etc*) grain *m*

Thailand ['taɪlænd] *n* Thaïlande *f*

Thames [tɛmz] *n*: **the ~** la Tamise

than [ðæn, ðən] *conj* que; (*with numerals*): **more ~ 10/once** plus de 10/d'une fois; **I have more/less ~ you** j'en ai plus/moins que toi; **she has more apples ~ pears** elle a plus de pommes que de poires

thank [θæŋk] *vt* remercier, dire merci à; **~s** *npl* (*gratitude*) remerciements *mpl* ♦ *excl* merci!; **~ you (very much)** merci (beaucoup); **~s to** grâce à; **~ God!** Dieu merci!; **~ful** *adj*: **~ful (for)** reconnaissant(e) (de); **~less** *adj* ingrat(e); **T~sgiving (Day)** *n* jour *m* d'action de grâce (*fête américaine*)

┌─ **Thanksgiving Day** ─┐

i Thanksgiving Day *est un jour de congé aux États-Unis, le quatrième jeudi du mois de novembre, commémorant la bonne récolte que les Pélerins venus de Grande-Bretagne ont eue en 1621; traditionnellement, c'est un jour où l'on remerciait Dieu et où l'on organisait un grand festin. Une fête semblable a lieu au Canada le deuxiéme lundi d'octobre.*

└─────────────────────┘

┌─ **KEYWORD** ─┐

that [ðæt] *adj* (*demonstrative: pl those*) ce, cet +*vowel or h mute*, cette *f*; **that man/ woman/book** cet homme/cette femme/ ce livre; (*not "this"*) cet homme-là/cette femme-là/ce livre-là; **that one** celui-là (celle-là)

♦ *pron* **1** (*demonstrative: pl those*) ce; (*not "this one"*) cela, ça; **who's that?** qui est-ce?; **what's that?** qu'est-ce que c'est?; **is that you?** c'est toi?; **I prefer this to that** je préfère ceci à cela *or* ça; **that's what he said** c'est *or* voilà ce qu'il a dit; **that is (to say)** c'est-à-dire, à savoir

2 (*relative: subject*) qui; (: *object*) que; (: *indirect*) lequel (laquelle), lesquels (lesquelles) *pl*; **the book that I read** le livre que j'ai lu; **the books that are in the library** les livres qui sont dans la bibliothèque; **all that I have** tout ce que j'ai; **the box that I put it in** la boîte dans laquelle je l'ai mis; **the people that I spoke to** les gens auxquels *or* à qui j'ai parlé

3 (*relative: of time*) où; **the day that he came** le jour où il est venu

♦ *conj* que; **he thought that I was ill** il pensait que j'étais malade

♦ *adv* (*demonstrative*): **I can't work that much** je ne peux pas travailler autant que cela; **I didn't know it was that bad** je ne savais pas que c'était si *or* aussi mauvais; **it's about that high** c'est à peu près de cette hauteur

└─────────────────────┘

thatched [θætʃt] *adj* (*roof*) de chaume; **~ cottage** chaumière *f*

thaw [θɔ:] *n* dégel *m* ♦ *vi* (*ice*) fondre; (*food*) dégeler ♦ *vt* (*food: also:* **~ out**) (faire) dégeler

┌─ **KEYWORD** ─┐

the [ði:, ðə] *def art* **1** (*gen*) le, la *f*, l' +*vowel or h mute*, les *pl*; **the boy/girl/ink** le garçon/la fille/l'encre; **the children** les enfants; **the history of the world** l'histoire du monde; **give it to the postman** donne-le au facteur; **to play the piano/ flute** jouer du piano/de la flûte; **the rich and the poor** les riches et les pauvres

2 (*in titles*): **Elizabeth the First** Elisabeth première; **Peter the Great** Pierre le Grand
3 (*in comparisons*): **the more he works, the more he earns** plus il travaille, plus il gagne de l'argent

theatre ['θɪətər] *n* théâtre *m*; (*also:* lecture ~) amphi(théâtre) *m*; (*MED: also:* **operating** ~) salle *f* d'opération; **~-goer** *n* habitué(e) du théâtre; **theatrical** [θɪ'ætrɪkl] *adj* théâtral(e)

theft [θeft] *n* vol *m* (*larcin*)

their [ðɛər] *adj* leur; (*pl*) leurs; *see also* **my**; **~s** *pron* le (la) leur; (*pl*) les leurs; *see also* **mine**[1]

them [ðɛm, ðəm] *pron* (*direct*) les; (*indirect*) leur; (*stressed, after prep*) eux (elles); *see also* **me**

theme [θi:m] *n* thème *m*; **~ park** *n* parc *m* (d'attraction) à thème; **~ song** *n* chanson principale

themselves [ðəm'sɛlvz] *pl pron* (*reflexive*) se; (*emphatic, after prep*) eux-mêmes (elles-mêmes); *see also* **oneself**

then [ðɛn] *adv* (*at that time*) alors, à ce moment-là; (*next*) puis, ensuite; (*and also*) et puis ♦ *conj* (*therefore*) alors, dans ce cas ♦ *adj*: **the ~ president** le président d'alors *or* de l'époque; **by ~** (*past*) à ce moment-là; (*future*) d'ici là; **from ~ on** dès lors

theology [θɪ'ɔlədʒɪ] *n* théologie *f*

theoretical [θɪə'rɛtɪkl] *adj* théorique

theory ['θɪərɪ] *n* théorie *f*

therapy ['θɛrəpɪ] *n* thérapie *f*

KEYWORD

there [ðɛər] *adv* **1**: **there is, there are** il y a; **there are 3 of them** (*people, things*) il y en a 3; **there has been an accident** il y a eu un accident
2 (*referring to place*) là, là-bas; **it's there** c'est là(-bas); **in/on/up/down there** là-dedans/là-dessus/là-haut/en bas; **he went there on Friday** il y est allé vendredi; **I want that book there** je veux ce livre-là; **there he is!** le voilà!

3: **there, there** (*esp to child*) allons, allons!

there: **~abouts** *adv* (*place*) par là, près de là; (*amount*) environ, à peu près; **~after** *adv* par la suite; **~by** *adv* ainsi; **~fore** *adv* donc, par conséquent; **~'s** = **there is; there has**

thermal ['θə:ml] *adj* (*springs*) thermal(e); (*underwear*) en thermolactyl ®; (*COMPUT: paper*) thermosensible; (: *printer*) thermique

thermometer [θə'mɔmɪtər] *n* thermomètre *m*

Thermos ® ['θə:məs] *n* (*also:* ~ **flask**) thermos ® *m or f inv*

thermostat ['θə:məustæt] *n* thermostat *m*

thesaurus [θɪ'sɔ:rəs] *n* dictionnaire *m* des synonymes

these [ði:z] *pl adj* ces; (*not "those"*): **~ books** ces livres-ci ♦ *pl pron* ceux-ci (celles-ci)

thesis ['θi:sɪs] (*pl* **theses**) *n* thèse *f*

they [ðeɪ] *pl pron* ils (elles); (*stressed*) eux (elles); **~ say that …** (*it is said that*) on dit que …; **~'d** = **they had; they would; ~'ll** = **they shall; they will; ~'re** = **they are; ~'ve** = **they have**

thick [θɪk] *adj* épais(se); (*stupid*) bête, borné(e) ♦ *n*: **in the ~ of** au beau milieu de, en plein cœur de; **it's 20 cm ~** il/elle a 20 cm d'épaisseur; **~en** *vi* s'épaissir ♦ *vt* (*sauce etc*) épaissir; **~ness** *n* épaisseur *f*; **~set** *adj* trapu(e), costaud(e)

thief [θi:f] (*pl* **thieves**) *n* voleur(-euse)

thigh [θaɪ] *n* cuisse *f*

thimble ['θɪmbl] *n* dé *m* (à coudre)

thin [θɪn] *adj* mince; (*skinny*) maigre; (*soup, sauce*) peu épais(se), clair(e); (*hair, crowd*) clairsemé(e) ♦ *vt*: **to ~ (down)** (*sauce, paint*) délayer

thing [θɪŋ] *n* chose *f*; (*object*) objet *m*; (*contraption*) truc *m*; (*mania*): **to have a ~ about** être obsédé(e) par; **~s** *npl* (*belongings*) affaires *fpl*; **poor ~!** le (la) pauvre!; **the best ~ would be to** le mieux serait de; **how are ~s?** comment ça va?

think [θɪŋk] (*pt, pp* **thought**) *vi* penser, réfléchir; (believe) penser ♦ vt (imagine) imaginer; **what did you ~ of them?** qu'avez-vous pensé d'eux?; **to ~ about sth/sb** penser à qch/qn; **I'll ~ about it** je vais y réfléchir; **to ~ of doing** avoir l'idée de faire; **I ~ so/not** je crois or pense que oui/non; **to ~ well of** avoir une haute opinion de; **~ over** vt bien réfléchir à; **~ up** vt inventer, trouver; **~ tank** n groupe m de réflexion

thinly ['θɪnlɪ] adv (cut) en fines tranches; (spread) en une couche mince

third [θəːd] num troisième ♦ n (fraction) tiers m; (AUT) troisième (vitesse) f; (BRIT: SCOL: degree) ≃ licence f sans mention; **~ly** adv troisièmement; **~ party insurance** (BRIT) n assurance f au tiers; **~-rate** adj de qualité médiocre; **the T~ World** n le tiers monde

thirst [θəːst] n soif f; **~y** adj (person) qui a soif, assoiffé(e); (work) qui donne soif; **to be ~y** avoir soif

thirteen [θəː'tiːn] num treize

thirty ['θəːtɪ] num trente

KEYWORD

this [ðɪs] adj (demonstrative: pl these) ce, cet +vowel or h mute, cette f; **this man/woman/book** cet homme/cette femme/ce livre; (not "that") cet homme-ci/cette femme-ci/ce livre-ci; **this one** celui-ci (celle-ci)

♦ pron (demonstrative: pl these) ce; (not "that one") celui-ci (celle-ci), ceci; **who's this?** qui est-ce?; **what's this?** qu'est-ce que c'est?; **I prefer this to that** je préfère ceci à cela; **this is what he said** voici ce qu'il a dit; **this is Mr Brown** (in introductions) je vous présente Mr Brown; (in photo) c'est Mr Brown; (on telephone) ici Mr Brown

♦ adv (demonstrative): **it was about this big** c'était à peu près de cette grandeur or comme ça; **I didn't know it was this bad** je ne savais pas que c'était si or aussi mauvais

---

thistle ['θɪsl] n chardon m

thorn [θɔːn] n épine f

thorough ['θʌrə] adj (search) minutieux(-euse); (knowledge, research) approfondi(e); (work, person) consciencieux(-euse); (cleaning) à fond; **~fare** n route f; **"no ~fare"** "passage interdit"; **~ly** adv minutieusement; en profondeur; à fond; (very) tout à fait

those [ðəuz] pl adj ces; (not "these"): **~ books** ces livres-là ♦ pl pron ceux-là (celles-là)

though [ðəu] conj bien que +sub, quoique +sub ♦ adv pourtant

thought [θɔːt] pt, pp of think ♦ n pensée f; (idea) idée f; (opinion) avis m; **~ful** adj (deep in thought) pensif(-ive); (serious) réfléchi(e); (considerate) prévenant(e); **~less** adj étourdi(e); qui manque de considération

thousand ['θauzənd] num mille; **two ~** deux mille; **~s of** des milliers de; **~th** num millième

thrash [θræʃ] vt rouer de coups; donner une correction à; (defeat) battre à plate couture; **~ about, ~ around** vi se débattre; **~ out** vt débattre de

thread [θrɛd] n fil m; (TECH) pas m, filetage m ♦ vt (needle) enfiler; **~bare** adj râpé(e), élimé(e)

threat [θrɛt] n menace f; **~en** vi menacer ♦ vt: **to ~en sb with sth/to do** menacer qn de qch/de faire

three [θriː] num trois; **~-dimensional** adj à trois dimensions; **~-piece suit** n complet m (avec gilet); **~-piece suite** n salon m comprenant un canapé et deux fauteuils assortis; **~-ply** adj (wool) trois fils inv

threshold ['θrɛʃhəuld] n seuil m

threw [θruː] pt of throw

thrifty ['θrɪftɪ] adj économe

thrill [θrɪl] n (excitement) émotion f, sensation forte; (shudder) frisson m ♦ vt (audience) électriser; **to be ~ed** (with gift etc) être ravi(e); **~er** n film m (or roman m or pièce f) à suspense; **~ing** adj saisissant(e),

thrive → tie

thrive [θraɪv] (*pt, pp* **thrived**) *vi* pousser, se développer; (*business*) prospérer; **he ~s on it** cela lui réussit; **thriving** *adj* (*business, community*) prospère

throat [θrəut] *n* gorge *f*; **to have a sore ~** avoir mal à la gorge

throb [θrɔb] *vi* (*heart*) palpiter; (*engine*) vibrer; **my head is ~bing** j'ai des élancements dans la tête

throes [θrəuz] *npl*: **in the ~ of** au beau milieu de

throne [θrəun] *n* trône *m*

throng [θrɔŋ] *n* foule *f* ♦ *vt* se presser dans

throttle ['θrɔtl] *n* (AUT) accélérateur *m* ♦ *vt* étrangler

through [θruː] *prep* à travers; (*time*) pendant, durant; (*by means of*) par, par l'intermédiaire de; (*owing to*) à cause de ♦ *adj* (*ticket, train, passage*) direct(e) ♦ *adv* à travers; **to put sb ~ to sb** (BRIT: TEL) passer qn à qn; **to be ~** (BRIT: TEL) avoir la communication; (*esp US: have finished*) avoir fini; **to be ~ with sb** (*relationship*) avoir rompu avec qn; **"no ~ road"** (BRIT) "impasse"; **~out** *prep* (*place*) partout dans; (*time*) durant tout(e) le (la) ♦ *adv* partout

throw [θrəu] (*pt* **threw**, *pp* **thrown**) *n* jet *m*; (SPORT) lancer *m* ♦ *vt* lancer, jeter; (SPORT) lancer; (*rider*) désarçonner; (*fig*) décontenancer; **to ~ a party** donner une réception; **~ away** *vt* jeter; **~ off** *vt* se débarrasser de; **~ out** *vt* jeter; (*reject*) rejeter; (*person*) mettre à la porte; **~ up** *vi* vomir; **~away** *adj* à jeter; (*remark*) fait(e) en passant; **~-in** *n* (SPORT) remise *f* en jeu

thru [θruː] (US) = **through**

thrush [θrʌʃ] *n* (*bird*) grive *f*

thrust [θrʌst] (*pt, pp* **thrust**) *n* (TECH) poussée *f* ♦ *vt* pousser brusquement; (*push in*) enfoncer

thud [θʌd] *n* bruit sourd

thug [θʌg] *n* voyou *m*

thumb [θʌm] *n* (ANAT) pouce *m* ♦ *vt*: **to ~ a lift** faire de l'auto-stop, arrêter une voi-

ture; **~ through** *vt* (*book*) feuilleter; **~tack** (US) *n* punaise *f* (*clou*)

thump [θʌmp] *n* grand coup; (*sound*) bruit sourd ♦ *vt* cogner sur ♦ *vi* cogner, battre fort

thunder ['θʌndəʳ] *n* tonnerre *m* ♦ *vi* tonner; (*train etc*): **to ~ past** passer dans un grondement *or* un bruit de tonnerre; **~bolt** *n* foudre *f*; **~clap** *n* coup *m* de tonnerre; **~storm** *n* orage *m*; **~y** *adj* orageux(-euse)

Thursday ['θəːzdɪ] *n* jeudi *m*

thus [ðʌs] *adv* ainsi

thwart [θwɔːt] *vt* contrecarrer

thyme [taɪm] *n* thym *m*

tiara [tɪ'ɑːrə] *n* diadème *m*

tick [tɪk] *n* (*sound: of clock*) tic-tac *m*; (*mark*) coche *f*; (ZOOL) tique *f*; (BRIT: *inf*): **in a ~** dans une seconde ♦ *vi* faire tic-tac ♦ *vt* (*item on list*) cocher; **~ off** *vt* (*item on list*) cocher; (*person*) réprimander, attraper; **~ over** *vi* (*engine*) tourner au ralenti; (*fig*) aller *or* marcher doucettement

ticket ['tɪkɪt] *n* billet *m*; (*for bus, tube*) ticket *m*; (*in shop: on goods*) étiquette *f*; (*for library*) carte *f*; (*parking ~*) papillon *m*, p.-v. *m*; **~ collector**, **~ inspector** *n* contrôleur(-euse); **~ office** *n* guichet *m*, bureau *m* de vente des billets

tickle ['tɪkl] *vt, vi* chatouiller; **ticklish** *adj* (*person*) chatouilleux(-euse); (*problem*) épineux(-euse)

tidal ['taɪdl] *adj* (*force*) de la marée; (*estuary*) à marée; **~ wave** *n* raz-de-marée *m* *inv*

tidbit ['tɪdbɪt] (US) *n* = **titbit**

tiddlywinks ['tɪdlɪwɪŋks] *n* jeu *m* de puce

tide [taɪd] *n* marée *f*; (*fig: of events*) cours *m* ♦ *vt*: **to ~ sb over** dépanner qn; **high/low ~** marée haute/basse

tidy ['taɪdɪ] *adj* (*room*) bien rangé(e); (*dress, work*) net(te), soigné(e); (*person*) ordonné(e), qui a de l'ordre ♦ *vt* (*also:* **~ up**) ranger

tie [taɪ] *n* (*string etc*) cordon *m*; (BRIT: *also:* **necktie**) cravate *f*; (*fig: link*) lien *m*; (SPORT: *draw*) égalité *f* de points; match nul ♦ vt (*parcel*) attacher; (*ribbon, shoelaces*) nouer ♦ vi (SPORT) faire match nul; finir à égalité de points; **to ~ sth in a bow** faire un nœud à or avec qch; **to ~ a knot in sth** faire un nœud à qch; **~ down** vt (*fig*): **to ~ sb down (to)** contraindre qn (à accepter); **to be ~d down** (*by relationship*) se fixer; **~ up** vt (*parcel*) ficeler; (*dog, boat*) attacher; (*prisoner*) ligoter; (*arrangements*) conclure; **to be ~d up** (*busy*) être pris(e) or occupé(e)

tier [tɪəʳ] n gradin m; (*of cake*) étage m

tiger ['taɪgəʳ] n tigre m

tight [taɪt] adj (*rope*) tendu(e), raide; (*clothes*) étroit(e), très juste; (*budget, programme, bend*) serré(e); (*control*) strict(e), sévère; (*inf: drunk*) ivre, rond(e) ♦ adv (*squeeze*) très fort; (*shut*) hermétiquement, bien; **~en** vt (*rope*) tendre; (*screw*) resserrer; (*control*) renforcer ♦ vi se tendre, se resserrer; **~fisted** adj avare; **~ly** adv (*grasp*) bien, très fort; (*rope*) n corde f raide; **~s** (BRIT) npl collant m

tile [taɪl] n (*on roof*) tuile f; (*on wall or floor*) carreau m; **~d** adj en tuiles; carrelé(e)

till [tɪl] n caisse (enregistreuse) ♦ vt (*land*) cultiver ♦ prep, conj = **until**

tiller ['tɪləʳ] n (NAUT) barre f (du gouvernail)

tilt [tɪlt] vt pencher, incliner ♦ vi pencher, être incliné(e)

timber ['tɪmbəʳ] n (*material*) bois m (de construction); (*trees*) arbres mpl

time [taɪm] n temps m; (*epoch: often pl*) époque f, temps; (*by clock*) heure f; (*moment*) moment m; (*occasion, also* MATH) fois f; (MUS) mesure f ♦ vt (*race*) chronométrer; (*programme*) minuter; (*visit*) fixer; (*remark etc*) choisir le moment de; **a long ~** un long moment, longtemps; **for the ~ being** pour le moment; **4 at a ~** 4 à la fois; **from ~ to ~** de temps en temps; **at ~s** parfois; **in ~** (*soon enough*) à temps; (*after some ~*) avec le temps, à la longue; (MUS) en mesure; **in a week's ~** dans une semaine; **in no ~** en un rien de temps; **any ~** n'importe quand; **on ~** à l'heure; **5 ~s 5** 5 fois 5; **what ~ is it?** quelle heure est-il?; **to have a good ~** bien s'amuser; **~ bomb** n bombe f à retardement; **~ lag** (BRIT) n décalage m; (*in travel*) décalage horaire; **~less** adj éternel(le); **~ly** adj opportun(e); **~ off** n temps m libre; **~r** n (TECH) minuteur m; (*in kitchen*) compte-minutes m inv; **~scale** n délais mpl; **~-share** n maison f/appartement m en multipropriété; **~ switch** (BRIT) n minuteur m; (*for lighting*) minuterie f; **~table** n (RAIL) indicateur m horaire; (SCOL) emploi m du temps; **~ zone** n fuseau m horaire

timid ['tɪmɪd] adj timide; (*easily scared*) peureux(-euse)

timing ['taɪmɪŋ] n minutage m; chronométrage m; **the ~ of his resignation** le moment choisi pour sa démission

timpani ['tɪmpənɪ] npl timbales fpl

tin [tɪn] n étain m; (*also: ~ plate*) fer-blanc m; (BRIT: can) boîte f (de conserve); (*for storage*) boîte f; **~foil** n papier m d'étain or aluminium

tinge [tɪndʒ] n nuance f ♦ vt: **~d with** teinté(e) de

tingle ['tɪŋgl] vi picoter; (*person*) avoir des picotements

tinker ['tɪŋkəʳ] n (*gipsy*) romanichel m; **~ with** vt fus bricoler, rafistoler

tinkle ['tɪŋkl] vi tinter

tinned [tɪnd] (BRIT) adj (*food*) en boîte, en conserve

tin opener (BRIT) n ouvre-boîte(s) m

tinsel ['tɪnsl] n guirlandes fpl de Noël (*argentées*)

tint [tɪnt] n teinte f; (*for hair*) shampooing colorant; **~ed** adj (*hair*) teint(e); (*spectacles, glass*) teinté(e)

tiny ['taɪnɪ] adj minuscule

tip [tɪp] n (*end*) bout m; (*gratuity*) pourboire m; (BRIT: for rubbish) décharge f; (*advice*) tuyau m ♦ vt (*waiter*) donner un pourboire à; (*tilt*) incliner; (*overturn: also:* **~ over**) renverser; (*empty: ~ out*) déverser; **~-off** n (*hint*) tuyau m; **~ped** (BRIT) adj (*cigarette*) (à bout) filtre inv

tipsy ['tɪpsɪ] (*inf*) *adj* un peu ivre, éméché(e)

tiptoe ['tɪptəu] *n*: **on ~** sur la pointe des pieds

tiptop [tɪp'tɔp] *adj*: **in ~ condition** en excellent état

tire ['taɪər] *n* (*US*) = **tyre** ♦ *vt* fatiguer ♦ *vi* se fatiguer; **~d** *adj* fatigué(e); **to be ~d of** en avoir assez de, être las (lasse) de; **~less** *adj* (*person*) infatigable; (*efforts*) inlassable; **~some** *adj* ennuyeux(-euse); **tiring** *adj* fatigant(e)

tissue ['tɪʃuː] *n* tissu *m*; (*paper handkerchief*) mouchoir *m* en papier, kleenex ® *m*; **~ paper** *n* papier *m* de soie

tit [tɪt] *n* (*bird*) mésange *f*; **to give ~ for tat** rendre la pareille

titbit ['tɪtbɪt] *n* (*food*) friandise *f*; (*news*) potin *m*

title ['taɪtl] *n* titre *m*; **~ deed** *n* (*LAW*) titre (constitutif) de propriété; **~ role** *n* rôle principal

TM *abbr* = **trademark**

KEYWORD

to [tuː, tə] *prep* **1** (*direction*) à; **to go to France/Portugal/London/school** aller en France/au Portugal/à Londres/à l'école; **to go to Claude's/the doctor's** aller chez Claude/le docteur; **the road to Edinburgh** la route d'Édimbourg

2 (*as far as*) (jusqu')à; **to count to 10** compter jusqu'à 10; **from 40 to 50 people** de 40 à 50 personnes

3 (*with expressions of time*): **a quarter to 5** 5 heures moins le quart; **it's twenty to 3** il est 3 heures moins vingt

4 (*for, of*) de; **the key to the front door** la clé de la porte d'entrée; **a letter to his wife** une lettre (adressée) à sa femme

5 (*expressing indirect object*) à; **to give sth to sb** donner qch à qn; **to talk to sb** parler à qn

6 (*in relation to*) à; **3 goals to 2** 3 (buts) à 2; **30 miles to the gallon** 9,4 litres aux cent (km)

7 (*purpose, result*): **to come to sb's aid** venir au secours de qn, porter secours à qn; **to sentence sb to death** condamner qn à mort; **to my surprise** à ma grande surprise

♦ **with** *vb* **1** (*simple infinitive*): **to go/eat** aller/manger

2 (*following another vb*): **to want/try/start to do** vouloir/essayer de/commencer à faire

3 (*with vb omitted*): **I don't want to** je ne veux pas

4 (*purpose, result*) pour; **I did it to help you** je l'ai fait pour vous aider

5 (*equivalent to relative clause*): **I have things to do** j'ai des choses à faire; **the main thing is to try** l'important est d'essayer

6 (*after adjective etc*): **ready to go** prêt(e) à partir; **too old/young to ...** trop vieux/jeune pour ...

♦ *adv*: **push/pull the door to** tirez/poussez la porte

toad [təud] *n* crapaud *m*

toadstool ['təudstuːl] *n* champignon (vénéneux)

toast [təust] *n* (*CULIN*) pain grillé, toast *m*; (*drink, speech*) toast ♦ *vt* (*CULIN*) faire griller; (*drink to*) porter un toast à; **~er** *n* grille-pain *m inv*

tobacco [tə'bækəu] *n* tabac *m*; **~nist** *n* marchand(e) de tabac; **~nist's (shop)** *n* (bureau *m* de) tabac *m*

toboggan [tə'bɔgən] *n* toboggan *m*; (*child's*) luge *f* ♦ *vi*: **to go ~ing** faire de la luge

today [tə'deɪ] *adv* (*also fig*) aujourd'hui ♦ *n* aujourd'hui *m*

toddler ['tɔdlər] *n* enfant *m/f* qui commence à marcher, bambin *m*

toe [təu] *n* doigt *m* de pied, orteil *m*; (*of shoe*) bout *m* ♦ *vt*: **to ~ the line** (*fig*) obéir, se conformer; **~nail** *n* ongle *m* du pied

toffee ['tɔfɪ] *n* caramel *m*; **~ apple** (*BRIT*) *n* pomme caramélisée

together [tə'geðər] *adv* ensemble; (*at same*

time) en même temps; **~ with** avec

toil [tɔɪl] *n* dur travail, labeur *m* ♦ *vi* peiner

toilet ['tɔɪlət] *n* (*BRIT: lavatory*) toilettes *fpl* ♦ *cpd* (*accessories etc*) de toilette; **~ bag** *n* nécessaire *m* de toilette; **~ paper** *n* papier *m* hygiénique; **~ries** *npl* articles *mpl* de toilette; **~ roll** *n* rouleau *m* de papier hygiénique

token ['təukən] *n* (*sign*) marque *f*, témoignage *m*; (*metal disc*) jeton *m* ♦ *adj* (*strike, payment etc*) symbolique; **book/record ~** (*BRIT*) chèque-livre/-disque *m*; **gift ~** bon-cadeau *m*

told [təuld] *pt, pp of* **tell**

tolerable ['tɔlərəbl] *adj* (*bearable*) tolérable; (*fairly good*) passable

tolerant ['tɔlərnt] *adj*: **~ (of)** tolérant(e) (à l'égard de)

tolerate ['tɔləreɪt] *vt* supporter, tolérer

toll [təul] *n* (*tax, charge*) péage *m* ♦ *vi* (*bell*) sonner; **the accident ~ on the roads** le nombre des victimes de la route

tomato [tə'mɑːtəu] (*pl* **~es**) *n* tomate *f*

tomb [tuːm] *n* tombe *f*

tomboy ['tɔmbɔɪ] *n* garçon manqué

tombstone ['tuːmstəun] *n* pierre tombale

tomcat ['tɔmkæt] *n* matou *m*

tomorrow [tə'mɔrəu] *adv* (*also fig*) demain ♦ *n* demain *m*; **the day after ~** après-demain; **~ morning** demain matin

ton [tʌn] *n* tonne *f* (*BRIT* = 1016kg; *US* = 907kg); (*metric*) tonne (= 1000 kg); **~s** *pl* (*inf*) des tas de

tone [təun] *n* ton *m* ♦ *vi* (*also:* **~ in**) s'harmoniser; **~ down** *vt* (*colour, criticism*) adoucir; (*sound*) baisser; **~ up** *vt* (*muscles*) tonifier; **~-deaf** *adj* qui n'a pas d'oreille

tongs [tɔŋz] *npl* (*for coal*) pincettes *fpl*; (*for hair*) fer *m* à friser

tongue [tʌŋ] *n* langue *f*; **~ in cheek** ironiquement; **~-tied** *adj* (*fig*) muet(te); **~twister** *n* phrase *f* très difficile à prononcer

tonic ['tɔnɪk] *n* (*MED*) tonique *m*; (*also:* **~ water**) tonic *m*, Schweppes ® *m*

tonight [tə'naɪt] *adv, n* cette nuit; (*this evening*) ce soir

tonsil ['tɔnsl] *n* amygdale *f*; **~litis** [tɔnsɪ'laɪtɪs] *n* angine *f*

too [tuː] *adv* (*excessively*) trop; (*also*) aussi; **~ much** *adv* trop ♦ *adj* trop de; **~ many** trop de; **~ bad!** tant pis!

took [tuk] *pt of* **take**

tool [tuːl] *n* outil *m*; **~ box** *n* boîte *f* à outils

toot [tuːt] *n* (*of car horn*) coup *m* de klaxon; (*of whistle*) coup de sifflet ♦ *vi* (*with car horn*) klaxonner

tooth [tuːθ] (*pl* **teeth**) *n* (*ANAT, TECH*) dent *f*; **~ache** *n* mal *m* de dents; **~brush** *n* brosse *f* à dents; **~paste** *n* (pâte *f*) dentifrice *m*; **~pick** *n* cure-dent *m*

top [tɔp] *n* (*of mountain, head*) sommet *m*; (*of page, ladder, garment*) haut *m*; (*of box, cupboard, table*) dessus *m*; (*lid: of box, jar*) couvercle *m*; (: *of bottle*) bouchon *m*; (*toy*) toupie *f* ♦ *adj* du haut; (*in rank*) premier(-ère); (*best*) meilleur(e) ♦ *vt* (*exceed*) dépasser; (*be first in*) être en tête de; **on ~ of** sur; (*in addition to*) en plus de; **from ~ to bottom** de fond en comble; **~ up** (*US* **~ off**) *vt* (*bottle*) remplir; (*salary*) compléter; **~ floor** *n* dernier étage; **~ hat** *n* haut-de-forme *m*; **~-heavy** *adj* (*object*) trop lourd(e) du haut

topic ['tɔpɪk] *n* sujet *m*, thème *m*; **~al** *adj* d'actualité

top: **~less** *adj* (*bather etc*) aux seins nus; **~-level** *adj* (*talks*) au plus haut niveau; **~most** *adj* le (la) plus haut(e)

topple ['tɔpl] *vt* renverser, faire tomber ♦ *vi* basculer; tomber

top-secret ['tɔp'siːkrɪt] *adj* top secret(-ète)

topsy-turvy ['tɔpsɪ'tɜːvɪ] *adj, adv* sens dessus dessous

torch [tɔːtʃ] *n* torche *f*; (*BRIT: electric*) lampe *f* de poche

tore [tɔːr] *pt of* **tear**¹

torment [*n* 'tɔːmɛnt, *vb* tɔː'mɛnt] *n* tourment *m* ♦ *vt* tourmenter; (*fig: annoy*) harceler

torn [tɔːn] *pp of* **tear**¹

tornado [tɔː'neɪdəu] (*pl* **~es**) *n* tornade *f*

torpedo [tɔː'piːdəu] (*pl* **~es**) *n* torpille *f*

torrent ['tɔrnt] *n* torrent *m*; **~ial** [tɔ'renʃl] *adj* torrentiel(le)

tortoise ['tɔːtəs] *n* tortue *f*; **~shell** *adj* en écaille

torture ['tɔːtʃər] *n* torture *f* ♦ *vt* torturer

Tory ['tɔːrɪ] (*BRIT: POL*) *adj, n* tory (*m/f*), conservateur(-trice)

toss [tɔs] *vt* lancer, jeter; (*pancake*) faire sauter; (*head*) rejeter en arrière; **to ~ a coin** jouer à pile ou face; **to ~ up for sth** jouer qch à pile ou face; **to ~ and turn** (*in bed*) se tourner et se retourner

tot [tɔt] *n* (*BRIT: drink*) petit verre; (*child*) bambin *m*

total ['təʊtl] *adj* total(e) ♦ *n* total *m* ♦ *vt* (*add up*) faire le total de, additionner; (*amount to*) s'élever à; **~ly** *adv* totalement

totter ['tɔtər] *vi* chanceler

touch [tʌtʃ] *n* contact *m*, toucher *m*; (*sense, also skill: of pianist etc*) toucher ♦ *vt* toucher; (*tamper with*) toucher à; **a ~ of** (*fig*) un petit peu de; une touche de; **to get in ~ with** prendre contact avec; **to lose ~** (*friends*) se perdre de vue; **~ on** *vt fus* (*topic*) effleurer, aborder; **~ up** *vt* (*paint*) retoucher; **~-and-go** *adj* incertain(e); **~down** *n* atterrissage *m*; (*on sea*) amerrissage *m*; (*US: FOOTBALL*) touché-en-but *m*; **~ed** *adj* (*moved*) touché(e); **~ing** *adj* touchant(e), attendrissant(e); **~line** *n* (*SPORT*) (ligne *f* de) touche *f*; **~y** *adj* (*person*) susceptible

tough [tʌf] *adj* dur(e); (*resistant*) résistant(e), solide; (*meat*) dur, coriace; (*firm*) inflexible; (*task*) dur, pénible; **~en** *vt* (*character*) endurcir; (*glass etc*) renforcer

toupee ['tuːpeɪ] *n* postiche *m*

tour ['tʊər] *n* voyage *m*; (*also*: **package ~**) voyage organisé; (*of town, museum*) tour *m*, visite *f*; (*by artist*) tournée *f* ♦ *vt* visiter; **~ guide** *n* (*person*) guide *m/f*

tourism ['tʊərɪzm] *n* tourisme *m*

tourist ['tʊərɪst] *n* touriste *m/f* ♦ *cpd* touristique; **~ office** *n* syndicat *m* d'initiative

tournament ['tʊənəmənt] *n* tournoi *m*

tousled ['taʊzld] *adj* (*hair*) ébouriffé(e)

tout [taʊt] *vi*: **to ~ for** essayer de raccrocher, racoler ♦ *n* (*also*: **ticket ~**) revendeur *m* de billets

tow [təʊ] *vt* remorquer; (*caravan, trailer*) tracter; **"on ~"** (*BRIT*) or **"in ~"** (*US*) (*AUT*) "véhicule en remorque"

toward(s) [tə'wɔːd(z)] *prep* vers; (*of attitude*) envers, à l'égard de; (*of purpose*) pour

towel ['taʊəl] *n* serviette *f* (de toilette); **~ling** *n* (*fabric*) tissu éponge *m*; **~ rail** (*US* **towel rack**) *n* porte-serviettes *m inv*

tower ['taʊər] *n* tour *f*; **~ block** (*BRIT*) *n* tour *f* (d'habitation); **~ing** *adj* très haut(e), imposant(e)

town [taʊn] *n* ville *f*; **to go to ~** aller en ville; (*fig*) y mettre le paquet; **~ centre** *n* centre *m* de la ville, centre-ville *m*; **~ council** *n* conseil municipal; **~ hall** *n* ≈ mairie *f*; **~ plan** *n* plan *m* de ville; **~ planning** *n* urbanisme *m*

towrope ['təʊrəʊp] *n* (câble *m* de) remorque *f*

tow truck (*US*) *n* dépanneuse *f*

toy [tɔɪ] *n* jouet *m*; **~ with** *vt fus* jouer avec; (*idea*) caresser

trace [treɪs] *n* trace *f* ♦ *vt* (*draw*) tracer, dessiner; (*follow*) suivre la trace de; (*locate*) retrouver; **tracing paper** *n* papier-calque *m*

track [træk] *n* (*mark*) trace *f*; (*path: gen*) chemin *m*, piste *f*; (: *of bullet etc*) trajectoire *f*; (: *of suspect, animal*) piste *f*; (*RAIL*) voie ferrée, rails *mpl*; (*on tape, SPORT*) piste; (*on record*) plage *f* ♦ *vt* suivre la trace ou la piste de; **to keep ~ of** suivre; **~ down** *vt* (*prey*) trouver et capturer; (*sth lost*) finir par retrouver; **~suit** *n* survêtement *m*

tract [trækt] *n* (*of land*) étendue *f*

traction ['trækʃən] *n* traction *f*; (*MED*): **in ~** en extension

tractor ['træktər] *n* tracteur *m*

trade [treɪd] *n* commerce *m*; (*skill, job*) métier *m* ♦ *vi* faire du commerce ♦ *vt* (*exchange*): **to ~ sth (for sth)** échanger qch (contre qch); **~ in** *vt* (*old car etc*) faire reprendre; **~ fair** *n* foire(-exposition) commerciale; **~-in price** *n* prix *m* à la reprise; **~mark** *n* marque *f* de fabrique; **~**

name *n* nom *m* de marque; **~r** *n* commerçant(e), négociant(e); **~sman** (*irreg*) *n* (*shopkeeper*) commerçant; **~ union** *n* syndicat *m*; **~ unionist** *n* syndicaliste *m/f*

tradition [trəˈdɪʃən] *n* tradition *f*; **~al** *adj* traditionnel(le)

traffic [ˈtræfɪk] *n* trafic *m*; (*cars*) circulation *f* ♦ *vi*: **to ~ in** (*pej: liquor, drugs*) faire le trafic de; **~ calming** *n* ralentissement *m* de la circulation; **~ circle** (*US*) *n* rond-point *m*; **~ jam** *n* embouteillage *m*; **~ lights** *npl* feux *mpl* (de signalisation); **~ warden** *n* contractuel(le)

tragedy [ˈtrædʒədɪ] *n* tragédie *f*

tragic [ˈtrædʒɪk] *adj* tragique

trail [treɪl] *n* (*tracks*) trace *f*, piste *f*; (*path*) chemin *m*, piste; (*of smoke etc*) traînée *f* ♦ *vt* traîner, tirer; (*follow*) suivre ♦ *vi* traîner; (*in game, contest*) être en retard; **~ behind** *vi* traîner, être à la traîne; **~er** *n* (*AUT*) remorque *f*; (*US*) caravane *f*; (*CINEMA*) bande-annonce *f*; **~er truck** (*US*) *n* (camion *m*) semi-remorque *m*

train [treɪn] *n* train *m*; (*in underground*) rame *f*; (*of dress*) traîne *f* ♦ *vt* (*apprentice, doctor etc*) former; (*sportsman*) entraîner; (*dog*) dresser; (*memory*) exercer; (*point: gun etc*): **to ~ sth on** braquer qch sur ♦ *vi* suivre une formation; (*SPORT*) s'entraîner; **one's ~ of thought** le fil de sa pensée; **~ed** *adj* qualifié(e), qui a reçu une formation; (*animal*) dressé(e); **~ee** [treɪˈniː] *n* stagiaire *m/f*; (*in trade*) apprenti(e); **~er** *n* (*SPORT: coach*) entraîneur(-euse); (: *shoe*) chaussure *f* de sport; (*of dogs etc*) dresseur(-euse); **~ing** *n* formation *f*; entraînement *m*; **in ~ing** (*SPORT*) à l'entraînement; (*fit*) en forme; **~ing college** *n* école professionnelle; (*for teachers*) ≈ école normale; **~ing shoes** *npl* chaussures *fpl* de sport

trait [treɪt] *n* trait *m* (de caractère)

traitor [ˈtreɪtə] *n* traître *m*

tram [træm] *n* (*BRIT*) (*also:* **~car**) tram(way) *m*

tramp [træmp] *n* (*person*) vagabond(e), clo-

chard(e); (*inf: pej: woman*): **to be a ~** être coureuse ♦ *vi* marcher d'un pas lourd

trample [ˈtræmpl] *vt*: **to ~ (underfoot)** piétiner

trampoline [ˈtræmpəliːn] *n* trampoline *m*

tranquil [ˈtræŋkwɪl] *adj* tranquille; **~lizer** (*US* **tranquilizer**) *n* (*MED*) tranquillisant *m*

transact [trænˈzækt] *vt* (*business*) traiter; **~ion** *n* transaction *f*

transatlantic [ˈtrænzətˈlæntɪk] *adj* transatlantique

transfer [*n* ˈtrænsfə, *vb* trænsˈfəː] *n* (*gen, also SPORT*) transfert *m*; (*POL: of power*) passation *f*; (*picture, design*) décalcomanie *f*; (: *stick-on*) autocollant *m* ♦ *vt* transférer; passer; **to ~ the charges** (*BRIT: TEL*) téléphoner en P.C.V.; **~ desk** *n* (*AVIAT*) guichet *m* de transit

transform [trænsˈfɔːm] *vt* transformer

transfusion [trænsˈfjuːʒən] *n* transfusion *f*

transient [ˈtrænzɪənt] *adj* transitoire, éphémère

transistor [trænˈzɪstə] *n* (~ *radio*) transistor *m*

transit [ˈtrænzɪt] *n*: **in ~** en transit

transitive [ˈtrænzɪtɪv] *adj* (*LING*) transitif(-ive)

transit lounge *n* salle *f* de transit

translate [trænzˈleɪt] *vt* traduire; **translation** *n* traduction *f*; **translator** *n* traducteur(-trice)

transmission [trænzˈmɪʃən] *n* transmission *f*

transmit [trænzˈmɪt] *vt* transmettre; (*RADIO, TV*) émettre

transparency [trænsˈpɛərnsɪ] *n* (*of glass etc*) transparence *f*; (*BRIT: PHOT*) diapositive *f*

transparent [trænsˈpærnt] *adj* transparent(e)

transpire [trænsˈpaɪə] *vi* (*turn out*): **it ~d that ...** on a appris que ...; (*happen*) arriver

transplant [*vb* trænsˈplɑːnt, *n* ˈtrænsplɑːnt] *vt* transplanter; (*seedlings*) repiquer ♦ *n* (*MED*) transplantation *f*

transport [*n* ˈtrænspɔːt, *vb* trænsˈpɔːt] *n*

transport *m*; (*car*) moyen *m* de transport, voiture *f* ♦ *vt* transporter; **~ation** ['trænspɔː'teɪʃən] *n* transport *m*; (*means of transportation*) moyen *m* de transport; **~ café** (*BRIT*) *n* ≃ restaurant *m* de routiers

trap [træp] *n* (*snare, trick*) piège *m*; (*carriage*) cabriolet *m* ♦ *vt* prendre au piège; (*confine*) coincer; **~ door** *n* trappe *f*

trapeze [trə'piːz] *n* trapèze *m*

trappings ['træpɪŋz] *npl* ornements *mpl*; attributs *mpl*

trash [træʃ] (*pej*) *n* (*goods*) camelote *f*; (*nonsense*) sottises *fpl*; **~ can** (*US*) *n* poubelle *f*; **~y** (*inf*) *adj* de camelote; (*novel*) de quatre sous

trauma ['trɔːmə] *n* traumatisme *m*; **~tic** [trɔː'mætɪk] *adj* traumatisant(e)

travel ['trævl] *n* voyage(s) *m(pl)* ♦ *vi* voyager; (*news, sound*) circuler, se propager ♦ *vt* (*distance*) parcourir; **~ agency** *n* agence *f* de voyages; **~ agent** *n* agent *m* de voyages; **~ler** (*US* **traveler**) *n* voyageur(-euse); **~ler's cheque** (*US* **traveler's check**) *n* chèque *m* de voyage; **~ling** (*US* **traveling**) *n* voyage(s) *m(pl)*; **~ sickness** *n* mal *m* de la route (*or* de mer *or* de l'air)

trawler ['trɔːlər] *n* chalutier *m*

tray [treɪ] *n* (*for carrying*) plateau *m*; (*on desk*) corbeille *f*

treacherous ['tretʃərəs] *adj* (*person, look*) traître(-esse); (*ground, tide*) dont il faut se méfier

treacle ['triːkl] *n* mélasse *f*

tread [tred] (*pt* **trod**, *pp* **trodden**) *n* pas *m*; (*sound*) bruit *m* de pas; (*of tyre*) chape *f*, bande *f* de roulement ♦ *vi* marcher; **~ on** *vt fus* marcher sur

treason ['triːzn] *n* trahison *f*

treasure ['treʒər] *n* trésor *m* ♦ *vt* (*value*) tenir beaucoup à; **~r** *n* trésorier(-ère); **treasury** *n*: **the Treasury,** (*US*) **the Treasury Department** le ministère des Finances

treat [triːt] *n* petit cadeau, petite surprise ♦ *vt* traiter; **to ~ sb to sth** offrir qch à qn

treatment *n* traitement *m*

treaty ['triːtɪ] *n* traité *m*

treble ['trebl] *adj* triple ♦ *vt, vi* tripler; **~ clef** *n* (*MUS*) clé *f* de sol

tree [triː] *n* arbre *m*

trek [trek] *n* (*long*) voyage; (*on foot*) (longue) marche, tirée *f*

tremble ['trembl] *vi* trembler

tremendous [trɪ'mendəs] *adj* (*enormous*) énorme, fantastique; (*excellent*) formidable

tremor ['tremər] *n* tremblement *m*; (*also*: **earth ~**) secousse *f* sismique

trench [trentʃ] *n* tranchée *f*

trend [trend] *n* (*tendency*) tendance *f*; (*of events*) cours *m*; (*fashion*) mode *f*; **~y** *adj* (*idea, person*) dans le vent; (*clothes*) dernier cri *inv*

trespass ['trespəs] *vi*: **to ~ on** s'introduire sans permission dans; **"no ~ing"** "propriété privée", "défense d'entrer"

trestle ['tresl] *n* tréteau *m*

trial ['traɪəl] *n* (*LAW*) procès *m*, jugement *m*; (*test: of machine etc*) essai *m*; **~s** *npl* (*unpleasant experiences*) épreuves *fpl*; **to be on ~** (*LAW*) passer en jugement; **by ~ and error** par tâtonnements; **~ period** *n* période *f* d'essai

triangle ['traɪæŋgl] *n* (*MATH, MUS*) triangle *m*; **triangular** [traɪ'æŋgjulər] *adj* triangulaire

tribe [traɪb] *n* tribu *f*; **~sman** (*irreg*) *n* membre *m* d'une tribu

tribunal [traɪ'bjuːnl] *n* tribunal *m*

tributary ['trɪbjutərɪ] *n* (*river*) affluent *m*

tribute ['trɪbjuːt] *n* tribut *m*, hommage *m*; **to pay ~ to** rendre hommage à

trick [trɪk] *n* (*magic ~*) tour *m*; (*joke, prank*) tour, farce *f*; (*skill, knack*) astuce *f*, truc *m*; (*CARDS*) levée *f* ♦ *vt* attraper, rouler; **to play a ~ on sb** jouer un tour à qn; **that should do the ~** ça devrait faire l'affaire; **~ery** *n* ruse *f*

trickle ['trɪkl] *n* (*of water etc*) filet *m* ♦ *vi* couler en un filet *or* goutte à goutte

tricky ['trɪkɪ] *adj* difficile, délicat(e)

tricycle ['traɪsɪkl] *n* tricycle *m*

trifle ['traɪfl] *n* bagatelle *f*; (*CULIN*) ≃ diplomate *m* ♦ *adv*: **a ~ long** un peu long;

trifling *adj* insignifiant(e)

trigger ['trɪgər] *n* (*of gun*) gâchette *f*; ~ **off**
vt déclencher

trim [trɪm] *adj* (*house, garden*) bien tenu(e);
(*figure*) svelte ♦ *n* (*haircut etc*) légère coupe; (*on car*) garnitures *fpl* ♦ *vt* (*cut*) couper légèrement; (*NAUT: a sail*) gréer; (*decorate*): **to ~ (with)** décorer (de); **~mings**
npl (*CULIN*) garniture *f*

trinket ['trɪŋkɪt] *n* bibelot *m*; (*piece of jewellery*) colifichet *m*

trip [trɪp] *n* voyage *m*; (*excursion*) excursion
f; (*stumble*) faux pas ♦ *vi* faire un faux
pas, trébucher; **on a ~** en voyage; ~ **up**
vi trébucher ♦ *vt* faire un croc-en-jambe à

tripe [traɪp] *n* (*CULIN*) tripes *fpl*; (*pej: rubbish*) idioties *fpl*

triple ['trɪpl] *adj* triple; **~ts** *npl* triplés(-
ées) **triplicate** ['trɪplɪkət] *n*: **in triplicate**
en trois exemplaires

tripod ['traɪpɔd] *n* trépied *m*

trite [traɪt] (*pej*) *adj* banal(e)

triumph ['traɪʌmf] *n* triomphe *m* ♦ *vi*: **to ~
(over)** triompher (de)

trivia ['trɪvɪə] (*pej*) *npl* futilités *fpl*; **~l** *adj*
insignifiant(e); (*commonplace*) banal(e)

trod [trɔd] *pt of* **tread**; **~den** *pp of* **tread**

trolley ['trɔlɪ] *n* chariot *m*

trombone [trɔm'bəun] *n* trombone *m*

troop [truːp] *n* bande *f*, groupe *m* ♦ *vi*: ~
in/out entrer/sortir en groupe; **~s** *npl*
(*MIL*) troupes *fpl*; (*: men*) hommes *mpl*,
soldats *mpl*; **~ing the colour** (*BRIT*) *n*
(*ceremony*) le salut au drapeau

trophy ['trəufɪ] *n* trophée *m*

tropic ['trɔpɪk] *n* tropique *m*; **~al** *adj* tropi-
cal(e)

trot [trɔt] *n* trot *m* ♦ *vi* trotter; **on the ~**
(*BRIT: fig*) d'affilée

trouble ['trʌbl] *n* difficulté(s) *f(pl)*, pro-
blème(s) *m(pl)*; (*worry*) ennuis *mpl*, soucis
mpl; (*bother, effort*) peine *f*; (*POL*) troubles
mpl; (*MED*): **stomach** *etc* ~ troubles gas-
triques *etc* ♦ *vt* (*disturb*) déranger, gêner;
(*worry*) inquiéter ♦ *vi*: **to ~ to do** prendre
la peine de faire; **~s** *npl* (*POL etc*) troubles
mpl; (*personal*) ennuis, soucis; **to be in ~**

avoir des ennuis; (*ship, climber etc*) être en
difficulté; **what's the ~?** qu'est-ce qui ne
va pas?; **~d** *adj* (*person*) inquiet(-ète);
(*epoch, life*) agité(e); **~maker** *n* élément
perturbateur, fauteur *m* de troubles;
~shooter *n* (*in conflict*) médiateur *m*;
~some *adj* (*child*) fatigant(e), difficile;
(*cough etc*) gênant(e)

trough [trɔf] *n* (*also:* **drinking ~**) abreuvoir
m; (*also:* **feeding ~**) auge *f*; (*depression*)
creux *m*

trousers ['trauzəz] *npl* pantalon *m*; **short
~** culottes courtes

trout [traut] *n inv* truite *f*

trowel ['trauəl] *n* truelle *f*; (*garden tool*) dé-
plantoir *m*

truant ['truənt] (*BRIT*) *n*: **to play ~** faire
l'école buissonnière

truce [truːs] *n* trêve *f*

truck [trʌk] *n* camion *m*; (*RAIL*) wagon *m* à
plate-forme; ~ **driver** *n* camionneur *m*; ~
farm (*US*) *n* jardin maraîcher

true [truː] *adj* vrai(e); (*accurate*) exact(e);
(*genuine*) vrai, véritable; (*faithful*) fidèle; **to
come ~** se réaliser

truffle ['trʌfl] *n* truffe *f*

truly ['truːlɪ] *adv* vraiment, réellement;
(*truthfully*) sans mentir; *see also* **yours**

trump [trʌmp] *n* (*also:* ~ **card**) atout *m*

trumpet ['trʌmpɪt] *n* trompette *f*

truncheon ['trʌntʃən] (*BRIT*) *n* bâton *m*
(d'agent de police); matraque *f*

trundle ['trʌndl] *vt, vi*: **to ~ along** rouler
lentement et bruyamment

trunk [trʌŋk] *n* (*of tree, person*) tronc *m*; (*of
elephant*) trompe *f*; (*case*) malle *f*; (*US:
AUT*) coffre *m*; **~s** *npl* (*also:* **swimming
~s**) maillot *m or* slip *m* de bain

truss [trʌs] *vt*: **to ~ (up)** ligoter

trust [trʌst] *n* confiance *f*; (*responsibility*)
charge *f*; (*LAW*) fidéicommis *m* ♦ *vt* (*rely
on*) avoir confiance en; (*hope*) espérer;
(*entrust*): **to ~ sth to sb** confier qch à qn;
to take sth on ~ accepter qch les yeux
fermés; **~ed** *adj* en qui l'on a confiance;
~ee [trʌs'tiː] *n* (*LAW*) fidéicommissaire *m/f*;
(*of school etc*) administrateur(-trice); **~ful,**

~ing *adj* confiant(e); **~worthy** *adj* digne de confiance

truth [truːθ] *n* vérité *f*; **~ful** *adj* (*person*) qui dit la vérité; (*answer*) sincère

try [traɪ] *n* essai *m*, tentative *f*; (*RUGBY*) essai ♦ *vt* (*attempt*) essayer, tenter; (*test: sth new: also:* ~ *out*) essayer, tester; (*LAW: person*) juger; (*strain*) éprouver ♦ *vi* essayer; **to have a** ~ essayer; **to** ~ **to do** essayer de faire; (*seek*) chercher à faire; ~ **on** *vt* (*clothes*) essayer; **~ing** *adj* pénible

T-shirt [ˈtiːʃəːt] *n* tee-shirt *m*

T-square [ˈtiːskwɛəʳ] *n* équerre *f* en T, té *m*

tub [tʌb] *n* cuve *f*; (*for washing clothes*) baquet *m*; (*bath*) baignoire *f*

tubby [ˈtʌbɪ] *adj* rondelet(te)

tube [tjuːb] *n* tube *m*; (*BRIT: underground*) métro *m*; (*for tyre*) chambre *f* à air

tuberculosis [tjubəːkjuˈləusɪs] *n* tuberculose *f*

TUC *n abbr* (*BRIT: Trades Union Congress*) confédération des syndicats britanniques

tuck [tʌk] *vt* (*put*) mettre; ~ **away** *vt* cacher, ranger; ~ **in** *vt* rentrer; (*child*) border ♦ *vi* (*eat*) manger (de bon appétit); ~ **up** *vt* (*child*) border; ~ **shop** (*BRIT*) *n* boutique *f* à provisions (*dans une école*)

Tuesday [ˈtjuːzdɪ] *n* mardi *m*

tuft [tʌft] *n* touffe *f*

tug [tʌg] *n* (*ship*) remorqueur *m* ♦ *vt* tirer (sur); **~-of-war** *n* lutte *f* à la corde; (*fig*) lutte acharnée

tuition [tjuːˈɪʃən] *n* (*BRIT*) leçons *fpl*; (: *private* ~) cours particuliers; (*US: school fees*) frais *mpl* de scolarité

tulip [ˈtjuːlɪp] *n* tulipe *f*

tumble [ˈtʌmbl] *n* (*fall*) chute *f*, culbute *f* ♦ *vi* tomber, dégringoler; **to** ~ **to sth** (*inf*) réaliser qch; **~down** *adj* délabré(e); ~ **dryer** (*BRIT*) *n* séchoir *m* à air chaud

tumbler [ˈtʌmbləʳ] *n* (*glass*) verre (droit), gobelet *m*

tummy [ˈtʌmɪ] (*inf*) *n* ventre *m*; ~ **upset** *n* maux *mpl* de ventre

tumour [ˈtjuːməʳ] (*US* **tumor**) *n* tumeur *f*

tuna [ˈtjuːnə] *n inv* (*also:* ~ **fish**) thon *m*

tune [tjuːn] *n* (*melody*) air *m* ♦ *vt* (*MUS*) accorder; (*RADIO, TV, AUT*) régler; **to be in/ out of** ~ (*instrument*) être accordé/ désaccordé; (*singer*) chanter juste/faux; **to be in/out of** ~ **with** (*fig*) être en accord/ désaccord avec; ~ **in** *vi* (*RADIO, TV*): **to** ~ **in (to)** se mettre à l'écoute (de); ~ **up** *vi* (*musician*) accorder son instrument; **~ful** *adj* mélodieux(-euse); **~r** *n*: **piano ~r** accordeur *m* (de pianos)

tunic [ˈtjuːnɪk] *n* tunique *f*

Tunisia [tjuːˈnɪzɪə] *n* Tunisie *f*

tunnel [ˈtʌnl] *n* tunnel *m*; (*in mine*) galerie *f* ♦ *vi* percer un tunnel

turbulence [ˈtəːbjuləns] *n* (*AVIAT*) turbulence *f*

tureen [təˈriːn] *n* (*for soup*) soupière *f*; (*for vegetables*) légumier *m*

turf [təːf] *n* gazon *m*; (*clod*) motte *f* (de gazon) ♦ *vt* gazonner; ~ **out** (*inf*) *vt* (*person*) jeter dehors

Turk [təːk] *n* Turc (Turque)

Turkey [ˈtəːkɪ] *n* Turquie *f*

turkey [ˈtəːkɪ] *n* dindon *m*, dinde *f*

Turkish [ˈtəːkɪʃ] *adj* turc (turque) ♦ *n* (*LING*) turc *m*

turmoil [ˈtəːmɔɪl] *n* trouble *m*, bouleversement *m*; **in** ~ en émoi, en effervescence

turn [təːn] *n* tour *m*; (*in road*) tournant *m*; (*of mind, events*) tournure *f*; (*performance*) numéro *m*; (*MED*) crise *f*, attaque *f* ♦ *vt* tourner; (*collar, steak*) retourner; (*change*): **to** ~ **sth into** changer qch en ♦ *vi* (*object, wind, milk*) tourner; (*person: look back*) se (re)tourner; (*reverse direction*) faire demi-tour; (*become*) devenir; (*age*) atteindre; **to** ~ **into** se changer en; **a good** ~ un service; **it gave me quite a** ~ ça m'a fait un coup; **"no left ~"** (*AUT*) "défense de tourner à gauche"; **it's your** ~ c'est (à) votre tour; **in** ~ à son tour; à tour de rôle; **to take ~s (at)** se relayer (pour or à); ~ **away** *vi* se détourner ♦ *vt* (*applicants*) refuser; ~ **back** *vi* revenir, faire demi-tour ♦ *vt* (*person, vehicle*) faire faire demi-tour à; (*clock*) reculer; ~ **down** *vt* (*refuse*) rejeter, refuser; (*reduce*) baisser; (*fold*) rabattre; ~ **in** vi (inf: go to bed) aller se coucher ♦ vt (fold) rentrer; ~ **off** vi (from road) tourner ♦ vt (light, radio etc) éteindre; (tap) fermer; (engine) arrêter; ~ **on** vt (light, radio etc) allumer; (tap) ouvrir; (engine) mettre en marche; ~ **out** vt (light, gas) éteindre; (produce) produire ♦ vi (voters, troops etc) se présenter; **to ~ out to be ...** s'avérer ..., se révéler ...; ~ **over** vi (person) se retourner ♦ vt (object) retourner; (page) tourner; ~ **round** vi faire demi-tour; (rotate) tourner; ~ **up** vi (person) arriver, se pointer (inf); (lost object) être retrouvé(e) ♦ vt (collar) remonter; (radio, heater) mettre plus fort; ~**ing** n (in road) tournant m; ~**ing point** n (fig) tournant m, moment décisif

turnip ['tə:nɪp] n navet m

turn: ~**out** n (of voters) taux m de participation; ~**over** n (COMM: amount of money) chiffre m d'affaires; (: of goods) roulement m; (of staff) renouvellement m, changement m; ~**pike** (US) n autoroute f à péage; ~**stile** n tourniquet m (d'entrée); ~**table** n (on record player) platine f; ~-**up** (BRIT) n (on trousers) revers m

turpentine ['tə:pəntaɪn] n (also: **turps**) (essence f de) térébenthine f

turquoise ['tə:kwɔɪz] n (stone) turquoise f ♦ adj turquoise inv

turret ['tʌrɪt] n tourelle f

turtle ['tə:tl] n tortue marine or d'eau douce; ~**neck (sweater)** n (BRIT) pullover m à col montant; (US) pullover m à col roulé

tusk [tʌsk] n défense f

tutor ['tju:tər] n (in college) directeur(-trice) d'études; (private teacher) précepteur(-trice); ~**ial** [tju:'tɔ:rɪəl] n (SCOL) (séance f de) travaux mpl pratiques

tuxedo [tʌk'si:dəu] (US) n smoking m

TV n abbr (= television) télé f

twang [twæŋ] n (of instrument) son vibrant; (of voice) ton nasillard

tweed [twi:d] n tweed m

tweezers ['twi:zəz] npl pince f à épiler

twelfth [twelfθ] num douzième

twelve [twelv] num douze; **at ~ (o'clock)** à midi; (midnight) à minuit

twentieth ['twentɪɪθ] num vingtième

twenty ['twentɪ] num vingt

twice [twaɪs] adv deux fois; ~ **as much** deux fois plus

twiddle ['twɪdl] vt, vi: **to ~ (with) sth** tripoter qch; **to ~ one's thumbs** (fig) se tourner les pouces

twig [twɪg] n brindille f ♦ vi (inf) piger

twilight ['twaɪlaɪt] n crépuscule m

twin [twɪn] adj, n jumeau(-elle) ♦ vt jumeler; ~**(-bedded) room** n chambre f à deux lits; ~ **beds** npl lits jumeaux

twine [twaɪn] n ficelle f ♦ vi (plant) s'enrouler

twinge [twɪndʒ] n (of pain) élancement m; **a ~ of conscience** un certain remords; **a ~ of regret** un pincement au cœur

twinkle ['twɪŋkl] vi scintiller; (eyes) pétiller

twirl [twə:l] vt faire tournoyer ♦ vi tournoyer

twist [twɪst] n torsion f, tour m; (in road) virage m; (in wire, flex) tortillon m; (in story) coup m de théâtre ♦ vt tordre; (weave) entortiller; (roll around) enrouler; (fig) déformer ♦ vi (road, river) serpenter

twit [twɪt] (inf) n crétin(e)

twitch [twɪtʃ] n (pull) coup sec, saccade f; (nervous) tic m ♦ vi se convulser; avoir un tic

two [tu:] num deux; **to put ~ and ~ together** (fig) faire le rapprochement; ~-**door** adj (AUT) à deux portes; ~-**faced** (pej) adj (person) faux (fausse); ~**fold** adv: **to increase ~fold** doubler; ~-**piece (suit)** n (man's) costume m (deux-pièces); (woman's) tailleur m) deux-pièces m inv; ~-**piece (swimsuit)** n (maillot m de bain) deux-pièces m inv; ~**some** n (people) couple m; ~-**way** adj (traffic) dans les deux sens

tycoon [taɪ'ku:n] n: **(business) ~** gros homme d'affaires

type [taɪp] n (category) type m, genre m, espèce f; (model, example) type m, modèle m; (TYP) type, caractère m ♦ vt (letter etc) taper (à la machine); ~-**cast** adj (actor) condamné(e) à toujours jouer le même rôle; **~face** n (*TYP*) œil m de caractère; **~script** n texte dactylographié; **~writer** n machine f à écrire; **~written** adj dactylographié(e)

typhoid ['taɪfɔɪd] n typhoïde f

typical ['tɪpɪkl] adj typique, caractéristique

typing ['taɪpɪŋ] n dactylo(graphie) f

typist ['taɪpɪst] n dactylo m/f

tyrant ['taɪərnt] n tyran m

tyre ['taɪəʳ] (*US* **tire**) n pneu m; **~ pressure** n pression f (de gonflage)

U, u

U-bend ['juːbend] n (*in pipe*) coude m

ubiquitous [juːˈbɪkwɪtəs] adj omniprésent(e)

udder ['ʌdəʳ] n pis m, mamelle f

UFO ['juːfəʊ] n abbr (= *unidentified flying object*) OVNI m

Uganda [juːˈɡændə] n Ouganda m

ugh [əːh] excl pouah!

ugly ['ʌɡlɪ] adj laid(e), vilain(e); (*situation*) inquiétant(e)

UHT abbr (= *ultra heat treated*): **UHT milk** lait m UHT or longue conservation

UK n abbr = **United Kingdom**

ulcer ['ʌlsəʳ] n ulcère m; (*also:* **mouth ~**) aphte f

Ulster ['ʌlstəʳ] n Ulster m; (*inf: Northern Ireland*) Irlande f du Nord

ulterior [ʌlˈtɪərɪəʳ] adj: **~ motive** arrière-pensée f

ultimate ['ʌltɪmət] adj ultime, final(e); (*authority*) suprême; **~ly** adv (*at last*) en fin de compte; (*fundamentally*) finalement

ultrasound ['ʌltrəsaʊnd] n ultrason m

umbilical cord [ʌmˈbɪlɪkl-] n cordon ombilical

umbrella [ʌmˈbrelə] n parapluie m; (*for sun*) parasol m

umpire ['ʌmpaɪəʳ] n arbitre m

umpteen [ʌmpˈtiːn] adj je ne sais combien de; **~th** adj: **for the ~th time** pour la nième fois

UN n abbr = **United Nations**

unable [ʌnˈeɪbl] adj: **to be ~ to** ne pas pouvoir, être dans l'impossibilité de; (*incapable*) être incapable de

unacceptable [ʌnəkˈseptəbl] adj (*behaviour*) inadmissible; (*price, proposal*) inacceptable

unaccompanied [ʌnəˈkʌmpənɪd] adj (*child, lady*) non accompagné(e); (*song*) sans accompagnement

unaccustomed [ʌnəˈkʌstəmd] adj: **to be ~ to sth** ne pas avoir l'habitude de qch

unanimous [juːˈnænɪməs] adj unanime; **~ly** adv à l'unanimité

unarmed [ʌnˈɑːmd] adj (*without a weapon*) non armé(e); (*combat*) sans armes

unattached [ʌnəˈtætʃt] adj libre, sans attaches; (*part*) non attaché(e), indépendant(e)

unattended [ʌnəˈtendɪd] adj (*car, child, luggage*) sans surveillance

unattractive [ʌnəˈtræktɪv] adj peu attrayant(e); (*character*) peu sympathique

unauthorized [ʌnˈɔːθəraɪzd] adj non autorisé(e), sans autorisation

unavoidable [ʌnəˈvɔɪdəbl] adj inévitable

unaware [ʌnəˈweəʳ] adj: **to be ~ of** ignorer, être inconscient(e) de; **~s** adv à l'improviste, au dépourvu

unbalanced [ʌnˈbælənst] adj déséquilibré(e); (*report*) peu objectif(-ive)

unbearable [ʌnˈbeərəbl] adj insupportable

unbeatable [ʌnˈbiːtəbl] adj imbattable

unbeknown(st) [ʌnbɪˈnəʊn(st)] adv: **~ to me/Peter** à mon insu/l'insu de Peter

unbelievable [ʌnbɪˈliːvəbl] adj incroyable

unbend [ʌnˈbend] (*irreg*) vi se détendre ♦ vt (*wire*) redresser, détordre

unbiased [ʌnˈbaɪəst] adj impartial(e)

unborn [ʌnˈbɔːn] adj à naître, qui n'est pas encore né(e)

unbreakable [ʌnˈbreɪkəbl] adj incassable

unbroken [ʌnˈbrəʊkən] adj intact(e); (*fig*) continu(e), ininterrompu(e)

unbutton [ʌnˈbʌtn] vt déboutonner

uncalled-for [ʌnˈkɔːldfɔːʳ] adj déplacé(e), injustifié(e)

uncanny [ʌnˈkænɪ] *adj* étrange, troublant(e)

unceremonious [ˌʌnsɛrɪˈməunɪəs] *adj* (*abrupt, rude*) brusque

uncertain [ʌnˈsəːtn] *adj* incertain(e); (*hesitant*) hésitant(e); **in no ~ terms** sans équivoque possible; **~ty** *n* incertitude *f*, doute(s) *m(pl)*

uncivilized [ʌnˈsɪvɪlaɪzd] *adj* (*gen*) non civilisé(e); (*fig: behaviour etc*) barbare; (*hour*) indu(e)

uncle [ˈʌŋkl] *n* oncle *m*

uncomfortable [ʌnˈkʌmfətəbl] *adj* inconfortable, peu confortable; (*uneasy*) mal à l'aise, gêné(e); (*situation*) désagréable

uncommon [ʌnˈkɔmən] *adj* rare, singulier(-ère), peu commun(e)

uncompromising [ʌnˈkɔmprəmaɪzɪŋ] *adj* intransigeant(e), inflexible

unconcerned [ʌnkənˈsəːnd] *adj*: **to be ~ (about)** ne pas s'inquiéter (de)

unconditional [ʌnkənˈdɪʃənl] *adj* sans conditions

unconscious [ʌnˈkɔnʃəs] *adj* sans connaissance, évanoui(e); (*unaware*): **~ of** inconscient(e) de ♦ *n*: **the ~** l'inconscient *m*; **~ly** *adv* inconsciemment

uncontrollable [ʌnkənˈtrəuləbl] *adj* indiscipliné(e); (*temper, laughter*) irrépressible

unconventional [ʌnkənˈvɛnʃənl] *adj* peu conventionnel(le)

uncouth [ʌnˈkuːθ] *adj* grossier(-ère), fruste

uncover [ʌnˈkʌvəʳ] *vt* découvrir

undecided [ʌndɪˈsaɪdɪd] *adj* indécis(e), irrésolu(e)

under [ˈʌndəʳ] *prep* sous; (*less than*) (de) moins de; au-dessous de; (*according to*) selon, en vertu de ♦ *adv* au-dessous, en dessous; **~ there** là-dessous; **~ repair** en (cours de) réparation; **~age** *adj* (*person*) qui n'a pas l'âge réglementaire; **~carriage** *n* (*AVIAT*) train *m* d'atterrissage; **~charge** *vt* ne pas faire payer assez à; **~coat** *n* (*paint*) couche *f* de fond; **~cover** *adj* secret(-ète), clandestin(e); **~current** *n* courant *m* sentiment sous-jacent; **~cut** (*irreg*) *vt* vendre moins cher que;

~dog *n* opprimé *m*; **~done** *adj* (*CULIN*) saignant(e); (*pej*) pas assez cuit(e); **~estimate** *vt* sous-estimer; **~fed** *adj* sousalimenté(e); **~foot** *adv* sous les pieds; **~go** (*irreg*) *vt* subir; (*treatment*) suivre; **~graduate** *n* étudiant(e) (qui prépare la licence); **~ground** *n* (*BRIT: railway*) métro *m*; (*POL*) clandestinité *f* ♦ *adj* souterrain(e); (*fig*) clandestin(e) ♦ *adv* dans la clandestinité, clandestinement; **~growth** *n* broussailles *fpl*, sous-bois *m*; **~hand(ed)** *adj* (*fig: behaviour, method etc*) en dessous; **~lie** (*irreg*) *vt* être à la base de; **~line** *vt* souligner; **~mine** *vt* saper, miner; **~neath** *adv* (*en*) dessous ♦ *prep* sous, au-dessous de; **~paid** *adj* souspayé(e); **~pants** *npl* caleçon *m*, slip *m*; **~pass** (*BRIT*) *n* passage souterrain; (*on motorway*) passage inférieur; **~privileged** *adj* défavorisé(e), économiquement faible; **~rate** *vt* sous-estimer; **~shirt** (*US*) *n* tricot *m* de corps; **~shorts** (*US*) *npl* caleçon *m*, slip *m*; **~side** *n* dessous *m*; **~skirt** (*BRIT*) *n* jupon *m*

understand [ʌndəˈstænd] (*irreg: like* **stand**) *vt, vi* comprendre; **I ~ that ...** je me suis laissé dire que ...; je crois comprendre que ...; **~able** *adj* compréhensible; **~ing** *adj* compréhensif(-ive) ♦ *n* compréhension *f*; (*agreement*) accord *m*

understatement [ˈʌndəsteɪtmənt] *n*: **that's an ~** c'est (bien) peu dire, le terme est faible

understood [ʌndəˈstud] *pt, pp of* **understand** ♦ *adj* entendu(e); (*implied*) sousentendu(e)

understudy [ˈʌndəstʌdɪ] *n* doublure *f*

undertake [ʌndəˈteɪk] (*irreg*) *vt* entreprendre; se charger de; **to ~ to do sth** s'engager à faire qch

undertaker [ˈʌndəteɪkəʳ] *n* entrepreneur *m* des pompes funèbres, croque-mort *m*

undertaking [ˈʌndəteɪkɪŋ] *n* entreprise *f*; (*promise*) promesse *f*

under-: **~tone** *n*: **in an ~tone** à mi-voix; **~water** *adv* sous l'eau ♦ *adj* sousmarin(e); **~wear** *n* sous-vêtements *mpl*;

(*women's only*) dessous *mpl*; ~**world** *n* (*of crime*) milieu *m*, pègre *f*; ~**write** *n* (*INSURANCE*) assureur *m*

undies ['ʌndɪz] (*inf*) *npl* dessous *mpl*, lingerie *f*

undiplomatic ['ʌndɪpləˈmætɪk] *adj* peu diplomatique

undo [ʌnˈduː] (*irreg*) *vt* défaire; ~**ing** *n* ruine *f*, perte *f*

undoubted [ʌnˈdautɪd] *adj* indubitable, certain(e); ~**ly** *adv* sans aucun doute

undress [ʌnˈdrɛs] *vi* se déshabiller

undue [ʌnˈdjuː] *adj* indu(e), excessif(-ive)

undulating ['ʌndjuleɪtɪŋ] *adj* ondoyant(e), onduleux(-euse)

unduly [ʌnˈdjuːlɪ] *adv* trop, excessivement

unearth [ʌnˈɜːθ] *vt* déterrer; (*fig*) dénicher

unearthly [ʌnˈɜːθlɪ] *adj* (*hour*) indu(e), impossible

uneasy [ʌnˈiːzɪ] *adj* mal à l'aise, gêné(e); (*worried*) inquiet(-ète); (*feeling*) désagréable; (*peace, truce*) fragile

uneconomic(al) ['ʌniːkəˈnɔmɪk(l)] *adj* peu économique

uneducated [ʌnˈɛdjukeɪtɪd] *adj* (*person*) sans instruction

unemployed [ʌnɪmˈplɔɪd] *adj* sans travail, en *or* au chômage ♦ *n*: **the** ~ les chômeurs *mpl*; **unemployment** *n* chômage *m*

unending [ʌnˈɛndɪŋ] *adj* interminable, sans fin

unerring [ʌnˈɜːrɪŋ] *adj* infaillible, sûr(e)

uneven [ʌnˈiːvn] *adj* inégal(e); (*quality, work*) irrégulier(-ère)

unexpected [ʌnɪksˈpɛktɪd] *adj* inattendu(e), imprévu(e); ~**ly** [ʌnɪksˈpɛktɪdlɪ] *adv* (*arrive*) à l'improviste; (*succeed*) contre toute attente

unfailing [ʌnˈfeɪlɪŋ] *adj* inépuisable; (*remedy*) infaillible

unfair [ʌnˈfɛər] *adj*: ~ **(to)** injuste (envers)

unfaithful [ʌnˈfeɪθful] *adj* infidèle

unfamiliar [ʌnfəˈmɪlɪər] *adj* étrange, inconnu(e); **to be** ~ **with** mal connaître

unfashionable [ʌnˈfæʃnəbl] *adj* (*clothes*) démodé(e); (*place*) peu chic *inv*

unfasten [ʌnˈfɑːsn] *vt* défaire; détacher; (*open*) ouvrir

unfavourable [ʌnˈfeɪvrəbl] (*US* **unfavorable**) *adj* défavorable

unfeeling [ʌnˈfiːlɪŋ] *adj* insensible, dur(e)

unfinished [ʌnˈfɪnɪʃt] *adj* inachevé(e)

unfit [ʌnˈfɪt] *adj* en mauvaise santé; pas en forme; (*incompetent*): ~ **(for)** impropre (à); (*work, service*) inapte (à)

unfold [ʌnˈfəuld] *vt* déplier ♦ *vi* se dérouler

unforeseen ['ʌnfɔːˈsiːn] *adj* imprévu(e)

unforgettable [ʌnfəˈgɛtəbl] *adj* inoubliable

unfortunate [ʌnˈfɔːtʃənət] *adj* malheureux(-euse); (*event, remark*) malencontreux(-euse); ~**ly** *adv* malheureusement

unfounded [ʌnˈfaundɪd] *adj* sans fondement

unfriendly [ʌnˈfrɛndlɪ] *adj* inimical(e), peu aimable

ungainly [ʌnˈgeɪnlɪ] *adj* gauche, dégingandé(e)

ungodly [ʌnˈgɔdlɪ] *adj* (*hour*) indu(e)

ungrateful [ʌnˈgreɪtful] *adj* ingrat(e)

unhappiness [ʌnˈhæpɪnɪs] *n* tristesse *f*, peine *f*

unhappy [ʌnˈhæpɪ] *adj* triste, malheureux(-euse); ~ **about** *or* **with** (*arrangements etc*) mécontent(e) de, peu satisfait(e) de

unharmed [ʌnˈhɑːmd] *adj* indemne, sain(e) et sauf (sauve)

UNHCR *n abbr* (= *United Nations High Commission for refugees*) HCR *m*

unhealthy [ʌnˈhɛlθɪ] *adj* malsain(e); (*person*) maladif(-ive)

unheard-of [ʌnˈhɜːdɔv] *adj* inouï(e), sans précédent

unhurt [ʌnˈhɜːt] *adj* indemne

unidentified [ʌnaɪˈdɛntɪfaɪd] *adj* non identifié(e), *see also* **UFO**

uniform ['juːnɪfɔːm] *n* uniforme *m* ♦ *adj* uniforme

uninhabited [ʌnɪnˈhæbɪtɪd] *adj* inhabité(e)

unintentional [ʌnɪnˈtɛnʃənəl] *adj* involontaire

union ['ju:njən] *n* union *f*; (*also:* **trade ~**) syndicat *m* ♦ *cpd* du syndicat, syndical(e); **U~ Jack** *n* drapeau du Royaume-Uni

unique [ju:'ni:k] *adj* unique

UNISON ['ju:nɪsn] *n* grand syndicat des services publics en Grande-Bretagne

unison ['ju:nɪsn] *n*: **in ~** (*sing*) à l'unisson; (*say*) en chœur

unit ['ju:nɪt] *n* unité *f*; (*section: of furniture etc*) élément *m*, bloc *m*; **kitchen ~** élément de cuisine

unite [ju:'naɪt] *vt* unir ♦ *vi* s'unir; **~d** *adj* uni(e); unifié(e); (*effort*) conjugué(e); **U~d Kingdom** *n* Royaume-Uni *m*; **U~d Nations (Organization)** *n* (Organisation *f* des) Nations unies; **U~d States (of America)** *n* États-Unis *mpl*

unit trust (*BRIT*) *n* fonds commun de placement

unity ['ju:nɪtɪ] *n* unité *f*

universal [ju:nɪ'və:sl] *adj* universel(le)

universe ['ju:nɪvə:s] *n* univers *m*

university [ju:nɪ'və:sɪtɪ] *n* université *f*

unjust [ʌn'dʒʌst] *adj* injuste

unkempt [ʌn'kempt] *adj* négligé(e), débraillé(e); (*hair*) mal peigné(e)

unkind [ʌn'kaɪnd] *adj* peu gentil(le), méchant(e)

unknown [ʌn'nəʊn] *adj* inconnu(e)

unlawful [ʌn'lɔ:ful] *adj* illégal(e)

unleaded ['ʌn'lɛdɪd] *adj* (*petrol, fuel*) sans plomb

unleash [ʌn'li:ʃ] *vt* (*fig*) déchaîner, déclencher

unless [ʌn'lɛs] *conj*: **~ he leaves** à moins qu'il ne parte

unlike [ʌn'laɪk] *adj* dissemblable, différent(e) ♦ *prep* contrairement à

unlikely [ʌn'laɪklɪ] *adj* (*happening*) improbable; (*explanation*) invraisemblable

unlimited [ʌn'lɪmɪtɪd] *adj* illimité(e)

unlisted ['ʌn'lɪstɪd] (*US*) *adj* (*TEL*) sur la liste rouge

unload [ʌn'ləʊd] *vt* décharger

unlock [ʌn'lɔk] *vt* ouvrir

unlucky [ʌn'lʌkɪ] *adj* (*person*) malchanceux(-euse); (*object, number*) qui porte malheur; **to be ~** (*person*) ne pas avoir de chance

unmarried [ʌn'mærɪd] *adj* célibataire

unmistak(e)able [ʌnmɪs'teɪkəbl] *adj* indubitable; qu'on ne peut pas ne pas reconnaître

unmitigated [ʌn'mɪtɪgeɪtɪd] *adj* non mitigé(e), absolu(e), pur(e)

unnatural [ʌn'nætʃrəl] *adj* non naturel(le); (*habit*) contre nature

unnecessary [ʌn'nɛsəsərɪ] *adj* inutile, superflu(e)

unnoticed [ʌn'nəʊtɪst] *adj*: **(to go** or **pass) ~** (passer) inaperçu(e)

UNO *n abbr* = **United Nations Organization**

unobtainable [ʌnəb'teɪnəbl] *adj* impossible à obtenir

unobtrusive [ʌnəb'tru:sɪv] *adj* discret(-ète)

unofficial [ʌnə'fɪʃl] *adj* (*news*) officieux(-euse); (*strike*) sauvage

unorthodox [ʌn'ɔ:θədɔks] *adj* peu orthodoxe; (*REL*) hétérodoxe

unpack [ʌn'pæk] *vi* défaire sa valise ♦ *vt* (*suitcase*) défaire; (*belongings*) déballer

unpalatable [ʌn'pælətəbl] *adj* (*meal*) mauvais(e); (*truth*) désagréable (a entendre)

unparalleled [ʌn'pærəlɛld] *adj* incomparable, sans égal

unpleasant [ʌn'plɛznt] *adj* déplaisant(e), désagréable

unplug [ʌn'plʌg] *vt* débrancher

unpopular [ʌn'pɔpjulər] *adj* impopulaire

unprecedented [ʌn'prɛsɪdɛntɪd] *adj* sans précédent

unpredictable [ʌnprɪ'dɪktəbl] *adj* imprévisible

unprofessional [ʌnprə'fɛʃənl] *adj*: **~ conduct** manquement *m* aux devoirs de la profession

UNPROFOR *n abbr* (= *United Nations Protection Force*) FORPRONU *f*

unqualified [ʌn'kwɔlɪfaɪd] *adj* (*teacher*) non diplômé(e), sans titres; (*success, disaster*) sans réserve, total(e)

unquestionably [ʌn'kwɛstʃənəblɪ] *adv* incontestablement

unravel [ʌnˈrævl] *vt* démêler

unreal [ʌnˈrɪəl] *adj* irréel(le); (*extraordinary*) incroyable

unrealistic [ˈʌnrɪəˈlɪstɪk] *adj* irréaliste; peu réaliste

unreasonable [ʌnˈriːznəbl] *adj* qui n'est pas raisonnable

unrelated [ʌnrɪˈleɪtɪd] *adj* sans rapport; sans lien de parenté

unreliable [ʌnrɪˈlaɪəbl] *adj* sur qui (*or* quoi) on ne peut pas compter, peu fiable

unremitting [ʌnrɪˈmɪtɪŋ] *adj* inlassable, infatigable, acharné(e)

unreservedly [ʌnrɪˈzɜːvɪdl] *adv* sans réserve

unrest [ʌnˈrest] *n* agitation *f*, troubles *mpl*

unroll [ʌnˈrəul] *vt* dérouler

unruly [ʌnˈruːlɪ] *adj* indiscipliné(e)

unsafe [ʌnˈseɪf] *adj* (*in danger*) en danger; (*journey, car*) dangereux(-euse)

unsaid [ʌnˈsed] *adj*: **to leave sth ~** passer qch sous silence

unsatisfactory [ˈʌnsætɪsˈfæktərɪ] *adj* peu satisfaisant(e)

unsavoury [ʌnˈseɪvərɪ] (*US* **unsavory**) *adj* (*fig*) peu recommandable

unscathed [ʌnˈskeɪðd] *adj* indemne

unscrew [ʌnˈskruː] *vt* dévisser

unscrupulous [ʌnˈskruːpjuləs] *adj* sans scrupules

unsettled [ʌnˈsetld] *adj* perturbé(e); instable

unshaven [ʌnˈʃeɪvn] *adj* non *or* mal rasé(e)

unsightly [ʌnˈsaɪtlɪ] *adj* disgracieux(-euse), laid(e)

unskilled [ʌnˈskɪld] *adj*: **~ worker** manœuvre *m*

unspeakable [ʌnˈspiːkəbl] *adj* indicible; (*awful*) innommable

unstable [ʌnˈsteɪbl] *adj* instable

unsteady [ʌnˈstedɪ] *adj* mal assuré(e), chancelant(e), instable

unstuck [ʌnˈstʌk] *adj*: **to come ~** se décoller; (*plan*) tomber à l'eau

unsuccessful [ʌnsəkˈsesful] *adj* (*attempt*) infructueux(-euse), vain(e); (*writer, proposal*) qui n'a pas de succès; **to be ~** (*in attempting sth*) ne pas réussir; ne pas avoir de succès; (*application*) ne pas être retenu(e)

unsuitable [ʌnˈsuːtəbl] *adj* qui ne convient pas, peu approprié(e); inopportun(e)

unsure [ʌnˈʃuər] *adj* pas sûr(e); **to be ~ of o.s.** manquer de confiance en soi

unsuspecting [ʌnsəsˈpektɪŋ] *adj* qui ne se doute de rien

unsympathetic [ˈʌnsɪmpəˈθetɪk] *adj* (*person*) antipathique; (*attitude*) peu compatissant(e)

untapped [ʌnˈtæpt] *adj* (*resources*) inexploité(e)

unthinkable [ʌnˈθɪŋkəbl] *adj* impensable, inconcevable

untidy [ʌnˈtaɪdɪ] *adj* (*room*) en désordre; (*appearance, person*) débraillé(e); (*person: in character*) sans ordre, désordonné

untie [ʌnˈtaɪ] *vt* (*knot, parcel*) défaire; (*prisoner, dog*) détacher

until [ənˈtɪl] *prep* jusqu'à; (*after negative*) avant ♦ *conj* jusqu'à ce que +*sub*; (*in past, after negative*) avant que +*sub*; **~ he comes** jusqu'à ce qu'il vienne, jusqu'à son arrivée; **~ now** jusqu'à présent, jusqu'ici; **~ then** jusque-là

untimely [ʌnˈtaɪmlɪ] *adj* inopportun(e); (*death*) prématuré(e)

untold [ʌnˈtəuld] *adj* (*story*) jamais raconté(e); (*wealth*) incalculable; (*joy, suffering*) indescriptible

untoward [ʌntəˈwɔːd] *adj* fâcheux(-euse), malencontreux(-euse)

unused[1] [ʌnˈjuːzd] *adj* (*clothes*) neuf (neuve)

unused[2] [ʌnˈjuːst] *adj*: **to be ~ to sth/to doing sth** ne pas avoir l'habitude de qch/de faire qch

unusual [ʌnˈjuːʒuəl] *adj* insolite, exceptionnel(le), rare

unveil [ʌnˈveɪl] *vt* dévoiler

unwanted [ʌnˈwɒntɪd] *adj* (*child, pregnancy*) non désiré(e); (*clothes etc*) à donner

unwelcome [ʌn'wɛlkəm] *adj* importun(e); (*news*) fâcheux(-euse)

unwell [ʌn'wɛl] *adj* souffrant(e); **to feel ~** ne pas se sentir bien

unwieldy [ʌn'wiːldɪ] *adj* (*object*) difficile à manier; (*system*) lourd(e)

unwilling [ʌn'wɪlɪŋ] *adj*: **to be ~ to do** ne pas vouloir faire; **~ly** *adv* à contrecœur, contre son gré

unwind [ʌn'waɪnd] (*irreg*) *vt* dérouler ♦ *vi* (*relax*) se détendre

unwise [ʌn'waɪz] *adj* irréfléchi(e), imprudent(e)

unwitting [ʌn'wɪtɪŋ] *adj* involontaire

unworkable [ʌn'wəːkəbl] *adj* (*plan*) impraticable

unworthy [ʌn'wəːðɪ] *adj* indigne

unwrap [ʌn'ræp] *vt* défaire; ouvrir

unwritten [ʌn'rɪtn] *adj* (*agreement*) tacite

KEYWORD

---

up [ʌp] *prep*: **he went up the stairs/the hill** il a monté l'escalier/la colline; **the cat was up a tree** le chat était dans un arbre; **they live further up the street** ils habitent plus haut dans la rue
♦ *adv* **1** (*upwards, higher*): **up in the sky/ the mountains** (là-haut) dans le ciel/les montagnes; **put it a bit higher up** mettez-le un peu plus haut; **up there** là-haut; **up above** au-dessus
2: **to be up** (*out of bed*) être levé(e); (*prices*) avoir augmenté *or* monté
3: **up to** (*as far as*) jusqu'à; **up to now** jusqu'à présent
4: **to be up to** (*depending on*): **it's up to you** c'est à vous de décider; (*equal to*): **he's not up to it** (*job, task etc*) il n'en est pas capable; (*inf: be doing*): **what is he up to?** qu'est-ce qu'il peut bien faire?
♦ *n*: **ups and downs** hauts et bas *mpl*

---

up-and-coming [ʌpənd'kʌmɪŋ] *adj* plein(e) d'avenir *or* de promesses

upbringing ['ʌpbrɪŋɪŋ] *n* éducation *f*

update [ʌp'deɪt] *vt* mettre à jour

upgrade [ʌp'greɪd] *vt* (*house*) moderniser; (*job*) revaloriser; (*employee*) promouvoir

upheaval [ʌp'hiːvl] *n* bouleversement *m*; branle-bas *m*

uphill ['ʌp'hɪl] *adj* qui monte; (*fig: task*) difficile, pénible ♦ *adv* (*face, look*) en amont; **to go ~** monter

uphold [ʌp'həuld] (*irreg*) *vt* (*law, decision*) maintenir

upholstery [ʌp'həulstərɪ] *n* rembourrage *m*; (*cover*) tissu *m* d'ameublement; (*of car*) garniture *f*

upkeep ['ʌpkiːp] *n* entretien *m*

upon [ə'pɔn] *prep* sur

upper ['ʌpə*] *adj* supérieur(e); du dessus ♦ *n* (*of shoe*) empeigne *f*; **~-class** *adj* de la haute société, aristocratique; **~ hand** *n*: **to have the ~ hand** avoir le dessus; **~most** *adj* le (la) plus haut(e); **what was ~most in my mind** ce à quoi je pensais surtout; **~ sixth** *n* terminale *f*

upright ['ʌpraɪt] *adj* droit(e); vertical(e); (*fig*) droit, honnête

uprising ['ʌpraɪzɪŋ] *n* soulèvement *m*, insurrection *f*

uproar ['ʌprɔː*] *n* tumulte *m*; (*protests*) tempête *f* de protestations

uproot [ʌp'ruːt] *vt* déraciner

upset [*n* 'ʌpsɛt, *vb, adj* ʌp'sɛt] (*irreg: like* **set**) *n* bouleversement *m*; (*stomach ~*) indigestion *f* ♦ *vt* (*glass etc*) renverser; (*plan*) déranger; (*person: offend*) contrarier; (: *grieve*) faire de la peine à; bouleverser ♦ *adj* contrarié(e); peiné(e); (*stomach*) dérangé(e)

upshot ['ʌpʃɔt] *n* résultat *m*

upside-down [ʌpsaɪd'daun] *adv* à l'envers; **to turn ~ ~** mettre sens dessus dessous

upstairs [ʌp'stɛəz] *adv* en haut ♦ *adj* (*room*) du dessus, d'en haut ♦ *n*: **the ~** l'étage *m*

upstart ['ʌpstɑːt] (*pej*) *n* parvenu(e)

upstream [ʌp'striːm] *adv* en amont

uptake ['ʌpteɪk] *n*: **to be quick/slow on the ~** comprendre vite/être lent à comprendre

uptight [ʌp'taɪt] (*inf*) *adj* très tendu(e), cris-

pé(e)
up-to-date [ˈʌptəˈdeɪt] *adj* moderne; *(information)* très récent(e)
upturn [ˈʌptəːn] *n (in luck)* retournement *m*; *(COMM: in market)* hausse *f*
upward [ˈʌpwəd] *adj* ascendant(e); vers le haut; **~(s)** *adv* vers le haut; **~(s) of 200** 200 et plus
urban [ˈəːbən] *adj* urbain(e); **~ clearway** *n* rue *f* à stationnement einterdit
urbane [əːˈbeɪn] *adj* urbain(e), courtois(e)
urchin [ˈəːtʃɪn] *n* polisson *m*
urge [əːdʒ] *n* besoin *m*; envie *f*; forte envie, désir *m* ♦ *vt*: **to ~ sb to do** exhorter qn à faire, pousser qn à faire; recommander vivement à qn de faire
urgency [ˈəːdʒənsɪ] *n* urgence *f*; *(of tone)* insistance *f*
urgent [ˈəːdʒənt] *adj* urgent(e); *(tone)* insistant(e), pressant(e)
urinal [ˈjuərɪnl] *n* urinoir *m*
urine [ˈjuərɪn] *n* urine *f*
urn [əːn] *n* urne *f*; *(also: tea ~)* fontaine *f* à thé
US *n abbr* = **United States**
us [ʌs] *pron* nous; *see also* **me**
USA *n abbr* = **United States of America**
use [*n* juːs, *vb* juːz] *n* emploi *m*, utilisation *f*; usage *m*; *(~fulness)* utilité *f* ♦ *vt* se servir de, utiliser, employer; **in ~** en usage; **out of ~** hors d'usage; **to be of ~** servir, être utile; **it's no ~** ça ne sert à rien; **she ~d to do it** elle le faisait (autrefois), elle avait coutume de le faire; **~d to: to be ~d to** avoir l'habitude de, être habitué(e) à; **~ up** *vt* finir, épuiser; consommer; **~d** [juːzd] *adj (car)* d'occasion; **~ful** [ˈjuːsful] *adj* utile; **~fulness** *n* utilité *f*; **~less** [ˈjuːslɪs] *adj* inutile; *(person: hopeless)* nul(le); **~r** [ˈjuːzəʳ] *n* utilisateur(-trice), usager *m*; **~r-friendly** *adj (computer)* convivial(e), facile d'emploi
usher [ˈʌʃəʳ] *n (at wedding ceremony)* placeur *m*; **~ette** [ʌʃəˈrɛt] *n (in cinema)* ouvreuse *f*
usual [ˈjuːʒuəl] *adj* habituel(le); **as ~** comme d'habitude; **~ly** [ˈjuːʒuəlɪ] *adv*

d'habitude, d'ordinaire
utensil [juːˈtɛnsl] *n* ustensile *m*
uterus [ˈjuːtərəs] *n* utérus *m*
utility [juːˈtɪlɪtɪ] *n* utilité *f*; *(also:* **public ~)** service public; **~ room** *n* buanderie *f*
utmost [ˈʌtməust] *adj* extrême, le (la) plus grand(e) ♦ *n*: **to do one's ~** faire tout son possible
utter [ˈʌtəʳ] *adj* total(e), complet(-ète) ♦ *vt (words)* prononcer, proférer; *(sounds)* émettre; **~ance** *n* paroles *fpl*; **~ly** *adv* complètement, totalement
U-turn [ˈjuːˈtəːn] *n* demi-tour *m*

V, v

v. *abbr* = **verse**; **versus**; **volt**; *(= vide)* voir
vacancy [ˈveɪkənsɪ] *n (BRIT: job)* poste vacant; *(room)* chambre *f* disponible; **"no vacancies"** "complet"
vacant [ˈveɪkənt] *adj (seat etc)* libre, disponible; *(expression)* distrait(e)
vacate [vəˈkeɪt] *vt* quitter
vacation [vəˈkeɪʃən] *n* vacances *fpl*
vaccinate [ˈvæksɪneɪt] *vt* vacciner
vacuum [ˈvækjum] *n* vide *m*; **~ cleaner** *n* aspirateur *m*; **~-packed** *adj* emballé(e) sous vide
vagina [vəˈdʒaɪnə] *n* vagin *m*
vagrant [ˈveɪɡrənt] *n* vagabond(e)
vague [veɪɡ] *adj* vague, imprécis(e); *(blurred: photo, outline)* flou(e); **~ly** *adv* vaguement
vain [veɪn] *adj (useless)* vain(e); *(conceited)* vaniteux(-euse); **in ~** en vain
valentine [ˈvæləntaɪn] *n (also: ~ card)* carte *f* de la Saint-Valentin; *(person)* bien-aimé(e) *(le jour de la Saint-Valentin)*; **V~'s day** *n* Saint-Valentin *f*
valiant [ˈvælɪənt] *adj* vaillant(e)
valid [ˈvælɪd] *adj* valable; *(document)* valable, valide
valley [ˈvælɪ] *n* vallée *f*
valour [ˈvæləʳ] *(US* **valor**) *n* courage *m*
valuable [ˈvæljuəbl] *adj (jewel)* de valeur; *(time, help)* précieux(-euse); **~s** *npl* objets

mpl de valeur

valuation [væljuˈeɪʃən] *n* (*price*) estimation *f*; (*quality*) appréciation *f*

value [ˈvæljuː] *n* valeur *f* ♦ *vt* (*fix price*) évaluer, expertiser; (*appreciate*) apprécier; **~ added tax** (*BRIT*) *n* taxe *f* à la valeur ajoutée; **~d** *adj* (*person*) estimé(e); (*advice*) précieux(-euse)

valve [vælv] *n* (*in machine*) soupape *f*, valve *f*; (*MED*) valve, valvule *f*

van [væn] *n* (*AUT*) camionnette *f*

vandal [ˈvændl] *n* vandale *m/f*; **~ism** *n* vandalisme *m*; **~ize** *vt* saccager

vanguard [ˈvæŋɡɑːd] *n* (*fig*): **in the ~ of** à l'avant-garde de

vanilla [vəˈnɪlə] *n* vanille *f*

vanish [ˈvænɪʃ] *vi* disparaître

vanity [ˈvænɪtɪ] *n* vanité *f*

vantage point [ˈvɑːntɪdʒ-] *n* bonne position

vapour [ˈveɪpəʳ] (*US* **vapor**) *n* vapeur *f*; (*on window*) buée *f*

variable [ˈvɛərɪəbl] *adj* variable; (*mood*) changeant(e)

variance [ˈvɛərɪəns] *n*: **to be at ~ (with)** être en désaccord (avec); (*facts*) être en contradiction (avec)

varicose [ˈværɪkəus] *adj*: **~ veins** varices *fpl*

varied [ˈvɛərɪd] *adj* varié(e), divers(e)

variety [vəˈraɪətɪ] *n* variété *f*; (*quantity*) nombre *m*, quantité *f*; **~ show** *n* (spectacle *m* de) variétés *fpl*

various [ˈvɛərɪəs] *adj* divers(e), différent(e); (*several*) divers, plusieurs

varnish [ˈvɑːnɪʃ] *n* vernis *m* ♦ *vt* vernir

vary [ˈvɛərɪ] *vt*, *vi* varier, changer

vase [vɑːz] *n* vase *m*

Vaseline ® [ˈvæsɪliːn] *n* vaseline *f*

vast [vɑːst] *adj* vaste, immense; (*amount, success*) énorme

VAT [væt] *n abbr* (= *value added tax*) TVA *f*

vat [væt] *n* cuve *f*

vault [vɔːlt] *n* (*of roof*) voûte *f*; (*tomb*) caveau *m*; (*in bank*) salle *f* des coffres; chambre forte ♦ *vt* (*also:* **~ over**) sauter (d'un bond)

vaunted [ˈvɔːntɪd] *adj*: **much-~** tant vanté(e)

VCR *n abbr* = **video cassette recorder**

VD *n abbr* = **venereal disease**

VDU *n abbr* = **visual display unit**

veal [viːl] *n* veau *m*

veer [vɪəʳ] *vi* tourner; virer

vegan [ˈviːɡən] *n* végétalien(ne)

vegeburger [ˈvɛdʒɪbəːɡəʳ] *n* burger végétarien

vegetable [ˈvɛdʒtəbl] *n* légume *m* ♦ *adj* végétal(e)

vegetarian [vɛdʒɪˈtɛərɪən] *adj*, *n* végétarien(ne)

vehement [ˈviːmənt] *adj* violent(e), impétueux(-euse); (*impassioned*) ardent(e)

vehicle [ˈviːɪkl] *n* véhicule *m*

veil [veɪl] *n* voile *m*

vein [veɪn] *n* veine *f*; (*on leaf*) nervure *f*

velocity [vɪˈlɔsɪtɪ] *n* vitesse *f*

velvet [ˈvɛlvɪt] *n* velours *m*

vending machine [ˈvɛndɪŋ-] *n* distributeur *m* automatique

veneer [vəˈnɪəʳ] *n* (*on furniture*) placage *m*; (*fig*) vernis *m*

venereal [vɪˈnɪərɪəl] *adj*: **~ disease** maladie vénérienne

Venetian blind [vɪˈniːʃən-] *n* store vénitien

vengeance [ˈvɛndʒəns] *n* vengeance *f*; **with a ~** (*fig*) vraiment, pour de bon

venison [ˈvɛnɪsn] *n* venaison *f*

venom [ˈvɛnəm] *n* venin *m*

vent [vɛnt] *n* conduit *m* d'aération; (*in dress, jacket*) fente *f* ♦ *vt* (*fig: one's feelings*) donner libre cours à

ventilator [ˈvɛntɪleɪtəʳ] *n* ventilateur *m*

ventriloquist [vɛnˈtrɪləkwɪst] *n* ventriloque *m/f*

venture [ˈvɛntʃəʳ] *n* entreprise *f* ♦ *vt* risquer, hasarder ♦ *vi* s'aventurer, se risquer

venue [ˈvɛnjuː] *n* lieu *m*

verb [vəːb] *n* verbe *m*; **~al** *adj* verbal(e); (*translation*) littéral(e)

verbatim [vəːˈbeɪtɪm] *adj*, *adv* mot pour mot

verdict [ˈvəːdɪkt] *n* verdict *m*

verge [vəːdʒ] *n* (*BRIT*) bord *m*, bas-côté *m*; "**soft ~s**" (*BRIT: AUT*) "accotement non stabilisé"; **on the ~ of doing** sur le point de faire; **~ on** *vt fus* approcher de

verify ['verɪfaɪ] *vt* vérifier; (*confirm*) confirmer

vermin ['vəːmɪn] *npl* animaux *mpl* nuisibles; (*insects*) vermine *f*

vermouth ['vəːməθ] *n* vermouth *m*

versatile ['vəːsətaɪl] *adj* polyvalent(e)

verse [vəːs] *n* (*poetry*) vers *mpl*; (*stanza*) strophe *f*; (*in Bible*) verset *m*

version ['vəːʃən] *n* version *f*

versus ['vəːsəs] *prep* contre

vertical ['vəːtɪkl] *adj* vertical(e) ♦ *n* verticale *f*

vertigo ['vəːtɪgəu] *n* vertige *m*

verve [vəːv] *n* brio *m*, enthousiasme *m*

very ['verɪ] *adv* très ♦ *adj*: **the ~ book which** le livre même que; **the ~ last** le tout dernier; **at the ~ least** tout au moins; **~ much** beaucoup

vessel ['vesl] *n* (*ANAT, NAUT*) vaisseau *m*; (*container*) récipient *m*

vest [vest] *n* (*BRIT*) tricot *m* de corps; (*US: waistcoat*) gilet *m*

vested interest *n* (*COMM*) droits acquis

vet [vet] *n abbr* (*BRIT: veterinary surgeon*) vétérinaire *m/f* ♦ *vt* examiner soigneusement

veteran ['vetərn] *n* vétéran *m*; (*also:* **war ~**) ancien combattant

veterinary surgeon ['vetrɪnərɪ-] (*BRIT*), **veterinarian** [vetrɪ'neərɪən] (*US*) *n* vétérinaire *m/f*

veto ['viːtəu] (*pl* **~es**) *n* veto *m* ♦ *vt* opposer son veto à

vex [veks] *vt* fâcher, contrarier; **~ed** *adj* (*question*) controversé(e)

via ['vaɪə] *prep* par, via

viable ['vaɪəbl] *adj* viable

vibrate [vaɪ'breɪt] *vi* vibrer

vicar ['vɪkəʳ] *n* pasteur *m* (*de l'Église anglicane*); **~age** *n* presbytère *m*

vicarious [vɪ'keərɪəs] *adj* indirect(e)

vice [vaɪs] *n* (*evil*) vice *m*; (*TECH*) étau *m*

vice- [vaɪs] *prefix* vice-

vice squad *n* ≈ brigade mondaine

vice versa ['vaɪsɪ'vəːsə] *adv* vice versa

vicinity [vɪ'sɪnɪtɪ] *n* environs *mpl*, alentours *mpl*

vicious ['vɪʃəs] *adj* (*remark*) cruel(le), méchant(e); (*blow*) brutal(e); (*dog*) méchant(e), dangereux(-euse); (*horse*) vicieux(-euse); **~ circle** *n* cercle vicieux

victim ['vɪktɪm] *n* victime *f*

victor ['vɪktəʳ] *n* vainqueur *m*

Victorian [vɪk'tɔːrɪən] *adj* victorien(ne)

victory ['vɪktərɪ] *n* victoire *f*

video ['vɪdɪəu] *cpd* vidéo *inv* ♦ *n* (*~ film*) vidéo *f*; (*also:* **~ cassette**) vidéocassette *f*; (*also:* **~ cassette recorder**) magnétoscope *m*; **~ tape** *n* bande *f* vidéo *inv*; (*cassette*) vidéocassette *f*; **~ wall** *n* mur *m* d'images vidéo

vie [vaɪ] *vi*: **to ~ with** rivaliser avec

Vienna [vɪ'enə] *n* Vienne

Vietnam ['vjet'næm] *n* Viêt-Nam *m*, Vietnam *m*; **~ese** [vjetnə'miːz] *adj* vietnamien(ne) ♦ *n inv* Vietnamien(ne); (*LING*) vietnamien *m*

view [vjuː] *n* vue *f*; (*opinion*) avis *m*, vue *f* ♦ *vt* voir, regarder; (*situation*) considérer; (*house*) visiter; **in full ~ of** sous les yeux de; **in ~ of the weather/the fact that** étant donné le temps/que; **in my ~** à mon avis; **~er** *n* (*TV*) téléspectateur(-trice); **~finder** *n* viseur *m*; **~point** *n* point *m* de vue

vigorous ['vɪgərəs] *adj* vigoureux(-euse)

vile [vaɪl] *adj* (*action*) vil(e); (*smell, food*) abominable; (*temper*) massacrant(e)

villa ['vɪlə] *n* villa *f*

village ['vɪlɪdʒ] *n* village *m*; **~r** *n* villageois(e)

villain ['vɪlən] *n* (*scoundrel*) scélérat *m*; (*BRIT: criminal*) bandit *m*; (*in novel etc*) traître *m*

vindicate ['vɪndɪkeɪt] *vt* (*person*) innocenter; (*action*) justifier

vindictive [vɪn'dɪktɪv] *adj* vindicatif(-ive), rancunier(-ère)

vine [vaɪn] *n* vigne *f*; (*climbing plant*) plante grimpante

vinegar ['vɪnɪɡər] *n* vinaigre *m*

vineyard ['vɪnjɑːd] *n* vignoble *m*

vintage ['vɪntɪdʒ] *n* (*year*) année *f*, millésime *m*; **~ car** *n* voiture *f* d'époque; **~ wine** *n* vin *m* de grand cru

viola [vɪ'əulə] *n* (MUS) alto *m*

violate ['vaɪəleɪt] *vt* violer

violence ['vaɪələns] *n* violence *f*

violent ['vaɪələnt] *adj* violent(e)

violet ['vaɪələt] *adj* violet(te) ♦ *n* (*colour*) violet *m*; (*plant*) violette *f*

violin [vaɪə'lɪn] *n* violon *m*; **~ist** [vaɪə'lɪnɪst] *n* violoniste *m/f*

VIP *n abbr* (= *very important person*) V.I.P. *m*

virgin ['vəːdʒɪn] *n* vierge *f* ♦ *adj* vierge

Virgo ['vəːɡəu] *n* la Vierge

virile ['vɪraɪl] *adj* viril(e)

virtually ['vəːtjuəlɪ] *adv* (*almost*) pratiquement

virtual reality ['vəːtjuəl-] *n* (COMPUT) réalité virtuelle

virtue ['vəːtjuː] *n* vertu *f*; (*advantage*) mérite *m*, avantage *m*; **by ~ of** en vertu *or* en raison de; **virtuous** *adj* vertueux(-euse)

virus ['vaɪərəs] *n* (COMPUT) virus *m*

visa ['viːzə] *n* visa *m*

visibility [vɪzɪ'bɪlɪtɪ] *n* visibilité *f*

visible ['vɪzəbl] *adj* visible

vision ['vɪʒən] *n* (*sight*) vue *f*, vision *f*; (*foresight, in dream*) vision

visit ['vɪzɪt] *n* visite *f*; (*stay*) séjour *m* ♦ *vt* (*person*) rendre visite à; (*place*) visiter; **~ing hours** *npl* (*in hospital etc*) heures *fpl* de visite; **~or** *n* visiteur(-euse); (*to one's house*) visite *f*, invité(e); **~or centre** *n* hall *m* or centre *m* d'accueil

visor ['vaɪzər] *n* visière *f*

vista ['vɪstə] *n* vue *f*

visual ['vɪzjuəl] *adj* visuel(le); **~ aid** *n* support visuel; **~ display unit** *n* console *f* de visualisation, visuel *m*; **~ize** *vt* se représenter, s'imaginer; **~ly-impaired** *adj* malvoyant(e)

vital ['vaɪtl] *adj* vital(e); (*person*) plein(e) d'entrain; **~ly** *adv* (*important*) absolument; **~ statistics** *npl* (*fig*) mensurations *fpl*

vitamin ['vɪtəmɪn] *n* vitamine *f*

vivacious [vɪ'veɪʃəs] *adj* animé(e), qui a de la vivacité

vivid ['vɪvɪd] *adj* (*account*) vivant(e); (*light, imagination*) vif (vive); **~ly** *adv* (*describe*) d'une manière vivante; (*remember*) de façon précise

V-neck ['viːnɛk] *n* décolleté *m* en V

vocabulary [vəu'kæbjulərɪ] *n* vocabulaire *m*

vocal ['vəukl] *adj* vocal(e); (*articulate*) qui sait s'exprimer; **~ cords** *npl* cordes vocales

vocation [vəu'keɪʃən] *n* vocation *f*; **~al** *adj* professionnel(le)

vociferous [və'sɪfərəs] *adj* bruyant(e)

vodka ['vɔdkə] *n* vodka *f*

vogue [vəuɡ] *n*: **in ~** en vogue *f*

voice [vɔɪs] *n* voix *f* ♦ *vt* (*opinion*) exprimer, formuler; **~ mail** *n* (*system*) messagerie *f* vocale; (*device*) boîte *f* vocale

void [vɔɪd] *n* vide *m* ♦ *adj* nul(le); **~ of** vide de, dépourvu(e) de

volatile ['vɔlətaɪl] *adj* volatil(e); (*person*) versatile; (*situation*) explosif(-ive)

volcano [vɔl'keɪnəu] (*pl* **~es**) *n* volcan *m*

volition [və'lɪʃən] *n*: **of one's own ~** de son propre gré

volley ['vɔlɪ] *n* (*of gunfire*) salve *f*; (*of stones etc*) grêle *f*, volée *f*; (*of questions*) multitude *f*, série *f*; (TENNIS *etc*) volée *f*; **~ball** *n* volley(-ball) *m*

volt [vəult] *n* volt *m*; **~age** *n* tension *f*, voltage *m*

volume ['vɔljuːm] *n* volume *m*

voluntarily ['vɔləntrɪlɪ] *adv* volontairement

voluntary ['vɔləntərɪ] *adj* volontaire; (*unpaid*) bénévole

volunteer [vɔlən'tɪər] *n* volontaire *m/f* ♦ *vi* (MIL) s'engager comme volontaire; **to ~ to do** se proposer pour faire

vomit ['vɔmɪt] *vt, vi* vomir

vote [vəut] *n* vote *m*, suffrage *m*; (*cast*) voix *f*, vote; (*franchise*) droit *m* de vote ♦ *vt* (*elect*): **to be ~d chairman** *etc* être élu président *etc*; (*propose*): **to ~ that** proposer que ♦ *vi* voter; **~ of thanks** discours *m* de remerciement; **~r** *n* électeur(-trice); **voting** *n* scrutin *m*, vote *m*

voucher ['vautʃə^r] *n* (*for meal, petrol, gift*) bon *m*

vouch for ['vautʃ-] *vt fus* se porter garant de

vow [vau] *n* vœu *m*, serment *m* ♦ *vi* jurer

vowel ['vauəl] *n* voyelle *f*

voyage ['vɔɪdʒ] *n* voyage *m* par mer, traversée *f*; (*by spacecraft*) voyage

vulgar ['vʌlɡə^r] *adj* vulgaire

vulnerable ['vʌlnərəbl] *adj* vulnérable

vulture ['vʌltʃə^r] *n* vautour *m*

W, w

wad [wɒd] *n* (*of cotton wool, paper*) tampon *m*; (*of banknotes etc*) liasse *f*

waddle ['wɒdl] *vi* se dandiner

wade [weɪd] *vi*: **to ~ through** marcher dans, patauger dans; (*fig: book*) s'évertuer à lire

wafer ['weɪfə^r] *n* (CULIN) gaufrette *f*

waffle ['wɒfl] *n* (CULIN) gaufre *f*; (*inf*) verbiage *m*, remplissage *m* ♦ *vi* parler pour ne rien dire, faire du remplissage

waft [wɒft] *vt* porter ♦ *vi* flotter

wag [wæɡ] *vt* agiter, remuer ♦ *vi* remuer

wage [weɪdʒ] *n* (*also:* **~s**) salaire *m*, paye *f* ♦ *vt*: **to ~ war** faire la guerre; **~ earner** *n* salarié(e); **~ packet** *n* (enveloppe *f* de) paye *f*

wager ['weɪdʒə^r] *n* pari *m*

wag(g)on ['wæɡən] *n* (*horse-drawn*) chariot *m*; (BRIT: RAIL) wagon *m* (de marchandises)

wail [weɪl] *vi* gémir; (*siren*) hurler

waist [weɪst] *n* taille *f*; **~coat** (BRIT) *n* gilet *m*; **~line** *n* (tour *m* de) taille *f*

wait [weɪt] *n* attente *f* ♦ *vi* attendre; **to keep sb ~ing** faire attendre qn; **to ~ for** attendre; **I can't ~ to ...** (*fig*) je meurs d'envie de ...; **~ behind** *vi* rester (à attendre); **~ on** *vt fus* servir; **~er** *n* garçon *m* (de café), serveur *m*; **~ing** *n*: **"no ~ing"** (BRIT: AUT) "stationnement inter-

dit"; **~ing list** *n* liste *f* d'attente; **~ing room** *n* salle *f* d'attente; **~ress** *n* serveuse *f*

waive [weɪv] *vt* renoncer à, abandonner

wake [weɪk] (*pt* **woke, waked**, *pp* **woken, waked**) *vt* (*also:* **~ up**) réveiller ♦ *vi* (*also:* **~ up**) se réveiller ♦ *n* (*for dead person*) veillée *f* mortuaire; (NAUT) sillage *m*

Wales [weɪlz] *n* pays *m* de Galles; **the Prince of ~** le prince de Galles

walk [wɔːk] *n* promenade *f*; (*short*) petit tour; (*gait*) démarche *f*; (*path*) chemin *m*; (*in park etc*) allée *f* ♦ *vi* marcher; (*for pleasure, exercise*) se promener ♦ *vt* (*distance*) faire à pied; (*dog*) promener; **10 minutes' ~ from** à 10 minutes à pied de; **from all ~s of life** de toutes conditions sociales; **~ out** *vi* (*audience*) sortir, quitter la salle; (*workers*) se mettre en grève; **~ out on** (*inf*) *vt fus* quitter, plaquer; **~er** *n* (*person*) marcheur(-euse); **~ie-talkie** *n* talkie-walkie *m*; **~ing** *n* marche *f* à pied; **~ing shoes** *npl* chaussures *fpl* de marche; **~ing stick** *n* canne *f*; **W~man** ® *n* Walkman ® *m*; **~out** *n* (*of workers*) grève-surprise *f*; **~over** (*inf*) *n* victoire *f* ou examen *m etc* facile; **~way** *n* promenade *f*

wall [wɔːl] *n* mur *m*; (*of tunnel, cave etc*) paroi *m*; **~ed** *adj* (*city*) fortifié(e); (*garden*) entouré(e) d'un mur, clos(e)

wallet ['wɒlɪt] *n* portefeuille *m*

wallflower ['wɔːlflauə^r] *n* giroflée *f*; **to be a ~** (*fig*) faire tapisserie

wallow ['wɒləu] *vi* se vautrer

wallpaper ['wɔːlpeɪpə^r] *n* papier peint ♦ *vt* tapisser

walnut ['wɔːlnʌt] *n* noix *f*; (*tree, wood*) noyer *m*

walrus ['wɔːlrəs] (*pl* **~** *or* **~es**) *n* morse *m*

waltz [wɔːlts] *n* valse *f* ♦ *vi* valser

wand [wɒnd] *n* (*also:* **magic ~**) baguette *f* (magique)

wander ['wɒndə^r] *vi* (*person*) errer; (*thoughts*) vagabonder, errer ♦ *vt* errer dans

wane [weɪn] *vi* (*moon*) décroître; (*reputation) décliner

wangle ['wæŋgl] (BRIT: inf) vt se débrouiller pour avoir; carotter

want [wɔnt] vt vouloir; (need) avoir besoin de ♦ n: **for ~ of** par manque de, faute de; **~s** npl (needs) besoins mpl; **to ~ to do** vouloir faire; **to ~ sb to do** vouloir que qn fasse; **~ed** adj (criminal) recherché(e) par la police; **"cook ~ed"** "on recherche un cuisinier"; **~ing** adj: **to be found ~ing** ne pas être à la hauteur

war [wɔːʳ] n guerre f; **to make ~ (on)** faire la guerre (à)

ward [wɔːd] n (in hospital) salle f; (POL) canton m; (LAW: child) pupille m/f; **~ off** vt (attack, enemy) repousser, éviter

warden ['wɔːdn] n gardien(ne); (BRIT: of institution) directeur(-trice); (: also: **traffic ~**) contractuel(le); (of youth hostel) père m or mère f aubergiste

warder ['wɔːdəʳ] (BRIT) n gardien m de prison

wardrobe ['wɔːdrəub] n (cupboard) armoire f; (clothes) garde-robe f; (THEATRE) costumes mpl

warehouse ['wɛəhaus] n entrepôt m

wares [wɛəz] npl marchandises fpl

warfare ['wɔːfɛəʳ] n guerre f

warhead ['wɔːhɛd] n (MIL) ogive f

warily ['wɛərɪlɪ] adv avec prudence

warm [wɔːm] adj chaud(e); (thanks, welcome, applause, person) chaleureux(-euse); **it's ~** il fait chaud; **I'm ~** j'ai chaud; **~ up** vi (person, room) se réchauffer; (water) chauffer; (athlete) s'échauffer ♦ vt (food) (faire) réchauffer, (faire) chauffer; (engine) faire chauffer; **~-hearted** adj affectueux(-euse); **~ly** adv chaudement; chaleureusement; **~th** n chaleur f

warn [wɔːn] vt avertir, prévenir; **to ~ sb (not) to do** conseiller à qn de (ne pas) faire; **~ing** n avertissement m; (notice) avis m; (signal) avertisseur m; **~ing light** n avertisseur lumineux; **~ing triangle** n (AUT) triangle m de présignalisation

warp [wɔːp] vi (wood) travailler, se déformer ♦ vt (fig: character) pervertir

warrant ['wɔrnt] n (guarantee) garantie f; (LAW: to arrest) mandat m d'arrêt; (: to search) mandat de perquisition; **~y** n garantie f

warren ['wɔrən] . n (of rabbits) terrier m; (fig: of streets etc) dédale m

warrior ['wɔrɪəʳ] n guerrier(-ère)

Warsaw ['wɔːsɔː] n Varsovie

warship ['wɔːʃɪp] n navire m de guerre

wart [wɔːt] n verrue f

wartime ['wɔːtaɪm] n: **in ~** en temps de guerre

wary ['wɛərɪ] adj prudent(e)

was [wɔz] pt of **be**

wash [wɔʃ] vt laver ♦ vi se laver; (sea): **to ~ over/against sth** inonder/baigner qch ♦ n (clothes) lessive f; (~ing programme) lavage m; (of ship) sillage m; **to have a ~** se laver, faire sa toilette; **to give sth a ~** laver qch; **~ away** vt (stain) enlever au lavage; (subj: river etc) emporter; **~ off** vi partir au lavage; **~ up** vi (BRIT) faire la vaisselle; (US) se débarbouiller; **~able** adj lavable; **~basin** (US **washbowl**) n lavabo m; **~cloth** (US) n gant m de toilette; **~er** n (TECH) rondelle f, joint m; **~ing** n (dirty) linge m; (clean) lessive f; **~ing machine** n machine f à laver; **~ing powder** (BRIT) n lessive f (en poudre); **~ing-up** n vaisselle f; **~ing-up liquid** n produit m pour la vaisselle; **~-out** (inf) n désastre m; **~room** (US) n toilettes fpl

wasn't ['wɔznt] = **was not**

wasp [wɔsp] n guêpe f

wastage ['weɪstɪdʒ] n gaspillage m; (in manufacturing, transport etc) pertes fpl, déchets mpl; **natural ~** départs naturels

waste [weɪst] n gaspillage m; (of time) perte f; (rubbish) déchets mpl; (also: **household ~**) ordures fpl ♦ adj (land, ground: in city) à l'abandon; (leftover): **~ material** déchets mpl ♦ vt gaspiller; (time, opportunity) perdre; **~s** npl (area) étendue f désertique; **~ away** vi dépérir; **~ disposal unit** (BRIT) n broyeur m d'ordures; **~ful** adj gaspilleur(-euse); (process) peu économique; **~ ground** (BRIT) n terrain m vague;

~paper basket *n* corbeille *f* à papier

watch [wɔtʃ] *n* montre *f*; (*act of ~ing*) surveillance *f*; guet *m*; (*MIL: guards*) garde *f*; (*NAUT: guards, spell of duty*) quart *m* ♦ *vt* (*look at*) observer; (: *match, programme, TV*) regarder; (*spy on, guard*) surveiller; (*be careful of*) faire attention à ♦ *vi* regarder; (*keep guard*) monter la garde; **~ out** *vi* faire attention; **~dog** *n* chien *m* de garde; (*fig*) gardien(ne); **~ful** *adj* attentif(-ive), vigilant(e); **~maker** *n* horloger(-ère); **~man** (*irreg*) *n see* **night**; **~strap** bracelet *m* de montre

water ['wɔːtəʳ] *n* eau *f* ♦ *vt* (*plant, garden*) arroser ♦ *vi* (*eyes*) larmoyer; (*mouth*): **it makes my mouth ~** j'en ai l'eau à la bouche; **in British ~s** dans les eaux territoriales britanniques; **~ down** *vt* (*milk*) couper d'eau; (*fig: story*) édulcorer; **~colour** (*US* **watercolor**) *n* aquarelle *f*; **~cress** *n* cresson *m* (de fontaine); **~fall** *n* chute *f* d'eau; **~ heater** *n* chauffe-eau *m*; **~ing can** *n* arrosoir *m*; **~ lily** *n* nénuphar *m*; **~line** *n* (*NAUT*) ligne *f* de flottaison; **~logged** *adj* (*ground*) détrempé(e); **~ main** *n* canalisation *f* d'eau; **~melon** *n* pastèque *f*; **~proof** *adj* imperméable; **~shed** *n* (*GEO*) ligne *f* de partage des eaux; (*fig*) moment *m* critique, point décisif; **~-skiing** *n* ski *m* nautique; **~tight** *adj* étanche; **~way** *n* cours *m* d'eau navigable; **~works** *n* (*building*) station *f* hydraulique; **~y** *adj* (*coffee, soup*) trop faible; (*eyes*) humide, larmoyant(e)

watt [wɔt] *n* watt *m*

wave [weɪv] *n* vague *f*; (*of hand*) geste *m*, signe *m*; (*RADIO*) onde *f*; (*in hair*) ondulation *f* ♦ *vi* faire signe de la main; (*flag*) flotter au vent; (*grass*) ondoyer ♦ *vt* (*handkerchief*) agiter; (*stick*) brandir; **~length** *n* longueur *f* d'ondes

waver ['weɪvəʳ] *vi* vaciller; (*voice*) trembler; (*person*) hésiter

wavy ['weɪvɪ] *adj* (*hair, surface*) ondulé(e); (*line*) onduleux(-euse)

wax [wæks] *n* cire *f*; (*for skis*) fart *m* ♦ *vt* cirer; (*car*) lustrer; (*skis*) farter ♦ *vi* (*moon*)

croître; **~works** *npl* personnages *mpl* de cire ♦ *n* musée *m* de cire

way [weɪ] *n* chemin *m*, voie *f*; (*distance*) distance *f*; (*direction*) chemin, direction *f*; (*manner*) façon *f*, manière *f*; (*habit*) habitude *f*, façon; **which ~? - this ~** par où? - par ici; **on the ~** (*en route*) en route; **to be on one's ~** être en route; **to go out of one's ~ to do** (*fig*) se donner du mal pour faire; **to be in the ~** bloquer le passage; (*fig*) gêner; **to lose one's ~** perdre son chemin; **under ~** en cours; **in a ~** dans un sens; **in some ~s** à certains égards; **no ~!** (*inf*) pas question!; **by the ~ ...** à propos ...; **"~ in"** (*BRIT*) "entrée"; **"~ out"** (*BRIT*) "sortie"; **the ~ back** le chemin du retour; **"give ~"** (*BRIT: AUT*) "cédez le passage"; **~lay** (*irreg*) *vt* attaquer

wayward ['weɪwəd] *adj* capricieux(-euse), entêté(e)

W.C. *n abbr* w.c. *mpl*, waters *mpl*

we [wiː] *pl pron* nous

weak [wiːk] *adj* faible; (*health*) fragile; (*beam etc*) peu solide; **~en** *vi* faiblir, décliner ♦ *vt* affaiblir; **~ling** *n* (*physically*) gringalet *m*; (*morally etc*) faible *m/f*; **~ness** *n* faiblesse *f*; (*fault*) point *m* faible; **to have a ~ness for** avoir un faible pour

wealth [wɛlθ] *n* (*money, resources*) richesse(s) *f(pl)*; (*of details*) profusion *f*; **~y** *adj* riche

wean [wiːn] *vt* sevrer

weapon ['wɛpən] *n* arme *f*

wear [wɛəʳ] (*pt* **wore**, *pp* **worn**) *n* (*use*) usage *m*; (*deterioration through use*) usure *f*; (*clothing*): **sports/babywear** vêtements *mpl* de sport/pour bébés ♦ *vt* (*clothes*) porter; (*put on*) mettre; (*damage: through use*) user ♦ *vi* (*last*) faire de l'usage; (*rub etc through*) s'user; **town/evening ~** tenue *f* de ville/soirée; **~ away** *vt* user, ronger ♦ *vi* (*inscription*) s'effacer; **~ down** *vt* user; (*strength, person*) épuiser; **~ off** *vi* disparaître; **~ out** *vt* user; (*person, strength*) épuiser; **~ and tear** *n* usure *f*

weary ['wɪərɪ] *adj* (*tired*) épuisé(e); (*dispirited*) las (lasse), abattu(e) ♦ *vi*: **to ~ of** se lasser de

weasel ['wi:zl] *n* (ZOOL) belette *f*

weather ['wɛðəʳ] *n* temps *m* ♦ *vt* (*tempest, crisis*) essuyer, réchapper à, survivre à; **under the ~** (*fig: ill*) mal fichu(e); **~-beaten** *adj* (*person*) hâlé(e); (*building*) dégradé(e) par les intempéries; **~cock** *n* girouette *f*; **~ forecast** *n* prévisions *fpl* météorologiques, météo *f*; **~ man** (*irreg*) (*inf*) *n* météorologue *m*; **~ vane** *n* = **weathercock**

weave [wi:v] (*pt* **wove**, *pp* **woven**) *vt* (*cloth*) tisser; (*basket*) tresser; **~r** *n* tisserand(e)

web [wɛb] *n* (*of spider*) toile *f*; (*on foot*) palmure *f*; (*fabric, also fig*) tissu *m*; **the (World Wide) W~** le Web

website ['wɛbsaɪt] *n* (COMPUT) site *m* Web

wed [wɛd] (*pt, pp* **wedded**) *vt* épouser ♦ *vi* se marier

we'd [wi:d] = **we had**; **we would**

wedding [wɛdɪŋ] *n* mariage *m*; **silver/ golden ~ (anniversary)** noces *fpl* d'argent/d'or; **~ day** *n* jour *m* du mariage; **~ dress** *n* robe *f* de mariée; **~ ring** *n* alliance *f*

wedge [wɛdʒ] *n* (*of wood etc*) coin *m*, cale *f*; (*of cake*) part *f* ♦ *vt* (*pack tightly*) enfoncer

Wednesday ['wɛnzdɪ] *n* mercredi *m*

wee [wi:] (SCOTTISH) *adj* (tout(e)) petit(e)

weed [wi:d] *n* mauvaise herbe ♦ *vt* désherber; **~killer** *n* désherbant *m*; **~y** *adj* (*man*) gringalet

week [wi:k] *n* semaine *f*; **a ~ today/on Friday** aujourd'hui/vendredi en huit; **~day** *n* jour *m* de semaine; (COMM) jour ouvrable; **~end** *n* week-end *m*; **~ly** *adv* une fois par semaine, chaque semaine ♦ *adj* hebdomadaire ♦ *n* hebdomadaire *m*

weep [wi:p] (*pt, pp* **wept**) *vi* (*person*) pleurer; **~ing willow** *n* saule pleureur

weigh [weɪ] *vt, vi* peser; **to ~ anchor** lever l'ancre; **~ down** *vt* (*person, animal*) écraser; (*fig: with worry*) accabler; **~ up** *vt* examiner

weight [weɪt] *n* poids *m*; **to lose/put on ~** maigrir/grossir; **~ing** *n* (*allowance*) indemni-

té *f*, allocation *f*; **~lifter** *n* haltérophile *m*; **~lifting** *n* haltérophilie *f*; **~y** *adj* lourd(e); (*important*) de poids, important(e)

weir [wɪəʳ] *n* barrage *m*

weird [wɪəd] *adj* bizarre

welcome ['wɛlkəm] *adj* bienvenu(e) ♦ *n* accueil *m* ♦ *vt* accueillir; (*also*: **bid ~**) souhaiter la bienvenue à; (*be glad of*) se réjouir de; **thank you - you're ~!** merci - de rien *or* il n'y a pas de quoi!

welder ['wɛldəʳ] *n* soudeur(-euse)

welfare ['wɛlfɛəʳ] *n* (*well-being*) bien-être *m*; (*social aid*) assistance sociale; **~ state** *n* État-providence *m*

well [wɛl] *n* puits *m* ♦ *adv* bien ♦ *adj*: **to be ~** aller bien ♦ *excl* eh bien!; (*relief also*) bon!; (*resignation*) enfin!; **as ~** aussi, également; **as ~ as** en plus de; **~ done!** bravo!; **get ~ soon** remets-toi vite!; **to do ~** bien réussir; (*business*) prospérer; **~ up** *vi* monter

we'll [wi:l] = **we will**; **we shall**

well: ~-behaved *adj* sage, obéissant(e); **~-being** *n* bien-être *m*; **~-built** *adj* (*person*) bien bâti(e); **~-deserved** *adj* (bien) mérité(e); **~-dressed** *adj* bien habillé(e); **~-heeled** (*inf*) *adj* (*wealthy*) nanti(e)

wellingtons ['wɛlɪŋtənz] *npl* (*also*: **wellington boots**) bottes *fpl* de caoutchouc

well: ~-known *adj* (*person*) bien connu(e); **~-mannered** *adj* bien élevé(e); **~-meaning** *adj* bien intentionné(e); **~-off** *adj* aisé(e); **~-read** *adj* cultivé(e); **~-to-do** *adj* aisé(e); **~-wishers** *npl* amis *mpl* et admirateurs *mpl*; (*friends*) amis *mpl*

Welsh [wɛlʃ] *adj* gallois(e) ♦ *n* (LING) gallois *m*; **the ~** *npl* (*people*) les Gallois *mpl*; **~ Assembly** *n* Parlement *m* gallois; **~man** (*irreg*) *n* Gallois *m*; **~woman** (*irreg*) *n* Galloise *f*

went [wɛnt] *pt of* **go**

wept [wɛpt] *pt, pp of* **weep**

were [wəːʳ] *pt of* **be**

we're [wɪəʳ] = **we are**

weren't [wəːnt] = **were not**

west [wɛst] *n* ouest *m* ♦ *adj* ouest *inv*, de *or* à l'ouest ♦ *adv* à *or* vers l'ouest; **the W~** l'Occident *m*, l'Ouest; **the W~ Coun-**

try (*BRIT*) ♦ *n* le sud-ouest de l'Angleterre; ~erly *adj* (*wind*) d'ouest; (*point*) à l'ouest; ~ern *adj* occidental(e), de *or* à l'ouest ♦ *n* (*CINEMA*) western *m*; W~ Indian *adj* antillais(e) ♦ *n* Antillais(e); W~ Indies *npl* Antilles *fpl*; ~ward(s) *adv* vers l'ouest

wet [wɛt] *adj* mouillé(e); (*damp*) humide; (*soaked*) trempé(e); (*rainy*) pluvieux(-euse) ♦ *n* (*BRIT: POL*) modéré *m* du parti conservateur; to get ~ se mouiller; "~ paint" "attention peinture fraîche"; ~ suit *n* combinaison *f* de plongée

we've [wiːv] = we have

whack [wæk] *vt* donner un grand coup à

whale [weɪl] *n* (*ZOOL*) baleine *f*

wharf [wɔːf] (*pl* wharves) *n* quai *m*

KEYWORD

what [wɔt] *adj* quel(le); what size is he? quelle taille fait-il?; what colour is it? de quelle couleur est-ce?; what books do you need? quels livres vous faut-il?; what a mess! quel désordre!
♦ *pron* 1 (*interrogative*) que, *prep* +quoi; what are you doing? que faites-vous?, qu'est-ce que vous faites?; what is happening? qu'est-ce qui se passe?, que se passe-t-il?; what are you talking about? de quoi parlez-vous?; what is it called? comment est-ce que ça s'appelle?; what about me? et moi?; what about doing ...? et si on faisait ...?
2 (*relative*: *subject*) ce qui; (: *direct object*) ce que; (: *indirect object*) ce +*prep* +quoi, ce dont; I saw what you did/was on the table j'ai vu ce que vous avez fait/ce qui était sur la table; tell me what you remember dites-moi ce dont vous vous souvenez
♦ *excl* (*disbelieving*) quoi!, comment!

whatever [wɔt'ɛvə^r] *adj*: ~ book quel que soit le livre que (*or* qui) +*sub*; n'importe quel livre ♦ *pron*: do ~ is necessary faites (tout) ce qui est nécessaire; ~ happens quoi qu'il arrive; no reason ~ pas la moindre raison; nothing ~ rien du tout

whatsoever [wɔtsəu'ɛvə^r] *adj* = whatever

wheat [wiːt] *n* blé *m*, froment *m*

wheedle ['wiːdl] *vt*: to ~ sb into doing sth cajoler *or* enjôler qn pour qu'il fasse qch; to ~ sth out of sb obtenir qch de qn par des cajoleries

wheel [wiːl] *n* roue *f*; (*also*: steering ~) volant *m*; (*NAUT*) gouvernail *m* ♦ *vt* (*pram etc*) pousser ♦ *vi* (*birds*) tournoyer; (*also*: ~ round*: person*) virevolter; ~barrow *n* brouette *f*; ~chair *n* fauteuil roulant; ~ clamp *n* (*AUT*) sabot *m* (de Denver)

wheeze [wiːz] *vi* respirer bruyamment

KEYWORD

when [wɛn] *adv* quand; when did he go? quand est-ce qu'il est parti?
♦ *conj* 1 (*at, during, after the time that*) quand, lorsque; she was reading when I came in elle lisait quand *or* lorsque je suis entré
2 (*on, at which*): on the day when I met him le jour où je l'ai rencontré
3 (*whereas*) alors que; I thought I was wrong when in fact I was right j'ai cru que j'avais tort alors qu'en fait j'avais raison

whenever [wɛn'ɛvə^r] *adv* quand donc ♦ *conj* quand; (*every time that*) chaque fois que

where [wɛə^r] *adv, conj* où; this is ~ c'est là que; ~abouts ['wɛərəbauts] *adv* où donc ♦ *n*: nobody knows his ~abouts personne ne sait où il se trouve; ~as [wɛər'æz] *conj* alors que; ~by *adv* par lequel (*or* laquelle *etc*); ~ver [wɛər'ɛvə^r] *adv* où donc ♦ *conj* où que +*sub*; ~withal ['wɛəwɪðɔːl] *n* moyens *mpl*

whether ['wɛðə^r] *conj* si; I don't know ~ to accept or not je ne sais pas si je dois accepter ou non; it's doubtful ~ il est peu probable que +*sub*; ~ you go or not que vous y alliez ou non

which [wɪtʃ] *adj* (*interrogative: direct, indirect*) quel(le); **which picture do you want?** quel tableau voulez-vous?; **which one?** lequel (laquelle)?; **in which case** auquel cas

♦ *pron* **1** (*interrogative*) lequel (laquelle), lesquels (lesquelles) *pl*; **I don't mind which** peu importe lequel; **which (of these) are yours?** lesquels sont à vous?; **tell me which you want** dites-moi lesquels or ceux que vous voulez

2 (*relative: subject*) qui; (: *object*) que, *prep* +lequel (laquelle); **the apple which you ate/which is on the table** la pomme que vous avez mangée/qui est sur la table; **the chair on which you are sitting** la chaise sur laquelle vous êtes assis; **the book of which you spoke** le livre dont vous avez parlé; **he knew, which is true/I feared** il le savait, ce qui est vrai/ce que je craignais; **after which** après quoi

whichever [wɪtʃˈevər] *adj*: **take ~ book you prefer** prenez le livre que vous préférez, peu importe lequel; **~ book you take** quel que soit le livre que vous preniez

while [waɪl] *n* moment *m* ♦ *conj* pendant que; (*as long as*) tant que; (*whereas*) alors que; bien que +*sub*; **for a ~** pendant quelque temps; **~ away** *vt* (*time*) (faire) passer

whim [wɪm] *n* caprice *m*

whimper [ˈwɪmpər] *vi* geindre

whimsical [ˈwɪmzɪkəl] *adj* (*person*) capricieux(-euse); (*look, story*) étrange

whine [waɪn] *vi* gémir, geindre

whip [wɪp] *n* fouet *m*; (*for riding*) cravache *f*; (POL: *person*) chef de file assurant la discipline dans son groupe parlementaire ♦ *vt* fouetter; (*eggs*) battre; (*move quickly*) enlever/sortir brusquement; **~ped cream** *n* crème fouettée; **~-round** (BRIT) *n* collecte *f*

whirl [wə:l] *vi* tourbillonner; (*dancers*) tour-noyer ♦ *vt* faire tourbillonner; faire tour-noyer; **~pool** *n* tourbillon *m*; **~wind** *n* tornade *f*

whirr [wə:r] *vi* (*motor etc*) ronronner; (: *louder*) vrombir

whisk [wɪsk] *n* (CULIN) fouet *m* ♦ *vt* fouetter; (*eggs*) battre; **to ~ sb away** or **off** emmener qn rapidement

whiskers [ˈwɪskəz] *npl* (*of animal*) moustaches *fpl*; (*of man*) favoris *mpl*

whisky [ˈwɪskɪ] (IRELAND, US **whiskey**) *n* whisky *m*

whisper [ˈwɪspər] *vt, vi* chuchoter

whistle [ˈwɪsl] *n* (*sound*) sifflement *m*; (*object*) sifflet *m* ♦ *vi* siffler

white [waɪt] *adj* blanc (blanche); (*with fear*) blême ♦ *n* blanc *m*; (*person*) blanc (blanche); **~ coffee** (BRIT) *n* café *m* au lait, (café) crème *m*; **~-collar worker** *n* employé(e) de bureau; **~ elephant** *n* (*fig*) objet dispendieux et superflu; **~ lie** *n* pieux mensonge; **~ paper** *n* (POL) livre blanc; **~wash** *vt* blanchir à la chaux; (*fig*) blanchir ♦ *n* (*paint*) blanc *m* de chaux

whiting [ˈwaɪtɪŋ] *n inv* (*fish*) merlan *m*

Whitsun [ˈwɪtsn] *n* la Pentecôte

whizz [wɪz] *vi*: **to ~ past** or **by** passer à toute vitesse; **~ kid** (*inf*) *n* petit prodige

who [hu:] *pron* qui; **~dunit** [hu:ˈdʌnɪt] (*inf*) *n* roman policier

whoever [hu:ˈevər] *pron*: **~ finds it** celui (celle) qui le trouve(, qui que ce soit), quiconque le trouve; **ask ~ you like** demandez à qui vous voulez; **~ he marries** quelle que soit la personne qu'il épouse; **~ told you that?** qui a bien pu vous dire ça?

whole [həul] *adj* (*complete*) entier(-ère), tout(e); (*not broken*) intact(e), complet(-ète) ♦ *n* (*all*): **the ~ of** la totalité de, tout(e) le (la); (*entire unit*) tout *m*; **the ~ of the town** la ville tout entière; **on the ~, as a ~** dans l'ensemble; **~food(s)** *n(pl)* aliments complets; **~hearted** *adj* sans réserve(s); **~meal** (BRIT) *adj* (*bread, flour*) complet(-ète); **~sale** *n* (vente *f* en) gros *m* ♦ *adj* (*price*) de gros; (*destruction*) systématique ♦ *adv* en gros; **~saler** *n* grossiste *m/f*; **~some** *adj* sain(e); **~wheat** *adj* = **wholemeal; wholly** [ˈhəulɪ] *adv* entièrement, tout à fait

whom [huːm] *pron* 1 (*interrogative*) qui; **whom did you see?** qui avez-vous vu?; **to whom did you give it?** à qui l'avez-vous donné?
2 (*relative*) que, *prep* +qui; **the man whom I saw/to whom I spoke** l'homme que j'ai vu/à qui j'ai parlé

whooping cough [ˈhuːpɪŋ-] *n* coqueluche *f*

whore [hɔːʳ] (*inf: pej*) *n* putain *f*

whose [huːz] *adj* 1 (*possessive: interrogative*): **whose book is this?** à qui est ce livre?; **whose pencil have you taken?** à qui est le crayon que vous avez pris?, c'est le crayon de qui que vous avez pris?; **whose daughter are you?** de qui êtes-vous la fille?
2 (*possessive: relative*): **the man whose son you rescued** l'homme dont *or* de qui vous avez sauvé le fils; **the girl whose sister you were speaking to** la fille à la sœur de qui *or* de laquelle vous parliez; **the woman whose car was stolen** la femme dont la voiture a été volée
♦ *pron* à qui; **whose is this?** à qui est ceci?; **I know whose it is** je sais à qui c'est

why [waɪ] *adv* pourquoi ♦ *excl* eh bien!, tiens!; **the reason ~** la raison pour laquelle; **tell me ~** dites-moi pourquoi; **~ not?** pourquoi pas?

wicked [ˈwɪkɪd] *adj* mauvais(e), méchant(e); (*crime*) pervers(e); (*mischievous*) malicieux(-euse)

wicket [ˈwɪkɪt] *n* (CRICKET) guichet *m*; terrain *m* (*entre les deux guichets*)

wide [waɪd] *adj* large; (*area, knowledge*) vas-

te, très étendu(e); (*choice*) grand(e) ♦ *adv*: **to open ~** ouvrir tout grand; **to shoot ~** tirer à côté; **~-awake** *adj* bien éveillé(e); **~ly** *adv* (*differing*) radicalement; (*spaced*) sur une grande étendue; (*believed*) généralement; (*travel*) beaucoup; **~n** *vt* élargir ♦ *vi* s'élargir; **~ open** *adj* grand(e) ouvert(e); **~spread** *adj* (*belief etc*) très répandu(e)

widow [ˈwɪdəu] *n* veuve *f*; **~ed** *adj* veuf (veuve); **~er** *n* veuf *m*

width [wɪdθ] *n* largeur *f*

wield [wiːld] *vt* (*sword*) manier; (*power*) exercer

wife [waɪf] (*pl* **wives**) *n* femme *f*, épouse *f*

wig [wɪg] *n* perruque *f*

wiggle [ˈwɪgl] *vt* agiter, remuer

wild [waɪld] *adj* sauvage; (*sea*) déchaîné(e); (*idea, life*) fou (folle); (*behaviour*) extravagant(e), déchaîné(e); **to make a ~ guess** émettre une hypothèse à tout hasard; **~erness** [ˈwɪldənɪs] *n* désert *m*, région *f* sauvage; **~life** *n* (*animals*) faune *f*; **~ly** *adv* (*behave*) de manière déchaînée; (*applaud*) frénétiquement; (*hit, guess*) au hasard; (*happy*) follement; **~s** *npl* (*remote area*) régions *fpl* sauvages

wilful [ˈwɪlful] (*US* **willful**) *adj* (*person*) obstiné(e); (*action*) délibéré(e)

will [wɪl] (*vt: pt, pp* **willed**) *aux vb* 1 (*forming future tense*): **I will finish it tomorrow** je le finirai demain; **I will have finished it by tomorrow** je l'aurai fini d'ici demain; **will you do it? - yes I will/no I won't** le ferez-vous? - oui/non
2 (*in conjectures, predictions*): **he will** *or* **he'll be there by now** il doit être arrivé à l'heure qu'il est; **that will be the postman** ça doit être le facteur
3 (*in commands, requests, offers*): **will you be quiet!** voulez-vous bien vous taire!; **will you help me?** est-ce que vous pouvez m'aider?; **will you have a cup of tea?** voulez-vous une tasse de thé?; **I won't put up with it!** je ne le tolérerai

pas!

♦ *vt*: **to will sb to do** souhaiter ardemment que qn fasse; **he willed himself to go on** par un suprême effort de volonté, il continua

♦ *n* volonté *f*; testament *m*

willing ['wɪlɪŋ] *adj* de bonne volonté, serviable; **he's ~ to do it** il est disposé à le faire, il veut bien le faire; **~ly** *adv* volontiers; **~ness** *n* bonne volonté

willow ['wɪləu] *n* saule *m*

willpower ['wɪl'pauər] *n* volonté *f*

willy-nilly ['wɪlɪ'nɪlɪ] *adv* bon gré mal gré

wilt [wɪlt] *vi* dépérir; (*flower*) se faner

win [wɪn] (*pt, pp* **won**) *n* (*in sports etc*) victoire *f* ♦ *vt* gagner; (*prize*) remporter; (*popularity*) acquérir ♦ *vi* gagner; **~ over** *vt* convaincre; **~ round** (*BRIT*) *vt* = **win over**

wince [wɪns] *vi* tressaillir

winch [wɪntʃ] *n* treuil *m*

wind[1] [wɪnd] *n* (*also MED*) vent *m*; (*breath*) souffle *m* ♦ *vt* (*take breath*) couper le souffle à

wind[2] [waɪnd] (*pt, pp* **wound**) *vt* enrouler; (*wrap*) envelopper; (*clock, toy*) remonter ♦ *vi* (*road, river*) serpenter; **~ up** *vt* (*clock*) remonter; (*debate*) terminer, clôturer

windfall ['wɪndfɔːl] *n* coup de chance

winding ['waɪndɪŋ] *adj* (*road*) sinueux(-euse); (*staircase*) tournant(e)

wind instrument [wɪnd-] *n* (*MUS*) instrument *m* à vent

windmill ['wɪndmɪl] *n* moulin *m* à vent

window ['wɪndəu] *n* fenêtre *f*; (*in car, train, also: ~ pane*) vitre *f*; (*in shop etc*) vitrine *f*; **~ box** *n* jardinière *f*; **~ cleaner** *n* (*person*) laveur(-euse) de vitres; **~ ledge** *n* rebord *m* de la fenêtre; **~ pane** *n* vitre *f*, carreau *m*; **~-shopping** *n*: **to go ~-shopping** faire du lèche-vitrines; **~sill** ['wɪndəusɪl] *n* (*inside*) appui *m* de la fenêtre; (*outside*) rebord *m* de la fenêtre

windpipe ['wɪndpaɪp] *n* trachée *f*

wind power [wɪnd-] *n* énergie éolienne

windscreen ['wɪndskriːn] *n* pare-brise *m* *inv*; **~ washer** *n* lave-glace *m* *inv*; **~**

wiper *n* essuie-glace *m* *inv*

windshield ['wɪndʃiːld] (*US*) *n* = **windscreen**

windswept ['wɪndswɛpt] *adj* balayé(e) par le vent; (*person*) ébouriffé(e)

windy ['wɪndɪ] *adj* venteux(-euse); **it's ~** il y a du vent

wine [waɪn] *n* vin *m*; **~ bar** *n* bar *m* à vin; **~ cellar** *n* cave *f* à vin; **~ glass** *n* verre *m* à vin; **~ list** *n* carte *f* des vins; **~ waiter** *n* sommelier *m*

wing [wɪŋ] *n* aile *f*; **~s** *npl* (*THEATRE*) coulisses *fpl*; **~er** *n* (*SPORT*) ailier *m*

wink [wɪŋk] *n* clin *m* d'œil ♦ *vi* faire un clin d'œil; (*blink*) cligner des yeux

winner ['wɪnər] *n* gagnant(e)

winning ['wɪnɪŋ] *adj* (*team*) gagnant(e); (*goal*) décisif(-ive); **~s** *npl* gains *mpl*

winter ['wɪntər] *n* hiver *m*; **in ~** en hiver; **~ sports** *npl* sports *mpl* d'hiver; **wintry** *adj* hivernal(e)

wipe [waɪp] *n*: **to give sth a ~** donner un coup de torchon/de chiffon/d'éponge à qch ♦ *vt* essuyer; (*erase: tape*) effacer; **~ off** *vt* enlever; **~ out** *vt* (*debt*) éteindre, amortir; (*memory*) effacer; (*destroy*) anéantir; **~ up** *vt* essuyer

wire ['waɪər] *n* fil *m* (de fer); (*ELEC*) fil électrique; (*TEL*) télégramme *m* ♦ *vt* (*house*) faire l'installation électrique de; (*also: ~ up*) brancher; (*person: send telegram to*) télégraphier à; **~less** (*BRIT*) *n* poste *m* de radio; **wiring** *n* installation *f* électrique; **wiry** *adj* noueux(-euse), nerveux(-euse); (*hair*) dru(e)

wisdom ['wɪzdəm] *n* sagesse *f*; (*of action*) prudence *f*; **~ tooth** *n* dent *f* de sagesse

wise [waɪz] *adj* sage, prudent(e); (*remark*) judicieux(-euse) ♦ *suffix*: **...wise**: **time-wise** etc en ce qui concerne le temps *etc*

wish [wɪʃ] *n* (*desire*) désir *m*; (*specific desire*) souhait *m*, vœu *m* ♦ *vt* souhaiter, désirer, vouloir; **best ~es** (*on birthday etc*) meilleurs vœux; **with best ~es** (*in letter*) bien amicalement; **to ~ sb goodbye** dire au revoir à qn; **he ~ed me well** il m'a souhaité bonne chance; **to ~ to do/sb to do**

désirer *or* vouloir faire/que qn fasse; **to ~ for** souhaiter; **~ful** *adj*: **it's ~ful thinking** c'est prendre ses désirs pour des réalités

wistful ['wistful] *adj* mélancolique

wit [wit] *n* (*gen pl*) intelligence *f*, esprit *m*; (*presence of mind*) présence *f* d'esprit; (*wittiness*) esprit; (*person*) homme/femme d'esprit

witch [witʃ] *n* sorcière *f*; **~craft** *n* sorcellerie *f*

⎡ KEYWORD ⎤

with [wið, wiθ] *prep* **1** (*in the company of*) avec; (*at the home of*) chez; **we stayed with friends** nous avons logé chez des amis; **I'll be with you in a minute** je suis à vous dans un instant

2 (*descriptive*): **a room with a view** une chambre avec vue; **the man with the grey hat/blue eyes** l'homme au chapeau gris/aux yeux bleus

3 (*indicating manner, means, cause*): **with tears in her eyes** les larmes aux yeux; **to walk with a stick** marcher avec une canne; **red with anger** rouge de colère; **to shake with fear** trembler de peur; **to fill sth with water** remplir qch d'eau

4: I'm with you (*I understand*) je vous suis; **to be with it** (*inf: up-to-date*) être dans le vent

withdraw [wið'drɔː] (*irreg*) *vt* retirer ♦ *vi* se retirer; **~al** *n* retrait *m*; **~al symptoms** *npl* (*MED*): **to have ~al symptoms** être en état de manque; **~n** *adj* (*person*) renfermé(e)

wither ['wiðə'] *vi* (*plant*) se faner

withhold [wið'həuld] (*irreg*) *vt* (*money*) retenir; **to ~ (from)** (*information*) cacher (à); (*permission*) refuser (à)

within [wið'ın] *prep* à l'intérieur de ♦ *adv* à l'intérieur; **~ his reach** à sa portée; **~ sight of** en vue de; **~ a kilometre of** à moins d'un kilomètre de; **~ the week** avant la fin de la semaine

without [wið'aut] *prep* sans; **~ a coat** sans manteau; **~ speaking** sans parler; **to go ~**

sth se passer de qch

withstand [wið'stænd] (*irreg*) *vt* résister à

witness ['witnis] *n* (*person*) témoin *m* ♦ *vt* (*event*) être témoin de; (*document*) attester l'authenticité de; **to bear ~ (to)** (*fig*) attester; **~ box** (*US* **witness stand**) *n* barre *f* des témoins

witty ['witi] *adj* spirituel(le), plein(e) d'esprit

wives [waivz] *npl* of **wife**

wizard ['wizəd] *n* magicien *m*

wk *abbr* = **week**

wobble ['wɔbl] *vi* trembler; (*chair*) branler

woe [wəu] *n* malheur *m*

woke [wəuk] *pt* of **wake**; **~n** *pp* of **wake**

wolf [wulf] (*pl* **wolves**) *n* loup *m*

woman ['wumən] (*pl* **women**) *n* femme *f*; **~ doctor** *n* femme *f* médecin; **~ly** *adj* féminin(e)

womb [wuːm] *n* (*ANAT*) utérus *m*

women ['wimin] *npl* of **woman**; **~'s lib** (*inf*) *n* MLF *m*; **W~'s (Liberation) Movement** *n* mouvement *m* de libération de la femme

won [wʌn] *pt, pp* of **win**

wonder ['wʌndə'] *n* merveille *f*, miracle *m*; (*feeling*) émerveillement *m* ♦ *vi*: **to ~ whether/why** se demander si/pourquoi; **to ~ at** (*marvel*) s'émerveiller de; **to ~ about** songer à; **it's no ~ (that)** il n'est pas étonnant (que +*sub*); **~ful** *adj* merveilleux(-euse)

won't [wəunt] = **will not**

wood [wud] *n* (*timber, forest*) bois *m*; **~ carving** *n* sculpture *f* en *or* sur bois; **~ed** *adj* boisé(e); **~en** *adj* en bois; (*fig*) raide; inexpressif(-ive); **~pecker** *n* pic *m* (*oiseau*); **~wind** *n* (*MUS*): **the ~wind** les bois *mpl*; **~work** *n* menuiserie *f*; **~worm** *n* ver *m* du bois

wool [wul] *n* laine *f*; **to pull the ~ over sb's eyes** (*fig*) en faire accroire à qn; **~len** (*US* **woolen**) *adj* de *or* en laine; (*industry*) lainier(-ère); **~lens** *npl* (*clothes*) lainages *mpl*; **~ly** (*US* **wooly**) *adj* laineux(-euse); (*fig: ideas*) confus(e)

word [wəːd] *n* mot *m*; (*promise*) parole *f*;

(*news*) nouvelles *fpl* ♦ *vt* rédiger, formuler; **in other ~s** en d'autres termes; **to break/keep one's ~** manquer à sa parole/tenir parole; **~ing** *n* termes *mpl*; libellé *m*; **~ processing** *n* traitement *m* de texte; **~ processor** *n* machine *f* de traitement de texte

wore [wɔːr] *pt of* **wear**

work [wɜːk] *n* travail *m*; (*ART, LITERATURE*) œuvre *f* ♦ *vi* travailler; (*mechanism*) marcher, fonctionner; (*plan etc*) marcher; (*medicine*) agir ♦ *vt* (*clay, wood etc*) travailler; (*mine etc*) exploiter; (*machine*) faire marcher *or* fonctionner; (*miracles, wonders etc*) faire; **to be out of ~** être sans emploi; **to ~ loose** se défaire, se desserrer; **~ on** *vt fus* travailler à; (*influence*) (essayer d')influencer; **~ out** *vi* (*plans etc*) marcher ♦ *vt* (*problem*) résoudre; (*plan*) élaborer; **it ~s out at £100** ça fait 100 livres; **~ up** *vt*: **to get ~ed up** se mettre dans tous ses états; **~able** *adj* (*solution*) réalisable; **~aholic** [wɜːkə'hɒlɪk] *n* bourreau *m* de travail; **~er** *n* travailleur(-euse), ouvrier(-ère); **~ experience** *n* stage *m*; **~force** *n* main-d'œuvre *f*; **~ing class** *n* classe ouvrière; **~ing-class** *adj* ouvrier(-ère); **~ing order** *n*: **in ~ing order** en état de marche; **~man** (*irreg*) *n* ouvrier *m*; **~manship** (*skill*) *n* métier *m*, habileté *f*; **~s** *n* (*BRIT: factory*) usine *f* ♦ *npl* (*of clock, machine*) mécanisme *m*; **~ sheet** *n* (*COMPUT*) feuille *f* de programmation; **~shop** *n* atelier *m*; **~ station** *n* poste *m* de travail; **~-to-rule** (*BRIT*) *n* grève *f* du zèle

world [wɜːld] *n* monde *m* ♦ *cpd* (*champion*) du monde; (*power, war*) mondial(e); **to think the ~ of sb** (*fig*) ne jurer que par qn; **~ly** *adj* de ce monde; (*knowledgeable*) qui a l'expérience du monde; **~wide** *adj* universel(le); **W~-Wide Web** *n* Web *m*

worm [wɜːm] *n* ver *m*

worn [wɔːn] *pp of* **wear** ♦ *adj* usé(e); **~-out** *adj* (*object*) complètement usé(e); (*person*) épuisé(e)

worried ['wʌrɪd] *adj* inquiet(-ète)

worry ['wʌrɪ] *n* souci *m* ♦ *vt* inquiéter ♦ *vi* s'inquiéter, se faire du souci

worse [wɜːs] *adj* pire, plus mauvais(e) ♦ *adv* plus mal ♦ *n* pire *m*; **a change for the ~** une détérioration; **~n** *vt, vi* empirer; **~ off** *adj* moins à l'aise financièrement; (*fig*): **you'll be ~ off this way** ça ira moins bien de cette façon

worship ['wɜːʃɪp] *n* culte *m* ♦ *vt* (*God*) rendre un culte à; (*person*) adorer; **Your W~** (*BRIT: to mayor*) Monsieur le maire; (: *to judge*) Monsieur le juge

worst [wɜːst] *adj* le (la) pire, le (la) plus mauvais(e) ♦ *adv* le plus mal ♦ *n* pire *m*; **at ~** au pis aller

worth [wɜːθ] *n* valeur *f* ♦ *adj*: **to be ~** valoir; **it's ~ it** cela en vaut la peine, ça vaut la peine; **it is ~ one's while (to do)** on gagne (à faire); **~less** *adj* qui ne vaut rien; **~while** *adj* (*activity, cause*) utile, louable

worthy ['wɜːðɪ] *adj* (*person*) digne; (*motive*) louable; **~ of** digne de

KEYWORD

would [wud] *aux vb* **1** (*conditional tense*): **if you asked him he would do it** si vous le lui demandiez, il le ferait; **if you had asked him he would have done it** si vous le lui aviez demandé, il l'aurait fait
2 (*in offers, invitations, requests*): **would you like a biscuit?** voulez-vous un biscuit?; **would you close the door please?** voulez-vous fermer la porte, s'il vous plaît?
3 (*in indirect speech*): **I said I would do it** j'ai dit que je le ferais
4 (*emphatic*): **it WOULD have to snow today!** naturellement il neige aujourd'hui! *or* il fallait qu'il neige aujourd'hui!
5 (*insistence*): **she wouldn't do it** elle n'a pas voulu *or* elle a refusé de le faire
6 (*conjecture*): **it would have been midnight** il devait être minuit
7 (*indicating habit*): **he would go there on Mondays** il y allait le lundi

would-be ['wudbiː] (*pej*) *adj* soi-disant

wouldn't ['wudnt] = **would not**
wound[1] [wu:nd] *n* blessure *f* ♦ *vt* blesser
wound[2] [waund] *pt, pp of* **wind**[2]
wove [wəuv] *pt of* **weave**; **~n** *pp of* **weave**
wrap [ræp] *vt* (*also:* **~ up**) envelopper, emballer; (*wind*) enrouler; **~per** *n* (BRIT: *of book*) couverture *f*; (*on chocolate*) emballage *m*, papier *m*; **~ping paper** *n* papier *m* d'emballage; (*for gift*) papier cadeau
wreak [ri:k] *vt*: **to ~ havoc (on)** avoir un effet désastreux (sur)
wreath [ri:θ] (*pl* **~s**) *n* couronne *f*
wreck [rɛk] *n* (*ship*) épave *f*; (*vehicle*) véhicule accidenté; (*pej: person*) loque humaine ♦ *vt* démolir; (*fig*) briser, ruiner; **~age** *n* débris *mpl*; (*of building*) décombres *mpl*; (*of ship*) épave *f*
wren [rɛn] *n* (ZOOL) roitelet *m*
wrench [rɛntʃ] *n* (TECH) clé *f* (à écrous); (*tug*) violent mouvement de torsion; (*fig*) déchirement *m* ♦ *vt* tirer violemment sur, tordre; **to ~ sth from** arracher qch à *or* de
wrestle ['rɛsl] *vi*: **to ~ (with sb)** lutter (avec qn); **~r** *n* lutteur(-euse); **wrestling** *n* lutte *f*; (*also:* **all-in wrestling**) catch *m*, lutte *f* libre
wretched ['rɛtʃɪd] *adj* misérable; (*inf*) maudit(e)
wriggle ['rɪgl] *vi* (*also:* **~ about**) se tortiller
wring [rɪŋ] (*pt, pp* **wrung**) *vt* tordre; (*wet clothes*) essorer; (*fig*): **to ~ sth out of sb** arracher qch à qn
wrinkle ['rɪŋkl] *n* (*on skin*) ride *f*; (*on paper etc*) pli *m* ♦ *vt* plisser ♦ *vi* se plisser; **~d** *adj* (*skin, face*) ridé(e)
wrist [rɪst] *n* poignet *m*; **~watch** *n* montre-bracelet *f*
writ [rɪt] *n* acte *m* judiciaire
write [raɪt] (*pt* **wrote**, *pp* **written**) *vt, vi* écrire; (*prescription*) rédiger; **~ down** *vt* noter; (*put in writing*) mettre par écrit; **~ off** *vt* (*debt*) passer aux profits et pertes; (*project*) mettre une croix sur; **~ out** *vt* écrire; **~ up** *vt* rédiger; **~-off** *n* perte totale; **~r** *n* auteur *m*, écrivain *m*
writhe [raɪð] *vi* se tordre

writing ['raɪtɪŋ] *n* écriture *f*; (*of author*) œuvres *fpl*; **in ~** par écrit; **~ paper** *n* papier *m* à lettres
wrong [rɒŋ] *adj* (*incorrect*) faux (fausse); (*morally*) mauvais(e); (*wicked*) mal; (*unfair*) injuste ♦ *adv* mal ♦ *n* tort *m* ♦ *vt* faire du tort à, léser; **you are ~ to do it** tu as tort de le faire; **you are ~ about that, you've got it ~** tu te trompes; **what's ~?** qu'est-ce qui ne va pas?; **you've got the ~ number** vous vous êtes trompé de numéro; **to go ~** (*person*) se tromper; (*plan*) mal tourner; (*machine*) tomber en panne; **to be in the ~** avoir tort; **~ful** *adj* injustifié(e); **~ly** *adv* mal, incorrectement; **~ side** *n* (*of material*) envers *m*
wrote [rəut] *pt of* **write**
wrought iron [rəut] *n* fer forgé
wrung [rʌŋ] *pt, pp of* **wring**
wt. *abbr* = **weight**
WWW *n abbr* (= *World Wide Web*): **the ~** le Web

X, x

Xmas ['ɛksməs] *n abbr* = **Christmas**
X-ray ['ɛksreɪ] *n* (*ray*) rayon *m* X; (*photo*) radio(graphie) *f*
xylophone ['zaɪləfəun] *n* xylophone *m*

Y, y

yacht [jɔt] *n* yacht *m*; voilier *m*; **~ing** *n* yachting *m*, navigation *f* de plaisance; **~sman** (*irreg*) *n* plaisancier *m*
Yank [jæŋk], **Yankee** ['jæŋkɪ] (*pej*) *n* Amerloque *m/f*
yap [jæp] *vi* (*dog*) japper
yard [jɑːd] *n* (*of house etc*) cour *f*; (*measure*) yard *m* (= 91,4 *cm*); **~stick** *n* (*fig*) mesure *f*, critères *mpl*
yarn [jɑːn] *n* fil *m*; (*tale*) longue histoire
yawn [jɔːn] *n* bâillement *m* ♦ *vi* bâiller; **~ing** *adj* (*gap*) béant(e)
yd. *abbr* = **yard(s)**

yeah [jɛə] (*inf*) *adv* ouais

year [jɪəʳ] *n* an *m*, année *f*; **to be 8 ~s old** avoir 8 ans; **an eight-~-old child** un enfant de huit ans; **~ly** *adj* annuel(le) ♦ *adv* annuellement

yearn [jə:n] *vi*: **to ~ for sth** aspirer à qch, languir après qch

yeast [ji:st] *n* levure *f*

yell [jɛl] *vi* hurler

yellow ['jɛləu] *adj* jaune

yelp [jɛlp] *vi* japper; glapir

yes [jɛs] *adv* oui; (*answering negative question*) si ♦ *n* oui *m*; **to say/answer ~** dire/répondre oui

yesterday ['jɛstədɪ] *adv* hier ♦ *n* hier *m*; **~ morning/evening** hier matin/soir; **all day ~** toute la journée d'hier

yet [jɛt] *adv* encore; déjà ♦ *conj* pourtant, néanmoins; **it is not finished ~** ce n'est pas encore fini *or* toujours pas fini; **the best ~** le meilleur jusqu'ici *or* jusque-là; **as ~** jusqu'ici, encore

yew [ju:] *n* if *m*

yield [ji:ld] *n* production *f*, rendement *m*; rapport *m* ♦ *vt* produire, rendre, rapporter; (*surrender*) céder ♦ *vi* céder; (*US: AUT*) céder la priorité

YMCA *n abbr* (= *Young Men's Christian Association*) YMCA *m*

yob [jɔb] (*BRIT: inf*) *n* loubar(d) *m*

yoghourt ['jɔugət] *n* yaourt *m*

yog(h)urt ['jɔugət] *n* = **yoghourt**

yoke [jəuk] *n* joug *m*

yolk [jəuk] *n* jaune *m* (d'œuf)

KEYWORD
---

you [ju:] *pron* **1** (*subject*) tu; (*polite form*) vous; (*plural*) vous; **you French enjoy your food** vous autres Français, vous aimez bien manger; **you and I will go** toi et moi *or* vous et moi, nous irons

2 (*object: direct, indirect*) te, t' +*vowel*, vous; **I know you** je te *or* vous connais; **I gave it to you** je vous l'ai donné, je te l'ai donné

3 (*stressed*) toi; vous; **I told YOU to do it** c'est à toi *or* vous que j'ai dit de le faire

4 (*after prep, in comparisons*) toi; vous; **it's for you** c'est pour toi *or* vous; **she's younger than you** elle est plus jeune que toi *or* vous

5 (*impersonal: one*) on; **fresh air does you good** l'air frais fait du bien; **you never know** on ne sait jamais

---

you'd [ju:d] = **you had**; **you would**

you'll [ju:l] = **you will**; **you shall**

young [jʌŋ] *adj* jeune ♦ *npl* (*of animal*) petits *mpl*; (*people*): **the ~** les jeunes, la jeunesse; **~er** [jʌŋgəʳ] *adj* (*brother etc*) cadet(te); **~ster** *n* jeune *m* (garçon *m*); (*child*) enfant *m/f*

your [jɔ:ʳ] *adj* ton (ta), tes *pl*; (*polite form, pl*) votre, vos *pl*; *see also* **my**

you're [juəʳ] = **you are**

yours [jɔ:z] *pron* le (la) tien(ne), les tiens (tiennes); (*polite form, pl*) le (la) vôtre, les vôtres; **~ sincerely/faithfully/truly** veuillez agréer l'expression de mes sentiments les meilleurs; *see also* **mine**[1]

yourself [jɔ:'sɛlf] *pron* (*reflexive*) te; (: *polite form*) vous; (*after prep*) toi; vous; (*emphatic*) toi-même; vous-même; *see also* **oneself**; **yourselves** *pl pron* vous; (*emphatic*) vous-mêmes

youth [ju:θ] *n* jeunesse *f*; (*young man: pl* ~s) jeune homme *m*; **~ club** *n* centre *m* de jeunes; **~ful** *adj* jeune; (*enthusiasm*) de jeunesse, juvénile; **~ hostel** *n* auberge *f* de jeunesse

you've [ju:v] = **you have**

YTS *n abbr* (*BRIT: Youth Training Scheme*) ≈ TUC *m*

Yugoslav ['ju:gəuslɑ:v] *adj* yougoslave ♦ *n* Yougoslave *m/f*

Yugoslavia ['ju:gəu'slɑ:vɪə] *n* Yougoslavie *f*

yuppie ['jʌpɪ] (*inf*) *n* yuppie *m/f*

YWCA *n abbr* (= *Young Women's Christian Association*) YWCA *m*

Z, z

zany ['zeɪnɪ] *adj* farfelu(e), loufoque

zap [zæp] *vt* (*COMPUT*) effacer

zeal [ziːl] *n* zèle *m*, ferveur *f*; empressement *m*

zebra ['ziːbrə] *n* zèbre *m*; ~ **crossing** (*BRIT*) *n* passage clouté *or* pour piétons

zero ['zɪərəu] *n* zéro *m*

zest [zɛst] *n* entrain *m*, élan *m*; (*of orange*) zeste *m*

zigzag ['zɪgzæg] *n* zigzag *m*

Zimbabwe [zɪm'bɑːbwɪ] *n* Zimbabwe *m*

Zimmer frame ['zɪmə-] *n* déambulateur *m*

zinc [zɪŋk] *n* zinc *m*

zip [zɪp] *n* fermeture *f* éclair ® ♦ *vt* (*also:* ~ **up**) fermer avec une fermeture éclair ®; ~ **code** (*US*) *n* code postal; ~**per** (*US*) *n* = **zip**

zit [zɪt] (*inf*) *n* bouton *m*

zodiac ['zəudɪæk] *n* zodiaque *m*

zone [zəun] *n* zone *f*

zoo [zuː] *n* zoo *m*

zoom [zuːm] *vi*: **to** ~ **past** passer en trombe; ~ **lens** *n* zoom *m*

zucchini [zuː'kiːnɪ] (*US*) *n(pl)* courgette(s) *f(pl)*

LE DICTIONNAIRE ET LA GRAMMAIRE

Bien qu'un dictionnaire ne puisse jamais remplacer une grammaire détaillée, il fournit néanmoins un grand nombre de renseignements grammaticaux. Le Robert & Collins Mini présente les indications grammaticales de la façon suivante:

Les catégories grammaticales

Elles sont données en italique immédiatement après la transcription phonétique des entrées. La liste des abréviations se trouve pages xi et xii.

Les changements de catégorie grammaticale au sein d'un article – par exemple, d'adjectif à adverbe, ou de nom à verbe intransitif à verbe transitif – sont indiqués au moyen de losanges – comme pour le mot français "large" et l'anglais "act".

Les adverbes

La règle générale pour former les adverbes en anglais est d'ajouter "-ly" à l'adjectif ou à sa racine. Ainsi:

$$\text{bad} > \text{badly}$$
$$\text{gentle} > \text{gently}$$

La terminaison en "-ly" est souvent l'équivalent du français "-ment":

$$\text{slowly} - \text{lentement}$$
$$\text{slyly} - \text{sournoisement}$$

Il faut toutefois faire attention car certains mots en "-ly" sont des adjectifs et non des adverbes. Par exemple: "friendly", "likely", "ugly", "silly". Ces mots ne peuvent pas être utilisés en tant qu'adverbes. Il faut donc bien vérifier la catégorie grammaticale du mot que vous voulez utiliser.

Les adverbes figurent soit dans les articles des adjectifs correspondants s'ils suivent ces adjectifs dans l'ordre alphabétique ("fortunately"), soit comme entrées à part entière s'ils précèdent alphabétiquement l'adjectif ("happily"). Si leur usage est moins fréquent, ils n'apparaissent pas du tout. Vous pouvez cependant les traduire facilement en français d'après la traduction de l'adjectif correspondant.

Le pluriel des noms en anglais

Normalement, on forme le pluriel des noms anglais en ajoutant un "-s" au singulier.

cat > cats

Le pluriel des noms qui finissent en "-o" est formé en ajoutant "-es" au singulier.

Tous les pluriels irréguliers sont donnés entre parenthèses et en caractères gras immédiatement après la transcription phonétique (v. "tomato").

Certains noms ont un pluriel irrégulier, comme "knife" et "man" en regard. Ces pluriels irréguliers apparaissent également en tant qu'entrées à part entière dans le texte et renvoient au singulier (v. "knives" et "men").

Les verbes irréguliers

Les verbes irréguliers sont clairement signalés dans ce dictionnaire: les formes du prétérit (*pt*) et du participe passé (*pp*) sont données en caractères gras entre parenthèses immédiatement après la transcription phonétique de l'entrée. Voir les verbes "to teach" et "to swim".

Par ailleurs les formes du prétérit et du participe passé des verbes irréguliers apparaissent elles-mêmes comme des entrées à part entière dans le dictionnaire et renvoient à l'infinitif du verbe. Voir "taught", "swam" et "swum".

De plus, vous avez la possibilité de vous référer rapidement à la liste des verbes irréguliers anglais pages 587 et 588 vers la fin de votre dictionnaire.

Enfin, pour ce qui est des verbes réguliers, vous remarquerez que leur prétérit et leur participe passé ne sont pas donnés. Ceci est dû au fait que ces formes ne présentent aucun problème puisqu'on ajoute toujours "-ed" à l'infinitif pour les obtenir (ou bien "-d" si l'infinitif se termine par la voyelle "-e").

		prétérit		**participe passé**
exemples:	to help	– helped	–	helped
	to love	– loved	–	loved

THE DICTIONARY AND GRAMMAR

While it is true that a dictionary can never be a substitute for a detailed grammar it nevertheless provides a great deal of grammatical information. If you know how to extract this information you will be able to use French more accurately both in speech and in writing.

The Collins French Dictionary presents grammatical information as follows.

Parts of speech

Parts of speech are given in italics immediately after the phonetic spellings of headwords. Abbreviated forms are used. Abbreviations can be checked on pages xi and xii.

Changes in parts of speech within an entry – for example, from adjective to adverb to noun, or from noun to intransitive verb to transitive verb – are indicated by means of lozenges - ♦ - as with the French 'large' and the English 'act'.

Genders of French nouns

The gender of each noun in the French-English section of the dictionary is indicated in the following way:

> *nm* = nom masculin
>
> *nf* = nom féminin

You will occasionally see *nm/f* beside an entry. This indicates that a noun – 'concierge', for example – can be either masculine or feminine.

Feminine and *irregular* plural forms of nouns are shown, as with 'chercheur' and 'cheval': the ending which follows the entry is substituted, so that 'chercheur' becomes 'chercheuse' in the feminine, and 'cheval' becomes 'chevaux' in the plural.

In the English-French section of the dictionary, the gender immediately follows the noun translation, as with 'grass'. Where a noun can be either masculine or feminine, this is shown by '*m/f*' if the form of the noun does not change, or by the bracketed feminine ending if it does change, as with 'graduate'.

So many things depend on your knowing the correct gender of a French noun – whether you use 'il' or 'elle' to translate 'it'; the way you spell and pronounce certain adjectives; the changes you make to past participles, etc. If you are in any doubt as to the gender of a noun, it is always best to check it in your dictionary.

581

Adjectives

Adjectives are given in both their masculine and feminine forms, where these are different. The usual rule is to add an '-e' to the masculine form to make an adjective feminine, as with 'noir'.

In the English-French section, an adjective's feminine form or ending appears immediately after it in brackets, as with 'soft'.

Some adjectives have identical masculine and feminine forms. Where this occurs, there is no 'e' beside the basic masculine form.

Many French adjectives, however, do not follow the regular pattern. Where an adjective has an irregular feminine or plural form, this information is clearly provided in your dictionary, usually with the irregular form being given in full. Consider the entries for 'net' and 'sec'.

Adverbs

The normal 'rule' for forming adverbs in French is to add '-ment' to the feminine form of the adjective. Thus:

> lent > lente > lentement

The '-ment' ending is often the equivalent of the English '-ly':

> lentement   – slowly
> sournoisement – slyly

Adjectives ending in '-ant' and '-ent' are slightly different:

> courant > couramment
> prudent > prudemment

In your dictionary some adverbs appear as a separate entry; others appear as subentries of adjective headwords; while others do not feature in the dictionary at all. Compare 'heureusement', 'froidement' and 'sournoisement'.

Where an adverb does not appear, this is usually because it is not a particularly common one. However, you should be able to work out a translation from the adjective once you have found that in the dictionary.

Information about verbs

A major problem facing language learners is that the form of a verb will change according to the subject and/or the tense being used. A typical French verb can take many different forms – too many to list in a dictionary entry.

Yet, although verbs are listed in your dictionary in their infinitive forms only, this does not mean that the dictionary is of limited value when it comes to handling the verb system of the French language. On the contrary, it contains much valuable information.

First of all, your dictionary will help you with the meanings of unfamiliar verbs. If you came across the word 'remplit' in a text and looked it up in your dictionary you wouldn't find it. You must deduce that it is part of a verb and look for the infinitive form. Thus you will see that 'remplit' is a form of the verb 'remplir'. You now have the basic meaning of the word you are concerned with – something to do with the English verb 'fill' – and this should be enough to help you understand the text you are reading.

It is usually an easy task to make the connection between the form of a verb and the infinitive. For example, 'remplissent', 'remplira', 'remplissons' and 'rempli' are all recognisable as parts of the infinitive 'remplir'. However, sometimes it is less obvious – for example, 'voyons', 'verrai' and 'vu' are all parts of 'voir'. The only real solution to this problem is to learn the various forms of the main French regular and irregular verbs.

And this is the second source of help offered by your dictionary. The verb tables on pages 585 to 586 of the Collins French Dictionary provide a summary of some of the main forms of the main tenses of regular and irregular verbs. Consider the verb 'voir' below where the following information is given:

1	voyant	– Present Participle
2	vu	– Past Participle
3	vois, voyons, voient	– Present Tense forms
4	voyais	– 1st Person Singular of the Imperfect Tense
5	verrai	– 1st Person Singular of the Future Tense
7	voie	– 1st Person Singular of the Present Subjunctive

The regular '-er' verb 'parler' is presented in greater detail. The main tenses and the different endings are given in full. This information can be transferred and applied to all verbs in the list. In addition, the main parts of the most common irregular verbs are listed in the body of the dictionary.

PARLER

1   parlant
2   parlé
3   parle, parles, parle, parlons, parlez, parlent
4   parlais, parlais, parlait, parlions, parliez, parlaient
5   parlerai, parleras, parlera, parlerons, parlerez, parleront
6   parlerais, parlerais, parlerait, parlerions, parleriez, parleraient
7   parle, parles, parle, parlons, parliez, parlent *impératif* parle!, parlez!

In order to make maximum use of the information contained in these pages, a good working knowledge of the various rules affecting French verbs is required. You will acquire this in the course of your French studies and your Collins dictionary will serve as a useful 'aide-mémoire'. If you happen to forget how to form the second person singular form of the Future Tense of 'voir' there will be no need to panic — your dictionary contains the information!

FRENCH VERB FORMS

1 Participe présent *2* Participe passé *3* Présent *4* Imparfait *5* Futur *6* Conditionnel *7* Subjonctif présent

acquérir *1* acquérant *2* acquis *3* acquiers, acquérons, acquièrent *4* acquérais *5* acquerrai *7* acquière

ALLER *1* allant *2* allé *3* vais, vas, va, allons, allez, vont *4* allais *5* irai *6* irais *7* aille

asseoir *1* asseyant *2* assis *3* assieds, asseyons, asseyez, asseyent *4* asseyais *5* assiérai *7* asseye

atteindre *1* atteignant *2* atteint *3* atteins, atteignons *4* atteignais *7* atteigne

AVOIR *1* ayant *2* eu *3* ai, as, a, avons, avez, ont *4* avais *5* aurai *6* aurais *7* aie, aies, ait, ayons, ayez, aient

battre *1* battant *2* battu *3* bats, bat, battons *4* battais *7* batte

boire *1* buvant *2* bu *3* bois, buvons, boivent *4* buvais *7* boive

bouillir *1* bouillant *2* bouilli *3* bous, bouillons *4* bouillais *7* bouille

conclure *1* concluant *2* conclu *3* conclus, concluons *4* concluais *7* conclue

conduire *1* conduisant *2* conduit *3* conduis, conduisons *4* conduisais *7* conduise

connaître *1* connaissant *2* connu *3* connais, connaît, connaissons *4* connaissais *7* connaisse

coudre *1* cousant *2* cousu *3* couds, cousons, cousez, cousent *4* cousais *7* couse

courir *1* courant *2* couru *3* cours, courons *4* courais *5* courrai *7* coure

couvrir *1* couvrant *2* couvert *3* couvre, couvrons *4* couvrais *7* couvre

craindre *1* craignant *2* craint *3* crains, craignons *4* craignais *7* craigne

croire *1* croyant *2* cru *3* crois, croyons, croient *4* croyais *7* croie

croître *1* croissant *2* crû, crue, crus, crues *3* croîs, croissons *4* croissais *7* croisse

cueillir *1* cueillant *2* cueilli *3* cueille, cueillons *4* cueillais *5* cueillerai *7* cueille

devoir *1* devant *2* dû, due, dus, dues *3* dois, devons, doivent *4* devais *5* devrai *7* doive

dire *1* disant *2* dit *3* dis, disons, dites, disent *4* disais *7* dise

dormir *1* dormant *2* dormi *3* dors, dormons *4* dormais *7* dorme

écrire *1* écrivant *2* écrit *3* écris, écrivons *4* écrivais *7* écrive

ÊTRE *1* étant *2* été *3* suis, es, est, sommes, êtes, sont *4* étais *5* serai *6* serais *7* sois, sois, soit, soyons, soyez, soient

FAIRE *1* faisant *2* fait *3* fais, fais, fait, faisons, faites, font *4* faisais *5* ferai *6* ferais *7* fasse

falloir *2* fallu *3* faut *4* fallait *5* faudra *7* faille

FINIR *1* finissant *2* fini *3* finis, finis, finit, finissons, finissez, finissent *4* finissais *5* finirai *6* finirais *7* finisse

fuir *1* fuyant *2* fui *3* fuis, fuyons, fuient *4* fuyais *7* fuie

joindre *1* joignant *2* joint *3* joins, joignons *4* joignais *7* joigne

lire *1* lisant *2* lu *3* lis, lisons *4* lisais *7* lise

luire *1* luisant *2* lui *3* luis, luisons *4* luisais *7* luise

maudire *1* maudissant *2* maudit *3* maudis, maudissons *4* maudissait *7* maudisse

mentir *1* mentant *2* menti *3* mens, mentons *4* mentais *7* mente

mettre *1* mettant *2* mis *3* mets, mettons *4* mettais *7* mette

mourir *1* mourant *2* mort *3* meurs, mourons, meurent *4* mourais *5* mourrai *7* meure

naître *1* naissant *2* né *3* nais, naît, naissons *4* naissais *7* naisse

offrir *1* offrant *2* offert *3* offre, offrons *4* offrais *7* offre

PARLER *1* parlant *2* parlé *3* parle, parles, parle, parlons, parlez, parlent *4* parlais, parlais, parlait, parlions, parliez, parlaient *5* parlerai, parleras, parlera, parlerons, parlerez, parleront *6* parlerais, parlerais, parlerait, parlerions, parleriez, parleraient *7* parle, parles, parle, parlions, parliez, parlent *impératif* parle, parlez

partir *1* partant *2* parti *3* pars, partons *4* partais *7* parte

plaire *1* plaisant *2* plu *3* plais, plaît, plaisons *4* plaisais *7* plaise

pleuvoir *1* pleuvant *2* plu *3* pleut, pleuvent *4* pleuvait *5* pleuvra *7* pleuve

pourvoir *1* pourvoyant *2* pourvu *3* pourvois, pourvoyons, pourvoient *4* pourvoyais *7* pourvoie

pouvoir *1* pouvant *2* pu *3* peux, peut, pouvons, peuvent *4* pouvais *5* pourrai *7* puisse

prendre *1* prenant *2* pris *3* prends, prenons, prennent *4* prenais *7* prenne

prévoir *comme voir* *5* prévoirai

RECEVOIR *1* recevant *2* reçu *3* reçois, reçois,

reçoit, recevons, recevez, reçoivent *4* recevais *5* recevrai *6* recevrais *7* reçoive

RENDRE *1* rendant *2* rendu *3* rends, rends, rend, rendons, rendez, rendent *4* rendais *5* rendrai *6* rendrais *7* rende

résoudre *1* résolvant *2* résolu *3* résous, résout, résolvons *4* résolvais *7* résolve

rire *1* riant *2* ri *3* ris, rions *4* riais *7* rie

savoir *1* sachant *2* su *3* sais, savons, savent *4* savais *5* saurai *7* sache *impératif* sache, sachons, sachez

servir *1* servant *2* servi *3* sers, servons *4* servais *7* serve

sortir *1* sortant *2* sorti *3* sors, sortons *4* sortais *7* sorte

souffrir *1* souffrant *2* souffert *3* souffre, souffrons *4* souffrais *7* souffre

suffire *1* suffisant *2* suffi *3* suffis, suffisons *4* suffisais *7* suffise

suivre *1* suivant *2* suivi *3* suis, suivons *4* suivais *7* suive

taire *1* taisant *2* tu *3* tais, taisons *4* taisais *7* taise

tenir *1* tenant *2* tenu *3* tiens, tenons, tiennent *4* tenais *5* tiendrai *7* tienne

vaincre *1* vainquant *2* vaincu *3* vaincs, vainc, vainquons *4* vainquais *7* vainque

valoir *1* valant *2* valu *3* vaux, vaut, valons *4* valais *5* vaudrai *7* vaille

venir *1* venant *2* venu *3* viens, venons, viennent *4* venais *5* viendrai *7* vienne

vivre *1* vivant *2* vécu *3* vis, vivons *4* vivais *7* vive

voir *1* voyant *2* vu *3* vois, voyons, voient *4* voyais *5* verrai *7* voie

vouloir *1* voulant *2* voulu *3* veux, veut, voulons, veulent *4* voulais *5* voudrai *7* veuille *impératif* veuillez

LE VERBE ANGLAIS

present	pt	pp	present	pt	pp
arise	arose	arisen	fall	fell	fallen
awake	awoke	awoken	feed	fed	fed
be (am, is, are; being)	was, were	been	feel	felt	felt
			fight	fought	fought
bear	bore	born(e)	find	found	found
beat	beat	beaten	flee	fled	fled
become	became	become	fling	flung	flung
begin	began	begun	fly (flies)	flew	flown
behold	beheld	beheld	forbid	forbade	forbidden
bend	bent	bent	forecast	forecast	forecast
beseech	besought	besought	forego	forewent	foregone
beset	beset	beset	foresee	foresaw	foreseen
bet	bet, betted	bet, betted	foretell	foretold	foretold
bid	bid, bade	bid, bidden	forget	forgot	forgotten
bind	bound	bound	forgive	forgave	forgiven
bite	bit	bitten	forsake	forsook	forsaken
bleed	bled	bled	freeze	froze	frozen
blow	blew	blown	get	got	got, (US) gotten
break	broke	broken			
breed	bred	bred	give	gave	given
bring	brought	brought	go (goes)	went	gone
build	built	built	grind	ground	ground
burn	burnt, burned	burnt, burned	grow	grew	grown
			hang	hung, hanged	hung, hanged
burst	burst	burst			
buy	bought	bought	have (has; having)	had	had
can	could	(been able)			
cast	cast	cast	hear	heard	heard
catch	caught	caught	hide	hid	hidden
choose	chose	chosen	hit	hit	hit
cling	clung	clung	hold	held	held
come	came	come	hurt	hurt	hurt
cost	cost	cost	keep	kept	kept
creep	crept	crept	kneel	knelt, kneeled	knelt, kneeled
cut	cut	cut			
deal	dealt	dealt	know	knew	known
dig	dug	dug	lay	laid	laid
do (3rd person: he/she/it does)	did	done	lead	led	led
			lean	leant, leaned	leant, leaned
draw	drew	drawn			
dream	dreamed, dreamt	dreamed, dreamt	leap	leapt, leaped	leapt, leaped
			learn	learnt, learned	learnt, learned
drink	drank	drunk			
drive	drove	driven	leave	left	left
dwell	dwelt	dwelt	lend	lent	lent
eat	ate	eaten	let	let	let

present	pt	pp	present	pt	pp
lie (lying)	lay	lain	speed	sped, speeded	sped, speeded
light	lit, lighted	lit, lighted			
lose	lost	lost	spell	spelt, spelled	spelt, spelled
make	made	made			
may	might	—	spend	spent	spent
mean	meant	meant	spill	spilt, spilled	spilt, spilled
meet	met	met			
mistake	mistook	mistaken	spin	spun	spun
mow	mowed	mown, mowed	spit	spat	spat
must	(had to)	(had to)	split	split	split
pay	paid	paid	spoil	spoiled, spoilt	spoiled, spoilt
put	put	put			
quit	quit, quitted	quit, quitted	spread	spread	spread
			spring	sprang	sprung
read	read	read	stand	stood	stood
rid	rid	rid	steal	stole	stolen
ride	rode	ridden	stick	stuck	stuck
ring	rang	rung	sting	stung	stung
rise	rose	risen	stink	stank	stunk
run	ran	run	stride	strode	stridden
saw	sawed	sawn	strike	struck	struck, stricken
say	said	said			
see	saw	seen	strive	strove	striven
seek	sought	sought	swear	swore	sworn
sell	sold	sold	sweep	swept	swept
send	sent	sent	swell	swelled	swollen, swelled
set	set	set			
shake	shook	shaken	swim	swam	swum
shall	should	—	swing	swung	swung
shear	sheared	shorn, sheared	take	took	taken
shed	shed	shed	teach	taught	taught
shine	shone	shone	tear	tore	torn
shoot	shot	shot	tell	told	told
show	showed	shown	think	thought	thought
shrink	shrank	shrunk	throw	threw	thrown
shut	shut	shut	thrust	thrust	thrust
sing	sang	sung	tread	trod	trodden
sink	sank	sunk	wake	woke	woken
sit	sat	sat	waylay	waylaid	waylaid
slay	slew	slain	wear	wore	worn
sleep	slept	slept	weave	wove, weaved	woven, weaved
slide	slid	slid			
sling	slung	slung	wed	wedded, wed	wedded, wed
slit	slit	slit			
smell	smelt, smelled	smelt, smelled	weep	wept	wept
			win	won	won
sow	sowed	sown, sowed	wind	wound	wound
speak	spoke	spoken	wring	wrung	wrung
			write	wrote	written

LES NOMBRES

NUMBERS

un(une)	1	one
deux	2	two
trois	3	three
quatre	4	four
cinq	5	five
six	6	six
sept	7	seven
huit	8	eight
neuf	9	nine
dix	10	ten
onze	11	eleven
douze	12	twelve
treize	13	thirteen
quatorze	14	fourteen
quinze	15	fifteen
seize	16	sixteen
dix-sept	17	seventeen
dix-huit	18	eighteen
dix-neuf	19	nineteen
vingt	20	twenty
vingt et un(une)	21	twenty-one
vingt-deux	22	twenty-two
trente	30	thirty
quarante	40	forty
cinquante	50	fifty
soixante	60	sixty
soixante-dix	70	seventy
soixante et onze	71	seventy-one
soixante-douze	72	seventy-two
quatre-vingts	80	eighty
quatre-vingt-un(-une)	81	eighty-one
quatre-vingt-dix	90	ninety
quatre-vingt-onze	91	ninety-one
cent	100	a hundred
cent un(une)	101	a hundred and one
trois cents	300	three hundred
trois cent un(une)	301	three hundred and one
mille	1 000	a thousand
un million	1 000 000	a million

premier (première), 1er	first, 1st
deuxième, 2e *or* 2ème	second, 2nd
troisième, 3e *or* 3ème	third, 3rd
quatrième	fourth, 4th
cinquième	fifth, 5th
sixième	sixth, 6th
septième	seventh

LES NOMBRES

huitième
neuvième
dixième
onzième
douzième
treizième
quatorzième
quinzième
seizième
dix-septième
dix-huitième
dix-neuvième
vingtième
vingt-et-unième
vingt-deuxième
trentième
centième
cent-unième
millième

Les Fractions etc

un demi
un tiers
deux tiers
un quart
un cinquième
zéro virgule cinq, 0,5
trois virgule quatre, 3,4
dix pour cent
cent pour cent

Exemples

il habite au dix
c'est au chapitre sept
à la page sept
il habite au septième (étage)
il est arrivé (le) septième
une part d'un septième
échelle au vingt-cinq millième

NUMBERS

eighth
ninth
tenth
eleventh
twelfth
thirteenth
fourteenth
fifteenth
sixteenth
seventeenth
eighteenth
nineteenth
twentieth
twenty-first
twenty-second
thirtieth
hundredth
hundred-and-first
thousandth

Fractions etc

a half
a third
two thirds
a quarter
a fifth
(nought) point five, 0.5
three point four, 3.4
ten per cent
a hundred per cent

Examples

he lives at number 10
it's in chapter 7
on page 7
he lives on the 7th floor
he came in 7th
a share of one seventh
scale one to twenty-five
thousand

L'HEURE

THE TIME

quelle heure est-il?

what time is it?

il est ...

it's ...

minuit	midnight
une heure (du matin)	one o'clock (in the morning), one (a.m.)
une heure cinq	five past one
une heure dix	ten past one
une heure et quart	a quarter past one, one fifteen
une heure vingt-cinq	twenty-five past one, one twenty-five
une heure et demie, une heure trente	half past one, one thirty
une heure trente-cinq, deux heures moins vingt-cinq	twenty-five to two, one thirty-five
deux heures moins vingt, une heure quarante	twenty to two, one forty
deux heures moins le quart, une heure quarante-cinq	a quarter to two, one forty-five
deux heures moins dix, une heure cinquante	ten to two, one fifty
midi	twelve o'clock, midday, noon
deux heures (de l'après-midi)	two o'clock (in the afternoon), two (p.m.)
sept heures (du soir)	seven o'clock (in the evening), seven (p.m.)

à quelle heure?

at what time?

à minuit	at midnight
à sept heures	at seven o'clock
dans vingt minutes	in twenty minutes
il y a quinze minutes	fifteen minutes ago